AMERICAN DEMOCRACY NOW

7TH EDITION

Brigid Callahan Harrison
Montclair State University

Jean Wahl Harris
University of Scranton

Michelle D. Deardorff
University of Tennessee at Chattanooga

AP CONTRIBUTOR

Rebecca Small
Fairfax County Public Schools

Mc
Graw
Hill

AMERICAN DEMOCRACY NOW: SEVENTH EDITION

3 4 5 6 7 8 9 LWI 24 23 22

ISBN 978-1-26-431913-8
MHID 1-26-431913-4

Senior Portfolio Manager: *Jason Seitz*
Product Development Manager: *Dawn Groundwater*
Senior Product Developer: *Sarah Colwell*
Senior Marketing Manager: *Michael Gedatus*
Content Project Managers: *Rick Hecker; George Theofanopolous*
Buyer: *Susan K. Culbertson*
Designer: *Beth Blech*
Content Licensing Specialist: *Carrie Burger*
Front Cover: *sborisov/iStock/Getty Images*
Back Cover: *McGraw Hill*
Compositor: *Aptara®, Inc.*

Library of Congress Cataloging-in-Publication Data

Names: Harrison, Brigid C., author. | Harris, Jean (Jean Wahl), 1960- author.
  | Deardorff, Michelle D., author.
Title: American democracy now / Brigid Callahan Harrison, Montclair State
  University, Jean Wahl Harris, University of Scranton, Michelle D.
  Deardorff, University of Tennessee at Chattanooga.
Description: Seventh edition. | New York, NY : McGraw Hill Education,
  [2022] | Includes index.
Identifiers: LCCN 2020031867 | ISBN 9781264319138
Subjects: LCSH: Political participation—United States—Textbooks. | United
  States—Politics and government—Textbooks.
Classification: LCC JK276 .A43 2022 | DDC 320.473—dc23
  LC record available at https://lccn.loc.gov/2020031867

Brief Contents

Table of Contents

3 FEDERALISM   108

UNIT 2 INTERACTIONS AMONG BRANCHES OF GOVERNMENT   152

4 CONGRESS   156

5 THE PRESIDENCY 196

6 THE JUDICIARY 240

7   THE BUREAUCRACY   282

UNIT 2   WRAP-UP   324

11 ECONOMIC POLICY 486

12 DOMESTIC POLICY 526

13 FOREIGN POLICY AND NATIONAL SECURITY 566

UNIT 4   WRAP-UP   613

▍Exam Practice   616

Multiple Choice Questions   616

Free Response Questions   622

UNIT 5   POLITICAL PARTICIPATION   624

▍What is Political Participation?   626

Big Ideas   626

Skills and Practices   627

14   CAMPAIGNS, ELECTIONS, AND VOTING   628

15 POLITICAL PARTIES 676

UNIT 5 WRAP-UP   829

Fully Aligned for AP Success

The 7th Edition of *American Democracy Now* has been thoroughly updated to fully align with the Advanced Placement® U.S. Government and Politics Curriculum Framework. The program is organized to follow the AP Course Framework, which features commonly taught units of study that provide a suggested sequence for the course. These units are based on content and conceptual understandings that colleges and universities typically expect students to master to qualify for college credit and/or placement. The content is grounded in Big Ideas, which are cross-cutting concepts that built conceptual understanding and spiral through the course.

Additionally, the course comprehensively incorporates AP Disciplinary Practices and Reasoning Processes, which are central to the study and understanding of government and politics. As laid out in the AP Course Framework, these skills are embedded in every chapter through features that incorporate AP Key Terms, Foundational Documents, and required Supreme Court cases.

The program engages students with current and compelling content and increases their sense of political efficacy by exciting them about the political conversations of the day. Integrated critical thinking activities help students to connect the past and present of politics with the future, and ask: What's next for our democracy? Dedicated chapters on The Media and Politics and Technology meet students where they are so they can truly connect with the relevance of politics in their everyday lives — this can lead to lively class discussions and activities that support Enduring Understandings such as balance of power, public opinion polling, and how the various forms of media inform and influence. Students learn how the fundamental principles of American democracy inform their understanding of the politics and policies of today so that they can think about, and participate in creating, the policies they would like to see take shape tomorrow.

At the heart of the *American Democracy Now* is a rich set of pedagogical tools designed around AP Big Ideas, using Enduring Understandings and Learning Objectives to meet the rigors of AP coursework and prepare students for success on the AP Exam. The instructional design is visually appealing, relevant, and written in an accessible voice to ensure all students, at all levels, are well supported as they garner a solid understanding of the key elements, institutions, and dynamics of American government.

Overview of Program Features

- **Unit Openers** present **AP Big Ideas** contextualized in real-world scenarios. The questions in the openers provide a framework for how to think about the readings and activities in the subsequent chapters and encourage students to identify unifying themes and concepts within these chapters to help them synthesize information and see the bigger picture.

- **Chapter Introductions** point students toward the learning ahead, helping to focus their study and highlighting the connections between past, present, and future.

- **AP Key Terms, Foundational Documents,** and **Supreme Court Cases** highlight required **AP Concepts, Documents,** and **Supreme Court Cases** with annotations for quick reference. A list of terms and documents are also provided in the **Chapter Wrap-Up** giving students the opportunity to review and check their understanding.

- *Then, Now, Next* provides ample practice in **applying political concepts and processes** to past, present, and future scenarios and to develop arguments in support of a position.

Fully Aligned for AP Success, *continued*

- ***Thinking Critically*** activities ask students to thoughtfully evaluate sources while applying AP disciplinary practices such as **concept application, argumentation,** and **source analysis.**
- **Data Analysis** activities help students consume political data in a meaningful way.
- **SCOTUS Application** activities help students understand **required AP Supreme Court Cases** and how they apply to other Court cases.
- A variety of **graphs, charts, illustrations, photos, political cartoons, text-based documents,** and **commentary** provide additional source analysis activities.
- **Chapter AP Test Practice** in the AP multiple choice and free response formats helps students test their knowledge while familiarizing themselves with AP exam – style questions.
- **Unit Wrap-Ups** revisit the AP Big Ideas from the Unit Openers, asking students to make connections between the chapters and encouraging them to seek continuities in U.S. political history, life, and ideologies.
- **AP Unit Exam Practice** allows students to test the knowledge gained and strengthens mastery of concepts in the cross-cutting AP Big Ideas.

AP-Aligned Units Engage Students and Connect to AP Big Ideas

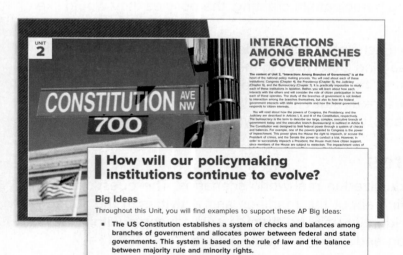

Unit Openers emphasize overarching themes and apply them to real-world scenarios.

Units are organized based on the AP Course Framework, which systematically builds knowledge through **Big Ideas** that frame that unit's subsequent chapters. The Unit Openers help students determine important themes and concepts as they proceed through course material, enhancing conceptual understandings.

Students are also given guidance and examples to better understand how to apply the **AP Reasoning Processes and Disciplinary Practices** they'll exercise in each chapter.

Chapters Designed Exclusively for the AP Classroom

Each chapter in *American Democracy Now* Seventh Edition has a **Chapter Introduction**, emphasizing the **AP Enduring Understandings**, which are related to the Big Ideas, to give students a foundation for understanding and putting the chapter content into AP context. By highlighting the Enduring Understandings that frame each chapter, students will be equipped to understand how the topics illustrate these statements and how they come together as a whole.

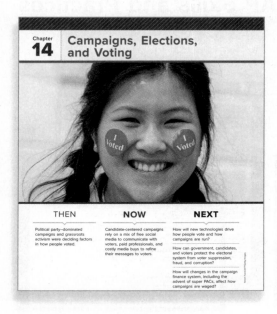

Chapter **14** Campaigns, Elections, and Voting

THEN	NOW	NEXT
Political party–dominated campaigns and grassroots activism were deciding factors in how people voted.	Candidate-centered campaigns rely on a mix of free social media to communicate with voters, paid professionals, and costly media buys to refine their messages to voters.	How will new technologies drive how people vote and how campaigns are run?
		How can government, candidates, and voters protect the electoral system from voter suppression, fraud, and corruption?
		How will changes in the campaign finance system, including the advent of super PACs, affect how campaigns are waged?

Chapters are organized with a unique ***Then, Now, Next*** structure designed to emphasize how the past informs the present, and how present-day issues and events might impact the future. Students are challenged to consider how their participation as citizens might help shape tomorrow's political culture, ideologies, and institutions.

Throughout each chapter, annotations call attention to **Key Terms** and **AP Required SCOTUS Cases** and **Foundational Documents**. These enhance student understanding of important topics as well as offering specific context for understanding both political history and present-day realities.

full faith and credit clause
The constitutional clause that requires states to comply with and uphold the public acts, records, and judicial decisions of other states.

Because of the ease of traveling between states as well as relocating from state to state, an important component of horizontal federalism stems from the full faith and credit clause of Article IV, Section 1, of the Constitution. The **full faith and credit clause** asserts that each state must recognize as legally binding (that is, valid and enforceable) the public acts, records, and judicial proceedings of every other state. For example, in March 2016, the Supreme Court cited the full faith and credit clause when it ruled that states must honor adoptions by same-sex parents who move across state lines.[8]

AP U.S. GOVERNMENT REQUIRED FOUNDATIONAL DOCUMENTS		
	Author(s)	Main ideas to look for/consider
Articles of Confederation	U.S. Continental Congress	Established a weak central government that lacked the power to tax and raise an army.
Federalist 10	James Madison	It is natural for citizens in a free society to form factions.
Federalist 51	James Madison	Federalism, separation of powers, and checks and balances established in the Constitution will control the effects of factions.
Brutus 1	Unknown	The Constitution provides too much elasticity and power to the national government, and if ratified, will render state governments irrelevant.

Tables also provide quick reference to encourage mastery of concepts in Foundational Documents.

Chapters Provide Deeper Application of AP Skills and Practices
Apply Disciplinary Practices and Develop Reasoning Skills

Each chapter also includes opportunities to apply **Disciplinary Practices** giving students the opportunity to learn and build critical thinking skills necessary for success on the **AP Exam**. These skills can be used to analyze both written and visual sources. Students are given the opportunity to build those skills in every chapter as they proceed through the course.

- **Argumentation** and **Concept Application** activities ask students to explore specific issues within larger conceptual understandings relating to the AP Big Ideas.
- **Comparison** activities challenge students to analyze how political phenomena and government institutions have changed over time, using concrete examples.
- **Data Analysis** activities use critical thinking questions to help students understand how to analyze statistics, as well as how to read visual representations of data. This feature helps students evaluate information they encounter every day and determine both the legitimacy of the source and the motivation or agenda of the source.
- **Source Analysis** activities give students direct practice in analyzing both written and visual sources for meaning, context, and perspective.

Interpreting Images questions challenge students to analyze photographs, political cartoons, and art for context, symbolism, and the perspective of the creator.

In-Depth Supreme Court Coverage and Activities are Presented in Print and Online

The program includes activities that take a deep dive into the required AP Supreme Court Cases. Annotations in the margins of each chapter provide additional information to help students understand the impact of these cases.

THE POWER TO REGULATE COMMERCE The landmark case of **McCulloch v. Maryland** (1819) exemplifies a Supreme Court ruling that established the use of the implied powers to expand the national government's enumerated authority.[9] The case stemmed from Congress's establishment of a national bank, and in particular a branch of that bank located in the state of Maryland, which the Maryland state authorities tried to tax. Maryland's attorneys argued that Congress

McCulloch v. Maryland
The 1819 case that established that the necessary and proper clause justifies broad understandings of enumerated powers.

SCOTUS APPLICATION *UNITED STATES V. LOPEZ (1995)*

In 1808, the government of New York granted a steamboat company a monopoly to operate its boats on the state's waters, which included bodies of water that stretched between states. Aaron Ogden held a license under this monopoly to operate steamboats between New Jersey and New York. Thomas Gibbons, another steamboat operator, competed with Aaron Ogden on this same route but held a federal coasting license issued by an act of Congress. Ogden filed a complaint in New York court to stop Gibbons from operating his boats, claiming that the monopoly granted by New York was legal even though he operated on shared, interstate waters. Gibbons disagreed, arguing that the U.S. Constitution gave Congress the sole power over interstate commerce, and he challenged Ogden's licensing in court.

The case eventually reached the Supreme Court, and in the ruling, the court held that the commerce clause of the Constitution grants the federal government the power to regulate the operation of steamboats between New York and New Jersey. Therefore, the license issued to Gibbons by Congress to operate a ferry service superseded the monopoly license to operate a ferry service issued to Ogden by the state of new York.

A. Identify the constitutional clause that was used in *U.S. v. Lopez* (1995) and *Gibbons v. Ogden* (1824).

B. Based on the constitutional clause identified in part A, explain why the facts of *Gibbons v. Ogden* led to a different holding than the holding in *U.S. v. Lopez*.

C. Describe an action that state governments could take if they disagree with the holding in *Gibbons v. Ogden* could take to limit its impact.

SCOTUS Application AP activities take an in-depth look into the SCOTUS Cases required by the AP Course Framework, challenging students to both understand the facts of the cases, as well as their impact on U.S. life and politics.

SCOTUS Comparison Free Response Questions ask students to compare required SCOTUS cases to non-required cases, further enhancing their skills of analysis and comparison.

▮ Free Response Questions

SCOTUS Comparison

In *U.S. Term Limits v. Thornton (1995)*, the state or Arkansas had adopted a state amendment imposing term limits for federally elected officials from the state of Arkansas would be ineligible to serve more than 3 terms and anyone elected to the U.S. Senate would be ineligible to serve more than 2 terms. In their ruling, the Supreme Court stated that the Constitution prohibits States from adopting Congressional qualifications in addition to those enumerated in the Constitution.

A. Identify the constitutional clause that is common to both *U.S. Term Limits v. Thornton (1995)* and *McCulloch v. Maryland (1819)*.

B. Based on the constitutional clause identified in part A, explain why the facts of *U.S. Term Limits v. Thornton* led to a different holding in *McCulloch v. Maryland*.

C. Explain an action citizens who disagree with the ruling in *U.S. Term Limits v. Thornton* could take to limit its impact.

The program also includes **SCOTUS AP Activities** through our robust digital resources. These interactive online activities dive deep into each case, providing students with the opportunity to analyze SCOTUS cases as primary sources, and to not only read synopses of the case, but the arguments and opinions themselves, and respond with their own reasoning and arguments.

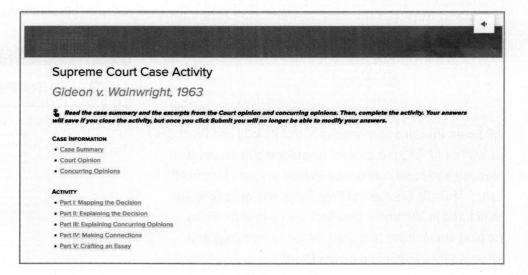

Supreme Court Case Activity

Gideon v. Wainwright, 1963

🔖 *Read the case summary and the excerpts from the Court opinion and concurring opinions. Then, complete the activity. Your answers will save if you close the activity, but once you click Submit you will no longer be able to modify your answers.*

CASE INFORMATION
- Case Summary
- Court Opinion
- Concurring Opinions

ACTIVITY
- Part I: Mapping the Decision
- Part II: Explaining the Decision
- Part III: Explaining Concurring Opinions
- Part IV: Making Connections
- Part V: Crafting an Essay

Chapter and Unit Wrap-Ups and AP Exam Practice Synthesize Knowledge for Retention and Success

▎Conclusion: Thinking Critically About What's Next for Federalism

Today's federalism (partisan federalism) is not the framers' federalism (dual federalism). James Madison and other framers argued that the national government's powers were limited by the Constitution and focused on foreign affairs and defense matters, while states' powers were expansive and covered domestic issues. However, the proper distribution of authority and balance of power between the national and state governments has always been controversial. Until recent decades, the Supreme Court's interpretations tended to favor an expansion of the national government's enumerated and implied powers into a growing number of domestic matters. However, the past few decades have witnessed inconsistency in the Court's interpretations. The Court protects and even expands national powers in some cases while protecting states' powers in other cases.

Each **Chapter Wrap-Up** includes a list of **Key Terms and Documents** with page numbers for quick reference.

▎Multiple Choice Questions

Questions 1 and 2 refer to the passage below.

"Ambition must be made to counteract ambition. The interest of the man must be connected with the constitutional rights of the place. It may be a reflection on human nature, that such devices should be necessary to control the abuses of government. But what is government itself, but the greatest of all reflections on human nature? If men were angels, no government would be necessary. If angels were to govern men, neither external nor internal controls on government would be necessary. In framing a government which is to be administered by men over men, the great difficulty lies in this: you must first enable the government to control the governed; and in the next place oblige it to control itself."

—Madison, *Federalist 51*

1. What is Madison's main arg
   A. The Constitution is a so
   B. Elected officials will be
      temptations of power
   C. The government's powe
      tyranny
   D. The nature of human b

2. Which of the following is an e
   A. Judicial review
   B. the Supremacy clause
   C. Implied powers
   D. The ratification process

▎Free Response Questions

SCOTUS Comparison

In *Martin v. Hunter's Lessee* (1816), Denny Martin, a British subject, had the land he inherited from his uncle seized by Virginia during the Revolutionary War in 1781. The next year, Virginia's state legislature granted part of the land seized from Denny Martin to a man named David Hunter. However, a federal treaty then required that the land be given back to Denny Martin. The Virginia Supreme Court sided with the Virginia legislature. Upon review, the U.S. Supreme Court sent the case back to the Virginia Supreme Court, stating that the federal treaty required the land should indeed be returned to Denny Martin. The Virginia Supreme Court argued that the U.S. Supreme Court did not have authority over cases originating in state court. The case returned to the U.S. Supreme Court and ended in the Court's final ruling that it **does** have authority to interpret federal law as established by its supremacy in matters of constitutional interpretation.

   A. Identify the constitutional principle that is common to both *Martin v. Hunter's Lessee* (1816) and *Marbury v. Madison* (1803).
   B. Based on the constitutional clause identified in part A, explain why the facts of *Martin v. Hunter's Lessee* led to the same ruling as in *Marbury v. Madison*.
   C. How was the ruling in *Martin v. Hunter's Lessee* similar to other rulings by the Marshall Court?

AP Exam Practice emphasizes both AP Skills and Practices as well as AP-aligned content for students to assess their learning and build confidence as they prepare for the AP Exam. Multiple Choice and Free Response questions are structured in alignment to reflect the current AP Exam, helping students be prepared for the terminology and phrasing they might find on the Exam.

Chapter Conclusions revisit AP Enduring Understandings laid out in Chapter Introductions. These help students review and reflect on concepts they've learned in each chapter, reinforcing their conceptual understandings.

CHAPTER 4 WRAP-UP	

▎Key Terms

agency review	171	markup	171
agenda setting	165	minority whip	175
attentive public	182	nuclear option	173
bill	168	ombudsperson	163
casework	163	pocket veto	174
cloture	172	politico	163
conference committee	173	pork barrel	163
congressional oversight	164	president pro tempore	177
discharge petition	171	reapportionment	166
earmark	163	redistricting	166
filibuster	172	report	171
hearings	171	Rules Committee	171
hopper	169	select committee	170
House majority leader	175	Senate majority leader	177
House minority leader	175	Senate minority leader	177
instructed delegate model	163	seniority system	170
joint committee	171	Speaker of the House	174
joint referral	170	standing committee	170
lead committee	170	subcommittee	171
logrolling	180	trustee model	162
majority whip	175	unanimous consent	172

AP Unit Wrap-Ups revisit AP Big Ideas and Enduring Understandings laid out in the AP Unit Openers and Chapter Introductions to ensure students' understanding and retention.

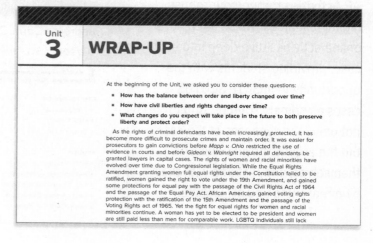

Unit 3	WRAP-UP

At the beginning of the Unit, we asked you to consider these questions:
- How has the balance between order and liberty changed over time?
- How have civil liberties and rights changed over time?
- What changes do you expect will take place in the future to both preserve liberty and protect order?

As the rights of criminal defendants have been increasingly protected, it has become more difficult to prosecute crimes and maintain order. It was easier for prosecutors to gain convictions before *Mapp v. Ohio* restricted the use of evidence in courts and before *Gideon v. Wainright* required all defendants be granted lawyers in capital cases. The rights of women and racial minorities have evolved over time due to Congressional legislation. While the Equal Rights Amendment granting women full equal rights under the Constitution failed to be ratified, women gained the right to vote under the 19th Amendment, and gained some protections for equal pay with the passage of the Civil Rights Act of 1964 and the passage of the Equal Pay Act. African Americans gained voting rights protection with the ratification of the 15th Amendment and the passage of the Voting Rights act of 1965. Yet the fight for equal rights for women and racial minorities continue. A woman has yet to be elected to be president and women are still paid less than men for comparable work. LGBTQ individuals still lack

AP Teacher Support

The **AP Teacher Manual** gives teachers the tools to help students navigate the AP U.S. Government and Politics course and succeed on the AP Exam. The content supports and deepens understanding of the content covered in the Student Edition, ensuring it will both engage and broaden the perspectives of students. The Teacher Manual, available in print and digital format, provides:

- Dynamic projects for each unit
- Overviews of chapter content
- Pacing Guides for each unit and chapter
- Engaging Chapter Activities that allow students to dive deeper into content
- Guides, answers, and responses for every AP feature, reinforcing the content and challenging students to think deeply about issues
- Key Terms, Foundational Documents, and Required SCOTUS Cases included in each chapter
- Answers and explanations for every question in the Chapter and Unit Practice Exams, as well as rubrics for each free response question
- Additional practice questions designed to prepare students for the AP Exam

Digital Resources Enrich Instruction and Extend the Learning

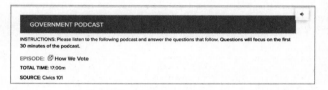

Podcast Activities offer a selection of podcast episodes that engage students in thinking about political concepts and U.S. institutions. Popular podcasts like Heightened Scrutiny, More Perfect, and Civics 101 are featured. Review questions accompany each podcast.

Supreme Court Case Activities and **Foundational Documents Activities** help students analyze required cases and documents by going in-depth into the historical context, arguments, and importance of these resources. These robust online resources deepen student understanding gained through the information and activities in the student edition.

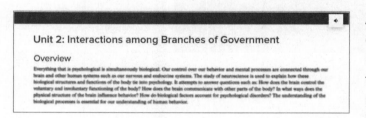

AP Unit Reviews challenge students to test their knowledge of AP content and concepts through self-directed study. Unit Reviews are thoroughly aligned with the AP Course Framework, touching on each element of the AP Unit Guides. Each Unit Review includes multiple-choice questions with feedback to help students master and retain content knowledge.

Concept Clips are engaging videos that walk students through the more difficult concepts in the AP U.S. Government and Politics course—such as the Electoral College, Supreme Court procedures, or how to evaluate a public opinion poll. After watching a short video, students respond to questions to evaluate their understanding of the topic.

Personalized, Adaptive, and Dynamic
Digital Resources

American Democracy Now delivers multimedia content that supports the course Framework and provides multiple opportunities for students to learn and apply their understanding of the disciplinary practices and reasoning processes to ensure course and Exam success. Students are led to content and concept mastery with resources such as Foundational Document and Supreme Court Case Activities, interactivities, Unit Reviews, and AP Test Practice.

Teachers can easily customize lessons, monitor student progress, and make data-driven decisions with the flexible, easy-to-navigate instructional tools.

Intuitive Design

Resources are organized at the chapter level. To enhance the core content, teachers can add assignments, activities, and instructional aids to any lesson.

The chapter landing page gives students access to:

- assigned AP activities

- AP test prep and practice

- interactive eBook

- adaptive, assignable *SmartBook*®

- interactive concept clips

- activities delving into key Supreme Court Cases and Foundational Documents

McGraw Hill

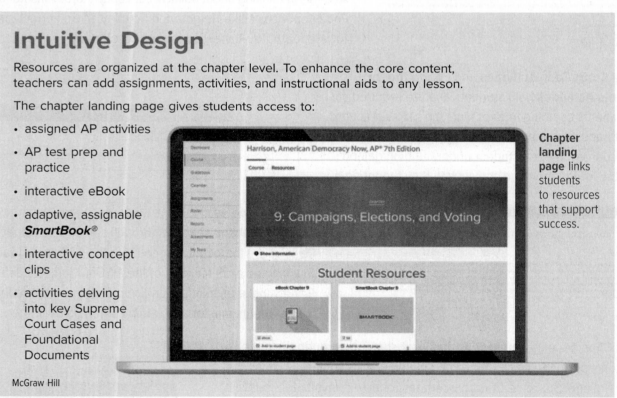

Chapter landing page links students to resources that support success.

 Mobile Ready Access to course content on-the-go is easier and more efficient than ever before with the *ReadAnywhere* mobile app.

Because learning changes everything.®

Adaptive Study Tools

SMARTBOOK® is the assignable, adaptive study tool. The interactive features personalize learning with self-guided tools that:

- assess proficiency and knowledge,
- track which topics have been mastered,
- identify areas that need more study,
- deliver meaningful practice with guidance and instant feedback,
- recharge learning with previously completed assignments and personalized recommendations,
- allow teachers to assign material at the topic level.

Highlighted content continuously adapts as students work through exercises.

Practice sets measure depth of understanding and present a personalized learning path based on student responses.

Teacher Resources

Teachers have access to the interactive eBook, adaptive *SmartBook®,* and a wealth of customizable chapter resources and powerful gradebook tools including:

- Online Teacher Manual with chapter outlines, teaching suggestions, and pacing guides
- Student performance reports to help teachers identify gaps, make data-driven decisions, and adjust instruction
- Customizable PowerPoint presentations
- Labeled visual aids and additional ideas for lecture enrichment

Searchable library makes it easy to find and assign resources.

Customizable assignments and quiz banks are automatically graded and populate easy-to-read reports.

McGraw Hill

Harness technology, unlock success with the digital resources for *American Democracy Now*
Visit My.MHEducation.com

Key Figures & Tables

Staying Current

This edition reflects the November 2020 election results.

CHAPTER 1 PEOPLE, POLITICS, AND PARTICIPATION

- Updated the discussion of the current political context to include the impact of the pandemic and the renewed Black Lives Matter movement; the relationship of the Trump presidency with the media; the ideological debates on such topics as the Green New Deal and health insurance; and the concerns over Russian interference in U.S. elections, trade policy with China, and ongoing threats of terrorism.
- Refocused Evaluating the Facts to feature the relationship between voter turnout and state voting options, such as vote by mail.
- Revised Thinking Critically feature to prompt students to more carefully evaluate facts they encounter in media related to recent issues.
- Added new data for Analyzing the Sources feature that frames the issue of partisanship in the United States by generation.
- Expanded discussion of progressivism to reflect its place in current issues such as the 2020 presidential primary campaign, Medicare for All, and the Green New Deal.
- Clarified definition of socialism and discussed the use of the term in the context of the Sanders presidential campaigns.
- Updated data about the U.S. population and U.S. families.

CHAPTER 2 THE CONSTITUTION

- Enhanced integration of key terms from Chapter 1.
- Provided greater focus on the political battles that transformed a British colony to a nation of "we the people."
- Created new Thinking Critically feature that asks whether the Electoral College should be abolished.
- Added three new tables to highlight the key (1) British policies that mobilized colonists to rebellion, (2) colonists' efforts to create a new nation, and (3) U.S. government actions to transition from a confederal to a federal system of government.
- Created new Analyzing the Sources that investigates the balance of powers between the three branches of national government.
- Revised numerous political inquiry questions in the annotated Constitution to focus on constitutional procedures used or questioned, and constitutional language debated during the past few years.

CHAPTER 3 FEDERALISM

- Wrote new chapter-opening story about the establishment of a legal voting age, and how local, state, and national governments interact and vary in doing so.
- Created new Analyzing the Sources that considers the population of each state and the number of local governments each has.
- Integrated the intergovernmental responses to the coronavirus.
- Created new Then, Now, Next feature on the census.

- Added new table highlighting the national government's constitutional obligations to the states.
- Enhanced the focus on states as laboratories of democracy.
- Added new table that summarizes the elements of public policy that are a framework for understanding intergovernmental relations and the models of federalism.
- Reorganized the discussion on the evolution of federalism in the United States.
- Updated data and graphics related to fiscal federalism.

CHAPTER 4 CONGRESS

- Added new research and data on congressional incumbency.
- Added a new discussion of congressional oversight of the president.
- Added a new discussion of a 2020 Supreme Court decision regarding redistricting.
- Updated and expanded discussion of the use of the "nuclear option" in the Senate.
- Updated the congressional leadership section.
- Added updates on the 2020 elections and the party composition of Congress.

CHAPTER 5 THE PRESIDENCY

- Examined the 2020 presidential election.
- Added new discussion of signing statements and, in particular, the CARES Act in the context of the pandemic.
- Added new discussion of the president's leadership during the pandemic and his use of emergency powers.
- Updated information on presidential vetoes.
- Added a new discussion of the president's role in managing the economy.
- Expanded discussion of the president's role as chief diplomat.
- Added new discussion of the president's role as civilian leader of the military.
- Added a new discussion of factors involved in selecting a vice president.
- Added new discussion of executive privilege in the context of President Trump's impeachment.
- Expanded discussion of the use of the bully pulpit.
- Included new comparative data on women and minorities appointed to presidential cabinets.
- Included new comparative data on presidential public approval.
- Examined discussion of the geographical variation in President Trump's popularity.
- Included a new discussion on President Trump's impeachment.
- Revised the discussion of women and the presidency in the context of the 2020 elections.
- Added information on the First Lady's priorities for her role.

CHAPTER 6 THE JUDICIARY

- Reorganized chapter to emphasize the importance of judicial legitimacy and the rule of law in a democratic society.
- Added new Analyzing the Sources feature on judicial legitimacy.
- Revised Then, Now, Next feature, "Supreme Court Diversity."
- Updated data on demographics of federal judges to include those confirmed during the Trump administration.
- Incorporated a discussion of President Trump's executive orders addressing COVID-19.
- Integrated a new discussion of the disagreement between President Trump and Chief Justice Roberts over the role and legitimacy of the federal courts.

CHAPTER 7 THE BUREAUCRACY

- Added new opening story on bureaucratic and red tape challenges to discovering and implementing quick, widespread testing following the coronavirus outbreak.
- Revised first section of the chapter to discuss the role of bureaucracy in a democracy.
- Added new table to highlight the characteristics of Weber's ideal bureaucracy.
- Reorganized the discussion on the bureaucrats who implement federal policies.
- Updated data throughout the chapter.
- Added new discussion of the courts holding the Department of Education and its secretary accountable to the Administrative Procedures Act.
- Added new discussion of the whistleblower who alleged misconduct by President Trump regarding conversations with the Ukrainian president.
- Created new Analyzing the Sources feature that asks whether evaluation of government performance is actually based on bureaucratic performance or partisanship.
- Updated discussion and analysis in section "Does Contracting-Out Improve Performance?"
- Added discussion of role of bureaucratic performance in containing the coronavirus.

CHAPTER 8 CIVIL LIBERTIES

- Updated statistics, data, and Supreme Court rulings from the previous edition.
- Included a new section on journalism and freedom of speech.
- Introduced decisions and policies of the Trump administration, as opposed to prior focus on the Obama administration.
- Added new features on excessive bail reform, privacy issues in the public sector, and symbolic speech.
- Moved focus from Millennials to Generation Z.
- Introduced a new section on facial recognition technology.

CHAPTER 9 CIVIL RIGHTS

- Updated statistics, data, and Supreme Court rulings from the previous edition.
- Incorporated new discussions of weight discrimination and voter suppression.
- Included a new discussion of housing discrimination by the federal government and an updated chart on wage disparities.
- Added a discussion of Fourth Wave Feminism.
- Updated all references and citations.

CHAPTER 10 POLITICAL SOCIALIZATION AND PUBLIC OPINION

- Added new Thinking Critically feature that asks whether the United States is a nation divided.
- Explored new data concerning the gender gap in political party identification between men and women.
- Evaluated new data about the policy priorities of men and women in the 2016 presidential election.
- Evaluated the gender gap in presidential vote choice in 2016.
- Updated information about the opinions of Millennials.
- Added new information on the politics of Generation Z.
- Included new discussion of the new "most important problem."
- Included new data concerning trust in government.

CHAPTER 11 ECONOMIC POLICY

- Created new Then, Now, Next feature that considers the increasing cost of the American dream.
- Added a table highlighting the traditional measures of a healthy economy.
- Created a new Analyzing the Sources feature that considers income inequality in the United States.
- Integrated information on the CARES Act as a response to the pandemic into the discussion of fiscal policy.
- Discussed deficit spending in the context of the pandemic.
- Discussed the economic responses of state and local governments to the pandemic.
- Added graphics on U.S. debt and which countries hold it.
- Expanded the discussion of deregulation with examples from the Trump administration.
- Updated data throughout the chapter.
- Analyzed the overall impact of the pandemic on the economy.

CHAPTER 12 DOMESTIC POLICY

- Created new Analyzing the Sources that compares policy priorities of several groups of Americans: (1) women and men, (2) Democrats and Republicans, and (3) younger voters and older voters.
- Discussed the Small Business Administration's response to the pandemic.
- Added material on unemployment compensation issues during the pandemic.
- Created new Thinking Critically feature called "Should the United States Postal Service Be Shut Down?"
- Added new discussion of the provision of information as a public policy tool.
- Added new Then, Now, Next feature on the sources of energy used in the United States.
- Added new section on national education policy, including college student loan-payment issues.
- Added new figure comparing TANF benefits across the states.
- Streamlined discussion of the Affordable Care Act.
- Updated data throughout the chapter.

CHAPTER 13 FOREIGN POLICY AND NATIONAL SECURITY

- Described the context for current foreign policy.
- Added new Analyzing the Sources feature that asks students to evaluate the Ukraine transcripts.
- Updated discussion of the creators and shapers of foreign policy.
- Updated coverage of the use of new technologies in foreign policy.
- Described future challenges in foreign policy, including post-pandemic globalism, trade policy, the renewed threat of terrorism, and Russian expansion and efforts to increase influence.

CHAPTER 14   CAMPAIGNS, ELECTIONS, AND VOTING

- Reorganized chapter to emphasize importance of new uses of balloting in the wake of COVID-19 and concerns about suppressing voter turnout during the pandemic.
- Expanded discussion of the importance of fair, independent elections.
- Expanded discussion of why election meddling matters.
- Included a new discussion of efforts at voter suppression.
- Revised discussion of voting by mail in the 2020 elections, particularly in the context of the pandemic.
- Included a new discussion of caucuses.
- Discussed 2020 ballot initiatives in the states.
- Examined impact of COVID-19 on campaigning in 2020 and on ability to gather signatures for ballot measures.
- Updated data concerning 2020 Electoral College vote.
- Updated data concerning age and presidential election turnout.
- Updated data concerning race and presidential elections.
- Included new research concerning how voters decide.
- Explained campaign finance regulations for the 2020 elections.
- Included new discussion of dark money in campaigns.

CHAPTER 15   POLITICAL PARTIES

- Included an updated discussion of "A Democratic Party Struggling to Define Itself."
- Included an updated discussion of "The Republican Party in the Era of President Trump."
- Added discussion of effect of the pandemic on party priorities.
- Updated data concerning Americans' opinions of the two political parties.
- Added new information about the role of the parties in the 2020 elections.
- Updated the discussion of the responsible party model.
- Added a new Analyzing the Sources feature that asks students to evaluate why Democrats and Republicans belong to each political party.
- Updated data on differences between Democrats and Republicans concerning policy priorities.

- Updated data on Americans' support for a third party.
- Added new discussion of the future of the Democrats and Republicans.

CHAPTER 16   INTEREST GROUPS

- Included a discussion of the effect of *Janus v. United States* on interest groups.
- Updated information the actions of foreign-policy interest groups in the United States.
- Included more detailed discussion of *Citizens United v. Federal Election Commission.*
- Updated data on political action committee contributions to congressional candidates by incumbency status.
- Added new data on top political action committee contributors.
- Added a new Analyzing the Sources feature demonstrating the importance of considering interest groups' perspective when evaluating interest group ratings.

CHAPTER 17   THE MEDIA

- Reframed the current debate about media accuracy.
- Revised the Analyzing the Sources feature that examines new data on confidence in the media.
- Added new data on the increasing diversity in newsrooms.
- Included new research on the demographics related to the increase in online news consumption.
- Expanded discussion of generational differences in media consumption.

CHAPTER 18   POLITICS AND TECHNOLOGY

- Updated data on Internet usage.
- Added new discussion of the use of technology in politics to inform, inflame, provoke, and confuse during the COVID-19 pandemic.
- Updated research on the use of technology in the 2020 elections.
- Added information on the use of social media as a tool of protests.
- Added new research on election infiltration.
- Updated discussion on the impact of technology on political life.
- Revamped discussion of the effects of FCC Chairman Ajit Pai's rollback of the net neutrality order.

Acknowledgments

We owe a debt of thanks to all of the people who contributed their thoughts and suggestions to the development of *American Democracy Now*.

Content Reviewers

Stephen Anthony, *Georgia State University*
Stephen Baker, *Jacksonville University*
Michael Baranowski, *Northern Kentucky University*
Kyle Barbieri, *Georgia Perimeter College*
Donna Bennett, *Trinity Valley Community College*
Amy Brandon, *El Paso Community College–Valle Verde*
Wendell Broadwell, *Georgia Perimeter College*
Monique Bruner, *Rose State College*
Joseph Campbell, *Rose State College*
Kathleen Collihan, *American River College*
Joe Corrado, *Clayton State University*
Vida Davoudi, *Lone Star College–Kingwood*
Julia Decker, *Texas State University–San Marcos*
William Delehanty, *Missouri Southern State University*
Jacqueline DeMerritt, *University of North Texas*
Kevin Dockerty, *Kalamazoo Valley Community College*
Cecil Dorsey, *San Jacinto College*
Walle Engedayehu, *Prairie View A&M University*
Matthew Eshbaugh-Soha, *University of North Texas*
Heather Evans, *Sam Houston State University*
Glen Findley, *Odessa College*
David Fistein, *Gulf Coast Community College*
John Forshee, *San Jacinto College*
Myrtle Freeman, *Tarrant County College–South*
Crystal Garrett, *Georgia Perimeter College*
Sandra Gieseler, *Palo Alto College*
Dana Glencross, *Oklahoma City Community College*
James Michael Greig, *University of North Texas*
Alexander Hogan, *Lone Star College–CyFair*
Richard Kiefer, *Waubonsee Community College*
Robert King, *Georgia Perimeter College–Dunwoody*
Melinda Kovacs, *Sam Houston State University*
Nancy Kral, *Lone Star College–Tomball*
Fred Lokken, *Truckee Meadows Community College*
Becky Lubbers, *Saint Clair County Community College*
Joseph Mancos, *Lenoir-Rhyne University*
Roger Marietta, *Darton College*
Vinette Meikle-Harris, *Houston Community College–Central*
Brooke Miller, *Middle Georgia State College*
Shea Mize, *Georgia Highlands College*
Fran Moran, *New Jersey City University*
Joseph Moskowitz, *New Jersey City University*

Yamini Munipalli, *Florida State College*
Kathleen Murnan, *Ozarks Technical Community College*
Martha Musgrove, *Tarrant County College–South*
Glynn Newman, *Eastfield College*
John Osterman, *San Jacinto College–Pasadena*
Cecil Larry Pool, *El Centro College*
Robert K. Postic, *University of Findlay*
Sean Reed, *Wharton County Junior College*
Shauna Reilly, *Northern Kentucky University*
Elizabeth Rexford, *Wharton County Junior College*
Sonja M. Siler, *Cuyahoga Community College*
Shyam Sriram, *Georgia Perimeter College*
Adam Stone, *Georgia Perimeter College*
Steve Tran, *Houston Community College*
Dennis Toombs, *San Jacinto College–North*
David Uranga, *Pasadena City College*
Ronald Vardy, *University of Houston–Houston*
Sarah Velasquez, *Fresno Community College*
Peter Wielhouwer, *Western Michigan University–Kalamazoo*
Robert Wilkes, *Atlanta Metropolitan State College*

American Government Symposia

Since 2006, McGraw Hill has conducted several symposia in American Government for instructors from across the country. These events offered a forum for instructors to exchange ideas and experiences with colleagues they might not have met otherwise. They also provided an opportunity for editors from McGraw Hill to gather information about what instructors of American Government need and the challenges they face. The feedback we have received has been invaluable and has contributed—directly and indirectly—to the development of *American Democracy Now*. We would like to thank the participants for their insights:

Melvin Aaron, *Los Angeles City College*
Yan Bai, *Grand Rapids Community College*
Leslie Baker, *Mississippi State University*
Evelyn Ballard, *Houston Community College*
Robert Ballinger, *South Texas College*
Nancy Bednar, *Antelope Valley College*
Jeffrey Birdsong, *Northeastern Oklahoma A&M College*
Madelyn Bowman, *Tarrant County College–South*

Amy Brandon, *San Jacinto College–North*

Jane Bryant, *John A. Logan College*

Dan R. Brown, *Southwestern Oklahoma State University*

Monique Bruner, *Rose State College*

Anita Chadha, *University of Houston–Downtown*

John Clark, *Western Michigan University–Kalamazoo*

Kathleen Collihan, *American River College*

Steven Collins, *Oklahoma State University–Oklahoma City*

Daphne Cooper, *Indian River State College, Central*

Andrew Crocker, *Ozarks Technical Community College*

John Davis, *Howard University*

Kevin Davis, *North Central Texas College*

Paul Davis, *Truckee Meadows Community College*

Vida Davoudi, *Lone Star College–Kingwood*

Robert De Luna, *Saint Philips College*

Jeff DeWitt, *Kennesaw State University*

Hien Do, *San Jose State University*

Kevin Dockerty, *Kalamazoo Valley Community College*

Cecil Dorsey, *San Jacinto College–South*

Jay Dow, *University of Missouri–Columbia*

Manar Elkhaldi, *University of Central Florida*

Emily Erdmann, *Blinn College, Bryan*

Henry Esparza, *University of Texas at San Antonio*

Karry Evans, *Austin Community College*

Jeffrey Ewen, *Ivy Technical Community College*

Kahlib Fischer, *Helms School of Government, Liberty University*

Marie Flint, *San Antonio College*

Reynaldo Flores, *Richland College*

Pearl Ford, *University of Arkansas–Fayetteville*

John Forshee, *San Jacinto College–Central*

Ben Riesner Fraser, *San Jacinto College*

Daniel Fuerstman, *Dutchess Community College*

Marilyn Gaar, *Johnson County Community College*

Jarvis T. Gamble, *Owens Community College*

Crystal Garrett, *Perimeter College at Georgia State University–Dunwoody*

Michael Gattis, *Gulf Coast Community College*

Patrick Gilbert, *Lone Star College–Tomball*

William Gillespie, *Kennesaw State University*

Dana K. Glencross, *Oklahoma City Community College*

Larry Gonzalez, *Houston Community College–Southwest*

Nirmal Goswami, *Texas A&M University–Kingsville*

Daniel Gutierrez, *El Paso Community College*

Richard Gutierrez, *University of Texas, El Paso*

Kenneth Gwyn, *Richland College*

Precious Hall, *Truckee Meadows Community College*

Michelle Kukoleca Hammes, *St. Cloud State University*

Cathy Hanks, *University of Nevada, Las Vegas*

Wanda Hill, *Tarrant County Community College*

Joseph Hinchliffe, *University of Illinois at Urbana–Champaign*

John Hitt, *North Lake College*

Mark Jendrysik, *University of North Dakota*

Brenda Jones, *Houston Community College–Central*

Franklin Jones, *Texas Southern University*

Lynn Jones, *Collin County Community College*

James Joseph, *Fresno City College*

Jason Kassel, *Valdosta State University*

Manoucher Khosrowshahi, *Tyler Junior College*

Rich Kiefer, *Waubonsee Community College*

Robert J. King, *Georgia Perimeter College*

Orin Kirshner, *Florida Atlantic University*

Melinda Kovacs, *Sam Houston State University*

Jordan Leising, *Tyler Junior College*

LaDella Levy, *College of Southern Nevada*

Chien-Pin Li, *Kennesaw State University*

Fred Lokken, *Truckee Meadows Community College*

Mary Louis, *Houston Community College*

Kenneth Mariano, *Rowan College at Burlington County*

Jan McCauley, *Tyler Junior College*

John Mercurio, *San Diego State University*

Janna Merrick, *University of South Florida*

Joe Meyer, *Los Angeles City College*

Eric Miller, *Blinn College*

Kent Miller, *Weatherford College*

Charles Moore, *Georgia State University*

Patrick Moore, *Richland College*

Eduardo Munoz, *El Camino College*

Kay Murnan, *Ozarks Technical Community College*

Carolyn Myers, *Southwestern Illinois College*

Sharon Navarro, *University of Texas at San Antonio*

Blaine Nelson, *El Paso Community College*

Theresa Nevarez, *El Paso Community College*

James A. Norris, *Texas A&M International University*

Mohsen Omar, *Northeast Lakeview College*

Kent Park, *U.S. Military Academy at West Point*

Sylvia Peregrino, *El Paso Community College*

Amy Perry, *Texas State University*

Andrea Peterson, *Chattahoochee Technical College*

Eric Rader, *Henry Ford Community College*

Elizabeth Rexford, *Wharton County Junior College*

Barbara Robertson, *Georgia State University*

Tara Ross, *Keiser University*

Carlos Rovelo, *Tarrant Community College–South*

Ryan Rynbrandt, *Collin County Community College*

Ray Sandoval, *Richland College*

Craig Scarpelli, *California State University–Chico*

Louis Schubert, *City College of San Francisco*

Edward Senu-Oke, *Joliet Junior College*

Mark Shomaker, *Blinn College*

Thomas Simpson, *Missouri Southern University*

Henry Sirgo, *McNeese State University*

Amy Smith, *North Lake College*

Daniel Smith, *Northwest Missouri State University*

John Speer, *Houston Community College–Southwest*

Jim Startin, *University of Texas at San Antonio*

Matt Stellges, *Blinn College, Bryan*

Sharon Sykora, *Slippery Rock University*

Tressa Tabares, *American River College*

Beatrice Talpos, *Wayne County Community College*
Alec Thomson, *Schoolcraft College*
Judy Tobler, *Northwest Arkansas Community College*
Steve Tran, *Houston Community College*
Beth Traxler, *Greenville Technical College*
William Turk, *University of Texas–Pan American*
Ron Vardy, *University of Houston*
Sarah Velasquez, *Fresno City College*
Ron VonBehren, *Valencia Community College–Osceola*
Albert C. Waite, *Central Texas College*
Natasha Washington, *Northwest Arkansas Community College*
Van Allen Wigginton, *San Jacinto College–Central*
Geoffrey Willbanks, *Tyler Junior College*
Charlotte Williams, *Pasadena City College*
Theodore Williams, *Kennedy-King College, City Colleges of Chicago*
Ike Wilson, *U.S. Military Academy*
Paul Wilson, *San Antonio College*
John Wood, *University of Central Oklahoma*
Robert Wood, *University of North Dakota*
Larry Wright, *Florida A&M University*
Ann Wyman, *Missouri Southern State University*
Kathryn Yates, *Richland College*

Personal Acknowledgments

We must thank our team at McGraw Hill: Katie Stevens, managing director; Jason Seitz, portfolio manager; Dawn Groundwater, product development manager; Michael Gedatus, marketing manager; Susan Messer, product developer; and David Tietz, photo researcher. We are extraordinarily grateful to all of you.

For their patience, understanding, and support, the authors also wish to thank: Paul Meilak; Caroline, Alexandra, and John Harrison; Rosemary Fitzgerald; Patricia Jillard; Kathleen Cain; Teresa Biebel; Thomas Callahan; Michael Harris; Audrey Wahl and the Wahl "girls"—Eileen Choynowski, Laura McAlpine, Audrey Messina, and Jaimee Conner; David Deardorff; Amy Donaldson; and Michael, Kelly, and Logan Donaldson, and Lauren Donaldson Block.

John and Rosemary Callahan, Jim and Audrey Wahl, and Earl and Fonda Donaldson first began the conversation of democracy with us, and we thank them and all of the students and colleagues, friends, and family members who continue that conversation now.

BRIGID CALLAHAN HARRISON
JEAN WAHL HARRIS
MICHELLE D. DEARDORFF

©Brigid Callahan Harrison   ©Eileen Notarianni   ©Jaimie Davis

From the Authors

Welcome to the seventh edition of *American Democracy Now*! In this program, we share our passion for politics while providing students with the foundation they need to become informed citizens in a rapidly changing democracy.

In creating the first edition of *American Democracy Now*, we merged our years of experience as classroom instructors and our desire to captivate students with the compelling story of their democracy into a student-centered program. We refined those goals with an integrated learning program for American government to maximize student performance in the second edition. The third edition revolutionized how we think about American democracy by incorporating for the first time a chapter on Politics and Technology, demonstrating the extent to which technology has become integral to how citizens participate in their democracy and how governments serve their citizenry. The fifth edition continued this tradition, tackling new ways in which technology is changing how politics happens—for both the good and the bad. In the sixth edition we sought to help students navigate the vast array of information that technology provides by strengthening their ability to evaluate information for accuracy. In this seventh edition, we write from the space of a "brave new world" of citizens who have faced a global pandemic. This catastrophe has altered how communication, information distribution, political participation, and governance take place for residents, citizens, voters, political leaders, and governments. And so, in this edition, we seek to help students evaluate which changes are temporary, which are permanent, and how they can use critical thinking skills to understand and navigate the new political context.

As technology has changed our polity, it has also transformed student learning. The seventh edition of *American Democracy Now* relies on technological advances to improve how we deliver information to students in a way that they can best understand, enjoy, and share our passion for political life. Informed by data garnered from tens of thousands of students, we have revised our program to ensure greater clarity in areas that have proven complex for past student readers. In this edition, we continue to integrate and highlight the increasing role technology is playing in politics. And we have continued our quest to create a student-centered program by examining how these students—in front of us in our classrooms, or in front of their computer screens—differ from previous generations of students. By meeting today's students where they are, then providing to them a framework that does not only explain the past and present of politics, we can ask them to think critically about the future: What's next for their democracy? In *American Democracy Now*, seventh edition, students learn how today's context, layered on the fundamental principles of American democracy, informs their understanding of politics and policies so they can think about the policies they would like to see take shape tomorrow. In short, they learn to inquire: How do *then* and *now* shape what's going to happen *next*? This "Then, Now, Next" approach to critical thinking serves as the basis for student participation.

As in previous editions, *American Democracy Now*, seventh edition, takes a broader, more contemporary view of participation than other programs. To us, participation encompasses a variety of activities from the modest, creative, local, or even personal actions students can take to the larger career choices they can make. And choosing how to participate makes American government matter.

Today's hyper-partisan politics and ever-changing technology provide challenges for those seeking to ensure that the rights guaranteed by the Constitution are protected, and they present opportunities for those striving to fulfill the responsibilities that come with living in a constitutional democracy. *American Democracy Now*, seventh edition, enables students to garner a solid understanding of the essential elements, institutions, and dynamics of national government and politics, while fostering critical thinking skills that are essential to meeting these novel challenges and realizing these new opportunities.

Facilitating success—as students, but also as citizens and participants—means honing their critical thinking skills, harnessing their energy, and creating tools that foster success in the American government course and in our polity. We know we have succeeded when students apply their knowledge and sharpened skills to consider the outcomes they—as students, citizens, and participants—would like to see.

Creating this success means joining increasingly diverse students where they are so that they can see the relevance of politics in their everyday lives. Instagram, YouTube, Snapchat, and Twitter are not only powerful social networking tools, but also powerful political and educational tools. New technologies help politicians to communicate with citizens, citizens to communicate with each other, and you to communicate with your students. The seventh edition of *American Democracy Now* further integrates technology into our students' study of politics so that their engagement with content is seamless.

We are excited to present you with the seventh edition of *American Democracy Now*, and we wish you and your students success.

BRIGID CALLAHAN HARRISON
JEAN WAHL HARRIS
MICHELLE D. DEARDORFF

BRIGID CALLAHAN HARRISON specializes in the civic engagement and political participation of Americans, especially the Millennial generation and Generation Z, the U.S. Congress, and the presidency. Brigid has taught American government for 25 years at Montclair State University in New Jersey. She takes particular pride in creating a learning experience in the classroom that shapes students' lifelong understanding of American politics, sharpens their critical thinking about American government, and encourages their participation in civic life. She enjoys supervising student internships in political campaigns and government and is a frequent commentator in print and electronic media on national and New Jersey politics. She is past president of the New Jersey Political Science Association and of the National Women's Caucus for Political Science. She received her B.A. from Stockton University; her M.A. from Rutgers, The State University of New Jersey; and her Ph.D. from Temple University. Harrison lives in Longport, New Jersey, with her husband, Paul Meilak, a retired New York City police detective. She has three children: Caroline (26), Alexandra (20), and John (18). Born and raised in New Jersey, Harrison is a fan of Bruce Springsteen and in her spare time, she enjoys reading on the beach, traveling, cycling, and binge-watching political thrillers on Netflix. Like her on Facebook at Brigid Callahan Harrison, and follow her on Twitter @BriCalHar.

JEAN WAHL HARRIS'S research interests include political socialization and engagement, federalism and intergovernmental relations, and the gendered nature and effects of U.S. politics. Jean has taught introductory courses in local, state, and national government and upper-level courses in public administration, public policy, and judicial politics for the Political Science Department at the University of Scranton for 33 years. She is also a founding mother and former director of the Women's & Gender Studies Program at the university. Since 2012, Jean has coordinated the university's Ready to Run Northeastern Pennsylvania program, which educates women about why it's important to have more women in government and how to run for office. In her academic career and her community service, Jean seeks to cultivate a high sense of political efficacy in everyone she encounters, empowering and inspiring them to engage in community, state, national, and/or international politics. Jean earned her B.A., M.A., and Ph.D. from the State University of New York at Binghamton. In 1994, the University of Scranton named her its CASE (Council for Advancement and Support of Education) professor of the year. She was an American Council on Education (ACE) Fellow during the 2007–2008 academic year. Jean lives in Nicholson, Pennsylvania, with her husband, Michael. She enjoys reading on her deck overlooking the Endless Mountains of Northeast Pennsylvania and the benefits of Michael's gardens.

MICHELLE D. DEARDORFF'S teaching and research focus on the constitutional and statutory protections surrounding gender, race, and religion. She particularly enjoys developing classes that allow students to apply their understandings of law, politics, and political theory to current events; she seeks to foster critical citizens prepared to participate in governing our communities and nation. Deardorff is currently head of Political Science and Public Service at the University of Tennessee at Chattanooga. Before coming to UTC, she spent 10 years teaching at Jackson State, a historically Black university in Mississippi, and another decade at Millikin University, a small private college in Illinois. She recently served on the Council of the American Political Science Association and is a founding faculty member of the Fannie Lou Hamer National Institute on Citizenship and Democracy, a coalition of academics who promote civic engagement and popular sovereignty through the study of the struggle for civil rights in the United States. She lives in Chattanooga with her husband, David, where they enjoy kayaking, hiking, live music, and reading in beautiful places.

AP CONTRIBUTOR REBECCA SMALL taught high school Advanced Placement Government & Politics for over twenty years, and was actively involved in the AP program as a member of the Test Development Committee, reader, and AP Summer Institute instructor. She is a published author of test preparation books, lesson plans and other resources for teachers. Rebecca earned a Doctorate of Education and Policy Studies from George Washington University in 2019 and currently serves as the High School Advanced Academics programs specialist for Fairfax County public schools where she supports AP instruction and professional development.

The Seventh Edition of *American Democracy Now* is dedicated to the memory of John P. Callahan and to those who lost their lives in the COVID-19 pandemic.

IN CONGRESS

timous Declaration of the thirteen

When in the course of human events, it becomes necessary for

to which the Laws of Nature and of N these tru

We the People

insure domestic Tranquility, provide for the co

and our Posterity, do ordain and establish this

Article 1.

FOUNDATIONS OF AMERICAN DEMOCRACY

The Constitution of the United States is over 200 years old and has remained the framework of our government. Throughout U.S history, debates over the proper role of government in our society have continued. Our first national government, under the Articles of Confederation, was so limited that some questioned whether it was a government at all. Because the Constitution provided mechanisms to strengthen the national government, it was initially viewed as too radical a document to ever be ratified, and opponents to the Constitution declared that national government powers under it dangerously threatened state sovereignty. Supporters of the Constitution argued that it was necessary to bring the nation out of the chaos that existed under the Articles of Confederation.

While arguments in the debate between supporters and opponents of the Constitution may sound extreme today in light of the Constitution's endurance, debates over the proper scope of federal power continue. In this AP U.S Government & Politics course, you will read the key arguments made by the framers of the Constitution at the time of its proposal, both in favor of the ratification of the Constitution (Federalist 10, 51) and against (Brutus 1). As you read these documents, consider the extent to which the debate over the power of central and state government persists today.

The U.S. Constitution established a federal system of government. Under the Articles of Confederation, the states were supreme, but under the Constitution, supremacy rests with the national government. As you will read in this unit, the balance of power between the national government and the state governments continues to shift over time. Shortly after the Constitution was ratified, the federal government gained power, but more recently, there has been a resurgence of state power. What examples do you find in this unit of increasing federal power over states? What examples do you find of state resurgence of power?

As an AP U.S. Government student, you will be reading several required Foundational Documents and Supreme Court cases. See the chart on the following page for the documents and court cases you will be introduced to in Unit I.

Required Foundational Document	Key Ideas
Declaration of Independence	What democratic ideals are reflected in the Declaration of Independence?
Articles of Confederation	What made the Articles of Confederation such a weak central government? Why were the founders motivated to make it so weak?
Federalist 10 & 51	What concerns about the new Constitution are presented, and how are those concerns answered? What are the strongest arguments made in favor of the new Constitution?
Brutus 1	What arguments against the Constitution are presented? To what extent did Brutus's concerns materialize when the Constitution was ratified?
The U.S. Constitution	How does the Constitution simultaneously protect majority rule and minority rights? Did the Constitution make the national government too powerful, as Brutus feared it would? What features of our Constitution enabled it to endure for 200 years?
McCulloch v. Maryland (1819)	In what ways did the ruling in this case make the national government more powerful?
U.S. v. Lopez (1995)	In what ways did this case cause a resurgence of state power?

What are the major components of the U.S. political system?

Big Ideas

Throughout this text, you will find rich examples to support these two AP Big Ideas:

- **A balance between government power and individual rights has been a hallmark of American political development,** *and*

- **The U.S. Constitution establishes a system of checks and balances among branches of government and allocates power between federal and state governments. This system is based on the rule of law and balance between majority rule and minority rights.**

As you read, consider the question: How has the balance of power between the national and state governments shifted over time, and what events have caused the shift? To answer these questions, you will need to have a clear understanding of the historical events and understand some commonly held conflicting beliefs about government, power, liberty, and equality that existed when the country was founded and remain today.

Representative democracies like the United States can take on several characteristics. In a *participatory democracy,* there is broad participation by individual citizens in the political process, while in a *pluralist democracy,* the most effective participation takes the form of group pressure. Finally, in an *elite democracy* there is limited participation from individual citizens, and a smaller number of elite groups and citizens control the political dialogue. Throughout your journey this school year, as you become a consumer of news and read this textbook, ask yourself: What form of democracy do I see? Is it the system I want? If not, what role might I play to facilitate change?

Skills and Practices

As you read through the following chapters, consider how the skills of description, analysis, comparison, and causation help you to make sense of the information. By the end of this unit, you should be able to answer questions such as:

- **What are the origins of federalism in the U.S?**

- **How was the Constitution written, and what were the major compromises that allowed it to be ratified?**

- **Compare and contrast the goals of the Federalists and Anti-Federalists.**

- **What is the social contract, and what is its role in the development of the American political system?**

- **Name two social contract theorists and discuss how their philosophies inform the political system in the United States today.**

- **What is political ideology, and how does it affect politics in the U.S?**

- **Provide examples of specific political ideologies and describe them.**

Chapter

1

People, Politics, and Participation

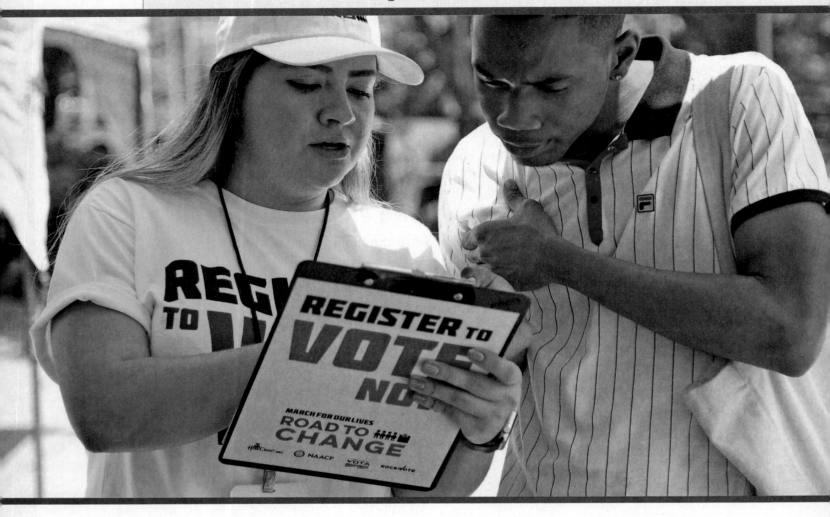

THEN

Cynicism, distrust, and apathy characterized Americans' relationship with their government for the past generation.

NOW

Polarization and anger characterize the segments of the American electorate, and mistrust is rampant. But new technologies and increasing participation among Millennials and Gen Z voters give some cause for optimism as the nation faces today's challenges, including recovery from a global pandemic as well as continued inequality and the threat of terrorism and violence.

NEXT

Will the present generation break the cycle of cynicism and, increasingly, anger that has pervaded the politics of the recent past?

Will new information technologies continue to facilitate and energize political participation?

Will our nation's increasing diversity continue to tear our nation apart or eventually create compassion, respect, and unity?

Annie Rice/AP Images

■ Chapter Introduction

As the COVID-19 epidemic raged in the United States in the summer of 2020, Americans remained divided about the role of government in containing the spread of the virus. While many Americans supported a requirement that people wear masks in public, citizens were divided about this requirement. Across the country, many governors, mayors, and top infectious disease experts urged Americans to wear masks in stores and other public spaces to contain the spread of the virus, but the nation was divided about both whether or not the government should require mask wearing and whether or not as individuals they should comply. The division in American society depends in part on attitudes about government power and individual choice, a common debate in American politics. For those opposed to a mask mandate, declining to wear a mask was a visible way to demonstrate individual personal liberties. For those who supported a mandate, wearing a mask was a way to protect the common good.

As stated in the Advanced Placement (AP) Curriculum and Exam Description (CED), *A balance between governmental power and individual rights has been a hallmark of American political development.* When considering this as you read Chapter 1, what examples do you find of the struggle to maintain a balance between liberty and order? While our democracy was founded on the ideas of limited government and individual liberty, in the context of containing an epidemic, it is a struggle for the government to maintain these values and protect the public good. In the AP U.S Government course, you will continue to return to this question of balancing liberty and order. As Big Idea 2 in the AP U.S. Government Course states, "Governmental laws and policies balancing order and liberty are based on the U.S. Constitution and have been interpreted differently over time."

Chapter 1 will provide you with an overview of our political system, including a discussion of common attitudes of our citizens and basic ideals of our democracy. You will learn about political culture in the United States, including the demographics of our population and common belief patterns. As you read, consider how our democratic ideals and population characteristics contribute to the ongoing political debate about the proper role of government in our nation.

Volurol/Shutterstock

y shd u stdy am dem now? Or, Why Should You Study American Democracy Now?

politics
The process of deciding who gets benefits in society and who does not.

Politics as practiced today is not your parents' brand of politics. **Politics**—the process of deciding who gets benefits in society and who does not—is a much different process today than it was even a decade ago. Advances in technology have altered the political landscape in many ways. In some countries, these advances have facilitated the overthrow of governments. In other countries, they are changing how voters and candidates communicate with each other, how governments provide information to individuals, how people get their news about events, and how governments administer laws. The political landscape has also changed because of world events.

How Technology Has Changed Politics

It would be difficult to overstate the influence of the technological revolution on politics as it is practiced today. During the COVID-19 epidemic, we saw firsthand how technology can be relied upon to track and provide information essential to our everyday lives. Even before the outbreak, however, it was common for the president to regularly rely on social media as a tool to communicate directly with the electorate. In this, the president is not alone.

Technology and Political Participation

THEN

(1970s)
50 percent of 18- to 29-year-olds voted in the 1976 presidential election.

People got their national news from nightly news broadcasts.

Many people participated in civic life, primarily through demonstrations, protests, and voting.

NOW

About 53 percent of 18- to 29-year-olds voted in the 2020 presidential election, breaking previous records.

People get their news from an array of sources, including Twitter feeds, Internet news services, and 24-hour news networks available on demand via computers and cell phones.

Internet activism is now main-stream: Online protests and petitions are commonplace, and social media groups have replaced many in-real-life (IRL) groups.

NEXT

- Will young voters continue to vote in record numbers?

- How might advancing media technologies further transform the ways that people consume their news?

- What new forms of civic participation will emerge?

In electoral politics, faster computers, the Internet, micro-targeting, and social media have revolutionized a process that, until the advent of the personal computer, the Internet, and cellular technology, was not very different in 1990 from the way it was carried out in 1890. Today, many voters get much of their information from Facebook, Twitter, and Internet-based news sites and blogs. Campaigns rely on e-mail and text messaging, and they use websites and social networking sites such as Instagram, Snapchat, Facebook, and Twitter to communicate with and organize supporters. State governments rely on computers to conduct elections, and cities use computers to provide services to their residents.

Because of these unprecedented shifts in the ways politics are conducted and how government is administered, Americans today face both new opportunities and new challenges. Evidence demonstrating Russia's efforts to influence the 2016 election using social media led many citizens to ask how we might use technology to ensure that elections are conducted fairly. How might the abundance and reach of media technology be directed toward informing and enriching us rather than overwhelming us or perpetuating the citizen cynicism of recent years? What privacy rights can we be sure of in the present digital age? Whatever your age, as a student, you are a member of one of the most tech-savvy groups in the country, and your input, expertise, and participation are vital to sorting out the opportunities and obstacles of this next stage of American democracy. Throughout this text, we examine the many ways in which people are using technology to link with each other and with the branches of government in an effort to influence those branches.

The Political Context Now

The political context today is defined by the aftermath of the COVID-19 virus, which caused massive loss of life across the globe, devastated people's livelihoods, upended economies, and in some cases, exacerbated already fraught political tensions. And while many Americans were thinking that their lives were hard, they were forcefully reminded that life is harder for some than for others as images of the murder of George Floyd, a black Minneapolis man, by a police officer went viral, sparking outrage and prompting protests throughout the country. Many people decried President Trump's response, which was to fan the tensions rather than to unify a struggling, wounded nation—one example of the growing questions about the role of the presidency moving forward. President Trump transformed this traditional institution into a thoroughly modern, if unpredictable, office. Gone are the days of well-crafted televised presidential addresses from the White House. Instead, during the Trump administration, Americans have grown accustomed to hearing their president speak for an hour during a daily press conference or a Fox News call-in program, or to reading, via Twitter, what was troubling the president the night before. Whether one views President Trump as hero or villain, for many the question is this: What's next for the institution of the presidency? Has Trump permanently transformed communication between the president and voters? Is his sidelining of the traditional apparatus that formulates foreign and domestic policy the new *modus operandi*? Or will future presidents embrace a more traditional view of the presidency and the policy-making bureaucracies of the executive branch?

Beyond the institution of the presidency, larger-scale debates about the appropriate role of government also dominate the political context today. As both the Republican and Democratic parties have felt more ideological pressure from their members, debate during the 2020 U.S elections centered on the role government should play in people's everyday lives. For example, should economic growth be fostered through tax cuts to corporations, in the hope that they will increase wages and create jobs, or should the federal government spend more money on services, like schools, that directly benefit people? Should the federal government create national standards for use of force by state and local police departments? Should the government take an aggressive role in tackling climate change, as promoted by proponents of the Green New Deal, or should it shy away completely from addressing climate change, as advocated by many conservatives who oppose increasing government regulations? Should the government create its own health care system and end private insurance, as advocated by those who want to see "Medicare for All," or should the reforms enacted during the Obama administration under the Affordable Care Act be repealed, lessening the federal government's role in health care?

Also part of the U.S. political context is a global environment characterized by uncertainty and instability on many fronts. Many Americans fear continuing Russian interference in U.S. elections, and some hold broader concerns about Russia's desire to increase its sphere of influence around the world. Uncertainty continues concerning North Korea and its nascent nuclear program. In the meantime, Trump administration policies regarding foreign trade—particularly with China—have led to unstable relationships between the United States and other nations, including China, but also with many countries traditionally thought of as U.S. allies.[1] These pressures continue within a global context that includes the threat of terrorism, often perpetrated by groups formed in the wake of the civil wars and political instability that arose in the Middle East after the retaliatory wars the United States fought in Afghanistan and Iraq following the September 11, 2001, terrorist attacks.

Americans' Efficacy

Since the early 1970s—a decade blemished by the intense unpopularity of the Vietnam War and by scandals that ushered in the resignation of President Richard Nixon in 1974—Americans' attitudes about government have been dismal.[2] Numerous surveys of the American public, including an ongoing Gallup poll, have demonstrated low levels of trust in government and of confidence in government's ability to solve problems. Today those levels have reached historically low numbers, with only 17 percent of Americans saying they trust the government to do what's right always or most of the time.[3] Young people's views have mirrored those of the nation as a whole.[4] Lack of **efficacy**, which is a person's belief that he or she has the ability to achieve something desirable and that the government genuinely listens to individuals, is prevalent among young people.

efficacy
Citizens' belief that they have the ability to achieve something desirable and that the government listens to people like them.

These attitudes are expressed through one of the most easily measured contexts: vote choice. Figure 1.1 shows that if the 2020 election were held only among young people, it would have been a Joe Biden landslide. Historically, majorities of young Americans typically have supported Democratic candidates for president, especially Barack Obama, whose 2008 candidacy generated record turnout and support among young Americans. Research shows that young voters are much more likely to participate when states have laws that encourage early voting and allow people to vote by mail, methods students attending college often use. The widespread use of those methods in 2020 because of COVID-19 meant a historic uptick in youth voter participation.

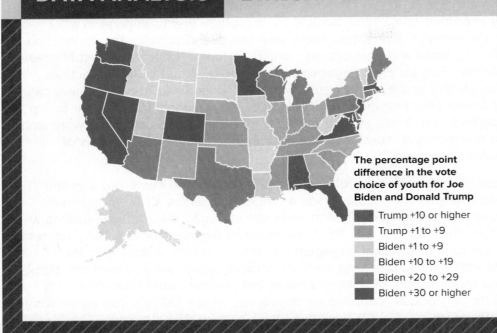

The percentage point difference in the vote choice of youth for Joe Biden and Donald Trump

- Trump +10 or higher
- Trump +1 to +9
- Biden +1 to +9
- Biden +10 to +19
- Biden +20 to +29
- Biden +30 or higher

FIGURE 1.1 ▪ **Youth Vote Choice in the 2020 Presidential Election** In the 2020 election, young voters overwhelmingly supported Joe Biden. What are the implications for future elections?

Source: Tufts University, Tisch College, CIRCLE.

Despite the complexity of the youth vote issue, there remain lingering media characterizations of a cynical, nonparticipatory youth electorate. But evidence indicates that many young people are actually enthusiastic participants in civic and political life.[5] Others are taking part in ways that have not traditionally been thought of, and measured as, participation, including Internet activism and using one's power as a consumer to send political messages. For many students, that foundation of political participation, volunteerism, or community action has already provided them with a rationale for increasing their knowledge of, and participation in, their communities.

Individuals who engage in politics and civic life experience many benefits. Engaged citizens are knowledgeable about public issues; actively communicate with policy-makers and others; press government officials to carry out the people's will; advocate for their own self-interest and the interests of others; and hold public officials accountable for their decisions and actions. You will find that advocating for your own interests or working with others in similar situations sometimes (perhaps to your surprise) leads to desired outcomes. This is efficacy in action. And you will discover that with experience you will become more effective at advocacy—the more you do, the better you get. Furthermore, you will derive social and psychological benefits from being civically engaged.

In addition, and equally important, local communities, states, and the nation benefit from an engaged populace. Governments are more effective when people voice their views. As we will see as we explore *American Democracy Now*, today's citizens and others have more opportunities to influence governmental action than at any other time in history.

Civic Engagement: Acting on Your Views

civic engagement
Individual and collective actions designed to identify and address issues of public concern.

One vitally important goal of this book is to encourage you to engage in a respectful, continuing conversation about your views and to make the connection between having ideas and opinions and acting on them. Political scientist Michael Delli Carpini has defined **civic engagement** as individual and collective actions designed to identify and address issues of public concern. Civic engagement can take many forms, from individual voluntarism to organizational involvement to electoral participation. It can include efforts to directly address an issue, work with others in a community to solve a problem, or interact with the institutions of representative democracy.[6]

political engagement
Citizen actions that are intended to solve public problems through political means.

The possibilities for citizen involvement are so broad and numerous that the idea of civic engagement encompasses a range of activities. Civic engagement might include everything from tutoring an underprivileged child to volunteering at a conservative think tank. In this book, we focus in particular on civic engagement that takes the form of **political engagement**—that is, citizen actions that are intended to solve public problems through political means. As you read this book, you will find that a variety of political actions are possible, from boycotting and *buycotting* (buying goods produced by companies whose policies you agree with) to running for office.

We hope that this book not only empowers you by teaching you about the institutions, policies, and processes of government but also inspires you to become civically and politically engaged. Today, many students stick their toes into the waters of political activism by using the Internet—by following an elected official on Instagram, for example. You have many ways of taking part in your democracy—by following a group on the Internet that's advocating for an issue you care about, organizing a fund-raising event, signing an e-petition, joining a volunteer group, volunteering for a campaign, or even participating in a protest march, to name just a few of the many options. Consider which potential volunteer activities pique your interest. Think about what might best suit your schedule, lifestyle, and personal and professional goals. By taking part, you will ensure that your voice is heard, and you will derive the satisfaction of knowing that your community and the nation benefit from your actions as well.

government
The institution that creates and implements policy and laws that guide the conduct of the nation and its citizens.

What Government Does

citizens
Members of the polity who, through birth or naturalization, enjoy the rights, privileges, and responsibilities attached to membership in a given nation.

In this section, we look at the nature of government and the functions a government performs. **Government** is an institution that creates and implements the policy and laws that guide the conduct of a nation and its citizens. **Citizens** are those members of a political community—town, city, state, or country—who, through birth or naturalization, enjoy the rights, privileges, and responsibilities attached to membership in a given nation. **Naturalization** is the process of becoming a citizen by means other than birth, as in the case of immigrants. Although governments vary widely in how well they perform, most national governments share some common functions.

naturalization
The process of becoming a citizen by means other than birth, as in the case of immigrants.

Facts Matter

Published by *The New York Times,* the Pentagon Papers demonstrated that successive presidents had "systematically lied, not only to the public but also to Congress" between 1945 and 1967. The Pentagon Papers caused a huge controversy at the time and undermined the confidence of the American people in their government, generally, and in the presidency, specifically. Since then, it seems that Americans have more to worry about than their government lying to them. Thanks to the Internet, information is abundant but often unreliable. And increasingly, those who disseminate misinformation appear to be doing so as a political tactic, a strategy made particularly effective with the advent of social media.

CONSIDER:

- During the 2019–2020 impeachment process, President Trump and many Republican allies continued to restate a debunked conspiracy theory that Ukraine interfered in the 2016 election, despite the fact that the entire U.S. intelligence community has found no evidence to support that claim.*

- During impassioned opposition to the U.S. policy of separating families attempting to cross into the United States over the border with Mexico, some Democrats tweeted out photos of children in steel cages. Some sources claimed that these were old photos and not related to Trump administration policy.

EVALUATE:

- *Tier One—Gut Check:* Using common sense, ask yourself: Is the information consistent with what I already know about the subject? Is the claim outlandish or implausible? Red flags for fake news include a multitude of exclamation marks, misspelled words, headlines in all capital letters, or claims of "Not a Hoax!"

- *Tier Two—Credibility Check:* Is the information current? Is the material copyrighted (typically indicated after the headline or at the bottom of a news story)? Is the website a legitimate one? Beware of slight adaptations of the URLs of traditional news outlets, and consult the Snopes list of fake news sites.

- *Tier Three—Accuracy Check:* Can the information be independently verified or corroborated? Look to see if multiple sources are independently reporting similar versions of events. Do sources contain links to verifiable data sources, independent accounts of events, or other verifying statements?

*https://www.cnn.com/2019/12/02/politics/senate-intelligence-ukraine-2016-election

>> Naturalized citizens are those members of a country who have become citizens by means other than birth, as in the case of immigrants. Naturalized citizens enjoy the rights, privileges, and responsibilities attached to membership in a given nation. What does the image here say about naturalized citizens in the United States? How might opponents of immigration portray naturalization differently?

Mario Tama/Getty Images

To get a clear sense of the business of government, consider the following key functions performed by government in the United States and many other nations:

- **To protect their sovereign territory and their citizenry and to provide national defense.** Governments protect their *sovereign territory* (that is, the territory over which they have the ultimate governing authority) and their citizens at home and abroad. Usually they carry out this responsibility by maintaining one or more types of armed services, but governments also provide for the national defense through counterterrorism efforts.

    In the United States, the armed services include the Army, Navy, Marines, Air Force, and Coast Guard. Governments also preserve order domestically. In the United States, domestic order is preserved through the National Guard and federal, state, and local law enforcement agencies.

- **To preserve order and stability.** Governments also preserve order by providing emergency services and security in the wake of disasters. Governments also maintain stability by providing a political structure that has **legitimacy**: a quality conferred on government by citizens who believe that its exercise of power is right and proper.[7]

- **To establish and maintain a legal system.** Governments create legal structures by enacting and enforcing laws that restrict or ban certain behaviors. In the United States, the foundation of this legal structure is the federal Constitution.[8] Governments also provide the means to implement laws through the actions of local police and other state and national law enforcement agencies. By means of the court system, governments administer justice and impose penalties.

- **To provide services.** Governments distribute a wide variety of services to their citizens. In the United States, government agencies provide services ranging from inspecting the meat we consume to ensuring the safety of our workplaces. Federal, state, and local governments provide roads, bridges, transportation, education, and health services. They facilitate communication, commerce, air travel, and entertainment.

    Many of the services governments provide are called **public goods** because their benefits, by their nature, cannot be limited to specific groups or individuals. For example, everyone enjoys national defense, equal access to clean air and clean water, airport security, highways, and other similar services. Because the benefits of these goods are extended to everyone, they are available through revenue collected by taxes.

- **To raise and spend money.** All the services that governments provide, from national protection and defense to health care, cost money.[9] Governments

legitimacy
A quality conferred on government by citizens who believe that its exercise of power is right and proper.

public goods
Goods whose benefits cannot be limited and that are available to all.

>> Children are socialized in the dominant political culture from a very early age. When children emulate police officers, for example, they begin the process of learning about the functions governments perform.

Huntstock/age fotostock

at all levels spend money collected through taxes. Depending on personal income, between 25 and 35 cents of every dollar earned by those working in the United States and earning above a certain level goes toward federal, state, and local income taxes. Governments also tax *commodities* (commercially exchanged goods and services) in various ways—through sales taxes, property taxes, "sin" taxes, and luxury taxes.

- **To socialize new generations.** Governments play a role in *socialization*, the process by which individuals develop their political values and opinions. Governments perform this function by, for example, providing funding for schools, establishing standards for curriculum, introducing young people to the various "faces" of government (perhaps through a police officer's visiting a school or a mayor's bestowing an honor on a student), and facilitating participation in civic life through institutions like libraries, museums, and public parks. In these ways, governments transmit cultural norms and values, such as patriotism, and build commitment to fundamental values, such as those we explore later in this chapter. For a detailed discussion of political socialization, see Chapter 10.

▌ Types of Government

When social scientists categorize the systems of government operating in the world today, two factors influence their classifications. The first factor is *who participates in governing or in selecting those who govern*. These participants vary as follows, depending on whether the government is a monarchy, an oligarchy, or a democracy:

- In a **monarchy**, a member of a royal family, usually a king or a queen, has absolute authority over a territory and its government. Monarchies typically are inherited—they pass down from generation to generation. Most modern monarchies, such as those in Great Britain and Spain, are *constitutional monarchies*, in which the monarch plays a ceremonial role but has little say in governance, which is carried out by elected leaders. In contrast, in traditional monarchies, such as the Kingdom of Saudi Arabia, the monarch is both the ceremonial and the governmental head of state.

monarchy
Government in which a member of a royal family, usually a king or queen, has absolute authority over a territory and its government.

oligarchy
Government in which an elite few hold power.

democracy
Government in which supreme power of governance lies in the hands of its citizens.

totalitarianism
System of government in which the government essentially controls every aspect of people's lives.

authoritarianism
System of government in which the government holds strong powers but is checked by some forces.

constitutionalism
Government that is structured by law, and in which the power of government is limited.

limited government
Government that is restricted in what it can do so that the rights of the people are protected.

- In an **oligarchy**, an elite few hold power. Some oligarchies are *dictatorships*, in which a small group, such as a political party or a military junta, supports a dictator. North Korea is a present-day example of an oligarchy.

- In a **democracy**, the supreme power of governance lies in the hands of citizens. The United States and most other modern democracies are *republics*, sometimes called *representative democracies*, in which citizens elect leaders to represent their views. We discuss the republic form of government in Chapter 2.

When classifying governments, social scientists also consider *how governments function* and *how they are structured*:

- Governments that rule according to the principles of **totalitarianism** essentially control every aspect of their citizens' lives. In these tyrannical governments, citizens enjoy neither rights nor freedoms, and the state is the tool of the dictator. Totalitarian regimes tend to center on a particular ideology, religion, or personality. North Korea is a contemporary example of a totalitarian regime.

- When a government rules by the principles of **authoritarianism**, it holds strong powers, but they are checked by other forces within the society. China and Cuba are examples of authoritarian states, because their leaders are restrained in their exercise of power by political parties, constitutions, and the military. Individuals living under an authoritarian regime may enjoy some rights, but often those rights are not protected by the government.

- **Constitutionalism**, a form of government structured by law, provides for **limited government**—a government that is restricted in what it can do so that the rights of the people are protected. Constitutional governments can be democracies or monarchies. In the United States, the federal Constitution created the governmental structure, and this system of government reflects both the historical experiences and the norms and values of the founders.

The Constitution's framers (authors) structured American government as a *constitutional democracy*. In this type of government, a constitution creates a representative democracy in which the rights of the people are protected. We can trace the roots of this modern constitutional democracy back to ancient times.

■ The Origins of American Democracy

The ancient Greeks first developed the concept of a democracy. The Greeks used the term *demokratia* (literally, "people power") to describe some of the 1,500 *poleis* ("city-states"; also the root of *politics*) on the Black and the Mediterranean Seas. These city-states were not democracies in the modern sense of the term, but the way they were governed provided the philosophical origins of American democracy. For example, citizens decided public issues using majority rule in many of the city-states. However, in contrast to modern democracies, the Greek city-states did not count women as citizens. The Greeks also did not count enslaved people as citizens. American democracy also traces some of its roots to the Judeo-Christian tradition and English common law, particularly the ideas that thrived during the Protestant Reformation.[10]

Democracy's Origins in Popular Protest: The Influence of the Reformation and the Enlightenment

We can trace the seeds of the idea of modern democracy almost as far back as the concept of monarchy—back to several centuries ago, when the kings and emperors who ruled in Europe claimed that they reigned by divine sanction, or God's will. The monarchs' claims reflected the political theory of the **divine right of kings**, articulated by Jacques-Benigne Bossuet (1627–1704), who argued that monarchies, as a manifestation of God's will, could rule absolutely without regard to the will or well-being of their subjects. Challenging the right of a monarch to govern or questioning one of his or her decisions thus represented a challenge to the will of God.

divine right of kings
The assertion that monarchies, as a manifestation of God's will, could rule absolutely without regard to the will or well-being of their subjects.

At odds with the theory of the divine right of kings was the idea that people could challenge the Crown and the church—institutions that seemed all-powerful. This idea took hold during the Protestant Reformation, a movement to reform the Catholic Church. In October 1517, Martin Luther, a German monk who would later found the Lutheran Church, affixed his *95 Theses*, criticizing the harmful practices of the Catholic Church, to a door of a church at Wittenberg Castle. The Reformation continued throughout the sixteenth century, during which time reform-minded Protestants (whose name is derived from *protest*) challenged basic tenets of Catholicism and sought to *purify* the church.

In England, some extreme Protestants, known as Puritans, thought that the Reformation had not gone far enough in reforming the church. Puritans asserted their right to communicate directly with God through prayer rather than through an intermediary such as a priest. This idea that an individual could speak directly with God lent support to the notion that the people could govern themselves. Faced with persecution in England, congregations of Puritans, known to us today as the Pilgrims, fled to America, where they established self-governing colonies, a radical notion at the time. Before the Pilgrims reached shore in 1620, they drew up the Mayflower Compact, an example of a **social contract**—an agreement between people and their leaders, whereby the people give up some liberties so that their other liberties will be protected. In the Mayflower Compact, the Pilgrims

social contract
An agreement between people and their leaders in which the people agree to give up some liberties so that their other liberties are protected.

≫ In his scientific work, Sir Isaac Newton demonstrated the power of science to explain phenomena in the natural world and discredited prevalent ideas based on magic and superstition. Newton's ideas laid the foundation for the political philosophers of the Enlightenment.

Pixtal/age fotostock

agreed to be governed by the structure of government they formed, thereby establishing the idea of consent of the governed.

In the late seventeenth century came the early beginnings of the Enlightenment, a philosophical movement that stressed the importance of individuality, reason, and scientific endeavor. Enlightenment scientists such as Sir Isaac Newton (1642–1727) drastically changed how people thought about the universe and the world around them, including government. Newton's work in physics, astronomy, math, and mechanics demonstrated the power of science and repudiated prevalent ideas based on magic and superstition. Newton's ideas about **natural law**, the assertion that the laws that govern human behavior are derived from the nature of humans themselves and can be applied universally, laid the foundation for the ideas of the political philosophers of the Enlightenment.

natural law
The assertion that standards that govern human behavior are derived from the nature of humans themselves and can be applied universally.

The Modern Political Philosophy of Hobbes and Locke

The difficulty of individual survival under the rule of an absolute monarch is portrayed in British philosopher Thomas Hobbes's book *Leviathan* (1651). Hobbes (1588–1679), who believed in the righteousness of absolute monarchies, argued that the strong naturally prey on the weak and that through a social contract, individuals who relinquish their rights can enjoy the protection offered by a sovereign. Without such a social contract and without an absolute monarch, Hobbes asserted, anarchy prevails, describing this state as one lived in "continuall feare, and danger of violent death; And the life of man, solitary, poore, nasty, brutish, and short."[11]

John Locke (1632–1704) took Hobbes's reasoning concerning a social contract one step further. In the first of his *Two Treatises on Civil Government* (1689), Locke systematically rejected the notion that the rationale for the divine right of kings is based on scripture. By providing a theoretical basis for discarding the idea of a monarch's divine right to rule, Locke paved the way for more radical notions about the rights of individuals and the role of government. In the second *Treatise*, Locke argued that individuals possess certain unalienable (or natural) rights, which he identified as the rights to life, liberty, and property, ideas that would prove pivotal in shaping Thomas Jefferson's articulation of the role of government and the rights of individuals found in the Declaration of Independence. Locke, and later Jefferson, stressed that these rights are inherent in people as individuals; that is, government can neither bestow them nor take them away. When people enter into a social contract, Locke said, they do so with the understanding that the government will protect their natural rights. At the same time, according to Locke, they agree to accept the government's authority; but if the government fails to protect the inherent rights of individuals, the people have the right to rebel.

popular sovereignty
The theory that government is created by the people and depends on the people for the authority to rule.

social contract theory
The idea that individuals possess free will, and every individual is equally endowed with the God-given right of self-determination and the ability to consent to be governed.

The French philosopher Jean-Jacques Rousseau (1712–1778) took Locke's notion further, stating that governments formed by social contract rely on **popular sovereignty**, the theory that government is created by the people and depends on the people for the authority to rule. **Social contract theory**, which assumes that individuals possess free will and that every individual possesses the God-given right of self-determination and the ability to consent to be governed, would eventually form the theoretical framework of the Declaration of Independence.

The Creation of the United States as an Experiment in Representative Democracy

The American colonists who eventually rebelled against Great Britain and who became the citizens of the first 13 states were shaped by their experiences of living under European monarchies. Many rejected the ideas of absolute rule and the divine right of kings, which had been central to rationalizing the monarchs' authority. The logic behind the rejection of the divine right of kings was that people could govern themselves.

In New England, where many colonists settled after fleeing England to escape religious persecution, a form of **direct democracy**, sometimes called a *participatory democracy,* a structure of government in which citizens discuss and decide policy through majority rule, emerged in *town meetings* (which still take place today). In every colony, the colonists themselves decided who was eligible to participate in government, and so in some localities, women and people of color who owned property participated in government well before they were granted formal voting rights under amendments to the federal Constitution.

direct democracy
A structure of government in which citizens discuss and decide policy through majority rule.

Beyond the forms of direct democracy prevalent in the New England colonies, nearly all the American colonies had councils structured according to the principle of representative democracy, sometimes called **indirect democracy**, in which citizens elect representatives who decide policies on their behalf. These representative democracies foreshadow important political values that founders such as Thomas Jefferson and James Madison would incorporate into key founding documents, including the Declaration of Independence and the Constitution.

indirect democracy
Sometimes called a *representative democracy,* a system in which citizens elect representatives who decide policies on behalf of their constituents.

■ Political Culture and American Values

American democracy rests on a set of ideals rooted in the founding of our republic—concepts of liberty, freedom, and equality that were born of the Enlightenment. These and other core values—capitalism; consent of the governed; and the importance of the individual, family, and community—shape our beliefs about government and inform our views as we react and reconsider our values and beliefs in our dynamic, rapidly changing society. While the importance we place on certain ideals may ebb and flow—for example, in an age of terrorism, some might consider security more important than liberty—their underpinnings remain constant. These ideals are part of American **political culture**—the people's collective beliefs and attitudes about government and the political process. Individuals' differing perception of these core values—and how they weigh the importance of each— affects not only the relationship citizens have with their federal government but also the relationship they have with each other. Indeed, much of the political division seen in recent times in the United States lies in individuals' differing concepts of our core values and the relative importance of these values.

political culture
The people's collective beliefs and attitudes about government and political processes.

Liberty

The most essential quality of American democracy, **liberty** is both freedom from government interference in our lives (limited government) and freedom to pursue happiness. Many of the colonies that eventually became the United States were

liberty
The most essential quality of American democracy; it is both the freedom from governmental interference in citizens' lives and the freedom to pursue happiness.

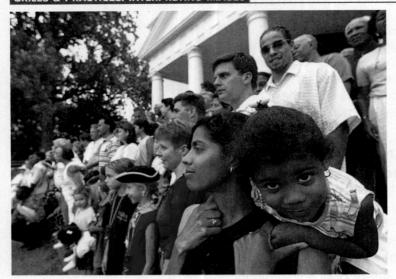

>> Thomas Jefferson's ideas about the role of government shaped the United States for generations to come. In 2008, descendants of Thomas Jefferson, including those he fathered with Sally Hemings, his wife's half-sister whom he enslaved, posed for a group photo at his plantation, Monticello, in Charlottesville, Virginia. How does the inclusion of the Hemings descendants change our perspective about the founding of the United States?

Paul J. Richards/AFP/Getty Images

founded by people who were interested in one notion of liberty: religious freedom. Those who fought in the War for Independence were intent on obtaining economic and political freedom. The framers of the Constitution added to the structure of the U.S. government many other liberties,[12] including freedom of speech, freedom of the press, and freedom of association.[13]

Throughout history and to the present day, liberties have often conflicted with efforts by the government to ensure a secure and stable society by exerting restraints on liberties. When government officials infringe on personal liberties, they often do so in the name of security, arguing that such measures are necessary to protect the rights of other individuals, institutions (including the government itself), or society as a whole. Such was the case when it was revealed that the National Security Agency had recorded information about 125 million cell phone communications in a 30-day period in 2013, including 3 million communications originating in the United States.

The meaning of liberty—how we define our freedoms—is constantly evolving. Today, technological innovation prompts new questions about individual privacy, including what information the government should be privy to. Should the government be permitted to collect metadata—data about communications data (the length of calls, for example)—of members of suspected terrorist cells? Should government officials be able to monitor phone calls and text messages to individuals in these cells? What if that person is suspected of plotting a terrorist attack—should officers be required to obtain a warrant first in that situation? Should law enforcement officers be allowed to track a person's movements using GPS (a global positioning system) if that person is suspected of a crime? Or should they be required to get a warrant first? What if one of the suspected plotters is not a U.S. citizen?

Equality

The Declaration of Independence states that "all men are created equal. . . ." But the founders' notions of equality were vastly different from those that prevail today. Their ideas of equality evolved from the emphasis the ancient Greeks placed on equality of opportunity. The Greeks envisioned a merit-based system in which educated freemen could participate in democratic government rather than inheriting their positions as a birthright. The Judeo-Christian religions also emphasize the idea of equality. All three major world religions—Christianity, Judaism, and Islam—stress that all people are equal in the eyes of God. These notions of equality informed both Jefferson's assertions about equality in the Declaration of Independence and, later, the framers' structuring of the U.S. government in the Constitution.[14]

The idea of equality evolved during the 19th and 20th centuries. In the early American republic, all women, as well as all men of color, were denied fundamental rights, including the right to vote. Through long, painful struggles—including the abolition movement to free enslaved people; the suffrage movement to gain women the right to vote; various immigrants' rights movements; and later the civil rights, Native American rights, and women's rights movements of the 1960s and 1970s (Chapter 5)—members of these disenfranchised groups won the rights previously denied to them. Several groups are still engaged in the struggle for legal equality today, notably those that advocate for equality in the criminal justice and legal systems, including groups that fight for reform of police procedures geared at reducing the number of cases of the use of excessive force, and those that advocate for the rights of transgender, bisexual, gay, and lesbian individuals, and of immigrants.

Beyond these questions of legal equality, today many arguments focus on issues of economic equality, a concept about which there is substantial disagreement. Many people in the United States believe that the government should do more to eliminate disparities in wealth—by taxing wealthy people more heavily than others, for example, or by providing more subsidies and services to the poor. Others disagree, however, and argue that although people should have equal opportunities for economic achievement, their attainment of that success should depend on factors such as education and hard work, and that success should be determined in the marketplace rather than through government intervention.

Capitalism

Although the founders valued the notion of equality, capitalism was enormously important to them. **Capitalism** is an economic system in which the means of producing wealth are privately owned and operated to produce profits. In a pure capitalist economy, the marketplace determines the regulation of production, the distribution of goods and services, wages, and prices. In this type of economy, for example, businesses pay employees the wage that they are willing to work for, without the government setting a minimum wage by law. Although capitalism is an important value in American democracy, the U.S. government does impose certain regulations on the economy. For example, it mandates a minimum wage, regulates and inspects goods and services, and imposes tariffs on imports and taxes on domestically produced goods that have an impact on pricing.

capitalism
An economic system in which the means of producing wealth are privately owned and operated to produce profits.

One key component of capitalism is **property**—anything that can be owned. There are various kinds of property: businesses, homes, farms, the material items we use every day, and even ideas are considered property. Property holds such a prominent position in American culture that it is considered a natural right, and the Constitution protects some aspects of property ownership.

property
Anything that can be owned.

What Is the Proper Role of Our Levels of Government During a Pandemic?

Which level of government is responsible for each type of COVID-19 response?

	Federal Government	State Governments
Guidelines for vulnerable populations	✓	
Housing assistance/ eviction moratorium		✓
Economic stimulus	✓	
School reopening		✓
Maintaining food safety	✓	
Election safety and types of voting available		✓

THE ISSUE: The COVID-19 pandemic dramatically altered life for all Americans. The national and state governments struggled with how to coordinate to contain the pandemic. The U.S. Constitution does not explicitly require the federal government to play a role in disease control. However, due to the spending clause of the Constitution, the federal government can leverage state policy through withholding of funding. The framers of the Constitution valued limited government power. National and state governments are often at odds on how to approach solving a problem, and there are frequent conflicts between Congress and the president on policy. Our decentralized system makes a coordinated response extremely difficult.

Practice Analytical Thinking: Concept Application

A. Based on your understanding of the Constitution, describe a power the president could use to address the impasse outlined in the scenario.

B. In the context of the scenario, explain how the use of presidential power in Part A can be affected by its interaction with Congress.

C. In the context of the scenario, explain how the interaction between Congress and the presidency can be affected by citizen pressure.

WHAT DO YOU THINK?

1. Which level of government should decide each of the following policies during a pandemic? Explain your response.

  a. Coordinate overall containment efforts

  b. Regulate mask wearing in public

  c. Fund testing

  d. Fund personal protective equipment (PPE) for health care workers

2. What should the penalty be for a citizen who does not obey a law to wear a mask in public?

3. How can states and the federal government cooperate in the overall effort to contain the virus?

Consent of the Governed

The idea that, in a democracy, the government's power derives from the consent of the people is called the **consent of the governed**. As we have seen, this concept, a focal point of the rebellious American colonists and eloquently expressed in Jefferson's Declaration of Independence, is based on John Locke's idea of a social contract. Implicit in Locke's social contract is the principle that the people agree to the government's authority, and if the government no longer has the consent of the governed, the people have the right to revolt.

The concept of consent of the governed also implies **majority rule**—the principle that, in a democracy, only policies with 50 percent plus one vote are enacted. Governments based on majority rule include the idea that the majority has the right of self-governance and typically also protect the rights of people in the minority. A particular question about this ideal of governing by the consent of the governed has important implications for the United States in the early 21st century: Can a democracy remain stable and legitimate if less than a majority of its citizens participate in elections?

consent of the governed
The idea that in a democracy, the government's power derives from the consent of the people.

majority rule
The idea that in a democracy, only policies with 50 percent plus one vote are enacted, and only candidates that win 50 percent plus one vote are elected.

Individual, Family, and Community

Emphasis on the individual is a preeminent feature of American democratic thought. In the Constitution, rights are bestowed on, and exercised by, the individual. The importance of the individual—an independent, hearty entity exercising self-determination—has powerfully shaped the development of the United States, both geographically and politically.

Family and community have also played central roles in the U.S. political culture, both historically and in the present day. Children first learn political behavior from their families, and in this way the family serves to perpetuate the political culture. From the earliest colonial settlements to Snapchat today, communities have channeled individuals' political participation. Indeed, the intimate relationship between individualism and community life is reflected in the First Amendment of the Constitution, which ensures individuals' freedom of assembly—one component of which is their right to form or join any type of organization, political party, or club without penalty.

▌ Ideology: A Prism for Viewing American Democracy

Besides focusing on the demographic characteristics of the U.S. population, we can also analyze political events and trends by looking at them through the prism of ideology. **Political ideology** is an integrated system of ideas or beliefs about political values in general and the role of government in particular. Political ideology provides a framework for thinking about politics, policy issues, and the role of government in society. In the United States, one key component of various ideologies is the *extent* to which adherents believe that the government should have a role in people's everyday lives. Table 1.1 summarizes the key ideologies we consider in this section.

political ideology
An integrated system of ideas or beliefs about political values in general and the role of government in particular.

Liberalism

Modern **liberalism** in the United States is associated with the ideas of liberty and political equality. Its advocates favor change in the social, political, and economic realms to better protect the well-being of individuals and to produce equality within society. They emphasize the importance of civil liberties, including freedom of speech, assembly, and the press, as outlined in the Bill of Rights. Modern liberals also advocate the separation of church and state, often opposing measures that bring religion into the public realm, such as prayer in the public schools. In addition, they support political equality, advocating contemporary movements that promote the political rights of such groups as gay and lesbian couples and voting rights for the disenfranchised.

TABLE 1.1 ▪ The Traditional Ideological Spectrum

	Socialism	Liberalism	Middle of Road (Moderate)	Conservatism	Libertarianism
Goal of Government	Equality	Equality of opportunity; protection of fundamental liberties	Nondiscrimination in opportunity; protection of some economic freedoms; security; stability	Traditional values; order; stability; economic freedom	Absolute economic and social freedom
Role of Government	Strong government control of economy	Government action to promote opportunity	Government action to balance the wants of workers and businesses; government fosters stability	Government action to protect and bolster the capitalist system; few limitations on fundamental rights	No governmental regulations of economy; no limitations on fundamental rights

The historical roots of modern liberalism reach back to the ideals of classical liberalism: freedom of thought and the free exchange of ideas, limited governmental authority, the consent of the governed, the rule of law in society, the importance of an unfettered market economy, individual initiative as a determinant of success, and access to free public education. These also were some of the founding ideals that shaped American democracy as articulated in the Declaration of Independence and the Constitution.

Modern liberalism, which emerged in the early 20th century, diverged from its classical roots in a number of ways. Most important, modern liberals expect the government to play a more active role in ensuring political equality and economic opportunity. Whereas classical liberals emphasized the virtues of a free market economy, modern liberals, particularly after the Great Depression that began in 1929, advocated government involvement in economic affairs. Today, we see this expectation in action when liberals call for prioritizing economic policies that benefit the poor and middle class, including job creation and tax policies. In

A Nation Divided?

The table below shows the partisan preferences of generations of Americans who voted in the 2018 midterm elections.

AGE	Democrat	Republican
18–24	68%	31%
25–29	66%	33%
30–39	59%	37%
40–49	52%	46%
50–64	49%	50%
65 and older	48%	50%

Practice Analytical Thinking

1. What is the trend with regard to partisan preference as one ages? Why do you think this is the case?

2. Historically, Baby Boomers (those born between 1946 and 1964) were known to be a liberal generation, but like previous generations, they became more conservative as they got older. Do you think this trend will continue with Gen Xers? With Millennials? Based on your view, what would this distribution look like in 20 years?

3. In the United States, most large cities tend to vote Democratic (liberal), while rural areas are more Republican (conservative). With these facts in mind, can you make any deductions about specific areas where young people are most likely to live?

modern times, liberals also are likely to advocate for universal health care; increases in social welfare programs such as Social Security, Medicare, and Medicaid; and government regulation of business and workplace conditions.

Conservatism

Advocates of **conservatism** recognize the importance of preserving tradition—of maintaining the status quo or keeping things the way they are. Conservatives emphasize community and family as mechanisms of continuity in society. Ironically,

conservatism
An ideology that emphasizes preserving tradition and relying on community and family as mechanisms of continuity in society.

some modern conservative ideals are consistent with the views of classical liberalism. In particular, the emphasis on individual initiative, the rule of law, limited governmental authority, and an unfettered market economy are key components of both classical liberalism and contemporary conservatism.

Traditionally, one of the key differences between modern liberals and conservatives has been their view of the role of government in regulating the marketplace and addressing social issues. In fact, one of the best ways of determining your own ideology is to ask yourself, "To what extent should the government be involved in people's everyday lives?" Modern liberals believe that the government should play a role in ensuring the public's well-being, whether through the regulation of industry or the economy, through antidiscrimination laws, or by providing an economic "safety net" for the neediest members of society. By contrast, conservatives believe that government should play a more limited role in people's everyday lives. They think that government should have a smaller role in regulating business and industry and that market forces, rather than the government, should largely determine economic policy. Conservatives believe that families, faith-based groups, and private charities should be more responsible than the government for protecting the neediest. When governments must act, conservatives prefer decentralized action by state governments rather than a nationwide federal policy.

Other Ideologies on a Traditional Spectrum: Progressivism, Socialism and Libertarianism

Although liberals and conservatives dominate the U.S. political landscape, other ideologies reflect the views of some Americans. In general, those ideologies tend to be more extreme than liberalism or conservatism. Advocates of certain of these ideologies call for *more* governmental intervention than modern liberalism does, and supporters of other views favor even *less* governmental interference than conservatism does.

progressives
A faction within the Democratic Party who emphasize the need for societal reform that results in greater economic and social equality.

For example, today **progressives**—those who emphasize the need for societal reform that results in greater economic and social equality—have become an increasingly vocal part of the Democratic Party. They advocate for both increased government support of society's most vulnerable and wide-scale reforms (including programs such as Medicare for All and the Green New Deal) that would transform power relations in society. In 2020 many progressives coalesced around the presidential candidacies of Senators Elizabeth Warren and Bernie Sanders, whose platforms advocated for these reforms. A central part of the progressive movement is an emphasis on grassroots participation.

socialism
An ideology that advocates economic equality, theoretically achieved by having the government or workers own the means of production (businesses and industry).

Some progressives advocate for a form of **socialism**—an ideology that, in its purest theoretical form, stresses economic equality achieved by having the government or workers own the means of production (businesses and industry). Most progressives would stop short of government ownership of the means of production, as socialism generally lies to the left of liberalism and progressivism on the political spectrum.[15] True, socialists play a very limited role in modern American politics, though Sanders, who identifies himself as a "democratic socialist," has brought new focus to this ideology during his 2016 and 2020 presidential campaigns.[16] In the early part of the 20th century, socialists had a good deal of electoral success, electing two members of Congress, more than 70 mayors of cities of various sizes, and numerous state legislators.

According to **libertarianism**, in contrast, government should take a "hands-off" approach in most matters. This ideology can be found to the right of conservatism on a traditional ideological spectrum. Libertarians believe that the less government intervention, the better. They dislike attempts by the government to foster economic equality or to promote a social agenda, whether that agenda is the equality espoused by liberals or the traditional values espoused by conservatives. Libertarians strongly support the rights of property owners and a *laissez-faire* (French for "let it be") capitalist economy.

libertarianism
An ideology whose advocates believe that government should take a "hands off" approach in most matters.

Multidimensional Political Models

A one-dimensional ideological continuum is limited, however, because it sometimes fails to reflect the complexity of many individuals' views. For example, although an individual may believe that government should play a strong role in regulating the economy, he or she may also believe that the government should allow citizens a high degree of personal freedom of speech or religion. Even the traditional ideologies do not always fit easily into a single continuum that measures the extent to which the government should play a role in citizens' lives. Liberals supposedly advocate a larger role for the government; however, although this may be the case in matters related to economic equality, liberals generally take a more laissez-faire approach when it comes to personal liberties, advocating strongly for privacy and free speech. And although conservatives support less governmental intervention in the economy, they sometimes advocate government action to promote traditional values, such as constitutional amendments to ban gay marriage, flag burning, and abortion, and supporting laws that mandate prayer in public schools. Scholars have developed various *multidimensional scales* that attempt to represent people's ideologies more accurately.[17]

Ideology is one of the most important factors influencing people's beliefs about the types of issues they prioritize and the solutions they see to various policy challenges. But ideology alone does not explain priorities and preferred solutions. Also important are the characteristics of who we are, as these characteristics often make us more likely to identify certain issues as important or render us more likely to favor one policy solution over another.

The Changing Face of American Democracy

Figure 1.2 shows how the U.S. population has grown since the first census in 1790. At that point, there were fewer than 4 million Americans. By 2020, the U.S population had reached more than 332 million. Immigrants have always been part of the country's population growth, and over the centuries they have made innumerable contributions to American life and culture.[18] Immigrants from lands all around the world have faced the kinds of struggles that today's undocumented immigrants encounter. Efforts to improve the lot of immigrant populations are not new either; Chinese Americans, for example, were instrumental in pioneering the West and completing the construction of the transcontinental railroad in the mid-19th century, but the Chinese Exclusion Act of 1881 prevented them from becoming U.S. citizens. Faced with the kinds of persecution that today would be considered hate crimes, Chinese Americans used civil disobedience to fight

FIGURE 1.2 ■ **Growth of the U.S. Population from 1800 to 2050** The U.S. population increased gradually, and it did not reach 100 million until the second decade of the 20th century. What factors caused the steep rise during the 20th century? How will these forces continue to affect the size of the U.S. population during this century?

Source: U.S. Census Bureau.

against the so-called Dog Tag Laws that required them to carry registration cards. In one incident, in 1885, they fought back against unruly mobs that drove them out of the town of Eureka, California, by suing the city for reparations and compensation.[19]

A Population That Is Growing—and on the Move

Between the 1960 census and the Census Bureau's 2017 Population Estimates (the latest available until the results of the 2020 census are made available), the population of the United States increased by more than 50 percent. As the population increases, measures of **demographics**—the characteristics of the American people in terms of race, gender, educational attainment, and other characteristics—have significant implications for the policies, priorities, values, and preferred forms of political participation of the people. All the factors contributing to U.S. population growth—including immigration, the birthrate, falling infant mortality rates, and longer life spans—influence both politics and policy.

demographics
The characteristics of the American people in terms of race, sex, educational attainment and other characteristics.

Accompanying the increase in population over the years has been a shift in the places where people live. Figure 1.3 shows that much of the population in the United States is concentrated in just a few densely populated areas: the Northeast, the Great Lakes states, the Carolinas, Florida, Texas, and California. Between 2000 and 2010, the South and West accounted for 84 percent of the country's increase in population. Though not shown in Figure 1.3, census data indicates that many of the states in the Midwest are facing an out-migration of population, particularly of younger residents who are moving to metropolitan areas seeking employment. Over the past 10 years, all of the 10 most populous metropolitan areas grew, as did 9 of the 10 most populous cities. In parts of the

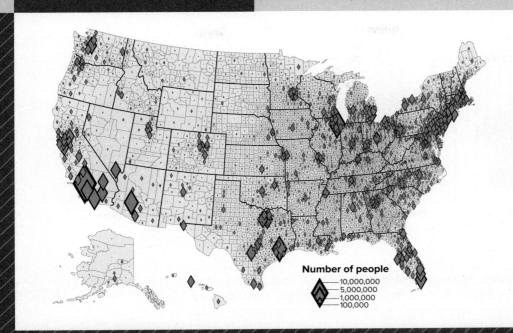

FIGURE 1.3 ■ **Population Distribution by County** The area of each diamond symbol is proportioned by the number of people in a county. The legend presents example symbol sizes from the many symbols shown on the map. Where are the largest population centers in the United States? What areas have comparatively sparse population?

Source: U.S. Census Bureau.

Number of people
— 10,000,000
— 5,000,000
— 1,000,000
— 100,000

rural Midwest, though, some of this out-migration is counterbalanced by migration into these areas by families and retirees attracted by the comparatively low cost of living characteristic of such places.

An Aging Population

As the U.S. population increases and favors new places of residence, it is also aging. Figure 1.4 shows the distribution of the population by age and by sex as a series of three pyramids for three different years. The 2000 pyramid shows the "muffin top" of the Baby Boomers, who were 36–54 years old in that year. A quarter century later, the echo boom of the Millennials, who will be between the ages of 30 and 55 in 2025, is clearly visible. The pyramid evens out and thickens by 2050, showing the effects of increased population growth and the impact of extended longevity, with a large number of people (women, in particular) expected to live to the age of 85 or older.

Some areas of the United States are well known meccas for older Americans. For example, the reputation of Florida and the Southwest as the premier retirement destinations in the United States is well earned, and many senior citizens also reside in a broad north-south band that runs down the United States's midsection. Older people are concentrated in the Midwest and Plains states because of the high levels of out-migration from these areas by younger Americans, who are leaving their parents behind to look for opportunity elsewhere.

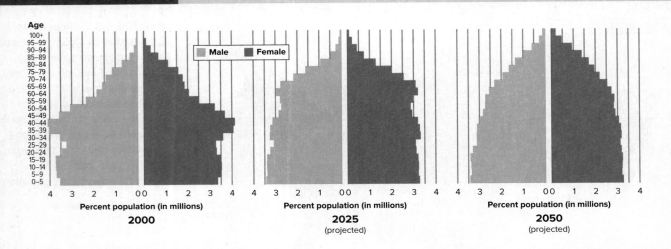

FIGURE 1.4 ■ **The Aging U.S. Population, 2000–2050** What effect will the changing age distribution of the U.S. population have on demand for services in 2025? In 2050? Given what you know about the racial composition of the Millennial generation, what will that mean for the racial composition of the U.S. population as it ages?

Source: U.S. Census Bureau.

A Changing Complexion: Race and Ethnicity in the United States Today

The population of the United States is becoming not only older but also more racially and ethnically diverse. Today, non-Hispanic whites constitute a majority of the population, with about 60 percent of Americans identifying themselves as "white alone." But according to the Census Bureau, by 2060, non-Hispanic whites will be only 44 percent of the U.S. population. Figure 1.5 shows the racial and ethnic composition of the U.S. population over time. Notice that Hispanics* now make up a greater proportion of the U.S. population than do black Americans.

Figure 1.5 also indicates that the percentage of Asian Americans has more than doubled in recent decades, from just over 3 percent of the U.S. population in 1990 to nearly 6 percent today, and is projected to increase to 9 percent by 2060. The Native American population remains just below 1 percent of the whole population. Figure 1.5 also shows the proportion of people reporting that they belonged to two or more racial groups—nearly 3 percent of the population today. How the Census Bureau has measured multi-racial backgrounds has changed over time,

*A note about terminology: When discussing data for various races and ethnicities to make comparisons, we use the terms *Black* and *Hispanic* because these labels are typically used in measuring demographics by the U.S. Census Bureau and other organizations that collect this type of data. In more descriptive writing that is not comparative, we use the terms *African American* and *Latinx*, which is the preferred gender-neutral term for *Latinos* and *Latinas* at this time. Although the term *Latinx* excludes Americans who came from Spain (or whose ancestors did), these people compose a very small proportion of this population in the United States.

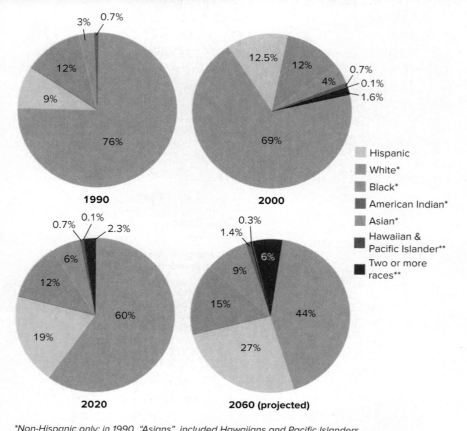

1990

- 0.7%
- 3%
- 12%
- 9%
- 76%

2000

- 12.5%
- 12%
- 0.7%
- 0.1%
- 1.6%
- 4%
- 69%

2020

- 0.1%
- 0.7%
- 2.3%
- 6%
- 12%
- 60%
- 19%

2060 (projected)

- 0.3%
- 1.4%
- 6%
- 9%
- 15%
- 44%
- 27%

Legend:
- Hispanic
- White*
- Black*
- American Indian*
- Asian*
- Hawaiian & Pacific Islander**
- Two or more races**

*Non-Hispanic only; in 1990 "Asians" included Hawaiians and Pacific Islanders.
**Option available for the first time in 2000 census.

FIGURE 1.5 ■ **Population by Race, 1990–2060** Consider the data presented in these graphs. Why does this style of visual representation effectively convey the data? Would presenting this data as a line or bar graph leave a different impression? When you think about the categories in the data, what kinds of information might be left out that would be helpful in analyzing race and ethnicity in the United States?

Sources: Social Science Data Analysis Network, University of Michigan; and U.S. Census Bureau.

as is reflected in the data. This category was not an option on the census questionnaire until 2000, and the population proportion of this group has nearly doubled since that time. It will double again to over 6 percent by 2060. The increasing diversity of the U.S. population can be seen too in the Census Bureau's population projections: by 2044, more than half of all Americans will belong to a minority group (any group other than non-Hispanic whites alone); and by 2060, nearly one in five of the nation's total population will be foreign born.[20]

As Figures 1.6 and 1.7 show, minority populations tend to be concentrated in different areas of the United States. Figure 1.6 shows the concentration of non-Hispanic black Americans. At 12 percent of the population, Black Americans are the largest racial minority in the United States. (Hispanics are an ethnic minority.) As the map illustrates, the black American population tends to be centered in urban areas and in the South where, in some counties, black Americans constitute a majority of the population.

Hispanics, in contrast, historically have tended to cluster in Texas, Arizona, and California along the border between the United States and Mexico and in the

FIGURE 1.6 ■ **Where African Americans Live** From this figure, we see that the African American population in the United States is centered in the South, along the Eastern Seaboard, and in major cities. Given that African American voters are a core constituency of the Democratic Party, how might the distribution of this group of voters affect electoral politics in these regions? Are there national implications for this trend?

Source: U.S. Census Bureau, Census Data Mapper.

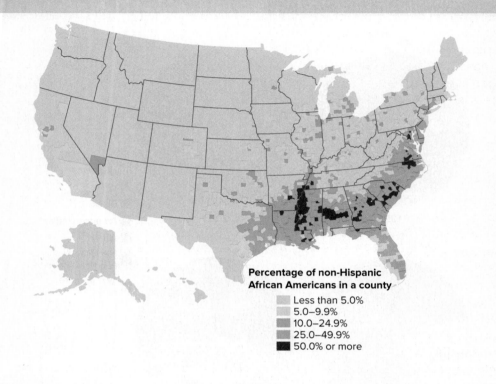

Percentage of non-Hispanic African Americans in a county

- Less than 5.0%
- 5.0–9.9%
- 10.0–24.9%
- 25.0–49.9%
- 50.0% or more

FIGURE 1.7 ■ **Where Hispanics Live** From this figure, we see that the Hispanic population in the United States is centered in the Southwest and the Eastern Seaboard. How might higher populations of Hispanics influence political culture in these regions? Do you think these Hispanic populations are homogeneous in their outlook? What policies might be priorities for the majority of Hispanics?

Source: U.S. Census Bureau, Census Data Mapper.

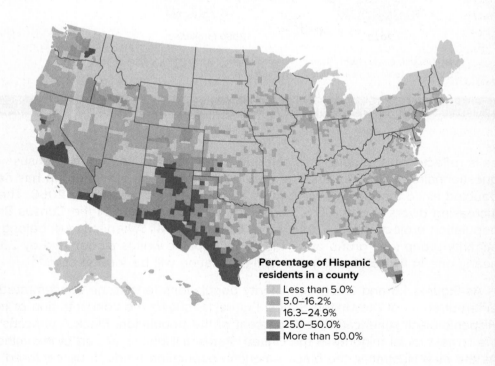

Percentage of Hispanic residents in a county

- Less than 5.0%
- 5.0–16.2%
- 16.3–24.9%
- 25.0–50.0%
- More than 50.0%

urban centers of New Mexico (as shown in Figure 1.7), but recent years have seen significant growth in the number of Hispanics living in the South. Since 2000, there have been sizable increases in Hispanic populations in Florida and the Northeast as well. Hispanics are the fastest-growing ethnic group in the United States, with over 18 percent of the U.S. population identifying themselves as Hispanic in 2020, an increase of over 180 percent since 1980. By 2060, the Hispanic population is projected to grow to over 110 million, an almost 80 percent increase from today. Among people of Hispanic ethnicity, Mexicans make up the largest number (about 7 percent of the total U.S. population), followed by Puerto Ricans and Cubans.

Changing Households: American Families Today

The types of families that are counted by the U.S. census are also becoming more diverse. The traditional nuclear family, consisting of a stay-at-home mother, a breadwinning father, and their children, was at one time the stereotypical "ideal family" in the United States. Many—though hardly all—American families were able to achieve that cultural ideal during the prosperous 1950s and early 1960s. Today, about 27 percent of children who live in a married-couple family have a stay-at-home mom; 1 percent have a stay-at-home dad. But more typically, since the women's liberation movement of the 1970s in which women sought equal rights with men, the American family has changed drastically. As a result, the proportion of single-person households has increased significantly (from 13 percent in 1960 to 28 percent in 2020). One explanation for this trend is that the proportion of young adults who are married has decreased. In 1978, 59 percent of young adults ages 18 to 34 were married, compared to 29 percent in 2018. In addition, as the population ages, increasing numbers of individuals are left widowed. The percentage of female householders without spouses (both with and without children) remained constant between 2000 and 2020 after a significant increase from 1970 through 1990. The proportion of male householders without spouses increased slightly, and men without a spouse are more likely to be raising children than they were in 1980. Finally, the proportion of the population living in nonfamily households, both those living alone and those living with others, rose slightly.

Why the Changing Population Matters for Politics and Government

Each of the changes to the U.S. population described here has implications for American democracy. As the nature of the electorate shifts, a majority of the nation's people may have different priorities, and various policies may become more or less important. For example, in recent years, we have seen increased demands for comprehensive immigration reform, often propelled by immigrants or families of immigrants with a vested interest in this reform. In addition, the swift growth in U.S. population means that demand for the services government provides—from schools to highways to health care—will continue to increase. The aging population will inevitably increase the burden on the nation's Social Security and government-supported health care systems, which will be forced to support the needs of that older, growing population.

THEN

KNOW-NOTHINGISM IN BROOKLYN.
"None but citizens of the United States can be licensed to engage in any employment in this city."
Brooklyn Board of Aldermen.

NOW

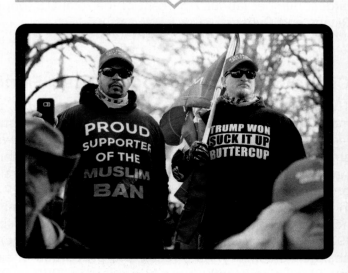

>> **The Chinese Exclusion Act of 1881 prevented Chinese Americans from becoming U.S. citizens, and local laws, including one in Brooklyn depicted here (left), banned them from employment. Faced with the kinds of persecution that today would be considered hate crimes, Chinese Americans used civil disobedience to fight against the so-called Dog Tag Laws that required them to carry registration cards. Today, other immigrant groups are subject to discrimination and persecution. What are the circumstances that cause increases in anti-immigrant sentiments in the United States?**

(l)Library of Congress, Prints and Photographs Division [LC-USZC2-761]; (r)Alex Milan Tracy/Sipa/AP Images

Changes in the population's racial and ethnic composition also matter, as does the concentration of racial minorities in specific geographic areas. The racial and ethnic makeup of the population (along with other influences) can significantly affect the nation's political culture and people's political attitudes, as can be seen both in the viewpoints of young Americans concerning the fairness of the judicial system and in the prioritization of issues associated with immigration by many Hispanics, particularly those who are themselves recent immigrants. It has implications too for who will govern, as more and more representatives of the country's various racial and ethnic groups become candidates for political office and as *all* political candidates must reach out to increasingly diverse groups of voters—or possibly pay the price at the ballot box for failing to do so.

Conclusion: Thinking Critically About What's Next in American Democracy

Now is an important, exciting time to study American democracy. As American society grapples with pressing questions that will shape our society for generations, participation in government and civic life is more vitally important than ever. Simultaneously, fast-paced changes in technology make participation easier than ever. The effects of participating in the continuing conversation of American democracy through both words and actions are unequivocally positive—for you, for others, and for the government—and can have large ripple effects.

Will the present generation break the cycle of cynicism, anger, and division that has pervaded the politics of the recent past? Today, the differing political viewpoints between generations of Americans will clearly have repercussions in our polity. Technology will continue to play a significant role in how we communicate and participate in politics and how government creates and administers policy. Major transformations have come to pass in the political realm, and there is no end to them in sight.

Demographic changes in American society—particularly the growing diversity and the aging of the U.S. population—are giving rise to new public policy demands and creating new challenges. Challenges mean opportunities for those who are ready for them, and citizens who respond to those challenges will have an impact on the future of the nation.

▮ References

1. Ken Thomas, "White House Sends Mixed Signals on Trade Fight; Markets Dive," *Associated Press*. April 8, 2018.

2. E. J. Dionne Jr., *Why Americans Hate Politics: The Death of the Democratic Process,* 2nd ed. (New York: Touchstone, 1992).

3. Gallup Poll, "Little Public Support for Reductions in Federal Government Spending."

4. www.people-press.org/2017/05/03/public-trust-in-government-remains-near-historic-lows-as-partisan-attitudes-shift/.

5. Barbara Roswell, "From Service-Learning to Service Politics: A Conversation with Rick Battistoni."

6. Michael Delli Carpini, Director Pew Charitable Trusts.

7. S. E. Finer, *The History of Government,* 3 vols. (London: Oxford University Press, 1997).

8. Martin A. Reddish, *The Constitution as Political Structure* (London: Oxford University Press, 1995).

9. Theodore Sky, *To Provide for the General Welfare: A History of the Federal Spending Power* (Newark: University of Delaware Press, 2003).

10. David Epstein, *The Political Theory of the Federalist* (Chicago: University of Chicago Press, 1984).

11. Thomas Hobbes, *Leviathan* (1651; New York: Oxford University Press, 1996), chap. 14.

12. Oscar Handlin and Mary Handlin, *The Dimensions of Liberty* (Cambridge, MA: Harvard University Press, 1961).

13. Richard Labunski, *James Madison and the Struggle for the Bill of Rights* (London: Oxford University Press, 2006).

14. Jack N. Rakove, *Original Meanings: Politics and Ideas in the Making of the Constitution* (New York: Knopf, 1996).

15. Clyde W. Barrow, *Critical Theories of the State: Marxist, Neo-Marxist, Post- Marxist* (Madison: University of Wisconsin Press, 1993).

16. Seymour Martin Lipset and Gary Marks, *It Didn't Happen Here: Why Socialism Failed in the United States* (New York: W. W. Norton, 2001).

17. Giovanni Sartori and Peter Mair, *Parties and Party Systems: A Framework for Analysis* (Oxford, England: European Consortium for Political Research, 2005).

18. Ira Katznelson and Martin Shefter, eds., *Shaped by War and Trade: International Influences on American Political Development* (Princeton, NJ: Princeton University Press, 2002).

19. *Wing Hing v. City of Eureka* (Calif.), 1886.

20. www.census.gov/content/dam/Census/ library/publications/2015/demo/p25-1143.pdf.

■ Key Terms

Multiple Choice Questions

Choose the best answer to each question.

1. An individual who advocates for affirmative action, increased government regulation of the economy, and separation of church and state is most likely to be a

   A. Conservative

   B. Libertarian

   C. Liberal

   D. Socialist

2. Which of the following is an accurate comparison of the political views of John Locke and Thomas Hobbes?

Locke	Hobbes
A. The government's role is to protect the people's natural rights	The life of man is nasty, brutish, and short
B. A direct democracy is the best form of government	Rulers receive their power to govern directly from God
C. Only a strong monarch can bring order to society	The people should enter into a social contract that relies on popular sovereignty
D. Government power should be separated into 3 branches	It is the government's job to ensure every citizen is entitled to life, liberty and property

3. All of the following are values of American political culture EXCEPT

   A. Success should depend on factors such as education and hard work rather than government policies ensuring successful outcomes

   B. The government should own the means of production and redistribute wealth to the middle class

   C. Government's power is derived from the consent of the people

   D. The people should have the liberty to speak freely and participate in politics

Questions 4 and 5 refer to the chart below: Voter Turnout in Presidential Elections (2004–2020) by Voter Age.

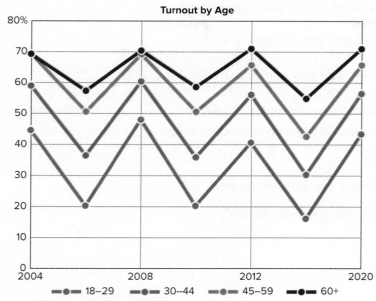

Source: United States Elections Project

4. Which of the following is an accurate statement about the information in the line graph?

  A. Voters aged 18–29 have the highest turnout among all age groups

  B. Voters aged 30–44 vote at higher rates due to an increase of education

  C. Voters of all age groups vote at higher rates during presidential election years

  D. Older voters tend to vote at higher rates due to increased levels of political efficacy

5. Based on the information in the line graph, which of the following is the most likely implication for political participation?

  A. Voter turnout overall is low due to low levels of trust in government

  B. Young people are finding ways other than voting to participate in the political system

  C. Candidates running for political office will focus their campaign messages on issues concerning older Americans

  D. Millennials overwhelmingly came out to vote for Hillary Clinton in 2016

6. Which of the following policies is likely to cause tension between the competing values of equality and capitalism?

  A. The government establishing a minimum wage

  B. Reducing environmental regulations

  C. Constitutional amendment protecting gay marriage

  D. School-sponsored prayer

7. Who is LEAST likely to vote in the next presidential election?

  A. a senior citizen

  B. a union employee

  C. a Millennial

  D. a lawyer

Questions 8–9 refer to the passage below:

"Civil government, so far as it is instituted for the security of property, is in reality instituted for the defence of the rich against the poor, or of those who have some property against those who have none at all."

—Adam Smith, *The Wealth of Nations*

8. Which of the following statements is most consistent with the author's argument in the passage?
   A. The government should actively redistribute wealth to ensure order in society
   B. Governments should seek to maintain order and stability through adherence to the social contract
   C. Individualism is a threat to social capital
   D. The practical purpose of government is to protect the elite in society

9. Which political thinker would most likely agree with the passage above?
   A. John Locke
   B. Thomas Hobbes
   C. Thomas Jefferson
   D. Jean-Jacques Rousseau

10. The United States is an example of which type of government?
    A. Constitutional monarchy
    B. Direct democracy
    C. Republic
    D. Oligarchy

■ Free Response Questions

Argument

Develop an argument that explains which of the two main ideologies—liberal or conservative—best achieves the founders' intent for the proper role of government in society and the economy. In your essay, you must:

- Articulate a defensible claim or thesis that responds to the prompt and establishes a line of reasoning.

- Support your claim with at least TWO pieces of accurate and relevant information:

  - At least ONE piece of evidence must be from one of the following foundational documents:

    — Declaration of Independence

    — U.S. Constitution

    — Brutus I

  - Use a second piece of evidence from another foundational document from the list or from your study of the electoral process

- Use reasoning to explain why your evidence supports your claim/thesis.

- Respond to an opposing or alternative perspective using refutation, concession, or rebuttal.

Quantitative Analysis

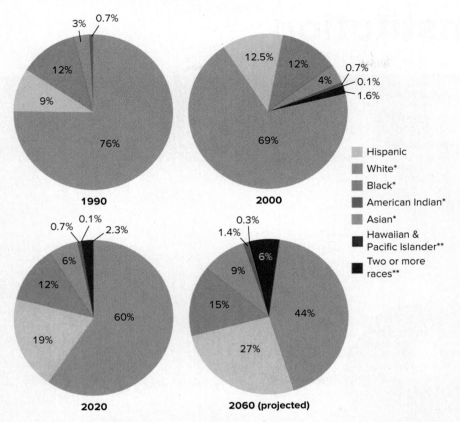

Population by Race, 1990–2060

*Non-Hispanic only; in 1990 "Asians" included Hawaiians and Pacific Islanders.
**Option available for the first time in 2000 census.

Sources: Social Science Data Analysis Network, University of Michigan; and U.S. Census Bureau

Use the information in the graphic above to answer the questions.

A. Identify the most common race in the United States.

B. Describe a similarity or difference in the racial composition of the United States as illustrated in the graphic, and draw a conclusion about that similarity or difference.

C. Explain how the racial composition of the United States as shown in the graphic demonstrates the impact race has on American democracy.

Concept Application

In 2014, Edward Snowden, a whistleblower at the National Security Agency (NSA), revealed that the agency had recorded information from about 125 million cell phone communications in a 30-day period, including 3 million communications originating in the United States. After reading the scenario, respond to A, B, and C below:

A. Specifically addressing American political culture, explain why some Americans were upset with the NSA's actions.

B. In the context of the scenario, explain how the NSA's recording of cell phone communication affects Americans' trust in government.

C. In the context of the scenario, explain how Locke's idea of a social contract and natural rights are affected by the NSA's actions.

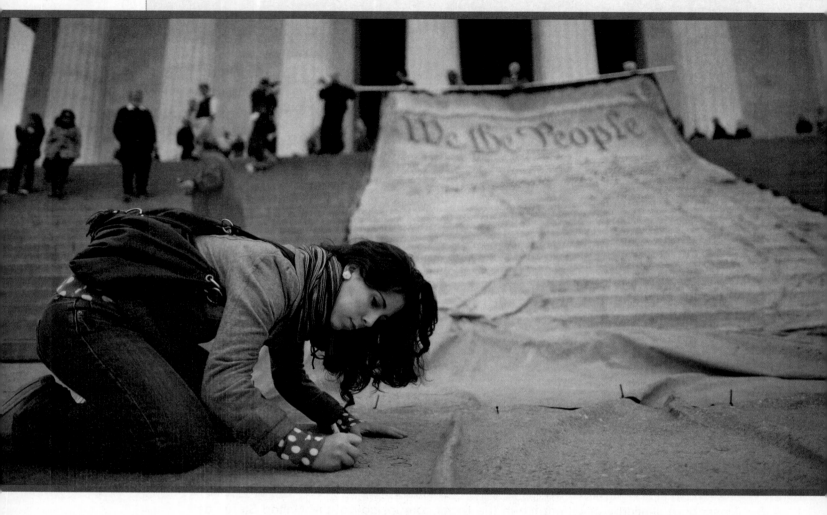

THEN

To establish a representative democracy that protects individual liberties, the Constitution's framers divided governmental power between the federal and the state governments and created checks and balances among the three separate branches of the national government.

NOW

Questions about the meaning of constitutionally established governing structures and procedures, rights, and liberties regularly end up at the doorstep of the U.S. Supreme Court as the nation continues to pursue a more perfect union.

NEXT

Will the courts' constitutional interpretations alter the balance of power between national and state governments?

Will the courts' interpretations of separation of powers and checks and balances change the balance of power among the branches of the national government?

How will the Constitution affect your pursuit of happiness?

Chip Somodevilla/Getty Images

■ Chapter Introduction

This chapter frames the history of the writing of the U.S. Constitution, a required foundational reading for all AP U.S. Government students. As you read the history of the ratification of the Constitution, allow this Enduring Understanding (EU) to center your thinking: *The Constitution emerged from the debate about the weaknesses in the Articles of Confederation as a blueprint for limited government.* The establishment of a weak central government under the Articles was a natural reaction against the centralization that existed under British rule. Considering the sentiment against centralized power at the time, it should not surprise you that an extraordinarily weak central government was created under the Articles. What is more surprising to learn about is the extraordinary ability of the Federalists to persuade others to adopt a Constitution that included a supremacy clause for national power and a necessary and proper clause for the national Congress. Both increased the power of the central government. The Anti-Federalists, including Brutus, opposed centralization and argued that the Constitution was a radical and dangerous document that should not be ratified.

In AP U.S. Government, you will read both the Federalists' arguments in favor of ratification and the Anti-Federalists' arguments against ratification. As you read these documents, consider the ways in which the debate over federal and state power under the Constitution endures to this day. Scholars attribute the Constitution's longevity to its vague and ambiguous language, which allows for interpretation and elasticity over time. For example, Article 1 gives Congress power to make "all Laws which shall be necessary and proper," and the Eighth Amendment bans cruel and unusual punishment. Debate over what laws are necessary and proper and what punishments are cruel and unusual, along with other debates about the meaning of the words of the Constitution, continue in American politics. As you read the U.S. Constitution, consider not only how the words leave room for interpretation but also how the document attempts to balance competing interests, including national and state power and majority rule with minority rights. Finally, consider how the Constitution limits national power with a system of checks and balances within the branches of the national government. When reading the Constitution and applying it to policy debates today, consider this EU: *The Constitution created a competitive policy-making process to ensure the people's will is represented and that freedom is preserved.*

AP U.S. GOVERNMENT REQUIRED FOUNDATIONAL DOCUMENTS		
	Author(s)	**Main ideas to look for/consider**
Articles of Confederation	U.S. Continental Congress	Established a weak central government that lacked the power to tax and raise an army.
Federalist 10	James Madison	It is natural for citizens in a free society to form factions.
Federalist 51	James Madison	Federalism, separation of powers, and checks and balances established in the Constitution will control the effects of factions.
Brutus 1	Unknown	The Constitution provides too much elasticity and power to the national government, and if ratified, will render state governments irrelevant.

THE U.S. CONSTITUTION

Article(s)	Topic(s)	Key Idea(s)
I, II, & III	Legislative, Executive, and Judicial branches of government	The powers of and constraints on legislative, executive, and judicial authority are defined in these articles.
IV	Relations among the states	Each state must give citizens of other states the same rights as its own citizens.
V	Process for amending the Constitution	It takes a supermajority vote of the national legislature or of state legislatures to propose an amendment.
VI	Constitutional supremacy	The Constitution and national laws are the supreme law of the land.
VII	Ratification	Ratification by nine out of thirteen states is necessary for the Constitution to take effect.

AMENDMENTS TO THE CONSTITUTION
The First Ten Amendments are the Bill of Rights

1	Freedom of Religion, Speech, Press, Assembly and Petition	12	Election of the President and Vice President
2	Right to Bear Arms	13	Abolition of slavery
3	Quartering of Soldiers	14	All born in the US are citizens, Equal Protection Clause
4	Right of citizens to be protected against unreasonable searches and seizures	15	African American voting rights
5	Right to a Grand Jury. Protections against double jeopardy and self-incrimination. Right to due process of law. Government power of eminent domain (aka the Takings Clause)	16	Income Tax
		17	Popular election of Senators
		18	Prohibition of liquor
		19	Women's voting rights
6	Right to an attorney, right to speedy trial	20	Presidential Term and Succession
7	Right to trial by jury of one's peers	21	Repeal of prohibition of liquor
8	Ban on cruel and unusual punishments and excessive fines	22	Two-term limit of the Presidency
		23	Presidential electors for DC
9	Non-enumerated rights are retained by the people	24	Abolition of poll taxes
10	Rights not given to national government are reserved to the states	25	Presidential disability and succession
		26	Right to vote at age 18
11	Suits against states	27	Congressional Compensation

■ What Is a Constitution?

A **constitution** presents the mission of the government that is described in the document, the fundamental principles that will guide the government's operations, and the foundational structures and procedures by which the government operates to fulfill its mission.

Typically, constitutions begin with a description of the mission of the government. For example, the first sentence in the Constitution of the United States, known as the Preamble, states:

We the People of the United States, in Order to form a more perfect Union, establish Justice, insure domestic Tranquility, provide for the common defence, promote the general Welfare, and secure the Blessings of Liberty to ourselves and our Posterity, do ordain and establish this Constitution for the United States of America.

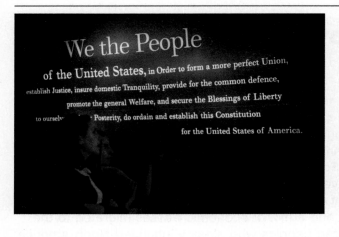

>> Visitors at the National Constitution Center read the first sentence of the U.S. Constitution, which is painted on glass panels over the main exhibit. The center, sitting on federal land, is a private, nonprofit organization chartered by Congress to "disseminate information about the U.S. Constitution on a nonpartisan basis." Although such a center was first proposed in 1887, during the Constitution's centennial celebration, it was not established until 1988 when President Ronald Reagan signed the Constitution Heritage Act. The Center opened on September 17, 2000. Why is September 17th celebrated as Constitution Day?

William Thomas Cain/Getty Images

After the Preamble, the first three articles (main sections) of the U.S. Constitution describe the structure of the national government. Specifically the articles describe three foundational government bodies—the legislative, executive, and judicial branches—and articulate the responsibilities of each body as well as the relationships among those bodies. The Constitution also details essential operating procedures, including those used to select national government officials, to make laws, and to formally amend the Constitution (by changing language in the document), as well as the process by which the Constitution itself was to be ratified. The Preamble and the Bill of Rights—that is, the first 10 amendments to the Constitution—are two sections where fundamental principles that guide the government's operations are identified.

When you read a constitution, in addition to finding the mission statement, fundamental principles, descriptions of foundational structures, and details of essential operating procedures, you will also find some vague and ambiguous language. For example, reread the Constitution's Preamble. What do you think "promote the general welfare" means? Does it mean that the government is responsible for ensuring that all people living in the nation have decent health care? Does it mean that everyone needs access to a good education and a job with a living wage so that they can be financially independent? Does it mean that the government needs to ensure that all people have sufficient and nutritious food and safe housing?

Debates over the meaning of constitutional language were taking place in living rooms, restaurants, government offices, courtrooms, and on the streets even before the states ratified the Constitution. Ultimately, the U.S. Supreme Court has the final word on the meaning of constitutional language. You will learn as you read the chapters in this book that members of the Supreme Court do not always agree on the meaning of constitutional language. Moreover, throughout U.S. history, as the members of the Supreme Court changed and the nation's economy, technology, and culture evolved, societal understanding of constitutional language changed, as did judicial interpretation of the language.

To comprehend today's debates about the meanings of constitutional language, we need to first develop an understanding of what the framers of the Constitution and the citizens who debated it were hoping to achieve. What was their vision of a more perfect union?

The Creation of the United States of America

In the 1600s, waves of Europeans made the dangerous sea voyage to America to start new lives. A few people with connections to the king of England received large grants of land and the authority to govern. Many others came to create communities with people of the same religion so that they could practice their faith without government interference. Some voyagers came as *indentured servants*, who would work for a number of years for a master who paid for their passage. Countless others—Africans brought to the colonies as slaves—came against their will. In short, a diversity of people and a mix of economic classes migrated to the colonies, joining the Native American peoples who already inhabited North America.

By the early 18th century, a two-tier system of governing the British colonies in America had evolved, with governance split between the colonies and Britain. The colonists elected local officials to colonial assemblies that had the authority to rule on day-to-day matters (including criminal law and civil law) and to set and collect taxes to implement laws regarding day-to-day matters. Back in England, Parliament, with no elected representatives from the colonies, and the king enacted laws with which the British government expected the colonists to comply. Governors appointed by the king oversaw the enforcement of British law in the colonies. For the colonists, this combination of colonial assemblies close to home and a faraway Parliament represented by an appointed governor living in the colonies worked well: Life went on without much interference from the British Parliament and Crown.

In the latter half of the 18th century, this relationship began to change. Parliament tried to raise additional revenue from the colonists to pay for its growing debt (due to war expenses in Europe and America). Parliament also enacted laws to confirm its sovereignty over the colonists. To accomplish these goals, Parliament approved legislation that put more and more restrictions on the colonists' freedoms and their pursuit of economic well-being. Colonists began to complain among themselves about the British government's damaging treatment of them. Eventually those conversations coalesced around their preference for a government by the people (popular sovereignty) and for the people (government established to protect the people's liberties). Criticism turned into rebellion, which became a revolution. In the process, a new country was born.

British Policies Incite Revolution in the Colonies

Between 1756 and 1763, Britain was engaged in the Seven Years' War in Europe, a military conflict that involved all the major European powers of the era. At the same time, British and French forces (and France's Native American allies) were battling in North America, in a conflict known as the French and Indian War. To help pay the costs of waging those wars and the postwar costs of maintaining peace in America, the British Parliament turned to the colonies for increased revenues and to provide support and housing for British soldiers. As colonists criticized and then protested the new laws, Parliament continued to enact additional laws that limited the colonists' liberties and pursuit of happiness (see Table 2.1). Eventually the colonists' protests turned to revolution.

TABLE 2.1 ■ British Policies Incite Revolution

1764	Sugar Act
1765	Stamp Act
1765	Quartering Act
1766	Repeal of Stamp Act
1767	Townshend Act
1770	Boston Massacre
1773	Tea Act
1774	Coercive (Intolerable) Act
1775	British troops move to seize guns and ammunition in Lexington and Concord

TAXATION WITHOUT REPRESENTATION In 1764, Parliament enacted the Sugar Act, which increased taxes on goods imported into the colonies and directed that all taxes collected be sent directly to Britain instead of to the colonial assemblies, as had been the practice.[1] Then, in 1765, Parliament passed the Stamp Act, which taxed the paper used for all legal documents, advertisements, and newspapers.[2]

Colonists condemned these laws and called for their repeal, claiming they had no obligation to pay the taxes because they had no representation in the Parliament that created them. The Daughters of Liberty and the Sons of Liberty, two secret organizations of political activists focused on protecting colonists' rights, formed in response to the Stamp Act. In addition, the colonists boycotted goods imported from Britain. Women, who substituted homegrown or homespun goods for the boycotted items, were key to the success of the boycotts, which, according to historian Glenna Matthews "proved to be the single most valuable tool, short of war, that the patriots possessed."[3]

To support the growing number of troops it was sending to the colonies as protests grew, Parliament enacted the Quartering Act in 1765. This act directed each colonial assembly to provide supplies to meet the basic needs of the British

>> Boycotts were a valuable tool of rebellion used by colonists. Participation by women, including the Daughters of Liberty, was essential to the success of the boycotts. What is a boycott? What explains why women's participation was essential to the success of boycotts?

Classic Image/Alamy Stock Photo

soldiers stationed in the colonies. An expansion of this act in 1766 required the colonial assemblies to ensure housing for the soldiers as well.[4] Many colonists viewed the Quartering Act as an indirect tax forcing them to pay some of the costs of the troops, whose presence the colonists saw as a threat to their liberties.[5]

In response to protests, Parliament repealed the Stamp Act in 1766. However, at the same time, it enacted the Declaratory Act, which confirmed Parliament's power to make laws that the colonists were legally required to follow.[6] The Townshend Act of 1767 confirmed Parliament's power to impose taxes that the colonists were obligated to pay. It also expanded the list of imported goods to be taxed.[7]

A "MASSACRE," A MONOPOLY, AND A TEA PARTY By 1770, thousands of British soldiers were quartered in the homes of the civilians living in Boston. To make matters worse, the British soldiers sought additional paid labor, competing with the colonists for jobs. Growing tensions came to a head in Boston on March 5, 1770, when an angry mob of nearly 1,800 struggling colonists clashed with British soldiers. The soldiers shot into the crowd, leaving five dead and six wounded.[8] Samuel Adams, a member of the Sons of Liberty, and an expert at "spinning" a news story, condemned the event as "the Boston Massacre." Colonists' calls for resistance and protests grew.

In 1772, Samuel Adams created the Massachusetts Committee of Correspondence, a group dedicated to encouraging and maintaining the free flow of information and the spread of calls for rebellion among the Massachusetts colonists. Angry and disaffected people in other colonies followed suit, creating their own correspondence committees to encourage and organize acts of resistance and protest.[9]

Adding fuel to the fire of rebellion, in 1773 Parliament passed the Tea Act, which gave the East India Tea Company a monopoly on importing tea into the colonies. The Sons of Liberty questioned the act's legitimacy, vowed they would block the Company's ships from docking in ports, and called for renewed boycotts of British goods. The Sons of Liberty successfully swayed public opinion and became the catalyst for the Boston Tea Party. In November 1773, the first post–Tea Act shipment of tea arrived in Boston Harbor on three East India Company ships. On the night of December 16, 1773, more than 100 colonists, dressed as Mohawk Indians, boarded the three ships, broke open hundreds of crates, and dumped thousands of pounds of tea into the harbor.[10] The Boston Tea Party had a

>> Five thousand people gathered at the Old South Meeting House in Boston on the morning of December 16, 1773. The topic of discussion was the imported cargo on several ships in Boston Harbor: tea. By that night, with Samuel Adams in the lead, hundreds of men destroyed the tea by dumping it into the harbor, while thousands watched. Only one man was caught and imprisoned for participating in this nonviolent, rebellious act. This photo shows markers on the graves of two of the 116 people documented as participants in the Boston Tea Party.

Elise Amendola/AP Images

cataclysmic effect, not only on the relationship between Britain and the colonies but also on relationships among the colonists themselves.

Parliament responded to the Boston Tea Party with the Coercive Acts (Intolerable Acts) in 1774, which closed the port of Boston with the intent of keeping it closed until the colonists paid for the lost tea. In addition, the act imposed martial law, shut down the colonial assembly, and banned virtually all town meetings, thus curtailing legal opportunities for Massachusetts colonists to engage in politics.[11]

THE FIRST CONTINENTAL CONGRESS: A DECLARATION OF RIGHTS AND GRIEVANCES Sympathy among the other colonies for Massachusetts's plight, along with colonists' rising concerns about the harm being done to their economy and lifestyle by the British government, reinforced the colonists' growing sense of community and their shared consciousness of the need to engage in collective political action. The Massachusetts and Virginia colonial assemblies requested a meeting of delegates from all thirteen colonies to develop a joint statement of concern they would send to the king. In September 1774, every colony but Georgia sent delegates to Philadelphia for what became known as the First Continental Congress. The delegates, elected by colonial legislatures or committees of correspondence, were elite men involved in politics and business.

The First Continental Congress adopted and sent to King George III the Declaration of Rights and Grievances. This document listed numerous rights to which the delegates argued the colonists were entitled. Some of the rights included in the list were life, liberty, and property; representation in Parliament; and consideration of their grievances and petitions to the king.[12] The Congress also adopted the Articles of Association, which put forth a plan for the colonies to work together.[13] Finally, the Congress scheduled a second meeting of delegates— the Second Continental Congress—to discuss the anticipated king's response to their declaration of rights and list of grievances.

King George III refused to respond to the First Continental Congress's declarations and grievances. Colonists' discussions about pursuing independence grew louder. On April 19, 1775, before the Second Continental Congress met, shots rang out at Lexington and Concord, Massachusetts, as British troops moved to seize the colonists' store of guns and ammunition. The rebellion—sparked by more than a decade's worth of Parliament's policies that threatened the life, liberties, and pursuit of happiness of the colonists—was now a military conflict, a revolutionary war for independence, that would last for eight years (1775–1783).

The Common Sense of Declaring Independence

On May 10, 1775, the Second Continental Congress convened. The assembled delegates, elected by state legislatures or correspondence committees, authorized the Congress to function as an independent government, a de facto national government, and to prepare for war with Britain. The Congress also appointed George Washington to command the to-be-created Continental Army.

In July 1775, the Second Continental Congress made one last effort to avert a full-blown war. It petitioned King George III to end hostile actions against the colonists. The king refused and sent even more troops to the colonies to put down the growing rebellion. Yet even as the Congress prepared for war, many colonists remained unsure about cutting their ties with Britain. A pamphlet written by Thomas Paine, a recently arrived radical from Britain, and published in January 1776, transformed many such wavering colonists into revolutionary patriots. Paine's *Common Sense* argued that war with Great Britain was not only necessary but also unavoidable. Only through independence would Americans attain civil and religious liberty.[14]

In May 1776, Richard Henry Lee, a Virginia delegate to the Congress, asserted "that these united Colonies are, and of right ought to be free and independent States, [and] that they are absolved from all allegiance to the British crown."[15] Lee's resolution also called for the drafting of a plan of union for the colonies, each of which would become an independent state. This "declaration of independence," which congressional delegates from other colonies subsequently echoed, led the Second Continental Congress to establish a committee to write a formal declaration of independence on behalf of all the colonies. The committee selected Virginia delegate Thomas Jefferson, a wealthy plantation owner, to draft the declaration.

Unanimously endorsed by the Second Continental Congress on July 4, 1776, Jefferson's Declaration of Independence was groundbreaking. It put forth three principles that at the time were radical. First, it claimed that all men are equal, with *natural rights* (also called *unalienable rights*), which are rights that all humans possess as a gift from nature, or God—not rights established by government. The Declaration stated that the natural rights that all men have are the rights to life, liberty, and the pursuit of happiness. Second, guided by social contract theory, it proposed that all governments must be based on the consent of the people they serve. Also guided by social contract theory, the third radical principle put forth in the Declaration stated that if a government is not protecting the rights of the people, then the people have the duty to abolish it and create a new government.

After establishing those three radical principles, the Declaration spelled out a list of grievances against King George III in an attempt to convince the colonists and the European powers that the colonists' break with Great Britain was necessary and justified. The Declaration won the hearts and minds of people in the colonies and abroad. Until this point, the colonists were united in their complaints against Britain but lacked a rallying point for moving forward. The Declaration provided that rallying point by envisioning a new government that would be based on the consent of the people, with liberty and equality as its central goals.

>> Today you can see an original copy of the U.S. Constitution and the inkwell used to sign the Declaration of Independence when you visit Independence Hall in Philadelphia, Pennsylvania. Within the walls of this historic building, the Second Continental Congress met, beginning in May 1775. The Continental Congress formed the committee to draft the first constitution of the United States in this hall in June 1776. The Declaration of Independence was adopted here on July 4, 1776. Because Congress had to evacuate Philadelphia twice due to British occupation, the Articles of Confederation were approved in York, Pennsylvania, on November 15, 1777, instead of in Independence Hall. During the summer of 1787, however, the Constitutional Convention worked on drafting the U.S. Constitution in Independence Hall, signing it on September 17, 1787.

Library of Congress, Prints & Photographs Division, photograph by Carol M. Highsmith [LC-DIG-highsm-12311]

The War for Independence (the American Revolutionary War), which began at Lexington and Concord in 1775, would end eight years later with the signing of a peace treaty in Paris (1783). However, the colonists could not wait until the end of the war to establish a new government. Even before the colonial delegates at the Second Continental Congress endorsed the Declaration of Independence, they encouraged the legislative assembly of each colony to write a constitution establishing a state government, independent of Great Britain. In addition, by 1777, the Second Continental Congress drafted and submitted to the states a proposed constitution, the Articles of Confederation and Perpetual Union, which designed a collaborative governing alliance among the independent, sovereign states.

The State Constitutions

Before Congress adopted the Declaration of Independence, four colonies had adopted their own constitutions. By the end of 1776, eight of the 13 colonies had ratified state constitutions. New York and Georgia followed suit in 1777. After four years of intense deliberation, Massachusetts adopted a state constitution in 1780. Connecticut and Rhode Island decided to operate under revised royal charters (governing documents from the British government with references to the king removed) until they enacted new constitutions in 1818 and 1843, respectively.[16]

The state constitutions were revolutionary for three primary reasons. First, each was a single, written document that specified the principles, structures, and operating procedures of a government established by the consent of the people. Second, they were adopted at a specific moment in time, unlike constitutions before them, which were accumulations of disparate laws written over time or created by judges through the years, based on customs and traditions.[17] Third, they transformed the legal status of people from that of "subjects" under the rule of a king, who was sovereign due to heredity not election by the people, into citizens sharing in popular sovereignty. Each state constitution, drafted and ratified by the elected members of the existing colonial assembly or by elected delegates to a constitutional convention, instituted government created by and for the people.[18]

FUNDAMENTAL PRINCIPLES The mission of each state government was to ensure natural rights. This is evident in the bills of rights in state constitutions, which limited government actions in order to prevent the government from infringing on individuals' liberties and pursuit of happiness. State constitutions adhered to the principle of constitutionalism, meaning that government is structured by law, and the power of government is limited. State bills of rights (1) affirmed that all government's power derives from the people; (2) endorsed rights such as trial by jury and religious freedom; and (3) included protections for free speech and press, protection from excessive fines and bail, and protection from unreasonable search and seizure. Hence, the inclusion of a written list of citizens' liberties, a *bill of rights*, limited government by ensuring that both the people and the government knew what freedoms the government could not violate.

BASIC STRUCTURES AND PROCEDURES The framers of the first state constitutions attempted to implement the principles of popular sovereignty and natural rights presented in the Declaration of Independence through the governing structures and procedures they instituted. Each state constitution established a **republic**, better known today as a representative democracy. Moreover, most state constitutions asserted explicitly that the people held the power—government was instituted by the consent of the people and was to serve the people. State governments included three governing bodies—the legislative, executive, and judicial branches. **Bicameral legislatures**, which are legislatures comprising two parts (or chambers), were the norm in the states. State legislators, who were elected directly by voters in most states, were delegated more governing powers than members of the other two branches, who were not typically elected by voters. The prevailing view of people of the time was that the legislature offered the best prospects for representative government that would ensure popular sovereignty and protection of life, liberty, and the pursuit of happiness.

> **republic**
> A government that derives its authority from the people and in which citizens elect government officials to represent them in the processes by which laws are made; a representative democracy.
>
> **bicameral legislature**
> Legislature comprising two parts, called *chambers*.

We must acknowledge that women, enslaved people, and indigenous (Native) Americans were excluded from the principles of popular sovereignty, social contract theory, and representative democracy as established in the state constitutions and, later, national constitutions. The political actors who wrote and ratified state constitutions, as was true of the political actors involved in the Continental Congresses, were white male elites. The constitutions they drafted and ratified perpetuated the societal norm that white adult males who owned a certain amount of land, possessed private property worth a designated amount of money, paid taxes, or some combination of these criteria, would have the right to vote. Men interested in being elected to state government offices typically had to own even more property than did men who had the right to vote.

Within this framework, the states of the newly forming union used their constitutions to guide them in handling day-to-day domestic matters. Meanwhile, members of the Second Continental Congress turned their attention to developing a system of government that would guarantee each state's independence and sovereignty while allowing the states to engage collectively in international affairs and providing for the common defense of all the states and their people.

The Articles of Confederation (1781–1788)

Because of the colonists' bitter experience under the British Crown, the people and their delegates to the Second Continental Congress distrusted a strong, distant central government; they preferred limited governments, close to home, which they established in their state constitutions. The congressional delegates nevertheless recognized the need for a unified authority to engage in international trade, foreign affairs, and defense. In June of 1776, while Jefferson worked on the Declaration of Independence and the colonies were drafting state constitutions, the Continental Congress established a committee to draft a document that would allow the states to continue to work together in their battle with Great Britain and other international matters.

The Second Continental Congress submitted to the states for ratification the Articles of Confederation and Perpetual Union (Articles) in 1777. The Articles established a **confederation**: a union of independent states in which each state retains its sovereignty—that is, its ultimate power to govern—and agrees to work collaboratively on matters the states expressly agree to delegate to a central (national) governing body. Through the Articles, the states created an alliance for mutual well-being in the international realm, yet continued to pursue independently their own self-interests within their own borders. Discussions and debates over the Articles took place in each state. Finally, in 1781, after Maryland became the 13th state to ratify it, the Articles of Confederation officially went into effect, with the War for Independence still raging. Table 2.2 presents key actions leading to the establishment of the United States of America.

confederation
A union of independent states in which each state retains its sovereignty, that is, its ultimate power to govern, and agrees to work collaboratively on matters the states expressly agree to delegate to a central governing body.

TABLE 2.2 ■ **Creation of the U.S. Confederation**

1774	First Continental Congress held
1775	Second Continental Congress held
1776	Eight state constitutions ratified
1776	Declaration of Independence signed
1777	Articles sent to states
1781	Articles ratified by states and go into effect
1783	War for Independence ends with signing of Peace Treaty

STRUCTURE AND AUTHORITY OF THE CONFEDERATION Unlike the state constitutions, with their separation of powers among three branches of government, the Articles created only one governing body in the national government, a congress. The Congress was a **unicameral legislature**, meaning that it had only one chamber, not a bicameral legislature as the majority of states had established. Each state selected from two to seven delegates to serve in Congress, and had the authority to determine how it would select its delegates. However, each state congressional delegation had only one vote on proposed policies, treaties, and constitutional amendments. Approving policies and ratifying treaties required an affirmative vote from nine of the state delegations in Congress. Amending the Articles required an affirmative vote from each of the 13 state delegations: a unanimous vote.

unicameral legislature
A legislative body with a single chamber

The Articles did not create a judicial branch, an executive branch, or a president. Congressional delegates would select one of their members to serve as president, to preside over the meetings of Congress. State courts would resolve legal conflicts, unless the dispute was between states, in which case Congress would resolve it. State governments would implement and pay for (if they agreed to congressional requests for money) policies approved by Congress.

The structure of national government instituted by the Articles was a product of its framers' experiences under the British government; the framers wanted to avoid structures and procedures they feared would lead to tyranny. Congress had very limited authority. Although it could approve policies relevant to foreign affairs, defense, and the coining of money, it was not authorized to raise revenue through taxation. Only state governments could levy and collect taxes. Therefore, to pay the national government's bills, Congress had to request money from each state. State governments, the governments closer to the people, with representatives elected by eligible voters, remained sovereign and more powerful than the national government.

WEAKNESSES OF THE CONFEDERATION The Articles of Confederation emphasized the sovereignty of individual, independent states at the expense of a powerful national government. Citizens' allegiance was to their states; no mass national conscience existed. Under the Articles, the states retained ultimate authority in matters of day-to-day life, commerce, and currency. There was no centralized economic policy. In addition, each state taxed goods coming into the state from foreign nations and from other states. Moreover, several states issued their own money and required the use of that currency for all business within the state. At the national level, Congress lacked authority to collect taxes and lacked the power to compel states to honor national policies and obligations, including state cooperation in building roads and canals, which were the infrastructure needed for a healthy economy that supports general welfare.

The cumulative effect of each state having its own economic policies was that interstate and international commerce was hampered, putting the nation's economic health in jeopardy.[19] At the same time, the national government had war debt to pay. Farmers (a substantial component of the economy) were struggling financially and losing their farms. Veterans of the Revolutionary War were waiting for pay. State governments threw debtors in jail. When petitions to state governments calling for them to address the problems of those suffering financially went unanswered, debt-burdened citizens protested and rebelled, some taking up arms. Rebellions occurred in most states, but the most serious, known as Shays's Rebellion, occurred in Massachusetts between 1786 and 1787.

Farmer and war veteran Daniel Shays led hundreds of debt-burdened rebels in protests at Massachusetts courthouses, closing them down and burning debtor records. As such protests spread to other states, Congress voted to establish a national army and requested that each state provide money to pay for it. Only the state of Virginia agreed to provide the requested money. At the same time, the Massachusetts state government enacted laws to criminalize protests against, and speech critical of, the government. In addition, the Massachusetts governor raised money from wealthy merchants to support a private militia to battle Shays's Rebellion. In the winter of 1787, the state militia crushed the rebellion.[20]

The weaknesses of the confederal system—including its barriers to the development of national economic policies and to defense against domestic uprisings—were becoming apparent to the nation's political and business leaders.

CALLS TO REMEDY DEFECTS OF THE ARTICLES OF CONFEDERATION As Congress faced an inability to pay the costs of governing, and as violent rebellions threatened peace and security in the states, five states sent delegates to Annapolis, Maryland, in 1786, to discuss ways to "remedy defects of the Federal Government," as the national government created by the Articles of Confederation was known at that time. The states charged their Annapolis delegates with considering the trade and commerce problems of the United States. However, in the report of their proceedings, the delegates noted that the "embarrassments which characterize the present State of our national affairs, foreign and domestic" suggested that trade and commerce were not the only problems of the federal government. Therefore, the delegates called for a future convention, to be attended by representatives from all 13 states, to devise amendments to the Articles of Confederation that would fix its weaknesses and to submit its proposals to "the United States in Congress assembled."[21]

Crafting the Constitution of the United States

The convention called to address the defects of the Articles of Confederation was held in Philadelphia from May 25 through September 17, 1787. All states except Rhode Island sent delegates. The delegates to this Constitutional Convention, elected by their state's legislature, were among the most elite Americans. Some 80 percent had served as members of the Continental Congresses, and most were lawyers, businessmen, or plantation owners. Many were engaged in highly lucrative international trade, and all were wealthy men. These elites contrasted sharply with the majority of the population, which included women, slaves, Native Americans, and the country's hard-pressed farmers, struggling local merchants, and those engaged in trade. In fact, historian Charles Beard contended in 1913 that the Constitution's framers succeeded in forging a government that protected their elite status.[22]

Although very early in the convention the delegates agreed on the need for a stronger national government than the Articles had created, there was conflict over how best to structure a stronger national government while incorporating principles of representative democracy and protecting liberties. Conflict also arose over the issue of slavery. In working through those conflicts to create compromises they could support, the delegates were pragmatic. They had to balance their preference for a strong central government with the citizens' distrust of a strong central government. Ultimately, the delegates framed a new constitution, instituting new foundational government structures and operating procedures in an effort to fulfill the principles laid out in the Declaration of Independence. Thereafter, proponents of the proposed new constitution won its ratification only after acknowledging the need to amend it quickly by adding a bill of rights to limit the power of the national government it created.

Areas of Consensus

Early in the convention, consensus developed on the need for dual sovereignty (a federal system of government) to address the Articles' weaknesses while at the same time winning the votes needed to support a new constitution. The delegates also reached quick consensus on the need to establish the new constitution as the supreme law of the country, with which the national and state governments must all comply. In addition, the delegates' views coalesced around the principle of distributing the basic governing functions among three branches of the national government, each with capabilities to monitor the other branches, a structure that was evident in the state constitutions.

A FEDERAL SYSTEM: DUAL SOVEREIGNTY According to the congressional charge to the convention, the convention delegates had to send their final proposal to the existing Congress for action. Remember that Congress, as structured by the Articles of Confederation (the constitution in effect at the time of the Constitutional Convention), was made up of representatives selected by each state. The convention delegates recognized that these representatives were not likely to ratify a document that created a strong central government at the expense of the existing state governments. Therefore, the framers had to balance a strong central government (national sovereignty) and existing state sovereignty. That balance hinged on delegating governing powers to the national government in the policy areas that were problematic under the Articles—interstate and international trade, foreign affairs, and defense—and leaving the remaining domestic matters with the states.

The framers created an innovative system of government with **dual sovereignty**—one in which ultimate governing authority is divided between two levels of government—a central government and regional governments—with each level having ultimate authority over different policy matters and different geographic areas. Today, we call this a *federal system* of government. Article I of the Constitution lists the matters over which the national legislature (Congress) has lawmaking authority, such as regulating interstate and foreign commerce, coining money, raising and funding an army, and declaring war. Article I also prohibits state governments from engaging in several specific activities, such as negotiating treaties. (Chapter 3 focuses on dual sovereignty and the constitutional distribution of power between the national and the state governments in the U.S. federal system of government.)

Although the Constitution's first three articles list powers and responsibilities of the national government, nowhere in the document that was drafted at the convention were states' powers and responsibilities listed. Therefore, the distribution of sovereignty in the federal system was not clearly articulated in the proposed Constitution.

CONSTITUTIONAL SUPREMACY The framers anticipated that this system of dual sovereignty would cause tension between the national government and the state governments. Therefore, they included in Article VI of the Constitution a **supremacy clause**, which states that the Constitution and the treaties and laws created by the national government in compliance with the Constitution are the supreme law of the land.

The framers did not include a list or even a vague outline of the matters over which the states had sovereignty. Citizens apprehensive of a strong central government, recollecting the colonists' experiences under the British government, would argue that this vacuum of information on state sovereignty was a major fault in the Constitution, because it would allow the national government to infringe on state sovereignty. The lack of a list of individual liberties to limit the power of the national government, a bill of rights such as each state constitution had, was also a major concern for citizens afraid of a strong central government.

SEPARATION OF POWERS WITH INTEGRATED CHECKS AND BALANCES The opinions of the framers also converged around the foundational structures of the new government they were creating. Borrowing from the state constitutions, the framers separated the primary governing functions among three branches of government— referred to as the **separation of powers**—so that no one group of officials controlled all the governing functions. Under the terms of the separation of powers, each branch of the government has specific powers and responsibilities that allow it to operate independently of the other branches: the legislative branch has authority to formulate policy; the executive branch has authority to implement policy; and the judicial branch has authority to resolve conflicts over the law.

Once the framers separated the primary functions, they established various mechanisms by which each branch can monitor and limit the functions of the other branches to ensure that no branch acts to the detriment of citizens' natural rights. These mechanisms collectively form a system of **checks and balances**. If one branch tries to move beyond its own sphere or to behave tyrannically, this arrangement ensures that the other branches can take action to stop it. For example, Congress formulates and approves legislation; however, before legislation becomes law, the president has the opportunity to approve or reject it (through the veto process). Although the president has authority to nominate top executive branch officials and federal judges, the Senate has the authority to confirm or reject the presidential nominees. Figure 2.1 shows how specific checks and balances contribute to the separation of powers.

The delegates spent most of the first two months of the Constitutional Convention arguing about the national legislature and focused primarily on the question of state representation in Congress. They devoted less than a month to the other issues before them, including the structure of the executive and judicial branches; the relationship between the federal and the state governments; the process for amending the new constitution, should the need arise to do so; the procedures for the Constitution's ratification; and perpetuation of the slave trade.[23]

Conflict and Compromise Over Representation

Among the delegates' top points of contention was representation in the national government. They engaged in intense political battles over how to implement popular sovereignty while also protecting individual rights and ensuring tranquility within the nation's borders. And they disagreed about how the government officials in each of the three branches of this newly formed republican national government should be selected and how the states should be represented in the national government. Slavery was another contentious issue that impacted representation as well as the implementation of the principle that "all men are created equal."

THE CONNECTICUT COMPROMISE Virginian James Madison arrived at the convention with a plan in hand for restructuring the national government. The **Virginia Plan**, drafted by Madison and proposed by the Virginia delegation, called for a radically restructured national government, consisting of three branches: a bicameral legislature (Congress), an executive elected by the Congress, and a separate national judiciary. Under the Virginia Plan, state representation in both chambers of Congress would be proportional, based on state population. The people would elect members to the lower house, and members elected by the people to the lower house would select the members of the upper house.

separation of powers
The Constitution's delegation of authority for the primary governing functions among three branches of government so that no one group of government officials controls all the governing functions.

checks and balances
A system in which each branch of government can monitor and limit the functions of the other branches.

Virginia Plan
The new governmental structure proposed by the Virginia delegation to the Constitutional Convention, which consisted of a bicameral legislature (Congress), an executive elected by the legislature, and a separate national judiciary; state representation in Congress would be proportional, based on state population; the people would elect members to the lower house, and members of the lower house would elect the members of the upper house.

Separation of Powers with Checks and Balances

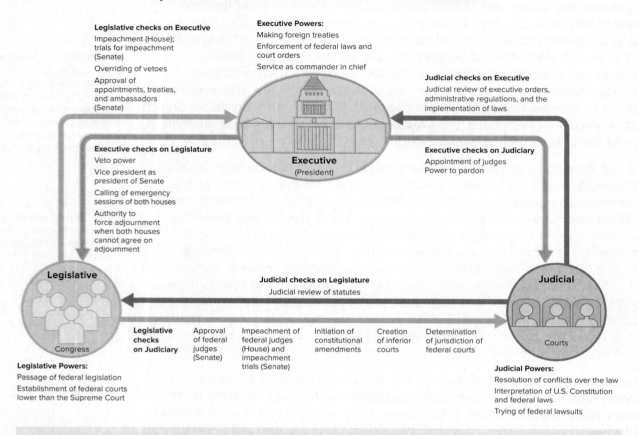

Legislative checks on Executive
Impeachment (House); trials for impeachment (Senate)
Overriding of vetoes
Approval of appointments, treaties, and ambassadors (Senate)

Executive Powers:
Making foreign treaties
Enforcement of federal laws and court orders
Service as commander in chief

Judicial checks on Executive
Judicial review of executive orders, administrative regulations, and the implementation of laws

Executive checks on Legislature
Veto power
Vice president as president of Senate
Calling of emergency sessions of both houses
Authority to force adjournment when both houses cannot agree on adjournment

Executive
(President)

Executive checks on Judiciary
Appointment of judges
Power to pardon

Legislative
Congress

Judicial checks on Legislature
Judicial review of statutes

Judicial
Courts

Legislative checks on Judiciary — Approval of federal judges (Senate) — Impeachment of federal judges (House) and impeachment trials (Senate) — Initiation of constitutional amendments — Creation of inferior courts — Determination of jurisdiction of federal courts

Legislative Powers:
Passage of federal legislation
Establishment of federal courts lower than the Supreme Court

Judicial Powers:
Resolution of conflicts over the law
Interpretation of U.S. Constitution and federal laws
Trying of federal lawsuits

FIGURE 2.1 ■ **Why Did the Constitution's Framers Separate Powers Among the Three Branches of the National Government?** What specific powers does each branch have? What is the purpose of the Constitution's checks and balances? For each branch of the government—legislative, executive, and judicial—name a specific check that it can exert on each of the other two. Which, if any, branch is the most powerful? Explain.

New Jersey Plan
The proposal presented in response to the Virginia Plan by the less populous states at the Constitutional Convention, which called for a unicameral national legislature in which all states would have an equal voice (equal representation), an executive office composed of several people elected by Congress, and a Supreme Court whose members would be appointed by the executive office.

Connecticut Compromise
The compromise between the Virginia Plan and the New Jersey Plan that created a bicameral legislature with one chamber's representation based on population and the other chamber having two members for each state (also known as the *Great Compromise*).

Under the Virginia Plan, states with larger populations would have more representatives, each with a vote, and therefore more votes. On behalf of the less populous states, William Paterson of New Jersey presented a series of resolutions known as the **New Jersey Plan**, which essentially reworked the Articles of Confederation. Under the New Jersey Plan, a unicameral national legislature would remain the centerpiece of the government, and all states would have equal representation in this legislature. The New Jersey Plan also called for Congress to elect several people to form a multi-member executive office, and the executive office had the authority to appoint members to a Supreme Court.

The disagreement and negotiation over the Virginia and the New Jersey Plans resulted in several compromises, most notably the **Connecticut Compromise** (also known as the *Great Compromise*). This compromise created today's bicameral Congress, with state representation in the House of Representatives based on state population and equal state representation in the Senate (two senators per state).

THE CONSTITUTION'S LIMITS ON REPRESENTATIVE DEMOCRACY At the heart of representative democracy is the participation of citizens in electing their government officials. Yet the framers allowed citizens, whose eligibility to vote was determined by state constitutions instead of the Constitution of the United States, to elect directly only the members of the House of Representatives, thereby placing tremendous limits on representative democracy. Existing state constitutions allowed only property-owning white men to vote. The one exception was New Jersey, where property-owning white women could also vote until 1807, when the state constitution was amended to deny all women the right to vote. Hence, all women (except in New Jersey from 1776 to 1807) and many men, including Native Americans and enslaved African Americans, were denied the right to vote under the new Constitution. The framers thus effectively limited voting rights to a small minority of citizens. Chapter 5 discusses the evolution of popular sovereignty (expansion of voting rights).

Until the Seventeenth Amendment was passed in 1913, state legislators selected the state's representatives in the national senate (U.S. senators). The Seventeenth Amendment gave eligible voters in each state the power to elect their representatives in the U.S. Senate.

The process that the framers devised for the election of the president and the vice president was a compromise between those supporting popular election and those supporting selection by officials elected to national or state legislatures. The conflicts over the best way to elect the president and the vice president are ongoing, as discussed in this chapter's "Thinking Critically" feature. The Constitution gives states the authority to select, using a method of each state's choosing, individuals (*electors*) to elect the president and the vice president. Each state selects the same number of electors as the number of representatives they elect to Congress. The electors from all states compose the **Electoral College**, the body of citizens that actually selects the president and the vice president. Before ratification of the Twelfth Amendment (1804), each elector would cast two votes for president. The candidate receiving the largest majority of electors' votes became president, and the candidate receiving the second largest number of votes became vice president. Since ratification of the Twelfth Amendment, each elector casts one vote for president and one vote for vice president.

Electoral College
The name given to the body of representatives elected by voters in each state to elect the president and the vice president.

Therefore, representative democracy in the national government was very limited under the Constitution as ratified in 1788. Most inhabitants could not vote, and those who could, voted to elect representatives to only one chamber of Congress, the House of Representatives.

Conflict and Compromise Over Slavery

Delegates to the Constitutional Convention disagreed on the "peculiar institution" (as Thomas Jefferson called it) of slavery. In 1790, enslaved persons made up 18 percent of the U.S. population, and most were enslaved in the southern states.[24] Delegates from those states, whose economies relied on the labor of enslaved people, feared that a strong central government would abolish slavery. Meanwhile, northern delegates, who were concerned that a weak national government would limit the United States's ability to engage in commerce and international trade, believed that the nation needed a more powerful central government. Ultimately, to get the southern states to agree to the strong central government established in the Constitution, the northern states compromised on the slavery issue by agreeing to a delay in debating the issue.

A provision in Article I, Section 9, of the Constitution postponed any debate on the legality of slavery by prohibiting Congress from addressing or discussing the importation of new enslaved people into the United States until January 1, 1808.

Moreover, Article IV, which deals with interstate relations, established the states' obligation to deliver all fugitive enslaved people back to their slaveholders. This measure aimed to ensure that people in free states would continue to respect the property rights of slaveholders—including their right to hold enslaved people, who were legally defined as property, not people with natural guaranteed rights.

Evolution of Representation in the National Government

	THEN	NOW	NEXT
	(1790)		■ Will those advocating for statehood of Washington, D.C., and Puerto Rico succeed? If so, what will be the number of congressional members and members of the Electoral College?
Number of voting members in the House	105*	435**	
Number of people represented by each House member	Approximately 34,000*	Approximately 710,000, with a high of 1 million in Montana and a low of 583,000 in Wyoming****	
Number of U.S. senators	22***	100	
Number of people represented by each senator	Varied; highest number was in Virginia, and lowest number was in Delaware*	Varies; highest is 38 million in California, and lowest is 583,000 in Wyoming****	■ Will calls to improve popular sovereignty by replacing the Electoral College with direct election of the president and vice president by citizen voters be acted upon? How would such a change be accomplished?
Who votes for U.S. House members?	Determined by the states; in all states, white men who owned property could vote	Citizens 18 years and older (per 15th, 17th, 19th, and 26th amendments to the Constitution)	
Who selects U.S. senators?	State legislatures (per Constitution of 1789)	Elected by voters in each state	
Who votes for president and vice president?	State-by-state selected electors; each elector had two votes	State-by-state selected electors; electors each have one vote for president and one vote for vice president (per 12th Amendment)	
	Presidential candidate with the most electoral votes wins the presidency; candidate with the second-most votes wins the vice presidency.		

*www.census.gov/prod/3/98pubs/CPH-s-US.PDF

**Reapportionment Act of 1929

***www.senate.gov/history/1787.htm

****www.census.gov/population/apportionment/files/Apportionment%20Population%202010.pdf

Should We Abolish the Electoral College?

THE ISSUE: In the world's oldest democracy, the reality is that the president of the United States might not be the choice of the majority of the voting population. Such was the case in the 2016 presidential election. According to the Federal Election Commission's election results, Democrat Hillary Clinton won the most votes, with 48 percent of the popular vote. Republican Donald Trump won 45.9 percent of the popular vote. This amounted to Clinton winning 2,868,518 more citizens' votes than Trump did.* In every other election for federal office, the candidate with the most popular votes wins that seat. But in the case of the president, the Constitution requires that the candidate be elected by the Electoral College. Essentially, the winner is determined by the cumulative results of 51 separate elections, one conducted in each state plus the District of Columbia, with the number of electoral votes determined in proportion to the size of the state's congressional delegation. Is the Electoral College system unfair? Should we abolish it?

YES: The Electoral College is exclusive and undemocratic. This system demands that candidates focus nearly exclusively on key swing states that will be pivotal to their election and on populous states that carry the most electoral votes. The system is undemocratic because it relies on plurality elections within the states. In a plurality, the candidate with the most Electoral College votes wins, even if that candidate does not receive a majority of the popular vote. In neither the 2000 nor the 2016 presidential election did the ultimate victory go to the candidate most people preferred. Instead, the winners were George W. Bush and Donald Trump. Due to the undemocratic nature of the Electoral College, it should be abolished.

NO: In structuring the Electoral College as they did, the Constitution's framers devised a way of representing the views of both the people who elect the electors and the states because of the state-based nature of the elections. If the Electoral College were abolished, the most populous geographical regions would dominate in presidential elections. Urban areas would have tremendous clout in presidential elections, and less densely populated rural areas would be virtually ignored. The current structure strengthens the power of the states and in this way ensures that our federal system remains strong.

OTHER APPROACHES: Because of the difficulty of abolishing the Electoral College, various schemes have been proposed that would make it almost impossible for the loser of the popular vote to win the presidency. These include awarding a state's electoral votes proportionally instead of on a winner-take-all basis, dividing electoral votes by congressional district (currently done in Maine and Nebraska), and awarding extra electoral votes to the winner of the popular vote. Legislation recently passed in Maryland, Hawaii, Illinois, and New Jersey would commit those states' electors to vote for the winner of the popular vote if states representing a 270-vote majority in the Electoral College enact similar legislation.

*https://transition.fec.gov/pubrec/fe2016/2016presgeresults.pdf.

WHAT DO YOU THINK?

1. Should the Electoral College be abolished, remain the same, or be reformed? Why? If your answer is "should be reformed," what changes would you implement?

2. If the Electoral College were abolished, what impact would the change likely have on voters in your home state? Does that scenario influence your view?

3. Americans revere the Constitution as a near-sacred document. Typically, citizens are reluctant to advocate amending the "supreme law of the land." What is your view concerning amending the Constitution?

Although enslaved people were legally considered property, Article I, Section 2 established a formula for "counting" enslaved persons for purposes of representation in the House of Representatives, apportionment of electors for the Electoral College, and the allocation of tax burdens among the states. This **Three-Fifths Compromise** counted each enslaved person as three-fifths of a free person. The southern states benefited from this compromise: They gained greater representation in the House and in the Electoral College than they would have if only free people were counted. The benefit to the northern states was that if the national government imposed a direct tax on the states based on their populations, southern states would pay more than they would if only non-enslaved people were counted. (The national government has never imposed such a direct tax on the states.)

James Madison, while deploring slavery, argued that the delegates' "compromise" over slavery was "in the spirit of accommodation which governed the Convention." He insisted that without the Three-Fifths Compromise, the Constitution would never have been signed.

So, at the Constitutional Convention, delegates resolved some disagreements through accommodations and compromises, such as the large state–small state conflict over congressional representation. They put on hold other differences, such as their divisions over slavery. In the end, the document that the framers sent to the states for ratification described a government structure that aimed to fulfill the principles of the Declaration of Independence, for a select group of people. Foremost among those principles was the idea that it is up to the people to create a government that protects their natural rights to life, liberty, and the pursuit of happiness.

To ensure those rights, which were initially meant only for white, property-owning men, the framers devised two key arrangements: the separation of powers with an integrated system of checks and balances, and a federal system in which the national and state governments had distinct, ultimate authorities. Although there was consensus on the mission of the new government, the conflict and arguments over the appropriate structure of government and government processes resulted in compromises and often vague language that the framers anticipated would be clarified in the future.

What About a Bill of Rights?

While the Declaration of Independence argued that governments were created by the people to protect their natural rights to life, liberty, and the pursuit of happiness, unlike state constitutions, the Constitution as drafted by the framers did not provide protections for these rights in the form of a list of limits on the national government. On September 12, 1787, George Mason, a delegate from Virginia, called for a bill of rights such as those found in state constitutions, which would list fundamental freedoms upon which the national government could not infringe. Roger Sherman, a delegate from Connecticut, argued that there was no need for one, because state constitutions included their own bills of rights. With hardly any discussion, the delegates decided not to add a bill of rights to the proposed constitution.[25] The lack of a bill of rights would become a main target for critics of the proposed constitution.

Three-Fifths Compromise
The negotiated agreement by the delegates to the Constitutional Convention to count each enslaved person as three-fifths of a free person for the purpose of representation and taxes.

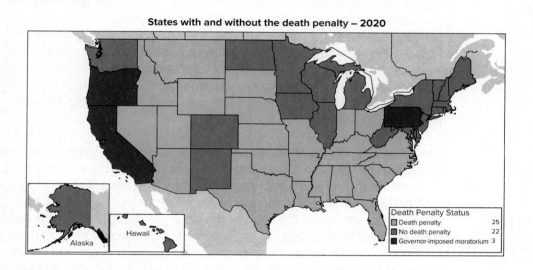

States with and without the death penalty – 2020

Death Penalty Status
Death penalty 25
No death penalty 22
Governor-imposed moratorium 3

Source: Death Penalty Information Center, https://deathpenaltyinfo.org/state-and-federal-info/state-by-state

Use the information in the graphic to answer the questions.

A. Identify the most common state death penalty policy.
B. Describe a similarity or difference in death penalty policy by state or region, as illustrated in the information graphic, and draw a conclusion about that similarity or difference.
C. Explain how death penalty policy as shown in the information graphic demonstrates the principle of federalism.

Congress Sends the Constitution to the States for Ratification

On September 17, 1787, thirty-nine convention delegates signed the Constitution. Following the amendment process in the Articles of Confederation, the delegates delivered their proposed constitution to the standing Congress. However, fearful that the document would not garner the approval of all 13 state legislatures as mandated by the Articles of Confederation's amendment process, the framers included in the proposed constitution a new ratification process that required just 9 of the 13 states to approve it for it to replace the Articles.

The framers requested that Congress send the proposed constitution to the states and that the state legislatures each establish a special, popularly elected convention to review and ratify the Constitution. One argument made to support this ratification process, which violated the Articles of Confederation, was that ratification by popularly elected conventions would validate the Constitution as the supreme law of the land, legitimized by the consent of the people. Congress acquiesced to the framers' request, and sent the proposed constitution to the states for ratification votes in special conventions.

The proposed constitution sent to the states was a product of conflict, deliberation, compromise, and pragmatism. In seven articles, the framers established a new national government with structures modeled after the state governments: separating the basic governing functions into three branches, giving each branch means to check the others, and establishing a radical new system of government—a federal system with dual sovereignty. Before exploring the states' debates and ratification of the Constitution, we review the blueprint of government embodied in the constitution sent to the states. To explore the entire Constitution, as amended since 1791, turn to the annotated Constitution that follows this chapter.

ARTICLE I: THE LEGISLATIVE BRANCH Article I of the Constitution delegates lawmaking authority to Congress, describes the structure of the legislative branch, and outlines the legislative process. Article I specifies that the legislature is bicameral, comprising the House of Representatives and the Senate. Each state is represented in the House based on its population, with each elected representative having one vote. To ensure representation based on state population, Article 1 also calls for a census every 10 years, to count all the people living in the country. In contrast, state representation in the Senate is equal, with each state having two senators, with one vote each.

According to Article I, a proposed piece of legislation—a *bill*—requires simple majority votes (50 percent plus one vote) in each chamber, the House and the Senate, to become a law. This requirement means that the House and the Senate can check each other in the legislative process, because even if one chamber garners a majority vote, the other chamber can kill the bill if its majority does not support the bill. Because all pieces of legislation supported by the majority of the House and the majority of the Senate go to the president for approval or rejection, the president has a check on the legislative authority of Congress.

ARTICLE II: THE EXECUTIVE BRANCH Article II of the Constitution describes the authority of the president. This article gives the president the obligation to ensure that the laws are faithfully executed, to appoint people to assist in administering the laws, to negotiate treaties, and to command the military. In addition to those executive functions, Article II allows the president several checks on the power of the other two branches of government.

All pieces of legislation approved by the House and the Senate must be forwarded to the president's desk. The president has 10 days to act on a bill, or it will automatically become law. Within those 10 days, the president can either sign the bill into law or **veto** it—that is, reject it, sending it back to Congress with his objections noted. Because Congress has primary responsibility for the legislative function, it can set aside the president's veto—that is, override the veto—with two-thirds of House members and two-thirds of the senators voting to approve the vetoed bill. Therefore, a bill can become law without the president's approval, once he has had the opportunity to approve it, but a bill cannot become law without the approval of at least a simple majority in each chamber of Congress.

With respect to the legislature's checks on the executive, the Constitution gives the Senate the power of **advice and consent**—the power to approve or reject—for treaties and presidential appointments. The Senate's advice and consent authority extends to the president's judicial nominees as well.

veto
The president's rejection of a bill, which is sent back to Congress with the president's objections noted.

advice and consent
The Senate's authority to approve or reject the president's top appointments and negotiated treaties.

Three Branches of Government: Are Their Powers Balanced?

The Federalist Papers are 85 essays published in New York City papers as well as in a two-volume book between October 1787 and May 1788. The essays criticized the government created by the Articles of Confederation and analyzed the innovative government proposed in the draft Constitution of the United States. Written and distributed as part of a propaganda campaign to win ratification of the Constitution in New York State, *The Federalist Papers* provided what is still viewed as the most authoritative interpretation of the Constitution.

One governing principle analyzed in *The Federalist Papers* is the separation of powers coupled with checks and balances, as discussed in the quotes below.

It will not be denied, that power is of an encroaching nature, and that it ought to be effactually restrained from passing the limits assigned it. After discriminating therefore in theory, the several classes of power, as they may in their nature be legislative, executive, or judiciary; the next and most difficult task, is to provide some practical security for each against the invasion of the others. What this security ought to be, is the great problem to be solved. (The Federalist No. 48: Madison)

The legislative department [branch] *derives a superiority in our governments . . .* (The Federalist No. 48: Madison)

Whoever attentively considers the different departments of power must perceive, that in a government in which they are separated from each other, the judiciary, from the nature of its functions, will always be the least dangerous to the political rights of the constitution . . . (The Federalist No. 78: Hamilton)

Now read Articles I, II, and III of the Constitution and review Figure 2.1. Based on these sources of information, complete the Practice Analytical Thinking exercise.

Practice Analytical Thinking: Source Analysis

1. Does the Constitution "effactually" restrain each branch of government from encroaching on the other branches? Provide examples of constitutional restraints. Can you propose any additional restraints that should be added to the Constitution?

2. Madison claims that the legislative branch is superior to the other branches. Provide evidence, from the Constitution, to support his claim. Provide constitutional evidence that disputes his claim.

3. Hamilton claims that it is clear to whomever "attentively considers" how the powers are separated among three branches that the judiciary is the branch we should worry about least. Provide constitutional evidence to support his claim. Provide constitutional evidence that disputes his claim.

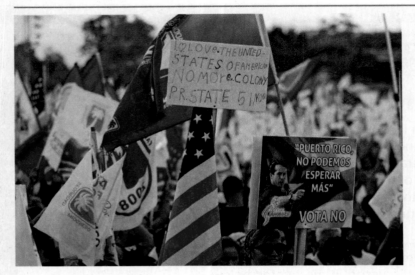

>> Congress has the authority to add new states to the union. Puerto Rico is not a state; it has been a U.S. territory since the end of the Spanish-American war in 1898. However, since the Jones-Shafroth Act (1917), people born in Puerto Rico are U.S. citizens. Although Puerto Ricans can vote in presidential primaries, unless they relocate to one of the 50 U.S. states, they cannot vote in presidential elections, nor do they vote to elect representatives to either the U.S. House or Senate. Puerto Ricans living on the island do elect a non-voting delegate to the U.S. House. In October 2019, Puerto Rico's House delegate, Jenniffer Gonzalez-Colon, introduced the Puerto Rico Statehood Admission Act that would fund a non-binding ballot referendum asking Puerto Rican voters if they want statehood. Even if the majority votes for statehood, in what would be the sixth statehood referendum since 1967, Congress could decide to do nothing. When was the last time Congress approved adding a new state to the union?

Ana Martinez/Reuters/Newscom

Marbury v. Madison
The 1803 Supreme Court case that established the power of judicial review, which allows the Court to strike down laws passed by the other branches that it views to be in conflict with the Constitution.

judicial review
Court authority to determine whether an action taken by any government official or governing body violates the Constitution; established by the Supreme Court in the 1803 *Marbury v. Madison* case.

ARTICLE III: THE JUDICIAL BRANCH Article III describes the judicial branch. More specifically, Article III establishes the U.S. Supreme Court, and it delegates to Congress the authority to establish other, inferior (lower) courts. The Supreme Court and the other federal courts established by Congress have the authority to resolve lawsuits arising under the Constitution, national laws, and international treaties. In 1803, in the case of **Marbury v. Madison**,[26] the Supreme Court interpreted Article III to mean that the Court has the authority to determine whether an action taken by any government official or governing body violates the supreme law of the land, the Constitution; this is the power of **judicial review**.

ARTICLE IV: STATE-TO-STATE RELATIONS The Constitution does not include a list of state powers, rights, or responsibilities as it does for the national government. However, in Article IV, the Constitution does describe how the states must respect the rights and liberties of the citizens of all states, as well as the legal proceedings and decisions of the other states. Article IV also establishes the means by which Congress can add new states to the union at the same time it prohibits Congress from changing state borders without consent of the affected states. Article IV also obligates the national government to ensure that all states are representative democracies.

ARTICLE V: THE AMENDMENT PROCESS The framers recognized that the Constitution was a compromise born of their attempts to resolve existing problems, and therefore future generations would want to, and need to, revise the document in light of their own experiences, circumstances, and problems. Therefore, the framers provided processes to amend the Constitution.

The Constitution's framers wanted to ensure that widespread deliberation among the American people would precede any and all changes in the written Constitution. Thus, they made it no easy matter to amend formally the U.S. Constitution—that is, to change its written language. Constitutional amendment is a two-step process, entailing, first, the proposal of the amendment and, second, the ratification of the proposed amendment. Article V describes two different

Amending the Constitution

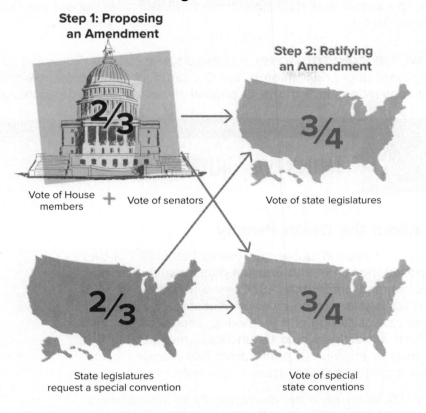

Step 1: Proposing an Amendment

2/3

Vote of House members + Vote of senators

2/3

State legislatures request a special convention

Step 2: Ratifying an Amendment

3/4

Vote of state legislatures

3/4

Vote of special state conventions

FIGURE 2.2 ■ In what two ways can an amendment be ratified? Who has the authority to ratify amendments to the Constitution? Why is the designation of this authority important to the balance of power between the national and state governments? Explain.

procedures for *proposing* an amendment (see Figure 2.2). The first method requires a two-thirds majority vote in each chamber, the House and the Senate, after which Congress sends the approved proposal to the states for ratification. The second method requires Congress to call a convention for proposing amendments if two-thirds of state legislatures petition Congress for such a convention. Today, an Article V Convention movement is pressing state legislatures to petition Congress to call a convention for proposing amendments. Twenty-eight states have applied for an Article V Convention for a balanced budget amendment. Fifteen states have applied for an Article V Convention for amendments that would limit the power of the federal government.[27]

Article V also outlines two avenues by which the second step, *ratification* of a proposed amendment, may occur. **Ratification** means that the proposal is formally confirmed, thereby becoming law. An amendment is ratified by a vote of approval in either three-quarters of the state legislatures or three-quarters of special state conventions.

ARTICLE VI: SUPREMACY OF THE CONSTITUTION Article VI proclaims that the new national government will be legally responsible for all debts incurred by the Congress of the United States established by the Articles of Confederation. In addition, the article states that the Constitution, and laws and treaties made in

ratification
The process by which constitutions and constitutional amendments are formally confirmed, thereby becoming law.

compliance with it by the national government, are the supreme law of the land. Moreover, all national and state government officials must uphold the Constitution of the United States.

ARTICLE VII: THE CONSTITUTIONAL RATIFICATION PROCESS According to Article VII of the Constitution, ratification of the Constitution required the affirmative vote of special conventions in 9 of the 13 original states. After the delegates signed

CONCEPT APPLICATION | THINKING CRITICALLY

Changing Public Opinion About the Death Penalty

The Eighth Amendment to the U.S. Constitution states, "Excessive bail shall not be required, nor excessive fines imposed, nor cruel and unusual punishments inflicted." The ban on cruel and unusual punishment under the U.S. Constitution is debated to this day. What does it mean for a punishment to be cruel or unusual? One punishment used in Colonial America was tarring and feathering, imposed to publicly humiliate a suspected criminal. Such a practice would be unconscionable today. The standards of what constitutes a cruel or an unusual punishment has changed over the course of history and with our communities' standards of decency.

The federal government and many U.S. states allow the death penalty as a punishment for capital crimes. In recent years, however, two Supreme Court cases, *Roper v. Simmons* (2005) and *Atkins v. Virginia* (2002), have defined imposing the death penalty on minors and on individuals with impaired mental capacity as cruel; and while the death penalty is still an option for federal crimes, many states have limited the death penalty or banned it entirely due to errors made in executions and numerous legal challenges that have arisen from botched executions and allegations of racism in sentencing.

Public opinion of the appropriateness of the death penalty has evolved over time. Opinions of people favoring the death penalty for individuals who commit murder have been on the decline since 1995. A May 2020 Gallup poll reported a record low percentage of Americans who find the death penalty morally acceptable, and many have come to support alternative punishments. According to the Death Penalty Information Center, the number of executions in the United States has been declining since the late 1990s.

Practices of other nations may have a role in the changing view of the death penalty in the United States, and the way the death penalty is applied in the United States may also influence views. The United States is unique among developed democracies in its use of the death penalty. The Death Penalty Information Center reports that Black defendants are disproportionately more likely to receive the death penalty than whites, and there have been several high profile exonerations of death row inmates. The 2019 film *Just Mercy* profiled the true story of an innocent man condemned to death who was ultimately released after a long and prolonged legal battle.

WHAT DO YOU THINK?

1. How you expect public opinion of the death penalty will evolve?

2. Is the death penalty cruel? Is the death penalty unusual?

3. Should the 8th Amendment's ban on cruel and unusual punishment include a ban on the death penalty?

the Constitution, the standing Congress forwarded it to the states, directing them to hold ratification conventions according to Article VII of the Constitution, instead of implementing the constitutional amendment process established in the Articles of Confederation (the constitution in effect at the time).

The Ratification Battle: Federalists versus Anti-Federalists

Two days after 39 delegates signed the Constitution, it was published in a special issue of a newspaper called the *Pennsylvania Packet*. Almost immediately, opponents of the proposed Constitution began to write letters, issue pamphlets, and make stirring speeches urging the state legislatures to reject the document. The debate developed as one between the Federalists and the Anti-Federalists. The **Federalists** supported the Constitution as presented by the convention delegates. The **Anti-Federalists** opposed the Constitution, arguing it gave the national government too much power—power that would erode states' authority, which was left undefined in the document, and endanger individual freedoms because it was not limited by a bill of rights. In the end, the success or failure of the ratification process hinged on the battle over a bill of rights.

Federalists
Individuals who supported the new Constitution as presented by the Constitutional Convention in 1787.

Anti-Federalists
Individuals who opposed ratification of the Constitution because they were deeply suspicious of the powers it gave to the national government and of the impact those powers would have on states' authority and individual freedoms.

THE ANTI-FEDERALISTS' CONCERNS WITH THE PROPOSED CONSTITUTION Numerous Anti-Federalists penned countless letters, speeches, and essays warning of the dangers of the proposed new constitution and urging Americans to reject it. Under the pen name "A Columbian Patriot," Mercy Otis Warren wrote several pieces critical of the proposed constitution, including her "Observations on the New Constitution, and on the Federal and State Conventions" (1788), which presented a comprehensive summary of the Anti-Federalist arguments against the proposed Constitution of the United States. The circulation of Warren's pamphlet was larger than that of *The Federalist Papers* written by James Madison, Alexander Hamilton, and John Jay to win support for ratification of the proposed constitution.[28]

The bottom line for Warren and the Anti-Federalists was that the foundational structures in the proposal threatened protection of citizens' natural rights in several ways. First, the Constitution delegated too much power to the executive branch at the expense of the legislative branch, which in a republic should have the most power because it is composed of representatives elected by the people (not by an Electoral College). Next, it gave too much power to the national government at the expense of the state governments, which were closer to the

≫ During the 18th century, the letters, plays, poems, and pamphlets of Mercy Otis Warren influenced the debates over declaring independence from Britain and ratifying the Articles of Confederation, the Constitution, and the Bill of Rights. Have you heard of her? One reason you may not have is that she was an Anti-Federalist (on the losing side of the ratification debate). Another reason you might not have heard about her is she was a politically engaged woman at a time when society believed women should not be involved in politics.

John Singleton Copley/Art Reserve/Alamy Stock Photo

people and therefore better understood their concerns and problems. Moreover, the Constitution lacked a bill of rights to limit the vague powers delegated to the national government, including Congress's ambiguous power to make all laws it deems necessary and proper to promote the general welfare. Without a bill of rights, there was no way of truly limiting the actions the national government might take to achieve its goals, actions that might threaten states' rights (sovereignty) and the liberties and rights of the people.

Articulating Anti-Federalist views, Thomas Jefferson, author of the Declaration of Independence, insisted that the inclusion of a bill of rights in the Constitution was essential to protecting citizens' rights. Federalist Alexander Hamilton countered that listing those rights might endanger the very kind of individual freedoms and rights they sought to safeguard. It was possible, Hamilton reasoned, that the list would be incomplete and that at some future time people might legitimately argue that because a given right was not specifically enumerated, it did not exist. Jefferson's response was that "half a loaf is better than no bread" and that "if we cannot secure all our rights, let us secure what we can."[29]

THE FEDERALIST PAPERS: IN SUPPORT OF THE CONSTITUTION The Federalists made their most famous arguments in support of the proposed constitution in a series of essays known as **The Federalist Papers.** The authors of *The Federalist Papers*, James Madison, Alexander Hamilton, and John Jay, knew that achieving ratification depended on convincing the public and state legislators that the Constitution would empower the new nation to succeed. They also understood that many of the Anti-Federalists' concerns centered on how much power the national government would have under the Constitution and how that authority would affect the states and individual freedoms. Consequently, they approached the ratification debate strategically, writing essays (in the form of letters to the citizens) to consider those specific issues.

With regard to protecting individual rights, in *Federalist* No. 10, Madison reassuringly details how the republican government created by the Constitution would ensure that many views would be heard and that a majority of the population would not be permitted to trample the rights of the numerical minority. Writing in *Federalist* No. 84, Hamilton argues that because "the people surrender nothing, and as they retain every thing" by way of the Constitution, there was no danger that the new government would usurp individual rights and liberties.

In *Federalist* No. 51, Madison explains that there is a "double security" for protecting individual rights and liberties. In the federal system, "the power surrendered by the people is first divided between two distinct governments," the national and the state, and each government will control the other. In addition, both levels of government are "subdivided among distinct and separate departments" (branches of government) that check each other.

With regard to loss of state power, James Madison argues in *Federalist* No. 45 that the states retain "a very extensive portion of active sovereignty" because "the powers delegated by the proposed Constitution to the federal government are few and defined. Those which are to remain in the State governments are numerous and indefinite." Therefore, the listed national powers are limited while the lack of a list of state powers means the states have fewer limits than does the national government.

For the Federalists, the foundational structures of the new government, which included the federal system of government (dual sovereignty), the separation of powers, and the system of checks and balances, would protect individual liberties

The Federalist Papers
A series of essays, written by James Madison, Alexander Hamilton, and John Jay, that argued for the ratification of the Constitution.

Did the Constitution create an overly centralized government, or did it properly limit federal power? Develop an argument that takes a position on how well the Constitution properly balances national and state power.

In your essay, you must:

- Articulate a defensible claim or thesis that responds to the prompt and establishes a line of reasoning.

- Support your claim with at least TWO pieces of accurate and relevant information:

  - At least ONE piece of evidence must be from one of the following foundational documents:

    - The U.S. Constitution

    - *Federalist* No. 10

    - Brutus 1

  - Use a second piece of evidence from another foundational document from the list or from your study of U.S. Government and Politics.

- Use reasoning to explain why your evidence supports your claim or thesis.

- Respond to an opposing or alternative perspective using refutation, concession, or rebuttal.

and states' rights. For the Anti-Federalists, those structures were not sufficient. An enumeration of limits on the national government was also essential to protect individual liberties and states' rights.

Ratification: Constitution (1788) and Bill of Rights (1791)

In the end, the concerns of the Anti-Federalists and the larger public conversation about states' rights and individuals' liberties placed significant pressure on the Federalists to reconsider the need for inclusion of a bill of rights. With the proviso that a bill of rights would be the first order of business for the new Congress, Massachusetts, Maryland, South Carolina, and New Hampshire—the last four states of the nine needed for ratification—ratified the Constitution in 1788. In 1790, Rhode Island was the last of the original 13 states to ratify the Constitution. Table 2.3 presents an overview of the creation of the federal system of U.S. government from the Constitutional Convention through the ratification of the Bill of Rights.

In the opening days of the first session of the newly constituted Congress in March 1789, Virginia congressman James Madison introduced a bill of rights. Comprising 12 amendments, this proposed addition to the Constitution powerfully reflected the public concerns voiced during the ratification debates by enumerating limits on the national government's right to infringe on the natural rights of life,

TABLE 2.3 ▪ Creation of the U.S. Federal System

May 25–September 17, 1787	Constitutional Convention occurs
June 21, 1788	Constitution replaces Articles of Confederation
February 4, 1789	First presidential election takes place
March 4, 1789	First Congress under Constitution convenes
April 6, 1789	Results of presidential election announced
June 8, 1789	James Madison proposes 12 amendments
September 25, 1789	Congress approves 12 proposed amendments
February 2, 1790	Supreme Court convenes for first time
December 15, 1791	Virginia is ninth state to ratify 10 of 12 amendments; Bill of Rights is ratified

Bill of Rights
The first 10 amendments to the Constitution, which were ratified in 1791, constituting an enumeration of the individual liberties with which the government is forbidden to interfere.

liberty, and the pursuit of happiness and by preserving the states' sovereignty. Congress passed all 12 proposed amendments and sent them to the states for ratification. By 1791, the required number of states had quickly ratified 10 of the 12 amendments, which we refer to today as the **Bill of Rights**.

The first eight amendments in the Bill of Rights establish the government's legal obligation to protect several specific liberties to which the Declaration of Independence referred when it stated that men were "endowed by their creator with certain unalienable rights." These natural rights became government-protected liberties, *civil liberties*, through the ratification process. With the Jefferson and Hamilton debate over the pros and cons of listing citizens' rights in mind, the Ninth Amendment indicates that the list of liberties in the first eight amendments is not exhaustive and therefore "shall not be construed to deny or disparage others retained by the people." (Chapter 8 discusses in depth the civil liberties established in the Bill of Rights.) The tenth and last amendment in the Bill of Rights preserves states' rights. The Tenth Amendment says that the powers not delegated to the national government by the Constitution "nor prohibited by it to the states, are reserved to the states respectively, or to the people." By listing rights of citizens and the states, the Bill of Rights addressed the core concerns raised by the Anti-Federalists by imposing limits on the national government.

The Constitution as a Living, Evolving Document

The authors of the Constitution were pragmatic men who were willing to compromise to resolve the problems confronting the new nation and to get a new constitution ratified.[30] To win the votes needed to move the document from first draft through ratification, the framers had to negotiate and compromise over constitutional language. As a result of this give-and-take, the Constitution is replete with vague and ambiguous phrases, which the framers expected would be reviewed and revised through both formal amendment of the Constitution and judicial interpretation.

According to James Madison's convention notes on the discussion of Article V, the formal amendment process, delegate "Elbridge Gerry noted that 'the novelty and difficulty of the experiment requires periodical revisions.'"[31] Thomas Jefferson even proposed during the discussion of Article V that a constitutional convention be called at the beginning of each new century.[32] At the time of his retirement, President George Washington (1789–1797) stated that he thought "the People (for it is with them to Judge) can as they will have the advantage of experience on their Side, decide with as much propriety on the alterations and amendments which are necessary [as] ourselves. I do not think we are more inspired, have more wisdom, or possess more virtue, than those who will come after us."[33]

Viewing the Constitution as a living document that should evolve along with the nation, through conventions and formal amendment, the framers also expected judges to interpret the Constitution, and laws made under its provisions, in light of the realities of their own time. Alexander Hamilton wrote in *Federalist* No. 78, "A constitution is in fact, and must be, regarded by judges as a fundamental law. It therefore belongs to them to ascertain its meaning as well as the meaning of any particular act proceeding from the legislative body. . . . The courts must declare the sense of the law. . . ."[34] As Supreme Court justice Charles Evans Hughes (1862–1948) later observed, "The Constitution is what the Judges say it is."[35]

The alteration of this document—through both the passage of formal amendments and judicial (re)interpretation of key clauses—derives from a continuing conversation among citizens about the core beliefs and principles of the framers and the generations that have followed them, including Americans today, and what those beliefs mean for contemporary realities. Hence, the Constitution continues to be a living and evolving document.

Formal Amendment of the Constitution

Every term, members of Congress introduce between 100 and 200 proposals for new constitutional amendments. Members of Congress who oppose a ruling by the U.S. Supreme Court or a law that creates a great deal of public debate may propose a constitutional amendment to supersede the Court ruling or the controversial law. Often, members of Congress introduce constitutional amendments knowing that the amendment will never be ratified but wanting to appease their core constituencies by at least instigating public conversation about how our government should function and what rights and freedoms individuals possess.

Only a tiny fraction of the thousands of proposed amendments have cleared Congress—in fact, only 33 have achieved the two-thirds vote necessary in both the House and the Senate—and, as noted, the states have ratified only 27 of those congressional proposed amendments. The amendments that the states have ratified fit into one of three categories: They have (1) extended civil liberties and civil rights (equal protection of laws for citizens), (2) altered the selection of officials or the operation of the branches of the national government, or (3) dealt with important policy issues. The annotated Constitution that follows this chapter indicates the three categories in which each constitutional amendment fits.

One possible explanation for the relatively low number of constitutional amendments is that the framers established a difficult amendment process (review Figure 2.2), requiring super-majority votes: two-thirds of the members in each

THEN

Corbis Historical/Getty Images

NOW

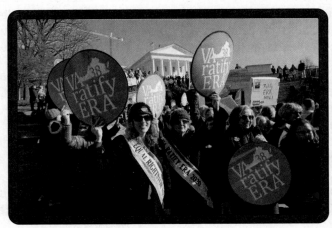

Steve Helber/AP Images

Source Analysis Alice Paul (left), a leader of the women's suffrage movement, toasts Tennessee's vote to ratify the proposed Susan B. Anthony Amendment. Tennessee's ratification was the last vote needed to add the 19th Amendment to the U.S. Constitution, guaranteeing women citizens the right to vote beginning in 1920. Because the ratification occurred during Prohibition, which was enacted by the 18th Amendment (1919) and repealed by the 21st Amendment (1933), she toasted with grape juice. Recognizing that the vote was just the first step in guaranteeing women equal rights and liberties, Paul drafted an Equal Rights Amendment (ERA) for the U.S. Constitution. First introduced in Congress in 1923, the ERA proposal was approved by Congress in 1972 and sent to the states for ratification. In 2020, the 100th anniversary of the 19th Amendment, Virginia became the 38th state, and last state needed, to ratify the ERA. However, the congressional established deadline for the ERA's ratification had passed in 1982. So, while supporters of the ERA celebrated, opponents argued the ratification was moot. What is the current status of the ERA?

chamber in Congress and three-quarters approval among the states. They did so to ensure that nationwide public discourse would take place before the written words in the Constitution, the supreme law of the land, could be changed.

Interpretation by the U.S. Supreme Court

Beyond the addition of formal amendments, the Constitution has changed over time through interpretation by the courts. This interpretation began with the U.S. Supreme Court's landmark *Marbury v. Madison* decision in 1803, in which the Court established the important power of judicial review—the authority of the courts to rule on whether acts of government officials and governing bodies violate the Constitution. Although the U.S. Supreme Court's interpretation is final, if the Supreme Court does not review constitutional interpretations made by lower federal courts, then the interpretations of those lower courts are the final word on the Constitution's meaning.

According to constitutional law scholars Laurence Tribe and Joshua Matz, a wealth of scholarly literature discusses the varied factors influencing judges' decisions that "define the framework of our fundamental law" as established in the Constitution. That literature indicates that when resolving a conflict over the meaning of constitutional language, the judges and justices "look to the Constitution's text, how it was understood when it was ratified, our national history, judicial precedent [previous court opinions and decisions], the Constitution's values, and the practical needs of our time."[36]

Judges and justices have interpreted and reinterpreted (changed previous judicial interpretations of) constitutional clauses regularly. Such interpretations and reinterpretations are discussed throughout this book, particularly in the chapters on civil liberties and civil rights.

Richard Beeman, a widely respected constitutional scholar, identifies three recurring themes evident in Supreme Court rulings: (1) the nature of the Constitution as a document that continues evolving as the courts interpret changing social norms, (2) the tensions created by the foundational structures established in the Constitution (separation of powers, checks and balances, and the dual sovereignty of our federal system), and (3) the clarification of fundamental rights guaranteed by the Bill of Rights.[37] With regard to changing societal norms, Court decisions reflect an expansion of the principle of equality, as well as of the liberties and rights granted by the Bill of Rights and subsequent amendments.

In most cases, the Court's rulings are in step with public opinion. Analysts note that the Court does not often lead public opinion—in fact, it more often follows it.[38] And even if the justices wanted to take some very controversial and unpopular action, the system of checks and balances forces them to consider how the other branches would react. Recall that the Court has the power to interpret the law; it does not have the power to implement or to enforce the law and must be concerned about how the other branches might retaliate against it for highly unpopular decisions. Therefore, for the most part, changes to the Constitution, both formal (constitutional amendment) and informal (court interpretation), are incremental and further the will of the people because they are the product of a government with separation of powers and a system of checks and balances, a written constitution that establishes fundamental law, and widespread public discourse—an ongoing conversation of democracy.

Conclusion: Thinking Critically About What's Next for the Constitution

The governing principles proclaimed in the Declaration of Independence successfully unified American colonists to fight the War for Independence. However, government created by the consent of the people with the mission of protecting the people's natural rights to life, liberty, and the pursuit of happiness has proven difficult. Economic upheaval and domestic uprisings experienced under the Articles of Confederation sparked the call for a convention to amend the constitution. The product of the convention to amend the Articles, a convention in which the "spirit of accommodation" governed, was a proposed new constitution replete with compromises over major issues (such as how to implement representative government and the right to enslave people) and vague language.

The foundational structures established by the Constitution (federal system, separation of powers with integrated system of checks and balances), the core governing procedures, and the values and principles articulated in the Preamble (mission) have been perpetually questioned, debated, clarified, and amended since day one of the new union. Indeed, the Constitution is an ever evolving and living document, just as the framers predicted.

In response to lawsuits, the courts continue to determine what is and is not constitutional through judicial review. In addition, citizens and elected officials continue to debate possible amendments to the Constitution. The framers' mission to create a more perfect union through the Constitution of the United States is still a work in progress.

■ References

1. "Sugar Act of 1764," www.u-s-history.com/pages/h1211.html.

2. "Great Britain: Parliament-The Stamp Act, March 22, 1765," http://avalon.law.yale.edu/18th_century/stamp_act_1765.asp.

3. Glenna Matthews, *The Rise of Public Woman: Women's Power and Women's Place in the United States 1630–1970* (New York: Oxford University Press, 1992), 56.

4. "Prelude to Revolution," www.historyplace.con/unitedstates/revolution/rev-prel.htm.

5. J. Alan Rogers, "Colonial Opposition to the Quartering of Troops During the French and Indian War," *Military Affairs* (1970): 7.

6. "Great Britain: Parliament—The Declaratory Act, March 18, 1766," http://avalon.law.yale.edu/18th_century/declaratory_act_1767.html.

7. America's Homepage, "The Townshend Act," http://ahp.gatech.edu/townshend_act_1767.html.

8. Russell Bourne, *Cradle of Violence: How Boston's Waterfront Mobs Ignited the American Revolution* (Hoboken, NJ: Wiley, 2006).

9. "Committees of Correspondence," www.u-s-history.com/pages/h675.html.

10. Boston Tea Party Ships & Museums, www.bostonteapartyship.com/.

11. "The Intolerable Acts," www.ushistory.org/declaration/related/intolerable.htm.

12. "The Declaration of Rights and Grievances," www.usconstitution.net/intol.html#Rights.

13. "The Articles of Association," www.usconstitution.net/assocart.html.

14. For further discussion of the impact of *Common Sense* on colonial attitudes and beliefs, see Edmund S. Morgan, *The Birth of the Republic: 1763–89* (Chicago: University of Chicago Press, 1992), 71–76.

15. "Lee's Resolutions," http://avalon.law.yale.edu/18th_century/lee.asp.

16. You can find these constitutions at Yale Law School's Avalon Project, http://avalon.law.yale.edu/subject_menus/18th.asp.

17. Jack N. Rakove, "A Tradition Born of Strife," in *American Politics: Classic and Contemporary Readings,* 6th ed., ed. Allan J. Cigler and Burdett A. Loomis (Boston: Houghton Mifflin, 2005), 4–5.

18. Constitutional Rights Foundation, "How the First State Constitutions Helped Build the U.S. Constitution," https://crf-usa.org/images/pdf/gates/First-States-Constitutions.

19. For an excellent discussion of how the Articles benefited the states, see Keith L. Dougherty, *Collective Action Under the Articles of Confederation* (New York: Cambridge University Press, 2001), 76–82.

20. "Shays Rebellion," www.government-and-constitution.org/history-us-political-parties/shays-rebellion.htm.

21. "Proceedings of Commissioners to Remedy Defects of the Federal Government: 1786," http://avalon.law.yale.edu/18th_century/annapoli.asp.

22. Charles Beard, *An Economic Interpretation of the Constitution of the United States* (New York: Macmillan, 1913).

23. "The Constitutional Convention," www.usconstitution.net/consttop_ccon.html.

24. Eddie Becker, "Chronology on the History of Slavery and Racism," http://innercity.org/holt/chron_1790_1829.html.

25. Richard Beeman, *The Penguin Guide to the United States Constitution* (New York: Penguin Books, 2010), 161.

26. *Marbury v. Madison,* 5 U.S. 137 (1803).

27. Jay Riestenberg, "U.S. Constitution Threatened as Article V Convention Movement Nears Success," March 2019, www.commoncause.gov/resource/u-s-constitution-threatened-as-article-v-convention-movement-nears-success.

28. Larry M. Lane and Judith J. Lane, "The Columbian Patriot: Mercy Otis Warren and the Constitution," in *Women, Politics, and the Constitution,* ed. Naomi B. Lunn (New York: Harrington Park Press, 1990), 17–31.

29. Thomas Jefferson, letter to James Madison on the Bill of Rights debate, March 15, 1789. Courtesy of *Eigen's Political & Historical Quotations.*

30. John P. Roche, "The Founding Fathers: A Reform Caucus in Action," *American Political Science Review,* LV (1961).

31. Larry J. Sabato, *A More Perfect Constitution: Why the Constitution Must Be Revised—Ideas to Inspire a New Generation* (New York: Walker Publishing Company, 2007), 315, fn 4.

32. Ibid., 218.

33. Ibid., 221.

34. Alexander Hamilton, "Federalist No. 78," *The Federalist Papers* (Cutchogue, NY: Buccaneer Books, 1992), 395–396.

35. "Charles Evans Hughes," http://c250.columbia.edu/c250_celebrates/remarkable_columbians/charles_hughes.

36. Laurence Tribe and Joshua Matz, *Uncertain Justice: The Roberts Court and the Constitution* (New York: Picador, 2014), 5.

37. Richard Beeman, *The Penguin Guide to the United States Constitution* (New York: Penguin Books, 2010), 190.

38. Thomas Marshall, "Representing Public Opinion: American Courts and the Appeals Process," *Politics and Policy,* 31 (December 2003): 726–739.

Key Terms

■ Multiple Choice Questions

Questions 1 and 2 refer to the passage below.

> "Ambition must be made to counteract ambition. The interest of the man must be connected with the constitutional rights of the place. It may be a reflection on human nature, that such devices should be necessary to control the abuses of government. But what is government itself, but the greatest of all reflections on human nature? If men were angels, no government would be necessary. If angels were to govern men, neither external nor internal controls on government would be necessary. In framing a government which is to be administered by men over men, the great difficulty lies in this: you must first enable the government to control the governed; and in the next place oblige it to control itself."
>
> —Madison, *Federalist 51*

1. What is Madison's main argument in the excerpt from *Federalist 51*?
   A. The Constitution is a social contract between the government and the governed
   B. Elected officials will be of the highest integrity and will not succumb to the temptations of power
   C. The government's power will be checked and balanced in order to prevent tyranny
   D. The nature of human behavior is often unpredictable and overly ambitious

2. Which of the following is an example of the controls Madison refers to in *Federalist 51*?
   A. Judicial review
   B. the Supremacy clause
   C. Implied powers
   D. The ratification process for the Constitution

3. Which explanation best describes why there are only 27 amendments to the United States Constitution?
   A. Congress and the courts can never agree on an amendment's procedural issues related to making changes to the Constitution
   B. The framers set up the Constitution to last no more than 10 years, making modern-day amendments difficult to add
   C. The U.S. Supreme Court has repeatedly struck down amendments because many of them have lacked legal standing
   D. It is difficult to get two-thirds of Congress to propose an amendment and three-fourths of state legislatures to ratify a constitutional amendment.

Questions 4 and 5 refer to the political cartoon below.

The Library of Congress

4. The political cartoon above demonstrates which of the following weaknesses of the Articles of Confederation?
A. The Congress's inability to tax
B. The Congress's reliance on the state militias to quell domestic uprisings
C. The Congress's inability to regulate interstate commerce
D. The Congress's lack of authority to compel states to honor national priorities such as infrastructure building

5. The importance of Shays's Rebellion to the development of the U.S. Constitution was that it
A. revealed the necessity of both adding the Bill of Rights to the Constitution and creating a new system of checks and balances.
B. demonstrated the intensity of anti-ratification sentiment within the 13 states.
C. indicated that a strong, constitutionally designed national government was needed to protect property and maintain order.
D. convinced the delegates attending the Constitutional Convention to accept the Connecticut plan Compromise.

6. Which of the following is an accurate comparison of the beliefs of Federalists and Anti-Federalists?

Federalists	Anti-Federalists
A. The executive would have too much power under the Constitution	The executive would not have enough power under the Constitution
B. Representatives will be too far away in the nation's capital to know the needs of their constituents	Representatives elected by the people would be able to communicate their constituents' needs to the federal government
C. States should maintain sovereignty	The Constitution should serve as the supreme law of the land
D. The Constitution does not need a Bill of Rights because internal and external control will prevent the government from infringing upon the rights of the people	A Bill of Rights would protect the rights of citizens from federal government overreach

7. Which of the following best represents popular sovereignty in the original Constitution as it was ratified in 1789?

    A.   Election of members of the House of Representatives

    B.   Election of members of the Senate

    C.   Election of the president

    D.   Ratification of treaties

■ Free Response Questions

SCOTUS Comparison

In *Martin v. Hunter's Lessee* (1816), Denny Martin, a British subject, had the land he inherited from his uncle seized by Virginia during the Revolutionary War in 1781. The next year, Virginia's state legislature granted part of the land seized from Denny Martin to a man named David Hunter. However, a federal treaty then required that the land be given back to Denny Martin. The Virginia Supreme Court sided with the Virginia legislature. Upon review, the U.S. Supreme Court sent the case back to the Virginia Supreme Court, stating that the federal treaty required the land should indeed be returned to Denny Martin. The Virginia Supreme Court argued that the U.S. Supreme Court did not have authority over cases originating in state court. The case returned to the U.S. Supreme Court and ended in the Court's final ruling that it **does** have authority to interpret federal law as established by its supremacy in matters of constitutional interpretation.

    A.   Identify the constitutional principle that is common to both *Martin v. Hunter's Lessee* (1816) and *Marbury v. Madison* (1803).

    B.   Based on the constitutional clause identified in part A, explain why the facts of *Martin v. Hunter's Lessee* led to the same ruling as in *Marbury v. Madison*.

    C.   How was the ruling in *Martin v. Hunter's Lessee* similar to other rulings by the Marshall Court?

Argumentation

Develop an argument that explains whether the fears and concerns of the Anti-Federalists regarding governmental tyranny are evident in today's government.

In your essay, you must:

- Articulate a defensible claim or thesis that responds to the prompt and establishes a line of reasoning.

- Support your claim with at least TWO pieces of accurate and relevant information:

    - At least ONE piece of evidence must be from one of the following foundational documents:

        — Federalist No. 51

        — Brutus 1

        — The Constitution, including the Bill of Rights and subsequent amendments

    - Use a second piece of evidence from another foundational document from the list or from your study of the Constitution.

    - Use reasoning to explain why your evidence supports your claim/thesis.

- Respond to an opposing or alternative perspective using refutation, concession, or rebuttal.

Quantitative Analysis

Amending the Constitution

Step 1: Proposing an Amendment

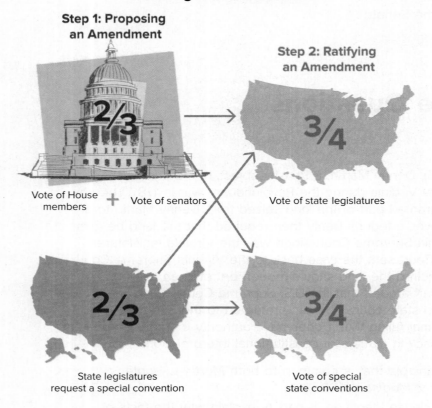

Step 2: Ratifying an Amendment

Vote of House members **+** Vote of senators

Vote of state legislatures

State legislatures request a special convention

Vote of special state conventions

Use the information in the graphic to answer the questions.

A. Identify the steps to add an amendment to the U.S. Constitution.

B. Describe a similarity or difference in the four methods used to ratify an amendment, and draw a conclusion about that similarity or difference.

C. Explain how the amendment process as illustrated in the information graphic demonstrates the principle of federalism.

The Constitution of the United States of America

■ Preamble

We the People of the United States, in Order to form a more perfect Union, establish Justice, insure domestic Tranquility, provide for the common defence, promote the general Welfare, and secure the Blessings of Liberty to ourselves and our Posterity, do ordain and establish this Constitution for the United States of America.

POLITICAL INQUIRY:

1. *Who was included in "we the people" who ordained and established the Constitution?*

2. *What did the people of the United States in the late 18th century mean by "secure the blessings of liberty to ourselves and our posterity"?*

3. *What are some of the debates among people of the United States today related to the goal of promoting the general welfare?*

The Preamble states that "the People" are creating a new government, which is described in the Constitution. The Preamble also decrees that it is the mission of this new government to serve the people better than did the government established by the Articles of Confederation, which had been in effect since before the end of the War for Independence. The major goals of governments in the United States are enumerated in the Preamble.

■ ARTICLE I. (Legislative Branch)

Section 1. (Bicameral Legislative Branch)

All legislative Powers herein granted shall be vested in a Congress of the United States, which shall consist of a Senate and House of Representatives.

POLITICAL INQUIRY:

1. *Why did the framers establish a bicameral legislature instead of a unicameral legislature such as existed under the Articles of Confederation?*

2. *In 1934, as a cost-cutting measure, the state of Nebraska adopted a unicameral legislature (one chamber) to replace its bicameral legislature. What are some advantages and disadvantages of a bicameral legislature compared to a unicameral (one chamber) legislature?*

3. *Given the reality of partisanship in today's Congress, would a unicameral legislature better serve the country? Explain your answer.*

Article I presents the organization, procedures, and authority of the lawmaking branch, the Congress, a bicameral (two-chamber) legislature comprising the House of Representatives and the Senate.

CLAUSE 1 House members are elected to serve a two-year term.

CLAUSE 2 The Constitution specifies only three qualifications to be elected to the House: You must be at least 25 years old; you must be a U.S. citizen for at least seven years (so a foreign-born, naturalized citizen can be a House member); and you must be a resident of the state you will represent. By tradition, House members live in the district that they represent.

CLAUSE 3 The "three-fifths" clause called on the government to count enslaved people as three-fifths of a person when conducting the decennial (every ten years) census, which measures how many people live in the country and where they live.

Census data is also used in the distribution of more than $600 billion in federal funds to state and local governments annually.

The population count is used to distribute the 435 House seats among the states—the goal being that each House member represents about the same number of constituents, which is 710,000 based on the 2010 Census. Congress set the number of House seats at 435 through the Reapportionment Act of 1929.

CLAUSE 4 Governors have the authority to call for a special election to fill any of their states' House seats that become vacant.

CLAUSE 5 House members select their presiding officer, the Speaker of the House. The Speaker is in line to succeed the president if both the president and the vice president are unable to serve.

Note that the Constitution does not mention the selection of a majority leader or a minority leader in the House. Those positions have been established by House rules.

The Constitution gives the House a check on officials of the executive and judicial branches through its power of impeachment: the power to accuse such officials formally of offenses such as treason, bribery, and other high crimes and misdemeanors. If the accused officials are subsequently found guilty in a trial held by the Senate, they are removed from office. Because the country had no national criminal code when the Constitution was written and ratified, the meaning of "high crimes and misdemeanors" is controversial, as witnessed in the most recent impeachment process.

Section 2. (The House of Representatives)

CLAUSE 1: The House of Representatives shall be composed of Members chosen every second Year by the People of the several States, and the Electors in each State shall have the Qualifications requisite for Electors of the most numerous Branch of the State Legislature.

CLAUSE 2: No Person shall be a Representative who shall not have attained to the age of twenty five Years, and been seven Years a Citizen of the United States, and who shall not, when elected, be an Inhabitant of that State in which he shall be chosen.

CLAUSE 3: Representatives and direct Taxes shall be apportioned among the several States which may be included within this Union, according to their respective Numbers, which shall be determined by adding to the whole Number of free Persons, including those bound to Service for a Term of Years, and excluding Indians not taxed, three fifths of all other Persons. The actual Enumeration shall be made within three Years after the first Meeting of the Congress of the United States, and within every subsequent Term of ten Years, in such Manner as they shall by Law direct. The Number of Representatives shall not exceed one for every thirty Thousand, but each State shall have at Least one Representative; and until such enumeration shall be made, the State of New Hampshire shall be entitled to chuse three, Massachusetts eight, Rhode-Island and Providence Plantations one, Connecticut five, New-York six, New Jersey four, Pennsylvania eight, Delaware one, Maryland six, Virginia ten, North Carolina five, South Carolina five, and Georgia three.

POLITICAL INQUIRY:

1. *Why is an accurate census important to citizens?*

2. *Why is an accurate census important to state and local governments?*

3. *An online census was one of several technological innovations the Census Bureau used in 2020 to respond to the challenges of counting an increasingly large and diverse society, while also complying with strict cost constraints that Congress imposed. How well did it work?*

CLAUSE 4: When vacancies happen in the Representation from any State, the Executive Authority thereof shall issue Writs of Election to fill such Vacancies.

CLAUSE 5: The House of Representatives shall chuse their Speaker and other Officers; and shall have the sole Power of Impeachment.

POLITICAL INQUIRY:

1. *What does the "sole power of impeachment" mean?*

2. *What presidents have the House impeached?*

3. *What were the charges presented in the Articles of Impeachment in the most recent impeachment of a president?*

Section 3. (The Senate)

CLAUSE 1: The Senate of the United States shall be composed of two Senators from each State, chosen by the Legislature thereof, for six Years; and each Senator shall have one Vote.

POLITICAL INQUIRY: *In the 1960s, the U.S. Supreme Court ruled that in state government the proper implementation of representative democracy must follow the principle of one person, one vote. This means that each elected representative in a state House should represent about the same number of constituents, and each elected state senator must represent about the same number of constituents. Based on the Great Compromise during the Constitutional Convention, representation in the U.S. Senate requires two senators per state. This means two senators represent Wyoming's 583,000 residents and two senators represent California's 38 million residents.*

1. *Do you support the Great Compromise or do you think that the principle of one person, one vote should be upheld, which would mean amending the Constitution? Justify your answer.*

2. *What are the chances that states with small populations, such as Wyoming, would support an amendment to apportion senators based on state population, as is done for the House of Representatives? Explain.*

CLAUSE 2: Immediately after they shall be assembled in Consequence of the first Election, they shall be divided as equally as may be into three Classes. The Seats of the Senators of the first Class shall be vacated at the Expiration of the second Year, of the second Class at the Expiration of the fourth Year, and of the third Class at the Expiration of the sixth Year, so that one third may be chosen every second Year; and if Vacancies happen by Resignation, or otherwise, during the Recess of the Legislature of any State, the Executive thereof may make temporary Appointments until the next Meeting of the Legislature, which shall then fill such Vacancies.

CLAUSE 3: No Person shall be a Senator who shall not have attained to the Age of thirty Years, and been nine Years a Citizen of the United States, and who shall not, when elected, be an Inhabitant of that State for which he shall be chosen.

CLAUSE 4: The Vice President of the United States shall be President of the Senate but shall have no Vote, unless they be equally divided.

CLAUSE 5: The Senate shall chuse their other Officers, and also a President pro tempore, in the Absence of the Vice President, or when he shall exercise the Office of President of the United States.

CLAUSE 6: The Senate shall have the sole Power to try all Impeachments. When sitting for that Purpose, they shall be on Oath or Affirmation. When the President of the United States is tried the Chief Justice shall preside: And no Person shall be convicted without the Concurrence of two thirds of the Members present.

Article I, Section 3

CLAUSE 1 Before the Seventeenth Amendment was passed (1913), state legislatures selected their state's two U.S. senators, each of whom served a 6-year term. Today, voters in each state elect their two U.S. senators.

CLAUSE 2 Today, every even-numbered year, congressional elections are held in which one-third of the Senate's 100 seats and all 435 House seats are up for election.

Thanks to the Seventeenth Amendment (1913), each state's governor is authorized to call for elections to fill a vacancy in a Senate seat; in addition, each state legislature is authorized to determine the process by which a vacant Senate seat will be temporarily filled until the election of a new senator.

CLAUSE 3 Senators must be at least 30 years old, either natural-born citizens or immigrants who have been citizens for at least nine years, and—like members of the House—residents of the state they are elected to represent.

CLAUSE 4 The vice president serves as the president of the Senate, with the authority to preside over meetings of the Senate and to vote when there is a tie.

CLAUSE 5 Although the first few vice presidents did preside over daily meetings of the Senate, the vice president rarely does so today.

Note that the Constitution does not mention the selection of a majority or minority leader in the Senate. Those positions are established through Senate rules.

CLAUSE 6 The Senate exercises a check on officials of the executive and judicial branches of the federal government by trying them once they have been impeached by the House of Representatives.

CLAUSE 7 If the Senate convicts an impeached official, he or she is removed from office and may be subject to prosecution in the criminal courts. The vote required to convict an impeached official is two thirds (67) of the senators.

Article I, Section 4
CLAUSE 1 Though states have the authority to organize and conduct elections, today they rely heavily on local governments to assist them. Congress has passed numerous laws to ensure constitutionally guaranteed voting rights. The first such law was passed shortly after ratification of the Fifteenth Amendment to criminalize attempts to deny black men their newly won right to vote. Congress has also enacted laws to make voter registration easier. For example, a 1996 federal law requires states to allow citizens to register to vote through the mail.

CLAUSE 2 The Twentieth Amendment (1933) changed the date on which the annual meeting of Congress must begin. Today, Congress must assemble beginning at noon on the 3rd day of January.

Article I, Section 5
CLAUSE 1 Each chamber decides whether the election of each of its members is legitimate. A majority of the members of each chamber must be present to conduct business: currently, 218 in the House; 51 in the Senate.

CLAUSE 2 After each congressional election, both the House and the Senate determine how they will conduct their business. The members of each chamber establish codes of behavior, which they use to judge and—if necessary—punish members' misconduct.

CLAUSE 7: Judgment in Cases of Impeachment shall not extend further than to removal from Office, and disqualification to hold and enjoy any Office of honor, Trust or Profit under the United States: but the Party convicted shall nevertheless be liable and subject to Indictment, Trial, Judgment and Punishment, according to Law.

POLITICAL INQUIRY:

1. *What was the vote in the 2020 impeachment trial of President Trump?*

2. *Who presided over the 2020 impeachment trial of the president?*

Section 4. (Congressional Elections)

CLAUSE 1: The Times, Places and Manner of holding Elections for Senators and Representatives, shall be prescribed in each State by the Legislature thereof; but the Congress may at any time by Law make or alter such Regulations, except as to the Places of chusing Senators.

POLITICAL INQUIRY: *To increase voter turnout (the percentage of eligible voters that vote on Election Day), states have enacted laws allowing voters to vote by mail, to register to vote on Election Day, and even to vote during a two-week window instead of only on Election Day (known as early voting). Within the last few years, several states have repealed early voting or shortened the time period for early voting.*

1. *Would you support or oppose allowing voters to vote by Internet? Explain your response.*

2. *What are some advantages of and some concerns raised by allowing voters to vote during a two-week window?*

3. *Does your state allow voters to vote by mail? to register to vote on Election Day? to vote during a two-week window instead of only on Election Day?*

CLAUSE 2: The Congress shall assemble at least once in every Year, and such Meeting shall be on the first Monday in December, unless they shall by Law appoint a different Day.

Section 5. (Powers and Responsibilities of each Chamber)

CLAUSE 1: Each House shall be the Judge of the Elections, Returns and Qualifications of its own Members, and a Majority of each shall constitute a Quorum to do Business; but a smaller Number may adjourn from day to day, and may be authorized to compel the Attendance of absent Members, in such Manner, and under such Penalties as each House may provide.

CLAUSE 2: Each House may determine the Rules of its Proceedings, punish its Members for disorderly Behaviour, and, with the Concurrence of two thirds, expel a Member.

CLAUSE 3: Each House shall keep a Journal of its Proceedings, and from time to time publish the same, excepting such Parts as may in their Judgment require Secrecy; and the Yeas and Nays of the Members of either House on any question shall, at the Desire of one fifth of those Present, be entered on the Journal.

CLAUSE 4: Neither House, during the Session of Congress, shall, without the Consent of the other, adjourn for more than three days, nor to any other Place than that in which the two Houses shall be sitting.

Section 6. (Rights of Congressional Members)

CLAUSE 1: The Senators and Representatives shall receive a Compensation for their Services, to be ascertained by Law, and paid out of the Treasury of the United States. They shall in all Cases, except Treason, Felony and Breach of the Peace, be privileged from Arrest during their Attendance at the Session of their respective Houses, and in going to and returning from the same; and for any Speech or Debate in either House, they shall not be questioned in any other Place.

CLAUSE 2: No Senator or Representative shall, during the Time for which he was elected, be appointed to any civil Office under the Authority of the United States, which shall have been created, or the Emoluments whereof shall have been increased during such time; and no Person holding any Office under the United States, shall be a Member of either House during his Continuance in Office.

Section 7. (The Legislative Process)

CLAUSE 1: All Bills for raising Revenue shall originate in the House of Representatives; but the Senate may propose or concur with amendments as on other Bills.

CLAUSE 2: Every Bill which shall have passed the House of Representatives and the Senate, shall, before it become a law, be presented to the President of the United States: If he approve he shall sign it, but if not he shall return it, with his Objections to that House in which it shall have originated, who shall enter the Objections at large on their Journal, and proceed to reconsider it. If after such Reconsideration two thirds of that House shall agree to pass the Bill, it shall be sent, together with the Objections, to the other House, by which it shall likewise be reconsidered, and if approved by two thirds of that House, it shall become a Law. But in all such Cases the Votes of both Houses shall be determined by Yeas and Nays, and the Names of the Persons voting for and against the Bill shall be entered on the Journal of each House respectively. If any Bill shall not be returned by the President within ten Days (Sundays excepted) after it shall have been presented to him, the Same shall be a Law, in like Manner as if he had signed it, unless the Congress by their Adjournment prevent its Return, in which Case it shall not be a Law.

CLAUSE 3: Every Order, Resolution, or Vote to which the Concurrence of the Senate and House of Representatives may be necessary (except on a question of Adjournment) shall be presented to the President of the United States; and before the Same shall take Effect, shall be approved

CLAUSE 3 The House and the Senate must keep and publish records of their proceedings, including a record of all votes for and against proposals, except those that they decide require secrecy. However, if one-fifth of the members of a chamber demand that a vote be recorded, it must be recorded. Congress publishes a record of its debates, called the Congressional Record.

CLAUSE 4 To close down business for more than three days during a session, or to conduct business at another location, each chamber needs to get approval from the other one. This ensures that one chamber cannot stop the legislative process by refusing to meet.

Article I, Section 6
CLAUSE 1 Today, each member of Congress earns at least $174,000 per year, paid by taxes collected by the national government. Members of Congress are protected from civil lawsuits and criminal prosecution for the work they do as legislators. They are also protected from arrest while Congress is in session except for a charge of treason, of committing a felony, or of committing a breach of the peace.

CLAUSE 2 To ensure the separation of basic governing functions, no member of Congress can hold another federal position while serving in the House or the Senate. Moreover, members of Congress cannot be appointed to a position in the executive or judicial branch that was created during their term of office.

Article I, Section 7 This section details the legislative process.

CLAUSE 1 Although all revenue-raising bills, such as tax bills, must originate in the House, the Senate reviews them and has the authority to make modifications; ultimately the House and the Senate must each approve the identical bill for it to become law.

CLAUSE 2 After the House and the Senate approve the identical bill by a simple majority vote in each chamber, it is sent to the president for approval or rejection. The president has 10 days in which to act, or the bill will automatically become law (unless Congress has adjourned, in which case the bill dies—a pocket veto). If the president signs the bill within 10 days, it becomes law. If the president rejects—vetoes—the bill, he or she sends it back to the chamber of its origin with objections. Congress can then rewrite the vetoed bill and send the revised bill through the legislative process. Or Congress can attempt to override the veto by garnering a super-majority vote of approval (two-thirds majority) in each chamber.

CLAUSE 3 The president must approve or veto everything that Congress approves, except its vote to adjourn or any resolutions that do not have the force of law.

by him, or being disapproved by him, shall be repassed by two thirds of the Senate and House of Representatives, according to the Rules and Limitations prescribed in the Case of a Bill.

Section 8. (The Lawmaking Authority of Congress)

CLAUSE 1: The Congress shall have Power To lay and collect Taxes, Duties, Imposts and Excises, to pay the Debts and provide for the common Defence and general Welfare of the United States; but all Duties, Imposts and Excises shall be uniform throughout the United States;

CLAUSE 2: To borrow Money on the credit of the United States;

POLITICAL INQUIRY:

1. *To whom does the national government owe $23 trillion?*

2. *What arguments are made to support a balanced budget amendment to the Constitution—that is, one that would prevent Congress and the president from approving more spending than the government can collect in revenues?*

3. *What national situations might require spending more money than is raised in a budget year?*

CLAUSE 3: To regulate Commerce with foreign Nations, and among the several States, and with the Indian Tribes;

CLAUSE 4: To establish an uniform Rule of Naturalization, and uniform Laws on the subject of Bankruptcies throughout the United States;

CLAUSE 5: To coin Money, regulate the Value thereof, and of foreign Coin, and fix the Standard of Weights and Measures;

CLAUSE 6: To provide for the Punishment of counterfeiting the Securities and current Coin of the United States;

CLAUSE 7: To establish Post Offices and post Roads;

CLAUSE 8: To promote the Progress of Science and useful Arts, by securing for limited Times to Authors and Inventors the exclusive Right to their respective Writings and Discoveries;

CLAUSE 9: To constitute Tribunals inferior to the supreme Court;

CLAUSE 10: To define and punish Piracies and Felonies committed on the high Seas, and Offences against the Law of Nations;

CLAUSE 11: To declare War, grant Letters of Marque and Reprisal, and make Rules concerning Captures on Land and Water;

CLAUSE 12: To raise and support Armies, but no Appropriation of Money to that Use shall be for a longer Term than two Years;

CLAUSE 13: To provide and maintain a Navy;

CLAUSE 14: To make Rules for the Government and Regulation of the land and naval Forces;

Article I, Section 8 This section specifies the constitutionally established congressional powers. These powers are limited to those listed and any other powers that Congress believes are "necessary and proper" for Congress to fulfill its listed powers. Congress has used the "necessary and proper" clause (Clause 18) to justify laws that expand its powers that are listed in Article I of the Constitution. Laws that appear to go beyond the listed powers can be challenged in the courts, with the Supreme Court ultimately deciding their constitutionality.

CLAUSE 1 The power to raise money and to authorize spending it for common defense and the general welfare is one of the most essential powers of Congress. The Sixteenth Amendment (1913) authorizes a national income tax, which was not previously possible given the "uniformity" requirement in Clause 1.

CLAUSE 2 Today, after years of borrowing money to pay current bills, the national government has a debt of over $23 trillion.

CLAUSE 3 With the Supreme Court's support, Congress has interpreted Clause 3 in a way that has allowed it to expand its involvement in the economy and the daily lives of U.S. citizens. However, state governments have frequently challenged Congress's expansion of power by way of the commerce clause when they believe that Congress is infringing on their constitutional authority.

CLAUSE 4 Congress has the authority to establish the process by which foreigners become citizens or bankruptcy is declared.

CLAUSE 5 Congressional authority to make and regulate money as well as to standardize weights and measures is essential to the regulation of commerce.

CLAUSE 8 is the constitutional basis for copyright laws, which protect people's rights to their intellectual products.

CLAUSE 9 Congress exercised its authority to create the federal court system, other than the Supreme Court, which was established under Article III of the Constitution.

CLAUSE 10 Every nation in the world possesses the authority to establish its own laws regarding crimes outside its borders and violations of international law.

CLAUSES 11 THROUGH 14 collectively delegate to Congress the authority to raise and support military troops, to enact rules to regulate the troops, to call the troops to action, and to declare war. However, the president as commander in chief (Article II) has the authority to wage war. Presidents have committed armed troops without a declaration of war, leading to disputes over congressional and presidential war powers. Clause 11 also provides Congress with the authority to hire an individual for the purpose of retaliating against another nation for some harm it has caused the United States—that is, to provide a letter of Marque, an outdated practice.

CLAUSE 15: To provide for calling forth the Militia to execute the Laws of the Union, suppress Insurrections and repel Invasions;

CLAUSE 16: To provide for organizing, arming, and disciplining, the Militia, and for governing such Part of them as may be employed in the Service of the United States, reserving to the States respectively, the Appointment of the Officers, and the Authority of training the Militia according to the discipline prescribed by Congress;

CLAUSE 17: To exercise exclusive Legislation in all Cases whatsoever, over such District (not exceeding ten Miles square) as may, by Cession of Particular States, and the Acceptance of Congress, become the Seat of the Government of the United States, and to exercise like Authority over all Places purchased by the Consent of the Legislature of the State in which the Same shall be, for the Erection of Forts, Magazines, Arsenals, dock-Yards and other needful Buildings;—And

---

POLITICAL INQUIRY: *Article IV of the Constitution delegates to Congress the authority to admit new states to the union. The citizens of Washington, D.C., the seat of national government over which Congress has legislative power, have petitioned Congress to become a state.*

1. *What would be the benefits to its residents if Washington, D.C., became a state? What would be the benefits for the rest of the nation?*

2. *What problems might arise for the residents of Washington, D.C., if it were to become a state? What problems might arise for the rest of the nation?*

CLAUSE 18: To make all Laws which shall be necessary and proper for carrying into Execution the foregoing Powers and all other Powers vested by this Constitution in the Government of the United States, or in any Department or Officer thereof.

Section 9. (Prohibitions on Congress)

CLAUSE 1: The Migration or Importation of such Persons as any of the States now existing shall think proper to admit, shall not be prohibited by the Congress prior to the Year one thousand eight hundred and eight, but a Tax or duty may be imposed on such Importation, not exceeding ten dollars for each Person.

CLAUSE 2: The Privilege of the Writ of Habeas Corpus shall not be suspended, unless when in Cases of Rebellion or Invasion the public Safety may require it.

CLAUSE 3: No Bill of Attainder or ex post facto Law shall be passed.

CLAUSE 4: No Capitation, or other direct, Tax shall be laid, unless in Proportion to the Census of Enumeration herein before directed to be taken.

CLAUSE 5: No Tax or Duty shall be laid on Articles exported from any State.

CLAUSE 6: No Preference shall be given by any Regulation of Commerce or Revenue to the Ports of one State over those of another: nor shall Vessels bound to, or from, one State, be obliged to enter, clear or pay Duties in another.

CLAUSES 15 AND 16 guarantee the states the right to maintain and train a militia (today's National Guard), but state control of the militia is subordinate to national control when the national government needs the support of these militias to ensure that laws are executed, to suppress domestic uprisings, and to repel invasion.

CLAUSE 17 Congress has the authority to govern Washington, D.C., which is the seat of the national government. Today, citizens living there elect local officials to govern the city with congressional oversight. The national government also governs federal lands throughout the states that are used for federal purposes, such as military installations.

CLAUSE 18 grants Congress authority to make all laws it deems necessary and proper to fulfill its responsibilities under the Constitution, including those listed in Section 8. This clause also authorizes Congress to pass laws it deems necessary to ensure that the other two branches are able to fulfill their responsibilities. Congress has used this clause to expand its powers.

Article I, Section 9 limits Congress's lawmaking authority, thereby protecting rights of the people, and mandates that Congress be accountable to the people in how it spends the public's money.

Without using the word "slave," Clause 1 barred Congress from passing laws to prohibit the slave trade until 1808 at the earliest. The Thirteenth Amendment (1865) made slavery illegal.

CLAUSES 2 AND 3 guarantee protections to those accused of crimes. Clause 2 establishes the right of imprisoned persons to challenge their imprisonment in court (through a writ of habeas corpus). It notes that Congress can deny the right to a writ of habeas corpus during times of a rebellion or invasion if public safety is at risk.

CLAUSE 3 prohibits Congress from passing laws that declare a person or a group of people guilty of an offense (bills of attainder). Only courts have the authority to determine guilt. Congress is also prohibited from passing laws that punish a person tomorrow for an action he or she took that was legal today (ex post facto laws).

CLAUSE 4 prohibits Congress from directly taxing individual people, such as imposing an income tax. The Sixteenth Amendment (1913) authorized congressional enactment of a direct income tax on individual people.

CLAUSE 5 Congress is prohibited from taxing goods that are exported from any state, either those sent to foreign lands or to other states.

CLAUSE 6 Congress cannot favor any state over another in its regulation of trade.

CLAUSE 7 The national government can spend money only as authorized by Congress through enacted laws (no more than authorized and only for the purpose authorized) and must present a public accounting of revenues and expenditures.

CLAUSE 8 Congress cannot grant individuals special rights, privileges, or a position in government based on their heredity (birth into a family designated as nobility), which is how kings, queens, and other officials were granted their positions in the British monarchy. In addition, federal officials cannot accept gifts from foreign nations except those Congress allows (which today are gifts of minimal value).

Article I, Section 10
CLAUSE 1 specifically prohibits states from engaging in several activities that the Constitution delegates to the national government, including engaging in foreign affairs and creating currency. It also extends prohibitions on the states that are imposed on Congress in Section 9 of this Article, including prohibitions on enacting a law that declares a person or group guilty of an offense (bill of attainder) or a law that punishes a person tomorrow for an action that was legal when the person took the action (ex post facto law).

CLAUSE 2 prevents states from interfering in foreign trade without congressional approval.

CLAUSE 3 States cannot, without congressional approval, levy import taxes, build an army, or keep war ships during times of peace; neither can they enter into interstate compacts with other states or agreements with other countries.

CLAUSE 7: No Money shall be drawn from the Treasury, but in Consequence of Appropriations made by Law; and a regular Statement and Account of the Receipts and Expenditures of all public Money shall be published from time to time.

POLITICAL INQUIRY: *Today the government has a secret budget (black budget) for some military operations, intelligence operations, and counterterrorism operations. The Trump administration asked Congress for an all-time high $81 billion for the 2019 "black budget." Some argue that the existence of the black budget violates the Constitution's requirement for "a regular Statement and Account of the Receipts and Expenditures of all public Money."*

1. *What justification does the federal government use for the black budget?*

2. *Are you comfortable with the existence of a black budget? Explain your answer.*

CLAUSE 8: No Title of Nobility shall be granted by the United States: And no Person holding any Office of Profit or Trust under them, shall, without the Consent of the Congress, accept of any present, Emolument, Office, or Title, of any kind whatever, from any King, Prince or foreign State.

POLITICAL INQUIRY: *Several lawsuits were filed that accused President Trump of violating the constitutional clause that restricts government officials from receiving gifts or emoluments (money payments for work done) from any King, Prince, or foreign government. The lawsuits claimed that Trump was receiving emoluments from foreign governments through his continued ownership of profit-making businesses, including hotels.*

1. *What do you think the framers were trying to prevent by prohibiting government officials from accepting gifts and emoluments from foreign governments?*

2. *Do you think President Trump has violated the Constitution by the fact that his hotels accept payments from foreign officials who use the services of the hotels he owns? Why or why not?*

Section 10. (Prohibitions on the States)

CLAUSE 1: No State shall enter into any Treaty, Alliance, or Confederation; grant Letters of Marque and Reprisal; coin Money; emit Bills of Credit; make any Thing but gold and silver Coin a Tender in Payment of Debts; pass any Bill of Attainder, ex post facto Law, or Law impairing the Obligation of Contracts, or grant any Title of Nobility.

CLAUSE 2: No State shall, without the Consent of the Congress, lay any Imposts or Duties on Imports or Exports, except what may be absolutely necessary for executing its inspection Laws: and the net Produce of all Duties and Imposts, laid by any State on Imports or Exports, shall be for the Use of the Treasury of the United States; and all such Laws shall be subject to the Revision and Control of the Congress.

CLAUSE 3: No State shall, without the Consent of Congress, lay any Duty of Tonnage, keep Troops, or Ships of War in time of Peace, enter into any Agreement or Compact with another State, or with a foreign Power, or engage in War, unless actually invaded, or in such imminent Danger as will not admit of delay.

■ ARTICLE II. (Executive Branch)

Section 1. (Executive Powers of the President)

CLAUSE 1: The executive Power shall be vested in a President of the United States of America. He shall hold his Office during the Term of four Years, and, together with the Vice President, chosen for the same Term, be elected, as follows:

CLAUSE 2: Each State shall appoint, in such Manner as the Legislature thereof may direct, a Number of Electors, equal to the whole Number of Senators and Representatives to which the State may be entitled in the Congress: but no Senator or Representative, or Person holding an Office of Trust or Profit under the United States, shall be appointed an Elector.

CLAUSE 3: The Electors shall meet in their respective States, and vote by Ballot for two Persons, of whom one at least shall not be an Inhabitant of the same State with themselves. And they shall make a List of all the Persons voted for, and of the Number of Votes for each; which List they shall sign and certify, and transmit sealed to the Seat of the Government of the United States, directed to the President of the Senate. The President of the Senate shall, in the Presence of the Senate and House of Representatives, open all the Certificates, and the Votes shall then be counted. The Person having the greatest Number of Votes shall be the President, if such Number be a Majority of the whole Number of Electors appointed; and if there be more than one who have such Majority, and have an equal Number of Votes, then the House of Representatives shall immediately chuse by Ballot one of them for President; and if no Person have a Majority, then from the five highest on the List the said House shall in like Manner chuse the President. But in chusing the President, the Votes shall be taken by States, the Representatives from each State having one Vote; a quorum for this Purpose shall consist of a Member or Members from two thirds of the States, and a Majority of all the States shall be necessary to a Choice. In every Case, after the Choice of the President, the Person having the greatest Number of Votes of the Electors shall be the Vice President. But if there should remain two or more who have equal Votes, the Senate shall chuse from them by Ballot the Vice President.

POLITICAL INQUIRY: *The Electoral College system is criticized for many reasons. Some critics argue that deciding the presidential election by any vote other than that of the citizens (the popular vote) is undemocratic and, therefore, the Electoral College system should be eliminated and replaced by direct popular election of the president and vice president.*

1. *What might be the benefits of eliminating the Electoral College?*

2. *What might be the potential harm to the nation of eliminating the Electoral College?*

3. *What presidents lost the popular vote yet won the electoral vote to become president?*

Article II outlines the authority of the president and the vice president and the process of their selection.

Article II, Section 1

CLAUSE 1 The Constitution delegates to the president the authority to administer the executive branch of the national government. The term of office for the president and the vice president is four years. No term limit was specified; until President Franklin D. Roosevelt (1933–1945), there was a tradition of a two-term limit. President Roosevelt served four terms. The Twenty-second Amendment (1951) limits the president to two terms.

CLAUSE 2 The Electoral College system was established as a compromise between those who wanted citizens to elect the president directly and others who wanted Congress to elect the president. Each state government has the authority to determine how their state's electors will be selected.

CLAUSE 3 Electors have the authority to select the president and the vice president. Citizens' votes determine who their state's electors will be. Electors have the authority to select the president and the vice president. Each state political party with a presidential and vice-presidential candidate on the ballot selects a slate of electors. The slate of electors for the party whose presidential and vice-presidential candidates win the popular vote in the state participates in the Electoral College vote for the state. Before passage of the Twelfth Amendment (1804), each elector had two votes. The candidate receiving the majority of votes won the presidency, and the candidate with the second highest number of votes won the vice presidency.

CLAUSE 4 Today, by law, national elections are held on the Tuesday following the first Monday in November, in even-numbered years. During presidential election years, the electors gather in their state capitals on the Monday after the second Wednesday in December to vote for the president and the vice president. When Congress convenes in January after the presidential election, its members count the electoral ballots and formally announce the newly elected president and vice president.

CLAUSE 5 The president (and the vice president) must be at least 35 years old and must have lived within the United States for at least 14 years. Unlike the citizenship qualification for members of the House and the Senate, the president and the vice president must be natural-born citizens; they cannot be immigrants who have become citizens after arriving in the United States.

CLAUSE 6 states that the powers and duties of the presidency are transferred to the vice president when the president is no longer able to fulfill them. It also states that Congress can pass legislation to indicate who shall act as president if both the president and the vice president are unable to fulfill the president's powers and duties. The "acting" president would serve until the disability is removed or a new president is elected. The Twenty-Fifth Amendment (1967) clarifies when the vice president acts as president temporarily—such as when the president undergoes surgery—and when the vice president actually becomes president.

CLAUSE 7 Currently the president's salary is $400,000 per year plus numerous benefits, including a nontaxable expense account.

Article II, Section 2
CLAUSE 1 The president is the commander of the military and of the National Guard (militia of the several states) when it is called to service by the president. When they are not called to service by the president, the state divisions of the National Guard are commanded by their governors.

The president is authorized to establish the cabinet, the presidential advisory body comprising the top officials (secretaries) of each department of the executive branch.

As the chief executive officer, the president can exercise a check on the judicial branch by decreasing or eliminating sentences and even pardoning (eliminating guilty verdicts of) federal prisoners.

CLAUSE 4: The Congress may determine the Time of chusing the Electors, and the Day on which they shall give their Votes; which Day shall be the same throughout the United States.

CLAUSE 5: No Person except a natural born Citizen, or a Citizen of the United States, at the time of the Adoption of this Constitution, shall be eligible to the Office of President; neither shall any person be eligible to that Office who shall not have attained to the Age of thirty five Years, and been fourteen Years a Resident within the United States.

CLAUSE 6: In Case of the Removal of the President from Office, or of his Death, Resignation, or Inability to discharge the Powers and Duties of the said Office, the Same shall devolve on the Vice President, and the Congress may by Law provide for the Case of Removal, Death, Resignation or Inability, both of the President and Vice President, declaring what Officer shall then act as President, and such Officer shall act accordingly, until the Disability be removed, or a President shall be elected.

POLITICAL INQUIRY: *The vice president's constitutional responsibilities are to act as president (temporarily or to complete the term, depending on the situation) and to be president of the Senate (see Article 1, Section 3). However, since Vice President Walter Mondale (1977–1981), vice presidents have been important, active members of presidential administrations. Yet, citizens do not get to vote for the vice president. Presidential candidates choose the person who will be their running mate; voters have one vote with which they elect a president and her/his selected vice president.*

1. *What responsibilities do you think are appropriate for the vice president?*

2. *Should the Constitution be amended to include an enumeration of vice presidential responsibilities and constraints? Why or why not?*

CLAUSE 7: The President shall, at stated Times, receive for his Services, a Compensation, which shall neither be increased nor diminished during the Period for which he shall have been elected, and he shall not receive within that Period any other Emolument from the United States, or any of them.

CLAUSE 8: Before he enter on the Execution of his Office, he shall take the following Oath or Affirmation:—"I do solemnly swear (or affirm) that I will faithfully execute the Office of President of the United States, and will to the best of my Ability, preserve, protect and defend the Constitution of the United States."

Section 2. (Powers of the President)

CLAUSE 1: The President shall be Commander in Chief of the Army and Navy of the United States, and of the Militia of the several States, when called into the actual Service of the United States; he may require the Opinion, in writing, of the principal Officer in each of the executive Departments, upon any Subject relating to the Duties of their respective Offices, and he shall have Power to Grant Reprieves and Pardons for Offences against the United States, except in Cases of Impeachment.

CLAUSE 2: He shall have Power, by and with the Advice and Consent of the Senate, to make Treaties, provided two thirds of the Senators present concur; and he shall nominate, and by and with the Advice and Consent of the Senate, shall appoint Ambassadors, other public Ministers and Consuls, Judges of the supreme Court, and all other Officers of the United States, whose Appointments are not herein otherwise provided for, and which shall be established by Law: but the Congress may by Law vest the Appointment of such inferior Officers, as they think proper, in the President alone, in the Courts of Law, or in the Heads of Departments.

CLAUSE 3: The President shall have Power to fill up all Vacancies that may happen during the Recess of the Senate, by granting Commissions which shall expire at the End of their next Session.

Section 3. (Responsibilities of the President)

He shall from time to time give to the Congress Information on the State of the Union, and recommend to their Consideration such Measures as he shall judge necessary and expedient; he may, on extraordinary Occasions, convene both Houses, or either of them, and in Case of Disagreement between them, with Respect to the Time of Adjournment, he may adjourn them to such Time as he shall think proper; he shall receive Ambassadors and other public Ministers; he shall take Care that the Laws be faithfully executed, and shall Commission all the Officers of the United States.

Section 4. (Impeachment)

The President, Vice President and all Civil Officers of the United States, shall be removed from Office on Impeachment for and Conviction of, Treason, Bribery, or other high Crimes and Misdemeanors.

■ ARTICLE III. (Judicial Branch)

Section 1. (Federal Courts and Rights of Judges)

The judicial Power of the United States, shall be vested in one supreme Court, and in such inferior Courts as the Congress may from time to time ordain and establish. The Judges, both of the supreme and inferior Courts, shall hold their Offices during good Behaviour, and shall, at stated Times, receive for their Services, a Compensation, which shall not be diminished during their Continuance in Office.

POLITICAL INQUIRY: *Calls to amend the Constitution by eliminating the life tenure of Supreme Court justices and replacing it with a fixed term of office (a specified number of years a justice could serve) are heard now and then when people do not like the decisions (constitutional interpretations) being made by the Supreme Court.*

1. *What argument can you make in support of a life term for Supreme Court justices?*

2. *What argument can you make for a fixed term for Supreme Court justices?*

CLAUSE 2 The Constitution provides a check on the president's authority to negotiate treaties and appoint foreign ambassadors, top officials in the executive branch, and Supreme Court justices by requiring that treaties be ratified and appointments be confirmed by the Senate. Congress can create additional executive branch positions and federal courts and can decree how these legislatively created positions will be filled.

CLAUSE 3 In 2014, the Supreme Court clarified when the president can make "recess appointments"—that is, appointments to fill vacancies that occur when the Senate is not in session and is therefore not available to confirm presidential appointees. In *National Labor Relations Board v. Noel Canning,* the Court found that the president can make recess appointments only during Senate recesses that last no fewer than 10 days. Such recess appointees serve through the end of the congressional session.

Article II, Section 3 As chief executive officer of the nation, the president is required to ensure that laws are properly implemented by overseeing the executive branch agencies to be sure they are doing the work of government as established in law. The president is required from time to time to give an assessment of the status of the nation to Congress and to make recommendations for the good of the country. This has evolved into the annual televised State of the Union Address, which is followed within days by the presentation of the president's budget proposal to Congress. The president can also call special sessions of Congress.

Article II, Section 4 Presidents, vice presidents, and other federal officials can be removed from office if the members of the House of Representatives formally accuse them of treason (giving assistance to the nation's enemies), bribery, or other vaguely defined abuses of power ("high Crimes and Misdemeanors") and two-thirds of the Senate members find them guilty of these charges.

Article III presents the organization and authority of the U.S. Supreme Court and delegates to Congress the authority to create other courts as its members deem necessary.

Article III, Section 1 To ensure that judges make neutral and objective decisions, and are protected from political influences, federal judges serve until they retire, die, or are impeached by the House and convicted by the Senate. In addition, Congress cannot decrease a judge's pay.

Article III, Section 2

CLAUSE 1 Federal courts have the authority to hear all lawsuits pertaining to national laws (including legislation and presidential executive orders), the Constitution of the United States, and treaties. They also have jurisdiction over cases involving citizens of different states and citizens of foreign nations. Note that the power of judicial review—that is, the power to declare acts of government officials or bodies unconstitutional—is not articulated in the Constitution.

CLAUSE 2 The Supreme Court hears cases involving foreign diplomats and cases in which states are a party. Today, such cases are rare. For the most part, the Supreme Court hears cases on appeal from lower federal courts.

CLAUSE 3 Defendants accused of federal crimes have the right to a jury trial in a federal court located in the state in which the crime was committed. Those accused of state crimes are tried in the state court system in which the alleged crime was committed.

Article III, Section 3

CLAUSE 1 Clause 1 defines treason as making war against the United States or helping its enemies. At least two witnesses to the crime are required for a conviction.

CLAUSE 2 This clause prevents Congress from redefining treason. Those found guilty of treason can be punished, but their family members cannot be (no "Corruption of Blood").

Article IV establishes the obligations states have to each other and to the citizens of other states.

Article IV, Section 1 States must respect one another's legal judgments and records, and a contract agreed to in one state is binding in the other states.

Article IV, Section 2

CLAUSE 1 No matter what state they find themselves in, all U.S. citizens are entitled to the same privileges and rights as the citizens of that state.

Section 2. (Jurisdiction of Federal Courts)

CLAUSE 1: The judicial Power shall extend to all Cases, in Law and Equity, arising under this Constitution, the Laws of the United States, and Treaties made, or which shall be made, under their Authority;—to all Cases affecting Ambassadors, other public ministers and Consuls;—to all Cases of admiralty and maritime Jurisdiction;—to Controversies to which the United States shall be a Party;—to Controversies between two or more States;—between a State and Citizens of another State;—between Citizens of different States;—between Citizens of the same State claiming Lands under Grants of different States, and between a State, or the Citizens thereof, and foreign States, Citizens or Subjects.

CLAUSE 2: In all Cases affecting Ambassadors, other public Ministers and Consuls, and those in which a State shall be Party, the supreme Court shall have original Jurisdiction. In all the other Cases before mentioned, the supreme Court shall have appellate Jurisdiction, both as to Law and Fact, with such Exceptions, and under such Regulations as the Congress shall make.

CLAUSE 3: The Trial of all Crimes, except in Cases of Impeachment, shall be by Jury; and such Trial shall be held in the State where the said Crimes shall have been committed; but when not committed within any State, the Trial shall be at such Place or Places as the Congress may by Law have directed.

Section 3. (Treason)

CLAUSE 1: Treason against the United States, shall consist only in levying War against them, or in adhering to their Enemies, giving them Aid and Comfort. No Person shall be convicted of Treason unless on the Testimony of two Witnesses to the same overt Act, or on Confession in open Court.

CLAUSE 2: The Congress shall have Power to declare the Punishment of Treason, but no Attainder of Treason shall work Corruption of Blood, or Forfeiture except during the Life of the Person attainted.

■ ARTICLE IV. (State-to-State Relations)

Section 1. (Full Faith and Credit of Legal Proceedings and Decisions)

Full Faith and Credit shall be given in each State to the public Acts, Records, and judicial Proceedings of every other State. And the Congress may by general Laws prescribe the Manner in which such Acts, Records and Proceedings shall be proved, and the Effect thereof.

Section 2. (Privileges and Immunities of Citizens)

CLAUSE 1: The Citizens of each State shall be entitled to all Privileges and Immunities of Citizens in the several States.

CLAUSE 2: A Person charged in any State with Treason, Felony, or other Crime, who shall flee from Justice, and be found in another State, shall on Demand of the executive Authority of the State from which he fled, be delivered up, to be removed to the State having Jurisdiction of the Crime.

CLAUSE 3: No Person held to Service or Labour in one State, under the Laws thereof, escaping into another, shall, in Consequence of any Law or Regulation therein, be discharged from such Service or Labour, but shall be delivered up on Claim of the Party to whom such Service or Labour may be due.

Section 3. (Admission of New States)

CLAUSE 1: New States may be admitted by the Congress into this Union; but no new State shall be formed or erected within the Jurisdiction of any other State; nor any State be formed by the Junction of two or more States, or Parts of States, without the Consent of the Legislatures of the States concerned as well as of the Congress.

CLAUSE 2: The Congress shall have Power to dispose of and make all needful Rules and Regulations respecting the Territory or other Property belonging to the United States; and nothing in this Constitution shall be so construed as to Prejudice any Claims of the United States, or of any particular State.

Section 4. (National Government Obligations to the States)

The United States shall guarantee to every State in this Union a Republican Form of Government, and shall protect each of them against Invasion; and on Application of the Legislature, or of the Executive (when the Legislature cannot be convened) against domestic Violence.

ARTICLE V. (Formal Constitutional Amendment Process)

The Congress, whenever two thirds of both Houses shall deem it necessary, shall propose Amendments to this Constitution, or, on the Application of the Legislatures of two thirds of the several States, shall call a Convention for proposing Amendments, which, in either Case, shall be valid to all Intents and Purposes, as Part of this Constitution, when ratified by the Legislatures of three fourths of the several States, or by Conventions in three fourths thereof, as the one or the other Mode of Ratification may be proposed by the Congress; Provided that no Amendment which may be made prior to the Year One thousand eight hundred and eight shall in any Manner affect the first and fourth Clauses in the Ninth Section of the first Article; and that no State, without its Consent, shall be deprived of its equal Suffrage in the Senate.

CLAUSE 2 If requested by a governor of another state, a state is obligated to return an accused felon to the state from which he or she fled.

CLAUSE 3 The Thirteenth Amendment (1865) eliminated a state's obligation to return slaves fleeing from their enslavement in another state.

Article IV, Section 3
CLAUSE 1 Congress can admit new states to the union, but it cannot alter established state borders without the approval of the states that would be affected by the change.

CLAUSE 2 The federal government has authority to administer all federal (public) lands wherever they are located, including national parks and historic sites as well as military installations. Today, the federal government administers about 640 million acres of public land, which is about 28% of all the land in the country. Most of these public lands are in Western states; almost half of the land in the eleven coterminous Western states is federally owned.

Article IV, Section 4 The national government must ensure that every state has a representative democracy, protect each state from foreign invasion, and assist states in addressing mass breaches of domestic tranquility. Under this section, Congress has authorized the president to send in federal troops to protect public safety. During the civil rights movement, for example, federal troops ensured the safety of black students attending newly desegregated high schools and colleges.

Article V details the process by which the Constitution can be amended.

Amendments can be proposed either by Congress or by a special convention called at the request of the states. States have the authority to ratify amendments to the Constitution; three-fourths of the state legislatures must ratify an amendment for it to become part of the Constitution. Every year dozens of constitutional amendments are proposed in Congress, yet only 27 have been ratified since 1789.

Article VI decrees that the Constitution is the supreme law of the land.

CLAUSE 1 This provision states that the new federal government created by the Constitution was responsible for the financial obligations of the national government created by the Articles of Confederation.

CLAUSE 2 The Constitution, and all laws made to fulfill its mission that are in compliance with it, are the supreme law of the land; no one is above the supreme law of the land.

CLAUSE 3 All national and state officials must take an oath promising to uphold the Constitution. This article also prohibits the national government from requiring officeholders to submit to a religious test or swear a religious oath, hence supporting a separation of government and religion.

Article VII outlines the process by which the Constitution will be ratified.

▌ARTICLE VI. (Supremacy of the Constitution)

CLAUSE 1: All Debts contracted and Engagements entered into, before the Adoption of this Constitution, shall be as valid against the United States under this Constitution, as under the Confederation.

CLAUSE 2: This Constitution, and the Laws of the United States which shall be made in Pursuance thereof; and all Treaties made, or which shall be made, under the Authority of the United States, shall be the supreme Law of the Land; and the Judges in every State shall be bound thereby, any Thing in the Constitution or Laws of any state to the Contrary notwithstanding.

CLAUSE 3: The Senators and Representatives before mentioned, and the Members of the several State Legislatures, and all executive and judicial Officers, both of the United States and of the several States, shall be bound by Oath or Affirmation, to support this Constitution; but no religious Test shall ever be required as a Qualification to any Office or public Trust under the United States.

▌ARTICLE VII. (Constitutional Ratification Process)

CLAUSE 1: The Ratification of the Conventions of nine States, shall be sufficient for the Establishment of this Constitution between the States so ratifying the same.

POLITICAL INQUIRY: *The framers of the Constitution developed a ratification process that violated the process of constitutional amendment established in the Articles of Confederation. Not only did their process allow for the new constitution to replace the constitution in effect since 1781 with nine votes of approval instead of a unanimous vote of approval, but they also suggested that special state conventions, not the state legislatures, vote to ratify the new constitution.*

1. *Do you think ratification of the Constitution would have occurred in just two years if ratification required approval by the existing state legislatures instead of special conventions? Explain your answer.*

2. *With the fact that no delegates from Rhode Island signed the proposed constitution, do you think ratification would have occurred in just two years (or at all) if the vote had to be unanimous (as called for in the Articles of Confederation)? Explain your answer.*

CLAUSE 2: Done in Convention by the Unanimous Consent of the States present the Seventeenth Day of September in the Year of our Lord one thousand seven hundred and Eighty seven and of the Independence of the United States of America the Twelfth. In witness whereof We have hereunto subscribed our Names,

G. Washington—President and deputy from Virginia

Delaware
George Read
Gunning Bedford, Jr.
John Dickinson
Richard Bassett
Jacob Broom

Maryland
James McHenry
Daniel of St. Thomas
  Jenifer
Daniel Carroll

Virginia
John Blair
James Madison, Jr.

North Carolina
William Blount
Richard Dobbs Spaight
Hugh Williamson

South Carolina
John Rutledge
Charles Cotesworth
  Pinckney
Charles Pinckney
Pierce Butler

Georgia
William Few
Abraham Baldwin

New Hampshire
John Langdon
Nicholas Gilman

Massachusetts
Nathaniel Gorham
Rufus King

Connecticut
William Samuel Johnson
Roger Sherman

New York
Alexander Hamilton

New Jersey
William Livingston
David Brearley
William Paterson
Jonathan Dayton

Pennsylvania
Benjamin Franklin
Thomas Mifflin
Robert Morris
George Clymer
Thomas FitzSimons
Jared Ingersoll
James Wilson
Gouverneur Morris

POLITICAL INQUIRY:

1. *What state did not send any delegates to the Constitutional Convention?*

2. *Why did this state not send any delegates?*

Amendments to the Constitution of the United States of America

POLITICAL INQUIRY: *As you read through the Bill of Rights and the other 17 amendments to the Constitution, consider the impact that these changes to the Constitution have had on your life.*

1. *What would your life look like without the Bill of Rights?*

2. *How does the Fifteenth, Nineteenth, and/or Twenty-Sixth Amendment benefit you?*

3. *What amendment has been the most beneficial to you? Explain your response.*

4. *What amendment has been harmful to you? Explain your response.*

Amendment I Government cannot make laws that limit freedom of expression, which includes freedom of religion, speech, and the press, as well as the freedom to assemble and to petition the government to address grievances. None of these individual freedoms is absolute, however; courts balance the protection of individual freedoms (as provided for in this Constitution) with the protection of public safety, including national security.

◆ Amendment I (1791)

Congress shall make no law respecting an establishment of religion, or prohibiting the free exercise thereof; or abridging the freedom of speech, or of the press; or the right of the people peaceably to assemble, and to petition the Government for a redress of grievances.

Amendment II Today, states and the federal government balance the right of the people to own guns with the need to protect the public.

◆ Amendment II (1791)

A well regulated Militia, being necessary to the security of a free State, the right of the people to keep and bear Arms, shall not be infringed.

POLITICAL INQUIRY: *Public debates and debates among government officials over Second Amendment rights and gun control are sparked every time people are killed in a mass shooting in the United States.*

1. *Is the right to own a gun absolute, or does the right have to be balanced with public safety and general welfare, as are the other individual rights established in the Constitution? Explain your answer.*

2. *Does your state allow colleges to prohibit weapons on their campuses?*

Amendment III Military troops cannot take control of private homes during peacetime.

◆ Amendment III (1791)

No Soldier shall, in time of peace be quartered in any house, without the consent of the Owner, nor in time of war, but in a manner to be prescribed by law.

◆ Amendment IV (1791)

The right of the people to be secure in their persons, houses, papers, and effects, against unreasonable searches and seizures, shall not be violated, and no Warrants shall issue, but upon probable cause, supported by Oath or affirmation, and particularly describing the place to be searched, and the persons or things to be seized.

POLITICAL INQUIRY: *Since the terrorist attacks on September 11, 2001, the national government has tried to balance the right of people to be secure in their person and property with public safety and national security.*

1. *What reasons have the president and members of Congress offered in defense of allowing intelligence agencies to bypass the requirement that they obtain judicial permission to conduct searches or seizures of phone records?*

2. *How valid are those reasons? In your opinion, can they be reconciled with constitutional protections?*

◆ Amendment V (1791)

No person shall be held to answer for a capital, or otherwise infamous crime, unless on a presentment or indictment of a Grand Jury, except in cases arising in the land or naval forces, or in the Militia, when in actual service in time of War or public danger; nor shall any person be subject for the same offence to be twice put in jeopardy of life or limb; nor shall be compelled in any criminal case to be a witness against himself, nor be deprived of life, liberty, or property, without due process of law; nor shall private property be taken for public use, without just compensation.

◆ Amendment VI (1791)

In all criminal prosecutions, the accused shall enjoy the right to a speedy and public trial, by an impartial jury of the State and district wherein the crime shall have been committed, which district shall have been previously ascertained by law, and to be informed of the nature and cause of the accusation; to be confronted with the witnesses against him; to have compulsory process for obtaining witnesses in his favor, and to have the Assistance of Counsel for his defence.

◆ Amendment VII (1791)

In Suits at common law, where the value in controversy shall exceed twenty dollars, the right of trial by jury shall be preserved, and no fact tried by a jury, shall be otherwise re-examined in any Court of the United States, than according to the rules of the common law.

Amendment IV Government officials must obtain approval before they search or seize a person's property. The approval must come either from the person whose private property they are searching or seizing or from a judge who determines that the government is justified in taking this action to protect public safety and who therefore signs a search warrant. Yet, the courts have established exceptions to the need for approval under certain circumstances.

Amendment V provides much more than the familiar protection against self-incrimination that we hear people who are testifying before Congress and the courts claim by "taking the Fifth." For example, before the government can punish a person for a crime (take away a person's life, liberty, or pursuit of happiness), it must follow certain procedures specified in law; it must follow due process of the law. The federal government guarantees those accused of federal crimes a grand jury hearing in which the government presents its evidence to a selected group of citizens who determine whether there is sufficient evidence to go to trial. If a defendant is found not guilty of a specific criminal offense, he or she cannot be brought to trial again by the same government for the same offense. If the government determines it needs private property for a public use, the owner is compelled to sell the land, and the government must pay a fair price based on the market value of the property.

Amendment VI outlines additional procedures that the government must follow before taking away a person's life, liberty, or pursuit of happiness. People accused of crimes have the right to know what they are accused of doing, to hear from witnesses against them, and to defend themselves in a trial that is open to the public within a reasonable amount of time after the accusations are made. An indigent (very poor) person is guaranteed a government-provided lawyer in serious criminal cases. It is assumed all others can afford to hire a lawyer.

Amendment VII Either party (the complainant or the person accused of causing harm or violating a contract) in a federal civil lawsuit involving more than $20 can demand a jury trial.

AMENDMENT KEY

◆ Amendments to Protect Civil Rights and Liberties

◇ Amendments Related to Selection of Government Officials or Government Operations

★ Amendments That Address a Specific Public Policy

Amendment VIII protects those accused of crimes as well as those found guilty from overly punitive decisions. Bail, a payment to the government that can be required to avoid incarceration before and during trial, cannot be set at an excessively high amount, unless the judge determines that freedom for the accused would jeopardize public safety or that he or she might flee. The punishment imposed on those convicted of crimes is expected to "fit" the crime: It is to be reasonable given the severity of the crime. Punishment cannot be excessive or cruel.

Amendment IX acknowledges that there are additional rights, not listed in the preceding eight amendments, that the government cannot deny to citizens. The Supreme Court has interpreted the First, Fourth, Fifth, and Ninth Amendments collectively to provide individuals with a right to privacy.

Amendment X acknowledges that state governments retain all authority they had before ratification of the Constitution that has not been delegated to the national government by the Constitution. This amendment was demanded by the Anti-Federalists, who opposed ratification of this Constitution. The Anti-Federalists feared that the national government would infringe on people's freedoms and on the authority of the state governments. The vagueness of the rights retained by the states continues to cause tensions and disputes between the state governments and the national government.

Amendment XI The courts have interpreted this amendment to mean that federal courts do not have the authority to hear lawsuits brought by citizens against their own state or against another state, or brought by foreigners against a state.

◆ Amendment VIII (1791)

Excessive bail shall not be required, nor excessive fines imposed, nor cruel and unusual punishments inflicted.

◆ Amendment IX (1791)

The enumeration in the Constitution, of certain rights, shall not be construed to deny or disparage others retained by the people.

POLITICAL INQUIRY: *Thomas Jefferson and Alexander Hamilton debated the need for a bill of rights. Hamilton argued that a list of rights would be incomplete and therefore, people might argue that because a given right was not listed, it did not exist.*

1. *How well do you think the Ninth Amendment addresses Hamilton's argument against a bill of rights? Explain.*

2. *The right to privacy is not enumerated in the Bill of Rights or anywhere else in the Constitution. Courts have claimed that such a right exists based on combining the principles established in several amendments in the Bill of Rights. What rights enumerated in the Bill of Rights did courts use to identify a foundational constitutional right to privacy?*

3. *What other rights has the Supreme Court identified that are not enumerated in the Constitution?*

◆ Amendment X (1791)

The powers not delegated to the United States by the Constitution, nor prohibited by it to the States, are reserved to the States respectively, or to the people.

POLITICAL INQUIRY: *Go back and read Article 1, Section 8, Clause 18, of the Constitution and compare its meaning with that of the Tenth Amendment.*

1. *How do these two sections of the Constitution make it difficult to distinguish between national authority to act and state authority to act?*

2. *Ultimately, who resolves the conflict when the national government claims that its action is "necessary and proper" and a state claims that the national action is unconstitutional because it violates its constitutionally reserved powers?*

◇ Amendment XI (1795)

The Judicial power of the United States shall not be construed to extend to any suit in law or equity, commenced or prosecuted against one of the United States by Citizens of another State, or by Citizens or Subjects of any Foreign State.

Amendment XII (1804)

The Electors shall meet in their respective states and vote by ballot for President and Vice-President, one of whom, at least, shall not be an inhabitant of the same state with themselves; they shall name in their ballots the person voted for as President, and in distinct ballots the person voted for as Vice-President, and they shall make distinct lists of all persons voted for as President, and of all persons voted for as Vice-President, and of the number of votes for each, which lists they shall sign and certify, and transmit sealed to the seat of the government of the United States, directed to the President of the Senate;—The President of the Senate shall, in the presence of the Senate and House of Representatives, open all the certificates and the votes shall then be counted;—The person having the greatest Number of votes for President, shall be the President, if such number be a majority of the whole number of Electors appointed; and if no person have such majority, then from the persons having the highest numbers not exceeding three on the list of those voted for as President, the House of Representatives shall choose immediately, by ballot, the President. But in choosing the President, the votes shall be taken by states, the representation from each state having one vote; a quorum for this purpose shall consist of a member or members from two-thirds of the states, and a majority of all the states shall be necessary to a choice. And if the House of Representatives shall not choose a President whenever the right of choice shall devolve upon them, before the fourth day of March next following, then the Vice-President shall act as President, as in the case of the death or other constitutional disability of the President—The person having the greatest number of votes as Vice-President, shall be the Vice-President, if such number be a majority of the whole number of Electors appointed, and if no person have a majority, then from the two highest numbers on the list, the Senate shall choose the Vice-President; a quorum for the purpose shall consist of two-thirds of the whole number of Senators, and a majority of the whole number shall be necessary to a choice. But no person constitutionally ineligible to the office of President shall be eligible to that of Vice-President of the United States.

POLITICAL INQUIRY: *Electors in the Electoral College have two votes: one vote for a presidential candidate and one vote for a vice presidential candidate. Citizens have just one vote; citizens vote for a ticket that includes both a presidential candidate and the vice presidential candidate selected by the presidential candidate.*

1. *What effect might each citizen having two votes as do the electors—one vote for a presidential candidate and one vote for a vice presidential candidate—have on presidential campaigns?*

2. *What effect might it have on the ability of the president to govern?*

Amendment XIII (1865)

SECTION 1. Neither slavery nor involuntary servitude, except as a punishment for crime whereof the party shall have been duly convicted, shall exist within the United States, or any place subject to their jurisdiction.

Amendment XII The presidential election in 1800 ended with a tie in Electoral College votes between Thomas Jefferson and Aaron Burr. Because the candidate with the most votes was to become president and the candidate with the second highest number of votes was to become vice president, the tie meant that the job of selecting the president was turned over to the House of Representatives. The House selected Jefferson. Calls to change the procedure were answered by the enactment of this amendment.

Today, each elector has two votes: one for a presidential candidate and one for a vice-presidential candidate. The presidential candidate who wins the majority of electoral votes wins the presidency, and the same is true for the vice-presidential candidate. If no presidential candidate wins a majority of the electoral votes, the House selects the president. If no vice-presidential candidate wins a majority of the electoral votes, the Senate selects the vice president.

Amendment XIII This amendment abolished slavery.

Amendment XIV This amendment extends the rights of citizenship to all those born in the United States and those who have become citizens through naturalization. States are prohibited from denying U.S. citizens their rights and privileges and must provide all people with due process before taking away their life, liberty, or pursuit of happiness. States must also treat all people equally and fairly. The courts have also used this section of the Fourteenth Amendment to require that states ensure citizens their protections under the Bill of Rights.

SECTION 2 This section of the Fourteenth Amendment is the first use of the term *male* in the Constitution. This section requires that if a state denies men over the age of 21 the right to vote, its representation in the House will be diminished accordingly. The Fifteenth Amendment makes this section unnecessary.

SECTION 3 The intent of this section was to prevent government officials who supported the Confederacy during the Civil War from serving in government. Congress voted in 1898 to eliminate this prohibition.

SECTION 4 This section allowed the national and state governments to refuse to pay debts of the Confederate Army as well as claims made by slaveholders whose slaves were freed by the Thirteenth Amendment.

SECTION 2. Congress shall have power to enforce this article by appropriate legislation.

◆ Amendment XIV (1868)

SECTION 1. All persons born or naturalized in the United States and subject to the jurisdiction thereof, are citizens of the United States and of the State wherein they reside. No State shall make or enforce any law which shall abridge the privileges or immunities of citizens of the United States; nor shall any State deprive any person of life, liberty, or property, without due process of law; nor deny to any person within its jurisdiction the equal protection of the laws.

POLITICAL INQUIRY: *In the debate over the proposed Equal Rights Amendment, opponents and proponents often discuss the Fourteenth Amendment. This is what the proposed ERA states: "Equality of rights under the law shall not be denied or abridged by the United States or by any State on account of sex."*

1. *How do opponents of the ERA use the Fourteenth Amendment to support their position?*

2. *How do proponents of the ERA use the Fourteenth Amendment to support their position?*

3. *Do you support or oppose adding the ERA to the Constitution? Justify your position.*

SECTION 2. Representatives shall be apportioned among the several States according to their respective numbers, counting the whole number of persons in each State, excluding Indians not taxed. But when the right to vote at any election for the choice of electors for President and Vice President of the United States, Representatives in Congress, the Executive and Judicial officers of a State, or the members of the Legislature thereof, is denied to any of the male inhabitants of such State, being twenty-one years of age, and citizens of the United States, or in any way abridged, except for participation in rebellion, or other crime, the basis of representation therein shall be reduced in the proportion which the number of such male citizens shall bear to the whole number of male citizens twenty-one years of age in such State.

SECTION 3. No person shall be a Senator or Representative in Congress, or elector of President and Vice President, or hold any office, civil or military, under the United States, or under any State, who, having previously taken an oath, as a member of Congress, or as an officer of the United States, or as a member of any State legislature, or as an executive or judicial officer of any State, to support the Constitution of the United States, shall have engaged in insurrection or rebellion against the same, or given aid or comfort to the enemies thereof. But Congress may by a vote of two-thirds of each House, remove such disability.

SECTION 4. The validity of the public debt of the United States, authorized by law, including debts incurred for payment of pensions and bounties for services in suppressing insurrection or rebellion, shall not be questioned. But neither the United States nor any State shall assume or pay any debt or obligation incurred in aid of insurrection or rebellion against the United States, or any claim for the loss or emancipation of any slave; but all such debts, obligations and claims shall be held illegal and void.

SECTION 5. The Congress shall have power to enforce, by appropriate legislation, the provisions of this article.

◆ Amendment XV (1870)

SECTION 1. The right of citizens of the United States to vote shall not be denied or abridged by the United States or by any State on account of race, color, or previous condition of servitude.

SECTION 2. The Congress shall have power to enforce this article by appropriate legislation.

★ Amendment XVI (1913)

The Congress shall have power to lay and collect taxes on incomes, from whatever source derived, without apportionment among the several States, and without regard to any census or enumeration.

◻ Amendment XVII (1913)

The Senate of the United States shall be composed of two Senators from each State, elected by the people thereof, for six years; and each Senator shall have one vote. The electors in each State shall have the qualifications requisite for electors of the most numerous branch of the State legislatures.

When vacancies happen in the representation of any State in the Senate, the executive authority of such State shall issue writs of election to fill such vacancies: Provided, That the legislature of any State may empower the executive thereof to make temporary appointments until the people fill the vacancies by election as the legislature may direct.

This amendment shall not be so construed as to affect the election or term of any Senator chosen before it becomes valid as part of the Constitution.

★ Amendment XVIII (1919)

SECTION 1. After one year from the ratification of this article the manufacture, sale, or transportation of intoxicating liquors within, the importation thereof into, or the exportation thereof from the United States and all territory subject to the jurisdiction thereof for beverage purposes is hereby prohibited.

SECTION 2. The Congress and the several States shall have concurrent power to enforce this article by appropriate legislation.

Amendment XV As interpreted by the courts, the Fifteenth Amendment guaranteed all male citizens meeting their state's minimum age requirement the right to vote.

Amendment XVI authorizes the national government to establish taxes on personal and corporate income.

Amendment XVII Representative democracy was enhanced by the Seventeenth Amendment, which changed the process by which U.S. senators were selected. Senators are now elected by the citizens in each state rather than by state legislatures. The amendment also allows each state legislature to establish the process by which vacancies in the Senate will be filled, either through special election or by gubernatorial appointment.

Amendment XVIII The "Prohibition" amendment—making it illegal to manufacture, sell, or transport alcoholic beverages in the United States—was widely disobeyed during the years it was in effect. This is the only amendment that has been repealed.

Amendment XIX All female citizens meeting their state's minimum age requirement are guaranteed the right to vote.

Amendment XX
SECTIONS 1 AND 2 The first two sections of the Twentieth Amendment establish new starting dates for the president's and vice president's terms of office (January 20) as well as for members of Congress (January 3). Section 2 also decrees that the annual meeting of Congress will begin on January 3 unless Congress specifies a different date.

SECTIONS 3 AND 4 of this amendment establish that if the president elect dies before his or her term of office begins, the vice president elect becomes president. If the president elect has not been selected or is unable to begin the term, the vice president elect serves as acting president until the president is selected or is able to serve.

SECTION 3. This article shall be inoperative unless it shall have been ratified as an amendment to the Constitution by the legislatures of the several States, as provided in the Constitution, within seven years from the date of the submission hereof to the States by the Congress.

◆ Amendment XIX (1920)

The right of citizens of the United States to vote shall not be denied or abridged by the United States or by any State on account of sex. Congress shall have power to enforce this article by appropriate legislation.

POLITICAL INQUIRY: *All male citizens gained the right to vote with the Fifteenth Amendment in 1870, 50 years before all women citizens did. Today, women's voter turnout is typically higher than is men's voter turnout and women voters lean more Democratic than men voters.*

1. *What does the fact that women did not win the vote until 1920 suggest about the status of women in the United States during the 19th and early 20th centuries?*

2. *What effect do you think women's voter turnout patterns have had on campaigns and public policy debates in the 21st century?*

3. *How has the legal status, social status, and economic status of women and men changed since 1920, when women citizens won the right to vote?*

◐ Amendment XX (1933)

SECTION 1. The terms of the President and Vice President shall end at noon on the 20th day of January, and the terms of Senators and Representatives at noon on the 3d day of January, of the years in which such terms would have ended if this article had not been ratified; and the terms of their successors shall then begin.

SECTION 2. The Congress shall assemble at least once in every year, and such meeting shall begin at noon on the 3d day of January, unless they shall by law appoint a different day.

SECTION 3. If, at the time fixed for the beginning of the term of the President, the President elect shall have died, the Vice President elect shall become President. If a President shall not have been chosen before the time fixed for the beginning of his term, or if the President elect shall have failed to qualify, then the Vice President elect shall act as President until a President shall have qualified; and the Congress may by law provide for the case wherein neither a President elect nor a Vice President elect shall have qualified, declaring who shall then act as President, or the manner in which one who is to act shall be selected, and such person shall act accordingly until a President or Vice President shall have qualified.

SECTION 4. The Congress may by law provide for the case of the death of any of the persons from whom the House of Representatives may choose a President whenever the right of choice shall have devolved upon them, and for the case of the death of any of the persons from whom the Senate may choose a Vice President whenever the right of choice shall have devolved upon them.

SECTION 5. Sections 1 and 2 shall take effect on the 15th day of October following the ratification of this article.

SECTION 6. This article shall be inoperative unless it shall have been ratified as an amendment to the Constitution by the legislatures of three-fourths of the several States within seven years from the date of its submission.

◆ Amendment XXI (1933)

SECTION 1. The eighteenth article of amendment to the Constitution of the United States is hereby repealed.

SECTION 2. The transportation or importation into any State, Territory, or possession of the United States for delivery or use therein of intoxicating liquors, in violation of the laws thereof, is hereby prohibited.

SECTION 3. This article shall be inoperative unless it shall have been ratified as an amendment to the Constitution by conventions in the several States, as provided in the Constitution, within seven years from the date of the submission hereof to the States by the Congress.

◻ Amendment XXII (1951)

SECTION 1. No person shall be elected to the office of the President more than twice, and no person who has held the office of President, or acted as President, for more than two years of a term to which some other person was elected President shall be elected to the office of the President more than once. But this Article shall not apply to any person holding the office of President, when this Article was proposed by the Congress, and shall not prevent any person who may be holding the office of President, or acting as President, during the term within which this Article becomes operative from holding the office of President or acting as President during the remainder of such term.

SECTION 2. This article shall be inoperative unless it shall have been ratified as an amendment to the Constitution by the legislatures of three-fourths of the several States within seven years from the date of its submission to the States by the Congress.

POLITICAL INQUIRY: *Critics of term limits in general argue that they are undemocratic because they may force out of office an official whom the voters want to keep in office as their representative.*

1. *What is an additional argument for eliminating the two-term limit for the presidency?*

2. *What is an argument against eliminating the two-term limit for the presidency (other than the argument that it is undemocratic)?*

Amendment XXI With this amendment, the Eighteenth Amendment's prohibition of the manufacture, sale, and transportation of alcoholic beverages was repealed. This is the only constitutional amendment that was ratified by special state conventions, not by state legislatures.

Amendment XXII This amendment establishes a two-term limit for the presidency, or in the case of a vice president succeeding to the presidency and then running for reelection, a maximum limit of 10 years in office.

Amendment XXIII Citizens living in Washington, D.C., are given the right to elect three voting members to the Electoral College. Before this amendment, these citizens were not represented in the Electoral College.

Amendment XXIV Governments are prohibited from requiring a person to pay a tax in order to vote.

Amendment XXV

SECTION 1 The vice president becomes president if the president resigns or dies.

SECTION 2 The president can nominate a person to fill a vice-presidential vacancy. Congress must approve the nominee. President Richard Nixon appointed and Congress confirmed Gerald Ford to the vice presidency when Vice President Spiro Agnew resigned. When President Nixon resigned, Vice President Ford, who had not been elected, became president. He subsequently appointed and Congress confirmed Nelson Rockefeller to be vice president.

SECTION 3 If the president indicates in writing to Congress that he or she cannot carry out the duties of office, the vice president becomes acting president until the president informs Congress that he or she is again fit to resume the responsibilities of the presidency.

◆ Amendment XXIII (1961)

SECTION 1. The District constituting the seat of Government of the United States shall appoint in such manner as the Congress may direct: A number of electors of President and Vice President equal to the whole number of Senators and Representatives in Congress to which the District would be entitled if it were a State, but in no event more than the least populous State; they shall be in addition to those appointed by the States, but they shall be considered, for the purposes of the election of President and Vice President, to be electors appointed by a State; and they shall meet in the District and perform such duties as provided by the twelfth article of amendment.

SECTION 2. The Congress shall have power to enforce this article by appropriate legislation.

◻ Amendment XXIV (1964)

SECTION 1. The right of citizens of the United States to vote in any primary or other election for President or Vice President, for electors for President or Vice President, or for Senator or Representative in Congress, shall not be denied or abridged by the United States or any State by reason of failure to pay any poll tax or other tax.

SECTION 2. The Congress shall have power to enforce this article by appropriate legislation.

POLITICAL INQUIRY: *Several states have enacted laws requiring voters to show a government-issued photo ID to vote. However, many elderly, poor, and urban residents do not have a government-issued photo ID and therefore would have to pay for one, or would be prevented from voting.*

1. *Is this a modern poll tax? Why or why not?*

2. *What is the explanation states provide for enacting laws requiring a government-issued photo ID to vote?*

◻ Amendment XXV (1967)

SECTION 1. In case of the removal of the President from office or of his death or resignation, the Vice President shall become President.

SECTION 2. Whenever there is a vacancy in the office of the Vice President, the President shall nominate a Vice President who shall take office upon confirmation by a majority vote of both Houses of Congress.

SECTION 3. Whenever the President transmits to the President pro tempore of the Senate and the Speaker of the House of Representatives his written declaration that he is unable to discharge the powers and duties of his office, and until he transmits to them a written declaration to the contrary, such powers and duties shall be discharged by the Vice President as Acting President.

SECTION 4. Whenever the Vice President and a majority of either the principal officers of the executive departments or of such other body as Congress may by law provide, transmit to the President pro tempore of the Senate and the Speaker of the House of Representatives their written declaration that the President is unable to discharge the powers and duties of his office, the Vice President shall immediately assume the powers and duties of the office as Acting President.

Thereafter, when the President transmits to the President pro tempore of the Senate and the Speaker of the House of Representatives his written declaration that no inability exists, he shall resume the powers and duties of his office unless the Vice President and a majority of either the principal officers of the executive department or of such other body as Congress may by law provide, transmit within four days to the President pro tempore of the Senate and the Speaker of the House of Representatives their written declaration that the President is unable to discharge the powers and duties of his office. Thereupon Congress shall decide the issue, assembling within forty-eight hours for that purpose if not in session. If the Congress, within twenty-one days after receipt of the latter written declaration, or, if Congress is not in session, within twenty-one days after Congress is required to assemble, determines by two-thirds vote of both Houses that the President is unable to discharge the powers and duties of his office, the Vice President shall continue to discharge the same as Acting President; otherwise, the President shall resume the powers and duties of his office.

◀▶ Amendment XXVI (1971)

SECTION 1. The right of citizens of the United States, who are eighteen years of age or older, to vote shall not be denied or abridged by the United States or by any State on account of age.

SECTION 2. The Congress shall have power to enforce this article by appropriate legislation.

◻ Amendment XXVII (1992)

No law varying the compensation for the services of the Senators and Representatives shall take effect, until an election of Representatives shall have intervened.

POLITICAL INQUIRY: *Now that you have read the Constitution, do you think three-quarters of state legislatures would ratify this document—even as amended—today? Why or why not?*

SECTION 4 If the vice president in concert with a majority of cabinet officials (or some other body designated by Congress) declares to Congress in writing that the president is unable to fulfill the duties of office, the vice president becomes acting president until the president claims he or she is again fit for duty. However, if the vice president and a majority of cabinet officials challenge the president's claim, then Congress must decide within three weeks if the president can resume office.

Amendment XXVI Citizens 18 years of age and older are guaranteed the right to vote.

Amendment XXVII Proposed in 1789, this amendment prevents members of Congress from raising their own salaries. Approved salary increases cannot take effect until after the next congressional election.

Chapter 3

Federalism

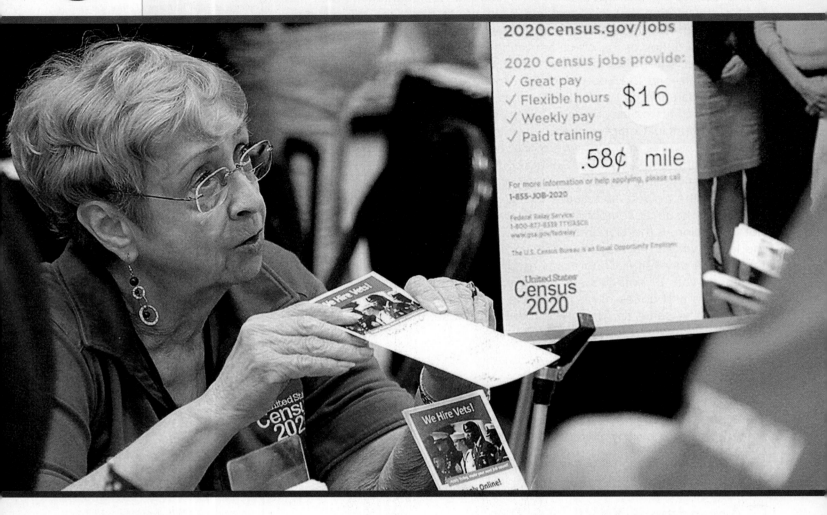

Randy Hoeft/The Yuma Sun/AP Images

THEN

The newly created national government and the preexisting state governments acted independently as they implemented the innovative federal system of government established in 1789.

NOW

National, state, and local governments challenge one another regularly over the proper interpretation of the Constitution's vague and ambiguous distribution of power in the federal system of U.S. government.

NEXT

Will Supreme Court justices continue to issue conflicting interpretations of the proper balance of power in the federal system of government?

Will state and local governments continue their policy experiments to find more effective means of addressing domestic problems?

Will partisan differences between state governments and the national government perpetuate lawsuits brought by each level of government?

▌ Chapter Introduction

In this chapter, you will learn about the dynamic system of federalism, supporting this *Enduring Understanding* from the Advanced Placement course: "*Federalism reflects the dynamic distribution of power between national and state governments.*" Federalism refers to the U.S. government structure of two levels of governing: the national government (also called the federal government) and state governments[i]. Under this system, each level of government has authority over a population and a set of policies. Citizens are governed by both levels of government—the state in which they live and the federal government. Under the U.S. Constitution, the federal government is given authority over certain policy matters (such as foreign affairs and raising an army) and all other policy matters (such as controlling crime and issuing domestic licenses) are left to the state governments.

The delineation of powers between our levels of government has been fluid and wrought with conflict. The fluidity stems in part from the vague language of the Constitution describing the authority of each level of government. For example, according to the Constitution, Congress can write laws which are "Necessary and Proper" within its enumerated powers, and the states have reserved powers. The powers of our national and state governments have changed over time. While early in our history, matters of education were solely the responsibility of the state, the national government has taken an increasing role in education policy in recent decades due in part to changing demands of society and the ability of the national government to leverage power under the spending clause of the Constitution. Because the national government provides funding to local public school systems, it can also dictate rules the local school systems must follow to be eligible for federal funding. Conflicts between state and federal law persist, such as the conflict over marijuana legalization.

The balance of power between the national and state governments has been interpreted differently over time by the U.S. Supreme Court, as illustrated by two required Supreme Court cases in the AP U.S. Government & Politics course: *McCulloch v. Maryland* (1819) and *U.S. v. Lopez* (1995). While in the *McCulloch v. Maryland* (1819) case the Supreme Court sided with the federal government, in the *U.S. v. Lopez* case, the Court sided with the states. In the *McCulloch v. Maryland* ruling, the Supreme Court relied on the *necessary and proper clause* of the Constitution, ruling that this clause encompassed the national government's creation of a national bank and ruling that the Supremacy Clause of the Constitution meant that the state of Maryland did not have the authority to tax the national government. Over 100 years later, in the *U.S. v. Lopez* (1995) case, the national government's attempt to expand its power was prevented by the Supreme Court when it ruled when the Supreme Court ruled that the commerce clause of the Constitution was not broad enough to encompass the national government's authority to write a federal guns-free school zone law.

In this chapter, you will read about how the balance of power between the national and state governments has shifted through national public policies designed to meet the needs of society. Essential Knowledge in the AP U.S. Government course is, "The distribution of power between federal and state governments to meet the needs of society changes, as reflected by grants, incentives, and aid programs including federal revenue sharing mandates,

[i]While federalism refers to the system of levels of government, the term "federal" government refers to the national government (federal government/national government are interchangeable terms).

categorical grants, and block grants." To support the Essential Knowledge, you will read about how the Great Depression prompted the national government to write New Deal legislation designed to alleviate poverty and unemployment, and in the process carved out a new role for the federal government. The chapter discusses several models of federalism, including dual federalism, centralized federalism, and new federalism. As you read, consider how these models provide illustrative examples of the dynamic distribution of power between national and state governments, or in other words, how the distribution of power between national and state governments has been fluid over time even though we still have a federal system of government in which the national government and the state governments have constitutionally distributed authority over a population and a set of policies.

An Overview of the U.S. Federal System

federal system
A governmental structure with two levels of government in which each level has sovereignty over different policy matters and geographic areas; a system of government with dual sovereignty.

The U.S. Constitution established an innovative and unique government structure, a federal system. A **federal system** has two constitutionally recognized levels of government, each with *sovereignty*—that is, ultimate governing authority, with no legal superior—over different policy matters and geographic areas. According to the Constitution, the national government has ultimate authority over some matters, and the state governments hold ultimate authority over different matters. In addition, the national government's jurisdiction covers the entire geographic area of the nation, and each state government's jurisdiction covers the geographic area within the state's borders. The existence of two levels of government, each with ultimate authority over different matters and geographic areas—an arrangement called *dual sovereignty*—is what distinguishes the federal system of government from the two other most common systems of government worldwide: the unitary system and the confederal system. The American colonists' experience with a unitary system, and subsequently the early U.S. citizens' life under a confederal system (1781–1788), led to the creation of the innovative federal system.

Unitary System

unitary system
A governmental system in which one central government is *the* sovereign government and it creates other, regional governments to which it delegates some governing powers and responsibilities; however, the central government retains ultimate authority (sovereignty).

Today, the majority of countries in the world have unitary governments. In a **unitary system**, the central government is *the* sovereign government. It can create other governments (regional governments) and delegate governing powers and responsibilities to them. In addition, the sovereign central government in a unitary system can unilaterally take away any governing powers and responsibilities it delegated to the regional governments it created. Ultimately, the sovereign central government can even eliminate the regional governments it created.

Indeed, under Britain's unitary system of government during the American colonial period, the British Crown (the sovereign central government) created colonial governments (regional governments) and gave them authority to handle day-to-day matters such as regulating marriages, resolving business conflicts, providing for public safety, and maintaining roads. As the central government in Britain (with no representatives from the colonies) approved tax and trade policies that harmed the colonists' quality of life, growing public discourse and dissension spurred the colonists to protest. The colonists' failed attempts to influence the central government's policies eventually sparked their declaration of independence from Great Britain.

Confederal System

When the colonies declared their independence from Great Britain in 1776, each colony became an independent sovereign state and adopted its own constitution. As a result, no state had a legal superior; each was *the* sovereign government for its geographic area. In 1777, delegates from every state except Rhode Island met in a convention and agreed to a proposed alliance of the 13 sovereign state governments. In 1781, the 13 independent state governments ratified the Articles of Confederation, the first constitution of the United States, which created a confederal system of government.

In a **confederal system**, several independent sovereign governments (such as the first 13 state governments in the case of the United States) agree to cooperate on specified policy matters while each sovereign state retains ultimate authority over all other governmental matters within its borders. The cooperating sovereign state governments delegate some governing responsibilities to a central governing body. However, the sovereign state governments retain ultimate authority and can modify or even eliminate governing responsibilities they agreed to delegate to the central government.

As detailed in Chapter 2, the effectiveness of the confederal system of government created by the Articles of Confederation quickly came into question due to economic problems and domestic rebellions. In 1787, the national Congress (the central governing body created by the sovereign states) called for a constitutional convention "for the sole and express purpose of revising the Articles of Confederation" in order to preserve the union. Clear-eyed about the failures of the unitary system they experienced as British colonies, and the confederal system, the citizens of the United States decided to experiment with a unique government system. The federal system created by the Constitution of the United States remains in place today, although it has evolved into a more complex web of intergovernmental relations than the framers of the Constitution envisioned.

confederal system
A government structure in which several independent sovereign states agree to cooperate on specified policy matters by creating a central governing body; each sovereign state retains ultimate authority over other governmental matters within its borders, so the central governing body is not a sovereign government.

Federal System

The state delegates who met in Philadelphia in 1787 drafted a new constitution that created the federal system with dual sovereignty. The Constitution's framers established dual sovereignty by detailing a new, sovereign national government for the United States and modifying the sovereignty of the existing state governments. The sovereign national government thus created has no legal superior on matters over which the Constitution gives it authority, and the sovereign state governments have no legal superior on the matters which the Constitution grants to them.

Such dual sovereignty does not exist in unitary or confederal systems, where sovereignty is held by one level of government (the central government in a unitary system and the regional governments in a confederal system). Figure 3.1 compares the three types of governing systems.

The federal system, as it works in the United States today, can be confusing—not only to citizens, but also to government officials. The confusion is a product of at least three factors. First, vague constitutional language that distributes sovereignty between the national government and the state governments fuels questions about which government is sovereign over specific matters. Second,

UNITARY SYSTEM

In a unitary system, the sovereign central government creates, delegates power to, and can eliminate regional governments, which are not sovereign governments.

CONFEDERAL SYSTEM

In a confederal system, the sovereign regional governments create, delegate power to, and can eliminate the central government, which is not a sovereign government.

FEDERAL SYSTEM

In a federal system, two levels of government are sovereign: central government as well as regional governments. Each of the two levels of sovereign governments (central and regional) is sovereign over different matters. Thus, dual sovereignty defines the federal system of government.

FIGURE 3.1 ■ Three Governing Systems What does it mean to be a sovereign government? Distinguish between the three systems of government by explaining what level, or levels, of government holds sovereignty in each system.

state governments have established tens of thousands of local governments—a third level of government—delegating some governing powers and responsibilities to them, to assist the state in serving its citizens. The relationship between a state government and the local governments it creates follows the *unitary system* of government; the sovereign state government retains ultimate authority over all the matters it delegates to its local governments, can remove power and responsibilities it delegates to its local governments, and ultimately can eliminate any local government it creates. Today the United States has more than 90,000 local governments. (See the "Source Analysis" feature for the number of local governments in each state.) The third factor adding to the confusion is the fact that today, most government services and benefits are a product of collaborative efforts by two or more governments. Therefore, it is often difficult to determine which government is responsible for what.

What the Federal System Means for U.S. Citizens

The majority of U.S. citizens live under the jurisdiction of at least five governments: national, state, county (called *borough* in Alaska and *parish* in Louisiana), municipal or township, and school district. Every one of those governments can enact laws with which the people living in its jurisdiction must comply and from which they may benefit.

Each of these governments can impose responsibilities on the people living in its jurisdiction. The most obvious responsibility is to pay taxes. These taxes can include the national personal income tax; state sales and personal income taxes; and county, municipal/township, and school district property taxes.

Each state and local government can enact laws to regulate behaviors, as long as the law does not violate rights and liberties established in the U.S. Constitution. For example, while some states have tight gun control laws, other states do not. In both Nelson and Kennesaw, Georgia, every head of household is required by their city's law to maintain a firearm and ammunition.[1]

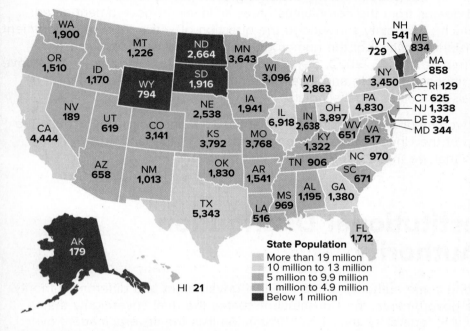

Thousands of Governments Serve U.S. Residents

State	Number
WA	1,900
OR	1,510
MT	1,226
ND	2,664
MN	3,643
ID	1,170
WI	3,096
NH	541
VT	729
ME	834
WY	794
SD	1,916
MI	2,863
NY	3,450
MA	858
NV	189
NE	2,538
IA	1,941
OH	3,897
PA	4,830
RI	129
CT	625
UT	619
IL	6,918
IN	2,638
NJ	1,338
CA	4,444
CO	3,141
KS	3,792
MO	3,768
WV	651
VA	517
DE	334
MD	344
KY	1,322
AZ	658
NM	1,013
OK	1,830
AR	1,541
TN	906
NC	970
SC	671
TX	5,343
MS	969
AL	1,195
GA	1,380
LA	516
FL	1,712
AK	179
HI	21

State Population
- More than 19 million
- 10 million to 13 million
- 5 million to 9.9 million
- 1 million to 4.9 million
- Below 1 million

Number of Local Governments in Each State

Sources: U.S. Census Bureau, "2017 Census of Governments"; U.S. Census, "2019 Census Estimates"

Practice Analytical Thinking

1. What might explain the range in the number of local governments that exist in the 50 states?

2. Do the states with the largest geographic area have the largest number of local governments?

3. Are there regional patterns?

4. Do states with smaller populations have fewer local governments?

5. How many local governments exist in your state?

6. Can you name all the governments under which you live?

In 1990, federal law established 18 years as the minimum age at which people could buy tobacco products. On January 1, 2016, Hawaii became the first state to raise the legal age for the purchase of tobacco products and electronic smoking devices from 18 years to 21 years. By the end of 2019, 20 states had increased the age to purchase tobacco products to 21 years. Several cities had also increased the legal age for purchasing tobacco products to 21 years, including New York City and Cleveland, Ohio.[2] So, depending on which state you lived in or even which city, the age to buy tobacco products was somewhere between 18 and 21 years. Then in December 2019, President Trump signed a national law that increased the purchase age for tobacco products to 21 years. Therefore, beginning in the summer of 2020, the minimum purchase age for tobacco products throughout the United States has been 21 years. State and local governments can establish an older age to purchase those products, but not a younger age.

The Constitution lists individual liberties and rights in the Bill of Rights. In addition, every state constitution has its own bill of rights, and some local governments offer further protections to their citizens. For example, the Pennsylvania constitution states: "The people have a right to clean air, pure water, and to the preservation of the natural, scenic, historic and esthetic" and that the state's "natural resources are the common property of all the people, including generations yet to come." The U.S. Constitution does not mention the environment or natural resources.

Clearly, people's rights and responsibilities vary depending on where they live in the United States (as discussed further in Chapter 4). Thus, the federal system can be confusing for citizens. It can also be confusing for the many governments created to serve the people. During the spring of 2020, as rates of infection and related deaths from the coronavirus grew, all levels of government acted. However, much uncertainty surrounded the question of which level of government was responsible for which of the numerous problems the pandemic caused. President Trump's April 13, 2020, declaration that he had total authority to remove restrictions imposed by state and local government officials was challenged by those officials as well as legal scholars.

Which government is responsible for what services and policies? Because the Constitution of the United States is the supreme law of the land, it is to the Constitution that we must turn to answer that question.

Constitutional Distribution of Authority

By distributing some authority to the national government and different authority to the state governments, the Constitution creates the dual sovereignty that defines the U.S. federal system. The Constitution lists the several matters over which the national government has ultimate authority, and it implies additional national authority. The Constitution spells out just a few matters over which the state governments have authority. The Constitution lacks detail on state authority in part because, at the time of the Constitution's drafting, the states expected to retain their authority, except for matters that, by way of the Constitution, they agreed to turn over to the newly created national government.

To fulfill their responsibilities to their citizens, both the national and the state governments have the authority to engage in basic governing functions inherent to all sovereign governments. The powers that are exercised by both the national and state governments are the first topic in this section.

Concurrent Powers

concurrent powers
Basic governing functions that are exercised by the national and state governments independently, and at the same time, including the power to make policy, raise revenue, implement policies, and establish courts.

To function, sovereign governments need basic governing powers such as the authority to make policy, raise and spend money, implement policies, and establish courts to resolve conflicts over the law. In the U.S. federal system, these basic governing powers are **concurrent powers** because the national government and all state governments exercise them, independently and at the same time. For example, national and state governments make their own public policies, and raise and spend their own revenues to implement their policies. In addition, the national court system resolves conflicts over national laws, including the U.S. Constitution, and each state has its own court system to resolve conflicts over its state laws. State governments delegate some concurrent powers to the local governments they create so that the local governments can govern. Table 3.1 lists concurrent powers of the national and state governments, powers that states may share with their local governments.

In addition to the basic governing powers that the national and state governments hold concurrently, in the federal system the national government and the state governments have sovereignty over different matters. We now consider the distinct sovereign powers of the national and state governments.

TABLE 3.1 ▪ Concurrent Powers of National and State Governments

Make policy
Raise and spend money
Borrow money
Implement policy
Charter banks and corporations
Establish courts
Take private property for public use (eminent domain)

National Sovereignty

The Constitution distributes powers to the national government's three branches (legislative, executive, and judicial) that are (1) enumerated, or specifically listed, and (2) implied. For example, Article I of the Constitution enumerates the matters over which Congress holds the authority to make laws, including regulation of interstate and foreign commerce, the system of money, general welfare, and national defense, including the authority to declare war. These matters are **enumerated powers** of the national government. The Constitution also gives Congress **implied powers**—that is, powers that are not described explicitly but that may be interpreted to be necessary to fulfill the enumerated powers. Congress specifically receives implied powers through the Constitution's **necessary and proper clause**, sometimes called the **elastic clause** because the national government uses this passage to stretch its enumerated authority. The necessary and proper clause in Article I, Section 8, of the Constitution states that Congress has the power to "make all Laws which shall be necessary and proper" for carrying out its enumerated powers.

Articles II and III of the Constitution also enumerate powers of the national government. Article II delegates to the president the responsibility to ensure the proper implementation of national laws and, with the advice and consent of the U.S. Senate, the authority to make treaties with foreign nations and to appoint foreign ambassadors. With respect to the U.S. Supreme Court and the lower federal courts, Article III enumerates jurisdiction over legal cases involving U.S. constitutional issues, national legislation, and treaties. The jurisdiction of the Supreme Court also extends to disagreements between two or more state governments, as well as to conflicts between citizens from different states. Figure 3.2 lists national powers enumerated in Articles I, II, and III of the Constitution.

enumerated powers
The powers of the national government that are listed in the Constitution.

implied powers
The powers of the national government that are not enumerated in the Constitution but that Congress claims are necessary and proper for the national government to fulfill its enumerated powers in accordance with the necessary and proper clause of the Constitution.

necessary and proper clause (elastic clause)
A clause in Article I, Section 8, of the Constitution that gives Congress the power to do whatever it deems necessary and constitutional to meet its enumerated obligations; the basis for the implied powers.

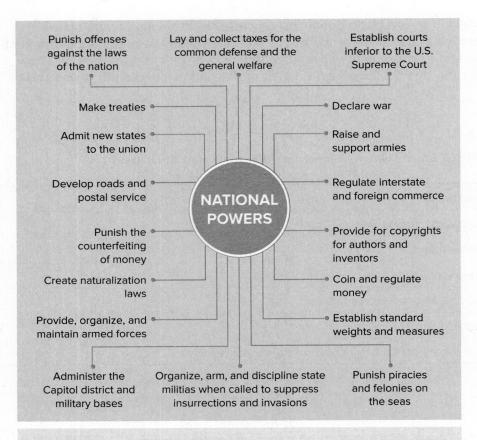

Punish offenses against the laws of the nation

Lay and collect taxes for the common defense and the general welfare

Establish courts inferior to the U.S. Supreme Court

Make treaties

Declare war

Admit new states to the union

Raise and support armies

Develop roads and postal service

NATIONAL POWERS

Regulate interstate and foreign commerce

Punish the counterfeiting of money

Provide for copyrights for authors and inventors

Create naturalization laws

Coin and regulate money

Provide, organize, and maintain armed forces

Establish standard weights and measures

Administer the Capitol district and military bases

Organize, arm, and discipline state militias when called to suppress insurrections and invasions

Punish piracies and felonies on the seas

FIGURE 3.2 ▪ **Enumerated Powers of National Government** Can you locate each enumerated power in the Constitution that precedes this chapter (by article, section, and clause)?

THE SUPREMACY CLAUSE The country's founders anticipated disagreements over the interpretation of constitutional language and prepared for them by creating the Supreme Court. The Court has mostly supported the national government when states, citizens, or interest groups have challenged Congress's use of the necessary and proper clause to take on new responsibilities beyond its enumerated powers. Unless the Supreme Court finds a national law to be outside of the enumerated or implied powers, that law is constitutional and hence the **supreme law of the land**, as defined by the supremacy clause in Article VI of the Constitution: "This Constitution, and the Laws of the United States which shall be made in Pursuance thereof; and all Treaties made, or which shall be made, under the Authority of the United States, shall be the supreme Law of the Land." State and local governments are thereby obligated to comply with national laws that implement national enumerated and implied powers, as well as with treaties— including treaties with Native American nations.

supreme law of the land
A clause in Article VI, by which the U.S. Constitution's ultimate authority is established; the clause states that all laws made by governments within the United States must comply with the Constitution.

NATIONAL TREATIES WITH INDIAN NATIONS Throughout U.S. history, the national government has signed treaties with Native American nations, which are legally considered sovereign foreign nations. As with all treaties, those made with Native American nations are supreme law with which the national, state, and local governments must comply. The core issue in the majority of these treaties is the provision of land (reservations) on which the native peoples resettled after non-Indians took their lands during the 18th and 19th centuries. Today, the federal government recognizes more than 573 Indian tribes. Although most Native Americans no longer live on reservations, 323 reservations remain, in 34 states.[3]

Even though Indian reservations lie within state borders, national treaties and national laws, not state or local laws, apply to the reservation populations and lands. State and local laws, including laws having to do with taxes, crime, and the environment, are unenforceable on reservations. Moreover, Native American treaty rights to hunt, fish, and gather on reservations and on public lands supersede national, state, and local environmental regulations.[4] However, tribes, states, and local governments frequently work together through agreements on matters of mutual concern such as environmental issues and law enforcement.

With the exception of Native American reservations that exist within their borders, state governments are sovereign over the lands and people living in the state for the matters the Constitution distributes to them. What are the matters that fall within state sovereignty?

State Sovereignty

The Constitution specifies only a few state powers. It provides the states with a role in national politics and gives them the final say on formally amending the U.S. Constitution. One reason for the lack of constitutional specificity regarding the matters over which state governments are sovereign is because, unlike the newly created national government, the state governments were already functioning when they ratified the Constitution. Other than those responsibilities that the states agreed to delegate to the newly created national government through their ratification of the Constitution, the states expected to retain their sovereignty over all the day-to-day matters internal to their borders that they were already handling. Yet the original Constitution did not speak of this state sovereignty explicitly.

POWERS RESERVED TO THE STATES The Constitution's limited attention to state authority caused concern among citizens of the early American republic. Many people feared that the new national government would meddle in matters for which states had been responsible, in that way compromising state sovereignty. Citizens were also deeply concerned about their own liberties. As described in Chapter 2, within two years of the states' ratification of the Constitution, they ratified the Bill of Rights (1791), the first 10 amendments to the U.S. Constitution, in response to those concerns.

The Tenth Amendment asserts that the "powers not delegated to the United States by the Constitution, nor prohibited by it to the States, are *reserved to the States* respectively, or to the people." This **reserved powers** clause of the Tenth Amendment acknowledged the domestic matters over which the states had exercised authority since the ratification of their own constitutions. These matters included the handling of the daily affairs of the people—laws regarding birth, death, marriage, intrastate commerce, crime, health, morals, and safety. The states' reserved powers to protect the health, safety, lives, and property of their citizens are their **police powers**. It was over these domestic matters, internal to each state, that the states retained sovereignty according to the Tenth Amendment.

Figure 3.3 summarizes the constitutionally reserved powers of the states at the time of the Tenth Amendment's ratification, as well as some of the few powers delegated to the states in the Constitution prior to ratification of the Tenth Amendment.

reserved powers
The matters referred to in the Tenth Amendment over which states retain sovereignty.

police powers
The states' reserved powers to protect the health, safety, lives, and properties of residents in a state.

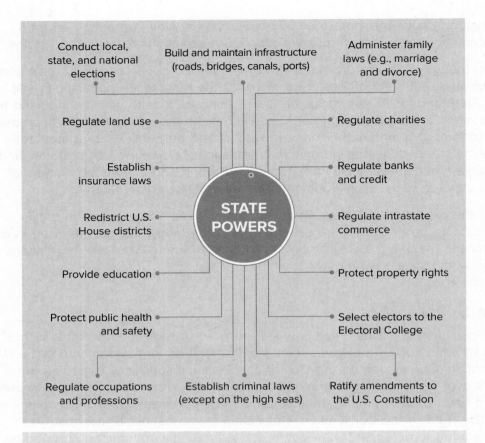

Conduct local, state, and national elections

Build and maintain infrastructure (roads, bridges, canals, ports)

Administer family laws (e.g., marriage and divorce)

Regulate land use

Regulate charities

Establish insurance laws

Regulate banks and credit

Redistrict U.S. House districts

STATE POWERS

Regulate intrastate commerce

Provide education

Protect property rights

Protect public health and safety

Select electors to the Electoral College

Regulate occupations and professions

Establish criminal laws (except on the high seas)

Ratify amendments to the U.S. Constitution

FIGURE 3.3 ■ **Constitutionally Delegated and Reserved Powers** Few of these powers are specified in the Constitution. Which of these state powers are listed (delegated) in the Constitution? Where do the other powers come from?

POWERS DELEGATED TO THE STATES Although the Constitution does not list all the specific powers reserved to the states, it does assign, or delegate, several powers to the states. These powers provide the states with a distinct voice in the composition and priorities of the national government. Members of Congress are elected by voters in their home states (U.S. senators) or their home districts (representatives in the U.S. House). Therefore, members of Congress are accountable to the voters in the state that elected them. State governments also have the authority to redraw the boundaries of the U.S. House districts within the state after each decennial census, which is a count of all the people living in the United States and is constitutionally mandated to occur every ten years. The "Then, Now, Next" feature provides additional information about the decennial census. In addition, each state government determines the procedure by which the state's Electoral College electors will be selected to participate in the state's vote for the president and vice president. Overall, state voters expect that the officials whom they elect to the national government will carefully consider their concerns when creating national policy.

In addition to establishing the various electoral procedures that give voice to state interests in the national policy-making process, the Constitution creates a formal means by which the states can ensure that the language in the Constitution is not changed in such a way that their sovereignty is threatened. Specifically, the Constitution stipulates that three-fourths of the states (through votes in either their

The Census

THEN

(2000)
Largely conducted by mail

Used a short form (10 questions) and a long form (45 questions)

Lawsuit successfully challenged plan to statistically adjust for undercounts and overcounts

Four states gained the most U.S. House seats and Electoral College votes: Texas, Florida, Georgia, and Arizona each gained two seats

Two states lost the most U.S. House seats and Electoral College votes: New York and Pennsylvania (2 seats)

32 states had no change in their number of U.S. House seats or Electoral votes

*Election Data Service

NOW

(2020)
For the first time, largely conducted online

For the second time, used only the short form (9 questions)

Lawsuit successfully challenged plan to add a citizenship question to the 2020 Census

Two states are forecast to gain the most U.S. House seats and Electoral College votes: Texas (3 seats) and Florida (2 seats)*

Ten states are forecast to lose the most U.S. House seats (1 seat): Alabama, California, Illinois, Michigan, Minnesota, New York, Ohio, Pennsylvania, Rhode Island, West Virginia*

33 states are forecast to have no change to their number of U.S. House seats or Electoral votes*

NEXT

- Will the long-term shift in population and political power from the Rust Belt (parts of northeastern and midwestern states) to the Sun Belt (southern states) continue based on the 2020 Census results, as forecast?

- Will the 2020 Census count be legally challenged in the courts due to concerns about cyber security issues?

- Will the largely online 2020 Census provide a more accurate count than previous censuses, or will the undercounting of racial minorities and overcounting of non-Hispanic whites continue?

---

legislatures or special conventions, as discussed in Chapter 2) must ratify amendments to the Constitution. By having the final say in whether the supreme law of the land will be changed formally through the passage of amendments to the U.S. Constitution, the states can protect their constitutional powers. Indeed, they did just that when they ratified the Tenth Amendment.

State-to-State Relations: Horizontal Federalism

In Article IV, the Constitution sets forth obligations that the states have to one another and to each other's citizens. Collectively, these state-to-state obligations and the intergovernmental relationships they mandate are forms of **horizontal federalism**. For example, state governments have the right to forge agreements with other states, known as **interstate compacts**. Congress must review and approve interstate compacts to ensure that they do not harm the states that are

horizontal federalism
The state-to-state relationships created by the U.S. Constitution.

interstate compacts
Agreements between states that Congress has the authority to review and reject.

>> The Rio Grande originates in Colorado and flows south into New Mexico and Texas. To resolve disputes over the three states' claims to water rights, Texas, New Mexico, and Colorado signed the Rio Grande Compact in 1938, an agreement that apportions the water of the Rio Grande Basin among the three states.

William Silver/Shutterstock

not party to them and the nation as a whole. States enter into interstate compacts to provide services and benefits for one another, such as monitoring paroled inmates from other states; sharing and conserving natural resources that spill over state borders, such as water; and decreasing pollution that crosses state borders.

extradition
The return of individuals accused of a crime to the state in which the crime was committed upon the request of that state's governor.

States also cooperate through a procedure called **extradition**, the legal process of sending individuals back to a state that accuses them of having committed a crime, and from which they have fled. The Constitution establishes a state governor's right to request the extradition of an accused criminal. Yet the courts have also supported governors' refusals to extradite individuals.

privileges and immunities clause
The Constitution's requirement that a state extend to other states' citizens the privileges and immunities it provides for its citizens.

The Constitution asserts, too, that each state must guarantee the same **privileges and immunities** it provides to its citizens to all U.S. citizens, including citizens from other states who visit or move into the state. This guarantee does not prohibit states from imposing reasonable requirements before extending rights to visiting or new state residents. For example, states can and do charge higher tuition costs to out-of-state college students. In addition, in many states, new state residents must wait 30 days before they can register to vote. Yet no state can deny new state residents who are U.S. citizens the right to register to vote once they meet a reasonable state residency requirement.

full faith and credit clause
The constitutional clause that requires states to comply with and uphold the public acts, records, and judicial decisions of other states.

Because of the ease of traveling between states as well as relocating from state to state, an important component of horizontal federalism stems from the full faith and credit clause of Article IV, Section 1, of the Constitution. The **full faith and credit clause** asserts that each state must recognize as legally binding (that is, valid and enforceable) the public acts, records, and judicial proceedings of every other state. For example, in March 2016, the Supreme Court cited the full faith and credit clause when it ruled that states must honor adoptions by same-sex parents who move across state lines.[5]

Supreme Court Interpretation of the Constitution

Vague language in the U.S. Constitution continues to spark disputes over what are the constitutional powers of the national government versus what are the constitutional powers of the state governments. Some constitutional clauses that the courts have had to interpret repeatedly include the *necessary and proper* powers of Congress and the powers of Congress to provide for the *general welfare* and to regulate *commerce among the several states*. In addition, the courts are continually interpreting and reinterpreting the meaning of the *reserved powers clause* of the Tenth Amendment. The U.S. Supreme Court has the final say over what constitutional language means. In the process of resolving conflicts by distinguishing among national enumerated and implied powers and the powers reserved for the states, the Court has given meaning to the supremacy clause of the Constitution and influenced the relationships among the national and state governments.

THE POWER TO REGULATE COMMERCE The landmark case of **McCulloch v. Maryland** (1819) exemplifies a Supreme Court ruling that established the use of the implied powers to expand the national government's enumerated authority.[6] The case stemmed from Congress's establishment of a national bank, and in particular a branch of that bank located in the state of Maryland, which the Maryland state authorities tried to tax. Maryland's attorneys argued that Congress did not have the constitutional authority to establish a national bank, noting it was not among the enumerated powers. They also argued that if the Court interpreted the Constitution such that the national government did have the implied power to establish a national bank, then Maryland had the concurrent power to tax the bank. Lawyers for the national government in turn argued that the Constitution did indeed imply federal authority to establish a national bank and that Maryland's levying a tax on the bank was unconstitutional, for it impinged on the national government's ability to fulfill its constitutional responsibilities by taking some of its financial resources.

The Supreme Court decided in favor of the national government. The justices based their ruling on their interpretation of the Constitution's necessary and proper clause and the enumerated powers of Congress to "lay and collect taxes, to borrow money . . . and to regulate commerce among the several states." The Court said that, combined, these enumerated powers implied that the national government had the authority to charter a bank and to locate a branch in Maryland. Moreover, the Court found that Maryland did not have the right to tax that bank, because taxation by the state would interfere with the exercise of national authority. This case set the precedent that continues today. No level of government can impose a tax on the property of another level of government; government properties are tax exempt.

In the *McCulloch* case, the Supreme Court established that the necessary and proper clause allows Congress to broadly interpret the enumerated powers of the national government. Moreover, the Court interpreted the national supremacy clause to mean that in the event of a conflict between national legislation (the law chartering the national bank) and state legislation (Maryland's tax law), the national law is supreme *as long as* it falls under the enumerated and implied powers that the Constitution distributes to the national government.

A few years later, in the case of *Gibbons v. Ogden* (1824), the Supreme Court again justified a particular national action on the basis of the implications of an enumerated power.[7] The *Gibbons* case was the first suit brought to the Supreme Court seeking clarification on the constitutional meaning of *commerce* in the Constitution's clause on the regulation of interstate commerce, commonly referred to as the **commerce clause**. The Court established a broad definition of commerce: "all commercial intercourse—meaning all business dealings." The conflict in this case concerned which government, New York State or the national government, had authority to regulate the operation of boats on the waterways

McCulloch v. Maryland
The 1819 case that established that the necessary and proper clause justifies broad understandings of enumerated powers.

commerce clause
Article I clause that delegates to Congress the power to regulate interstate and international commercial interactions.

>> Which government has the authority to regulate navigation on the waterways between the states of New York and New Jersey? That was the question the U.S. Supreme Court answered in *Gibbons* v. *Ogden* (1824). Which constitutional clauses did the Court interpret to resolve the conflict between the two states? What was the Court's decision?

Vitaly Edush/iStock/Getty Images

between New York and New Jersey. The Court ruled that regulation of commerce implied regulation of navigation and therefore the national government had authority to regulate it, not New York State.

Not until the Great Depression (1930s) did the national government begin to justify new laws by arguing that they were necessary to fulfill its enumerated power to regulate interstate commerce. After some initial conflicts, the Court has more often agreed than disagreed with Congress's broad understanding of what its enumerated powers implied it could do through legislation. In addition to expanding its power through implications of the regulation of interstate commerce clause, Congress has also successfully used the general welfare clause to take on new matters, hence expanding its authority.

THE POWER TO PROVIDE FOR THE GENERAL WELFARE The national government's landmark Social Security Act of 1935 was a response to the Great Depression's devastating impact on the financial security of countless Americans. The congressional vote to establish Social Security was overwhelmingly favorable. Yet several states challenged the constitutionality of this expansive program shortly after its passage, claiming it infringed on their reserved police powers. In 1937, the Supreme Court had to decide: Was Social Security indeed a matter of general welfare for which Congress is delegated the authority to raise and spend money? Or was Social Security a matter for the state governments to address? The Court found the national policy to be constitutional—a reasonable congressional interpretation, the justices wrote, of the enumerated and implied powers of the national government.[8]

The Supreme Court's decisions in the *McCulloch, Gibbons,* and Social Security cases set the stage for the expansion of national power in domestic policy matters by combining the necessary and proper clause with such enumerated powers as the regulation of commerce and providing for the general welfare. Although throughout U.S. history, particularly since the 1930s, the Court has typically supported Congress's enactment of laws dealing with matters implied by—but not specifically enumerated in—the Constitution, Congress does not always get its way. For example, in ***United States v. Lopez*** (1995), the Supreme Court rejected the national government's claim that its Gun-Free School Zones Act of 1990 was a necessary and proper means to regulate interstate commerce. The Court found the act unconstitutional because it was not related to an enumerated

United States v. Lopez
Case in which the U.S. Supreme Court ruled the national Gun-Free School Zones Act unconstitutional and affirmed that state governments have the right to establish gun-free school zones.

In 1808, the government of New York granted a steamboat company a monopoly to operate its boats on the state's waters, which included bodies of water that stretched between states. Aaron Ogden held a license under this monopoly to operate steamboats between New Jersey and New York. Thomas Gibbons, another steamboat operator, competed with Aaron Ogden on this same route but held a federal coasting license issued by an act of Congress. Ogden filed a complaint in New York court to stop Gibbons from operating his boats, claiming that the monopoly granted by New York was legal even though he operated on shared, interstate waters. Gibbons disagreed, arguing that the U.S. Constitution gave Congress the sole power over interstate commerce, and he challenged Ogden's licensing in court.

The case eventually reached the Supreme Court, and in the ruling, the court held that the commerce clause of the Constitution grants the federal government the power to regulate the operation of steamboats between New York and New Jersey. Therefore, the license issued to Gibbons by Congress to operate a ferry service superseded the monopoly license to operate a ferry service issued to Ogden by the state of New York.

A. Identify the constitutional clause that was used in *U.S. v. Lopez* (1995) and *Gibbons v. Ogden* (1824).

B. Based on the constitutional clause identified in part A, explain why the facts of *Gibbons v. Ogden* led to a different holding than the holding in *U.S. v. Lopez*.

C. Describe an action that state governments could take if they disagree with the holding in *Gibbons v. Ogden* to limit its impact.

power, nor was it implied by the interstate commerce clause. In addition, the national law infringed on states' reserved police powers; state governments have authority to create gun-free school zones, and they can extend that authority to their local governments.[9]

In addition to establishing dual sovereignty and creating two independently operating levels of government, the Constitution enumerates some obligations that the national government has to the states. These obligations, identified in Table 3.2, include guaranteeing a republican form of government, protecting states from foreign invasion and domestic violence, and prohibiting the national government from changing state boundaries without consent of the states concerned.

Judicial Federalism

The Fourteenth Amendment authorizes the national government to ensure that the state governments (1) follow fair procedures (due process) before taking away a person's life, liberties, or pursuit of happiness and (2) guarantee all people the

TABLE 3.2 ■ National Government Obligations to the States

The National Government
* Must treat states equally in matters of the regulation of commerce and the imposition of taxes
* Must guarantee a republican form of government
* Must protect states from foreign invasion
* Must, at their request, protect states against domestic violence
* Cannot approve the creation of a new state from the property of an existing state without the consent of the states concerned
* Cannot change state boundaries without the consent of the states concerned

same rights (equal protection of the laws) to life, liberties, and pursuit of happiness without arbitrary discrimination. In addition, the amendment guarantees the privileges and immunities of U.S. citizenship to all citizens in all states.

The rights and privileges guaranteed by the U.S. Constitution are minimums; all governments in the United States must comply with the Constitution. However, state and local governments can guarantee additional rights and privileges to the people in their jurisdictions. Indeed, state and local governments have enacted laws that provide more rights and privileges than found in the Constitution.

For example, the California state constitution protects freedom of speech and expression in privately owned properties, such as shopping centers. The U.S. Constitution's guaranteed freedom of expression does not extend to privately owned properties.[10] And in numerous municipalities and counties across the country, laws prohibit some forms of discrimination due to a person's sexual orientation, though the U.S. Constitution does not prohibit such discrimination.

Historically, state courts turned to the U.S. Constitution when deciding civil rights and liberties cases. However, beginning in the 1970s, state courts increasingly based these decisions on their own state constitutions, which guaranteed more extensive rights to their citizens than did the U.S. Constitution. For example, after the U.S. Supreme Court's 1973 ruling that the equal protection clause of the Fourteenth Amendment did not require equal funding of schools in Texas,[11] state courts in 15 states ruled that their state constitutions required equal funding of schools.[12] Political scientists refer to the reliance of state courts on their state constitutions as **judicial federalism**.

judicial federalism
State courts' use of their state constitutions to determine citizens' rights, particularly when state constitutions guarantee greater protections than does the U.S. Constitution.

States as Laboratories of Democracy

In a 1932 case, U.S. Supreme Court Justice Louis Brandeis wrote, "It is one of the happy incidents of the federal system that a single courageous state may, if its citizens choose, serve as a laboratory; and try novel social and economic experiments without risk to the rest of the country."[13] In this statement, Brandeis was acknowledging that under the Constitution, state governments have the right to try innovative policies to address public problems, without interference from the national government. Obviously, state experiments must not violate the Constitution. Local governments may also experiment with innovative policies, as long as they comply with both the U.S. Constitution and their own state's laws. Of course, the national government also experiments with public policies.

Governments pay attention to such policy experiments, and one government often adopts a successful policy experiment of another government. For example, California has been the major laboratory for innovative environmental policies adopted by other states and localities. Also, in 1996, the federal government made major changes to its existing income security program for low-income families based on successful welfare policy experiments in numerous states. And, as discussed earlier, state and local governments experimented with raising the purchase age for tobacco products to 21 years, and the national government then did the same.

In 2019, youth activists in Oregon succeeded in getting the state legislature and governor to enact a law that expanded excused school absences to include "mental health days." Oregon has a suicide rate 40 percent higher than the national average; suicide is Oregon's second-leading cause of death among those of ages 10 to 34. The youth leaders drafted and advocated for the "mental health days" law to address their state's mental health crisis. With the national suicide rate on the rise, climbing by 30 percent since 1999, the Oregon policy experiment will be watched and possibly adopted by other states,[14] a benefit of the U.S. federal system.

Evolution of Intergovernmental Relations in the U.S. Federal System

Constitutional language establishing the U.S. federal system of government, with dual sovereignty, remains essentially as it was in 1791. However, how the federal system is currently administered day-to-day differs considerably from how it functioned in 1791. In *Federalist* No. 45, James Madison (1788) stated that the powers delegated to the national government in the Constitution are "few and defined" and primarily focused on "external objects" such as war and peace, foreign relations, and commerce. He also noted that the powers reserved for the states are "numerous and indefinite," extending to matters affecting the daily "lives, liberties and properties of the people; and the internal order, improvement, and prosperity of the state [police powers]."[15]

Gary Gerstle, a respected scholar of American government, agrees with Madison's claims: As written, the Constitution anticipated that the national government would be limited in its roles and responsibilities and the state governments would be expansive. In his book *Liberty and Coercion* (2015), Gerstle argues that the Tenth Amendment's reserved powers grant the state governments "a staggering freedom of action." When balancing the enumerated powers of the federal government and the police powers reserved for the states, Gerstle claims that the federal system as established in the Constitution clearly gave dominant power to the states. However, according to Gerstle, presidents, congresses, and the U.S. Supreme Court have twisted the meaning of the Constitution over the course of U.S. history so that today, the federal government dominates. Therefore, today's federal system is not the system of government envisioned by the framers of the Constitution.[16]

Most government services and benefits today are products of collaborative efforts by two or more governments. To serve its people, a government must have the authority to formulate and approve a plan of action (policy statement), to raise and spend money to finance the plan (policy financing), and to hire workers who put the plan into action (policy implementation). Therefore, all public policies have three elements: the policy statement, the policy financing, and the policy implementation (see Table 3.3). In the U.S. federal system today, the responsibility for these three elements may rest entirely with one level of government (national, state, or local) or may be shared in a collaborative effort by two or more of these levels. Political scientists label the interactions of two or more governments (national, state, and local) in their collective efforts to provide goods and services to the people they serve **intergovernmental relations (IGR)**. Today, IGR is a dominant characteristic of the U.S. federal system of government.

intergovernmental relations (IGR)
The interactions of two or more governments (national, state, and local) in their collective efforts to provide goods and services to the people they each serve.

TABLE 3.3 ▬ Elements of Government Action

Element	Definition
Policy statement	Plan of government action to address a public problem
Policy financing	Identification of government(s) that will pay the costs of policy implementation
Policy implementation	Employment of staff who will put the policy into action

Models of Federalism

To understand the intergovernmental relations of today's federal system and the expansion of federal power since 1789, we need to first survey several models of federalism, each of which characterizes different roles, responsibilities, and relationships between the national and state governments in the United States. Then we will review the policy tools of intergovernmental relations.

DUAL FEDERALISM Initially, the dual sovereignty of the U.S. federal system was implemented in such a way that the national and state governments acted independently of each other. The national government raised its own money and spent it on policies it created, paid for, and implemented. Each state government also raised its own money and spent it on policies it created, paid for, and implemented. Political scientists give the name **dual federalism** to this model of administering the federal system; the national government takes care of its enumerated powers and the states independently take care of their reserved powers. From 1789 through 1932, dual federalism was the dominant pattern of intergovernmental relations. Congresses and presidents did enact some laws that states argued infringed on their powers, and the U.S. Supreme Court typically found in favor of the states in those cases. Yet, as the 1819 *McCulloch* case shows, sometimes the Supreme Court ruled in favor of the national government.

dual federalism
The initial model of national and state relations in which the national government takes care of its enumerated powers while the state governments independently take care of their reserved powers.

COOPERATIVE FEDERALISM Passage of the Sixteenth Amendment (1913) powerfully enhanced the ability of the national government to raise money. The amendment granted Congress the authority to collect income taxes from workers and corporations

SOURCE ANALYSIS | CONCEPT APPLICATION

As you read the passage, consider how you would describe the author's claim(s), perspective, evidence and reasoning.

Excerpt from: Opening the Third Century of American Federalism: Issues and Prospects

By Daniel Elazar

Strong forces for centralization continue to operate in the American federal system; however, especially since the election of President Ronald Reagan in 1980, countervailing forces have worked to promote decentralization and even restore noncentralization in the federal system. . . . The potential for greater noncentralization is being reinforced by changing socioeconomic conditions that place a greater emphasis on networks of relationships rather than on traditional hierarchies.

. . . By its decisive actions in so many fields, the Reagan administration demonstrated that it was still possible to take hold of the reins of government and begin to reverse seemingly irreversible trends, including the at least seventy-year-long thrust toward greater government permeation of society. Yet fulfilling Reagan's promise to strengthen the state within that system, and thereby strengthen the system as a whole, has not been easy.

. . . Especially during the first postwar generation (194-76), there was an environmental basis for centralization. . . . The civil rights revolution led to substantial federal intervention in the legal and educational systems.

A. Describe the author's claim in the passage above about federalism.

B. Identify evidence that might support the author's claim of strong state government.

C. Identify evidence that would support a claim of state resurgence after 1980.

Elazar, Daniel J. "Opening the Third Century of American Federalism: Issues and Prospects." The Annals of the American Academy of Political and Social Science 509 (1990): 11–21.

without apportioning the taxes among the states on the basis of population (which the Constitution had required before this amendment). With the capacity to raise more revenue, the national government could financially assist states.

To help the state governments deal with the domestic problems spawned by the global economic depression that began in 1929 (the Great Depression), Congress and President Franklin D. Roosevelt (1933–1945) approved numerous policies, collectively called the New Deal. **Grants-in-aid**—transfers of money from one government (the national government) to another government (state and local governments) that need not be paid back—became a main mechanism of President Roosevelt's New Deal programs. State and local governments welcomed the national grants-in-aid, which assisted them in addressing the domestic matters that fell within state sovereignty while allowing states and their local governments

grant-in-aid (intergovernmental transfer)
The transfer of money from one government to another government that does not need to be paid back.

to make most of the specific program decisions to implement the policies. Through grants-in-aid, dual federalism was replaced by **cooperative federalism** in numerous policy matters. Collaborative intergovernmental relations was a product of cooperative federalism, which dominated national and state government relations from the New Deal era to the early 1960s.

cooperative federalism
Intergovernmental relations in which the national government supports state governments' efforts to address the domestic matters reserved to them.

CENTRALIZED FEDERALISM By the time of Lyndon Johnson's presidency (1963–1969), a new pattern of national-state relations was developing. In this new form of federalism, the national government imposed its own policy preferences on state and local governments. Specifically, in **centralized federalism**, directives in national legislation, including grant-in-aid programs with ever-increasing conditions or strings attached to the money, force state and local governments to implement a particular national policy. Therefore, in centralized federalism, the national government dominates intergovernmental relations, imposing its policy preferences on state and local governments.

centralized federalism
Intergovernmental relations in which the national government imposes its policy preferences on state and local governments.

NEW FEDERALISM Presidents since Richard Nixon (1969–1974) have fought against this centralizing tendency in intergovernmental relations by proposing to return policy responsibilities (policy making, policy financing, and policy implementation) to state and local governments. Presidents Nixon and Ronald Reagan (1981–1989) gave the name *new federalism* to these efforts, and today we use the term **devolution** to refer to the return of power to state and local governments.

devolution
The process whereby the national government returns policy responsibilities to state or local governments.

Today, Republicans and Democrats (including presidents, members of Congress, and state and local lawmakers) broadly support selective devolution, though they engage in partisan battles over *what policies* to devolve and over *which elements of a policy* should be devolved (policy statements, policy financing, and/or policy implementation). The results of these partisan battles is a new model of federalism.

PARTISAN FEDERALISM Whether the national government or state governments take precedence in any given policy matter is determined by the political party that wins the policy battle. That is, the winners of policy battles institute the model of federalism that they believe will most likely lead to their preferred policy outcome. Scholar Jessica Bulman-Pozen labels this phenomenon **partisan federalism**—that is, a preference for state or national government action (hence, a preference for dual federalism, cooperative federalism, or centralized federalism) that depends on policy substance and partisan makeup of government at the other levels.[17]

partisan federalism
The phenomenon of preference for state or national government action (hence, preference for dual federalism, cooperative federalism, or centralized federalism) depending on policy substance and partisan makeup of government at the other levels.

When Congress is gridlocked, and therefore, a vacuum exists in a policy matter salient to states, state governments will step up and enact their preferred policies. With Democrats controlling government in some states and Republicans in others, state-level policies may conflict with each other, and some will conflict with the national government's priorities. In addition, when a state government is dominated by one party and Congress or the presidency is controlled by the other major party, the state may act on its own, fulfilling its policy preferences. Scholar Bulman-Pozen argues that the U.S. federal system "provides durable and robust scaffolding for partisan conflict," which allows states and local governments to challenge national policies when the national government is controlled by the opposing party.[18]

Traditionally, since the New Deal, Democrats have supported federal government expansion in domestic policy matters. Republicans have been viewed as the party that supports states' rights (protects states' reserved powers) over national expansion. However, in today's era of partisan federalism, government officials at all levels of government and from both major political parties will support action by whichever level of government supports their policy preferences; state governments will support national action when it is in line with their preferences or state action when the national government opposes their preferences. The partisans in national government act this way, too. If they cannot obtain what they want through national action, they will support state action. According to a report from the Congressional Research Service, "the historical record suggests that for members of both political parties, regardless of their personal ideological preferences, federalism principles often lose out when in conflict with other policy goals."[19]

Partisan federalism was evident during the spring of 2020 as national, state, and local governments responded to the coronavirus. President Trump moved from claiming the state governments should be in charge of governmental responses (and the cost of responding) to claiming total authority over states' responses when he wanted states to reopen businesses in April and May. States with Republican governors were more supportive of Trump's calls to open up, while those with Democratic governors pushed back and argued that it was their decision when to reopen.

Although conflicts between the states and the national government have been a reality throughout U.S. history, contemporary scholarship on U.S. federalism notes increased "volume and intensity" in intergovernmental tensions.[20] During the 21st century, state governments have filed lawsuits against the national government over national health care policy, immigration policy, education policy, and environmental protection.[21] The national government has filed lawsuits against state and local governments over immigration policy, environmental protection, and voting rights.[22] States have increasingly acted to invalidate (nullify) national laws by enacting state laws that conflict with or modify national laws.[23] During the Obama administration, the Republican governor of Texas even publicly mentioned secession.[24]

The pace of lawsuits filed by state attorneys general against the national government has become extraordinary. According to political scientist Paul Nolette, Republican state attorneys general filed five partisan briefs with the Supreme Court during President Clinton's administration. They filed 97 partisan briefs during the first seven years of Obama's presidency.[25] During the first seven months of Trump's presidency, "State attorneys from Massachusetts to New York to California, often working together, . . . brought more than 40 legal actions against the Trump administration . . . an average of one lawsuit or legal motion every five days since Trump's inauguration, not including many more letters, legal threats and formal comments to federal agencies." The chair of the Republican Attorneys General Association was concerned that the lawsuits were less about the law and more about opposing the president. At the same time, Democratic attorneys general claimed their legal actions were based on merit.[26]

For example, on January 1, 2018, the California Values Act went into effect. This state law "restricts state authorities from cooperating with federal immigration agents, and places limits on agents entering schools, churches, hospitals or courthouses to detain undocumented immigrants."[27] Although the law is inconsistent with the national government's efforts to detain and possibly deport undocumented immigrants, other states have also proposed laws to limit the role their local police officers can play in national immigration policy enforcement. In response to such state and local immigrant "sanctuary" initiatives, the Trump

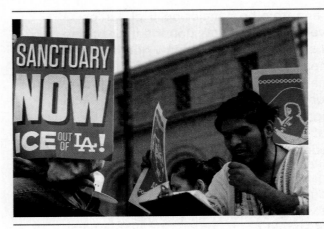

≫ A good example of partisan federalism is the tension some state and local governments, such as the city of Los Angeles and the state of California, have had with the national government over rights of undocumented immigrants and the sovereignty of state governments with regard to law enforcement. Explain how this tension exemplifies partisan federalism during the Trump presidency.

Ronen Tivony/NurPhoto/Getty Images

administration announced in February 2020 that it would send specially trained border control agents to assist Immigration and Customs Enforcement (ICE) officers in sanctuary cities across the country. In the same month, the Department of Justice filed suit against state and local governments in California, New Jersey, and Washington over sanctuary policies.[28]

In 2009, with Democrat Barack Obama in the White House, the U.S. attorney general announced that the federal government would not prosecute individuals for dispensing marijuana or using it in compliance with state laws in states that legalized such activity. Then in 2013, as states began to legalize recreational marijuana use, the Department of Justice issued a policy memo that acknowledged marijuana as an illegal drug according to federal law, yet instructed federal prosecutors to deprioritize marijuana-related prosecutions in states that had enacted laws decriminalizing recreational marijuana use (except in cases that were gang related or where marijuana was sold to children).[29] In 2018, however, with Republican Donald Trump in the White House, the Department of Justice rescinded the Obama administration's policy, hence freeing federal prosecutors to enforce national marijuana laws in states whose policies are inconsistent with (nullify) the national laws.[30]

The dual sovereignty established in the Constitution has evolved into a complex, often confusing, web of relationships among the national, state, and state-created local governments in the United States. A review of the tools used by the national government helps to understand the complex intergovernmental relations of today's federal system of government.

Tools of Intergovernmental Relations

Although the national government shared its revenue surplus with the states in the form of grants-in-aid in 1837, it did not make a habit of offering grants-in-aid until the Great Depression of the 1930s. Today, federal grants-in-aid are 17 percent of the national government's annual spending, and they provide about one-third of total state government revenue.[31] Table 3.4 presents data on the state and local government-administered programs receiving the largest federal grants-in-aid.

Census data is the foundation the federal government uses to determine the distribution of hundreds of billions of grant dollars among state and local governments to help cover costs such as highway construction as well as health care and housing for the elderly, low-income adults and children, and persons

TABLE 3.4 ■ Fiscal Federalism: Largest Federal Intergovernmental Transfers (2019)

Program	Cost (In Billions)
Medicaid	$409
Highways	45
Child Nutrition	23
Tenant Based Rental Assistance (Section 8 Vouchers)	22
Children's Health Insurance Fund	18
Temporary Assistance to Needy Families	16
Accelerating Achievement and Ensuring Equity (Education for the Disadvantaged)	16
Special Education	13
State Children and Families Services Programs	11
Urban Mass Transportation Grants	11
TOTAL OUTLAYS FOR GRANTS TO STATES AND LOCALS	$721

Federal grants-in-aid provide approximately one-third of state and local government revenues. What information about each of these grant programs would you need to determine whether the program fits into the cooperative federalism model or the centralized federalism model?

Source: Office of Management and Budget, *Historical Tables,* "Table 12.3: Total Outlays for Grants to State and Local Governments by Function, Agency and Program."

with disabilities. The dollars for federal grants come from taxpayers in each state, which the federal government then transfers back to state governments. The total amount of money paid in federal taxes by people in a dozen states is much more than the grants-in-aid received by their states, as shown in Table 3.5. This situation is often criticized in the states that pay more than they receive in return.

The pervasiveness of intergovernmental transfers of money has led political scientists to the study of **fiscal federalism**—the intergovernmental relationships that develop from the grants of money the national government provides to state and local governments. Sometimes the relationships are positive. Other times the intergovernmental relationships are tense.

CATEGORICAL GRANTS Historically, the most common type of grant-in-aid has been the **categorical formula grant**—a grant of money from the federal government to state and local governments for a narrow purpose, as defined by the federal government. The legislation that creates such a grant includes a formula determining how much money will be available to each grant recipient. The formula is typically based on factors related to the purpose of the grant, such

fiscal federalism
The relationship between the national government and state and local governments whereby the national government provides grant money to state and local governments.

categorical formula grant
A grant-in-aid for a narrowly defined purpose, whose dollar value is based on a formula.

TABLE 3.5 ▪ States That Pay More in Federal Taxes Than They Get Back

TAXPAYERS IN 12 STATES PAY MORE TO THE FEDERAL GOVERNMENT THAN THEY RECEIVE IN RETURN THROUGH FEDERAL GRANTS.

State	How much more is paid than is received in grants	How much more the average state resident paid than they received
New Jersey	$24.7 billion	$2,748
New York	$24.1 billion	1,216
Illinois	$14.8 billion	1,158
California	$13.7 billion	348
Massachusetts	$10.5 billion	1,532
Minnesota	$6.0 billion	1,078
Connecticut	$4.4 billion	1,242
New Hampshire	$749 million	558
Nebraska	$267 million	139
Utah	$236 million	76
Wyoming	$169 million	291

Source: Hillary Hoffower, "States Pay More in Federal Taxes than They Get Back," *Business Insider*, January 14, 2019, www.businessinsider.com/federal-taxes-federal-services-differences-by-state-2019-1.

mandate
Clauses in legislation, including legislation that establishes grants-in-aid programs, that direct state and local governments to comply with national rules, standards, and other legislative directives.

as the number of people in the state in need of the program's benefits. Categorical grants come with strings attached—that is, rules and regulations with which the recipient government must comply. Strings attached to grants-in-aid are one form of a **mandate**.

matching funds requirement
A grant requirement that obligates the government receiving the grant to spend some of its own money to match a specified percentage of the grant money provided.

One typical string is a **matching funds requirement**, which obligates the government receiving the grant to spend some of its own money to match a specified percentage of the grant money provided. Matching funds requirements allow the national government to influence the budget decisions of state and local governments by forcing them to spend some of their own money on a national priority, which may or may not also be a state priority, in order to receive national funding. Medicaid, a health insurance program the national government created for low-income citizens, is jointly funded by federal and state money due to a matching funds requirement. Put into action primarily by state and local governments, this is one example of a national categorical formula grant program with strings attached.

categorical project grant
A grant-in-aid for a narrowly defined purpose for which governments compete with each other by proposing specific projects.

Since the 1960s, the national government has also offered categorical project grants. Like the categorical formula grant, a **categorical project grant** covers a narrow purpose (program area), but unlike the formula grant, a project grant does not include a formula specifying how much money a recipient will receive. Instead, state and local governments interested in receiving such grants must compete for them by writing proposals detailing what programs they wish to implement and what level of funding they need. A categorical project grant has strings attached to it and typically offers less funding than a categorical formula grant.

BLOCK GRANTS Another type of formula-based intergovernmental transfer of money, the **block grant**, differs from categorical formula and categorical project grants in that the matters for which state and local governments can use the money are not narrowly defined, thus allowing state and local governments more discretion to decide how to spend the money. Whereas a categorical grant might specify that the money is to be used for a child care program, a block grant gives the recipient government more discretion to determine how it will be used within a broad policy area such as assistance to economically needy families with children. In 1996, the national government eliminated Aid to Families with Dependent Children (AFDC), its most well-known income assistance program to low-income families, which was a categorical formula grant program for states. It replaced AFDC with a block grant program for the states, Temporary Assistance to Needy Families (TANF).

block grant
A grant-in-aid for a broadly defined policy area, whose funding amount is typically based on a formula.

When first introduced by the Nixon administration in the 1970s, block grants had fewer strings attached to them than did categorical grants. Today, however, the number and specificity of conditions included in block grants are increasing, which means increased limits on state and local government discretion in policy making and program implementation.

State and local governments have grown dependent on national financial assistance, and so grants are an essential tool of national power to direct state and local government activity. Although the states welcome federal grant money, they do not welcome the federally imposed requirements or mandates.

MANDATES National mandates are statements in national laws, including the strings attached to grants-in-aid, that require state and local governments to do something specified by the national government. Many national mandates relate to ensuring citizens' constitutional rights. For example, the Equal Employment Opportunity Act of 1972 extended the prohibitions against discrimination in employment established in the Civil Rights Act of 1964 to state and local government employment. In this case, the national government enacted the law to fulfill its constitutional responsibilities and imposes it on state and local governments.

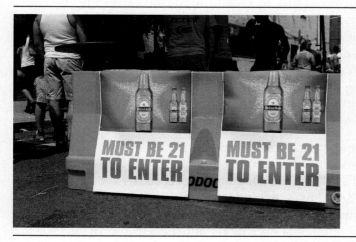

>> In 1987 the Supreme Court found the drinking-age mandate to be constitutional because it was attached to a grant. However, in 2012 the Court found a grant mandate attached to the national Affordable Care Act of 2010 to be unconstitutional. What did the Affordable Care Act mandate require of states? What model of federalism do these two divergent Court decisions support?

B Christopher/Alamy Stock Photo

When the national government assumes the entire cost of a mandate it imposes on a state or local government, it is a *funded mandate*. However, more often than not, the national government does not cover the entire cost of its mandates. Often, it does not cover any of the cost, forcing states to pick up the bill. When the state or local government must cover all or some of the cost, it is an *unfunded mandate*. Because grants-in-aid are voluntary—that is, state and local governments can decide to accept or reject a grant-in-aid—state and local governments can determine whether they can afford to accept the grant and hence its mandate. Although state and local governments have always opposed the strings attached to grants, the attaching of mandates to grant money has come under increasing fire.

In the 1923 case *Massachusetts v. Mellon*,[32] one of the first cases in which state governments questioned the national government's right to attach mandates to grant money, the Supreme Court found the mandates in national grants-in-aid to be constitutional, arguing that grants-in-aid are voluntary cooperative arrangements. By voluntarily accepting the national grant, the justices ruled, the state government agrees to the grant conditions. The Court's decision did not, however, end states' challenges to grant mandates.

In 1987, South Dakota challenged a 1984 national transportation law that penalized states whose legal drinking age was lower than 21 years. The intent of the national law was to decrease driving while intoxicated (DWI) car accidents. States with legal drinking ages lower than 21 years would lose 5 percent of their national grant money for transportation. South Dakota argued that Congress was using grant conditions to put a law into effect that Congress could not achieve through national legislation because the law dealt with a power reserved to the states—determining the legal age for drinking alcoholic beverages.

In its decision in *South Dakota v. Dole*, the Court confirmed that setting a drinking age is indeed a reserved power of the states.[33] However, the Court found that the national government could *encourage* states to set a drinking age of 21 years by threatening to decrease their grants-in-aid for transportation. Ultimately, the national policy goal of a drinking age of 21 was indeed accomplished by 1988—not through a national law but through a condition attached to national highway funds offered to state governments, funds on which the states depend.

In the summer of 2012, the U.S. Supreme Court found unconstitutional a mandate in the Affordable Care Act of 2010 (ACA)—specifically, the one that required states accepting Medicaid grants to extend Medicaid coverage to additional lower-income citizens.[34] The act mandated that if a state did not expand its coverage to additional citizens, it would lose all its Medicaid grant money—not just forfeit the new ACA grant money available to them for coverage expansion. Therefore, although state governments "voluntarily" participate in the Medicaid program by accepting Medicaid categorical grants, this ruling appears to limit the "financial penalty" the national government can impose through a grant's mandate.

As a result of the Court's ruling, states have a choice to expand Medicaid coverage or not; it is not required. Initially, some states—mostly those with Democratic governors—expanded Medicaid coverage, while states with Republican governors were less apt to do so. However, many Republican-controlled states expanded their coverage after they received from the national government **waivers** that exempted them from some additional conditions attached to the ACA.

waivers
Exemptions from particular conditions normally attached to grants.

THEN

NOW

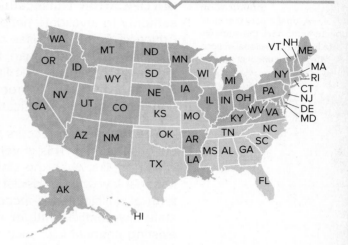

States that expanded
Medicaid eligibility

>> In 2012, the U.S. Supreme Court found the ACA mandate for states to increase the income eligibility level for Medicaid coverage unconstitutional. At that time, seven states and Washington D.C. had already expanded their Medicaid coverage, as shown in the Then image. Since 2012, 29 additional states decided to expand their coverage, bringing to 36 the number of states with expanded Medicaid coverage, as shown in the Now image. This includes both Democratic- and Republican-dominated states.

Presidents have used waivers to appease those who do not support mandates in a specific law in order to gain their support for the law's passage. Waivers can soften partisan opposition to a law with mandates.

PREEMPTION Another means the national government can use to direct the actions of state and local governments is preemption. **Preemption** means that a national policy supersedes a state or local policy because it deals with an enumerated or implied national power. Therefore, people must obey, and states must enforce, the national law even if the state or local government has its own law on the matter.

Preemption is common in environmental policy. Although states have been able to enact and enforce laws with greater protections than are established in national environmental law, they cannot do less than what is called for in the national law. However, the Trump administration challenged this historical pattern of states regulating the air quality more strictly than the federal government does. For example, the 1970 Clean Air Act granted California the right to set stricter environmental rules than the new federal law called for because California had clean air legislation in place before the federal Clean Air Act was enacted. In the fall of 2019, President Trump attempted to revoke California's authority to set auto

preemption
The constitutionally based principle that allows a national law to supersede state or local laws.

135

emissions rules that are stricter than the federal rules. Richard L. Revesz, a professor of environmental law at New York University, noted that no administration has ever revoked a state government's authority to regulate its own air quality.[35]

California and 22 other states, Washington, D.C., and the cities of Los Angeles and New York joined in a suit challenging the Trump administration's revocation of California's right to set stricter emissions rules.[36]

nullification
A legal theory that state governments have the authority to invalidate national actions they deem unconstitutional

NULLIFICATION Nullification is a legal theory that state governments have the authority to invalidate national actions they deem unconstitutional. (The "Thinking Critically" feature focuses on the theory of nullification.) Federalism scholars Adam Olson, Timothy Callaghan, and Andrew Karch investigated more than 2,500 state legislative proposals that fit into three categories of nullification activity from 2010 through 2016.[37] Their three categories of nullification are: true nullification, non-acquiescence nullification, and inconsistent legislation nullification.

True nullification occurs when a state law explicitly declares the national law unconstitutional. This is very rare. More common is *non-acquiescence nullification*, which occurs when the state law claims the state will not cooperate with a national law without declaring the national law unconstitutional. The most common form of nullification is *inconsistent legislation nullification*, which occurs when the state law conflicts with or attempts to alter the rules or procedures enacted in an existing national law, such as state laws that legalize marijuana use.

According to Olson, Callaghan, and Karch, "contemporary American federalism is characterized by unusually high tensions. These [nullification] bills appeared in every state, and their policy goals spanned the ideological spectrum." They also write that the "new partisan alignment at the national level [that began with Trump's inauguration in January 2017] also represents an opportunity to assess whether state-level Republicans' embrace of nullification during the Obama administration was principled or opportunistic."[38] If principled, then proposing nullification follows the tradition in which Republicans support states' rights. If opportunistic, then proposing nullification indicates that Republicans were opposing the policy preferences of a Democratic president and using nullification to that end, not merely to support states' rights—an example of partisan federalism.

The United States's experiment with a federal system of government has lasted more than 225 years. What began as a system of government with dual sovereignty implemented through a model of dual federalism has evolved into a system of government with dual sovereignty implemented through a model of partisan federalism. In addition, although the national government works independently on some policy matters (such as national defense and foreign policy), and state governments work independently on others (such as land use and the regulation of occupations and professions), most domestic matters are addressed through mutual efforts of at least two, if not three, levels of government, through intergovernmental relations.

The dual sovereignty established in the Constitution has evolved into a complex web of relationships among the national, state, and state-created local governments in the United States. Intergovernmental cooperation exists alongside intergovernmental tension. And questions continue about the constitutional distribution of sovereignty between the national and state governments; many of these questions end up before the courts. Reviewing the more than 225 years of experience with dual sovereignty, one can identify both advantages and disadvantages in the federal system of government as it functions today.

Can State Governments Nullify National Laws?

THE ISSUE: Nullification is the theory that states have the authority to invalidate national laws. By 2018, 30 states and the District of Columbia had legalized marijuana in some form. Eight states and the District of Columbia enacted laws legalizing marijuana for recreational use. These states are nullifying national law that criminalizes the growth, sale, possession, and use of marijuana. Do state governments have the constitutional authority to nullify national laws?

YES: The Tenth Amendment allows a state to nullify a national law that exceeds the enumerated powers of the national government. If the national government enacts a law relevant to a matter that is reserved for the states, the states have the right to declare it void. One benefit of the federal system touted by the framers was that two levels of government exist to doubly protect citizens' rights and liberties. When states believe a national law or court ruling infringes on citizens' rights or liberties, states have an obligation to nullify it. In addition, the Constitution is a compact among the states. The states had to ratify it for it to go into effect. That means the states gave power to the national government, and they can reclaim it.

NO: In a federal system, neither the state governments nor the national government can nullify laws enacted by other governments because neither is sovereign over the other. Article VI of the Constitution establishes that the Constitution and national laws made in compliance with it are the supreme law of the land. All governments in the United States must comply with the supreme law of the land.

OTHER APPROACHES: The power of judicial review allows courts to determine whether government actions, including enacted legislation, comply with the Constitution. If states believe that an action of the national government violates the states' constitutional authority, they can file a lawsuit against the national government. The proper interpretation of the enumerated powers, necessary and proper clause, the supremacy clause, and the Tenth Amendment are vital to the health of the union. If the debate over constitutionality of national or state laws gets too heated, the ultimate means of clarification is through a constitutional convention, which states can call for according to Article V of the Constitution.

Is there a proper balance between national and state power in the United States today? The nullification debate is just one example of a question about the proper scope of federal/state power within our federal system of government. As an AP Government student, you will likely be asked to analyze the nature of federalism itself on your AP exam in the form of a source analysis question. In a source analysis question, you will be presented with a passage and will have to apply what you have learned in the course to the passage when answering questions.

WHAT DO YOU THINK?

1. Do you think a constitutional convention to clarify constitutional language will resolve the perpetual conflicts over state and national authority? Explain.

2. Some people are concerned that recent growth in the number of laws among the states that contradict each other as well as national law will spark domestic upheavals. Do you share this concern? Why or why not?

3. Are the conflicting marijuana laws among states and the national government a good case study for partisan federalism?

4. What is your answer to the question of whether states can nullify national laws? Support your position.

Advantages and Disadvantages of Today's Federalism

When political scientists discuss the advantages and disadvantages of the federal system, what one person argues is an advantage may look like a disadvantage to another. For example, a frequently stated advantage of the federal system is the numerous access points for citizens to participate in their governments. Citizens can engage with national, state, county, municipal, and school district governments. They elect representatives to multiple governments that can be responsive to their needs and protect their rights.

For citizens, however, the availability of so many access points might be confusing and time-consuming. Which government is the one with the legal responsibility to solve the problem you want addressed? Which elected official or government has the authority and resources to solve a specific problem? Vague constitutional language does not make these easy questions for either citizens or government officials to answer.

Moreover, each election requires citizens to research candidates running for office. Who has the time? Each year, every state has a primary election day and a general election day. On any given election day, a citizen may be asked to vote for a handful of government officials or dozens. Voters elect more than 500,000 government officials to serve them in the three levels of government. Some political scientists argue that voter turnout would be higher if there were fewer elections.

Another proclaimed advantage of the federal system is that it offers flexibility that makes for more efficient, effective, and responsive government. For example, because of their proximity, local and state governments can respond more quickly, and with a better understanding, to regional problems and needs than can the national government. In addition, what is a problem in one location may not be a problem elsewhere in the nation. Therefore, a national policy may not be appropriate. Moreover, the solution (policy) supported by citizens in one area may not be supported by citizens in a different area. One-size-fits-all national policies are not necessarily effective for all or supported by all.

Yet, some problems and needs cross state borders and affect the entire nation. As a result, we need national policies for some matters, state policies for other matters, and local policies for still others. A federal system provides for policies at all three levels. However, it also allows for problems to fall through the cracks, as each level points to another level as the government that is responsible for addressing the problem. While the finger pointing continues, no government is addressing the problem.

On the flip side, governments may duplicate each other's efforts as they enact policies that address the same concern of their overlapping citizens. Duplication of effort is costly to taxpayers and inefficient. On the other hand, multiple governments enacting different policies to address the same problem allows for experimentation and innovation in the search for the best solution. Governments observing other governments' efforts to solve a problem can then adopt the policy they deem best for their citizens. State and local governments are laboratories for public policies.

One clear disadvantage to the federal system is that it creates inequalities in services and policies; some state or local governments provide their citizens with better public services or more rights than citizens elsewhere. Today, legal rights and privileges (such as the right to legal use of marijuana or to lower in-state college tuition) depend on the state in which you live. Such inequalities may satisfy those who support state laws on given matters, but they dissatisfy those who do not support the laws and want the same rights as citizens in other states. Vague constitutional language also allows states to enact policies that may infringe on national sovereignty, and it allows the national government to enact policies that may infringe on state sovereignty. Conflicts over sovereignty can disrupt domestic tranquility (via protests and demonstrations) and lead to costly lawsuits. They may also fuel distrust and dissatisfaction with all the governments.

Today, we see hostility and tension between state governments and the national government over numerous issues, including immigration reform, the right to bear arms and gun control, the right to abortion, the expansion of Medicaid eligibility, and the proper implementation of the Affordable Care Act. Some observers have begun to discuss a new states' rights movement, as state governments that do not agree with a national policy enact their own laws that may conflict with national laws.[39]

Polarization in Congress, which leads to gridlock, is fueling the states' rights movement. When Congress cannot agree on policies to solve problems, state governments step into the silence and pass their own policies. The result can be conflicting state policies and state policies that infringe on national sovereignty. Ultimately, the courts have to resolve these conflicts.

Conclusion: Thinking Critically About What's Next for Federalism

Today's federalism (partisan federalism) is not the framers' federalism (dual federalism). James Madison and other framers argued that the national government's powers were limited by the Constitution and focused on foreign affairs and defense matters, while states' powers were expansive and covered domestic issues. However, the proper distribution of authority and balance of power between the national and state governments has always been controversial. Until recent decades, the Supreme Court's interpretations tended to favor an expansion of the national government's enumerated and implied powers into a growing number of domestic matters. However, the past few decades have witnessed inconsistency in the Court's interpretations. The Court protects and even expands national powers in some cases while protecting states' powers in other cases.

The national government has created a complex web of intergovernmental relations (IGR) through its application of the Fourteenth Amendment, as well as grants-in-aid, mandates, and preemption. IGR makes it difficult to determine what governments are in charge of making policy, financing policy, and implementing policy; therefore, it can be hard to know which government can solve your particular problem.

Today, we see increasing differences among state policies enacted to address similar needs and concerns of their residents. State governments' differing responses to the coronavirus provide clear examples of this. States are experimenting to find effective policies that their citizens support. Because of years of gridlock in Congress over several policy matters that traditionally were the purview of the national government, we also are witnessing an increase in state and local laws enacted to fill in the national policy silences. Moreover, state governments are enacting laws that often seem to conflict with national laws. IGR and partisan federalism are today's reality in the U.S. federal system of government.

References

1. Powell Leighton, Leah Fleming, and Adam Ragusea, "In Some Georgia Cities, a Requirement to Bear Arms," GPB Radio News, April 16, 2018, www.gpbnews.org/post/some-georgia-cities-requirement-bear-arms.

2. Andrew Blake, "Hawaii Becomes First State to Raise Legal Smoking Age to 21," *The Washington Times,* January 5, 2016.

3. U.S. Bureau of Indian Affairs, "Frequently Asked Questions," https://www.bia.gov/frequently-asked-questions.

4. Dennis L. Dresang and James J. Gosling, *Politics and Policy in American States and Communities,* 4th ed. (New York: Pearson Longman, 2004).

5. *V.L. v. E.L., et al.* 136 S. Ct. 1017 (2016).

6. *McCulloch v. Maryland,* 17 U.S. 316 (1819).

7. *Gibbons v. Ogden,* 22 U.S. 1 (1824).

8. *Helvering v. Davis,* 301 U.S. 619 (1937).

9. *United States v. Lopez,* 514 U.S. 549 (1995).

10. *Pruneyard Shopping Center & Fred Sahadi v. Michael Robins et al.,* 447 U.S. 74, 100 S. Ct. 2035.

11. *San Antonio Independent School District v. Rodriguez,* 411 U.S. 1 (1973).

12. G. Alan Tarr, *Judicial Process and Judicial Policymaking,* 6th ed. (Boston, MA: Cengage Learning, 2014), 309.

13. *New State Ice Co. v. Liebmann,* 285 U.S. 262, (1932).

14. Sarah Zimmerman, "For Oregon students, 'Sick Days' Expanding," *Scranton Times-Tribune,* July 23, 2019.

15. James Madison, "Federalist No. 45," *The Federalist Papers* (Cutchogue, NY: Buccaneer Books, 1992), 236.

16. Gary Gerstle, *Liberty and Coercion: The Paradox of American Government From the Founding to the Present* (Princeton, NJ: Princeton University Press, 2015).

17. Jessica Bulman-Pozen, "Partisan Federalism," *Harvard Law Review* 124, no. 4 (2014): 1077–1146.

18. As quoted in Greg Goelzhauser and S. Rose, "The State of American Federalism 2016–2017: Policy Reversals and Partisan Perspectives on Intergovernmental Relations," *Publius: The Journal of Federalism* 47, no. 3 (2017): 285–313.

19. Robert Jay Dilger, *Federal Grants to State and Local Governments: A Historical Perspective on Contemporary Issues* (Washington, DC: Congressional Research Service, 2017), 39.

20. Greg Goelzhauser and S. Rose, "The State of American Federalism 2016–2017: Policy Reversals and Partisan Perspectives on Intergovernmental Relations," *Publius: The Journal of Federalism* 47, no. 3 (2017): 285–313; Adam Olson, T. Callaghan, and A. Karch, "Return of the 'Rightful Remedy': Partisan Federalism, Resource Availability, and Nullification Legislation in the American States," *Publius: The Journal of Federalism 48, no. 3 (2018), 1–28.*

21. Goelzhauser and Rose, "The State of American Federalism 2016–2017."

22. Daniel C. Vock, "At Odds," *Governing* (June 2016): 24–31.

23. Olson, Callaghan, and Karch, "Return of the 'Rightful Remedy.'"

24. Vock, "At Odds."

25. Alan Greenblatt, "The Pruitt Backlash," *Governing* (February 2017): 9.

26. Steve Peoples, "Dem Attorneys General Escalate Fight vs. Trump," *Times-Tribune*, August 14, 2017, p. B9.

27. Tim Arango, "In Clash between California and Trump, It's One America versus Another," *New York Times,* January 7, 2018.

28. Caitlin Dickerson and Zolan Kanno-Youngs, "Border Patrol Will Deploy Elite Tactical Agents to Sanctuary Cities," *New York Times,* February 14, 2020.

29. "Justice Department Announces Update to Marijuana Enforcement Policy," August 29, 2013, www.justice.gov/opa/pr/2013/August/13-opa-974.html.

30. Charlie Savage and Jack Healy, "Trump Administration to Move to Weaken Marijuana Legalization Movement," *New York Times,* January 4, 2018, https://nyti.ms/2E6rxbE.

31. Dilger, *Federal Grants to State and Local Governments.*

32. *Massachusetts v. Mellon,* 262 U.S. 447 (1923).

33. *South Dakota v. Dole,* 483 U.S. 208 (1987).

34. *National Federation of Independent Business v. Sebelius,* 567 U.S. _____, 132 S. Ct. 2566 (2012).

35. Coral Davenport, "Trump to Revoke California's Authority to Set Stricter Auto Emissions Rules," *New York Times*, September 17, 2019.

36. Tony Barboza and Anna M. Phillips, "California sues Trump again for revoking state's authority to limit auto emission," *LA Times,* November 15, 2019.

37. Olson, Callaghan, and Karch, "Return of the 'Rightful Remedy.'"

38. Olson, Callaghan, and Karch, "Return of the 'Rightful Remedy.'"

39. Dylan Scott, "The United States of America: In the Absence of Strong Federal Policies, States Have Become More Active—and More Divergent—Than They've Been in Decades," *Governing* (June 2013): 42–47; Peter Harkness, "Shall We Overcome? After 50 Years, a New No-Holds Barred States' Rights Movement Has Emerged," *Governing* (November 2013): 18–19.

■ Key Terms

Multiple Choice Questions

Questions 1 and 2 are based on the map below.

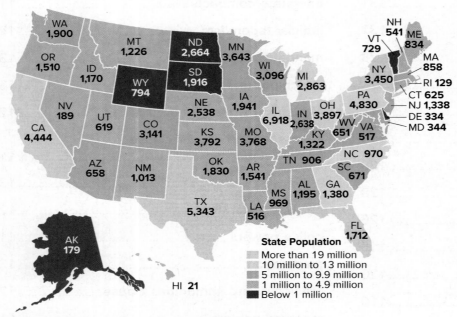

Number of Local Governments in Each State

1. Which of the following accurately describes the information based on the map above?

   A. States with Democratic governors tend to have more governments

   B. New England states have the most governments per capita because they are the oldest

   C. Federalism allows the states to retain sovereignty and create numerous local governments

   D. Unitary systems such as Britain also have multiple governments

2. Which of the following is a practical consequence of a federal system based on the information in the map above?

   A. Confusion among citizens and government officials regarding government powers and responsibilities

   B. Increased efficiency in the delivering of good and services by the government to its citizens

   C. Increased accountability among government institutions

   D. The abuse of interstate compacts

3. Which of the following is an example of concurrent powers?

   A. regulating interstate commerce

   B. raising revenue

   C. minting coins

   D. raising an army

4. The ruling in *McCulloch v. Maryland* is based on which constitutional clause?
   A. Commerce clause
   B. Due process clause
   C. Equal protection clause
   D. Necessary and proper clause

5. Which of the following is an accurate comparison of dual and cooperative federalism?

Dual Federalism	Cooperative Federalism
A. The dominant pattern of national-state relations from 1945–1970	The dominant pattern of national-state relations from 1789–1920
B. Results in decreased efficiency	Results in increased efficiency
C. States should follow the direction of the federal government	States should maintain sovereignty
D. Caused by the belief that the national government takes care of its enumerated powers and the states independently take care of their reserved powers	Caused by the complexity of the Great Depression and New Deal which demanded closer cooperation between federal and state governments

6. Which of the following actions by the federal government is an example of an unfunded mandate?
   A. Requiring states to raise their income tax rate
   B. Requiring states and municipalities to make all public buildings accessible to people with disabilities
   C. Requiring states to balance their budget each year
   D. Requiring states and municipalities to privatize public universities

7. Which of the following accurately aligns the powers of the state government to the powers of the national government?

National powers	State powers
A. Negotiate treaties	Ratify treaties
B. Raise an army	Grant marriage licenses
C. Ratify amendments to the U.S. Constitution	Regulate intrastate commerce
D. Develop a postal service	Provide for copyrights

■ Free Response Questions

SCOTUS Comparison

In *U.S. Term Limits v. Thornton (1995),* the state of Arkansas had adopted a state amendment imposing term limits for federally elected officials from the state of Arkansas. Specifically, anyone elected to the U.S. House of Representatives from

Arkansas would be ineligible to serve more than 3 terms and anyone elected to the U.S. Senate would be ineligible to serve more than 2 terms. In their ruling, the Supreme Court stated that the Constitution prohibits states from adopting congressional qualifications in addition to those enumerated in the Constitution.

A. Identify the constitutional clause that is common to both *U.S. Term Limits v. Thornton (1995)* and *McCulloch v. Maryland (1819)*.

B. Based on the constitutional clause identified in part A, explain why the facts of *U.S. Term Limits v. Thornton* led to a different holding in *McCulloch v. Maryland*.

C. Explain an action citizens who disagree with the ruling in *U.S. Term Limits v. Thornton* could take to limit its impact.

Concept Application

In 1990, Congress passed the Americans with Disabilities Act (ADA), which prohibited discrimination based on disability. The Act required states and local employers to provide funding to make changes to existing buildings and facilities, making sure that these buildings and facilities would be accessible to people with disabilities. Employers were also required to accommodate any employees with disabilities.

After reading the scenario, respond to A, B, and C below:

A. Describe an action the federal government could take to offset the costs of the ADA on the states.

B. In the context of the scenario, explain how the use of the federal government's power described in part A can be affected by its interaction with the states.

C. In the context of the scenario, explain how the interaction between the federal government and the states can be affected by federalism.

Argumentation

Develop an argument that explains whether dual or cooperative federalism is most similar to the framers' original intention for the relationship between the federal government and the states.

In your essay, you must:

- Articulate a defensible claim or thesis that responds to the prompt and establishes a line of reasoning.

- Support your claim with at least TWO pieces of accurate and relevant information:

  - At least ONE piece of evidence must be from one of the following foundational documents:

    — The Constitution of the United States (including the Bill of Rights and subsequent Amendments)

    — Brutus 1

    — Federalist No. 10

- Use a second piece of evidence from another foundational document from the list or from your study of the electoral process

- Use reasoning to explain why your evidence supports your claim/thesis

- Respond to an opposing or alternative perspective using refutation, concession, or rebuttal

At the beginning of this unit, we introduced you to these two AP Big Ideas:

- *A balance between government power and individual rights has been a hallmark of American political development,* and

- *The U.S. Constitution establishes a system of checks and balances among branches of government and allocates power between federal and state governments. This system is based on the rule of law and balance between majority rule and minority rights.*

We also asked these questions:

- **What form of democracy best represents American democracy today (participatory, pluralist or elite)?**

- **How has the balance of power between the national and state governments shifted over time? What events have caused the shift? What examples do you find of state resurgence of power?**

In the context of the reading, how can we answer these questions? In Chapter 1 we learned that in colonial New England, a direct democracy formed. New England was ruled through majority rule in town meetings, which still take place today; however, as the demographics of the United States continue to become more diverse, the diversity of our elected officials has not always reflected changes in our population. In the Interest Group chapter later in this text, you will find evidence to support the pluralist and elitist models of democracy. Is this what you want? If not, what role might you play to facilitate change?

The proper balance of power between national government and state governments was debated vigorously when the Constitution was being written. The Articles of Confederation provided a weak central government unable to solve problems. When Shays's Rebellion broke out in Massachusetts and began to spread to surrounding states, the central government under the Articles was unable to stop it, leading to calls to strengthen the central government, which in turn, eventually led to meetings in which the Constitution was written and proposed to a skeptical public. The Constitution provided for a much stronger central government, including a supremacy clause and an elastic clause, allowing Congress to make all laws "necessary and proper." The elastic clause was of concern to Anti-Federalists such as Brutus who argued that the new constitution would, in effect, make state power meaningless.

As we learned in Chapter 3, after the ratification of the U.S. Constitution, national power continued to expand, as demonstrated by the ruling in *McCulloch v. Maryland* which resulted in a holding that allowed the national government to create a bank and forbid states from taxing the national government. About a hundred years later, the Supreme Court ruling of *U.S. v. Lopez* shifted the balance of power back towards state power. The *Lopez* case resulted in the Supreme Court striking down a federal law on the grounds that the central government had exceeded its authority under the commerce and necessary and proper clauses.

▌Multiple Choice Questions

1. Which of the following accurately describes an irony of political efficacy in the United States?

    A. People believe they can make a difference in government, yet don't participate in the political process

    B. People are cynical about government, yet they participate in large political demonstrations

    C. In polls, citizens report they don't approve of Congress as a whole, but they support their individual Congressperson

    D. In polls, citizens report distrusting the federal government overall, but they report high levels of trust in state government

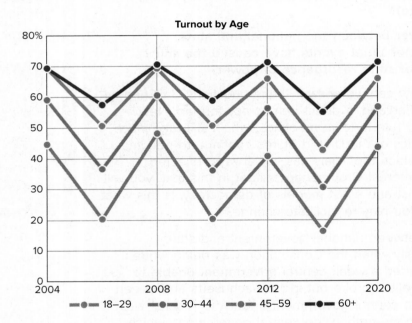

2. Which of the following is supported by the information in the chart above?

    A. Voter turnout in presidential elections fluctuates.

    B. Voter turnout is higher in mid-term elections than in presidential elections.

    C. People over 60 vote at higher rates than other ages.

    D. Voter turnout among 18–29-year-olds is increasing.

3. Scenario: a presidential candidate is accused by a political opponent of not being born in the United States and thus being ineligible to be elected. The accusations call into question which of the following about the candidate?

    A. Demographics

    B. Efficacy

    C. Legitimacy

    D. Social Contract

4. Which of the following is a correct comparison between national and state powers?

	Power of the National Government	Power of the State Governments
A.	Regulate interstate commerce	Naturalize citizens
B.	Administer family laws	Regulate land use
C.	Declare war	Conduct elections
D.	Negotiate treaties	Admit new states to union

TABLE 1.1 ▦ **The Traditional Ideological Spectrum**

	Socialism	Liberalism	Middle of Road (Moderate)	Conservatism	Libertarianism
Goal of Government	Equality	Equality of opportunity; protection of fundamental liberties	Nondiscrimination in opportunity; protection of some economic freedoms; security; stability	Traditional values; order; stability; economic freedom	Absolute economic and social freedom
Role of Government	Strong government control of economy	Government action to promote opportunity	Government action to balance the wants of workers and businesses; government fosters stability	Government action to protect and bolster the capitalist system; few limitations on fundamental rights	No governmental regulations of economy; no limitations on fundamental rights

5. Based on the table above, which of the following ideologies favors the smallest government?
   A. Liberalism
   B. Moderate
   C. Conservatism
   D. Libertarianism

6. Which of the following is an accurate comparison of goals of liberalism and conservatism?

	Liberalism	Conservatism
A.	Strict separation of church and state	Preserving rights of those traditionally disenfranchised
B.	Preserving limited government	Preserving the rule of law
C.	Economic equality	Preserving tradition
D.	Emphasis on free market	Government as an agent to help the poor

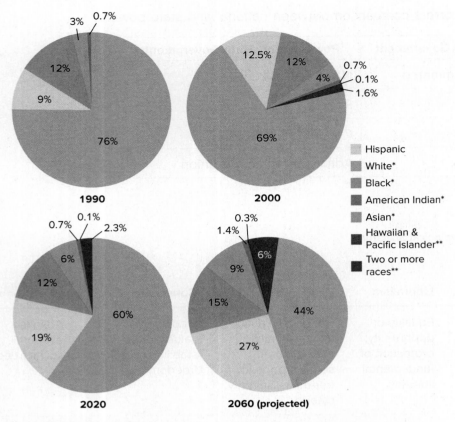

*Non-Hispanic only; in 1990 "Asians" included Hawaiians and Pacific Islanders.
**Option available for the first time in 2000 census.

7. Which of the following can be concluded from the graph above?
  A. The United States is a multicultural nation
  B. The percentage of whites in the U.S. population has been decreasing each decade
  C. The percentage of Hispanics in the U.S. population has fluctuated each decade
  D. The U.S. population is increasing each decade

...It appears from these articles that there is no need of any intervention of the state governments, between the Congress and the people, to execute any one power vested in the general government, and that the constitution and laws of every state are nullified and declared void, so far as they are or shall be inconsistent with this constitution, or the laws made in pursuance of it, or with treaties made under the authority of the United States . . .

Brutus 1

---

8. Which of the following clauses of the Constitution was Brutus most concerned about?
  A. The privileges and immunities clause
  B. The habeas corpus clause
  C. The necessary and proper clause
  D. The commerce clause

Amending the Constitution

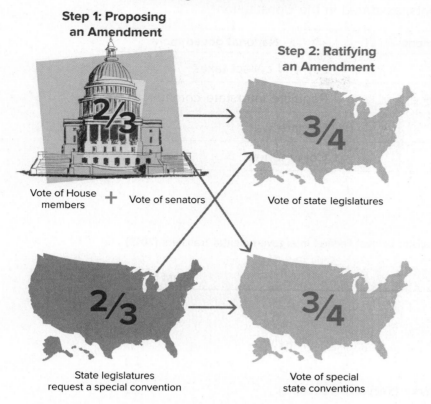

Step 1: Proposing an Amendment

Step 2: Ratifying an Amendment

2/3 — Vote of House members + Vote of senators

3/4 — Vote of state legislatures

2/3 — State legislatures request a special convention

3/4 — Vote of special state conventions

9. Which of the following can be concluded from the infographic above which describes the steps involved in amending the Constitution?

A. The most common method of amending the Constitution is by ⅔ of Congress followed by a ¾ vote of state legislatures

B. Two supermajority votes are required to successfully amend the Constitution, and there are four paths to amending the Constitution

C. The Constitution is rarely ratified

D. For the Constitution to be ratified, the president must initiate an amendment proposal

10. Which of the following is a main idea of *Federalist* No. 10?

A. A powerful president will provide stability under the Constitution

B. The Constitution will effectively control the effects of factions

C. State sovereignty will be protected and preserved under the Constitution

D. The role of the courts will provide a strong rule of law

11. The Declaration of Independence draws inspiration from which of the following thinkers?

A. Hamilton

B. Madison

C. Locke

D. Hobbes

12. Which of the following is an accurate comparison of division of power between the state and national governments, as stated in the Constitution?

	State government	National government
A.	Negotiate treaties	Lay and collect taxes
B.	Develop a postal service	Regulate interstate commerce
C.	Schedule elections	Declare war
D.	Establish courts	Coin money

TABLE 3.4 ▪ Fiscal Federalism: Largest Federal Intergovernmental Transfers (2019)

Program	Cost (In Billions)
Medicaid	$409
Highways	45
Child Nutrition	23
Tenant Based Rental Assistance (Section 8 Vouchers)	22
Children's Health Insurance Fund	18
Temporary Assistance to Needy Families	16
Accelerating Achievement and Ensuring Equity (Education for the Disadvantaged)	16
Special Education	13
State Children and Families Services Programs	11
Urban Mass Transportation Grants	11
TOTAL OUTLAYS FOR GRANTS TO STATES AND LOCALS	$721

Federal grants-in-aid provide approximately one-third of state and local government revenues. What information about each of these grant programs would you need to determine whether the program fits into the cooperative federalism model or the centralized federalism model?

Source: Office of Management and Budget, *Historical Tables*, "Table 12.3: Total Outlays for Grants to State and Local Governments by Function, Agency and Program."

13. Which of the following can be concluded from the data above?
  A. The amount of federal intergovernmental transfers is increasing
  B. Medicaid is over half of the total outlays for federal grants to states
  C. Urban Mass Transportation Grants was the highest category in 2019
  D. The amount the federal government spends on highways has been decreasing

> We hold these truths to be self-evident, that all men are created equal, that they are endowed by their Creator with certain unalienable Rights, that among these are Life, Liberty and the pursuit of Happiness.

14. The excerpt above is from which of the following foundational documents in the AP US Government & Politics course?

A. Declaration of Independence

B. Articles of Confederation

C. *Federalist* No. 10

D. Brutus 1

15. The excerpt above derives its main idea from which of the following thinkers?

A. Locke

B. Hobbes

C. Montesquieu

D. Voltaire

16. A voter agrees with liberal political ideology on issues related to the role of government on moral issues, but agrees with the conservative ideology on issues related to the role of government on economic issues. This voter aligns most closely with which of the following?

A. progressive

B. populist

C. laissez-faire

D. libertarian

17. The majority opinion in *U.S. v. Lopez* (1995) rejected the national government's Gun-Free School Zones Act of 1990 because the national government exceeded its authority under which of the following clauses to the U.S. Constitution?

A. The due process of law clause

B. The equal protection clause

C. The commerce clause

D. The eminent domain clause

18. The effect of the ruling in *U.S. v. Lopez* was which of the following?

A. A shift in power to the states away from the national government

B. An increase in presidential power

C. An increase in power of the National Rifle Association

D. A decrease in ability of state and local governments to regulate school safety

19. Both *McCulloch v. Maryland* and *U.S. v. Lopez* were about which of the following?

A. Judicial review

B. Amendment

C. Separation of powers

D. Federalism

20. Which of the following is a reason why the framers separated powers among the three branches of government?

A. To allow greater citizen participation in the political process

B. To allow a voice to state governments in national policy

C. To prevent one branch of government from having excessive authority

D. To allow greater rule of law

CONSTITUTION AVE
NW

700

INTERACTIONS AMONG BRANCHES OF GOVERNMENT

The content of Unit 2, "Interactions Among Branches of Government," is at the heart of the national policy-making process. You will read about each of these institutions: Congress (Chapter 4), the Presidency (Chapter 5), the Judiciary (Chapter 6), and the Bureaucracy (Chapter 7). It is practically impossible to study each of these institutions in isolation. Rather, you will learn about how each interacts with the others and will consider the role of citizen participation in how each of these operates. The study of the branches of government is not limited to interaction among the branches themselves, but also includes how the federal government interacts with state governments and how the federal government responds to citizen interests.

You will read about how the powers of Congress, the presidency, and the judiciary are described in Articles I, II, and III of the Constitution, respectively. The bureaucracy is the term to describe our large, complex, executive branch of government today, and the executive branch (bureaucracy) is outlined in Article II. The Constitution was designed to limit the power of each branch of government through a system of checks and balances. For example, one of the powers granted to Congress is the power of impeachment. This power gives the House the right to impeach, or accuse the president of crimes, and the Senate the power to conduct a trial. However, in order to successfully impeach a president, the House must have citizen support, since members of the House are subject to reelection.

Checks and balances limit the power of each branch of government and create a policy-making process that is cautious, deliberate, and responds to many interests. You will learn about the formal checks and balances system outlined in the U.S. Constitution as well as how the powers have evolved beyond what is stated in the Constitution. For example, while the Constitution describes the process of filling a Supreme Court vacancy via presidential appointment and Senate confirmation, the role of politics has changed how the Senate evaluates nominees.

Presidential power has grown considerably since the Constitution was written. Today, we judge our presidents through their success in implementing a successful legislative agenda. The Supreme Court, the highest court in our judicial branch of government, has also achieved a degree of power in the policy-making process through judicial review, a power not stated in the Constitution.

You will also learn about the role of citizen interaction with each of the branches. Members of Congress and the president are subject to reelection and therefore should be responsive to citizen inquiry. Theoretically, a citizen can contact the president of the United States, but due to our population size, it is difficult for an average citizen to get the president's ear. While citizens can directly contact their members of Congress with a public policy concern, the other branches of government are more elusive. While federal bureaucrats have influence over policy through administrative discretion, they are unelected officials. The way for a citizen to have influence over the bureaucracy is through Congress and Congress's power to oversee the bureaucracy. The judiciary is a passive branch of government, meaning citizens must bring legitimate cases to the court for it to act.

In addition to the interaction between Congress, the presidency, the courts, and the bureaucracy, consider how the branches of government respond to citizens, interest groups, and state governments.

Political scientists use quantitative and qualitative methods to study political behaviors and our institutions of government. Quantitative analysis involves gathering data and drawing conclusions from that data, while qualitative analysis involves narrative observations and descriptions. In the branches of government chapters, you will find quantitative data with questions for you to consider. For example, in Chapter 4, you will find a figure that shows the party breakdown in the House and Senate in various election years, and you will be asked to identify trends. In Chapter 5, you will find a table that shows both the number of vetoes and percentage of presidential vetoes overridden by Congress in each presidency. Such data allow political scientists to analyze trends in American politics which are useful for explaining political change or the lack of political change.

How will our policy-making institutions continue to evolve?

Big Ideas

Throughout this unit, you will find examples to support these AP Big Ideas:

- **The U.S. Constitution establishes a system of checks and balances among branches of government and allocates power between federal and state governments. This system is based on the rule of law and the balance between majority rule and minority rights.**

- **Governmental laws and policies balancing order and liberty are based on the U.S. Constitution and have been interpreted differently over time.**

- **Popular sovereignty, individualism, and republicanism are important considerations of U.S. laws and policymaking and assume citizens will engage and participate.**

- **Multiple actors and institutions interact to produce and implement public policies.**

- **Using various types of analyses, political scientists measure how U.S. political behavior, attitudes, ideologies, and institutions are shaped by several factors over time.**

While the paragraphs above have illustrated some ways in which the five Big Ideas interact with the content in this unit, as students of government, we consider what the trend will be in the policy-making process in the coming decades. How have the institutions outlined in the Constitution evolved over time, and where does the balance of power lie today between Congress, the president, the judiciary, and the bureaucracy? The answer to this question requires historical analysis and an understanding of how the Constitution has been interpreted over time.

Skills and Practices

As you read through these four chapters, consider how the skills of description, analysis, comparison, and causation help you to make sense of the information. By the end of this unit, you should be able to answer questions such as:

- **What has historically caused the power of the presidency to increase?**

- **Will executive power continue to increase, as it has in recent decades?**

- **What factors have shaped the conflict between the president and the Senate over the appointment of new federal judges?**

- **What might be the policy-making impact of those new appointments?**

- **Will the Supreme Court's power of judicial review continue to have strong influence over public policies?**

Chapter 4 | Congress

Chip Somodevilla/Getty Images

THEN

The framers granted to Congress both explicit powers and implied powers, by which the national government strengthened and broadened its authority.

NOW

A much more demographically diverse but ideologically polarized Congress exercises wide powers, its decision making influenced by shifting constituencies in a changing nation.

NEXT

Will increased polarization of Republicans and Democrats in Congress continue to define the congressional agenda?

Will the competition between the president and Congress continue to define Congress as the weaker of the two branches?

Will the composition and policymaking of Congress more broadly reflect the changing face of the United States?

■ Chapter Introduction

In the AP US Government and Politics course, the Congress unit centers on this Enduring Understanding: *The republican ideal in the U.S. is manifested in the structure and operation of the legislative branch.* The Congress chapter in this text addresses both the structure and the operation of Congress. However, the operation of the Congress (the legislative branch) does not always function according to the republican ideals that reject a ruling class. For example, earlier in U.S. History Supreme Court nominations often passed easily in the Senate; now the nomination process has become increasingly politicized.

Historically, when Supreme Court appointments were considered and debated in the Senate, the nominee's judicial and legal qualifications were most important considerations for senators. Legally qualified judicial nominees were typically confirmed even when the president was from a different political party than the Senate majority. More recently, a judge's ideology has taken on increased importance in the confirmation battle. The political parties no longer defer to the other side, and are contentious when there is divided government, and when there is not, the nominations pass easily.

At the end of President Trump's first term, the Senate was controlled by the Republican Party and President Trump was also a Republican. Approximately six weeks before the election for Trump's possible second term, Supreme Court Justice Ginsburg passed away. Justice Ginsburg was a champion to the political left, having been nominated by President Clinton and arguing for gender equality in her opinions during her tenure on the Court. Under Trump, because the same party controlled the presidency and the Senate, the confirmation of Trump's nominee proceeded smoothly. In fact, most Republicans announced they would support President Trump's nominee before Trump had named the person he intended to appoint. In contrast, at the end of Obama's second term, when a Supreme Court vacancy had occurred, Obama (a Democrat) had a Republican-controlled Senate. Senate leadership under Obama refused to hold hearings or a vote on Obama's Supreme Court nominee, arguing it was too close to the election.

The recent history of Supreme Court justice battles left many in the public wondering: why do a different set of rules apply when a president faces the opposite party in control of the Senate? Why has the Court, an institution designed to be free from politics, become so politicized? These controversial questions seem to be in direct conflict with the Enduring Understanding we explored earlier: *The republican ideal in the U.S. is manifested in the structure and operation of the legislative branch.* In this context, "republican ideal" refers to American values including democracy, rule of law, and rejection of a ruling class. For decades, Supreme Court justices who were well qualified were confirmed, regardless of whether there was divided party control of the presidency and Senate. In recent years, each political party seems to view nominees through the lens of party, vote accordingly, and is willing to thwart efforts of the opposite party to fill Court vacancies.

As you read this chapter, consider the EU language which states that "structure and operation of the legislative branch" supports the ideal of republicanism. You will read about how bicameral structure of Congress both provides differing forms of representation for the people and mechanisms that ensure a cautious and deliberate lawmaking process. Regularly scheduled elections ensure a level of stability in American politics, and the ability of American citizens to vote separately for members of Congress and the president means that as people split their ticket, there are frequent divided government election patterns, in which one party controls the White House and the opposite party controls one or both houses of Congress. Historically, divided governments have led elected officials to compromise in order to pass legislation.

The lawmaking process is also a structure that supports republicanism. As you read about the lawmaking process, however, keep in mind that it is rare for a bill to follow each step exactly as it is demonstrated in the flowchart. Often, politics gets in the way as lawmakers face unexpected obstacles, including pressure from special interest groups, **logrolling** attempts by colleagues, pressure from constituencies, and inter- or intra-party pressure that can cause the steps outlined in the text to be derailed. As you read subsequent chapters, you will continue to build an understanding of the complexity of the policy-making process, and throughout the text, you will return to Big Idea 4 in AP US Government: *Multiple actors and institutions interact to produce and implement possible policies.*

■ The Origins of Congress

For the United States' founders, creating the Congress was a crucially important task. Fearful of a powerful executive, but having endured the problems stemming from the weak confederal government under the Articles of Confederation, the framers of the Constitution believed that the legislature should be the key branch of the newly formed government. In their vision, the Congress would be the institution responsible for making laws that would create effective public policy. In structuring the Congress, the framers strove to create a legislative branch that was at once powerful enough to govern and to check the power of the president and yet not so powerful that the legislature itself would exercise tyrannical rule.

As they debated the shape of the Congress, the Constitution's framers had to balance the desires of representation of two opposing groups. The Constitution created a bicameral, or two-house, legislature in which one chamber, the House of Representatives, would be based on population, and the other chamber, the Senate, would be based on state representation.[1] The constitutionally specified duties of each house of Congress reflect the framers' views of the essential nature of the two chambers and the people who would serve in them.

The House of Representatives, with the smallest constituencies of any federal office (currently about 711,000 people reside in each congressional district), is the chamber closer to the people. As such, the framers intended the House to closely represent the people's views. The Constitution thus requires, for example, that all revenue bills (bills that would impose taxes) must originate in the House of Representatives. In the framers' eyes, unwarranted taxation was an egregious offense. By placing the power to tax in the hands of the members of the House of Representatives—the officials who face more frequent federal elections—the framers sought to avoid the types of unpopular, unfair taxes that had sparked the American Revolution. A short electoral cycle, they reasoned, would allow disfavored politicians to be voted out of office. Like all other bills, revenue bills must be passed in identical form by both the House and the Senate to become law, but requiring revenue bills to originate in the House reflected a victory by the large states at the Constitutional Convention. (Smaller states wanted taxation power to reside with the Senate.)

The framers viewed the House of Representatives as the "people's chamber," and they conceived the Senate to be a more elite, more deliberative institution, one not subject to the whims of mass politics like its lower-house counterpart. Today, because of its smaller size and because its members face elections less frequently than do House members, the Senate remains a more deliberative body than the House. In addition, because of the specific constitutional duties mandated to the upper house, particularly the requirement that treaties must be ratified in the Senate, many U.S. senators have specialized in foreign policy issues. (See "The House and the Senate Compared" later in this chapter for further discussion of differences between the two chambers.)

The framers' vision was to structure the Congress to embody republican principles, ensuring that in its central policy-making responsibilities the national legislature would be responsive to the needs and the will of the people. Both historically and continuing in the present day, civically engaged citizens have exerted a strong influence on the outcome of the policy-making process.

▪ Powers of Congress

The primary source of congressional authority is the U.S. Constitution. As shown in Table 4.1, the Constitution enumerates to Congress a number of powers. The nature of these responsibilities reveals that the Constitution is both very specific in describing congressional powers (as in punishing illegal acts on the high seas), yet at the same time quite vague (as in its language establishing the federal court system). Many of the specific duties of Congress reflect Americans' bitter experience in the colonial era, in that the framers granted powers to Congress that they did not want to place in the hands of a strong executive. For example, the economic powers granted to Congress, including the ability to tax and spend, to establish tariffs, and to borrow money, all limit the power of the president.

Among the most important powers granted to Congress is the power of impeachment (see more in Chapter 5), the power of Congress to accuse the president (or the vice president or federal judges) of crimes, and to conduct a trial. In recent years, many of President Trump's detractors criticized Congress for failing to pursue articles of impeachment against him following former FBI Director Robert Mueller's investigation of Russian interference in the 2016 presidential election. Congress was the subject of further criticism and scorn in 2019 when the House of Representatives voted to impeach President Trump following the revelation that he had leveraged foreign aid to Ukraine and asked the Ukrainian president to investigate his political rival, former vice president Joe Biden. While the Democratically controlled House voted to impeach, the Senate, controlled by Republicans, did not convict Trump, which could have resulted in him being censured or removed from office.

TABLE 4.1 ■ Enumerated Powers of the Congress

Judicial Powers
Establish the federal court system
Punish counterfeiters
Punish illegal acts on the high seas
Impeach the president, vice president, and federal judges

Economic Powers
Impose taxes
Establish import tariffs
Borrow money
Regulate interstate commerce
Coin and print money; determine the value of currency

National Security Powers
Declare war
Raise and regulate national armed forces
Call up and regulate state national guard
Suppress insurrections
Repel invasions

Regulatory Powers
Establish standards of weights and measures
Regulate copyrights and patents

Administrative Powers
Establish procedures for naturalizing citizens
Establish post offices
Govern the District of Columbia

Impeachment is one of the most significant congressional powers because it gives Congress the means to actually change the composition of the other two branches of government by removing someone from office. Other powers specifically granted to Congress may be more mundane, but they still have a distinct impact on our everyday lives. For example, Congress regulates currency, establishes weights and measures, and administers post offices. As we have seen, the connection between Congress, particularly the House, and the people was crucial to the framers, and so the Constitution requires that all taxation and spending measures originate in the House. This was because the framers believed the House would be nearer to the people, and that its members' actions would therefore express the people's will.

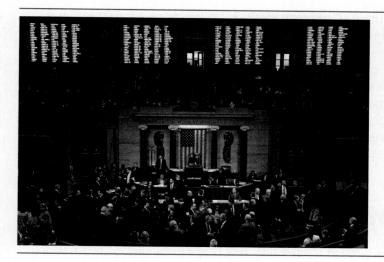

>> In 2019, the U.S. House of Representatives voted to pass two articles of impeachment against President Donald Trump on charges of abuse of power and obstruction of Congress.

Chip Somodevilla/Getty Images

The Constitution moreover imbues the Congress with an additional source of power, one that has proved important in the expansion of legislative authority over time. As discussed in Chapter 2, the necessary and proper—or elastic—clause states that the Congress shall have the power to "make all Laws which shall be necessary and proper for carrying into Execution the foregoing powers, and all other Powers vested by this Constitution in the Government of the United States, or in a Department or Officer thereof." This clause has been responsible for Congress's ability to legislate in many matters not described in the enumerated powers. Reforming our nation's health care system, determining the powers of law enforcement in investigating terrorism, and overhauling our system of immigration are all examples of powers not enumerated in the Constitution but that Congress exercises because of the broad scope of authority provided by the necessary and proper clause.

In recent years, particularly during the Trump administration, Congress has faced significant criticism from scholars and voters who contend that Congress is shirking a fundamental duty to exercise oversight of the president. The perception, for example, that the Republican-controlled Senate would acquit President Trump no matter what the allegations were against him contributed to the sentiment that Congress was prioritizing loyalty to the president and their party over their own constitutional responsibilities.

Another area in which Congress has faced criticism concerns its oversight of the president in military operations. Constitutionally, only Congress has the power to declare war, but in the immediate aftermath of the terrorist attacks on September 11, 2001, Congress passed the Authorization for Use of Military Force (AUMF), which allowed the president to "use all necessary and appropriate force against those nations, organizations, or persons he determines planned, authorized, committed, or aided the terrorist attacks that occurred on September 11, 2001, or harbored such organizations or persons, in order to prevent any future acts of international terrorism against the United States by such nations, organizations, or persons." Since its passage, presidents have used the AUMF as a mechanism to wage attacks without congressional authorization against those not involved in 9/11. For example, presidents have targeted missile and drone strikes against Yemeni forces and Syrian government fighter aircraft, using AUMF as their legal justification. This broad use has prompted many lawmakers to demand that the AUMF be reevaluated so that it more clearly specifies situations when the president can use military force without congressional authorization.

In addition to the Constitution, Congress derives power from Supreme Court decisions, the media, and the people. Supreme Court decisions often uphold the constitutionality of a law, in a sense verifying Congress's ability to create policy on a given subject. The media grant Congress power by providing members with a forum in which to communicate with constituents, sway public opinion, and create a favorable climate for the passage of legislation. The people are a key source of congressional power through civic participation in the electoral and legislative processes. Citizens communicate their views and priorities to their representatives, who then can claim public support in their endeavors to enact policy.

▮ Functions of Congress

The Constitution is far more explicit in defining the responsibilities of the national legislature than it is in describing the function of the other branches of the government.[2] In its shaping of congressional functions, the Constitution's concerns with limited government, checks and balances, the separation of powers, and the creation of a federal system are all readily apparent. Today, Congress has a number of functions beyond lawmaking, including representation, oversight, agenda setting, and managing social conflict.

Representation Comes in Many Forms

In delineating the composition of the federal legislature and the procedures for electing its members, the Constitution shapes the congressional function of representation in several ways. Representation traditionally involves a House or Senate member's articulating and voting for the position that best represents the views of his or her constituents.[3] Sometimes, though, a member of Congress may speak for other constituencies as well. For example, a feminist legislator might "represent" feminists nationwide,[4] and a gay legislator might "represent" the collective interests of LGBTQ people across the United States.

Often, Congress's policy-making function is at odds with its representation function. A legislator may be pressured—by his or her political party or own conscience—to vote for a policy that clashes with constituents' interests or views. In representing constituents, legislators frequently follow one of two models of representative behavior.

trustee model
A model of representation in which a member of the House or the Senate follows his or her own conscience when deciding issue positions.

MODELS OF REPRESENTATION According to the **trustee model** of representation, a member of the House or the Senate follows his or her own conscience when deciding issue positions and determining how to vote. Sometimes a legislator relying on the trustee model will act contrary to the views of his or her constituents. This model was espoused by British political theorist Edmund Burke (1729–1797), who served in Parliament as a representative of Bristol, England. Explaining his conception of representation, Burke emphasized to his constituents that a member of Parliament "is not a member of Bristol, he is a member of Parliament."[5] Burke accordingly argued that a member of Parliament should follow his conscience when making decisions in the legislature: "Your representative owes you, not his industry only, but his judgment; and he betrays, instead of serving you, if he sacrifices it to your opinion."[6] In this trustee view, a legislator may act in opposition to the clear wishes of his or her constituents, such as in cases where an action is "for their own good" or the good of society.

Another model of representation is the **instructed delegate model,** the idea that a legislator, as a representative of his or her constituents, should vote in keeping with the constituents' views, *even if those views contradict the legislator's personal views*. This model of representation conceives of legislators as the agents of their constituents. A legislator hewing to the instructed delegate model faces a dilemma when his or her constituency is evenly divided on an issue.

Given these two different models of representation, which one do legislators typically follow? Most analyses of representation indicate that legislators are likely to merge the two models into a hybrid model, called **politico,** in which legislators act as instructed delegates when deciding important or high-profile issues, but for more mundane matters about which their constituents are less likely to be aware or to hold a strong position, they rely on the trustee model.

PORK BARREL AND EARMARKS Members of Congress also represent their constituencies through pork barrel politics. **Pork barrel** (also called simply *pork*) refers to legislators' appropriations of funds for special projects located within their congressional districts. Because pork brings money and jobs to a particular district, legislators who are seeking reelection work aggressively to secure monies for their states or districts—to "bring home the bacon."[7] Traditionally, members have used transportation bills as a means of creating pork barrel projects for their districts.[8] Members of Congress also use **earmarks**—designations within spending bills that provide for specific expenditures—as a means of representing constituent interests. In 2010, Republicans in Congress sought to eliminate earmarks as part of a larger effort to rein in government spending, and Republicans in both chambers endorsed a two-year moratorium on earmarks. But over time, that moratorium has fallen by the wayside, and members of Congress have resumed the practice, securing 163 earmarks in the 2017 fiscal budget, costing taxpayers $6.8 billion.[9]

CASEWORK A special form of representation called **casework** refers to providing representation in the form of personal aid to a constituent or a group of constituents, typically by getting the government to do something the constituent wants done. Members of Congress and their staffs commonly assist constituents in dealing with bureaucratic agencies. In doing so, they serve in the capacity of an **ombudsperson,** an elected or appointed representative who acts as a citizens' advocate by listening to their needs and investigating their complaints with respect to a particular government agency. For example, a member of Congress might intervene with U.S. Citizenship and Immigration Services to request that a constituent's relative in a foreign country be granted a visa to travel to the United States.

According to political scientist Morris Fiorina, casework is a valuable tool for legislators. Fiorina points out that serving constituents is relatively easy for members of Congress, because bureaucrats—who depend on Congress for their funding—typically respond quickly to the requests of legislators.[10] The loyalty derived from assisting constituents is one aspect of the incumbency advantage that makes current members of Congress more likely to be elected than their challengers, who do not enjoy that source of constituent loyalty.

Casework benefits constituents when, for example, a member of Congress's staff works with a local branch of a Veterans Administration clinic to secure services for a retired veteran, whose family members derive a sense of efficacy—a feeling that they can get things done and that the government works for people like them.

instructed delegate model
A model of representation in which legislators, as representatives of their constituents, should vote in keeping with the constituents' views, even if those views contradict the legislator's personal views.

politico
A hybrid model of representation in which legislators vote in keeping with constituents' views on important or high-profile matters but rely on the trustee model for more mundane matters.

pork barrel
Legislators' appropriations of funds for special projects located within their congressional districts.

earmark
A designation within a spending bill that provides for a specific expenditure.

casework
Personal work by a member of Congress on behalf of a constituent or group of constituents, typically aimed at getting the government to do something the constituent wants done.

ombudsperson
A role in which an elected or appointed leader acts as an advocate for citizens by listening to and investigating complaints against a government agency.

They perceive that their individual member of Congress genuinely represents them and protects their interests, with the result that these constituents not only feel engaged but also are likely to advocate for their member's reelection bid.

Policymaking: A Central Responsibility

Each year, Congress considers laws determining everything from whether background checks should be required for gun purchases, to what law enforcers can do when they suspect someone of being a terrorist, to whether the nation's immigration policy should be overhauled. Many of these laws are passed by Congress and signed into law by the president, thus becoming the nation's policy. While all areas of congressional policymaking are not explicitly listed in the Constitution (see discussion of the elastic clause in Chapter 2), it does invest Congress with some specific policy-making powers, including the authority to tax and spend, declare war, establish courts, and regulate the armed forces. This policy-making function is the central responsibility that the Congress carries out, and nearly all its other functions are related to its policy-making role. Congressional policy-making power also extends to the operations and priorities of governmental departments and agencies.

Oversight: A Check on the Executive Branch

congressional oversight
The process by which the legislative branch "checks" the executive branch to ensure that the laws Congress has passed are being administered in keeping with legislators' intent.

In creating a system of checks and balances in the Constitution, the framers established the key congressional function of oversight.[11] **Congressional oversight** is the process by which Congress "checks" the executive branch to ensure that the laws Congress passes are being administered in keeping with legislators' intentions. Congressional oversight is a check on the executive branch because the federal bureaucracy that implements laws is part of the executive branch. For example, oversight was important in the 2018 midterm elections, when many Democrats ran for seats in the House of Representative arguing that they would exercise more vigorous congressional oversight of the Trump administration than the Republican-led Congress had up to that point.

In carrying out their oversight function, members of Congress use a variety of tools, some of which are listed here:

- Congressional hearings, in which government officials, bureaucrats, and interest groups testify as to how a law or a policy is being implemented and examine the impact of its implementation. Such was the case in 2019 during the impeachment hearings of President Trump, when several career diplomats with the State Department testified before the House concerning the leveraging of foreign aid to Ukraine

- Confirmation hearings on presidential appointees to oversee executive departments or government agencies

- Investigations to determine whether a law or a policy is being implemented the way Congress intended it to be, and inquiries into allegations of wrongdoing by government officials or bureaucrats

- Budgetary appropriations that determine funding of an executive department or a government agency

These tools ensure that Congress has some say in how the executive branch administers the laws Congress creates. Members of Congress increasingly have viewed their role of checking the executive branch as crucially important. One especially significant form of oversight is impeachment, a formal charge that the president has violated the law, as discussed previously in this chapter.

Agenda Setting and Civic Engagement

Congress engages continuously in **agenda setting:** determining which public policy issues the federal legislature should consider.[12] Indeed, political scientists such as Gary Cox and Mathew McCubbins assert that agenda setting relieves the pressure that parties face in getting their members to vote with the party.[13] At the beginning of a congressional term, House and Senate leaders announce their goals for the coming session. In setting the national agenda, Congress serves as a key agent in molding the scope of civic engagement and discourse, as people learn about, discuss, and form positions about issues. Frequently, agenda setting is itself influenced by public discourse, as when constituents complain to a member of Congress about a problem that needs to be solved or when an interest group contacts a legislator about a policy its membership would like to see implemented. Such was the case when students and family members of victims passionately advocated Congress for gun-safety laws in the wake of a mass shooting at Marjory Stoneman Douglas High School in Parkland, Florida, in February 2018. The students succeeded in setting the agenda for many of the mid-term congressional elections in 2018 and then again in 2020, particularly in some districts where incumbent legislators had accepted large campaign contributions from the National Rifle Association, which opposed the students' efforts.

agenda setting
The determination by Congress of which public issues the government should consider for legislation.

Managing Societal Conflict

Congress also has a significant influence in managing the societal conflict inherent in a divided society such as the United States. Americans are divided in many ways, and in the past several years, ideological divisions have become greatly apparent as congressional district maps facilitate the election of staunchly ideological candidates.

Issues also divide Americans: Some citizens want higher wages, while others advocate for more "pro-business" policies. Some want policies that benefit rural areas, and others give higher priority to urban areas. Some want more money for programs for senior citizens; others seek funding for children's programs. With respect to abortion policy, some people are pro-life, and others are pro-choice. In addition, there are divisions related to social class, race, geography, gender, sexual orientation, religion, and so on. Congress manages these conflicts by representing a wide range of views and interests, by taking stands on these positions, and then finally by negotiating and compromising on these issues.

■ The House and the Senate Compared

Although the House of Representatives and the Senate share numerous functions, the two chambers of Congress differ in significant ways. As President Woodrow Wilson remarked, the "House and Senate are naturally unalike."[14] Constitutionally, the two houses are conceived as unique organizations, and the framers designated

TABLE 4.2 ■ Differences Between the House and the Senate

House	Senate
Larger (435 members)	Smaller (100 members)
Shorter electoral cycle (2-year term)	Longer electoral cycle (6-year term)
Narrow constituency (congressional districts)	Broad constituency (states)
Less prestigious	More prestigious
Originates all revenue bills	Ratifies treaties; confirms presidential nominees
Less reliant on staff	More reliant on staff
Power vested in leaders and committee chairs	Power distributed more evenly

their duties to match the strengths and expertise of the people who would come to hold office in each chamber. Table 4.2 highlights these major differences. As discussed earlier in this chapter, the Constitution empowers the House of Representatives, as the legislative body closer to the people, with initiating any bills that result in taxes; whereas it empowers the Senate, as the more deliberative house, to give the president advice and consent on appointments and the ratification of treaties. The differences between the House and the Senate are not limited merely to their functions, however. The electoral and legislative structures are also sources of differences between the two houses.

reapportionment
Reallocation of seats in the House of Representatives to each state based on changes in state populations since the last census.

redistricting
The redrawing of congressional district boundaries within each state, based on the reapportionment from the census.

Each of the 435 current members of the House of Representatives represents a legislative district determined by the **reapportionment** and **redistricting** process that occurs every 10 years, based on data from the U.S. Census. In more populated areas, these congressional districts are often homogeneous, cohesive units in which a House member's constituency is likely to have fairly unified positions on many issues.[15] Senators, however, are elected by the population of an entire state, and although the political culture in some states is somewhat cohesive (for example, Vermont voters are more liberal on most issues than are Kansas voters), in many states there are notable differences in constituents' views, ideologies, and policy priorities. One of the best examples of this vast diversity of views is California. Although it is typically viewed as having a very liberal political culture, California senators must advocate for the interests of more conservative voters in the eastern part of the state as well as the more liberal voters in the western coastal areas. Sometimes, moreover, constituents' interests divide in complex ways over a given issue. In California, for example, environmental activists and fishers have argued against programs that divert water from lakes and streams so that it can be used for irrigation on commercial farms, whereas affluent agribusinesses advocate water diversion. A U.S. senator must balance such conflicting positions when making policy decisions.

Government scholars often note, "The rules of election determine outcomes". In other words, with different rules, elections will turn out differently. This idea is offensive to those who believe elections reflect the will of the majority, not a set of rules. To what extent is this idea true? If it is true, what rules are manipulating the outcome of elections? One such rule in Congressional elections is the process of drawing district lines. In the United States, each state is responsible for drawing legislative district lines for both state and federal legislatures. The question argued in the Supreme Court case *Baker v. Carr* was whether federal courts could rule on the way states drew their state legislative district lines. As populations in the U.S. began to shift from rural areas to cities and states did not redistrict, the result was districts unequal in population size. Voters filed lawsuits alleging inequity between districts with small and large populations, but the courts routinely dismissed the lawsuits. The cases were believed to be viewed as "political questions" not proper for a court to decide. Consider how the facts and decision in the *Baker* case apply to the *Wesberry* case below.

Wesberry v. Sanders (1964)

James Wesberry resided in a Georgia congressional district with a population two to three times greater than that of other congressional districts in the state. Wesberry argued that his vote was debased as a result of the state's failure to reapportion the districts with equal population sizes. The constitutional question argued before the Supreme Court was whether or not Georgia's congressional districts violated the 14th Amendment.

In a 6-3 decision for Wesberry, the Court held that congressional districts must have roughly equal population sizes when this is feasible and that legislative apportionment was justiciable.

A. Identify the constitutional clause that is common to both *Wesberry v. Sanders* and *Baker v. Carr.*

B. Explain the difference in the holdings of *Wesberry* and *Baker.*

C. Identify one limit to state's redistricting power based on the holding of *Wesberry* and identify how states still have power to manipulate legislative districts.

The differing lengths of representatives' and senators' terms of service affect how members of each chamber of Congress relate to their constituents. Given their short two-year terms, members of the House of Representatives naturally are reluctant to defy the will of the electorate on a given issue because of the likelihood that their opposition will be used against them during their reelection campaign. As the framers structured it, the House remains "the people's house," the chamber in which civically engaged individuals can effectively have their interests represented. And although U.S. senators naturally also want to please their constituents, they recognize that voting against their constituents' will on a particular issue might be less significant than such an action would be for a House member, especially if the issue arises early in their term and is not important enough for people to hold against them six years down the road. When the Republican members of the U.S. Senate, with only one exception—Senator Mitt Romney (R-Mass.)—voted not to convict President Trump on the impeachment charges of abuse of power and obstruction of Congress, 23 of those senators faced reelection in 2020.

The size of the chambers and the length of terms also affect the relative prestige of each chamber. In general, the smaller Senate is considered more prestigious than the House of Representatives, although some individual House members may enjoy more prestige than some senators.

Although the House and the Senate differ in their constitutionally determined duties, both must pass any piece of legislation before it can become law. The way in which legislation is considered and voted on, however, differs in each house of Congress.

The larger size of the House of Representatives, with its 435 members, necessitates a more formal legislative structure to prevent unruliness. The House, for example, generally has more, and more formal, rules guiding debate than the Senate. Despite the differences between the two chambers, the legislative process is remarkably similar in both.

■ The Legislative Process

bill
A proposed piece of legislation.

Article I, Section 1, of the Constitution states, "All Legislative Powers herein granted shall be vested in a Congress of the United States, which shall consist of a Senate and House of Representatives." A **bill** is a proposed piece of legislation. As shown in Figure 4.1, every bill must be approved by *both houses* (the House and the Senate) *in identical form*. In general, bills must pass through five steps to become law:

1. **Introduction.** A member of the House of Representatives or the Senate formally proposes the bill.

2. **Committee review.** Subgroups within the House and the Senate, composed of legislators who have expertise in the bill's subject matter, review the bill.

3. **House and Senate approval.** If the bill makes it out of committee, a majority of members in the House and the Senate must approve it.

4. **Conference committee reconciliation.** A conference committee reconciles the bill when different versions have passed in the House and the Senate.

5. **Presidential approval.** If the president signs the bill, it becomes law. But even after this arduous process, a presidential veto can kill the bill.

Introducing a Bill

Bills are introduced differently in each chamber of Congress. In the House of Representatives, a member of a legislator's staff drafts the proposed legislation,

The Legislative Process

Concept for legislative consideration

Bill introduced in House	**Bill introduced in Senate**

Bill assigned to committee, then usually referred to subcommittee

Subcommittee	Subcommittee
Committee	Committee
Rules Committee schedules debate	Senate leadership schedules debate
Floor action	Floor action
House bill	Senate bill

Differences?

Yes → Conference committee → Conference bill → Floor action

No

Presidential approval?

Yes → **Bill becomes law**

No → Veto → **Override veto?** → Yes → **Bill becomes law**

Override veto? → No → **Start legislative process again**

FIGURE 4.1 ■ **The Legislative Process** Where are there similarities between the House and the Senate in the legislative process? How do the Senate and the House resolve differences in versions of a bill passed in each chamber? What outcomes are possible once a bill goes to the president for approval?

and the House member puts the bill into the **hopper,** a wooden box that sits on a desk at the front of the House chamber. Upon introduction, a bill is referred to as "H. R.," meaning House of Representatives, followed by a number that indicates the order in which it was introduced in a given legislative session, for example, "H. R. 207."

hopper
A wooden box that sits on a desk at the front of the House of Representatives, into which House members place bills they want to introduce.

In the Senate, the process is less formal. Here, senators can announce proposed legislation to colleagues in a speech on the Senate floor. Alternatively, a senator can submit a written draft of the proposed legislation to an official known as the Senate clerk, or sometimes a senator will propose legislation simply by offering it as an amendment to an already pending piece of legislation. Once a bill is introduced in the Senate, it is referred to as "S.," or "Senate," followed by its number reflecting the order in which it was introduced in a given legislative session—for example, "S. 711."

joint referral
The practice, abolished in the 104th Congress, by which a bill could be referred to two different committees for consideration.

lead committee
The primary committee considering a bill.

Before 1995, a bill introduced in the House of Representatives could be subject to **joint referral,** the practice of referring the bill simultaneously to two different House committees for consideration. But the 104th Congress abolished joint committee referrals. Today, bills introduced in the House are referred to one committee, called the **lead committee.** Occasionally, when the substance of a bill warrants additional referrals to other committees that also have jurisdiction over the subject of the bill, the bill might be subsequently referred to a second committee.[16] In the Senate, bills typically are referred to only one committee.

The Bill in Committee

After introduction by a member of the House or the Senate, a bill is read into the *Congressional Record*, a formal record of all actions taken by Congress. Because of the large number of bills introduced, both chambers rely on an extensive committee structure that facilitates the consideration of so high a volume of bills.[17] Most bills that are introduced "die" in committee. That is, a committee does not consider the bill (sometimes because the committee does not have the time in a legislative session to take up the measure) or declines to forward the bill to the full chamber.

Each congressional committee and subcommittee is composed of a majority of members of the majority party in that chamber. For example, if 218 or more members (a majority in the House) elected to the House of Representatives are Republicans, then every committee and subcommittee in the House has a majority of Republicans. The parties in each chamber decide members' committee and subcommittee assignments.

seniority system
The system in which the member with the longest continuous tenure on a standing committee is given preference when the committee chooses its chair.

Though the selection of committee chairs varies between chambers and parties, committee chairs are often chosen using the **seniority system,** by which the member with the longest continuous tenure on a standing committee receives preference when the committee chooses its chair. The committee chairs run committee meetings and control the flow of work in each committee. Although the seniority system is an institution in Congress, it is an informal system, and seniority does not always determine who will be the committee chair.[18] Chairs are chosen by a secret ballot, and in recent years, junior members sometimes have won out over senior committee members.

standing committee
A permanent committee in Congress, with a defined legislative jurisdiction.

Standing committees are permanent committees with a defined legislative jurisdiction. The House and the Senate each have 20 standing committees. The House Appropriations Committee and the Senate Armed Services Committee are examples of standing committees.

select committee
A congressional committee created to consider specific policy issues or address a specific concern.

Select committees are specially created to consider a specific policy issue or to address a particular concern, including the U.S. House Select Committee on the Climate Crisis, formed in 2019. This select committee is charged with recommending a set of public policy proposals to Congress with the goal of reducing pollution and other factors that contribute to the climate crisis. Other select committees have also grappled with controversial issues of the times, including climate change, the response to Hurricane Katrina, and homeland security and terrorism. Congress currently has one permanent Select Committee on Intelligence, which is concerned with the nation's intelligence apparatus.

Joint committees are bicameral committees composed of members of both chambers. Congress currently has five joint committees. One is concerned with issues of taxation, another with the solvency of pension plans, another with economic issues, and another with printing. Sometimes these committees offer administrative or managerial guidance of various kinds. For example, one joint committee supervises the administration of the Library of Congress.

In addition to the congressional committees, the House has 102 subcommittees, and the Senate has 67. **Subcommittees** typically handle specific areas of the committees' jurisdiction. For example, the House Energy and Commerce Committee is a standing committee, and within the committee there are six subcommittees: Communications and Technology, Digital Commerce and Consumer Protection, Energy, Environment, Health, and Oversight and Investigations. Each subcommittee handles bills relevant to its specified jurisdiction.

When a committee or a subcommittee favors a measure, it usually takes four actions:

1. **Agency review.** During **agency review,** the committee or subcommittee asks the executive agencies that would administer the law for written comments on the measure.

2. **Hearings.** Next the committee or subcommittee holds **hearings** to gather information and views from experts, including interest groups, concerned citizens, and policy experts involved with the issue.

3. **Markup.** During **markup,** the committee "marks up" the bill with suggested language changes and amendments. The committee does not actually alter the bill; rather, members recommend changes to the full chamber. In a typical bill markup, the committee may eliminate a component of the proposal or amend the proposal in some way.

4. **Report.** After agreeing to the wording of the bill, the committee issues a **report** to the full chamber, explaining the bill and its intent. The bill may then be considered by the full chamber.

In the House of Representatives, a special measure known as a **discharge petition** is used to extract a bill from a committee to have it considered by the entire House. A discharge petition requires the signature of a majority (218) of the members of the House.

Debate on the House and Senate Floor

Table 4.3 compares the legislative processes in the House and the Senate. For example, if a House bill is "discharged," or makes it out of committee, it then goes to the **Rules Committee,** one of the most important committees in the House, which decides on the length of debate and the scope of amendments that will be allowed on a bill. The Rules Committee sets the structure for the debate that ensues in the full House. For important bills, the Rules Committee tends to set strict limits on the types of amendments that can be attached to a bill. In general, the Rules Committee also establishes limits to floor debate in the House.

joint committee
A bicameral committee composed of members of both chambers of Congress.

subcommittee
A subordinate committee in Congress that typically handles specific areas of a standing committee's jurisdiction.

agency review
Part of the committee or subcommittee process of considering a bill, wherein committee members ask executive agencies that would administer the law for written comments on the measure.

hearings
Sessions held by committees or subcommittees to gather information and views from experts.

markup
The process by which the members of legislative committees "mark up" a bill with suggested language for changes and amendments.

report
A legislative committee's explanation to the full chamber of a bill and its intent.

discharge petition
A special tactic used to extract a bill from a committee to have it considered by the entire House.

Rules Committee
One of the most important committees in the House, which decides the length of debate and the scope of amendments that will be allowed on a bill.

TABLE 4.3 ■ Differences Between the Legislative Process in the House and Senate

House	Senate
Bill introduced by member placing bill in hopper	Bill introduced by member
Relies on Rules Committee to schedule debate on House floor and to establish rules for amendments	Relies on unanimous consent agreements to determine rules for debate and amendments
Has a rule barring nongermane amendments	No rule banning nongermane amendments
Does not allow filibusters	Allows filibusters
Discharge petition can be used to extract a bill from a committee	Does not allow discharge petitions

What are the root causes of the differences between the House and Senate? Which chamber has a greater number of rules and procedures? Why do you think this is the case?

---

unanimous consent
An agreement by every senator to the terms of debate on a given piece of legislation.

filibuster
A procedural move by a member of the Senate to attempt to halt passage of a bill, during which the senator can speak for an unlimited time on the Senate floor.

cloture
A procedural move in which a supermajority of 60 senators agrees to end a filibuster.

The Senate does not have a committee to do the work of the Rules Committee, but the Senate's small size allows members to agree to the terms of debate through **unanimous consent** agreements. Unanimous consent must be just that: Every senator needs to agree to the terms of debate (including time limits on debate), and if even one senator objects, unanimous consent does not take effect. Senators do not look favorably on objections to unanimous consent, and so such objections are rare. Objecting to unanimous consent agreements can potentially undermine a senator's ability to get legislation passed by provoking the ire of other senators.

If the Senate does not reach unanimous consent, the possibility of a **filibuster** arises—a procedural move that attempts to halt passage of the bill.[19] Sometimes the mere threat of a filibuster is enough to compel a bill's supporters to alter a bill's content. During a filibuster, a senator can speak for an unlimited time on the Senate floor. A filibuster can end by a vote of **cloture,** in which a supermajority of 60 senators agrees to end debate. Cloture is initiated if 16 senators sign a cloture petition. Filibustering senators do not need to restrict themselves to speaking only on the subject of the bill—they just need to keep talking. Some senators have read the Bible or cookbooks, and in 2013, Senator Ted Cruz even read Dr. Seuss's *Green Eggs and Ham* into the *Congressional Record*. Former senator Strom Thurmond (R-S.C.) holds the Senate record for the longest filibuster. In an attempt to block passage of the Civil Rights Act of 1957, Thurmond filibustered for 24 hours and 18 minutes.

During his administration, President Trump repeatedly expressed his frustration with this procedural maneuver, which sometimes stymied his ability to win legislative votes. In 2018, he tweeted, "With the ridiculous Filibuster Rule in the Senate, Republicans need 60 votes to pass legislation, rather than 51. Can't get votes, END NOW!"[20] The filibuster practice briefly became an issue in the 2020 presidential campaign when Senator Elizabeth Warren (D-Mass.) advocated abolishing it, but on the whole, senators in both political parties have expressed reluctance to end the filibuster rule.[21]

In 2017, facing significant Democratic opposition, Republicans exercised the so-called **nuclear option,** in which the Senate majority leader overrides a standard rule of the Senate. The nuclear option is based on a 1957 opinion drafted by then-vice president Richard M. Nixon, who asserted that the Constitution grants the presiding officer of the Senate the power to override Senate rules. Nuclear options—characterized as such because they are explosive procedural maneuvers likely to leave toxic political fallout for years in the future— have been used in the past to require a simple majority of 51 votes to end debate in the Senate, rather than the traditional 60, or to reduce the amount of time allowed for debate of presidential nominations. As an example of the latter, in 2019, Senate Majority Leader Mitch McConnell reduced the debate time allowed for presidential judicial nominations from 30 hours to 2 hours in order to expedite the appointment of some of President Trump's judicial appointments.

nuclear option
A maneuver exercised by the presiding officer in the Senate in which a standard rule of the Senate is overridden.

Although Supreme Court confirmation hearings traditionally had been exempt from the nuclear option, in 2017 Republicans used it to confirm Neil Gorsuch as President Donald Trump's nominee to the Supreme Court, a historic progression in the evolution of the nuclear option. In 2013, Democrats in charge of the Senate had changed Senate rules so that filibusters on appointments and nominations could be subjected to a simple majority vote. Then-Senate majority leader Harry Reid (D-Nev.) argued that a backlog of appointments to the Obama administration and the federal courts was a result of Republican opposition to President Obama's administration overall rather than a reflection of the qualifications of individuals nominated to various positions, an argument that resurfaced during Gorsuch's confirmation. The deep divisions between the political parties in the Senate are illustrated by the fact that the nuclear option has been a mechanism to force the confirmation of nominations three times in just six years.

After a bill is debated by the full chamber, the members vote on it. Before a bill can become law, identical versions of the bill must pass in both the House and the Senate. If only one chamber passes a bill during a congressional term, the bill dies. If both the House and the Senate pass bills on the same topic but with differences between the bills, the bills are then sent to a **conference committee,** a bicameral, bipartisan committee composed of legislators whose job is to reconcile the two versions of the bill. After the committee develops a compromise version of the bill, the bill then goes back to both chambers for another vote. If the bill does not pass in both chambers during a congressional term, the bill is dead, although it can be reintroduced in the next session. If both chambers approve the bill, it then goes to the president for signature or veto.

conference committee
A bicameral, bipartisan committee composed of legislators whose job is to reconcile two versions of a bill.

Presidential Action

When both the House and the Senate manage to pass a bill in identical form, it proceeds to the president, who may take one of three actions. First, the president may sign it, in which case the bill becomes a law. Second, the president may choose to do nothing. If the president does nothing and Congress is in session, the bill becomes law after 10 days without the president's signature. A president may take this route if he or she does not support the bill but knows that Congress would override a veto. If, however, Congress has adjourned (that is, the bill was passed at the end of a legislative session), then the president may exercise a pocket veto. A **pocket veto** occurs when Congress has adjourned and the president waits 10 days without signing the bill; the president effectively "puts the bill in his pocket," and the bill dies. Finally, a president may exercise the executive power of a *veto*: rejecting the bill and returning it to Congress with a message explaining why the bill should not become law. Congress can vote to override the veto by a two-thirds vote in both houses, in which case the bill becomes law. But overriding a presidential veto is a difficult and rare achievement.

pocket veto
A special presidential veto of a bill passed at the conclusion of a legislative session, whereby the president waits 10 days without signing the bill, and the bill dies.

■ Congressional Leadership

In earlier eras, forceful politicians rose to the position of majority leader in both houses and strongly influenced congressional priorities and legislation.[22] But allegiance to party leaders in these institutions has dwindled, a function of the decreasing role that political parties play in individual members' election to Congress.[23] Today's congressional power brokers face members whose loyalty to the party and the leadership is tempered by the increase in the number of highly ideological members hailing from safe congressional districts and the increasing need to please constituencies that themselves are less loyal to the parties than in bygone times.[24] The era has long passed in which individuals could essentially control what members of Congress do through their assertive personalities.[25] Nonetheless, despite the evolution in the role of congressional leader, partisanship remains a strong aspect of congressional politics.

Leadership in the House of Representatives

Although Article I, Section 2, of the Constitution states, "The House of Representatives shall choose their Speaker and other Officers," and all members of the House vote for the Speaker, it is really the members of the majority party who select their **Speaker of the House.** Second in the line of presidential succession (after the vice president), the Speaker serves as the presiding officer and manager of the House. In this capacity, the Speaker chairs floor debates, makes majority party committee assignments, assigns members to the powerful Rules Committee, negotiates with members of the minority party and the White House, and guides legislation through the House.[26] But the Speaker is also the leader of his or her party in the House, and a key duty associated with this role is helping party members to get reelected. Finally, the Speaker is himself or herself an elected member of the House.

Speaker of the House
The leader of the House of Representatives, chosen by the majority party.

The House leadership—which, in addition to the Speaker, includes the majority leader, the minority leader, and the party whips—is chosen at the beginning of each session of Congress through a conference also known as a *caucus*. During a caucus, all the members of the political party meet and elect their chamber leaders, approve committee assignments, and elect committee chairpersons. Party leaders also may call a party caucus during a legislative session to shore up support on an issue being voted upon or to formulate the party's position on an issue on the agenda.[27]

The Speaker relies on the **House majority leader** to help develop and implement the majority party's legislative strategy, to work with the minority party leadership, and to encourage unity among majority party legislators. In this last task, the Speaker and the House majority leader are assisted by the **majority whip,** who acts as a go-between with the leadership and the party members in the House. The term *whip* comes from the English hunting term *whipper-in*, a hunter whose job is to keep the foxhounds in the pack and to prevent them from straying during a fox hunt. Similarly, the job of the party whip is to keep party members together, encouraging them to vote with the party on issues and preventing them from straying off into their own positions. The minority party in the House also elects leaders, the **House minority leader** and the **minority whip,** whose jobs mirror those of their majority-party colleagues but without the power that comes from holding a majority in the House.

In 2019, Nancy Pelosi (D-Calif.) took the helm as Speaker of the House of Representatives following the 2018 congressional elections, in which Democrats took over a majority of House seats. Pelosi, who is the only woman in U.S. history to serve in this position, had previously served as Speaker from 2007 to 2011. She regained the position in 2019 because many new Democrats had wrested seats from Republican control during the mid-term elections, which were largely viewed as a mandate on the Trump presidency. For many months, Pelosi steered the House cautiously, aware that many of her "frontline" members would have to win reelection in competitive districts in 2020, and so she was reluctant to push the chamber, particularly with regard to impeachment. But in the fall of 2019, revelations surfaced concerning a phone call between President Trump and the president of Ukraine in which President Trump seemed to leverage the release of aid to Ukraine with a request to the Ukrainian president to investigate Trump's political rival, former vice president Joe Biden. In response, several newly elected House members, nearly all of them veterans of the armed forces, wrote an op-ed in the *Washington Post* urging impeachment proceedings. The signal from those members, who had sworn oaths to their country twice and who seemed prepared to face the potential wrath of constituents, was all Pelosi needed. In October 2019, the House voted to begin an impeachment inquiry, a fact-finding investigation that led to two charges of impeachment against Trump. Since that time, Pelosi has become a national symbol—reviled by Trump supporters and idolized by his detractors.

But Pelosi has not been without critics within her own party. In particular, young progressive Democrats have often taken exception to Pelosi's moderate tendencies. For example, she has sometimes been at odds with members of "the Squad," a group of four women elected to the House in 2018, including Alexandria Ocasio-Cortez (D-N.Y.), Ilhan Omar (D-Minn.), Ayanna Pressley (D-Mass.), and Rashida Tlaib (D-Mich.). While the Squad was the subject of negative Tweets and targeting by President Trump, back-biting social media posts have also displayed the fissures between Pelosi and the more progressive members of her caucus.

Pelosi assumed the speakership after a similar period of factionalism within the Republican Party. In September 2015, John Boehner (pronounced BAY-ner) (R-Ohio), then the Speaker of the House of Representatives, shocked many by announcing his resignation. Boehner, a moderate Republican who had served at the helm since 2010, was a victim of the factionalism that has plagued the Republican Party since that time. While Pelosi faces a push toward more liberal policies by dissenters within her Democratic caucus, Boehner had difficulty reining

House majority leader
The leader of the majority party, who helps the Speaker to develop and implement strategy and who works with other members of the House of Representatives.

majority whip
The go-between with the majority leadership and party members in the House of Representatives.

House minority leader
The leader of the minority party, whose job mirrors that of the majority leader but without the power that comes from holding a majority in the House of Representatives.

minority whip
The go-between with the minority leadership, whose job mirrors that of the majority whip but without the power that comes from holding a majority in the House of Representatives.

THEN

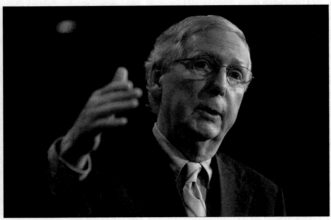

Chip Somodevilla/Getty Images

NOW

Saul Loeb/AFP/Getty Images

>> Senator Mitch McConnell (R-Ky.) was elected Senate majority leader when the Republicans took control of the Senate in 2014. When they maintained their majority in the chamber in 2016 and 2018, McConnell was reelected to that role but an evenly-divided Senate was elected in 2020, and Vice President Kamala Harris is now the tie-breaking vote. With Harris' support Sen. Chuck Schumer (D-NY) became Majority Leader in 2021. Representative Nancy Pelosi (D-Ca; left) has served as Speaker of the House since 2019, and previously from 2007 to 2011. She is the highest-ranking woman elected official in U.S. history and is the only woman to have ever served as Speaker. Since 2019, she has faced pressure from more progressive members of her party, including Representative Alexandria Ocasio-Cortez (D-NY; right). In your view, do more ideologically extreme members of a party make the House and Senate leaders' jobs harder or easier? Why?

in the conservative Freedom Caucus. For example, in 2013 Boehner could not corral conservatives to compromise with Democrats on the budget, resulting in a 16-day shutdown of the federal government. In 2015, Freedom Caucus members, their numbers bolstered by the 2014 mid-term elections, threatened to shut down the government again by withholding votes on a budget measure, prompting Boehner's resignation.

When Boehner resigned as Speaker, House Republicans floundered for a short time in deciding upon his successor. They sought someone who could unify but who was also conservative enough to placate the intra-party rumblings that had caused Boehner's downfall. Paul D. Ryan (R-Wis.) emerged as that consensus candidate, winning all but nine of the Republican House votes. When he was elected, he acknowledged the challenge he faced: reforming an institution that he characterized as "broken,"[28] with deep divisions between Republicans and Democrats and within the Republican Party itself. After President Trump's inauguration in 2017, Ryan enjoyed the advantage of having a president of his party in the White House, but that also presented many challenges, as President Trump's priorities and positions often diverged greatly from those in Ryan's caucus. The reluctant Speaker, who often seemed disturbed by President Trump's behavior, also faced factionalism within his caucus. When it became evident that the Democrats might gain enough seats in the 2018 mid-term elections to take control of the House, Ryan announced that he was retiring from Congress.

Leadership in the Senate

In the Senate, the vice president of the United States serves as the president of that body, according to the Constitution. But in actual practice, vice presidents preside over the Senate only rarely. They do, however, have one power in the Senate that, although rarely exercised, is enormously important. If a vote in the upper house of Congress is tied, the vice president breaks the tie. Vice President Mike Pence cast a record number of tie-breaking votes in the Senate, including the deciding vote on a plan that allows states to block funding for Planned Parenthood and the deciding vote on the nomination of Betsy DeVos to be secretary of education.

The majority party in the Senate elects a Senate leader called the **president pro tempore.** Meaning "president for the time," this position is often referred to as "president pro tem." The job of the president pro tem is to chair the Senate in the vice president's absence. Historically, this position has been honorary, with the majority-party senator who has the longest record of continuous Senate service being elected to the office. Although the position is honorary, the Senate's president pro tem is third in the line of presidential succession (following the vice president and the Speaker of the House). Senator Patrick Leahy (D-VT), who was first elected to the Senate in 1974, has served as the president pro tem since 2021.

president pro tempore
Also called *president pro tem*; theoretically, the chair of the Senate in the vice president's absence; in reality, an honorary title, with the senator of the majority party having the longest record of continuous service being elected to the position.

The real power in the U.S. Senate is held and wielded by the **Senate majority leader,** whose job is to manage the legislative process so that favored bills are passed; to schedule debate on legislation in consultation with his or her counterpart in the minority party, the **Senate minority leader;** and to act as the spokesperson for the majority party in the Senate. The majority and the minority leaders both play crucial roles in ushering bills through the Senate, and the majority leader facilitates the numerous negotiations that arise when senators bargain over the content of a given piece of proposed legislation.[29]

Senate majority leader
The most powerful position in the Senate; the majority leader manages the legislative process and schedules debate on legislation.

Senate minority leader
The leader of the minority party in the Senate, who works with the majority leader in negotiating legislation.

Senate Majority Leader Mitch McConnell (R-Ky.) was elected after the Republicans won a majority of seats in the 2014 Senate elections and was reelected in 2016, when the Republicans retained control of the Senate. McConnell had previously served as minority leader. As majority leader, McConnell initially faced pressure both from more conservative members of his party and from the Trump administration on an array of issues. Although McConnell forcefully went toe to toe with President Trump early in the president's tenure,[30] he gradually evolved into an important Trump ally, both blocking the Democratic agenda put forth by the House of Representatives and providing support for Trump, particularly during both impeachment votes. In January 2021, McConnell became Senate minority leader. Senator Charles Schumer (D-N.Y.) was the new Senate majority leader.

Decision Making in Congress: The Legislative Context

When deciding whether to "toe the party line" on a legislative vote, members of Congress do not operate independently and in isolation. Throughout the legislative process, they face a variety of external pressures that influence their views. Some of these pressures are subtle; others are more pronounced. Moreover, the effectiveness of the pressure varies according to the timing and type of legislation being considered. For example, political scientist Barry C. Burden has noted that the personal experiences of legislators sometimes have a bearing on their policy stances on issues.[31] Among the most important influences on members of Congress with respect to the legislative process are political parties, members' colleagues and staff, interest groups, the president, and of course their constituents—the people who elected them to serve as their representatives in our system of republican government.

Political Parties and Partisanship in Decision Making

Figure 4.2 shows the party breakdown in Congress since 1993. The data show that 1994 was a pivotal year, ending Democratic control in the House and the

DATA ANALYSIS   PATTERNS AND TRENDS

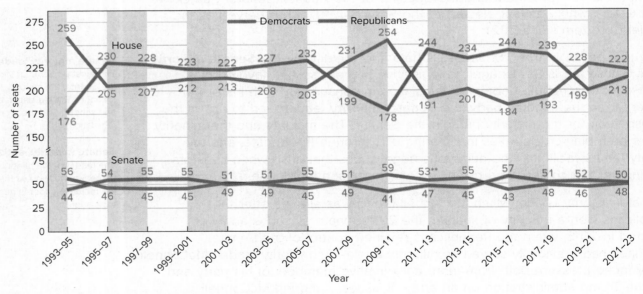

Party Breakdowns in the House and Senate, 1993–2023*

*At the time of publication, runoff elections were scheduled for both U.S. Senate seats in Georgia.

FIGURE 4.2   Party Representation Trends What trends does this graph show with respect to party representation in the House of Representatives since 1993? What trends does it indicate for the Senate? Generally speaking, do the patterns for the House resemble those for the Senate?

Senate. For nearly all of the next 12 years, Republicans retained control over both the House and the Senate. (Republicans lost their narrow majority in the Senate in 2001 when one Republican senator switched parties, but they regained control in the 2002 elections.) But in 2006, the balance of power shifted back to the Democrats, who won majorities in both houses, squeaking out a majority in the Senate with a one-member lead. That year, Democratic candidates benefited from Republican President George W. Bush's unpopularity and the public's weariness with the war in Iraq. In 2008 the Democrats continued to increase their majorities in both houses as a result of voters' continuing dislike of Bush's policies, and—for some Democratic congressional candidates—from Barack Obama's coattails. But this trend was reversed in 2010, when Republicans won a majority of seats in the House of Representatives and increased their numbers in the U.S. Senate. In the 2012 elections, in which President Obama topped the Democratic ticket, Democrats increased their margins slightly in both the House and the Senate, but again, this trend reversed itself in 2014, with Republicans increasing their majority in the House and winning a majority in the U.S. Senate. In 2016, Republicans lost several seats but maintained control of the House of Representatives. In 2018, Democrats succeeded in recapturing the House by flipping over 30 seats, many in affluent, suburban areas. In 2020, Democrats did not see the predicted anti-Trump "blue wave," and lost seven seats in the House, but retained their majority, winning 222 seats. The Senate is evenly divided with 50 seats held by Republicans and 50 by Democrats—but because Senate rules say that the Vice President is the tie-breaker in that chamber, the Democrats effectively have a majority.

The partisan breakdown of Congress is important because most major legislative votes cast are "party votes," meaning that most members of one political party vote one way, and most members of the other party vote the other way. In some cases, this divide is due to differing ideologies. In other instances, party voting is

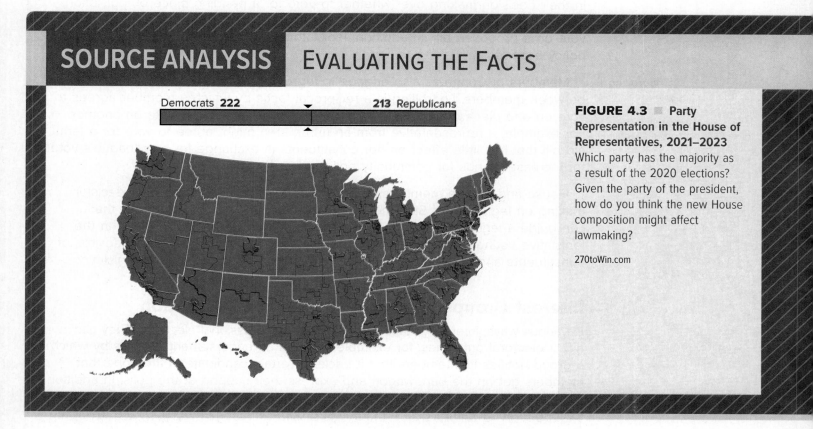

SOURCE ANALYSIS   EVALUATING THE FACTS

Democrats **222**   **213** Republicans

FIGURE 4.3 ■ **Party Representation in the House of Representatives, 2021–2023**
Which party has the majority as a result of the 2020 elections? Given the party of the president, how do you think the new House composition might affect lawmaking?

270toWin.com

simply pure partisanship: Democrats vote against something because Republicans vote for it, and vice versa. Partisan voting increased after the Watergate scandal in the 1970s, rose again after the 1994 congressional elections when Republicans took control of Congress, and then increased again when the conservative Tea Party members of Congress began flexing their political muscle after the 2010 elections. This trend continued after 2018, when Democrats took control of the House of Representatives while Republicans held the Senate. Partisan voting tends to be particularly acrimonious immediately before congressional and presidential elections. It occurs more often when members are voting on domestic policy issues, including environmental policies, economic regulatory policies, or policies concerning entitlement programs. Policy decisions such as these tend to crystallize ideological differences between the parties, as the Affordable Care Act did.

The increasingly sophisticated ability of mapmakers to draw congressional districts that offer partisan advantage to one party means that partisanship has increased in the House of Representatives. But many scholars assert that a similar bifurcation of political ideology has not occurred in the Senate. They claim that, because state populations as a whole tend to be more ideologically diverse and less homogeneous than House districts, U.S. senators often must temper their views to reflect the wider range of their constituents' perspectives. Thus, senators tend to be more willing than their House counterparts are to compromise and to take a more moderate stance in negotiating with the opposing party. Nonetheless, other scholars note that on some issues, the Senate is increasingly divided strongly along partisan lines, as was demonstrated during the 2020 impeachment votes in the Senate.[32]

Colleagues and Staff: Trading Votes and Information

Congressional colleagues provide cues for members of the House and the Senate in their decision making over whether to vote for a pending piece of legislation. Members may seek the opinions of like-minded colleagues in determining how to vote on a proposed bill. In addition, legislators may consult with peers who are policy experts.

logrolling
The practice of members of Congress agreeing to vote for a bill in exchange for their colleague's vote on another bill.

Members of Congress also engage in **logrolling,** the practice of trading votes between members. Logrolling is a reciprocal tactic by which a member agrees to vote on one piece of legislation in exchange for a colleague's vote on another. For example, a representative from an urban area might agree to vote for a farm aid bill that has little effect on her constituents in exchange for a colleague's vote for increased funds for community policing in cities.

House and Senate members also rely on their staffs to inform their decision making on legislation.[33] Staff members frequently have policy expertise that can guide a legislator's decision on an upcoming vote. They also figure in the legislative voting process by communicating with legislators about the desires of constituents and interest groups with respect to a pending piece of legislation.

Interest Groups: Influence Through Organization

In various ways, interest groups also influence congressional elections. They can affect electoral outcomes, for example, through an endorsement process by which a group notifies its members that it backs a certain candidate in the hope that members get on the bandwagon and express their support at the polls. In addition, through their political action committees, interest groups make financial contributions to congressional campaigns. And interest groups whose memberships are mobilized to support or oppose a candidate often provide grassroots activists to political campaigns.[34] Interest groups also shape the legislative process. They make their mark by influencing congressional campaigns, by providing information to members of Congress as they try to decide whether to vote for a particular piece of legislation, and by lobbying members of Congress to support or oppose legislation.[35]

The President's Effect on Decision Making

As we have seen, the president determines whether to sign or veto legislation that reaches his or her desk. But often, before a bill reaches the signing stage, the president's position on it carries enough influence to sway members of Congress, particularly members of the president's political party, to vote for or against the proposed legislation.

President Biden has succeeded in convincing lawmakers to pass his America Rescue Act plan to address COVID relief, just as President Trump succeeded in shepherding his federal tax plan through Congress. Trump was also able to pressure lawmakers into breaking with tradition and use the "nuclear option" (described earlier in this chapter) to confirm his nominees for the U.S. Supreme Court, Neil Gorsuch, and later, Brett Kavanaugh. But he had less success with other measures, including repealing the Affordable Care Act, securing funding to build a wall between the United States and Mexico, and reforming immigration policy. Where he had less success, it is in part because members of Congress were pressured by other entities, including their constituents.[36]

CONCEPT APPLICATION   THINKING CRITICALLY

In 2009, Republican Anh "Joseph" Cao was elected to Congress. In a stunning and unexpected victory, he would represent a heavily Democratic district in New Orleans. Congressman Cao was the first Vietnamese American elected to Congress and was a deeply religious Catholic representing a district that was largely African American. Many in Cao's district lacked health insurance. When the House voted on the Affordable Care Act, Representative Cao faced pressure from both sides. President Obama courted his vote and promised to help Cao's district with federal funding if he did so, but the Republican leadership pressured him to stick with his party. The uninsured in Cao's district might gain if health insurance became easier to obtain. Cao voted yes, becoming the only Republican to vote with Democrats. However, in a later version of the Affordable Care Act, the revised bill diluted language prohibiting funds being spent on abortions, and Cao voted no on that version.

A. Describe how the president attempted to influence Congressman Cao's vote.

B. In the context of the scenario, describe Congressman Cao's chosen voting model.

C. In the context of the scenario, explain how Cao's voting behavior can be influenced by a political party.

Source: https://www.washingtonpost.com/wp-dyn/content/article/2009/11/08/AR2009110815740.html

181

Constituents: The Last Word

Of all the players with a voice in the legislative process, congressional constituents—the people whom the members of Congress represent—wield perhaps the strongest, if indirect, influence with respect to congressional decision making. Most members of Congress want to be reelected, and representing constituents' views (and being able to convince voters that their views are represented well) is a major avenue to reelection to Congress. Thus, constituents influence the legislative process by ensuring that their representatives in Congress work hard to represent the constituents' perspectives and policy interests, whether those concerns are over environmental pollution, crime, or the soaring cost of higher education.

Some research shows that the public's "potential preferences" can motivate legislators to espouse a policy position likely to be embraced by constituents.[37] But other research shows that most voters are not especially vigilant when it comes to monitoring their elected officials in Congress. In fact, only a very small percentage of voters, sometimes called the **attentive public,** pay careful attention to the public policies being debated by Congress and to the votes cast by their representatives and senators. But the fact that the attentive public is a relatively

attentive public
The segment of voters who pay careful attention to political issues.

Partisanship in Congress

THEN

(1980s)
Congress was divided; Democrats controlled the House of Representatives, and Republicans controlled the Senate.

Although incumbents enjoyed a considerable advantage, many congressional districts were a mix of constituents of both major parties.

Partisan voting was evident, but legislators were often forced to base their positions on constituent preferences in addition to their own party loyalty.

NOW

Congress is divided; Democrats control the House of Representatives, and Republicans control the Senate.

Fewer congressional districts are competitive. Many districts are more homogeneous because district boundaries can be drawn with sophisticated computer programs.

With the advent of less competitive districts, legislators are more partisan than their predecessors.

NEXT

- Has the outcome of the 2020 elections increased or decreased party tensions, in your view? Why?

- In recent years, partisanship has increased when there has been a president of one party and a Congress of another. Does such a scenario exist today? What implications does that have for the future of partisanship in Congress for the next several years?

- Increases in technological sophistication could make redistricting an even more exact science. What effect would this change have on partisanship in Congress?

small minority does not mean that votes taken in Congress are insignificant as far as constituents' opinions go. Indeed, if a member of Congress should disregard constituents' views in voting on a major issue, it is quite likely that an opposing candidate or political party will bring this misstep to the public's attention during the individual's next congressional campaign.

The People and Their Elected Representatives

Although members of Congress may make it a priority to represent the viewpoints and interests of their constituents, demographically speaking, they do not represent the American public at large. As Table 4.4 shows, Congress, especially the Senate, is older, whiter, more educated, and more likely to be male than the population as a whole. That said, Congress is not designed to be a perfect sampling of American demographics.[38] Yet Congress is more diverse today than at any other point in history, with recent elections ushering in a slew of historic "firsts" among elected House members, including Representatives Sharice Davids (D-Kans.) and Deb Haaland (D-N.M.), the first Native American women elected to the House of Representatives.

Women in Congress

The year 2020 saw a record number of women's candidacies for Congress and a particularly large number of Democratic women running against Republican House members. In many of these cases, the women candidates said that they were motivated to run because of their objection to President Trump's rhetoric and behavior toward women and because of the policy stances of their Republican representatives, a trend we saw continuing through the 2020 elections. Many women candidates opposed the repeal of the Affordable Care Act. The candidacies also were part of a larger women-centered social movement born in the aftermath of President Trump's election, spawned through marches after his inauguration, kindled by the #MeToo social media protests surrounding sexual harassment, and nurtured through anti–gun violence demonstrations that occurred in the wake of school shootings.

Because of the strong advantage associated with incumbency, many women candidates were not successful, but in some cases, the threat of their candidacies alone caused an unprecedented occurrence: faced with sometimes well-financed and formidable challengers (and several in the wake of allegations of sexual harassment), large numbers of incumbent members of Congress decided to retire. These changes were particularly evident in Republican districts: in 2018, nine House Democrats outright retired (that is, they did not retire in order to pursue a U.S. Senate seat) compared to 25 House Republicans. These retirements presented opportunities for many women candidates in those districts.

Most states have women as part of their congressional delegations. While Congress as a whole is becoming increasingly diverse and a record number of women won seats in 2020, the proportion of women in Congress is not nearly equal to their proportion in the national population. In 2020, 117 women were elected to the House of Representatives, constituting 27 percent of the 435 members. In addition, 24 women (or 24 percent of the 100 members) serve

TABLE 4.4 ▪ Demographic Characteristics of the 115th Congress Compared to the U.S. Population

	House (%)	Senate (%)	Population (%)
Party			
Democrat	53	45	27
Republican	45	53	28
Independent/Unaffiliated	0.2	2	42
Average Age	58 years	63 years	39 years
Sex			
Male	77	74	49
Female	23	26	51
Race			
White	78	93	60
Black	12	3	12
Hispanic (any race)	10	5	19
Asian/Pacific Islands	4	3	8
Native American	1	0	.72
Education			
Bachelor's degree	95	100	30
Master's degree	23	18	9
Law degree	37	53	>1
Ph.D.	5	4	>1
M.D.	5	4	>1

Source: Jennifer E. Manning, *Membership of the 115th Congress: A Profile* (Washington, DC: Congressional Research Service), and U.S. Census Bureau, *Population Estimates,* and The Gallup Organization.

in the Senate. Despite an upward trend, the United States lags behind many industrialized democracies with respect to the proportion of women serving in the national legislature.

Racial and Ethnic Diversity in Congress

As with women, African Americans have historically been underrepresented in Congress. To date, only 10 African Americans have served in the Senate, including two, Hiram Revels and Blanche Bruce, who served during the Reconstruction era that followed the Civil War. After Bruce left the Senate in 1881, no other African American would be elected to that chamber until 1967, when Senator Edward

Brooke (R-Mass.) was elected for one term. More recently, Senator Carol Moseley Braun (D-Ill.) was elected in 1992 and served for one term, and Barack Obama was elected from the state of Illinois in 2004. From 2011 through 2013, no African Americans served in the U.S. Senate, but in 2013, Cory Booker (D-N.J.) was elected to fill the remainder of the term vacated when Senator Frank Lautenberg passed away. Booker was reelected to a full six-year term in 2014, and another in 2020. Booker was joined in the Senate by Tim Scott (R-S.C.), the first African American to be elected that year to the Senate from the South since the Reconstruction era. Before being elected Vice President in 2020, in 2016 California's Kamala Harris became the first mixed race senator. (Harris is Black and Asian American.)

Figure 4.4 traces the increasing success of African Americans in getting elected to the House of Representatives. The figure shows that, as in the Senate, African Americans' initial service in the House came about in the Reconstruction period. But the successes of that era were short-lived, and the numbers of African Americans in Congress would not match those of the immediate post-Reconstruction period until after the civil rights movement of the 1960s. Today, as is the case for women, more African Americans serve in Congress than at any other point in U.S. history, and with each election history continues to be made.

Latinx have seen marked success in gaining representation in Congress in recent years. In 2020, at least six new Latinx legislators were elected to the House, joining 35 incumbents and bringing the total number of representatives of Hispanic heritage to at least 41. Elected in 2020, Sen. Ben Ray Luján (D-N.M.) was elected to the Senate joining four current Latinx members: Senators Catherine Cortez Masto (D-Nev.), Robert Menendez (D-N.J.), Marco Rubio (R-Fla.), and Ted Cruz (R-Tex.). Many states, including New Mexico, California, Texas, and Arizona,

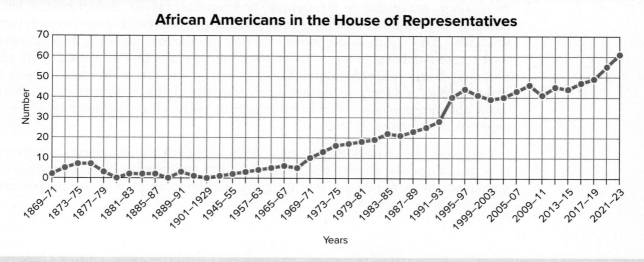

DATA ANALYSIS   PATTERNS AND TRENDS

African Americans in the House of Representatives

FIGURE 4.4 ▪ **African Americans Elected to the House** What explains the rise in African American representation in the House from 1871 through 1887? Why did African Americans' representation fall after 1887? What pattern do you see since the late 1960s, and what political and social changes explain it?

are seeing rising numbers of Latinx elected to state legislatures, providing a pool of candidates who could move on to run for Congress. As women, African Americans, and ethnic minorities make up an increasing proportion of the eligibility pool—the group of people deemed qualified for office—diversity in Congress is sure to grow.

Conclusion: Thinking Critically About What's Next in Congress

Congress is an ever-evolving institution. The national legislature is shaped by the framers' vision that created it; by the groups and individuals that seek to, and do, influence it; and by the broader electorate who vote for the representatives who serve in it. The Constitution's framers ingeniously created a strong legislative system designed to dominate the national government. In doing so, they simultaneously—and significantly—checked the power of the executive. In recent years, Congress has abdicated some of its powers to forceful presidents, which seems to be a result of not only the deep partisanship dividing the chambers but also the intra-party strife that has often forced leaders to fend off attacks from both inside and outside their own parties.

The framers ensured that the legislative branch of the federal government would be responsive to changing times. Today, Congress is more demographically diverse than ever before in history. In recent years, it has also responded to modern challenges, including internal struggles and low approval ratings. Congressional decision making today is influenced by shifting constituencies in a country that is rapidly growing more diverse. How will continued increasing diversity affect congressional decision making in the future?

With Congress well-structured to respond to constituents' needs, ongoing technological advances and the spread of inexpensive technology to more and more citizens mean that members of Congress and their staffs should be increasingly accessible to the people. And representatives' district offices will continue to provide constituents another easily accessed channel through which to convey their needs and interests to their representatives—and through which their representatives, in turn, can monitor the opinions of their constituents so that they may better represent them. But technology also has driven the process of congressional redistricting, rendering more highly partisan districts and creating a more polemic legislature that often prioritizes party issues, sometimes at the expense of the national interest.

Congress has proved itself to be a remarkably flexible institution, responding to changes in society, shifting constituencies, and increasingly diverse members, particularly in recent times. That Congress will become even more diverse over time is certain.

■ References

1. See, for example, David E. Price, *The Congressional Experience: A View from the Hill* (Boulder, CO: Westview, 1992).

2. Samuel Kernell, ed., *James Madison: The Theory and Practice of Republican Government* (Stanford, CA: Stanford University Press, 2003), 5.

3. Richard F. Fenno Jr., *Congressional Travels* (New York: Pearson Longman, 2007).

4. Sue Thomas, *How Women Legislate* (New York: Oxford University Press, 1994).

5. Edmund Burke, *Speeches at His Arrival at Bristol,* November, 3, 1774, http://books.google.com.

6. Ibid.

7. Diana Evans, *Greasing the Wheels: Using Pork Barrel Projects to Build Majority Coalitions in Congress* (New York: Cambridge University Press, 2004).

8. Bret Schulte, "A Bridge (Way) Too Far," *U.S. News and World Report,* 139:5, August 8, 2005, p. 26.

9. www.cagw.org/reporting/pig-book.

10. See, for example, Bruce Cain, John Ferejohn, and Morris Fiorina, *The Personal Vote: Constituency Service and Electoral Independence* (Cambridge, MA: Harvard University Press, 1987).

11. Walter J. Oleszek, *Congressional Procedures and the Policy Process,* 7th ed. (Washington, DC: CQ Press, 2007).

12. See Janet M. Martin, *Lessons from the Hill: The Legislative Journey of an Education Program* (New York: St. Martin's, 1994).

13. Gary Cox and Mathew D. McCubbins, *Setting the Agenda* (Cambridge: Cambridge University Press, 2004).

14. Woodrow Wilson, *Constitutional Government in the United States* (New York: Columbia University Press, 1911), 87.

15. David Butler and Bruce Cain, *Congressional Redistricting: Comparative and Theoretical Perspectives* (New York: Macmillan, 1992).

16. Christopher J. Deering and Steven S. Smith, *Committees in Congress,* 3rd ed. (Washington, DC: Congressional Quarterly, 1997).

17. Garrison Nelson, *Committees in the U.S. Congress, 1947–1992,* 2 vols. (Washington, DC: CQ Press, 1993).

18. Steven S. Smith, Jason M. Roberts, and Ryan J. VanderWielen, *The American Congress,* 5th ed. (New York: Cambridge University Press, 2007).

19. Lawrence C. Dodd and Bruce I. Oppenheimer, *Congress Reconsidered,* 8th ed. (Washington, DC: CQ Press, 2004).

20. https://twitter.com/realDonaldTrump/status/908640949605163010?.

21. www.youtube.com/watch?time_continue=4&v=6NjDrnCWW84.

22. Sarah H. Binder, *Minority Rights, Majority Rule: Partisanship and the Development of Congress* (New York: Cambridge University Press, 1997).

23. David W. Brady and Mathew D. McCubbins, *Party, Process, and Political Change in Congress: New Perspectives on the History of Congress* (Stanford, CA: Stanford University Press, 2002).

24. Gary W. Cox, *Legislative Leviathan: Party Government in the House* (Berkeley: University of California Press, 1993).

25. Joseph Martin Hernon, *Profiles in Character: Hubris and Heroism in the U.S. Senate, 1789–1990* (Armonk, NY: M. E. Sharpe, 1997).

26. Ronald M. Peters Jr., *The American Speakership: The Office in Historical Perspective,* 2nd ed. (Baltimore: Johns Hopkins University Press, 1997).

27. Susan Webb Hammond, *Congressional Caucuses in National Policy Making* (Baltimore: Johns Hopkins University Press, 2001).

28. Mike DeBonis, "Paul Ryan Elected House Speaker," *The Washington Post,* October 29, 2015.

29. Barbara Sinclair, *Majority Leadership in the US House and the Transformation of the US Senate* (Baltimore: Johns Hopkins University Press, 1990).

30. www.cnn.com/2018/03/20/politics/mitch-mcconnell-mueller-defense-schumer/index.html.

31. Barry C. Burden, *Personal Roots of Representation* (Princeton, NJ: Princeton University Press, 2007).

32. Sean Theriault, "Party Polarization in Congress" (paper presented at the annual meeting of the American Political Science Association, Washington, DC, September 1, 2005).

33. Michael J. Malbin, *Unelected Representatives: Congressional Staff and the Future of Representative Government* (New York: Basic Books, 1980).

34. Burdett A. Loomis, *The Contemporary Congress,* 3rd ed. (Boston: Bedford/St. Martin's, 2000).

35. John R. Wright, *Interest Groups and Congress* (New York: Allyn and Bacon, 1996).

36. www.dispatch.com/news/20170202/for-legislators-now-pressures-on-to-meet-constituents.

37. R. Douglas Arnold, *The Logic of Congressional Action* (New Haven, CT: Yale University Press, 1990).

38. For a discussion of the potential goals of demographic representation, see, for example, David T. Canon, "Representing Racial and Ethnic Minorities," in *The Legislative Branch,* eds. Paul J. Quirk and Sarah A. Binder (New York: Oxford University Press, 2005).

▌Key Terms

▪ Multiple Choice Questions

1. Which of the following is an accurate comparison of the House and the Senate?

House	Senate
A. 435 members with representation based on population	100 members with representation equal per state
B. Less formal and structured rules	More formal and structured rules
C. Does not allow discharge petitions	Allows discharge petitions
D. Allows filibusters	Does not allow filibusters

2. Which of the following is an accurate comparison of the trustee and instructed delegate models of representation?

Trustee	Instructed Delegate
A. Legislators should vote based on constituents' views	Legislators should vote contrary to their constituents if they feel it is in the best interests of the country
B. Legislators should follow their conscience when voting	Legislators should act as agents of their constituency
C. Legislators should vote based on their party	Legislators should vote as their staff instructs them to
D. Legislators should vote based on how the president trusts them to vote	Legislators should vote based on PAC campaign contributions

Questions 3 and 4 are based on the graphic below.

The Legislative Process

3. Since the 104th Congress, the following practice was abolished
   A. Hearings
   B. Unanimous consent
   C. Logrolling
   D. Joint referral

4. According to Senate procedure, committee chairs are usually chosen using

    A. Trustee model

    B. Agenda setting

    C. Seniority system

    D. Filibuster

Majority Minority Districts

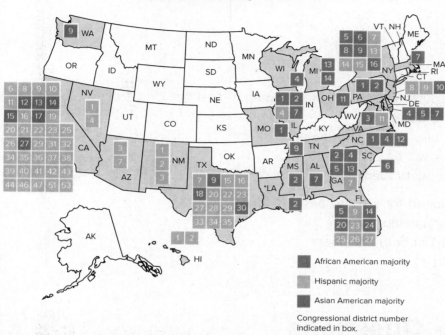

Source: Bell, Peter, and David Wasserman. "Since 1982, Minority Congressional Districts Have Tripled." National Journal, April 13, 2012.

5. The election results in the map above are most likely a result of which of the following Supreme Court rulings?

    A. *Baker v. Carr*

    B. *Shaw v. Reno*

    C. *Brown v. Board of Education*

    D. *Regents of the University of California v. Bakke*

6. Congress derives a significant amount of its power from

    A. necessary and proper clause

    B. ex post facto clause

    C. executive orders

    D. inherent powers clause

7. Which of the following statements about partisanship in Congress is true?

    A. President Trump's leadership has ushered in a new era of bipartisanship

    B. Members of Congress who engage in logrolling further contribute to partisanship

    C. Partisanship is usually at its height before congressional and presidential elections

    D. Divided government frequently leads to more consensus in Congress

	Democrats	Republicans	Other
House	232	198	5
Senate	45	53	2

Use the data above to answer questions 8 & 9.

8. Which term below is a label for the government above?
   A. Divided government
   B. Coalition government
   C. Pork-barrel government
   D. Log-roll government

9. Assuming the president is a Republican, which of the following is most likely to be true?
   A. Legislation will be filibustered easily
   B. The president's revenue bills will be introduced
   C. The president's nominees will be confirmed
   D. Presidential vetos will be overridden

10. Which of the following is required for a bill to become law?
    A. Conference committee proceedings
    B. Passage in identical forms in both chambers
    C. Discharge petition
    D. Cloture

■ Free-Response Questions

Argumentation

Develop an argument in which you decide which model of representation—trustee, instructed delegate, or politico—best achieves the founders' intent for adequate representation of citizens.

In your essay, you must:

- Articulate a defensible claim or thesis that responds to the prompt and establishes a line of reasoning.

- Support your claim with at least TWO pieces of accurate and relevant information:

  - At least ONE piece of evidence must be from one of the following foundational documents:

    — The Constitution of the United States (including the Bill of Rights and subsequent Amendments)
    — Brutus 1
    — *Federalist* No. 51

- Use a second piece of evidence from another foundational document from the list or from your study of civil liberties

- Use reasoning to explain why your evidence supports your claim/thesis

- Respond to an opposing or alternative perspective using refutation, concession, or rebuttal

Concept Application

President Barack Obama signed the budget agreement covering federal spending for the remainder of the current fiscal year on Friday, bringing an end to any remaining fears of a government shutdown.

The bipartisan deal, which won approval Thursday from both the House and Senate, cuts $38.5 billion in spending while funding the government through September 30.

In a White House statement, Obama expressed his objection to two sections of the agreement, which prohibit the use of funds to transfer Guantanamo detainees into the United States and to move detainees into the custody of foreign countries unless specific conditions are met.

"Despite my continued strong objection to these provisions, I have signed this act because of the importance of avoiding a lapse in appropriations for the federal government, including our military activities, for the remainder of fiscal year 2011," the president said.

"Nevertheless, my administration will work with the Congress to seek repeal of these restrictions, will seek to mitigate their effects, and will oppose any attempt to extend or expand them in the future."

The measure passed the Republican-controlled House on a 260-167 vote. The bill would not have passed, however, without support from members of both parties. Fifty-nine members of the GOP majority opposed it, showing the challenge faced by House Speaker John Boehner, R-Ohio, in keeping his conservative Tea Party-infused caucus unified amid politically perilous tax and spending negotiations with the Democrats.

The House vote also reflected growing liberal angst and anger over the impending spending reductions. Only 81 Democrats backed the measure; House Minority Leader Nancy Pelosi, D-California, voted no.

In the Democratic-controlled Senate, the final vote was 81-19.

CNN.com April 15, 2011

After reading the scenario, respond to A, B, and C below:

A. In the context of the scenario, describe a power the president has in the budget process.

B. In the context of the scenario, explain how the use of congressional power described in Part A can be affected by its interaction with the presidency.

C. In the context of the scenario, explain how the interaction between Congress and the presidency can be affected by divided government.

Quantitative Analysis

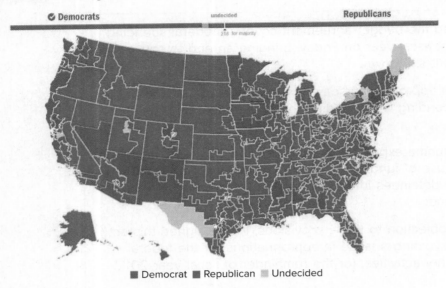

☑ Democrats   undecided   Republicans

218 for majority

■ Democrat ■ Republican ■ Undecided

Use the information graphic above to answer the questions.

A. Identify which party controls a majority of the seats in the House of Representatives.

B. Describe a similarity or difference in party representation in the House across the United States, as illustrated in the information graphic, and draw a conclusion about that similarity or difference.

C. Explain how party representation as shown in the map demonstrates the principle of gerrymandering.

THEN

Presidential power grew over the centuries to "imperial" proportions and then ebbed in the late 20th century in the wake of scandals.

NOW

President Biden seeks to heal a divided nation and guide the nation's recovery from COVID-19.

NEXT

Will President Biden unify a divided American electorate?

Will future presidents use technology in an unfettered and unfiltered manner?

Did President Trump forever change the presidency, or will it revert to the traditional institution it once was?

Carolyn Kaster/AP Images

Chapter Introduction

This Enduring Understanding—*The Presidency has been enhanced beyond its expressed constitutional powers*—will frame your reading of this chapter. You will consider how modern presidents wield considerably greater power than early presidents, despite the fact that President Biden has nearly identical constitutional powers as George Washington did. But the presidency itself has evolved, with a large bureaucracy enabling presidents to assert more power and impressive staffs creating the impression an a "imperial" office.

The tools of presidential power stem from both formal and informal powers. Formal powers are powers expressly delineated to the president in the U.S. Constitution, and informal powers are powers the president enjoys that are not explicitly written in the Constitution. Formal power of the president include vetoing legislation and serving as commander-in-chief of the armed services; informal powers include agenda setting, the president's role in diplomacy, in managing the economy, and in serving as party leader. Both formal and informal presidential powers have expanded throughout our history. For example, in the area of war early in our history when a president deployed troops, it was expected that the Congress had used its power under the Constitution to declare war. Today, presidents deploy troops into hostile situations without formal congressional declarations of war. Today, we also expect the president to lead the congressional agenda and to manage the economy of the United States, though neither of those roles is explicitly written in the Constitution.

While presidential power has expanded greatly, presidents continue to face political battles with the Congress, particularly when there is a divided government, or the president faces a Congress controlled by the opposite political party. Because members of Congress today are highly likely to vote with their party and to oppose a president's initiative in Congress in a divided government, presidents often face obstacles in enacting their legislative agenda in Congress. When facing a Congress reluctant to enact policy, presidents often rely increasingly on executive orders which have the force of law but are not passed through Congress. Presidents can issue executive orders to manage and control agencies within the executive branch of government.

Presidential Elections

The relationship between Americans and their president begins well before a president takes the oath of office. In presidential election years, nonstop campaigning provides ample opportunities for the public to learn about candidates and their positions on issues, as we could see during the 2020 campaign, which offered 11 debates between Democratic candidates in the primaries alone, plus nearly nonstop coverage of the Trump and Biden campaigns. Campaigns are opportunities for voters to familiarize themselves with the policy stances and personal traits of candidates. Campaigns also present many avenues for participation by the people—for example, by volunteering in or contributing to candidates' campaigns or even just by debating candidates' views around the water cooler or on Twitter. Although these opportunities for citizen engagement are especially abundant during a presidential election year, similar chances to get involved arise well before, because potential candidates typically position themselves years in advance of Election Day to secure their party's nomination and to win the general election.

Citizens in each state who vote in their party's primary election choose the delegates to the national conventions, where the parties' nominees are officially chosen. After the nominees have been decided, typically by late August, they and their vice presidential running mates begin their general election campaign. Usually, the parties' choice of nominee is a foregone conclusion by the time of the convention, as was the case in 2020 when Senator Bernie Sanders (I-VT) dropped out of the race in early April, leaving former Vice President Joe Biden the presumptive Democratic nominee. The votes tallied on Election Day determine which presidential candidate's slate of electors will cast their ballots, in accordance with state law. There are 538 electors in the Electoral College, because the number of electors is based on the number of members of Congress—435 in the House of Representatives, 100 in the Senate—plus 3 electors who represent the people of the District of Columbia, though these elected officials are not the actual electors. A presidential candidate today needs a simple majority of electoral votes (270) to win the presidency. On the Monday following the second Wednesday of December, the slate of electors chosen in each state meets in their respective state capitals and casts their electoral votes. The results are then announced in a joint session of Congress in early January. In most presidential elections, however, the winner is known on election night because analysts tabulate the outcome in each state and predict the electoral vote. The winner takes the oath of office as president in inaugural ceremonies on January 20.

■ Presidential Roles and Responsibilities

Newly elected presidents quickly discover that they need to perform a variety of functions each day. Many of these are closely related to the president's constitutionally ascribed duties, including the role of commander in chief of the U.S. armed forces, and others relate to the president's role as chief diplomat. Other roles reflect the growth of the presidency in modern times,[1] whether it was Donald Trump's desire to bring industrial jobs back to the United States, Barack Obama's desire to overhaul health care, George W. Bush's priority of reforming schools, or all presidents' need to keep the economy sound and growing. Presidents also must conduct the "politics" of the job: they must interact with Congress and serve as the leader of their party.[2]

Chief of State

The president's role as chief of state reflects the chief executive's embodiment of the values and ideals of the nation, both within the United States and abroad. The function of chief of state is similar to the ceremonial role played by the constitutional monarch in parliamentary systems such as Great Britain's. In the United States, the role of symbolic leader of the nation enhances the president's image and authority and promotes national unity. We may experience this sense that we are one indivisible nation when, for example, the president, as chief of state, makes a formal state visit to another nation or hosts U.S. Olympic medalists at the White House.

The President's Role in Congressional Agenda Setting

Although the separation of powers precludes the president from actually creating laws, presidents nonetheless have significant legislative power.[3] Presidents can influence Congress by lobbying its members to support or oppose pending legislation and by defining the congressional agenda in the annual presidential State of the Union message, a constitutionally required address to Congress. Presidents also "legislate" when they submit the budget for the entire federal government to Congress annually, although Congress ultimately passes the spending plan.

Today, one of the most important legislative tools at a president's disposal is the authority either to sign legislation into law or to veto it,[4] as described in Chapter 2. Although a **veto** allows the president to check the power of Congress, it also provides Congress with the opportunity to check presidential power by overriding the veto with a two-thirds majority vote.[5] In giving the president the right to veto laws, the Constitution essentially integrates the executive into the legislative process.[6]

veto
The president's constitutional right to reject a law passed by Congress.

The veto has several variations. During a regular legislative session, if the president does not sign or veto a bill within 10 days after receiving it from Congress, the bill becomes law even without the president's consent. But if the president receives a congressional bill to sign and Congress is scheduled to adjourn within 10 days, the president can exercise a **pocket veto**, in which the bill is vetoed if the president takes no action at all.

pocket veto
An indirect veto of legislation wherein the executive retains the bill until it is too late for the legislature to deal with it during their current session.

Figure 5.1 shows that the use of the veto varies widely from president to president. Modern presidents are generally much more likely to veto legislation than their predecessors were. A primary determinant of whether a president will regularly exercise veto power is whether the president's party has a majority in Congress. For example, President Trump did not veto any measures passed by the Republican-controlled Congress in the first two years of his term. However, in 2018, after Democrats won control of the House of Representatives, he vetoed six measures, including three separate Senate resolutions sponsored by Senator Robert Menendez (D-N.J.) that would have prohibited the sale of various weapons and military support systems to Saudi Arabia, the United Arab Emirates, and other nations. Similarly, when Democrats had control of Congress during President Obama's administration, he issued only two vetoes, neither of which was controversial. But after Republicans took control of Congress in 2014, Obama went on to veto 10 additional measures, including a controversial one, the Keystone XL pipeline bill, which would have allowed construction of an oil pipeline running from Alberta, Canada, to Steele City, Nebraska, where it would join an existing pipe. Obama also vetoed another measure that would have repealed his own health care act.

An exception to this trend was the presidency of Franklin D. Roosevelt. As Figure 5.1 shows, during his 12-year term in the White House, Roosevelt issued 372 vetoes, or 12 percent of all presidential vetoes. Roosevelt chalked up this exceptional record despite having strong Democratic majorities in Congress throughout his tenure. But Roosevelt used the veto much differently than most presidents do. Because he was such a strong president, he exercised his veto power to prevent the passage of even small pieces of legislation with which he disagreed. Most presidents save the veto for important legislative matters, because they are unwilling to offend members of Congress over smaller laws that they do not favor.

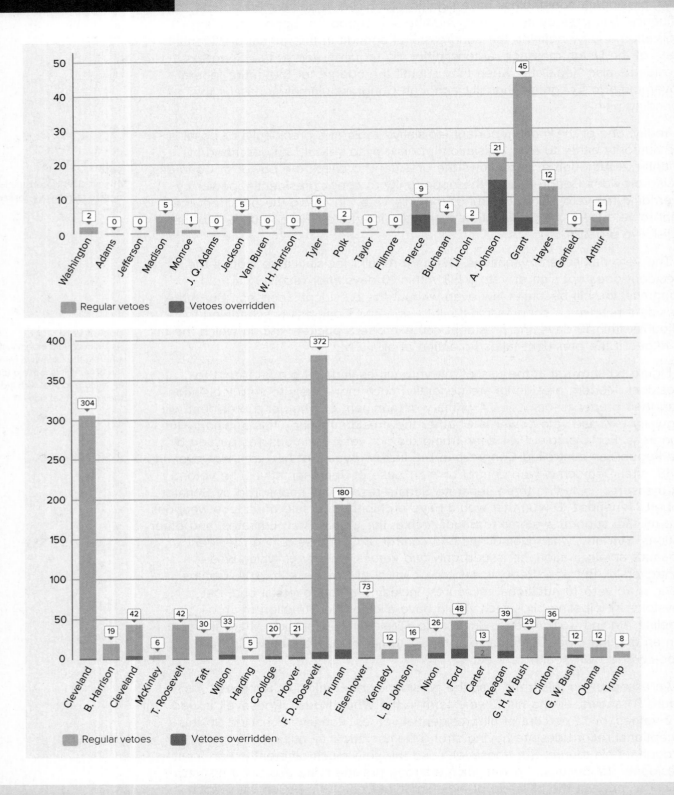

FIGURE 5.1 ■ **Presidential Vetoes, 1789–2020** What does this graph generally indicate about the use of the presidential veto over time? What trend is evident in presidents' use of the veto from the administration of Franklin D. Roosevelt to the present? Why do you think a president is more likely to veto legislation when one party controls Congress and the other controls the presidency?

But presidents today use a different tactic—the signing statement—to influence how policies are to be administered during their tenure in office (see "Thinking Critically" on the following page). A presidential **signing statement** is a written message that the president issues when signing a bill into law. A presidential signing statement may, for example, direct executive departments in how they should implement a law, taking into account constitutional or political considerations. President Trump used this technique frequently to push back against congressional oversight of various pieces of legislation—in effect, attempting to negate legislative intent. For example, when Congress passed the Coronavirus Aid, Relief, and Economic Security Act (the CARES Act), the $2 trillion coronavirus relief bill, President Trump railed against Democratic efforts to oversee how the relief was administered, saying that those provisions presented "constitutional concerns" that interfered with his ability to direct and control the executive branch. Specifically, Democrats wanted to ensure that monies allocated to what they characterized as a corporate "slush fund" were being spent properly, so they legislated the appointment of a special inspector general who would ensure legislative oversight by making regular reports to Congress. But Trump used his signing statement to refuse, stating, "I do not understand, and my administration will not treat, this provision as permitting the [special inspector general for pandemic recovery (SIGPR)] to issue reports to the Congress without the presidential supervision" required by the Constitution.[7]

signing statement
A written message that the president issues upon signing a bill into law.

The use of the controversial practice that constrains congressional decision-making began during the administration of George W. Bush, who used the signing statement frequently despite criticism that he was modifying the intent of the laws by asserting unconstitutional legislative authority. But President Obama actually increased the use of signing statements. During almost every year of Obama's presidency, Congress included a provision in the nation's Defense Authorization Act that sought to ban the transfer of detainees in Guantánamo Bay, Cuba—which at one time held more than 800 individuals the United States identified as potential terrorists—to the United States. President Obama had vowed to close the facility early in his administration but faced significant resistance in Congress and among the public, which led to the inclusion of the bans in the bills. Each year, Obama signed the defense measure but issued a signing statement objecting to Congress's attempts to constrict his efforts to close the facility, saying, "Any attempt to deprive the executive branch of that tool undermines our nation's counterterrorism efforts and has the potential to harm our national security."[8]

Manager of the Economy

Although the Constitution makes no mention of presidential responsibilities with respect to the economy, we can see the enormous power presidents have in this regard by examining priorities of the Trump administration. During the height of the COVID-19 epidemic, a clear priority for President Trump was reopening the economy as soon as possible, despite the opinions of medical experts who called for continued social distancing to decrease the spread of the disease. Even in more mundane times, the president's role in the economy could be seen in President Trump's decision to impose tariffs, or import taxes, on several raw and manufactured goods, including solar panels, washing machines, aluminum, and steel coming from China, in an effort to recover American jobs that had been lost because lower-priced imports were available. Despite the president's intentions, the independent Tax Foundation concluded these tariffs reduced economic

Do Signing Statements Violate Constitutional Checks and Balances?

THE ISSUE: Increasingly, when signing a bill into a law, presidents are using signing statements—written messages that direct executive departments or agencies as to how a law should be implemented. Sometimes the purpose of a signing statement is relatively benign, conveying why the president agrees or disagrees with a bill and contextualizing the bill in light of the president's overall agenda. Sometimes a signing statement seeks to clarify ambiguities written into the bill—that is, to direct the executive branch in how they should implement a law that is not written clearly. But in other cases, the president seemingly circumvents Congress by directing the executive branch to implement a bill in a way that is counter to congressional intention. President Monroe used the first signing statement to highlight his views on legislation, but today this tool is used for policy making. Many scholars and members of Congress have asked this question: Do signing statements usurp power from Congress and erode our system of checks and balances?

YES: Article I of the Constitution grants Congress the power to make law, and the president must abide by the Constitution and not attempt to circumvent the will and authority of Congress. Presidents have the power to veto legislation, and they should use that constitutionally granted power—not a signing statement—if they want to prevent a bill from becoming law. In addition, signing statements that sometimes neutralize one aspect of a law are akin to line item vetoes, which the U.S. Supreme Court declared unconstitutional in *Clinton v. New York*, 524 U.S. 417 (1998).

NO: Because the Constitution does not mention signing statements, it doesn't prohibit them. Instead, the Constitution says that the president has the power to veto any bill passed by Congress (Article 1, section 7) and the authority to confirm that the laws are faithfully executed (Article 2, section 3). Because the president has a constitutional obligation to confirm that the laws are faithfully executed, signing statements offer a logical means of doing so because they direct the executive branch in how laws are to be implemented.

OTHER APPROACHES: It is true that the Constitution makes no mention of signing statements, but that alone is not grounds for either allowing or prohibiting them. The reality is that the president is the ultimate decider in *how* laws are administered, unless implementation of the laws results in a judicial challenge. Therefore, the signing statement is a valid means for a president to direct the executive branch in implementation, but only if it seeks to proscribe how laws are administered rather than circumventing congressional intent. Thus, signing statements should be used only in limited circumstances.

WHAT DO YOU THINK?

1. Do you think signing statements violate checks and balances? Would you support a constitutional amendment prohibiting the practice?

2. Do the judicial or legislative branches have any means to check the president after a signing statement has been issued? How can Congress or the judiciary draw the line to limit the circumstances for using the signing statement?

3. Does your view of whether signing statements violate the Constitution vary depending on which president is using them?

≫ One way presidents try to affect the nation's economy is through the appointment of the Fed chair, who oversees the Federal Reserve Board—a body that plays a crucial role in managing the economy. In 2017, President Trump replaced Obama appointee Janet Yellen with Jerome Powell. Powell was sometimes on the receiving end of criticism from Trump, but he garnered widespread praise for how the Fed handled the economic response to the coronavirus in 2020.

Chip Somodevilla/Getty Images

growth, lowered wages, and decreased employment. Political reaction to the tariffs was somewhat mixed, with many Republicans and most economists criticizing the move and some Democrats supporting the tariffs, hoping they would restore some jobs. But no matter the view, the strong influence of the president on the nation's economy was apparent.

This influence could also be seen in the 2018–2019 federal budget process, during which President Trump and his administration lobbied for and won key changes to the U.S. tax code. Supporters note that some Americans will pay less in taxes for the five years following the budget cycle, but critics point out the serious increase in the national debt and the negative consequences that could have on the national economy. (See Chapter 11 for further discussion of economic policy.) By submitting a budget to Congress, President Trump, like all presidents before him, affects where federal tax dollars are spent and thereby sets the economic priorities of the legislative agenda. Presidents also help to establish the regulatory and economic environment in which businesses must operate, and in that way they can influence economic growth and employment levels.

Central in presidents' oversight of economic performance is the appointment of the Federal Reserve Board ("the Fed") and its chair, who play a crucial role in managing the economy. The position of Fed chair tends to be less partisan than many other appointments, and a given chair often serves under presidents of both political parties. In 2018, President Trump surprised many by choosing not to renominate Janet Yellen, who President Obama had appointed as Fed chair, as presidents often renominate chairs from previous administrations if the economy is growing. But Trump chose Jerome Powell, a member of the Fed since Obama nominated him in 2012, to be the new chair. While Powell enjoys a reputation as a bipartisan consensus builder, for years he evoked criticism and scorn from President Trump, who said that he regretted appointing Powell to the post. But in the wake of the coronavirus, Powell was widely praised for the Fed's swift and large-scale reaction to the economic component of the crisis. For example, the Fed quickly made congressionally authorized money available to loan to businesses and state and local governments to speed the economic recovery.

The appointment of a Fed chair has a lot to do with consumer confidence, as well as with support from economically influential individuals on Wall Street, including investment bankers, stockbrokers, and mortgage lenders. The fact that a Fed action (such as increasing the interest rate that banks charge one another for loans, which affects other interest rates charged to private individuals and businesses) can send the stock market plummeting sheds light on why presidential appointments to the Fed are watched so closely.

Chief Diplomat

Serving in the capacity of chief diplomat, the president (along with advisers) shapes and administers the nation's foreign policy. Supported by a wide array of foreign policy resources, including the State Department, the National Security Council, the Central Intelligence Agency, and the various branches of the U.S. military, the president creates and administers foreign policy. In setting foreign policy, the president can act more unilaterally than with most domestic policies. Members of Congress, who, in reflection of their constituents' main interests, tend to be concerned primarily with domestic policy issues, are much less likely to challenge presidents in the foreign policy arena.

As chief diplomat, the president, in conjunction with his or her staff, negotiates treaties and other international agreements with foreign nations and represents the United States at international summits. The president also has the authority to enter into an **executive agreement,** a kind of international agreement. Executive agreements are based on the constitutional authority vested in the president and, unlike treaties, they may not be binding on future presidents, nor do they require Senate approval.

The Constitution also empowers the president to appoint **ambassadors** to other nations. As high-ranking diplomats, ambassadors are the official representatives of the United States in their host nation. Ambassadors' duties vary widely, depending on the locale of their appointment.

Members of the diplomatic corps tend to be background players, developing decades of expertise and deep understanding of the specific regions in their portfolio. But in 2019, a spotlight was shone on their world when several career diplomats were called to testify in the impeachment hearing concerning allegations that President Trump had leveraged U.S. aid to Ukraine in order to force an investigation of Joe Biden, his political rival. Following their testimony, several diplomats became objects of scorn in presidential tweets, a marked contrast with the respect presidents typically pay to the diplomatic corps.

Civilian Leader of the Military

As commander in chief, the president is the supreme military commander of the U.S. Army, Navy, Air Force, Marines, and Coast Guard. Counseled by advisers, the president decides when to send troops into battle and sets military strategy in times of both peace and war.[9]

While the Constitution grants the president the power to be commander in chief, the president is constrained by the powers granted to other branches, specifically the power of Congress to declare war. At various times, Congress has granted the president extraordinary latitude in using the military, but at other times it has sought to rein in the unchecked use of force.

executive agreement
An international agreement between the United States and other nations, not subject to Senate approval and in effect only during the administration of the president who negotiates the agreement.

ambassadors
Official representatives of the United States in host nations.

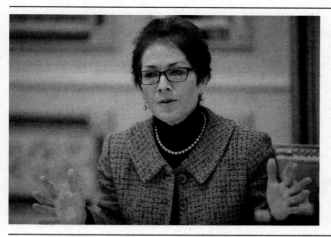

>> The diplomatic corps took center stage in 2019, when several career diplomats, including former U.S. Ambassador to Ukraine Marie Yovanovitch, testified in the impeachment hearing of President Trump concerning allegations that Trump had leveraged U.S. aid to Ukraine in order to force an investigation of Joe Biden. In general, however, diplomats tend to be background players, developing decades of expertise and deep understanding of the specific regions in their portfolio.

photowalking/Shutterstock

Party Leader

One of the most important domestic roles for the president is political: the function of party leader. Such a role is sometimes difficult, particularly given the fractured nature of both political parties. But President Trump assumed the role of party leader and succeeded in attracting candidates willing to embrace his agenda and message. While President Trump's popularity was high in some areas of the country, in other areas Republican members of the House and Senate faced constituencies who had low opinions of the president and so sometimes attempted to distance themselves from him. During Trump's first campaign in 2016, many in the Republican Party establishment were at odds with Trump, leading to concern about his ability to lead the party that he had vocally criticized and whose members had often criticized him. But Trump seized control of the GOP, effectively silencing many of his critics within the Republican Party.

As chief of one of the two main parties, the president is a symbolic leader for the party members and asserts influence in the party's operations by selecting the national party chair and serving as the party's premier fund raiser. The presidential function of party leader has become even more significant in recent White House administrations, with presidents working ever more aggressively to promote the reelection of candidates from their party by ensuring that enough money is available for their campaigns.

The president also acts as party head in the day-to-day operations of the executive branch, because many of the staff appointments to the White House office, cabinet, subcabinet, ambassadorships, and judiciary typically come from party ranks. Finally, at the end of a president's term, the president likely campaigns on behalf of the party's new presidential nominee.

Chief Executive

As the nation's leader in domestic and foreign policy initiatives, the president serves as chief executive. In this capacity, the president appoints the *secretaries* (top administrators) of the cabinet—the 15 departments of the federal government—as well as the heads of other federal government agencies charged with developing and implementing the administration's policy. As chief executive, the president also appoints other staff members and numerous advisers, including staff in the Executive Office of the President. In the capacity of chief executive, the president determines how the bureaucracy will implement the laws Congress has passed and which policies—those concerning education, crime, social welfare, and so on—will be emphasized.[10]

The President and the Executive Branch

As chief executive, the president is constitutionally charged with ensuring that the "laws be faithfully executed." Today, this responsibility means that the president oversees a bureaucracy of more than four million government employees, including the members of the military, while presiding over an astonishing annual federal budget of nearly *$4 trillion*. In addition, as we now consider, the president is the leader of the executive branch of government, which includes the vice president, the cabinet, the offices within the White House, and the entire federal bureaucracy.

The Vice President's Role

Benjamin Franklin once supposedly referred to the vice president as "his superfluous excellency."[11] This observation on the vice presidential office matches the perceptions of many Americans fairly well. But although the media and the public tend to ignore the vice presidency and to marginalize the responsibilities of the second-in-command, vice presidents have an enormously important function. They are first in the line of succession to the presidency if the president should die or become incapacitated. Only eight presidents have died while in office, and although presidential succession may not be the foremost consideration in selecting a running mate for many presidential candidates, it can be an issue. Bill Clinton, in describing his selection of Tennessee Senator Al Gore as his running mate, explained that his choice of Gore in part reflected Clinton's belief that Gore would make a good president "if something happened to me."[12]

THE VICE PRESIDENT'S JOB Many vice presidents serve a largely ceremonial function, performing such activities as attending state dinners, visiting foreign nations, and attending the funerals of foreign dignitaries. But vice presidents may have more substantive responsibilities, depending on their skills and the needs of the administration. Sometimes, for example, a vice president acts as legislative liaison with Congress, particularly if the vice president has more experience in dealing with the legislative branch than the president. For example, before being elected governor of Indiana, Vice President Mike Pence served a dozen years in Congress, including a stint as chair of the House Republican Conference, where he forged deep relationships with fellow Republicans, and these relationships benefited the Trump administration. In other instances, vice presidents' policy expertise is a crucial resource for the administration. In the case of Vice President Dick Cheney, experience in foreign policy and national security determined the pivotal role he played in developing the foreign policy of George W. Bush's administration.

>> When presidential nominees select a running mate, they often strive to increase their own chances of being elected to the presidency and of being able to govern effectively after taking office. Joe Biden chose an historic running mate: the nation's first female, first Black, and first Indian-American vice president.

Paul Kitagaki Jr./Zuma Wire/Alamy Stock Photo

Although vice presidents are only "a heartbeat away" from the presidency, their own election to the presidency (should they decide to run) is not ensured when their term as second-in-command has ended. It is true that several vice presidents—among them, George H. W. Bush and Lyndon B. Johnson—have won election to the presidency in their own right, but many other former vice presidents have failed to win the highest office.[13] Notably, Al Gore, Walter Mondale, and Gerald Ford (the vice presidents of Bill Clinton, Jimmy Carter, and Richard Nixon, respectively) all went down to defeat at the polls in their bids for the White House.

CHOOSING A VICE PRESIDENT In selecting a vice presidential running mate, traditionally, presidential candidates take into account several considerations. Would-be presidents strive for a **balanced ticket;** that is, to broaden their appeal to the electorate and increase their chances of getting elected, they select a running mate who brings diversity of ideology, geographic region, age, gender, race, or ethnicity to the slate. Such was the case in 2020, when Democrat Joe Biden chose Kamala Harris. Early in the presidential campaign, Biden had promised to select a female running mate, and the choice of Harris was also designed to bring other constituencies, including Black voters and younger voters, into the Democratic fold. Similarly, when Republican presidential nominee Donald Trump chose Indiana Governor Mike Pence in 2016, many party supporters were heartened to have an experienced, conservative politician on the ticket who could balance Trump's lack of political experience. Back in 2008, the selection of Joe Biden as vice president was designed to counterbalance Barack Obama in terms of age (Biden was 65 years old, compared with Obama's 47), experience (Biden had served in the Senate since 1972, Obama since 2000), and expertise (Biden was chair of the Senate Foreign Relations Committee; Obama had faced media criticism about his lack of foreign policy experience).

balanced ticket
The selection of a running mate who brings diversity of ideology, geographic region, age, gender, race, or ethnicity to the slate.

The Cabinet

Since George Washington's presidency, every president has depended on the advice of a **cabinet,** the group of experts chosen by the president to serve as advisers on running the country. These advisers serve as the heads of each of the executive departments. Figure 5.2 shows the 15 departments of the cabinet and their respective websites. Each cabinet member except the head of the Department of Justice is called the *secretary* of that department. The head of the Department of Justice is called the attorney general.

cabinet
The group of experts chosen by the president to serve as advisers on running the country.

FIGURE 5.2 **The Departments of the President's Cabinet** The presidential cabinet consists of the 15 departments shown in the figure. Which department is concerned with finding alternatives to the use of fossil fuels? Which one addresses the problems of the dedicated men and women who served in Afghanistan and Iraq? Which department arose as a result of the September 11, 2001, terrorist strikes?

President George W. Bush created the newest department, the Department of Homeland Security, in 2002. This department is charged with increasing the nation's preparedness, particularly with respect to catastrophic events like terrorist attacks and natural disasters. George Washington's cabinet consisted of the heads of only four departments—justice, state, treasury, and war. (The last is now called the Department of Defense.) Subsequent presidents added other departments.

Each president may also designate cabinet rank to other advisers whose agencies are not permanent cabinet departments. Typically, presidents have specified that their national security adviser, director of the Office of Management and Budget, and administrator of the Environmental Protection Agency be included in their administration's cabinet. In addition to these advisers, President Trump included the Small Business Administrator in his cabinet.

Today, presidents and the public typically scrutinize presidential cabinet appointments to determine whether, in the words of Bill Clinton, they "look like America." As the data in Table 5.1 confirm, this is a relatively new gauge, since only three women and two members of ethnic minority groups had served in presidential cabinets until the Carter administration. Although President Trump's cabinet was less diverse than those of recent presidents, before his tenure, presidential cabinets were becoming increasingly diverse, with significant strides made during President Bill Clinton's administration.[14] Clinton became the first president to appoint a woman to any of the "big four" posts when he named Janet Reno attorney general and Madeleine Albright secretary of state. George W. Bush named Colin Powell the first black secretary of state, and when Powell resigned, Bush replaced him with Condoleezza Rice, an African American woman who had served previously as national security adviser.

TABLE 5.1 ■ Women and Minorities Appointed to Presidential Cabinets

President	Number of Women* Cabinet Members	Number of Minority** Cabinet Members	Tenure
Trump	6	4	2017–2021
Obama	14	15	2009–2017
G.W. Bush	7	10	2001–2009
Clinton	13	11	1993–2001
G.H.W. Bush	4	3	1989–1993
Reagan	4	2	1981–1989
Carter	4	1	1977–1981
Ford	1	1	1974–1977
Nixon	0	0	1969–1974
Johnson	0	1	1963–1969
Kennedy	0	0	1961–1963
Eisenhower	1	0	1953–1961
Truman	0	0	1945–1953
F. Roosevelt	1	0	1933–1945

*Includes cabinet and cabinet-level appointments.

**Includes African Americans, Latinos/as, and Asian Americans.

Sources: Brigid C. Harrison, *Women in American Politics: An Introduction* (Belmont, CA: Wadsworth Publishing, 2003); the Center for the American Woman and Politics, National Information Bank on Women in Public Office, Eagleton Institute of Politics, Rutgers University.

The Obama administration continued the trend of increasing diversity. During his two terms, President Obama appointed 14 female cabinet members, including several to "big four" posts: Hillary Clinton served as secretary of state during his first term, and Loretta Lynch served as attorney general during his second. Obama also appointed a record number of racial and ethnic minorities to cabinet posts. President Trump's cabinet was less diverse than his immediate predecessors': Secretary of Housing and Urban Development Benjamin S. Carson Sr. was the only African American, and Secretary of Labor Alexander Acosta was the only Hispanic. Then-Secretary of Transportation Elaine L. Chao is Asian American, and she was joined by Secretary of Education Betsy DeVos and CIA Director Gina Haspel (the first woman to serve in that position) in the Trump cabinet. Other women to serve included Secretary of Homeland Security Kirstjen Nielsen and Small Business Administrator Linda McMahon, both of whom resigned their posts in 2019, as well as United Nations Ambassador Nikki Haley, who left the administration in 2018.

The Executive Office of the President

Executive Office of the President (EOP)
The offices, councils, and boards that help the president to carry out his day-to-day responsibilities.

Whereas the cabinet usually functions as an advisory board for the president, the **Executive Office of the President (EOP)** typically is the launchpad for the implementation of policy. The offices, councils, and boards that compose the EOP help the president to carry out the day-to-day responsibilities of the presidency and similarly assist the first lady and the vice president in their official activities. The EOP also coordinates policies among different agencies and departments.

Among the EOP offices, several are particularly important, including the White House Office, the National Security Council, the Office of Management and Budget, and the Council of Economic Advisers. These offices are crucial not only because of the prominent issues with which they deal but also because of their strong role in developing and implementing policy in these issue areas.[15]

White House Office (WHO)
The office that develops policies and protects the president's legal and political interests.

THE WHITE HOUSE OFFICE Playing a pivotal role in most presidential administrations, **White House Office (WHO)** staff members develop policies favored by the presidential administration and protect the president's legal and political interests. They research policy and keep the president informed about policy issues on the horizon. WHO staffers also regularly interact with members of Congress, their primary goal being to get presidential policy priorities enacted into law. They strive to ensure that those policies, once passed into law, are administered in keeping with the president's expectations.

chief of staff
Among the most important staff members of the White House Office (WHO); serves as both an adviser to the president and the manager of the WHO.

press secretary
The president's spokesperson to the media.

White House counsel
The president's lawyer.

Because of the enormous influence of staff members in the White House Office, presidents take pains to ensure their loyalty and trustworthiness. Among the top staff members of the White House Office is the **chief of staff,** who serves as both an adviser to the president and the manager of the WHO. Other staff members with clout include the **press secretary** (the president's spokesperson to the media) and the **White House counsel** (the president's lawyer). The president's secretary and appointments secretary are also influential WHO employees; they act as gatekeepers by controlling access to the president by other staffers and by members of Congress and the cabinet.

NATIONAL SECURITY COUNCIL The president consults members of the **National Security Council (NSC)** on domestic and foreign matters related to national security. Since its creation in 1947 during the Truman administration,[16] the NSC has advised presidents on key national security and foreign policy decisions and assisted in the implementation of those decisions by coordinating policy administration among different agencies. For example, once the president has decided on a specific policy, the NSC might coordinate its implementation among the Department of State, the Central Intelligence Agency, various branches of the military, and diplomatic officials.

The president officially chairs the National Security Council. Its other regular members include the vice president, the secretary of defense, the secretary of state, the secretary of the treasury, and the assistant to the president for national security affairs, often called the **national security advisor,** who is responsible for administering the day-to-day operations of the NSC and its staff. Other administration officials serve the NSC in advisory capacities or are invited to meetings when matters concerning their area of expertise are being decided.

OFFICE OF MANAGEMENT AND BUDGET Once part of the Department of the Treasury, the **Office of Management and Budget (OMB**—originally called the Bureau of the Budget) has been a separate office within the EOP since 1939. Its chief responsibility is to create the president's annual budget, which the president submits to Congress each January. The budget outlines all of the anticipated revenue that the government will receive in the next year, usually from taxes and fees paid by businesses and individuals. The budget also lists the anticipated expenditures for the coming year, detailing how much money the various departments and agencies in the federal government will have available to spend on salaries, administrative costs, and programs. The OMB is among the president's most important agencies for policy making and policy implementation.

The director of the Office of Management and Budget, a presidential appointee confirmed by the Senate, has a staff of about 600 career civil servants. In recent decades, the OMB director has figured prominently in presidential administrations and typically has been designated a member of the cabinet. The director's job is complex. He or she interacts extensively with Congress, trying to ensure that the budget that passes resembles the president's proposed budget as closely as possible. The director also lobbies members of Congress with the goal of ensuring that the key provisions of the budget that are important to the president remain intact in the congressionally approved version.

Once Congress approves the budget, the director of the OMB turns attention to its implementation, because it is the job of the OMB staff to manage the budget's execution by federal departments and agencies—to ensure that monies are spent on their designated purposes and that fraud and financial abuse do not occur. This managerial responsibility of the OMB was the reasoning behind the change in the office's name (from the Bureau of the Budget) in 1970.

National Security Council (NSC)
Consisting of top foreign policy advisers and relevant cabinet officials, this is an arm of the Executive Office of the President that the president consults on matters of foreign policy and national security.

national security advisor
The assistant to the president for national security affairs, advisor to the president on national security policy, and administrator over the day-to-day operations of the National Security Council.

Office of Management and Budget (OMB)
The office that creates the president's annual budget.

■ Presidential Succession

No examination of the executive branch would be complete without considering the question, What happens if the president dies? Presidential succession is determined by the Presidential Succession Law of 1947. But sometimes incapacitation other than death prevents presidents from fulfilling their duties. In such cases, the Twenty-Fifth Amendment, ratified in 1967, determines the course of action.

When the President Dies in Office

When the president dies, the course of action is clear in most cases: The vice president assumes the presidency. Such was the situation when Harry S Truman became president upon Franklin D. Roosevelt's death from natural causes in 1945 and when Lyndon B. Johnson was sworn in as president after the assassination of John F. Kennedy in 1963. Vice presidents sometimes fill the unexpired term of their president for reasons other than the president's death, as when Gerald Ford acceded to the presidency upon the resignation of Richard Nixon after the Watergate scandal.

The Presidential Succession Law of 1947 determines presidential succession if the vice president also dies or is unable to govern. Table 5.2 shows that after the vice president, the next in line for the presidency is the Speaker of the House of Representatives, then the president pro tem of the Senate, followed by a specified order of the members of the cabinet. Notice that as new cabinet departments have been established, their secretaries have been added to the bottom of the line of succession. As a precaution, at the State of the Union address each year, one cabinet member is chosen not to attend the president's speech before Congress, but rather, to stay behind at the White House. This measure ensures that if a catastrophe should occur in Congress during the address, someone in the line of succession will be able to assume the duties of the president.

>> When a president dies in office, the line of presidential succession is clear. Crowds watched the funeral procession for President Franklin D. Roosevelt, who died in office in 1945 and was succeeded by his vice president, Harry S Truman (1945–1953).

George Skadding//Time Life Pictures/Getty Images

TABLE 5.2 ▪ The Line of Presidential Succession

1.	Vice president	10.	Secretary of commerce
2.	Speaker of the House of Representatives	11.	Secretary of labor
3.	President pro tem of the Senate	12.	Secretary of health and human services
4.	Secretary of state	13.	Secretary of housing and urban development
5.	Secretary of the treasury	14.	Secretary of transportation
6.	Secretary of defense	15.	Secretary of energy
7.	Attorney general	16.	Secretary of education
8.	Secretary of the interior	17.	Secretary of veterans affairs
9.	Secretary of agriculture	18.	Secretary of homeland security

When the President Cannot Serve: The Twenty-Fifth Amendment

What happens when a president is alive but unable to carry out the responsibilities of the office? Until the ratification of the Twenty-Fifth Amendment in 1967, the course of action was not clear. Such was the case in 1881, when an assassin shot President James Garfield, and yet Garfield lived two and a half months before succumbing to his injuries. In another such instance, President Woodrow Wilson was so ill during his last months in office that he was incapacitated. First Lady Edith Wilson assumed some of his responsibilities and decision making. Questions about presidential health also arose toward the end of Franklin D. Roosevelt's tenure, and during Dwight D. Eisenhower's administration, the president authorized Vice President Richard Nixon to determine whether Eisenhower, who was battling a series of illnesses, was competent to govern. President John F. Kennedy, who suffered from a host of physical ailments, including severe, chronic back pain and Addison's disease, similarly empowered Vice President Lyndon B. Johnson. In an informal agreement, the men arranged that if Kennedy was physically unable to communicate with Johnson, Johnson was authorized to assume the presidency.

After Kennedy's assassination, the ratification of the Twenty-Fifth Amendment (1967) finally put codified procedures in place for dealing with an incapacitated president. According to the Twenty-Fifth Amendment, if a president believes he or she is unable to carry out the duties of the office, the president must notify Congress, and the vice president becomes the acting president until the president can resume authority. The amendment would apply in the case when a president is anesthetized for surgery, for example, or perhaps recuperating from a debilitating illness.

In other situations, a president might be incapable of carrying out the duties of office and also incapable of notifying Congress. In such a case, the Twenty-Fifth Amendment requires that the vice president and a majority of the cabinet notify Congress, and the vice president becomes the acting president. If a question arises as to whether the president is fit to reassume the duties of office, a two-thirds vote of Congress is required for the acting president to remain.

■ Sources of Presidential Power

The presidency that Joe Biden assumed on January 20, 2021, scarcely resembled George Washington's presidency in the 1790s. From the late 18th century to today, the powers of the president have evolved, reflecting the expansion of the federal government, changes in public attitudes about the proper role of government, and the personalities and will of those who have served as president.

In describing the powers that would guide presidents for centuries to come, the framers of the Constitution created a unique office. These visionary authors had lived through a repressive era in which an authoritarian monarch had exercised absolute power. They subsequently had witnessed the new American nation's struggles under the ineffectual Articles of Confederation, in which the federal government had too little power and the states too much. Thus, the framers sought to establish an office that would balance the exercise of authority with the preservation of the rights and the will of the people.

Given their colonial experience, it was no surprise that the framers granted the president both *expressed powers* and *inherent powers* in the Constitution. Congress grants presidents additional powers, called *statutory powers*, through congressional action. We consider these various powers in this section.

Additional presidential powers have emerged over time. These newer authorities reflect both changes in the institution of the presidency and shifts in popular views on the appropriate role of government and the president. These powers include emergency powers granted in Supreme Court decisions and powers that, though not formalized, are given to presidents by the public through election mandates, presidential popularity, or unified public opinion on a particular issue or course of action.

The Constitution: Expressed Powers

The primary source of presidential power comes from the Constitution in the form of the **expressed powers,** which are those enumerated in the Constitution. Article II, Sections 2 and 3, list the following powers of the president:

commander in chief
The president's role as supreme officer in charge of the country's armed forces.

- ■ Serve as **commander in chief** of the armed forces.

- ■ Appoint heads of the executive departments, ambassadors, Supreme Court justices, people to fill vacancies that occur during the recess of the Senate, and other positions.

- ■ Pardon crimes, except in cases of impeachment.

- ■ Enter into treaties, with two-thirds consent of the Senate.

- ■ Give the State of the Union address to Congress.

- Convene the Congress.

- Receive ambassadors of other nations.

- Commission all officers of the United States.

The expressed powers outlined in the Constitution provide a framework for presidential responsibilities and an outline of presidential power. They also shape how presidents themselves develop their authority.

The Constitution: Inherent Powers

One of the principal ways by which the Constitution provides for presidents themselves to assert additional powers, beyond those expressed in the Constitution, is the **take care clause,** which states that "the executive Power shall be vested in a President of the United States of America" and that the president "shall take Care that the Laws be faithfully executed." On the basis of that clause, presidents throughout U.S. history have asserted various **inherent powers,** which are powers that are not expressly granted by the Constitution but are inferred.

take care clause
The constitutional basis for inherent powers, which states that the president "shall take Care that the Laws be faithfully executed."

President Thomas Jefferson exercised inherent powers in his far-reaching Louisiana Purchase in 1803. Jefferson authorized this $15 million purchase of 800,000 square miles of land, even though the Constitution did not authorize any such action on the part of a president. Interestingly, in the civic discourse over the Constitution, Jefferson, an Anti-Federalist, had argued for states' rights and against a strong central government and a powerful presidency. Jefferson had believed that the powers enumerated in the Constitution defined the powers of the government. But Jefferson thought that the purchase of the Louisiana Territory was of crucial strategic and economic importance. He believed that the deal was key to the United States averting war with France and to securing the port of New Orleans, which was essential for the new American republic's fortunes in trade. Jefferson could not wait for a constitutional amendment to authorize the transaction, and so he forged ahead with the purchase. Congress and many Americans of the day agreed with his actions, and so there were no negative consequences to them.

President Franklin D. Roosevelt also drew on the inherent powers when he expanded the size of the federal government in the 1930s to administer his New Deal programs, designed to relieve the economic and human distress of the Great Depression. Beginning in 2002, President George W. Bush used the inherent powers when he suspended the civil liberties of foreign nationals being held in a military prison at the U.S. naval base at Guantánamo Bay, Cuba, as part of the administration's war on terror. The individuals at Guantánamo Bay were detained indefinitely for questioning about their possible terrorist activities. These instances of presidents' exercise of inherent powers generated varying degrees of controversy among Americans of the times.

President Obama also exercised his inherent powers by again expanding the scope of the federal government through passage of the Patient Protection and Affordable Care Act of 2010, also known as Obamacare. This health care reform act, which was approved by the Democrat-controlled Congress at President Obama's behest, expanded Medicaid, subsidized health insurance premiums for middle-income families, offered incentives for employers to provide health care to their employees, and mandated that uninsured individuals purchase government-approved health insurance. The measure, which has been vehemently opposed by many Republicans in Congress since its passage, marked the entrance of the federal government into previously uncharted territory.

Statutory Powers

statutory powers
Powers explicitly granted to presidents by congressional action

The Constitution's expressed and inherent powers provided a foundation for presidential power that has evolved over time. Those powers have been supplemented by additional powers, including **statutory powers,** which are explicitly granted to presidents by congressional action.

An example of such a grant of statutory powers is the 1996 Line Item Veto Act, which gave the president the power to strike down specific line items on an appropriations bill while allowing the rest of the bill to become law. In 1997 the Supreme Court declared the line-item veto unconstitutional on the grounds that the congressional action violated the separation of powers.

Special Presidential Powers

Presidents also have special powers that have evolved from various sources, including the Constitution and Supreme Court decisions. These powers, which numerous presidents have exercised, have come to be regarded as accepted powers and privileges of the presidency. They include *executive orders, emergency powers,* and *executive privilege.*

Evolution of the Modern Presidency

THEN

(1970s)
The presidency had become an increasingly powerful institution, shaped by the predecessors of Richard Nixon, who assumed office in 1969.

The presidency supplanted Congress as the epicenter of power in the federal government.

Backlash against abuses of executive power in the Nixon administration paved the way for the election of Jimmy Carter, a comparatively weak president.

NOW

President Trump relied on unprecedentedly bold tactics to act as a unilateral actor.

Presidential exercise of authority in the foreign policy realm serves to limit Congress's ability to rein in presidential power.

While Democrats decried President Trump's uses of executive power, even members of his own party sometimes objected to his actions.

NEXT

- Will a parallel backlash against President Trump's exercise of authority occur, like the one seen in the post-Nixon era?

- What public policy issues will likely dominate in the months and years to come? How will these issues influence the ways presidential power is exercised?

- What conditions facilitate the creation of "imperial" presidencies? Do these conditions exist now?

EXECUTIVE ORDERS The president has the power to issue **executive orders** that have the force of law. Executive orders carry the same weight as congressional statutes and have been used in a variety of circumstances to guide the executive branch's administrative functions.[17] Executive orders have very few limitations and stipulations, though one limitation is that presidents cannot use them to create new taxes or appropriate funds, because the Constitution reserves those powers for Congress. In general, executive orders:

- Direct the enforcement of congressional statutes or Supreme Court rulings.

- Enforce specific provisions of the Constitution.

- Guide the administration of treaties with foreign governments.

- Create or change the regulatory guidelines or practices of an executive department or agency.

Executive orders can be an important strategic tool, because they convey the president's priorities to the bureaucracy that implements the laws. For example, in 1948 President Harry Truman signed Executive Order 9981, which states, "It is hereby declared to be the policy of the President that there shall be equality of treatment and opportunity for all persons in the armed services without regard to race, color, religion, or national origin."[18] This executive order effectively banned segregation in the U.S. military. Why would Truman issue an executive order instead of working for congressional passage of a statute that would desegregate the military? Many analysts think that Truman, who ardently believed that the military should be desegregated, not only doubted that Congress would pass such a measure but also faced pressure from early civil rights activists who had pledged an African American boycott of military service if the military was not desegregated.

EMERGENCY POWERS Broad powers that a president exercises during times of national crisis have been invoked by presidents since Abraham Lincoln's claim to **emergency powers** during the Civil War. Lincoln used emergency powers during the war to suspend the civil liberties of alleged agitators, to draft state militia units into national service, and to federalize the governance of southern states after the war. One hundred and fifty years later, President Trump used emergency powers to declare a national state of emergency during the coronavirus epidemic, thus enabling the federal government to coordinate a response through the Federal Emergency Management Agency and to allocate money to help with both disease control and economic recovery, including the authorization of funds to aid state and local governments.

In 1936, the U.S. Supreme Court acknowledged the existence of presidential emergency powers in *United States v. Curtiss-Wright Export Corp.*[19] In this case, the U.S. government charged the Curtiss-Wright Corporation with conspiring to sell 15 machine guns to Bolivia, in violation of a joint resolution of Congress and a presidential proclamation. Without congressional approval, President Franklin D. Roosevelt had ordered an embargo on the machine-gun shipment. The Court supported Roosevelt's order, ruling that the president's powers, particularly in foreign affairs, are not limited to those powers expressly stated in the Constitution. The justices also stated that the federal government is the primary actor in foreign affairs and that the president, in particular, has inherent powers related to the constitutionally derived duties in foreign relations.

executive order
The power of the president to issue orders that carry the force of law.

emergency powers
Broad powers exercised by the president during times of national crisis.

EXECUTIVE PRIVILEGE Presidents also can exercise **executive privilege,** the authority of the president and other executive officials to refuse to disclose information concerning confidential conversations or national security to Congress or the courts. In invoking executive privilege, presidents draw on the idea that the Constitution's framework of separation of powers justifies the withholding of certain information from Congress or the judiciary,[20] a claim initially asserted when George Washington refused to grant Congress access to all documents pertaining to treaty negotiations. Typically, presidents claim executive privilege so that they can get advice from aides without fear that such conversations might be made public or scrutinized by members of Congress or the judiciary. Presidents also have invoked executive privilege when negotiating foreign policies with other heads of state, to shield these leaders from having sensitive negotiations examined by the other branches of the federal government.

On occasion, the judicial branch of the federal government has successfully challenged executive privilege. For example, when President Richard Nixon refused to turn over tapes of Oval Office conversations to a special prosecutor investigating the Watergate scandal in 1974, the Supreme Court intervened. In *United States v. Richard M. Nixon*, the Court asserted that although executive privilege does exist, it was not applicable regarding the tapes because President Nixon's claim of executive privilege concerning the tapes was too broad.[21]

In general, the courts have allowed executive privilege in cases where a clear issue of separation of powers exists—as with respect to international negotiations and conversations regarding matters of policy or national security. The courts have tended to limit the use of executive privilege when presidents have exercised it in an effort to prevent the revelation of misdeeds by members of the executive branch. During the Monica Lewinsky scandal, when Bill Clinton evoked executive privilege to prevent White House aides from testifying before special prosecutor Kenneth Starr, the courts ruled that executive privilege did not apply, and his aides were compelled to testify. (Clinton was accused of having extramarital relations with Lewinsky, a White House intern.)

During the 2019 impeachment hearings, President Trump used the claim of executive privilege to withhold information from Congress, asserting that his aides could not be compelled to testify before Congress or to turn over documents. He also repeatedly instructed both current and past staff members to refuse to comply with congressional subpoenas. Trump's exercise of this claim to withhold evidence from Congress formed the basis for the House's second article of impeachment, "obstruction of Congress." While the Democratically controlled House voted to impeach President Trump, the Senate, controlled by Republicans, voted to acquit him of those charges.

The People as a Source of Presidential Power

One of the most important sources of presidential power today comes from the people. Although one president generally will have the same formal powers as the next, presidents' ability to wield their power, to control the political agenda, and to get things done typically is a function of political skill, charisma, and what political scientist Richard Neustadt has called "the power to persuade."[22]

The President and the Bully Pulpit

Modern presidents work to persuade the public on a virtually continuous basis. They know that if they win popular support for their views and political agenda, they will have an easier time getting their policy priorities through Congress. In their efforts to persuade the people, they exploit the power of their office, using the presidency as a forum from which to speak out on any matter—and to have their views listened to. This ready access to the public ear and broad power of the president to communicate led President Theodore Roosevelt to exclaim, "I have got such a bully pulpit!"[23]

In using their **bully pulpit,** the ability of presidents to speak out and be listened to by voters, presidents seek to communicate that their stances on important issues are the right choices and that their actions, particularly controversial decisions, should be supported. Presidents also strive to persuade the public that they are doing a good job on key policy fronts, such as economic and foreign policy. Sometimes presidents seek to mobilize the public to take specific actions or to adopt certain beliefs. For example, although President Trump faced stern criticism (from both his supporters and detractors), his mastery of Twitter, the modern bully pulpit, illustrated his ability not only to inform the public but also to single-handedly determine the national agenda, often steering media coverage toward one issue or another simply through a 280-character message.

> **bully pulpit**
> The ability of presidents to speak out and be listened to by voters.

The reason presidents work so tirelessly to win public support for their agenda is that they understand that getting Congress to act on policy priorities, to approve budgets, and to pass favored legislation depends heavily on the perception that the public supports presidential initiatives. Indeed, political scientist Richard Neustadt argues that the modern institution of the presidency is weak and that presidents in fact must rely on public and congressional support in order to enact their agendas.[24] Getting Congress to do what the president wants is more difficult when a president faces a divided government, a situation in which the president belongs to one political party and Congress is controlled by a majority of members of the other party, or when the president must deal with a truncated government, in which the president and one house of Congress are controlled by one party, but the other house of Congress is controlled by the other.

But beyond partisan differences, presidents' ability to get things done in Congress depends on their powers of bargaining and persuasion. These abilities to cajole and convince members of Congress to do something they might not be inclined to do is also a function of their popularity with the people. A popular president can use that clout to persuade members of Congress that favored positions are the right ones; an unpopular president, or one distracted by issues not related to policy, will face greater obstacles in getting Congress's cooperation to enact the preferred legislative agenda.

The President and Public Approval

When presidents are sworn in to office, they are typically met with a time of hope and optimism on the part of the public who elected them. The advantage of this **honeymoon period,** a time early in a new president's administration characterized by optimistic approval by the public, varies in strength from president to president (see "Data Analysis: Presidential Job Approval"). But during this time a president's **approval rating,** the percentage of survey respondents who say they "approve" or "strongly approve" of the way the president is doing the job, is often above 55 percent.

> **honeymoon period**
> A time early in a new president's administration characterized by optimistic approval by the public.

> **approval ratings**
> The percentage of survey respondents who say that they "approve" or "strongly approve" of the way the president is doing his job.

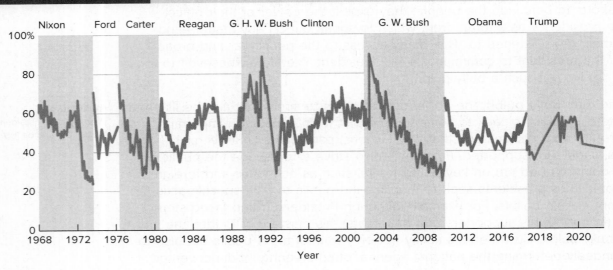

Source: Gallup

Measuring presidential job approval is relatively simple: Pollsters ask survey respondents whether they approve or disapprove of the job the president is doing. But these ratings are also a powerful indicator of how the public views the president and how much they support the president's agenda. Presidential approval ratings are also an indicator of power in and of themselves—that is, Congress will be reluctant to defy an extremely popular president, while they may perceive little harm in resisting an unpopular president's priorities or agenda.

Practice Analytical Thinking

1. Which presidents enjoyed the highest approval ratings? When did these high ratings occur? What prompted the American people to be so supportive of these presidents in those times?

2. In general, in looking at the approval trend of modern presidents, how do two-term presidents differ in their overall approval trend from one-term presidents?

3. Compare President Trump's approval ratings with President Obama's and with those of President George W. Bush. Which president enjoyed the highest approval ratings? Which had the lowest? Whose approval was the most even?

While some presidents, on average, are more popular than others, the approval ratings for many presidents varies a great deal during their terms in office. Take, for example, President George W. Bush: After the September 11, 2001, terrorist attacks and President Bush's rapid and dignified response to them, Bush enjoyed record high approval ratings. Immediately after September 11, President Bush's approval ratings hovered in the high 80s, occasionally reaching 90 percent, meaning that 90 percent of those surveyed indicated that they approved of the way the president was handling his job. (In contrast, the average presidential approval rating since the Franklin D. Roosevelt administration was 56 percent.) During this time, Bush had enormous legislative successes. These included the passage of the USA PATRIOT Act of 2001, which gave law enforcement officers greater authority in handling suspected terrorist acts, and the congressional declaration of a "war on terror." When Bush's popularity subsequently waned because of the people's dissatisfaction with the rate of progress in the war in Iraq, the high number of casualties in the war, and continued weakness in the American economy, so, too, did support decrease for the continuation of the war, the president's economic policies, and a proposed extension of the USA PATRIOT Act.

While President Obama's approval ratings did not show the same enormous variations, we can see that he enjoyed a strong and sustained honeymoon period, followed by a gradual decline in approval, with an uptick during his reelection campaign in 2012.

In general, presidential approval ratings reveal that some presidents are simply more popular than others. For example, Presidents Ronald Reagan and Bill Clinton tended to enjoy high approval ratings, with President Clinton's second-term ratings running particularly high, despite the Monica Lewinsky scandal and the subsequent impeachment proceedings against him. When the United States engages in a short-term military action or is the subject of an attack by terrorists, we see similar peaks in approval ratings, sometimes referred to as the **rally 'round the flag effect**. A president rarely sustains high public approval continuously. Once achieved, however, high ratings help the chief executive succeed by demonstrating the people's support of the presidential agenda.[25]

rally 'round the flag effect
The peaks in presidential approval ratings during short-term military action.

Scratching beneath the surface, however, it is apparent that while high approval ratings can bolster presidential power, lower approval ratings can sometimes signal something other than universally low regard. Take, for example, President Trump's approval rating. As it did throughout his presidency, Trump's approval rating in 2020 varied greatly from state to state, as shown in Figure 5.3. At one point, for example, only 29 percent of Vermonters approved of the president's job performance, but 61 percent of West Virginians did. All in all, President Trump received approval ratings above 50 percent in 17 states, while he received ratings below 40 percent in 12 states. These figures demonstrate the polarized nature of opinion of President Trump, but they also demonstrate his efforts to build and maintain support in certain areas of the country.

Technology and the Media as Tools of Presidential Influence

Just as President Trump transformed the presidency by using social media to convey his priorities and views to the American people, so too have his predecessors embraced technological innovation as a means of wielding influence. In the 1930s, Franklin D. Roosevelt changed the relationship between the president and his constituents by using radio to communicate directly with the American people. President Kennedy would replicate this transformation using the medium of television in the 1960s. (See Chapter 18 for further discussion of the president's use of technology.)

PATTERNS AND TRENDS

FIGURE 5.3 ■ Approval of President Donald Trump Varied from State to State

Geographically, in which states was President Trump the most popular? The least popular? Assess President Trump's popularity in the states with the largest populations.

Source: Gallup

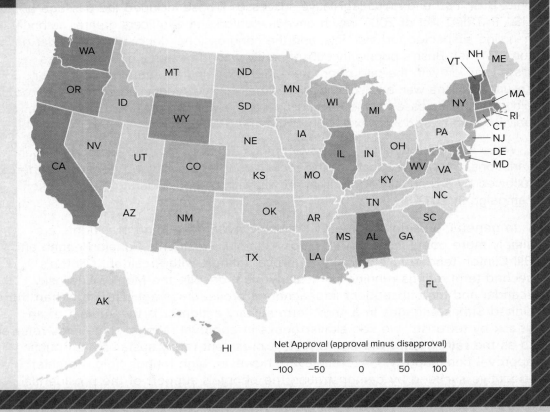

For every president, technology and the media can be used as a tool of influence, as the expertise of the White House communications office can "spin" news in a favorable light for the administration. In particular, the White House can manage direct communication using new technologies by releasing videos on the president's Facebook page or YouTube channel or by holding "office hours" on Twitter. Relying on traditional media, the communication director forges relationships with the most prominent media outlets by providing access, exclusive interviews, and scoops on breaking stories to reporters considered friendly to the administration.

Although the nature of presidential press conferences and other media forums has evolved over time, the mass media have served as a key avenue by which modern presidents have communicated directly to the population at large. Because the nature of the president's relationship with his constituency is constantly evolving, so, too, is presidential power.

■ The Evolution of Presidential Power

Although the constitutional powers of the presidency have changed little over time, the power of the presidency has evolved a great deal.[26] This development stems in part from some presidents' skillful use of powers not granted by the

Constitution, such as the powers to persuade and to assert authority. But the political environment within which presidents have governed has also contributed to the evolution of presidential power.[27]

The history of the early republic saw an incremental expansion of the power of the presidency, whereas the Great Depression of the 1930s and the election of Franklin D. Roosevelt in 1932 spawned an enormous growth in presidential authority.[28] As successor presidents inherited the large bureaucracy that Roosevelt built, presidential powers have expanded further—gradually creating what historian Arthur Schlesinger, Jr., has called the **imperial presidency,** a term used to describe some modern presidencies because of the enormous powers the office has gained through assertion, the size of the bureaucracy, and the presence of staff loyal to an individual president.

Early Presidents and the Scope of Presidential Power

Thomas Jefferson's election to the presidency in 1801 marked one of the earliest expansions of presidential power. Jefferson broadened the powers of the office despite his Anti-Federalist reluctance to delegate too much power to the national government. Jefferson increased presidential power in two significant ways. First, as we have seen, Jefferson established the principle of inherent powers of the presidency by undertaking the Louisiana Purchase. Second, Jefferson's tenure in office witnessed the first time that a president had to act as party leader. Jefferson had no choice but to assume this role. If he had not, he would not have been elected president, given the dominance of the Federalist Party during this era (see Chapter 6).

Twenty-five years later, Andrew Jackson would also adopt the role of president-as-party-leader, but he would add a new twist. Jackson's emphasis on *populism*, a political philosophy that emphasizes the needs of the common person, spawned a new source of presidential power, because Jackson was the first president to derive real and significant power from the people. Whereas earlier politics had mostly emphasized the needs of the elite, Jackson's populism mobilized the masses of common people who traditionally had not been civically engaged. This populism augmented the power of the presidency by increasing the popularity of that office and investing the president with power that came from the people's goodwill.

In the 20th century, the nature and scope of presidential power changed as a consequence of the prevailing political environment. One of the most extraordinary shifts in the nature of the presidency occurred during Franklin D. Roosevelt's administration, which lasted from 1932 until his death in 1945. (Roosevelt was elected to an unprecedented four terms; the **Twenty-Second Amendment** to the Constitution, which allows only two elected presidential terms, was ratified six years after his death.)

Having come to power during the Great Depression, Roosevelt engineered a significant change in the function of the federal government. He called for a New Deal for the American people, a series of social welfare programs that would provide employment for many of the nation's unemployed workers. Roosevelt's New Deal was based on the ideas of economist John Maynard Keynes, who argued for temporary deficit spending by the government (that is, going into debt) to spur the economy during economic downturns.

Roosevelt's primary weapon in his New Deal arsenal was the **Works Progress Administration (WPA)**, a federal government program that employed 8.5 million people at a cost of more than $11 million between 1935 and 1943. The idea was that government-funded employment would create economic growth in the private sector because those employed by the government would have the money to buy goods and services, thus creating spiraling demand. The rising demand for goods and services would mean that the private sector could then employ more people, and the cycle of recovery and growth would continue. For example, if during the 1930s the government employed your great-great-grandfather to work on a road-building project in his town, he might have put his paycheck toward buying more bread and other baked goods than he previously could have afforded. If enough people in town could have similarly patronized the bakery, then the baker might have had to hire an assistant to keep up with demand, and consequently the assistant would have had money to spend on, say, new shoes for his children. In that way, the increased demand for products and services would continue, creating additional economic growth.

Roosevelt's New Deal was important to the presidency for two reasons. First, it dramatically changed people's views of the role of the federal government. Many people now tend to think of the federal government as the provider of a "safety net" that protects the most vulnerable citizens—a safeguard that did not exist before the New Deal, when those needing assistance had to rely on the help of family, friends, churches, and private charities. Second, this popular perception and the programs that emerged—the WPA, unemployment insurance, Social Security—meant that the federal government would have to grow larger in order to administer these programs. As a result, the president's role as chief executive of a large federal bureaucracy would become much more important to modern presidents than it had been to those who served before Roosevelt.[29]

The Watershed 1970s: The *Pentagon Papers*, Watergate, and the "Imperial Presidency"

Americans' penchant for strong presidents modeled after Roosevelt diminished drastically in the 1970s. In 1971, Daniel Ellsberg, a Defense Department employee, leaked a classified, top-secret 7,000-page history of the nation's involvement in and thinking on Vietnam dating from the Truman administration in 1945 to the Nixon administration then in the White House. Called the *Pentagon Papers*, the work first appeared as a series of articles in *The New York Times*. When the Nixon

>> William Frazee, the chief of the presses for the *Washington Post*, makes the victory sign after learning of the Supreme Court's decision allowing newspapers to publish the *Pentagon Papers*. Applause broke out in the press room as the first print run began rolling.

Bettmann/Getty Images

administration in 1971 successfully petitioned the Department of Justice to prevent the publication of the remainder of the articles, the *Washington Post* assumed publication of them. When the Department of Justice sued the *Post*, the *Boston Globe* resumed their publication. Two weeks later, in an expedited appeals process, the U.S. Supreme Court ruled in *The New York Times Co. v. The United States* that the government "carries a heavy burden of showing justification for the imposition of such a restraint" and that the government had failed to meet that burden, thus allowing the continued publication of the papers.[30]

The *Pentagon Papers* tainted the public's view of the presidency. The published work revealed miscalculations by policymakers in presidential administrations from Truman's to Nixon's, as well as arrogance and deception on the part of policymakers, cabinet members, and presidents. Specifically, the *Pentagon Papers* revealed that the federal government had repeatedly lied about or misrepresented the fact of increasing U.S. military involvement in Southeast Asia. In particular, the analysis in the *Pentagon Papers* indicated not only that U.S. marines had conducted offensive military maneuvers well before the public was informed but also that the U.S. military had engaged in other actions, including air strikes over Laos and military raids throughout the North Vietnamese coastal regions. The Nixon administration's legal wrangling to prevent the release of the *Pentagon Papers* cast a dark cloud over the public's perception of the presidency.

Cynicism about the presidency continued to grow in light of the **Watergate** scandal that took place a year later. In 1972, men affiliated with President Nixon's reelection campaign broke into the headquarters of the Democratic National Committee (located in the Watergate Hotel in Washington, D.C.) to retrieve wiretaps that they had previously installed to monitor their opponents. *Washington Post* reporters Bob Woodward and Carl Bernstein, in a groundbreaking series of stories, traced the burglaries and the subsequent cover-up to high-level officials in the Nixon administration. This crime, and the Nixon administration's attempts at cover-ups, became known as the Watergate scandal. A Senate investigation revealed that President Nixon had secretly taped conversations in the Oval Office that would shed light on "what the president knew [about the break-in] and when he knew it."[31] Nixon claimed executive privilege and refused to turn over the tapes to a special prosecutor who had been appointed to investigate the scandal. When the U.S. Supreme Court ruled in *United States v. Richard Nixon* that Nixon must provide the tapes to the special prosecutor, one key tape was found to have a gap of almost 20 minutes where someone, reportedly his secretary, Rosemary Woods, had erased part of the recording.

Meanwhile, all the Watergate burglars had pleaded guilty and been sentenced, and only one refused to name the superiors who had orchestrated the break-in. But the testimony of burglar James W. McCord, Jr., linked the crime to the Committee to Re-Elect the President (CREEP), to Nixon's campaign organization, and to high-ranking Nixon White House officials. The disclosure prompted John Dean, Nixon's White House counsel, to remark, "We have a cancer within, close to the presidency, that is growing."[32] With indictments handed down for many of Nixon's top aides, and with a Senate investigation and a special prosecutor's investigation in progress, the House Judiciary Committee took up the matter of impeachment. The committee handed down three articles of impeachment against Nixon—one for obstruction of justice, a second for abuse of power, and a third for contempt of Congress. When a newly released tape documented that Nixon had planned to block the investigations by having the Federal Bureau of Investigation

Watergate
During the Nixon administration, a scandal involving burglaries of material on Democratic political opponents and the subsequent cover-up by high-level administration officials.

and the Central Intelligence Agency falsely claim that matters of national security were involved, the tape was referred to as a "smoking gun."[33] Nixon lost the support of his few loyalists in Congress, and on August 8, 1974, he announced that he would resign from office the following day.

Watergate might seem like a relatively insignificant event in the history of the American presidency, but the impact of the Watergate scandal on the presidency has been enormous. Watergate badly wounded the trust that many Americans held for their president and for their government. Combined with the unpopularity of the Vietnam War and the release of the *Pentagon Papers*, it created a deep cynicism that pervades many Americans' perception of their government even today—a pessimistic attitude that has passed from generation to generation.

Watergate also dramatically demonstrated how enormously the presidency had changed. Modern presidents had supplanted Congress as the center of federal power, and in so doing had become too powerful. Historian Arthur Schlesinger, Jr., and other presidential scholars have decried the problem of the growth of the executive branch and, in particular, the imperial "courts"—the rising number of Executive Office of the President staff members, many of whom are not subject to Senate confirmation and share a deep loyalty to the person who is president rather than to the institution of the presidency. In juxtaposition with an attitude like that expressed by Richard Nixon in his comment that "when the president does it, that means it is not illegal,"[34] the imperial presidency left much room for abuse.

The Post-Watergate Presidency

With the election of Jimmy Carter to the White House in 1976, many observers believed that the era of the imperial presidency had passed. Carter, the mild-mannered governor of Georgia and thus a Washington outsider, seemed to be the antidote the nation needed after the display of power-run-amok during Nixon's tenure. But given the significant challenges Carter faced during his term, many people believed that he did not exercise *enough* authority—that he acted weakly when faced with various crises. Ronald Reagan's election in 1980 in some ways represented a return to a more powerful, "imperial" presidency. Reagan, a former actor, was Hollywood swagger personified, speaking tough talk that many Americans found appealing. His administration was not unlike an imperial court, featuring a group of advisers with deep loyalties to Reagan. Many would argue that the George W. Bush administration was best at re-creating a form of an imperial presidency. Bush was able to exercise strong authority because of the fear created both among the citizenry and in Congress after the September 11, 2001, terror attacks. And given President Bush's activist foreign policy, he exercised great authority in that realm, with Congress having little ability to check him. Ironically, many critics of the Bush administration would assert that he was assisted in creating a modern imperial presidency by many of the same staff members who were part of the Nixon administration. But administration supporters would note that a strong presidency was necessary at this critical juncture in the nation's history.

Many Democrats were frustrated by President Obama's comparative lack of assertiveness when exercising presidential power in the early years of his first term. Many analysts faulted his conciliatory, consensus-building nature as an impediment to exercising strong authority. These abilities, however, enabled the president to get the hallmark achievement of his administration passed: the Affordable Care Act of 2010. After the congressional elections later that year, which saw a Republican majority elected in the House, many viewed Obama's powers as dissipating. In particular, the Republican majority in the Senate served as a heavy check on the latter portion of his first term. After the government shutdown in 2013, President Obama seemed more willing to exert strong authority in exercising presidential duties, oftentimes while circumventing Congress. But in 2014, Republicans also won control of the U.S. Senate, and Obama faced even more roadblocks to his policy proposals and initiatives. The check provided by Republicans in the Congress thwarted any prospect of the Obama administration becoming an imperial one.

President Trump's election in 2016 marked a return to the imperial presidency in a way that few thought possible in modern times. Trump's administration resembled Reagan's in that the president's advisers were deeply loyal to him. But in contrast with other presidents who surrounded themselves with party members with experience and loyalty to a shared ideology, many on Trump's staff came to the White House and the executive branch with minimal government or political experience. And given Trump's propensity to fire staff who disagreed with him, the ultimate defining characteristic of his staff was a dedication to Trump personally, rather than a loyalty to the office or the party, characteristic of other "imperial" presidents.

Impeachment: A Check on Abuses of Presidential Power

Although presidential powers are flexible and can be shaped by the individuals holding the office, these powers do not go unchecked. One crucial check on presidential power is **impeachment,** the power of the House of Representatives to formally accuse the president (and other high-ranking officials, including the vice president and federal judges) of crimes. The Constitution specifically refers to charges of "Treason, Bribery, or other high Crimes and Misdemeanors," an appropriately vague description of the potential offenses a president could commit. An impeachment can be thought of as an indictment: If a majority of the members of the House of Representatives vote to impeach the president, they forward the charges against the president, called the **articles of impeachment,** to the Senate. The Senate then tries the president and, in the event of conviction for the offenses, determines the penalty. In convicting a president, the Senate has the authority to punish the president by removing him from office.

Although the Senate can force a president to step down, it has never done so in practice, and only three presidents have been impeached by the House of Representatives. The first was Andrew Johnson, who succeeded Abraham Lincoln as president in 1865 upon the latter's assassination. When he assumed the presidency, Johnson faced not only a divided nation but also a government in turmoil. The 11 articles of impeachment against him had to do primarily with his removal of the secretary of war, Edwin Stanton, who was working with Johnson's congressional opponents to undermine Johnson's reconstruction policies in the South. The so-called Radical Republicans in the House believed that Johnson's policies were too moderate, and they sought to treat the Confederate states as conquered territories and to confiscate the land of slaveholders. Those same House members wanted to protect their ally Stanton and prevent him from being removed from office. The Senate ultimately recognized the politically motivated nature of the articles of impeachment against Johnson and acquitted him on all counts.

During the Watergate scandal that rocked Richard Nixon's presidency, the House Judiciary Committee in 1974 approved articles of impeachment against the president and sent them to the full House for a vote. Republican members of Congress convinced Nixon that the House would vote to impeach him and that the Senate would convict him and remove him from office. Faced with the inevitable, Nixon became the first president to resign from office before the House could vote to impeach him.

impeachment
The power of the House of Representatives to formally accuse the president (and other high-ranking officials, including the vice president and federal judges) of crimes.

articles of impeachment
Charges against the president during an impeachment.

In *Federalist* No. 70, Hamilton argues in favor of the strong executive that the Constitution provides. He opposed the weak executive that existed under the Articles of Confederation. Hamilton envisioned a strong presidency that the people could unify behind. He argued that "energy in the executive is the leading character in the definition of good government" and a strong executive is essential to "the protection of the community against foreign attacks . . . to the steady administration of the laws, to the protection of property . . . to justice; [and] to the security of liberty . . ."

At the time the Constitution was being written, there were fears that a single executive would be too powerful, in the same way the British monarch was too powerful. Some called for a co-presidency or a presidency checked by a council, but Hamilton defended the single executive. He argued that the single executive would be "far more safe" because disagreement among a multiple executive system would weaken central authority.

Develop an argument that takes a position on whether or not the American president has become too powerful.

In your essay, you must:

- Articulate a defensible claim or thesis that responds to the prompt and establishes a line of reasoning

- Support your claim with at least TWO pieces of accurate and relevant information:

  - At least ONE piece of evidence must be from one of the following foundational documents:

    - *Federalist* No. 70

    - U.S. Constitution

  - Use a second piece of evidence from another foundational document or from your study of the informal powers of the president

- Use reasoning to explain why your evidence supports your claim/thesis

- Respond to an opposing or alternative perspective using refutation, concession, or rebuttal

The second president to be impeached was Bill Clinton, when the House of Representatives approved two articles of impeachment in 1998. On the basis of an investigation by a special prosecutor, the House impeached Clinton for lying to a grand jury about his relationship with White House intern Monica Lewinsky and for obstructing justice. The Senate acquitted Clinton on both counts.

The most recent occurrence was in 2019–2020, when the House of Representatives approved two articles of impeachment against President Trump. The first article, abuse of power, centered on allegations that Trump unlawfully sought to have Ukrainian government officials influence the 2020 presidential election. The second charge, obstruction of Congress, concerned Trump's direction to members of his staff not to comply with the House investigation, as discussed previously in this chapter. In a 51–49 vote, the Senate blocked witnesses from testifying, thus paving the way for an acquittal of Trump by the Senate.

■ Women and the Presidency

In 2020, six women candidates sought the Democratic nomination for president. Although none garnered the traction necessary to win the nomination, Senator Elizabeth Warren (D-Mass.) led the field at several points during the primary. Still, the desire of many to see a woman in the highest office of the land was so compelling that the eventual nominee, Joe Biden, promised to choose a female running mate. And indeed, in selecting Kamala Harris, Biden acknowledged that for some voters, this would be a "make or break" issue.

In 2016, many believed that Hillary Clinton would be elected the first woman president of the United States. Clinton's candidacy was historic, but her loss represented a stark political reality concerning how difficult it would be for any woman to win the most powerful position in the world, a reality that was reinforced in 2020. Of the three branches of government, the executive branch has been the most challenging for women to enter as formal participants. Historically, part of that struggle stems from the fact that sizable portions of Americans have been unwilling to vote for a qualified woman for president, as shown in Figure 5.4. For example, in 1937, only 33 percent of Americans said they would cast their presidential ballot for a qualified woman, although that figure has risen steadily over the years. By 2013, the number of Americans who claimed they

>> In 2020, six women candidates—clockwise from left: U.S. Senator Amy Klobuchar (D-MN); U.S. Senator Elizabeth Warren (D-MA); U.S. Senator Kamala Harris (D-CA), author Marianne Williamson; Representative Tulsi Gabbard (D-HI); and U.S. Senator Kirsten Gillibrand (D-NY)—sought the Democratic nomination for president.

(Top left): Sheila Fitzgerald/Shutterstock; (Top middle): Paul Boucher/Shutterstock; (Top right): Sheila Fitzgerald/Shutterstock; (Bottom left): Ron Adar/Shutterstock; (Bottom middle): Kessler Bowman/Shutterstock; (Bottom right): Sheila Fitzgerald/Shutterstock;

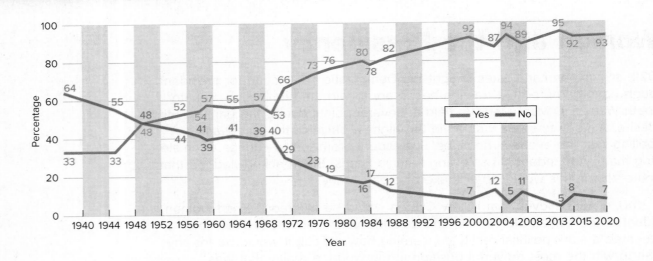

FIGURE 5.4 ■ **America's Willingness to Vote for a Woman President** What has been the trend since the late 1930s in the American electorate's willingness to vote for a woman president? What factors do you think explain this shift?

Sources: Roper Center for Public Opinion Research and Gallup

>> In 2020, Joe Biden selected Sen. Kamala Harris (D-CA) as his running mate. Harris's nomination was historic: She was the first Black woman, the first Southeast Asian-American, and the third woman to be selected as the vice-presidential nominee for a major party ticket.

Erin Schaff/The New York Times/Redux

were willing to vote for a woman for president had reached 95 percent. In 2015, with the prospect of a Hillary Clinton candidacy emerging, the percentage showed a slight down-tick, presumably because some respondents viewed Clinton as that likely woman candidate, and she was unpopular with some groups of constituents. In 2020,

93 percent said they would vote for a qualified woman. While the trend is positive, it remains disconcerting that a statistically significant proportion of the American electorate—indeed, many presidential elections are determined by less than 7 percent of the vote—would be unwilling to vote for a qualified woman for president. Also at issue is how these numbers have borne out: While voters say they are willing to vote for a woman candidate, when presented with a qualified female candidate, they often seem to find a reason not to, many times questioning a female candidate's "likability," a characteristic over which few male candidates seem to lose votes.

The First Lady

Much like the presidency itself, the role of the president's spouse has been defined by the individuals who have occupied it. Melania Trump, a modern mother who once worked as a model, shaped the office to suit her own personality and her marriage. Historically, some first ladies have preferred to take a very hands-on approach when it comes to politics and policy, while others stay out of the spotlight. That the American people typically accept both types of first spouses is evidence of the open-mindedness with which the American people view the role.

Some first ladies have used their proximity to the chief executive to influence policy concerns broadly and forcefully. Several have acted "behind the scenes," as was the case with Edith Wilson, the wife of Woodrow Wilson. Others have taken a more public role. Eleanor Roosevelt, the wife of Franklin D. Roosevelt, fought for many causes during her husband's administration, including human rights and civil rights for African Americans. Hillary Clinton transformed the office of first lady by serving, at her husband's appointment, as the chair of a presidential task force on health care reform. Her role in the task force, and indeed throughout the Clinton administration, proved to be a lightning rod for critics who thought that a first lady should not be so prominent.

>> Virginia "Bess" Truman, Edith Wilson, and Eleanor Roosevelt were modern first ladies of their era. Wilson assumed some presidential responsibilities and decision making while her husband, Woodrow, was ill. Truman was recognized as a strong campaign asset, and Roosevelt is widely regarded as being the first modern feminist first lady. Today, Dr. Jill Biden is a thoroughly modern first lady, who announced her decision to continue in her profession while during her husband's term as president—the first First Lady to do so.

(Left): Bettmann/Getty Images; (Right): Crush Rush/Shutterstock

Laura Bush, Hillary Clinton's successor, by contrast was a more reserved and less public first lady, a persona that Michelle Obama later seemed to emulate. Both shunned the policy-oriented role that Hillary Clinton had forged, though each had causes to which they drew attention. For Bush, that issue was reading and libraries (Bush was a schoolteacher and a librarian before serving as first lady), while Obama prioritized the issue of childhood obesity, using her status to bring attention to the problem and to shape policy affecting it. By and large, though, Obama preferred to focus on raising the Obamas' daughters, Malia and Sasha, and on the more ceremonial aspect of serving as first lady.

Similar to Michelle Obama, Melania Trump embraced a traditional interpretation of the role, shying away from the policy and politics some former first ladies have pursued. Instead, she participated in the ceremonial duties associated with the position and has also focused on raising the Trumps' young son, Barron, who was just 10 years old when his father was elected president. Melania Trump has also prioritized the issue of cyber-bullying, advocating for more civility on the Internet, particularly in regard to children.

Conclusion: Thinking Critically About What's Next in the Presidency

The American presidency is a dynamic institution, one that is molded by the individuals who serve and by the American people—by their changing interests, viewpoints, struggles, and needs. The presidency has a symbiotic relationship with the larger culture in which it exists; it is at once shaped by, and shapes, the culture.

The executive branch of the federal government is also flexible, incorporating the needs of diverse constituencies and participants, particularly in recent times. The continued evolution of the presidency as a more diverse institution is relatively ensured. How will this evolution take place in the next several decades?

The presidency is a product of both the design of the framers and the desires of the citizenry. As the country's need for stronger presidents has increased, the resources and authority of presidents have grown to accommodate new powers. Since the activist administration of Franklin D. Roosevelt, the characterization of the presidency as an "imperial" institution has dogged numerous presidents, most recently President Trump. But divided government has meant that modern presidents are increasingly "checked" in their efforts to expand presidential authority by Congress.

Looking ahead, how will the citizens of the future view the scope of presidential power? The answer will depend in large part on the people themselves, particularly those who vote. It will depend on whom citizens elect to the highest office in the land; on how the people's opinions shape (or, in some cases, fail to shape) presidential actions; and on how the people's relationships with their presidents develop. Although the Constitution created a system in which presidential powers can be checked institutionally, the framers did not foresee the most significant checks on modern presidents: the will of the people and a ruthlessly investigatory media, both of which ensure that presidential power is never unrestrained.[35]

References

1. Jean Reith Schroedel, *Congress, the President, and Policymaking: A Historical Analysis* (Armonk, NY: M. E. Sharpe, 1994).

2. William W. Lammers, *The Presidency and Domestic Policy: Comparing Leadership Styles, FDR to Clinton* (Washington, DC: CQ Press, 2000).

3. Andrew Rudalevige, *Managing the President's Program: Presidential Leadership and Legislative Policy Formulation* (Princeton, NJ: Princeton University Press, 2002).

4. Richard A. Watson, *Presidential Vetoes and Public Policy* (Lawrence: University of Kansas Press, 1993).

5. Robert J. Spitzer, *The Presidential Veto: Touchstone of the American Presidency* (Albany: SUNY Press, 1988).

6. Sidney M. Milkis and Michael Nelson, *The American Presidency: Origins and Development, 1776–1998,* 4th ed. (Washington, DC: CQ Press, 2003).

7. https://www.whitehouse.gov/briefings-statements/statement-by-the-president-38/.

8. Statement by the President on H.R. 1540, December 31, 2011.

9. Louis Fisher, *Presidential War Power* (Lawrence: University of Kansas Press, 1995).

10. Cornell G. Hooton, *Executive Governance: Presidential Administrations and Policy Change in the Federal Bureaucracy* (Armonk, NY: M. E. Sharpe, 1997).

11. Valerie Haeder, "His Superfluous Excellency: Tales of the Vice Presidency," *Library of Congress*, https://blogs.loc.gov/headlinesandheroes/2019/02/his-superfluous-excellency-tales-of-the-vice-presidency/

12. Bill Clinton, *My Life* (New York: Knopf, 2004), 414.

13. Stephen Skowronek, *The Politics Presidents Make: Leadership from John Adams to George Bush* (Cambridge, MA: Belknap Press, 1997).

14. MaryAnne Borrelli, *The President's Cabinet: Gender, Power, and Representation* (Boulder, CO: Lynne Rienner, 2002).

15. Joel D. Aberbach and Mark A. Peterson, eds., *The Executive Branch* (New York: Oxford University Press, 2005).

16. William E. Leuchtenburg, *In the Shadow of FDR: From Harry Truman to Ronald Reagan* (Ithaca, NY: Cornell University Press, 1989).

17. Kenneth R. Mayer, *With the Stroke of a Pen: Executive Orders and Presidential Power* (Princeton, NJ: Princeton University Press, 2002).

18. Executive Order 9981, www.trumanlibrary.org/9981.htm.

19. *United States v. Curtiss-Wright Export Corp.,* 229 U.S. 304 (1936).

20. Mark J. Rozell, *Executive Privilege: Presidential Power, Secrecy, and Accountability,* 2nd ed. rev. (Lawrence: University of Kansas Press, 2002).

21. *United States v. Richard M. Nixon,* 418 U.S. 683 (1974).

22. Richard Neustadt, *The Power to Persuade* (New York: Wiley, 1960).

23. *Outlook,* February 27, 1909.

24. Richard E. Neustadt, *Presidential Power and the Modern President* (New York: The Free Press, 1990).

25. George C. Edwards III with Alec M. Gallup, *Presidential Approval: A Sourcebook* [Eisenhower to Reagan] (Baltimore: Johns Hopkins University Press, 1990).

26. Harry A. Bailey Jr. and Jay M. Shafritz, *The American Presidency: Historical and Contemporary Perspectives* (Pacific Grove, CA: Brooks/Cole, 1988).

27. Marc Landy and Sidney M. Milkis, *Presidential Greatness* (Lawrence: University of Kansas Press, 2000).

28. Harold J. Laski, *The American Presidency* (New York: Harper & Row, 1940).

29. William M. Goldsmith, *The Growth of Presidential Power: A Documented History,* 3 vols. (New York: Chelsea House, 1974).

30. *New York Times Co. v. United States,* 403 U.S. 713 (1971).

31. Statement of Senator Howard Baker (R-Tenn.) during the Senate Committee investigation.

32. John Dean, the Nixon presidential transcripts, March 21, 1973.

33. Watergate Special Prosecution Force (WSPF) conversations, Nixon Presidential Library and Museum.

34. David Frost, *I Gave Them a Sword* (New York: William Morrow, 1978).

35. Charles C. Thach Jr., *The Creation of the Presidency, 1775–1789: A Study in Constitutional History* (Baltimore, MD: Johns Hopkins University Press, 1969).

▮ Key Terms

■ Multiple-Choice Questions

1. One reason presidents use executive agreements over negotiating a treaty is that
   A. Executive agreements have more support with the public
   B. Senate ratification is not required
   C. Executive agreements do not require funding from Congress
   D. Executive agreements have more legal authority than treaties

2. A fundamental source of presidential influence lies in the use of
   A. executive privilege
   B. photo opportunities
   C. the bully pulpit
   D. spin control

3. Which of the following is an accurate comparison of the president's expressed and inherent powers?

Expressed Powers	Inherent Powers
A. Include powers such as the ability to purchase land	The power to protect the borders and regulate immigration
B. Include powers such as the ability to suspend civil liberties	The power to tax
C. Executive Orders	Executive agreements
D. The ability to command the armed forces	President Obama's extension of health care through the Affordable Care Act

Questions 4 and 5 are based on the graph below.

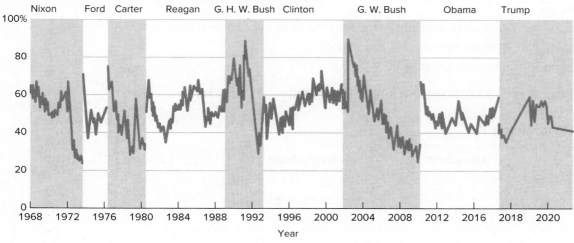

Source: Gallup

4. Which of the following is true of the information provided in the graph?

 A. Presidents tend to be most popular at the end of their term in office

 B. Presidential approval tends to dip near midterm elections

 C. Presidential approval increases throughout a president's term

 D. Presidential approval is always highest at the beginning of a president's term

5. Which president saw the steepest decline in their approval between the time they took office to the time they left office?

 A. Nixon

 B. Reagan

 C. Ford

 D. Clinton

Questions 6 and 7 are based on the excerpt below.

"Energy in the Executive is a leading character in the definition of good government. It is essential to the protection of the community against foreign attacks; it is not less essential to the steady administration of the laws; to the protection of property against those irregular and high-handed combinations which sometimes interrupt the ordinary course of justice; to the security of liberty against the enterprises and assaults of ambition, of faction, and of anarchy.

A feeble Executive implies a feeble execution of the government. A feeble execution is but another phrase for a bad execution; and a government ill executed, whatever it may be in theory, must be, in practice, a bad government."

—*Federalist* No. 70

6. All of the following are arguments for a strong executive as stated by Hamilton in *Federalist* No. 70 EXCEPT

 A. Only a strong and vigorous leader can steer the country to success

 B. A plural executive would lead to a more efficient execution of the laws

 C. An energetic president would be able to thwart the influence of factions

 D. A strong president would have the tools to protect the citizens' natural right to property

7. Which of the following would serve as a check on an energetic executive?

 A. Executive privilege

 B. Congress's use of the necessary and proper clause to limit executive orders

 C. Requirement to deliver a State of the Union address

 D. Congressional impoundment of funds

8. In which of the following scenarios is impeachment and removal from office most likely to occur?

 A. **Hypothetical Government A**

	Democrat	Republican
President	X	
House	250	185
Senate	48	52

B. **Hypothetical Government B**

	Democrat	Republican
President	X	
House	250	185
Senate	55	45

C. **Hypothetical Government C**

	Democrat	Republican
President	X	
House	250	185
Senate	51	49

D. **Hypothetical Government D**

	Democrat	Republican
President	X	
House	185	250
Senate	33	67

9. A president seeking to influence how legislation is carried out may use which of the following?

A. statutory powers
B. executive privilege
C. signing statement
D. emergency powers

10. Which of the following identifies a correct formal and informal power of the president?

	Formal	Informal
A.	Veto	Head of executive branch
B.	Party Leader	Chief of State
C.	Commander in Chief	Chief Diplomat
D.	Agenda Setter	Manager of the Economy

■ Free Response Questions

Quantitative Analysis

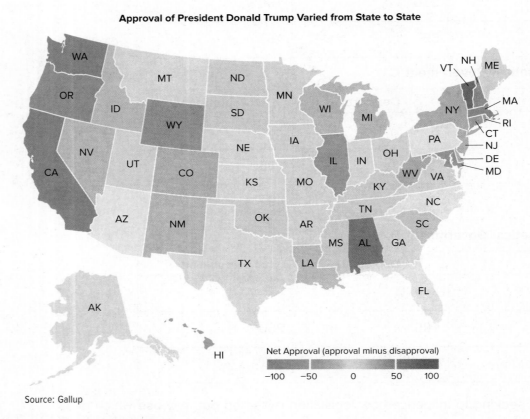

Approval of President Donald Trump Varied from State to State

Net Approval (approval minus disapproval)

−100 −50 0 50 100

Source: Gallup

Use the map above to answer the questions.

A. Identify a region where Trump is least popular.

B. Describe a similarity or difference in the approval ratings of Donald Trump, as illustrated in the information graphic, and draw a conclusion about that similarity or difference.

C. Explain at least two factors that influence presidential approval ratings.

Argumentation

Develop an argument in which you decide whether modern presidents' increasing reliance on informal powers creates an imperial presidency.

In your essay, you must:

- Articulate a defensible claim or thesis that responds to the prompt and establishes a line of reasoning.
- Support your claim with at least TWO pieces of accurate and relevant information:
  - At least ONE piece of evidence must be from one of the following foundational documents:
    - The Constitution of the United States (including the Bill of Rights and subsequent Amendments)
    - *Federalist* No. 70
    - *Federalist* No. 51

- Use a second piece of evidence from another foundational document from the list or from your study of the interactions of the institutions

- Use reasoning to explain why your evidence supports your claim/thesis

- Respond to an opposing or alternative perspective using refutation, concession, or rebuttal

Concept Application

Scenario: A Republican president is governing with a slim Republican majority in the U.S. Senate and a slim Democratic majority in the House of Representatives. Just prior to the mid-term elections, a Supreme Court justice announces his retirement, paving the way for the president to fill the seat. The president chooses a jurist known for conservative rulings on lower federal courts to be the nominee. Shortly after his selection, a credible news source reports that the nominee has a record of sexually harassing multiple women he worked with over the course of his career. This revelation galvanizes Democrats against the nomination and Republicans for the nomination into national campaigns.

After reading the scenario, respond to A, B, and C below:

A. In the context of the scenario, describe a power the president has in shaping the decisions of the Supreme Court.

B. In the context of the scenario, explain how the use of presidential power described in Part A can be affected by its interaction with Congress.

C. In the context of the scenario, explain how the interaction between Congress and the presidency can be affected by divided government.

The Judiciary

THEN

The federal judiciary did not affect the daily lives of citizens due to its limited jurisdiction as established by the Judiciary Act of 1789.

NOW

All major policy issues—social, economic, and political— eventually end up in the courts, where judges interpret laws; therefore, courts make policies that affect the daily lives of citizens.

NEXT

Will calls to reform the term of office of federal judges and justices succeed?

Will the partisan battles over judicial appointments and over the Senate's advice and consent powers continue?

Will the judiciary retain its legitimacy in our democracy?

■ Chapter Introduction

The AP U.S. Government and Politics Enduring Understanding for the judicial branch chapter is: *The design of the judicial branch protects the Supreme Court's independence as a branch of government, and the emergence of judicial review remains a powerful practice.* In the AP Opener for the Congress chapter, we explored how the appointment of Supreme Court justices has become politicized. Given that discussion, it may seem ironic to learn that the judicial branch is designed to be independent. Unlike many state judges, all federal judges are appointed and are given lifelong terms in the Constitution. The purpose of lifelong terms was to free judges from concern over the popularity of their decisions, since they are not subject to re-election. Instead, judges are to focus solely on the law. Federal judges are appointed by the president and confirmed by the Senate, both branches are elected to office and perceive that appointing judges with similar policy views to the federal courts as an effective means of advancing their own policy agendas. While the appointment power can influence the composition of the federal courts, the power of judicial review allows the courts to remain independent and check or limit the power of the elected branches. Judicial review is the power of the courts to determine the constitutionality of actions of the other branches of government and empowers the courts to interpret the Constitution, laws, and other governmental actions.

Article III of the Constitution specifies the design of the federal courts and the life tenure of federal judges. Article III is brief when compared to Articles I and II which describe Congress and the presidency respectively. Article III does not specify that there must be 9 Supreme Court justices, nor does it mention that the Court has the power of judicial review. Article III explicitly gives "judicial power" to the Supreme Court, gives federal judges lifelong appointments, gives Congress the power to create federal courts, and outlines cases of original jurisdiction in the Supreme Court. No explicit power of judicial review is granted. The first time the Supreme Court exercised the power of judicial review was in the case of *Marbury v. Madison* (1803). The paragraphs that follow describe the *Marbury v. Madison* case in detail. *Marbury v. Madison* is a required Supreme Court case in the AP U.S. Government and Politics course.

Marbury v. Madison (1803)

John Adams, a member of the Federalist political party, was in the final days of his presidency (known as the **lame duck** period), having lost the election of 1800 to Thomas Jefferson, who was a member of the Democratic-Republican party. Congress, which was controlled by the Federalists, passed a last-minute law giving President Adams the power to appoint justices of the peace for the District of Columbia. During the lame duck period, Adams appointed over 40 judges and the Senate confirmed them. However, not all of the commissions (letters of appointment) were delivered to the new appointees before the transition to the next administration. When Thomas Jefferson became president, the Democratic-Republicans took control of Congress. Congress abolished the court positions created by the Federalists, and Jefferson signed into law the measure abolishing the positions. The Jefferson administration refused to deliver the commissions to the judges who had not received them from the Adams administration.

Marbury did not receive his commission, and took his case to the Supreme Court requesting a writ of mandamus—an order requiring a government official to carry out a specific duty. Marbury wanted to force Secretary of State James Madison to deliver his commission, and Marbury argued that the Judiciary Act, passed by Congress in 1789, gave the Supreme Court the power to issue a writ of mandamus.

Chief Justice Marshall had to consider not only the Judiciary Act of 1789 but also Article III, Section 2, of the Constitution:

> In all cases affecting ambassadors, other public ministers, and consuls, and those in which a state shall be a party, the Supreme Court shall have original jurisdiction. In all the other cases before mentioned, the Supreme Court shall have appellate jurisdiction, both as to law and fact, with such exceptions, and under such regulations as the Congress shall make.
>
> *—Article III, Section 2, U.S. Constitution*

> The Supreme Court…shall have power to issue…writs of mandamus, in cases warranted by the principles and usages of law, to any courts appointed, or persons holding office under the authority of the United States.
>
> *—Judiciary Act of 1789*

Marshall declared the Court's right to interpret laws by stating, "It is emphatically the province…of the judicial branch to say what the law is." Then, he interpreted Article III, Section 2, of the Constitution in a narrow, literal way. He said that Section 2 granted the Supreme Court original jurisdiction only in those instances expressly mentioned, and the writ of mandamus was not among them. Therefore, the attempt by the Judiciary Act of 1789 to extend the Court's original jurisdiction to include a writ of mandamus was in direct conflict with the Constitution. The statute was therefore unconstitutional. Marshall reasoned that the Constitution was superior and not to be changed by ordinary congressional action.

The ruling in *Marbury v. Madison* was important because it was the first time the Supreme Court used the power of **judicial review**, a power not explicitly stated in the Constitution although practiced in English and colonial law. The power of judicial review would shape the role and power of the Supreme Court for decades. Judicial review gives the Supreme Court a role in the policy-making process.

■ What Do Courts Do?

Our democratic system is based on separation of powers and checks and balances. The judiciary plays a very significant role in limiting the actions of the other branches of government. This role includes interpreting the meaning of laws and policies, evaluating the constitutionality of the actions of other branches, resolving conflicts between political actors and other individuals, and ensuring that laws are applied consistently and fairly.

dual court system
The existence of 50 independently functioning state judicial systems, each responsible for resolving legal disputes over its state laws, and one national judicial system, responsible for resolving legal disputes over national laws.

In our federal system, both the national government and the state governments are sovereign, each having its own authority to make, execute, and resolve conflicts over its laws (as explained in Chapters 2 and 3). One characteristic of this dual sovereignty is that the federal government establishes national law, and each state government establishes its own state laws. A second characteristic of dual sovereignty is the **dual court system,** in which each state has a judicial

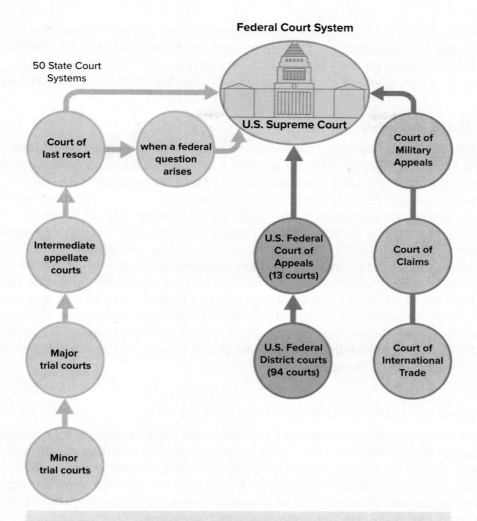

Federal Court System

50 State Court Systems

U.S. Supreme Court

Court of last resort

when a federal question arises

Intermediate appellate courts

U.S. Federal Court of Appeals (13 courts)

Court of Military Appeals

Major trial courts

U.S. Federal District courts (94 courts)

Court of Claims

Minor trial courts

Court of International Trade

FIGURE 6.1 ■ **Jurisdiction in the Dual Court System** In the dual court system, the cases that state courts have authority to hear differ from those that the federal courts have authority to hear. What cases are within the jurisdiction of a state's court system? How does this chart demonstrate federalism and our structure of government? How does this structure reflect the value of rule of law? When can a case that began in a state court system move into the federal court system?

system that is responsible for resolving legal disputes over the state's laws, while the federal judicial system is responsible for resolving legal disputes over national laws and between state governments (Figure 6.1).

Unlike the legislative and executive branches, which proactively respond to citizens' needs and demands by formulating, approving, funding, and implementing laws, judges (and the courts in which they work) are reactive. Judges must wait for someone to file a lawsuit (a legal dispute) or engage in litigation before they can do their work. In addition, while elected legislators and executives represent their constituents, judges do not have constituents to represent. Judges are responsible for resolving disputes over whether accused persons have harmed society or another person by their actions or inactions, as well as determining the constitutionality of laws and their applications. Therefore, in our democracy we expect elected legislators and executives to be partial to the majority of their constituents—the principle of majority rule. At the same time, we expect judges to be independent—that is, impartial to individuals or groups—and uphold the Constitution and laws that comply with it. Because federal judges and many state judges are not elected, they must ensure that citizens perceive the courts as legitimate, in turn granting them the authority to decide conflicts and controversies.

The Rule of Law

rule of law
Belief that a country should be governed by consistently applied and legitimately adopted policies and statutes, not by the will of an individual.

The United States—like many democracies—is governed by the **rule of law.** Instead of being ruled by arbitrary decisions of leaders, a country like ours is grounded in the expectation that all citizens—powerful and destitute—are governed by authoritatively adopted and consistently applied laws that are publicly announced before they are enforced. As judicial scholar Walter F. Murphy noted, "[a]t its core, rule of law implies governance through regulations that apply not only to rulers and ruled but also equally among the ruled."[1] Our belief in this fundamental assumption explains why many of us are so disappointed when the powerful seem to play by different rules and why we have high expectations of our legal process and judges. Rule of law protects us from tyranny and gives us a shared definition of fairness and justice. It requires an independent judiciary that is not beholden to a political party or a specific president or governor. Without rule of law and a strong independent judiciary that the public trusts, democracy is threatened.

Sources of Law in the United States

law
A body of rules established by government officials that bind governments, individuals, and nongovernment organizations.

Law is a body of rules established by government officials that bind governments, individuals, and nongovernment organizations. A goal of law is to create a peaceful, stable society by establishing rules of behavior that government enforces, with punishments imposed on those whom the government finds guilty of violating the law. Another goal of law is to create processes by which conflicts about the rules and expected behaviors can be resolved. The United States has a variety of sources for its laws—including constitutions, pieces of legislation, executive orders, rules and regulations made by administrative bodies, and judicial decisions—all of which must comply with the U.S. Constitution.

common law
Judge-made law grounded in tradition and previous judicial decisions, instead of in written law.

doctrine of *stare decisis*
From the Latin for "let the decision stand," a common-law doctrine that directs judges to identify previously decided cases with similar facts and then apply to the current case the rule of law used by the courts in the earlier cases.

precedents
Previous cases with similar facts that judges identify for use in a new case they are deciding; judges apply the legal principles used in the precedent cases to decide the legal dispute they are currently resolving.

JUDICIAL DECISIONS: COMMON LAW Common law is judge-made law grounded in tradition and previous judicial decisions. When there is no written law for judges to apply when resolving disputes, the judges use their understanding of the societal norms of justice and fairness to resolve conflicts. The legal principle established by the court (common law) is binding on other judges when resolving later cases with similar facts. The common-law **doctrine of *stare decisis*** (Latin for "let the decision stand") directs judges to identify previously decided cases with similar facts, called **precedents.** Judges use these precedent cases to decide new controversies, thus ensuring the law stays consistent in its meaning.

The United States inherited, and then built on, a system of common law from England. When a newly established court in the United States had no written law to guide its decision, it typically referred to British common law, and then eventually U.S. common law. Common law was the predominant form of law in the United States in the 19th century, before the volume of state and national legislation, rules, and regulations expanded. Eventually, many of the legal rules and principles developed by judges to resolve disputes over property, contracts, and harm caused by another person's negligent behavior were enacted in written laws by legislative bodies.

Although the doctrine of *stare decisis* directs judges to ground their decisions in precedents, judges do have the discretion to step away from precedent if there are contradictory precedents, or if they believe the earlier decision was wrong (that is, if it misinterpreted or misapplied the law). Ultimately, common law gives judges the responsibility for interpreting law, especially if there are few precedents to guide them.[2]

CONSTITUTIONS: CONSTITUTIONAL LAW Constitutions regulate the behavior of governments and the interactions of governments with their citizens. The body of law established in constitutions is **constitutional law.**

In the United States, the U.S. Constitution is the supreme law of the land. All other laws and government actions must comply with the U.S. Constitution. National laws and treaties cannot violate the Constitution. State constitutions and laws, likewise, cannot violate the Constitution. Throughout U.S. history, courts have had to resolve disputes over the meaning of the language in the U.S. Constitution. For example, in 1974 the Supreme Court had to resolve a conflict arising from President Nixon's claim of constitutionally established executive privilege—the right to withhold information from other branches of the government. As the Court stated in *United States v. Nixon*, "In the performance of assigned constitutional duties, each branch of the Government must initially interpret the Constitution, and the interpretation of its powers by any branch is due great respect from the others. [President Nixon's] counsel, as we have noted, reads the Constitution as providing an absolute privilege of confidentiality for all Presidential communications. Many decisions of this Court, however, have unequivocally reaffirmed the holding of *Marbury v. Madison* (1803), that '[i]t is emphatically the province and duty of the judicial department to say what the law is.'"[3]

> **constitutional law**
> The body of law that comes out of the courts in cases involving the interpretation of the Constitution.

>> President Nixon, with his daughter at his side, says farewell to members of the cabinet and White House staff after resigning from the presidency in August 1974. Nixon's resignation came after the U.S. Supreme Court ruled that presidential executive privilege did not extend to his refusal to provide material subpoenaed in a criminal case. The Court found that constitutional due process rights of the accused prevailed over Nixon's use of executive privilege to withhold tapes of phone conversations he had in his possession.

National Archives and Records Administration [ARC ID 194597]

LEGISLATION: STATUTES By the early 20th century, rapid changes in society and the economy forced legislators in Congress and the states to create laws to regulate the behavior of individuals and organizations to further the public good and protect individual liberties and rights. Laws written by legislatures are called legislation, acts, and statutes. Legislation may be consolidated in one document, such as the **U.S. Code,** a compilation of all the laws ever passed by the U.S. Congress.

> **U.S. Code**
> A compilation of all the laws passed by the U.S. Congress.

penal code
The compilation of a state's criminal law—legislation that defines crime—into one document.

The U.S. Code has 53 sections spanning a range of issues, including agriculture, bankruptcy, highways, the postal service, and war and defense. At the state level, each state has a **penal code,** which is the compilation of all its criminal law.

EXECUTIVE ORDERS Article II, Section 1, of the U.S. Constitution states that "the executive Power shall be vested in a President of the United States of America." This power has been interpreted to allow the president to issue orders that create and guide the bureaucracy in implementing policy as well as orders that establish commissions. A president can enact an executive order without input from the other branches of government, though executive orders are subject to judicial review and depend on the legislature for funding. Because executive orders have the force and effect of law, they represent a crucial tool in the president's lawmaking toolbox. Because executive orders are not laws, they can be easily reversed or replaced by the next presidential administration.

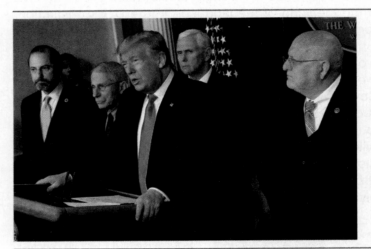

>> When the COVID-19 pandemic began, President Donald Trump was able to respond with executive orders that the government could implement without congressional approval. For new budgetary allocations, however, the Constitution requires Congress to participate in the passing of legislation. Why would the principle of separation of powers require this?

Alex Wong/Getty Images

Executive orders can be an efficient way to deal with crises and immediate issues. Reacting to state concerns and stock market declines from the COVID-19 pandemic, on March 18, 2020, the president used his authority to issue Executive Order 1309, "Prioritizing and Allocating Health and Medical Resources to Respond to the Spread of COVID-19." This order evoked emergency powers. While also recognizing that the local, state, and federal governments had already taken actions to slow the spread of the virus, President Trump gave the federal government authority to set health priorities and allocate health and medical resources. This declaration provided access to some emergency funds and loans for small businesses and states, and it also allowed the IRS and Department of the Treasury to grant extensions to citizens for the filing of their tax returns.[4] Immediately after, additional orders were given to prevent the hoarding of health and medical resources (March 23), to use the Defense Production Act to expand the domestic production of ventilators and personal protective equipment (March 27), and to authorize the Secretaries of Defense and Homeland Security to activate the members of the Ready Reserves in the military branches (March 27).[5] All of these actions could be subject to judicial review if contested in court.

ADMINISTRATIVE RULES AND REGULATIONS: ADMINISTRATIVE LAW Legislation that creates policies and programs also delegates discretion to the bureaucrats in the executive branch whose job it is to implement them. Applying their administrative discretion, bureaucrats determine the best means to achieve the goals of the policies they execute. In the lawmaking process known as administrative rule making, bureaucrats use their administrative discretion to establish specific rules, regulations, and standards necessary for the effective and efficient implementation of policy. The rules, regulations, and standards made by bureaucrats through administrative rule making have the force of law.

An example of administrative law is the standards established by the Social Security Administration to determine eligibility for Social Security disability benefits. Once established, bureaucrats in the Social Security Administration offices apply the standards case-by-case in their review of medical documentation to determine which applicants are qualified to receive disability benefits. Conflicts over the application of the standards can end up in a courtroom for resolution.

Resolving Legal Disputes

To resolve legal disputes, courts in the United States have an **adversarial judicial system,** in which the two sides (parties) each present its set of facts. At the end of a lawsuit, one party will win, and the other party will lose. Two kinds of legal disputes are brought to courts: questions of facts are resolved in trial courts, and questions of interpretation and application of law are resolved in appellate courts.

TRIAL COURTS **Trial courts** have **original jurisdiction,** which means they are the first courts to hear a case. Trial courts resolve lawsuits by determining the truth of what occurred—the facts of the case. The dispute in a trial court may involve the claim that a defendant harmed society by violating criminal law, or it may involve the claim that a defendant caused harm to an individual, a group, or an organization by violating civil law.

Trials include the questioning of witnesses by lawyers for both parties and the presentation of evidence. The accused usually has the choice between a bench trial and a jury trial. In a **jury trial,** a group of citizens selected to hear the evidence determines guilt or liability. Each juror (member of the jury) is expected to be impartial and neutral and base her or his decision on the facts presented in the courtroom. In a **bench trial,** the judge who presides over the court proceedings decides guilt or liability; there is no jury. In federal trial courts, the jurors must unanimously agree on the verdict.

CRIMINAL LAW **Criminal law** is the body of law dealing with conduct considered harmful to the peace and safety of society as a whole, even when directed against an individual. Each state establishes its own criminal law, compiled in its penal code. In addition, Congress has established national criminal law; however, the vast majority of crimes are defined by state legislation, not national legislation. Therefore, state courts resolve the overwhelming majority of criminal lawsuits. The government whose criminal statute was violated—either the national or state government— files the lawsuit, as the prosecutor against the defendant. For example, when a government arrests and accuses a person of setting a house on fire (arson), it is the state in whose territory the crime occurred that has the authority to bring a lawsuit, charging the person with violating its criminal law. At times, an act may violate both state and federal criminal law. In that situation, the state government and the national government can each prosecute based on its own law.

In a criminal case, the government as prosecutor has the burden to prove its case against the defendant **beyond a reasonable doubt,** which means there is no

adversarial judicial system
A judicial system in which two parties in a legal dispute each present its case and the court must determine which side wins the dispute and which loses.

trial court
Court with original jurisdiction in a legal dispute that decides guilt or liability based on its understanding of the facts presented by the two disputing parties.

original jurisdiction
Judicial authority to hear cases for the first time and to determine guilt or liability by applying the law to the facts presented.

jury trial
A trial in which a group of people selected to hear the evidence presented decides on guilt or liability

bench trial
A trial in which the judge who presides over the trial decides on guilt or liability.

criminal law
The body of law dealing with conduct so harmful to society as a whole that it is prohibited by statute, and is prosecuted and punished by the government.

beyond a reasonable doubt
The standard of proof the government must meet in criminal cases; the government must convince the judge or the jury that there is no reasonable doubt that the defendant committed the crime.

reasonable doubt in the mind of the judge (bench trial) or the jury that the defendant is guilty of violating the criminal law as charged. When a court finds a criminal defendant guilty, typically the judge (even where there is a jury) determines the punishment. However, because the overwhelming majority of defendants charged with criminal offenses plead guilty before trial through plea bargaining, most criminal cases never go through a trial. In criminal cases, punishments can range from community service to capital punishment, depending on the severity of the crime.

Criminal defendants who go to trial have a variety of constitutional rights to guarantee due process before the government infringes on their life, liberty, or pursuit of happiness through punishment. Some of these rights include the right to a speedy trial; to exclusion of evidence that law enforcement gained through an unreasonable search or seizure; to assistance of counsel, including counsel paid for by the government for indigent defendants accused of serious crimes; and to protection from cruel and unusual punishment. Defendants found guilty have the legal right to an appeal, although the overwhelming majority do not appeal guilty verdicts. Because the Constitution protects people from double jeopardy, which is the trying of a person again for the same crime he or she has been cleared of in court, the government does not have the right to appeal not-guilty verdicts.

SOURCE ANALYSIS COMPARATIVE

THEN

NOW

Source Analysis While historically the law was applied through civil and criminal litigation, resulting in the trials most Americans are familiar with through television and movies, in the past decade the number of trials has dwindled. Today, *only about 1%* of grievances or charges actually go to trial. The vast majority of criminal cases are resolved via plea bargaining, and in civil cases, the majority are resolved via settlements, arbitration, or contractual obligations not to sue.

(*Left*): Heide Benser/The Image Bank/Getty Images; (*Right*): fizkes/iStock/Getty Images

State and federal courts resolve criminal cases. However, both levels of government spend much more time resolving the larger volume of civil cases brought to them.

CIVIL LAW **Civil law** is the body of law dealing with private rights and obligations that are established by voluntary agreements (written and oral contracts) or laws.[6] Civil lawsuits involve disputes between individuals, between an individual and a corporation, between corporations, and between individuals or corporations and a government. In civil law disputes, one party (the plaintiff or complainant) alleges that some action or inaction by the other party (the respondent) has caused harm to his or her body, property, psychological well-being, reputation, or civil rights or liberties.

When the harm is to a person's body or property and is caused by another person's negligence or other wrongful act it is known as a **tort.** Well-publicized tort lawsuits include medical malpractice suits (disputes over claims that negligence of medical professionals caused harm) and product liability lawsuits (disputes over claims that a product, from toys to makeup to medicine, caused harm). The most common civil lawsuits stem from traffic accidents. Divorce and other family conflicts are also resolved in civil lawsuits, because these disputes deal with obligations and rights created by a marriage contract.

Courts have a range of procedures that the variety of civil lawsuits must follow. However, some common practices are seen across civil suits. For example, the complainant who files the lawsuit has the burden to prove that the respondent caused the harm. The burden of proof used in civil lawsuits is lower than that used in criminal trials. In civil trials, the complainant must prove that the **preponderance of evidence** is on his or her side—that is, the evidence indicates that the respondent is more likely than not to have caused the harm and is therefore liable.

Unlike criminal defendants, the respondents in civil suits do not have a constitutional right to the assistance of counsel. Nor do the complainants. This may explain why so many people who are harmed by the action or inaction of another, and have grounds to file a civil lawsuit, decline to do so; they often cannot afford a lawyer. In addition, the overwhelming majority of civil lawsuits are settled (resolved) before trial. Respondents found liable for causing harm are not punished like those found guilty in criminal cases, but instead are required to remedy the harm, which often means paying monetary damages to the complainant. (See Table 6.1 for a summary comparison of criminal and civil trials.)

civil law
The body of law dealing with disputes between individuals, between an individual and corporations, between corporations, and between individuals and their governments over harms caused by a party's actions or inactions.

tort
Situation when a person's body or property is harmed by another person's negligence or other wrongful act, other than the violation of a contract.

preponderance of evidence
The standard of proof used in civil cases; the evidence must show that it is more likely than not that the accused caused the harm claimed by the complainant.

TABLE 6.1 ■ Comparison of Criminal and Civil Law

Characteristic	Criminal law	Civil law
The accusation	Defendant harmed the peace and safety of society by violating the criminal law	Respondent's action or inaction caused harm to an individual or group
Accuser	State or federal government whose criminal law was alleged violated (prosecutor)	Individual or group that alleges harm (complainant)
Standard of proof	Beyond a reasonable doubt	Preponderance of evidence
Verdict	Guilty or acquitted (not guilty)	Liable or not liable
Outcome	Punishment	Remedy

Verdicts in both criminal and civil trials may be appealed to correct errors in the interpretation or application of law made by the judge presiding over the trial. We now turn to differentiating appellate procedures from trial procedures.

courts of appeal
Courts with authority to review cases heard by other courts to correct errors in the interpretation or application of law.

appellate jurisdiction
Judicial authority to review the interpretation and application of the law in previous decisions reached by another court in a case.

APPELLATE COURTS Courts of appeal have **appellate jurisdiction,** which means they are responsible for identifying and correcting errors made by judges in lower trial courts. Often, courts of appeal must clarify laws to determine if the judge(s) in the previous trial or hearing properly interpreted and applied the relevant laws to the case. At other times, courts of appeal must navigate between conflicting laws. In the process of clarifying laws and navigating conflicting laws, courts of appeal determine what the law is, and in so doing, they make law.

Appellate court cases do not include the questioning of witnesses, nor do they use juries. Instead, each party to the legal dispute submits a legal brief that presents the facts as it understands them, the relevant law, and any favorable precedent cases. The goal of each party's legal brief is to persuade the court to rule in its favor. A panel of judges reviews the legal briefs as well as the transcripts from the trial court and any previous appellate court hearings from the case. Judges may allow each party to make a brief oral argument, which may be interrupted by questions from the panel; each party is typically allocated about 20 minutes. The panel decides the case (with a simple majority vote) based on the review of the briefs, oral arguments when allowed, and deliberations among themselves and their law clerks. Appellate courts often write, announce, and publish opinions that provide the legal rationale for the court's decision. Table 6.2 summarizes the differences between trial and appellate courts.

TABLE 6.2 ■ Comparison of Trial and Appellate Courts

Characteristic	Trial Courts	Appellate Courts
Type of jurisdiction	Original	Appellate
Conflict to be resolved	Is the accused guilty or not guilty?	Did an error of interpretation or application of law occur?
Evidence	Witnesses testify to facts.	Legal briefs and court transcripts are reviewed.
Who decides?	Judge in bench trial; jury in jury trial	Panel of judges

JUDICIAL REVIEW In resolving disputes, courts are responsible for ensuring that the U.S. Constitution is not violated. In the landmark case *Marbury v. Madison* (1803), the Supreme Court, led by Chief Justice John Marshall, grabbed for itself the power of judicial review.[7] *Judicial review* is the Court's authority to determine whether an action taken by any government official or governing body violates the Constitution (see Chapter 2). In the *Marbury* case, the Supreme Court ruled that a section of the Judiciary Act of 1789 was unconstitutional. In its ruling, the U.S. Supreme Court argued something it had never argued before: that it had the power not only to review acts of Congress and the president, but also to decide whether those acts (including laws enacted) were consistent with the Constitution and to strike down laws that conflicted with constitutional principles.

Legal scholar Joel B. Grossman observes that in *Marbury*, "[Chief Justice John] Marshall made it abundantly clear that the meaning of the Constitution was rarely self-contained and obvious and that those who interpreted it—a role he staked out for the federal courts but one that did not reach its full flowering until the mid-twentieth century—made a difference."[8] Judicial review is the most significant power the Supreme Court exercises. Over time, the Court has extended this power to apply not only to acts of Congress, the president, and federal bureaucrats, but also to laws passed by state legislatures and executives, as well as to state court rulings and acts of state and local bureaucrats. Today, all courts in the United States, federal and state, have judicial review authority. We now turn to an examination of the federal judicial system.

The Structure of the Federal Court System

Article III of the Constitution established that "Judicial power of the United States shall be vested in one supreme Court and in such inferior Courts as the Congress may from time to time ordain and establish." Article III also states that the power of the national judiciary extends to all disputes over the U.S. Constitution, national laws, and treaties. While the Constitution provides for the basic structure of the U.S. Supreme Court and power of the federal judiciary, it is through legislation that Congress established inferior courts and special courts with distinctive jurisdiction. In addition, through legislation and judicial decision making, the authority of the federal courts has evolved.

The federal court system is a three-tier hierarchical system. At the bottom, in the first tier, are the U.S. district courts, which are the federal trial courts with original jurisdiction over a case. In the middle tier of the federal system are the U.S. courts of appeals, which have appellate jurisdiction. At the top of the federal court hierarchy, in the top tier, is the U.S. Supreme Court. The U.S. Supreme Court has appellate jurisdiction and rarely used, very limited, original jurisdiction. The U.S. Supreme Court is the federal **court of last resort.**

court of last resort
The highest court in a court system.

One twist to the independent functioning of state and federal courts in the U.S. dual court system, as presented in Figure 6.1, is that a lawsuit that began in a state court can end up in the federal court system. Specifically, if a state court case raises questions about federal laws (typically about U.S. constitutional rights during an appeal), then the case may be brought to a federal appeals court after the state court of last resort, the highest court in the state's court system, has an opportunity to hear the case.

Congress has complemented the three-tier system of Article III courts (district courts, courts of appeals, and the U.S. Supreme Court) with specialized courts. Congress established the specialized courts through legislation grounded in its authority under Article I of the Constitution to "constitute tribunals inferior to the Supreme Court," and so the specialized courts are known as Article I courts.

Article I Courts

Congress establishes **Article I courts** to administer and resolve conflicts regarding specific federal laws.[9] Article I courts include U.S. Bankruptcy Courts, the U.S.

Article I courts
Courts created by Congress under constitutional authority provided in Article I that help administer and resolve conflicts over specific federal legislation.

Court of Military Appeals, and the U.S. Tax Court. Unlike the judges sitting on the benches in Article III courts, who are appointed to **life terms,** the judges who preside over Article I courts are appointed to serve for fixed terms.

life term (life tenure)
Judicial appointment that will last until the judge dies.

Probably the most well known Article I court is the Foreign Intelligence Surveillance Act (FISA) court. Established by Congress, FISA empowers the government to conduct secret searches where necessary to protect national security, and it significantly broadened the powers of law enforcement agencies to engage in such investigations. Agencies must go before the FISA court to justify secret searches.[10] After the impeachment of President Trump, the Justice Department's independent inspector, Michael E. Horowitz, looked into the FBI's Russia investigation. His report revealed that the secrecy of the FISA process had allowed for abuses that spread well beyond investigations of the Trump administration.[11] For example, in Spring 2020, an audit of FBI applications to the FISA court for surveillance revealed a broadened pattern of sloppiness in the FBI's use of powerful tools to eavesdrop on American soil in national security cases. In response, the FBI implemented greater training of its officers and new checklists that officers must follow in filing FISA applications.[12]

U.S. District Courts

There are 94 federal district courts with 673 judgeships. Each state has between one and four district courts, and Washington, D.C., and Puerto Rico each have a district court. These **district courts** do the bulk of the work of the federal judiciary because these trial courts have original **mandatory jurisdiction,** which means they must hear every case filed with them. A judge presides over the trial court. The judge, or a jury if the defendant chooses a jury trial, decides what happened in the case, based on the application of the law to the facts presented in the courtroom. It is in the trial court that two parties to the lawsuit present evidence and witnesses testify. Congress, through legislation, can modify the jurisdiction of district courts as well as change the number of district court judgeships.

district courts
The federal trial courts with mandatory jurisdiction.

mandatory jurisdiction
The requirement that a court hear all cases filed with it.

Defendants who lose in the district courts have the right to appeal their cases to a federal court of appeals if they believe the presiding judge misinterpreted or misapplied the law. However, the majority of cases decided by the district courts are not appealed. Therefore, the overwhelming majority of federal lawsuits that go to trial are resolved in the district courts.

U.S. Courts of Appeals

federal courts of appeals (circuit courts)
Federal courts with mandatory, appellate jurisdiction.

At the middle level of the federal judicial hierarchy are 13 **federal courts of appeals,** also called **circuit courts**, with a total of 179 congressionally created judgeships. The First through Twelfth Circuit Courts each has a geographic area over which it has appellate jurisdiction. Each of these circuit courts hears appeals from the district courts in its geographic area (circuit). The Twelfth Circuit is better known as the D.C. Circuit because that is the area its jurisdiction covers, which includes appeals stemming from federal administrative agencies located in Washington, D.C.

The Thirteenth Circuit is better known as the Federal Circuit. The jurisdiction of the Federal Circuit Court is not geographically based; it is issue based. The Federal Circuit Court handles appeals of cases that cover specific federal matters such as international trade, government contracts, and patents. Judges on the courts of appeals work in panels of three to review cases. Similar to the U.S. district courts, the U.S. courts of appeals have mandatory jurisdiction; therefore, they hear all cases that are filed with them. Losing parties can appeal to the U.S. Supreme Court; however, only a very small percentage do. Therefore, the courts of appeals are in fact the last court to hear most cases appealed from the district courts.

The U.S. Supreme Court

At the top of the federal judicial hierarchy sits the **U.S. Supreme Court.** Although the Court has a very limited original jurisdiction, it hears appeals from both the federal courts and the state courts of last resort when cases involve a conflict over the constitution, federal law, or treaties (known as a federal question). The framers limited the Supreme Court's original jurisdiction to those cases that concern ambassadors, public ministers, and consuls, and those involving two or more states. But over time, Congress, in cooperation with the Court, has decided that the Court should retain original jurisdiction only in cases involving suits between two or more states.

The U.S. Supreme Court's appellate jurisdiction is **discretionary jurisdiction,** which means the justices choose the cases they will hear from among all the cases appealed to the Court. Ultimately, the justices select to hear only a fraction of the cases appealed to the Supreme Court each term.

Since legislation enacted in 1869, nine judges, called justices, sit on the Supreme Court. One of these justices has been specially selected by a president to serve as the **chief justice,** the judge who provides both organizational and intellectual leadership on the Court. Each of the remaining eight justices is an **associate justice.** Political scientists distinguish periods of court activity by changes in the chief justices; therefore, Supreme Courts are named for the chief justice. Today, we have the Roberts Court, named for the current chief justice, John Roberts, whom President George W. Bush nominated and the Senate confirmed in 2005.

U.S. Supreme Court
The court of last resort for conflicts over the U.S. Constitution and national laws; in addition to its appellate jurisdiction, the Court has limited original jurisdiction.

discretionary jurisdiction
The authority of a court to select the cases it will hear from among all the cases appealed to it.

>> Chief Justice John Roberts has been dedicated to maintaining the legitimacy of the federal courts. Recently, he has been more outspoken than in the past, as when President Donald Trump, critical of unfavorable federal court opinions, complained about an "Obama judge." Roberts responded, stating, "We do not have Obama judges or Trump judges, Bush judges or Clinton judges. What we have is an extraordinary group of dedicated judges doing their level best to do equal right to those appearing before them." Could such challenges affect how the public perceives the federal courts? How does the photo—from the State of the Union address—demonstrate why this matters? How would you describe the relationships demonstrated in this photo?

Leah Millis/Getty Images

▮ Appointing Federal Judges

judicial independence
Insulating judges from the need to be accountable to voters or elected officials so that they can make impartial decisions based on the law.

The framers wanted to ensure **judicial independence** so that federal judges could make impartial decisions based on the law, protected from the need to win the votes of citizens or support from elected officials to keep their job. To foster judicial independence, the framers stated that Article III judges "shall hold their offices during good behavior," which has been interpreted to mean their term extends until they resign, retire, or pass away, or until Congress removes them through the impeachment process. In addition, Article III states that judges "shall at stated times, receive for their services, a compensation, which shall not be diminished during their continuance in office." Their salary cannot be cut by a president or Congress unhappy with their decisions. The goal of judicial independence is to allow the courts to rule "without fear or favor" and to not be dangerously reliant on other branches or overly responsive to partisan demands.[13]

Article II of the Constitution establishes the president's authority to appoint, with the advice and consent of the Senate, Supreme Court justices and other federal officers, including federal judges. Therefore, the power to appoint federal judges is a power shared by the president and the Senate. Presidents and senators are aware of the long-term effect a judge, particularly a Supreme Court justice, can have on constitutional interpretation and public policies. However, the Constitution does not establish qualifications for judgeships. Therefore, presidents are left to use their own discretion when nominating judges, and senators also use their discretion when providing advice and consent. What criteria do presidents and senators use in the judicial appointment process?

Selection Criteria

Presidents seek competent nominees who will win Senate consent. In addition, presidents since at least Jimmy Carter have also considered demographic characteristics in efforts to make federal courts more representative of the nation's growing diversity. Unfortunately, as judicial scholars Christoper P. Banks and David M. O'Brien claim, "because the meaning of senatorial 'advice and consent' has never been settled, the political self-interest of presidents and senators makes the federal judicial appointment process politically contentious."[14] The lack of constitutionally enumerated judicial qualifications opens the door even wider to a politically contentious process.

JUDICIAL COMPETENCE What knowledge, skills, and capacities make a judge competent? Constitutionally, federal judges are not required to have a law degree, nor do Supreme Court justices need to have prior judicial experience. Today, a law degree is expected, and judicial experience has also become a means to assess competence of judicial nominees. Prior to President Dwight Eisenhower's presidency (1953–1961), about one-third of Supreme Court nominees were sitting judges. Since 1953, more than two-thirds of the nominees have been sitting judges.[15] Of the justices currently on the Court, only one, Justice Elena Kagan, was not a sitting judge when appointed.

In addition to legal education and experience, presidents and senators look for candidates who evidence professional and personal integrity, and solid oral and written communication skills. President Obama calculated that Elena Kagan's reputation as a skilled peacemaker and experienced **Solicitor General** who could bring divergent ideological sides together outweighed her lack of experience on the bench when he nominated her to the Supreme Court in 2010.

Solicitor General
The person appointed to represent the federal government in all appeals before the Supreme Court.

Supreme Court Diversity

Characteristic	THEN (1981)	NOW (2020)	NEXT
Sex	First woman appointed	Second, third, and fourth woman serving	**A.** Identify one change in demographic characteristic of the Supreme Court between 1981 and 2020.
Race	First African American man serving	Second African American man and first Latina serving	**B.** Describe a pattern in demographic diversity of the Supreme Court between 1981 and 2020.
Religion	3 Episcopalian 3 Presbyterian 1 Lutheran 1 Methodist 1 Roman Catholic	6 Catholic 3 Jewish	**C.** Explain how the data in the chart may influence the legitimacy of the Supreme Court.
Average age	67 years	68 years	
Age range	51 to 75 years	53 to 87 years	
Party affiliation of appointing president	5 Republican 4 Democrat	5 Republican 4 Democrat	
Law schools	4 Harvard 1 Howard 1 Northwestern 1 Stanford 1 William Mitchell 1 Yale	4 Harvard 4 Yale 1 Columbia	
Prior judicial experience	3 justices had no prior judicial experience	1 justice has no prior judicial experience	
Chief justice	15th chief 15th white man	17th chief 17th white man	

REPRESENTATION OF DEMOGRAPHIC GROUPS The impulse to diversify the Court's membership serves the goal of **descriptive representation,** which is representation on governing bodies of the country's leading demographic groups in proportion to their representation in the population at large. There is an implicit assumption that a justice will better understand and serve the concerns of the racial, ethnic, gender, or other groups to which he or she belongs, thereby offering

descriptive representation
The attempt to ensure that governing bodies include representatives of major demographic groups—such as women, African Americans, Latinas, Jews, and Catholics—in proportions similar to their representation in the population at large.

substantive representation; that is, the Latina justice will take the perspective of Latinas, the male justice will consider the policy preferences of men, and so on. However, the representation may be more symbolic than real because not all men have the same views, nor do all women, even if they are of the same race or ethnicity. Therefore, one female or Latino judge cannot represent the diversity of views of the people they look like. Nevertheless, many public figures and citizens say that the Court should mirror as closely as possible the main contours of the national demographic profile, because such descriptive representation offers **symbolic representation,** which indicates that our democracy is functioning appropriately by offering equal opportunity to all to influence government as a government official.

Some presidents appear more concerned than others with enhancing diversity on the federal bench. Table 6.3 suggests that, compared to Republican presidents, Democratic presidents have been more concerned about descriptive representation.

TABLE 6.3 ■ Demographics of Federal Judges as a Percentage of Those Confirmed

Characteristic	Carter	Reagan	G.H.W. Bush	Clinton	G.W. Bush	Obama	Trump
Total appointees	261	364	188	372	324	324	194*
Hispanic	6%	4%	4%	6%	9%	9%	4%
Black	14%	2%	7%	17%	7%	19%	4%
White	78%	94%	89%	76%	82%	64%	85%
Female	16%	8%	19%	29%	22%	42%	25%
Male	84%	92%	81%	71%	78%	58%	75%
Median age	54.6	52	50.8	50.4	51	52.8	48.2

*Trump's appointees through July 15, 2020.

Sources: Pew Research Center, "How Trump compares with other recent presidents in appointing federal judges," July 15, 2020. Russell Wheeler. "Judicial appointments in Trump's first three years: myths and realities," Brookings Institution, January 28, 2020.

POLITICAL IDEOLOGY In February 2016, just 10 days before Associate Justice Antonin Scalia died, Chief Justice John Roberts criticized the Supreme Court confirmation process, noting it "is not functioning very well." More specifically, Roberts stated, "Look at my more recent colleagues, all extremely well qualified for the court, and the votes were, I think, strictly on party lines for the last three of them, or close to it, and that doesn't make any sense. That suggests to me that the process is being used for something other than ensuring the qualifications of the nominees."[16]

Judges and justices need to be perceived, as Chief Justice Roberts indicates, as more loyal to the law and Constitution than to the party that nominated them, in order for the courts to maintain legitimacy. However, presidents and political parties have goals that often are in opposition to those of the federal judiciary.

Mindful that federal judges typically serve far beyond the tenure of the presidents who appoint them, presidents often regard these nominations as a way of cementing their own legacies (see Data Analysis: Evaluating the Facts). Using party affiliation and previous decisions on the bench to assess a nominee's political ideology, presidents nominate judges, including Supreme Court justices, with whom they are ideologically compatible. Liberal presidents nominate liberal judges, and conservative presidents nominate conservative judges.

President Trump set as an administrative goal to transform the judiciary by appointing as many young ideologically conservative judges as possible to the federal bench. By early 2020, he had appointed more court of appeals judges than any predecessor and more federal judges overall than any recent president besides President Jimmy Carter. Trump had an impact through his appointments; when he came to office in 2017, Republican-appointed circuit judges held 40 percent of posts, and in early 2020, they had 54 percent. However, on the district courts, he mostly replaced Republican-appointed retiring judges.[17] President Trump prioritized this goal even during the early months of the COVID pandemic in 2020, naming nominees even when Congress was in recess. The Republican Senate Majority Leader Mitch McConnell has also seen this as a personal priority, noting publicly in an interview addressing court appointments, "My motto for the rest of the year is 'leave no vacancy behind.'"[18]

The Senate's Role: Advice and Consent

Article II of the Constitution gives the president the authority, with the advice and consent of the Senate, to appoint federal judges. This sharing of power, with the president nominating judges and the Senate confirming them, operates in accordance with our system of checks and balances.

In practice, the Senate's power of advice and consent for presidential nominations to federal offices and judgeships involves the tradition of **senatorial courtesy;** the Senate will not confirm a nominee if a senator from the nominee's home state opposes the nominee. In the case of federal judicial appointments, the Senate Judiciary Committee sends to the nominee's home-state senators a form called a "blue slip," so called because it is printed on blue paper, on which the senator can indicate support or opposition to a judicial nominee. At the discretion of the Senate Judiciary Committee chairperson, if one of the home-state senators does not support the nominee, or does not return the blue slip, then the nomination may not move forward in the confirmation process. Today, senatorial courtesy is considered in the selection of district court and courts of appeals judges.

senatorial courtesy
A custom whereby the Senate will not confirm a presidential nominee if the nominee is opposed by one (or both) senators from the nominee's home state.

The Senate Judiciary Committee gathers information on and interviews judicial nominees. Then, the Committee votes on whether to recommend the nominees to the full Senate. The full Senate uses this vote to signal whether a nominee is acceptable. Sometimes the judiciary committee does not make a recommendation about a nominee, as when members split their vote 7–7 on the nomination of Clarence Thomas to the U.S. Supreme Court in 1991. The full Senate followed this split recommendation with a 52–48 vote to confirm Thomas.

President Obama, like Presidents Bill Clinton and George W. Bush before him, ran into problems with many of his judicial nominees, particularly those nominated to the courts of appeals. Sparked by partisanship, senators from both

Should There Be a Retirement Age for Supreme Court Justices?

THE ISSUE: In 2021 five justices qualify for Social Security; their ages will range from 66 to 83. Calls for justices to retire are not unusual, although the call is typically sparked by ideological disagreements. However, as the average age of retirement for justices has risen from 68 before 1971 to 79 today, calls for a mandatory retirement age have grown louder. This debate intensified following the death of Justice Ruth Bader Ginsburg at the age of 87 in September 2020.

YES: The justices that sit on the Supreme Court are responsible for solving some of the most controversial legal disputes that are dividing our nation today. We cannot afford to leave these vital decisions to justices who may be experiencing even normal, age-related cognitive decline. Although mandatory retirement was made illegal in 1986, there are some exceptions to the law. Most state governments have taken advantage of this and established mandatory retirement ages for their judges; most set the retirement age between 70 and 75. The legitimacy of the Court is at stake.

NO: Americans are living longer and healthier lives with each generation. Life expectancy at birth for people born in 1900 was 49 years; for people born in 1950 it was 68 years. For people born in 2012, life expectancy is 79 years. People should not be forced to retire simply because of the number of years they have lived. Retirement should be voluntary unless an employer can prove the employee is no longer competent to do the job. If there is evidence that a justice is declining cognitively and is no longer competent, the justice can be encouraged to retire. If the justice chooses not to retire, then impeachment might be an option; lack of good behavior could be the accusation. This approach serves fairness and due process.

OTHER APPROACHES: The federal government should establish successful programs already piloted. For example, the Ninth Circuit Court of Appeals offers a series of mental health assessments, hosts educational programs with neurological experts, and has a hotline for staff and judges to report signs of cognitive decline of judges. Another approach would be to offer an incentive for justices to accept "senior status," which is a form of semi-retirement available to judges at a certain combination of years served and age. Constitutional scholars have suggested another approach: Establish an 18-year term for federal judges.

WHAT DO YOU THINK?

1. A constitutional amendment is needed to establish an age of retirement or a fixed term for justices. Do you think that Congress and three-quarters of state legislatures would support either amendment? Why or why not?

2. Do you think the statement that justices "shall hold their offices during good behavior" means that they serve a life term until they retire, die, or get impeached? Could it mean "shall keep their job as long as they are competent"? Justify your answer.

3. Would such a policy affect the independence of the judiciary? Would it affect its legitimacy? Explain why or why not.

political parties have used the filibuster to block votes on judicial nominees to promote partisan bias on specific courts. In November 2013, after repeated filibustering of President Obama's nominees, the Democratic majority in the U.S. Senate argued that the Republican minority had gone too far in its efforts to thwart the president. Without one vote from the Republican minority, the Democratic majority approved a filibuster rule change, called the nuclear option, prohibiting the use of the filibuster to block votes on presidential nominees to executive branch positions and all judicial positions except those for the U.S. Supreme Court. In the 2017 confirmation of Justice Gorsuch, the Senate Republicans voted to prohibit the use of the filibuster to block his confirmation to the Supreme Court.

Once Supreme Court justices and other Article III judges are confirmed by the Senate, they serve for as long as they want, or until death, or conviction by the Senate of an impeachable offense. Although lifetime tenure is controversial, as debated in the "Thinking Critically" feature, it also means that such appointees often are the longest-lasting legacies of the presidents who appoint them.

How the U.S. Supreme Court Functions

As a **collegial court,** the Supreme Court is made up of a panel of justices who must work closely together to evaluate a case and decide, with a simple majority vote, the outcome. Collegially, they decide what cases to hear, resolve each case heard, and develop the legal reasoning that, as presented in the Court's written opinion, will persuade the public that the Court's decision is correct. The *correct decision* means the justices upheld the legal principles found in the Constitution. Today's reality is that it is common for Supreme Court cases to be decided by a 5–4 vote, which indicates that the justices do not all agree on the same interpretation of constitutional language and its legal principles.

collegial court
A court made up of a group of judges who must evaluate a case together and decide on the outcome; compromise and negotiation take place as members try to build a majority coalition.

The overwhelming majority of cases decided by the U.S. Supreme Court are appeals. Therefore, we focus on how the Court processes the appeals that are filed with it.

Choosing Cases for Review

Between 7,000 and 8,000 *certiorari* **petitions** are filed with the Court each year, each asking for the review of a case already decided. Ultimately, the justices agree to review about 80 cases in each annual term that begins in October and typically runs through the following June or July.[19] For the thousands of cases the Court decides not to hear, the decision made by the last court to hear the case stands. How do the justices decide which cases to hear? Like the other stages of the decision-making process, "deciding to decide," as Supreme Court scholar H. W. Perry puts it, is a joint activity.[20]

***certiorari* petition**
A petition submitted to the Supreme Court requesting review of a case already decided by a lower court.

The decision to place a case on the Supreme Court's docket (schedule of cases it will review) is a collaborative one, with the nine justices and their law clerks (four clerks per associate justice, and five for the chief justice) working together. Most Supreme Court justices pool their law clerks so that only one clerk reviews a *certiorari* petition and writes a **cert memo,** which includes a description of the facts of the case, the pertinent legal arguments, and a recommendation as to whether the Court should hear the case. The clerk's cert memo is shared with all the justices. After reviewing the cert memos, the chief justice distributes a list of possible cases, the discuss list. The associate justices may add cases to the discuss list based on their own reviews of cert memos.

On Fridays throughout the Court's term, the justices meet in conference to discuss the cases on the discuss list.[21] At this point, they vote on whether to issue a writ of *certiorari*—a Latin term roughly translated as "a request to make certain"—for specific cases. The **writ of *certiorari*** is a higher court's order to a lower court to make available the records of a past case so that the higher court can review the case.[22] A writ of *certiorari* is sent when the justices, using their discretionary jurisdiction, agree to hear a case. The justices determine which cases to hear according to a practice known as the **Rule of Four,** under which the justices will hear a case if four or more of the nine justices decide they want to hear it. They do not need to give reasons for wanting or not wanting to hear a case—they simply must vote.

Considering Legal Briefs and Oral Arguments

When the justices agree to put a case on the docket, the parties in the litigation shift into high gear (see Figure 6.2). The petitioner (the party that sought the Court's review) files with the Court a brief—a document detailing the legal argument for the desired outcome. After the filing of this brief, the opposing party files its own brief with the Court.

Today, *amicus curiae* briefs are a common part of Supreme Court litigation. Filed by a person or group that is not a party to the lawsuit, an ***amicus curiae* brief,** or **"friend of the court" brief,** is written to influence the Court's decision in a specific case. Controversial cases with the potential to affect public policy trigger the filing of many *amicus* briefs. In 2013, the 136 *amicus* briefs submitted in the lawsuit challenging parts of the Affordable Care Act was the highest number filed in one case up to that date. Then, in 2015, 148 *amicus* briefs were filed in the same-sex marriage case *Obergefell v. Hodges*. One of those 148 briefs was filed on behalf of 370 businesses.[23]

In comparison with the legal briefs filed by the two parties involved in the legal dispute, *amicus curiae* briefs typically put forth new legal arguments and discuss broader societal effects of potential Court decisions (not just the effect on the litigants). Justices do not legally have to consider the information provided in *amicus curiae* briefs. However, research indicates that justices often use the information or the legal arguments contained in *amicus curiae* briefs to help them decide cases.[24] Judicial scholar Paul Collins found that no type of interest group dominated *amicus* activity, but instead "*amicus* participation in the Court is pluralistic."[25] Associate Supreme Court justice Stephen Breyer argues that the participation of organized interests in the judicial decision-making process provides an avenue for citizen engagement and civic discourse, which support a healthy democracy.[26]

Cases on the U.S. Supreme Court's docket

Original jurisdiction

Applications for review by appeal or writ of *certiorari* from federal and state courts (justices use Rule of Four to determine docket)

1 Briefs submitted by both sides; *amicus curiae* briefs filed by interested parties

2 Oral arguments presented by attorneys for each side

3 Justices' conference: cases discussed; nonbinding votes taken; opinion writing assigned

4 Justices' opinions drafted and circulated for comment

5 Court's final decision announced

FIGURE 6.2 ■ **Decision Making on the Supreme Court**

In addition to reviewing legal briefs, justices listen to oral arguments—attorneys' formal spoken arguments that lay out why the Court should rule in their client's favor. Heard in the Supreme Court's public gallery, oral arguments give the justices the opportunity to ask the parties and their lawyers specific questions about the arguments in their briefs. To assist in their preparation for oral argument, justices typically have their law clerks prepare **bench memos,** which summarize the case and outline relevant facts and issues presented in the case documents and the legal briefs. The bench memos may also suggest questions for the justices to ask during oral arguments.[27]

In typical cases, each side's lawyers have 30 minutes to make a statement to the Court and to answer the justices' questions. However, the justices can provide more time for oral argument, as they did in 2012 when they scheduled six hours of oral argument, over the course of three days, for the case challenging the constitutionality of the Patient Protection and Affordable Care Act (2010). The justices frequently interrupt the attorneys during their oral arguments by asking questions and sometimes seem to ignore the lawyers entirely, instead talking with one another. Chief Justice Roberts points out that the justices do not discuss the cases before oral argument. "When we get out on the bench, it's really the first time we start to get some clues about what our colleagues think. So we are often using questions to bring out points that we think our colleagues ought to know about."[28] Associate Justice Kagan notes that "part of what oral argument is about is a little bit of the justices talking to each other with some helpless person standing at the podium who you're talking through."[29] This discourse takes place entirely in public view, and transcripts and even audiotapes are readily available to the public.

After the oral arguments, the justices meet in a private, justice-only conference to deliberate; no law clerks are present, and no information is shared with the public. The justices take a nonbinding vote on the case. If the chief justice votes with the majority, he chooses whether he wants to write the opinion that will provide the legal reasoning for the Court's decision or if he will assign the task to one of the other justices in the likely majority. If the chief justice is not with the majority, the senior member of the majority decides whether to write the opinion or assign the opinion to another justice. The assignment of the majority opinion is crucial to the resolution of the case because, in writing the opinion, the justice may persuade some justices to change their votes, making for a larger majority or possibly turning the majority into the minority, turning the losing party (based on the nonbinding conference vote) into the winning party.

Resolving the Legal Dispute: Deciding How to Vote

How does each justice decide how to vote in a particular case? Judicial scholars offer several judicial decision-making models. The **legal model** focuses on legal norms and principles as the guiding force in judicial decision making. Specifically, according to the legal model, judges consider existing precedents, relevant constitutional and statutory law, and the intent of those who wrote the relevant laws, when deciding cases. Law schools train lawyers, and therefore judges, to follow the legal model. The **attitudinal model** indicates that judges allow their policy and ideological preferences to influence their decisions. In fact, evidence suggests that Supreme Court justices are for the most part ideologically consistent in their own decision making.[30] Constitutional law professor Dale Carpenter notes, "There's evidence that the justices do vote against their policy preferences from time to time, enough to disrupt the general narrative that they just vote their ideological preferences. But that doesn't stop the general story from being true."[31]

bench memo
Written by a justice's law clerk, a summary of the case, outlining relevant facts and issues presented in the case documents and briefs, that may also suggest questions to be asked during oral arguments.

legal model
Judicial decision-making model that focuses on legal norms and principles as the guiding force in judicial decision making, including existing precedents, relevant constitutional and statutory law, and the lawmakers' intent.

attitudinal model
Judicial decision-making model that claims judicial decision making is guided by policy and ideological preferences of individual judges.

strategic model

Judicial decision-making model that states that the primary guide for judges is their individual policy preferences; however, their preferences are tempered by their consideration of institutional factors, as well as concern over the legitimacy of the court system.

According to the **strategic model,** "while justices' decisions are primarily motivated by policy concerns (thus accepting the attitudinal model), institutional constraints exist that limit the ability of the justices to vote in a manner that is compatible with their attitudes and values in every case."[32] The institutional constraints identified by proponents of the strategic model include the preferences of Congress, the president, and other justices sitting on the collegial Court, as well as concern for maintaining the legitimacy of the court system. If the Court makes decisions that are too far afield from societal norms, the public might begin to question the legitimacy of the Court in our democracy.

Research on the decision making of the Supreme Court justices suggests that none of these models explains every aspect of judicial decision making. Indeed, the three models must be combined to better understand these decision makers. Judicial scholars Bryan W. Marshall, Richard L. Pacelle, Jr., and Christine Ludowise argue that "the behavior of the Supreme Court is governed by the personal preferences of the justices, but that is tempered by the need to attend to precedent as well as the institution's sense of duty and obligation to the law and the Constitution."[33]

Legal Reasoning: Writing the Opinions

After the conference at which the nonbinding vote to decide a case occurs, justices and their law clerks begin writing opinions. The justices' law clerks often write the first draft of their opinions and frequently take the lead in communicating with the other justices through their law clerks. In fact, judicial scholar Artemus Ward states: "Modern justices now see themselves and their clerks as comprising an opinion writing team."[34]

concurring opinion

A judicial opinion agreeing with the majority decision in the case but disagreeing with at least some of the legal interpretations or conclusions reached in the majority opinion.

The justice assigned the majority opinion will circulate a draft and revise it based on input from the other justices. Revisions are made to strengthen the legal reasoning, to win new votes from justices who were in the minority, or to keep the votes of justices in the majority. Other justices, with their clerks, will draft and circulate opinions with their legal reasoning. Some of these drafts may become concurring opinions; others may become dissenting opinions. **Concurring opinions** agree with the majority decision in the case but disagree with at least some of

---

INTERPRETING IMAGES

>> The Supreme Court began audio recording oral arguments in 1955, but to date it does not allow video recording or even photographs during oral arguments. Therefore, the only images we have of Supreme Court cases are artists' sketches. The public can download the audio files or listen to the recordings on the Court's website or on oyez.com. The National Archives serves as the repository for the Court's recordings.

Interpret: Why would the presence of video recordings or photographs affect the work of the Court? What might be the motivation for continuing to allow only sketches like this one? What message do these images send?

Dana Verkouteren/AP Images

the legal reasoning or conclusions reached in the majority opinion. **Dissenting opinions** not only disagree with the legal reasoning but also reject the underlying decision in the case.

After the opinions are written and signed off on, the Court announces the decision by publishing it. On rare occasions, the justices read their opinions from the bench. In 2007, Justice Ginsburg read her dissenting opinion in the *Ledbetter v. Goodyear Tire & Rubber*[35] case to bring immediate attention to a decision that she believed would have great, negative consequences, especially on women. Ginsburg's reading was a catalyst for Congress to formulate and enact the Lilly Ledbetter Fair Pay Act in 2009, which overruled the Court's interpretation of a piece of the 1964 Civil Rights Act.

In the *Ledbetter* case, the Court decided that when Ledbetter finally found out about her discriminatory pay, 19 years after her first discriminatory paycheck, it was too late for her to sue. The majority of justices interpreted the 1964 Civil Rights Act as limiting the time to file a lawsuit to no more than 180 days after the first discriminatory paycheck was issued. However, the Fair Pay Act of 2009 states that the 180-day statute of limitation to file an equal pay lawsuit established in the 1964 law resets after each new discriminatory paycheck. The Fair Pay Act is now the law the Supreme Court must apply in discrimination cases.

Although the U.S. Supreme Court is the court of last resort, it does not always have the final word. As in the *Ledbetter* case, Congress can write new legislation to overrule the Court's interpretation of law. In this way, the U.S. Supreme Court is part of an ongoing dialogue, with officials in the other branches and levels of government, on laws and policies.

■ Judges as Policymakers

Courts make law—common law—by deciding cases and establishing legal principles that guide future litigants and judges. The lawmaking function of courts ensures that judges have a powerful role as public policymakers, because the decisions they make profoundly affect not only the parties in the case but also society, the economy, and politics.

Law professor Tom Ginsburg, who compares constitutions from across the globe adopted since 1787, notes that the U.S. Constitution is briefer and covers fewer topics than do more recently approved constitutions. It also does not cover contemporary issues and topics because it was ratified over 225 years ago and has been amended only 27 times. This means that the U.S. Constitution leaves more room for courts to fill in gaps. According to Ginsburg, "all of these factors perversely empower the Supreme Court and make the court much more likely to engage in public policy."[36]

From Judicial Review to Judicial Policymaking

The Court's decision in *Marbury v. Madison* (1803) claimed the power of judicial review for the courts, making the courts a major policymaker. The courts determine what government actions are constitutional. In 1896, the Supreme Court decided in *Plessy v. Ferguson*[37] that the Fourteenth Amendment did not prohibit segregation of people based on race and color in public accommodations, specifically train cars. The Court in *Plessy* established the common-law legal principle of separate but equal. That decision allowed state and local governments to enact laws that permitted, and in some cases even required, segregation by race in a variety of venues, from movie theaters to housing developments to public schools. Then the Court struck a blow to segregation policies with its decision in *Brown v. Board of Education of Topeka, Kansas* (1954).[38] In *Brown*, using the common-law principle of judicial review, the Court reinterpreted the Fourteenth Amendment's equal protection clause, ruling the legal principle of separate but equal unconstitutional, and found segregation laws unconstitutional. The Court took its decision further, calling for integration of public schools with all deliberate speed. Clearly, the Court was engaged in policymaking, and the policy has had a tremendous effect on society, the economy, and politics.

Former Supreme Court Justice Sandra Day O'Connor argues that the *Brown* case was a catalyst for lawsuits in which litigants claim violations of their constitutional rights to equal protection of the law and due process. O'Connor notes that prior to the *Brown* case, conflicts over the separation of powers within the national government and the distribution of powers between the national and state governments dominated the Supreme Court's docket. However, since the *Brown* case, "the Supreme Court's decisions on individual rights have recognized for the first time many of the freedoms that most Americans today assume as our birthrights. Among them are the right to speak freely and advocate for change, the right to worship as we please, and the privilege of political participation."[39] Therefore, judicial policymaking includes defending and creating individual rights through the courts' interpretations of laws.

Judicial Activism, Living Constitution, Judicial Restraint, and Originalism

When considering the courts' role as policymakers, politicians and the popular media often categorize judges and justices as exercising either judicial activism or judicial restraint. **Judicial activism** refers to the courts' willingness to strike down laws made by elected officials as well as to step away from precedents, thereby creating new laws and policies. It reflects the notion that the role of the courts is to check the power of the federal and state executive and legislative branches when those governmental entities exceed their authority or violate the Constitution. In contrast, some judges reject the idea that the courts' role is to actively check legislative and executive authority. Noting that people elect officials to those branches to carry out the people's will, these judges observe **judicial restraint**—the limiting of their own power as judges. Practitioners of judicial restraint believe that the judiciary, as the least democratic (unelected) branch of government, should not check the power of the democratically elected executive and legislative branches unless their actions clearly violate the Constitution.[40]

During the Warren Court (the tenure of Chief Justice Earl Warren, 1953–1969), using the doctrine of judicial review, the Supreme Court took an activist stance, most notably in rejecting the constitutionality of racial segregation. By barring southern states from segregation in a variety of contexts—including schools and other public facilities—the Warren Court powerfully bolstered the efforts of civil rights activists. The activism of the Warren Court also shaped the modern rights of the accused and the modern definitions of the privacy rights of individuals, which later formed the framework for the Court's thinking about abortion rights. Supported by presidents who enforced its rulings, the Warren Court took on a

judicial activism
An approach to judicial decision making whereby judges are willing to strike down laws made by elected officials as well as step away from precedents.

judicial restraint
An approach to judicial decision making whereby judges defer to the democratically elected legislative and executive branches of government.

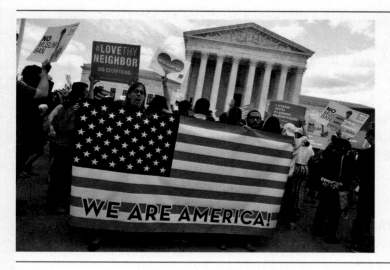

>> The Supreme Court is a backdrop for public protest on issues of interest to both liberals and conservatives. While the federal courts face criticism from all who disagree with their decisions, their authority to make such decisions traditionally has not been challenged. Do you believe President Trump's record of criticizing the courts threatens separation of powers or checks and balances?

Mandel Ngan/AFP/Getty Images

leadership role in changing the nature of U.S. society. Therefore, the majority on the Warren Court, in racial segregation cases and with regard to due process in the criminal justice system, treated the Constitution as a **living constitution;** that is, their legal interpretations took into consideration changes in social customs and norms.

Judicial activism is also used to further conservative causes. In fact, judicial scholar Thomas Keck labeled the Rehnquist Court (1986–2005) "the most activist Supreme Court in history."[41] The Rehnquist Court's conservative-leaning activism is evident in cases in which the Court overturned laws enacted by Congress such as the Gun-Free School Zones Act[42] and a section of the Violence Against Women Act that created a right for victims of sexual misconduct to sue in federal courts.[43] For some, the ultimate judicial activism occurred during the 2000 presidential election, when the U.S. Supreme Court overturned the Florida Supreme Court's interpretation of Florida election law on counting votes.[44]

Originalism (textualism), the judicial principle that the Constitution means no more or less than what it meant to those who wrote it, is often coupled with judicial restraint when characterizing a justice's judicial decision making. Presented as the opposite of those who acknowledge the Constitution as a living document, originalists try to interpret constitutional language based on the time, culture, norms, and customs at the time of its writing. However, even the most well-known originalist and advocate for judicial restraint, former Supreme Court justice Antonin Scalia, was not always faithful to the "original" meaning of the Constitution. For example, in the majority opinion he wrote in *District of Columbia v. Heller*,[45] Scalia used legislative history (not the public understanding from 1789) to justify, for the first time in U.S. history, that the Second Amendment protects an individual's right to keep and bear arms for self-defense.[46] (See Chapter 8 for a longer discussion of the evolution of the Second Amendment.)

Today, political scientists argue that "judicial activism simply means that the courts make public policy when the elected branches cannot or will not, often by declaring the actions of other political actors to be unconstitutional."[47] But, as noted, the term *judicial activism* is also applied to judges who view the Constitution as a living, evolving document. However, people also often use the term to criticize judges when they disagree with a decision, thereby limiting its utility in explaining judicial decisions. As judicial scholar Thomas Keck has

ARGUMENTATION | THINKING CRITICALLY

Develop an argument taking a position on whether or not the Supreme Court has achieved judicial independence as intended by the framers of the Constitution. Consider not only the decisions made by the Court, but also the confirmation process of the individual justices.

In your essay, you must:

- Articulate a defensible claim or thesis that responds to the prompt and establishes a line of reasoning

- Support your claim with at least TWO pieces of accurate and relevant information:

  - At least ONE piece of evidence must be from one of the following foundational documents:

    — *Federalist* No. 78
    — Article II of the U.S. Constitution
    — Article III of the U.S. Constitution

  - Use a second piece of evidence from another foundational document from the list or from your study of the process of appointing federal judges

- Use reasoning to explain why your evidence supports your claim/thesis

- Respond to an opposing or alternative perspective using refutation, concession, or rebuttal

observed in reference to "activist" decisions, "if [they] provoke a wide range of responses on the part of other policymakers, it is misleading to characterize such decisions as calling an end to democratic deliberation and debate."[48]

Constraints on Judicial Policymaking

The U.S. judiciary is a powerful institution. Nonetheless, judges and justices face checks and constraints that limit how they decide cases, make law, and act as policymakers. Among the most important checks on the judiciary's power are the other branches of government. But lawyers, interest groups, and individual citizens also check the courts and constrain their activism. Moreover, judges and justices are trained to, and actively attempt to, make good law by correctly interpreting the Constitution.[49]

CHECKS AND BALANCES Article II of the Constitution explicitly gives the legislative and executive branches crucial checks on the structure of the courts. It grants Congress the power to create all federal courts other than the Supreme Court. It also gives the president and the U.S. Senate important powers in determining who sits on all federal courts, providing the president and the Senate with significant control over the judiciary.

Beyond giving the president a check on the judiciary through the power to nominate judges, the Constitution also empowers the president and the executive branch because the courts must rely on the executive branch to enforce their decisions. Specifically, if presidents fail to direct the bureaucracy to carry out judicial decisions, those decisions carry little weight. Frequently, it is executive implementation that gives teeth to the judiciary's decisions.

The Constitution also creates a legislative check on the judiciary because the framers established only the Supreme Court and left it up to Congress to create the lower federal courts. In addition, the Constitution allows Congress to control the Supreme Court's jurisdiction. Congress also can control, through legislation, the number of judges or justices who serve in the federal judiciary. Historically, Congress has been willing to increase the number of judges only when its majority is of the same party affiliation as the incumbent president, who will have the authority to nominate judges to the newly created judgeships. During the Democratic presidential primaries, candidates such as Pete Buttigieg and activists advocated for the expansion of the Supreme Court to 15 seats, with five being recommended by Democrats, five by Republicans, and five selected in a nonpartisan fashion.[50]

The two houses of Congress, moreover, have a central role in deciding whether to impeach federal judges. The House issues the articles of impeachment, and the Senate conducts the impeachment trial. Finally, Congress initiates the process of constitutional amendment and can attempt to change the Constitution to overrule a Court decision with which it disagrees. In fact, in several cases Congress has embarked on constitutional amendment procedures in direct response to a Court decision with which members of Congress or their constituencies have disagreed. For example, the Twenty-Sixth Amendment (1971), which standardized the voting age to 18 years, came about after the Supreme Court ruled that states could set their own age limits for state elections.[51]

Although the courts can check the lawmaking (and hence policy-making) power of the legislative and executive branches by exercising judicial review, the legislature and the executive can check the courts' power of judicial review through the creation of new laws. For example, as discussed earlier in this chapter, in response to the Supreme Court's interpretation of a piece of the Civil Rights Act of 1964 in *Ledbetter v. Goodyear Tire & Rubber* in 2007, Congress approved and President Obama signed the Lilly Ledbetter Fair Pay Act in 2009, which overruled the Court's interpretation of law.

PUBLIC ACCOUNTABILITY Public opinion seems to have a distinct influence on what the courts do, especially appellate courts such as the U.S. Supreme Court. The Court rarely issues a decision that is completely out of step with the thinking of the majority of the population. In part, this is because the federal courts depend on the elected branches of government—which are directly responsive to public opinion—for the enforcement of their edicts. When the Court does break with public opinion, it opens itself up to harsh criticism by the president, Congress, interest groups, and/or the general public.

But sometimes in the case of a landmark decision that is out of touch with public sentiment, the Court's ruling and people's opinions align over time. This shift can occur either because later courts adjust the original, controversial decision or, less commonly, because the Supreme Court's decision changes public opinion. One example of the interplay between public opinion and judicial

Citizens' Approval of the Supreme Court and Its Work

U.S. Supreme Court Job Approval

Do you approve or disapprove of the way the Supreme Court is handling its job?

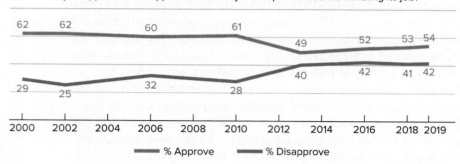

U.S. Supreme Court Job Approval, by Party ID

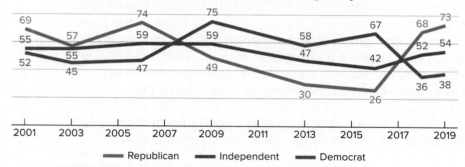

Source: Lydia Saad, Politics, October 2, 2019, Gallup.

Practice Analytical Thinking

1. Look at the first chart regarding public approval of the Supreme Court. What trends do you see? For context, trust in the judiciary averaged in the low 70s prior to President Richard Nixon's impeachment.

2. For comparison, trust in the presidency has averaged around 54 percent overall, trust in the legislative branch has averaged 50 percent, and trust in the judiciary has been at 64 percent. Why do you think the judiciary is the most trusted of the three federal branches? Which factors might cause people to trust it more or less?

3. In looking at the second chart, what factors might have influenced changes in trust of the judiciary?

4. What happened in 2008 and 2016 that might explain the large shifts in partisan valuing of the judiciary in 2009 and 2018?

5. Why would new presidential administrations affect public perception of the courts if the court's personnel is static until the new president begins appointing new judges or justices?

6. Why does it matter if approval of the judiciary is tied to presidential elections? How does the concept of judicial legitimacy help explain this relationship?

decisions can be seen in the *Brown v. Board of Education* Court ruling. Initially, many southern state legislatures and even judges in federal district and appellate courts in the South did not comply with the Court's call to integrate schools. Not only did some school districts continue to segregate, but more than 100 southern legislators signed the "Southern Manifesto," a document that claimed the U.S. Supreme Court had overstepped its authority. By the 1970s, some progress in integrating schools had been made. However, legal conflicts over segregation and integration are ongoing.

Citizens can also constrain the courts by threatening to ignore their rulings. When members of the public disagree with judicial decisions, or with any law for that matter, they can engage in civil disobedience. In acts of civil disobedience, individuals or groups flout the law to make a larger point about its underlying unfairness. Keep in mind that the courts have little ability to enforce their decisions, and if people refuse to recognize those decisions and the other branches of the government fail to enforce them, the courts risk losing their authority and power. Fear of losing authority may explain in part why judicial decisions rarely fall out of step with the larger public stance on an issue. Like legislators, executives, and their colleagues sitting on the bench, citizens can impose significant constraints on courts and probably limit how judges handle cases and interpret laws. These constraints may not be written into the U.S. Constitution as the checks by the other branches are, but they are nonetheless very powerful and have a significant impact on how judges decide cases.

INTERNAL CONSTRAINTS Judges and justices also face powerful internal constraints on their judicial actions. Law schools train lawyers, and hence judges, to focus on the facts of the case and the relevant legal principles (found in law and precedent cases) when deciding cases. For lower-court judges, precedents from higher courts, as well as earlier decisions made by the court itself, impose limitations through the common-law doctrine of *stare decisis.* In addition, federal district court and appeals court judges do not diverge far from Supreme Court precedent because if they did so, they would risk having their decisions overturned by the Supreme Court. According to judicial scholar Paul Collins, "Judges are concerned with making good law: attempting to determine the *most* legally appropriate answer to the controversy."[52]

■ Judicial Legitimacy and Public Trust

President Donald Trump was an atypical president in many ways, but his relationship to the federal courts has challenged many traditional norms and expectations, often via his use of social media.

- When a U.S. district judge blocked his administration's effort to withhold federal funding from cities offering sanctuary for undocumented immigrants, the president tweeted (referencing the wrong court) that it was a "ridiculous" ruling and that the Ninth Circuit "has a terrible record of being overturned (close to 80%). They used to call this 'judge shopping!' Messy system."[53]

- While the president's friend Roger Stone was being prosecuted for lying to Congress and obstructing an inquiry into potential collaboration between Donald Trump's campaign and Russia during the 2016 election, the president tweeted this about the presiding judge: "I think almost any judge in the

Country . . . would order a new trial, I'm not so sure about Judge Jackson, I don't know."[54] He also tweeted, "Is this the Judge that put Paul Manafort [his former campaign chair] in SOLITARY CONFINEMENT, something that not even mobster Al Capone had to endure? How did she treat Crooked Hillary Clinton? Just asking!"[55]

- After a federal judge temporarily blocked enforcement of his 2017 ban prohibiting travelers from selected Muslim countries, President Trump tweeted, "The opinion of this so-called judge, which essentially takes law-enforcement away from our country, is ridiculous and will be overturned!"[56]

- At other times, President Trump has referred to decisions as "disgraceful" and biased because the president who appointed the presiding judge was a Democrat, and he suggested that Justices Ruth Bader Ginsburg and Sonia Sotomayor should recuse themselves from every decision addressing his administration.[57]

Public criticism of judicial decisions by presidents is not unheard of or unusual. After the 2010 *Citizens United v. FCC*[58] decision, President Obama was very outspoken in his evaluation of the new doctrine. What has made President Trump's approach atypical is that he did not limit himself to expressing disappointment or disagreement with a judicial ruling that was contrary to his administration's policy preferences; instead, his attacks targeted the legitimacy of the courts to make these rulings and the integrity of the federal judges who make them. As you have learned earlier in this chapter, life tenure protects these justices and judges from being removed from the bench because a president or Congress doesn't like their rulings.[59]

In fact, judges and justices have been so concerned about President Trump's assessment of the federal courts that they have responded publicly. In Advisory Opinion 116, passed in 2019, the committee that regulates the judicial code of conduct for federal judges recommended that judges consider whether an organization is "viewed by the public as having adopted a consistent political or ideological point of view equivalent to the type of partisanship often found in political organizations" before participating in that group's activities.[60] Chief Justice Roberts has been particularly concerned about judicial legitimacy as it interferes with the ability of the courts to uphold the rule of law.[61]

INTERPRETING IMAGES

>> How does this picture demonstrate the ways in which the federal courts have become more politicized? What does it mean for the legitimacy of the courts when justices participate in activities perceived to be partisan or have action figures that appeal to a specific ideology?

Max Oden/Sipa USA/AP Images

TABLE 6.4 ■ The Roberts Court

Considering the age of the Supreme Court justices nominated by President Barack Obama, what do you think will be President Obama's long-term effect on the decision making of the Court? What might explain the pattern of change in confirmation votes from 1991 through 2020? How many justices do you predict President Biden will be able to appoint?

Justice	Year Appointed	Nominating President	Confirmation Vote	Year of Birth
Clarence Thomas	1991	George H. W. Bush (R)	52–48	1948
Stephen G. Breyer	1994	Bill Clinton (D)	87–9	1938
John G. Roberts	2005	George W. Bush (R)	78–22	1955
Samuel Anthony Alito	2006	George W. Bush (R)	58–42	1950
Sonia Sotomayor	2009	Barack Obama (D)	68–31	1954
Elena Kagan	2010	Barack Obama (D)	63–37	1960
Neil Gorsuch	2017	Donald Trump (R)	54–45	1967
Brett Kavanaugh	2018	Donald Trump (R)	50–48	1963
Amy Coney Barrett	2020	Donald Trump (R)	52–48	1972

Source: U.S. Supreme Court

The courts have always understood that citizens must be confident that the rule of law is the basis of our government and that the courts uphold it fairly. Even when it does not work perfectly, this guarantee promises us something to work and aspire toward. So while judges and justices are human and have personal preferences and political ideologies, they have historically worked hard not to have identifiable partisan alignments. Some justices do not vote in primary elections so that their party identification remains private. Further, we have the concept of the **cult of the robe,** which refers to the deliberate mystification of the courts, and the Supreme Court in particular, through the wearing of black robes, the practice of sitting on high benches, the exclusion of cameras, and the internal policy of not providing additional justification for decisions outside the official opinions. These trappings of office are designed to make judges and justices appear less political as a body and more trustworthy in their administration of law. And judicial norms reinforce the ideal that judges and justices avoid partisan or overtly political commentary or actions.[62] But despite these concerted efforts to avoid engaging in partisan politics, the judiciary is still a political branch generating policy decisions that impact "who gets what, when, and how."[63]

cult of the robe
The trappings of judicial office (robe, high bench, no filming, private deliberations) that separate the judicial branch from the elected bodies to make it appear to be outside partisan politics.

271

In recent years, this barrier between the judiciary and the public has slipped. Justices Alito, Thomas, and Kavanaugh have regularly spoken publicly at the Federalist Society, a conservative interest group. Justice Ginsburg, known as RBG, had a cult following of liberal fans who identify with her and her dissents on issues they care about, and she was celebrated in two movies and a plethora of merchandise. She slipped at times and publicly commented in a partisan fashion.

What does it mean for the rule of law if the courts are just another partisan branch? Scholarship shows that at all levels of the appellate judiciary, there are a large percentage of cases on which panels of judges rule unanimously or that are untouched by partisan rancor.[64] Only in the most visible and highly contested cases, on issues that affect citizens personally—abortion, health care, same-sex marriage, campaign finance, as examples—where parties have a stake and Congress has been unwilling or unable to make clear policy, do we see these close, split opinions along partisan lines. But these are the only opinions that most Americans know about. These are the opinions that the mainstream media covers. These relatively rare opinions frame Americans' understanding of the judicial branch, possibly to our detriment.

Conclusion: Thinking Critically About What's Next for the Judiciary

Rooted in a common-law tradition and framed by the Constitution, the American judiciary in its early form strongly reflected its English heritage, with its emphasis on law made by judges. Over the past two-plus centuries, the judiciary has evolved powerfully to accommodate a broad spectrum of societal changes in a continuously developing country. Today the policy-making role of the courts is acknowledged, if not appreciated, by political scientists, government officials, and most citizens.

The judicial activism practiced by all justices, as they apply the doctrine of judicial review, feeds concerns that the courts are engaged in partisan policymaking, just like the other two branches of government. Although judges strive to make decisions that are legally correct and grounded in the fundamental rights found in the U.S. Constitution and statutory law, the reality of divided decisions indicates that we do not always agree on the meaning of the Constitution. As the nation becomes increasingly polarized along partisan lines, as politics is primarily perceived through a partisan lens, and as elected branches see the courts as a means of achieving their political agendas, people's faith in the courts has likewise polarized.

Although many people criticize appellate courts for judicial activism when they disagree with a court decision, citizens trust the nonelected policymakers (judges and justices) of the federal judicial branch more than they trust their elected federal representatives in the executive and legislative branches. A Gallup October 2019 poll showed that 68 percent of Americans had a "great deal" or a "fair amount" of trust in the judicial branch. However, additional research demonstrates deep partisan divides in our trust in the federal judiciary.[65] Belief in the judiciary seems contingent on whether your preferred party occupies the White House and therefore has the ability to appoint people who may support your own ideology. Will the courts maintain their legitimacy and be able to fairly support the rule of law if they are perceived as merely another partisan branch? Will Chief Justice Roberts be able to lead the federal judiciary in demonstrating that their allegiance to the Constitution and to the rule of law is sustained even as they make decisions with political and policy implications?

References

1. Walter F. Murphy, *Constitutional Democracy: Creating and Maintaining a Just Political Order* (Baltimore, MD: Johns Hopkins University Press, 2007), 12.

2. Brian L. Porto, *May It Please the Court: Judicial Processes and Politics in America* (New York: Longman, 2001), 4.

3. *United States v. Nixon,* 418 U.S. 683 (1974).

4. "President Trump Declares State of Emergency for COVID-19," National Conference of State Legislatures, March 25, 2020.

5. 2020 Donald Trump Executive Orders, *Federal Register*, https://www.federalregister.gov/presidential-documents/executive-orders/donald-trump/2020.

6. G. Alan Tarr, *Judicial Process and Judicial Policymaking*, 6th ed. (Boston: Wadsworth/Cengage Learning, 2014).

7. Charles D. Shipan, *Designing Judicial Review* (Ann Arbor: University of Michigan Press, 1997).

8. Joel B. Grossman, "Paths to the Bench: Selecting Supreme Court Justices in a 'Juristocratic' World," in *The Judicial Branch,* ed. Kermit L. Hall and Kevin T. McGuire (Oxford: Oxford University Press, 2005), 143.

9. Porto, *May It Please the Court,* 32.

10. 50 U.S.C. §§1801-1811, 1821-29, 1841-46, and 1861-62.

11. Charlie Savage, "We Just Got a Rare Look at National Security Surveillance: It Was Ugly," *The New York Times*, December 11, 2019.

12. Charlie Savage, "Problems in FBI Wiretap Applications Go beyond Trump Aide Surveillance, Review Finds," *The New York Times*, March 31, 2020.

13. Mary L. Volcansek, *Comparative Judicial Politics* (Lanham, MD: Rowman & Littlefield, 2019), 76.

14. Christopher P. Banks and David M. O'Brien, *Courts and Judicial Policymaking* (Upper Saddle River, NJ: Pearson Prentice Hall, 2008), 130.

15. Adam Liptak, "Suggestions on a Successor: Scalia Urged a More Varied Membership," *The New York Times*, February 16, 2016: A1, A13.

16. Adam Liptak, "Roberts Had Criticized Supreme Court Confirmation Process," *The Times-Tribune*, March 22, 2016: A7.

17. Russell Wheeler, "Judicial Appointments in Trump's First Three Years: Myths and Realities," Brookings Institution, January 28, 2020.

18. Hugh Hewitt, transcript of an interview, "Senate Majority Leader Mitch McConnell," March 31, 2020.

19. Robert M. Yablon, "Justice Sotomayor and the Supreme Court's Certiorari Process," 123 *Yale L. J. F.* 551 (2014).

20. H. W. Perry Jr., *Deciding to Decide: Agenda Setting in the United States Supreme Court* (Cambridge, MA: Harvard University Press, 1994).

21. Bob Woodward, *The Brethren: Inside the Supreme Court* (New York: Simon & Schuster, 2005).

22. Henry J. Abraham, *The Judicial Process* (New York: Oxford University Press, 1998).

23. Nina Totenberg, "Record Number of Amicus Briefs Filed in Same-Sex-Marriage Cases," *NPR*, April 28, 2015.

24. Benjamin N. Cardozo, *The Nature of the Judicial Process* (Mineola, NY: Dover, 2005); Paul Collins Jr., *Friends of the Supreme Court: Interest Groups and Judicial Decision Making* (New York: Oxford University Press, 2008); and Allison Orr Larsen, "The Trouble with Amicus Facts," *Virginia Law Review* 100, no. 8 (December 2014).

25. Collins, *Friends of the Supreme Court*, 71–72.

26. Stephen Breyer, *Active Liberty: Interpreting Our Democratic Constitution* (New York: Vintage Books, 2006).

27. Artemus Ward, "Sorcerers' Apprentices: U.S. Supreme Court Law Clerks," in *Exploring Judicial Politics,* ed. Mark C. Miller (New York: Oxford University Press, 2009), 159.

28. Adam Liptak, "A Most Inquisitive Court? No Argument There," *The New York Times*, October 8, 2013.

29. Ibid.

30. Bryan W. Marshall, Richard L. Pacelle Jr., and Christine Ludowise, "A Court of Laws or a Superlegislature? An Integrated Model of Supreme Court Decision Making," in *Exploring Judicial Politics,* ed. Mark C. Miller (New York: Oxford University Press, 2009), 194.

31. Eric Black, "Something Changed: Picking a Supreme Court Justice Is Now a Partisan Battle," *MinnPost*, November 26, 2012.

32. Collins, *Friends of the Supreme Court,* 12.

33. Marshall, Pacelle, and Ludowise, "A Court of Laws or a Superlegislature?"

34. Ward, "Sorcerers' Apprentices," 168.

35. *Ledbetter v. Goodyear Tire & Rubber,* 550 U.S. 618 (2007).

36. Quoted in Eric Black, "How the Supreme Court Has Come to Play a Policymaking Role," MinnPost.com, November 20, 2012.

37. *Plessy v. Ferguson,* 163 U.S. 537 (1896).

38. *Brown v. Board of Education of Topeka, Kansas,* 347 U.S. 483 (1954).

39. Sandra Day O'Connor, *The Majesty of the Law: Reflections of a Supreme Court Justice* (New York: Random House, 2003), 266.

40. Antonin Scalia, *A Matter of Interpretation: Federal Courts and the Law* (Princeton, NJ: Princeton University Press, 1998).

41. Thomas M. Keck, *The Most Activist Supreme Court in History: The Road to Modern Judicial Conservatism* (Chicago: University of Chicago Press, 2004).

42. *U.S. v. Lopez,* 514 U.S. 549 (1995).

43. *U.S. v. Morrison,* 529 U.S. 598 (2000).

44. *Bush v. Gore,* 531 U.S. 98 (2000).

45. *District of Columbia v. Heller,* 554 U.S. 570 (2008).

46. Sheldon Whitehouse, "Conservative Judicial Activism: The Politicization of the Supreme Court Under Chief Justice Roberts," *Harvard Law & Policy Review*, March 18, 2015.

47. Mark C. Miller, "The Interactions between the Federal Courts and the Other Branches," in *Exploring Judicial Politics,* ed. Mark C. Miller (New York: Oxford University Press, 2009), 278–279.

48. Thomas M. Keck, *Judicial Politics in Polarized Times* (University of Chicago Press, 2014), 253.

49. Richard H. Fallon Jr., *Law and Legitimacy in the Supreme Court* (Cambridge, MA: Belknap/Harvard University Press, 2018), 130–131.

50. David A. Graham. "The Democrats Discover the Supreme Court," *The Atlantic*. June 4, 2019. Page 531

51. *Oregon v. Mitchell,* 400 U.S. 112 (1970).

52. Collins, *Friends of the Supreme Court*, 175.

53. Louis Nelson, "Trump attacks judiciary for blocking order on sanctuary cities," *Politico.com*, April 26, 2017.

54. Dan Mangan and Kevin W. Breuninger. "Trump Pushes for New Roger Stone Trial as Judges Call Emergency Meeting on Political Pressure," CNBC, February 18, 2020.

55. Brett Samuels. "Trump Swipes at Resigned Prosecutors, Judge in Roger Stone Case," *The Hill*, February 11, 2020.

56. Amy Wang, "Trump Lashes Out at 'So-Called Judge' Who Temporarily Blocked Travel Ban: The Tweets Came Hours after a Federal Judge in Washington State Temporarily Blocked Enforcement of President Trump's Executive Order," *Washington Post*, February 4, 2017.

57. Eli Okun, "Trump Calls for Sotomayor, Ginsburg to Recuse Themselves from Cases Dealing with His Administration," *Politico*, February 25, 2020.

58. *Citizens United v. FCC,* 558 U.S. 310 (2010).

59. Amy Steigerwalt. "He Won't Be Smiling: How Federal Judges Could Be Donald Trump's Worst Nightmare," *National Interest*, February 29, 2020.

60. Dennis Rendleman, "Undue Influence? Special Interest Groups Sponsor Judicial Education," American Bar Association, April 2019.

61. Adam Liptak, "Politics Has No Place at the Supreme Court, Chief Justice Roberts Says," *The New York Times*, September 25, 2019.

62. Barbara Perry, *The Priestly Tribe: The Supreme Court's Image in the American Mind* (New York: Praeger, 1999).

63. Harold Lasswell, *Politics: Who Gets What, When, How* (New York: Whittlesey House, 1936).

64. Cass R. Sunstein, David Schkade, Lisa M. Ellman, and Andres Sawicki, *Are Judges Political? An Empirical Analysis of the*

Federal Judiciary (Washington, DC: Brookings Institution, 2006.)

65. Jeffrey Jones, "Trust in Judicial Branch Up, Executive Branch Down," *News Gallup,* September 20, 2017.

■ Key Terms

▌Multiple-Choice Questions

1. A significant constraint to the United States Supreme Court's authority lies in its inability to
   A. overturn previous Supreme Court rulings
   B. use previous dissents for future court decisions
   C. add to their docket emergent cases carrying national consequences
   D. rely on Congress, the president, or the states to enforce its more unpopular rulings

2. Which of the following best describes an example of *amicus curiae*?
   A. An argument challenging the president's constitutional authority to seize steel mills
   B. The NAACP's legal brief in support of a black girl's request to attend an all-white school
   C. The Court's ruling that all persons have the right to a court-appointed attorney
   D. The Court's ruling that burning a United States flag is a protected form of speech

3. Which of the following is an accurate comparison of judicial restraint and judicial activism?

Judicial Restraint	Judicial Activism
A. The decision in *Brown v. Board* to overturn the precedent established in *Plessy v. Ferguson*	The Warren Court
B. The Burger Court	The Rehnquist Court
C. An approach to judicial decision making whereby judges are reluctant to strike down laws	An approach to judicial decision making whereby judges strike down laws
D. The Court's decision in 2000 to overturn the Florida Supreme Court's interpretation of Florida election law	A strict adherence to *stare decisis*

4. Which of the following is an accurate comparison of trial courts and courts of appeals?

Trial Courts	Courts of Appeals
A. Original jurisdiction	Appellate jurisdiction
B. Panel of judges decides the case	A jury of peers decides the case
C. Legal briefs and court transcripts are reviewed	Evidence is presented and facts are considered
D. Errors in the application of law are decided	Guilt or innocence is decided

Questions 5 and 6 are based on the chart below.

TABLE 6.4 ▇ The Roberts Court

Considering the age of the Supreme Court justices nominated by President Barack Obama, what do you think will be President Obama's long-term effect on the decision making of the Court? What might explain the pattern of change in confirmation votes from 1991 through 2020? How many justices do you predict President Biden will be able to appoint?

Justice	Year Appointed	Nominating President	Confirmation Vote	Year of Birth
Clarence Thomas	1991	George H. W. Bush (R)	52–48	1948
Stephen G. Breyer	1994	Bill Clinton (D)	87–9	1938
John G. Roberts	2005	George W. Bush (R)	78–22	1955
Samuel Anthony Alito	2006	George W. Bush (R)	58–42	1950
Sonia Sotomayor	2009	Barack Obama (D)	68–31	1954
Elena Kagan	2010	Barack Obama (D)	63–37	1960
Neil Gorsuch	2017	Donald Trump (R)	54–45	1967
Brett Kavanaugh	2018	Donald Trump (R)	50–48	1963
Amy Coney Barrett	2020	Donald Trump (R)	52–48	1972

Source: U.S. Supreme Court

5. Based on the chart above, which of the following is an accurate description of Article III courts?

A. Courts created by Congress that help administer and resolve conflicts over specific federal legislation

B. Courts created with the power to decide only those cases over which the Constitution gives them authority

C. Federal trial courts with mandatory jurisdiction

D. Federal courts with mandatory, appellate jurisdiction

6. Which of the following is the most important source of the Supreme Court's caseload?

A. Original jurisdiction

B. Cases referred from state supreme courts

C. Appellate jurisdiction

D. Cases directly referred to the Court by the president

7. The doctrine of *stare decisis* refers to

A. The authority of the Court to declare certain actions by the federal government to be unconstitutional

B. A person's right not to be prosecuted a second time for the same crime

C. The Court's commitment to applying previous precedents and decisions to a current case

D. The power of the higher court to review and, when necessary, overturn a lower court's decision

TABLE 6.3 ▪ Demographics of Federal Judges as a Percentage of Those Confirmed

Characteristic	Carter	Reagan	G.H.W. Bush	Clinton	G.W. Bush	Obama	Trump
Total appointees	261	364	188	372	324	324	194*
Hispanic	6%	4%	4%	6%	9%	9%	4%
Black	14%	2%	7%	17%	7%	19%	4%
White	78%	94%	89%	76%	82%	64%	85%
Female	16%	8%	19%	29%	22%	42%	25%
Male	84%	92%	81%	71%	78%	58%	75%
Median age	54.6	52	50.8	50.4	51	52.8	48.2

*Trump's appointees through July 15, 2020.

Sources: Pew Research Center, "How Trump compares with other recent presidents in appointing federal judges," July 15, 2020. Russell Wheeler. "Judicial appointments in Trump's first three years: myths and realities," Brookings Institution, January 28, 2020.

8. Which of the following is an accurate statement about the information in the table?
   A. The demographics of federal judges matches the demographics of the United States
   B. The percentage of female federal judges has been declining over time
   C. President G.H.W. Bush appointed the highest percentage of Hispanic judicial nominees when compared to the other presidents on the table
   D. President Obama appointed the highest percentage of Black judicial nominees when compared to the other presidents on the table

9. Based on the information in the table, which of the following is correct?
   A. The percentage of women and minority judicial nominees is increasing over time
   B. Most judicial nominees have law degrees and experience working in government
   C. African American nominees are more likely to be appointed by Republican presidents than Democratic presidents
   D. Republican presidents are more likely to appoint female nominees than Democratic presidents

10. Which is an accurate statement about the data in the table?

    A. From 1993–2005, Supreme Court justice nominees were confirmed by supermajority votes

    B. From 1954–1963 most Supreme Court justice nominees were not confirmed by the Senate

    C. President Clinton's Supreme Court nominees were the most controversial of any in the table

    D. President George W. Bush appointed the most Supreme Court nominees of any in the table

■ Free Response Questions

Argument

Develop an argument in which you decide whether lifetime tenure for federal judges harms democracy.

In your essay, you must:

- Articulate a defensible claim or thesis that responds to the prompt and establishes a line of reasoning.

- Support your claim with at least TWO pieces of accurate and relevant information:

  - At least ONE piece of evidence must be from one of the following foundational documents:

    - The Constitution of the United States (including the Bill of Rights and subsequent Amendments)
    - *Federalist* No. 78
    - *Federalist* No. 51

- Use a second piece of evidence from another foundational document from the list or from your study of interaction among the branches of government

- Use reasoning to explain why your evidence supports your claim/thesis

- Respond to an opposing or alternative perspective using refutation, concession, or rebuttal

Quantitative Analysis

TABLE 6.3 ■ Demographics of Federal Judges as a Percentage of Those Confirmed

Characteristic	Carter	Reagan	G.H.W. Bush	Clinton	G.W. Bush	Obama	Trump
Total appointees	261	364	188	372	324	324	194*
Hispanic	6%	4%	4%	6%	9%	9%	4%
Black	14%	2%	7%	17%	7%	19%	4%
White	78%	94%	89%	76%	82%	64%	85%
Female	16%	8%	19%	29%	22%	42%	25%
Male	84%	92%	81%	71%	78%	58%	75%
Median age	54.6	52	50.8	50.4	51	52.8	48.2

*Trump's appointees through July 15, 2020.

Sources: Pew Research Center, "How Trump compares with other recent presidents in appointing federal judges," July 15, 2020. Russell Wheeler. "Judicial appointments in Trump's first three years: myths and realities," Brookings Institution, January 28, 2020.

Use the chart above to answer the questions.

A. Identify a trend regarding the demographic characteristics of judicial nominees.

B. Describe a similarity or difference in the demographic characteristics of judicial nominees by president, as illustrated in the information graphic, and draw a conclusion about that similarity or difference.

C. Explain how the courts are still limited by public opinion despite the demographic differences between judges and the public.

SCOTUS Comparison

In the midst of the Watergate investigation, the special prosecutor assigned to the case issued a subpoena to obtain audio recordings made by President Nixon. Nixon claimed that he was not required to turn over the tapes, citing executive privilege.

In a unanimous opinion, the Supreme Court ordered the president to obey the subpoena and turn over the tapes. Further, the Court argued that the president could not make unqualified claims of executive privilege.

A. Identify the constitutional principle that is common to both *U.S. v. Nixon (1974)* and *Marbury v. Madison (1803)*.

B. Based on the constitutional principle identified in part A, explain why the facts of *U.S. v. Nixon (1974)* led to a similar holding in *Marbury v. Madison (1803)*.

C. Explain an action Congress could take to limit the ruling in *U.S. v. Nixon*.

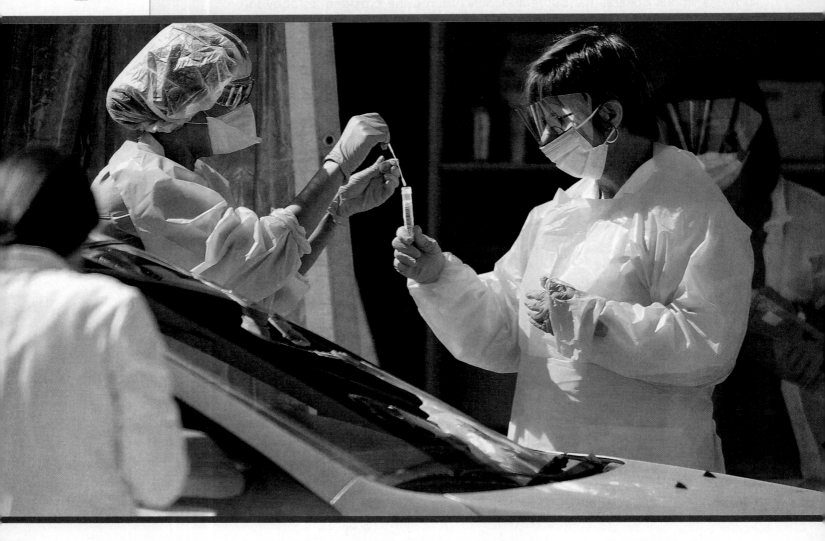

THEN

The federal bureaucracy under President George Washington had three departments and two offices staffed with public servants engaged in mostly clerical work, serving a national population of 4 million.

NOW

Approximately 4 million national bureaucrats—plus at least 13 million state and local bureaucrats, and private for-profit and nonprofit shadow bureaucrats—implement national public policies that serve the country's population of over 330 million.

NEXT

Will the best and the brightest respond to the call to serve while elected officials denigrate the work and independence of federal bureaucrats?

Will the federal government address the transparency and accountability concerns raised by its use of contracts and shadow bureaucrats to implement public policies?

Josh Edelson/AFP/Getty Images

■ Chapter Introduction

The AP U.S. Government and Politics Enduring Understanding to frame this chapter is: *The federal bureaucracy implements federal policies.* The first question to answer in tackling this EU is: What is the federal bureaucracy? The second question to tackle is: How does the federal bureaucracy implement federal policies? Next, we will need to explore the policy-making role of the federal bureaucracy. By exploring the policy-making role of the federal bureaucracy we will return to Big Idea 4: *Multiple actors and institutions interact to produce and implement possible policies.* We have examined the role of Congress and the president in the policy-making process, and now we will examine the role of the bureaucracy here.

The federal bureaucracy is part of the executive branch of government. The bureaucracy is a large, complex network of government agencies that are created by congressional legislation or presidential executive order. These agencies are created in order to carry out federal law, and there are hundreds of them. As an AP U.S. government student, you will not be required to know about all of the agencies, but it is helpful to be able to identify a handful of government agencies and understand how those agencies implement federal policies. See the chart on the next page to identify the specific government agencies you will need to know about on the AP U.S. Government and Politics exam.

Answering the second question of *how* the federal bureaucracy implements federal policies is a little more complex. Agencies within the bureaucracy are created to carry out laws passed by Congress. In the process of carrying out laws, sometimes the actions of the bureaucracy have a policy-making effect because bureaucrats have discretionary authority, meaning they can make decisions that have the effect of policy. For example, when writing auto-safety legislation, Congress may lack the engineering expertise needed to direct the industry, and as a result, will rely on the U.S. Department of Transportation (DOT) to follow up on the legislation by writing regulations. In the process, some discretion is given to the experts at the DOT.

Discretionary authority of the bureaucracy can potentially be problematic in a democracy because citizens are entitled to have a say in government policies. Typically, such say occurs through elections. When citizens don't like laws passed by government leaders, they can vote these leaders out of office. The potential problem is that bureaucrats are unelected officials. However, it is the responsibility of Congress to control the bureaucracy's discretionary authority. Congress can control the bureaucracy by holding hearings and by writing laws that give the bureaucracy less discretion when appropriate. Congressional oversight of bureaucracy is not an easy job, in part because our bureaucracy has grown so large and is so complex.

This chapter will describe the intricacies and complexities of our federal bureaucracy, including the various types of agencies and how they function. For example, Cabinet agencies are designed to answer to the president, but independent regulatory agencies are not. Finally, to return to Big Idea 4: *Multiple actors and institutions interact to produce and implement possible policies.* Keep in mind that the federal bureaucracy is one of the multiple actors and institutions that produce and implement policies.

The bureaucracy is controlled both by Congress and the president. The president can direct certain agencies within the bureaucracy through executive order, and

Congress has the power to create, organize, and fund the bureaucracy through legislation. Because the bureaucracy is staffed by unelected officials, sometimes the bureaucracy is reluctant to carry out the will of either the president or Congress. Because the bureaucracy is unelected, it is somewhat isolated from partisan politics, but in order to influence the bureaucracy's implementation of policy, a citizen can attempt to lobby Congress to request that Congress oversee the bureaucracy.

Government Agencies that are Essential Knowledge (EK) on the AP U.S. Government & Politics Exam

Government Agency Name	Type of Agency	Mission	Examples of Policies Agency Implements
Department of Homeland Security	Cabinet	Keep the nation safe from foreign and domestic threats, including in aviation and border security.	■ 9-11 Commission Act ■ Disaster Relief Act
Department of Transportation	Cabinet	Ensure our nation has the safest, most efficient, and modern transportation system.	■ Air Traffic Control ■ Automobile child safety
Department of Veterans Affairs	Cabinet	Serving and honoring the men and women who are America's veterans.	■ Veterans' health care benefits ■ Veterans' education benefits
Federal Election Commission	Independent Regulatory	Administer and enforce federal campaign finance law for campaigns for the U.S. House, Senate and president/vice president.	■ Public disclosure of funds raised and spent to influence federal elections ■ Restrict contributions and expenditures made to influence federal elections ■ Manage the public financing option of of presidential election campaigns
Securities and Exchange Commission	Independent Regulatory	Protect investors, maintain fair, orderly, and efficient markets and facilitate capital formation.	■ Securities Act of 1933 (requires that investors receive information about securities for sale; prohibits fraud in the sale of securities)

■ Democracy and Bureaucracy

People turn to their governments to solve individual and societal problems. In a representative democracy, citizens elect government officials to make policy for them. Elected officials determine what societal problems the government should address. They negotiate and compromise as they develop a plan of action (policy) to solve each problem. Then they authorize the spending of money to put the policy into action (policy implementation). In the process of making policy, elected officials make value judgments; they decide what problems to address and what problems not to address; they decide who will and will not be served by government actions; they decide who will pay for government services and benefits (through tax policies) and who will not pay. Citizens can hold elected officials accountable at the ballot box; if the electorate is unhappy with the decisions made by elected officials, they can decide not to reelect them. That is how democracy is expected to work.

In the national government, after Congress and the president agree on what societal problems to address, approve policies to address them, and fund policy implementation, millions of **bureaucrats**, non-elected government employees hired to implement public policies, take on the work of putting those policies into action. Elected officials delegate to bureaucrats the responsibility of competently and neutrally (without biases or preferences) implementing public policies.

bureaucrats
Non-elected government employees hired to implement public policy; public administrators; public servants.

For their trillions of tax dollars, Americans expect the millions of bureaucrats working in the **bureaucracy**, which is the term for the collection of all executive branch units in a government, to provide services and benefits efficiently (without wasting resources, including tax dollars) and effectively (successfully addressing the societal problem). Americans also expect equal treatment from bureaucrats and bureaucracies as well as accountability, which includes knowing who to blame when policies are not efficient or effective. That is how bureaucracy is expected to work.

bureaucracy
The collection of all executive branch organizations in a government.

Bureaucrats are the government employees with whom citizens interact regularly; they are the faces of government. It is the daily implementation of public policies by bureaucrats working in the bureaucracy that citizens focus on when they evaluate government performance.

The national bureaucracy is replete with **red tape**: rules and procedures that are viewed as inefficient and dehumanizing, and that require tedious paperwork. The national bureaucracy also has many agencies that at times appear to have less-than-harmonious relationships with each other. Red tape and division of responsibilities among agencies characterize all bureaucratic organizations and, believe it or not, are in place to foster equal treatment, accountability, efficiency, and effectiveness.

red tape
Bureaucratic rules and procedures that are viewed as inefficient, dehumanizing, and requiring tedious paperwork.

Max Weber (1864–1920), the "father of sociology," is famous for creating an ideal model of a bureaucracy. Weber's **bureaucratic structure** had the following features: a division of labor, specialization of job tasks, hiring and promotion systems based on worker competency, hierarchy with a vertical chain of command, and reliance on standard operating procedures, rules, and regulations (see Table 7.1). For Weber, the bureaucratic structure was the best way to ensure that the public interest would be fulfilled in a fragmented government directed by an aristocracy (a small, elite ruling class). Today, government agencies as well as large, nongovernmental organizations typically conform to this bureaucratic structure. Review Figure 7.1 to identify bureaucratic structures in the national government.

bureaucratic structure
A large organization with the following features: a division of labor, specialization of job tasks, hiring systems based on worker competency, hierarchy with a vertical chain of command, and standard operating procedures.

TABLE 7.1 ■ **Characteristics of Weber's Ideal Bureaucracy**

- Division of labor
- Specialization of job tasks
- Hiring systems based on worker competence
- Hierarchy with a vertical chain of command
- Standard operating procedures, rules, and regulations

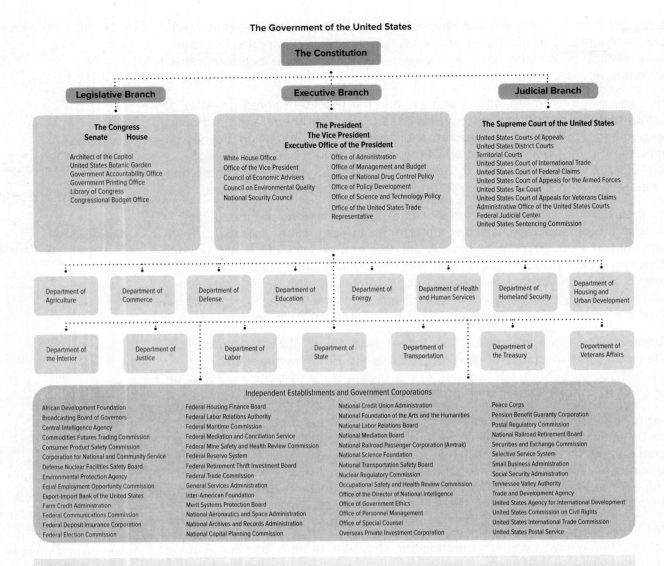

FIGURE 7.1 ■ **U.S. Government Organizational Chart** How is the federal bureaucracy's division of labor evident in the national government organizational chart? How is the vertical chain of command evident in the chart? What other characteristics of Weber's ideal bureaucracy can you identify in this organizational chart?

Colleges and universities (public and private) are good examples of organizations with bureaucratic structures. They have a division of labor with specialization of tasks. Consider the various academic departments, each specializing in a different discipline. They hire employees (such as professors, computer technicians, and student affairs staff) with the knowledge, skills, and abilities essential to doing their jobs well. Colleges and universities also have a hierarchy with a vertical chain of command: faculty members report to chairpersons, who report to a dean, who reports to the vice president for academic affairs, who reports to the president, who makes final decisions. University employees implement standardized procedures, rules, and regulations to register students for classes, determine financial aid eligibility, and punish violations of the conduct code.

For most people, the word *bureaucracy* conjures up the image of a large government organization with red tape: rules and procedures that are inefficient and dehumanizing, and that require tedious paperwork. They visualize long lines at the Department of Motor Vehicles as uncaring workers, who they believe the government cannot fire, slowly process mounds of forms. Taxpayers are not the only people who think and speak negatively of the bureaucracy. Even our presidents and congressional members—who rely on bureaucrats to implement their policy promises—do not hesitate to criticize bureaucrats. Are the negative images and criticisms fair? The reality is that much of the red tape is a product of the bureaucratic structure—and the expectations we have for equal treatment and government accountability.

Although most people think of government when they hear the word *bureaucracy*, as noted above regarding colleges and universities, a bureaucracy is *any* organization with Weber's bureaucratic structure. Yet in this chapter, as is appropriate to our study of American national government, we focus on the departments and agencies that compose the national government bureaucracy. And even though most people think of government employees when they hear the term *bureaucrat*, non-government employees, as we will see, may also be paid with taxpayer money to serve the public, and so it is appropriate that we consider these shadow bureaucrats, too.

The U.S. national government is the largest bureaucracy in the world, employing approximately 4.2 million people: 2.8 million civilian bureaucrats and 1.4 million uniformed military personnel.[1] Those numbers don't include the millions of private-sector employees contracted to provide public services. Who are all these bureaucrats?

The Bureaucrats Who Implement Federal Policies

Very few children say they want to be bureaucrats when they grow up. Bureaucrats themselves prefer the label *public servant* because that phrase captures how they see themselves and their essential job goal. Yet millions aspire to careers through which they can serve the public good, including as teachers, police officers, health care professionals, epidemiologists, scientists, and lawyers. In 2018, public-sector jobs (national, state, and local government jobs) accounted for 14 percent of total

>> From A (air traffic controller) to Z (zookeeper), and every occupation in between, whatever your career aspiration, you can do it as a bureaucrat. As a matter of fact, some occupations are available only as government jobs. Can you think of one or two occupations for which only governments hire? Can you think of a (legal) occupation for which the government does not hire?

Space photo: Monty Rakusen/Cultura/ Getty Images; *Zoo photo:* Holly Hildreth/ McGraw-Hill Education

Federal Civil Servant Hiring Process

THEN

(2000)

Majority of job applications require lengthy essays and extensive job application forms and questionnaires.

Many applicants experience a "black hole," never receiving a response to their applications.

Majority of applicants apply directly to the Office of Personnel Management (OPM).

usajobs.gov lists open positions for which OPM accepts applications.

NOW

(2020)

Almost all job applications require the uploading of a résumé and cover letter; no lengthy essays, application forms, or questionnaires.

www.usajobs.gov allows applicants to follow the flow of their applications through the hiring process.

Majority of applicants apply directly to the agency with the open position.

All federal agencies must post their job openings on usajobs.gov; many also post them on their own websites.

NEXT

- Will perpetually changing technology, which leads to increased efficiency in the usajobs.gov application process, make it easier for the federal government to recruit and hire the best and the brightest?

- Will partisan politics and the fear of future government shutdowns affect federal hiring?

- What effect, if any, will the result of the 2020 presidential election have on the hiring of bureaucrats for departments and agencies that were targets for severe presidential criticism during 2018 and 2019?

---

civilian employment in the United States,[2] which includes approximately 3 million national bureaucrats, 4 million state bureaucrats, and 11 million local bureaucrats.[3]

Political scientists distinguish among federal bureaucrats according to several factors, including the processes by which they are hired, the procedures by which they can be fired, and the grounds for which they can be fired. On the basis of these factors, we examine three categories of national civilian bureaucrats: political appointees, Senior Executive Service appointees, and civil servants. Then we consider the role of state, local, and non-government employees in national policy implementation.

Political Appointees

patronage system
A personnel system in which the chief executive officer (CEO) can appoint whomever he or she wants to top bureaucratic positions, without the need for open competition for applicants; those hired through patronage typically serve at the pleasure of the CEO who hired them

In 1863, President Abraham Lincoln, suffering from smallpox, told his secretary to "send all the office seekers in here. I finally have something I can give to them all." Indeed, before the creation of the federal civil service system in 1883, presidents had the authority to hire bureaucrats, selecting whomever they wanted and establishing whatever qualifications they desired, through the **patronage system** of hiring. Under the patronage system, hordes of men seeking government jobs presented themselves to the president after each election.

Now, after each presidential election, the federal government publishes the **plum book**, which lists thousands of top jobs in the federal bureaucracy to which the president will appoint people through the patronage system. There is no standard process for assessing the knowledge, skills, and abilities needed for appointive positions, nor is there open competition for these patronage jobs. Further, because citizens expect presidents to be responsive and accountable to them, and presidents rely on their political appointees to meet those expectations, presidents tend to appoint people who support their policy preferences, which typically means they are affiliated with the same political party as the president. Most top-level patronage positions come with a downside for the appointees: no job security. The president not only hires but also can fire most political appointees at his or her pleasure.

Today, presidents are able to hire approximately 3,000 political appointees through the patronage system. These appointees serve under the president, in the top several layers in the federal executive branch's hierarchy (vertical chain of command). Below the layers of political appointees are members of the Senior Executive Service (SES), and below them are the civil servants.

Senior Executives

The keystone of the Civil Service Reform Act of 1978 was the creation of the **Senior Executive Service (SES)**.[4] The SES is composed of the top managerial, supervisory, and policy positions that link the political appointees to the rest of the federal bureaucracy.

The SES bureaucrat is a hybrid of the political appointee and the civil servant. At least 90 percent of SES bureaucrats are career appointees hired based on merit through an open, competitive process. These employees can be moved from job to job and from agency to agency, as can political appointees. However, unlike political appointees, they cannot be fired at the discretion of the president. To fire an SES career appointee, the government must prove that the employee is not performing the job, is performing it poorly, or is performing it in a manner that violates agency rules or the law.

The remaining 10 percent of SES bureaucrats are non-career and temporary appointees hired without open, competitive procedures, similar to political appointees. Their appointments are approved by the Office of Personnel Management (the federal government's central personnel office) and the White House Office of Presidential Personnel, and they can be removed at the pleasure of the president.[5]

Civil Servants

During the first century of U.S. history, all federal bureaucrats were hired through the patronage system. Then in 1883, after the assassination of President James Garfield by a man who did not get the patronage position he sought, Congress and President Chester Arthur (1881–1885) approved the Pendleton Civil Service Act. The goal of the act was to eliminate the expectation that government jobs were the spoils of an electoral victory, distributed by the winning candidate. The act established a **merit-based civil service** in the national government. The hiring principles of this system included open competition, competence, and political neutrality, which would ensure the independence and integrity of civil servants. **Civil servants** are bureaucrats hired through the merit-based personnel system established by the Pendleton Act and reinforced by the 1978 Civil Service Reform Act.

plum book
A publication that lists the top jobs in the bureaucracy to which the president will appoint people through the patronage system.

Senior Executive Service (SES)
A unique personnel system for top managerial, supervisory, and policy positions offering less job security but higher pay than the merit-based civil service system.

merit-based civil service
A personnel system in which bureaucrats are hired on the basis of the principles of competence, equal opportunity (open competition), and political neutrality; once hired, these public servants have job protection.

civil servants
Bureaucrats hired through a merit-based personnel system and who have job protection.

THEN

NOW

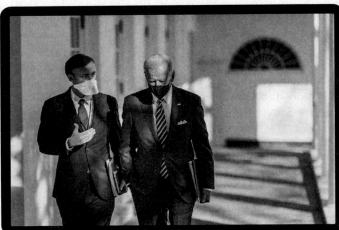

>> Presidents have the authority to appoint, without the need for Senate confirmation, a national security advisor (NSA), who serves as a presidential aide in the Executive Office of the President (EOP). The NSA serves at the pleasure of the president. During his eight years in office, President Obama appointed a total of three NSAs. His third and last NSA was Susan Rice (shown at left). Obama's successor, President Trump, appointed four NSAs and three acting NSAs in his first three years of office. President Biden appointed Jake Sullivan (right), at the beginning of his term in 2021. What are the advantages and disadvantages of having a long-serving NSA versus a series of short-serving NSAs? How might this affect the larger national security establishment?

(*Left*): Andrew Harrer/Pool/Getty Images; (*Right*): GM/Current Affairs/Alamy Stock Photo

By the 1970s, there was widespread criticism of federal government performance. As President Jimmy Carter (1977–1981) said in 1978, "The public suspects that there are too many government workers, that they are underworked, overpaid, and insulated from the consequences of incompetence."[6] To address the criticisms, Carter proposed the Civil Service Reform Act (CSRA). The CSRA reaffirmed and expanded the merit principles established by the Pendleton Act, established the SES, and reorganized the management of the national civil service.

OPEN COMPETITION, COMPETENCE, AND EQUAL OPPORTUNITY Today, merit-based civil service jobs, which compose the majority of the federal bureaucracy, are open and accessible to all citizens who wish to compete for a position. The competition requires that candidates prove their competence to do the job (their merit). This may be done by evaluation of the applicants' education and work experiences, written exams, or some other examination of their knowledge, skills, and abilities that are relevant to job performance.

The Office of Personnel Management (OPM), the central personnel office for the federal government, determines which positions it will evaluate candidates for and for which positions individual agencies can conduct their own evaluations. Regarding the positions for which it conducts evaluations, the OPM analyzes and ranks them on the basis of the knowledge, skills, and abilities needed to do the job competently. A job's rank determines its salary. The pay scales are expected to offer equal pay for jobs of equal worth. (Table 7.2 presents the pay scales and education requirements for white-collar federal government jobs evaluated by the OPM.)

As the proportion of jobs that require the hiring of professionals has increased, the OPM has delegated to a growing number of agencies more control over hiring processes and establishing salaries.

TABLE 7.2 ■ Education Requirements and Salary Ranges for White-Collar Federal Civil Servants (2020)

Level	Salary Range	Qualifying Education
GS-1	$19,543–$24,448	No high school diploma required
GS-2	$21,974–27,653	High school graduation or equivalent
GS-3	$23,976–$31,167	One academic year above high school
GS-4	$26,915–$34,988	Two academic years above high school, or associate's degree
GS-5	$30,113–$39,149	Four academic years above high school leading to a bachelor's degree, or a bachelor's degree
GS-6	$33,5676–$43,638	Experience required in addition to the stated level of education
GS-7	$37,301–$48,488	Bachelor's degree with superior academic achievement or one academic year of graduate education or law school
GS-8	$41,310–$53,703	Experience required in addition to the stated level of education
GS-9	$45,627–$59,316	Master's (or equivalent graduate degree) or two academic years of progressively higher level graduate education
GS-10	$40,246–$65,321	Experience required in addition to the stated level of education
GS-11	$55,204–$71,764	PhD or equivalent degree or three academic years of progressively higher level graduate education
GS-12	$66,167–$86,021	Completion of all requirements for a doctoral or equivalent degree (for research positions only)
GS-13	$78,681–$102,288	Appropriate specialized experience
GS-14	$92,977–$120,868	Appropriate specialized experience
GS-15	$109,366–$142,180	Appropriate specialized experience

Source: 2020 Base GS Pay Scale, https://www.federalpay.org/gs/locality.

Several national laws that mandate equal opportunities have helped to make today's civil servants, as a group, look more like the U.S. population at large than they did in the past. Title VII of the 1964 Civil Rights Act, as amended, prohibits employers, including governments, from making personnel decisions based on factors irrelevant to job competence, such as sex, race, color, ethnicity, age, and disabilities that can be reasonably accommodated. The merit principles of the CSRA reiterate this prohibition against discrimination in personnel practices. The Title VII and CSRA bans against discrimination do not apply to the positions of elected officials or political appointees.

Title VI of the 1964 Civil Rights Act prohibits discrimination based on race, color, religion, and ethnicity in educational opportunities offered by institutions receiving federal funding. Title IX, which was added to the act in 1972, extended this prohibition to sex-based discrimination. Enforcement of these laws has increased the diversity of people who are able to gain the education and experience needed to do government jobs competently. Titles VI, VII, and IX, combined with the merit principles of the Pendleton Act and the CSRA, have fostered movement toward a **representative bureaucracy**, which means that bureaucrats, as a group, resemble the larger population whom they serve in demographic characteristics such as race, age, ethnicity, sex, religion, and economic status. Figure 7.2 presents some demographic data of federal bureaucrats.

representative bureaucracy
A bureaucracy in which the people serving resemble the larger population whom they serve in demographic characteristics such as race, age, ethnicity, sex, religion, and economic status.

POLITICAL NEUTRALITY Civil servants cannot be fired merely because someone with different political beliefs is elected or appointed to supervise them. They can be fired for poor quality of work (misfeasance), or for nonperformance of their work (nonfeasance), or for violating the law or the rules and regulations that guide their work (malfeasance). The merit-based civil service system thus gives competent civil servants job protection and does not require them to adhere to the president's policy preferences (unlike political appointees). Hence, the civil

American Indian/
Alaska Native
2%

More than one race
1%

Hispanic/Latino
9%

Asian/Pacific
Islander
7%

Black
18%

White
63%

FIGURE 7.2 ■ **Race/National Origin of Federal Bureaucrats**

Sources: U.S. Office of Personnel Management, Data, Analysis & Documentation Federal Employment Reports, "Executive Branch Employment by Gender and Race/National Origin" service system supports political neutrality in hiring and retaining competent bureaucrats. To bolster political neutrality, the federal government limits through the Hatch Act the rights of bureaucrats to run for partisan office and participate in campaigning during work hours. The expectation is that civil servants hired through the merit system will be competent and will make work decisions that are nonpartisan and that serve the public good.

MANAGING THE FEDERAL CIVIL SERVICE The CSRA of 1978 established three new independent administrative agencies—the Office of Personnel Management (OPM), the Merit System Protection Board (MSPB), and the Federal Labor Relations Authority (FLRA)—to replace the old Civil Service Commission created by the Pendleton Act. Today, the OPM, as the central personnel office, is responsible for developing and implementing merit-based civil service personnel policies and procedures. The MSPB ensures proper implementation of the merit system by investigating allegations of improper implementation. The CSRA, which legislated for the collective bargaining rights (unionization rights) of national civil servants, created the FLRA to monitor relations between unionized bureaucrats and the federal government.

UNIONIZED CIVIL SERVANTS Thirty-one percent of U.S. federal civil servants are represented by unions. By comparison, 32 percent of state bureaucrats and 43 percent of local bureaucrats are represented by unions. The percentage of private-sector employees represented by unions is only seven percent.[7] Whereas the majority of U.S. Postal Service employees are union members, the level of union membership among bureaucrats in the State Department is close to zero.

Unionized civil servants have leverage to negotiate certain conditions of work. For example, they may bargain for improved training opportunities and enhanced due process protections in disciplinary matters. Federal civil service employee unions cannot negotiate salaries or work hours, however. And unlike private-sector unions, federal civil servant unions do not have the legal right to strike. The prohibition of strikes by federal civil servants is typically justified by the fact that these workers provide services that are vital to public safety. A strike by these workers would therefore threaten public safety and health.

In 2018, President Trump signed three executive orders aimed at limiting the power of federal employee unions. The unions responded with a court challenge that proved unsuccessful. Thus, in spring 2020, federal agencies began to implement these three orders, which exempt adverse personnel actions (such as disciplinary decisions) from grievance procedures; streamline collective bargaining negotiations; reduce the number of hours union members can spend on union business during work hours; and decrease the length of performance-improvement plans, which shortens the time period for an employee to improve her job performance before being fired.[8]

State, Local, and Shadow Bureaucrats

When it comes to implementing federal policies, joining the national bureaucrats are state and local bureaucrats and **shadow bureaucrats**—employees on the payroll of private for-profit businesses and private nonprofit organizations that have received government contracts and grants. Through a process of **contracting-out** (also called outsourcing), the government signs work contracts with these private organizations to assist in implementing national policy as well

shadow bureaucrats
People hired and paid by private for-profit and nonprofit organizations that implement public policy through a government contract.

contracting-out
Also called *outsourcing;* a process by which the government contracts with a private for-profit or nonprofit organization to provide public services, such as disaster relief, or resources needed by the government, such as fighter planes.

as producing certain resources needed to serve the public. In other words, shadow bureaucrats do some of the work of government, but they do not receive government paychecks.

Examples of outsourcing include the federal government's contracting with Lockheed Martin, General Dynamics, and Boeing for the production of defense resources such as helmets, fighter planes, and laser-guided missiles. Traditionally, the government also undertakes large capital projects such as the construction of roads and government buildings through contracts with private businesses. Furthermore, the federal government outsources medical as well as social research to cure diseases and address the ills of society. And through government contracts, the Red Cross has dispensed disaster relief for decades. The federal government's contracts totaled $559 billion in 2018, with 67 percent of that spending ($373 billion) paying for Pentagon contracts. The $559 billion was the most the government spent on contracts since 2010, when the government spent $562 billion.[9]

The federal government expects that contracting-out will reduce the expense of government by eliminating the overhead costs (including employee benefits and basic operating costs) of producing public goods and services. Outsourcing also provides a means by which the government can hire experts and specialists only when they are needed. Proponents of outsourcing argue that private- and nonprofit-sector employees and organizations are more efficient and effective than government bureaucracies. However, as we discuss later in this chapter, the benefits of contracting-out are debatable.

Political scientist John Dilulio estimates that at least 10 million shadow bureaucrats and 3 million state and local bureaucrats receive paychecks that are at least partially funded by federal tax dollars due to contracts and grants-in-aid.[10] As discussed in Chapter 3, the federal government has devolved greater responsibility for financing and administering national public policies to state and local governments, putting the implementation of national policy in the hands of state and local bureaucrats. Either through grants-in-aid conditions or unfunded mandates in federal laws, state and local bureaucrats implement national policies. In cases where federal law preempts (takes precedence over) state and local law, state and local bureaucrats may have to implement federal policy instead of state or local policies if their policies are weaker than the federal policy, or if they have no policy on the matter.

Even with the increased use of state, local, and shadow bureaucrats, the federal bureaucracy is neither small nor streamlined. It is composed of thousands of executive units with a variety of names and organizational structures. The federal bureaucracy continues to grow in complexity even as it contracts out and devolves more of its work.

The Evolution of the Federal Bureaucracy

Four million people resided in the United States in 1789, the year George Washington was sworn in as the first president. Most of them lived off the land and were self-sufficient; they expected few services from the federal government. The federal bureaucracy consisted of the Department of War, Department of

Foreign Affairs, Treasury Department, Attorney General's Office, and Postal Services Office. Those three departments and two offices handled the core functions demanded of the national government at that time: respectively, providing defense, managing foreign affairs, collecting revenues and paying bills, resolving lawsuits and legal questions, and delivering mail. With the exception of defense, the work of public servants was mostly clerical in nature.

Since the nation's founding, Congresses and presidents have enacted laws creating hundreds of executive branch bureaucracies. The size, scope, and complexity of today's federal bureaucracy are products of elected officials' efforts to respond to the ever-changing needs and growing demands of U.S. citizens. Elected policymakers rely on the federal bureaucracy to faithfully execute the laws they enact, providing a range of services and benefits that would shock George Washington.

Today, with the U.S. population of 330 million, hundreds of federal executive branch units, employing more than 4 million civilian and active-duty military personnel, implement volumes of national policies. The number of bureaucrats is comparable to the nation's total population in 1789. Figure 7.3 presents the growth in the size of federal, state, and local workforces since 1965. Figure 7.4 shows the growth in cost of the national bureaucracy since 1960. The "Thinking Critically" feature debates whether the federal government is too big.

DATA ANALYSIS PATTERNS AND TRENDS

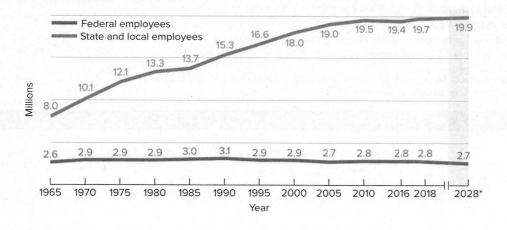

FIGURE 7.3 ▪ **Growth in Civilian Workforce** What has been the trend regarding federal employees since 1965? What has been the pattern for the growth regarding state and local bureaucrats over the same period? What helps to explain these patterns?

Sources: U.S. Census Bureau. *Statistical Abstracts of the United States.* 1965, Table 476; 1968, Table 567; 1978, Table 504; 1990, Table 487; 2012, Table 461. 2016 data source: U.S. Bureau of Labor Statistics, Employment Projections program, Table 2.1 Employment by major industry sector, 2006, 2016, and projected 2026; .U.S. Bureau of Labor Statistics, Employment Projections program, Table 2.1 Employment by major industry sector, 2008, 2018, and *projected 2028.

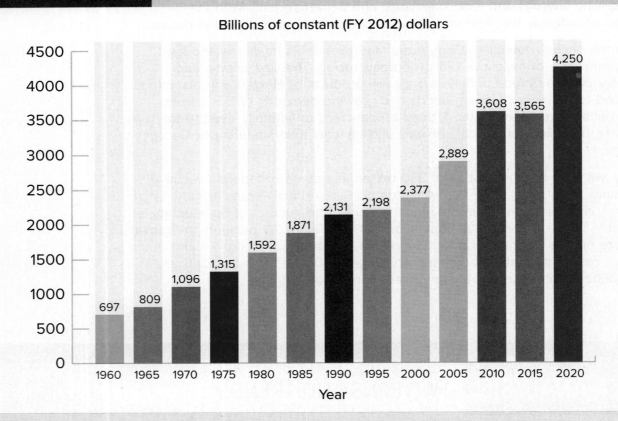

Billions of constant (FY 2012) dollars

FIGURE 7.4 ▪ **Trends in Federal Expenditures** What has been the overall trend in federal government spending since 1960? What has the pattern been since 2000? Consider the data in Figure 7.3. Clearly, increases in the federal labor force do not account for the budget increases. What factors (new societal problems) might explain the trend in federal spending since 2000?

Source: Office of Management and Budget. *Historical Tables*, "Table 1.3—Summary of Receipts, Outlays, and Surpluses or Deficits in Current Dollars, Constant (FY 2012) Dollars, and as Percentages of GDP: 1940–2025."

Political scientists distinguish among five categories of executive branch organizations based on their structure and the type of work they perform: (1) departments, (2) independent administrative agencies, (3) independent regulatory commissions, (4) government corporations, and (5) agencies in the Executive Office of the President. Within each category there is much variation in size, structure, and function. When Congress and the president authorize a new policy, they must decide whether they will assign its implementation to an existing agency or create a new agency. If they choose the latter option, they must determine which type of agency to create.

Is the Federal Government Too Big?

THE ISSUE: Many taxpayers complain that the federal government is too big. For some, this means the government spends too much money. For others, it means the government is doing things that individuals or businesses should do. For still others, "too big" means too involved in their daily lives. Is the federal government too big?

YES: The federal government spends close to $4 trillion per year, which is almost one-quarter of the value of all goods and services produced in the country each year. In contrast, total spending by the 50 states is less than $2 trillion per year. The national government has many more employees and contractors than any state government. To pay its bills, the national government must continuously borrow money, because it cannot cover its annual costs with the revenue it collects each year. The federal government has taken on too many responsibilities. It should hand over many of its domestic policies to the states and their local governments; this is how the framers expected our federal system to function.

NO: The amount of money the federal government spends does not tell you how big the government is. The largest single expense in the federal budget is Social Security, which is a transfer of money to individuals that does not require the employment of large numbers of people. Elimination of Social Security would decrease the cost of government, but it would not have a significant impact on the number of federal bureaucrats. Almost half of all full-time federal civilian bureaucrats work to implement defense and homeland security policies. These policies are the responsibility of the federal government, per the Constitution. They cannot be handed over to the state and local governments, which already engage in implementing numerous national policies.

OTHER APPROACHES: According to the PEW Research Center, 29 percent of Democrats think the government is doing too many things that are better left to businesses and individuals. At the same time, 71 percent of Republicans hold this view. This partisan gap in perception of scope of government (which relates to size of budget and number of employees) suggests that there is no consensus opinion on what is the "right" size for the federal government. Even those who say the federal government is too big don't necessarily agree on what programs or costs can be cut to shrink it, a sentiment that can be summarized as "Cut government spending, but don't cut my services or benefits."

WHAT DO YOU THINK?

1. How should the size of the federal government be measured: cost, number of employees, number of citizens served? Is there some other measure you can justify?

2. If the federal government devolved domestic policies to the state governments, would people begin to complain about the size of state governments? If so, what would stop state governments from devolving more responsibilities to their local governments? Would devolution actually decrease costs for taxpayers or merely lead to increases in state and local taxes?

3. Are there public programs, services, or goods the federal government provides that the majority of people will agree to shrink or eliminate? How likely are people willing to give up a benefit they currently receive?

Develop an argument that takes a position on whether Congress should pass legislation to decrease the size of the federal bureaucracy.

In your essay, you must:

- Articulate a defensible claim or thesis that responds to the prompt and develops a line of reasoning.

- Support your claim with at least TWO pieces of accurate and relevant information:

  - At least ONE piece of evidence must be from one of the following foundational documents:

    - U.S. Constitution

    - Brutus 1

    - *Federalist* No. 51

  - Use a second piece of evidence from another foundational document from the list or from your study of the bureaucracy.

Departments

department
One of 15 executive branch units responsible for a broadly defined policy area and whose top administrator (secretary) is appointed by the president, is confirmed by the Senate, and serves at the discretion of the president.

The Department of Homeland Security, established in 2002, is the newest of 15 federal **departments**, each responsible for one broadly defined policy area. The president holds the 15 departments accountable through the appointment of a head official. *Secretary* is the title of this top political appointee in all departments except the Department of Justice, where the head is the attorney general. Although the Senate must confirm them, these top appointees report to the president and serve at the president's pleasure. In addition to appointing the department secretaries, the president names bureaucrats to positions in several levels of the hierarchy below the secretaries. These political appointees have titles such as *deputy secretary, assistant deputy secretary, agency director,* and *deputy director.* Table 7.3 lists the 15 departments, from oldest to newest.

Collectively, the secretaries of all the departments, the attorney general, the vice president, and other top political appointees selected by the president compose the cabinet. As discussed in Chapter 5, the cabinet is an advisory board for the president.

independent administrative agency
An executive branch unit created by Congress and the president that is responsible for a narrowly defined function and whose structure is intended to be protected from partisan politics.

Independent Administrative Agencies

Whereas each executive branch department has authority for a broadly defined policy area, a host of **independent administrative agencies** are each responsible for a more narrowly defined function of the national government. Congress and the president create these agencies to fulfill one of several purposes. Some of them, such as the Smithsonian Institution, were established

TABLE 7.3 ■ **Establishment of Cabinet Departments**

What do the names of the departments indicate about the concerns and interests that have won federal policymakers' attention over the country's history? What mobilized the government to establish the Department of Homeland Security? Do you have an area of national concern for which you would advocate Congress create a department? Is there a department you think we no longer need? If so, explain why it is no longer needed.

Department	Year Established
State	1789
Treasury	1789
War	1789
Army	1798
Navy	1798
Interior	1859
Justice (Attorney General's Office, 1789)	1870
Agriculture	1889
Commerce and Labor	1903
Commerce (separated from Commerce and Labor)	1913
Labor (separated from Commerce and Labor)	1913
Defense (pulled War, Army, and Navy into one department)	1947
Health, Education, and Welfare	1953
Housing and Urban Development	1965
Transportation	1966
Energy	1977
Health & Human Services (separated from Health, Education, and Welfare)	1979
Education (separated from Health, Education, and Welfare)	1979
Veterans Affairs	1988
Homeland Security	2002

>> James Smithson, a French citizen who never visited the United States, donated his estate to establish an educational institution in Washington, D.C. His donation was used to establish the Smithsonian Institution in 1846, the first independent administrative agency created by the federal government. Today, the Smithsonian includes 19 museums and galleries. The newest addition to the Smithsonian is the Museum of African American Culture, pictured here, which opened in 2016.

Jahi Chikwendiu/The Washington Post/Getty Images

to handle new governmental functions that did not easily fall within the scope of responsibilities of existing departments. Other independent administrative agencies support the work of existing departments and agencies, including recruiting and training employees (Office of Personnel Management) and managing government properties and records (General Services Administration). Still others, such as the National Science Foundation and the National Aeronautics and Space Administration, focus on research and preservation of national resources.

These agencies are "independent" because Congresses and presidents place them outside the cabinet departments, which means they do not report to a cabinet secretary. In addition, some independent administrative agency heads serve fixed terms, making their agencies independent from the president. In other agencies, the heads serve at the pleasure of the president, but the president must have a cause (such as misconduct) to remove them. In yet other agencies, the president can remove the head without specifying a cause. Although the structures of independent administrative agencies are expected to make them "independent" of partisan politics, ultimately such agencies still need to earn the support of those who authorize the spending of money and who have authority to restructure the agency or its mission—Congress and the president.

Independent Regulatory Commissions

independent regulatory commission
An executive branch unit outside of cabinet departments, responsible for developing standards of behavior within specific industries and businesses, monitoring compliance with these standards, and imposing sanctions on violators.

Over time, Congresses and presidents have recognized the need for expertise in regulating the country's diverse economic activities and in evaluating their impact on the overall economy, workers, consumers, and the environment. Acknowledging their own lack of such expertise, they have created numerous **independent regulatory commissions**, bureaucracies outside of the cabinet departments with the authority to develop standards of behavior for specific industries and businesses, to monitor compliance with these standards, and to impose sanctions on those it finds guilty of violating the standards.

Initially, government regulation centered on *economic regulation*—matters such as setting the prices of goods and services and ensuring competition in the marketplace. The first independent regulatory commission, the Interstate Commerce Commission, was set up in 1887 to oversee the prices and services of the railroad industry. By the 1970s, Congress had turned more in the direction of *social regulation*, establishing regulatory commissions that focused on how business practices affected the environment, and the health and safety of consumers and workers. For example, Congress and the president created the Consumer Product Safety Commission in 1972.

Independent regulatory agencies are under the direction of bipartisan boards whose members do not need to be loyal to the president's preferences. Typically, the president nominates and the Senate confirms an odd number of board members. Board members serve staggered fixed terms. This structure allows the agency to make decisions based on the expertise of its board members, not on the preferences of the president or Congress. Still, the agencies need both presidential and congressional support to survive.

Government Corporations

Like private businesses, **government corporations** sell a service or a product and compete for customers; but unlike private businesses, they are government owned. Congress and the president create government corporations when they believe it is in the public interest for the federal government to engage in a commercial activity, such as selling stamps to pay for the cost of delivering mail. Unlike the other categories of bureaucracies, government corporations, such as the U.S. Postal Service, are expected to make enough money to cover their costs, instead of being funded by tax dollars.

government corporation
An executive branch unit that sells a service and is expected to be financially self-sufficient.

A bipartisan board typically directs each government corporation. The president appoints the board members to serve for staggered fixed terms. Typically, the Senate is not required to confirm the board members. Like regulatory commissions and administrative agencies, government corporations are independent of cabinet departments.

Executive Office of the President

By 1939, the federal bureaucracy had grown tremendously in size and diversity of responsibilities. Acknowledging that the president, who serves as the chief executive of the bureaucracy, needed help to manage this constellation of departments, independent administrative agencies, independent regulatory commissions, and government corporations, President Franklin Roosevelt and Congress created the Executive Office of the President (EOP).

The EOP is composed of dozens of offices and councils that assist the president in managing the complex and sprawling executive branch of the bureaucracy. The president appoints the top-level bureaucrats in EOP units, and the majority of these appointments are not subject to Senate confirmation. The president has the authority to fire these appointees at his pleasure. Therefore, the EOP serves the president; it is in fact the presidential bureaucracy. (See Chapter 5 for a detailed discussion of the EOP.)

As the U.S. government organizational chart (Figure 7.1) indicates, the legislative branch has several offices supporting its work (including the Government

Accountability Office, the Government Printing Office, and the Library of Congress). In addition, there are offices in the judicial branch supporting the work of the courts (the Administrative Office of the United States Courts, the Federal Judicial Center, and the United States Sentencing Commission). Federal bureaucrats employed in these legislative and judicial bodies support the formulation, implementation, and evaluation of public policies.

■ The Work of Bureaucrats

Although the primary work of bureaucrats is policy implementation—putting public policy into action—bureaucrats play an active, vital role in all six stages of the public policy cycle. These stages are (1) agenda setting, (2) policy formulation, (3) policy approval, (4) appropriation approval, (5) policy implementation, and (6) policy evaluation. (Figure 7.5 presents an example of how the Affordable Care Act of 2010 is working through the six-stage policy cycle.)

politics-administration dichotomy
The concept that elected government officials, who are accountable to the voters, create and approve public policy, and then competent, politically neutral bureaucrats implement the public policy.

According to the **politics-administration dichotomy**, there is a clear line between *politics* (deciding what government should accomplish, enacting those goals into laws, and allocating money to pay to execute laws) and the *administration* of public policy (the real work of putting the laws into action). The dichotomy says that elected officials (whom citizens hold accountable through the ballot box) have authority for politics and that competent bureaucrats (hired through merit-based civil service) have authority for policy administration. Theoretically, this arrangement fosters not only government by and for the people (representative democracy) but also efficient and effective public services.

The politics-administration dichotomy may sound good, but the reality of public policy processes does not allow for such a clean separation between those who "do politics" and those who administer policy. Although bureaucrats are hired to implement policy made by elected officials, elected officials tap the expertise of bureaucrats throughout the other five stages of the policy process, allowing bureaucrats to influence and even make policies themselves, as we now shall see.

Agenda Setting

In the first stage of the public policy cycle, elected officials decide what issues they want to discuss and possibly address by placing them on their lists of items to work on, their policy agendas. Bureaucrats play an instrumental role in helping to set the policy agenda. Because their focus is to implement public policy at the street level, bureaucrats have a clear view of the societal problems that citizens expect the government to address and strong views on how best to address those problems. Political scientists use the term *iron triangle* to describe long-term collaborative efforts among bureaucrats in a government agency, the members of an interest group, and the members of a legislative committee to get their mutual concerns on the agenda and then addressed through approved public policies. *Issue networks*, which are temporary collaborations among bureaucrats, elected officials, and the members of numerous interest groups, also work to set the agenda as well as to influence policy formulation and approval. For more about iron triangles and issue networks, see Chapter 16.

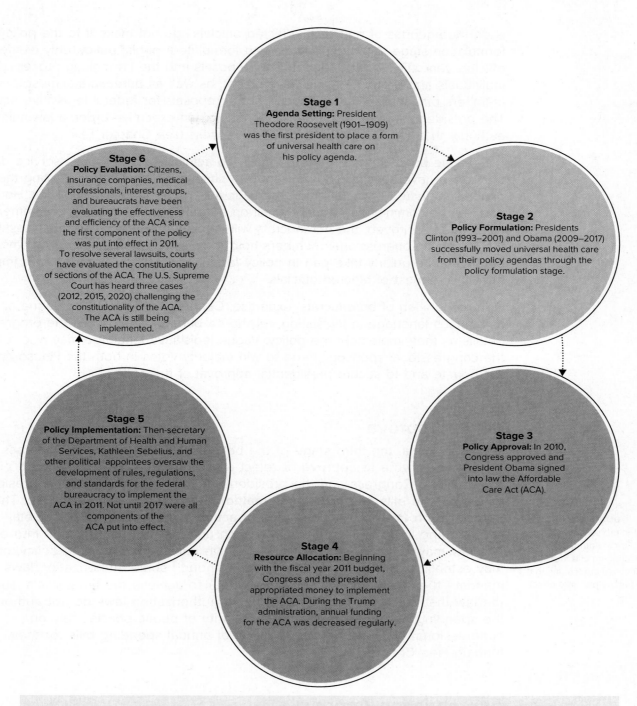

Stage 1
Agenda Setting: President Theodore Roosevelt (1901–1909) was the first president to place a form of universal health care on his policy agenda.

Stage 2
Policy Formulation: Presidents Clinton (1993–2001) and Obama (2009–2017) successfully moved universal health care from their policy agendas through the policy formulation stage.

Stage 3
Policy Approval: In 2010, Congress approved and President Obama signed into law the Affordable Care Act (ACA).

Stage 4
Resource Allocation: Beginning with the fiscal year 2011 budget, Congress and the president appropriated money to implement the ACA. During the Trump administration, annual funding for the ACA was decreased regularly.

Stage 5
Policy Implementation: Then-secretary of the Department of Health and Human Services, Kathleen Sebelius, and other political appointees oversaw the development of rules, regulations, and standards for the federal bureaucracy to implement the ACA in 2011. Not until 2017 were all components of the ACA put into effect.

Stage 6
Policy Evaluation: Citizens, insurance companies, medical professionals, interest groups, and bureaucrats have been evaluating the effectiveness and efficiency of the ACA since the first component of the policy was put into effect in 2011. To resolve several lawsuits, courts have evaluated the constitutionality of sections of the ACA. The U.S. Supreme Court has heard three cases (2012, 2015, 2020) challenging the constitutionality of the ACA. The ACA is still being implemented.

FIGURE 7.5 ◼ **Stages of the Policy Process** This flowchart shows how the Affordable Care Act (ACA) continues to work through the policy cycle. In reality, the stages of the cycle often overlap. Today, additional rules and regulations are being established as the ACA is implemented. At the same time, critics and supporters continue to evaluate the ACA, as are government agencies and courts. In 2021 the Supreme Court will again rule on the constitutionality of the ACA. In the meantime, calls for reform to the act may force it back to the agenda-setting stage, which could lead to the formulation of new legislation revising or even repealing it.

Policy Formulation

The second stage of the policy process, policy formulation, involves defining a problem that has made it to an agenda and developing a plan of action (a policy) to address the problem. Many issues that reach an elected official's agenda—or even the agendas of numerous elected officials—do not make it to the policy formulation stage. Although anyone can formulate a public policy, only elected officials can officially introduce policy proposals into the lawmaking process. Thus individuals and groups outside government, as well as bureaucrats, must identify members of Congress to introduce policy proposals for federal legislative action. The president can also make policy by issuing an executive order, a lawmaking authority that lies outside the legislative process (see Chapter 5).

Because bureaucrats are the people who actually provide public service daily, they often have specialized knowledge of societal problems. Recognizing their expertise, elected officials rely on bureaucrats when formulating policies. House and Senate committees frequently call on bureaucrats to review and comment on bills that, if approved, the bureaucrats will implement. Bureaucrats often testify at the hearings congressional members hold to investigate and study problems. Thus bureaucrats regularly take part in policy formulation, whether at their own impetus or at the request of elected officials.

In recognition of bureaucrats' expertise, Congress often includes vague or ambiguous language in legislation, relying on bureaucrats to fill in the program details as they implement the policy. Vague legislative language may also reflect the congressional sponsors' need to win majority votes in both the House and the Senate and to secure presidential approval of the policy.

Policy Approval

Policy approval, the third stage of the policy cycle, occurs when Congress and the president vote to approve or reject a bill that presents a formulated public policy. When Congress and the president, or Congress alone over a president's veto, approve bills, the laws thus created authorize government action. These **authorization laws** provide the plan of action to address a given societal concern and identify the executive branch unit that will put the plan into effect. The law may authorize an existing executive unit to carry out the policy, or it may establish a new unit to do the job. Although some authorization laws mandate the spending of money every year to achieve the law's goals, such as the law that created Social Security, most authorization laws do not authorize the spending of money. Instead, the majority of public policies rely on congressional and presidential approval of annual spending bills for their funding (see Chapter 11).

authorization law
A law that provides the plan of action to address a given societal concern and identifies the executive branch unit that will put the plan into effect.

Appropriation Approval

In the next phase of the policy process, appropriation, Congress and the president specify how much money each bureaucracy is authorized to spend during the budget year. Through the budget process (see Chapter 11), Congress and the president formulate appropriation bills, which are plans for the distribution of government revenue to government entities, including bureaucracies, legislative bodies, and judicial bodies. Approved appropriation bills—**appropriation laws**—give bureaucracies the legal authority to spend money during a specific fiscal year.

appropriation law
A law that gives bureaucracies and other government entities the legal authority to spend money.

Bureaucrats play three key roles in the budget process. First, at the request of the president, bureaucrats develop an annual budget request for their agencies.

Second, Congress calls on bureaucrats to justify their budget requests. In turn, bureaucrats lobby members of Congress to allocate to their agencies the funds they requested. With limited money available, bureaucracies typically do not receive all the funding they request. Therefore, bureaucracies compete with one another for their piece of the limited budget pie. Once Congress and the president approve the appropriation bills, bureaucrats take on their primary public policy role; they put public policy into action.

Policy Implementation

Policy implementation, the second-to-last stage of the policy cycle, is the main work of bureaucrats. To put policy into action, bureaucrats must first interpret the authorization law and then carry it out. Congress and the president delegate to bureaucrats the authority to determine the best way to implement the policy; this authority is called **administrative discretion**. Applying administrative discretion, bureaucrats use their expertise and best judgment to interpret vague laws, establish programs and procedures aimed at achieving the policy goals, and make the day-to-day decisions necessary to execute public policy. Elected officials risk the loss of control over the content of public policy when they delegate administrative discretion to bureaucrats. However, they have numerous tools to hold bureaucrats accountable, which we discuss later in this chapter.

administrative discretion
The authority delegated to bureaucrats to use their expertise and judgment when determining how to implement public policy.

Bureaucrats use administrative discretion to establish programs, rules, regulations, and standards necessary for the effective and efficient implementation of policy. **Administrative rule making** is the process by which upper-level bureaucrats use their administrative discretion to create rules, regulations, and standards that the bureaucracy will then enforce. For example, recognizing its lack of expertise in the specifics of how to prevent air and water pollution, Congress delegated to the Environmental Protection Agency (EPA) the authority to establish policy. The EPA sets specific pollution emissions standards to implement the Clean Water and Clean Air Acts. Although Congress does not approve these EPA administrative standards, the standards have the force of law.

administrative rule making
The process by which an independent commission or agency fills in the details of a vague law by formulating, proposing, and approving rules, regulations, and standards that will be enforced to implement the policy.

Agencies involved in administrative rule making also engage in **administrative adjudication**; they have the authority to determine if their rules are violated and to impose penalties on the violators. Citizens who disagree with an agency's application of its administrative rules or those whom an agency finds guilty of violating its rules may challenge the agency's decisions through a lawsuit. For example, if the Social Security Administration denies an individual benefits, that person can appeal the decision through Social Security Administration procedures. Once she has exhausted those administrative procedures, if the denial is upheld, she can file a lawsuit challenging it.

administrative adjudication
The process by which agencies resolve disputes over the implementation of their administrative rules.

Policy Evaluation

The last stage of the policy process is policy evaluation—the assessment of the intended and unintended effects of policy implementation. As mentioned earlier, people assess government by determining the effectiveness and efficiency of public services and benefits delivered. Therefore, the implementation of policy by bureaucrats, that is, bureaucratic performance, is the key to citizens' satisfaction with government, and the key to government success.

In 1973, political scientists Jeffrey L. Pressman and Aaron B. Wildavsky published their study of a federally funded economic development program, which concluded that it is "amazing that federal programs work at all" given the hurdles bureaucrats encounter.[11] Their landmark research fueled outcries for increased transparency and evaluations of public policies. As a result, policy evaluation has become a larger component of the workload of legislators and bureaucrats.

Because elected officials and citizens want proof of the efficiency and the effectiveness of implemented policies, agencies must document what they do and the impact of their work. Because citizens do not elect bureaucrats, they do not have the opportunity to fire public servants whose performance is unsatisfactory. Therefore, citizens defer the responsibility for bureaucratic accountability to members of Congress, the president, and the judges who preside over the courts because these elected and appointed government officials have legal means to monitor bureaucrats' work and to hold them accountable.

■ Bureaucratic Accountability

When it comes to public service, everyone is watching. The courts, through the mechanism of lawsuits, review the actions of the executive and legislative branches to ensure that they are constitutional and legal. Congress and the president, as the creators and funders of bureaucracies, can threaten to revamp or eliminate any bureaucratic organization, or to decrease its funding, if its performance falls short of expectations. In his budget proposal for 2021, President Trump called for the elimination of 11 Education Department programs that his administration deemed wasteful.[14] Congress and the president not only structure bureaucracies to foster efficient, effective, and accountable public service, but they also pass laws to increase self-policing by bureaucrats.

sunshine laws
Legislation that opens up government functions and documents to the public.

People outside government, including many ordinary citizens, also keep a close eye on bureaucracies. **Sunshine laws** open up government activities and documents to the public, fostering transparency and supporting the public's right to know about government actions and decision making. However, laws, including sunshine laws, are effective only if citizens know about them and take advantage of them.

Accountability to the People

One of the first national sunshine laws was the Administrative Procedure Act (APA) of 1946. The APA responded to citizens' and interest groups' concerns about the fast growth in the number of agencies involved in administrative rule making and the lack of transparency and accountability of the bureaucratic rule makers. The APA standardized rule-making procedures, and all federal agencies except those specifically excluded by their authorization legislation must comply with them. These procedures include requiring bureaucracies to publicize their proposed rules in the *Federal Register*, a daily national government publication, which is now online (www.federalregister.gov). Agencies also must publish an invitation for people to offer comments on their proposals.

To facilitate this open process, www.regulations.gov, the national government website, posts proposed administrative rules and accepts electronically submitted comments on the rules. In this way, people can have a voice in administrative rule making. Such citizen input is essential to democracy because bureaucrats propose and approve more administrative rules each year than Congress proposes and approves pieces of legislation. Once the agency collects and reviews the comments that people have submitted, it must publish its approved rules in the *Federal Register*.

The Freedom of Information Act (FOIA), a 1966 amendment to the APA, requires national agencies to give citizens access to government documents on request and at a reasonable cost. Today, the act also requires all federal executive units to proactively post on their websites information of interest to the public, without the need for a FOIA request.

The Government in the Sunshine Act of 1976 requires all multi-headed national agencies, except those in the Executive Office of the President, to conduct open, public meetings where citizens can testify and present their concerns about these agencies' procedures as well as their past, current, and potential actions.

These days, all levels of government are using the Internet to offer services to citizens more efficiently and cost effectively and to foster accountability. In September 2000, the General Services Administration (GSA) launched the national government's one-stop portal to national, state, local, and tribal government agency websites. The site, www.usa.gov, puts government information and services at your fingertips, including the ability to apply for federal government jobs.

In a democracy, bureaucrats, like elected officials, operate in a fishbowl. Working face-to-face or computer screen–to–computer screen, with the people whom they serve, they are in full view of anyone interested in monitoring them. Sunshine laws and e-government provide citizens with the means to find out what is going on in the bureaucracy. When citizens or watchdog groups identify a problem with bureaucratic operations, they frequently turn to the media to bring public attention to the issue, because the media are always ready to report on bureaucratic inefficiency and impropriety. A more expensive option for citizen and interest group action against bureaucratic waste and misconduct is the filing of a lawsuit.

Accountability to the Courts

Through the litigation process, the U.S. judicial system seeks to ensure that bureaucrats and bureaucracies comply with the law, including the authorization laws that create them, the appropriation laws that fund them, constitutional protections for due process and equal treatment, the Administrative Procedures Act, sunshine laws, and any other laws Congress applies to them. If an individual or group believes that a bureaucrat or bureaucracy has violated the law, they can file a lawsuit. For example, people or organizations have filed lawsuits against the National Security Administration because they believed NSA employees violated the Fourth Amendment's protection against unreasonable search and seizure when collecting cell phone data.

In 2018, attorneys general from 18 states and the District of Columbia sued Department of Education Secretary Betsy DeVos after she froze implementation of the Borrower Defense to Repayment rule. This rule was written to help students receive debt forgiveness if they were cheated by their college, as measured by not finding gainful employment after graduation. A federal judge found that DeVos's freezing of the rule was "arbitrary and capricious."[15] Then, in January 2020, the American Federation of Teachers, one of the largest teachers' unions

Red tape and regulations prevented quick, widespread testing for the coronavirus after the first confirmed case in the United States was reported in late January 2020.[12] Early, widespread testing would have allowed for containment when the outbreak began.

Starting in the fall of 2019 and continuing into 2020, Dr. Helen Y. Chu, an infectious disease expert, and her team at the University of Washington were collecting nasal swabs in the Seattle area for their research project on the flu. Once the first U.S. case of coronavirus was confirmed, Chu and her team repeatedly requested that state and federal government officials allow them to repurpose their tests for monitoring the new disease. Eventually, Washington State's epidemiologist contacted the chief of the national Centers for Disease Control and Prevention's (CDC) epidemiology and prevention branch, requesting that Chu's study be used to test for the coronavirus. The CDC's National Center for Immunization and Respiratory Disease responded that the national Food and Drug Administration (FDA) would have to approve this request. The FDA replied that it could not give approval because Chu's lab was not certified as a clinical lab, but rather as a research lab. The lab could apply to the Centers for Medicare and Medicaid for reclassification; however, that process could take months.

As Chu's team fought unsuccessfully for permission to perform coronavirus testing, the CDC was developing and shipping its own test kits to public labs. But after using these CDC kits, the public labs found that the results were invalid. In response, the Association of Public Health Laboratories requested that the FDA commissioner use his discretion to allow state and local public health laboratories to develop their own coronavirus tests. The commissioner's response was that state and local labs could submit their tests to the FDA for emergency authorization. Around the same time, the FDA relaxed rules and regulations, making it easier for clinical labs to use their own coronavirus tests as long as the labs submitted evidence to the FDA that the tests worked.

The initial coronavirus-related goal of governments throughout the United States was containment—isolating the sick and quarantining the people they contacted. But without widespread testing early in the outbreak, the new goal became mitigation—taking steps to minimize deaths from the disease and slow its spread so that hospitals could keep up with the volume of patients.[13]

A. Describe a power Congress could use to address the red tape and regulations described in the scenario.

B. In the context of the scenario, explain how the use of congressional power described in Part A can be affected by its interaction with the presidency.

C. In the context of the scenario, explain how the interaction between Congress and the presidency can be affected by state governments.

in the nation, sued DeVos after the Education Department repealed the Borrower Defense to Repayment rule. The lawsuit claimed the department had not followed the proper procedures, under the Administrative Procedures Act, to repeal the rule.[14]

Accountability to Congress

Bureaucrats must always keep in mind the preferences of Congress if they want to survive because Congress approves the legislation that creates (and eliminates), regulates, and funds bureaucracies. The Senate has an additional mechanism for promoting bureaucratic accountability in that more than one-quarter of the president's appointees are subject to Senate confirmation. The confirmation process for political appointees gives senators a degree of influence over the leadership and direction of executive departments and agencies.

Another means by which Congress encourages bureaucratic accountability is through the monitoring of bureaucracies' policy implementation, a form of legislative oversight. When the media, citizens, or interest groups bring concerns about a bureaucracy's policy implementation to the attention of legislators, Congress might launch an investigation. If, consequently, Congress and the president are dissatisfied with that bureaucracy's performance or behavior, they can cut its budget, modify its legal authority, or even eliminate the agency.

Congress can force itself to evaluate a bureaucracy's performance by including a **sunset clause** in the authorization law that establishes an agency or a program. A sunset clause creates an expiration date for a program or policy, meaning the program or policy will end unless Congress and the president reauthorize it through new legislation.

sunset clause
A clause in legislation that sets an expiration date for an authorized program or policy unless Congress reauthorizes it.

Accountability to the President

The president also has several tools for holding bureaucracies accountable. Like Congress, the president can use the legislative process to ensure accountability by approving or vetoing authorization and appropriation bills. In addition, because most top political appointees serve at the president's pleasure, they are responsive to the president's policy preferences—and in this way, they and their agencies are accountable to the president.

Today, the Office of Management and Budget (OMB), an EOP agency, is the key lever in the president's efforts to hold the bureaucracy accountable. The OMB evaluates bureaucratic performance for the president. The OMB also spearheads the development of the president's budget, controls the implementation of appropriation laws, and regulates administrative rule making. Through its Office of Information and Regulatory Affairs, the OMB ensures that regulations created by executive branch agencies through the administrative rule-making processes are not "unnecessarily costly"[15] and that they support the president's policy preferences.

Internal Accountability

The president, Congress, the courts, and ordinary citizens have multiple means by which to hold bureaucrats accountable. But bureaucrats, who themselves are taxpayers, also worry about inefficiency and waste in public service. Legislated codes of behavior, whistleblower protections, and inspectors general help foster accountability from within bureaucracies.

ETHICS IN GOVERNMENT ACT The Ethics in Government Act of 1978 established the Office of Government Ethics (OGE), which is charged with preventing conflicts

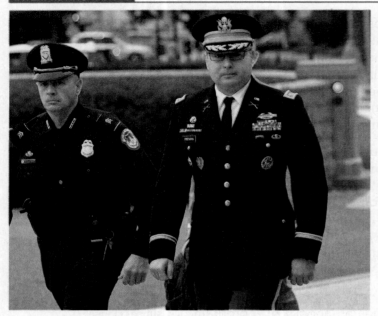

>> In 2020, shortly after the U.S. Senate voted down the impeachment charges brought against the president, Trump removed Army Lieutenant Colonel Alexander Vindman (above, right) from his position as Director for European Affairs for the U.S. National Security Council. Vindman had testified in the House impeachment inquiry that actions of the president were "inappropriate and had nothing to do with national security." Does the Constitution require bureaucrats to be accountable to or loyal to the president?

Interpret: Is a military bureaucrat like Col. Vindman perceived differently in his public service role than a civilian? How does the image of a uniformed military officer testifying before Congress affect public perception differently than that of a civilian public servant?

Mandel Ngan/AFP/Getty Images

---

conflict of interest
In the case of public servants, the situation in which they can personally benefit from a decision they make or an action they take in the process of doing their jobs.

of interest by bureaucrats (political appointees, SES bureaucrats, and civil servants). A **conflict of interest** arises when a public servant is in a position to make a work decision or take a work action from which he or she can personally benefit. In such a situation, the public servant's private interest is in conflict with his or her responsibility to serve the public interest.

In 1992, the OGE published a comprehensive set of ethical standards for federal bureaucrats, which provides guidelines for ethical, efficient, and effective behavior. Some agencies also have their own codes of behavior. Moreover, many of the professions in which bureaucrats are members (lawyers, doctors, nurses, accountants, engineers, and so on) also have established codes of behavior. Importantly, however, codes of behavior are just guidelines. They do not stipulate what a bureaucrat should do in a given situation. Thus bureaucrats must use discretion when applying such codes to their daily work of providing public service.

whistleblower
A bureaucrat or private party who discloses to the government mismanagement, fraud, waste, corruption, or threats to public health and safety.

WHISTLEBLOWER PROTECTIONS AND INSPECTORS GENERAL **Whistleblowers** are people who disclose government misconduct, waste, mismanagement, abuse of authority, or threat to public health or safety. They can be bureaucrats or private parties. To enhance bureaucratic accountability, the 1978 Civil Service Reform Act provided some protections to civil servants who are whistleblowers, including the establishment of the Office of Special Counsel to protect the jobs of public servants who blow the whistle. Congress strengthened whistleblower protections with the 1989 Whistleblower Protection Act and the 2012 Whistleblower Enhancement Act.

In the fall of 2019, a whistleblower filed a "Disclosure of Urgent Concern Form" with the Intelligence Community Office of the Inspector General, alleging misconduct by President Trump in a phone call with Ukraine's President Zelensky.

The whistleblower filing led the U.S. House of Representatives to an investigation that ended in the impeachment of President Trump. Initially, however, in response to the news of this filing, questions were raised about the rights of whistleblowers. The form filed by the whistleblower provides two assurances that his or her confidentiality will be protected. First, the information is protected by the 1974 Privacy Act, a law enacted after President Nixon attempted to gain information about a whistleblower. Second, whistleblower confidentiality is mandated by the Inspector General Act of 1978.[16]

Congress approved the Inspector General Act to ensure the integrity of public service by creating government watchdogs, called **inspectors general**, appointed by the president and embedded in government agencies to monitor policy implementation and investigate alleged misconduct. The law requires the appointment of the inspectors general without regard to their political affiliation and strictly based on their abilities in accounting, auditing, or investigation. Today, 72 federal agencies have inspectors general. "We're supposed to check our politics at the door and call things as we see them. If we uncover things that reflect badly on the government, we're legally and morally obliged to report it. We're obliged to do that for the good of the country." So explained Clark Ervin, who held the position of inspector general at the Departments of State and Homeland Security.[17]

inspectors general
Political appointees who work within a government agency to ensure the integrity of public service by investigating allegations of misconduct by bureaucrats.

The country has laws, rules, regulations, and structures in place to ensure that bureaucrats (those millions of non-elected government officials as well as shadow bureaucrats) serve the public well (efficiently, effectively, equally) and are responsible to the elected officials who make policy. However, in their daily decision-making, bureaucrats have considerable discretion that elected officials delegate to them. No law or rule is written with such detail that it can tell bureaucrats what to do in every interaction they have with the people they serve. As Bernardo Zacka states in his book, *When the State Meets the Street: Public Service and Moral Agency*, in their daily decision-making bureaucrats "are responsible not only for assessing facts and selecting appropriate procedures; they must also weigh competing values and goals against one another and give countenance to objectives that are often vague."[18]

In summary, codes of ethics, whistleblower protection laws, and inspectors general enhance the ability of the bureaucrats themselves to police the agencies in which they work, and sunshine laws give government outsiders various instruments for monitoring the bureaucracy. But many citizens and government officials believe that more needs to be done to improve bureaucrats' record of performance.

Can Bureaucratic Performance Be Improved?

In the United States, bureaucrats perform every job imaginable. They generally do their jobs so well that we rarely think about how their work positively affects us around the clock. We and our elected officials are nevertheless quick to bash the bureaucracy at the slightest hint of inefficiency. Similarly, the media seize upon any opportunity to report on problems with bureaucrats and bureaucracies. When was the last time you heard a news report or were involved in a friendly conversation that praised a public servant?

Yet the U.S. Postal Service delivers hundreds of millions of pieces of mail six days a week, and rarely is a letter or a package lost. Thousands of planes safely take off from and land at U.S. airports every hour, guided by federal bureaucrats in the person of air traffic controllers. Millions of senior citizens receive a Social Security benefit on time every month.

Policy scholar Charles Goodsell has found that two-thirds to three-fourths of Americans report their encounters with government bureaucrats and bureaucracy as "satisfactory."[19] However, Pew Research Center surveys show that Americans' views on government performance are mixed and can change quickly.[20] Figure 7.6 presents public views on a select group of federal agencies. The following Data Analysis feature shows how partisanship may affect and explain the changing viewpoints on government performance.

The Best-Performing Bureaucracies

Research consistently shows that some federal agencies perform better than do others. Political scientists William T. Gormley and Steven Balla reviewed national performance data and summarized the characteristics of federal agencies that

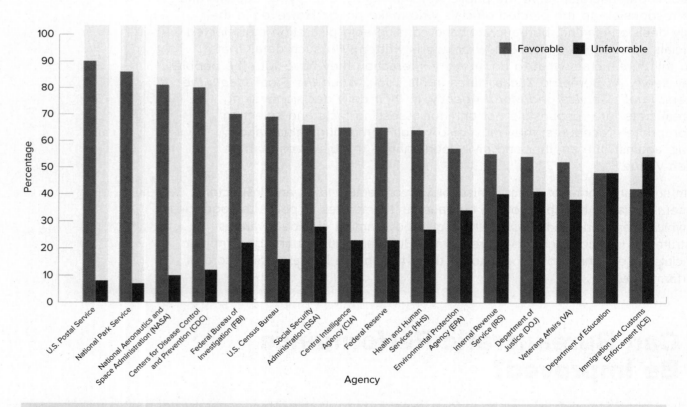

FIGURE 7.6   Public Views on Select Federal Agencies The data in this figure was collected in September 2019. Based on actions of the listed agencies since September 2019, for which agencies can you argue their favorable percentage has declined? For which agencies can you argue their favorable percentage has increased?

Source: Pew Research Center, "Public Expresses Favorable Views of a Number of Federal Agencies," October 1, 2019.

Is It Government Performance or Partisanship?

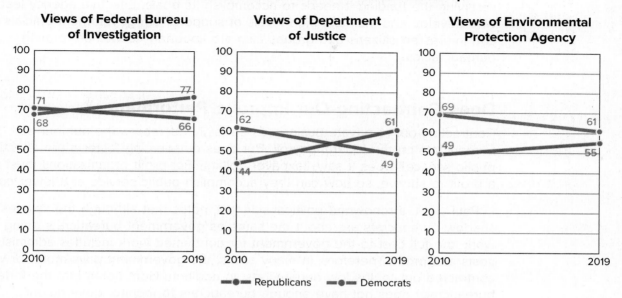

Source: Pew Research Center, "Public Expresses Favorable Views of a Number of Federal Agencies," October 1, 2019.

When surveys ask citizens their views on government performance, the expectation is that respondents are assessing the quality of services provided. The data above comes from Pew Research Center surveys conducted nine years apart. This data reports the percentage of Democratic and Democratic-leaning respondents (one category) and Republican and Republican-leaning respondents (a second category) who have a favorable opinion of the identified agency. Use the data in your analysis.

Practice Analytical Thinking

1. Summarize the shifts in the opinions in each chart. What events between 2010 and 2019 might have contributed to these shifts?

2. If you were a bureaucrat in the Federal Bureau of Investigation (FBI), Department of Justice (DOJ), or Environmental Protection Agency (EPA), what would you take away from these survey results?

3. What does this data suggest about citizens' satisfaction survey results?

perform well.[21] They found several characteristics common among better-performing bureaucracies. They include language in the agency's authorization legislation that clearly states what the agency is expected to accomplish and that delegates high levels of administrative discretion, which allows bureaucrats to determine the best way to achieve the agency's goal. Better-performing bureaucracies tend to be those with easily measured goals, especially goals that include providing resources to citizens (such as Social Security benefits) as opposed to taking resources (tax collection). Another factor correlated with good performance is high levels of support for the agency's mission from elected officials, the media, and diverse groups of citizens. High levels of support typically result in an agency's receiving the funding it needs to accomplish its goals. Effective agency leaders who develop and maintain high levels of support from government officials and interested citizens and groups also are important to well-performing bureaucracies.

Does Contracting-Out Improve Performance?

Contracting-out to private businesses certainly decreases the number of bureaucrats on the federal payroll. But does outsourcing foster more effective public service? Does it save taxpayer dollars? For-profit organizations must make a profit to survive, so how can they accomplish public service at a lower cost?

Paul Light, a renowned political scientist, notes that although the salaries of shadow bureaucrats are about the same as government bureaucrats doing similar work, the full cost to the government for contracted work includes administrative costs and profit. Therefore, in many cases, the government pays more for work contracted out to shadow bureaucrats. In addition, Light notes that the federal bureaucracy does not have enough bureaucrats to monitor government contractors,[22] which means that holding contractors accountable for delays, cost overruns, and quality of results is difficult.

The problems the Internal Revenue Service (IRS) encountered with contracting out collection of late payments in 1996 and 2006 provide a good study. The contracted debt collectors were paid up to 25 percent of what they collected. However, due to cost overruns and concerns about abuses of taxpayer rights, the IRS abandoned the use of contractors. According to the IRS, the outsourcing cost the government millions more than it actually collected from taxpayers. Yet, in 2017, following a provision in a 2015 law and a congressional order, the IRS began contracting with debt collectors again.[23]

In his review of the status of federal contracting-out, Peter Schuck, professor of law emeritus at Yale University, found that "the vast amount of contracting reduces accountability and transparency, and raises serious questions about agencies' ability to manage these contracts effectively and measure contractors' performance."[24] The lack of accountability for the results of contractors' work is a growing concern for the Government Accountability Office (GAO), the independent agency that functions as Congress's watchdog for bureaucratic performance and use of taxpayer money. The GAO has determined contract management to be a high-risk function for numerous federal agencies.[25]

In 2018, the Senate Homeland Security and Government Affairs Committee and the House Oversight and Government Reform Committee both initiated investigations of the Federal Emergency Management Agency's (FEMA) handling of a failed contract. The $156 million contract to provide 300 million emergency meals to hurricane victims in Puerto Rico was canceled after the contractor was unable to fulfill the contract. Senators stated that the contract was "further evidence of systemic weaknesses in FEMA's contracting practices."[26]

Unlike government bodies, private businesses, including those with government contracts, can legally function behind closed doors—unless and until concerned citizens, watchdog groups, the media, and government officials force the doors open through congressional investigations or lawsuits. In 1986, the federal government strengthened the False Claims Act, which originated during the Civil War in response to fraud committed against the military. This law allows a private party with information about fraud against a government program committed by a person or a company (typically a federal contractor) to file a lawsuit on behalf of the government. If the government wins such a lawsuit and recovers money, the whistleblower is eligible to receive 15 to 30 percent of the recovered money.

In 2018 the Department of Justice reported obtaining more than $2.8 billion in settlements and judgments from cases involving fraud and false claims against the national government. Of this total, $2.5 billion was recovered from the health care industry, including drug and medical device manufacturers, hospitals, pharmacies, laboratories, and physicians. This was the ninth year in a row that the DOJ recovered at least $2 billion from the health care industry. In addition to the federal dollars recovered, the DOJ also recovered millions of state dollars spent on their Medicaid programs.[27]

Citizens' Role in Bureaucratic Performance

Citizens turn to the government to provide services and solve problems. Unfortunately, the solutions to many societal problems are not known. How can government prevent crime? How can government solve homelessness and poverty? Can government find a cure for cancer or the coronavirus? Often several potential solutions are offered, but elected officials might not agree on what potential solution to try. This is why political scientists describe a policy cycle: a circular, ongoing process that typically yields incremental changes while attempting to improve current policies based on policy evaluations.

As we have discussed, the national government's success in serving the people well depends on many factors. The president and Congress play key roles in providing the resources bureaucrats and bureaucracies need to perform well so citizens are satisfied. They must appoint good leaders who hire competent civil servants, legislate clear policy goals, delegate ample administrative discretion, and fund agencies and programs at sufficient levels. Ultimately, even if all other factors correlated with a well-performing bureaucracy are in place, the bureaucracy will fail without the participation and compliance of the people it serves.

The effectiveness of public policies depends on people's knowledge of and compliance with the law. It depends on their applying for the government programs for which they qualify. It depends on their conformity to the rules, regulations, standards, and directions of bureaucrats. This symbiotic relationship is essential to the success of government. On March 15, 2020, the CDC recommended that no gatherings of more than 50 people, and for organizations serving at-risk people no gatherings of more than 10 people, be held for the next eight weeks. This recommendation included weddings, parades, conferences, sporting events, and so on. The CDC said its recommendation was made "in an attempt to reduce introduction of the [corona]virus into new communities, and to slow the spread of infection in communities already affected by the virus."[28] Some state and local governments set the maximum gathering size at 10 people and mandated the closing of schools, non-essential businesses, and places of worship. Throughout the summer of 2020, the CDC continued to urge people to keep a distance of six feet from each other in public spaces and to wear masks as states began to allow the reopening of businesses and gatherings of larger numbers of people. How important was citizen, state, and local government compliance with the CDC recommendations to the governments' ability to address the coronavirus pandemic?

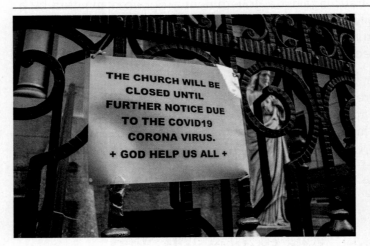

>> By late May 2020, all states were easing restrictions on businesses and gatherings that they had imposed based on guidelines the national Centers for Disease Control and Prevention (CDC) had published to contain and mitigate the spread of the coronavirus. At the same time, the Trump administration disagreed with the CDC's guidelines for reopening places of worship, arguing they were too strict. This disagreement offers just one example of tension between elected officials (doing politics) and bureaucrats attempting to provide competent and effective public services.

Bill Tompkins/Getty Images

Conclusion: Thinking Critically about What's Next in the Bureaucracy

Ultimately, for citizens to be satisfied with their governments, elected officials must "do politics" well by formulating and agreeing to enact sound solutions to societal problems, and by appropriating the funds necessary to properly and fully implement public policies. To be successful in "doing politics," elected officials must rely on the expertise, competence, and neutrality of bureaucrats who participate in every stage of the policy cycle, with their primary responsibility being the provision of public goods and services (administering policy) daily.

Although bureaucrat bashing pervades the media and is a common practice among candidates and elected officials, surveys consistently find that the majority of citizens are satisfied with their interactions with bureaucrats and with how the national bureaucracy is addressing their top areas of concern. However, there are always challenges to the efficiency, effectiveness, and accountability of the bureaucracy, as well as opportunities to make improvements.

Citizens' satisfaction with their governments depends on the performance of bureaucrats and the bureaucracies. The success of bureaucrats depends on numerous factors out of their control: from authorization legislation to funding to leadership to citizen knowledge of available services to cooperation of people with bureaucrats. Democracy and bureaucracy succeed or fail based on the ability of people to make good decisions and work together.

■ References

1. Congressional Research Service, "Federal Workforce Statistics Sources: OPM and OMB," October 24, 2019.

2. U.S. Bureau of Labor Statistics, *Employment Projections*, "Table 2.1 Employment by major industry sector," September 4, 2019.

3. U.S. Census Bureau, *2018 Government Employment & Payroll Tables*, March 2018, census.gov/data/tables/2018/econ/apes/annual-apes.html.

4. Office of Personnel Management, "Senior Executive Service Overview and History."

5. Office of Personnel Management, "Senior Executive Service Overview and History."

6. Jimmy Carter, "Federal Civil Service Reform Remarks Announcing the Administration's Proposals to the Congress: March 2, 1978."

7. U.S. Bureau of Labor Statistics, *Economic News Release*, "Table 3: Union Affiliation of Employed Wage and Salary Workers by Occupation and Industry," January 20, 2020.

8. Katherine McIntire Peters, "Agencies May Now Enforce Trump's Controversial Workforce Orders," *Government Executive*, October 2, 2019, https://www.govexec.com/management/2019/10/agencies-may-enforce-trumps-controversial-workforce-orders/160320.

9. Andrew Eversden, "New Data Shows the Soaring Cost of Government Contracts," *Federal Times*, August 1, 2019, https://www.federaltimes.com/newsletters/acquisition-update/2019/08/01/government-spent-nearly-560-billion-on-contracts-in-2018/.

10. George Will, "'Big Government' Is Ever Growing, on the Sly," *National Review*, February 25, 2017.

11. Jeffrey L. Pressman and Aaron Wildavsky, *Implementation: How Great Expectations in Washington Are Dashed in Oakland: Or, Why It's Amazing That Federal Programs Work at All* (Berkeley and Los Angeles: University of California Press, 1973).

12. Eric Katz, "11 Major Agency Reforms in Trump's 2021 Budget," *Government Executive*, February 11, 2020, https://www.govexec.com/management/2020/02/11-major-agency-reforms-2021-budget/163049.

13. Sheri Fink and Mike Baker, "'It's Just Everywhere Already': How Delays in Testing Set Back the U.S. Coronavirus Response," *The New York Times*, March 10, 2020, https://nyti.ms/39SdV3K.

14. Denise Grady, "U.S. Health Experts Say Stricter Measures Are Required to Limit Coronavirus's Spread," *The New York Times*, March 8, 2020, https://nyti.ms/21w3ved.

15. Katie Lobosco, "Betsy DeVos Loses Lawsuit after Delaying Student Loan Protection Rule," *CNN Politics*, September 12, 2018, www.cnn.com/2018/09/13/politics/betsy-devos-loses-lawsuit/index.html.

16. Cory Turner, "Teachers Union Lawsuit Claims DeVos 'Capriciously' Repealed Borrower Protections," *NPR*, January 22, 2020, https://www.npr.org/2020/01/22/798128256/teachers-union-lawsuit-devos-capriciously-repealed-borrower-protections.

17. William T. Gormley Jr. and Steven J. Balla, *Bureaucracy and Democracy: Accountability and Performance* (Washington, DC: CQ Press, 2004), 67.

18. Stephen Kohn, "Setting the Record Straight on the Legal Protections for the Ukraine Whistleblower: 'No One Volunteers for the Role of Social Pariah,'" *The National Law Review*, December 31, 2019, https://www.natlawreview.com/article/setting-record-straight-legal-protections-ukraine-whistleblower-no-one-volunteers.

19. Matt Kelley, "Probes at NASA Plummet Under Its Current IG," *USA Today*, January 11, 2008.

20. Bernardo Zacka, *When the State Meets the Street: Public Service and Moral Agency* (Cambridge, MA: Belknap Press of Harvard University Press, 2017), 35.

21. Charles T. Goodsell, *The Case for Bureaucracy: A Public Administration Polemic*, 4th ed. (Washington, DC: CQ Press, 2004), 54.

22. PEW Research Center, "Public Expresses Favorable Views of a Number of Federal Agencies," https://www.people-press.org/2019/10/01/public-expresses-favorable-views-of-a-number-of-federal/agencies/.

23. Gormley and Balla, *Bureaucracy and Democracy*, 164–178.

24. Paul Light, "Contractors in Federal Workforce," November 12, 2013, www.c-spanvideo.org/program/CostofCo.

25. Stacy Cowley and Jessica Silver-Greenberg, "Outside Collectors for I.R.S. Are Accused of Illegal Practices," *The New York Times*, June 23, 2017, https://nyti.ms/2tXfXdC.

26. Peter H. Schuck, *Why Government Fails So Often: And How It Can Do Better* (Princeton and Oxford: Princeton University Press, 2014), 325.

27. Peter H. Schuck, *Why Government Fails So Often: And How It Can Do Better* (Princeton and Oxford: Princeton University Press, 2014), 325.

28. Charles S. Clark, "FEMA Meals Contractor's Proposal Was Rife with False Claims, Senators Allege," *Government Executive*, February 23, 2018.

29. Department of Justice, "Justice Department Recovers over $2.8 Billion from False Claims Act Cases in Fiscal Year 2018," *Department of Justice News*, December 21, 2018, https://www.justice.gov/opa/pr/justice-department-recovers-over-28-billion-false-claims-act-cases-fiscal-year-2018.

30. "CDC Gives New Guidelines, New York to Close Restaurants and Schools and Italian Deaths Rise," *The New York Times*, March 15, 2020, https://nyti.ms/3aYn5vT.

CHAPTER 7 WRAP-UP

∎ Key Terms

■ Multiple-Choice Questions

1. Congress can check the bureaucracy's powers through which of the following actions?
   A. Appropriation and oversight
   B. Rule making and discretion
   C. Implementation and approval
   D. Agenda setting and policy formation

2. All of the following are characteristic of political appointees EXCEPT
   A. Senior executive positions that are won as the result of campaign contributions
   B. Supervisory positions that are eliminated by the new/incoming presidential administration
   C. Ambassadorships won in exchange for voting support during the presidential campaign
   D. Agency experts hired on the basis of elite educational attainment and specialized skills

3. Which of the following is an accurate comparison of independent administrative agencies and independent regulatory commissions?

Independent administrative agencies	Independent regulatory commissions
A. An executive branch unit that sells a service and is expected to be financially self-sufficient	Composed of dozens of offices and councils that assist the president in managing the bureaucracy
B. Created by Congress and the president; responsible for a narrowly defined function and whose structure is intended to be protected from partisan politics	An executive branch unit responsible for developing standards of behavior within specific industries and businesses
C. Responsible for a broadly defined policy area	Created by Congress to assist with specific policy areas
D. Directors are appointed for a limited time and purpose	Directors are appointed for life

Questions 4–5 are based on the graph below:

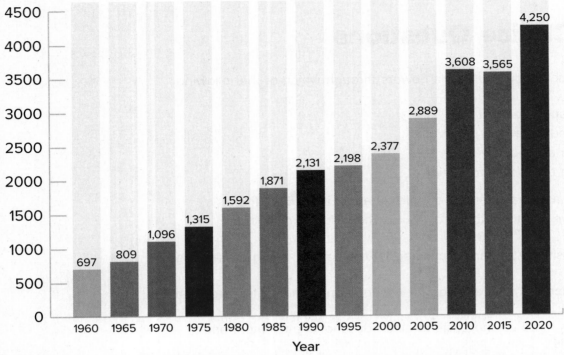

Billions of constant (FY 2012) dollars

Source: Office of Management and Budget. *Historical Tables,* "Table 1.3—Summary of Receipts, Outlays, and Surpluses or Deficits in Current Dollars, Constant (FY 2012) Dollars, and as Percentages of GDP: 1940–2025."

4. What has been the overall trend in federal government spending since 1960?
   A. Government spending continues to decrease due to tax cuts
   B. Republican administrations in the 1980s cut social programs to balance the budget
   C. Spending has continued to increase
   D. Spending has increased strictly due to military expenditures

5. Which of the following factors might explain the trend in federal spending since 2000?
   A. The creation of the Department of Homeland Security and costs associated with the war on terror
   B. The president's increased use of executive orders to fund counterterrorism
   C. Additional congressional investigations into executive branch wrongdoing
   D. Increased population due to immigration

6. Which of the following is considered to be the first step of the public policy process?
   A. Resource allocation
   B. Policy implementation
   C. Agenda setting
   D. Policy approval

7. Which of the following is true of devolution as related to government bureaucracy?
   A. It distributes power from federal to state legislatures
   B. It shifts control from state to federal bureaucracies
   C. It shifts control away from federal bureaucracies to state bureaucracies
   D. It strives to equalize federal and state control of a bureaucracy

8. Which of the following correctly pairs information about cabinet departments with information about independent regulatory agencies?

	Cabinet Departments	**Independent Regulatory Agencies**
A.	Sell a service or product to customers	Funded by Congress
B.	Develop standards of behavior for businesses	Write regulations
C.	Leaders are appointed by the president and confirmed by the Senate	Leaders serve fixed terms
D.	Are created by acts of Congress	Are governed by executive order

9. Which of the following make up an iron triangle?
- A. Governors, members of Congress, and members of independent regulatory agencies
- B. The Supreme Court, the president, and the Senate
- C. Congress, state legislatures, and the bureaucracy
- D. State Department, congressional committees, and private lobbying groups

10. Which of the following is an example of an agency exercising discretionary authority?
- A. A member of the Securities and Exchange Commission testifies in a congressional committee hearing
- B. The Secretary of Veterans Affairs appears in a CNN interview
- C. An engineer at the Department of Transportation writes a regulation increasing requirements for automobile safety
- D. A member of the Social Security Administration discusses a citizen's Social Security benefits with her

■ Free-Response Questions

Quantitative Analysis

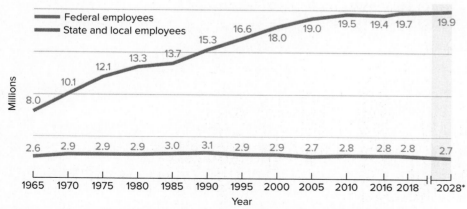

Sources: U.S. Census Bureau. *Statistical Abstracts of the United States*. 1965, Table 476; 1968, Table 567; 1978, Table 504; 1990, Table 487; 2012, Table 461. 2016 data source: U.S. Bureau of Labor Statistics, Employment Projections program, Table 2.1 Employment by major industry sector, 2006, 2016, and projected 2026; U.S. Bureau of Labor Statistics, Employment Projections program, Table 2.1 Employment by major industry sector, 2008, 2018, and *projected 2028.

Use the graph on the previous page to answer the questions.

A. Identify a trend regarding national civilian bureaucrats since 1965.

B. Describe a similarity or difference in the number of federal and state and local employees, as illustrated in the information graphic, and draw a conclusion about that similarity or difference.

C. Explain how the number of federal and state and local employees as shown in the graph demonstrates devolution.

Concept Application

"Last December, the FCC under Republican Chairman Ajit Pai voted to roll back the rules. Pai, who had been a commissioner when the rules were approved, is a longtime critic of the policy. He has argued that the regulations are too restrictive on businesses and discourage them from investing in network upgrades that could make your Internet service faster and better.

The end of the bans on blocking, slowing and paid prioritization means your Internet providers will be free to engage in that activity without legal repercussions, so long as they disclose it to the public on their own websites or to the FCC."

—*Washington Post, June 11, 2018*

After reading the scenario above, respond to A, B, and C below:

A. In the context of the scenario, describe a power the president has in shaping the actions of bureaucratic agencies such as the FCC.

B. In the context of the scenario, explain how the use of presidential power described in Part A can be affected by its interaction with Congress.

C. In the context of the scenario, explain how the interaction between Congress and the presidency can be affected by linkage institutions.

WRAP-UP

At the beginning of this unit, we asked you to consider what the evidence suggests for answers to the questions below, which address the central question: How will our policy-making institutions continue to evolve?

- **What has historically caused the power of the presidency to increase?**
- **Will executive power continue to increase, as it has in recent decades?**
- **What factors have shaped the conflict between the president and the Senate over the appointment of new federal judges?**
- **What might be the policy-making impact of those new appointments?**
- **Will the Supreme Court's power of judicial review continue to have strong influence over public policies?**

In Chapter 5, we learned that the power of the president has expanded far beyond the powers outlined in the U.S. Constitution. The heart of presidential power today resides in the "informal" roles of the president, including serving as chief diplomat and manager of the economy. We also learned that the formal powers of the president, such as the presidential veto, are a very strong check on congressional power. Because such a small percentage of vetoes are overridden by Congress, the veto threat is a powerful tool at the disposal of the president. Contemporary presidents have power to persuade through use of the bully pulpit, a role that has evolved through the use of social media.

In Chapter 4, we learned that the president and Senate continue to have contentious battles over Supreme Court nominees when there is a divided government, but when there is a unified government the nominees are confirmed easily. This indicates that partisan politics, rather than judicial philosophy, plays a more important role than in decades past. In Chapter 6 we learned that the Supreme Court plays an extraordinary role in the policy-making process, as a Supreme Court ruling is often the final stop for a public policy. While Supreme Court rulings can be overturned by either a subsequent ruling or an amendment to the Constitution, such instances are quite rare.

Use the following images to answer questions 1–4.

Bettmann/Getty Images

Source: U.S. Department of the Interior

1. The image on the left is a political cartoon. Which of the following best describes the message in the cartoon?
   A. Congressional districts lines are drawn to favor one candidate over another.
   B. Party politics have become increasingly partisan.
   C. The method of drawing district lines is antiquated.
   D. There are no winners in congressional elections due to the drawing of district lines.

2. Which of the following Supreme Court rulings is most relevant to the topic in the cartoon?
   A. *Brown v. Board of Education*
   B. *Citizens United v. Federal Election Commission*
   C. *Baker v. Carr*
   D. *New York Times v. United States*

3. The map on the right is a modern congressional district in the United States. Which of the following key terms describes the way in which the district was drawn?
   A. Filibuster
   B. Cloture
   C. Logroll
   D. Gerrymander

4. Which of the following is a leading factor that contributes to district lines being drawn like the one above?
   A. Census Bureau results
   B. Partisanship
   C. Demographics
   D. Supreme Court rulings

5. When a member of Congress votes strictly on the basis of the wishes of his or her constituents, the member of Congress is adhering to which of the following?

A. The principle of majoritarianism
B. The politico model
C. The trustee model
D. The delegate model

	Popular vote total	Popular vote percentage	Number of Electoral Votes
Democrat	65,853,514	48	227
Republican	62,984,828	46%	304
Independent candidates	293,000	6%	0

6. An opponent of the Electoral College may use the election results above to make which of the following arguments?

A. The Electoral College rewards independent candidates in the election
B. The will of the people is not reflected in election results
C. The framers of the Constitution opposed the Electoral College
D. The Electoral College limits the power of the states in the presidential election

7. Assume the presidential election results above. Which of the following is true?

A. Since no candidate won a majority of the vote, the election will be held in the House of Representatives
B. Without the independent candidates, there would have been a clear election mandate for the winner
C. The Democratic candidate won the election
D. The Republican candidate won the election

The Legislative Process

Concept for legislative consideration

Bill introduced in House

Bill introduced in Senate

Bill assigned to committee, then usually referred to subcommittee

Subcommittee

Subcommittee

Committee

Committee

Rules Committee schedules debate

Senate leadership schedules debate

Floor action

Floor action

House bill

Senate bill

Differences?

Yes → Conference committee → Conference bill → Floor action

No

Presidential approval?

Yes → **Bill becomes law**

No

Veto

Override veto?

Yes → Bill becomes law

No → **Start legislative process again**

8. At which stage of the legislative process above would a presidential signing statement be used?

   A. Bill introduction

   B. Committee

   C. Conference Committee

   D. Bill becomes law

9. Which of the following is true about the use of the presidential veto?
   A. Most bills vetoed by the president are overridden by Congress
   B. The number of vetos per president has been steadily increasing over time
   C. Most presidents veto fewer than 50 bills in their terms in office
   D. The number of vetos overridden by Congress has sharply decreased

10. Based on the information in the figure, what is the implication of the presidential veto power?
    A. In a divided government, vetos are less likely
    B. The longer a president is in office, the fewer veto overrides there are
    C. Vetos happen every day Congress is in session
    D. Once a bill is vetoed, it is unlikely to be overridden by Congress

11. Which of the following is most appropriately handled by an agency in the federal bureaucracy?
    A. State criminal matter
    B. Dispute between two states
    C. Citizen did not receive entitlement payment
    D. School board seeks to hire new school superintendent

12. Which of the following is most likely to occur after there are allegations of fraud within an agency of the federal bureaucracy?
    A. Congress holds hearings to investigate
    B. The Supreme Court will grant judicial review
    C. The state legislatures will hold investigations
    D. The president will issue an executive order to close the agency

13. Which of the following is an example of patronage in the federal bureaucracy?
    A. Department of Veterans Affairs provides housing benefits to veterans
    B. The Security and Exchange Commission regulates a bank
    C. The president chooses a political donor to serve as secretary of a federal agency
    D. Promotion of a bureaucrat based on merit

14. Which of the following was not included within Max Weber's theory of bureaucracy?
    A. Bureaucratic discretion
    B. Division of labor
    C. Specialization of tasks
    D. Hiring based on merit

Federal Court System

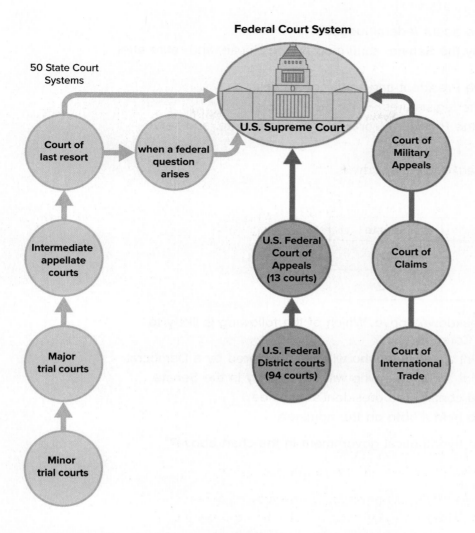

15. Which of the following constitutional principles is demonstrated in the diagram of the court system above?
  A. Due process of law
  B. Separation of powers
  C. Federalism
  D. Habeas corpus

16. When a Supreme Court justice rules in accordance with the line of thought in a previous ruling, he or she is practicing which of the following doctrines?
  A. Amicus curiae
  B. Judicial restraint
  C. In loco parentis
  D. Stare decisis

17. Which of the following was declared unconstitutional in the *Marbury v. Madison* ruling?
  A. An act of ordinary legislation, in effect amended the Constitution
  B. Congress creating a national bank within the state of Maryland
  C. A congressional district of an unusual shape and size
  D. Separate but equal schooling for children of different races

18. Which of the following is true about federal judges?

    A. They are appointment by the Senate, confirmed by the House, and retire after 10 years

    B. They are selected by the President and serve for 10 years

    C. They are elected by state legislatures

    D. They are appointed by the President, confirmed by the Senate, and serve life-long terms

19. *Hypothetical government breakdown by party:*

President: Republican

	House	Senate
Democrat	277	48
Republican	158	52

Assume the government breakdown above. Which of the following is likely to occur if there is a Supreme Court vacancy?

    A. The president will appoint a nominee who will be filibustered by a Democrat

    B. The president will appoint a nominee who will pass swiftly in the Senate

    C. The House will refuse to confirm the president's nominee

    D. The House will refuse to hold a vote on the nominee

20. What key term describes the hypothetical government in the chart above?

    A. Coalition government

    B. Divided government

    C. Gridlock government

    D. Bi-partisan government

■ Free Response Questions

Concept Application

> In 2020 the novel coronavirus raged in the United States, with over 200,000 deaths in 7 months, and a public divided over whether or not mask-wearing should be mandatory. Throughout the United States, governors took different approaches to minimizing the effects of the virus, with some imposing travel bans, closing public establishments and schools, and requiring masks, while others took very few actions.

After reading the scenario, respond to A, B, and C below:

A. Describe a power Congress could use to address the scenario.

B. In the context of the scenario, explain how the use of congressional power described in part A can be affected by its interactions with the presidency.

C. In the context of the scenario, explain how interaction between Congress and the presidency can be affected by actions of the state(s).

Quantitative Analysis

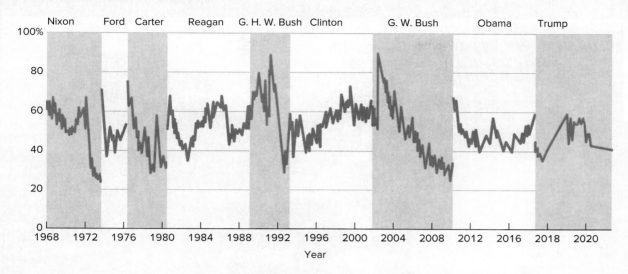

A. Identify a president that had a high approval rating at the beginning of his term.
B. Describe a similarity or difference in presidential approval ratings between administrations and draw a conclusion about that similarity or difference.
C. Explain how presidential approval ratings as shown in the graph demonstrate the importance of informal powers of the president.

Argumentation

Develop an argument that explains which of the three branches of government is most powerful over the policy-making process: Congress, the president, or the Supreme Court.

In your essay, you must:

- Articulate a defensible claim or thesis that responds to the prompt and establishes a line of reasoning.

- Support your claim with at least TWO pieces of accurate and relevant information:

  - At least ONE piece of evidence must be from one of the following foundational documents:

    — *Federalist* No. 70

    — *Federalist* No. 78

    — The U.S. Constitution

  - Use a second piece of evidence from another foundational document from the list or from your study of the policy-making process.

- Use reasoning to explain why your evidence supports your claim/thesis

- Respond to an opposing or alternative perspective using refutation, concession, or rebuttal.

JOSE LUIS MAGANA/Getty Images

CIVIL LIBERTIES AND CIVIL RIGHTS

In the summer of 2020, there was a nationwide debate over the power police should be able to wield to maintain public order. George Floyd, a Black man, was killed by a police officer during an arrest and his death was caught on camera. Footage of the killing was broadcast around the world and his death sparked large-scale protests in cities across the United States to demand greater accountability for police who use deadly force. Public protests over the use of excessive police force have ironically been met with force by police, including use of tear gas and batons to subdue protesters. In the photo on the previous page, police used tear gas in response to protesters in front of the White House in Washington, D.C., demanding an end to police brutality. These clashes between police and protesters have led to calls for defunding of police departments and have revived the debate over how much force is necessary to maintain order.

▌ What is the Balance Between Order and Liberty?

Big Ideas

The AP U.S. Government Big Ideas addressed in Unit 3 are:

Big Idea 1: Constitutionalism: (The) Constitutional system is based on the rule of law and the balance between majority rule and minority rights.

Big Idea 2: Liberty and Order: Governmental laws and policies balancing order and liberty are based on the U.S. Constitution and have been interpreted differently over time.

Big Idea 3: Civic participation in a representative democracy: Citizens engage and participate in the political process.

Big Idea 4: Competing policy-making interests: Multiple actors and institutions interact to produce and implement possible policies.

As you read, consider the following questions:

- **How has the balance between order and liberty changed over time through both court rulings and legislation?**
- **How have civil liberties and rights changed over time?**
- **What changes do you expect will take place in the future to both preserve liberty and protect order, and why do you have those expectations?**

Governmental laws and policies balancing order and liberty have been interpreted differently over time. The U.S. Constitution attempts to balance the need for order with the right of individual liberties. In this unit you will learn how the Bill of Rights in the U.S. Constitution protects citizens from government power, as well as how national laws have been passed to give governments the power to enforce laws protecting individuals. Chapter 8 will address changing interpretations of many aspects of the Bill of Rights.

As we discussed in Unit I, the Constitution is an elastic document, meaning its interpretation has changed over time. The Supreme Court often has the final say in how the Constitution is interpreted. This topic will be filled with Supreme Court rulings including the 15 required Supreme Court cases in the AP U.S. Government and Politics course in Chapter 8: Civil Liberties. For example, interpretation of the First Amendment's establishment clause has led to a ban on prayer by school officials in public schools (*Engel v. Vitale)*. While most Americans consider themselves Christian, the Constitution explicitly allows freedom of religion, protecting the right of minority faiths to be free from religious coercion, and interpretation of the free exercise clause has allowed certain religious sects to stop public education of their children beyond the eighth grade (*Wisconsin v. Yoder*). The Second Amendment right to bear arms was recently interpreted to mean that state governments cannot ban an individual from possessing a firearm (*McDonnell v. Chicago*). Civil liberties protected in the U.S. Constitution were not always enforced by national or state governments. The ratification of the Fifteenth Amendment, which guaranteed Black voting rights, was not followed by many southern states. Instead, southern states enacted Jim Crow laws which barred most Black Americans from voting. The Constitution alone does not provide the mechanisms needed to protect civil liberties; rather, laws must be passed to enforce the Constitution. Civil rights legislation, including the civil rights Act of 1964 and the Voting Rights Act of 1965, was passed in response to the Civil Rights movement. The movement included mass protests led by the National Association for the Advancement of Colored People (NAACP) for an end to public segregation. The Voting Rights Act provided Congress with the ability to enforce the Fifteenth Amendment.

AP U.S. Government & Politics Required Supreme Court Cases discussed in Unit 3

Case name	Topic	Pages
Engel v. Vitale	First Amendment – Establishment Clause	358
Wisconsin v. Yoder	First Amendment – Free Exercise Clause	359
Tinker v. Des Moines	First Amendment – Free Speech Clause	350
New York Times v. U.S.	First Amendment – Prior Restraint	354
Schenck v. U.S.	First Amendment – Clear and Present Danger	347
Gideon v. Wainright	Sixth Amendment – Right to Counsel	366
Roe v. Wade	Right of Privacy	361
McDonald v. Chicago	Second Amendment – Right to Bear Arms	344
Brown v. Board of Education	Fourteenth Amendment – Equal Protection Clause	395
Citizens United v. FEC	First Amendment – Campaign Finance	352

Skills & Practices

As you read through the following chapters, consider how the skills of description, analysis, comparison, and causation help you to make sense of the information. By the end of this unit, you should be able to answer questions such as:

- **Why were civil liberties included in the Constitution?**

- **What kinds of rights are guaranteed by the Constitution and what kinds are not?**

- **How have the rights and liberties in the Constitution evolved over time?**

- **How do the institutions in the U.S. government work to either expand or limit the liberties and rights in the U.S. Constitution?**

Kevin Frayer/Getty Images

THEN

The Bill of Rights was designed to protect citizens' rights to speak and act without undue monitoring by or interference from the national government; however, Congress soon legislated exceptions to those protections.

NOW

Ideas about liberty in the context of such areas as religion and privacy often conflict with one another, resulting in tensions that legislatures and courts must resolve.

NEXT

Will the nation find ways to balance the Second Amendment's guarantee of a protected individual right to bear arms with concerns about security and the increased occurrence of mass shootings?

As biometric techniques like facial recognition technology evolve, how will we balance the competing demands of crime and disease control (security) and personal privacy (liberty)?

■ Chapter Introduction

As you read this chapter, consider the following Enduring Understandings in the AP U.S. Government & Politics course:

- *Provisions of the U.S. Constitution's Bill of Rights are continually being interpreted to balance the power of government and the civil liberties of individuals.*

- *Protections of the Bill of Rights have been selectively incorporated by way of the Fourteenth Amendment's due process clause to prevent state infringement of basic liberties.*

This chapter addresses how interpretations of the Bill of Rights, the first ten amendments to the Constitution, have evolved over time. Questions the reading will address stem from the Bill of Rights and include:

- Under what circumstances is speech dangerous, and thus warrants government limitations? (First Amendment)

- Does the Constitution's provision of free exercise of religion allow religious groups to break laws in the name of their religion? (First Amendment)

- Is a state government's ban on the personal possession of firearms in order to maintain order and stability an excessive infringement on personal liberty? (Second Amendment)

Other rights in the Bill of Rights discussed in this chapter include the right to counsel (Sixth Amendment), protection against unreasonable searches (Fourth Amendment), and the exclusionary rule which bars evidence obtained illegally from court proceedings (due process clause of the Fifth Amendment).

Interpretations of the free speech clause of the First Amendment have changed over time. Government attempts to balance liberty and order (Big Idea) is also a theme in this topic: while the First Amendment provides freedom of speech and places no explicit limits to speech, the Supreme Court has ruled that speech that creates a clear and present danger to others may have government limitations (*Schenck v. U.S.*). Interpretations of the free exercise clause have also changed over time. While early Court interpretations of the free exercise clause did not allow religious groups to break basic laws, more recently the Court interpreted the free exercise clause to allow a religious group to exempt their children from public school for religious reasons (*Wisconsin v. Yoder*).

The Bill of Rights did not always apply to actions of the state government, until the Fourteenth Amendment's due process clause was interpreted by the Supreme Court to apply some of the protections in the Bill of Rights to the states. This chapter will explain how interpretation of the applicability of the Bill of Rights to state governments changed with a process known as selective incorporation, a key concept in the AP U.S. Government & Politics course. Because the Fourteenth Amendment states, "no *state* shall deprive its citizens of life, liberty, or property without due process of law," the Court began to selectively apply parts of the Bill of Rights to state governments in a case-by-case fashion (see Table 8.1). Through selective incorporation, parts of the Bill of Rights were applied to state governments, including most recently, the Second Amendment right to bear arms. A Chicago law that banned handgun ownership outright was overturned in the case *McDonald v. Chicago.* The Supreme Court ruled that the Fourteenth

Amendment's due process clause incorporated the Second Amendment's right to bear arms to state government, overturning the city's handgun ban. The Second Amendment debate is a further example of how government attempts to balance the need for order with the right of individual liberty (Big Idea).

This chapter includes most of the required Supreme Court cases in the AP U.S. Government & Politics course discussed in context. There are 15 required Supreme Court cases in the course. This chapter discusses 9 of those, and Chapter 9 discusses the 10th. See the chart on page 334 listing these 10 cases and where they are found in Unit 3.

Civil Liberties in the American Legal System

Civil liberties are individual liberties established in the Constitution and safeguarded by state and federal courts. We also refer to civil liberties as *personal freedoms* and often use the concepts of "liberty" and "freedom" interchangeably.

civil liberties
Constitutionally established guarantees that protect citizens, opinions, and property against arbitrary government interference.

Civil liberties differ from civil rights. **Civil liberties** are constitutionally established guarantees that protect citizens, opinions, and property *against* arbitrary government interference. In contrast, civil rights (the focus of Chapter 9) reflect positive acts of government (in the form of constitutional provisions or statutes) *for* the purpose of protecting individuals against arbitrary or discriminatory actions. For example, the freedom of speech, a liberty established in the First Amendment to the U.S. Constitution, protects citizens against the government's censorship of their words, particularly when those words are politically charged. In contrast, the constitutionally protected right to vote requires the government to step in to ensure that all citizens be allowed to vote, without restriction by individuals, groups, or government officials.

The Freedoms Protected in the American System

The U.S. Constitution, through the Bill of Rights, and state constitutions explicitly recognize and protect civil liberties. As demonstrated in the Constitution in Chapter 2, the first 10 amendments to the Constitution explicitly limited the power of the legislative, executive, and judicial branches of the national government.

The Bill of Rights established freedoms essential to individuals' and groups' free and effective participation in the larger community. Without these protections, citizens could not freely express their opinions through rallies, speeches, protests, letters, pamphlets, tweets, blogs, e-mail, and other forms of civic engagement. The Constitution's framers, who had been denied these liberties under British rule, saw them as indispensable to forming a new democratic republic.

The meanings of these precious freedoms have shifted over the course of U.S. history, as presidents, legislators, judges, and ordinary citizens have changed their minds about how much freedom the people should have. When Americans have not perceived themselves as being under some external threat, they generally have adopted an expansive interpretation of civil liberties. During those times, citizens tend to believe that the government should interfere as little as necessary in individuals' lives, strongly supporting people's right to gather with others and to speak their minds. When the nation has been under some perceived threat, citizens have often allowed the government to limit protected freedoms.[1] (See "Analyzing the Sources.") Limits have also extended to many **due process** protections—legal safeguards that prevent the government from arbitrarily depriving people of life, liberty, or property without adhering to strict legal procedures. In this chapter, we consider not only the historical context of our civil liberties but also recent changes in how Congress, the president, and the courts interpret these liberties.

> **due process**
> The legal safeguards that prevent the government from arbitrarily depriving citizens of life, liberty, or property; guaranteed by the Fifth and Fourteenth Amendments.

The Historical Basis for American Civil Liberties: The Bill of Rights

The framers vividly remembered the censorship and suppression of speech that they had suffered under British rule. Colonists had been harshly punished, often by imprisonment and confiscation of their property and even death, if they criticized the British government, through both speech and the publication of pamphlets. The framers understandably viewed liberty as a central principle guiding the creation of a new democratic republic. Federalists such as Alexander Hamilton saw the Constitution itself as a bill of rights because it delegated specific powers to the national government and contained specific provisions designed to protect citizens against an abusive government.

DATA ANALYSIS · ANALYZING THE SOURCES

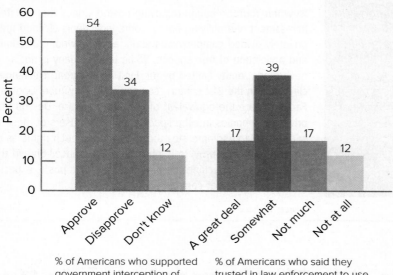

Balancing the Tension Between Liberty and Security

% of Americans who supported government interception of suspects' email in 2001

- Approve: 54
- Disapprove: 34
- Don't know: 12

% of Americans who said they trusted in law enforcement to use facial recognition technology responsibly in 2019

- A great deal: 17
- Somewhat: 39
- Not much: 17
- Not at all: 12

Source: (1) https://www.pewresearch.org/internet/2001/04/02/main-report-23/ April 2001(2)https://www.pewresearch.org/internet/2019/09/05/more-than-half-of-u-s-adults-trust-law-enforcement-to-use-facial-recognition-responsibly/ September 2019

Practice Analytical Thinking

1. The use of technology in law enforcement and crime control has changed over time. How has the American public's support of it changed?

2. What significance is there, if any, in the difference between these two survey questions?

3. What do these surveys tell us about the tension between liberty and security?

Some constitutional protections were designed to protect people from being punished, imprisoned, or executed for expressing political beliefs or opposition. These are noted on the annotated Constitution in Chapter 2. However, the Anti-Federalists still stressed the need for a written bill of rights. As we saw in Chapter 2, the ratification of the Constitution stalled because citizens feared that the government might use its expanded powers to limit individual freedoms, particularly those associated with political speech and engagement. The First Amendment, which ensures freedom of religion, the press, assembly, and speech, was essential to political speech and to discourse in the larger society.

The freedoms embodied in the Bill of Rights are broad principles rather than specific prohibitions against governmental action. From the nation's beginnings, the vagueness of the Bill of Rights led to serious disagreement about how to interpret its amendments. For example, the First Amendment's establishment clause states simply that "Congress shall make no law respecting an establishment of religion." Some commentators, most notably Thomas Jefferson, argued that the clause mandated a "wall of separation between church and state" and barred any federal support of religion. Others interpreted the clause more narrowly as barring only the establishment of a national religion or the requirement that all public officials swear an oath to some particular religion.

Other freedoms, too, have been subject to differing interpretations, including the First Amendment guarantees of freedom of speech, assembly, and the press. These conflicting interpretations often arise in response to public crises or security concerns. Security concerns also affect the protections offered to those accused of threatening the safety of the nation. Civil liberties advocates worry that fear is causing Americans to give up their most precious freedoms.

This video has been removed for violating YouTube's policy on harassment and bullying.
Learn more

>> When YouTube began removing posted videos that violated their harassment and bullying policy, some individuals claimed the privately owned company was engaged in viewpoint discrimination and a violation of free speech. While the company is not a government entity limited by the First Amendment, challengers claim that in the 21st century, companies like YouTube, Google, and Facebook are the equivalent of the public square. Do you think private companies in cyberspace should give users of these large social media conglomerates the same free speech rights as the government must provide in physical public space? Should they also engage in fact checking the premises of public posts, especially for fallacious posts that could impact election outcomes?

Source: YouTube

Incorporation of the Bill of Rights to Apply to the States

The framers intended the Bill of Rights to restrict the powers of only the *national government*. They did not see the Bill of Rights as applicable to the state governments. In general, there was little public worry that the states would curtail civil liberties, because most state constitutions included their own bill of rights that protected the individual against abuses of state power. Further, it was generally

Scenario: In response to the police killing of George Floyd, protests occurred in cities across the country that numbered in the thousands. Protesters carried a variety of signs, with messages such as "I can't breathe" which were the words of Floyd before his death, and "Defund the Police". Some of the protests turned violent and included protesters hurling Molotov cocktails and rioting. The police responded to some of these actions with tear gas and used batons in an attempt to quell the violence.

After reading the scenario, respond to A, B, and C below:

A. Describe how the Constitution protects the protesters in the scenario.

B. In the context of the scenario, explain how the constitutional protection you described in part A can be affected by the state legislature.

C. In the context of the scenario, explain how the balance between order and liberty can be affected by a social movement.

believed that because the state governments were geographically closer to the people than the national government, they would be less likely to encroach upon individual rights and liberties.

Through most of early U.S. history, the Bill of Rights applied to the national government but not to the states. That assumption is illustrated by the case of *Barron v. Baltimore* (1833), in which a wharf owner named Barron sued the city of Baltimore, Maryland. Barron claimed that the city had violated the "takings clause" of the Fifth Amendment, which bars the taking of private property for public use without just compensation. Barron argued that by paving its streets, the city of Baltimore had changed the natural course of certain streams, and that the resulting buildup of silt and gravel in the harbor made his wharf unusable. In *Barron,* the Supreme Court determined that the Fifth Amendment applies only to actions taken by the federal government and not to state or local actions.[2]

In 1868, three years after the Civil War ended, the Fourteenth Amendment was added to the U.S. Constitution. The Fourteenth Amendment reads as if it was meant to extend the protections of the Bill of Rights to citizens' interactions with *state governments*:

No State shall make or enforce any law which shall abridge the privileges or immunities of citizens of the United States; nor shall any State deprive any person of life, liberty, or property, without due process of law; nor deny to any person within its jurisdiction the equal protection of the laws.

total incorporation
The theory that the Fourteenth Amendment's due process clause requires the states to uphold *all* freedoms in the Bill of Rights; rejected by the Supreme Court in favor of selective incorporation.

selective incorporation
The process by which, over time, the Supreme Court applied those freedoms that served *some* fundamental principle of liberty or justice to the states, thus rejecting total incorporation.

Although this language sounds like an effort to protect citizens' rights and liberties from arbitrary interference by state governments, the Supreme Court rejected the doctrine of **total incorporation**: that is, the application of *all* the protections contained in the Bill of Rights to the states. Instead, beginning with a series of cases decided by the Court in the 1880s, the justices formulated a narrower approach known as **selective incorporation**.[3] This approach considered each protection individually, one case at a time, for possible incorporation into the Fourteenth Amendment and application to the states. The Court determined that due process mandates the incorporation of those rights that serve the fundamental principles of liberty and justice, those that were at the core of the "very idea of free government" and that were unalienable rights of citizenship.

As Table 8.1 shows, it was not until 1925 that the Court gradually began the process of incorporation, starting with the First Amendment protections most central to democratic government and civic engagement. That year, in the case of *Gitlow v. New York*, the Court held that freedom of speech is "among the fundamental personal rights and 'liberties' protected by the due process clause of the Fourteenth Amendment from impairment by the states."[4] In 1931, in its decision in *Near v. Minnesota*, the Court added freedom of the press, and in 1937 it added freedom of assembly to the list of incorporated protections.[5]

Incorporation progressed further with the landmark case of *Palko v. Connecticut* (1937), in which the Court laid out a formula for defining fundamental rights that later courts have used time and time again in incorporation cases, as well as in due process cases more generally. The justices found that fundamental rights were rooted in the traditions and conscience of the American people. Moreover, if those rights were eliminated, the justices argued, neither liberty nor justice could exist.[6] In case after case, the justices have considered whether such a right is fundamental—that is, rooted in the American tradition and conscience and essential for liberty and justice—and they have been guided by the principle that citizen participation in government and society is necessary for democracy in gauging the importance of each constitutionally protected right.

Freedoms in Practice: Controversy over the Second Amendment and the Right to Bear Arms

The fierce debate today over gun control illustrates much about the conflicts surrounding the civil liberties protected in the United States. Americans disagree about how to interpret the Second Amendment of the Constitution, but they do agree to have their disputes settled through laws and court rulings rather than armed conflict. Private citizens and political interest groups use their First Amendment freedoms of speech and assembly to voice their opinions about the place of guns in society. They also work behind the scenes to influence elected officials through campaign contributions and lobbying (see Chapter 16). At the heart of this debate is the question of the role of guns in creating a safe and free society and negotiating the tension between personal liberty and community security.

DATA ANALYSIS PATTERNS AND TRENDS

TABLE 8.1 ▪ Selective Incorporation of the Bill of Rights

The process of selective incorporation has been very slow. While a Supreme Court decision in 1897 was later understood to incorporate a right to the state, the Supreme Court did not deliberately begin the process until 1925, and it continues today. What trends do you see in the incorporation of the Bill of Rights to the states? What categories of rights were more quickly applied to the states under the Fourteenth Amendment, and which ones took longer? Do you think those amendments that have not been currently incorporated might be in the future? Why or why not?

Date	Liberty	Amendment	Key Case
1897	Right to just compensation (for property taken by *government*)	V	*Chicago, B&Q RR Co. v. Chicago*
1925	Freedom of speech	I	*Gitlow v. New York*
1931	Freedom of the press	I	*Near v. Minnesota*
1937	Freedom of assembly and petition	I	*DeJonge v. Oregon*
1940	Freedom to practice religion	I	*Cantwell v. Connecticut*
1947	Freedom from government-established religion	I	*Everson v. Board of Education*
1948	Right to a public trial	VI	*In re Oliver*
1949	No unreasonable searches and seizures	IV	*Wolf v. Colorado*
1961	Exclusionary rule	IV	*Mapp v. Ohio*
1962	No cruel and unusual punishments	VIII	*Robinson v. California*
1963	Right to counsel in criminal cases	VI	*Gideon v. Wainwright*
1964	No compulsory self-incrimination	V	*Malloy v. Hogan*
1965	Right to confront witnesses	VI	*Pointer v. Texas*
1966	Right to an impartial jury	VI	*Parker v. Gladden*
1967	Right to a speedy trial	VI	*Klopfer v. North Carolina*
1968	Right to a jury in criminal trials	VI	*Duncan v. Louisiana*
1969	No double jeopardy	VII	*Benton v. Maryland*
2010	Right to bear arms	II	*McDonald v. City of Chicago*
2019	No excessive fines or bail	VIII	*Timbs v. Indiana*
	No quartering of soldiers	III	Not incorporated
	Right to grand jury indictment	V	Not incorporated
	Right to a jury in civil trials	VII	Not incorporated

Changing Interpretations of the Second Amendment

Over the last decade, the Supreme Court has changed its interpretation of the Second Amendment, which reads

> A well-regulated Militia, being necessary to the security of a free State, the right of the people to keep and bear Arms, shall not be infringed.

The Second Amendment was initially interpreted by the Supreme Court as ensuring that state militias could support the government in maintaining public order; under this interpretation, the right to bear arms is a group right subject to regulation by Congress and the states.[7]

McDonald v. Chicago
This Supreme Court decision requires the states to guarantee their own citizens the Second Amendment's protection of an individual's right to own guns.

In 2008, the Supreme Court ruled in the *District of Columbia v. Heller* that the Second Amendment confers an individual right to possess a firearm for lawful purposes, such as self-defense.[8] In the 2010 case of **McDonald v. Chicago**, the Court incorporated the Second Amendment to the states, requiring states to respect this new individual constitutional right when they regulated citizen access to guns.[9] This forced many states to change their laws to allow individuals to carry concealed weapons, though there remains a great deal of variation in how these laws are implemented.

Citizens Engaged: Fighting for a Safer Nation

The U.S. gun death rate (homicides and suicides) decreased in 2018 and early 2019 after a period of increase.[10] The increased occurrence of mass shootings—such as those in or at Virginia Tech; Sandy Hook Elementary School; the Aurora movie theater; the church in Charleston; the Orlando nightclub; Las Vegas; Parkland; the El Paso Walmart—has kept the question of domestic security visible. Some activists, like the interest group The Coalition to Stop Gun Violence, argue that stricter weapons laws are necessary for a safe society.

Other groups, like the National Rifle Association, believe that if more law-abiding citizens can carry weapons, fewer violent crimes will be committed. Both groups have joined vocally in the public debate, exercising their freedom of speech and assembly to influence opinions about guns in the United States and by working to influence policy.

By 2014, every state allowed for some form of concealed-carry protection, permitting citizens to have weapons on them or in close proximity. In addition, the nation has been debating the wisdom of "Stand Your Ground" laws, allowing individuals who feel threatened to fire their weapons in self-defense. The shooting death of Trayvon Martin, a 17-year-old African American high school student, in February 2012 in Stanford, Florida, galvanized many critics of Stand Your Ground laws. George Zimmerman, a 28-year-old neighborhood watch coordinator, claimed that he felt threatened by the unarmed Martin. Later that year, the shooting of Jordan Davis, another unarmed 17-year-old high school student at a Florida convenience store, by Michael David Dunn, sparked protests against liberal gun laws. Dunn objected to the volume of the music playing in the car in which Davis was riding. Unlike Zimmerman, Dunn was convicted of murder and sentenced to life in prison and another 90 years for three counts of attempted murder. Critics argued that the mere perception of a threat does not constitute one, while many civil rights groups contend that Stand Your Ground laws ultimately result in the deaths of innocent, young African American men, like Martin and Davis, who are more likely to be unfairly stereotyped as a threat.

Should the United States Have Stricter Gun Safety Laws?

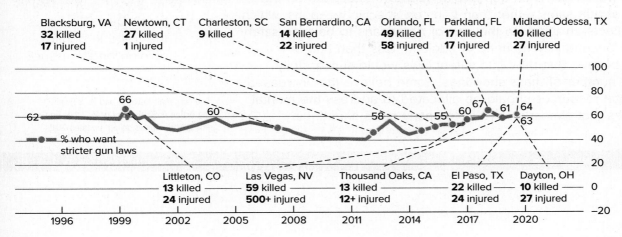

THE ISSUE: Public debate on gun safety laws is contentious, and reflects existing geographic, partisan, and cultural divides. In recent years, numerous polls indicate that a majority of Americans support stricter gun control, but they differ acutely in levels of support for various policies. While some policies garner overwhelming support, a relatively small proportion of the population ranks gun safety as a salient issue that would determine their choice of candidate.

Support for Stricter Gun Laws

YES: Support for stricter gun control continues to increase, with more than 64 percent of Americans in favor. Fully 90 percent of Democrats support stricter gun laws. In addition, some policies—including universal background checks—garner almost unanimous support of all Americans (96 percent of Americans support this policy). While other policies may not garner unanimous approval, support is strong for a 30-day waiting period for all gun sales (supported by 75 percent of Americans) and a regulation that would require all guns to be registered with local police (70 percent support).

NO: Today, the partisan gap in support of stricter gun laws is greater than ever: only 33 percent of Republicans support increased gun control, creating a 57 percent difference between the proportion of Republicans versus Democrats supporting it. This difference is greater than even the gap between gun owners versus non-gun owners, which tends to hover between a 25- and 38-percentage-point difference. In addition, Americans show little support for banning

WHAT DO YOU THINK?

1. Do you support increased gun safety laws in general? Do you support specific reforms, including requiring universal background checks, a 30-day waiting period for all gun sales, and the registration of all guns with local police? Do you support banning semiautomatic assault weapons? Handguns?

2. Are your views consistent with your partisan identity? Are they consistent with your status as a gun owner or non-gun owner?

3. Do you believe that stricter gun laws will decrease the number of mass shootings? According to the specific types of guns: Less than a majority (47 percent) support banning semiautomatic assault weapons, while only 29 percent support a ban on handguns.

OTHER APPROACHES: Data appears to support restrictions on the conditions of gun sales rather than bans on specific weapons, which perhaps reflects an effort on the part of Americans to balance safety against the Second Amendment. In addition, less than half of Americans believe that new gun safety laws would successfully reduce the number of mass shootings. Some believe that increased governmental resources should be allocated to address the mental health issues that almost always accompany mass shootings.

graph, what effect do mass shootings have on public opinion concerning support of increased gun safety laws? Overall, what is the trend in public opinion on this issue?

Source: Frank Newport and R. J. Reinhart, "Direction From the American Public on Gun Policy," http://news.gallup, updated 2019.

By 2019, numerous states had passed campus carry laws allowing weapons (with an appropriate permit) on public campuses, and others sought to arm trained teachers and security personnel in public schools. After several shootings on military bases, federal legislation allowing soldiers to remain armed on bases has been introduced to Congress, despite dissent from the Pentagon. Advocates of these policies believe that introducing personal firearms into these previously gun-free spaces will deter additional mass shootings. Opponents think it will only increase the likelihood of additional casualties due to the lax regulations of who may legally carry a firearm and the potential increases of suicide on bases.

Freedoms of Speech, Assembly, and the Press: Supporting Civic Discourse

Civic discourse and free participation in the political process have certain requirements. As we consider in this section, an individual must be able to express his or her political views through speech, assembly, and petition. Freedom of speech, assembly, petition, and the press is essential to an open society and to democratic rule. These freedoms ensure that individuals can discuss the important issues facing the nation and try to agree about how to address these matters without government censorship. Scholars have referred to this sharing of contrasting opinions as the **marketplace of ideas**. It is through the competition of ideas—some of them radical, some even loathsome—that solutions emerge. Freedom of the press allows for the dissemination and discussion of these varying ideas and encourages consensus building.

marketplace of ideas
A concept at the core of the freedoms of expression and press, based on the belief that true and free political discourse depends on a free and unrestrained discussion of ideas.

The marketplace of ideas enables people to voice their concerns and views freely and allows individuals to reconsider their ideas on important national and local issues. The centrality of the freedom of political expression to the First Amendment reflects the founders' belief that democracy would flourish only through robust discussion and candid debate.

The First Amendment and Political Instability

Over time, the Supreme Court has distinguished between political expression that the First Amendment protects and expression that the government may limit or even prohibit. The government has tried to limit speech, assembly, and the press during times of national emergency, when it has viewed that expression as more threatening than it would be in normal times.

THE TENSION BETWEEN FREEDOM AND ORDER A fundamental tension exists between the Bill of Rights, with its goal of protecting individual freedoms, and the government's central goal of ensuring order. Not even a decade had gone by after the Constitution's ratification when Congress passed the Alien and Sedition Acts (1798). These laws placed the competing goals of freedom and order directly in conflict. The Sedition Act criminalized all speech and writings judged to be critical of the government, Congress, or the president. This was just the first of many times in U.S. history that lawmakers sacrificed free speech and freedom of the press in an effort to ensure national security and order. For example, President Abraham Lincoln (1861–1865) attempted to silence political dissidents during the Civil War by mandating that they be tried in military courts, without the due process protections afforded in a civilian court. Lincoln also suspended the writ of **habeas corpus** (Latin, meaning "you have the body"), an ancient right and constitutional guarantee that protects an individual in custody from being held without the right to be heard in a court of law.[11] Again, political dissidents were targeted for indefinite detention without trial. Whenever the nation has perceived itself under attack or threat, pressure has been placed on the government by some citizens to limit individual freedom to ensure societal order, and other citizens have pressured the government to maintain freedom while securing order.

The struggle for a balance between freedom and order continues today as the United States fights a global war on terrorism. Part of the 1798 Alien and Sedition Acts, known as the Alien Enemies Act, empowered the president to deport any non-citizen suspected of threatening the nation's security or to imprison them indefinitely.[12] Soon after assuming office in January 2017, President Donald J. Trump signed an executive order that identified countries from which the United States would not accept immigrants or visitors and expanded the basis on which immigrants could be deported.[13] A federal district judge determined the order to be biased against Muslims and a constitutional violation of the First Amendment; a revised executive order has been litigated in the federal courts.[14]

THE HISTORICAL CONTEXT FOR FREE SPEECH LAWS The Supreme Court's willingness to suppress or punish political speech has changed over time in response to perceived internal and external threats to the nation. During World War I, the Court upheld the conviction of socialist and war protester Charles Schenck for distributing a pamphlet to recently drafted men urging them to resist the draft.[15] For the first time, the Court created through its ruling a test to evaluate such government actions, called the clear and present danger test. Under this standard, the government may silence speech or expression only when there is an evident and immediate danger that such speech will bring about some harm that the government has the power to prevent. In the *Schenck v. United States* case, the Court noted that the circumstances of war permit greater restrictions on the freedom of speech than would be allowable during peacetime. The justices ruled that Schenck's actions could endanger the nation's ability to carry out the draft and prosecute the war.

habeas corpus
An ancient right that protects an individual in custody from being held without the right to be heard in a court of law.

Schenck v. U.S.
Established the clear and present danger test whereby the government may silence speech or expression when there is a clear and present danger that this speech will bring about some harm that the government has the power to prevent

Soon after the *Schenck* case, a majority of the justices adopted a far more restrictive test that made it easier to punish citizens for the content of their speech. This test, known as the **bad tendency test**, was extended in the case of ***Gitlow v. New York***, which concerned Benjamin Gitlow, who was convicted of violating a New York State criminal anarchy law by publishing pamphlets calling for a revolutionary mass action to create a socialist government.[16] The political context of Gitlow's conviction is revealing: A so-called red scare—fears that the socialist revolution in the Soviet Union would spread to other nations with large populations of workers—was sweeping the nation. Gitlow's lawyer contended that there was no proof that Gitlow's pamphlet created a clear and present danger of a violent uprising. The Court disagreed, however, ruling that any speech that had a likelihood of inciting crime or disturbing the public peace could be silenced.

This highly restrictive test required only that the government demonstrate that some speech may at some time help to bring about harm. The threat did not need to be immediate or even direct. The test sacrificed the freedoms of speech and the press to concerns about public safety and protection of the existing order. The bad tendency test lasted only a short while; by the late 1930s, the Court had reverted to the clear and present danger test, which the justices interpreted more broadly to protect speech and participation. The relative peace and stability of the period between the two world wars is apparent in the Court's handling of speech and press cases, as the justices required government officials to demonstrate that the speech obviously posed a danger to public safety.

Even after the Court returned to the clear and present danger test, however, it still allowed concerns about national security to control its handling of First Amendment cases. In the wake of World War II, a war of conflicting ideologies emerged between the United States and the Soviet Union. Termed the *Cold War* because it did not culminate in a direct military confrontation between the countries, this development nevertheless created a climate of fear and insecurity in both nations. Concerns about the spread of communism in the United States led to prosecutions of individuals deemed to be sympathetic to communism and socialism under the Smith Act of 1940. This federal law barred individuals from advocating or teaching about "the duty, necessity, desirability, or propriety of overthrowing or destroying any government in the United States by force or violence."

In the most important case of this period, the Supreme Court upheld the conviction of several individuals who were using the writings of German philosophers Karl Marx and Friedrich Engels, along with those of Soviet leaders

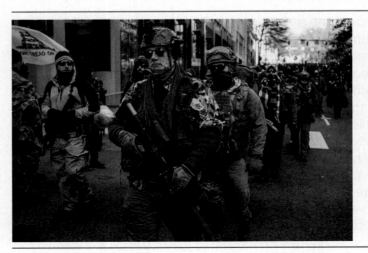

>> On January 20, 2020, approximately 22,000 people, many armed, came to the Virginia capitol in Richmond to rally for gun rights. The rally was peaceful despite concerns regarding violence and the heavy police presence. Why is the right to assemble so important in a democracy? What kind of impact do mass protests have on policymaking?

Zach Gibson/Getty Images

Vladimir Lenin and Josef Stalin, to teach about socialism and communism.[17] In upholding the convictions, the justices found that although the use of these writings did not pose a risk of imminent danger to the government, it created the *probability* that such harm would result. The seriousness of the evil was key to the test that came out of this ruling, known as the **clear and probable danger test**. Because the government was suppressing speech to avoid the gravest danger, an armed takeover of the United States, the Supreme Court majority ruled that it was justified in its actions—even if the risk or probability of this result was relatively remote.

As the Cold War subsided and concerns diminished about a potential communist takeover of the United States, the Court shifted to a broader interpretation of the First Amendment speech and press protections. Beginning with *Brandenburg v. Ohio* (1969), the Court signaled that it would give more weight to First Amendment claims and less to government concerns about security and order. In this case, the Court considered the convictions of the leaders of an Ohio Ku Klux Klan group who were arrested after they made a speech at a televised rally, during which they uttered racist and anti-Semitic comments and showed guns and rifles. Local officials charged them with violating a state law that banned speech that disturbed the public peace and threatened armed overthrow. In overturning the convictions, the Court reverted to a strict reading of the clear and present danger test. The justices held that government officials had to demonstrate that the speech they sought to silence went beyond mere advocacy, or words, and that it created the risk of immediate disorder or lawlessness.[18]

THE STANDARD TODAY: THE IMMINENT LAWLESS ACTION TEST The *Brandenburg* test, known as both the **imminent lawless action test** and the **incitement test**, altered the clear and present danger test by making it even more stringent. Specifically, after the *Brandenburg* decision, any government in the United States—national, state, or local—trying to silence speech would need to show that the risk of harm from the speech was highly likely and that the harm was imminent or immediate. The imminent lawless action test is the standard the courts use today to determine whether speech is protected from government interference.

Even though the *Brandenburg* test is well established, the issue of whether speech is protected continues to be debated. For example, public attention has increasingly focused on websites operated by terrorists and terrorist sympathizers, especially members of militant Islamic groups and those of the alternative right. Do First Amendment guarantees protect sites on which posters threaten those who disagree with them and equip their followers for violence? What about websites threatening violence against white supremacists or those who are accused of committing sexual assault? Courts examining these questions must determine not only whether the speech intends to bring about a bad result—most would agree that intent exists—but also whether the speech incites lawless action that is imminent.

Freedom of Speech

The freedom to speak publicly, even critically, about government and politics is central to the democratic process. Citizens cannot participate fully in a political system if they are unable to share information, opinions, advice, and calls to action. Citizens cannot hold government accountable if they cannot criticize government actions or demand change.

PURE SPEECH VERSUS SYMBOLIC SPEECH The Supreme Court has made a distinction between pure speech that is "just words" and advocacy that couples

clear and probable danger test
A standard established in the 1951 case *Dennis v. U.S.* whereby the government could suppress speech to avoid grave danger, even if the probability of the dangerous result was relatively remote; replaced by the imminent lawless action (incitement) test in 1969.

imminent lawless action test (incitement test)
A standard established in the 1969 *Brandenburg v. Ohio* case, whereby speech is restricted only if it goes beyond mere advocacy, or words, to create a high likelihood of immediate disorder or lawlessness.

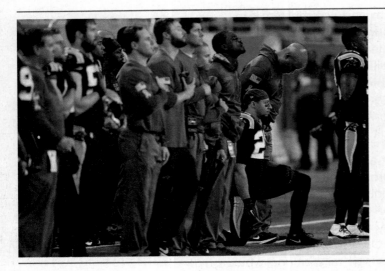

>> In 2016, Colin Kaepernick, an NFL player for the San Francisco 49ers, began "taking a knee" during the national anthem that is played at the beginning of games. This was an act of symbolic speech to protest the killing of unarmed African Americans by police. He was booed, and he left football after he was unable to find a position on another team. This act was seen as very divisive, but as shown above, others "took a knee" for social justice in athletic competitions across the country. President Trump called for everyone in the NFL who didn't stand for the anthem to be fired. Why is symbolic speech so powerful? What makes it so divisive?

Paul Sancya/AP Images

symbolic speech
Nonverbal "speech" in the form of an action such as picketing, flag burning, or wearing an armband to signify a protest.

words with actions. With respect to civic discourse, both are important. When speech moves beyond words into the realm of action, it is considered to be **symbolic speech**, nonverbal "speech" in the form of an action such as picketing or wearing an armband to signify a protest.

Unless words threaten imminent lawless action, the First Amendment will likely protect the speaker. But in civic discourse, words are often combined with action. For example, in the 1960s, antiwar protesters were arrested for burning their draft cards to demonstrate their refusal to serve in Vietnam, and public high school students were suspended from school for wearing black armbands to protest the war. When the two groups brought their cases to the Supreme Court, the justices had to determine whether their conduct rose to the level of political expression and merited First Amendment protection. Together, these cases help to define the parameters for symbolic speech.

In the first of these cases, *U.S. v. O'Brien*, the justices considered whether the government could punish several Vietnam War protesters for burning their draft cards in violation of the Selective Service Act, which made it a crime to "destroy or mutilate" those cards. The Court balanced the free expression guarantee against the government's need to prevent the destruction of the cards. Because the cards were critical to the nation's ability to raise an army, the Court ruled that the government had a compelling interest in preventing their destruction. Moreover, because the government had passed the Selective Service Act to facilitate the draft and not to suppress speech, the impact of the law on speech was incidental. When the justices balanced the government's interest in making it easy to raise an army against the incidental impact that this law had on speech, they found that the government's interest overrode that of the political protesters.[19]

Tinker v. Des Moines
The Supreme Court decision protecting the political speech of school children in public schools as long as it does not interfere with the educational process.

In contrast, when the Court considered the other symbolic speech case of this era, ***Tinker v. Des Moines***, they found that the First Amendment did protect the speech in question. In this case, the justices ruled that the political expression in the form of the students' wearing black armbands to school to protest the Vietnam War was protected.[20] On what basis did the justices distinguish the armbands in the *Tinker* case from the draft cards in the *O'Brien* case? They cited legitimate reasons for the government to ban the burning of draft cards in a time of war; but there were no comparable reasons to ban the wearing of armbands, apart from the school district's desire to curb or suppress political expression on school grounds. School officials could not show that the armbands had disrupted

>> Mary Beth Tinker was an eighth-grade student when she was suspended from high school, along with fellow student Chris Ekert, for wearing a black armband to school to protest the Vietnam War. Tinker's mother (pictured above with Mary Beth and her brother) was a civil rights activist and supported ending the war peacefully as well as her daughter's right to free speech. With help from the American Civil Liberties Union, Tinker's case eventually reached the United States Supreme Court, which ruled in favor of Tinker, holding that "students do not shed their Constitutional rights to freedom of speech or expression at the schoolhouse gate." The Court ruled students maintain their First Amendment rights in school, as long as it does not disrupt learning, a standard that is applied time and time again to subsequent cases involving free speech for schoolchildren. Today, Mary Beth Tinker is an activist and frequently speaks to students about their rights. She can be reached at: https://tinkertourusa.org/

Interpret: What does the above image tell you about Mary Beth Tinker and her family? How are images used to sway public opinion one way or the other? Do you think children should have the same civil liberties as adults? Does Mary Beth Tinker's case affect the way you think about the balance between liberty and order?

normal school activities.[21] For that reason, the Court argued, the symbolic speech in *Tinker* warranted more protection than that in *O'Brien*.

The highly controversial case of *Texas v. Johnson* (1989) tested the Court's commitment to protecting symbolic speech of a highly unpopular nature. At issue was a man's conviction under state law for burning the American flag during the Republican National Convention in 1984 to emphasize his disagreement with the policies of the administration of President Ronald Reagan (1981–1989). The Supreme Court overturned the man's conviction, finding that the flag burning was political speech worthy of protection under the First Amendment.[22] After the *Johnson* decision, Congress quickly passed the Flag Protection Act in an attempt to reverse the Court's ruling. Subsequently, however, in the case of *U.S. v. Eichman* (1990), the Court struck down the new law by the same 5–4 majority as in the *Johnson* ruling.[23]

The decisions in these flag-burning cases were very controversial and prompted Congress to pursue the only remaining legal avenue to enact flag protection statutes—a constitutional amendment. Every other year from 1995 to 2006, the proposed amendment received the two-thirds majority necessary for approval in the U.S. House of Representatives, but it failed to achieve the same constitutionally required supermajority vote in the U.S. Senate. This issue has apparently been resolved in favor of liberty, for although this proposed amendment is still introduced regularly, it has not left the judiciary committee for a full debate since 2006.

NOT ALL SPEECH IS CREATED EQUAL: UNPROTECTED SPEECH The Supreme Court long ago rejected the extreme view that all speech should be free in the United States. Whereas *political speech* tends to be protected against government suppression, other forms of speech can be limited or prohibited.

The courts afford **commercial speech**, that is, advertising statements, limited protection under the First Amendment. According to the Supreme Court, commercial speech may be restricted as long as the restriction "seeks to implement a substantial government interest, directly advances that interest, and goes no further than necessary to accomplish its objective." Restrictions on tobacco advertising, for example, limit free speech in the interest of protecting the

commercial speech
Advertising statements that describe products.

Citizens United v. Federal Election Commission
The Supreme Court decision in which the First Amendment's free speech clause was found to include corporate spending during election cycles.

libel
False written statements about others that harm their reputation

slander
False verbal statements about others that harm their reputation.

obscenity
Indecent or offensive speech or expression.

fighting words
Speech that is likely to bring about public disorder or chaos; the Supreme Court has held that this speech may be banned in public places to ensure the preservation of public order.

health of society. In 2010, the Supreme Court, in the controversial **Citizens United v. Federal Election Commission** decision, revised its previous rulings and determined that the First Amendment also protected corporate spending during elections as a form of free speech. Legislation that limits such spending was an unconstitutional banning of political speech.[24]

Other forms of speech, including libel and slander, receive no protection under the First Amendment. **Libel** (written statements) and **slander** (verbal statements) are false statements that harm the reputation of another person. To qualify as libel or slander, the defamatory statement must be made publicly and with fault, meaning that reporters, for example, must undertake reasonable efforts to verify allegations. The statement must extend beyond mere name-calling or insults that cannot be proven true or false. Those who take a legal action on the grounds that they are victims of libel or slander, such as government officials, celebrities, and people involved with specific public controversies, are required to prove that the defendant acted with malice—with knowledge that the statement was false or that they recklessly disregarded the accuracy of the statement.

Obscenity, indecent or offensive speech or expression, is another form of speech that is not protected under the First Amendment. After many unsuccessful attempts to define obscenity, in 1973 the Supreme Court developed a three-part test in *Miller v. California*.[25] The Court ruled that a book, a film, or another form of expression is legally obscene if

- The average person applying contemporary standards finds that the work taken as a whole appeals to the prurient interest—that is, tends to excite unwholesome sexual desire.

- The work depicts or describes, in an obviously offensive way, a form of sexual conduct specifically prohibited by an anti-obscenity law.

- The work taken as a whole lacks serious literary, artistic, political, or scientific value.

Of course, these standards do not guarantee that people will agree on what materials are obscene. What is obscene to some may be acceptable to others. For that reason, the Court has been reluctant to limit free speech, even in the most controversial cases.

The Court may also ban speech known as **fighting words**—speech that inflicts injury or results in public disorder. The Court first articulated the fighting-words doctrine in *Chaplinsky v. New Hampshire* (1942). Walter Chaplinsky was convicted of violating a New Hampshire statute that prohibited the use of offensive, insulting language toward persons in public places after he made several inflammatory comments to a city official. The Court, in upholding the statute as constitutional, explained the limits of free speech: "These include the lewd and obscene, the profane, the libelous, and the insulting or fighting words—those which by their very utterance inflict injury or tend to incite an immediate breach of the peace."[26] Thus the Court ruled that, like slander, libel, and obscenity, "fighting words" do not advance the democratic goals of free speech. Cross burning, for example, has been a form of symbolic speech that in the United States has come to represent racial violence and intimidation against African Americans and other vulnerable groups. In 2005, in *Virginia v. Black,* the Supreme Court found that a state could ban cross burning when it was used to threaten or attempt to silence other individuals, but that the state law could not assume all cross burnings attempt to communicate that message.[27]

Even the types of "unprotected speech" we have looked at enjoy broad protection under the law. For example, although cigarette ads are banned from television, many products are sold through every media outlet imaginable. Though a tabloid such as the *National Inquirer* sometimes faces lawsuits for the false stories it prints, most celebrities do not pursue legal action because of the high burden of proving that the paper knew the story was false, intended to damage the subject's reputation, and in fact caused real harm. Even though network television is censored for broadcasting objectionable material, the Supreme Court has ruled that the government cannot ban (adult) pornography on the Internet or on paid cable television channels.[28] And despite continued reaffirmation of the fighting-words doctrine, the Supreme Court has declined to uphold any convictions for fighting words since *Chaplinsky.* In short, the Court is reluctant to do anything that might limit the content of adults' free speech and expression, even when that speech is unpopular or offensive.

Freedom of Assembly and Redress of Grievances

The First Amendment says that people have the freedom to assemble peaceably and to seek redress of (compensation for) grievances against the government; yet, there are limits placed on assembly. As the Supreme Court has considered free assembly cases, it has been most concerned about ensuring that individuals and groups can gather to discuss their concerns and that they can take action in the public arena that advances their political goals.

The Court is keenly aware of the need for order in public forums and will clamp down on speech that is intended and likely to incite public unrest and anger. That is one reason the Court has reaffirmed the fighting-words doctrine. Although officials cannot censor speech before it occurs, they can take action to limit speech once it becomes apparent that public disorder is going to erupt. In its rulings, the Court has also allowed content-neutral **time, place, and manner restrictions**—regulations regarding when, where, or how expression may occur. Such restrictions do not target speech based on content, and to stand up in court, they must be applied in a content-neutral manner. For example, people have the right to march in protest, but not while chanting into bullhorns at four o'clock in the morning in a residential neighborhood.

time, place, and manner restrictions
Regulations regarding when, where, or how expression may occur; must be content neutral.

The Court's rulings in these various cases illustrate how the government is balancing the freedom of public assembly against other concerns, notably public safety and the right of an individual to be left alone. Further, the Court is carefully weighing the freedoms of one group of individuals against another and attempting to ensure the protection of free public expression.

The young people of Generation Z (born 1997–2012) make up 27 percent of the U.S. population (see Chapter 7), and as they make their voices heard, we are seeing their interest in the power of assembly and the right to protest. The most ethnically and racially diverse generation of Americans, Gen Z has—even in their teen years—used social media to organize and assert the right to assemble as a means of protesting the two issues that concern them most: gun violence and climate change. Because their school years have been marked with mass school shootings and the response-training attached to the fear of shootings, gun violence has become a high-profile focus for many of them. Also, as evidenced by the youthful leadership of the global Climate Strike in September 2019, concern for the environment and for world leaders' policy response to climate-related issues demonstrates Generation Z's use of new technology to engage in traditional feet-in-the-street protest.

Freedom of the Press

Throughout American history, the press has played a crucial role in the larger debate about political expression. Before the War for Independence, when the British monarchy sought to clamp down on political dissent in the colonies, the king and Parliament quickly recognized the urgency of silencing the press. A free press is essential to democratic ideals, and democracy cannot survive when a government controls the press. The First Amendment's guarantees of a free press ensure not only that American government remains accountable to its constituents but also that the people hear competing ideas about how to deal with matters of public concern. Increasingly, ordinary citizens share their views on important political issues on social media.

Ensuring a free press can complicate the work of government. As was seen during the Trump administration, the White House cannot control its press coverage. While this has been a source of frustration for most presidents, President Trump often responded with public expressions of anger and irritation. For instance, in 2019, the White House prevented four journalists from covering a dinner between North Korea's Supreme Leader Kim Jong Un and President Trump because they asked unsolicited questions of the president. Also, the administration justified the president's use of Twitter as a way of communicating directly to the public and avoiding a media he perceived to be biased against him. The Committee to Protect Journalists noted its concern that such White House rhetoric "undermines the media in the U.S. and emboldens autocratic leaders around the world."[29]

Certain well-established principles govern freedom of the press in the United States. First and foremost, the courts almost never allow the government to engage in prior restraint. **Prior restraint** means censorship—the attempt to block the publication of material that is considered to be harmful. The Supreme Court established this rule against censorship in 1931 in the landmark case of *Near v. Minnesota*. After editor Jay Near wrote a story in the *Saturday Press* alleging that Jews were responsible for corruption, bribery, and prostitution in Minneapolis, a state judge barred all future sales of the newspaper. The Court overturned the state judge's ruling, finding that the sole purpose of the order was to suppress speech. Because freedom of the press has strong historical foundations, the Court concluded, censorship is clearly prohibited.

In the *Near* ruling, however, the Court also recognized that there might be times when government officials *could* limit the publication of certain stories. Specifically, such censorship might be justified under extraordinary circumstances related to ensuring public safety or national security or in cases involving obscenity. In reality, though, the Court has disallowed prior restraint in the vast majority of cases. For example, in the most important case examining the national

security exception, ***New York Times v. U.S.***, the Court rejected the government's attempt to prevent publication of documents that detailed the history of the United States' involvement in Vietnam. In this case, also known as the *Pentagon Papers* case, the government argued that censorship was necessary to prevent "irreparable injury" to national security. But the Court dismissed that argument, asserting that full disclosure was in the interest of all Americans and that publication of the documents could contribute to the ongoing debate about the U.S. role in the Vietnam War.[30] In their ruling, the justices recognized that some materials are clearly necessary for full and fair discussion of issues facing the nation, whereas others are far less important to political discourse.

Freedoms of Religion, Privacy, and Criminal Due Process: Encouraging Civic Engagement

The Constitution's framers understood that the government they were creating could use its powers to single out certain groups for either favorable or unfavorable treatment. They realized, too, that unequal treatment of that kind could interfere with the creation of community—and with citizens' engagement within that community. The founders' commitment to community building and citizens' engagement lies at the heart of several constitutional amendments in the Bill of Rights. Specifically, these are the amendments establishing the freedom of religion, the right to privacy, and the right to due process for individuals in the criminal justice system.

The First Amendment and the Freedom of Religion

The religion clauses of the First Amendment—the establishment clause and the free exercise clause—essentially do two things. First, they bar the government from establishing or supporting any one religious sect over another, and second, they ensure that individuals are not hindered in the exercise of their religion. While the establishment clause requires that the government be neutral toward religious institutions, favoring neither one specific religion over others nor all religious groups over nonreligious groups, the free exercise clause prohibits the government from taking action that is hostile toward individuals' practice of their religion. As we now consider, there is tension between these two clauses.

THE ESTABLISHMENT CLAUSE Stating only that "Congress shall make no law respecting an establishment of religion," the **establishment clause** does little to clarify what the relationship between church and state should be. The Constitution's authors wanted to ensure that Congress could not create a national religion, as a number of European powers (notably France and Spain) had done. Further, many colonists had emigrated to America to escape religious persecution in Europe, and although many were deeply religious, uncertainty prevailed about the role that government should play in the practice of religion. That uncertainty, too, is reflected in the brevity of the establishment clause. The question arises, does the clause prohibit the government from simply preferring one sect over another, or is it broader, preventing any kind of government support of religion?

> **establishment clause**
> The First Amendment clause that bars the government from passing any law "respecting an establishment of religion"; often interpreted as a separation of church and state, but this is increasingly challenged.

This is a crucial question, because religious institutions have always been important forums for community building and engagement in the United States. Americans continue to be a very religious people. In 2016, over 75 percent of Americans surveyed said religion was fairly or very important in their lives.[31] But even given their strong religious affiliations, most Americans believe in some degree of separation between religious organizations and the government. The actual debate has been about how much separation the establishment clause requires.

Over time, scholars and lawyers have considered three possible interpretations of the establishment clause. One interpretation, called separationism, is that the establishment clause requires a *strict separation of church and state* and bars most or all government support for religious sects. Supporters of the strict separationist view invoke the writings of Thomas Jefferson, James Madison, and others that call for a "wall of separation" between church and state.[32] They also point to societies outside the United States in which religious leaders dictate how citizens may dress, act, and pray as examples of what can happen without strict separation.

A second, and more flexible, interpretation allows the government to offer support to religious sects as long as that support is neutral and not biased toward any one sect. This interpretation, known as *neutrality* or the *preferential treatment standard,* would permit government support provided that this support extended to all religious groups. The third interpretation is the most flexible and reads the establishment clause as barring only establishment of a state religion. This interpretation, known as *accommodationism,* allows the government to offer support to any or all religious groups, provided that this support does not rise to the level of recognizing an official religion.[33]

Which of these three vastly different interpretations of the establishment clause is correct? Over time, the Supreme Court has shifted back and forth in its opinions, usually depending on the kind of government support in question. Overall, the courts have rejected the strictest interpretation of the establishment clause, which would ban virtually any form of aid to religion. Instead, they have allowed government support for religious schools, programs, and institutions if the support advances a secular (nonreligious) goal (such as teaching mathematics) and does not specifically endorse a particular religious belief.

For example, in 1974, the Court upheld a New Jersey program that provided funds to the parents of parochial school students to pay for bus transportation to and from school.[34] The Court reasoned that the program was necessary to help students to get to school safely and concluded that if the state withdrew funding for any of these programs for parochial school students, it would be impossible to operate these schools. The impact would be the hindrance of the free exercise of religion for students and their parents.

In another landmark case, *Lemon v. Kurtzman* (1971), however, the Court struck down a state program that used cigarette taxes to reimburse parochial schools for the costs of teachers' salaries and textbooks. The Court found that subsidizing parochial schools furthered a process of religious teaching and that the "continuing state surveillance" that would be necessary to enforce the specific provisions of the laws would inevitably entangle the state in religious affairs.[35]

In the *Lemon* case ruling, the Court refined the establishment clause standard to include three considerations.

- Does the state program have a secular, as opposed to a religious, purpose?

- Does it have as its principal effect the advancement of religion?

- Does the program create an excessive entanglement between church and state?

This three-part test is known as the **Lemon test**. The programs most likely to withstand scrutiny under the establishment clause are those that have a secular purpose, have only an incidental effect on the advancement of religion, and do not excessively entangle church and state.

More recently, the Court upheld an Ohio program that gave vouchers to parents to offset the cost of parochial schooling.[36] The justices ruled that the purpose of the program was secular, not religious, because it was intended to provide parents with an alternative to the Cleveland public schools. Any aid to religious institutions—in this case, mostly Catholic schools—was indirect, because the primary beneficiaries were the students themselves. Finally, there was little entanglement between the church and state, because the parents received the vouchers based on financial need and then were free to use these vouchers as they pleased. There was no direct relationship between the religious schools and the state.

If a government program offers financial support, the Court has tended to evaluate the program by using either the preferential treatment standard or the accommodationist standard. If a program or policy involves prayer in the schools or issues related to the curriculum, however, the Court has adopted a standard that looks more like strict separatism.

SOURCE ANALYSIS COMPARATIVE

THEN

NOW

Source Analysis Throughout the first decades of the 21st century, the Supreme Court wrestled with protecting the free exercise of religion while ensuring that the establishment clause is not violated. Then in 2005, in *Van Orden v. Perry*, the Supreme Court ruled that the establishment clause did not prohibit a monument to the Ten Commandments on the state capitol grounds, where it resided with 17 monuments and 21 historical markers. Later, in 2019, the Supreme Court determined that a 40-foot cross honoring soldiers who died in World War I could stay on state property because it was not primarily a religious message. Does the Court's reasoning make sense to you? How do you differentiate between primarily religious art and something like a monument that invokes religious imagery? Do you think this kind of public art is perceived differently by people who do not belong to the majority religious culture?

(Left): Jana Birchum/Getty Images; *(Right):* Mark Gail/The Washington Post/Getty Images

A series of cases beginning with **Engel v. Vitale** (1962) has barred formalized prayer in the public schools, finding that such prayer has a purely religious purpose and that prayer is intended to advance religious, as opposed to secular, ideals.[37] For that reason, the Court has barred school-organized prayer in public elementary and secondary schools on the grounds that it constitutes a state endorsement of religion. Student-organized prayer is constitutional because the state is not engaging in any coercion by mandating or encouraging student participation.

THE FREE EXERCISE CLAUSE The tension between the establishment and free exercise clauses arises because the establishment clause bars the state from helping religious institutions, whereas the **free exercise clause** makes it illegal for the government to enact laws prohibiting the free practice of religion by individuals. Establishment clause cases often raise free exercise claims, and so courts must frequently consider whether, by banning state aid, they are interfering with the free exercise of religion.

How Does the Changing Religious Affiliation of Americans Affect the First Amendment?

THEN

NOW

NEXT

	2000	2020
Protestant	54%	46.6%
Catholic	24	20.8
Jewish	2	1.9
Islam/Muslim	N/A	.9
Other faith	5	3.5
None	14	22.8

- As Americans' religious affiliations continue to slowly decline, what might be the implications for the First Amendment? Will the battles around the free exercise clause and the establishment clause become more intense or less relevant?

- The Millennial generation had the highest levels of nonaffiliation of any previous generation, and Generation Z appears to be even less religious. What might the consequences of this be for debates surrounding the First Amendment?

Source: All data derived from the General Social Survey: The Association of Religion Data Archive, Pew Research Center, "2014 U.S. Religious Landscape Study."

Although free exercise and establishment cases raise many of the same concerns, they are different kinds of cases, whose resolution depends on distinct legal tests. Because establishment clause cases often center on state aid to religious schools, many involve the Roman Catholic Church, which administers the largest number of private elementary and secondary schools in the country. In contrast, free exercise clause cases tend to involve less-mainstream religious groups, among them Mormons, Jehovah's Witnesses, Christian Scientists, and Amish. These groups' practices tend to be less well known—or more controversial. For example, free exercise clause cases have involved the right to practice polygamy, use hallucinogens, refuse conventional medical care for a child, sacrifice animals, and refuse to salute the flag.

The Supreme Court has refused to accept that the government is barred from *ever* interfering with religious exercise. Free exercise claims are difficult to settle because they require that courts balance the individual's right to free practice of religion against the government's need to adopt some policy or program. First and foremost, the Court has always distinguished between religious beliefs, which government may not interfere with, and religious actions, which government is permitted to regulate. In **Wisconsin v. Yoder**, the Supreme Court agreed with the Amish that their free exercise of religion allowed them to remove their children from school after eighth grade, despite the state's interest in having educated citizens.[38] On the other hand, although adults may refuse lifesaving medical care on the basis of their own religious beliefs, they may not refuse medical procedures required to save the lives of their children.[39] More recently, debates over mandatory vaccination laws for students enrolling in public schools have been challenged as a violation of the free exercise of religion protected in the First Amendment. Lower federal courts have found these regulations to be a lawful exercise of the police power.[40] Unless there is conflict among the lower courts over this issue, the Supreme Court most likely will not hear this controversy.

Wisconsin v. Yoder
The Supreme Court found that an individual's interest in the free exercise of religion outweighs the state's interest in requiring education after the eighth grade.

In assessing those laws that interfere with religiously motivated action, the Court has distinguished between laws that are neutral and generally applicable to all religious sects and laws that single out one sect for unfavorable treatment. In *Employment Division, Department of Human Resources v. Smith* (1990), the Court allowed the state of Oregon to deny unemployment benefits to two substance-abuse counselors who were fired from their jobs after using peyote as part of their religious practice. Oregon refused to provide benefits because the two men had been fired for engaging in an illegal activity. The Court concluded that there was no free exercise challenge, because Oregon had good reason for denying benefits to lawbreakers who had been fired from their jobs. The justices concluded that the state was simply applying a neutral and generally applicable law to the men as opposed to singling them out for bad treatment.[41] One consequence of this case was that several states, including Oregon, passed laws excluding members of the Native American Church, who smoke peyote as part of traditional religious rites, from being covered by their controlled-substance laws.

One major change in the free exercise clause has been the extension of the First Amendment constitutional rights to corporations. The 2014 case of *Burwell v. Hobby Lobby* was an appeal of the Affordable Care Act's (Obamacare) requirement that family-owned corporations pay for insurance coverage of birth control for its employees.[42] The two companies, Hobby Lobby and Conestoga Wood Specialties, were owned by families who claimed that they try to run their businesses on Christian principles and that providing contraception coverage burdened their religious liberty. The Court agreed with the companies, but noted the decision applied only to "closely held" for-profit companies run on religious principles. The dissenting justices noted this was the first time the constitutional protection of religious freedom was extended to the commercial world, and more litigation will follow.

In summary, people are free to hold and profess their own beliefs, to build and actively participate in religious communities, and to allow their religious beliefs to inform their participation in politics and civil society. However, individual *actions* based on religious beliefs may be limited if those actions conflict with existing laws that are neutrally applied in a nondiscriminatory fashion. The extension of these rights to some corporations means that our understanding of religious liberty will continue to evolve.

The Right to Privacy

right to privacy
The right of an individual to be left alone and to make decisions freely, without the interference of others.

So far in this section, we have explored the relationship between civil liberties and some key themes of this book: civic participation, inclusiveness, community building, and community engagement. We now shift our focus somewhat to consider the **right to privacy**, the right of an individual to be left alone and to make decisions freely, without the interference of others. Privacy is a core principle for most Americans, and the right to make decisions, especially about intimate or personal matters, is at the heart of this right. Yet the right to privacy is also necessary for genuine inclusiveness and community engagement, because it ensures that each individual is able to act autonomously and to make decisions about how they will interact with others.

The right to privacy is highly controversial and the subject of much public debate. In large part, the reason is that this right is tied to some of the most divisive issues of our day, including abortion, aid in dying, and sexual orientation. The right to privacy is also controversial because, unlike the freedoms of speech, the press, assembly, and religion, it is not mentioned explicitly anywhere in the Constitution. A further reason for the debate surrounding the right to privacy is that the Supreme Court has only recently recognized it.

unreasonable search and seizure
Search and seizure of property by law enforcement that violates the Fourth Amendment to the Constitution. This includes searches done without a warrant or without probable cause except in very narrow circumstances.

THE EMERGENT RIGHT TO PRIVACY For more than 100 years, Supreme Court justices and lower-court judges have concluded that the right to privacy is implied in all the other liberties spelled out in the Bill of Rights. Not until the landmark Supreme Court case *Griswold v. Connecticut* (1965) did the courts firmly establish the right to privacy. The issue in this case may seem strange to us today: whether the state of Connecticut had the power to prohibit married couples from using birth control. In their decision, the justices concluded that the state law violated the privacy right of married couples by preventing them from seeking access to birth control, and the Court struck down the Connecticut prohibition. The Court argued that the right to privacy was inherent within many of the constitutional guarantees, most importantly in the First Amendment freedom of association, the Third Amendment right to be free from the quartering of soldiers, the Fourth Amendment right to be free from **unreasonable searches and seizures,** the Fifth Amendment protection against self-incrimination, and the Ninth Amendment assurance of rights not explicitly listed in the Bill of Rights. Justice William O. Douglas and his colleagues effectively argued that a zone of privacy surrounded every person in the United States and that government could not pass laws that encroached upon this zone.[43]

In its ruling, the Court asserted that the right to privacy existed quite apart from the law. It was implicit in the Bill of Rights and fundamental to the American system of law and justice. The right to privacy hinged in large part on the right of individuals to associate with one another, and specifically the right of marital partners to engage in intimate association.

In a 1984 case, the Supreme Court ruled that the Constitution protects two kinds of freedom of association: (1) intimate associations and (2) expressive associations.[44] The protection of intimate associations allows Americans to maintain private human relationships as part of their personal liberty. The protection of expressive associations allows people to form associations with others and to practice their First Amendment freedoms of speech, assembly, petition, and religion.

THE RIGHT TO PRIVACY APPLIED TO OTHER ACTIVITIES The challenge for the Court since *Griswold* has been to determine which activities fall within the scope of the privacy right, and that question has placed the justices at the center of some of the most controversial issues of the day. For example, the first attempt to extend the privacy right, which raised the question of whether the right protected abortion, remains at least as controversial today as it was in 1973, when the Court decided the first abortion rights case, ***Roe v. Wade***.[45] In *Roe,* and in the many abortion cases the Court has heard since, the justices have tried to establish whether a woman's right to abortion takes precedence over any interests the state may have in either the woman's health or the fetus's life. Over time, the Court has adopted a compromise position by rejecting the view that the right to abortion is absolute and by attempting to determine when states can regulate, or even prohibit, access to abortion. In 1992, the Court established the "undue burden" test, which asks whether a state abortion law places a "substantial obstacle in the path of a woman seeking an abortion before the fetus attains viability."[46] The Court, in 2016, found that some state requirements, such as requiring doctors to have admitting rights at local hospitals or that abortions could occur only at surgical centers, imposed such an undue burden without significantly protecting women's health.[47] Although the Court used this standard to strike down spousal notification requirements, it has upheld other requirements imposed by some states, including waiting periods, mandatory counseling, and parental consent.

The Court has also stepped gingerly around other privacy rights, such as the right to choose one's sexual partners and the right to terminate medical treatment or engage in physician-assisted suicide. Both of these rights have been presented to the Court as hinging on the much broader right to privacy. With respect to the right to terminate medical treatment, the Court has been fairly clear. Various Court decisions have confirmed that as long as an individual is competent to terminate treatment, the state may not stop him or her from taking this action, even if stopping treatment will lead to the person's death.[48]

The Court has been less clear in its rulings when an incompetent person's right is advanced by another individual, such as a spouse, a parent, or a child. In these circumstances, the Court has accepted the state's argument that before treatment may be terminated, the state may require that the person seeking to end life show that his or her loved one would have wanted that course of action.[49] When a person's wishes are not clear, loved ones may wage legal battles over whether to discontinue life support.

Roe v. Wade
The Supreme Court decision that expanded the right of privacy to include a woman's right to have an abortion, balanced by the state's concern to protect the health of the woman and the potential of human life.

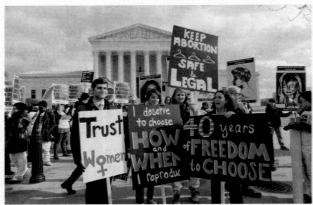

>> Public debate over abortion was not settled by the Supreme Court's 1973 decision in *Roe v. Wade.* In these photos taken more than four decades later, pro-life and pro-choice activists hold signs supporting their differing viewpoints. Abortion rights advocates frame the issue in terms of a pregnant person's right to privacy and to control their own body without interference from the government. Abortion rights opponents view abortion as murder and frame the issue in terms of the rights of an unborn child. Do you think that arguing the case on privacy grounds was the best case for legalizing abortion? Is there a better constitutional argument?

(Top): Olivier Douliery/Getty Images; (Bottom): B Christopher/Alamy Stock Photo

In cases involving the right to engage in consensual sexual activities with a partner of one's choosing, the Supreme Court has also employed a less than absolute approach. For many years, the Court allowed states to criminalize homosexual activity, finding that the right to engage in consensual sexual activity did not extend to same-sex partners.[50] In a 2003 case, *Lawrence v. Texas,* the Court changed course by ruling that the right to engage in intimate sexual activity was protected as a liberty right, especially when the activity occurred inside one's home, and that states could not criminalize this activity.[51] Since that decision, rights activists have worked through the courts and state and federal legislatures to secure for same-sex partners the same rights that heterosexual couples enjoy, including benefits provided by group health insurance and marriage. In the 2015 decision of *Obergefell v. Hodges,* the Supreme Court found that same-sex couples possessed the fundamental right to marry under the Fourteenth Amendment.[52] (See Chapter 9 for further discussion of the ruling.) Despite these rulings, states are still free to prohibit a range of sexual activities, including prostitution, child sexual abuse, and sex in public places.[53] In the Court's view, these activities can be prohibited primarily because they are not consensual or do not take place in the home, a place that accords special protection by the privacy right.

The right to privacy remains very controversial. Cases brought under the right to privacy tend to link this right with some other civil liberties, such as the protection against unreasonable search and seizure, the right to free speech, or the protection against self-incrimination. In other words, the privacy right, which the justices themselves created, seems to need buttressing by other rights that the Bill of Rights *explicitly* establishes. The explanation for this development may be the contentiousness of Americans' civic discourse about abortion, aid in dying, and other privacy issues. In short, continuing civic disagreement may have forced the Court to fall back on rights that are well established and more widely accepted.

GOVERNMENT USE OF SOCIAL MEDIA IN INVESTIGATIONS Public discourse about privacy is constantly evolving as people voluntarily share more and more information about themselves through online networking sites like Facebook, Pinterest, Twitter, LinkedIn, and Instagram. Users of such sites and bloggers share stories, photos, and videos of themselves—as well as of others, who may be unaware that they are the subject of a posting, a blog, or a video. Civil libertarians worry about the misuse and theft of personal information in a high-tech society where people's financial, employment, consumer, legal, and personal histories are so easily accessible.

In 2013, global media organizations disclosed evidence that the National Security Agency had tracked and reviewed international and domestic phone calls, text messages, and e-mails of an unknown number of Americans without first obtaining a warrant.[54] Social media platforms operated by such entities as Facebook, Apple, Microsoft, LinkedIn, Twitter, and Google are seeking to provide greater transparency as to their cooperation with governmental requests for user information.[55] However, in 2019, Facebook reported an unprecedented number of governmental demands for personal data. The U.S. government made the most requests, with two-thirds accompanied by a gag order that forbade Facebook from telling the user about the search.[56] Without legislation to determine when and if social media organizations may deny warrantless requests, and without legislation that mandates public disclosure of the scope of inquiries, no clear limits exist on the government.

The Fourth, Fifth, Sixth, and Eighth Amendments: Ensuring Criminal Due Process

The last category of civil liberties that bear directly on civic engagement consists of the criminal due process protections established in the Fourth, Fifth, Sixth, and Eighth Amendments. Does it surprise you that so many of the Bill of Rights amendments focus on the rights of individuals accused of crimes? The context for this emphasis is the founders' concern with how the British monarchy had abused its power and used criminal law to impose its will on the American colonists. The British government had used repeated trials, charges of treason, and imprisonment without bail to stifle political dissent. The founders therefore wanted to ensure that there were effective checks on the power of the federal government, especially in the creation and enforcement of criminal law. As we have seen, the Bill of Rights amendments were incorporated to apply to the states and to their criminal codes through the process of selective incorporation. Thus, criminal due process protections are the constitutional limits imposed on law enforcement personnel.

These four amendments together are known as the **criminal due process rights** because they establish the guidelines that the government must follow in investigating, bringing to trial, and punishing individuals who violate criminal law. Each amendment guides the government in administering some facet of law enforcement, and all are intended to ensure justice and fairness in the administration of the law. Criminal due process is essential to guarantee that individuals can participate in the larger society and that no one person is singled out for better or worse treatment under the law. Like the First Amendment, due process protects political speech and freedom. Without these liberties, government officials could selectively target those who disagree with the laws and policies they advocate.

criminal due process rights
Safeguards for those accused of crime; these rights constrain government conduct in investigating crimes, trying cases, and punishing offenders.

Moreover, without these rights, there would be little to stop the government from using criminal law to punish those who want to take action that is protected by the other amendments we have examined in this chapter. For example, what good would it do to talk about the freedom of speech if the government could isolate or punish someone who spoke out critically against it without having to prove in a public venue that the speech threatened public safety or national security? The criminal due process protections are essential to ensuring meaningful participation and engagement in the larger community and to safeguarding justice and fairness.

THE FOURTH AMENDMENT AND THE PROTECTION AGAINST UNREASONABLE SEARCHES AND SEIZURES The Fourth Amendment requires police to get a warrant before engaging in a search and guides law enforcement personnel in conducting criminal investigations and in searching an individual's body or property. It has its roots in colonial history—specifically, in the British government's abuse of its law enforcement powers to prosecute and punish American colonists suspected of being disloyal to England.

The Fourth Amendment imposes significant limits on law enforcement. In barring police from conducting any unreasonable searches and seizures, it requires that they show probable cause that a crime has been committed before they can obtain a search warrant. The warrant ensures that police officers can gather evidence only when they have probable cause. Further, a judicially created ruling known as the **exclusionary rule** compels law enforcers to carry out searches properly. Established for federal prosecutions in 1914, the exclusionary rule forbids the courts to admit illegally seized evidence during trial.[57] In the Supreme Court decision of *Mapp v. Ohio* (1961), the exclusionary rule was extended to state court proceedings.[58] Here, the Court overturned an Ohio court's conviction of Dollree Mapp for the possession of obscene materials. Police had found pornographic books in Mapp's apartment after searching it without a search warrant and despite the defendant's refusal to let them in. Critics of the exclusionary rule note that securing a warrant is not always necessary or feasible and that guilty people sometimes go free because of procedural technicalities. They argue that reasonable searches should not be defined solely by the presence of a court-ordered search warrant.[59]

What are "reasonable" and "unreasonable" searches under the Fourth Amendment? Over time, the U.S. Supreme Court has established criteria to guide both police officers and judges hearing cases. In the strictest definition of reasonableness, a warrant is always required: Where there is no warrant, the search is considered to be unreasonable. However, the Supreme Court has ruled that even without a warrant, some searches would still be reasonable. In 1984, for example, the Court held that illegally obtained evidence could be admitted at trial if law enforcers could prove that they would have obtained the evidence legally anyway.[60] In another case the same year, the Court created a "good faith" exception to the exclusionary rule by upholding the use of evidence obtained with a technically incorrect warrant, because the police officer had acted in good faith.[61]

More broadly, a warrantless search is valid if the person subjected to it has no reasonable expectation of privacy in the place or thing being searched. From colonial times to the present, the assumption has been that individuals have a reasonable expectation of privacy in their homes. Where there is no reasonable expectation of privacy, however, there can be no unreasonable search, and so the

exclusionary rule
The criminal procedural rule stating that evidence obtained illegally cannot be used in a trial.

police are not required to get a warrant before conducting the search or surveillance. Since the 1990s, the Court has expanded the situations in which there is no reasonable expectation of privacy and hence no need for a warrant. For example, there is no reasonable expectation of privacy in one's car, at least in those areas that are in plain view, such as the front and back seats. There is also no expectation of privacy in public places like parks and stores because it is reasonable to assume that a person knowingly exposes his or her activities to public view in those places. The same is true of one's trash: Because there is no reasonable expectation of privacy in the things that one discards, police may search this material without a warrant.[62]

In instances when there is a reasonable expectation of privacy, individuals or their property may be searched if law enforcement personnel acquire a warrant from a judge. To obtain a warrant, the police must provide the judge with evidence that establishes probable cause that a crime has been committed. Also, the warrant must be specific about the place to be searched and the materials that the agents are seeking. These requirements limit the ability of police simply to go on a "fishing expedition" to find some bit of incriminating evidence.

As society changes, expectations of privacy change as well. For example, technological innovation has given us new technology, such as e-mail and the Internet, and Fourth Amendment law has had to adapt to these inventions. As an example, in 2015, the Supreme Court ruled in *Torrey Dale Grady v. North Carolina* that the placement of a GPS tracking device on a convicted felon in order to monitor his movements is an unlawful search and violation of the Fourth Amendment.[63] Is there a reasonable expectation of privacy in our movements in public spaces? This is an important question, especially in light of citizens' heightened concerns about terrorism and security.

THE FIFTH AND SIXTH AMENDMENTS: THE RIGHT TO A FAIR TRIAL AND THE RIGHT TO COUNSEL The Fifth and Sixth Amendments establish the rules for conducting a trial. These two amendments ensure that criminal defendants are protected at the formal stages of legal proceedings. Although less than 10 percent of all charges result in trials, these protections have significant symbolic and practical importance, because they hold the state to a high standard whenever it attempts to use its significant power to prosecute a case against an individual.

The Fifth Amendment bars **double jeopardy** and compelled self-incrimination. These safeguards mean, respectively, that a person may not be tried twice for the same crime or forced to testify against himself or herself when accused of a crime. These safeguards are meant to protect people from persecution, harassment, and forced confessions. A single criminal action, however, can lead to multiple trials if each trial is based on a separate offense.

double jeopardy
The trying of a person again for the same crime that he or she has been cleared of in court; barred by the Fifth Amendment.

The Sixth Amendment establishes the rights to a speedy and public trial, to a trial by a jury of one's peers, to information about the charges against oneself, to the confrontation of witnesses testifying against oneself, and to legal counsel. The protection of these Fifth and Sixth Amendment liberties is promoted by the **Miranda rights**, based on the Supreme Court decision in *Miranda v. Arizona* (1966).[64] In the *Miranda* case, the Court outlined the requirement that "prior to questioning, the person must be warned that he has a right to remain silent, that any statement he does make may be used against him, and that he has a right to the presence of an attorney, either retained or appointed." Later cases have created some exceptions to *Miranda* (see Table 8.2).

Miranda rights
A criminal procedural rule, established in the 1966 case *Miranda v. Arizona*, requiring police to inform criminal suspects, on their arrest, of their legal rights, such as the right to remain silent and the right to counsel; these warnings must be read to suspects before interrogation.

TABLE 8.2 ■ Cases Weakening Protection Against Self-Incrimination

Year	Case	Ruling
1986	*Moran v. Burbine*	Confession is not inadmissible because police failed to inform suspect of attorney's attempted contacts.
1991	*Arizona v. Fulminante*	Conviction is not automatically overturned in cases of coerced confession if other evidence is strong enough to justify conviction.
1994	*Davis v. U.S.*	Suspect must unequivocally and assertively state his right to counsel to stop police questioning.
2013	*Salina v. Texas*	Accused must explicitly invoke the Fifth Amendment for it to apply.

Together, the Fourth, Fifth, and Sixth Amendments ensure the protection of individuals against abuses of power by the state, and in so doing they promote a view of justice that the community widely embraces. Because these rights extend to individuals charged with violating the community's standards of right and wrong, they promote a broad sense of inclusiveness—a respect even for persons who allegedly have committed serious offenses, and a desire to ensure that the justice system treats all people fairly.

The Court has considered the community's views in reaching its decisions in cases brought before it. For example, through a series of Supreme Court cases culminating with **Gideon v. Wainwright** (1963), the justices interpreted the **right to counsel** to mean that the government must provide lawyers to individuals who are too poor to hire their own.[65] The justices adopted this standard because they came to believe that the community's views of fundamental fairness dictated this result. Before this decision, states had to provide attorneys only in cases that could result in capital punishment.

THE EIGHTH AMENDMENT: PROTECTION AGAINST CRUEL AND UNUSUAL PUNISHMENT The meaning of *cruel* and *unusual* has changed radically since the Eighth Amendment was ratified, especially with regard to the imposition of capital punishment—the death penalty. Moreover, Americans have always disagreed among themselves about the death penalty itself. Throughout the country's history, citizens and lawmakers have debated the morality of capital punishment as well as the circumstances under which the death penalty should be used. Central to the public debate have been the questions of which crimes should be punished by death and how capital punishment should be carried out.

Generally, the Court has supported the constitutionality of the death penalty. An exception was the landmark case *Furman v. Georgia* (1972), in which, in a 5–4 decision, the Court suspended the use of the death penalty.[66] Justices Brennan and Marshall believed the death penalty to be "incompatible with evolving standards of decency in contemporary society." The dissenting justices argued in turn that capital punishment had always been regarded as appropriate under the

Gideon v. Wainwright
The Supreme Court determined that the Sixth Amendment's guarantee to the right of counsel requires that the government provide an attorney for people who cannot afford to hire one.

right to counsel
A right enumerated in the Sixth Amendment to the Constitution that has been interpreted to require the government to provide a lawyer to anyone charged with a crime who is too poor to pay for their own.

cruel and unusual punishment
Punishment considered unacceptable under the Eighth Amendment to the Constitution. This includes torture, humiliation, and punishment considered too severe for the crime committed.

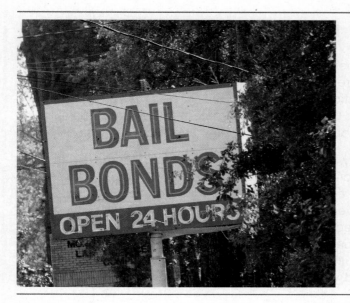

>> The Constitution's Eighth Amendment prohibits excessive bail when people who are accused of crimes are held before trial. The United State has the highest rate of incarceration in the world—one reason being the large number of people who cannot make bail while waiting for their trials. In 2019, many states passed bail reform laws, though these have been controversial, with disputed crime figures at the center of the dispute. Why would bail reform be so controversial? What role might the bail-bond lobby play in this dispute?

JLFCapture/iStockphoto/Getty Images

Anglo-American legal tradition for serious crimes and that the Constitution implicitly authorized death penalty laws because of the Fourteenth Amendment's reference to the taking of "life." The decision came about as a result of concurring opinions by Justices Stewart, White, and Douglas, who focused on the arbitrary nature with which death sentences had been imposed. The Court's decision forced the states and the national legislature to rethink their statutes for capital offenses to ensure that the death penalty would not be administered in a capricious or discriminatory manner. After states changed their laws regarding the death penalty in order to address legal processes that were unfair or arbitrary, the Court allowed the death penalty to be reinstated in the states (*Gregg v. Georgia,* 1976).[67]

Over time, the courts have also interpreted the Eighth Amendment as requiring that executions be carried out in the most humane and least painful manner. Public discourse and debate have strongly influenced thinking about which methods of execution are appropriate.

Recent studies, however, suggest that states' administration of the sedative sodium pentothal has left individuals conscious and in agony but paralyzed and thus unable to cry out while they are dying. But in 2008, the Supreme Court ruled in a 7–2 decision that lethal injection does not constitute cruel and unusual punishment,[68] paving the way for 10 states, which had halted lethal injections pending the case's outcome, to resume executions. This 2008 decision of *Baze v. Rees* marked the first time the Supreme Court reviewed the constitutionality of a method of execution since 1878, when the Court upheld Utah's use of a firing squad.[69]

In 2014, after the execution of Clayton Lockett using a three-drug lethal injection resulted in a 40-minute conscious death, Oklahoma created a new death protocol. One remaining option was a drug used in the Lockett execution—midazolam. Twenty-one inmates on death row argued that the use of midazolam violated the Eighth Amendment. The Court found that the Eighth Amendment did not guarantee a pain-free execution and that medical evidence did not demonstrate that midazolam created a risk of severe pain in light of Oklahoma's new safeguards.[70]

■ Civil Liberties Now

Public discussion about the proper balance of individual freedom with public action extends from First Amendment freedoms to gun laws to the rights of the accused. Debate has intensified as the nation struggles with the threat of terrorism and a growing protest culture at home. Citizens and government leaders are rethinking their beliefs about the proper scope of governmental power.

Over the course of U.S. history, liberty and security have coexisted in a state of tension. This tension has become more acute as the federal, state, and local governments have taken certain actions that directly intrude on individual freedoms. New technologies have increased the government's capacity to invade citizens' privacy, and a heightened fear of internal and external threats has been used to justify such invasions. The government and many citizens argue that these actions are necessary to protect life and property. But civil libertarians shudder at what they see as unprecedented violations of individual freedoms and rights.

Perceived Intrusions on Freedom of the Press

Freedom of the press is a key component of democracy because it ensures our government's accountability through the scrutiny of organizations and individuals that the government does not control or employ. In fact, Bright Line Watch, an ongoing survey of 2,000 political scientists and members of the general public regarding current threats to the values and practice of democracy, noted that one of the 28 core democratic principles is that "Government does not interfere with journalists and news organizations."[71] Moreover, Freedom House, an "independent watchdog" of democracy and individual freedom globally, noted in a 2017 report that freedom of the press has been in decline worldwide for the previous 13 years.

While the United States has always been a stalwart force in defending freedom of the press, as it possesses some of the most robust constitutional and cultural protections, it also has experienced the decline of this important liberty due to a number of factors unrelated to the priorities of the president in office. The Freedom House report argued that the expansion of the internet and social media undermines the financial viability of traditional media, resulting in the declining coverage of local news and inhibiting the investigative journalism necessary for governmental accountability. In addition, polarization and the development of explicitly partisan media outlets have led to a decline in public trust. The Obama administration began suppressing federal officials who leaked information to the press, and the Trump administration severely limited its access to the media.[72]

The Trump White House was unusually and explicitly negative in its treatment of the press, although most administrations can be frustrated with critical reporting. But in a tweet, President Trump called the press "the ENEMY OF THE PEOPLE"[73] and repeatedly referenced unfavorable media coverage as "fake news."[74] Of even greater concern, in December 2019 the American Civil Liberties Union, which sees its job as defending the interest of liberty against all security challenges, filed a lawsuit against the Department of Homeland Security (DHS) for targeting journalists who were reporting on issues related to immigration and the migrant caravans to the U.S. border with Mexico. The journalists claim that DHS targeted them for greater scrutiny at border crossings (detaining them, interrogating them, and searching their devices); collaborated with the Mexican government to track them; and created a secret database with dossiers including their personal details, information from social media accounts, and descriptions of their work.[75] The concern, according to free press advocates, is that such scrutiny can silence the speech of "vital watchers of democracy."[76]

Perceived Intrusions on Criminal Due Process

Attacks in Europe and across the globe, isolated attacks in the United States from people claiming sympathies with terrorist organizations, and numerous mass shootings have meant many Americans are willing to accept some infringement on their freedoms if it makes them safer. These citizens are more afraid of potential street crime than they are of potential government abuse of crime-control technology that can target politically unpopular groups or those critical of a presidential administration. Surveillance technology is developing quickly, and it is increasingly being used in the context of law enforcement and investigations. But the rush to ensure safety may sacrifice citizens' privacy and liberty in new ways. For example, how do we know which groups the federal government is using its powers to investigate and whether the focus on those groups is legitimate? How do we know that this new technology is justifiably targeting particular individuals rather than collecting data more broadly than necessary? What costs to personal privacy are we willing to pay to feel secure?

One of the most prevalent new crime-control techniques is facial recognition technology (FRT). This technology uses a computer program to track a "template" of an image of an individual face and then compares this template to a database of identified photographs, such as those from drivers' licenses, passports, mugshots, or even social media accounts like Instagram. Law enforcement officials believe that this technology can provide leads that identify criminals and therefore increase public safety, pointing out that once the algorithms are developed and the databases set up, the cost per use is very inexpensive, unlike DNA testing. Critics of this so-called biometric policing are concerned by the potential harm to civil liberties, noting the manner in which China, for example, uses this technology to control citizens who violate its country's social norms, such as dressing inappropriately in public. The technological advancements in contact tracing that have arisen with the COVID-19 pandemic have also raised civil liberties concerns. The point is that technology expands faster than we can regulate it or assess its effectiveness; new policing is in place before we have determined the acceptable lines between liberty and security.

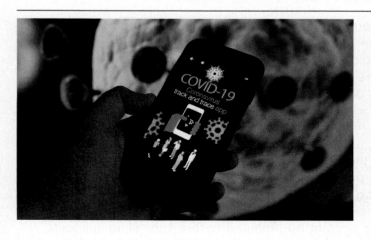

>> Nations have attempted to stop the spread of COVID-19 by using smart phones to trace the contacts infected people have had with others. Civil libertarians are concerned that personal liberty could be compromised if no limitations are placed on the storage of this data and the companies or government agencies that could have access to it. Federal and state legislation regulating this technology is being debated.

Niall Carson/PA Images/Getty Images

While FRT's capacity for accurate identification is high when the photograph being used is clear and well lit (about 0.3 percent error rate), in the more typical case of surveillance footage (for example, from an ATM machine), identification is more difficult. Grainy footage, poor lighting, ball caps, sunglasses, and low resolution all limit the effectiveness of FRT. Studies estimate that approximately 50 percent of all Americans are in a searchable database. The FBI has reported that it has two FRT programs: (1) Next Generation Identification (NGI), which pulls all mugshots (these are photographs of people who have been arrested but not necessarily convicted), fingerprints, and criminal history records, and (2) Facial Analysis, Comparison, and Evaluation (FACE) Services Unit, which uses facial images available in both state and federal databases—those on drivers' licenses, passports, and so on. NGI can be accessed by authorized local, state, tribal, and federal law enforcement, while FACE is used only to support ongoing FBI investigations. In congressional testimony in June 2019, the FBI, while noting the careful processes in their use surrounding these systems and the regular audits they conduct to prevent abuse, also recognized that they have no control over how other agencies use their database and findings.[77]

Advocates of biometric technology point to the cases that have been closed, the criminals who have been identified, and the ability to identify missing incapacitated individuals or those with dementia. They note the many times they have had recorded images of crimes but have not been able to identify the culprit until FRT provided a new lead for their investigation. Critics are concerned that this technology has exploded without any governmental oversight, judicial interpretation of investigatory techniques, or ongoing assessment of accuracy. They are concerned that prosecutors need not inform defendants when they have used FRT to identify them, undermining the ability of the defense to see if there are others suspects who are potentially culpable. How do we utilize these technologies to increase our security without ignoring that they have the same limitations as fingerprints, bite marks, ballistics, and blood splatter?[78] A "Face Recognition Vendor Test" completed in December 2019 by the Department of Commerce confirmed that these programs generated more false positives for women, the elderly, children, and any faces with darker skin. They found fewer false positives with East Asian faces and hypothesized this was because so many of the algorithms are created in China.[79] We know that this technology will become more effective and accurate over time as artificial intelligence continues to improve and as face image databases (such as state drivers' licenses) are more extensively connected. However, in the meantime, concerns about the potential of innocent people being convicted by this evidence abound.

Many states and local governments have invested in this technology, and private companies have eagerly pursued this growing market. States and localities are primarily using the technology for crimes like shoplifting, identification fraud, and check forgery.[80] But some are finding their security cameras are not compatible with the software or that their bandwidth is too slow to work effectively. As cities invest in increased bandwidth, this limitation may become increasingly irrelevant. In the meantime, San Francisco and Oakland (California) have banned the use of FRT, and Massachusetts, Michigan, and New York are seeking to pause the use of the technology until it is better understood and regulated. In response to the protests surrounding police brutality in 2020, many companies previously pursuing this technology—for example, Facebook and Microsoft—have withdrawn their investments. Moreover, pressure has grown on Congress to require that a warrant be obtained before surveilling suspects using FRT, thus treating FRT like other forms of surveillance, such as cell phone searches, wiretaps, or geotracking. Other biometric techniques are in development—for example, the "smart pavement," which can track people's movement based on their walking stride, or a new laser the Department of Defense has developed that can identify people in crowds based on their heartbeat. Although relatively experimental, these new biometric technologies point to the ongoing tension we will continue to see between privacy and security.[81]

Another area of concern regarding intrusion on criminal due process has surrounded unjustified police killings of civilians. In part because of the visibility of the Black Lives Matter movement (see Chapter 9 for a more detailed discussion) and cell phone videos made public over social media, the public has called for greater police accountability in their use of deadly force. After the police shooting of Michael Brown in Ferguson, Missouri, in 2014, the accompanying protests, and a Department of Justice investigation of local police practices, the arguments for police accountability expanded beyond the Black and Latino communities where they originated and became part of a national discussion. And as activists recorded similar fatalities across the country, a disproportionate pattern of officers killing persons of color was evident. Specifically, the police murders of George Floyd, Breonna Taylor, and Rayshard Brooks in the spring of 2020 led to global protests challenging police violence against people of color and invigorated a national debate regarding racism and the need for policy and budgetary changes in all levels of governments.

In response to such claims of systemic racism and police abuse, police officers in many communities are required to wear body cameras. Moreover, because of federal and state police task forces, beginning in November 2019, federal agents must wear body cameras when collaborating with local officers, easing these cooperative ventures. While these policies have the stated intention of protecting vulnerable populations, no national guidelines exist regarding how the body cameras should be used. Because FRT can increasingly be used on the civilian footage retrieved from these cameras, civil liberties watchdogs are concerned that this recording of civilians (but not of police actions) could simply become a means of government surveillance, absent careful regulations.[82] As this technology becomes integrated into local law enforcement communities, this question becomes increasingly significant: How can we ensure that it improves the quality of policing and relationships with citizens without enabling police to target people of color?

Free Speech on Campus

In light of our very polarized political system, some of the nation's elite public universities struggle with the meaning and requirements of free speech on campus. Student bodies are more ethnically, racially, and socioeconomically diverse than in previous generations, and these student groups seek to have a voice on campus. Universities are pressured to intellectually welcome traditionally marginalized student voices and value their perspectives on campus, a place from which they had historically been excluded. At the same time, a newly empowered conservative movement, particularly those on the alt-right who are galvanized by white supremacy and threatened by a more diverse and multicultural society, are calling for greater visibility on college campuses. Using the First Amendment to protect their speech, they have challenged public universities to allow their voices to be heard. Students of color and their allies feel they can't be silent because the alt-right is an "existential threat" seeking to destroy their very existence.[83]

In March 2019, President Donald Trump signed the "Executive Order on Improving Free Inquiry, Transparency, and Accountability at Colleges and Universities." He was explicit that one of his intents was to "promote free and open debate on college and university campuses." In 2017, Tennessee became the first state to pass related legislation, instructing public universities that it "is not the proper role of an institution to attempt to shield individuals from free speech, including ideas and opinions they find offensive, unwise, immoral, indecent, disagreeable, conservative, liberal, traditional, radical or wrong-headed."[84] Critics have claimed that we do not have a free speech crisis, just a few well-publicized conflicts on a few elite campuses and that partisans are using these high-visibility moments to justify distrust against institutions of higher education.[85]

What should college campuses do? How can they balance (1) the demands for free speech and student exposure to ideas that challenge their perception of the world with (2) the desire to ensure that all student perspectives are heard and valued? Is this an appropriate focus for state legislation? Have you experienced these challenges at your own school? If so, in what fashion?

SCOTUS APPLICATION | *US v. O'BRIEN (1968)*

Public protests against the U.S. war in Vietnam were at a peak in the late 1960s. David O'Brien protested the war by burning his draft card at a Boston courthouse. He was convicted under a federal law that made the destruction of draft cards a crime. O'Brien claimed that the burning of a draft card was symbolic speech and therefore protected under the First Amendment and challenged his conviction. The case, *United States v. O'Brien,* was argued and decided by the U.S. Supreme Court. The question argued was whether the law that convicted O'Brien infringed on protections guaranteed in the U.S. Constitution.

Justice Warren delivered the majority opinion of the Court, holding in favor of the government, stating "a government regulation is sufficiently justified if it is within the constitutional power of the Government; if it furthers an important or substantial government interest…"

A. Identify the constitutional clause that is common to both *U.S. v. O'Brien* and *Tinker v. Des Moines.*

B. Based on the constitutional clause identified in part A, explain why the facts of the *U.S. v. O'Brien* led to a different holding than the holding in *Tinker v. Des Moines.*

C. Describe an action that members of the public-school system who disagree with the holding in *Tinker* could take to limit its impact.

Conclusion: Thinking Critically About What's Next for Civil Liberties

At the core of the U.S. political and legal system lies a strong belief in individual liberties and rights. This belief is reflected in the Bill of Rights, the first 10 amendments to the Constitution. The freedoms therein are at the heart of civic engagement and ensure that individuals can freely participate in the political and social life of their communities. But these freedoms are also malleable, and at times the government has strictly limited them, as when officials perceive a threat to national security.

The inevitable tension between freedom and order is heightened as Americans and their government struggle to protect essential liberties while guarding the nation against future terrorist attacks and internal violence. Debates over enhanced Second Amendment rights in a culture of increasing mass shootings remain unresolved and continue to mobilize groups to protest and campaign. Privacy continues to be a concern of citizens as social media create new services that consumers both demand and desire. Tension between national security and personal freedom is reflected in contemporary debates over the role of journalists in our society.

Meanwhile, governmental mining of private information through warrantless surveillance of social media sites, increased reliance on facial recognition technology and police body cameras, and police violence against people of color raise new questions regarding the limits of liberty. The issues we confront will continue to evolve as we struggle to maintain the commitment to liberty that defines our nation while preserving the country itself.

References

1. For a history of civil liberties in wartime, see Geoffrey R. Stone, *Perilous Times: Free Speech in Wartime From the Sedition Act of 1798 to the War on Terrorism* (New York: W. W. Norton, 2004).

2. *Barron v. Baltimore,* 32 U.S. 243 (1833).

3. See *Hurtado v. California,* 110 U.S. 516 (1884) and *Turning v. New Jersey,* 211 U.S. 78 (1908) for a discussion of the standard the Court uses to determine whether a particular liberty should be incorporated into the Fourteenth Amendment.

4. *Gitlow v. New York,* 268 U.S. 652 (1925).

5. *Near v. Minnesota,* 283 U.S. 697 (1931).

6. *Palko v. Connecticut,* 302 U.S. 319 (1937).

7. For a detailed look at evolution of our constitutional understanding of the Second Amendment, see Michael Waldman, *The Second Amendment: A Biography* (New York: Simon & Schuster, 2014).

8. *District of Columbia v. Heller,* 554 U.S. (2008).

9. *McDonald v. City of Chicago,* 561 U.S. 3025 (2010).

10. F. B. Ahmad and B. Bastian, "Quarterly Provisional Estimates for Selected Indicators of Mortality, 2016–Quarter 4, 2017." National Center for Health Statistics. National Vital Statistics System. 2018.

11. Presidential Proclamation of September 24, 1862, by President Abraham Lincoln, suspending the writ of *habeas corpus.*

12. For two detailed accounts of the acts, see John C. Miller, *Crisis in Freedom: The Alien and Sedition Acts* (Boston: Little, Brown, 1951); and James Morton Smith, *Freedom's Fetters: The Alien and Sedition Laws and American Civil Liberties* (Ithaca, NY: Cornell University Press, 1956).

13. Liz Robbins, Fernando Santos, and Jennifer Medina, "Trump's Immigration Policies Explained," *New York Times*, February 21, 2017 and "President Donald J. Trump Restores Responsibility and the Rule of Law to Immigration," The White House Fact Sheets, September 5, 2017.

14. Garrett Epps, "The Supreme Court's Travel Ban Off-Ramp," *The Atlantic*, December 24, 2017.

15. *Schenck v. United States,* 249 U.S. 47 (1919).

16. *Gitlow v. New York,* 268 U.S. 652 (1925).

17. *Dennis v. U.S.,* 341 U.S. 494 (1951).

18. *Brandenburg v. Ohio,* 395 U.S. 444 (1969).

19. *U.S. v. O'Brien,* 391 U.S. 367 (1968).

20. *Tinker et al. v. Des Moines Independent Community School District et al.,* 393 U.S. 503 (1969).

21. For a discussion of *Tinker* and similar cases, see Jamin B. Baskin, *We the Students: Supreme Court Cases for and About Students,* 3rd ed. (Washington, DC: CQ Press, 2008).

22. *Texas v. Johnson,* 491 U.S. 397 (1989).

23. *U.S. v. Eichman,* 496 U.S. 310 (1990).

24. *Citizens United v. Federal Election Commission,* 558 U.S. 310 (2010).

25. *Miller v. California,* 413 U.S. 15 (1973).

26. *Chaplinsky v. New Hampshire,* 315 U.S. 568 (1942).

27. *Virginia v. Black,* 538 U.S. 343 (2003).

28. *Reno v. ACLU,* 521 U.S. 844 (1997); and *U.S. v. Playboy Entertainment Group,* 529 U.S. 803 (2000).

29. Martin Pengelly and Joanna Walters, "Trump Accused of Encouraging Attacks on Journalists with CNN Body-Slam Tweet," *The Guardian*, July 2, 2017, and Jacey Fortin, "Rough Treatment of Journalists in the Trump Era," *New York Times*, May 25, 2017.

30. *New York Times v. U.S.,* 403 U.S. 713 (1971).

31. Gallup poll, "Religion," www.gallup.com/poll/1690/Religion.aspx.

32. The phrase "wall of separation" first appeared in Thomas Jefferson's 1802 letter to the Danbury Baptist Association. This letter is available at the Library of Congress website: www.loc.gov/loc/lcib/9806/danpre.html.

33. For a discussion of the doctrine of accommodationism, see Kenneth D. Wald, *Religion and Politics in the United States,* 3rd ed. (Washington, DC: CQ Press, 1997). For a discussion of neutrality, see Robert Booth Fowler, Allen D. Hertzke, and Laura R. Olson, *Religion and Politics in America: Faith, Culture, & Strategic Choices,* 2nd ed. (Boulder, CO: Westview Press, 1999).

34. *Everson v. Board of Education,* 330 U.S. 1 (1947).

35. *Lemon v. Kurtzman,* 403 U.S. 602 (1971).

36. *Zelman v. Simmons-Harris,* 539 U.S. 639 (2002).

37. *Engel v. Vitale,* 370 U.S. 421 (1962).

38. *Wisconsin v. Yoder,* 406 U.S. 205 (1972).

39. *Prince v. Massachusetts,* 321 U.S. 158 (1944).

40. See for instance, *Phillips v. City of New York,* 14-2156-CV, 2015 (2nd Circuit); and *Schenker v. County of Tuscarawas,* 5:12 CV 1020, 2012 (E.D., Ohio).

41. *Employment Division, Department of Human Resources of the State of Oregon et al. v. Smith,* 494 U.S. 872 (1990).

42. *Employment Division, Department of Human Resources of the State of Oregon et al. v. Smith,* 494 U.S. 872 (1990).

43. *Griswold v. Connecticut,* 381 U.S. 479 (1965).

44. *Roberts v. U.S. Jaycees,* 468 U.S. 609 (1984).

45. *Roe v. Wade,* 410 U.S. 113 (1973).

46. *Planned Parenthood v. Casey,* 505 U.S. 833 (1992).

47. *Whole Women's Health v. Hellerstedt,* 579 U.S. _____ (2016).

48. *Cruzan v. Director, Missouri Department of Health,* 497 U.S. 261 (1990).

49. Ibid.

50. *Bowers v. Hardwick,* 478 U.S. 186 (1986).

51. *Lawrence v. Texas,* 539 U.S. 558 (2003).

52. *Obergefell v. Hodges,* 576 U.S. _____ (2015).

53. This is a point of agreement among the Court's opinion, the concurring opinion, and the dissenting opinion issued in *Lawrence v. Texas,* 539 U.S. 558 (2003).

54. American Civil Liberties Union, "NSA Documents Released to the Public Since June 2013".

55. Global Government Surveillance Reform, www.reformgovernmentsurveillance.com/.

56. Alfred Ng, "Google Reports All-Time High of Government Data Requests," *C/Net*, September 28, 2017.

57. *Weeks v. U.S.,* 232 U.S. 383 (1914).

58. *Mapp v. Ohio,* 367 U.S. 643 (1961).Page 155

59. See Chief Justice Warren E. Burger's dissent in *Coolidge v. New Hampshire,* 403 U.S. 443, 1971.

60. *Segura v. U.S.,* 468 U.S. 796 (1984).

61. *U.S. v. Leon,* 468 U.S. 897 (1984).

62. *California v. Greenwood,* 486 U.S. 35 (1988).

63. *Grady v. North Carolina,* 575 U.S. 606 (2015).

64. *Grady v. North Carolina,* 575 U.S. 606 (2015).

65. *Gideon v. Wainright,* 312 U.S. 335 (1963).

66. *Furman v. Georgia,* 408 U.S. 238 (1972).

67. *Gregg v. Georgia,* 428 U.S. 153 (1976) was the first of many such cases.

68. *Baze v. Rees,* 553 U.S. 35 (2008).

69. *Wilkerson v. Utah,* 99 U.S. 130 (1878).

70. *Glossip v. Gross,* 576 U.S. 863 (2015).

71. https://brightlinewatch.org/democratic-transgressions-and-constitutional-hardball-bright-line-watch-october-2019-surveys/.

72. Freedom House. 2017. "Freedom of the Press," https://freedomhouse.org /report/freedom-press/freedo-press-2017

73. http://thehill.com/homenews/administration/437610-trump-calls-press-the-enemy-of-the-people April 5, 2019.

74. https://www.factcheck.org/2019/12/another-dubious-trump-attack-on-fake-news/December 12, 2019.

75. https://www.aclu.org/blog/free-speech/freedom-press/government-detaining-and-interrogating-journalists-and-advocates-us March 7, 2019.

76. Center for Democracy and Technology, https://cdt.org/insights/dhs-should-stop-surveilling-activists-journalists-and-lawyers/May 3, 2019.

77. Deputy Assistant Director Kimberly J. Del Greco, "Facial Recognition Technology, "Statement before the House Oversight and Reform Committee" June 4, 2019.

78. Hannah Fry, 2018. *Hello World: Being Human in the Age of Algorithms*. W.W. Norton: 158-173 (electronic).

79. U.S. Department of Commerce. 2019. "Face Recognition Vendor Test (FRVT) Part 3: Demographic Effects." https://nvlpubs.nis .gov/nistpubs/ir/2019/NIST.I .8280.pdf December.

80. Jennifer Valentino-Devries, 2020. "How Police Use Facial Recognition and How it Falls Short," *New York Times*, January 12. https://www.nytimes.com/2020/01/12/technology/facial-recognition-police.html

81. Jason Tashea, 2019. "As facial recognition software becomes more ubiquitous, some governments slam on the brakes," *ABA Journal*. September 24. http://www.abajournal.com/web/article/facial-recog-bans

82. National Institute of Justice, "Research on Body-Worn Cameras and Law Enforcement," December 5, 2017.

83. Steve Kolowich, "Hey, Look Over Here!" *The Chronicle of Higher Education*, November 15, 2017.

84. State of Tennessee, "Campus Free Speech Protection Act." Amends TCA Title 49, Pub. Ch. No. 336. 2017.

85. Lee Bollinger, "Free Speech on Campus Is Doing Just Fine, Thank You,"*The Atlantic*, June 12, 2019; and, Tom Lindsay, "New Report: Most College Students Agree that Campus Free Speech Is Waning," *Forbes*, May 31, 2019.

▌Key Terms

▌ Multiple-Choice Questions

1. The free exercise clause of the First Amendment to the Constitution can be limited when actions
   A. Conflict with long-standing traditions and laws
   B. Advance the religion of one group over another
   C. Create heightened constitutional scrutiny
   D. Prohibit a religious group from forming

2. Which of the following is true about selective incorporation?
   A. It has been a key enumerated component of the Constitution
   B. It incorporates state constitutions to the national government
   C. It requires that the Bill of Rights be applied to the states on a case-by-case basis
   D. It requires that all aspects of the Bill of Rights be applied to the states

3. Which of the following is an accurate comparison of civil rights and civil liberties?

Civil Rights	Civil Liberties
A. Actions the government takes to protect individuals from discrimination	Protect citizens from government interferences
B. Established by the Bill of Rights	Established through law
C. Personal freedoms	Government restrictions
D. The right to free speech and assembly	Voting Rights Act of 1965

Questions 4 and 5 refer to the cartoon below.

THANKYOU FOR CALLING CIVIL LIBERTIES— YOUR CALL MAY BE RECORDED...

Clive Goddard/www.CartoonStock.com

4. Which of the following best describes the message in the political cartoon?
   A. The right to privacy is not protected by the Constitution
   B. Calls may be recorded by the government in order to prevent threats to public safety
   C. Citizens' civil liberties may be abridged by the government if the government can provide a compelling reason
   D. The government should increase funding for surveillance programs

5. Which of the following Supreme Court cases is most relevant to the topic of the cartoon?
   A. *Burwell v. Hobby Lobby*
   B. *Engel v. Vitale*
   C. *New York Times v. Sullivan*
   D. *Roe v. Wade*

Source: Harley Schwadron/CartoonStock

6. Which of the following best describes the message in the political cartoon?

   A. The federal government is making every effort to combat police brutality taking place in response to public protest

   B. The police and the government are aligned, making it difficult to combat police brutality in response to protest

   C. The Constitution allows protesters to speak out against police brutality

   D. The Constitution restrains the power of the police making excessive force unlikely

7. Which of the following constitutional amendments is most relevant to the topic of the cartoon?

   A. First

   B. Third

   C. Fourth

   D. Eighth

8. Which of the following is an accurate comparison of the two court cases?

	Engel v. Vitale	*Wisconsin v. Yoder*
A.	Holding was based on the establishment clause	Holding was based on the free exercise clause
B.	Involved school-aged children whose families removed them from school	Involved school prayer
C.	Involved free exercise of religion for members of the Jehovah's Witnesses church	Decided that state-sponsored prayer in school violated the establishment clause
D.	Allowed more free exercise of religion in public schools	Provided an avenue for schoolchildren to participate in religious-based clubs

9. Which of the following is true about the Eighth Amendment's ban on cruel and unusual punishment?

A. The death penalty has been banned under the Eighth Amendment

B. Interpretations of the death penalty have changed over time

C. Cruel and unusual punishments are banned by the federal government but not banned at the state level

D. Death penalty cases lack the right to a speedy trial

10. Which of the following is the mechanism by which the Supreme Court **selectively incorporated** parts of the Bill of Rights?

A. equal protection clause

B. free exercise clause

C. establishment clause

D. due process clause

▌Free Response Questions

Quantitative Analysis

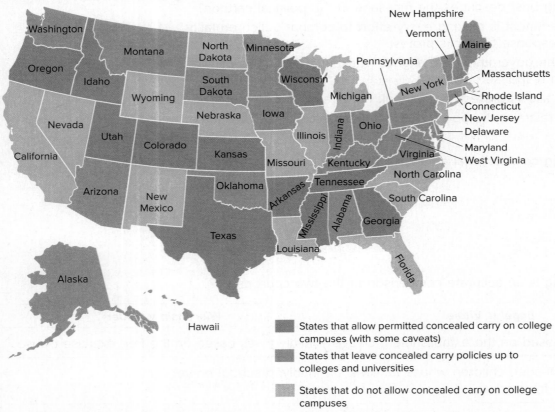

Source: "An Updated List of States That Allow Concealed Guns on Campus." Campus Safety Magazine. February 20, 2020. https://www.campussafetymagazine.com/university/list-of-states-that-allow-concealed-carry-guns-on-campus/

Use the map to answer the questions.

A. Identify the most common type of concealed carry laws on college campuses in the United States.

B. Describe a similarity or difference in concealed carry laws by state or region, as illustrated in the information graphic, and draw a conclusion about that similarity or difference.

C. Explain how concealed carry laws on college campuses as shown in the information graphic demonstrates the principle of federalism.

SCOTUS Comparison

In *The Church of Lukumi Babalu Aye v. City of Hialeah* (1993), congregants of The Church of Lukumi Babalu Aye practiced Santeria, which uses animal sacrifice as a form of worship. The City of Hialeah passed a city ordinance prohibiting possession of animals for sacrifice or slaughter, with specific exemptions for state-licensed activities.

In their ruling, the Supreme Court stated that the city ordinance singled out the activities of the Santeria faith and were neither neutral nor generally applicable. In passing the ordinance, the city of Hialeah targeted religious behavior.

A. Identify the constitutional clause that is common to both *The Church of Lukumi Babalu Aye v. City of Hialeah* (1993) and *Wisconsin v. Yoder* (1972).

B. Based on the constitutional clause identified in part A, explain why the facts of *The Church of Lukumi Babalu Aye v. City of Hialeah* led to the same holding as in *Wisconsin v. Yoder*.

C. Current U.S. law bans bigamy and polygamy despite the fact that it is practiced by some religious groups. Using the ruling from the cases above, explain why these laws have been upheld by the Supreme Court.

Argumentation

Develop an argument in which you decide whether the government is justified in taking actions limiting the freedom of citizens to ensure order.

In your essay, you must:

- Articulate a defensible claim or thesis that responds to the prompt and establishes a line of reasoning.

- Support your claim with at least TWO pieces of accurate and relevant information:

  - At least ONE piece of evidence must be from one of the following foundational documents:

    — The Constitution of the United States (including the Bill of Rights and subsequent amendments)
    — Brutus 1
    — *Federalist* No. 51

- Use a second piece of evidence from another foundational document from the list or from your study of civil liberties

- Use reasoning to explain why your evidence supports your claim/thesis

- Respond to an opposing or alternative perspective using refutation, concession, or rebuttal

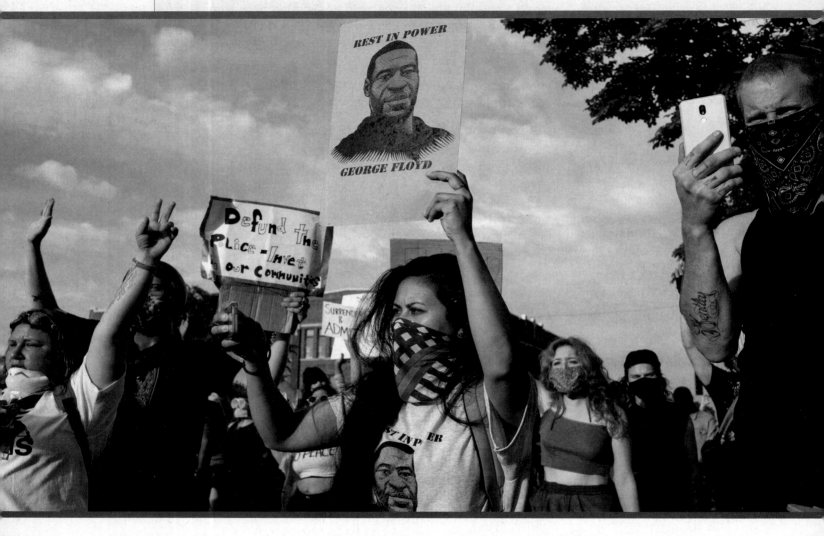

THEN

African Americans, women, Native Americans, Latinos, and other groups struggled to achieve equality in the United States.

NOW

State-sanctioned attempts to control the voting population are being challenged as civil rights violations.

Changing understandings of gender identity and sexual orientation are altering our definition of civil rights.

Communities of color are protesting abuses from law enforcement through the Black Lives Matter movement.

NEXT

What protections will the nation be willing to extend to undocumented immigrants and their children?

What will be the impact of new movements such as "Fat Rights" on our understanding of civil rights?

Should quality, affordable housing and child care be considered civil rights?

Stephen Maturen/Getty Images

■ Chapter Introduction

In Chapter 8, Civil Liberties, you considered how the Bill of Rights is continually being incorporated into government. This chapter on civil rights will further that conversation by examining how laws passed by Congress enforce the Bill of Rights through the federal bureaucracy. You will also delve into how social movements can influence government leaders to further protect citizens through federal legislation.

These three Big Ideas are themes of this chapter:

- Big Idea 1: Constitutionalism: In what ways does the Constitution attempt to limit abuse of government powers?

- Big Idea 3: Civic Participation in a Representative Democracy: How can individuals and groups help protect civil rights?

- Big Idea 4: Competing Policy Making Interests: Why have Supreme Court decisions about civil rights changed over time?

The citizen protections in the Bill of Rights alone did not prove to be enough to provide equality for women of all races and racially marginalized people. Decades after the Fifteenth Amendment was ratified, laws in many southern states prevented African Americans from voting. When you read about the Jim Crow laws, consider why the Fifteenth Amendment alone did not protect the right of African Americans to vote in southern states. In theory, the Constitution is the highest law of the land, but in practice, state legislative power can be a powerful mechanism to prevent the implementation of various aspects of the Constitution. It was not until the national Congress passed the Voting Rights Act of 1965 that the federal government had the power to enforce the Fifteenth Amendment through agencies in the federal bureaucracy. Today there are ongoing concerns that African Americans and others will be barred from voting as states continue to enact laws that make voting more challenging.

This reading will support the following Enduring Understandings:

- The Fourteenth Amendment's equal protection clause as well as other constitutional provisions have often been used to support the advancement of equality.

- Public policy promoting civil rights is influenced by citizen-state interactions and constitutional interpretation over time.

The civil rights movement, the women's movement, the movement to support LGBT rights, as well as the pro-life movement are evidence that citizen mobilization can lead to policy changes. Implementing policy changes can be complicated both by our system of checks and balances and our system of federalism, and this complexity is an example of the competing policy-making interests (PMI) in our government. For example, our system of federalism gives lawmaking powers at two levels: state and federal. In the case of the Jim Crow laws, southern states passed laws making it very difficult for African Americans to vote in spite of the Fifteenth Amendment to the U.S. Constitution, which explicitly granted voting rights to African Americans.

The Supreme Court's interpretation of the Constitution has changed over time in a manner — both to restrict minority rights and to advance minority rights. For example, in the *Plessy v. Ferguson* case, the Supreme Court restricted rights, only to overturn the decision decades later in the case of *Brown v. Board of Education*. While the Constitution did not change, interpretation of the Constitution changed.

In *Plessy*, the Court ruled that laws requiring separate rail cars for Black and white travelers did not violate the equal protection clause of the Constitution. The reasoning by the Court in the *Plessy* case was that so long as conditions were equal, separation of the races did not violate equal protection under the law. In *Brown*, the court ruled that separate schooling for Black and white students was 'inherently' unequal, overturning the line of reasoning and ruling in the *Plessy* case.

civil rights
The rights and privileges guaranteed to all citizens under the equal protection and due process clauses of the Fifth and Fourteenth Amendments; the idea that individuals are protected from discrimination based on characteristics such as race, national origin, religion, and sex.

equal protection clause
Part of the Fourteenth Amendment to the U.S. Constitution guaranteeing protection under the laws of the country.

The Meaning of Equality Under the Law

Although the issue of protecting civil liberties was in the forefront at the nation's founding, as we discussed in Chapter 8, the issue of guaranteeing civil rights reached the national agenda much later.[1] When we talk about **civil rights** in the United States, we mean the rights and privileges guaranteed by the government under the **equal protection** and due process clauses of the Fifth and Fourteenth Amendments and the privileges and immunities clause of the Fourteenth Amendment. These rights are based on the idea that the government should

Fighting for Their Rights: How Groups and Issues Change

THEN	NOW	NEXT
(1960s and 1970s) African Americans, women, Native Americans, Latinos, and the elderly fought for equal treatment under the law.	In addition to the earlier list, Asian citizens, citizens with disabilities, citizens who identify as fat, and lesbian, gay, bisexual, nonbinary, and transgender citizens fight for equal treatment under the law.	▪ What groups will begin to seek ways of achieving their civil rights?
Key strategies included nonviolent civil disobedience, protests, and seeking remedy through the judicial and legislative processes.	Protests, lobbying, and lawsuits remain important strategies, but today's activists also use social media to organize supporters and political theater to bring attention to their causes.	▪ How will emerging technologies change the strategies and tactics that civil rights activists use?
Important issues included equal access to schools, public accommodations, voting rights, and equal pay.	Important issues include rights for nonbinary persons, ensured access to adequate housing and health care, voting rights, and immigration policy.	▪ What issues will be at the forefront of the civil rights agenda in the future?

protect individuals from discrimination that results from inherent characteristics. **Inherent characteristics** are individual characteristics that are part of a person's nature, such as race, religion, national origin, and sex. Some of these rights are extended only to citizens (such as the right to vote), but there is a significant debate around what protections are extended to other individuals.[2]

> **inherent characteristics**
> Individual attributes such as race, national origin, religion, and sex.

The Constitution imposes constraints (civil liberties) and responsibilities (civil rights) on governments, which includes government officials and employees, but *not* on private individuals or organizations. However, governments can write laws that prohibit private individuals and organizations from infringing on civil liberties and civil rights. For example, the national government enacted the Civil Rights Act of 1964, which prohibited private businesses and organizations from discriminating in hiring decisions based on the inherent characteristics of race, color, religion, national origin, and sex.

Most people agree that no government, private individual, or organization should treat people differently because of these inherent characteristics. The courts have determined that treating citizens differently based on their inherent characteristics is unfair, arbitrary, and in most situations illegal. However, people and even government officials, including judges, disagree about whether the list of inherent characteristics should include such factors as age, physical and mental disabilities, and sexual identity. For example, should people whose

>> Historically, people have encountered discrimination because of their ethnicity, race, or gender. In some places, Irish citizens were barred from applying for jobs, African Americans attending theaters were forced to use separate entrances (here with the ironic promise of "good shows in comfort"), and help-wanted ads were segregated based on gender.

Interpret: How do these historical examples of discrimination compare with current types? What kinds of language is used today to indicate discrimination in hiring, housing, or public spaces? How do these changing norms demonstrate the way in which civil rights movements have altered our understanding of equality?

poster: Everett Collection/SuperStock; *theater:* New York Times /Hulton Archive/Getty Images; *newspaper:* History Archives/Alamy Stock Photo gender identity does not match their birth sex have the right to determine their own gender? Within all of these classifications, there are debates over if and when the government should allow differential treatment in order to encourage greater equality.

As we explored in Chapter 8, no civil liberty is absolute; there are situations in which the government may infringe on an individual's liberty. For example, the government may infringe on an individual's freedom of speech if it views her speech as violating the imminent lawless action test (or incitement test)—that is, if the risk of harm from the speech is highly likely and the harm is imminent or immediate. Civil rights are also not absolute. The national courts have established "tests" that the government uses to determine when unequal protection under the law (that is, differential or discriminatory treatment) is legal.

strict scrutiny test
Guidelines the courts use to determine the legality of suspect classification-based discrimination; on the basis of this test, discrimination is legal if it is a necessary means by which the government can achieve a compelling public interest.

heightened scrutiny test (intermediate scrutiny test)
The guidelines used most frequently by the courts to determine the legality of sex-based discrimination; on the basis of this test, sex-based discrimination is legal if the government can prove that it is substantially related to the achievement of an important public interest.

ordinary scrutiny test (rational basis test)
On the basis of this test, sex-based discrimination is legal if it is a reasonable means by which the government can achieve a legitimate public interest.

suspect classifications
Distinctions based on race, religion, and national origin, which are assumed to be illegitimate.

Today, the courts use three tests—**strict scrutiny**, **heightened scrutiny**, and **ordinary scrutiny**—to determine when unequal treatment is legal. Which test the court uses depends on the inherent characteristic that is the basis for differential treatment. For example, courts view race, ethnic origin, and religion to be **suspect classifications**, meaning that judges will assume that the laws treating individuals differently because of these inherent characteristics are unconstitutional and violate the equal protection clauses. When the courts hear a challenge to laws with suspect classifications, they use the *strict scrutiny test*, which requires the government to show that the differential treatment is necessary for it to achieve a compelling public interest for which it is responsible. Using the strict scrutiny test in *Loving v. Virginia* (1967), the Supreme Court determined that laws barring interracial marriage violated the Constitution because there was no compelling public interest for which the government was responsible; hence, the laws were not necessary.[3] Therefore, today it is illegal to deny interracial couples the right to marry.

The courts do not consider the inherent characteristic of sex to be a suspect classification, and therefore laws that allow differential treatment of women and men do not need to pass the strict scrutiny test when challenged. Instead, the courts apply the *heightened scrutiny test* (also known as the *intermediate scrutiny test*) in sex-based discrimination cases, which requires the government to show that the sex-based differential treatment is substantially related to an important public interest for which the government is responsible. The heightened scrutiny test is a weaker test, making it easier for the government to justify sex-based discrimination than discrimination based on race, religion, or ethnic origin. Therefore, today women in the military do not have the same opportunities in combat roles (and hence combat-related benefits) as military men do.

The weakest test the courts use when determining if a law allowing discriminatory treatment is legal is the *ordinary scrutiny test* (also called the *rational basis test*). Using the ordinary scrutiny test, courts require governments to show that the differential treatment is a rational means to achieve a legitimate public interest for which the government is responsible. State governments have established minimum ages for numerous legal rights, such as the right to marry, the right to get a driver's license, and the right to purchase alcoholic beverages. Many states have also established a retirement age (a maximum age) for state judges. These are areas of life where the courts, applying the ordinary scrutiny test, have determined age-based discrimination to be legal. Differential treatment based on age is a reasonable way to achieve some legitimate public interests.

Can you determine what the public interests are in each of these age-based differential treatment situations?

For most of our nation's history, the law not only allowed unequal treatment for different racial, ethnic, and religious groups as well as for men and women but also *required* this unequal treatment for a majority of the population. Women were not granted the right to vote until 1920, and they faced a wide variety of discriminatory practices. Ethnic and religious groups also faced widespread discrimination, some as a matter of law. For example, more than 120,000 people of Japanese ancestry were forcibly interned in camps during World War II. Mainstream America has most recently become aware of the **invidious discrimination** that has been exercised against individuals based on their sexual orientation and identity and against women through sexual harassment and violence.

invidious discrimination
Occurs when a class of people are treated in a manner that is malicious, hostile, or damaging.

A new arena of civil rights activism is developing to protect against weight discrimination in the workplace. Such claims are not covered by the Civil Rights Act of 1964, Title VII, which bars workplace discrimination based on race, ethnicity, sex, or religion. Nor are they covered by the Americans with Disabilities Act, unless weight is directly tied to a specific disability. However, today 40 percent of Americans are classified as obese, based on their body mass index (BMI), and research has consistently demonstrated that experiences of discrimination in the workplace increase with higher weights and that women experience more discrimination than men based on weight.[4] Research has also demonstrated that while bias based on race has decreased in the past decade by 37 percent and on sexuality by 50 percent, negative attitudes based on weight have declined only 15 percent.[5]

In response to the public's concern, San Francisco and Washington, D.C., have passed antidiscrimination laws based on weight or appearance, and Michigan (2014) and Washington State (2019) have such laws on record; Massachusetts is considering similar regulations. But most individuals in the United States are not protected by such statutes. Critics argue that weight is under the control of the individual and therefore falls into a different category than race or gender. They also fear that such protective laws will prevent workplaces from encouraging weight loss to lower insurance premiums or force them to neglect concerns about safety in the workplace. Advocates claim that a focus on healthy behaviors, as opposed to weight management, provides the same benefits for employers without discrimination. They also point to the fact that a higher weight rarely affects job performance but that it does have a clear relationship to lower pay and fewer promotions.[6]

Do you see this issue as similar to civil rights struggles of the past, or is it a new category? Is this something that the federal or state governments should address, or is it a private business matter? What factors should determine if something becomes a civil rights issue?

■ Slavery and Its Aftermath

The most egregious example of civil rights violations in U.S. history is slavery. This practice was protected under the law, and enslaved people were considered to be the property of their owners. When it was first written, the Constitution implicitly endorsed the unequal and discriminatory treatment of African Americans.[7] Some of the most important provisions of the new constitution treated people of African descent as property, allowing states to continue to permit them to be enslaved and to be sold in open markets. Although the movement to abolish slavery was in its early stages in 1787, the year the Constitution was completed, by the early to mid-1800s, it had gained significant momentum in the North, largely because of the activism of various religious and humanitarian groups.[8]

Slavery in the United States

Many African Americans today are the descendants of Africans who were forcibly brought to the New World. In 1619, twenty Africans arrived in Jamestown as *indentured servants*, workers with a fixed term of service. But by the mid-1600s, slavery began to replace indentured servitude.

OPPOSITION TO SLAVERY Some chafed at the hypocrisy of those who sought freedom and equality but kept slaves. Among the first to challenge slavery were former slaves, who staged both peaceful protests and armed insurrections throughout the late 1700s and early 1800s. These activists successfully rallied support in the North for the gradual abolition of slavery by 1804. They argued forcefully against the injustice of the slave system, moving the opponents of slavery to action by their horrifying firsthand accounts of the treatment of slaves. By 1860, many northern states had abolished slavery.

Despite those arguments, the U.S. Congress, wary of the divisiveness caused by the slavery issue, sought to balance the antislavery position of the abolitionist states with the proslavery sentiments of the slaveholding states. One such attempt was the Missouri Compromise, passed by Congress in 1820. The compromise regulated slavery in the newly acquired western territories: Slavery was prohibited north of the 36° 30′ north parallel, except within the state of Missouri.

The abolitionists objected to the efforts of Congress to accommodate the slaveholding states and called for the emancipation of all slaves. Black and white dissenters to slavery were actively engaged in **civil disobedience**, which is nonviolent refusal to comply with laws or government policies that are morally objectionable. Specifically, American Anti-Slavery Society members actively supported the Underground Railroad, a series of safe houses that allowed escaping slaves to flee to the northern states and Canada. But in 1850, the U.S. Congress—in an attempt to stall or prevent the secession, or separation, of southern states from the Union—passed the Fugitive Slave Act. The law required federal marshals to return runaway slaves or risk a $1,000 fine (over $20,000 in today's dollars); private citizens who harbored or abetted runaway slaves could be imprisoned for six months and fined $1,000. Passage of this law meant that "conductors" on the Underground Railroad operated in clear violation of the statute, risking their own livelihoods and property.

civil disobedience
Active, but nonviolent, refusal to comply with laws or governmental policies that are morally objectionable, while accepting the consequences of violating these laws.

THE CIVIL WAR ERA Abolitionists were bolstered in their efforts when Harriet Beecher Stowe's popular book *Uncle Tom's Cabin* was published in 1852. Vividly depicting the harsh reality of slavery in the United States, this work inspired many to actively challenge slavery. By the late 1850s, the widespread distribution of *Uncle Tom's Cabin*, as well as the trial and execution of John Brown, a white abolitionist who tried to ignite a slave insurrection in Harpers Ferry, in what was then Virginia and is now West Virginia, had convinced some northerners that slavery was immoral.

Yet the U.S. Supreme Court ruled otherwise. In 1857, Dred Scott, an African American enslaved by a surgeon in the U.S. Army, sued for his freedom, arguing that because he had lived in both a free state (Illinois) and a free territory (the Wisconsin Territory, now Minnesota), he had become a free man and as such he could not be re-enslaved when he moved to Missouri. The Supreme Court rejected Scott's claim and in *Dred Scott v. Sandford* ruled that the Missouri Compromise of 1820 was unconstitutional because the U.S. Congress lacked the authority to ban slavery in the territories.[9] It also ruled that Scott was not a U.S. citizen, asserting that because of their race, African Americans were not citizens with **standing to sue**, or the legal right to bring lawsuits in court. Although the *Dred Scott* decision appeared to be a victory for slaveholding states, it was also pivotal in mobilizing the abolitionist movement and swaying public opinion in favor of a war to prevent secession.

standing to sue
The legal right to bring lawsuits in court.

Certain that their way of life was under siege and alarmed by the election of Abraham Lincoln as president in 1860, southern states decided that they should secede from the Union. By May 1861, eleven southern states had declared their independence and created the Confederate States of America. A long and bloody civil war followed as the North fought to bring the southern states back into the Union.

An important turning point of the Civil War was the Emancipation Proclamation, issued by Abraham Lincoln in April 1862. This order abolished slavery in the states that had seceded from the Union. The Union army and navy were charged with implementing the order. The proclamation had several purposes: It decreed that the abolition of slavery was a goal of the war, and by doing so it effectively prevented Britain and France from intervening in the war on the southern side, because those countries had both renounced the institution of slavery. When the South finally surrendered in April 1865, it did so knowing that its economic way of life, which depended on slave-based plantation farming, was over. At the end of the war, nearly 4 million slaves in the United States were freed. The states then ratified three constitutional amendments to codify the victories won on the battlefield:

- Thirteenth Amendment (1865), which ended slavery throughout the United States and prohibited it in the future.

- Fourteenth Amendment (1868), which defines *citizens* as "all persons born or naturalized in the United States" and mandates the same privileges and immunities for all citizens and due process and equal protection for all people, overturning the *Dred Scott* decision.

- Fifteenth Amendment (1870), which decrees that every man has the right to vote, regardless of color.

Reconstruction and the First Civil Rights Acts

After the North won the war and Lincoln was assassinated in April 1865, members of Congress and others in government disagreed about the best way to proceed in the South. Many Republicans thought that the South should be stabilized and quickly brought back into the political fold. Like Lincoln, these moderates endorsed a plan that would enable the southern states to be quickly represented in Congress. Others, however, took a more radical view and argued that all those who had ever supported the Confederacy should be kept out of national and state politics. As the 1860s drew to a close, many of these more radical Republicans had come to power and had strictly limited the people in southern states who could participate in politics. As a result of their activities, during the **Reconstruction era** between 1866 and 1877—when the institutions and the infrastructure of the South were rebuilt—freed slaves, who could easily say they had never supported the Confederacy, made up a sizable portion of both the electorate and the candidate pool in the southern states. Federal troops provided protection that facilitated their participation. During this decade, African American voters made the most of their position in the South and elected a substantial number of other African Americans to legislative offices in the local, state, and federal governments. In some places, such as South Carolina, African American legislators outnumbered whites, giving them a majority during the Reconstruction years.

Between 1865 and 1875, Congress passed a series of laws designed to solidify the rights and protections outlined in the Thirteenth, Fourteenth, and Fifteenth Amendments. Congress needed to spell out the rights of African Americans because of the pervasiveness of **Black Codes**, laws passed immediately after the Civil War by the former Confederate states that limited the rights of "freemen," or those formerly enslaved. These codes prevented freemen from voting, owning property, or bringing suit. To remedy that situation, Congress passed laws that sought to negate the Black Codes. One law, the Civil Rights Act of 1866, extended the definition of *citizen* to anyone born in the United States (including freemen) and granted all citizens the right to sue, own property, bear witness in a court of law, and enter into legal contracts. The Enforcement Act of 1870 bolstered the Fifteenth Amendment by establishing penalties for interfering with the right to vote. The Civil Rights Act of 1872, also known as the Anti–Ku Klux Klan Act, made it a federal crime to deprive individuals of their rights, privileges, or immunities protected by the Constitution. Although the Reconstruction-era Congress sought to remedy the new forms of inequality that emerged after the Civil War, its efforts would be short-lived.

Backlash: Jim Crow Laws

In 1877, the inauguration of President Rutherford Hayes (1877–1881) brought the Reconstruction era to a decisive end, almost immediately rolling back the gains African Americans had achieved in education and political participation. Under Hayes, the federal troops that had protected African Americans from physical reprisals were withdrawn. State and local governments throughout the South mandated racial segregation by enacting what came to be known as **Jim Crow laws**. These laws required the strict separation of racial groups, with whites and "nonwhites" going to separate schools, being employed in different jobs, and using segregated public accommodations, such as transportation and restaurants. **De jure segregation**, legally mandated separation of the races, became the norm in much of the South. The North, on the other hand, manifested **de facto segregation** in employment and housing, resulting in educational segregation.

The idea behind the Jim Crow laws was that whites and nonwhites should occupy separate societies and have little to do with each other. Many whites

Reconstruction era
The time after the Civil War between 1866 and 1877 when the institutions and infrastructure of the South were rebuilt.

Black Codes
Laws passed immediately after the Civil War by the former Confederate states that limited the rights of "freemen" (people formerly enslaved).

Jim Crow laws
Laws requiring the strict separation of racial groups, with whites and "nonwhites" required to attend separate schools, work in different jobs, and use segregated public accommodations, such as transportation and restaurants.

de jure segregation
Segregation mandated by law.

de facto segregation
Segregation maintained by practice

feared that racial mixing would result in interracial dating and marriage, which would inevitably lead to the decline of their superior position in society; thus in many southern states, miscegenation laws, which banned interracial marriage, cohabitation, or sex, were passed and severe penalties imposed for those who violated them.

State and local governments in the South also found creative ways to prevent African Americans from exercising their right to vote. They relied on several tactics:

- The **white primary** was a primary election in which only white people were allowed to vote. Because Democrats dominated politics so heavily in the post–Civil War South, the only races that really mattered were the primary races that determined the Democratic nominees. But southern states restricted voting in these primaries to whites only.

- The **literacy test** determined eligibility to vote. Literacy tests were designed so that few voters would stand a chance of passing the exam administered to African American voters, whereas the test for white voters was easy to pass. Typically, white voters were exempt from literacy tests because of a grandfather clause. (Slaves had been barred from learning to read and write.)

- A **poll tax**, a fee levied for voting, often presented an insurmountable obstacle to poor African Americans. White voters were often exempt from poll taxes because of a grandfather clause.

- The **grandfather clause** exempted individuals from conditions on voting (such as poll taxes or literacy tests) if they or their ancestors had been eligible to vote before 1870. Because African Americans did not have the right to vote in southern states before the Civil War, the grandfather clause was a mechanism to protect the voting rights of whites.

white primary
A primary election in which a party's nominees for general election were chosen but in which only white people were allowed to vote.

literacy test
A test to determine eligibility to vote; designed so that few African Americans would pass.

poll tax
A fee for voting; levied to prevent poor African Americans in the South from voting.

grandfather clause
A clause exempting individuals from voting conditions such as poll taxes or literacy tests if they or their ancestors had voted before 1870, thus sparing most white voters.

These laws were enforced not only by government agents, particularly police, but by nongovernmental groups as well. Among the most powerful was the Ku Klux Klan (KKK). During the late 1800s and into the 1900s, the Klan was dreaded and hated throughout the southern states, and in some northern states. It used violence to threaten and intimidate those African Americans and whites who dared to question its core principle: that whites are in every way superior to African Americans. The Klan's brand of intimidation, the burning cross and the lynching noose, was reviled throughout the southern and border states, but few could dispute the power of the Klan there.

Governmental Acceptance of Discrimination

The federal government too had seemingly abandoned African Americans and the quest for equality under the law. In the *Civil Rights Cases* of 1883, the Supreme Court ruled that Congress lacked the authority to prevent discrimination by private individuals and organizations. Rather, Congress's jurisdiction, the Court claimed, was limited to banning discrimination in official acts of state or local governments. The Court also declared that the Civil Rights Act of 1875, which had sought to mandate "full and equal enjoyment" of a wide variety of facilities and accommodations, was unconstitutional.

In 1896, the Court struck what seemed to be the final blow against racial equality. In 1890, Louisiana passed a law that required separate accommodations for Black and white travelers on railroad trains. Several citizens of New Orleans sought to test the constitutionality of the law and enlisted Homer Plessy, who was one-eighth African American (but still considered "Black" by Louisiana state law) to serve as plaintiff. The choice of Plessy, who could pass for white, was intended to show the arbitrary nature of the statute. On June 7, 1892, Plessy boarded a railroad car designated for whites only. Plessy was asked to leave the whites-only car, and he refused. He was then arrested and jailed, charged with violating the state law. In 1896, the U.S. Supreme Court heard **Plessy v. Ferguson,** in which Plessy's attorneys argued that the Louisiana state law violated the *equal protection clause* of the Fourteenth Amendment, which states that no state shall "deny to any person within its jurisdiction the equal protection of the laws."

Plessy v. Ferguson
1896 Supreme Court ruling creating the separate but equal doctrine.

In a 7–1 decision, the Court rejected Plessy's arguments, claiming that segregation based on race was not a violation of the equal protection clause. Rather, the Court made this argument:

We consider the underlying fallacy of the plaintiff's argument to consist in the assumption that the enforced separation of the two races stamps the colored race with a badge of inferiority. If this be so, it is not by reason of anything found in the act, but solely because the colored race chooses to put that construction upon it.[10]

separate but equal doctrine
Established by the Supreme Court in *Plessy v. Ferguson*, it said that separate but equal facilities for whites and nonwhites do not violate the Fourteenth Amendment's equal protection clause.

In its decision, the Court created the **separate but equal doctrine**, declaring that separate but equal facilities do not violate the Fourteenth Amendment's equal protection clause. Under this doctrine, the Court upheld state laws mandating separation of the races in schools and all public accommodations such as businesses, public transportation, restaurants, hotels, swimming pools, and recreational facilities. The only condition the Court placed on these segregated facilities was that the state had to provide public facilities for both whites and nonwhites. The Court paid little attention to whether the school systems or public accommodations were comparable in quality. As long as the state had some kind of facilities in place for both whites and nonwhites, the segregation was permitted. This doctrine would become the legal backbone of segregationist policies for more than five decades to come.

Governmental Enforcement of Discrimination

The role of federal, state, and local governments in maintaining segregation extended far beyond the South. Richard Rothstein's 2017 book, *The Color of Law*, carefully documents how the government at all levels and in all regions of the country required and enforced housing discrimination from 1940 to 1970.[11] To begin with, the Federal Housing Administration prohibited African American (and in some regions of the country, Hispanic) families from buying homes in new subdivisions and in suburbs—ensuring they would never gain equity or accumulate the wealth of white families. Also, the government designated certain neighborhoods as white and only made or insured loans that kept Black homeowners in Black neighborhoods. This practice was known as **redlining**, after the color these neighborhoods were designated on maps. These practices were only deemed illegal after the 1968 Fair Housing Act, but enforcement continues to be a problem today.[12] Other scholars have demonstrated how discriminatory federal policies and the local distribution of resources kept African American families from accessing veterans' benefits, Social Security, and other governmental programs that benefited most white families.[13]

redlining
An illegal practice in which banks or insurance companies refuse or limit loans, mortgages, or insurance within specific geographic areas, often inner-city neighborhoods.

SCOTUS COMPARISON — *PLESSY V. FERGUSON* (1896)

The Supreme Court has at times allowed the restriction of the civil rights of minority groups and at other times has protected those rights (AP U.S. Government Learning Objective). In the *Plessy v. Ferguson* case, the Supreme Court ruled that separate facilities for blacks and whites did not necessarily violate the equal protection clause of the Constitution, reasoning that so long as the separate facilities were equal, blacks and whites could be separated under the Constitution. Justice Harlan dissented in the *Plessy* case, arguing that segregation violated the Fourteenth Amendment because the law sanctioned inequality between the races. Later, in the *Brown v. Board of Education* case, Harlan's dissent became the basis for the majority opinion in *Brown*. In the *Brown* case, Chief Justice Warren writing for the majority argued, " . . . we conclude that in the field of public education the doctrine of 'separate but equal' has no place. Separate educational facilities are inherently unequal."

Brown v. Board of Education was a watershed case in American history because it affected how millions of schoolchildren would be educated. Decades after *Brown,* the debate over how to advance the rights of minorities ensued. One example of this ongoing debate is a policy called **affirmative action**. In simple terms, affirmative action is a policy which promotes, supports or favors a group that is traditionally underrepresented in society. Affirmative action policies have been implemented by colleges and universities as well as by the federal government. Affirmative action policies are controversial in part because there are limited spaces for admission to any college, and affirmative action can give minorities an advantage. The debate on affirmative action includes justices who insist that the Constitution is colorblind and those who maintain that it forbids only racial classifications designed to harm minorities, not help them (AP U.S. Government Essential Knowledge).

The University of Michigan considers a number of factors when admitting students, including grades, test scores, alumni relationships, and underrepresented minorities. Beginning in 1998, the university began using a point system in which students were awarded an extra two points for being a member of an underrepresented minority.

Two students (Jennifer Gratz and Patrick Mamacher) applied to the university; both were of Caucasian descent, and both were denied admission. The students argued that the admission procedure discriminated against certain racial and ethnic groups and violated the Fourteenth Amendment and the Civil Rights Act. The question before the Supreme Court was, *Did the University of Michigan's use of racial preferences in undergraduate admission violate the equal protection clause of the Fourteenth Amendment and the Civil Rights Act of 1964?* The Supreme Court ruled that the university policy did violate the law.

A. Identify the constitutional clause that is common to both *Gratz v. Bollinger* and *Brown v. Board of Education.*

B. Based on the constitutional clause identified in part A, explain how the facts of *Gratz v. Bollinger* led to a different outcome than the holding in *Brown v. Board of Education.*

C. Describe an action members of the public who disagree with the holding in *Gratz* could take to limit its impact.

Source: https://www.oyez.org/cases/1979/76-811

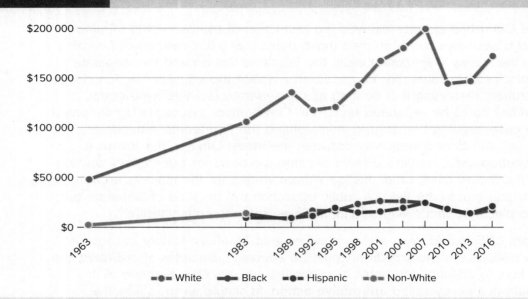

FIGURE 9.1 ▪ **Median Family Wealth by Race/Ethnicity, 1963–2016** In looking at the graph, consider how these long-term differences in wealth might result from race-based federal policy in the areas of housing, veterans benefits, Social Security, and other federal benefits. What kind of policy interventions could change this trend over time? What obligation, if any, do you believe the federal government has to disrupt this trend? Which elements of your political ideology explains your response to the questions above?

Notes: 2016 dollars. No comparable data are available between 1963 and 1983. Black/Hispanic distinction within nonwhite population available only in 1983 and later. For more, visit http://urbn.is/wealthcharts

Sources: Urban Institute calculations from Survey of Financial Characteristics of Consumers 1962 (December 31); Survey of Changes in Family Finances 1963; and Survey of Consumer Finances 1983–2016.

One consequence of this history is that many African American and Latino families missed the opportunity to move into the middle class and accumulate wealth, unlike many white families in the mid-twentieth century (see Figure 9.1).[14]

▪ The Modern Civil Rights Movement

In the early decades of the 20th century, African Americans continued their struggle for equal protection of the laws. Though the movement enjoyed some early successes, the century was nearly half over before momentous victories by civil rights activists finally began to change the status of African Americans in revolutionary ways. These victories were the result of strong leadership at the helm of the movement, the effective strategies used by activists, and new national media.

Fighting Back: Early Civil Rights Organizations

In the early years of the 20th century, the political climate was open to reform, with activists in the Progressive and Black Women's Club movements calling for an end to government corruption, reforms to labor laws, and an expansion of rights, including the right of women to vote and the civil rights of African Americans (see Chapter 15 for more on the Progressive movement). In 1909, W. E. B. Du Bois (an influential African American writer and scholar, who is today acknowledged as a father of social science) joined many other prominent African American and white male and female activists to form the National Association for the Advancement of Colored People (NAACP). One of the targets of the NAACP for the next several decades was the separate but equal doctrine, which remained in place.

Citing the lack of graduate and professional schools for African Americans, the NAACP argued that the states had violated the equal protection clause by failing to make such schools available to African Americans. During the 1930s, lawsuits brought by the NAACP in several states ended discriminatory admissions practices in professional schools.[15] Momentum in the movement for equality continued to grow, fueled in part by the growing political activism of African American soldiers returning home after fighting against fascism abroad during World War II. Many of these soldiers began to question why they were denied freedom and equality in their own country, and they mobilized for civil rights in their communities. Although the U.S. Supreme Court had not yet overturned the separate but equal doctrine, by 1950 it had ruled that segregating classrooms, dining rooms, or library facilities in higher education was unconstitutional.

Taking cues from those court decisions, by the 1950s the NAACP and other groups had changed their tactics. Instead of arguing that states had to provide equivalent education for African Americans and whites, these groups began to argue that segregation itself was a violation of the equal protection clause. But it was not until 1954 that the U.S. Supreme Court struck down the separate but equal doctrine, finding it inherently unequal and unconstitutional under the Fourteenth Amendment.

The End of Separate but Equal

In the fall of 1951, Oliver Brown, a welder at the Santa Fe Railroad yard in Topeka, Kansas, sought to have his daughter Linda enrolled in the third grade in an all-white public school seven blocks from their home. The act was not accidental; it was a calculated step in an NAACP legal strategy that would result in sweeping changes to the nation's public school system, effectively shattering the segregated school system dominant in the South.[16] The Browns lived in an integrated neighborhood in Topeka, and Topeka schools were segregated, as allowed (but not required) under Kansas state law. The Topeka NAACP persuaded them to join a lawsuit against the Topeka Board of Education. Brown agreed and was directed to attempt to register Linda at the all-white public school. Linda was denied admission.

Thurgood Marshall, who later became the first African American to sit on the U.S. Supreme Court, argued the case, and in a unanimous decision in 1954 the Supreme Court ruled in **Brown v. Board of Education of Topeka** that segregated schools violate the equal protection clause of the Fourteenth Amendment.[17] In one stroke, the Court concluded that "separate but equal"

Brown v. Board of Education of Topeka
This 1954 Supreme Court decision ruled that segregated schools violated the equal protection clause of the Fourteenth Amendment.

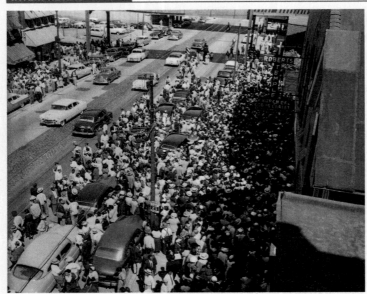

>> The 1955 Chicago funeral of Emmett Till, a teenager who was tortured and killed in Mississippi, attracted national attention. His mother insisted on an open casket funeral because she "wanted the whole world to see" what racism had done to her son.

Interpret: What can you learn from a photo like this? How do photos portraying grief or mourning impact public perception? Why might the national media attention on this murder have mobilized a generation of young people to push for radical social change in the 1960s? What are similar images that have contributed to more recent civil rights movements?

Bettmann/Getty Images

schools were inherently unequal, because they stamped African American children with a "badge of racial inferiority" that stayed with them throughout their lives.

The Movement Gains National Visibility

Civil rights activists were buoyed by the *Brown* decision, but white supremacists were mobilized.[18] In 1955, a 14-year-old African American Chicago teen who was visiting his uncle in Mississippi was kidnapped, tortured, and killed because a white female shopkeeper claimed he made offensive comments to her.[19] His mother ensured the nation saw his mutilated corpse by allowing a photograph to run in *Jet* magazine. His white killers, who later confessed in another national magazine, *Life*, were quickly acquitted.

Although African Americans had boycotted segregated public transportation throughout the South since the late 19th century, it would not be until 1955 that this protest would help to spark a national movement. In Montgomery, Alabama, and throughout the South, buses were segregated, with white riders boarding in the front and sitting front to back and African American riders sitting in the rear of the bus.[20] In December, Rosa Parks was on a bus returning home from work. The bus driver asked the 43-year-old African American woman to give up her seat for a white man; Parks refused and was arrested for violating a local segregation law.

The Montgomery chapter of the NAACP, of which Parks was a leader, had sought a test case to challenge the constitutionality of the state's Jim Crow laws. Parks agreed to participate in the case, and her arrest came at a pivotal time in the civil rights movement. Momentum favored the civil rights activists in the South, and their cause was bolstered when civil rights and religious leaders in Montgomery chose a 27-year-old minister, named Martin Luther

King, Jr., to lead a bus boycott to protest Parks's arrest and segregated public facilities.[21]

Local Organizing and Civil Disobedience Strategies

The year-long bus boycott garnered national media attention, and King became a national symbol for the civil rights movement. King's leadership skills were put to the test during the battle: He was arrested. His home was bombed. Death threats were made against him. But for 381 days, the buses of Montgomery remained virtually empty, representing a serious loss in revenue to the city and causing the NAACP to be banned in the state of Alabama. Finally, in December 1956, the U.S. Supreme Court ruled that segregated buses were unconstitutional.[22] The bus boycott was a success on many fronts: its justness was confirmed by the Supreme Court, the protests garnered national media attention and evoked public sympathy, and the civil rights movement had gained a powerful leader who was capable of unifying and motivating masses. King advocated protesting government-sanctioned discrimination through civil disobedience, peaceful boycotts, and marches. African American students, as well as white students and national civil rights activists, adopted these tactics to challenge the policies of segregation.

Other groups, including the Student Non-violent Coordinating Committee (SNCC) and the Congress of Racial Equality (CORE), advocated the use of more direct action nonviolent strategies—voter registration drives and sit-ins—in the most violent of the southern states, Mississippi and Georgia. In 1961, SNCC and CORE joined the NAACP and Martin Luther King's Southern Christian Leadership Conference (SCLC) under the umbrella organization of COFO (Coalition of Federated Organizations) to focus on common goals. SNCC, CORE, and the NAACP emphasized building leadership skills of local African American citizens in southern communities based on the groundwork laid by WWII veterans. Emphasizing voter registration and education, one of COFO's most nationally visible endeavors was the 1964 Summer Project in which northern college students came down to work with local communities in Freedom Schools and voter registration drives. One outcome of this work was the establishment of the racially integrated Mississippi Freedom Democratic Party at the 1964 Democratic National Convention, which forced presidential candidate Lyndon Johnson and the Democratic Party to refuse to seat future all-white delegations (see "Source Analysis: Analyzing Visual Sources").[23]

Besides political protest, activists from all these groups engaged in mass marches to draw public attention to their challenge to Jim Crow segregation and racial inequality. The violence in such places as Birmingham and Montgomery (Alabama), Jackson (Mississippi), and Albany (Georgia) televised on the evening news kept white America aware of the aims of the protesters. One famous series of marches occurred in early March 1965 from Selma to Montgomery, Alabama. On Sunday, March 7, about 600 civil rights activists began a march out of Selma, protesting the policies of intimidation and violence that prevented African Americans from registering to vote. The demonstrators walked only six blocks to the Edmund Pettus bridge, where law enforcement officials were waiting.[24] When the protesters peacefully attempted to cross the bridge, law enforcement officers brutally attacked them, using tear gas, bull whips, and nightsticks. Dubbed "Bloody Sunday," the march and the beatings were televised nationally and were

Bettmann/Getty Images

A Famous Image from the Civil Rights Era

In this photograph, Fannie Lou Hamer, a former sharecropper from Mississippi who became an activist with the Student Non-violent Coordinating Committee, testifies before the Democratic National Convention (DNC) held in Atlantic City in 1964. Local Mississippians and civil rights activists joined together in the interracial Mississippi Freedom Democratic Party (MFDP) to challenge the all-white Democratic Party in Mississippi. Mrs. Hamer told the nation of her attempts to register to vote and how, as a result, she and other women were severely beaten in a Winona, Mississippi, jail, and she was thrown off the plantation where she and her husband worked. She asked that the MFDP be seated and that the all-white Mississippi delegation be sent home. President Lyndon Johnson, who was running for reelection, offered to seat two of the MFDP delegates and determined that beginning in 1968 all national convention state delegations had to reflect the demographics of their state, including race, gender, and age. In 1972, the Republican Party made the same ruling.

Practice Analytical Thinking

1. What makes this picture unusual in terms of how we see official governmental actions? Would most Americans have heard stories like Mrs. Hamer's from the people who experienced them? What does this tell us about the power of the media to change democratic society?

2. In 1964, there were only three television networks, so when a national event like the DNC aired, all stations would cover it. Mrs. Hamer spoke during prime evening hours when the viewing audience was the largest. President Johnson attempted to interrupt it with a national address of his own. Why do you think this testimony had such an important impact?

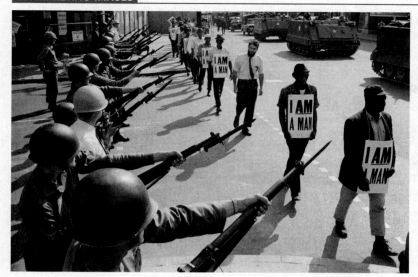

>> African American sanitation workers in Memphis, Tennessee, went on strike in 1968 to protest against dangerous working conditions and for better pay. They organized under the slogan "I Am a Man." Martin Luther King Jr. was in Memphis supporting the strike as part of his Poor People's Campaign when he was assassinated.

Interpret: What stands out to you about this photograph? How does the claim of "I Am a Man" resonate with the promises of our founding documents?

Bettmann/Getty Images

instrumental in swaying public opinion in favor of civil rights. The marches sparked a renewed focus on the lack of voting rights for African Americans and ultimately helped to pressure Congress to pass the Voting Rights Act in 1965.[25]

Although the violence used against protesters generated positive opinions of the civil rights movement, another form of violence, urban rebellions, eroded feelings of white goodwill. For five days in 1965, rioting in the Watts neighborhood of Los Angeles resulted in 34 deaths, more than 1,000 injuries, and over 4,000 arrests. Although the immediate cause of the violence was an altercation between white police officers and an African American man who had been arrested for drunk driving, the frustration and anger that spilled over had long been brewing in this poor, predominantly African American neighborhood.

On April 4, 1968, Martin Luther King, Jr., was in Memphis, Tennessee, in support of African American sanitation workers who were striking for equal treatment and pay with white workers. Standing on a balcony at the Lorraine Motel, King was killed by an assassin's bullet. Heartbreak, hopelessness, and despair followed King's assassination—a feeling manifested in part by further rioting in over 100 cities. Many Americans, both Black and white, objected to the looting depicted in nightly news broadcasts. But some noted that because of the accumulated injustices against African Americans, the government and the rule of law had lost legitimacy in the eyes of those who were rioting.[26]

The Government's Response to the Civil Rights Movement

The civil rights movement is credited not only with ending segregation in public schools but also with the desegregation of public accommodations such as buses, restaurants, and hotels and with promoting universal suffrage. As a result of the movement, Congress passed the 1965 Voting Rights Act, which aggressively sought to counter nearly 100 years of disenfranchisement, as well as the 1964 Civil Rights Act, which bars racial discrimination in accommodations and private employment, and the 1968 Civil Rights Act, which prohibits racial discrimination in housing.

The Civil Rights Act of 1964

Simultaneously expanding the rights of many Americans and providing them with important protections from discrimination based on race, sex, religion, or ethnicity, the Civil Rights Act of 1964 includes provisions that mandate equality on numerous fronts. The law requires equality in public accommodations, including hotels, restaurants, and theaters, as well as in employment and access to public facilities. It bars government agencies from discriminating and allows the federal government to sue to desegregate public schools. The last part of the act, Title VII, which establishes the equality standard in employment opportunity, provides the legal foundation for a body of law that regulates fair employment practices. Specifically, Title VII bans discrimination in employment based on inherent characteristics—race, national origin, religion, and sex. Title VII also established the Equal Employment Opportunity Commission (EEOC), a government body that still administers Title VII today.

The Voting Rights Act of 1965

Many civil rights leaders believed that legislation beyond the Civil Rights Act was necessary to protect the voting rights of African Americans in the South because they had been so systematically intimidated and prevented from participating.[27] In some southern counties, less than a third of all eligible African Americans were registered to vote, whereas nearly two-thirds of eligible white voters were registered in the same counties.

During the summer of 1964, thousands of civil rights activists, including many college students, worked to register Black voters in southern states where Black voter registration was dismal. Within months, a quarter of a million new voters had registered. However, because of violent attacks on civil rights activists and citizens, including the murders of activists in Mississippi in the summer of 1964, Congress determined that it needed to enact a federal law to eliminate discriminatory local and state government registration and voting practices.

The Voting Rights Act of 1965 (VRA) banned voter registration practices such as literacy tests. Moreover, if a county wanted to implement any law that would impact voting procedures—for example, by redrawing districts—and less than 50 percent of that county's eligible voters were registered, the VRA required the county to get approval from the Justice Department. In 2013, the Supreme Court in *Shelby County v. Alabama* found this portion of the law to be unconstitutional. Disagreement on the Court, and in the nation as a whole, centered around whether racial minorities continue to confront barriers to exercising the ballot in states with a history of racial animus.[28]

Impact of the Civil Rights Movement

The culmination of many acts of resistance by individuals and groups, the civil rights movement has had a momentous impact on society by working for the

Letter from Birmingham Jail

Martin Luther King, Jr., wrote *Letter from Birmingham Jail* from a jail cell in Birmingham, Alabama, after he and others were arrested for protesting peacefully. At the time, Birmingham was one of the most segregated cities and there was a ban on protesting.

After King's arrest, a letter was published in a local newspaper article entitled, "White Clergymen Urge Local Negros to Withdraw from Demonstrations" in which King and others were encouraged to slow down their efforts, to wait and end the strategy of civil disobedience. Ironically, the clergy who authored the letter in the newspaper were supporters of King's cause, but expressed disagreement with the strategy, arguing that segregation should be resolved through government actions rather than protest. Here are excerpts from King's letter. In the first excerpt, King responds to the calls by white clergymen in the newspaper to wait.

> ". . . [W]hen you have seen vicious mobs lynch your mothers and fathers at will and drown your sisters and brothers at whim; when you have seen hate-filled policemen curse, kick, brutalize, and even kill your black brothers and sisters with impunity; when you see the vast majority of your twenty million Negro brothers smothering in an airtight cage of poverty in the midst of an affluent society; when you suddenly find your tongue twisted and your speech stammering as you seek to explain to your six-year-old daughter why she cannot go to the public amusement park . . . when you are humiliated day in and day out . . . then you will understand why we find it difficult to wait."

King argued that "injustice anywhere is injustice everywhere" and that "A just law is a manmade code that squares with the moral law or the law of God. An unjust law is a code that is out of harmony with the natural law." In other words, individuals have the right to break laws that are unjust, so long as they are peaceful.

King argued that a primary obstacle to overcoming segregation and racism was not just the racists, but those who sympathized with the civil rights cause but took no actions. King wrote, "I have reached the regrettable conclusion that the Negro's great stumbling block in the stride toward freedom is not the White Citizens Councillor or the Ku Klux Klanner, but the white moderate who is more devoted to 'order' than justice . . . "

The *Letter from Birmingham Jail* became the inspiration for the Civil Rights Act of 1964 and the Voting Rights Act of 1965, and the ideas in the letter inspire those seeking greater justice through peaceful protest.

Note: *The Letter from Birmingham Jail is a required foundational document in the AP U.S. Government & Politics course; AP students should read and annotate the article in its entirety to prepare for the AP exam.*

Critical Thinking Questions:

1. How does *Letter from Birmingham Jail* draw on the ideas of John Locke?

2. How does King seek to change the conversation from a focus on law and order to a focus on justice?

3. In what circumstances (if any) is it acceptable for individuals to break a law?

laws and rulings that bar discrimination in employment, public accommodations, education, and housing. The movement has also had a profound impact on voting rights by establishing the principle that the laws governing voter registration and participation should ensure that individuals are permitted to vote regardless of their race. As a result of the Voting Rights Act, in Mississippi, for example, the percentage of African Americans registered to vote jumped from 7 percent in 1965 to 72 percent in 2006, up to 90 percent in 2012 and down to 77.9 percent in 2018. Today, in some states, including Georgia, Mississippi, and South Carolina, a greater percentage of African Americans are registered than whites. In addition, all states, especially those in the South, have seen an increase in the number of African Americans elected to serve in offices at the state, county, and municipal levels and in school districts. Indeed, more African Americans serve in local elective office in Mississippi than in any other state, and all southern states are among those with the highest numbers of African American local elected officials. Despite these advances in representation, Mississippi has not elected an African American official to a statewide office since Reconstruction.

In addition to having a profound effect on race relations and civil rights law, the civil rights movement soon came to be regarded by other groups as a model of political engagement. Women, ethnic minorities, and persons with disabilities have adopted many tactics of the movement in their own quest to secure their civil rights.

■ Black Lives Matter

The killing of Michael Brown, an unarmed Black 18-year-old, by Darren Wilson, a white police officer in Ferguson, Missouri, initiated the Black Lives Matter movement in Fall 2014. Following reports that Brown was holding his hands over his head when he was shot, "Hands Up, Don't Shoot" became a cry of advocates who gathered in Ferguson to protest the killing of Black people, particularly by representatives of the state such as law enforcement. While such violence has been an ongoing reality for the African American community, a new challenge to this state-sanctioned violence emerged around Ferguson.

While subsequent investigations by the Department of Justice (DOJ) found Wilson's shooting of Brown justified, it also found continuous violations of the rights of Black citizens in Ferguson by the local police. The report from the DOJ demonstrated various ways the local government had systematically oppressed its African American citizenry—through excessive and compounding fines, racist attitudes, bias in law enforcement, and the use of targeted excessive force. Here is what the DOJ report noted:

Our investigation indicates that this disproportionate burden on African Americans cannot be explained by any difference in the rate at which people of different races violate the law. Rather, our investigation has revealed that these disparities occur, at least in part, because of unlawful bias against and stereotypes about African Americans.[29]

This report reinforced what many African Americans had assumed about American law enforcement and documented for white America what many

>> The protests resulting from the police killings of George Floyd and Breonna Taylor built on a longer history of conflict between the state and communities of color in the U.S. Protestors employed tactics and rhetoric developed over decades of resistance.

Interpret: How does this image compare to those from the earlier African-American civil rights movement? How have the tactics and resources available to police changed over the last century? Do these contribute to community trust and safety?

Jose Luis Magana/Getty Images

communities of color experience. A long and continuous history of state-sanctioned violence against Black citizens related earlier in this chapter reinforces the belief of African Americans that lives of Black citizens are of lesser value in white America.

The use of social media to provide a more Afrocentric interpretation of political events and popular culture led to support from other communities of color who share similar fears of law enforcement and concerns that their lives also matter less. Because the movement had no central organizing structure—unlike many civil rights groups of the past—activists challenging perceived injustices from throughout the country simply identified with #BlackLivesMatter.

Future of the Movement

In May of 2020, two police killings of African American people—George Floyd in Minneapolis and Breonna Taylor in Louisville—and the immediate absence of criminal prosecution of the accused officers led to social media protests and, eventually, public protests. Even in the midst of the pandemic and concerns regarding social distancing, protests spread quickly across the nation, with some police supporting protesters by kneeling with them and others arresting and shooting them. When property damage accompanied some protests, President Donald Trump stated that "when the looting starts, the shooting starts" and mobilized the military to stop the protests. Many protesters viewed this move to mean that property damage was more important to the government than the lives of people of color. However, state and federal legislatures have responded to the police killings and the protesters' message by reconsidering their stance on militarization of police and the presence of resource officers in the schools.

As Chapter 8 discusses, the Black Lives Matter movement has resulted in the rethinking of strategies and training for police in their interaction with communities of color and in new policies relative to body cameras and protocol during potential violent scenarios. However, these high-profile deaths of civilians of color at the hands of police, and the hesitation around state prosecution of these officers, has meant continued frustration, anger, fear, and grief in communities of color.

The Movement for Women's Civil Rights

As already noted, the pronouncement in the Declaration of Independence that "all men are created equal" initially applied only to white men, and usually only to those who owned property. Not only did the concept of equal protection of the laws not apply to nonwhite male citizens, until the Civil War amendments to the Constitution and subsequent pieces of national legislation such as the Voting Rights and Civil Rights Acts, it also did not apply to female citizens—white or nonwhite. Like African American men, women had to wait until the Constitution was amended and civil rights legislation was adopted, in response to the women's rights movement, for equal protection of the laws.

Advocates for women's civil rights began their efforts in the mid-1800s, initially focusing on gaining the right to vote for women citizens. That endeavor, the first of three waves of the women's rights movement, won suffrage for women in 1920.

The First Wave of the Women's Rights Movement

The segregation of the women delegates at the 1840 World Anti-Slavery Conference in London was a defining moment for the first wave of the U.S. women's rights movement. Forced to sit in the balcony behind a drawn curtain, Lucretia Mott and Elizabeth Cady Stanton recognized that without improving their own legal and political status, women were not going to be successful in fighting for the legal rights of other groups of people.

In 1848, Mott and Stanton organized a meeting at Seneca Falls, New York, to talk about the lack of legal rights of U.S. citizens who happened to be born female. At the end of the convention, the participants signed the Declaration of Sentiments. This Declaration, modeled after the Declaration of Independence, listed many rights and opportunities that the law did not guarantee women, including the right to vote, educational and employment opportunities equal to those of white men, and married women's rights to own property as well as legal standing to sue. At the end of the convention, the participants signed the Declaration of Sentiments.

Clearly, John Adams and the other architects of the Constitution had ignored Abigail Adams's request to her husband and his colleagues to "remember the ladies" when they created the new system of government. Adams warned her husband that not only would women not feel bound to obey laws in which they had no say but also the ladies would "foment a rebellion" if they were not provided a voice in government.

The signatories of the Declaration of Sentiments began Adams's forecasted rebellion. The document they signed insisted "that [women] have immediate admission to all rights and privileges which belong to them as citizens of these United States." For those women and men who joined this new movement for women's civil rights, the right to vote became the focal point. They recognized that this right was the foundational right that would enable women to win the other rights and privileges of citizenship.

Because the Constitution initially reserved for the states the authority to determine who had the right to vote, as well as to be employed and obtain the best possible education, many of the initial battles for women's rights took place at the state level of government. Eventually, as the national government's responsibilities expanded through court interpretations of the Constitution, especially the Fourteenth Amendment, the federal government's role in guaranteeing civil rights expanded.

STATE-LEVEL RIGHTS Even after ratification of the Fourteenth Amendment (1868) guaranteeing equal protection of the laws for all people, women's educational and work opportunities were limited by social norms as well as state laws. Education for girls prepared them to be good wives and mothers, not to be economically independent. By the late 1800s, a few colleges began to admit women, and several women's colleges were established. Yet most colleges did not offer women the same educational opportunities as men, and women who graduated and aspired to a career were limited in two ways. First, by choosing a career, these educated women gave up the possibility of marriage. They were not legally banned from marriage, but societal norms prevented them from having both a career and a husband. Second, their career choices were limited: teaching, the developing professions of nursing and social work, or missionary work.

In 1873, Myra Bradwell challenged women's limited career choices when she sued the state of Illinois over its refusal to let her practice law.[30] In this case, the Supreme Court found that women's God-given destiny was to "fulfill the noble and benign offices of wife and mother" and that allowing women to practice law would impinge on that destiny. The *Bradwell* case established the precedent for the Court to justify allowing women to be treated differently than men are (sex-based discrimination) if the different treatment was deemed a *rational* means by which the government could fulfill a *legitimate* public interest. In the *Bradwell* case, the Court applied the *ordinary scrutiny* test, deeming it legitimate for the government to protect the role of women as wives and mothers, and, to accomplish that protection, it was rational to deny them equal employment opportunities.

In 1875, Virginia Minor of Missouri (actually her husband, because she, like all married women, did not have standing to sue) challenged the constitutionality of the Missouri law that guaranteed the right to vote only to male U.S. citizens. In this case, *Minor v. Happersett,* the Supreme Court acknowledged that women were citizens, yet it also decreed that state governments established voting rights, not the U.S. Constitution.[31] Therefore, the justices argued that the Fourteenth Amendment's privileges and immunities clause did not give women rights not established in the Constitution, hence it did not extend to women the right to vote.

THE NINETEENTH AMENDMENT TO THE CONSTITUTION The American Women's Suffrage Association (AWSA), directed by Lucy Stone, had been leading the battle

>> A line of women march for women's suffrage in Chicago in 1916; these are members of the Alpha Suffrage Club, an organization of African American women.

Interpret: How does this image challenge the way we typically conceive of the activists seeking the right to vote for women? How might we understand the history of voting rights differently if we focus on the experiences of Black women?

Afro Newspaper/Gado/Archive Photos/Getty Images

to extend the right to vote to women in the states since 1869. Simultaneously, the National Women's Suffrage Association (NWSA), directed by Susan B. Anthony and Elizabeth Cady Stanton, had been fighting to extend to women all rights of citizenship, including but not limited to the right to vote. In 1890, frustrated by their lack of success in the battle to extend suffrage to women, the AWSA and the NWSA joined forces, creating the National American Women's Suffrage Association (NAWSA). The NAWSA focused its efforts on amending the U.S. Constitution. African American women seeking to obtain the right to vote joined both organizations and formed their own regional societies.[32]

In 1916, Alice Paul founded the National Women's Party, which adopted more radical tactics than the NAWSA had been willing to use in its fight for suffrage. Noting the lack of support on the part of national officials for suffrage, Paul's organization called on voters in the 1916 election not to vote for candidates who opposed women's suffrage, including President Woodrow Wilson (1913–1921), who was running for reelection. In 1917, after President Wilson was reelected, Paul and other suffragists chained themselves to the White House fence and called on Wilson to support the suffrage amendment. Arrested, jailed, and force-fed when they engaged in a hunger strike, the women gained media attention, which in turn brought national attention to their struggle for suffrage and the president's opposition. After several months and persistent media pressure, President Wilson called on the House and the Senate to approve the women's suffrage amendment.

Congress approved this amendment in June 1919, and by the following year 36 states had ratified it. The Nineteenth Amendment prohibited the national and state governments from abridging or denying citizens the right to vote on account of sex. The right to vote was extended to another group of citizens in 1971 when the states ratified the Twenty-Sixth Amendment. This amendment guarantees citizens 18 years of age and older the right to vote.

The Second Wave of the Women's Rights Movement

After the Nineteenth Amendment was added to the Constitution, the push for women's rights ceased to be a mass movement. Women were still organized in groups and lobbied the government for women's civil rights, but the many women's organizations were no longer working collectively toward a single goal, such as the right to vote. Another mass women's movement did not arise until the 1960s. Several factors account for the mobilization of the second wave of the women's movement in the 1960s, which focused this time on the plethora of rights related to the social, economic, and political status of women, many of the same rights originally demanded in the Declaration of Sentiments.

By the 1960s, large numbers of women were working outside the home in the paid labor force. Working women talked with one another about their work and family lives and came to recognize common concerns and problems, including discrimination in educational opportunities, employment opportunities, and pay; lack of child care; domestic violence; the problem of rape, for which *they* were often blamed; and their inability to obtain credit (borrow money) without having a male cosign on the loan. Women recognized that as a class of citizens they did not have equal protection of the laws.

In 1961, at the prodding of Esther Peterson, the director of the Women's Bureau in the Department of Labor, President John F. Kennedy (1961–1963) established a Commission on the Status of Women, chaired by Eleanor Roosevelt. In 1963, the commission reported that women in the United States were discriminated against in many areas of life, including education and employment. In its report, the commission argued that women needed to pursue lawsuits that would allow the Supreme Court to interpret properly the Fourteenth Amendment's equal protection clause, hence prohibiting discrimination against women.

By the mid-1960s, the women's rights movement was rejuvenated with a second wave of mass activity. The goal of this second wave was equal legal rights for women. The means to achieve that goal included public demonstrations, legislation, litigation, and an as yet unsuccessful attempt to enact the Equal Rights Amendment (ERA), which had been written by Alice Paul and first introduced in Congress in 1923.

FEDERAL LEGISLATION AND WOMEN'S RIGHTS In 1955, Edith Green (D-Oreg.) introduced into Congress the first piece of national legislation written specifically to protect women, the Equal Pay Act. Enacted into law in 1963, the Equal Pay Act prohibited employers from paying women less than men were paid for the same job, which was the standard employment practice at the time. There are still concerns that a gender wage gap continues (see Figure 9.2).

The 1964 Civil Rights Act as initially drafted prohibited discrimination in education, employment, and public accommodations based on race, ethnicity, and religion. Yet because of congressional women's efforts, Title VII of the

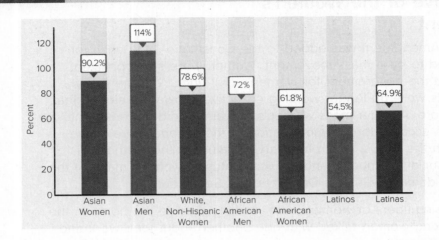

FIGURE 9.2 ■ The Wage Gap, by Gender and Race White, non-Hispanic men (not shown on the chart) are at 100 percent, and the bars show the percentage of that amount other demographic groups make. Recent surveys show that the gap has narrowed among younger workers. How do these data demonstrate the intersectionality discussed by Third Wave Feminists? What hypotheses can you generate to explain the differences in earnings—across education levels and types of jobs—based on race and gender? Why is the gap closing for younger workers? Why might civil rights legislation not have remedied this issue? Are these disparities something the government should be concerned about? Why or why not?

Source: U.S. Census Bureau, Current Population Survey. 2019. "PINC-05. Work Experience-People 15 Years Old and Over, by Total Money Earnings, Age, Race, Hispanic Origin, Sex, and Disability Status, https://www.census.gov/data/tables/time-series/demo/income-poverty/cps-pinc/pinc-05.html#par_textimage_0 (accessed September 10, 2019).

proposed act was rewritten to prohibit discrimination in all personnel decisions based on *sex* as well as the other inherent characteristics. Initially, the EEOC, the federal agency responsible for monitoring Title VII implementation, did not take sex-based discrimination complaints seriously.

To take advantage of Title VII's promise of equal employment opportunities, women needed to pursue educational opportunities on an equal basis with men. Yet Title VI of the 1964 Civil Rights Act does not prohibit sex-based discrimination in institutions that receive federal funds, including educational institutions. By 1972, women's rights advocates won an amendment to the 1964 Civil Rights Act, Title IX, which prohibits sex-based discrimination in educational institutions receiving federal funds.

The Equal Pay Act, Title VII, and Title IX are landmark pieces of national legislation that provide equal protection of the law for women. At the same time that Congress was enacting laws prohibiting sex-based discrimination, the courts were reinterpreting the equal protection clause of the Fourteenth Amendment.

WOMEN'S RIGHTS AND THE EQUAL PROTECTION CLAUSE In 1971, in the case of *Reed v. Reed,* the Supreme Court for the first time in history used the equal protection clause of the Fourteenth Amendment to find a law that discriminated against women unconstitutional.[33] In the *Reed* case, the Supreme Court found that an Idaho state law giving automatic preference to men to administer the estate of a deceased person who had not named an administrator was not a rational means to fulfill a legitimate government interest. Hence, using the ordinary scrutiny test established in the 1873 *Bradwell* case, the court ruled this discriminatory treatment of women was unconstitutional.

Then, in 1976, the Supreme Court developed a new test for the legality of sex-based discrimination. Oklahoma law allowed women 18 years of age to buy beer with 3.2 percent alcohol content. Yet men in Oklahoma had to be 21 years of age to purchase 3.2 percent beer. Men challenged the law, asking the Court to decide if this sex-based discrimination was constitutional. In this case, *Craig v. Boren*, the Court established the heightened scrutiny test for sex-based discrimination cases: Different treatment is legal if it is substantially related to an important government interest.[34] The Court used this test in the *Craig* case to find the Oklahoma law unconstitutional. The Court also used the heightened scrutiny test in the 1996 *United States v. Virginia* case.[35] In this case, the Court found the male-only admissions policy of the Virginia Military Institute unconstitutional. Justice Ruth Bader Ginsburg noted in her opinion that the state of Virginia had not shown that this discriminatory admissions policy was substantially related to the important government objective of training soldiers.

Today, courts typically use the heightened scrutiny test when deciding sex-based discrimination cases. Proponents of an ERA argue that the strict scrutiny test, which is used in race-, religion-, and ethnic-based discrimination cases, should also be used in sex-based discrimination cases, but that this will not happen until the Constitution is amended to explicitly guarantee equality of rights under the law regardless of gender.

THE PROPOSED EQUAL RIGHTS AMENDMENT During the 1970s, as the Supreme Court was reinterpreting the implications of the Fourteenth Amendment for sex-based discrimination, lobbying for the Equal Rights Amendment increased. In 1972, Congress approved the ERA, which states that "equality of rights under the law shall not be denied or abridged by the United States or by any State on account of sex." Finally, 49 years after it was first introduced in Congress, the ERA was sent to the states for ratification.

Opponents of the ERA argued it was a duplication of the Fourteenth Amendment and therefore was not needed. Opponents also claimed that passage of the amendment would make women subject to the military draft; would lead to the integration of all single-sex institutions, including schools and public bathrooms; and would result in the legalization of and public funding for all abortions. Moreover, they argued that the ERA was not needed because Congress was passing laws that guaranteed women equal protection in employment and education. Whether or not the claims of its opponents were accurate, they successfully defeated the ERA, which was not ratified by enough states by the deadline of 1982. By 2020, 38 states had finally ratified the amendment; however, since 1982, five states have passed resolutions rescinding their previous approval. Most likely the federal courts will determine whether advocates of the amendment must start again or whether it has met the threshold to be adopted.

The Third Wave of the Women's Rights Movement

Although the first two waves of the women's movement advocated for formal equality or identical legal treatment with men, by the 1990s, feminists realized that a good deal still needed to be done to realize these goals in practice. Despite legal and constitutional change, women still battle inequities, including unequal pay, sexual harassment, and the glass ceiling (aspiring to higher-level jobs but being unable to win them). Moreover, although the situation for women has greatly improved, not all women have benefited equally from gains in women's rights. Third-wave feminism recognizes that women have unequal access to legal rights owing to differences in race, class, sexual orientation, gender identity, ethnicity, and religion. For example, although *Roe v. Wade* secured a woman's right to an abortion, many women cannot afford one. (Abortions can cost anywhere from a few hundred dollars to many thousands of dollars.) Third-wave organizations, such as the Chicago Abortion Fund, seek to overcome economic barriers to reproductive rights by helping women fund abortions. Another key issue has been the ending of sexual violence, particularly that against women; the #MeToo movement has called to the ways sexual violence and harassment limit women's opportunities.

Women of color face the intertwined challenges of race and gender, which civil rights laws do not recognize, particularly in the area of employment discrimination. For instance, under the Civil Rights Act of 1964, women of color must challenge employment discrimination as being based on either their gender or their race; there is no legal recognition of the ways in which perceptions of their race and gender could create difficulties in the workplace. If the white women in the workplace are not similarly mistreated, then it is not gender discrimination, and if the men of color are not similarly mistreated, then it is not considered racial discrimination. Third-wave feminists refer to this as *intersectionality*, the experience of multiple forms of oppression simultaneously. Low-income and working-class women of all ethnicities seek solutions to such problems as affordable child and health care. Lesbian, bisexual, and transgender women are examining the intersection between gender discrimination and oppression based on their sexual identity.

Third-wave feminism has focused on expanding the political and economic gains made for women in the 1970s and 1980s to all women.[36] Third-wave feminism is a broader movement seeking redress on multiple and more individualized fronts—not merely legal and political, but cultural and economic as well.

The Fourth Wave: Sexual Violence Promotes Inequality

Private individuals can engage in unlawful discrimination, such as in cases of sexual harassment and assault, as can the government or public agencies through unequal policies and laws. While initially, most gender-equity activism focused on equal treatment under the law, by the late 20th century, the focus was on how the law could prevent or punish private behavior that harmed women based on their gender.

Originated by activist Tarana Burke in 2006, the #MeToo Movement was intended to remind survivors of sexual violence in communities of color that they were not alone. This movement gained momentum and visibility in the fall of 2017 after a year in which women accused prominent men (including Hollywood producers, directors, and actors; journalists; politicians; photographers; and chefs) of using sexual violence, the threat of violence, or sexual exposure (nakedness or masturbation) to intimidate or coerce women who were politically or economically weaker. Many women claimed that they had to comply with this coercion, or the "gatekeepers" to their professions could harm their careers and opportunities. While many of the allegations made were not criminal, the movement continues to demonstrate the scope of the problem in society and the limited options women have to challenge powerful people who coerce others and abuse their power.[37]

This focus on violence against women and their bodily autonomy is characteristic of the fourth wave, as is concern about economic inequalities. While intersectionality remains a clear theme as in the third wave, many note that the fourth wave is more inclusive of the lesbian, gay, bisexual, trans, plus other communities (LGBT+). What also makes this wave different is the heavy reliance on digital media and the tendency to be fronted by celebrities. It has not replaced the third wave, but has evolved into something broader and potentially more engaged with other social movements.[38]

■ Evolution of Civil Rights

Today, discriminatory treatment is still a reality for many groups of citizens. The civil rights acts notwithstanding, discrimination in employment, education, housing, and due process still occurs. Moreover, battles for civil rights continue. Unfortunately, we cannot discuss all the civil rights movements that have occurred or are ongoing in the United States. Therefore, we will explore the civil rights battles of just a few groups of citizens: Native Americans, Latinos (Latinx), Asian Americans, and citizens with disabilities. The hard-fought victories and aspirations of these groups offer an overview of both the history and the breadth of contemporary civil rights movements.

Lesbian, Gay, Bisexual, and Transgender Citizens

Lesbian, gay, bisexual, and **transgender** people, and those questioning their sexual identity or who identify as "queer"—a group often referred to with the abbreviation LGBTQ+—are redefining gender norms as well as actively seeking equal civil rights. Included in this classification are people who identify as non-binary—meaning they are neither "male" or "female." These communities are using many of the same strategies other groups have used to obtain legal and social equality. Some of the specific rights LGBTQ+ persons have organized to fight for focus on employment, housing, marriage, and protection from violence.

transgender
Individuals whose gender identity does not match the sex they were assigned at birth.

RIGHTS FOR TRANSGENDER PEOPLE Hate crimes continue to be a problem for members of the LGBTQ+ community as well as for communities of color—and especially for those who belong to both—and they have been particularly

>> Delegate Danica Roem, second from left, takes her oath of office at the opening ceremonies of the 2018 session of the Virginia House of Delegates at the Capitol in Richmond, Virginia. She is the first openly transgender elected official to serve in a state legislature in the United States.

Interpret: How might the presence of more transgender Americans in elected office impact policies at the state and federal level: How important is it in a representative system of government that elected officials reflect the intersectionality of their constituencies? Do elected bodies in the United States truly represent the demographics of the country?

Steve Helber/AP Images

hate crime
A crime committed against a person, property, or society, in which the offender is motivated, in part or in whole, by his or her bias against the victim because of the victim's race, religion, disability, sexual orientation, or ethnicity.

underreported in the trans community. The national government enacted its first hate crime law in 1969. Since then, it has expanded the inherent characteristics for which the law guarantees protection. Today, under federal law, a **hate crime** is one in which the offender is motivated in part or entirely by her or his bias against the victim because of the victim's actual or perceived race, color, religion, nationality, ethnicity, gender, sexual orientation, gender identity, or disability. Forty-six states and the District of Columbia also have hate crime laws, but the inherent characteristics covered by those laws vary.[39]

intersectionality
The experience of multiple forms of oppression (based on race, gender, class, sexual orientation, or sexual identity) simultaneously.

Violence against transgender people has been a continuous concern. For the first time, in 2014, the FBI released data on violence based on sexual identity of the victim, finding that hate crimes had decreased overall, but had increased based on sexual identity. The Human Rights Campaign found that at least 26 transgender people were killed in 2019;[40] however, this type of data is difficult to accurately gather. As with many groups, **intersectionality** complicates this issue. Those who are from communities of color, are poor, or are women often face greater violence and risk than those who are white or wealthy, or are male.

GROWTH OF THE MOVEMENT Several LGBT civil rights organizations were founded after the Stonewall Rebellion. In June 1969, groups of gay men and lesbians clashed violently with police in New York City, protesting the routine harassment by law enforcement of members of the lesbian and gay community. This influential conflict, which started at the Stonewall bar, marked the first time that members of this community acted collectively and in large numbers to assert their rights. Shortly after this event, in 1970, Lambda Legal, a national organization fighting for full recognition of the civil rights of LGBT citizens, was founded. Within a few years, gays and lesbians began to hold gay pride marches, and many new groups, such as the Human Rights Campaign and the National Gay and Lesbian Task Force, began advocating for LGBT rights.

As a result of organized educational and lobbying efforts by the gay community, during the 1980s a number of state and local governments adopted laws prohibiting discrimination in employment, housing, public accommodations, and employee benefits—that is, guaranteeing equal protection of some laws— for LGBT persons. Yet during the same decade, numerous states had laws on the books prohibiting sex between mutually consenting adults of the same sex, typically forbidding sodomy. In the 1986 case of *Bowers v. Hardwick*, the U.S. Supreme Court upheld Georgia's anti-sodomy law.[41] In 2003, another lawsuit challenging the constitutionality of a state anti-sodomy law came before the Supreme Court in the case of *Lawrence v. Texas*.[42] This time, the Court overturned the 1986 *Bowers* decision, finding that the Fourteenth Amendment provides due process and equal protection for sexual privacy, and therefore the Texas law was unconstitutional.

Before June 2020, LGBTQ+-based discrimination was allowed in the private-sector workplace. However, the Supreme Court decision of *Bostick v. Clayton County, Georgia*[43] interpreted the prohibition against sex discrimination in Title VII of the Civil Rights Act of 1964 as including sexual orientation and gender identity. This means that employers who fire LGBT employees solely because of their sexual identity now violate federal law.

Several states did however pass legislation affirming the religious liberty of business owners to refuse service to lesbians, gay men, and transgender people. These types of religious liberties have been interpreted to preclude individuals, religious organizations, or small businesses from being compelled to provide services they perceive as contrary to their beliefs. Some examples come from religiously affiliated schools that have fired women who were unmarried and pregnant, pharmacists who refused to fill birth control prescriptions, bakeries and photographers who refused services to same-sex weddings, and graduate students who abstained from counseling gay clients. How do we protect personal religious liberties while simultaneously advancing civil rights?

SAME-SEX MARRIAGE The issue of marriage has been a focal point for gay and lesbian activists in recent years. With marriage comes a host of advantages, including inheritance rights, taxation benefits, rights to governmental benefits, and hospital-visitation rights. Like other struggles for civil rights, the movement for marriage equality has relied on court action, bills in state legislatures, public referenda, and other strategies.

The 2013 Supreme Court case of *United States v. Windsor* paved the way for many states to change their laws when it determined that the federal Defense of Marriage Act (DOMA) defining marriage as inherently heterosexual was unconstitutional under the equal protection clause of the Fifth Amendment.[44]

In 2015, the U.S. Supreme Court decided the landmark case of *Obergefell v. Hodges*, which ruled that the due process clause of the Fourteenth Amendment protects the right to marry as a fundamental liberty—for same-sex couples identically to opposite-sex couples.[45] Denial of this right to marry, according to Justice Kennedy's majority opinion, violates the equal protection clause. The Court made it clear that while the free exercise clause of the First Amendment (Chapter 8) allows religious organizations to refrain from endorsing same-sex unions, it does not allow states to discriminate against their citizens. Although the LGBTQ+ community is winning many of its civil rights battles, the challenge continues. For example, in the area of family law, issues involving adoption rights and child custody as well as divorce and property rights are now battlegrounds.

Native Americans' Rights

At first, the fledgling nation recognized the native residents of the land that became the United States as members of sovereign and independent nations with inherent rights. The federal government entered into more than 370 treaties with Native American tribes between 1778 and 1870.[46] Most of those treaties promised land to tribes that agreed to move, and almost all those promises were empty, with the government reneging on most of the agreements. In addition, in 1830, Congress passed the Indian Removal Act, which called for the forced relocation of all native peoples to lands west of the Mississippi. In the end, most Native Americans were dispossessed of their lands and wound up living on reservations. The federal government treated Indians as subhumans, relegating them to second-class status, as they had African Americans.

Until Congress passed the Indian Citizenship Act in 1924, Native Americans had virtually no rights to U.S. citizenship, and even the laws that allowed immigrants to become citizens did not apply to Native Americans. The Indian Rights Association, founded in 1882 and active in lobbying Congress and the state legislatures until the 1930s, was one of the most important of the early groups that actively campaigned for full suffrage for native peoples, in the belief that enfranchisement would help to "civilize" them. The early 1900s also saw the founding of the Society of American Indians and the American Indian Defense Association, both of which fought for citizenship for Native Americans and then for their civil rights. However, for more than 40 years after passage of the Indian Citizenship Act, the basic rights enumerated in the Bill of Rights were not granted to Native Americans. In the 1960s, Indian activists became more radical, occupying government buildings, picketing, and conducting protests. In 1968, the American Indian Movement (AIM) was founded. In the same year, Congress passed the Indian Civil Rights Act, which ensured that Native Americans would have the full protection of the Bill of Rights both on and off their reservations. Although this law had significant symbolic impact, it lacked an enforcement mechanism, and so native peoples continued to be deprived of basic due process protections and equal education and employment opportunities. The National Indian Education Association (NIEA), founded in 1969, continues to confront the lack of quality educational opportunities for Native Americans and the loss of native culture and values.

During the 1970s, Native American organizations began a new effort to force the federal government to honor treaties granting Indians fishing and hunting rights as well as rights to the natural resources buried in their lands. Indians in New York, Maine, and elsewhere sued for land taken from them decades or even a century ago in violation of treaties. Starting with the 1975 Indian Self-Determination and Education Assistance Act, the national government has enacted laws that support greater autonomy for Indian tribes and give them more control of their assets.

THEN

NOW

≫ In both 1969 (left) and 2019 (right), Native Americans occupied Alcatraz Island. Calling themselves "Indians of All Tribes," their purpose was to bring attention to the injustices facing Native Americans based on long-standing federal policy--in their words, to "wake up the conscience of America." When peaceful protest doesn't bring about change, what options do people with social justice claims have? Do you believe that those who are experiencing state oppression ever have the right to occupy property or violate laws? If so, when? If not, what other options should they exercise?

(Left): Ralph Crane/The LIFE Picture Collection/Getty Images; (Right): Liu Guanguan/China News Service/VCG/Getty Images

The 1988 Indian Gaming Regulatory Act is the best known of the federal laws enacted to support Indian self-determination. This law authorizes Indian tribes to establish gaming operations on their property and requires them to negotiate compacts with the states in which their lands are located. The compacts typically include a profit-sharing understanding that requires the Indian tribe to give a proportion of its profits to the state government and possibly to contiguous local governments. The act mandates that the money made through gaming operations be used for education, economic development, infrastructure (for example, roads and utilities), law enforcement, and courts. By 2016, the National Indian Gaming Commission, the independent agency that regulates Indian gaming, reported that more than 247 of the federally recognized 562 Indian tribes operate more than 520 gaming establishments in 29 states. The gross revenues for these gaming activities totaled $33.7 billion in 2018.[47] Clearly, one goal of the Gaming Act was to generate resources that would increase the educational and employment opportunities on Indian reservations.

Even with gaming profits, however, the prospects for many Native Americans today remain bleak. According to race and ethnic relations scholars Joe R. Feagin and Clairece Booher Feagin, "Native Americans have endured the longest Depression-like economic situation of any U.S. racial or ethnic group."[48] They are among the poorest, least educated U.S. citizens. Native women face some of the highest levels of violence, in part because until 2015 non-Native people were immune from prosecution in tribal courts. Under the Violence Against Women Act reauthorization, tribal sovereignty has now been expanded to cover prosecution of these offenders. Like many other groups of U.S. citizens, Native Americans continue to fight in the halls of government, in the courtrooms, and in the public arena for their constitutionally guaranteed rights and privileges.

Citizens of Latin American Descent

U.S. citizens of Latin American descent (Latinos or Latinx) include those whose families hail from Central America, South America, or the Caribbean. Latinos are the largest minority group in the United States; almost 60 million people trace their heritage to Latin America and Spain. Sixty-seven percent of this Latino population is composed of natural-born U.S. citizens, and the majority of growth in the population is from U.S.-born children, not new immigrants.[49]

In the 2020 presidential election, Latinos had 32 million eligible voters and are the largest racial/ethnic minority in the United States.[50] So far, the elections that have occurred in the 21st century have been followed by numerous lawsuits claiming that individual citizens, organized groups, and local governments have prevented eligible Latino voters from voting. Limited English proficiency can create barriers to voting and equal educational and employment opportunities for many U.S. citizens, including Latino citizens. We focus here on U.S. citizens of Mexican origin—the largest Latino population in the United States today.

EARLY STRUGGLES OF MEXICAN AMERICANS In 1846, because of land disputes sparked by white immigrants from the United States encroaching on Mexican territory, the United States declared war on Mexico. By the terms of the 1848 Treaty of Guadalupe Hidalgo, which ended the war, Mexico ceded territory to the United States for $15 million. According to the treaty, Mexicans who stayed on their land would become U.S. citizens, and their civil rights would be protected. Although nearly 77,000 Mexicans chose to do so, their civil rights were *not* protected.[51] Thus began a long and continuing history of discrimination against U.S. citizens of Mexican descent.

At the turn of the 20th century, Mexican Americans organized to protest the various forms of discrimination they were experiencing, which included segregated schools, inequities in employment opportunities and wages, discrimination by law enforcement officers, and barriers to their voting rights such as poll taxes and English-only literacy tests. In 1929, several Mexican American organizations combined to create the League of United Latin American Citizens (LULAC).[52]

In 1945, LULAC successfully challenged the segregated school systems in California, which provided separate schools for Mexican children that were of poorer quality than the schools for white children. In this case, *Mendez v. Westminister*, the federal court set an important precedent by using the Fourteenth Amendment to guarantee equal educational opportunities.[53] In 1954, the U.S. Supreme Court followed this lower court's precedent when it ended legal race-based segregation in public schools throughout the nation

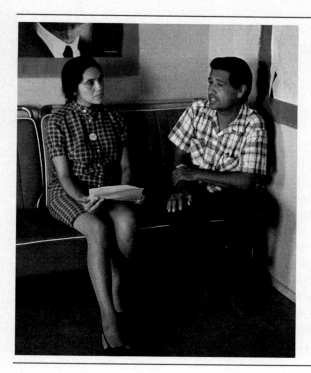

Cesar Chavez began his civil rights work as a community organizer in 1952 by encouraging Mexican Americans to vote and use their civil rights. Together with Dolores Huerta, he founded the United Farm Workers. From the early 1960s until his death in 1993, Chavez was the leading voice for and organizer of migrant farmworkers in the United States. Huerta was a prominent Chicana labor leader, developing other leaders and advocating for the rights of immigrant workers, women, and children.

Arthur Schatz/The LIFE Picture Collection/Getty Images

in the *Brown v. Board of Education of Topeka* case. The Supreme Court unanimously agreed in 1954 that Mexican Americans and all nationalities were guaranteed equal protection under the Fourteenth Amendment.[54] Mexican Americans were not explicitly protected under *Brown v. Board of Education* as a minority group until 1971.[55]

THE CHICANO MOVEMENT In addition to the women's rights movement and the civil rights movement for African American rights, the 1960s witnessed the birth of the Chicano Movement, the mass movement for Mexican American civil rights. The Chicano Movement was composed of numerous Latino organizations focusing on a variety of issues, including rights to equal employment and educational opportunities. One of the most widely recognized leaders in the Chicano Movement was Cesar Chavez.

Cesar Chavez began his civil rights work as a community organizer in 1952, encouraging Mexican Americans to vote and educating them about their civil rights. In the early 1960s, Chavez, along with Jessie Lopez and Dolores Huerta, founded the Agricultural Workers Organizing Committee (AWOC) and the National Farm Workers Association (NFWA). Under Chavez's leadership, the AWOC and the NFWA merged to form the United Farm Workers (UFW) in 1966. The UFW organized successful protests and boycotts to improve working conditions and pay for farmworkers.[56]

IMMIGRATION AND OTHER CIVIL RIGHTS ISSUES Approximately 10.5 million undocumented immigrants live in the United States, which is 3.2 percent of the U.S. population. The typical unauthorized immigrant has lived in the United States for 15 years, and approximately 47 percent of these undocumented immigrants are Hispanic.[57] In 2003, as part of the new Department of Homeland Security, U.S. Immigration and Customs Enforcement (ICE) was created to enforce immigration laws by rounding up and deporting individuals and families in the country illegally.

What Is the Impact of Illegal Immigration?

THE ISSUE: Approximately 10.5 million illegal immigrants live in the United States. These individuals, their impact on the country, and their fate have generated significant political debate in the United States over such issues as legal status, deportation, benefits, criminality, and education. In tandem, governmental and nongovernmental organizations have compiled massive amounts of data on these issues, and these numbers are open to multiple interpretations. How can we best evaluate data we encounter and know which interpretations to trust? Evaluating data and using them to determine policy are particularly difficult when advocates focus on different aspects of the problem. The two authors below use different data sets and come up with opposite conclusions from their studies. Is it possible that people in Arizona and Texas behave this differently, or is one of the studies flawed? How do we determine which arguments are more important?

Undocumented Immigrants Are More Likely to Commit Crimes

Lott, John R., Undocumented Immigrants, U.S. Citizens, and Convicted Criminals in Arizona (February 10, 2018). Available at SSRN: https://ssrn.com/abstract=3099992.

This author examined the crime rates of illegal versus legal residents of Arizona, using data on prisoners in the state prison system between January 1985 and June 2017. He presents the following numbers: "Undocumented immigrants are at least 142% more likely to be convicted of a crime than other Arizonans. They also tend to commit more serious crimes and serve 10.5% longer sentences, [are] more likely to be classified as dangerous, and [are] 45% more likely to be gang members than U.S. citizens." The author further concluded that these numbers underrepresented the amount of crime committed by undocumented immigrants, noting particularly that undocumented immigrants between 15 and 35 years of age make up 2 percent of the Arizona general population and 8 percent of the Arizona prison population. He also found that the crimes committed by undocumented immigrants tended to be more violent than crimes committed by citizens and documented immigrants. Based on his data, the author concludes that if "undocumented immigrants committed crime nationally as they do in Arizona, in 2016 they would have been responsible for over 1,000 more murders, 5,200 rapes, 8,900 robberies, 25,300 aggravated assaults, and 26,900 burglaries."

WHAT DO YOU THINK?

1. Both authors rely on governmental data for their information and have well-documented research, but they come to opposite conclusions. What might explain the difference?

2. The first author's position has implications against expansion of immigration or amnesty for the children of illegal immigrants. What questions does he not answer in his analysis? What else do you want to know?

3. The second author is arguing for the expansion of immigration and the amnesty for children of illegal immigrants. What questions does he not answer in his analysis? What else do you want to know?

4. Do an internet search and see what you can find about the sources of both articles. Is one more legitimate than the other? What do critics of each analysis say about the research and conclusions? How have these arguments been used in policy debates?

Undocumented Immigrants Are Less Likely to Commit Crimes

Alex Nowrasteh, "Criminal Immigrants in Texas in 2017: Illegal Immigrant Conviction Rates," *Cato Institute*, August 27, 2019.

"Texas is an ideal state to study criminality by immigration status for multiple reasons: it borders Mexico; it has the second-largest illegal immigrant population of any state; it is a politically conservative state governed by Republicans; in 2017 it did not have jurisdictions that limited its cooperation with federal immigration enforcement; and it has a law-and-order reputation for severely and strictly enforcing its criminal laws. In 2017 in Texas, 399,155 native-born Americans, 16,275 illegal immigrants, and 18,235 legal immigrants were convicted of crimes. Thus, 1,702 natives were convicted for every 100,000 [native-born people], 899 illegal immigrants [were convicted] for every 100,000 legal immigrants. As a percentage of their respective subpopulations, illegal immigrants were over 47 percent less likely to be convicted of a crime than native-born Americans. Legal immigrants were about 65 percent less likely to be convicted of a crime than native-born Americans."

5. To come up with your own stance on immigration, what information do you want? What is most important to you—crime rates, economic impact, or some other factor? What sources do you trust, and why?

Immediately after his inauguration, President Donald J. Trump (2017–2021) issued an executive order that expanded the grounds of who could be considered "removable aliens" well beyond the previous 2014 focus on convicted felons and those who are safety threats.[58] Beginning in July 2019, ICE deported 267,258 individuals in the following 12 months.[59]

Over the past several years, four primary approaches have been discussed nationally to address illegal immigration: implementing mass deportations; offering pathways to citizenship for families with children born in the United States; providing temporary reprieves from deportation without a pathway to citizenship; and/or providing refugee status to the increasing numbers of unaccompanied minors fleeing their home countries. Criticism of the Trump administration has escalated over Homeland Security policy of detaining refugee families at the Mexican border and separating children from parents. Protestors asserted that due process was being denied and that the health of detainees was threatened due to poor conditions and limited health care. Upon his election, President Biden vowed to repeal many of the Trump administration immigration policies and vowed to work on comprehensive immigration reform.[60]

Citizens of Asian Descent

Asian American citizens come from, or have ancestors from, a number of different countries with diverse cultures, religions, histories, and languages. Today, the largest percentage of Asian Americans have Chinese origins, followed by those of Filipino, Asian Indian, Vietnamese, Korean, and Japanese ancestry. Large numbers of immigrants from Japan came to the United States around the turn of the 20th century, but it was not until the 1940s that the flow of immigrants from other Asian countries began to increase, beginning with the Philippines. In the 1960s, the number of immigrants from Korea and India began to increase significantly, and in the 1970s—as the Vietnam War ended—immigrants from Vietnam began to arrive in large numbers. Today, 5.6 percent of the U.S. population is of Asian descent. These 20 million people trace their roots to 19 different origin groups from Southeast Asia, East Asia, and the Indian subcontinent.[61]

Like other U.S. citizens with significant nonwhite ancestry, Asian Americans have had to fight continually for their civil rights, specifically for equal protection under the law and particularly for equal access to educational and employment opportunities as well as citizenship. Asian immigrants and Asian Americans created organizations to fight for citizenship and equal protection of the law. One successful result of those efforts was the 1952 Immigration and Nationality Act, which allowed Asian immigrants to become citizens for the first time. Before passage of this law, only U.S.-born children of Asian immigrants could be citizens.

INTERNMENT OF JAPANESE AMERICANS DURING WORLD WAR II One of the most egregious violations of the civil rights of Asian American citizens occurred during World War II when Americans of Japanese ancestry were forced to move to government-established camps. Under President Franklin Roosevelt's Executive Order 9066, over 120,000 Japanese Americans, two-thirds of whom were native-born U.S. citizens, were relocated from the West Coast of the United States after Japan's attack on Pearl Harbor. During that same period, the federal government also restricted the travel of Americans of German and Italian ancestry who were living on the West Coast (the United States was also fighting against Germany and Italy), but those citizens were not relocated. Many relocated Japanese Americans lost their homes and businesses.

Activists fought for decades to obtain reparations for the citizens who were interned and for the repeal of a section of the 1950 Internal Security Act that allowed the government to imprison citizens deemed enemy collaborators during a crisis. Congress repealed the section of the 1950 law targeted by interest groups, and in 1987 President Ronald Reagan signed a bill providing $1.2 billion in reparations.[62]

CONTEMPORARY ISSUES FOR ASIAN AMERICANS During the 1960s and 1980s, the number of organizations and coalitions pressing for the civil rights of Asian Americans grew as large numbers of new immigrants from Asian countries arrived in the United States in response to changes in U.S. immigration laws. During the 1960s, Asian Americans on college campuses organized and fostered a group consciousness about the need to protect their civil rights. During the 1980s, Asian American organizations began to pay more attention to voting rights as well as to hate crimes and employment discrimination. Then in 1996, numerous organizations, each representing Asian Americans with ancestry from one country, joined to form the National Council of Asian Pacific Americans (NCAPA), which presses for equal protection of the law for all Asians.

Asian Americans have the highest median income compared with the population as a whole, but this varies greatly within Asian origin groups (see Figure 9.3).[63] Asian Americans are also twice as likely as the population as a whole to earn a bachelor's degree or higher but are less likely to own a home.[64] Moreover, Asian Americans are better represented in professional and managerial positions than any other racial or ethnic group, including white Americans. Yet like women, Asian American citizens appear to hit a glass ceiling, for they are not represented in the very top positions in the numbers that their high levels of educational achievement

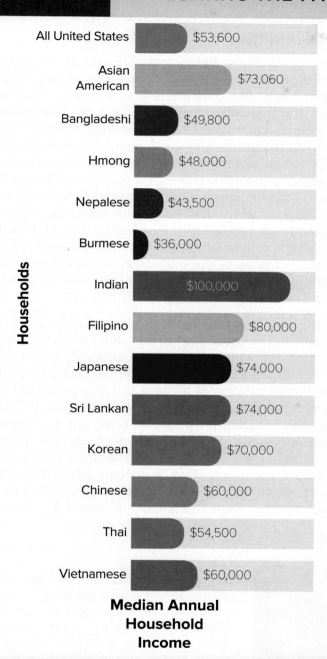

Households

Origin Group	Median Annual Household Income
All United States	$53,600
Asian American	$73,060
Bangladeshi	$49,800
Hmong	$48,000
Nepalese	$43,500
Burmese	$36,000
Indian	$100,000
Filipino	$80,000
Japanese	$74,000
Sri Lankan	$74,000
Korean	$70,000
Chinese	$60,000
Thai	$54,500
Vietnamese	$60,000

Median Annual Household Income

FIGURE 9.3 ▪ **Comparative Asian American Household Incomes** This chart shows wide variation in the household incomes of Asian American origin groups. While Asian American groups have the highest median income compared to the population as a whole, how do the numbers in this table clarify this generalization? What might explain the disparities among these origin groups?

Source: Lopez, Gustavo, Neil G. Ruiz and Eileen Patten. Key facts about Asian Americans, a Diverse and Growing Population. Pew Research Center, September 8, 2017.

would seem to predict. Therefore, those advocating for Asian American civil rights are increasingly concentrating their efforts on discrimination in employment. Professor Don T. Nakanishi, an expert on Asian Americans, points out that Asian Americans are becoming "more organized, more visible and more effective as participants and leaders in order to advance—as well as to protect—their individual and group interests, and to contribute to our nation's democratic processes and institutions."[65] Andrew Yang, technology entrepreneur, entered the 2020 race for the U.S. presidency, becoming the country's first Asian American presidential candidate. Today, more than 4,000 Asian Americans serve as elected or appointed officials in all levels of government throughout the nation.[66]

Citizens with Disabilities

The civil rights movements of the 1960s and 1970s made society more aware of the lack of equal protection of the laws for diverse groups of citizens, including people with disabilities. The first law to mandate equal protection for people with physical and mental disabilities was the 1973 Rehabilitation Act, which prohibited discrimination against people with disabilities in federally funded programs. In 1990, people with disabilities achieved a significant enhancement of this earlier victory in their fight to obtain protection of their civil rights. The Americans with Disabilities Act (ADA), enacted in that year, extends the ban on discrimination against people with disabilities in education, employment, health care, housing, and transportation to all programs and organizations, not just those receiving federal funds. The ADA defines a disability as any "physical or mental impairment that substantially limits one or more of the major life activities of the individual." The ADA does not enumerate every disability that it covers, resulting in much confusion over which conditions it covers and which it excludes.

A series of U.S. Supreme Court rulings in the late 1990s and early 2000s narrowed the interpretation of "disability," decreasing the number of people benefiting from the ADA. For example, the Court determined that if an individual can take an action to mitigate an impairment (such as taking medication to prevent seizures), then the impairment is not a disability protected by the ADA. In response, disability advocates, including the National Coalition of Disability Rights and the ADA Watch, successfully lobbied Congress to propose an act restoring the broader interpretation of the term "disability" and, hence, increasing the number of people benefiting from the ADA. The Americans with Disabilities Act Amendments of 2008 went into effect in January 2009. The act applies to the equal protection guaranteed in the Rehabilitation Act (1973) and the ADA (1990). It does not change the written definition of "disability" that is in the ADA,

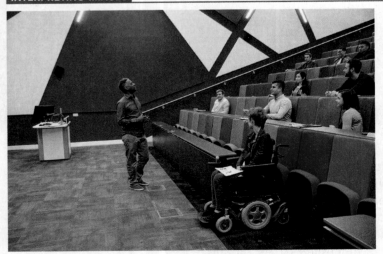

>> Federal law requires that schools make the same kinds of accommodations that the ADA requires of employers. That is, when reasonable adjustments to policy or process can allow a student access to education, school boards and institutions of higher education are obligated to make such changes.

Interpret: What do the photo and the ADA tell us about how we pursue equality in the United States? Is a learning environment like this one accessible? Is your classroom accessible? What does it mean for a space to be accessible?

Monkey Business Images/Shutterstock

Has the U.S. system of federalism advanced or inhibited civil rights? Write an essay that develops an argument that responds to this prompt and establishes a line of reasoning.

In your essay, you must:

- Articulate a defensible claim or thesis that responds to the prompt and establishes a line of reasoning

- Support your claim with at least TWO pieces of accurate and relevant information:

    - At least ONE piece of evidence must be from one of the following foundational documents

        - *Letter from Birmingham Jail*

        - The United States Constitution

        - *Federalist* No. 10

- Use a second piece of evidence from another foundational document from the list or from your study of the civil rights movement.

- Use reasoning to explain why your evidence supports your claim/thesis.

- Respond to an opposing or alternative perspective using refutation, concession, or rebuttal.

but broadens what "substantially limits" and "major life activities" mean, and no longer considers actions taken to mitigate impairments as relevant to determining if employers and educational institutions must accommodate a person's mental or physical disability in public facilities and housing.[67]

The ADA has enhanced the civil rights of citizens with disabilities—both visible and invisible. Before the ADA was enacted, people with disabilities who were fired from their jobs or denied access to schools, office buildings, or other public places had no recourse. Cities were under no obligation to provide even the most reasonable accommodations to people with disabilities who sought employment or the use of public transportation systems. And employers were under no obligation to make even the most minor modifications to their workplaces for employees with disabilities. For example, if a qualified job applicant used a wheelchair, an employer did not have to consider installing ramps or raising desks to accommodate the wheelchair but could simply refuse to hire the individual. The ADA requires employers, universities, schools, and governmental organizations to make it possible for people with disabilities to participate meaningfully in their communities through reasonable accommodations.

When Is Voter Suppression a Threat to Civil Rights?

Voter suppression is the attempt to control the outcome of an election by preventing or discouraging voting among certain categories of people, such as college students, felons, poor people, people of color, or the elderly. Such suppression can be legal or illegal and may use laws, administrative policies, or political tactics to prevent eligible voters from registering or casting a ballot.

Access to the ballot has been a challenging issue in American politics since our very founding as a nation, and for good reason.[68] In a representative democracy, like ours, those who elect political officials are the ones who determine public policy. Over time, the nation has extended the right to vote to groups regardless of gender, race, national origin, native language, literacy, religion, and property-ownership status. One reason the right to vote has been a contentious issue is the inherent conflict within American political thought over the relationship between voting and citizenship. Is the vote a right of citizenship or is it a privilege? A person who believes that voting is a right secured by citizenship argues that access to the ballot is fundamental and must be strongly protected by the law. For these individuals, any barrier to the ballot—be it the need to obtain an identification card, complete a complicated registration processes, or manage the commute to an distant polling place—is a badge of "second-class citizenship" and a threat to democracy. On the other hand, individuals who assume that voting is a privilege, which only certain citizens should exercise as a reward for their civic virtue or community investment, will believe that barriers to the franchise are appropriate. These advocates will support such policies as necessary to prevent potential fraud and to ensure that only the most committed and well-informed individuals determine the nation's course.[69]

Recent Examples of Voter Suppression

During the 2018 midterm elections, claims arose regarding significant voter suppression in states with highly competitive races—such as Texas, Florida, Georgia, and North Dakota. Some investigators found evidence that people were challenged when registering to vote, names were purged from voter rolls, overly strict rules regarding voter IDs were applied, voters were intimidated and harassed, polls were closed early or waiting times to vote were unreasonable, voting equipment malfunctioned, political activists were prevented from voting, and districts had been gerrymandered.[70] More recently, voter-suppression activities have been directed at college students, who are becoming an influential voting bloc. A 2019 story in *Inside Higher Education* noted that students voting near Sacred Heart University in Connecticut were confronted by poll workers who called them "stupid" and told them to go back to school, questioned them extensively about their state residency, and challenged the identification they provided.[71] This type of intimidation is not new and considered borderline voter suppression. Other states have made it difficult for students to demonstrate local residency and some, like Virginia, have moved polling places farther from campuses so that they are difficult to access.

The Question of Voter Fraud

One primary argument for limiting access to the ballot has been the desire to prevent voter fraud. Policies such as implementing voter ID laws, limiting voter-registration periods, and purging voter rolls are all designed for the stated purpose of preventing voter fraud or the casting of a ballot illegally. While this sounds like a good reason to limit the right to vote, the problem is that no research has ever uncovered contemporary evidence of voter fraud. Many public claims have been made of voter fraud after the 2016 and 2018 elections, but "extensive research reveals that fraud is very rare, voter impersonation is virtually nonexistent, and many instances of alleged fraud are, in fact, mistakes by voters or administrators."[72] In fact, President Trump created a Presidential Advisory Commission on Election Integrity in May 2017 to investigate charges of voter fraud, many of which the president himself made. However, he dissolved the commission in January 2018 before it could issue a final report.

Partisanship and Voter Suppression

In the past several years, a complicating factor regarding charges of voter suppression is that most of them have been aimed at the Republican Party because the citizens who are being prevented from voting tend to be Democrats. Why might this be? One potential explanation is that growing numbers of racial and ethnic minorities, as well as larger numbers of Millennial and Gen Z voters, have benefited the Democratic party, Republicans need to either appeal to new voters or change who is in the voting pool. In December 2019, a senior political advisor to the Trump reelection campaign, Justin Clark, was recorded while discussing voter-suppression efforts at a state chapter meeting of the Republican National Lawyers Association. When his comments were made public, he said that he was talking about the false claims of Republican activities. As noted, the partisanship surrounding this issue has certainly complicated efforts to challenge potential voter suppression.[73]

Who should have the right to vote, and when can states and municipalities legitimately limit access to the ballot or suppress the right to vote? Are there any circumstances in which a U.S. citizen should be barred from voting?

| Conclusion: Thinking Critically About What's Next in Civil Rights

For most of U.S. history, the law allowed, and in some cases even required, discrimination against people based on inherent characteristics such as race, ethnicity, and sex. This discriminatory treatment meant that the U.S. government did not guarantee all citizens equal protection of their civil rights. The long and continuing battles for civil rights of African Americans, Native Americans, and women are only part of the story. Latinos, Asian Americans, citizens with disabilities, and LGBTQ+ citizens are all currently engaged in political, legal, and civic activities aimed at guaranteeing equal protection of their civil rights. Numerous other groups are working to gain their civil rights as well. These include older Americans, poor Americans, and children born in the United States to parents who are in the country illegally. The Fourteenth Amendment extends citizenship, and hence civil rights, to these children.

In addition, questions of voter suppression have again raised concerns about what citizenship entails and what rights are guaranteed. As our national demographics continue to change, as the ethnic and racial profile of voters changes, and as our political system responds, how should we view voting? Is it a right bestowed by citizenship or a privilege limited to particular qualifications?

As individuals whose interests were not previously considered in discussions of civil rights intensify their challenges to oppression, the nation will continue to struggle with the scope and meaning of civil rights. Activists are raising access to affordable and safe housing, health care, and drinking water as civil and human rights demands.

■ References

1. David Schultz, John R. Vile, and Michelle D. Deardorff, *Constitutional Law in Contemporary America, Volume II: Civil Rights and Liberties* (Minneapolis: West Academic, 2017).

2. Joseph Landau, "Due Process and the Non-Citizen: A Revolution Reconsidered," *Connecticut Law Review* 47 (2015): 879–936.

3. *Loving v. Virginia,* 388 U.S. 1 (1967).

4. J. Spahlholz et al., "Obesity and Discrimination—A Systematic Review and Meta-Analysis of Observational Studies," Obesity Review (January 2016): 43–55.

5. Association for Psychological Studies, "Implicit Attitudes Can Change over the Long Term," January 2019, https://www.psychologicalscience.org/news/releases/implicit-attitudes-long-term-change.html.

6. Rebecca Puhl, "Weight Discrimination Is Rampant: But in Most Places It's Still Legal," Washington Post, June 21, 2019, https://www.washingtonpost.com/outlook/weight-discrimination-is-rampant-yet-in-most-places-its-still-legal/2019/06/21/f958613e-9394-11e9-b72d-d56510fa753e_story.html.

7. Timothy S. Huebner, *Liberty and Union* (Lawrence: University Press of Kansas, 2016).

8. John Hope Franklin and Evelyn Higginbotham, *From Slavery to Freedom,* 9th ed. (New York: McGraw-Hill, 2010).

9. *Dred Scott v. Sandford,* 60 U.S. 393 (1857).

10. *Plessy v. Ferguson,* 163 U.S. 537 (1896).

11. Richard Rothstein, *The Color of Law: A Forgotten History of How Our Government Segregated America* (New York: Liveright Press, 2017).

12. Walter F. Mondale, "The Civil Rights Law We Ignored," The New York Times, April 10, 2018, https://www.nytimes.com/2018/04/10/opinion/walter-mondale-fair-housing-act.html.

13. Ira Katznelson, *When Affirmative Action Was White: An Untold History of Racial Inequality in Twentieth-Century America* (New York: Liveright Press, 2005).

14. Kian Nassre, 2020. "Mapping Software Explores the Legacy of Redlining," The Tartan, February 2. http://thetartan.org/2020/2/3/scitech/housing

15. Michael Klarman, *From Jim Crow to Civil Rights* (New York: Oxford University Press, 2004).

16. Richard Kluger, *Simple Justice: The History of* Brown v. Board of Education *and Black America's Struggle for Equality* (New York: Knopf, 1976).

17. *Brown v. Board of Education,* 347 U.S. 483 (1954).

18. Klarman, 2004.

19. Timothy B. Dyson, *The Blood of Emmett Till* (New York: Simon & Schuster, 2017).

20. Jo Ann Robinson, *The Montgomery Bus Boycott and the Women Who Started It* (Knoxville: University of Tennessee Press, 1987).

21. Taylor Branch, *Parting the Waters: America during the King Years, 1954–1963* (New York: Simon & Schuster, 1988).

22. *Browder v. Gale,* 352 U.S. 903 (1956).

23. John Dittmer, *Local People: The Struggle for Civil Rights in Mississippi* (Champaign: University of Illinois Press, 1995).

24. Robert A. Pratt, *Selma's Bloody Sunday: Protest, Voting Rights, and the Struggle for Racial Equality* (Baltimore: Johns Hopkins University Press, 2016).

25. David J. Garrow, *Protest at Selma: Martin Luther King, Jr., and the Voting Rights Act of 1965* (New Haven, CT: Yale University Press, 2015).

26. Michael Honey, *Going Down Jericho Road: The Memphis Strike, Martin Luther King's Last Campaign* (New York: W. W. Norton, 2008).

27. Charles S. Bullock III and Ronald Keith Gaddie, *The Rise and Fall of the Voting Rights Act* (Norman: University of Oklahoma Press, 2016).

28. *Shelby County, Alabama v. Holder,* 570 U.S. 2 (2013).

29. U.S. Department of Justice, Civil Rights Division, *Investigation of the Ferguson Police Department*, March 4, 2015: 5.

30. *Bradwell v. Illinois,* 83 U.S. 130 (1873).

31. *Minor v. Happersett,* 88 U.S. 162 (1875).

32. Rosalyn Terborg-Penn, *African American Women in the Struggle for the Vote, 1840-1920* (Bloomington: Indiana University Press, 1998).

33. *Reed v. Reed,* 404 U.S. 71 (1971).

34. *Craig v. Boren,* 429 U.S. 190 (1976).

35. *U.S. v. Virginia,* 518 U.S. 515 (1996).

36. Jennifer Baumgardner, *F'em: Goo Goo, Gaga, and Some Thoughts on Balls* (New York: Seal Press, 2011).

37. Emily Sugerman, "MeToo: Why Are Women Sharing Stories of Sexual Assault and How Did It Start?" Independent, October 17, 2017.

38. See such works as: Rebecca Solnit, *Men Explain Things to Me* (Chicago: Haymarket Books, 2014); Chimamanda Ngozi Adichie, *We Should All Be Feminists* (New York: Anchor Books, 2015); and Roxanne Gay, *Bad Feminist* (New York: HarperCollins, 2014).

39. U.S. Department of Justice, "Hate Crimes: Laws and Policies," https://www.justice.gov/hatecrimes/laws-and-policies.

40. Human Rights Campaign, A National Epidemic: Fatal Anti-Transgender Violence in the United States in 2019, 2020, https://www.hrc.org/resources/a-national-epidemic-fatal-anti-trans-violence-in-the-united-states-in-2019.

41. *Bowers v. Hardwick,* 478 U.S. 186 (1986).

42. *Lawrence and Garner v. Texas,* 539 U.S. 558 (2003).

43. Movement Advancement Project, "Local Non-Discrimination Ordinances," 2020, https://www.lgbtmap.org/equality-maps/non_discrimination_ordinances.

44. *United States v. Windsor,* 570 U.S. 12, 2013.

45. *Obergefell v. Hodges,* 576 U.S. 644 (2015).

46. Joe R. Feagin and Clairece Booher Feagin, *Racial and Ethnic Relations* (Upper Saddle River, NJ: Prentice Hall, 2003), 135.

47. National Indian Gaming Commission, "2016 Indian Gaming Revenues Increase 4.4 Percent," July 17, 2017.

48. Feagin and Feagin, *Racial and Ethnic Relations,* 135.

49. Luis Noe-Bustamante, "Key Facts about U.S. Hispanics and Their Diverse Heritage," Pew Research Center, September 16, 2019, https://www.pewresearch.org/fact-tank/2019/09/16/key-facts-about-u-s-hispanics/.

50. Luis Noe-Bustamante, Abby Budiman, and Mark Hugo Lopez, "Where Latinos Have the Most Eligible Voters in the 2020 Election," Pew Research Center, January 31, 2020.

51. League of Latin American Citizens, "LULAC History—All for One and One for All," http://lulac.org/about/history/.

52. League of Latin American Citizens, "LULAC History—All for One and One for All," http://lulac.org/about/history/.

53. *Mendez v. Westminister,* 64 F. Supp. 544 (1946).

54. *Hernandez v. Texas,* 347 U.S. 475 (1954).

55. *Corpus Christi Independent School District v. Cisneros,* 330 F. Supp 1377 (S.D. Texas, 1977).

56. Feagin and Feagin, *Racial and Ethnic Relations,* 218.

57. Jeffrey S. Passel and D'Vera Cohn, "Mexicans Decline to Less than Half the U.S. Unauthorized Immigrant Population for the First Time," Pew Research Center, June 12, 2019, https://www.pewresearch.org/fact-tank/2019/09/16/key-facts-about-u-s-hispanics/.

58. Donald J. Trump, "Executive Order [13,768]: Enhancing Public Safety in the Interior of the United States," January 25, 2017.

59. U.S. Immigration and Customs Enforcement, *FY 2017 ICE Removal Operations Enforcement Report*, December 13, 2017.

60. Donald J. Trump, "Executive Order [13,767]: Border Security and Immigration Enforcement Improvements," January 25, 2017.

61. Abby Budiman, Anthony Cilluffo, and Neil G. Ruiz, "Key Facts About Asian origin groups in the U.S.," Pew Research Center, May 22, 2019.

62. Eric K. Yamamoto, *In the Shadow of Korematsu: Democratic Liberties and National Security* (Oxford: Oxford University Press, 2018).

63. Budiman, Cilluffo, Ruiz, 2019.

64. Budiman, Cilluffo, Ruiz, 2019.

65. Marisa Osorio, "New Edition of National Asian Pacific American Political Almanac Examines Group's Growing Impact," UCLA Newsroom, June 28, 2000.

66. Don T. Nakanishi and James Lai, *National Asian Pacific American Political Almanac, Fifteenth Edition* (Los Angeles: UCLA Asian Pacific American Center Press, 2016).

67. U.S. Equal Employment Opportunity Commission, "The Americans with Disabilities Act Amendments Act of 2008."

68. Alexander Keyssar, *The Right to Vote: The Contested History of Democracy in the United States* (New York: Basic Books, 2000); Michelle D. Deardorff, "Symposium Keynote: Constructing the Franchise: Citizenship Rights versus Privileges and their Concomitant Policies," Mississippi College Law Review 33 (2014): 161–180.

69. See such arguments as: D.B. Gantz, "Should All Voters Be Allowed to Vote?" The Blaze, February 14, 2014, www.the-blaze.com/contributions/should-all-voters-be-allowed-to-vote/; Jason Brennan, "The Right to Vote Should Be Restricted to Those with Knowledge," Aeon, September 29, 2016.

70. Danielle Root and Aadam Barclay, "Voter Suppression During the 2018 Midterm Elections," Center for American Progress, November 20, 2018.

71. Greta Anderson, "Tug-of-War Over Students' Votes," Inside Higher Education, November 12, 2019.

72. Justin Levitt, The Truth about Voter Fraud. Brennan Center for Justice, 2007, https://www.brennancenter.org/sites/default/files/2019-08/Report_Truth-About-Voter-Fraud.pdf.

73. Ken Tenbarge, "In Leaked Audio, a Top Trump Adviser Said the Republican Party Has 'Traditionally' Relied on Voter Suppression," Business Insider, December 21, 2019.

▮ Key Terms

Multiple-Choice Questions

Questions 1 and 2 are based on the chart below.

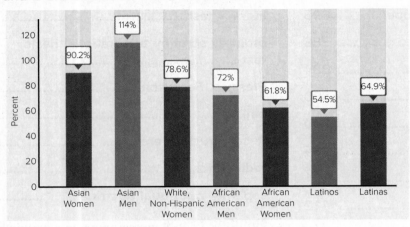

The Wage Gap by Gender and Race

Source: U.S. Census Bureau, Current Population Survey. 2019. "PINC-05. Work Experience-People 15 Years Old and Over, by Total Money Earnings, Age, Race, Hispanic Origin, Sex, and Disability Status <https://www.census.gov/data/tables/time-series/demo/income-poverty/cps-pinc/pinc-05.html#par_textimage_0> (accessed September 10, 2019).

1. Assuming that white, non-Hispanic men are at 100%, which of the following groups is most affected by the wage gap?
   A. Asian men
   B. Hispanic men
   C. White women
   D. Hispanic women

2. Which of the following is the most likely cause for the differences found in the chart?
   A. The failure to ratify the Equal Rights Amendment
   B. Lack of enforcement of Title VI of the Civil Rights Act of 1964
   C. The Supreme Court's ruling in *Reed v. Reed*
   D. A lack of women in Congress

3. All of the following methods were used in attempts to keep Black people from voting EXCEPT:
   A. Poll taxes
   B. Literacy tests
   C. Heightened scrutiny test
   D. Grandfather clauses

4. Which of the following scenarios is an accurate comparison of de jure and de facto segregation?

De jure segregation	De facto segregation
A. Laws requiring segregation of schools	Laws requiring segregation of public buses
B. Poll tax	School rules mandating separate locker rooms for Black and white athletes
C. The KKK's use of intimidation and violence to threaten African Americans	The ruling in *Plessy v. Ferguson*
D. Jim Crow laws	Blacks and whites choosing to live in separate neighborhoods

5. The "separate but equal" precedent referred to above was established by which of the following cases?
A. *Dred Scott v. Sandford,* 1857
B. *Plessy v. Ferguson,* 1896
C. *Youngstown Sheet and Tube Company v. Sawyer,* 1952
D. *Engel v. Vitale,* 1962

6. Which of the following is an example of a legal affirmative action policy?
A. A sports team's desire to have an all-female basketball squad
B. A firehouse with a quota system that only selects minority candidates
C. An airline's requirement that all flight attendants be over 5 feet tall
D. A university's use of race as one factor of consideration for admittance to its law school

7. Which of the following clauses of the Constitution was instrumental to the holding in *Brown v. Board of Education*?
A. Due process
B. Equal protection
C. Commerce
D. Habeas corpus

8. The Civil Rights Act of 1964 did which of the following?
A. Protected individuals from discrimination based on sexual orientation
B. Required equality in public accommodations
C. Integrated public schools
D. Banned literacy tests

9. Which of the following protects women from discrimination?
A. Equal Pay Act
B. Equal Rights Amendment to the Constitution
C. Gender equality act
D. Women's affirmative action act

10. Only in recent years has federal hate crime legislation been expanded to protect individuals on the basis of:

A. Race

B. Religion

C. Sexual orientation

D. National origin

■ Free Response Questions

SCOTUS Comparison

Allan Bakke, a white man, had applied to the University of California at Davis medical school on two separate occasions and was denied admission each time. As part of the medical school's affirmative action program, 16 spaces were set aside for minorities in each incoming class. Although Allan Bakke's qualifications were higher than the two separate classes of the 16 admitted minorities, he was still denied admission. In the ensuing case, *Regents of the University of California v. Bakke (1978),* Bakke contended that he was rejected each time because of his race. The Supreme Court agreed with Bakke and ruled that racial quotas are unconstitutional, but that race can be one of several criteria considered for admission.

A. Identify the constitutional clause that is common to both *Regents of the University of California v. Bakke* (1978) and *Brown v. Board of Education* (1954).

B. Based on the constitutional clause identified in part A, explain why the facts of *Regents of the University of California v. Bakke* (1978) led to a similar holding in *Brown v. Board of Education* (1954).

C. Explain an action an interest group could take if they disagreed with the ruling in *Bakke.*

Argumentation

Develop an argument in which you decide whether the use of strict scrutiny would be an appropriate test to determine the legality of sex-based discrimination.

In your essay, you must:

- Articulate a defensible claim or thesis that responds to the prompt and establishes a line of reasoning.

- Support your claim with at least TWO pieces of accurate and relevant information:

  - At least ONE piece of evidence must be from one of the following foundational documents:

    — The Constitution of the United States (including the Bill of Rights and subsequent amendments)

    — *Federalist* No. 78

- Use a second piece of evidence from another foundational document from the list or from your study of civil rights

- Use reasoning to explain why your evidence supports your claim/thesis

- Respond to an opposing or alternative perspective using refutation, concession, or rebuttal

Concept Application

"A federal appeals court upheld Texas' voter identification law on Friday, saying that it does not discriminate against black and Hispanic voters. The original law, which was known as Senate Bill 14 and was passed by the Republican-dominated Texas Legislature in 2011, required voters to show a driver's license, passport or other government-issued photo ID before casting a ballot. The law took effect in 2013, and it was found by the same federal appellate court to have a discriminatory effect on black and Hispanic voters, many of whom lack government-issued photo ID. One of the most contentious issues with the new law is that it creates criminal penalties for those who make false statements in their sworn affidavits, a move that critics of the law believe confuses and frightens potential voters."

New York Times, April 27, 2018

After reading the scenario, respond to A, B, and C below:

A. Describe a power Congress could use to address the comments outlined in the scenario.

B. In the context of the scenario, explain how the use of congressional power described in Part A can be affected by its interaction with the federal courts.

C. In the context of the scenario, explain how the interaction between Congress and the federal courts can be affected by linkage institutions.

At the beginning of the Unit, we asked you to consider these questions:

- **How has the balance between order and liberty changed over time?**

- **How have civil liberties and rights changed over time?**

- **What changes do you expect will take place in the future to both preserve liberty and protect order?**

As the rights of criminal defendants have been increasingly protected, it has become more difficult to prosecute crimes and maintain order. It was easier for prosecutors to gain convictions before *Mapp v. Ohio* restricted the use of evidence in courts and before *Gideon v. Wainright* required all defendants be granted lawyers in capital cases. The rights of women and racial minorities have evolved over time due to Congressional legislation. While the Equal Rights Amendment granting women full equal rights under the Constitution failed to be ratified, women gained the right to vote under the 19th Amendment, and gained some protections for equal pay with the passage of the Civil Rights Act of 1964 and the passage of the Equal Pay Act. African Americans gained voting rights protection with the ratification of the 15th Amendment and the passage of the Voting Rights act of 1965. Yet the fight for equal rights for women and racial minorities continue. A woman has yet to be elected to be president and women are still paid less than men for comparable work. LGBTQ individuals still lack protections under the law, including in housing and employment discrimination.

The advancements for both women and minorities were preceded by large social movements and protests that placed pressure on elected officials to make changes. What will the future hold? While it is impossible to know for certain, it seems that there is potential for the protests over excessive use of force by the police to lead to change in the same way that social movements and pressure for change for women and minorities eventually led to legal changes.

Multiple Choice Questions

In response to the coronavirus pandemic, virtual criminal hearings have become a new necessity for an expeditious court process. However, virtual hearings are creating new inequities. Not all have access to high-speed internet to appear in court with an attorney. While the attorneys can appear in court virtually, poor clients often lack the ability to do so. The Constitution states that all citizens are to have equal protection under the law, yet digital legal hearings have not kept that promise. Virtual hearings protect the wealthy from exposure to coronavirus, leaving the poor behind.

1. Which of the following best summarizes the argument in the passage above?
   A. Individuals in rural America improve their ability to defend themselves over the internet
   B. Virtual criminal hearings are efficient during a pandemic but are also inequitable
   C. Virtual hearings improve access to the justice system
   D. Poor rural Americans refuse to access the online judicial system

2. Which of the following amendments protects a right discussed in the passage?
   A. First Amendment
   B. Second Amendment
   C. Fourth Amendment
   D. Sixth Amendment

3. Which of the following Supreme Court cases is most related to the concern expressed in the passage?
   A. *Engel v. Vitale*
   B. *Wisconsin v. Yoder*
   C. *Tinker v. Des Moines*
   D. *Gideon v. Wainwright*

4. Based on the text, which of the following would the author most likely agree with?

A. The Constitution forbids online court hearings

B. Online court hearings, so long as counsel is provided, are fair

C. The legal system discriminates against low income citizens

D. The internet is a tool to make criminal proceedings more transparent and fair

THANKYOU FOR CALLING CIVIL LIBERTIES — YOUR CALL MAY BE RECORDED...

CartoonStock.com

Clive Goddard/CartoonStock

5. Which of the following best describes the message in the political cartoon above?

A. Civil liberties are widely protected through voice recordings

B. Americans dislike conversations about civil liberties

C. Americans often lack privacy with their personal information

D. Voice mail is outdated technology

6. Which of the following Supreme Court cases is most relevant to the topic of the cartoon?

A. *Roe v. Wade*

B. *Schenck v. United States*

C. *New York Times v. U.S.*

D. *McDonald v. Chicago*

7. The establishment clause of the Constitution does which of the following?

A. Prevents the Congress from creating a nationally recognized religion

B. Allows the establishment of public schools at the state level

C. Requires the establishment of a free independent press

D. Provides for the general welfare

8. The free exercise clause of the Constitution does which of the following?

A. Allows individuals to openly criticize government leaders
B. Allows individuals to choose any religion
C. Requires freedom of movement
D. Provides an open market

9. Which of the following was a result of the *Engel v. Vitale* Supreme Court ruling?

A. A religious group was allowed to opt their children out of school after the 8th grade for religious reasons
B. Formal prayer by school leaders was barred in public schools
C. Right to counsel meant that a lawyer must be provided to those who cannot afford one
D. Students have the right to protest so long as the protest is not substantially disruptive

10. Which of the following correctly matches an amendment with the Supreme Court case that interpreted that amendment?

	Amendment	Case
A.	1st	*Gideon v. Wainright*
B.	2nd	*McDonald v. Chicago*
C.	4th	*Schenck v. U.S.*
D.	5th	*Tinker v. Des Moines*

11. Which of the following scenarios would most likely violate the ban on unreasonable searches and seizures?

A. A police officer tickets an individual for contraband in plain sight
B. A school official announces all lockers will be searched the next day
C. A police officer enters a home to search for contraband without a warrant
D. A search checkpoint is established along the U.S.-Mexico border

12. Which of the following actions by public school students would most likely be protected speech?

A. Private prayer by students
B. Student-led prayer over the PA during morning announcements
C. Wearing a T-shirt advocating illegal activity
D. Holding a sign at a school parade with profane messages

13. Which of the following was used by the Supreme Court to selectively incorporate parts of the Bill of Rights?

A. Equal protection clause
B. Due process clause
C. Habeas corpus clause
D. Privileges and immunities clause

14. Which of the following did Congress provide for under the Civil Rights Act of 1964?

A. Voting rights

B. Protections from discrimination based on race and sex

C. Gender identity protection

D. Right to protest

15. White, non-Hispanic men (not shown in the chart) are at 100% and the bars show the percentage that other demographic groups make up.

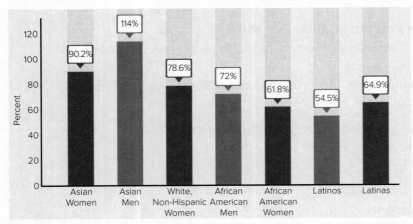

Source: U.S. Census Bureau, Current Population Survey. 2019. "PINC-05. Work Experience-People 15 Years Old and Over, by Total Money Earnings, Age, Race, Hispanic Origin, Sex, and Disability Status <https://www.census.gov/data/tables/time-series/demo/income-poverty/cps-pinc/pinc-05.html#par_textimage_0> (accessed September 10, 2019).

Which of the following conclusions can be drawn from the bar graph above?

A. White non-Hispanic men have the highest overall income when compared to other demographic groups.

B. Latinas are the lowest-earning demographic group

C. The income of all demographic groups has decreased over time

D. Across demographic groups, women earn less than men of the same demographic group

16. Which of the following increased women's rights nationwide?

A. The Equal Rights Amendment to the Constitution

B. The 19th Amendment

C. The 15th Amendment

D. *Brown v. Board of Education*

"A glass ceiling?... Don't be ridiculous. The sign works just fine."

Loren Fishman/CartoonStock

17. Which of the following best describes the main idea of cartoon above?
   A. Women's opportunities for career advancement are limited
   B. Women are often not allowed to socialize in all-male lounge areas at work
   C. Women and men often argue in the workplace
   D. Women are slowly breaking through the glass ceiling

18. Which of the following laws is most relevant to the cartoon above?
   A. Americans with Disabilities Act
   B. Affordable Care Act
   C. Voting Rights Act
   D. Equal Pay Act

19. Which of the following is a main idea expressed in *Letter from Birmingham Jail?*
   A. Due process of law is important for African American liberty
   B. Injustice anywhere is injustice everywhere
   C. Everyone has a right to trial by a jury of one's peers
   D. Right to an attorney will provide greater justice

20. The holding in *Brown v. Board of Education* relied on which of the following clauses of the Constitution?
   A. Commerce
   B. Supremacy
   C. Equal protection
   D. Due process

▉ Free Response Questions

Argumentation

Is there a proper balance between liberty and order? Develop an argument that answers this question.

In your essay, you must:

- Articulate a defensible claim or thesis that responds to the prompt and establishes a line of reasoning

- Support your claim with at least TWO pieces of accurate and relevant information:

  - At least ONE piece of evidence must be from one of the following foundational documents:
    — *Letter from Birmingham Jail*

    — The U.S. Constitution

  - Use a second piece of evidence from another foundational document from the list, from federal law(s), and your study of social movements

- Use reasoning to explain why your evidence supports your claim/thesis

- Respond to an opposing or alternative perspective using refutation, concession, or rebuttal

SCOTUS Comparison

A. Identify a similarity between the holding in *Timbs v. Indiana* and the holding in *Gideon v. Wainwright*.

B. Describe how the different facts in *Timbs* and *Gideon* led to different outcomes in the two cases.

C. Describe how the *Timbs* and *Gideon* holdings may limit the government's ability to maintain order.

Source: https://www.oyez.org/cases/2018/17-1091

Concept Application

"New Political Party Platform"

The new political party goals:

- Challenge the Democratic and Republican Parties as a viable third party and win elections

- Promote full employment

- End police brutality

- End racism and sexism

After reading the scenario above, respond to A, B, and C below:

A. Describe a power Congress could use to address an element of the "New Political Party Platform" as described above.

B. In the context of the scenario, explain how Congress's action you identified above may be affected by its interaction with the federal bureaucracy.

C. In the context of the scenario, explain how the interaction between Congress and the bureaucracy can be affected by linkage institutions.

AMERICAN POLITICAL IDEOLOGIES AND BELIEFS

This unit will explore American political ideologies and beliefs. In Chapter 10: Political Socialization and Public Opinion, you will learn about "political socialization," or the process by which citizens acquire beliefs about government, and how those beliefs are shaped. While there are great variations within all demographic groups, data tells us that there are patterns among groups: young people are more liberal and likely to vote Democratic, for example, while older Americans tend to be more conservative and are more likely to support Republican candidates.

In addition to studying demographic trends in attitudes, you will learn about widely held political beliefs in the U.S., which are referred to as political culture. The process by which we acquire political beliefs is called political socialization. In this chapter, we evaluate the many ways in which we we are socialized to our political beliefs, whether that is through our friends, our parents, or a YouTube influencer. We also analyze how being socialized today is different that how your parents were socialized to their beliefs.

To learn about trends in American attitudes, political scientists take surveys of populations, also known as public opinion polls. You will learn about the types of public opinion polls and characteristics of a valid poll. Because public opinion is constantly in motion, a poll is only a snapshot in time, and all polls, even those considered by political scientists to be "valid," will have a margin of error. While poll results have become more precise in recent years, ironically polls today are more difficult to conduct due to cell phone technology, which makes it more difficult to accurately measure the opinion of a given population.

Poll results often guide elected leaders to tackle public policy problems. In this chapter, we will explore American public opinion: what the people think of their leaders, and what they think the most important problem facing our nation is. We also will explore some similarities and differences in the views of various demographic groups in the United States.

Aaron Roeth Photography

How Do Widely Held Political Ideologies Shape Policy Debates and Choices in American Politics?

Big Ideas

In this unit, you will explore how citizen beliefs shape economic, domestic, and foreign/national security policy. Unit 4, American Political Ideologies and Beliefs, includes the following chapters:

Chapter 10: Political Socialization and Public Opinion

Chapter 11: Economic Policy

Chapter 12: Domestic Policy

Chapter 13: Foreign Policy and National Security

The AP U.S. Government Big Ideas addressed in Unit 4 are:

Big Idea 4: Competing Policy-making Interests: Multiple actors and institutions interact to produce and implement possible policies.

Big Idea 5: Methods of Political Analysis: Using various types of analyses, political scientists measure how U.S. political behavior, attitudes, ideologies, and institutions are shaped by a number of factors over time.

In these policy chapters, you will learn about the role of political ideology in shaping public policies and will consider how public opinion and political behavior influence the various institutions of government to produce policies in these broad categories.

Questions to consider as you read the material in this unit include:

- **What are the ways in which political scientists organize and display data? What are limitations of data and data presentations?**

- **What are the relationships among demographic characteristics and political beliefs/behaviors? What are the implications of the trends?**

- **How do ideologies shape policy outcomes, and what are the implications of how ideologies shape outcomes, considering ideological breakdown in the U.S.?**

Skills and Practices

When political scientists study ideologies and beliefs of a population, they often publish a summary of findings in charts, graphs, and tables, and as a student of government and politics, you will find yourself analyzing data generated by political scientists. Skills that AP U.S. Government and Politics students will develop include accurately describing quantitative data, connecting trends in data to political science concepts, and drawing conclusions about data. This unit has a strong connection to Big Idea 5.

As you read through the following chapters, consider how the skills of description, analysis, comparison, and causation help you to make sense of the information. By the end of this unit, you should be able to answer questions such as:

- **Why do so many demographic groups in the U.S. vote as a bloc?**

- **Why has trust in the national government waned in the last 50 years?**

- **How does public opinion affect policy?**

- **How does a person's perspective and life experience impact his or her political ideology?**

Political Socialization and Public Opinion

Nicholas Kamm/AFP/Getty Images

THEN

Families and schools were the most important influences on children as they developed their political views.

NOW

Families and schools remain influential, but the media have increased their multiple roles in developing the political views of members of the Millennial generation and Generation Z.

NEXT

How will technology affect the socialization of new generations of Americans?

How will polling organizations harness the power of the Internet to measure public opinion more accurately?

How will government officials reconcile differences in public opinion between generations of Americans?

■ Chapter Introduction

Our examination of Public Opinion and Socialization in this chapter sets the stage for studying the kinds of policies that policy-makers in the United States decide on, whether those policies concern domestic, economic or foreign policy matters. That is because governing — including the very important process of policy-making — takes place with in a constantly evolving political context, and that context is the subject of our focus in this chapter.

Political socialization (the process by which we acquire our political viewpoints) is shifting drastically as technology places an increasingly important role in our lives. While your parents and grandparents were likely primarily influenced most by the traditional ways in which we are socialized to our political views — things like family, school, peers, the church, and the media, today the media — more accurately social media — places a disproportionate role in the socialization of young people. But through all of the ways in which we acquire our views (these ways are called "agents of socialization," and will be discussed in much greater detail in this chapter), those viewpoints cumulatively become the aggregate of public opinion.

Public opinion, or what the people think about any number of different issues, is important because government leaders, especially elected government leaders, want to please their constituents. And so, the connection between public opinion and policy-making is strong: oftentimes it is the people who demand that issues be placed on the public agenda. Think, for example, to the summer of 2020 when two issues, dealing with the COVID-19 pandemic and the #BlackLivesMatter protests, captured the American people's attention and sparked calls for increased leadership concerning both issues. Public opinion on these issues was not necessarily unified, but there was widespread agreement that political leaders should do *something*. Other times, political leaders look to the America people for direction on *what* should be done, and take their policymaking directives from the will of the people.

Throughout this chapter, we will examine the changing ways in which Americans are acquiring their political viewpoints, and we'll examine some of the more traditional ways in which we still become socialized to politics. Finally, we'll explore some key trends regarding American's viewpoints: what they think of the various branches of government, what they identify are the most pressing concerns for policymakers should be, and finally, we'll look at some similarities and differences in the viewpoints of various subsets of Americans on these issues.

Political Socialization and Civic Participation

How do we acquire our political views? Although an infant would be hard pressed to evaluate the president's job performance, children begin to acquire political opinions at an early age, and this process continues throughout adulthood. As noted earlier, the process by which we develop our political values and opinions is called **political socialization.** As we develop our political values, we form the bedrock of what will become our political ideology, our integrated system of general political values. As this ideology emerges, it shapes how we view most political subjects: what side we take on public issues, how we evaluate candidates for office, and what our opinions on policies will be.

Although many people tend to think that political socialization occurs only as they approach voting age, in reality this process begins at home in very early childhood. Core tenets of our belief system—including our political ideology, our beliefs about people of different races and sexes, even our party identification—are often firmly embedded before we have completed elementary school.

A key aspect of political socialization is whether children are socialized to participate in politics. Simply put, civically engaged parents often have civically engaged children. Parents who engage in active forms of participation, such as volunteering on a campaign, and passive forms, such as staying informed and discussing important events, watching the news, or reading a newspaper, demonstrate to children what matters to them. Parents who change the channel to a rerun of *The Office* during an important presidential news conference are also socializing their children to their values. Children absorb the political views of their parents as well: A parent's subtle (or sometimes not so subtle!) comments about the president, a political news story, or a policy debate contribute to a child's political socialization by shaping that child's views.

The Process of Political Socialization

The beliefs and values we learn early in life also help shape how we view new information. Although events may change our views, we often choose to perceive events in a way that is consistent with our earlier beliefs. For example, people's evaluation of which candidate "won" a debate often coincides strongly with their party identification. Thus, the process of political socialization tends to be cumulative.

Historically, most social scientists have agreed that family and school have the strongest influence on political socialization. Our families teach us that it is—or is not—valuable to be an informed citizen and coach us in the ways in which we should participate in the civic life of our communities. For example, if your mother is active in Republican Party politics in your town, you are more likely to be active in that party than someone whose parents are not involved. Is your father active in charitable organizations such as the local food bank? He might ask you to run in a 5K race to raise money to buy food for the upcoming holiday season. Schools also influence our political socialization by teaching us shared cultural values. And in recent times, the omnipresent role that the media play in everyday life warrants their inclusion as one of the prime agents of political socialization.

political socialization
The process by which we develop our political values and opinions.

Participating in Civic Life

Studies indicate that children whose parents are active in politics or in their community are more likely to be active themselves. Schools also play an important role in socializing young people to become active in civic life; college students are more likely to participate than young people of the same age who are not attending school, and the longer people continue their education, the more likely they will be active in their communities.[1]

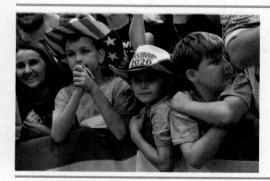

>> Children are socialized to the views of their parents at a very early age. What opinions were you socialized to as a young child?

Mandel Ngan/AFP/Getty Images

From our families and schools we also learn the value of becoming informed. Parents and schools, along with the media and the other agents of socialization that are discussed in the next section, provide us with important information that we can use to make decisions about our political actions. People who lack political knowledge, by contrast, tend not to be actively involved in their communities.[2] In fact, research indicates that when young people use any source of information regularly, including newspapers, radio, television, magazines, and the Internet, they are more likely to engage in all forms of civic participation. There is also a strong link between being informed and voting behavior. According to the results of one survey that measured civic engagement among young people, "youth who are registered to vote are more informed than their non-registered peers. Eighty-six percent of young registered voters answered at least one of the knowledge questions (measuring political knowledge) correctly as opposed to 78 percent of youth who are not registered to vote."[3]

An increasingly common observation about American political life is that deep divisions exist in American society, and that these divisions between groups tamp down participation in civic life, as individuals get turned off by the negativity and divisiveness. This is particularly true of the partisan divide that exists between Democrats and Republicans (see "Thinking Critically").

■ Agents of Socialization

Learning, culture, and socialization occur through **agents of socialization,** the individuals, organizations, and institutions that facilitate the acquisition of political views. Among the most important agents of socialization are family, the media, schools, churches, peers, and political and community leaders. Our political views are also shaped by who we are; our race, ethnicity, gender, and age all influence how we become socialized to political and community life.

agents of socialization
The individuals, organizations, and institutions that facilitate the acquisition of political views.

Family Influences on Attitudes, Opinions, and Actions

Family takes one of the most active roles in socializing us to politics and influencing our political views and behaviors. We learn whether our family

A Nation Divided?

THE ISSUE: Many Americans bemoan the "us versus them" nature of American society today. They argue that the differences between Democrats and Republicans are so serious that they are tearing apart the fabric of our country and that the divides are so deep and rancorous that we are increasingly unlikely to be characterized as "one nation, indivisible." Are we living in a nation divided?

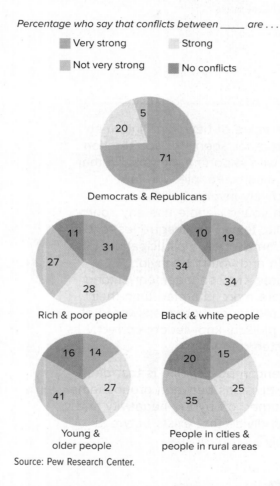

Percentage who say that conflicts between _____ are . . .

■ Very strong ■ Strong
■ Not very strong ■ No conflicts

Democrats & Republicans

Rich & poor people   Black & white people

Young & older people   People in cities & people in rural areas

Source: Pew Research Center.

YES: The data suggest that real, serious differences exist between Democrats and Republicans and that these differences reflect conflicting core values. More specifically, Democrats and Republicans differ in their policy priorities. Partisan support for one party or the other solidifies these very real differences. In turn, these differences have created a polarized structure in society, where even family dinners turn into brawls, and political intolerance is the norm.

NO: While deep divisions exist between Democrats and Republicans, these divisions are limited to one sector of our society—politics. In reality, on a day-to-day basis, the public perceives few sources of

---

WHAT DO YOU THINK?

1. Do you think the United States is becoming increasingly divided? Do you think the divide that exists reflects serious divisions, or that it comes from small minorities of people who are loudly vocalizing their views?

2. According to the data, besides the differences associated with political party affiliation, where do people perceive the greatest conflict? How might that conflict relate to partisan differences?

3. Examine the data concerning perception of differences between the old and young and between people in cities versus rural areas. Did the people who responded to this poll perceive a significant conflict between those groups?

conflict between other groups. For example, few see evidence of divisions between Black and white people, old and young people, or rural and urban people. Politics is supposed to reflect differences, and the divide between Democrats and Republicans does not mean that the nation itself is fractured.

OTHER APPROACHES: The data regarding partisan divisions are troubling, and while many strong disagreements clearly exist between Democrats and Republicans, the increased rancor and divisiveness stem in large part from very vocal extremists within each party. While many Democrats and Republicans disagree with each other, their disagreement can still be healed. The vitriol and division come from a small minority of individuals making a lot of noise and seeking to increase those divides.

members value civic activism by observing their actions and listening to their views. The children of political activists are taught to be engaged citizens. They may see their parents attend city council meetings, host Democratic or Republican club meetings in their home, or help local candidates for office by volunteering to campaign door to door on a weekend afternoon. Other parents may teach different forms of political engagement—some young children might attend protests or demonstrations with their parents or boycott a particular product for political reasons. When political activists discuss their own involvement, they often observe that "politics is in my blood." In reality, political activism is passed from one generation to the next *through example*.

In other homes, however, parents are not involved in politics or their communities. They may lack the time to participate in political activities, or they may fail to see the value of doing so. They may have a negative opinion of people who participate in politics, making such comments as "all politicians are corrupt," "they're just in it for themselves," or "it's all about ego." Such opinions convey to children that politics is not valued and may in fact be frowned on. A parent's political apathy need not necessarily sour a son or a daughter on politics or civic engagement permanently, however. Instead, first-generation activists often point to external influences such as school, the media, friends, and public policies, any of which can cause someone to become involved in civic life, regardless of family attitudes.

Our families influence not only whether or not we are civically active participants in the political process, but also what we believe. While parents or older siblings may discuss specific issues or policies, their attitudes and outlook also shape

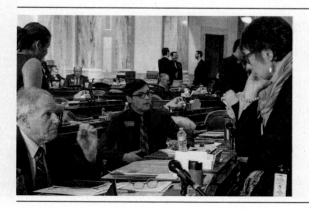

≫ In 2016, Jacob Bachmeier (center), age 18, won a seat in the Montana House of Representatives, becoming the youngest person in U.S. history elected to public office.

Bobby Caina Calvan/AP Images

children's general political attitudes and ideology. Children absorb their parents' beliefs—whether their parents think the government should have a larger or smaller role in people's lives, whether they value equality between the sexes and the races, whether they consider people in government to be trustworthy, and even specific opinions they have about political leaders. In fact, we can see evidence of how strongly parents' views are transmitted to their children in one of the best predictors of the results of presidential elections: Each election year until the publication folded in 2012, the *Weekly Reader*, a current events magazine that many school districts subscribed to, conducted nonrandomized polls of its readers. Since 1956, the first-grade through twelfth-grade student poll had correctly predicted the outcome of 90 percent of all presidential elections. Children know for whom their parents will vote and mimic that behavior in their responses to the poll.

The Media's Ever-Increasing Role in Socialization

An almost ever-present fixture in the lives of young Americans today, the media contribute to the political socialization of Americans in many ways. Television, radio,

---

SOURCE ANALYSIS   ANALYZING SECONDARY SOURCES

News that is generated by a media outlet that is designed to deceive the public while pretending to be legitimate news is referred to today as fake news. The ability of anyone to disseminate fake news widely has never been greater—as fake news is now routinely generated through social media and websites curated by individuals to look like real news. Misinformation spread through fake news can distort election campaigns, affect public perceptions, or shape human emotions.

You will respond to scenario-based questions on the free response section of the AP exam. How would you respond to the questions below?

Scenario: In 2016 there were organized efforts to disseminate several fake news stories, including Pope Francis endorsing Donald Trump for president, Hillary Clinton selling weapons to ISIS, and "Pizzagate." Pizzagate was a fake news story that alleged that sexually abused children were hidden in a pizza parlor and that Clinton knew about the ring. The fake conspiracy known as Pizzagate resulted in an individual with an assault weapon (who was later arrested) driving to find the children in the pizza parlor.

After reading the scenario, respond to A, B, and C below.

A. Explain the role of the media as a linkage institution in the scenario above.

B. Considering free speech protections, how can lawmakers address the issue of 'fake news'?

C. In the context of the scenario, explain how the interaction between the media and Congress and the president as described in this scenario may have affected the election of 2016.

Source: https://www.brookings.edu/research/how-to-combat-fake-news-and-disinformation/

---

social media, the Internet, and various forms of electronic entertainment and print media help shape Americans' political perspectives. First, the media help shape societal norms. In our early lives, the media impart norms and values on children's shows such as *Sesame Street*, *Barney*, and *Peppa Pig*, which teach about diversity. These shows and others reflect changing societal standards and values. The media also reinforce core democratic values. Television programs like *Dancing with the Stars*, *Survivor*, and *The Biggest Loser* incorporate the principle of voting: through telephone, online, or texted votes, viewers decide which contestant stays or goes.

Second, the media also help determine the national agenda. Whether they are covering the elections, the latest economic news, or congressional policy debates, the media focus the attention of the American public. This attention may then have spillover effects as people demand action on a policy issue.

Third, the media educate the public about policy issues. Local and national news programs, newsmagazine shows, and even comedies such as *Full Frontal with Samantha Bee* or *Saturday Night Live*'s "Weekend Update," inform viewers about current events, the actions of policymakers, and public policy challenges in communities, states, and the nation.

Schools, Patriotism, and Civic Participation

As early as preschool, children in the United States are socialized to believe in democracy and express patriotism. Schools socialize children to the concept of democracy by making the idea tangible for them. Leading up to Election Day, children might vote for their favorite snack and wait for the results at the end of the day. Or they might compare varieties of apples or grapes, or books, and then vote for a favorite. Lessons such as these introduce children to processes associated with democracy at its most basic level: They learn about comparing attributes, choosing a favorite, voting, and winning and losing.

Children also are taught patriotism as they recite the Pledge of Allegiance every day, sing patriotic songs, and learn to venerate the "founding fathers," especially George Washington, and other American heroes, including Ben Franklin, Abraham Lincoln, and Dr. Martin Luther King, Jr. Traditionally, elementary and high schools in the United States emphasized the "great men in great moments" form of history, a history that traditionally concentrated solely on the contributions of men in formal governmental or military settings. Today, however, the curriculum often includes contributions by women and racial and ethnic minorities, including African Americans and Latinx.

Education also plays a pivotal role in determining *who* will participate in the political affairs of the community. Research indicates that higher levels of education are associated with higher levels of political activism, which is passed through generations. In a book on civic voluntarism, Sidney Verba, Kay Schlozman, and Henry Brady wrote: "Well-educated parents are more likely to also be politically active and to discuss politics at home and to produce children who are active in high school. Growing up in a politicized household and being active in high school are associated with political engagement."[4]

Religious Institutions: Faith as an Agent of Socialization

The influence of religious institutions and religion in general on one's political socialization varies a great deal from individual to individual. For some people, faith communities formed at a church, temple, or mosque play a key, defining role in the development of their political beliefs. For some, the body of beliefs their religion conveys are the fundamental building blocks of all other beliefs and actions in their life, including their political views and behaviors. For others, religious institutions and faith are irrelevant.

For many years, political scientists have examined the effect that religious affiliation—whether one is Catholic or Jewish, Protestant or Muslim—has on political preferences. For example, religion is related to how people view various issues, especially the issue of abortion. But more recent analysis shows that a better predictor of the impact of religion on voting is not so much which religion an individual practices but how regularly he or she practices it. In general, it seems that those who regularly attend religious services are more likely to share conservative values—and support Republican candidates in general elections.

Research also shows that this relationship between frequency of church attendance and identification with the Republican Party is particularly strong among white Protestants but less so among Catholics, who are generally more Democratic, and among African Americans. African American voters are even more likely than Catholics to vote for a Democratic candidate but are also likely to have high levels of religiosity, as measured by frequency of attending services.

Figure 10.1 shows the breakdown in party affiliation by religiosity. The results are based on how frequently respondents attend church. Note in this figure that a majority—58 percent—of those who frequently attend church and other religious services voted Republican in the 2018 midterm elections. Those who attend religious services less regularly are less likely to have voted Republican: Of those who attended services a few times a month, 46 percent voted Republican. And that percentage dropped to 37 percent among those who attended services a few times a year, and 30 percent among those who never attended services. Conversely, individuals' likelihood of voting Democratic increased among those who attended

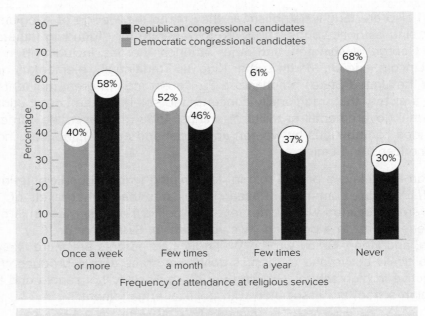

FIGURE 10.1 Candidate Preference of Religious and Non-Religious Americans

Source: www.pewresearch.org/fact-tank/2018/11/07/how-religious-groups-voted-in-the-midterm-elections/

services less regularly, as indicated in Figure 10.1. Although a strong link exists between religiosity and political party, the differences between the proclivities of religious and nonreligious voters are applicable only to white voters—as discussed later in this chapter. African Americans are likely to be Democrats no matter how religious they are; only 10 percent of very religious African Americans identify themselves as Republican. And although religious Latinos and Asian Americans are more likely to be Republican, by and large, majorities of both groups identify as Democrats. Nonetheless, the relationship among religiosity, party voting, and party identification is an important factor in American politics, particularly to the extent that religiosity shapes political views on social issues—abortion or gay marriage, say—and renders them moral imperatives for voters, rather than mere opinions.

Peers and Group Norms

Friends, neighbors, coworkers, and other peers influence political socialization. Through peers, we learn about community and the political climate and values of the area in which we live. For example, your neighbors might inform you that a particular member of the city council is a strong advocate for your neighborhood on the council, securing funds for recreational facilities or increased police protection in your area. Or a coworker might let you know what your member of Congress is doing to help save jobs in the industry in which you work. Keep in mind, however, that much research indicates that the primary function of peers is to reinforce our already-held beliefs and values. Typically, the people with whom you are acquainted are quite similar to you. Although diversity exists in many settings, the norms and values of the people you know tend to be remarkably similar to your own.

Political and Community Leaders: Opinion Influencers

Political and community leaders also help to socialize people and influence public opinion. Positions advocated by highly regarded government leaders hold particular sway, and the president plays an especially important role in shaping the views of Americans. Consider, for example, the national debate that occurred when then-presidential candidate Donald Trump proposed "building a wall" between the United States and Mexico to prevent people from entering the country illegally. Suddenly, what once had been considered a fringe idea was embraced by a sizable proportion of the population. But political leaders are not the only ones who can influence public opinion. Consider, for example, the influence that student activists from Marjory Stoneman Douglas High School had on public opinion and in compelling action regarding the issue of gun safety after the mass shooting at their high school in 2018. And chances are that in your town, the views of community leaders—elected and not—influence the way the public perceives local policies. Perhaps the fire or police chief endorses a candidate for city council, or the popular football coach for the Police Athletic League makes the funding of a new football field a policy priority in your town. Often we rely on the recommendations and priorities of well-respected leaders who have earned our trust.

Demographic Characteristics: Our Politics Are a Reflection of Us

Who we are often influences our life experiences, which shape our political socialization and therefore what we think. The racial and ethnic groups to which we belong, our gender, our age and the events that have shaped our lives, and where we live all play a role in how we are socialized to political and community life, our

FIGURE 10.2 Candidate Support by Racial and Ethnic Group Which racial group had the highest proportion of Trump supporters? Of Biden supporters? Which racial or ethnic group was the most unified? Which was the most divided?

Source: Pew Research Center

Legend: Biden | Trump | Other/Won't say

Whites: 42% / 57% / 1%
Blacks: 87% / 12% / 1%
Latinx: 66% / 32% / 2%
Asian: 63% / 31% / 6%
Other/Multiracial: 58% / 40% / 2%

values and priorities, and even whom we vote for. Demographic characteristics also shape our levels of civic involvement and may even help determine the ways in which we contribute to the civic life of our communities and our nation.

RACE AND ETHNICITY In general, whites, African Americans, Latinos, and Asian Americans prefer different candidates, hold different political views, and have different levels of civic involvement. Among the most salient of these differences are candidate preferences, which are reflective of party affiliation and ideology.

When analyzing candidate support by various racial and ethnic groups in the 2020 election, we can see that there are significant differences in the levels of support given to the Democratic and Republican candidates for president among African Americans and non-Hispanic whites, though of course there is variation within these groups. As shown in Figure 10.2, Black voters, Latinx voters and Asian voters were much more likely to support President Biden and Vice President Kamala Harris over Donald Trump and Mike Pence. The data in figure 10.2 are consistent with previous election years, which show the strongest support for Democrats among Black voters, though Biden increased the vote share among white voters (up from 37 percent in 2016) in 2020.

TABLE 10.1 ■ Latinx Party Identification by National Origin

Which Latinx nationality is most likely to identify as Democratic? Which as Republican? Which groups are the least Republican?

National Origin	PARTY IDENTIFICATION		
	Republican	Democratic	Independent
Puerto Rican	22%	57%	21%
Mexican	22	55	23
Cuban	33	48	19
Dominican	7	80	13
Salvadoran	12	52	36
Other	15	41	44

Source: Pew Research Center Survey Of Hispanic Adults, May 24–July 28, 2013, Pew Research Center.

But significant differences exist even within racial and ethnic groups.[5] Table 10.1 shows how the various categories of Latinx differ in terms of party identification. As the table shows, majorities of Latinx who identify themselves as Puerto Ricans, Dominicans, Salvadorans, and Mexican Americans (who constitute the largest nationality of all Hispanic Americans) identify as Democrats; Cubans, however, identify more strongly as Republicans. In fact, in 2016, 54 percent of Cuban American voters cast ballots for Donald Trump, compared to only 26 percent of Latinx of other national origins, a trend that proved pivotal in Trump's winning the state of Florida in 2020.[6]

Party affiliation among ethnic groups within the Asian American community also varies somewhat. In general, about 60 percent of all Asian Americans are registered Democrats. South Asians are most likely to be Democrats, and majorities of Chinese and Koreans are Democrats as well. A quarter to a third of all Korean, Southeast Asian, Filipino, and Chinese Americans are unaffiliated with either party.[7]

GENDER Public opinion polls and voting behavior indicate that men and women have very different views on issues, have different priorities when it comes to public issues, and often favor different candidates, particularly in national elections. This difference in men's and women's views and voting preferences is called the **gender gap**, the measurable difference in the way women and men vote for candidates and in the way they view political issues. Eleanor Smeal, who at the time was president of the National Organization for Women, first noticed the gender gap. In the 1980 presidential election, Democrat incumbent Jimmy

gender gap
The measurable difference in the way women and men vote for candidates and in the way they view political issues.

>> Eleanor Smeal, president of the Feminist Majority and a former president of the National Organization for Women, coined the term "gender gap" after the 1980 presidential election. Smeal noticed that in poll after poll, women favored Democratic incumbent Jimmy Carter over Republican challenger Ronald Reagan. Was there a gender gap in the 2020 presidential election?

Lawrence Jackson/Associated Press/AP Images

Carter lost to Republican challenger Ronald Reagan, but Smeal noticed that in poll after poll, women favored Carter.

Since that watershed 1980 election, the gender gap has been a factor in every subsequent presidential election, and in every presidential election, women are more likely than men to favor Democratic candidates—a fact that is representative of the differing partisan leanings of men and women, as shown in Figure 10.3. The gender gap is particularly pronounced among members of the Millennial generation: While both male and female Millennials are more likely to favor the Democratic Party than other age cohorts, Millennial women overwhelmingly lean Democrat, with 70 percent

DATA ANALYSIS   EVALUATING THE FACTS

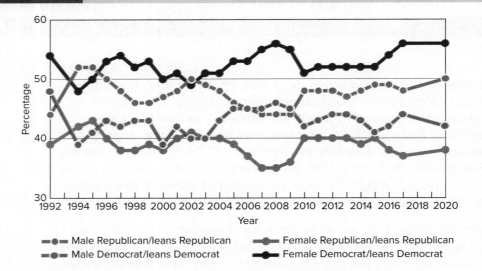

Male Republican/leans Republican
Male Democrat/leans Democrat
Female Republican/leans Republican
Female Democrat/leans Democrat

FIGURE 10.3 ◼ Party Identification Among Men and Women

1. In general, what has been the trend regarding men's party identification?
2. When has the gender gap been the largest? Why do you think there were such differences between men's and women's party identification then?
3. When has the gender gap been the smallest among Democrats? Among Republicans? What do you think explains the decrease in the gap at these times?

Source: Pew Research Center

of Millennial women compared to 49 percent of Millennial men favoring the Democrats. That 21 percent gap is far larger than in other generations: Among Gen Xers, there is an 11-point difference, and among members of the Silent Generation, women are 8 points more favorable to Democrats. Among Boomers, it's 10 points.[8] Race, too, plays an important role in the gender gap. In the 2020 presidential election, white women were only slightly more likely to vote Democrat (43 percent of white women compared to 40 percent of white men), but the gap was much greater among Black voters (91 to 80) and Latinx (70 to 61).

In addition to party affiliation, voting turnout patterns increase the effect of the gender gap. Women in most age groups—except those under age 25—are more likely to vote than their male counterparts. In addition, on average, women also live longer than men, so older women constitute an important voting bloc. The difference in women's candidate preferences and their higher likelihood of voting mean that the gender gap is a political reality that any candidate seeking election cannot ignore.

Women's and men's opinions also differ on public policy issues, although often in unexpected ways. One important way is that men and women differ in the extent to which they *prioritize* various issues. Figure 10.4 shows the top policy issue priorities for men and women during the 2020 presidential election. From this figure, we can see great disparities in the issues men and women identify as "very important." And so while similar percentages of men and women identified infrastructure, terrorism, the economy, and Social Security as very important, a sizably greater proportion of women identified gun policy and climate change as very important issues. Also, women were much more likely than men to identify health care costs, the poor and needy, jobs, and the environment as very important issues. And men were much more likely than women to identify the budget deficit, immigration, and trade policy as very important issues.

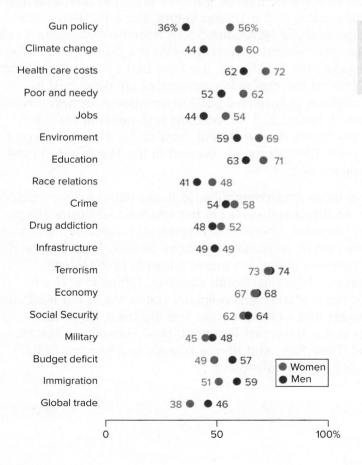

FIGURE 10.4   **Percentage of Registered Voters Saying Issue Should be a Top Priority**

Source: Pew Research Center.

But in addition to sometimes differing priorities, men and women sometimes differ on their viewpoints on issues. For example, women are more likely to believe that a lack of pay equity exists in the United States.[9] Men and women also differ on the issue of the death penalty, as men are about 10 percent more likely than women to favor capital punishment.[10] And men's and women's views on the optimal role of government vary greatly: 66 percent of young women believe that government should do more to solve problems (versus 60 percent of young men), whereas only 27 percent of women believe that government does too many things better left to businesses and individuals, as opposed to 35 percent of men.[11]

GEOGRAPHIC REGION Since the nation's founding, Americans have varied in their political attitudes and beliefs and how they are socialized to politics, depending on the region of the United States from which they come. These differences stem in part from historical patterns of immigration: Irish and Italian immigrants generally settled on the northeastern seaboard, influencing the political culture of Boston, New York, Philadelphia, and Baltimore. Chinese immigrants, instrumental in building the transcontinental railroad in the 19th century, settled in California and areas of the Pacific Northwest and have had a major influence on the political life of those areas.

Among the most important regional differences in the United States is the difference in political outlook between those who live in the Northeast and those in the South. The differences between these two regions predate even our nation's founding. During the Constitutional Convention in 1787, northern and southern states disagreed as to the method that should be used to count slaves for the purposes of taxation and representation. The differences between these two regions were intensified in the aftermath of the Civil War—the quintessential manifestation of regional differences in the United States. Since the Republican Party was the party of Lincoln and the North, the South became essentially a one-party region, with all political competition occurring *within* the Democratic Party. The Democratic Party dominated the South until the later part of the 20th century, when many Democrats embraced the civil rights movement (as described in Chapter 9). Differences in regional culture and political viewpoints between North and South remain, as shown in Figure 10.5. In most modern national elections, Republicans tend to carry the South, the West, and most of the Midwest, except for large cities in these regions. Democrats are favored in the Northeast, on the West Coast, and in most major cities.

Figure 10.6 illustrates one factor that contributes to these differences in regional political climate: religiosity. As discussed earlier in this chapter, religiosity affects political viewpoints, and the regional differences in levels of religiosity mean that those differences are manifested as regional differences as well. From Figure 10.6, we can see that the most religious states are found primarily in the South (Mississippi, Alabama, Louisiana, Arkansas, South Carolina, Tennessee, North Carolina, and Georgia), and none of the most religious states are in the Northeast or on the West Coast. Contrast that with where we find the least religious states: Nearly all are found in the Northeast (Vermont, New Hampshire, Maine, Massachusetts, Connecticut, New York, and Rhode Island), and four are in the West (Alaska, Oregon, Nevada, and Washington).

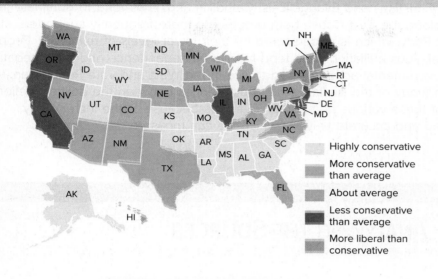

FIGURE 10.5 ☐ **Ideology in the States**

Source: Jones, Jeffrey M. Conservatives Greatly Outnumber Liberals in 19 U.S. States, Gallup, February 22, 2019.

Highly conservative

More conservative than average

About average

Less conservative than average

More liberal than conservative

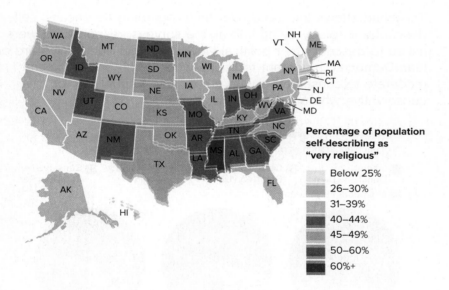

FIGURE 10.6 ☐ **Levels of Religiosity in the United States**

Source: Newport, Frank J. New Hampshire Now Least Religious State in U.S. Gallup, February 4, 2016.

Percentage of population self-describing as "very religious"

Below 25%

26–30%

31–39%

40–44%

45–49%

50–60%

60%+

1. Where are most conservative states located? Where are most liberal states located?

2. Do you think each state has a dominant ideology, or do you think ideological differences exist within the states?

3. Is your ideology and that of your classmates consistent with the ideology in your state? Why might substantial differences exist within a state?

The regional differences in levels of religiosity are compounded by the differences in the dominant religious denominations in each area. The South is much more Protestant than other regions of the United States. Not surprisingly, Republicans dominate in this area, particularly among the most religious Protestants, born-again Christians and Evangelicals. Catholics and Jews tend to dominate in the Northeast along the East Coast; both groups are more frequently supporters of the Democratic Party, which is underscored by their lower levels of religiosity. People without a religious affiliation, who tend to value independence and have negative views of governmental activism, tend to live in the West and vote Republican. We can discern many of the similarities and differences between the political beliefs of members of these various demographic groups because of the increasingly sophisticated and accurate ways in which we can measure public opinion.

DATA ANALYSIS | ANALYZING THE SOURCES

Practice Analytical Thinking

1. What does the graph indicate about the ideology of the total population? Examine the ideological composition of Democrats versus Republicans. Which party is more "ideological" (i.e., less moderate)?

2. Describe the trend with regard to ideology and age. What is the biggest difference between older and younger Americans in terms of their ideology?

3. Do you think that these trends will continue into the future? In your view, will Millennials remain as liberal as they are, or will they become more conservative as they age?

Examining Americans' Ideology

This chart shows the trend over time regarding Americans' self-described ideology by age. In all the surveys, respondents were asked to describe their political views as either liberal who are or lean Democrat; moderate to liberal who are or lean Democrat; moderate to conservative who are or lean Republican; or conservative who are or lean Republican.

Partisan and ideological differences by age

% of each generation who are...

Liberal Dem/Lean Dem
Cons/Mod Dem/Lean Dem
Moderate/Lib Rep/Lean Rep
Conservative Rep/Lean Rep
Independent/No Lean

Source: Pew Research Center, www.pewresearch.org/wp-content/uploads/2017/03/FT_17.03.16_ generations_ideology_2016.png?w=640

AGE AND EVENTS Differences in the candidates voters prefer—including the party, sex, and/or age of the candidates themselves—are one reflection of age and political opinions. People's opinions are also influenced by the events they have lived through and by their political socialization; an epic event may lead to a widespread change in political views (see "Source Analysis"). The **generational effect** (sometimes called the *age-cohort effect*) is the influence of a significant external event in shaping the views of a generation. Typically, generational effects are felt most strongly by young people. Think, for example, of those who lived through the terror attacks of September 11, 2001. For many people, the events that day galvanized a sentiment of patriotism. The major events that occur while we grow up affect our socialization by shaping our viewpoints and our policy priorities. One of the strongest examples of the generational effect is the Great Depression, which lasted from 1929 through 1939. Those who came of age during the era of Democratic president Franklin D. Roosevelt's New Deal social programs were, throughout their lives, most likely to vote Democratic.

generational effect
The impact of an important external event in shaping the views of a generation.

The Socialization and Opinions of Young Americans

Today, two diverse and different young generations—the Millennials, born between 1980 and 2000, and Generation Z, born after 2000—are making an imprint on the fabric of American political life. The Millennial generation in the United States is an important population politically simply because of their size—now numbering 80 million. Characterized as a "ripple boom"—many are the children of post–World War II Baby Boomers—Millennials are now the largest generation in the United States, comprising about one-third of the population. In addition, research has shown that many Millennials have a strong generational identity.[12] But as the oldest members of Generation Z have entered college and begun voting, it is apparent that Gen Zers and Millennials have some things in common.

Several "externalities" have shaped the political development of Millennials. Among the most important is that they are the first generation of Americans born after birth control became widely available. Thus, by and large, they are unique in that a sweeping majority of them were "wanted" by their parents. This reality has informed various spin-off characteristics: the concepts that they have been "helicopter parented" and socialized in a child-centric era during which unique child-rearing patterns—including hyper-scheduled "leisure" activities (play-dates, lessons, sports) and the psychology of "specialness"—prevailed.[13] In addition, American Millennials are the most educated generation in history; 40 percent have graduated with baccalaureate degrees, and their attendance in graduate school also surpasses previous generations.

Finally, Millennials are a very diverse generation of Americans. Many—about 15 percent—are themselves immigrants; others are first-generation Americans whose parents came to the United States as part of a new wave of immigration that followed World War II, and recent waves of Eastern European, Hispanic, and Asian immigration and increasing intermarriage between races. Forty-three percent of Millennials are nonwhite. This trend—both the reality of "being diverse" and the exposure to both racial and cultural diversity—also has a bearing on the formation of attitudes and opinions. One result of this diversity is consistently demonstrated

THEN

NOW

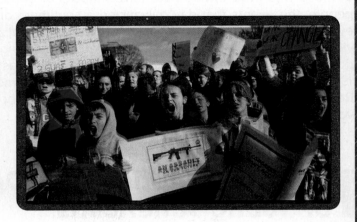

≫ Millennials (left), born between 1980 and 2000, are making a lasting imprint on American political life because of their size and because of their passionate advocacy and oftentimes cohesiveness around key issues, including their support of same-sex marriage. Generation Z, born after 2000, are following in their older brothers' and sisters' footsteps, and show strong support of gun violence prevention measures and criminal justice reform.

(Left): Brendan Smialowski/Stringer/Getty Images; *(Right):* Saul Loeb/AFP/Getty Images

in research: Millennials tend to be the most tolerant of all generations of Americans,[14] embracing what can be considered a "live and let live" philosophy. We can see this ideal of political tolerance manifested in several ways. One example is the overwhelming support of Millennials for gay rights: Millennials supported same-sex marriage earlier than other generations, and greater proportions of Millennials have always supported same-sex marriage.

Another example of Millennials' political tolerance is their support of marijuana legalization. Like same-sex marriage, the issue of marijuana legalization is one in which Millennials appear to be trail-blazing, as their support has been both earlier and more cohesive than among other generations. As shown in Figure 10.7, today, 76 percent of Millennials support legalization, with support more than doubling in less than a decade. (Millennials support of legalization stood at 34 percent in 2006.) Other generations also are increasingly supporting legalization, but Millennials' support of legalization has foreshadowed other cohorts' changing opinions. Among Gen Xers, 65 percent agree that marijuana should be legalized (up from 34 percent in 2006), and 63 percent of Baby Boomers say it should (up from 34 percent). Members of the Silent Generation (those born between 1928 and 1945) remain largely opposed, with only 35 percent favoring legalization.

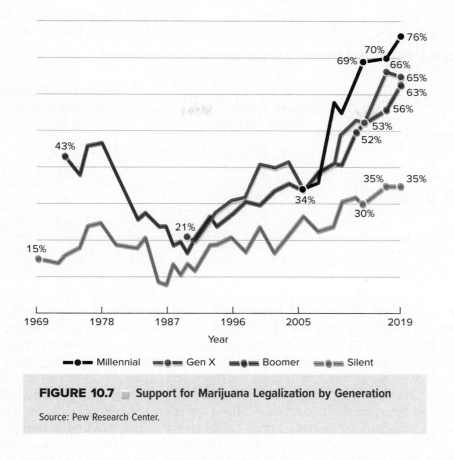

FIGURE 10.7 ▨ **Support for Marijuana Legalization by Generation**

Source: Pew Research Center.

A final issue in which we see a "live and let live" philosophy driving opinions among Millennials is immigration reform. Millennials are the cohort most likely to support reforms that include a path to citizenship for undocumented immigrants. And 79 percent of Millennials say immigrants strengthen rather than burden the country, compared to 66 percent of Gen Xers, 56 percent of Boomers, and 47 percent of members of the Silent Generation. Millennials' positive views of immigrants carry into specific policies concerning immigration: 72 percent of Millennials oppose expanding the border wall between Mexico and the United States, while 60 percent of Gen Xers oppose it, compared to 48 and 46 percent of Boomers and members of the Silent Generation, respectively.[15] Again, the issue positions of Millennials reflect the worldview to which they have been socialized: a tolerant, global, multicultural environment.

As with other generations, externalities also have played an important role in the political socialization of Millennials. For them, the terrorist attacks of September 11, 2001, and the ripple effects throughout the United States provided an event-centered, cohesive experience, jolting the nation and altering the context that shaped their political socialization. But another, more recent event also appears to be driving many Millennials' opinions and behaviors: the Great Recession. The results of the Great Recession were borne disproportionately by Millennials, who came of age facing higher levels of student loan debt, higher levels of unemployment, higher poverty rates, and lower levels of personal income and accumulated wealth than previous generations.[16] Those economic realities seem to have affected other attitudes and behaviors as well. Millennials are more likely to support federal government policies that reduce income inequality, including increasing the minimum hourly wage to $15, and are more likely to support "bigger government providing more services" than other generations, as shown in Table 10.2.

TABLE 10.2 ■ Preferences for Size of Government by Generation

	Percentage Favoring "Smaller Government, Fewer Services"	Percentage Favoring "Big Government, More Services"
Millennials	42%	50%
Gen X	44	51
Baby Boomers	53	44
Silent	51	43

Source: Pew Research Center.

While the oldest members of Generation Z are just coming of age politically, research demonstrates that the opinions of this generation are quite similar to those of Millennials. On issues like the proper role of government, the need to address racial equality, and the importance of climate change, the views of Gen Z mirror those of their Millennial brothers and sisters.[17] Characteristic of both generations has been the ability to tackle seemingly intransigent issues, make them part of the national agenda, and then transform public opinion on them, creating the impetus for policy changes. We saw this occur when Millennials embraced same-sex marriage and other LGBTQ+ rights. Millennials were the first generation to cohesively support these issues, and their views—perhaps over many impassioned discussions during family dinners—seemed to transform the views of older Americans. And this shift in views laid the groundwork for long-fought-for policy in this area. In addition, the views of Millennials regarding legalization of marijuana have transformed views on this issue among older generations, as depicted in Figure 10.7, as well as the current federal policy debate occurring in Washington, D.C.

Today, we see a similar phenomenon as members of Gen Z rally around the issue of gun violence prevention. The post-Columbine generation, who grew up participating in "active shooter" drills throughout elementary and high school, created a nationwide social movement in the aftermath of the particularly deadly school shooting at Marjory Stoneman Douglas High School in Parkland, Florida. From that shooting, seemingly overnight, March for Our Lives (MFOL) emerged as a collaborative movement of urban, suburban, and rural young people fed up with the gun violence that had shaped their childhoods; wreaked havoc on their communities; and, in some cases, injured them or their family members, friends, or classmates. MFOL working in concert with other gun violence prevention organizations has brought this issue to the forefront of the national political agenda.

In addition to their ability to sway the opinions and priorities of older generations, Generation Z is similar to Millennials in terms of its diversity. Indeed, Gen Z is surpassing Millennials as the most diverse generation, and as we saw with Millennials, diversity tends to breed tolerance. Members of Generation Z are more likely to have positive feelings about diversity, and in general, are opposed to policies or practices that discriminate against immigrants or people of different races, religions, or ethnic groups.[18] Some members of this generation have grown up in same-sex households, and as a whole, they are overwhelmingly supportive of same-sex marriage. They are also more supportive of transgender rights and are more likely to know someone who prefers gender-neutral pronouns such as "they," "them," or "ze," compared to Millennials. And more than 33 percent of Gen Zers strongly agree that gender does not define a person as much as it used to, compared to 23 percent of Millennials.[19]

■ Measuring Public Opinion

Public opinion consists of the public's expressed views about an issue at a specific point in time. Public opinion and ideology are inextricably linked because ideology is the prism through which people view all political issues; hence their ideology informs their opinions on a full range of political issues. Indeed, the growing importance of public opinion has even led some political scientists, such as Elizabeth Noelle-Neumann, to argue that public opinion itself is a socializing agent in that it provides an independent context that affects political behavior.[20] Although we are inundated every day with the latest public opinion polls, and while recent elections have raised questions about their accuracy, public opinion has played an important role historically in American politics.

Public opinion is manifested in various ways: demonstrators protesting on the steps of the state capitol; bloggers posting their opinions; citizens communicating directly with government officials, perhaps by telling their local city council members what they think of the town's plan to increase taxes or by calling their members of Congress to indicate their opinion on a current piece of legislation. One of the most important ways public opinion is measured is through the act of voting, which will be discussed further in Chapter 14. But another important tool that policymakers, researchers, and the public rely on as an indicator of public opinion is the **public opinion poll,** a survey of a given population's opinion on an issue at a particular time. Policymakers, particularly elected officials, care about public opinion because they want to develop and implement policies that reflect the public's views.[21] Such policies are more likely to attract support from other government leaders, who are also relying on public opinion as a gauge, but they also help ensure that elected leaders will be reelected, because they are representing their constituent's views.[22]

public opinion
The public's expressed views about an issue at a specific point in time.

public opinion poll
A survey of a given population's opinion on an issue or a candidate at a particular point in time.

How Public Opinion Polls Are Conducted

In politics, public opinion polls are used for many reasons.[23] As political scientist Herbert Asher noted, "Polling plays an integral role in political events at the national, state, and local levels. In any major event or decision, poll results are sure to be a part of the news media's coverage and the decision maker's deliberations."[24] (See earlier "Analyzing the Sources" to consider how decision makers might evaluate voters' ideology when thinking about policy positions.) In addition, public opinion polls help determine who those decision makers will be. Candidates for public office use polls to determine their initial name recognition, the effectiveness of their campaign strategy, their opponents' weaknesses, and how potential voters are responding to their message. Once elected to office, policymakers often rely on public opinion polls to gauge their constituents' opinions and to measure how well they are performing on the job.

population
In a poll, the group of people whose opinions are of interest and/or about whom information is desired.

The process of conducting a public opinion poll consists of several steps. Those conducting the poll first need to determine the **population** they are targeting for the survey—the group of people whose opinions are of interest and about whom information is desired. For example, if your neighbor were considering running for the U.S. House of Representatives, she would want to know how many people recognize her name. But she would be interested only in those people who live in your congressional district. Furthermore, she would probably narrow this population by looking only at those people in the district who are registered to vote. She might even want to narrow her target population further by limiting her survey to likely voters, perhaps those who have voted in past congressional elections.

SAMPLING Once the target population is determined and the survey measurement instrument, or poll, is designed, pollsters then must select a sample that will represent the views of this population. Because it is nearly impossible to measure all the opinions of any given population, pollsters frequently rely on **random sampling,** a scientific method of selection in which each member of the population has an equal chance of being included in the sample. Relying on random sampling helps to ensure that the sample is not skewed so that one component of the population is overrepresented.

random sampling
A scientific method of selection in which each member of the population has an equal chance of being included in the sample.

To demonstrate this point, suppose the dean of students asks your class to conduct a public opinion survey that will measure whether students believe that parking facilities are adequate at your school. In this case, the population you need to measure is the entire student body. But clearly, how you conduct the sampling will affect the responses. If you ask only students in your 8:00 a.m. American government class, you might find that they have little trouble parking because the campus is not crowded at that hour. If you ask students who attend classes only during peak hours, you might get different, yet not necessarily representative, views as well because these students may have more difficulty parking than average. How then would you obtain a random sample? The best way would be to ask the registrar for a list of all students, determine your sample size, randomly select every nth student from the list, contact each nth student, and ask for his or her views.

Researchers have noted, however, that one problem with polls is that even those conducted using random samples may not provide the accurate data needed to illuminate political opinions and behaviors. Consider that today, many people use cell phones exclusively. One standard method for conducting telephone surveys is to use random-digit dialing of telephones.[25] Although most major polling organizations now include cell phone users in order to create an accurate sample of Americans, some polling organizations still exclude cellular lines from their population.[26] Today, less than 50 percent of the U.S. population relies exclusively on cell phones and has no landline phone.[27] But even those polling organizations that include cell phone subscribers face a high rate of nonresponse because of the nearly universal use of caller ID, and the transportable nature of cell phones that makes their owners less likely to answer calls when involved in other activities.[28] In fact, one study found that those who are willing to respond to pollsters' questions are more politically engaged than those who hit "ignore." One way pollsters attempt to address these types of concerns is through the use of a **quota sample,** a more scientifically sophisticated method of sampling than random sampling. A pollster using this method structures the sample so that it is representative of the characteristics of the target

quota sample
A method by which pollsters structure a sample so that it is representative of the characteristics of the target population.

population. Let's say that your mother is running for mayor of your town, and you would like to conduct a poll that measures opinions of her among various constituencies. From Census data, you learn that your town is 40 percent white, 35 percent African American, 20 percent Latinx, and 5 percent Asian. Therefore, when conducting a poll you structure your sample so that it reflects the proportions of the population. With a sample of 200 voters, you would seek to include 80 white respondents, 70 African Americans, 40 Latinx, and 10 Asians. Pollsters routinely rely on quota sampling, though often they may not ask participants about their demographic characteristics until the end of the poll.

Another method used to address problems in sampling is **stratified sampling,** in which the national population is divided into fourths and certain areas within these regions are selected as representative of the national population. Although some organizations still rely on quota sampling, larger organizations and media polls now use stratified sampling, the most reliable form of random sampling. Today, nearly every major polling organization relies on U.S. Census data as the basis of their four sampling regions. Stratified sampling is the basis for much of the public opinion data used by political scientists and other social scientists, in particular the General Social Survey (GSS) and the American National Election Study.

stratified sampling
A process of random sampling in which the national population is divided into fourths and certain areas within these regions are selected as representative of the national population.

SAMPLING ERROR As we have seen, to accurately gauge public opinion, pollsters must obtain an accurate sample from the population they are polling. A sample need not be large to reflect the population's views. In fact, most national polling organizations rarely sample more than 1,500 respondents; most national samples range from 1,000 to 1,500. To poll smaller populations (states or congressional districts, for example), polling organizations routinely use samples of between 300 and 500 respondents.

The key is having a sample that accurately reflects the population. Let's say that your political science instructor offers extra credit if you attend a weekly study group. The group initially convenes immediately after your regular class session. At the conclusion of the study group, the leader asks if this is a convenient time for everyone to meet. Because everyone present has attended the study group, chances are that the time is more convenient for them than it is for those students who did not attend—perhaps because they have another class immediately after your political science class, or they work during that time period, or they have child care responsibilities. In other words, the composition of the sample—in this case, the students in the study group—will skew the responses to this question. Similarly, if a poll is administered to a nonrepresentative sample of a population—for example, if the sample underestimates a block of voters, as occurred in the 2016 presidential election polling—the responses will not accurately reflect the population's views.

Internet polls present their own set of obstacles, including the ability of some individuals to complete surveys (or vote for their favorite reality show contestant) repeatedly.[29] Nonetheless, market research firms, public opinion polling organizations, and even political candidates are increasingly relying on the Internet as a survey research tool.[30] To adjust for problems with sampling, every poll that relies on a sample has a **sampling error** (sometimes called a margin of error), which is a statistical calculation of the difference in results between a poll of a randomly drawn sample and a poll of the entire population. Most polls have a sampling error of ±3 percentage points ("plus or minus 3 percentage points"). This means that 3 percentage points should be added and subtracted from the poll results to find the range for the population. With Internet polls, sampling errors

sampling error
Also called *margin of error*; a statistical calculation of the difference in results between a poll of a randomly drawn sample and a poll of the entire population.

When evaluating survey research data, it is important to consider how the wording of questions may affect responses. Consider the Gallup polls below which intentionally asked people's views on the matter of physician assisted suicide using different phrasing. With two different question wordings, Gallup got different results. A media outlet that supports assisted suicide may choose to publish the results of Form A, while a media outlet against the practice may use the results of Form B. While Form B still indicates an overall support for assisted suicide, the results are far less convincing than they are on Form A. Gallup asked, "When a person has a disease that cannot be cured and is living in severe pain, do you think the doctors should or should not be allowed by law to assist the patient to commit suicide if the patient requests it?" and "When a person has a disease that cannot be cured, do you think the doctors should be allowed by law to end the patient's life by some painless means suicide if the patient and his or her family requests it?" The results shown predictably indicate that when the process is referred to in softer language ("end patient's life by some painless means") there is greater support than when the term "suicide" is used. Unless the news consumer knows how much the wording of the question can impact people's responses, she may place more confidence in the results of the survey than is deserved. Even when a news consumer is aware of the flaws of polls, she may not read the poll question carefully and may jump to incorrect conclusions.

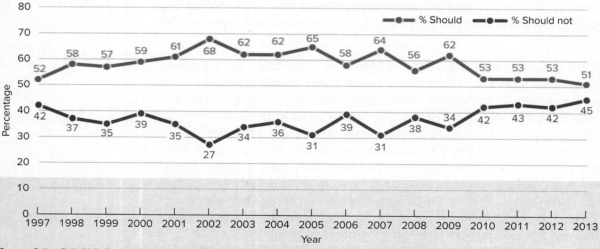

Source: Gallup Poll, "U.S. Support for Euthanasia Hinges on How It's Described." https://news.gallup.com/poll/162815/support-euthanasia-hinges-described.aspx

Data analysis is a skill that is tested on the Free Response section of the AP U.S. Government and Politics exam. Using the information in the infographic, answer the following:

A. Identify a level of support for physician-assisted suicide as demonstrated in the table.

B. Describe a similarity or difference in the attitudes for physician-assisted suicide from two question wordings and draw a conclusion about the similarity or difference.

C. Explain how opinion of physician-assisted suicide as shown in the graph above demonstrates what we know about conducting public opinion polls.

can run as high as ±5 percent. This means that as much as 10 percentage points could be added or subtracted from the poll results to find the range for the population. For example, if an Internet poll indicates that 70 percent of Americans favor cannabis legalization, and the margin of error is ±5 percent, that means that between 65 and 75 percent of Americans favor the legislation.

Types of Political Polls

The process of measuring political opinions has evolved drastically over the years.[31] Today, political candidates, parties, and news organizations rely on several types of polls, depending on their goals and objectives. These include tracking polls, push polls, and exit polls.

- **Tracking polls** measure changes in public opinion over the course of days, weeks, or months by repeatedly asking respondents the same questions over time and measuring changes in opinion. During the 2020 Democratic presidential primaries, when many candidates faced poll numbers that showed declining support, they withdrew from the race. Tracking polls can indicate the effectiveness of a media strategy in both the long term and short term, assess the success of a day's worth of campaigning, or measure whether the campaign has gotten its message across during a specific period of time.

- **Push polls** are a special type of poll that both attempts to skew public opinion about a candidate and provides information to campaigns about candidate strengths and weaknesses. Sometimes this is done by presenting survey respondents with a hypothetical situation and then asking them to gauge the importance of the hypothetical issue in determining their vote. For example, a push-pollster might ask: "If you knew that Congresswoman Jackson lives outside the district, how would that affect your vote?" At their best, push polls help gauge voter priorities so that a campaign can better target its message. The campaign can then determine whether to accentuate that message. But push polls have an unsavory reputation, because some campaigns and organizations have used them to smear an opponent, using hypothetical scenarios to make baseless accusations against an opponent without having to substantiate the charges.

tracking polls
Polls that measure changes in public opinion over the course of days, weeks, or months by repeatedly asking respondents the same questions and measuring changes in their responses.

push polls
A special type of poll that both attempts to skew public opinion about a candidate and provides information to campaigns about candidate strengths and weaknesses.

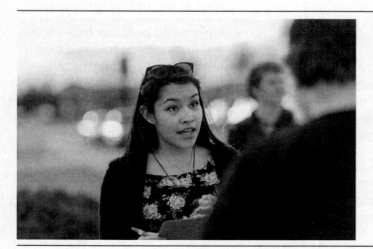

≫ An important type of poll is the exit poll, conducted on Election Day. From these polls, we learn about why voters voted for their candidates.

Marc Romanelli/Blend Images/Getty Images

exit polls
Polls conducted at polling places on Election Day to project the winner of an election before the polls close.

■ **Exit polls** are conducted at polling places on Election Day to project the winner of an election before the polls close. News organizations frequently sponsor exit polls, which help them predict the outcome of gubernatorial, congressional, and presidential elections. Because of exit polls, news organizations can frequently predict the outcome of a given election shortly after the polls have closed. Exit polls also provide the media, candidates, and political parties with information about why voters voted the way they did.

■ What Americans Think About Politics

Public opinion research is the means by which individuals can convey their opinions and priorities to policymakers. Consequently, polls connect Americans to their government.[32] Through public opinion polls, whether conducted by campaigns or media organizations, government officials come to know and understand the opinions of the masses.[33] Through polls, leaders learn what issues are important to people, which policy solutions they prefer, and whether they approve of the way government officials are doing their jobs.[34] The role of opinion polls in shaping citizens' involvement with their government is also circular: Polls play a pivotal role in shaping public opinion, and the results of polls, frequently reported by the media, provide an important source of information for the American public.

Public Opinion Polling

THEN	NOW	NEXT
(1970s) Telephone polls replaced mail-in and door-to-door polling, because most American households had landlines.	Internet polls are at the cutting edge of public opinion research, but anonymity and multiple responses from the same person can damage a poll's accuracy.	■ How will technologies such as YouTube and social networking sites shape polling in the future?
Early telephone polls overrepresented the views of homemakers and retirees, who were more likely to answer the phone during the day.	In the 2020 campaigns, pollsters strived to address their failure to accurately predict the outcome of the 2016 election.	■ How might pollsters overcome the obstacles associated with Internet polls, in particular, the problem of anonymous respondents giving false answers or responding to the same poll multiple times?
Pollsters remedied nonrepresentative sampling through quota sampling.	Pollsters rely on stratified sampling to ensure the most representative sample of the population they are targeting.	■ How will cell phones and text messaging change the way in which public opinion is measured in the future?

The Most Important Problem

Several polling organizations routinely ask respondents to identify (either from a list or in their own words) what they view as "the most important problem" facing the country. In 2020, 32 percent of respondents said that dissatisfaction with government/poor leadership was the most important problem, marking the second year in a row that this response was identified as the top concern of Americans. In previous years, economic issues, including the economy in general, unemployment, and income inequality dominated, but in 2020, just 11 percent of Americans identified economic issues as their top concern, with immigration (11 percent) and health care (10 percent) also ranking as important concerns.

Public Opinion About Government

Analysts of public opinion, government officials, and scholars of civic engagement are all concerned with public opinion about the government at all levels, in particular about the institutions of the federal government. For decades, public opinion researchers have measured the public's trust in government by asking survey respondents to rate their level of trust in the federal government's ability to handle domestic and international policy matters and to gauge their amount of trust and confidence in the executive, legislative, and judicial branches of government.

The responses to these questions are important for several reasons. First, although these measures indicate public opinion about institutions rather than individuals, individual officeholders nonetheless can use the data as a measure of how well they are performing their jobs. Lower levels of confidence in the institution of the presidency, for example, tend to parallel lower approval ratings of specific presidents.[35] Second, trust in government is one measure of the public's sense of efficacy, their belief that the government works for people like them, as discussed in Chapter 1. If people trust their government, they are more likely to believe that it is responsive to the needs of citizens. In Chapter 3, we examined the issue of citizens' trust in local, state, and federal governments. Here, we delve further into Americans' trust of the federal government—which branches they view as the most trustworthy, and in which policy areas.

As indicated by the results of a Gallup poll, the public's trust in the ability of the federal government to handle both international affairs and domestic problems had in general declined over the years after rebounding slightly between 2009 and 2016. Many analysts attributed the decline to widespread dissatisfaction with the war in Iraq and the economic downturn during the George W. Bush administration, the temporary rebound caused by optimism during President Obama's first term, and then frustration with many of Obama's policies, particularly concerning the terrorist group ISIS.

As shown in Figure 10.8, the public's trust in government to handle international problems reached a record high immediately after the September 11, 2001, terror attacks, with 83 percent of those surveyed indicating a great deal or a fair amount of trust, and it has reached record lows during the Trump presidency. The public's trust in government to handle international problems declined steadily from 2004 through 2007, reaching 51 percent in 2007, as the war in Iraq dragged on. The effect of President George W. Bush's "surge strategy" in Iraq and then the optimism generated by the election of President Obama accounted for a temporary increase in trust, but as the war in Afghanistan dragged on, trust declined again, hitting 57 percent in late 2011. Faith in Obama's ability to handle

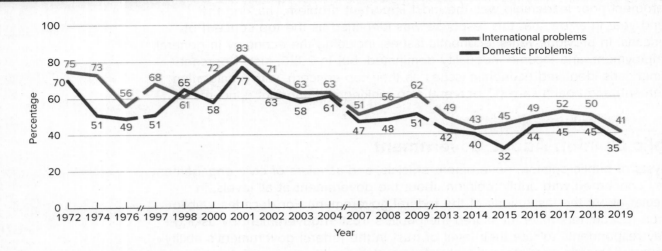

FIGURE 10.8 ■ **Trust in Government to Handle International and Domestic Problems** Public trust in the government's ability to deal with international problems decreased significantly between 2018 and 2019. Why do you think this was the case even before the COVID-19 pandemic? Trust in the government's ability to handle domestic problems is at a near-record low. To what do you attribute these low levels of trust?

* Jeffrey M. Jones "Trust in Government," Gallup.

international problems increased to 66 percent leading up to the 2012 election, but then declined to record lows in 2014 after the administration's early bungled response to the ISIS terror threat. Comparatively low levels of trust concerning the government's ability to handle international problems—pegged at 49 percent in 2016—continued to plague the remainder of Obama's tenure in office. But the Trump administration saw even more serious challenges to the perception that it could handle both international and domestic problems. After President Trump's election, trust concerning the handling of international problems dropped to 41 percent, the lowest of any presidential administration, while faith in its ability to handle domestic problems dropped to 35 percent.

The public's trust in the government's ability to handle domestic matters also peaked in 2001. From Figure 10.8, we can see that in 2007, worries about the economy dominated the public's thinking, and trust in government to handle domestic problems dropped to 47 percent, a figure that rivaled the record-low confidence levels of 51 percent to 49 percent seen in the period between 1974 and 1976, following the Watergate scandal. An uptick registered in 2009, coinciding with the start of Barack Obama's presidency. During his years in office, the skepticism and frustration many Americans felt concerning implementation of the Affordable Care Act plagued the public's trust in government to handle domestic matters. But President Trump fared worse; as noted, he garnered a 35 percent confidence rating in his administration's ability to handle domestic issues. He also faced significant opposition from portions of the general public who opposed some of his top domestic policy priorities, including tougher immigration laws and the construction of a wall between the United States and Mexico. Moreover, farmers and blue collar workers—a core component of his electoral base—became increasingly skeptical when they saw the negative impact of some of his policies, including his trade policy with China, which hampered the exporting of goods to the world's largest economy.

The effect of external events is reflected in the public's trust in specific institutions. For example, as shown in Figure 10.9, trust in the executive branch hit a near-record-high mark in 2002, when fully 72 percent of Americans voiced a great deal or fair amount of trust, as they rallied around President George W. Bush in the aftermath of the September 11, 2001, terror attacks. But the subsequent weariness with the war in Iraq, the Great Recession, the optimism following Barack Obama's election as president, the ultimate disappointment in his administration, and the continued dissatisfaction during the Trump administration is reflected in the downward slope of the trust in executive figures. As noted previously, the decline in trust in the institution of the presidency is closely related to public approval of individual presidents: In 2007, only 36 percent of those surveyed approved of the way President Bush was handling his job. Similarly, in 2009, trust in the executive branch spiked up to 61 percent, mirroring Barack Obama's higher approval ratings during that time. By 2014, Obama's popularity

DATA ANALYSIS   EVALUATING THE FACTS

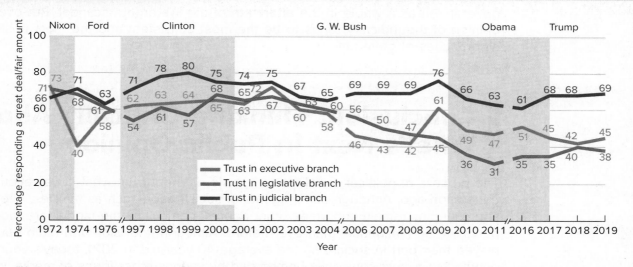

"How much trust and confidence do you have at this time in the executive branch headed by the president, the judicial branch headed by the U.S. Supreme Court, and the legislative branch, consisting of the U.S. Senate and House of Representatives—a great deal, a fair amount, not very much, or none at all?"

FIGURE 10.9 ■ **Trust in the Branches of Government** How do you think trust in government has changed since the COVID-19 pandemic? Since the 2020 elections?

Jeffrey M. Jones "Trust in Government," Gallup.

had diminished, and correspondingly, trust in the executive branch plummeted to a record low rating of 40 percent in 2014, marking the lowest level of public trust in the executive branch ever measured, including trust in the executive before Richard Nixon resigned the presidency.[36] By 2015, Americans' trust in the executive branch had rebounded to 45 percent, a small improvement that continued throughout both Obama presidencies, and then continued through President Trump's administration into 2020.

Congress, too, faces ups and downs in terms of its public approval rate, but in general the legislative branch has struggled to maintain approval ratings comparable with the other branches of government. While Congress enjoyed widespread popularity until the early 2000s, since that time the legislative branch has failed to win approval from the majority of Americans, as shown in Figure 10.9. From 2006 through 2010, increasing dissatisfaction with the Democrats in Congress was apparent, and this dissatisfaction culminated in the Republican takeover of the House of Representatives in 2010. But since that time, Republicans have fared no better: Often only one-third of Americans approve of the way Congress is handling its job. This is the case today, where we see Congress's approval rating at 38 percent. Nonetheless, this figure is an improvement from its record low of 28 percent in 2014, which reflected the widespread dissatisfaction with partisan bickering within the legislature and between Congress and the president.

The judicial branch of government consistently scores higher in levels of public trust than do the other two branches. Figure 10.9 shows that confidence in the judiciary typically hovers between 65 percent and 75 percent, sometimes climbing into the high 70s (or even 80 percent in 1999). The judiciary's lowest rating came in 1976, when there was widespread dissatisfaction with government as a whole in the aftermath of the Watergate scandal. But overall, opinion of the judiciary tends to be the most consistent and the most positive of all branches of government.

Conclusion: Thinking Critically About What's Next in Public Opinion

The process of political socialization is quite different from what it was even a generation ago. Although some agents of socialization such as families, peers, and churches remain important, other agents, particularly the media, are more pervasive and influential than ever before. Although television and radio have played their part in socializing the average 40-year-old in 2021, today's younger people are almost constantly bombarded by various other forms of media, which may influence their viewpoints, priorities, behaviors, and opinions.

Technology has also drastically changed the way public opinion is measured. The advent of the computer alone—from powerful mainframes to personal computers—has revolutionized the data-collection process; today, computers facilitate near-instant access to polling data. The catch-22, however, has been the pervasiveness of public opinion polls. People's opinions are solicited by every kind of survey from cheesy Internet polls to reputable polling organizations. As a result, the public has become poll weary, dubious of the value of the pollster's next set of questions. Will increasing weariness with

Internet polling result in less representative samples? How might pollsters overcome this challenge? How will the universality of cell phones revolutionize the process of public opinion polling?

Technology has provided—and will continue to provide—ways to solve the problems that technology itself has generated in accurately measuring public opinion. Stratified samples and other increasingly sophisticated microsampling techniques have improved the ability of reputable pollsters to gauge public opinion. And pollsters are incorporating new technologies, including text messaging and cell phone surveys, as they work to develop new ways to accurately measure and convey the public's views to candidates, to policymakers, and, through the media, to the public itself.

■ References

1. J. Foster-Bey, *Do Race, Ethnicity, Citizenship and Socio-economic Status Determine Civic-Engagement?* (College Park, MD: CIRCLE: The Center for Information and Research on Civic Learning & Engagement, 2008), 4.

2. Mark Hugo Lopez, Peter Levine, Deborah Both, Abby Kiesa, Emily Kirby, and Karlo Marcelo, *The 2006 Civic and Political Health of the Nation: A Detailed Look at How Youth Participate in Politics and Communities* (College Park, MD: CIRCLE: The Center for Information and Research on Civic Learning and Engagement, 2006), 4.

3. Ibid.

4. Sidney Verba, Kay Lehman Schlozman, and Henry E. Brady, *Voice and Equality: Civic Voluntarism in American Politics* (Cambridge, MA: Harvard University Press, 1995), 439.

5. David L. Leal, Matt A. Barreto, Jongho Lee, and Rodolfo O. de la Garza, "The Latino Vote in the 2004 Election," *PS: Political Science and Politics* (2005): 46.

6. www.pewresearch.org/fact-tank/2016/11/15/unlike-other-latinos-about-half-of-cuban-voters-in-florida-backed-trump/

7. National Asian American Survey, Post Election Survey of Asian Americans and Pacific Island Voters in 2012.

8. Lopez et al., *The 2006 Civic and Political Health of the Nation,* 20–21.

9. www.gallup.com/poll/185213/working-women-lag-men-opinion-workplace-equity.aspx.

10. David W. Moore, "Death Penalty Gets Less Support from Britons, Canadians Than Americans," Gallup News Service, February 20, 2006.

11. Karlo Barrios Marcelo, Mark Hugo Lopez, and Emily Hoban Kirby, *Civic Engagement Among Young Men and Women* (College Park, MD: CIRCLE: The Center for Information and Research on Civic Learning and Engagement, 2007), 12.

12. H.-W. Charng, J. A. Piliavin, and A. P. Callero, "Role Identity and Reasoned Action in the Prediction of Repeated Behavior," *Social Psychology Quarterly,* 1988: 303–317.

13. R. Alsop, *The Trophy Kids Grow Up: How the Millennial Generation Is Shaking Up the Workplace* (New York: John Wiley & Sons, 2008).

14. J. M. Twenge and S. M. Campbell, "Who Are the Millennials? Empirical Evidence for Generational Differences in Work Values, Attitudes and Personality," *Managing the New Workforce: International Perspectives on the Millennial Generation,* 2012, 1-19; B. J. Kowske and J. Wiley, "Millennials' (Lack of) Attitude Problem: An Empirical Examination of Generational Effects on Work Attitudes," *Journal of Business and Psychology,* 2010: 265–279; S. Gonzalez, "Religion and Ethics Newsweekly," *PBS,* November 7, 2014.

15. www.people-press.org/2018/03/01/4-race-immigration-same-sex-marriage-abortion-global-warming-gun-policy-marijuana-legalization/.

16. Don Peck, *Pinched: How the Great Recession Has Narrowed Our Futures and What We Can Do about It* (New York: Broadway Books, 2012).

17. https://www.pewsocialtrends.org/2019/01/17/generation-z-looks-a-lot-like-millennials-on-key-social-and-political-issues/#fn-25640-1.

18. www.nielsen.com/us/en/insights/news/2017/youth-movement-gen-z-boasts-the-largest-most-diverse-media-users-yet.html.

19. www.jwtintelligence.com/2016/03/gen-z-goes-beyond-gender-binaries-in-new-innovation-group-data/.

20. Elizabeth Noelle-Neumann, *The Spiral of Silence: Public Opinion—Our Social Skin,* 2nd ed. (Chicago: University of Chicago Press, 1993).

21. Susan Herbst, *Numbered Voices: How Opinion Polling Has Shaped American Politics* (Chicago: University of Chicago Press, 1993).

22. Robert S. Erikson, Gerald C. Wright, and John P. McIver, *Statehouse Democracy: Public Opinion and Policy in the American States* (New York: Cambridge University Press, 1994).

23. Herbert Asher, *Polling and the Public: What Every Citizen Should Know* (Washington, DC: CQ Press, 2001).

24. Ibid., 2.

25. Randolph Grossman and Douglas Weiland, "The Use of Telephone Directories as a Sample Frame: Patterns of Bias Revisited, *Journal of Advertising* 7 (1978): 31–36.

26. Stephen J. Blumberg and Julian V. Luke, "Coverage Bias in Traditional Telephone Surveys of Low-Income and Young Adults," *Public Opinion Quarterly* 71 (2007): 734–749.

27. www.statista.com/chart/2072/landline-phones-in-the-united-states/.

28. Clyde Tucker, J. Michael Brick, and Brian Meekins, "Household Telephone Service and Usage Patterns in the United States in 2004: Implications for Telephone Samples," *Public Opinion Quarterly* 71 (2007): 3–22.

29. George Terhanian and John Bremer, "Confronting the Selection-Bias and Learning Effects Problems Associated with Internet Research," Harris Interactive white paper, August 16, 2000.

30. G. Terhanian, R. Smith, J. Bremer, and R. K. Thomas, "Exploiting Analytical Advances: Minimizing the Biases Associated with Internet-Based Surveys of Non-Random Samples," *ARF/ESOMAR: Worldwide Online Measurement* 248 (2001): 247–272.

31. Irving Crespi, *Pre-Election Polling: Sources of Accuracy & Error* (New York: Russell Sage Foundation, 1988).

32. Benjamin I. Page and Robert Y. Shapiro, *The Rational Public: Fifty Years of Trends in Americans' Policy Preferences* (Chicago: University of Chicago Press, 1992). Page 225

33. Frank Newport, *Polling Matters: Why Leaders Must Listen to the Wisdom of the People* (New York: Warner Books, 2004).

34. James A. Stimson, *Tides of Consent: How Public Opinion Shapes American Politics* (Cambridge: Cambridge University Press, 2004).

35. Jeffrey M. Jones and Joseph Carroll, "National Satisfaction Level Dips to 25%, One of Lowest Since 1979; Iraq War Remains Top Problem in Americans' Eyes," *The Free Library.* 2007. Gallup Organization.

36. David W. Moore, "Top Ten Gallup Presidential Approval Ratings," Gallup press release, September 24, 2001.

■ Key Terms

▋ Multiple-Choice Questions

Questions 1 and 2 are based on the chart below.

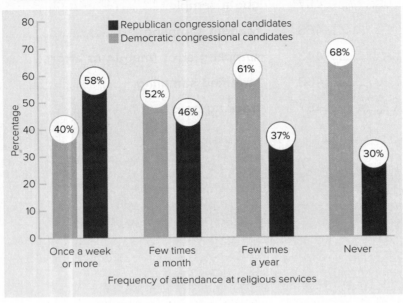

Candidate Preference of Religious and Non-Religious Americans

Source: https://www.pewresearch.org/fact-tank/2018/11/07/how-religious-groups-voted-in-the-midterm-elections/

1. Which of the following accurately describes the information based on the information graphic above?
   A. Democrats are most likely to be religious
   B. Republicans are most likely to be religious
   C. Independents do not have strong religious views
   D. Religion does not play a role in political affiliation

2. Which of the following accurately portrays the influence of religion on political affiliation?
   A. Catholics have the highest percentage of voter turnout
   B. Those who attend church more regularly are more likely to be Democrats
   C. The differences between the proclivities of religious and non-religious voters are applicable only to white voters
   D. Religious Latinos and Asian Americans are more likely to be Republicans

Questions 3 and 4 are based on the graph below.

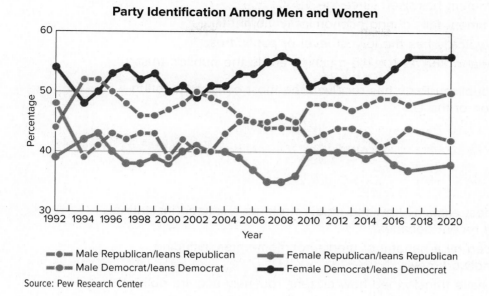

Party Identification Among Men and Women

Source: Pew Research Center

3. In general, what has been the trend regarding men's party identification?
  A. Men are becoming more independent
  B. Men are more liberal than women
  C. Men are becoming increasingly more likely to support the Republican Party than women
  D. Men tended to be more conservative in 2008.

4. Which of the following is a reason for the gender gap as illustrated in the graph above?
  A. It was started by President Carter when he ran against Ronald Reagan in 1980
  B. Difference in policy positions among men and women
  C. Men are more likely than women to choose formal political forms of activism such as voting
  D. Women are more likely to be pro-life

5. Which of the following scenarios is an accurate comparison of exit polls and push polls?

Exit polls	Push polls
A. Generally inaccurate and unreliable as evidenced in 2016	Accurately measures public opinion to determine voter preferences
B. Conducted by phone to likely voters	Conducted in person to registered voters
C. Project the winner of an election before the polls close	Attempts to skew public opinion
D. Uses random sampling	Uses stratified sampling

6. Which of the following is true about public trust in government?

A. Public trust in government has risen since the 1960s

B. Public trust in government falls during economically vibrant times

C. The judicial branch typically has the lowest level of public trust

D. The Watergate scandal of the 1970s did much to erode the public's trust

7. Since the 1960s, the Republican Party has received the most consistent voting support from which region of the U.S.?

A. the Northeast

B. the Midwest

C. the Southeast

D. the Plains

8. Which of the following best explains how the media's role as a linkage institution has been transformed in recent decades?

A. Citizens are influenced by a handful of media conglomerates including 24-hour news and network news

B. Advances in media have transformed how citizens routinely acquire political information

C. There is so much news to consume, that the average American shies away from reading news stories

D. The media's role as a linkage institution is diminishing because of lack of trust in the reliability of news stories

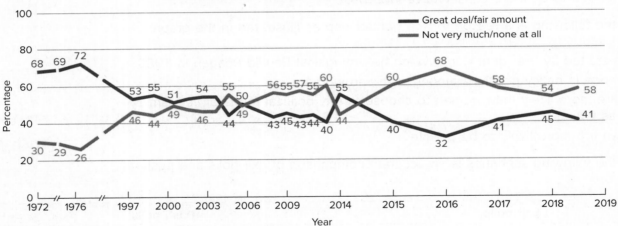

Americans' Trust in the Mass Media Edges Down

Source: Gallup. https://news.gallup.com/poll/267047/americans-trust-mass-media-edges-down.aspx

9. The trend in the chart above can be best explained by which of the following:

A. Increase in fake news

B. Increase in partisanship

C. Decrease in respect for the military

D. Decrease in popularity of the president

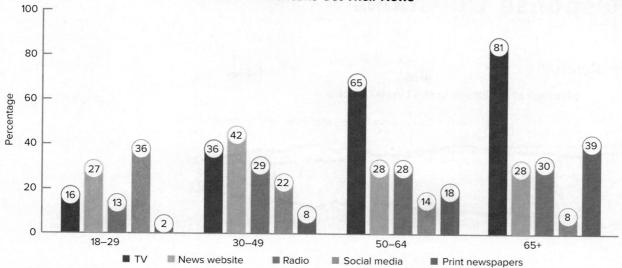

Where Americans Get Their News

Source: Pew Research Center.

10. If you were using the data in the table above to advise a candidate on how to improve standing with the elderly demographic in his or her reelection campaign, which of the following ad strategies would you recommend targeting?

A. Television
B. News websites
C. Radio
D. Social media

■ Free-Response Questions

Quantitative Analysis

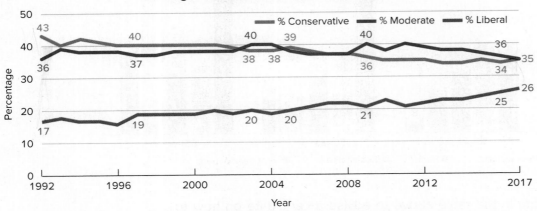

Ideological Affiliation in the United States

Source: Gallup. "Conservative Lead in U.S. Ideology Is Down to Single Digits". https://news.gallup.com/poll/225074/conservative-lead-ideology-down-single-digits.aspx.

Use the graphic above to answer the questions.

A. Identify a trend in the political views of Americans from 1992-2017.

B. Describe a similarity or difference in the political views of Americans, as illustrated in the information graphic, and draw a conclusion about that similarity or difference.

C. Identify and explain a possible limitation of the data provided in the information graphic.

Concept Application

> "The results of Tuesday's presidential election came as a surprise to nearly everyone who had been following the national and state election polling, which consistently projected Hillary Clinton as defeating Donald Trump. Relying largely on opinion polls, election forecasters put Clinton's chance of winning at anywhere from 70% to as high as 99%, and pegged her as the heavy favorite to win a number of states such as Pennsylvania and Wisconsin that in the end were taken by Trump.
>
> How could the polls have been so wrong about the state of the election?"
>
> *Pew Research Center, November 9, 2016*

After reading the scenario, respond to A, B, and C below:

A. Identify and describe a reason why the polls incorrectly forecasted the winner of the 2016 presidential election.

B. In the context of the scenario, explain how the media may have exacerbated the extent of the incorrect forecasts of the polls.

C. In the context of the scenario, explain how the interaction between the media and polling creates horserace journalism.

Quantitative Analysis

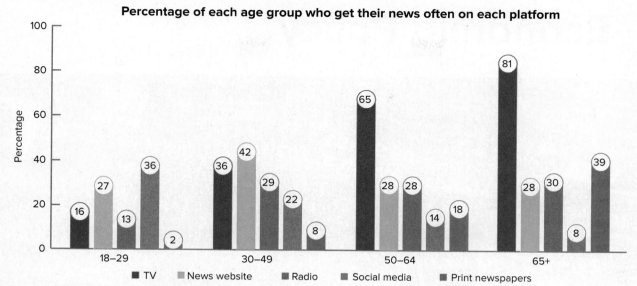

Percentage of each age group who get their news often on each platform

Source: Pew Research Center.

Use the information in the graphic to answer the questions.

A. Identify how most young people (18–29) access their news.

B. Describe a similarity or difference in how young people access their news when compared to one other age demographic and draw a conclusion about that similarity or difference.

C. Explain news consumption as shown in the graphic demonstrates the changing role of the media as a linkage institution.

Argumentation

Develop an argument that explains whether the increase in media outlets in recent decades facilitates or impedes competitive presidential elections in the U.S.

In your essay, you must:

- Articulate a defensible claim or thesis that responds to the prompt and establishes a line of reasoning

- Support your claim with at least TWO pieces of accurate and relevant information:

  - At least ONE piece of evidence must be from one of the following foundational documents:

    — Article I of the U.S. Constitution

    — The First Amendment to the U.S. Constitution

  - Use a second piece of evidence from another foundational document from the list or from your study of the electoral process

- Use reasoning to explain why your evidence supports your claim/thesis

- Respond to an opposing or alternative perspective using refutation, concession, or rebuttal

Economic Policy

THEN

Citizens and government officials agreed that the government should play a very limited role in the national economy.

NOW

The federal government intentionally makes taxing, spending, regulatory, and monetary policies aimed to create and maintain a healthy national economy, and it persistently borrows money to balance the federal budget.

NEXT

Will the coronavirus pandemic have a long-term negative effect on the national economy?

Will the call for a balanced budget amendment to the Constitution grow louder despite the economic challenges posed by the pandemic?

Will your generation and future generations achieve the American dream?

Mark Abramson/The New York Times/Redux

■ Chapter Introduction

In the wake of the COVID-19 pandemic, vast economic uncertainty emerged as first President Trump then President Biden sought to head off an economic depression. Both presidents signed massive economic stimulus bills into law, totaling over $4 trillion. The Federal Reserve (the Fed), the nation's central banking system, did its part to prevent the pandemic from devastating the economy by lowering interest rates and implementing new debt-buyback programs to protect businesses and keep markets functioning. As the Fed stated, "Aggressive efforts must be taken across the public and private sectors to limit the losses of jobs and incomes and to promote a swift recovery once the disruptions abate."[1]

Unlike the Great Recession (2007–2009), which was born out of decisions made by profit-making financial institutions in the United States, the economic disaster that began in March 2020 was sparked by national, state, and local government actions intended to contain and mitigate the public health damage of the coronavirus pandemic. As it did with the Great Recession, the national government used its taxing and spending authorities to offer some financial support to individuals, families, businesses, and state and local governments. The goal of the Coronavirus Aid, Relief, and Economic Security Act of 2020 (CARES Act) was to stabilize and then stimulate the economy at a time when a record-breaking 10 million people filed for unemployment in just the last two weeks of March and as local and state governments shut down schools, all but essential (life-sustaining) businesses, and gatherings of more than 10 people.

Americans expect their governments to protect life, liberty, and the pursuit of happiness. A healthy economy is necessary to (but not sufficient for) these aspirations. What can, and what should, the national government do to ensure a healthy economy? Since the birth of the United States, debates have ensued among elected and appointed officials at all levels of government, and among economists, business leaders, interest groups, and taxpayers, about the proper role of the national government in creating and maintaining a healthy economy.

This chapter explores how national policies affect the U.S. economic system. In the exploration, we consider various measures of economic health, economic theories about the proper role for government in maintaining a healthy economy, fiscal policy (government taxing and spending), monetary policy (actions of the Fed), regulatory policy, and trade policy.

The Enduring Understanding for you to consider during this chapter is: *Widely held political ideologies shape policy debates and choices in American policies.* This chapter will address how various ideologies view the proper role of government in economic policy, including liberals, and conservatives. As you read about the clash of ideas, consider how the two major political parties managed to come together and pass three economic stabilization bills during the pandemic. Assuming the economy rebounds, how might the political debate shape the conversation during a rebound? What do you expect to occur?

The American Dream and the American Economy

The American national government seeks a healthy economy so that it can raise the revenue it needs to serve the people in compliance with the mission laid out in the Preamble to the Constitution: to establish justice, ensure domestic tranquility, provide for the common defense, promote the general welfare, and secure the blessings of liberty today and in the future. On a more personal level, many U.S. citizens desire a healthy economy so that they can achieve the American dream.

The American Dream

It was during the Great Depression (1929-1939) that historian James Truslow Adams coined the term "American dream." In his book *The Epic of America* (1931), Adams argued that what made America a unique nation was its inhabitants' "dream of a better, richer, and happier life" for all people based on "equal opportunity for each according to his [or her] ability or achievement."[2]

The Pew Research Center[3] reports that the majority of people (82 percent) believe they have already achieved the American dream (36 percent) or they are on their way to achieving it (46 percent). The people who are most apt to see the American dream as out of their reach are those with only a high school degree or less than a high school degree (24 percent). The survey asked about the American dream as each respondent defined it; the survey did not provide a definition of the phrase.

The desire for enough money to buy not only what we require to meet our basic needs (food, shelter, and clothing) but also what many people would consider luxuries seems natural to most Americans. In developed countries such as the United States, "luxuries" typically include owning a home instead of renting, owning a car or two, dining at a nice restaurant now and then, taking vacations, and sending children to good schools. U.S. citizens and many immigrants to the United States seek a financially secure, happy, and healthy life, with upward mobility attained through an individual's hard work and persistence, and an even better life for their children. These beliefs and desires are known collectively as the **American dream.**

American dream
The belief that in the United States hard work and persistence will reap a financially secure, happy, and healthy life, with upward mobility.

Clearly, it takes money to live the American dream. For some, being born into a wealthy family or just dumb luck (winning the lottery!) may provide the means to live the American dream. For most individuals, however, the ability to earn enough money to attain the American dream is the product of several factors, including their education level, their work ethic, and the availability of well-paying jobs and health insurance.

Why do people attend college? Do they take classes to develop their intellectual capacities? To better understand themselves and the world around us? To get a better-paying job so they can live the American dream? If you read any college's mission statement, you will find that these institutions hope to facilitate all those accomplishments. (Read the "Thinking Critically" feature for a discussion of whether college tuition should be free.)

Although you may be able to increase your level of education, and you have control over your work ethic, the availability of well-paying jobs commensurate

Costs of the American Dream

	THEN	NOW	NEXT
Costs of the American Dream	**2000**	**2020**	
Tuition and fees at private college	$16,294	$41,426	
Tuition and fees at public college (out-of-state tuition)	$9,639	$27,120	
Tuition and fees at public college (in-state tuition)	$3,508	$11,260	
Average cost of a new home	$119,600	$245,334	
Median household income	$40,597	$65,666	

NEXT

- Will tuition for public colleges be free within the next decade?
- Will tuition for private colleges continue to increase at a rate greater than the rate of inflation?
- Will the proportion of families who own homes remain stable, decrease, or increase?
- Will the American Dream continue to be attainable?

Sources: Briana Boyington and Emma Kerr, "20 Years of Tuition Growth at National University," *U.S. News*, September 19, 2019; www.cnbc.com; Townhall Finance, "Median Household Income Reaches an All-Time High," February 7, 2020; "Here's How Much Housing Prices Have Increased in the Last 50 Years," June 23, 2017, www.cnbc.com; How Much the Average Home Costs in 2020, January 29, 2020, www.cnbc.com.

with your level of education is not within your control. The health of the national economy determines the availability of jobs and affects their compensation (pay and benefits). So, although achieving the American dream depends on individual attributes and opportunities to develop those attributes, the health of the national economy also plays a major role.

A healthy national economy supports a nation's ability to raise sufficient revenue to serve its people. The better the economy's performance, the greater the **tax base**: the overall *wealth* (income and assets, such as property) of citizens and corporations that governments tax to raise revenue to pay the costs of providing public goods and services.

tax base
The overall *wealth* (income and assets of citizens and corporations) that the government can tax to raise revenue.

The U.S. Economy

In the United States and other countries, national government policies influence the **economy**—the system for producing, selling, buying, and using goods and services. **Economic policy** is a collection of public policies that affect the health of the economy, which includes taxing and spending policies (fiscal policy), monetary policy, regulatory policy, and trade policy. Economists view a healthy economy as one in which unemployment is low, the prices of consumer goods are relatively stable, and the productivity of individual workers and the economy as a whole is increasing.

economy
A system for producing, selling, buying, and using goods and services.

economic policy
A collection of public policies that affect the health of the economy, which includes taxing and spending policies (fiscal policy), monetary policy, regulatory policy, and trade policy.

Should College Tuition Be Free?

THE ISSUE: Although a college degree is viewed as a path to the American dream, many people have a tough time paying for it. College costs keep increasing, and at a rate that is more than the rate of inflation. This is especially problematic for middle-class families, who are typically ineligible for most of the government scholarship and grant programs that are available for lower-income families and that wealthier families do not need. Graduates are delaying marriage and home purchases while they pay down their college debt from student loans. Many are asking whether college should be free.

YES: Today, a college degree has replaced a high school degree as the path to the American Dream and a middle-class lifestyle. Moreover, it is not only a private good for individuals, allowing them to become financially self-sufficient; it is also a public good. When more people earn college degrees, our workforce is more highly skilled and better educated, and therefore, our economy is more productive and competitive. Free college tuition is good for the individual and for the economy.

NO: Free tuition is not really free. Taxpayers will need to pay more (national and state taxes) to cover the cost for everyone, including the wealthy, who can afford to pay for their own tuition. The increased cost to taxpayers might lead to decreased access to college as the actual cost of a college education will keep increasing (due to increasing salaries and benefits for employees and the need to keep up with technology), while the ability and willingness of taxpayers to pay ever more in taxes are limited. If taxpayers cannot keep up with the increasing cost, then the quality of the education will be harmed. The current system, in which financial assistance is available based on financial need, is the best way to finance higher education.

OTHER APPROACHES: Deferring a proportion of tuition payments until after graduation would increase access and affordability for low- and middle-income families. Repayment plans could be based on the graduate's earnings. Payments could be a percentage of money earned; that is, as salary increases, so do the payments.

WHAT DO YOU THINK?

1. Is a college degree essential or important to achieving the American dream? Explain your answer.

2. Currently, a majority of students at community colleges (where tuition is on average the lowest among colleges) have to take remedial courses to succeed. Should we improve the quality and access to elementary and secondary education before (or at the same time as) we consider increasing access to college by making it more affordable?

Although labeled as a capitalist economic system, the U.S. economy is not an example of pure capitalism. In a **pure capitalist economy,** private individuals and companies own the modes of producing goods and services, and the government does *not* enact laws aimed at influencing the marketplace transactions that distribute those goods and services. In other words, a **pure capitalist economy** has a government-free marketplace. Although private ownership of the modes of production dominates the U.S. marketplace, it is not a government-free marketplace. National government policies in some cases encourage, and in other cases mandate, certain business practices that the government deems essential to sustain a healthy economy as well as a clean environment and a safe and productive citizenry. Because of the many national policies enacted to influence the economy, the U.S. economy is an example of a **regulated capitalist economy (mixed economy),** not a pure capitalist economy.

People around the world want their governments to engage in actions that ensure a healthy economy. Yet the actions a government takes to ensure a healthy economy depend on the economic theories its lawmakers follow. In the United States, Democrats and Republicans traditionally disagree on economic policies, each justifying their preferences with different economic theories. Before we survey several economic theories that have influenced U.S. national economic policy in various historical periods, we need to discuss how to measure the health of a nation's economy.

■ Measuring Economic Health

Economists and government officials describe a healthy economy as one that has the following characteristics: an increasing domestic product (GDP), low unemployment rate, and low inflation rate. These traditional measures of economic health together provide a useful snapshot of how the national economy is doing. Other measures of economic health focus on the general standard of living of the people by accounting for factors such as rates of poverty and literacy and the financial situation of households. Among less traditional measures of economic health are the United Nations Human Development Index, poverty rate, median household income, and income inequality.

Traditional Measures of Economic Health

Most economists assume that growth in the gross domestic product translates into a prosperous nation with improving living standards—hence progress toward living the American dream. **Gross domestic product (GDP)** is the total market value of all goods and services produced within a country's borders. Rising GDP is a sign of an expanding economy, which means the production of more goods and services—and thus the availability of more goods and services for consumers. Economists view annual GDP growth of 2–3 percent as evidence of a healthy economy.

Economists also expect a healthy economy to correlate with a low level of **inflation,** which is a decreased value of money as evidenced by increased prices. When inflation occurs, consumers' purchasing power falls and they cannot buy as much this year with the same amount of money they spent last year. The U.S. Bureau of Labor Statistics publishes the **consumer price index (CPI),** which measures the average change in prices over time of a "market basket" of goods and services, which includes food, clothing, shelter, fuel, transportation costs, and selected medical costs. The CPI is the most commonly used measure of the impact of inflation on people. According to economists, when the economy is healthy, the inflation rate (measured by the change in CPI) ranges between 1 and 3 percent. The Federal Reserve, the nation's central bank, targets a 2 percent inflation rate year-to-year.

pure capitalist economy
An economy in which private individuals and companies own the modes of producing goods and services, and the government does not enact laws aimed at influencing the marketplace transactions that distribute those goods and services.

regulated capitalist economy (mixed economy)
An economy in which private ownership of the modes of production dominates and the government enacts policies to influence the health of the economy.

gross domestic product (GDP)
The total market value of all goods and services produced by labor and properties within a country's borders.

inflation
The decreased value of money as evidenced by increased prices.

consumer price index (CPI)
The most common measure of inflation, it gauges the average change in prices over time of a "market basket" of goods and services including food, clothing, shelter, fuel, transportation costs, and selected medical costs.

TABLE 11.1 ■ **Evidence of a Healthy Economy**

> Unemployment rate lower than or equal to 5%

> Inflation rate between 1% and 3%

> Gross domestic product (GDP) growth of about 2%

A low unemployment rate, 5 percent or less, is also characteristic of a healthy economy, according to economists. When more people are working, the financial situation of families overall should improve. In addition, in a growing economy with falling unemployment, government revenues should increase because there is more corporate and personal income to tax, and government spending for social welfare programs should decrease because fewer people should need public assistance to meet their basic needs. These trends create a healthier financial situation for government.

In sum, a high or rising GDP, low inflation rate, and low unemployment rate suggest a healthy national economy. Table 11.1 summarizes these traditional measures of a healthy economy. Yet as the U.S. Department of Commerce's Bureau of Economic Analysis points out, "While the GDP is used as an indicator of economic progress, it is not a measure of well-being."[4] Therefore, we next describe other measures that attempt to assess the well-being of individuals and households, which most people expect is a product of a healthy economy and is correlated with achieving the American dream.

Other Measures of Economic Health

Although the GDP is a measure of a nation's economic output, it is not a good measure of how much the residents of a nation benefit from the economy. For example, it does not represent the well-being, or standard of living, of a nation's residents. People's standard of living is affected by the levels of wealth and poverty, access to material goods and services, employment and educational opportunities, and other necessities available to them.

Human Development Index (HDI)
A UN-created measure to determine how well a country's economy is providing for a long and healthy life, educational opportunity, and a decent standard of daily living.

The United Nations (UN) created the **Human Development Index (HDI)** to measure the standard of living of the people in various nations. The HDI assesses three components of human development that people in prosperous nations are expected to enjoy: a long and healthy life, educational opportunities, and a decent standard of daily living. Thus, the HDI sheds light on something quite different from the traditional measures of national economic health that we have just discussed.

Table 11.2 presents the countries with the five highest HDI scores and those with the five lowest HDI scores in the Human Development Reports of 2019. With an HDI score of .920 (1.0 is the highest score possible), the United States ranked 15th out of 189 countries.[5] How do we know what this rank means to American households, their standard of living, and their ability to live the American dream? Additional measures—the level of poverty within the population, household income, and income inequality—can help us answer these questions.

TABLE 11.2 ■ Human Development Index Rankings: 2019

On which continent(s) are the top five countries located? On which continent(s) are the bottom five countries located? The United States is ranked 15th out of 189 nations. Does that surprise you? Explain.

Top Five Countries 2019	Bottom Five Countries 2019
1. Norway (.954)	185. Burundi (.423)
2. Switzerland (.946)	186. South Sudan (.413)
3. Ireland (.942)	187. Chad (.401)
4. Germany (.939)	188. Central African Republic (.381)
5. Hong Kong, China (.939)	189. Niger (.377)

Sources: United Nations Development Programme, "2019 HDI Ranking," *Human Development Report 2019.*

The ideal healthy economy would ensure that all workers earn enough to stay out of **poverty**—the condition of lacking sufficient income to purchase the necessities for an adequate living standard. The **poverty rate** is the percentage of the population with income below the nationally designated poverty level. In 2018, the U.S. poverty rate was 11.8 percent, or 38.1 million people living in poverty in the United States.[6] The U.S. Census Bureau calculates the poverty rate by using its **poverty thresholds**—an annually updated set of income measures (adjusted for family size) that define who is living in poverty. According to the poverty thresholds for 2019,[7] a family of four, with two children under the age of 18 years, earning less than $25,926 was living in poverty. In 2019, one person under 65 years of age earning less than $13,300 was living in poverty, according to the Census Bureau. What quality of life would you have if you earned $13,301 a year, just $1 over the poverty threshold?

Household income is the total pretax earnings of all residents over the age of 15 living in a home. **Median household income** is the income level in the middle of all household incomes; 50 percent of the households have incomes less than the median and 50 percent have incomes greater than the median. An increase in median household income should characterize a healthy, expanding economy if we assume that increases in workers' productivity will translate into increases in workers' incomes. In 2018, the median household income was $63,179.[8]

poverty
The condition of lacking the income sufficient to purchase the necessities for an adequate living standard.

poverty rate
The proportion of the population living below the poverty line as established by the national government.

poverty thresholds
The U.S. Census Bureau's annually updated set of income measures (adjusted for family size) that define who is living in poverty.

household income
The total pretax earnings of all residents over the age of 15 living in a home.

median household income
The middle of all household incomes—50 percent of households have incomes less than the median and 50 percent have incomes greater than the median.

Is there too much income inequality in the United States?

According to the Pew Research Center,* the majority of Americans (61 percent) say that there is too much income inequality in the United States today. Among Democrats and those who lean Democratic, the majority (78 percent) say there is too much inequality. Among Republicans and those who lean Republican, a minority (41 percent) say this. People's view of income inequality also correlates with their income level, though the pattern differs within the two political parties. The overwhelming majority (93 percent) of upper-income Democrats and the majority of lower-income Democrats (65 percent) say there is too much inequality. Among Republicans, those with lower incomes are more apt than those with upper incomes to believe there is too much income inequality (48 percent versus 34 percent). Use the two accompanying graphs to answer the "Practice Analytical Thinking" questions.

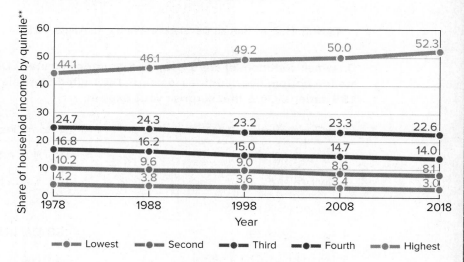

Share of Household Income by Quintile**

*Katherine Schaeffer, "6 Facts about Economic Inequality in the U.S.," *FacTank News in the Numbers,* Pew Research Center, February 7, 2020.

**Jessica Semega, Melissa Kollar, John Creamer, and Abinash Mohanty, U.S. Census Bureau, Current Population Reports, P60-266, *Income and Poverty in the United States: 2018* (Washington, DC: U.S. Government Printing Office, 2019).

Practice Analytical Thinking

1. What can you conclude about the trend in the share of household income earned by each quintile over the past 50 years?

2. What can you conclude about the trend in mean household income for each quintile over the past 50 years?

3. Look at mean household income data for 1998 and compare it to the data for 2008. How does the trend for the highest quintile differ from that of the other four quintiles? What does this indicate about the effect of the Great Recession that began in 2007?

4. In terms of the amount of income inequality in the United States, do you agree with the majority of Americans and Democrats, or with the majority of Republicans?

Mean Household Income by Quintile**

Mean household income by quintile**

Year	1978	1988	1998	2008	2018
Highest	138,431	161,179	196,911	203,925	233,895
Fourth	77,538	84,426	93,054	93,045	101,570
Third	52,930	55,351	60,167	58,611	63,572
Second	32,056	33,393	35,958	34,510	37,293
Lowest	13,053	13,231	14,241	13,628	13,775

—●— Lowest   —●— Second   —●— Third   —●— Fourth   —●— Highest

Source: Jessica Semega, Melissa Kollar, John Creamer, and Abinash Mohanty, U.S. Census Bureau, Current Population Reports, P60-266, *Income and Poverty in the United States: 2018* (Washington, DC: U.S. Government Printing Office, 2019).

To determine whether people at all income levels are benefiting from a healthy economy, the government measures changes in **income inequality,** which is the gap in the proportion of national income held by the richest compared to that held by the poorest. Governments and economists use several measures to assess income inequality. One measure calculates the percentage of the total national income possessed by households in five income groups, five *quintiles*, each comprised of 20 percent of the households in the nation, based on total household income. The bottom quintile comprises the 20 percent of households with the lowest incomes, and the top quintile comprises the 20 percent of households with the highest incomes. In 2018, the lowest quintile held 3 percent of the money income, while the highest quintile held 52 percent of the total money income.[9] Changes in the percentage of the total income held by each quintile over time indicate whether income inequality is growing or shrinking. The ideal is to see a shrinking of income inequality as the national economy expands. See "Analyzing the Sources" for additional consideration of income inequality in the United States.

income inequality
The gap in the proportion of national income held by the richest compared to that held by the poorest.

We have seen that not only traditional economic measures such as GDP, inflation, and unemployment rates serve as indicators of national economic health, but also other measures shed light on the quality of life of people in the United States. With this context in mind, we next explore some economic theories that influence the policies elected officials support to maintain a healthy economy.

Economic Theories That Shape Economic Policy

Today's debates about the proper role of the national government in the economy are nothing new. It was the lack of an economic role for the national government and the poor health of the economy under the Articles of Confederation that sparked rebellions and the call for a constitutional convention in 1787. The framers of the new system of government established by the Constitution envisioned a national government more involved in the economy. Citizens initially supported a limited role for the government in the economy—a **laissez-faire** economic policy. However, as the national economy evolved and experienced ups and downs, citizens and corporations sought greater government involvement in creating and maintaining a healthy economy. In addition, economists developed new theories about the proper role for governments in the economy: Keynesian economics, supply-side economics, and monetarism.

laissez-faire
The hands-off stance of a government in regard to the marketplace.

Laissez-Faire Economics: An Unrealized Policy

Until the late 1800s, a majority of the American people believed that the national government should take a relatively *laissez-faire,* or "hands-off," stance with regard to the marketplace. That is, they thought that the government should neither encourage nor discourage (through its laws) business practices that affected economic health. In his *Wealth of Nations* (1776), economist Adam Smith described the principles underlying the theory of laissez-faire economics. Smith's classical capitalist argument emphasized that the most effective means of supporting a strong and stable economy in the long term is to allow unregulated competition in the marketplace. According to Smith, people's pursuit of their self-interest in an unregulated marketplace would yield a healthy economy. Although it supported a hands-off approach in general, the national government became involved in economic activity as early as 1789, when Congress approved and President George Washington signed the first import tariff (tax on imported goods).

INTERPRETING IMAGES

>> In the late 19th and early 20th centuries, very low wages forced many American families to rely on the income brought home by their children, who worked in mines, glass and textile factories, agriculture, canneries, and home industries such as cigar making. Today, child labor is illegal in the United States and most countries in the world.

Interpret: How would an image like this support an argument against child labor? Did all families have to send their children to work? What economic realities can be understood if we think about the use of child labor? What kinds of economic forces might lead child labor to become unpopular?

Art Reserve/Alamy Stock Photo

As a manufacturing economy replaced the farming-dominated economy during the 19th century, the general laissez-faire stance of the national government disappeared. Technological advances fueled industrialization and the movement of workers from farms to manufacturing jobs in the cities. As immigrants flocked to the United States in search of the American dream, the supply of cheap labor ballooned. Giant corporations formed, and individuals with money to invest accumulated great wealth. Monopolies and trusts also developed, limiting competition in a variety of industries. Although the economy grew (with increased productivity) and unemployment was low, income inequality was a reality; "a huge gap between rich and poor defined the Gilded Age" (1870–1900), when 80 percent of workers "who toiled twelve to sixteen hours a day, stayed poor."[10] The quality of life for most working-class citizens deteriorated as additional family members, including children, needed to work to pay for life's basic necessities. As fewer and fewer people achieved the American dream, even with all family members working, many Americans began to look to the federal government to improve working and living conditions.

In the late 19th century, the federal government began to respond to workers' demands for better wages and working conditions and to business owners' calls for uniform (national) rules for business practices. Moreover, by the early 20th century, the national government took steps to protect public health by passing laws regulating the processing of foods and drugs and the cleanliness and safety of manufacturing plants. Though not directed at the health of the economy, such regulations increased the costs of doing business and, hence, affected the economy.

Clearly, the national government never fully implemented a laissez-faire economic policy. Moreover, as the national economy grew with industrialization, Americans accepted and even called for a mixed economy featuring regulated capitalism. Today, consensus exists on the need for some level of government involvement in the marketplace to ensure a healthy and sustainable economy, environment, and standard of living. But debate continues over how much government involvement is appropriate and what specific policies governments should enact.

Keynesian Economics

Before the Great Depression of the 1930s, government officials and economists believed that a **balanced budget** was important for a healthy economy. When the budget is balanced, the government's expenditures (costs of providing goods and services) are equal to or less than its revenues (money raised from taxes and other sources excluding borrowing). Yet government officials and economists recognized that during wartime the government might need to engage in **deficit spending,** spending more than is raised during the budget year, to pay for the military effort.

During the Great Depression of the 1930s, when unemployment rates soared to 25 percent, President Franklin D. Roosevelt and Congress supported deficit spending to address the severe economic depression that engulfed the nation. The Roosevelt administration implemented numerous economic regulations and a number of innovative work and public assistance programs. Those policies drove up government spending at a time of shrinking government revenues. A key objective of the government's increased spending was to trigger economic growth by lowering unemployment rates, thereby increasing demand for goods because more employed people means more people with money to spend. Deficit

balanced budget
A budget in which the government's expenditures are equal to or less than its revenues.

deficit spending
Government expenditures costing more than is raised in taxes during the budget year, leading to borrowing and debt.

spending, Roosevelt said, was a temporary emergency measure to solve the American people's economic woes by boosting the national economy.

The new economic theory of John Maynard Keynes supported Roosevelt's unprecedented peacetime deficit spending. **Keynesian economics** recommends that during a **recession**—an economic downturn during which unemployment is high and the production of goods and services is low—the national government should decrease taxes and increase its spending to create jobs so that people have more money to spend to stimulate the economy. Based on this theory, deficit spending is also justified during a **depression,** which is a long-term and severe recession. During times of rapid economic growth—an **economic boom,** when unemployment is low and productivity is increasing rapidly—Keynesian theory recommends cutting government spending and possibly increasing taxes. These actions, in turn, may create a budget surplus, which means money could be left over (not needed to pay the bills) at the end of the 12-month budget year. In the long term, deficit spending during recessions and depressions and collecting a surplus when the economy is booming should lead to a balanced budget. Hence Keynesian economic theory advocates using **fiscal policy,** the combination of tax policy and spending policy, to ensure a healthy economy. Fiscal policy is one type of economic policy.

In response to the Great Recession (2007–2009), President George W. Bush used fiscal policy to stimulate the economy. In February 2008, Congress and President Bush approved the Economic Stimulus Act, which included tax refunds for citizens totaling $168 billion along with tax cuts for select businesses. Later the same year, Congress and the president approved the Emergency Economic Stabilization Act, which included $300 billion to rescue three giant mortgage, insurance, and financial services companies from financial disaster and $700 billion to bail out faltering Wall Street financial institutions.

President Barack Obama and Congress continued to stimulate the sagging economy by enacting the American Recovery and Reinvestment Act (ARRA) in February 2009, which authorized $787 billion in combined tax cuts and federal spending. The goals of the ARRA, better known as the "stimulus package," were to create and save jobs, jump-start the nation's economy, and build the foundation for long-term economic growth. Although the success of the stimulus package was debated due to the slow pace of recovery from the Great Recession, most economists agree that the recession would have been even worse without the ARRA.[11]

During the summer of 2019, talk of an impending recession began to circulate among economists. Although unemployment was very low, manufacturing productivity was down and the agriculture sector was experiencing hard times. Many economists agreed that the U.S. economy was "slowing" after a healthy 2018.[12] Some economists pointed to the import taxes that the Trump administration imposed, particularly on China (a form of protectionist policy discussed later), as a partial explanation for the slowing in the manufacturing sector. Others considered the 2017 corporate tax cuts as a possible explanation. However, before the government began an in-depth discussion of the slowing economy, the coronavirus hit China.

On March 27, 2020, President Trump signed the $2.2 trillion Coronavirus Aid, Relief, and Economic Security (CARES) Act. *The New York Times* reported that the CARES Act "is unparalleled in its scope and size, touching on every aspect of the country in an effort to send help to desperate Americans, provide aid to hospitals combating the disease, and bolster an economy forced to slow or shut down

THEN

NOW

Source Analysis: In February 2009 (left), in response to the Great Recession (2007-2009), President Obama signed the American Recovery and Reinvestment Act (ARRA). The ARRA authorized tax cuts and targeted federal spending to stimulate the sagging national economy. In the summer of 2019, economists were predicting another economic recession. Then, in February 2020, the coronavirus hit the United States, causing businesses to shut down and leading to a swift economic downturn with rapidly growing unemployment (recession). Many feared an outcome rivaling the Great Depression of the 1930s. Following smaller measures by President Trump to head off a depression, in March, 2021, President Biden signed a massive $1.9 trillion stimulus act, the American Rescue Plan. Although the causes of the two recessions differed, in both cases Congress and the president turned to fiscal policy to reestablish a healthy national economy. How does political ideology affect government intervention in the economy? Do governments from different political parties approach stimulus spending in different ways?

(Left): Saul Loeb/AFP/Getty Images; *(Right):* AP Photo/AndrewHarnik/APWorld Wide Photos.

altogether to minimize the pandemic."[13] The CARES Act was a package of tax changes and targeted spending to provide economic relief to individuals, families, small businesses, large corporations, and state and local governments. Following President Biden's election, concerns continued to grow about the long-term economic impacts of the COVID-19 pandemic. Biden also faced pressure from many in his party to address concerns about infrastructure, and race- and income-based inequalities. In response, in March 2021, he signed the American Rescue Plan, a $1.9 trillion stimulus package. The goal: keep the economy from tanking. The means: fiscal policy.

Supply-Side Economics

supply-side economics
The theory that advocates the government cutting taxes and deregulating business to stimulate the economy.

Not all administrations have embraced Keynesian economics. President Ronald Reagan (1981–1989) stepped away from Keynesian theory and introduced the nation to **supply-side economics,** which advocates tax cuts and a decrease in government regulation to stimulate the economy in times of recession. Supply-siders argue that the government collects so much money in income taxes from workers that they are discouraged from working more than they absolutely need to (because any extra effort will just mean they pay more in taxes). In addition, supply-siders argue that high taxes drain the economy because they diminish people's ability to save and corporations' ability to invest to increase productivity. Therefore, the theory goes, if the government cuts taxes, workers will be more productive and corporations will have more money to invest, thus stimulating economic growth. Supply-siders also argue that, because government regulation increases the cost of producing goods, **deregulation**—reduction or elimination of government rules that businesses must follow—will reduce production costs.

deregulation
The reduction or elimination of government rules and regulations (laws) that businesses and industries must follow.

President Donald Trump entered office sounding like a supply-sider. The 2017 Tax Cuts and Jobs Act that he signed into law included several reforms to decrease the taxes paid by corporations; the most talked about was the cut in the top corporate tax rate from 35 percent to 21 percent. The Trump administration argued that revenue losses from the corporate tax cuts would be offset by increased revenue from a quick economic expansion. However, by July 2018, the Trump administration acknowledged that the economic expansion had not occurred and the federal deficit was growing faster than economists had predicted.[14] At the same time, Trump's administration was rolling back regulations, the second component of supply-side economics, which is discussed later in this chapter.

Monetarism

monetarism
The theory that says the government's proper economic role is to control the rate of inflation by controlling the amount of money in circulation.

Economist Milton Friedman, a one-time supporter of Keynesian economics, is today best known for yet another economic theory, **monetarism,** which advocates that the government's proper role in promoting a healthy economy is through its regulation of the amount of money circulating in the economy (including coin, currency, and bank deposits). By controlling the amount of money in the economy, the government tries to ensure that the rate of inflation remains low, which typically means unemployment also remains low.

monetary policy
The body of Federal Reserve actions aimed at adjusting the amount of money (coin, currency, and bank deposits) in the economy to maintain a stable, low level of inflation.

Monetarists believe that *too much* money in circulation leads to a high inflation rate, which slows economic growth as people buy less because of higher prices. In addition, as the rate of inflation increases, investors begin to worry about the health of the economy, and investments may decline as a result, ultimately limiting economic growth. On the flip side, the monetarists say, *too little* money in circulation means there is not enough for new investments and that consequently new jobs are not created; this situation, too, retards economic growth. Today, monetarists target an inflation rate of 1–3 percent per year to ensure an adequate money supply for a healthy economy. They believe that the national government must use its **monetary policy,** which is the body of Federal Reserve actions (discussed later in this chapter) aimed at adjusting the amount of money in the economy to maintain a stable, low level of inflation. Indeed, during the Great Recession, and again as the economy began to slow in 2019, the Federal Reserve did take actions to increase the amount of money in circulation and hence prevent an economic downturn.

Source: Jessica Semega, Melissa Kollar, John Creamer, and Abinash Mohanty, U.S. Census Bureau, Current Population Reports, P60-266, *Income and Poverty in the United States: 2018* (Washington, DC: U.S. Government Printing Office, 2019).

What conclusions can you draw about income inequality in the figure above?

Consider how each of the ideologies below would respond to income inequality:

    Conservative
    Liberal
    Laissez-faire

How might each of the policies below be used to address income inequality?

    Fiscal policy
    Monetary policy
    Supply-side economics
    Keynesian policy

What do you believe is the proper role of government in managing the economy? In what cases (if any) should government use a tool to respond to economic changes? Justify your answer.

On the AP U.S. Government exam free response section, you will be asked to read a scenario and respond to the scenario in context. How would you answer the scenario FRQ below?

In the fall of 2020, the coronavirus pandemic caused local governments to shut down schools and all but essential businesses and to prohibit gatherings of more than 10 people. As a result of the shutdowns, a record 10 million people filed for unemployment in the last two weeks of March.

After reading the scenario, respond to A, B, and C below:

A. Describe a power Congress could use to address the economic downturn described in the scenario.

B. In the context of the scenario, explain how the use of congressional power described in Part A can be affected by its interaction with the presidency.

C. In the context of the scenario, explain how interaction between Congress and the presidency can be affected by linkage institutions.

Should One Economic Theory Predominate?

Although economists, government officials, and citizens broadly agree that the government should act to ensure a healthy economy, there is perpetual debate over the proper level of government involvement in the economy and what specific policy actions it should take. Where people stand in this debate depends on which economic theory they advocate. Each theory supports the use of different government policies to promote a healthy economy.

Democrats and Republicans traditionally disagree on economic policies, each justifying their preferences with different economic theories. Since Reagan, Republicans have advocated policies based on supply-side economics, and Democrats have advocated policies more in line with Keynesian economics. Whether the president is a Democrat or Republican, the Federal Reserve, which is expected to be nonpartisan, continues to adjust monetary policy in attempts to maintain a healthy economy.

■ Fiscal Policy

As noted earlier, fiscal policy comprises a government's spending and tax policies. The national government, through its budget process, annually approves a 12-month plan for raising revenue and spending revenue. The 12-month accounting period for revenue raising and spending is known as a **fiscal year (FY).** The national government's fiscal year runs from October 1 through September 30 of the following calendar year and is named for the calendar year in which it ends. Therefore, the federal FY 2022 runs from October 1, 2021, through September 30, 2022.

fiscal year (FY)
The 12-month accounting period for revenue raising and spending, which for the national government begins on October 1 and ends on September 30 of the following year.

Although government spending certainly can create jobs, its primary goal is to provide the goods and services necessary to fulfill the Constitution's mission. The other side of the coin, tax policy, raises revenue needed by the national government to serve the people. Although the main goal of tax policy is to collect revenue, taxation also decreases the amount of money taxpayers have to spend in the marketplace and corporations have to invest. Hence, taxation may reduce consumer demand for goods and services, with possible effects on the unemployment rate as well as company profits. It may also affect investment, which contributes to economic growth. Thus tax policy, like spending policy, powerfully affects the economy.

Tax Policy

The Constitution delegates the power of the purse to Congress. By the authority of the Constitution, Congress formulates and approves (and then sends to the president for approval or rejection) *tax laws* to raise money along with *appropriations laws*—legislation that authorizes the spending of government money for a fiscal year. The Constitution specifies that the House must introduce revenue-raising bills before the Senate can consider them. The House Ways and Means Committee and the Senate Finance Committee are the congressional standing committees from which tax bills emerge.

Figure 11.1 presents the tax mix for the FY 1969 and FY 2019 budgets. Today, the national tax on individual income is the largest revenue source for the national

FIGURE 11.1 ■ **Federal Revenues and Expenditures: 1969 and 2019** Compare the revenue sources of 1969 and 2019 and summarize the differences. Compare the expenditures for 1969 with those of 2019 and summarize the differences. What stands out to you about the shift in revenue sources? What stands out to you about the shift in expenditures?

Photo: U.S. Mint

Source: Office of Management and Budget, Historical Tables, Table 2.2: Percentage Composition of Receipts by Source: 1934–2025.

government. The federal individual income tax is imposed on each individual's *earned income* (salaries and wages) and *unearned income* (profits made from investments).

The second-largest revenue category, social insurance and retirement receipts, includes taxes collected for Social Security and Medicare. Because employers deduct from workers' paychecks the amount they owe for social insurance taxes, these taxes are referred to as **payroll taxes.** The federal government's third-largest revenue source is corporate income taxes. The national government also collects *excise taxes*, which are taxes levied against a specific item such as gasoline or liquor, *estate and gift taxes*, and *customs duties* (import taxes).

Taxes levied by the federal government do not affect the income of all taxpayers in the same way. The national income tax is a **progressive tax** because it takes a larger percentage of the income of wealthier taxpayers and a smaller percentage of the income of less-well-off taxpayers. Most taxpayers view a

payroll taxes
Taxes employers deduct from workers' paychecks that pay for social insurance programs including Social Security and Medicare.

progressive tax
A tax that takes a larger percentage of the income of wealthier taxpayers and a smaller percentage of the income of lower-income taxpayers.

progressive tax as fair. However, some people believe that a **proportional tax (flat tax),** which takes the same percentage of each taxpayer's income, is fairer than a progressive tax. A flat tax of 10 percent would equal $3,500 for a person earning $35,000 and $13,500 for a person earning $135,000. Although these two taxpayers pay a different amount of money in taxes, the *proportion* of their income collected is the same—hence the name proportional tax. Taxes can also be regressive. A **regressive tax** takes a greater percentage of the income of lower-income earners than of higher-income earners. States' sales taxes are the prime example of a regressive tax because lower-income households spend a larger proportion of their income to pay for sales taxes than do wealthier households when the two are purchasing the same items.

Taxes may also affect various taxpayers differently because the government grants **tax expenditures** (better known as *tax breaks* or *tax loopholes*). These are government financial incentives, in other words, a decreased tax burden, that encourage individuals and corporations to behave in a way that promotes the public good. For example, to encourage home ownership, the government gives tax breaks to individuals paying interest on a home mortgage. The government also offers tax breaks to businesses for job creation and worker retraining.

Tax expenditures and tax cuts, such as the cuts established in the Tax Cuts and Jobs Act of 2017, would not be a concern if the government raised enough money to balance its budget. Unfortunately, the national government spends more than it raises in annual revenues. How is the government spending all this money?

Spending Policy

Decisions the federal government makes about spending significantly affect both the national economy and the ability of individuals to achieve the American dream. Although setting the budget is an annual process, with Congress and the president approving a spending plan one fiscal year at a time, not all national government spending is approved annually.

For the government to spend money, Congress and the president must enact laws that establish **budget authority,** which is the legal authority for agencies to spend federal money. Programs granted budget authority each year are **discretionary spending** programs. There are two categories of discretionary spending programs: defense programs and nondefense programs. As Figure 11.1 indicates, in FY 2019, discretionary defense spending was the same proportion of the budget pie as discretionary nondefense spending. Nondefense spending covers the majority of domestic programs, including the administration of justice, agriculture, education, energy, environment, health, housing, income security for those who are poor and disabled, and transportation.

Annual appropriations acts are pieces of legislation that define how much money can be spent in the fiscal year. Congress and the president deliberate each year over how much budget authority to include in these acts for discretionary spending programs. Typically, Democrats and Republicans differ on their priorities for such programs.

The share of the budget spent on discretionary spending has been shrinking due to the growth in **mandatory spending,** spending required by the authorization legislation that created a government program (see Figure 11.1). Social Security (income security for retired Americans and people with certain disabilities), Medicare (health insurance for elderly individuals), and Medicaid (health insurance for low-income individuals) are prime examples of mandatory spending programs. The government is obligated to pay for these entitlement programs every year, whatever the cost may be, for as long as the program exists. Because the government is legally obligated to pay back money it borrows, payments for the national debt also fall within the category of mandatory spending.

In the annual budget process, Congress and the president do not make annual decisions about most of the money spent by the national government because most expenditures are mandatory. Other than interest payments on the debt, mandatory spending could be controlled by Congress and the president by rewriting the legislation that established these open-ended budget obligations. For example, eligibility for receiving Social Security could be changed so that very wealthy retired individuals would not receive Social Security. However, recent attempts to rewrite the legislation that created the Social Security retirement program have shown that mandatory programs are difficult to change. This is partly because elected officials fear the impact such changes would have on their reelection prospects and partly because of partisanship. Therefore, most mandatory spending is considered **politically uncontrollable spending.** Not only do Democrats and Republicans disagree on the proper reforms, but also members of each party disagree among themselves on specific reforms. Without major reforms to programs like Social Security and Medicare, mandatory spending will continue to grow as a percentage of the federal budget.

politically uncontrollable spending
Spending on programs that are so popular that elected officials are not willing to change the laws that authorize the programs for fear of the effect on their reelection prospects.

National Budget Process: Creating Fiscal Policy

The federal government creates its policies and programs through authorization legislation that specifies policy goals and establishes whether the policy will be funded through budget authority obligated for the life of the program (open-ended, mandatory spending) or budget authority that must be set annually (discretionary spending). In an annual appropriations process, Congress and the president establish yearly funding for discretionary spending programs and possibly change tax policy to increase revenue raised—to pay the bills—or to cut taxes in an effort to stimulate the economy. This process begins in the executive branch.

THE PRESIDENT'S EXECUTIVE BUDGET The budget process officially starts about a year and a half before the beginning of the fiscal year for which budget authority will be obligated. For example, work on the budget for FY 2022 (which covers the spending period of October 1, 2021, through September 30, 2022) began during the spring of 2019. The process begins when the Office of Management and Budget (OMB) sends the president's budget priorities (policy and financing preferences) to the executive branch agencies. Executive branch agencies use the president's guidelines to formulate their funding requests. Typically, these requests are incremental changes (small increases) to their current fiscal year's budget authority.

The agencies' budget requests work their way back up the executive branch hierarchy to the OMB. The OMB reviews the budget requests, conducts hearings in which the agencies justify their requests, and analyzes the requests in light of economic forecasts. The OMB then submits its budget recommendations to the president, who works with the OMB to create a proposed fiscal plan for the entire national government for the upcoming fiscal year. The OMB drafts a budget document and a budget message, collectively labeled the **executive budget,** which explains the president's fiscal plan. The president is to submit the executive budget to Congress by the first Monday in February, eight months before the fiscal year begins.

executive budget
The budget document and budget message that explains the president's fiscal plan.

CONGRESSIONAL ACTION Once Congress receives the president's executive budget, the Congressional Budget Office (CBO), the legislative branch's counterpart to the OMB, swings into action. The CBO analyzes the executive budget in light of economic forecasts and predicted government revenues. The House Budget Committee and the Senate Budget Committee use the CBO's analysis, along with reports from other congressional committees, to develop the concurrent budget resolution. The **concurrent budget resolution** establishes a binding expenditure ceiling (the maximum amount that can be spent) and a binding revenue floor (the minimum amount that must be raised) as well as proposed expenditure levels for major policy categories. The House and the Senate must both agree to the concurrent budget resolution. This agreement is to occur by April 15, less than six months before the fiscal year begins.

After approval of the concurrent budget resolution, the House Appropriations Committee and the Senate Appropriations Committee each draft 12 appropriations bills to provide budget authority for all the discretionary spending for the upcoming fiscal year. To comply with the concurrent budget resolution, Congress may also need to revise the legislation that authorized selected government programs to stay below the expenditure ceiling, or it may have to agree to changes in tax legislation to meet the revenue floor. **Budget reconciliation** is the process of rewriting authorization legislation to comply with the concurrent budget resolution. The deadline for completion of the reconciliation process is June 15, less than four months before the fiscal year begins.

Congress has until the end of June to approve the 12 appropriations bills that fund discretionary spending for the upcoming fiscal year. This timetable leaves two months for the president to approve all 12 bills so that by October 1 the national government can begin the new fiscal year with budget authority.

The nature of the annual budget process is such that, at any given time, some government body in the executive or legislative branch is preparing a future budget, even as the executive branch is implementing the current budget. At the same time, the Government Accountability Office (GAO), a congressional office, is evaluating the implementation of the previous fiscal year's budget. Thus budgeting is a perpetual government activity, one that takes up a great deal of national officials' time.

Today's Federal Budget Realities

Although the budget process just outlined was established through legislation beginning with the 1974 Congressional Budget and Impoundment Control Act, the process is not often followed. By the 21st century, the federal budget process included these realities:

1. Appropriations bills that were not approved by October 1

2. Continuing resolutions were approved to fund some, if not all, of the fiscal year

3. Efforts to shrink annual deficit spending by establishing spending caps on annual discretionary spending

4. Regular increases to the debt ceiling to pay for debt already incurred

CONTINUING RESOLUTIONS If Congress and the president fail to approve one or more of the appropriations bills before the new fiscal year begins on October 1, Congress needs to approve a **continuing resolution** to authorize spending for

---

concurrent budget resolution

A document approved by the House and the Senate at the beginning of their budget processes that establishes binding expenditure ceilings and a binding revenue floor as well as proposed expenditure levels for major policy categories.

budget reconciliation

The annual process of rewriting authorization legislation to comply with the expenditure ceiling and revenue floor of the concurrent budget resolution for the upcoming fiscal year.

continuing resolution

An agreement of the House and Senate that authorizes agencies not covered by approved appropriation laws to continue to spend money within their previous budget year's levels.

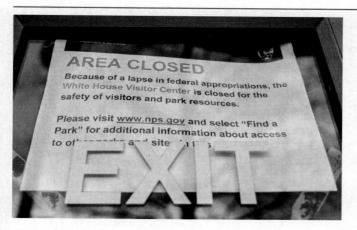

>> Since 1976, the federal government has experienced 21 funding gaps—meaning, instances in which not all government operations received budget authority. Beginning in 1980, based on the legal interpretation of then-Attorney General Benjamin Civiletti, such funding gaps have forced government shutdowns. During the Trump administration, two government shutdowns occurred, including the longest one ever: 35 days.

agencies and programs not covered by the approved appropriations bills. Typically, the level of spending authority approved in a continuing resolution is the same level as in the previous fiscal year, with adjustments for inflation. If a program or agency is not extended budget authority through either an appropriation law or a continuing resolution, then it cannot operate and must shut down until Congress and the president approve its budget authority.

For FY 2018, Congress approved five continuing resolutions (CRs) between October 1, 2017, and February 8, 2018, to fund the national government. During that period, the government shut down for 2.5 days between the approval of CR 3 and CR 4. It also shut down for a few hours between the approval of CR 4 and CR 5. Then, on March 23, 2018, just hours before another shutdown, Congress passed and the president signed $1.3 billion of appropriations for the remainder of FY 2018, which would end on September 30, 2018.

The longest government shutdown due to lack of appropriation laws occurred from December 22, 2018, through January 25, 2019. It was the second government shutdown involving furloughs during the Trump presidency.

DEFICIT SPENDING AND SPENDING CAPS Most Americans highly value the ideal of a balanced budget, in which the government spends no more than the revenues that it raises. Although the nation had a **budget surplus** (money left over when all expenses are paid) for several years at the end of the 1990s, **budget deficits** (more money spent than collected through revenues) recurred as the first decade of the 21st century unfolded. Indeed, over the past two decades, deficit spending has been the norm, not the exception (see Figure 11.2).

budget surplus
Money left over after all expenses are paid.

budget deficit
More money spent than collected through revenues.

The Budget Control Act of 2011 set caps on annual federal discretionary funding for 2012–2021 in an attempt to decrease (and eventually eliminate) budget deficits. The caps limited how much discretionary spending could be increased in each fiscal year. However, for most fiscal years since 2011, Congress has agreed to increase the established caps, and so deficit spending continues.

NATIONAL DEBT A government that engages in deficit spending borrows money and hence goes into debt. The **national debt** is the total amount of money the national government owes to all the creditors (individuals and groups) that loaned

national debt
The total amount of money the government owes to all the individuals and groups that loaned it money.

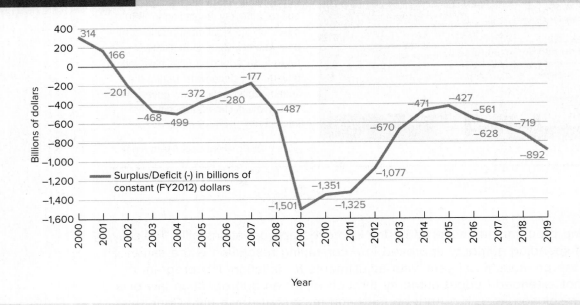

FIGURE 11.2 ■ **Deficit Spending Since Last Surplus Years** What accounts for the huge increase in the deficit in 2009? How might the 2020 Coronavirus Aid, Relief, and Economic Security Act (CARES Act) affect the deficit? What actions can the national government take to decrease annual deficits?

Source: Office of Management and Budget, Historical Tables, Table 1.3—Summary of Receipts, Outlays, and Surpluses or Deficits (–) in Current Dollars, Constant (FY2012) Dollars, and as Percentages of GDP: 1940–2025.

it money. Figure 11.3 indicates who these creditors are and the percentage of the debt owed to each creditor group. The figure also indicates the proportion of the debt owed by other nations. The long-term impact of debt is the legal obligation to pay back not only the money initially borrowed (the *principal*) but also interest, an additional amount of money equal to a percentage of the amount initially borrowed. In the case of government borrowing, future generations must pay back the debt of their parents and grandparents. On April 4, 2020, to pay off the $23.7 trillion national debt, each citizen (man, woman, and child) would have had to chip in $71,913.[15] Even as politicians, some economists, and many concerned citizens call for a balanced budget, deficit spending continues, and so the national debt grows.

Democrats and Republicans battle annually over what taxing and/or spending policies they should change to decrease annual deficits, moving the government toward a balanced budget. These battles grow more intense and bitter as the proportion of the budget that goes to mandatory spending grows.

debt ceiling
The legal borrowing limit for the national government.

To pay its annual financial obligations, including debt already incurred, Congress and the president have to regularly increase the **debt ceiling,** the legal borrowing limit for the national government. Congresses and presidents have raised the debt ceiling almost 100 times since it was first established in 1917.[16] Democrats and Republicans battle regularly about raising the debt ceiling, even

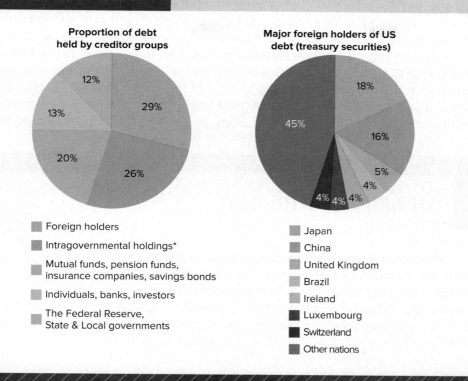

Proportion of debt held by creditor groups

- 12%
- 29%
- 13%
- 20%
- 26%

Legend:
- Foreign holders
- Intragovernmental holdings*
- Mutual funds, pension funds, insurance companies, savings bonds
- Individuals, banks, investors
- The Federal Reserve, State & Local governments

Major foreign holders of US debt (treasury securities)

- 18%
- 16%
- 45%
- 5%
- 4%
- 4%
- 4%
- 4%

Legend:
- Japan
- China
- United Kingdom
- Brazil
- Ireland
- Luxembourg
- Switzerland
- Other nations

FIGURE 11.3 ■ **Who Owns the $24 Trillion U.S. Debt?** Which creditor group do you think Americans are most worried about owing money to? Why?

Source: The Balance

*Intragovernmental holdings is the portion of the debt owed to 230 federal agencies.

though a decision not to raise the debt ceiling would leave the national government unable to pay all its financial obligations—a *default*. Countries around the globe worry that a U.S. government default on its debt would spark a global financial and economic disaster.

Elected officials fear that citizens harmed by spending cuts and tax increases will not vote for them on Election Day; therefore, attempts to shrink annual deficits often fail. While elected officials struggle with budget decisions and their impact on reelection hopes, appointed officials, whom citizens cannot hold accountable through the ballot box, make monetary policy that, like fiscal policy, affects the national economy.

Monetary Policy: The Federal Reserve System

The federal government seeks to influence the value of money by controlling its availability. When more money is in circulation, it is lower in value; consequently, consumers need to spend more money to keep buying the same goods and services. Inflation is at work. The costs of running a business also increase with inflation. As a result of increased costs and decreased sales (because fewer people can maintain their levels of spending), businesses may choose to lay off workers. To avert these potential problems, the Federal Reserve, the nation's central banking system, works to maximize employment, ensure stable prices (keep inflation low), and moderate long-term interest rates.

Congress and President Woodrow Wilson established the Federal Reserve System (the Fed) in 1913. The Fed is composed of the Board of Governors (a government agency whose seven members the president nominates and the Senate must confirm), 12 Federal Reserve banks, and the Federal Open Market Committee (FOMC). The Board of Governors, the president of the Federal Reserve Bank of New York, and the presidents of four of the other Federal Reserve banks, who serve on a rotating basis, make up the FOMC. Today, the Fed's responsibilities include (1) setting *monetary policy*—the body of government policies aimed at

ARGUMENTATION THINKING CRITICALLY

Differences of opinion on the proper role of government in economic matters are at the heart of differences between the Democratic and Republican Parties. Compare how the two major political parties articulate economic policy: The Democratic Party Platform of 2020 advocates raising the federal minimum wage, government spending to stimulate the economy, and a more progressive tax system. The Republican Party Platform (2016) mentions none of these measures, and instead advocates simplifying the tax code, lowering taxes to stimulate the economy, and deregulating the market.

What is the proper role of government in managing the economy? You will be asked to consider this question in the practice Argumentation FRQ at the end of this chapter.

Develop an argument that explains the proper response of the national government to an economic downturn.

Sources: https://democrats.org/where-we-stand/party-platform/building-a-stronger-fairer-economy/https://prod-cdn-static.gop.com/docs/Resolution_Platform_2020.pdf

In your essay, you must:

- Articulate a defensible claim or thesis that responds to the prompt and establishes a line of reasoning

- Support your claim with at least TWO pieces of accurate and relevant information:

  - At least ONE piece of evidence must be from one of the following foundational documents:

    — Article I of the U.S. Constitution
    — Article II of the U.S. Constitution

  - Use a second piece of evidence from another foundational document from the list or from your study of economic policy

- Use reasoning to explain why your evidence supports your claim/thesis

- Respond to an opposing or alternative perspective using refutation, concession, or rebuttal

maintaining price stability; (2) supervising and regulating banking institutions; (3) maintaining the stability of financial markets; and (4) providing financial services to depository institutions, the national government, and foreign official institutions—central banks of other nations, and international organizations such as the International Monetary Fund.

The Fed has three primary tools for setting monetary policy. It can raise or lower the *reserve requirement*—the amount of money that financial institutions must keep out of circulation. In times of high inflation, the Fed may raise the reserve requirement to decrease the amount of money available through credit, thus, decreasing the money supply. The Fed can also raise or lower the *discount rate*—the interest charged to financial institutions that borrow money from the Federal Reserve banks—and thereby make it more or less costly to borrow money. The Fed action that most influences the money supply, however, is its decision to buy or sell Treasury securities (bills, notes, and bonds, which represent loans of money to the government). The Fed sells Treasury securities when it wants to decrease the money supply and buys them to increase the supply.

On March 16, 2020, the Federal Reserve announced that it was taking emergency actions to support the national economy during the coronavirus pandemic. In addition to decreasing its discount rate to near zero, the Fed stated that it would buy Treasury securities. These actions were aimed at keeping financial markets functioning and making it easier for small businesses to borrow money to stay in business.[17]

■ Regulatory Policy

Marketplace competition among private entities, each trying to make a profit, may threaten economic health as well as public safety, people's health, and the environment. Consider, for example, the unsafe products, including dangerous food and drugs, which may be manufactured and sold to make a profit. Think about production and manufacturing processes that may pollute the air, water, and land, creating conditions that are injurious to public health. Competition may also lead firms to cut salaries and benefits to ensure their profits, or their very survival. Such cuts decrease workers' ability to earn wages and benefits that keep them in the middle class, or even out of poverty. Unsafe and unhealthful working conditions may be another "cost" that workers "pay" so that firms can hold down or reduce production costs. Moreover, if marketplace competition results in a few firms driving out their competition, they then have the power to raise prices or produce goods of lower quality, harming consumers.

In the U.S. economy today, the government regulates marketplace practices to protect the public and the economy. This regulation occurs in two broad categories: business regulation and social regulation. **Business regulation** includes government policies that aim to preserve competition in the marketplace. **Social regulation** refers to government policies directed at protecting workers, consumers, and the environment from the harm caused by marketplace competition. In Chapter 7, we surveyed the administrative rule-making process by which executive branch agencies establish business and social regulations. In this discussion, we trace the evolution of these two types of regulatory policy.

business regulation
Government rules, regulations, and standards directed at preserving competition in the marketplace.

social regulation
Government rules, regulations, and standards aimed at protecting workers, consumers, and the environment from market failure.

Business Regulation

The federal government created the first agency for the purpose of regulating business, the Interstate Commerce Commission (ICC), in 1887. The ICC initially regulated the prices of and services provided by the railroad industry to ensure that farmers could transport their goods to distant markets. Next, in 1914, the federal government established regulations to prevent large corporations from engaging in business practices that harmed marketplace competition and established the Federal Trade Commission (FTC) to oversee these regulations.[18] In 1934, during the Great Depression, the government created the Securities and Exchange Commission (SEC) to regulate and make transparent the nation's stock markets and financial markets.

More recently, the United States experienced a failure in the financial market because of risky decisions by numerous financial and banking institutions. Loans and credit lines were extended to people without the means to repay the borrowed money. Ultimately, this sparked an increase in the number of people who could not pay their mortgages and therefore lost their homes. Hundreds of billions of dollars' worth of mortgages could not be repaid by the fall of 2008, and several large, prominent financial and banking companies collapsed. President Bush and Congress began discussions about the need for new regulations for the banking and financial industries to prevent similar market failures in the future.

Congress and President Obama's administration continued those discussions, focusing on protecting consumers of the banking and financial industries. In the summer of 2010, President Obama signed the Dodd-Frank Wall Street Reform and Consumer Protection Act (Dodd-Frank Act). Among other things, this legislation established the Consumer Financial Protection Bureau (CFPB), an independent unit within the Fed. The CFPB has the authority to regulate a wide range of financial products, including mortgages and credit cards, and to collect and monitor consumer complaints about the financial and banking industries. The CFPB also has a responsibility to educate consumers about financial products and services.

The Dodd-Frank Act also imposed new regulations on banks and financial institutions. One such provision of the law required banks to pass "stress tests" that measured their ability to survive a severe economic downturn. In May 2018, Congress agreed to President Trump's request to roll back some of the regulations put on banks through the Dodd-Frank Act. Congressional members who supported the deregulation argued it would boost the economy.[19]

Social Regulation

The national government also uses social regulatory policy—which aims to protect the public's health and safety—to safeguard workers, consumers, and the environment from the potential harm created by the competitive quest for profits in the marketplace. Like business regulation, social regulation has an economic impact because it increases the costs of doing business.

The federal government first established social regulation when it passed two 1906 laws that protected *public* health—the Pure Food and Drug Act and the Meat Inspection Act. In his novel *The Jungle,* author Upton Sinclair described the dangerous and unsanitary conditions in the Chicago meatpacking industry, motivating President Theodore Roosevelt (1901–1909) to sign those two laws. The Pure Food and Drug Act created the Food and Drug Administration (FDA) and charged it with testing all foods and drugs produced for human consumption. It also requires individuals to present prescriptions from licensed physicians to purchase certain drugs and mandates the use of warning labels on habit-forming drugs. The Meat Inspection Act requires government inspection of animals that are slaughtered and processed for human consumption and establishes standards of cleanliness for slaughterhouses and meat processing plants.

The federal government first addressed working conditions that jeopardized *workers'* health and general welfare when it enacted the Fair Labor Standards Act (FLSA) in 1938. The FLSA established standards for a legal workweek, overtime pay for those working more than the standard workweek, a minimum wage, record keeping of workers' hours, and limits on child labor. President Franklin D. Roosevelt characterized the law as the "most far-reaching, far-sighted program to the benefit of workers ever adopted."[20]

In the 1960s, the government focused anew on growing concerns about product quality and safety. In his 1965 book *Unsafe at Any Speed*, attorney and consumer advocate Ralph Nader warned that "a great problem of contemporary

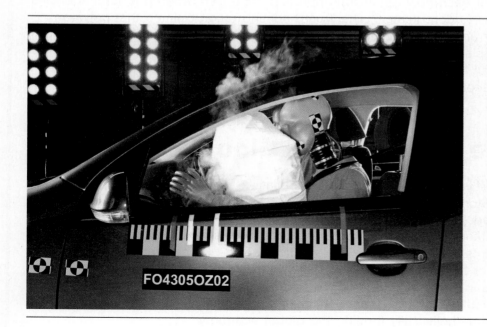

FO4305OZ02

life is how to control the power of economic interests which ignore the harmful effects of their applied science and technology."[21] Although Nader's book targeted the unsafe cars rolling off the assembly lines of the U.S. auto industry, his warning was equally relevant to the countless American industries that were discharging chemicals and toxins into the environment. Nader's book helped ignite an environmental movement and a consumer safety movement.

Lobbying by concerned citizens and interest groups led to passage of the Consumer Product Safety Act (CPSA) of 1973. The federal Consumer Product Safety Commission (CPSC), created through the CPSA, is charged with protecting the public from unreasonable risk of injury associated with more than 15,000 consumer products, including toys and other products for children, products for inside and outside the home, and products made for sports and recreation. The CPSC can recall such products if it deems them unsafe, just as the FDA can recall food and prescription medicines it judges to be unsafe. To better serve the public today, there is a website, www.recall.gov, that provides the latest information on recalls.

The Benefits and Costs of Regulation

Business and social regulation has unquestionably lowered the risk of harm to citizens and the environment caused by marketplace competition. It also has cushioned economic downfalls. But the burden of government regulations has driven up the cost of doing business and of government expenditures, and in the end, consumers pay for this cost. In many industries, this increased cost poses greater problems for smaller firms than for larger ones. The higher costs caused by compliance with government regulations may also put U.S. industries and firms at a competitive disadvantage in the global marketplace, because many other countries do not have such business or social regulations. Therefore, the production costs of firms in other countries are often lower than those in the United States.

President Obama "was among the most prolific authors of major regulations in presidential history."[22] His successor, President Trump, declared that rolling back regulations would be a defining theme of his presidency. He put this declaration into action by signing an executive order that called for the elimination of two regulations for each new regulation approved.[23] He also ordered federal agencies to form teams to deregulate.[24] The Trump administration claimed that between January 2017 and January 2018, they had "delayed, withdrawn or made inactive nearly 1,600 planned regulatory actions."[25] Trump's persistent deregulation efforts, combined with the tax cuts he signed into law in 2017, indicate that he supports supply-side economics.

■ Trade Policy in the Global Economy

The next time you are shopping, try to purchase only American-made products. Is it possible? Stores in the United States offer products that are domestic (that is, American made) as well as imported (made overseas by American or foreign companies). Moreover, many American-made products have imported components and ingredients. For example, U.S. International Trade Commission data show that ingredients for food products are imported from more than 100 countries.[26] Today, marketplaces in every country offer products grown and produced in countries from throughout the world. Hence, national economies are integrated and interdependent—holistically forming the **global economy.**

global economy
The worldwide economy created by the integration and interdependence of national economies.

To navigate in this global economy, each nation creates its own **trade policy**—a collection of tax laws and regulations that support the country's international commerce. In addition, international organizations whose mission is to establish trade rules for all nations to follow have created a global trade policy. The goal of trade policy, like the other economic policies we have discussed, is ostensibly to promote prosperous economies.

A government's trade policy may take one of two basic forms—free trade or protectionism—or it may be a combination of the two. **Protectionist trade policy** aims at sheltering domestic producers and businesses from foreign competition through tariffs and nontariff trade barriers. A **tariff** is a special tax on imported goods paid by the importer. **Nontariff trade barriers** include government business regulations (such as limits on the number of imports allowed into a country or bans on the sale of imports that a government deems unsafe). **Government subsidies**—tax breaks or another kind of financial support that encourages behaviors the government deems beneficial to the public good—are another form of nontariff barriers. Most subsidies are given to producers or distributors of goods to promote economic growth. Proponents of national government subsidies to U.S. farmers argue that to decrease these subsidies would place the farmers at a competitive disadvantage because European farmers receive even larger subsidies from their governments.

Opponents of protectionist policy argue that prices of domestic goods increase as a result of limited competition. In addition, the price of imported goods increases due to tariffs. Proponents of protectionist policy argue that businesses benefit from the limited competition, and workers' salaries benefit as business profits increase. Therefore, wealth remains in the country.

From the 1790s until the 1930s, protectionism was the aim of U.S. trade policy. The first secretary of the Treasury, Alexander Hamilton, argued successfully that taxes on imported goods could be set high enough to protect American-made products in the domestic marketplace. In 1930, even as the American economy was failing, Congress hiked tariffs 20 percent—so high that it set off an international tariff war. This tariff hike fueled the Great Depression, the economic toll of which was global.

After World War II, the United States and its international partners gradually shifted toward **free trade policy,** which aims at lowering or eliminating tariffs and nontariff barriers to trade. Free trade policies decrease the costs of bringing products to markets throughout the world and, in this way, open markets to a greater diversity of products and brisker competition. When other nations eliminate tariffs, American companies can participate in the global marketplace at a lower cost. These opportunities encourage an increase in the supply of U.S. goods and thus lead to an expansion of the U.S. economy. By the same token, when the United States eliminates its tariffs, more foreign products make their way into the American marketplace, increasing the diversity of consumer goods and producer competition and decreasing consumer prices in the United States. Opponents of free trade claim that the increased competition decreases profits of domestic businesses, and therefore, unemployment increases. Proponents counter that in the long term, poorer countries will develop healthier economies due to increased competition and increased employment opportunities and will become new consumers for the products of wealthier countries. Therefore, proponents argue, in the long term, all countries benefit from free trade policy.

trade policy
A collection of tax laws and regulations that support the country's international commerce.

protectionist trade policy
The establishment of trade barriers to shelter domestic goods from foreign competition.

tariff
A special tax on imported goods paid by the importer.

nontariff trade barriers
Business and social regulations as well as government subsidies aimed at creating a competitive advantage in trade.

government subsidy
A tax break or another kind of financial support that encourages behaviors the government deems beneficial to the public good.

free trade policy
The elimination of tariffs and nontariff trade barriers so that international trade is expanded.

In 1947, the United States and 23 other nations signed the General Agreement on Tariffs and Trade (GATT), which advocated for free trade and punishment of protectionism. This multilateral agreement on guidelines for conducting international trade had three basic objectives. First, the signatory countries would not discriminate against one another in trade matters. Second, the signatory countries would work toward eliminating all tariff and regulatory barriers to trade among their countries. Third, the signatory countries would consult and negotiate with one another to resolve any trade conflicts or damages caused by trading activities of another signatory country. Through multilateral negotiations, the GATT established the guidelines for international trade and resolved trade disputes from 1947 to 1995. Then, in 1995, the World Trade Organization (WTO) came into being. The WTO continues the GATT's advocacy of free trade and punishment of protectionism. Specifically, the WTO monitors adherence to international trade rules and resolves charges of rule violations raised by any of its over 150 member countries, of which the United States is one.

INTERPRETING IMAGES

≫ In 2016, the majority of British voters supported Brexit, the exit of Britain from the European Union (EU). Some Brexit supporters viewed the EU as a multinational financial and trade organization that failed to address the 2008 global recession and thus harmed Britain's economy. Some supporters also view multinational organizations such as the EU as a threat to Britain's sovereignty. In contrast, many economists view Brexit as a setback to free-trade efforts.

Interpret: How does patriotism play into support or opposition for global trade policy? What kinds of issues must policymakers consider when writing or deciding whether to support trade deals? Is there an ideological difference between unilateral and multilateral trade deals? How does this play out in the United States?

Jack Taylor/Getty Images

Today, most economists view tariffs as "mutually harmful to all nations involved."[27] However, after decades of trade agreements among countries that opened up trade markets and fostered globalization, a backlash to free trade was evident beginning in 2016. Both the United Kingdom's vote to leave the European Union in 2016 and U.S. presidential candidate Donald Trump's campaign were calls to revert back to protectionist trade policies. In 2018, President Trump imposed tariffs on steel and aluminum shipments to the United States from Canada, Mexico, and the European Union. Then he imposed tariffs on Chinese products. China responded by imposing tariffs on U.S. products. American farmers and manufacturers, and hence the U.S. economy, were harmed by these actions.

The American Dream in Today's Economy

According to a December 2019 Gallup Poll, 84 percent of Americans stated that the 2020 presidential candidates' positions on the economy were very important or extremely important to their voting decisions.[28] And a Pew Research Center poll conducted in January 2020 found that 67 percent of Americans believed that the economy should be a top priority for President Trump and Congress.[29] This high level of concern for the U.S. economy predated the historic damage caused by the coronavirus pandemic.

At the end of 2019, in fact, the national economy was considered healthy—not booming, but healthy. The growth in GDP in 2019 was 2.3 percent—lower than the 2.9 percent growth in 2018 but higher than the average growth of 2 percent since the Great Recession.[30] The average annual unemployment rate in 2019 was 3.7 percent.[31] From January 2017 through December 2019, the unemployment rate had been below 4 percent; in September 2019 it was 3.5 percent, the lowest rate since May 1969.[32] And the rate of inflation, as measured by the change in CPI from December 2018 through December 2019, was 2.3 percent.[33] If you compare this data with the information in Table 11.1, you will see why economists viewed the U.S. economy as healthy at the end of 2019.

Beginning in February 2020, as state and local governments attempted to contain and mitigate the impact of the coronavirus pandemic on public health, the national government employed its fiscal, monetary, and (de)regulatory policies to support the financial health of individuals, families, businesses, and hence, the nation.

Clearly, the national government has many tools it can use to create and maintain a healthy economy and support each individual's pursuit of the American dream. Typically, there is no consensus on the spending policies, tax policies, regulatory policies, trade policies, or monetary policies that will achieve that goal. However, in times of economic recession and depression, Democrats and Republicans have been able to build bipartisan consensus on policies aimed at creating and maintaining a healthy economy.

Conclusion: Thinking Critically About What's Next in Economic Policy

Governments throughout the world seek to maintain healthy economies using economic policy. U.S. economic policy comprises taxing and spending policies (fiscal policy), monetary policy, regulatory policy, and trade policy. Today, the realities of globalization influence economic decisions made by the president, Congress, and the Fed. As the coronavirus made clear, economic crises can come in unexpected ways. Whatever the cause, governments have to respond to crises that harm the economy. But economic policies frequently do not have immediate results; months or years may pass before fiscal, monetary, or regulatory policies show their effects on the health of the economy.

The state and local government responses to the coronavirus included stay-at-home orders and the closing of nonessential businesses. Such policies drastically affected the national economy. How long will these impacts be felt? Will the nation return to the debates about closing annual budget deficits through a balanced budget amendment to the Constitution? Will the American dream be attainable for your generation and future generations?

References

1. Jeanna Smialek, "The Fed Goes All In With Unlimited Bond-Buying Plan,"*The New York Times*, March 23, 2020, https://www.nytimes.com/2020/03/23/business/economy/coronavirus-fed-bond-buying.html

2. Quoted in David Kamp, "Rethinking the American Dream," *Vanity Fair,* April 2009.

3. Samantha Smith, "Most Think the 'American Dream' Is within Reach for Them," Pew Research Center, October 31, 2017, www.pewresearch.org/fact-tank/2017/10/31/most-think-the-american-dream-is-within-reach-for-them/.

4. U.S. Bureau of Economic Analysis, "Measuring the Economy: A Primer on GDP and the National Income and Product Accounts," September 2007.

5. United Nations Development Programme, "2019 HDI Ranking," *Human Development Report 2019,* www.hdr.undp.org/en/content/2019-human-development-index-ranking.

6. U.S. Census Bureau, *Newsroom,* "Income, Poverty & Health Insurance Coverage in the United States: 2018," September 10, 2019.

7. U.S. Census Bureau, *Data,* "Poverty Thresholds by Size of Family and Number of Children: 2019".

8. U.S. Census Bureau, *Data,* "Poverty Thresholds by Size of Family and Number of Children: 2019".

9. Jessica Semega, Melissa Kollar, John Creamer, and Abinash Mohanty, U.S. Census Bureau, Current Population Reports, P60-266, Income and Poverty in the United States: 2018, Table A-4: Selected Measures of Household Income Dispersion 1967–2018 (Washington, DC: U.S. Government Printing Office, 2019).

10. Charles Derber, *People Before Profit* (New York: Picador, 2002), 48.

11. David Leonhardt, "Judging Stimulus by Job Data Reveals Success," *The New York Times,* February 17, 2010.

12. Katie Rogers and Emily Cochrane, "Trump Urges Limits amid Pandemic, but Stops Short of National Mandates," *The New York Times,* March 16, 2020.

13. Emily Cochrane and Sheryl Gay Stolbert, "$2 Trillion Coronavirus Stimulus Bill is Signed into Law," *The New York Times,* March 27, 2020.

14. Jim Tankersley, "How the Trump Tax Cut Is Helping to Push the Federal Deficit to $1 Trillion," *The New York Times,* July 25, 2018.

15. "U.S. National Debt Clock," www.usdebtclock.org.

16. Ariana Eunjung Cha, "What's in the Debt Ceiling, and Why Is Everyone in Washington Talking About It?" *The Washington Post,* April 18, 2011.

17. Christoper Rugaber, "Fed takes steps to slash rates, ease bank rules," Associated Press, March 16, 2020.

18. Sherman Antitrust Act (1890); Clayton Antitrust Act (1914).

19. Alan Rappeport and Emily Flitter, "Congress Approves First Big Dodd-Frank Rollback," *The New York Times,* May 22, 2018.

20. "United States History: Fair Labor Standards Act," www.u-s-history.com/pages/h1701.html.

21. Ralph Nader, *Unsafe at Any Speed: The Designed-in Dangers of American Automobiles* (New York: Grossman Publishing, 1965), ix.

22. Steve Eder, "Neomi Rao, the Scholar Who Will Help Lead Trump's Regulatory Overhaul," *The New York Times,* July 9, 2017.

23. Binyamin Appelbaum and Jim Tankersley, "The Trump Effect: Business, Anticipating Less Regulation Loosens Purse Strings," *The New York Times,* January 1, 2018.

24. Danielle Ivory and Robert Faturchi, "Secrecy and Suspicion Surround Trump's Deregulation Teams," *The New York Times,* August 7, 2017.

25. Appelbaum and Tankersley, "The Trump Effect: Business, Anticipating Less Regulation, Loosens Purse Strings."

26. Alexei Barrionuevo, "Globalization in Every Loaf," *The New York Times,* June 16, 2007.

27. Paul Wiseman, "For world, a taxing situation," Associated Press, June 3, 2018.

28. Zach, Hrynowski, "Several Issues Tie as Most Important in 2020 Election," Gallup News, January 13, 2020.

29. Pew Research Center, "As Economic Concerns Recede, Environmental Protection Rises on the Public's Policy Agenda," Pew Research Center: U.S. Politics & Policy, February 13, 2020.

30. Courtney Brown and Dion Rabouin, "U.S. GDP slows to 2.3% in 2019," Axios.com, January 31, 2020.

31. U.S. Bureau of Labor Statistics, *Labor Force Statistics from the Current Population Survey,* "Latest Numbers," www.bls.gov/cps/.

32. White House, "U.S. Unemployment Rate Falls to a 50-year Low," October 4, 2019, https://www.whitehouse.gov/articles/u-s-unemployment-rate-falls-50-year-low/.

33. U.S. Inflation Calculator, "Current U.S. Inflation Rates: 2009–2020," https://www.usinflationcalculator.com/inflation/current-inflation-rates/.

■ Key Terms

Multiple Choice Questions

1. United States economic policy includes all of the following EXCEPT
   A. Fiscal
   B. Regulatory
   C. Trade
   D. Distributive

2. Which of the following is true about the federal budget?
   A. The percentage of discretionary spending is increasing while the percentage of mandatory spending is decreasing
   B. Economists project that by 2020 the federal budget will be totally consumed by mandatory spending
   C. Across the board spending cuts to all spending is the only remedy for balancing the budget
   D. The percentage of mandatory spending is increasing while the percentage of discretionary spending is decreasing

Questions 3 and 4 are based on the graph below.

Mean Household Income by Quintile

**Source: Jessica Semega, Melissa Kollar, John Creamer, and Abinash Mohanty, U.S. Census Bureau, Current Population Reports, P60-266, *Income and Poverty in the United States: 2018* (Washington, DC: U.S. Government Printing Office, 2019).

3. What is the overall pattern of income inequality over the past few decades?
   A. There is a growing divide between the rich and the poor
   B. The lowest income level is quickly closing the gap between it and the second lowest income level
   C. The highest income group has experienced the smallest increase in wealth
   D. The third highest income group has remained steady over time

4. Which of the following is an action Congress could take to address income inequality?
   A. Pass a budget that includes tax cuts for the highest income level
   B. Increase discretionary spending
   C. Increase taxes on the highest income level
   D. Reform entitlement programs by adding stricter regulations

Questions 5 and 6 are based on the graph below.

Surplus/Deficit in Billions of Constant (2012) Dollars

Year

Source: Office of Management and Budget, Historical Tables, Table 8.3: Table 8.2—Outlays by Budget Enforcement Act Category in Constant (FY 2012) Dollars: 1962–2025.

Deficit Spending Since Last Surplus Years

5. How did the 2009 American Recovery and Reinvestment Act affect the deficit?
   A. It created a surplus that was used to pay down foreign debt
   B. It created a large deficit which was used to stimulate the sluggish economy
   C. It stimulated new investments in American enterprises
   D. It led to higher unemployment due to record deficits

6. Which of the following actions can the national government take to decrease annual deficits?
   A. Raise the debt ceiling
   B. Pressure the Federal Reserve to increase interest rates to control inflation
   C. Cut spending on discretionary items such as defense
   D. Pass continuing resolution instead of fiscal year annual budgets

7. Examples of monetary policy include all of the following except
   A. Distributing nationwide tax refunds
   B. Invoking greater bank reserve requirements
   C. Purchasing and selling government securities
   D. Increasing federal funds rate

Questions 8 and 9 apply to the scenario below.

8. In the wake of a pandemic and a sharp economic downturn, the president and Congress pass an economic reform bill that includes an increase in government spending to stimulate the economy. Which of the following ideologies is most likely to support this approach to the downturn?
A. Conservatives
B. Liberals
C. Libertarians
D. Laissez-faire liberals

9. Which of the following terms describes the policy used by the president and Congress?
A. Keynesian
B. Supply-side
C. Monetary
D. Laissez-faire

10. Which of the following correctly pairs a government agency with a tool it uses to stimulate the economy?

	Government Agency	Economic Tool
A.	Treasury Department	Introduce budget legislation
B.	Federal Reserve Board	Win elections
C.	Department of Commerce	Raise interest rates
D.	Securities and Exchange Commission	Authorize increased government spending

■ Free Response Questions

Quantitative Analysis

Federal Revenues and Expenditures: 1969 and 2019

Photos: U.S. Mint. Source: Office of Management and Budget, Historical Tables, Table 2.2: Percentage Composition of Receipts by Source: 1934–2025.

Use the charts above to answer the questions.

A. Identify a trend regarding federal spending and revenues.

B. Describe a similarity or difference in the federal revenue and spending for FY 1969 and FY 2019, as illustrated in the information graphic, and draw a conclusion about that similarity or difference.

C. Explain how deficit spending will affect spending on net interest in the future.

Concept Application

Scenario: A global pandemic caused a once robust U.S. economy to nosedive. In response to the pandemic, many Governors forced businesses to close due to limitations on large indoor gatherings. As a result, unemployment reached record highs, particularly in the service industry. With unemployment at a high, many Americans were unable to pay rent and began defaulting on personal loans.

After reading the scenario, respond to A, B, and C below:

A. In the context of the scenario, describe a power the president has in shaping fiscal policy.

B. In the context of the scenario, explain how the use of presidential power described in Part A can be affected by its interaction with Congress.

C. In the context of the scenario, explain how the interaction between Congress and the presidency can be affected by linkage institutions.

Data Analysis

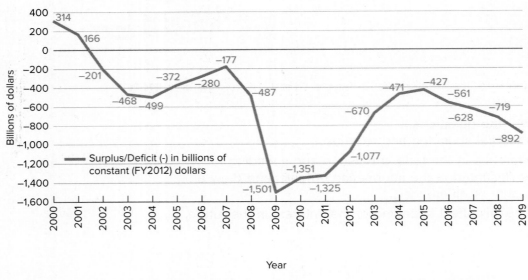

Source: Office of Management and Budget, Historical Tables, Table 8.3: Table 8.2—Outlays by Budget Enforcement Act Category in Constant (FY 2012) Dollars: 1962–2025.

Deficit Spending Since Last Surplus Years

Use the information graphic to answer the questions.

A. Identify a trend in deficit spending since the last surplus years.

B. Describe how deficit spending has changed over time and draw a conclusion about how those changes may be influenced by political ideology.

Argumentation

Develop an argument that explains the proper response of the national government to an economic downturn.

In your essay, you must:

- Articulate a defensible claim or thesis that responds to the prompt and establishes a line of reasoning

- Support your claim with at least TWO pieces of accurate and relevant information:

  - At least ONE piece of evidence must be from one of the following foundational documents:

    — Article I of the U.S. Constitution
    — Article II of the U.S. Constitution

  - Use a second piece of evidence from another foundational document from the list or from your study of economic policy

- Use reasoning to explain why your evidence supports your claim/thesis

- Respond to an opposing or alternative perspective using refutation, concession, or rebuttal

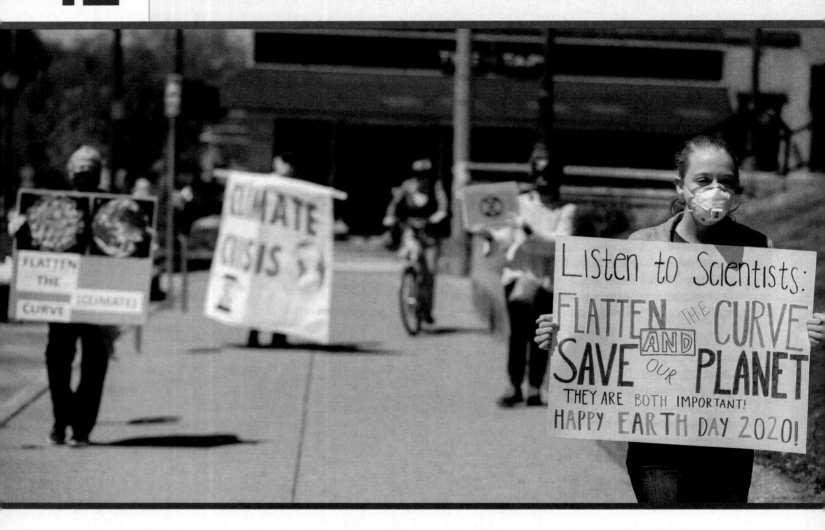

THEN

Before the Great Depression, state and local governments dominated domestic policy matters; the federal government had limited engagement in citizens' daily lives.

NOW

The federal government is responsible for a host of domestic policy issues that it implements in coordination with state and local governments, and that affect the lives of every U.S. resident daily.

NEXT

Will the national government's environmental and energy policies continue to be in tension with each other?

Will Congress rein in federal safety-net programs to ensure they are available for our posterity?

Will immigration policy continue to be a source of tension between the national, state, and local governments?

Jeremy Hogan/Echoes Wire/Barcroft Media/Getty Images

■ Chapter Introduction

Domestic policy includes a range of policies related to issues within the United States—including health care, education, and the environment. Domestic policy-making differs from foreign policymaking because in domestic policy, typically the president and Congress must work together to pass legislation while often in foreign policy, the president can negotiate or dictate policy without congressional approval. Because domestic policymaking is dependent on the cooperation between the president and Congress, the president's domestic policy agenda is often constrained when compared to foreign policy. This constraint exists even when the president is of the same political party as the Congress. For example, in the first two years of President Obama's term, he governed with a Democratic-controlled Congress, and still had difficulty passing the Affordable Care Act due to inter-party differences. Some Democrats opposed the Affordable Care Act because they did not believe the law went far enough to guarantee health care for all Americans, and other Democrats thought the coverage proposed under the law was too broad because it initially included abortion. In the beginning of the legislative journey, Obama did not have the votes needed from his own party to pass the bill. Eventually the Affordable Care Act passed with only Democratic votes; however, there were over 30 Democrats in the House that voted against the Affordable Care Act in its final stage.

In the area of domestic policy, the AP U.S. Government Curriculum & Exam Description (CED) focuses specifically on social policy. Social policy consists of government actions designed to improve quality of life, including welfare, health care, criminal justice, education, and labor. The Enduring Understanding from the AP CED that frames this chapter is: *Widely held political ideologies shape policy debates and choices in American policies.*

As you learn how ideologies shape domestic policies, as an AP Learning Objective, you should be able to: *Explain how political ideologies vary on the role of government in addressing social issues.* Democrats—closely aligned with the liberal ideology—tend to support the view that the government should play a larger role in people's everyday lives, including more governmental regulation in the marketplace. For example liberals would support programs at the federal level that would increase regulations to protect the environment or ensure access to clean water. Liberals also have a broader view of what the government should be doing to foster economic and social equality, and thus favor health care for all, and increased spending for food security and housing. Historically, liberals have favored programs at the federal government level, arguing that all Americans have the right to basic human needs. On the other hand, Republicans—aligned with the conservative ideology—tend to advocate for a lesser role for government, viewing the protection of personal liberty as a more important value than social and economic equality. Conservatives often oppose programs that they view as an expansion of government services. For conservatives, smaller government and fewer services means lower taxes, freeing individuals to use their income how they see fit, rather than by paying for government-run programs. Historically, conservatives have argued for less government, but when government intervention is necessary, they would prefer that states intervene, rather than the federal government. While a less commonly held view, libertarian ideologies believe that there should as little government as possible. Indeed many libertarians view the sole role of government as protecting individual liberty and private property. In this chapter, we will examine how these ideologies view and prioritize various domestic policies.

These views of ideologies about the role of government extend into the area of personal privacy, a key component of the AP U.S, Government CED. In general, liberals tend to believe that protections of personal privacy from government interference should be greater (except in the areas of religious and educational freedom). Modern conservatives are more likely to emphasize law and order, and support policies that strengthen the federal government's ability to combat terrorism, including domestic surveillance.

Citizen Engagement and Domestic Policy

The Constitution established a government that is by and for the people. Previous chapters have explored the many ways in which individuals and groups engage with government officials and political processes to influence what government does and does not do. Yet a widespread national affliction is the **NIMBY, or "not-in-my-backyard," syndrome**. People with the NIMBY syndrome often are not inspired to participate in politics until a government action or inaction threatens them directly. Lobbying government officials is a common first step in citizen engagement, and it may be as basic as making a phone call, sending an e-mail, or writing a letter. Additional modes of participation include joining public protests and demonstrations, attending open government meetings, and testifying at government hearings. Citizens may also use lawsuits to press government officials to focus on issues of concern and to eventually address them through policy-making. The most common form of political participation among citizens is voting.

Complicating the work of elected U.S. policymakers is the diversity of citizens' needs and expectations for government action. Almost every call for action sparks a call for either a different action or no action. The diversity of citizens' needs and priorities, the constantly changing priorities of citizens, and the range of political ideologies among citizens make for ongoing public conversations and legislative debates over which policies warrant government spending and who will pay the taxes to cover the bills. To explore the plurality of citizens' priorities, the "Data Analysis: Analyzing the Sources" feature presents the differing policy priorities of several groups of people.

social policy
Government actions designed to improve quality of life, including welfare, health care, criminal justice, education, and labor

safety net programs
A collection of public policies aimed at ensuring that citizens' basic physiological needs are met.

With regard to **social policy**—government actions designed to improve quality of life, including welfare, health care, criminal justice, education, and labor, in general Democrats are liberal in inclination. They tend to support **safety net programs**—public policies aimed at ensuring that citizens' basic physiological needs (food, water, shelter, health care, and a clean environment) are met. Republicans more commonly have a conservative ideology and focus more on public safety and national security issues. A growing plurality of citizens do not affiliate with either major party, and their collective views sometimes mirror Democratic tendencies, sometimes mirror Republican tendencies, and at still other times are distinct from both major parties. Ultimately, elected officials—who typically want to get reelected—find it much easier to add new policies and programs than to eliminate programs or to decrease existing program costs. Hence, the federal government's breadth of domestic responsibilities has grown, as has its costs (as discussed in Chapter 11).

What are the Policy Priorities of Americans?

Citizens in representative democracies expect their elected officials to listen to their concerns and then enact policies that address them. However, citizens do not speak with one voice. The policy priorities of citizens differ due to their differing life experiences.

A survey conducted by the Pew Research Center in January 2020 found that overall, Americans rated the following societal issues as their top priorities for the national government: terrorism (74 percent), the economy (67 percent), health care costs (67 percent), education (67 percent), and the environment (64 percent). However, when we compare the responses of women and men, of younger and older individuals, and of people with more liberal and more conservative leanings, the identified top priorities change.

For a complete picture, consider the list of priorities respondents were given to consider: budget deficit, climate change, crime, drug addiction, economy, education, environment, global trade, gun policy, health care costs, immigration, infrastructure, jobs, military, poor and needy, race relations, Social Security, and terrorism.

TOP FIVE PRIORITIES BY GENDER

Women	Men
1. Terrorism (73%)	1. Terrorism (74%)
2. Health care costs (72%)	2. Economy (68%)
3. Education (71%)	3. Social Security (64%)
4. Environment (69%)	4. Education (63%)
5. Economy (67%)	5. Health care costs (62%)

TOP FIVE PRIORITIES BY AGE GROUP:

Younger Voters (18–29)	Older Voters (65 plus)
1. Environment (77%)	1. Terrorism (81%)
2. Education (74%)	2. Social Security (74%)
3. Economy (66%)	3. Health care costs (73%)
4. Climate change (61%)	4. Crime (68%)
5. Health care costs (61%)	5. Immigration (65%)

Source: "As Economic Concerns Recede, Environmental Protection Rises on the Public's Policy Agenda," Pew Research Center, February 13, 2020.

TOP FIVE PRIORITIES BY PARTY IDENTIFICATION:

Democrat/Dem Leaning	Republican/ Rep Leaning
1. Environment (85%)	1. Terrorism (87%)
2. Education (80%)	2. Economy (74%)
3. Health care costs (80%)	3. Immigration (73%)
4. Climate change (78%)	4. Military (66%)
5. Poor and needy (68%)	5. Social Security (65%)

Practice Analytical Thinking

1. Within the three comparison groups—that is, women and men; younger and older; Democrat and Republican—which shows the most overlap in priorities? Which comparison group has the most divergent priorities?

2. If you were a member of Congress and the data presented here represented the priorities of your constituents, what would be your top five priorities? Explain your selections.

3. How do you think the coronavirus pandemic would have affected the survey results if it had been administered in the summer of 2020?

4. Compare liberal (Democratic) and conservative (Republican) priorities. Are there are any similarities? what do you think the priorities of libertarians would be?

As we have seen in preceding chapters, the government makes policy in several ways. For one, Congress and the president set policy by approving authorization bills, which establish a policy and identify who will implement it, and appropriations bills, which authorize the spending of national revenue to pay for policies (see Chapters 5, 6, and 11). As discussed in Chapter 7, federal, state, local, and shadow bureaucrats also make policy, through both the administrative rule-making process and their daily use of administrative discretion as they implement policies. In addition, the presidential power of the executive order amounts to making policy, because it gives the president the authority to tell bureaucrats how to carry out a national policy (see Chapter 5). Finally, as explored in Chapter 6, the federal courts resolve conflicts over the meaning and proper implementation of laws and, in doing so, make policy. In summary, each of the three branches of the national government has policy-making authority that it uses to fulfill the government's constitutionally established mission to serve present generations and their posterity.

Since 1789, the national government's scope of responsibility for addressing domestic matters has gradually expanded as individuals and groups have lobbied for their interests. Federal authority now covers a diverse collection of public policies. The national budget lists 12 functions of the federal government. The data in Table 12.1 show that today, most federal government functions are directed at (and most government spending goes toward) **domestic policies**, which are policies addressing the problems, needs, and relations of people residing within the country's borders, as opposed to matters involving relations with other countries and nations. In 2019, about 75 percent of federal expenditures paid for domestic policies and 12 percent paid for international affairs and defense policies. The remaining 8 percent of expenditures paid for interest on the national debt incurred by past borrowing to cover deficit spending.[1]

domestic policies
Policies addressing the problems, needs, and relations of people residing within the country's borders.

Because it would be impossible for us to examine every domestic policy program, we limit our focus in this chapter to a subset of national domestic policies. Specifically, we concentrate on national policies that address the most basic of human needs and are essential to sustaining life, liberty, and opportunities to pursue happiness: environmental, energy, educational, and income security policies. We also look at the controversial policy area of immigration, defined by some as a national security concern, by others as an economic issue, and by still others as a humanitarian cause reflecting the United States' roots and highest ideals.

■ Tools of Domestic Policy

The national government attempts to address citizens' problems and to provide benefits and services to the people by using various policy tools. Domestic policy tools include laws and regulations, direct provision of public goods, cash transfer payments, loans, loan guarantees, insurance, grants-in-aid to state and local governments, contracting-out the provision of public goods to nongovernmental entities (shadow bureaucracies and bureaucrats, as discussed in Chapter 7), and the provision of information to people.

Laws and Regulations

At the federal, state, and local levels, governments strive to accomplish their domestic policy goals by creating laws and regulations that require individuals and

TABLE 12.1 ▪ Percentage of FY 2019 Total Expenditures ($4.5 trillion) by Functions (rounded to the nearest percentage point)

Social Security	24%
Medicare	15%
National defense	15%
Health	13%
Income security	12%
Net interest	8%
Education, training, employment, and social services	3%
Veterans benefits and services	5%
Administration of justice	2%
Transportation	2%
International affairs	1%
Natural resources and environment	1%
Community and regional development	1%
General science, space, and technology	1%
Agriculture	1%
General government	1%
Energy	<1%
Commerce and housing credit	−1%
Undistributed offsetting receipts	−2%

Source: Office of Management and Budget, *Historical Tables*, "Table 3.1—Outlays by Superfunction and Function: 1940–2025." Percentages calculated by author.

organizations to do some things or refrain from doing others. Those who do not comply can be sanctioned or punished by the government. Tax laws, environmental standards, and public health regulations are just three examples. As discussed in Chapter 11, business regulations are aimed at preserving competition in the marketplace so that the economy stays healthy, and social regulations are directed at protecting workers, consumers, and the environment from the harms caused by marketplace competition.

The overwhelming majority of people and organizations comply with most laws and regulations. But because some individuals and organizations fail to do so, the government must monitor compliance with law enforcement personnel and inspectors. For example, the FDA hires inspectors to ensure that meat, poultry, and eggs are processed according to government safety regulations and, thus, are safe to consume. The government counts on citizens, interest groups, and the media to assist in overseeing compliance with laws and regulations by identifying violators.

Direct Provision of Public Goods

direct provision
A policy tool whereby the government that creates a policy hires public servants to provide the service.

Governments also provide services and benefits directly to people. Using the domestic policy tool of **direct provision,** governments hire public servants—bureaucrats who receive a government paycheck—to dispense public services and benefits. For example, veterans' hospitals hire doctors, nurses, and physical therapists to administer health care to veterans; the U.S. Postal Service hires mail carriers, postal clerks, and postal processing machine operators to deliver billions of pieces of mail each week. The workers hired by the national government to provide these services directly are on the payroll of the national government. (See "Argumentation: Thinking Critically" to explore the debate about direct provision of postal services.)

Cash Transfers

cash transfer
The direct provision of cash (in forms including checks, debit cards, and tax breaks) to eligible individuals or to providers of goods or services to eligible individuals.

in-kind assistance
A cash transfer in which the government pays cash to those who provide goods or services to eligible individuals.

Another instrument of government policy is the **cash transfer**—the direct provision of cash (in various forms) to eligible individuals or to those who provide goods or services to eligible individuals. Social Security is the most costly cash-transfer program; eligible people receive a check (a direct bank deposit) from the federal government. **In-kind assistance** is a form of a cash transfer in which the government pays those who provide goods or services to eligible individuals. The Supplemental Nutrition Assistance Program (SNAP; better known by its old name, the food stamp program) is an example of in-kind assistance. That is, the government provides cash to stores that accept the SNAP debit card for food purchases. Approximately 70 percent of the money spent by the national government goes toward cash transfers to citizens.[2] Nearly half of the American population lives in a household that receives a cash transfer.[3]

direct subsidy
A cash transfer from general revenues to particular persons or private companies engaged in activities that the national government believes support the public good.

With a **direct subsidy**, another type of cash transfer, the government provides financial support, often through tax breaks, to specific persons or organizations that engage in activities that the government believes benefit the public good. Individual farmers and agricultural corporations, for example, receive money from the government to grow specified crops or to limit how much they grow. Homeowners who are paying a mortgage (a loan to purchase a home) receive a tax break when paying their federal income taxes.

Loans, Loan Guarantees, and Insurance

To encourage behaviors that accomplish its goals, the national government also loans money to individuals and organizations, and it guarantees loans made by private businesses. Some examples are government loan programs to assist individuals in purchasing homes, reflecting the widespread belief that home ownership promotes the general welfare and domestic tranquility, and direct loans for college students and their parents. During the coronavirus pandemic, the Small Business Administration (SBA) provided billions of dollars in loans to keep small businesses alive. In some cases, small businesses did not have to repay the loans if they kept all their employees on their payroll during the early stages of the pandemic. The SBA also provides government-backed loan guarantees on loans made through private banks, credit unions, and other lenders. These loan guarantees make it easier for entrepreneurs who are beginning or expanding small businesses to acquire credit because lenders' risks are limited by the government's promise to pay back some of the borrowed money if the entrepreneur is unable to pay it back.

ARGUMENTATION | THINKING CRITICALLY

Should the United States Postal Service Be Shut Down?

THE ISSUE: The United States Postal Service (USPS) administers one of the first domestic services the national government ever provided to U.S. residents. As a public corporation, the USPS does not rely on taxpayer money. It is expected to be financially self-sufficient, raising the money it needs to operate through selling its services. To send an item through the USPS you must pay postage. However, if postage and other revenue sources are not sufficient to balance its budget, then Congress must appropriate taxpayer dollars to ensure its survival. The problem is that the USPS is not able to balance its budget. In fiscal year 2018, it had a deficit of just under $4 billion.* If the USPS cannot balance its budget, should the government shut it down?

YES: If the USPS cannot balance its budget without huge increases in prices or taxpayer support, then it should be shut down. Originally, the USPS was a necessary and trusted way to deliver important messages and communicate across the expanse of the country. Today, no one uses the USPS to deliver urgent messages; they call, text, or e-mail. Originally, USPS was the only provider available. Now we have FedEx, UPS, and other delivery businesses.

NO: The USPS is legally obligated to deliver mail to all postal addresses throughout the country at a flat rate. The postal rate is not established by the USPS, nor is it based on the cost of delivering mail to specific locations; it is more expensive to deliver mail to remote communities than to urban communities. The Federal Communications Commission reports that almost 15 million people in rural areas lack broadband (for Internet and e-mail). Rural residents, the elderly, and persons with disabilities rely on USPS for mail and often delivery of pharmaceuticals. In addition, the USPS is vital to our democracy. Since its founding, the USPS has been a means to inform the electorate. Beginning with ballots from military personnel in the Civil War, the USPS has delivered votes by mail. In 2000, Oregon became the first of a growing number of states to conduct all elections by mail. In the 2016 presidential election, one-quarter of ballots were cast through the USPS. At present, the coronavirus pandemic mobilized millions of Americans to vote by mail. Moreover, voting by mail saves state and local governments money and fosters higher voter turnout.

OTHER APPROACHES: The largest portion of the USPS budget covers personnel costs. If the USPS delivered mail fewer days per week, it could manage with fewer employees; it could create incentives for retirement, and thus, cut personnel and costs. Furthermore, the Postal Accountability and Enhancement Act (2006) requires the postal service to pre-fund its pension plan for 75 years. USPS is the only government agency that must do this. This requirement accounted for $55 billion of the agency's $62 billion losses from 2007-2016.* If Congress repealed this pension pre-funding requirement, USPS would not be in the financial trouble it is in currently.

WHAT DO YOU THINK?

1. As late as the 1970s, Congress gave the USPS an annual appropriation because it viewed it as fulfilling a "public service obligation." Is delivery of mail to every postal address an essential public service that the national government should provide? Explain your answer.

2. Do calls for expanding use of mail-in ballots for elections boost the need for government-provided mail delivery to every postal address at a flat rate in order to ensure equal opportunity to vote, or is there another way to ensure equal opportunity to vote?

3. What would be the policy stance of liberals, conservatives, and libertarians when it comes to the issue of closing the Postal Service?

*Kevin Kosar, "The Postal Service Is in Deep Trouble: Here's One Way to Get It Out," politico.com, April 16, 2020.

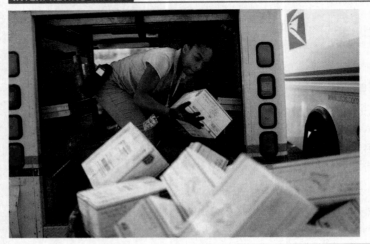

>> The United States Postal Service (USPS) was established by the Second Continental Congress in 1775. In its April 2020 mission statement, the USPS says that it plays a vital role in the commerce (and hence economy) of the nation and in national security. It also claims that it is "a trusted face of the federal government in every community." Do you agree with these characterizations? What evidence supports your view?

Interpret: Historically, government jobs like those at the USPS were considered good jobs that could support middle-class lifestyles. Who are most government workers today? How have perceptions about government work evolved over the last few decades?

Joe Raedle/Getty Images

The national government is also in the insurance business. The Federal Deposit Insurance Corporation (FDIC) is one example of a national insurance program. The FDIC insures bank deposits up to $250,000 in member banks to encourage people to save money not only for their own sake but also for the good of the national economy.

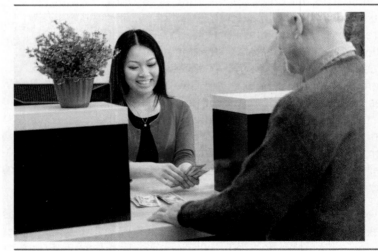

>> If you deposit money in a financial institution insured by the Federal Deposit Insurance Corporation (FDIC), the federal government guarantees that if the bank fails, the government will pay you the money you deposited (normally up to $250,000). Would you put your money in a bank that is not FDIC insured? To learn if your bank is thus insured, look for FDIC signs.

YinYang/E+/Getty Images

Grants-in-Aid and Contracting-Out

State and local governments and private-sector organizations implement a growing proportion of national government policies. Through funded and unfunded mandates as well as grants-in-aid (explored in Chapter 3), the federal government requires and encourages state and local governments to carry out national policies. We see these forms of intergovernmental relations in policies as diverse as homeland security, primary and secondary education, and environmental protection.

The government also contracts with private and nonprofit organizations to produce essential resources or to deliver services. One example of contracting-out, or outsourcing (see Chapter 7), is the government's contracts with corporations such as Lockheed Martin and Boeing to build the planes and missiles it needs to defend the country. Another example is medical research funded by the government and conducted by private companies and institutions of higher education.

The Provision of Information

Governments also try to persuade people to behave in preferred ways by providing them with information that may influence their decisions. For example, the government requires health warnings on packs of cigarettes and other tobacco products and labels on alcoholic beverages. When educating people through the provision of information does not accomplish behavioral changes, and public health and safety are threatened, governments may enact laws and regulations. For example, as the coronavirus spread, governments provided information about social distancing, mask wearing, and other behavioral modifications people could make to protect themselves and others. As the virus continued to spread, some state and local governments went beyond providing information; they enacted regulations that required restaurants to provide food only through pick-up and delivery services, and nonessential businesses and schools were required to close down. Violators of such government regulations could be fined.

By means of such tools as well as the others we have surveyed in this chapter, the government delivers goods and services to its citizens. In the rest of this chapter, we examine how government uses these tools to implement overall policy in several domestic policy areas, including environmental protection, energy, income security, health care, and immigration.

■ Environmental Policy

Providing for the general welfare means at the least ensuring that people have the basic necessities for sustaining life. These needs include clean and drinkable water, breathable air, and unpolluted land on which to grow food that is safe for consumption. No one argues against a clean environment. Yet there is no consensus on how to achieve and maintain one. In addition, appeals for environmental protection often conflict with demands for ample supplies of energy, particularly when burning fossil fuels is the key means of energy production.

The national government first acknowledged environmental degradation as a problem in the 1960s. In the 1970s, national environmental protection laws were enacted to address air, land, and water pollution. Also in the 1970s, public and government attention was drawn to the U.S. supply of energy and the nation's dependence on foreign oil supplies. Environmental protection policy and energy policy have been in tension ever since. As concern for environmental protection became a global focus in the 1990s, countries enacted their own policies as they also negotiated international agreements to address environmental concerns. The common target was reduction of emissions from burning fossil fuels.

Environmental Degradation

Since the 1940s, farmers have used chemicals to destroy insects, weeds, fungi, and other living organisms that harm their crops. The threats such pesticides pose to air, water, and land became the focus of public concern and political debate after the publication of scientist Rachel Carson's eye-opening best seller *Silent Spring* in 1962. Carson's book documented how pesticides were contaminating the environment and getting into human food. The use of chemicals, she warned, threatened the existence not only of birds—whose extinction would mean a silent spring—but of humankind itself.

Then, in 1969, those growing environmental apprehensions became a spectacular reality when the heavily polluted Cuyahoga River in Ohio caught fire. Around the same time, arsenic was found in the Kansas River, and millions of fish went belly-up in major waterways such as Lake Superior, killed by the chemicals and untreated waste emitted by industrial plants and local sewage systems. In response, state and local governments banned fishing in many polluted waterways.

The mounting environmental crises and additional governmental studies brought amplified calls to action from both citizens' groups and elected officials during the 1960s and 1970s. In 1965, 12 percent of citizens listed this as one of their top three political priorities; by 1970, 53 percent of citizens listed it as one of their top three priorities.[4]

U.S. senator Gaylord Nelson (D-Wisc.) responded to citizens' growing concerns by proposing a national teach-in that he hoped would mobilize the government to establish an environmental protection agenda. Nelson's vision became a reality through the first Earth Day, held April 22, 1970. More than 200,000 people gathered on the National Mall in Washington, D.C., and 20 million more congregated across the country.[5] Every year, millions of people around the globe celebrate Earth Day, which helps to keep concerns about environmental degradation on public policy agendas throughout the world.

greenhouse effect
The heating of the earth's atmosphere as a result of humans' burning of fossil fuels and the resultant buildup of carbon dioxide and other gases.

global warming
The rising temperature of the earth as a result of pollution that traps solar heat, keeping the air warmer than it would otherwise be.

climate change
A pattern of significant changes in regional and/or global temperature, precipitation, wind patterns, and other measures of climate that occur over several decades.

Since the 1990s, scientists and governments throughout the world have been raising concerns about air pollution, particularly emissions of carbon dioxide. Mounting evidence indicates that air pollution caused by burning fossil fuels (to create energy) produces a **greenhouse effect**, which is the heating of the earth's atmosphere as carbon dioxide and other gases build up and trap solar heat in the earth's atmosphere. The greenhouse effect causes **global warming**, the rising temperature of the earth. Today, people who discuss global warming often refer to the phenomenon of **climate change**: that is, significant changes in regional and/or global temperature, precipitation, wind patterns, and other measures of climate that occur over several decades.

Climate change is evident globally in more frequent and extreme weather: heat waves, droughts, floods, tornadoes, and hurricanes. The result of more frequent weather extremes is damage to water supplies, food supplies, health, standards of living, and rising sea levels.[6] The U.S. Department of Defense argues that "global climate change will aggravate problems such as poverty, social tensions, environmental degradation, ineffectual leadership and weak political institutions that threaten stability in a number of countries."[7]

Environmental Protection

In 1969, Congress passed the Environmental Protection Act, which established the Environmental Protection Agency (EPA) to oversee implementation of laws protecting the quality of air, water, and land. Then a cascade of national environmental protection legislation followed the first Earth Day.

CLEAN AIR The landmark Clean Air Act of 1970 delegates authority to the EPA to establish standards for regulating emissions of hazardous air pollutants. The act also mandated each state to develop and implement plans to meet EPA standards. Today, states typically delegate some of their enforcement responsibilities to local governments. If states and their local governments do not enforce compliance with the national standards or their own stricter standards, then the EPA can take over, enforcing national law through preemption (discussed in Chapter 3). To bolster compliance with the Clean Air Act, the law gives citizens the right to sue those who are violating the standards. Citizens also have the right to sue the EPA if it does not enforce the Clean Air Act. Citizens and environmental interest groups have availed themselves of their right to sue, pushing the government and industries to comply with the law.

Since 1992, United Nations negotiators have held annual meetings aimed at developing a global climate change treaty. In 1997, world leaders signed the Kyoto Protocol, which established binding targets for cutting greenhouse gases in the world's largest economies in developed countries, but the U.S. Senate never ratified the Kyoto Protocol.

In 2015, the Obama EPA enacted the Clean Power Plan, the first U.S. climate change policy. The plan established new regulations designed to reduce greenhouse gases emitted by power plants. Under the plan, the EPA set emission targets for each state, and each state could develop its own strategies to meet its target. If a state did not develop a plan, then the EPA could impose one on it.

Internationally, the Obama administration's Clean Power Plan was viewed as a sign that the United States was ready to join the international efforts to reduce carbon dioxide emissions. In December 2015, 195 nations (including the United States and China, the top two greenhouse-gas-emitting countries) reached a landmark international agreement, the Paris Accord, which commits each nation to decreasing its emission of greenhouse gases. The accord was touted as a turning point for climate change.

However, 2016 presidential candidate Donald Trump, a known climate change denier, promised to withdraw the United States from the Paris Accord and to repeal the Obama administration's environmental initiatives.[8] And on November 4, 2019, the first day on which countries that had agreed to the Paris Accord could begin the process of withdrawing from it, the United States became the first, and so far only, country to follow that path. The U.S. withdrawal was completed on November 4, 2020, the day after the U.S. presidential election.

In addition to eliminating more than 100 EPA regulations, Trump's EPA proposed the repeal of the Clean Power Plan in 2012. And in June 2019, the EPA repealed the Clean Power Plan, replacing it with the Affordable Clean Energy Rule (ACE), which has new "standards of performance to reduce carbon dioxide (CO_2) emissions from existing coal-fired EGUs [electric utility generating units]."[9] The standards are lower than those established in the Clean Power Plan.

CLEAN WATER The 1972 Federal Water Pollution Control Act (Clean Air Act), with the goal of making waterways clean enough to swim in and to eat fish from, authorizes the EPA to set water quality standards and to require permits for anyone discharging contaminants into any waterway. Under the act, state and local governments must monitor water quality, issue permits to those discharging waste into waterways, and enforce the national standards. If states and localities fail to carry out these mandated responsibilities, the EPA can step in and do the job. The law also provides for federal loans to local governments, funneled through state governments, for building wastewater treatment plants.

The Safe Drinking Water Act of 1974 authorizes the EPA to establish purity standards for drinking water. Because states or localities typically operate water systems, this act effectively requires the EPA to regulate state and local governments. The act provides for national grants to state and local governments for research and for improving their water systems. It also requires frequent testing of water samples from public water systems.

INTERPRETING IMAGES

>> In October 2018, city officials in Newark, New Jersey, provided water filters to some residents. The city did this in response to a lawsuit claiming that city and state officials had violated the Safe Drinking Water Act (1974). In August 2019, the federal EPA required the city and state governments to provide bottled water to certain city residents. This situation is a good example of the intergovernmental relations of environmental policy.

Interpret: Where have you seen recent examples of problems with water regulation? Who is most affected by this and how do they seek to solve these problems?

Bryan Anselm/Redux

Due to required testing of public water systems, Newark, New Jersey, began to tackle the problem of lead in its water in 2015. By March 2016, Newark Public Schools shut off 400 sources of drinking water in 30 schools. Water samples tested in 2012 and 2018 continued to find lead at levels above the federal maximum allowable, and a 2018 study tracked the lead contamination to old pipes. The city responded by providing 40,000 residents with filters. In the summer of 2019, the national EPA ordered Newark to give bottled water to its residents after a report found that the filters were not effective (possibly due to improper installation by residents). In September 2019, with city, county, and federal government funds, the city began to replace lead pipes. By March 2020, the city had replaced almost half of the 18,000 lead service lines. However, people in Newark are still drinking water that they should not be drinking.[10]

CLEAN LAND The Resource Conservation and Recovery Act of 1976, administered by the EPA, regulates the disposal of household, industrial, and manufacturing solid and hazardous wastes, and encourages recycling. Although this act authorized the cleanup of toxic waste sites, thousands of which the government identified in the 1970s, no national funding was made available for the cleanup. Then in 1980, just as Congress was focused on the crisis at Love Canal, New York, where 833 families had to be relocated because of health problems tied to the toxic waste buried below their homes and school, an abandoned site for the storage, treatment, and disposal of hazardous waste in Elizabeth, New Jersey, exploded. Shortly thereafter, Congress approved the Comprehensive Environmental Response, Compensation and Liability Act of 1980 (known as the Superfund law) to pay for cleanup of the nation's most toxic waste dumps.

The Superfund has protected human health and the environment by improving the identification and cleanup of hazardous waste sites. It has also increased the accountability of the parties responsible for creating hazardous waste problems. However, close to two thousand identified sites must still be cleaned, and new sites continue to be added to the list.[11]

Citizens with resources, including money and the time to organize, can fight to prevent the location of undesirable land uses (such as landfills, industrial plants, and toxic waste sites) in their communities. Lower-income communities are more likely than more affluent communities to bear the burden of land uses with negative environmental impacts. **Environmental racism** is the term used to describe the higher incidence of environmental threats and subsequent health problems in lower-income communities, which frequently are also communities populated by people of color.[12]

environmental racism
The term used to describe the higher incidence of environmental threats and subsequent health problems in lower-income communities, which frequently are also communities dominated by people of color.

ENVIRONMENTAL PROTECTION, ENERGY PRODUCTION, AND JOBS Although no one argues against a clean environment, tensions persist between the need for environmental protection and other policy areas. Energy production, both extraction of resources from the earth and the burning of fossil fuels, damages the environment and human health.

Efforts to reduce greenhouse emissions affect energy production businesses, particularly plants that burn fossil fuels such as coal and natural gas. Hence, environmental protection bumps up against economic health in terms of jobs. This tension was evident in the seven-year battle over the proposal to build the 1,700-mile Keystone XL pipeline from Alberta, Canada, through the United States to Texas. Proponents of the pipeline argued it would create jobs. Opponents argued it would harm the environment. In November 2015, President Obama rejected the pipeline's construction. In 2020, President Trump reversed that decision, approving its construction.

Today, as the nation and the world act to address environmental degradation, particularly global warming, exploration and development of renewable energy sources are ongoing. Renewable energy sources are those that do not get depleted or can be replenished within a generation, such as solar, wind, biomass, hydropower, and geothermal. This kind of exploration and development is good for the environment and also creates green jobs.

■ Energy Policy

Energy creation—the production of electricity and heat, as well as fuels to power automobiles, trucks, planes, trains, and other transport vehicles—is essential to the prosperity of the U.S. economy and to the American way of life. The high energy demands of the U.S. economy and the lifestyle of U.S. residents are problematic for several reasons, as we shall see.

In 1973 the Organization of Petroleum Exporting Countries (OPEC) refused to sell oil to the United States and Western European nations. The OPEC oil embargo caused oil and gas prices in United States to skyrocket. OPEC's actions focused national government attention on U.S. dependence on foreign oil as an economic, quality of life, and national security concern. In response, the national government

SOURCE ANALYSIS   COMPARATIVE

THEN

NOW

>> By 1905, when the THEN photo of coal miners at the bottom of a mine shaft in Scranton, Pennsylvania, was taken, coal had become the dominant source of energy in the United States. Coal continued to be the primary energy source through the middle of the 20th century, when petroleum overtook it as the primary source. Today, although the percentage of energy produced by petroleum is decreasing, it remains the dominant source of energy (36%). Natural gas is the number two source of energy (31%). Texas produces the most oil and natural gas in the United States. Texas also produces the most energy from wind turbines, one of the smallest sources of U.S. energy (about 3%).

Coal miners: Universal History Archive/UIG/Getty Images; *wind turbines:* Michael Mcmurray/Getty Images

Sources of Energy Used in the United States

THEN NOW NEXT

2000
- 6%
- 8%
- 39%
- 24%
- 23%

2020
- 12%
- 8%
- 36%
- 31%
- 13%

Legend:
- Renewable
- Nuclear
- Petroleum
- Natural gas
- Coal

Source: Pew Research Center, "Renewable energy is growing fast in the U.S., but fossil fuels still dominate," Factank: News in the Numbers, January 15, 2020.

- Most Americans say it's more important to develop alternative renewable energy sources, such as solar and wind power, than to produce more fossil fuel power. What policies can the federal government enact to increase development of alternative energy sources?

- In 2018, the total amount of energy used in the United States—including for lighting and heating homes, cooking, driving cars, fueling factories, and powering cell phones—hit the highest level since record keeping began in 1949. What policies can the federal government enact to encourage energy conservation?

- According to a Washington Post–Kaiser Family Foundation poll (July 9–August 5, 2019), the majority of Americans believe climate change is a major problem or a crisis (76 percent). Will the president and Congress be influenced by public opinion and enact legislation to support more rapid development of alternative energy sources and/or create incentives for energy conservation?

began to develop energy policy aimed at reducing the nation's dependence on foreign oil.

In 1975, the national government established the Strategic Petroleum Reserve, a store of crude oil to mitigate the security consequences of any future interruption in the supply of imported oil. The government also enacted legislation encouraging energy conservation and providing funding for research and development of alternative energy sources (such as solar, wind, and geothermal). Legislation created fuel efficiency standards for passenger cars and light trucks, the Corporate Average Fuel Economy (CAFE) standards. Then in 1976, the federal government created the Department of Energy to develop and oversee a comprehensive national energy plan.

In 1977, President Jimmy Carter declared an "energy crisis" and called for energy conservation and for research and development into alternative energy. Toward that end, the United States established a national speed limit of 55 miles per hour, Daylight Saving Time, weatherization assistance programs, tax incentives to insulate homes, and building codes related to energy efficiency.

Since the 1970s, with energy independence as its goal, U.S. energy policy has swung back and forth between (1) a focus on conservation, research on alternative renewable energy sources, and tax breaks supporting that research and (2) calls for increased use of coal and other domestic fossil fuel resources.

In December 2016, newly elected President Trump announced his administration's National Security Strategy (NSS) document, stating that "Access to domestic sources of clean, affordable, and reliable energy underpins a prosperous, secure, and powerful America for decades to come. . . . Unleashing these abundant energy resources—coal, natural gas, petroleum, renewables, and nuclear—stimulates the economy and builds a foundation for future growth."[13] In support of his energy plan, Trump approved the Keystone XL and Dakota Access Pipelines, opened much of the Atlantic and Pacific coasts to offshore drilling, lifted restrictions on coal mining on federal lands, and repealed the Obama Clean Power Plan.

Since the 1973 OPEC oil embargo, the national government's efforts to ensure energy independence have bounced between increasing production of fossil fuels and researching and developing renewable energy sources. In the view of environmental activists, energy independence must be achieved through the development of renewable energy sources because clean air, clean water, and clean land are foundational to the pursuit of happiness and quality of life of all Americans. Another condition important to those goals is affordable access to quality education, which we explore next.

■ Education Policy

Everyone agrees that high-quality education is important to both a healthy national economy and personal financial security (see Figure 12.1). At the same time, many people are critical of the quality of education in American primary and secondary schools. A few of the major criticisms surrounding kindergarten to 12th-grade education focus on government funding levels, school safety, school choice programs such as charter schools and voucher programs, standardized testing, and teacher salaries. Although Democratic and Republican presidents since George W. Bush (2001–2009) have been key voices and actors in education reform to address many of these criticisms, education is a responsibility that the U.S. Constitution reserves for the states.

Federal Education Policies

The federal government made its first comprehensive venture into primary and secondary education when it passed the 1965 Elementary and Secondary Education Act (ESEA). The ESEA, part of President Lyndon Johnson's war on poverty, primarily focused on enhancing funding for schools with higher numbers of low-income students. In 2002 the ESEA was reauthorized as the No Child Left Behind Act, which was reauthorized in 2015 as the Every Student Succeeds Act (ESSA).[14] Essential to these education policies is federal funding for primary and secondary education (currently covering approximately 8 percent of the total cost of educating children)[15] to ensure equal educational opportunities for all children in institutions receiving federal funding. Without attaching its policy preferences to funding (grants-in-aid), the federal government would have no authority in primary and secondary education. In addition to targeting funds toward schools that serve large numbers of financially disadvantaged students, the federal government prohibits discrimination in educational opportunities in schools receiving federal funds. Legislation exists to bar discrimination based on race, color, national origin, and religion (Title VI of the 1964 Civil Rights Act); sex (1972 Educational Amendments to the Civil Rights Act, known as Title IX); and disability (Individuals

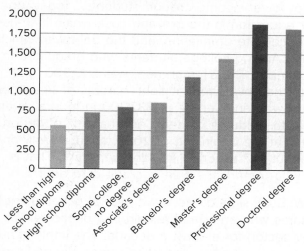

Median Weekly Earnings for Full-Time Workers, by Education Level

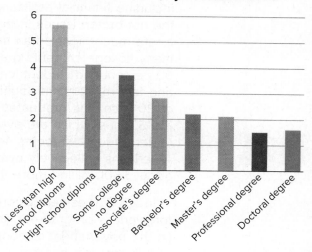

Unemployment Rate for Persons 25 Years and Over, by Education Level

FIGURE 12.1 ■ **Benefits of Educational Attainment (2018).** Explain how the two graphs support the claim that high-quality education is important to both a healthy national economy and personal financial security.

Source: U.S. Bureau of Labor Statistics, "Unemployment Rates and Earnings by Educational Attainment," *Employment Projections,* September 4, 2019.

with Disabilities Education Act of 1990, which replaced the 1975 Education for all Handicapped Children Act).

In 2002, one of the most significant federal educational policies was passed by Congress and signed into law by President George W. Bush. Importantly, Bush, a Republican, signed the No Child Left Behind Act, which expanded federal involvement in U.S. educational policy by increasing federal mandates that must be implemented by the states. For example, under the law, states are required to test students in reading and math annually in grades 3 through 8 and once in high school. While the bill had bi-partisan support when it was passed in Congress, many conservatives nationally balked at the federal government's expansion what was once a policy area controlled by the states. Liberals, on the other hand, have been critical of the the lack of funding provided by the federal government to the state in order to implement the policy.

The U.S. Department of Education was created under President Jimmy Carter in 1978. Since its birth, the need for this department has been questioned, particularly by Republican presidential candidates, presidents, and congressional members. President Ronald Reagan, who beat Carter in his 1980 bid for reelection, put forth the standard argument, still made today, to eliminate the department: "Welfare and education are two functions that should be primarily carried out at the state and local levels."[16] However, since 1965, federal funding and mandates have been vital to providing equal primary and secondary educational opportunities for all children.

Federal Policy and College Student Debt

In addition to passing the ESEA in 1965, Congress enacted the 1965 Higher Education Act, which authorized assistance for post-secondary education, including financial assistance for lower-income college students.[17] Today, one of the hot-button issues in higher education is the growing cost, which increases at a rate much higher than the annual rate of inflation, and the debt with which so many college students graduate. Among college students who graduated in 2019, 69 percent had student loans to repay. The average debt was $29,900 (both private and federal debt). In addition to their own student debt, parents of 14 percent of 2019 college graduates also owed an average of $37,200 in federal direct PLUS loans, which are available to graduate students and parents of dependent undergraduate students. In total, at the beginning of 2020, about 45 million Americans collectively owed about $1.7 trillion in student loan debt. That is about $600 billion more than what Americans owe in credit card debt.[18]

In 2007, President George W. Bush signed into law a federal government loan-forgiveness program for graduates who enter and remain in a public service career (in the government or nonprofit sector) for at least a decade. The implementation of this program has been extensively criticized due to its complexity and the poor quality of information provided to potential beneficiaries by loan service organizations with whom the federal government contracts to process payments and assist people through the process. The rejection rate for the first 73,000 people who applied for loan forgiveness (beginning in 2012) was 99 percent.[19]

The 2007 law also expanded repayment plans for federal student loans, using formulas based on a proportion of the graduate's discretionary income (income minus basic living expenses, which are defined by the federal poverty line). These repayment plans also included forgiveness of the remainder of a student loan after 20 years of repayment. In 2010, Congress eliminated the private bank loan guarantee programs. Under these programs, students borrowed money from private lenders, and the government guaranteed the lenders 95 percent of unpaid loan balances if the student defaulted. Since then, all new federal loans are direct loans from the government and eligible for a forgiveness program.[20]

As employers recruit and hire a generation of students crippled with debt, some are helping their employees repay their loans. According to the Society of Human Resource Management, by the end of 2019, about 8 percent of employers were offering their employees assistance with this debt, and the percentage of employers offering such a benefit is growing. Some employers offer to match employee payments, with a cap on the total amount of financial assistance they will provide. Other employers offer a flat contribution amount. Employers report that this employee benefit assists them in recruiting and retaining younger workers.[21]

■ Income Security Programs

Before the Great Depression of the 1930s, Americans who could not provide for their basic needs relied on relief from family, friends, charities, and local or state governments. During the Depression, however, the excessively weak economy left one-quarter of the U.S. labor force unemployed. Families lost jobs, savings, and homes. Charities were overwhelmed. State and local governments lacked the resources needed to assist the millions of people without incomes. Citizens, as well as state and local governments, looked to the federal government for assistance.

Within his first hundred days in office, President Franklin D. Roosevelt proposed a sequence of revolutionary bills to stimulate and regulate sectors of the depressed economy and to provide income to those in need. The model of a liberal vision of government, New Deal policies, placed the national government at the center of issues it had historically left to local and state governments, including income security for retired citizens and a safety net for people in financial need. Many of the New Deal programs are still in place today, though in modified form.

Social Security

The Social Security Act of 1935, a centerpiece of the New Deal, established a range of landmark income security programs. To this day, these programs provide financial assistance to individuals who are elderly, disabled, dependent, and unemployed.

OLD-AGE AND SURVIVORS INSURANCE (OASI) The Social Security Act established the Old-Age and Survivors Insurance (OASI) program, which initially provided income to individuals or families when a worker covered by the program retired. This is a **contributory cash-transfer program (social insurance program)**, a program paid for with tax revenues collected specifically for it. OASI is the traditional retirement insurance component of Social Security. OASI is also an **entitlement program**, meaning the government guarantees the program's benefits to all who meet the eligibility criteria. Each year, the federal government establishes the amount of earnings subject to the 12.4 percent Social Security tax (6.2 percent paid by employee and 6.2 percent paid by employer). In 2020, an individual's earned income up to $137,700 was subject to the tax.[22]

> **contributory cash-transfer program (social insurance program)**
> A program paid for with tax revenues collected specifically for it.
>
> **entitlement program**
> A program for which the government guarantees benefits to all who meet the eligibility criteria.

The 1937 Federal Insurance Contribution Act (FICA) established the pay-as-you-go funding mechanism for OASI. Through FICA contributions, tax dollars collected from current workers and employers are deposited in the Social Security Trust Fund. The government uses the money contributed today to pay today's beneficiaries. The money left over after today's payments are made is invested so that the trust fund will grow; income from investments will be combined with future FICA revenues to pay for future Social Security checks.

The government began to use money in the trust fund reserve to pay OASI benefits in 2020. If Congress does not legislate changes to the program that increase revenues, decrease costs, or do both, the trust fund reserves will be gone by 2034.[23]

AMENDMENTS TO THE SOCIAL SECURITY ACT Congress amended the Social Security Act in 1939 to provide benefits to the dependents and surviving spouse of a deceased worker. In 1956, the act was further amended to assist workers who, because of physical or mental disabilities, had to stop working after age 50 but before the OASI-designated retirement age. The new benefit program thus created, called Social Security Disability Insurance (SSDI), provides income to those covered by the Social Security program and to their families if they meet the guidelines for disability. Similar to OASI, SSDI is a contributory (social insurance) program.

> **noncontributory program**
> A program that benefits a targeted population and is paid for by a portion of the general revenue collected from all taxpayers.

In 1972, Congress again amended the Social Security Act by establishing the Supplemental Security Income (SSI) program, a **noncontributory program**, which is a

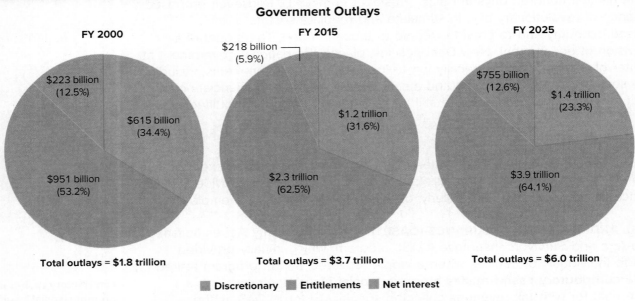

Government Outlays

FY 2000

$223 billion (12.5%)

$615 billion (34.4%)

$951 billion (53.2%)

Total outlays = $1.8 trillion

FY 2015

$218 billion (5.9%)

$1.2 trillion (31.6%)

$2.3 trillion (62.5%)

Total outlays = $3.7 trillion

FY 2025

$755 billion (12.6%)

$1.4 trillion (23.3%)

$3.9 trillion (64.1%)

Total outlays = $6.0 trillion

■ Discretionary ■ Entitlements ■ Net interest

Source: U.S. Chamber of Commerce. https://www.uschamber.com/above-the-fold/fiscal-follies-closer-look-entitlement-spending-interest

Entitlement spending, including Social Security and Medicare, take up an increasing percentage of federal government spending every year. This is due in part to our aging population—more Americans are drawing benefits for longer than ever before, and fewer citizens are paying taxes in proportion to the number of beneficiaries. Entitlement spending is more difficult to cut in our budgetary process because it cannot be negotiated in a given budget year; rather, changes must be projected into future years. Entitlement spending increases is just one factor that has led to U.S. deficit spending and a ballooning national debt. What can we do to reduce the debt? Should we cut spending? Raise taxes? Both? What will decreases in entitlement spending mean for senior citizens and others dependent on entitlement spending?

A. Identify the most common category of government spending.

B. Describe a trend in government spending and draw a conclusion about that spending.

C. Explain how the trend you identified in (B) may be affected by differences between ideologies of the two major political parties.

means-tested benefit
A benefit for which eligibility is based on having an income below a government-specified amount, typically based on a percentage of the poverty guideline.

program that benefits a targeted population and is paid for by a portion of the general revenue collected from all taxpayers. Recipients of SSI include low-income elderly people whose Social Security benefits are so low they cannot provide for themselves, individuals with disabilities, and blind people. Unlike other Social Security programs, SSI is a **means-tested benefit**, meaning that the eligibility criteria to receive the benefit include a government-specified income level, which is very low.

Unemployment Compensation

The Federal-State Unemployment Insurance Program, created by the Social Security Act of 1935, requires each state government to administer its own unemployment insurance program within guidelines established by federal law. Through this program, employees who lose their jobs through no fault of their own, and meet other eligibility requirements established by their state, can collect unemployment compensation from the state for up to 26 weeks. Employees fired for cause (based on their own behavior) cannot receive unemployment compensation. In general, the benefit received is based on a percentage of an individual's most recent earnings.

During economic recessions, such as the coronavirus-related recession that began in 2020, the national government has sometimes extended the 26-week benefit period if the unemployment rate remains high for a long time. When the federal government extends the benefit period in times of high, long-term unemployment, it (not the states) pays for the additional benefits.

Minimum Wage

When President Franklin D. Roosevelt asked Frances Perkins to serve as his secretary of labor in 1933, Perkins told him she would join his cabinet only if he agreed to establish a minimum wage.[24] He agreed, she became the first woman to serve as a department secretary, and the minimum wage became law through the 1938 Fair Labor Standards Act.

The aim of the minimum wage was to guarantee most employed workers a **living wage**—a wage high enough to keep them out of poverty. Yet, there have always been some workers not guaranteed the federal minimum wage. Today these include full-time students, youths under 20 years of age for the first 90 days of their employment, workers who earn tips, commissioned sales employees, farm laborers, and seasonal and recreational workers. For workers guaranteed the minimum wage, employers must pay overtime (equal to one and a half times an employee's regular hourly rate) for all hours over 40 worked during a workweek.

living wage
A wage high enough to keep workers and their families out of poverty and to allow them to enjoy a basic living standard.

>> Frances Perkins, the first woman to serve in the cabinet, was secretary of labor from 1933 to 1945. As chair of the President's Committee on Economic Security, she led the development of the Social Security Act (1935), which created the programs for Old-Age and Survivors Insurance (OASI, or Social Security retirement income) and Aid to Dependent Children. In addition, she was instrumental in establishing the minimum wage and the other worker benefits provided by the 1938 Fair Labor Standards Act. Here we see her standing behind President Roosevelt as he signs the Social Security Act.

FPG/Archive Photos/Getty Images

FIGURE 12.2 ◼ **Minimum Wage by State, January 1, 2020.** Identify the minimum wage rate for your home state. Then calculate the annual earnings of a minimum-wage worker (before taxes) if they work 40 hours per week for 52 weeks per year. Compare that annual wage to the poverty guideline annual earnings level shown in Table 12.2 to determine if the minimum wage is a "living wage."

Source: National Council of State Legislatures, *State Minimum Wages/ 2020 Minimum Wage by State,* January 6, 2020, https://www.nscl.org/research/labor-and-employment/state-minimum-wage-chart.aspx.

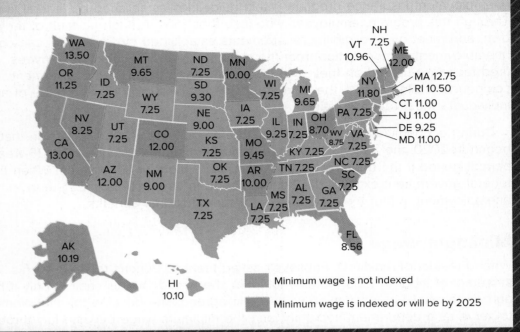

Legend:
- Minimum wage is not indexed
- Minimum wage is indexed or will be by 2025

In 1938, the government set the federal minimum wage at 25 cents per hour. Because the federal minimum wage is not an **indexed benefit**—that is, a benefit with an automatic cost-of-living increase based on the inflation rate—increases in the wage must be enacted through legislation, and so congressional battles to increase the minimum wage occur regularly. In 2009, Congress increased the minimum wage to $7.25. Since then, there have been numerous unsuccessful efforts to have Congress increase the minimum wage.

State and local governments can establish a minimum wage higher than the federal minimum for covered workers, and they can extend a minimum wage to workers not covered by the federal minimum wage. Figure 12.2 presents information on state minimum wage rates. At the beginning of 2019, 39 states and the District of Columbia had minimum wages higher than the federal level. In addition, 20 states have enacted laws to index their minimum wage, which means they have a system of automatic annual adjustments tied to a measure of inflation.[25] But even with these more generous benefits, many minimum-wage workers still live in poverty. Hence, today's minimum wage is not necessarily a living wage. To reduce the financial hardship on minimum and low-wage workers, the national government established the Earned Income Tax Credit program in 1975 and the Child Tax Credit in 1997.

indexed benefit
A government benefit with an automatic cost-of-living increase based on the rate of inflation.

Earned Income Tax Credit and Child Tax Credit

In addition to providing cash transfers and regulating wages, the government supports income security through programs offering tax breaks such as the Earned Income Tax Credit (EITC) and the Child Tax Credit (CTC) programs. The

EITC offers a tax credit to working citizens with low to moderate earned income who file an income tax return. Working parents are eligible for larger EITC credits than are workers without children. The amount of the tax credit decreases (eventually reaching zero) as earned income increases. The CTC is worth up to $2,000 per child for working families. Because the EITC and CTC reward work by supplementing the earnings of workers, there is broad bipartisan support for both programs. According to the Center on Budget and Policy Priorities, a research organization concerned with the status of poor people, in 2018 the EITC and the CTC lifted an estimated 10.6 million people out of poverty, including 5.5 million children.[26]

Temporary Assistance for Needy Families

The Social Security Act established Aid to Dependent Children (ADC), which evolved into Aid to Families with Dependent Children (AFDC) and was then replaced by Temporary Assistance for Needy Families (TANF). These income security programs target families with children and no or very low income (a means test).

ADC supported stay-at-home single widows with children. AFDC evolved into a program that supported one- and two-parent families with children. Federal grants and state funds paid for the ADC and AFDC noncontributory cash transfer entitlement programs. A formula in the national law determined what percentage of each state's annual program costs the federal government would cover. The federal law also gave each state discretion to determine the level of benefits as well as the eligibility criteria for program recipients in that state.

Beginning in the late 1950s, the number of households headed by women with children living in poverty began to increase, a development referred to as the **feminization of poverty**. Although the overwhelming majority of AFDC beneficiaries were children, myths about a poor work ethic and irresponsible sexual practices on the part of their typically single mothers fueled many calls for reform. Although AFDC was modified several times over the next few decades, a major reform did not occur until the 1990s.

feminization of poverty
The phenomenon of increasing numbers of unmarried, divorced, and separated women with children living in poverty.

In 1996, President Bill Clinton signed the Personal Responsibility and Work Opportunity Reconciliation Act (PRWORA), which radically changed both the nature and the provision of income security for low-income families with children. PRWORA replaced the AFDC entitlement program and several other grant assistance programs for low-income families with one block grant: Temporary Assistance for Needy Families (TANF). Unlike AFDC, TANF is not an entitlement program. The focus moreover has changed from one of encouraging women to stay home with their children to one of requiring recipients to work (those in both single- and dual-parent households) and requiring fathers (particularly those not living with their children) to take on greater financial responsibilities for their children.

TANF is designed to foster self-sufficiency among families with children by providing financial assistance for basic needs (like food, housing, and clothing), job training, childcare, and transportation, among other needs. States receive block grants from the federal government that give them discretion in determining TANF eligibility, benefits, and programs (see Figure 12.3). The grants also come with several very specific regulations. For example, a family can receive benefits only for two consecutive years and a lifetime maximum of five years. Moreover, program beneficiaries must work or be enrolled in an educational or training

FIGURE 12.3 ■ **Maximum TANF Benefit for a Family of Three by State: 2018.** The figure presents the average of the 2012 and 2018 maximum allowable TANF benefit (dollar amounts) for a family of three in each state. It also indicates the share of the federal poverty level the benefit represents in deciles (indicated by color). Do you see any geographic patterns to TANF benefits? What is your home state's maximum benefit and decile?

Source: Center on Budget and Policy Priorities, *State Fact Sheets: Trend in State TANF-to-Poverty Ratios,* "TANF State-by-State Fact Sheets," March 4, 2020, https://www.cbpp.org/research/family-income-support/state-fact-sheets-trends-in-state-tanf-to-poverty-ratios.

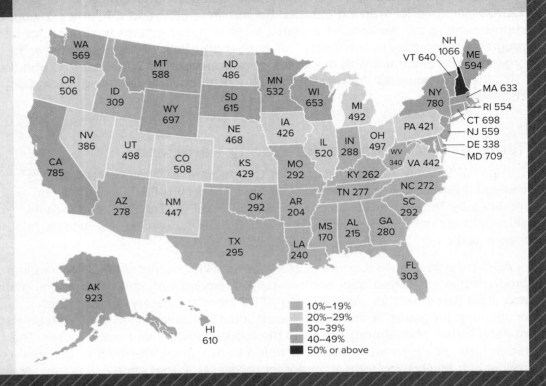

program that prepares them for work. Ultimately, the success of TANF depends on the availability of jobs that pay well and offer benefits; hence, its success depends on the overall health of the U.S. economy.

Other Safety Net Programs

Despite the various income security programs we have considered, in 2018, almost 40 million people in the United States, including millions who worked full time, lived in *poverty*[27]—the condition of lacking sufficient income to purchase the necessities for an adequate living standard. Millions of others are one problem away from poverty, meaning that a health emergency, significant car repair, family relations issue, or job layoff could land them in poverty. The government defines poverty using two measures: **poverty thresholds** and **poverty guidelines**.

Since the 1960s, the U.S. Census Bureau has used the gauge of **poverty thresholds**—an annually updated set of income measures adjusted for family size that define who is living in poverty (see Chapter 11). The government uses these thresholds to collect data on how many families and individuals are living in poverty.

Government agencies that offer additional safety-net programs beyond those we have considered so far do not use the Census Bureau's poverty thresholds to determine eligibility. Instead, many use **poverty guidelines** established by the Department of Health and Human Services (HHS). The guidelines are a version of the poverty thresholds simplified for administrative use (see Table 12.2).

poverty thresholds
The U.S. Census Bureau's annually updated set of income measures (adjusted for family size) that define who is living in poverty

poverty guidelines
A simplified version of the U.S. Census Bureau's poverty thresholds developed each year by the Department of Health and Human Services; used to set financial eligibility criteria for benefits

TABLE 12.2 ■ Department of Health and Human Services Poverty Guidelines for the 48 Contiguous States and Washington, DC, 2020 ($ per year)

What quality of life could you, as a single person, achieve at the income of 100 percent of the poverty guidelines? What quality of life could you, as a single person, achieve at the income of 185 percent of the poverty guidelines?

Persons in Household	100 Percent of Poverty	185 Percent of Poverty*
1	12,760	23,606
2	12,240	31,894
3	21,720	40,182
4	26,200	48,470
5	30,680	56,758
6	35,160	65,046
7	39,640	73,334
8	44,120	81,622

*Calculated from the HSS poverty guidelines; 185% is the means test, or value, HHS typically uses when determining eligibility for benefits.

Source: U.S. Department of Health and Human Services, "2020 Poverty Guidelines."

Most in-kind assistance safety-net programs allow families with incomes of a certain percentage above the HHS poverty guidelines (typically, 185 percent) to receive benefits. Programs that use the HHS poverty guidelines as the basis for determining eligibility include SNAP and the National School Lunch Program. These programs target the problem of **food insecurity**, the situation in which people have limited or uncertain ability to obtain, in socially acceptable ways, enough nutritious food to sustain a healthy and active life.

Housing insecurity—the condition in which people have limited or uncertain ability to obtain, in socially acceptable ways, housing that is affordable, safe, of decent quality, and permanent—is another problem for a proportion of the U.S. population. To assess the number of homeless people in the country, the U.S. Department of Housing and Urban Development (HUD) conducts a count one night each January. In January 2019, HUD's volunteers counted 567,715 persons experiencing homelessness.[28] However, advocates for the homeless question the validity of this one-night-in-January count, arguing that it misses many homeless persons.[29]

President Trump's 2021 budget proposal requested $2.8 billion to "assist the fight to end homelessness."[30] The most costly federal housing assistance

food insecurity
The situation in which people have a limited or an uncertain ability to obtain, in socially acceptable ways, enough nutritious food to live a healthy and active life.

housing insecurity
The situation in which people have limited or uncertain ability to obtain, in socially acceptable ways, affordable, safe, and decent-quality permanent housing.

programs come in the form of the tax breaks for homeowners, developers, and property owners who rent to low-income householders. However, the programs that are most in the public eye are means-tested public housing and housing-choice-voucher (Section 8 rent subsidy) programs for which low-income households can apply. Even with these programs, the nation has an affordable-housing crisis. The National Low Income Housing Coalition reports that the United States needs at least 7.2 million more affordable housing units.[31]

Health Care Policy

Lack of health insurance is an additional problem for low-income households, although the 2010 Patient Protection and Affordable Care Act (Affordable Care Act, or ACA) attempted to ensure that everyone has health insurance. According to the U.S. Census Bureau, in 2018 about 9 percent of the U.S. population was without health insurance. This represents the first year-to-year increase in the percentage of uninsured in the U.S. since 2008–2009. Of those with insurance, 67 percent had private insurance (55 percent of private insurance was employer-based), and 34 percent were covered by government health programs: 18 percent Medicare, 18 percent Medicaid.[32] These two programs were established in 1965 as part of President Lyndon B. Johnson's (1963–1969) Great Society plan, which included government programs to address the effects of poverty during a time of national economic prosperity. Medicare and Medicaid are entitlement programs and part of today's safety net.

Medicaid

Title XIX, added to the Social Security Act in 1965, created Medicaid—a joint federal-state entitlement program providing health care to people meeting a means test. Because the national legislation delegates substantial discretion to state governments regarding eligibility and benefits, there are really 50 different Medicaid programs.

In this cash transfer program, state governments pay health care providers, and then the national government reimburses the states for a percentage of those bills. The national government's share of each state's cost is based on a formula that takes into account the state's per capita income. The national government pays at least 50 percent of the Medicaid bill in high-income states and a greater percentage in low-income states.

The State Children's Health Insurance Program (SCHIP), established in 1997, covers medical costs for low-income uninsured children under the age of 19 who are not eligible for Medicaid. In this joint federal-state cash transfer program, eligibility is based on a family income that is generally less than 200 percent of the HHS poverty guidelines.

The 2010 Affordable Care Act allows states to expand Medicaid and SCHIP eligibility for children, pregnant women, parents, and other adults who were excluded previously from the programs by decreasing the income requirements. Specifically, it allows states to extend Medicaid to low-income individuals and adults in families with incomes up to 133 percent of the federal poverty level.[33]

Traditionally, although most of those who benefit from Medicaid are women and children, the bulk of Medicaid spending pays for nursing home and long-term care services, which Medicare does not cover.

Medicare

In 1965, President Lyndon Johnson signed legislation enacting Medicare, a program that provides health insurance to persons over age 65 and those under 65 who have been receiving SSDI for at least two years. Today, Medicare has four components.

- *Part A*, Medicare's Hospital Insurance Program, is a social insurance and entitlement program funded by a 1.45 percent tax paid by employees and employers that helps to cover hospital stays. (This tax and the Social Security tax make up the "FICA" deduction from your paychecks.)

- *Part B*, Medicare's Supplemental Medical Insurance, covers a percentage of physician costs and other outpatient health care expenses, such as laboratory fees and ambulance services.

- *Part C*, Medicare 1 Choice, allows Medicare beneficiaries to choose private health plans that provide them with the same coverage found in Medicare Parts A and B.

- *Part D* is a prescription drug plan that took effect in 2006.

The Affordable Care Act extended several preventive services to Medicare recipients at no cost, including cholesterol screening, mammograms, diabetes screening, and screening for colorectal, prostate, and cervical cancers. The act also filled in a prescription coverage gap in the Medicare Part D program.[34]

The Patient Protection and Affordable Care Act (ACA)

On March 23, 2010, President Obama signed into law the Patient Protection and Affordable Care Act (ACA), which had been approved by Congress without a single vote from a Republican congressional member. The ACA has several goals, including expanding consumers' protections in their dealings with health insurance companies, improving the quality and lowering the costs of health care, and increasing access to affordable health care.

The ACA regulations (1) prohibit insurance companies from denying coverage based on preexisting conditions, from discontinuing coverage when a customer gets sick, and from charging higher rates due to a person's sex or health status; (2) require insurance companies to allow young adults to be covered by their parents' insurance until they turn 26 years old and to spend at least 80 percent of all premium dollars on benefits and quality improvements; and (3) eliminate any lifetime dollar limits on insurance coverage.

Under the ACA, the federal government makes subsidies available to individuals with incomes between 133 percent and 400 percent of the federal poverty level to help them pay for insurance. Moreover, employers with more than 50 employees must provide health insurance to 95 percent of their full-time employees or pay a penalty to the Internal Revenue Service (IRS).[35]

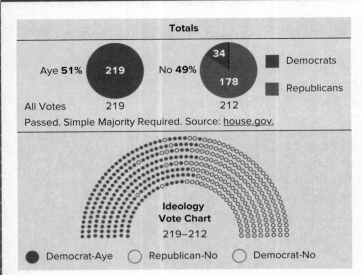

Totals

Aye **51%** 219

No **49%** 34 / 178

■ Democrats
■ Republicans

All Votes 219 212

Passed. Simple Majority Required. Source: house.gov.

Ideology Vote Chart

219–212

● Democrat-Aye ○ Republican-No ○ Democrat-No

UNITED STATES SENATE	
Roll Call Vote 111th Congress - 1st Session	
Vote Summary	
Question:	On Passage of the Bill (H.R. 3590 as Amended)
Vote Number:	396
Vote Date:	December 24, 2009, 07:05 AM
Required For Majority:	1/2
Vote Result:	Bill Passed
Measure Number:	H.R. 3590 (Patient Protection and Affordable Care Act)
Measure Title:	An act entitled the Patient Protection and Affordable Care Act.
Vote Counts:	YEAs 60 / NAYs 39 / Not Voting 1

*Information compiled through Senate LIS by the Senate bill clerk under the direction of the secretary of the Senate

(House Vote) Source: GovTrack. "H.R. 3590 (111th): Patient Protection and Affordable Care Act". https://www.govtrack.us/congress/votes/111-2010/h165.; (Senate Vote) Source: United States Senate. "Roll Call Vote 111th Congress - 1st Session". https://www.senate.gov/legislative/LIS/roll_call_lists/roll_call_vote_cfm.cfm?congress=111&session=1&vote=00396

President Obama made health care reform a legislative priority in the first two years of his presidency. In his first two years, Obama had strong Democratic control of Congress, but passing the Affordable Care Act legislation was a struggle, nevertheless. The Affordable Care Act proposal sought to provide more Americans with health insurance coverage through state-run insurance exchanges that individuals could purchase, and sought to end some insurance practices of dropping clients when they got sick or refusing to cover individuals with pre-existing conditions. The Affordable Care Act included provisions to provide low-income individuals with a subsidy to purchase insurance and requiring uninsured Americans with higher incomes to carry basic insurance.

When the Affordable Care Act came before Congress, there were demonstrations against the bill in the hundreds of thousands. Protesters argued that the bill was socialist and equated to a government takeover of private insurance. President Obama not only faced criticism over the proposal from Republicans, but from within the Democratic Party as well. Some Democrats wanted a more aggressive bill that would have essentially provided government insurance for all Americans and rejected the bill because it did not go far enough; others in the Democratic Party rejected the bill because they thought the proposal went too far, including its coverage of women's reproductive health.

In the Senate, Obama had 60 Democratic senators at the start of his term, and one version of the Affordable Care Act was passed through the Senate. In the middle of negotiations over the House version of the bill, Senator Ted Kennedy (D-MA) died, and in a special election, Kennedy's seat was filled by a Republican, leaving Obama with 59 Democrats. At this point, the bill was bound to be filibustered by Republican senators, and Democrats lacked the 60 votes needed for cloture. The only way Obama could pass the bill after Kennedy's death was to take the version of the bill that passed prior to Kennedy's death for a vote in the House (the Constitution requires that a bill pass both chambers in identical form and be signed by the president to become law), which he did. The vote breakdown on the Affordable Care Act is displayed in the charts on the preceding page. No Republicans voted for the bill and in the House, 39 Democrats voted against the bill. After the bill became law, it was challenged in the U.S. Supreme Court. In the *National Federation of Independent Businesses v. Sebelius* (2012), most of the act was upheld, but court challenges to the Affordable Care Act continue.

Critical Thinking: *Is legislation passed by one party less legitimate than legislation that is passed by a bipartisan vote? Why or why not?*

Is legislation that is challenged in court less legitimate if the court does not strike the law down?

Practice Quantitative Analysis:

A. Describe the party vote breakdown on the Affordable Care Act in the House and Senate.

B. Describe a similarity or difference in the vote when comparing the House vote to the Senate vote, and draw a conclusion about the implications of the similarity or difference.

C. Explain how the health care vote as shown in the data demonstrates the complexity of the lawmaking process.

▪ Immigration Policy

U.S. immigration policy has traditionally been a collection of laws that specify which people the government will authorize to emigrate to the United States and the processes by which people can apply for authorization. Approximately 45 million immigrants live in the United States today. Figure 12.4 shows that legal immigrants come from all around the globe. Among those immigrants are approximately 10.5 million unauthorized immigrants.[36] To decrease the number of unauthorized immigrants entering the country, President Trump made the construction of a wall at the United States–Mexico border a new component of U.S. immigration policy.

AUTHORIZED IMMIGRATION Federal immigration policy determines who may emigrate to the United States as permanent residents ("green card" recipients) and as temporary visitors (officially labeled non-immigrant admissions, including tourists, students, diplomats, businessmen and businesswomen, and guest workers). Immigrants with a green card can work, live, own property, attend public schools and colleges, and apply for citizenship when they meet the eligibility criteria. Non-immigrant visitors are legally obligated to leave the country when their temporary visas expire.

FIGURE 12.4 ▪ Where U.S. Lawful Permanent Residents Come From, 2018 What world region is the source of most U.S. immigrants today? With respect to the Americas, what country or larger geographical unit is the source of most immigrants to the United States? From what area of the world do you think most Americans believe the largest proportion of immigrants come to the United States? Do you think these statistics would surprise most Americans?

Source: Department of Homeland Security, Lawful Permanent Residents: 2018 Data. "Lawful Permanent Residents Data Table: Table 2." https://www.dhs.gov/immigration-statistics-permanent-residents.

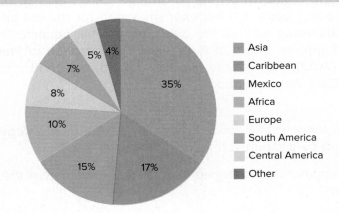

- Asia
- Caribbean
- Mexico
- Africa
- Europe
- South America
- Central America
- Other

Since the Immigration and Nationality Act of 1965, the largest category of immigrants authorized to come to the United States permanently is those seeking to reunify with immediate family members who are either U.S. citizens or authorized permanent residents. U.S. citizens can sponsor immediate family members—spouses, minor children, and parents—for visas, and the government has placed no limit on the number of these that they can issue. Approximately 49 percent of new lawful permanent residents in 2019 entered the country through this program.[37]

The second-largest category of new permanent residents are siblings and adult children of U.S. citizens, who receive preferences under a program that offers a limited number of visas each year to citizens' relatives. Immigrants with green cards can also apply for visas for their spouses and children. In 2019, 20 percent of new lawful permanent residents entered the country under this sponsorship program.[38]

In 2019, the third-largest category—about 14 percent of those admitted—was composed of individuals welcomed into the country for their employment skills; this group includes highly skilled professionals and wealthy entrepreneurs expected to invest in job creation. The fourth-largest category of authorized immigrants in 2019 was composed of refugees, meaning persons to whom the United States offers humanitarian protection from persecution, and likely persecution, because of race, religion, nationality, membership in a particular social group, or political views. An additional 5 percent of immigrants are admitted through the State Department's diversity lottery. The diversity lottery awards permanent residency to people from identified countries with low rates of immigration to the United States.

Those who are not eligible for permanent authorized immigration to the United States include foreigners who do not fall within one of the categories described previously; foreign nationals perceived to be anarchists or political extremists; and foreigners who the government perceives as security or terrorist threats, who have a criminal history, who have previously been removed from the United States, or who present a health risk.[39]

Unauthorized Immigration

Why do immigrants enter the United States without authorization each year? This question has several answers. One is that the United States may offer more economic opportunities than does the home country. Yet, unless an individual fits into one of the categories for authorized immigration, he or she has no basis on which to apply for permanent, legal entry into the United States. In addition, there are backlogs in processing applications for authorized immigration. These backlogs occur because family-sponsored and employment-based applications are capped each year, and the U.S. will not allow citizens of any one country to make up more than seven percent of the total number of applicants in these categories combined per year. The result is a backlog of more than 4 million applications, which may mean up to a 20-year wait for authorized immigration.[40]

What most people do not realize is that the main source of unauthorized immigrants is travelers who overstay their temporary visas. According to Robert Warren, a demographer who estimated visa-overstay by using data collected by the U.S. Census Bureau, "twice as many people [unauthorized immigrants] came in with a visa than came across the border illegally in recent years." Visa over-stayers make up almost half of the 10.5 million unauthorized immigrants in the United States today.[41]

Proposed Immigration Policy Reforms

Congress has been debating immigration reforms since the last major immigration reform law was enacted in 1986. Disagreement among congressional members (typically along party lines) has resulted in no new immigration policy legislation since then. Thus, presidents from Reagan to Trump have used their power of executive order to direct immigration policy in alignment with their priorities. In addition, state and local governments have stepped into the gap left by Congress, enacting their own policies to address concerns about undocumented immigrants. In turn, courts have had to resolve conflicts over the constitutionality of state and local policies, as well as presidential executive orders.

Federal judges and justices have ruled that state and local governments cannot craft their own immigration policies because they infringe on the federal government's constitutional authority over such matters. However, federal courts have also found that the Constitution does not allow the federal government to "commandeer local officials into federal service."[42] Indeed, several states have enacted laws that bar state and local government officials from cooperating with federal immigration-enforcement efforts—hence, the existence of sanctuary states and sanctuary cities, which were discussed in Chapter 3.

President Obama, through executive orders, established programs to protect targeted groups of unauthorized immigrants. In 2012, he established the Deferred Action for Childhood Arrivals (DACA) program to allow children and young adults who were brought to the United States illegally as children to apply for temporary deportation relief. A 2014 Obama executive order expanded the DACA program and created a new program, Deferred Action for Parents of Americans and Lawful Permanent Residents (DAPA). DAPA allowed undocumented immigrants who are the parents of U.S. citizens or of lawful permanent residents to be shielded from deportation and allowed to apply for work permits.[43] DACA and DAPA have been challenged in the courts by several states.

In his 2018 State of the Union address, President Trump outlined four pillars of his plan for immigration reform: protection for DACA recipients; an end to family reunification immigration; an end to the diversity lottery; and full funding for the border wall he has been calling for since his presidential campaign, which is estimated to cost $25 billion over 10 years.[44]

President Trump's efforts to lower the number of authorized and unauthorized immigrants, particularly those coming through the United States–Mexico border, include (1) requiring asylum seekers to apply for asylum before entering the United States as opposed to once they arrive, as specified in legislation; (2) allowing only immigrants who have officially been denied asylum in another country or who have been victims of human trafficking to apply for asylum in the United States; and (3) separating parents and their children when they arrive in the United States. These efforts have been successfully challenged in the courts as violations of federal law and international asylum laws.[45] The construction of a wall at the U.S.–Mexico border is also being challenged in the courts because the project in some locations conflicts with federal environmental and conservation laws as well as Native American tribal rights.[46]

Within his first two months in office, President Biden began to reverse Trump administration immigration policies.[47] Two examples include lifting the Trump-era requirement that asylum seekers had to stay in Mexico until their claims for asylum could be heard and the restriction that created huge reductions in the number of visas issued to immigrants. Instead of eliminating the diversity lottery, as proposed by the Trump administration, Biden's administration wants to increase the annual number of diversity visas. The Biden administration is also interested in increasing the number of refugees admitted into the country. Contrary to Trump's policies, Biden's policy proposals would allow more authorized immigrants into the United States. He is also interested in creating a pathway to legal immigration status for millions of unauthorized immigrants already in the country, including the DACA recipients, or "Dreamers," who have been protected from deportation since the Obama administration.

Conclusion: Thinking Critically About What's Next in U.S. Domestic Policy

A healthy environment is essential to human health, happiness, and survival. Reliance on nonrenewable energy sources, specifically fossil fuels, combined with the production of huge volumes of waste by the world's growing population harm the global environment. Today, people across the globe agree that countries must decrease their reliance on fossil fuels to limit climate change and its harmful effects. However, debates in the United States continue on how to accomplish this while not harming economic development and while increasing economic independence.

Ensuring a healthy and safe society in which citizens can live their lives freely, in pursuit of their happiness, means more than protecting air, water, and land quality. Today, the ever-increasing cost of ensuring a just and safe society is forcing U.S. policymakers to take a hard look at education, income security, food security, housing security, and health care policies. There is bipartisan concern about the growing costs of several safety net policies, particularly OASI, Medicare, and Medicaid. However, there is not bipartisan agreement on how to address the financial problems so that the benefits program recipients currently enjoy will also be available to their posterity.

The national government regularly works with state and local governments to provide the phenomenal range of domestic policies from which citizens benefit. Only through a unity of effort, which requires clear communication and cooperation, can intergovernmental relations succeed, whether the goal is protecting the environment, establishing energy independence, or maintaining a safety net that ensures life, liberties, and the pursuit of happiness. Today, healthy intergovernmental relations are key elements of effective and efficient national domestic policies. However, in several policy areas, including environmental protection and immigration, intergovernmental tension is growing as many state and local governments move in directions at odds with that of the national government. Intergovernmental cooperation and intergovernmental tension are both realities in U.S. domestic policy today.

References

1. Office of Management and Budget, *Historical Tables,* "Table 3.1—Outlays by Superfunction and Function: 1940–2025," www.whitehouse.gov/omb/historicals.

2. Office of Management and Budget, *Historical Tables,* "Table 11.1: Summary of Outlays for Payments for Individuals: 1940–2025," www.whitehouse.gov/omb/historical-tables/.

3. U.S. Census Bureau, "Measuring America," December 12, 2013.

4. "Gaylord Nelson and Earth Day—Introduction: The Earth Day Story and Gaylord Nelson," nelsonearthday.net/earth-day/index.htm.

5. Ibid.

6. Michael E. Mann and Tom Toles, *The Madhouse Effect: How Climate Change Denial Is Threatening Our Planet, Destroying Our Politics, and Driving Us Crazy* (New York: Columbia University Press, 2016).

7. Department of Defense , "DoD Releases Report on Security Implications of Climate Change," July 29, 2015, http://www.defense.gov/news/newsarticle.aspx?id5129366.

8. Michael E. Kraft, *Environmental Policy and Politics,* 7th ed. (New York: Routledge. 2018), 112.

9. EPA, Fact Sheet: The Affordable Clean Energy Rule (ACE); Fact Sheet: Overview of the final ACE rule, June 19, 2019, https://www.epa.gov/stationary-sources-air-pollu-tion/fact-sheet-overview-final-ace-rule.

10. Lauren Aratani, "'Damage Has Been Done': Newark Water Crisis Echoes Flint," *The Guardian*, August 25, 2019; and Rebecca Natanson, "Newark's Lead Crisis Isn't Over: 'People Are Still Drinking Water That They Shouldn't,'" *The Intercept*, March 15, 2020, www.intercept.com/2020/03/15/newark-new-jersey-lead-water-crisis.

11. https://www.epa.gov/superfund/search-superfund-sites-where-you-live.

12. David Hosansky, *The Environment A to Z* (Washington, DC: CQ Press, 2001), 80–81.

13. Michael T. Klare, "Donald Trump's Extract-Everything Energy Policy Dooms Us All," *The Nation*, February 12, 2018.

14. National Conference of State Legislatures, "A Primer: Every Student Succeeds Act (ESSA)," Education, October 2016.

15. New America, "Federal Spending on Early Care and Education: Past, Present, and Future," blog post, https://www.newamer-ica.org/education-policy/edcentral/federal-spending-early-care-and-education-past-present-and-future.

16. Dan Bauman and Brock Read, "A Brief History of GOP Attempts to Kill the Education Department," *The Chronicle of Higher Education,* June 21, 2018.

17. U.S. Department of Education, "The Federal Role in Education," May 5, 2012, https://www2.ed.gov/about/overview/fed/role.html.

18. Student Loan Hero, "A Look at the Shocking Student Loan Debt Statistics for 2020," January 15, 2020, https://studentloanhero.com/student-loan-debt-statistics/.

19. Kevin Carey, "It's Easy to Forget, but a Program to Forgive Student Loans Already Exists," *The New York Times,* July 24, 2019.

20. Ibid.

21. Sarah Skidmore Sell, "Employers offering student loan help," *Scranton Times-Tribune,* October 20, 2019.

22. Social Security Administration, "2020 Social Security Changes," *Fact Sheet: Social Security,* https://www.ssa.gov/news/press/factsheets/colafacts2020.pdf.

23. Center on Budget and Policy Priorities, "Policy Basics: Understanding the Social Security Trust Funds," *Policy Futures,* https://www.cbpp.org/research/social-security/policy-basics-understanding-the-social-security-trust-funds.

24. Jim Dwyer, "Exhausted Workers Recall Minimal Efforts to Enforce a Minimum Wage Law," *The New York Times,* November 7, 2013.

25. Raise the Minimum Wage, "Wage Data for all States," *Minimum Wage by State,* January 4, 2019.

26. Center on Budget and Policy Priorities, "Child Tax Credit and Earned Income Tax Credit Lifted 10.6 Million People out of Poverty," *Off the Charts: Policy Insight Beyond the Numbers*, October 31, 2019.

27. U.S. Census Bureau, "Income, Poverty and Health Insurance Coverage in the United States: 2018," *Newsroom*, September 10, 2019, Release Number CB19-141.

28. Department of Housing and Urban Development, "HUD Releases 2019 Annual Homeless Assessment Report," January 7, 2020, https://www.hud.gov/press/press-re-leases_media_advisories/HUD_No_20_003.

29. Maria Foscarinis, "Homeless Problem Bigger Than Our Leaders Think: Report Misleads on Those Without Shelter," *USA Today,* January 16, 2014.

30. U.S. Department of Housing and Urban Development, "Trump Administration Proposes 2021 HUD Budget," February 10, 2020, https://www.hud.gov/press/press_release_media_advisories/HUD_No_20_022.

31. National Low Income Housing Coalition, "The GAP: A Shortage of Affordable Homes," March 2018, https://nlihc.org/sites/default/files/gap/Gap-Report_2018.pdf.

32. U.S. Census Bureau, "Income, Poverty, and Health Insurance Coverage in the United States: 2018," September, 10, 2019, Release Number CB19-141, https://www.census.gov/newsroom/press-releases/2019/income-poverty.html.

33. Centers for Medicare and Medicaid, "Timeline: The Affordable Care Act Becomes Law," www.medicaid.gov/AffordableCareAct/Timeline/Timeline.html.

34. U.S. Department of Health and Human Services, "Key Features of the Affordable Care Act by Year," www.hhs.gov/healthcare/facts/timeline/timeline-text.html#Page_4.

35. Sachi Barreiro, "Is My Employer Required to Provide Health Care Coverage?", https://www.nolo.com/legal-encyclopedia/is-my-employer-required-to-provide-health-care.html.

36. Jeanne Batalova, Brittany Blizzard, and Jessica Bolter, "Frequently Requested Statistics on Immigrants and Immigration in the United States," *Migration Information Source,* February 14, 2020.

37. Department of Homeland Security, "Legal Immigration and Adjustment of Status Report Fiscal Year 2019, Quarter 4," March 4, 2020, https://www.dhs.gov/immigration-statistics//special-reports/legal-immigration.

38. Ibid.

39. "Inadmissibility: When the U.S. Can Keep You Out," *NOLO Law for All,* www.nolo.com/legal-encyclopedia/us-deny-entry-inadmissibility-reasons-29715.html.

40. Batalova, Blizzard, and Bolter, "Frequently Requested Statistics on Immigrants and Immigration in the United States."

41. Miriam Jordan, "Who Are America's Undocumented Immigrants? You Might Not Recognize Them," *The New York Times*, December 1, 2019.

42. Josh Gerstein, "Trump Administration Goes on Offense, Sues California over Sanctuary Laws," *Politico.com,* March 6, 2018.

43. U.S. Immigration and Customs Enforcement, "Deferred Action for Childhood Arrivals (DACA) and Deferred Action for Parents of Americans and Lawful Permanent Residents (DAPA)," www.ice.gov/daca.

44. Sheryl Gay Stolberg, "Senate Begins 'Wild' Week of Debate on Immigration, Outcome Unknown," *The New York Times*, February 12, 2018.

45. Miriam Jordan and Zolan Kanno-Youngs, "Trump's Latest Attempt to Bar Asylum Seekers is Blocked After a Day of Dueling Rulings," *The New York Times,* July 24, 2019.

46. Simon Romero, "Tribal Nation Condemns 'Desecration' to Build Border Wall," *The New York Times,* February 26, 2020.

47. Jens Manuel Krogstad and Ana Gonzalez-Barrera, "Key facts about U.S. immigration policies and Biden's proposed changes," *FACTANK: News in the Numbers,* March 22, 2021, https://www.pewresearch.org/fact-tank/2021/03/22/key-facts-about-u-s-immigration-policies-and-bidnes-proposed-changes/.

■ Key Terms

CHAPTER 12 EXAM PRACTICE

▌ Multiple-Choice Questions

1. Which of the following accurately compares social policy views of liberals versus conservatives?

	Liberal	Conservative
A.	Environmental regulations should be left to the states	Increase national environmental regulations
B.	Medicare and Medicaid are sufficient health care policies	Healthcare is a national responsibility
C.	Education policy should have national standards	Leave education policy up to the states
D.	Decrease temporary assistance to needy families	Increase temporary assistance to needy families

2. Which of the following reflects liberal ideology on government surveillance?
  A. Personal privacy protects individuals from government surveillance in most circumstances
  B. The need for security outweighs the need for personal privacy from some government surveillance
  C. All individuals have the right to be free from government surveillance
  D. Government surveillance is not needed except to protect private property

3. The policy priorities of citizens vary due to all of the following factors EXCEPT:
  A. Life experiences
  B. Political ideology
  C. Demographics
  D. Media

4. Which of the following is an accurate comparison of Medicare and Medicaid?

	Medicare	Medicaid
A.	Provides health insurance to persons over age 65	Provides health insurance to people meeting a means test
B.	Includes SCHIP to cover medical costs for children	Funded through FICA and Social Security deductions
C.	Allowed states to expand coverage for women and children	Includes Part D prescription drug coverage
D.	Provides for patient protection and affordable care	Provides temporary insurance for the unemployed

5. The biggest percentage of the budget spent by the national government goes toward
   A. Discretionary expenditures
   B. Entitlements
   C. National defense
   D. Deficit reduction

6. Which of the following is a means-tested benefit?
   A. Social Security
   B. Medicare
   C. Food stamps
   D. Earned income tax credit

7. Domestic agencies such as the Environmental Protection Agency and the Department of Homeland Security have emerged
   A. As the result of concern related to the general welfare of United States citizens
   B. Whenever the budget surplus allows for the national government to improve quality of life issues for U.S. citizens
   C. Each time the party out of power assumes renewed political control, and rewards the American people
   D. When the American electorate has shifted as a result of a critical election

8. Which of the following policies would be most difficult for a president?
   A. Opening dialogue with a leader of another country
   B. Creating an executive agreement to establish a new military base
   C. Passing a new healthcare law
   D. U.S. representation at the United Nations

Questions 9 and 10 are based on the following graphs.

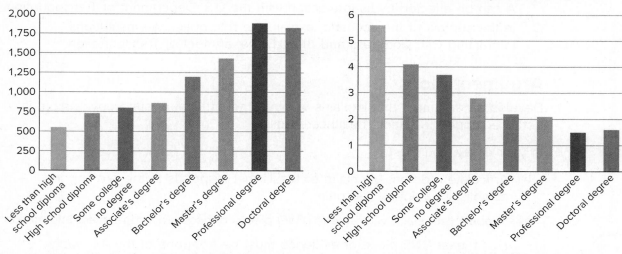

Unemployment Rates and Earnings by Educational Attainment

Median Weekly Earnings for Full-Time Workers, by Education Level

Unemployment Rate for Persons 25 years and over, by Education Level

Source: U.S. Bureau of Labor Statistics, "Unemployment Rates and Earnings by Educational Attainment," *Employment Projections,* September 4, 2019.

9. Which of the following is true, based on the data in the graphs above?
   A. The unemployment rate is highest for those with less than a high school diploma
   B. The rate of unemployment increases with the number of degrees a person holds
   C. Individuals with a professional degree earn the most when compared to other degree levels
   D. Individuals with associate's degrees earn the least when compared to other degree levels

10. Which of the following is a conclusion that might be drawn about the data in the graphs?
   A. There is no relationship between degree and weekly earnings
   B. There is an inverse relationship between degree and weekly earnings
   C. Education is important to personal financial security
   D. Taking out a loan to finance education pays off financially in the long run

■ Free Response Questions

Concept Application

Scenario: Automobile accidents exposed a lack of safety for children in automobiles. In response to this concern, Congress passed strict automobile safety legislation targeting new rules to be implemented by the U.S. Department of Transportation for child safety seats. While the new rules were welcomed by the public, the automobile industry argued that they were overly cumbersome and would cause the cost of automobiles to rise unnecessarily.

After reading the scenario, respond to A, B, and C below:

A. Describe a power Congress has to address the scenario.
B. In the context of the scenario, explain how Congress's power described in part A can be affected by its interaction with the U.S. Department of Transportation.
C. In the context of the scenario, explain the role of linkage institutions interacting with Congress and the U.S. Department of Transportation.

Argumentation

Develop an argument that explains whether the national or state government is better equipped to handle healthcare policy.

In your essay, you must:

- Articulate a defensible claim or thesis that responds to the prompt and establishes a line of reasoning

- Support your claim with at least TWO pieces of accurate and relevant information:

  - At least ONE piece of evidence must be from one of the following foundational documents:

    — Articles I-IV of the Constitution
    — The Bill of Rights

- Use a second piece of evidence from another foundational document from the list or from your study of social policymaking.

- Use reasoning to explain why your evidence supports your claim/thesis

- Respond to an opposing or alternative perspective using refutation, concession, or rebuttal

Quantitative Analysis

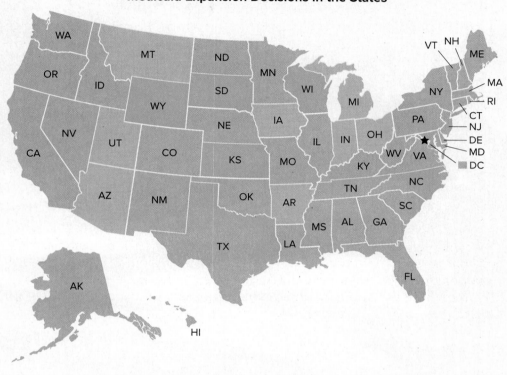

Medicaid Expansion Decisions in the States

▨ 12 states are not expanding Medicaid
▨ 31 states (count includes Washington, DC) are expanding Medicaid
▨ 8 states are expanding Medicaid, but using an alternative to traditional expansion through an 1115 waiver

Source: National Academy for State Health Policy. https://www.nashp.org/states-stand-medicaid-expansion-decisions/

Use the information graphic above to answer the questions.

A. Identify the most common decision regarding state expansion of Medicaid.

B. Describe a similarity or difference in ACA Medicaid expansion by state or region, as illustrated in the information graphic, and draw a conclusion about that similarity or difference.

C. Explain how ACA expansion is an example of federalism.

Chapter
13 Foreign Policy and National Security

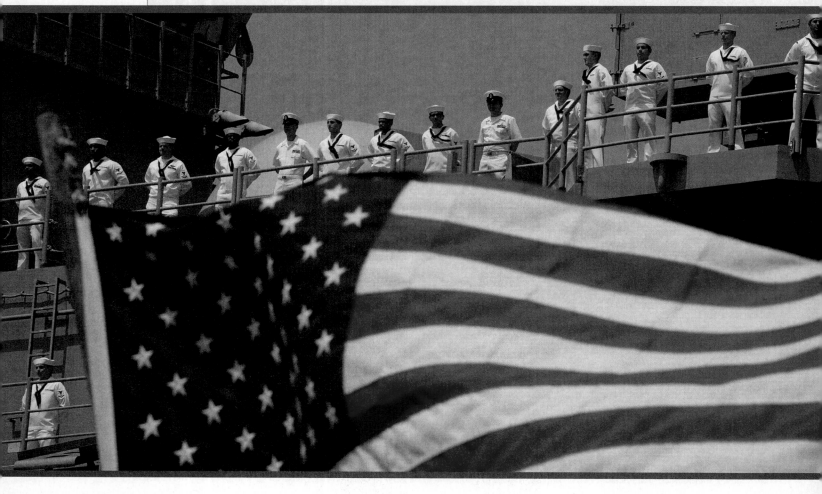

THEN

The emergence of the United States as a superpower and the Cold War dominated U.S. foreign policy in the aftermath of World War II.

NOW

Unpredictability and uncertainty characterize U.S. foreign and national security policy in a rapidly changing context that includes a global pandemic, the continued threat of terrorism, and global economic uncertainty.

NEXT

What will be the long-term repercussions of the COVID-19 pandemic on international relations and the global economy?

How will the continuing threat of terrorism against the United States and other Western democracies influence foreign and national security policy in the future?

Will U.S. foreign policy in the coming years increasingly reflect a clash of civilizations between Western democracies and fundamentalist Islamic actors?

Timothy A. Clary/AFP/Getty Images

■ Chapter Introduction

A previously unfathomable disaster overwhelmed the world in 2020: a global pandemic that halted day-to-day international relations and put nearly every other political crisis on the back burner. With the World Health Organization's declaration of COVID-19 as a pandemic, nearly every country in the world sealed its borders and economies went on lockdown. As COVID-19 devastated public health and wreaked havoc on the global economy, it also challenged governments and disrupted democracies in unprecedented ways. Public health has become a heightened global priority, changing international relations.

As we discussed in the domestic policy chapter, in foreign policy, presidents have more latitude to act in foreign policy matters than they do in domestic policy matters. Upon President Biden's election to the presidency, he announced to the world that "America is back," alluding to his desire to reforge old, neglected alliances and for the United States to resume its role as a key actor on the global stage. The Enduring Understanding from the AP CED that frames this chapter is: *Widely held political ideologies shape policy debates and choices in American policies.* In general, public opinion tends to play a less influential role in shaping specific foreign policies than it does domestic ones. People tend to be less concerned and less interested in foreign policy overall. But while public opinion make take a backseat, ideology does shape the foreign policy process. For example, liberals are more likely to favor lenient trade policies that protect U.S. workers, while conservatives generally would be more supportive of free trade.

The ability of the president to conduct foreign policy is an informal power of the president. The power of the president to conduct foreign policy stems from powers in the Constitution, including the power of the president to serve as commander in chief of the armed forces and the power to negotiate treaties. Essential Knowledge in the AP U.S. Government course is: *Foreign policy — both formal (commander-in-chief and treaties) and informal (executive agreements) powers that influence relations with foreign nations.*

■ The Tools of U.S. Foreign Policy

Government officials use a variety of instruments to shape foreign policy. That is, in creating foreign policy, policymakers rely on a variety of tactics to get foreign nations to bend to the will of the United States. Among these tools are diplomacy, trade and economic policies, and military options. Often, policymakers rely on more than one tool in their dealings with foreign nations.

Diplomacy

Covering a gamut of situations, diplomacy is often foreign policymakers' tool of choice. **Diplomacy** can generally be defined as the conduct of international relations, particularly involving the negotiation of treaties and other agreements between nations. It can include an occurrence as attention-grabbing as a Twitter war between two heads of state or as mundane as the communication between

diplomacy
The conduct of international relations, particularly involving the negotiation of treaties and other agreements between nations.

two embassies when a citizen of one country commits a crime in another. Or it can involve an event as significant as a major summit attended by world leaders. When diplomacy works, we typically do not hear about it.

Among the central figures in the diplomatic arena are **foreign service officers,** the diplomatic and consular staff at American embassies abroad. Foreign service officers, who are employees of the Department of State, conduct formal communications among nations. They are frequently responsible for negotiating many types of international agreements, including economic and trade policies.

Trade and Economic Policies

Almost a century ago, President Woodrow Wilson made this observation: "A nation that is boycotted is a nation that is in sight of surrender. Apply this economic, peaceful, silent, deadly remedy and there will be no need for force. It does not cost a life outside the nation boycotted, but it brings a pressure upon the nation which, in my judgment, no modern nation could resist."[1] It is within this context that U.S. foreign policymakers rely on trade policies, economic aid (foreign aid), and economic penalties to compel foreign governments to conform to the United States's will. Consider President Trump's 2018 decision to impose steep tariffs on steel and aluminum imports: In an effort to save American jobs in those industries, Trump sought to drive up the price of imported steel and aluminum, hoping to increase demand for domestically produced steel and aluminum. Opposition to the president's plan was swift and fierce, with members of his own party being his harshest critics, as Republicans traditionally have favored pro-business free-trade policies. Both Republicans in Congress and a clear consensus of economists argued that imposing tariffs would compel other nations to retaliate by imposing tariffs on goods produced in the United States but sold abroad. In response to those concerns, President Trump tweeted that "trade wars are good, and easy to win." But critics argue that in the past, trade wars have contributed to global recessions. Indeed, the Smoot-Hawley Tariffs of 1930, which imposed large tariffs on imported goods in the early days of the Great Depression, led to retaliatory trade wars that were viewed as exacerbating global economic decline. With that knowledge, the goal of most presidential administrations has been to broadly confer **normal trade relations (NTR) status,** meaning that a country grants a particular trading partner the same, least restrictive trade conditions (that is, the lowest tariff rates) that the country offers to its other favored trading partners—its "most favored nations." U.S. foreign policymakers can bestow most favored nation status on a country to influence it to enact policies the United States prefers. Conversely, they can withhold this status to punish a nation that does not institute policies supportive of the United States's goals.

Governments also use trade agreements as a tool of foreign policy. Among the most important of these agreements in the United States was the North American Free Trade Agreement (NAFTA), whose members included the United States, Mexico, and Canada. NAFTA eliminated barriers to trade and financial investments across the economies of the three nations, but after being a focal point of criticism by President Trump, it was replaced with a renegotiated agreement, the United States–Mexico–Canada Agreement (USMCA). One key component of that agreement was to bolster the automotive parts industry, so starting in 2020, a car or truck must have 75 percent of its components manufactured in Canada, Mexico, or the United States to qualify for zero tariffs, an increase over the 62.5 percent required under NAFTA. Trump administration officials also were able to increase the amount of U.S. dairy products that will be exported to Canada.

Beyond trade policy, American diplomats frequently use economic enticements in the form of foreign aid to pressure other countries into enacting and enforcing policies that the United States supports. Using foreign aid to compel a foreign government to take a specific action became a quite controversial measure during the Trump administration (see "Source Analysis"). But overall, using foreign aid to pursue national interests is not uncommon; for example, in the aftermath of the terrorist attacks of September 11, 2001, the George W. Bush administration sought the cooperation of the Pakistani government in Operation Enduring Freedom, the U.S. military offensive in neighboring Afghanistan.

At that time, the United States sought to overthrow the Islamic fundamentalist Taliban regime, which had harbored and provided training grounds for terrorists, and to capture 9/11 mastermind Osama bin Laden, who was believed to have been hiding in Afghanistan. Before the 9/11 terrorist strikes on domestic U.S. targets, Pakistan had received comparatively little aid from the United States—only about $3.4 million in 2001. But in 2002, Pakistan received more than $1 billion in U.S. aid. This amount tapered off in subsequent years, and in 2018, President Trump announced that the United States was temporarily suspending aid to that country amid allegations that Pakistan was aiding and harboring anti-American terrorist organizations.[2] In 2019, the budget contained $223 million in civilian assistance and $114 million in military aid to Pakistan,[3] but this was contingent on Pakistan taking action "to address areas of national divergence," including ceasing to provide safe haven to terrorists. It also authorized $350 million to support security-enhancement activities along Pakistan's western border, subject to certification requirements that were not met. In 2020, aid to Pakistan was decreased again from the previous year, with an allocation of $70 million for civilian and security aid, though $450 million did go to reimburse Pakistan for logistical and operational support of U.S.-led military operations.[4]

Increasingly, world leaders have recognized that economic policy must be coupled with other types of policies to effectively compel or deter desired actions. For example, after Iranian state media reported that the nation had begun the uranium-enrichment process, President Obama announced that the United States and its allies were developing a host of **sanctions**—penalties that halt economic exchanges (and that may include boycotts and a suspension of cultural exchanges)—on Iran. However, as former senator Christopher Dodd (D-Conn.), who chaired the Banking, Housing, and Urban Affairs Committee, noted: "Economic sanctions are a critical element of U.S. policy toward Iran. But sanctions alone are not sufficient. They must be used as effective leverage, undertaken as part of a coherent, coordinated, comprehensive diplomatic and political strategy which firmly seeks to deter Iran's nuclear ambitions and other actions which pose a threat to regional stability."[5] Under economic pressure from the United States, Great Britain, China, Russia, Germany, and the member states of the European Union, Iran agreed to halt its uranium-enrichment activities in a deal implemented in January 2014. In return, the United States and other nations agreed to lift some sanctions on Iran. The sanctions had effectively crippled Iran's economy, pressuring its leaders to negotiate with the United States and the other nations. After the International Atomic Energy Agency (IAEA) certified that it had succeeded in restricting Iran's sensitive nuclear activities, some sanctions were lifted. Specifically, the deal allowed Iran to export petrochemicals and to import goods and services for its automotive manufacturing and civilian aviation sectors, and to trade in gold and other precious metals. But in 2018, President Trump announced that the United States would withdraw from the deal, opening the possibility that sanctions and bans on imported goods could be unilaterally reinstated by the United States.

sanctions
Penalties that halt economic exchanges.

The Ukraine Transcripts

In 2019, President Trump had a telephone conversation with Ukraine's newly elected president, Volodymyr Zelensky. It was this conversation that led to charges of impeachment being leveled against President Trump for abuse of power. Critics contend that after Zelensky stated that Ukraine needed to buy Javelin anti-tank missiles from the United States, Trump turned the conversation to Ukraine doing "a favor" and subsequently asked Zelensky to have Hunter Biden, the son of President Trump's political rival Joe Biden, investigated. Read the transcript of Trump and Zelensky's call, and then analyze the content.

Declassified by order of the President

September 24, 2019

MEMORANDUM OF TELEPHONE CONVERSATION

SUBJECT: Telephone Conversation with President Zelenskyy* of Ukraine

PARTICIPANTS: President Zelenskyy of Ukraine

NOTETAKERS: The White House Situation Room

DATE, TIME   July 25, 2019, 9:03–9:33 a.m. EDT
AND PLACE: Residence

The President: Congratulations on a great victory. We all watched from the United States and you did a terrific job. The way you came from behind, somebody who wasn't given much of a chance, and you ended up winning easily. It' a fantastic achievement. Congratulations.

President Zelenskyy: You are absolutely right Mr. President. We did win big and we worked hard for this. We worked a lot but I would like to confess to you that I had an opportunity to learn from you. We used quite a few of your skills and knowledge and were able to use it as an example for our elections and yes it is true that these were unique elections. We were in a unique situation that we were able to achieve a unique success. I'm able to tell you the following; the first time, you called me to congratulate me when I won my presidential election, and the second time you are now calling me when my party won the parliamentary election. I think I should run more often so you can call me more often and we can talk over the phone more often.

The President: [laughter] That's a very good idea. I think your country is very happy about that.

President Zelenskyy: Well yes, to tell you the truth, we are trying to work hard because we wanted to drain the swamp here in our country. We brought in many many new people. Not the old politicians, not the typical politicians, because we want to have a new format and a new type of government. You are a great teacher for us and in that.

The President: Well it's very nice of you to say that I will say that we do a lot for Ukraine. We spend a lot of effort and a lot of time. Much more than the European countries are doing and they should be helping you more than they are. Germany does almost nothing for you. All they do is talk and I think it's something that you should really ask them about. When I was speaking to Angela Merkel she talks Ukraine, but she doesn't do anything. A lot of the European countries are the same way so I think it's something you want to look at but the United States has been very very good to Ukraine. I wouldn't say that it's reciprocal necessarily because things are happening that are not good but the United States has been very very good to Ukraine.

President Zelenskyy: Yes you are absolutely right not only 100%, but actually 1000% right. I can tell you the following; I did talk to Angela Merkel and I did meet with her. I also met and talked with Macron and I told them that they are not doing quite as much as they need to be doing on the issues with the sanctions. They are not enforcing the sanctions. They are not working as much as they should work for Ukraine. It turns out that even though logically, the European Union should be our biggest partner but technically the United States is a much bigger partner than the European Union and I'm very grateful to you for that because the United States is doing quite alot for Ukraine. Much more than the European Union especially when we are talking about sanctions against the Russian Federation. I would also like to thank you for your great support in the area of defense. We. are ready to continue to cooperate for the next steps, specifically we are almost ready to buy more Javelins from the United States for defense purposes.

The President: I would like you to do us a favor though because our country has been through a lot and Ukraine knows a lot about it. I would like you to find out what happened with this whole situation with Ukraine, they say Crowdstrike . . . I guess you have one of your wealthy people. The server, they say Ukraine has it. There-are a lot. of things that went on, the whole situation. I think you're surrounding yourself with some of the same people. I would like to have the Attorney General call you or your people and I would like you to get to the bottom of it. As you saw yesterday, that whole nonsense ended with a very poor performance by a man named Robert Mueller, an incompetent performance, but they say a lot of it started with Ukraine. Whatever you can do, it's very important that you do it if that's possible.

President Zelenskyy: Yes it is very important for me and everything that you just mentioned earlier. For me as a President, it is very important and we are open for any future cooperation. We are ready to open a new page on cooperation in relations between the United States and Ukraine. For that purpose, I just recalled our ambassador from United States and he will be replaced by a very competent and very experienced ambassador who will work hard on making sure that our two nations are getting closer. I would also like and hope to see him having your trust and your confidence and have personal relations with you so we can cooperate even more so. I will personally tell you that one of my assistants spoke with Mr. Giuliani just recently and we are hoping very much that Mr. Giuliani will be able to travel to Ukraine and we will meet once he comes to Ukraine. I just wanted to assure you once again that you have nobody but friends around us. I will make sure that I surround myself with the best and most experienced people. I also wanted to tell you that we are friends. We are great friends and you Mr. President have friends in our country so we can continue our strategic partnership. I also plan to surround myself with great people and in addition to that investigation, I guarantee as the President of Ukraine that all the investigations will be done openly and candidly. That I can assure you.

The President: Good because I heard you had a prosecutor who was very good and he was shut down and that's really unfair. A lot of people are talking about that, the way they shut your very good prosecutor down and you had some very bad people involved. Mr. Giuliani is a highly respected man. He was the mayor of New York City, a great mayor, and I would like him to call you. I will ask him to call you along with the Attorney General. Rudy very much knows what's happening and he is a very capable guy. If you could speak to him that would be great. The former ambassador from the United States, the woman, was bad news and the people she was dealing with in the Ukraine were bad news so I just want to let you know that. The other thing, There's a lot of talk about Biden's son, that Biden stopped the prosecution and a lot of people want to find out about that so whatever you can do with the Attorney General would be great. Biden went around bragging that he stopped the prosecution so if you can look into it . . . It sounds horrible to me.

President Zelenskyy: I wanted to tell you about the prosecutor. First of all I understand and I'm knowledgeable about the situation. Since we have won the absolute majority in our Parliament, the next prosecutor general will be 100% my person, my candidate, who will be approved, by the parliament and will start as a new prosecutor in September. He or she will look into the situation, specifically to the company that you mentioned in this issue. The issue of the investigation of the case is actually the issue of making sure to restore the honesty so we will take care of that and will work on the investigation of the case. On top of that, I would kindly ask you if you have any additional information that you can provide to us, it would be very helpful for the investigation to make sure that we administer justice in our country with regard to the Ambassador to the United States from Ukraine as far as I recall her name was Ivanovich. It was great that you were the first one who told me that she was a bad ambassador because I agree with you 100%. Her attitude towards me was far from the best as she admired the previous President and she was on his side. She would not accept me as a new President well enough.

The President: Well, she's going to go through some things. I will have Mr. Giuliani give you a call and I am also going to have Attorney General Barr call and we will get to the bottom of it. I'm sure you will figure it out. I heard the prosecutor was treated very badly and he was a very far prosecutor so good luck with everything. Your economy is going to get better and better I predict. You have a lot of assets. It's a great country. I have many Ukrainian friends, they're incredible people.

President Zelenskyy: I would like to tell you that I also have quite a few Ukrainian friends that live in the United States. Actually last time I traveled to the United States, I stayed in New York near Central Park and I stayed at the Trump Tower. I will talk to them and I hope to see them again in the future. I also wanted to thank you for your invitation to visit the United States, specifically Washington DC. On the other hand, I also want to ensure you that we will be very serious about the case and will work on the investigation. As to the economy, there is much potential for our two countries and one of the issues that is very important for Ukraine is energy independence. I believe we can be very successful and cooperating on energy independence with United States. We are already working on cooperation. We are buying American oil but I am very hopeful for a future meeting. We will have more time and more opportunities to discuss these opportunities and get to know each other better. I would like to thank you very much for your support.

The President: Good. Well, thank you very much and I appreciate that. I will tell Rudy and Attorney General Barr to call. Thank you. Whenever you would like to come to the White House, feel free to call. Give us a date and we'll work that out. I look forward to seeing you.

President Zelenskyy: Thank you very much. I would be very happy to come and would be happy to meet with you personally and get to know you better. I am looking forward to our meeting and I also would like to invite you to visit Ukraine and come to the city bf Kyiv which is a beautiful city. We have a beautiful country Which would welcome you. On the other hand, I believe that on Septermber I we will be in Poland and we can meet in Poland hopefully. After that, it might be a very good idea for you to travel to Ukraine. We can either take my plane and go to Ukraine or we can take your plane, which is probably much better than mine.

The President: Okay, we can work that out. I look forward to seeing you in Washington and maybe in Poland because I think we are going to be there at that time.

President Zelenskyy: Thank you very much Mr. President.

The President: Congratulations on a fantastic job you've done. The whole world was watching. I'm not sure it was so much of an upset but congratulations.

President Zelenskyy: Thank you Mr. President bye-bye.

End of Conversation

Source: The White House, September 2019.

*This White House transcript uses the international spelling of Zelenskyy, sometimes also translated as Zelenskiy, but officially Zelenskyi. We use the common anglicized Zelensky.

Practice Analytical Thinking

1. Much has been made of the president's use of the word "though," as in the sentence, "I would like you to do us a favor though." Given the preceding sentence, what does the word imply?

2. President Trump faced criticism for directing Zelensky to deal with Rudy Guiliani, the president's personal attorney, who held no formal governmental position. What is the problem with relying on nongovernmental officials when dealing with foreign nations?

3. President Trump asked the Ukrainian president to investigate Joe Biden's son, Hunter Biden. Why might relying on a foreign government to investigate the son of a political foe be problematic? What measures should Trump have taken instead if he believed Hunter Biden had engaged in wrongdoing?

The Military Option

When the United States and its allies, France and Great Britain, conducted a series of strategic air strikes in Syria in 2018, they targeted chemical weapons factories in response to an alleged chemical weapon attack by the Syrian government in the rebel-held town of Douma. This move was one in a series of actions by the U.S. government over the course of the presidencies of Donald Trump and his predecessor, Barack Obama, in which the United States and its allies flexed some muscle in the Syrian civil war, but also demonstrated an unwillingness to become involved in a full-on ground war. For example, in 2016, President Obama sent 300 U.S. military personnel to Syria to combat the insurgent group **ISIS,** the Islamic State in Iraq and Syria, a radical international fundamentalist terror organization. ISIS had gained a foothold in Syria in the wake of an anti-government uprising, and while U.S. efforts succeeded in thwarting ISIS's efforts, the conflict has escalated into a full-scale civil war, which has seen the displacement of over 11 million people.

ISIS
The Islamic State in Iraq and Syria, a radical international fundamentalist terror organization.

THE USE OF THE MILITARY OPTION AFTER THE 9/11 TERROR ATTACKS The military action in the Middle East today is a consequence of foreign policy in the aftermath of the September 11, 2001, terrorist strikes, and the subsequent U.S. government reactions, demonstrating how the creators of foreign policy use the military option as an instrument of foreign policy. Hungry for an enemy after the 2001 deadly attacks on American soil, the United States targeted

Afghanistan's Taliban regime. The Taliban had supported and harbored members of al-Qaeda ("The Base"), the radical Islamic fundamentalist terrorist organization that took credit for the 9/11 bloodshed. Foreign intelligence had pointed to Osama bin Laden, a Saudi millionaire living in Afghanistan, as the engineer of the attacks. U.S. military presence in Afghanistan has continued through 2019, with insurgent violence escalating and the United States responding with increased numbers of U.S. troops, in an attempt to quell concern that the Taliban regime will continue to allow anti-U.S. terrorist organizations to operate training camps in unsecured areas of the nation, camps that could train terrorists for missions outside Afghanistan.

A NEW BRAND OF ENEMY: NON-STATE ACTORS That fear is grounded in the reality that world terrorist activity today transcends national borders. Like ISIS militants today, the September 11 terrorists themselves were not citizen-soldiers of any one country but were nationals from countries across the globe. They had trained in various nations, including Afghanistan, and had been supported by citizens of still other countries. Thus, no single, clear nation-state was the enemy. Without a concrete enemy (over which a victory could be defined and declared), the Bush administration requested, and Congress passed, a formal declaration of a "war on terror."

One part of that war on terror included an invasion of Iraq, though that nation had not played a part in the September 11 attacks. But the George W. Bush administration, particularly then-secretary of state Colin Powell, made a case to the United Nations and to the American people alleging that U.S. intelligence indicated that the Saddam Hussein regime in Iraq was harboring **weapons of mass destruction (WMDs)**—nuclear, chemical, and biological weapons.[6] In response to what at the time appeared to be a credible threat, American troops invaded Iraq on March 20, 2003. The military strike toppled the Hussein regime, which the United States had supported for years through foreign aid.[7] Following the invasion, weapons inspectors conducted a thorough search of suspected weapons sites, but no WMDs were ever found, leaving many critics of the Bush administration to question the administration's motives and to ask whether the intelligence community had been pressured by administration officials to find intelligence rationalizing the war in Iraq.[8] From 2003 to 2016, over 4,500 U.S. troops died in Iraq, along with hundreds of other coalition forces and 500,000 Iraqi civilians, a figure that is increasing as insurgent violence continues. In the power vacuum that existed after American troops left Iraq, ISIS was able to seize control in many areas of the nation.

THE GOAL OF THE MILITARY OPTION When military conflict occurs on a grand scale—for the United States, that would include the wars in Afghanistan and Iraq, as well as the Gulf War (1990–1991), the Vietnam War (1965–1975), the Korean War (1950–1953), and the two world wars (1914–1918 and 1939–1945), the goal often is **regime change,** the replacement of a country's government with another government by facilitating the deposing of its leader or leading political party. That is, rather than attempting to change another nation's policies, historically wars were typically fought to end the reign of the enemy nations' leaders. On the other hand, most military action by the United States in the past century has occurred on a smaller scale, as policymakers have sought to change the policy in another country, as has been the case with the U.S. air strikes on Syrian targets.

weapons of mass destruction (WMDs)
Nuclear, chemical, and biological weapons.

regime change
The replacement of a country's government with another government by facilitating the deposing of its leader or leading political party.

Who Decides? The Creators and Shapers of Foreign Policy

In the United States, the executive and legislative branches are the primary foreign policymakers, with the president and the executive branch playing the dominant role. However, a variety of interests—from the media, to interest groups, to other nations, and even private individuals—provide the context of the foreign policy process and contribute to shaping the policy outcomes of that process.

The President and the Executive Branch

The president of the United States is the foremost foreign policy actor in the world. This vast power derives in part from the president's constitutionally prescribed duties, particularly the role of commander in chief of the U.S. armed forces. Presidents' foreign policy powers also have roots in the way the institution of the presidency has evolved and continues to evolve. Other government institutions, especially the U.S. Congress, have some ability to rein in the president's foreign policy authority. But U.S. presidents in the 21st century remain the central figures in the foreign policy arena, owing to presidential resources such as cabinet departments and the national intelligence community, as well as the executive prestige that supplements presidents' legal and administrative powers.

THE DEPARTMENTS OF STATE AND DEFENSE In the executive branch, the Departments of State and Defense take the lead in advising the president about foreign and military policy issues. Typically, these relationships tend to be cooperative, with members of the permanent bureaucracy carrying out informed policies prioritized by a particular president. During the Trump administration, however, the relationship between the president and administration officials, on the one hand, and non-political members of the State Department, on the other, were often at odds, as bureaucrats accustomed to carrying out deliberative policy sometimes found themselves being circumvented by administration officials. But the foreign policy bureaucracy is a vast one: Specifically, the Department of State, headed by the secretary of state, has more than 30,000 employees located both within the United States and abroad. (State Department employees work at more than 300 U.S. consular offices around the world.) These staff members are organized according to topical specialty (trade policy, environmental policy, and so on) and geographic area specialty (the Middle East or Southeast Asia, for example). Political appointees hold many of the top ambassadorial posts. These ambassadors and the career members of the foreign service who staff each **country desk**—the official operation of the U.S. government in each country with diplomatic ties to the United States—help to shape and administer U.S. foreign policy in those countries.

country desk
The official operation of the U.S. government in each country that has diplomatic ties to the United States.

The Department of Defense, often referred to as the Pentagon for its five-sided headquarters, is headed by the secretary of defense. The modern Department of Defense traces its history to the end of World War II, although it is the successor of the Department of War established at the nation's founding. The Defense Department is the cabinet department that oversees all branches of the U.S. military. Thus, although the Army, Navy, Marines, Air Force, and Coast Guard operate independently, administratively they are part of the Department of Defense. The commanding officers of each branch of the military, plus a chairperson and a vice chairperson, make up the Joint Chiefs of Staff, important military advisers to the president. Increasingly, both the State and the Defense Departments rely on private contractors to perform some functions typically associated with these respective departments, particularly overseas.

THE NATIONAL SECURITY COUNCIL AND THE INTELLIGENCE COMMUNITY As discussed in Chapter 5, the National Security Council, consisting of the vice president, the secretary of state, the secretary of the treasury, the secretary of defense, and the national security adviser, advises and assists the president on national security and foreign policy.

Through the input of the National Security Council, the president's administration considers the country's top security matters. The National Security Council also coordinates foreign policy approaches among the various government agencies that will implement them. A recent addition to the foreign policy apparatus, the national security adviser has traditionally competed with the secretary of state for influence over foreign policy—and for influence over the president as well. The tension between the two advisers also stems from the differing approaches each agency takes in shaping foreign policy. Frequently, the State Department has a long-term view of world affairs and advocates for foreign policies in keeping with long-term goals. In contrast, the National Security Council focuses more on short-term crises and objectives.

A key resource in presidential foreign policy making is the intelligence community. Chief among the agencies in this community is the Central Intelligence Agency (CIA). This independent agency of the federal government is responsible for collecting, analyzing, evaluating, and disseminating foreign intelligence to the president and senior national policymakers. Like the National Security Council, the modern CIA was created by the National Security Act of 1947 at the dawn of the Cold War to monitor the actions of the expansionist Soviet Union. During the Cold War, the CIA expanded its mission, using agents to penetrate the governments of foreign countries, influence their politics, and foment insurrections when the president deemed such tactics necessary to promote American interests. At times, particularly after September 11, 2001, critics have argued that the agency, along with the Federal Bureau of Investigation (FBI), had failed in their duty to avert the terrorist strikes. Congress scrutinized both agencies for lapses in intelligence and apprehension. Because the CIA and the FBI had been seriously understaffed in Arabic translators, neither agency had the means to interpret intercepted messages that might have enabled them to prevent the tragedy.

director of national intelligence (DNI)
The person responsible for coordinating and overseeing all the intelligence agencies within the executive branch.

Spurred by the 9/11 Commission's findings, President Bush announced in 2005 the appointment of a national intelligence czar, called the **director of national intelligence (DNI).** This individual is responsible for coordinating and overseeing all the intelligence agencies within the executive branch.

Congress

Along with the president, Congress enjoys significant constitutional authority in foreign policy making. The constitutional provisions that outline congressional authority with respect to foreign relations include, prominently, Congress's power to declare war. In modern times, however, presidential administrations have circumvented this congressional power by using U.S. troops without a formal congressional declaration of war. Such was the case in the Vietnam War, for example.

Does the President have too much power in foreign policymaking?

The Constitution designed foreign policymaking to be shared between the president and Congress, making the president commander in chief and giving the Congress the power to declare war, and by providing the president with the power to negotiate treaties and the Senate the power to ratify them.

The power of the president to conduct foreign policy unilaterally has been expanding for decades. The last time the U.S. declared war was in World War II, yet troops have been dispatched into hostile situations overseas on many occasions, creating a situation in which some question whether or not the war declaration power of Congress will ever be utilized again. Presidents can also freely negotiate with other countries without Senate involvement via executive agreements.

Develop an argument about whether presidents have too much power in foreign policymaking.

In your essay, you must:

- Articulate a defensible claim or thesis that responds to the prompt and establishes a line of reasoning

- Support your claim with at least TWO pieces of accurate and relevant information:

  - At least ONE piece of evidence must be from one of the following foundational documents:

    — *Federalist* No. 78
    — The U.S. Constitution

  - Use a second piece of evidence from another foundational document from the list or from your study of foreign policymaking

- Use reasoning to explain why your evidence supports your claim/thesis

- Respond to an opposing or alternative perspective using refutation, concession, or rebuttal

---

In response to this presidential tactic, Congress in 1973 passed the **War Powers Act.** This law limits presidential use of military forces to 60 days, with an automatic extension of 30 days if the president requests such an extension. But the War Powers Act quickly became less effective than it was in the days of traditional warfare, since most modern warfare is measured in weeks rather than months (the wars in Iraq and Afghanistan being exceptions). In the aftermath of the 9/11 attacks, Congress passed the Authorization for Use of Military Force

War Powers Act
A law that limits presidential use of military forces to 60 days, with an automatic extension of 30 additional days if the president requests such an extension.

(AUMF), which weakened the War Powers Act by essentially giving the president broad authority to use the Armed Forces. As the AUMF states, "the President is authorized to use all necessary and appropriate force against those nations, organizations, or persons he determines planned, authorized, committed, or aided the terrorist attacks that occurred on September 11, 2001, or harbored such organizations or persons in order to prevent any future acts of international terrorism against the United States by such nations, organizations or persons."

Three successive presidents (G.W. Bush, Obama, and Trump) have used the AUMF to justify the use of military force. In 2020, President Trump used the AUMF to rationalize his decision to assassinate Iranian Major General Qassim Soleimani, the director of the regional military Quds Force and a popular leader in Iran, who Trump said was planning an attack on the United States or allies in the Middle East. In the aftermath of the assassination, tensions between the United States and Iran escalated because Soleimani had been a government official, and fears in Congress were that Trump's decision could lead to war if Iran retaliated in a drastic fashion. With this escalation, some in Congress called for revisiting the AUMF, so Congress could reclaim the constitutional power to declare war that it had previously handed to the president.

But Congress's ability to shape foreign policy does not rest merely with its authority to declare war. Congressional powers with respect to foreign relations also include the authority of the U.S. Senate to ratify treaties, as well as to confirm presidential appointees to ambassadorial posts and to cabinet positions (including those of the secretaries of defense and state). Furthermore, one of Congress's greatest powers is its control of the purse strings. This control means that although the president can order troops into action, the members of Congress must authorize spending for such an operation.

The Military-Industrial Complex

In his farewell address, President Dwight D. Eisenhower (1953–1961), Supreme Allied Commander of Europe during World War II, warned the nation of the influence of the expanding military-industrial complex. Eisenhower stressed that the American people and their representatives in government must "guard against the acquisition of unwarranted influence" and noted that "only an alert and knowledgeable citizenry can compel the proper meshing of the industrial and military machinery of defense with our peaceful methods and goals so that security and liberty may prosper together."[9]

Eisenhower was describing the mutually advantageous—and potentially corrupting—collusion among the U.S. armed forces, the defense industry, and Congress. These three entities have the potential to develop "unwarranted influence" over foreign policy in general and defense spending in particular, for several reasons. First, the goals of the military and the goals of the defense industry often intersect. Consider, for example, the military's need to supply soldiers with the appropriate equipment to fight wars. Both the military complex and the defense industry benefit from doing so: The military wants to protect its troops and help ensure their success on the battleground, and the defense industry seeks to sell such goods to the military—and reap a healthy profit.

A second reason that the military-industrial complex has the potential to be so highly influential is the close personal and professional relationships that flourish between the individuals in the military and their counterparts in the defense industry. These relationships are similar to the associations that develop in the case of iron triangles. Indeed, many retired military personnel often put their military expertise to work in "retirement jobs" with defense contractors or as congressional lobbyists.

For many congressional districts throughout the United States, spending by the federal government for military bases, personnel, and defense contracts represents an important infusion of money into the local economy. When this economic influence is combined with the clout members of the military, veterans, their interest groups, and their families can wield, we can see why many members of Congress support the military-industrial complex.

SOURCE ANALYSIS   ANALYZING VISUAL SOURCES

©Jeff Stahler/Distributed by Universal Uclick for UFS via CartoonStock.com

Jeff Stahler/CartoonStock

Source Analysis is one of the required skills in AP US Government, to include political cartoons. when presented with a political cartoon to analyze, you will need to be able to:

- Describe the authors claim(s), perspective, evidence, and reasoning.

  To do this, you will need to describe the characters, objects, and actions in the cartoon. What is the cartoon above about? There is text in the cartoon above. How does the text contribute to the message the author is attempting to convey?

- Explain how the implications of the author's argument or perspective may affect political principles, institutions, processes, policies and behaviors.

  To do this for the cartoon above, what perspective is the cartoonist supporting about foreign policy? What alternative perspectives exist? Finally, what is the implication of the cartoonist's argument?

The Media and New Technologies

Because of the pervasiveness and reach of the media, foreign policy decisions provide prime fodder for news reporting. But the media and new technologies go well beyond monitoring and reporting on foreign policy; they also frequently play a role in shaping the country's foreign policy and in influencing the conduct of that policy.

Since the beginning of the 20th century, the U.S. government has used the news media in an organized way to promote its foreign policy priorities. During World War I, newspapers ran ads calling on Americans to take all kinds of actions to help the war effort, from cleaning their plates and planting "victory gardens" (to conserve food supplies for soldiers) to buying war bonds to help finance the war. By World War II, filmmakers spurred Americans to action, from enlisting in the armed services to conserving food fats and saving scrap metal for the war effort. In those various wartime initiatives, the media worked hand in hand with the government and generally took a highly patriotic and supportive stance. By the era of the Vietnam War, however, journalists, particularly television reporters stationed among U.S. troops in the faraway Asian country, painted a grimmer, more realistic canvas, focusing on the ravages of war that most Americans had never before seen. Today, new technologies can provide a check both on the government and on the media, as private citizens now have the ability to communicate directly with news and Internet platforms, enabling the whole world to watch events across the globe unfold. In this way, citizen activists rely on social media outlets to organize and mobilize across geographic borders.

The news media and technology influence the conduct and substance of foreign policy by increasing public awareness and thus by shaping the foreign policy agenda. President Trump's use of Twitter provides the perfect example, as one tweet heightens awareness of foreign policy positions, whether concerning North Korea, China, Iran, or even relations with U.S. allies. By focusing public attention on a certain area of the world or on a particular aspect of foreign policy, the media shape the priorities of, and the policies made by, the foreign policy apparatus.

New technologies have also been used as a tool for foreign policymakers, specifically as a means of surveillance against foreign governments, including U.S. allies, but other forms of new technologies, specifically unmanned drones, also have been used in conducting attacks against targets in Afghanistan, Pakistan, Somalia, and Yemen. According to investigative journalist sources, nearly 14,000 U.S. drone attacks have killed as many as 16,500 individuals, 2,300 of them civilians, and as many as 484 children.[10] The media also play a powerful role by serving as a watchdog to ensure that the actions of men and women who implement foreign policy "in the trenches" are consistent with the intentions of policymakers who craft the policies.

Public Opinion

In general, public opinion tends to play a less influential role in shaping specific foreign policies than it does in domestic issues. The public might voice strong opinions and call for politicians to fight terrorism in the wake of the saturated media reporting after a terrorist attack. But in general, people tend to be less concerned, less informed, and less interested in foreign policy matters than in domestic issues. Thus, the public at large is likely to accept the views and actions of the individuals who make their country's foreign policy.

Public opinion plays a comparatively small role in shaping foreign policy for several reasons. First, foreign policy is made incrementally, over years and decades, and keeping up with international developments in different parts of the world is not something that many individuals or even news organizations do. Often, international issues must reach crisis proportions before media coverage becomes significant and exerts an impact on public opinion.

Many Americans also feel less connected to foreign policy decisions than they do to domestic policy issues. While individuals may feel empathy for the victims of the refugee crisis, foreign policy crises typically have less bearing on their own lives than, say, whether their mortgage payments will increase because of Federal Reserve policy or whether more student loans will be available to pay their tuition. Despite this disconnect between most people's everyday lives and pressing issues in foreign policy, individuals nonetheless can and do influence foreign policy decisions, as we now consider.

Private Citizens

Individuals can have an impact on the foreign policy process. Consider the various educational exchange programs that arrange for students from one country to visit another. In effect, such visitors act as **public diplomats**—individuals who promote their country's interests by shaping the host country's perception of their homeland, not only through educational but also through business or entertainment initiatives that advance mutual understanding.

public diplomat
An individual outside government who promotes his or her country's interests and thus helps to shape international perceptions of the nation

>> Sometimes soccer is more than just a sport. At the "Korean Derby"—FIFA's World Cup 2022 qualifier—South Korea's Hwang Hee-chan (L) tries to shoot the ball against North Korea. Sports figures sometimes act as public diplomats, advancing understanding of their nation and shaping perceptions of their homeland.

Yonhap News/YNA/Newscom

World events can become an influence in American foreign policy, too, when individuals take personal causes that are related to their ethnic origins to the White House and Congress. The influence of domestic interests on foreign policy, called **intermestics,** plays a distinct part in foreign policy making.

intermestics
The influence of domestic interests on foreign policy.

A powerful example of intermestics involves the large number of Cuban immigrants in Florida, many of whom are refugees or descendants of refugees from the regime of Fidel Castro. This influential group effectively swayed U.S. policy toward imposing the embargo against the Castro government and keeping it in effect since 1962. Many of them also encouraged tightened travel and currency restrictions between the United States and Cuba. But as the revolution generation of immigrants has aged, many younger Cuban Americans hold less pronounced hostility toward Cuba, and they believe that normalizing relations with Cuba will both improve the lot of the Cuban people and bring proximity to openness and democracy, which might in turn plant seeds for reforms that isolationism has failed to bring about.

U.S. Foreign Policy in Historical Context

As those who make and shape U.S. foreign policy continue to confront contemporary challenges, they can look back on two broad historical traditions with respect to American foreign relations: isolationism and intervention. Historically, an initial policy of **isolationism,** a foreign policy characterized by a country's unwillingness to participate in international affairs, gave way to **interventionism,** the willingness of a country to take part and intervene in international situations, including another country's affairs.

isolationism
A foreign policy characterized by a nation's unwillingness to participate in international affairs.

interventionism
A foreign policy characterized by a nation's willingness to participate and intervene in international situations, including another country's affairs.

The Constitutional Framework and Early Foreign Policy Making

In drafting the Constitution, the founders sought to remove the United States from international affairs. They reasoned that it was best for the new American republic to stay out of the deadly wars that had plagued Europe for centuries and because of which many Americans had left their native lands. Because of that isolationist outlook, the founders structured the Constitution so that responsibility for conducting foreign affairs rests exclusively with the national government rather than with the states.

THE CONSTITUTION AND FOREIGN POLICY POWERS The Constitution provides for shared responsibility for foreign policy making in the national government between the executive and the legislative branches. The Constitution grants the president very specific powers. These include powers related to the role of commander in chief, to making treaties, and to appointing and receiving ambassadors. In comparison, Congress's powers in foreign policy making are broader. Moreover, the Constitution structures executive and legislative powers as complementary. Note that the Constitution provides for checks and balances: although the president is commander in chief, Congress declares war and raises and supports an army and navy. Political scientist Roger Davidson has termed the give-and-take between presidential and congressional power "an invitation to struggle," reflecting the founders' attempt to ensure that neither entity dominates the process.[11]

EARLY ISOLATIONISM In keeping with the founders' emphasis on isolationism, President George Washington's Farewell Address in 1796 warned the young government against involving the United States in entangling alliances. Washington feared that membership in such international associations would draw a war-weary people and a war-weakened nation into further conflicts. He refused to accept the advice of either his secretary of state, Thomas Jefferson, who favored an alliance with France, or his treasury secretary, Alexander Hamilton, who wanted stronger ties to Great Britain. As a general who knew firsthand about the ravages of war and who also was the first American leader to connect foreign and defense policy, Washington set the tone for the United States' role in the world for the next 200 years.

>> *Burning of the Frigate Philadelphia in the Harbor of Tripoli, February 16, 1804,* a painting by Edward Moran (1829–1901), shows the USS Philadelphia aflame in Tripoli Harbor during the Barbary Wars.

Universal History Archive/UIG/Getty images

FOREIGN TRADE AND THE EROSION OF U.S. ISOLATIONISM During Washington's tenure as president and in the next several successive administrations, the United States' primary activity in the international arena was trade. Rich in natural resources and blessed with an industrious labor force, the United States sought to increase its wealth by selling raw materials and supplies to all sides in the Napoleonic Wars (1792–1815), the latest in the never-ending series of European conflicts. The French Empire took exception to the United States' provision of supplies to its enemies, and when France captured ships that it alleged were bound for enemy ports, the United States was forced into an undeclared naval war with France in the 1790s.

Neutral international trade was a difficult feat to accomplish in the American republic's early years. American ships had to cross sea lanes where neutrality was not the governing principle; instead, pirates, warring nations, and the allies of warring nations controlled the seas, and nationality counted for little. When pirates off the Barbary Coast of Africa seized ships and their crews, which they held for ransom, the United States fought the Barbary Wars (1801–1805 and 1815) against the North African Barbary states (what are now Morocco, Algeria, Tunisia, and Libya).

Throughout the early part of the 19th century, the seas proved a difficult place for American sailors. During that time, the British Navy began the practice of **impressment,** or forcing merchant sailors off U.S. ships—in effect, kidnapping them—on the spurious grounds that American sailors were "deserters" from the British Navy. In protest of this policy, Congress passed the Embargo Act of 1807, which forced U.S. ships to obtain approval from the American government before departing for foreign ports. But the British continued impressments and the Embargo Act seriously curtailed the amount of U.S. goods being exported. Overall, the Embargo Act harmed the U.S. economy, as the decline in trade spurred more economic woes.

The tensions between the United States and Great Britain escalated as the practice of impressment continued. When the United States sought to increase its

impressment
The forcible removal of merchant sailors from U.S. ships on the spurious grounds that the sailors were deserters from the British Navy.

territory northward into Canada (then still part of the British Empire), the United States and Great Britain fought the War of 1812 over the United States' desire to annex portions of Canada and to put a halt to the practice of impressments. The war was relatively short-lived, ending with the signing of the Treaty of Ghent in 1814, when the British decided that their military resources could be better used against France in the Napoleonic Wars.

Hegemony and National Expansion: From the Monroe Doctrine to the Roosevelt Corollary

After the conclusion of the War of 1812 in 1814 and of the Napoleonic Wars in 1815, peace settled over the United States and Europe. Still, some American politicians feared that European nations—especially France, Spain, and Russia—would attempt to assert or reassert their influence in the Western Hemisphere. Thus, the view arose in American foreign policy-making circles that the United States should establish **hegemony**—a form of imperial geographic dominance—over its own hemisphere. In 1823, President James Monroe declared that "the American continents by the free and independent condition which they have assumed and maintain, are henceforth not to be considered as subjects for future colonization by any European power." Known as the **Monroe Doctrine,** this policy attempted to prevent European nations from colonizing any nations in North or South America. Monroe's declaration, however, sounded more like bravado than policy because the United States was still too weak militarily to chase a European power away from South America, Central America, or the Caribbean. But the United States' interest in preventing the colonization of the Americas was consistent with the interest of the British, who did not want to see European rivals dominating in the Americas. Thus, Monroe's doctrine had the backing of the still-formidable British fleet.

With the Americas out of play, European countries were expanding their colonial empires in Africa and the Middle East during the first half of the 19th century. Meanwhile, the United States also extended its territories westward and solidified its borders. Supporters of the theory of **manifest destiny**—the idea that it was the United States's destiny to expand throughout the North American continent—used this concept to rationalize the spread of U.S. territory. As the philosophy of manifest destiny took hold on the popular imagination, the United States expanded west to the Pacific Ocean, as well as south and southwest.

During this era, too, the United States became increasingly active in profitable international trade, particularly with China and Japan. To facilitate this Pacific trade—which was a primary goal of American policymakers—the United States acquired the islands of Hawaii, Wake, and Midway and part of Samoa in the 1890s. In 1898, on the pretext of ending Spanish abuses in Cuba and instigated by a jingoistic (extremely nationalistic and aggressive) President William McKinley and press, the United States decided to fight Spain, which by then was the weakest of the colonial powers. The United States won the Spanish-American War handily, and the victory increased the country's international prestige.

Theodore Roosevelt, who later became president, achieved enormous national popularity during the Spanish-American War for his leadership of the Rough Riders, a cavalry regiment. Their charge up San Juan Hill in Cuba in 1898 was the war's bloodiest and most famous battle. As spoils, the United States obtained the Philippines, Guam, Puerto Rico, and—temporarily—Cuba from Spain. Roosevelt supported the United States's entry into the war and later, as president (1901–1909), added his own

hegemony
A form of imperial geographic dominance.

Monroe Doctrine
President James Monroe's 1823 declaration that the Americas should not be considered subjects for future colonization by any European power.

manifest destiny
The idea that it was the United States's destiny to spread throughout the North American continent; used to rationalize the expansion of U.S. territory.

famous dictum to the Monroe Doctrine: the **Roosevelt Corollary.** He announced that to ensure stability in the region, the United States had the right to act as an "international police power" and intervene in Latin America—and indeed, the entire Western Hemisphere—if the situation in any country warranted the intervention of a "civilized society."

After Roosevelt became president, the United States intervened in Panama, where U.S.-backed revolutionaries won independence from Colombia in 1903. The United States then immediately began construction on the Panama Canal in 1904. The canal improved the flow of trade by reducing the length of time ships took to travel between the Atlantic and Pacific Oceans.

World War I and the End of U.S. Isolationism

Encouraged by its successful efforts at colonization and strong enough by this time to ignore George Washington's admonition about avoiding foreign entanglements, the nation became embroiled in two major European wars in the 20th century: World War I and World War II. The United States's isolation from the world ended with these two wars, even though strong isolationist forces in Congress and the White House continued to play a role during the first half of the 20th century.

World War I came about primarily because of the balance of power system that dominated the world's foreign policy decisions from the end of the Napoleonic Wars in 1815 until the conclusion of World War I in 1918. The **balance of power system** was a system of international alliances that, in theory, would balance the power of one group of nations against the power of another group and thus discourage war. So, for example, when it was perceived that England was becoming too powerful in this European balance of power in the 1770s, France, Spain, and Holland assisted the colonial forces in the American Revolution in an effort to bring the British down a notch. For nearly a century, that attempt to bring order to international relations worked, and Europe enjoyed a long period of peace. But a flaw of the balance of power system was that a relatively small skirmish could escalate into a major international incident because of agreements for **collective defense**—the idea that allied nations agree to defend one another in the face of invasion—that were inherent in the system. Such was the case in 1914 in Sarajevo when a young Bosnian Serb student assassinated Archduke

Roosevelt Corollary
The idea, advanced by President Theodore Roosevelt, that the United States had the right to act as an "international police power" in the Western Hemisphere to ensure stability in the region.

balance of power system
A system of international alliances that, in theory, would balance the power of one group of nations against the power of another group and thus discourage war.

collective defense
The concept that allied nations agree to defend one another in the face of an invasion.

Ferdinand, heir to the Austro-Hungarian throne. The assassin was a member of a group seeking Bosnia's independence from the Austro-Hungarian Empire. The empire demanded that Serbia respond to the assassination, and when it determined that Serbia had not responded, it declared war. Austria-Hungary's declaration of war led to a sweeping domino effect that had the European continent in full-scale war within weeks of that initial declaration because of those alliances and collective defense obligations between nations.

The United States entered World War I in 1917, three years after the conflict began and largely at the behest of Britain. U.S. participation led President Woodrow Wilson to formulate the first conceptual framework for world governance that had ever been articulated. The most effective way to maintain peace, Wilson believed, was through **collective security**—the idea that peace could be achieved if nations agreed to collectively oppose any nation that attacked another country. By using this approach, nations at peace could prevent war by working together to restrain the lawlessness inherent in more unstable parts of the world.

collective security
The idea that peace could be achieved if nations agreed to collectively oppose any nation that attacked another country.

Internationalism and the League of Nations

League of Nations
A representative body founded in the aftermath of World War I to establish the collective security of nations.

In negotiating the end of World War I at the Paris Peace Conference, Wilson sought to organize a **League of Nations,** a representative body that would ensure the collective security of nations. Wilson was successful in convincing representatives at the Paris meetings of the need for such an organization. But he was less successful in convincing Congress of the merits of the League of Nations. In 1918, the Republican-controlled Senate (Wilson was a Democrat) refused to ratify the Treaty of Versailles, which included among the terms for ending World War I the formation of the League of Nations. Without the United States, the League died a natural death before being replaced near the end of World War II by the United Nations.

In the dawning days of World War I, the United States was still heeding George Washington's call to avoid entangling alliances. At the war's conclusion, isolationism remained a key tenet of U.S. foreign policy. In the years immediately following the war, trade reasserted itself as the key component of U.S. foreign policy. The Industrial Revolution was in full swing, and the United States depended on the import of raw materials and the export of manufactured goods to grease the wheels of its prosperous economy in the 1920s. During this time, however, Europe was healing from the ravages of World War I, and growth in its manufacturing sector meant serious competition for American industry.

The U.S. economy suffered another blow in 1929 when the stock market crashed, marking the beginning of the Great Depression. And the trade war that resulted from the Smoot-Hawley Tariff exacerbated the Depression, causing industrialists, as well as citizens who saw the economic impact of an isolated United States, to question the isolationism that had characterized U.S. foreign policy to date—from the era of Washington to the era of Smoot-Hawley.

World War II: U.S. Foreign Policy at a Crossroads

World War I was supposed to be the "war to end all wars." In hindsight, however, many observers believed that the victors only sowed the seeds of World War II (1939–1945). By impoverishing the defeated Germany through the imposition of huge reparations (compensation paid by a defeated nation to the victors for war damages) and the loss of 13 percent of its territory, the Treaty of Versailles (1919) created the environment that gave Adolf Hitler, the fascist leader of Germany, the opportunity to succeed politically. With his aggressive foreign policy, Hitler aimed to expand the German homeland at the expense of non-Germanic populations.

Influenced by a strong isolationist group in Congress, the United States waited until two years after the official start of the war in 1939 to declare war. Following a deadly Japanese attack on the U.S. naval base at Pearl Harbor, Hawaii, in December 1941, the United States declared war first on Japan and then on the other Axis powers (Germany and Italy) after those countries declared war on the United States. Following years of fighting on multiple fronts, in August 1945 the United States dropped two atomic bombs on the Japanese cities of Hiroshima and Nagasaki. Those devastating attacks ended the war.

The question remains whether the United States would have joined the efforts of the Allies (the United States, England, France, China, and the Soviet Union) sooner had policymakers known about the **Holocaust**—the murder by Hitler and his subordinates of 6 million Jews, along with political dissidents, Catholics, homosexuals, Roma, and individuals with disabilities. Newspapers did not report the genocide until 1943, well after the war was under way. The experience of fighting World War II and dealing with its aftermath forced U.S. policymakers to reassess the country's role in the world, as well as the policies that governed its entire approach to foreign affairs.

Holocaust
The genocide perpetrated by Adolf Hitler and the Nazis of 6 million Jews, along with political dissidents, Catholics, homosexuals, individuals with disabilities, and Roma.

The Postwar Era: The United States as Superpower

The post-World War II era saw the emergence of two of the Allied victors, the United States and the Soviet Union, as **superpowers**—leader nations with dominating influence in international affairs. The United States's role as superpower in a new international system, and the relationship between these superpowers, would shape America's foreign policy for the remainder of the 20th century. Increasingly important in this new era was the role that **multilateral** (many-sided, or supported by numerous nations) organizations and agreements would play.

superpowers
Leader nations with dominating influence in international affairs.

multilateral
Many-sided; having the support of numerous nations.

International Agreements and Organizations

In the aftermath of World War II, the United States was intent on avoiding the mistakes of the Treaty of Versailles, which many policymakers felt had led directly to the conditions that produced the war. They proceeded to address those mistakes one by one, often forming international organizations equipped to respond to the public policy challenges confronting the postwar world.

A key component of the postwar recovery effort was the **Marshall Plan.** Named for Secretary of State George Marshall, the program provided the funds necessary for Western European countries—even the United States's enemies during World War II—to rebuild. War-ravaged nations, including defeated (West) Germany, soon became economic powerhouses, thanks to initial help from the Marshall Plan. Ironically, by forcing the Germans to demilitarize as a condition of their surrender, the Allies freed Germany from spending large amounts of its own tax money on defense, thus enabling the German people to devote more of their resources to

Marshall Plan
The U.S. government program that provided funds necessary for Western European countries to rebuild after World War II.

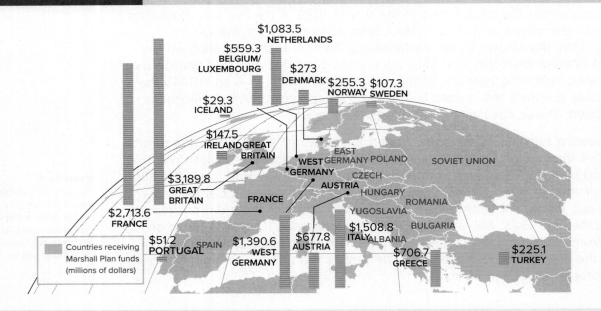

FIGURE 13.1 ■ **Recipients of Marshall Plan Aid, 1948–1951.** What were the effects of the Marshall Plan? How does this approach to postwar foreign policy differ from more modern examples?

Source: CNN, Cold War 3/24, Marshall Plan

economic development. Other countries impoverished by war also benefited from the Marshall Plan (Figure 13.1), creating new markets for U.S. products. Eastern European nations, now securely under Soviet influence, were prevented from participating. Because of the plan's success in Western Europe, the United States recognized that economic development and peace were intertwined, that economic stability was critical if future wars were to be prevented, and that an international approach was preferable to isolationism in foreign policy.

THE UNITED NATIONS The Allied victors of World War II recognized the need for a structure to ensure collective security. In that spirit, U.S. officials organized a meeting in San Francisco in 1945 with 50 U.S. allies, all of whom agreed to create the **United Nations (UN).** Participants hoped that this international body, through collective security, would develop the capacity to prevent future wars. The charter of the United Nations created these components:

United Nations (UN)
An international body established in 1945 in order to prevent future wars by achieving collective security and peace.

- *United Nations (UN):* established in 1945, an international body intended to prevent future wars by achieving collective security and peace.

- *Security Council:* 11 members, 5 of which—including the United States, the Soviet Union (now Russia), China, Great Britain, and France—are permanent members with the power to veto any action taken by the council. Today, the Security Council consists of 15 members, with the permanent members and their veto power remaining unchanged.

- *General Assembly:* consisting of all the member nations, each with a single vote. (In 1945, there were 51 member nations; today there are 193.)

- *Secretariat:* headed by a secretary-general with a staff at UN headquarters in New York City. The secretary-general in 2020 is Antonio Guterres of Portugal.

- Several specialized organizations to handle specific public policy challenges, including the Economic and Social Council, the Trusteeship Council, and the International Court at The Hague.

The United Nations' mission includes the promotion of economic and social development. Since its founding, it has added peacekeeping to its functions and has had some limited success in that endeavor in areas of the former Yugoslavia, the Middle East, and Africa. But in the immediate post-World War II era, the ability of the United Nations in general, and of the Security Council in particular, to provide for collective security was seriously undermined by the Soviet Union's presence on the Security Council. Because the Soviet Union was a permanent member with veto power, any attempt by the Security Council to thwart Soviet aggression was blocked by the Soviets' veto.

NATO It did not take long for the United States and the Western democracies to be disappointed by the inability of the United Nations to provide for collective security. The UN's failure to halt the militaristic expansion of the Soviet sphere of influence particularly troubled them. Their frustrations led the United States and its Western allies to attempt to bring order to international relations through the creation of regional security alliances. **Regional security alliances** typically involve a superpower and nations that are ideologically similar in a particular area of the world.

The first regional security alliance was the **North Atlantic Treaty Organization (NATO).** Established in 1949, NATO created a structure for regional security for its 15 member nations through a declaration that "an armed attack against one or more NATO nations . . . shall be considered an attack against them all."[12] Through the formation of NATO, the United States made a specific commitment to defend Western Europe in the event of a Soviet attack. In response to the creation of NATO, the Soviet Union and its seven satellite states in Eastern Europe formed a similar regional security alliance, the **Warsaw Pact,** in 1955.

Both NATO and the Warsaw Pact reflected the tensions and the rivalry that existed between the United States and the Soviet Union. They also reflected the failure of the United Nations to provide for collective security, that is, the security of *all* nations. Instead, the regional security alliances more closely resembled the balance of power alliances established after the Napoleonic Wars.

NATO's role as a structure for regional security was highlighted in 2014, when Russia annexed Crimea, which had been part of Ukraine. Stationing 40,000 troops along the border with Ukraine, Russia evoked fears that it intended to annex more of Ukraine, or even parts of Eastern European and Baltic nations. In response to Russia's actions in Crimea, NATO ceased practical cooperation with Russia and drew up plans to reinforce NATO's defenses in NATO member states in the area.

INTERNATIONAL FINANCIAL ORGANIZATIONS In addition to establishing the United Nations and NATO for the purposes of conflict management and security, the United States recognized the need to relinquish a great deal of its own economic

regional security alliance
An alliance typically between a superpower and nations that are ideologically similar in a particular region.

North Atlantic Treaty Organization (NATO)
An international mutual defense alliance formed in 1949 that created a structure for regional security for its 15 member nations.

Warsaw Pact
A regional security structure formed in 1955 by the Soviet Union and its seven satellite states in Eastern Europe in response to the creation of the North Atlantic Treaty Organization (NATO).

power in exchange for the economic stability that would come from international financial institutions. Doing so would benefit the global economy in general but also the U.S. economy in particular.

To that end, in 1944, an international agreement made in Bretton Woods, New Hampshire—the Bretton Woods Agreement—established the **International Monetary Fund (IMF).** The meeting delegates charged the newly created international financial institution with regulating monetary relationships among nations. One of the IMF's key purposes was to establish exchange rates for currencies, determining, for example, how many dollars a British pound or a Japanese yen was worth. To the present day, IMF member states provide the resources the IMF needs to operate through a formula by which nations pay amounts roughly proportional to the size of their economies. Based on these IMF contribution quotas, nations are allocated votes proportional to their contributions. Thus, the IMF perpetuates the dominance of the high-contributing economic powerhouses. Today, the United States has more than 17 percent of the IMF votes. The Bretton Woods agreement also established the institution that would become the **World Bank,** which initially focused on lending money to countries devastated in World War II. Today, the World Bank lends money to developing nations to help them become self-sufficient.

Still reeling from the effects of high tariffs on international trade during the Depression, the United States also encouraged an international agreement that would heal the economies of nations by lowering tariffs and promoting international trade. In 1948, 23 nations signed the General Agreement on Tariffs and Trade (GATT). The GATT is based on the most-favored nation principle.

In 1995, the **World Trade Organization (WTO)** replaced the GATT. Whereas the GATT was a series of agreements among nations, the WTO is an actual organization that negotiates, implements, and enforces international trade agreements. Today, the WTO consists of 159 member nations. Although it has a one-nation, one-vote policy, this policy is moot because the largest economies have the greatest say. The organization's goal—to remove all types of trade barriers, including obstacles to investment—is more ambitious than that of the GATT.

The Cold War: Superpowers in Collision

During World War II, the United States, Great Britain, and the Soviet Union were allies against the Nazis. But events at the wartime Yalta Conference in 1945 sowed the seeds of what would become known as the Cold War. The **Cold War** refers to the political, ideological, and military conflict that lasted from 1945 until 1990 between the Soviet Union and its allies, and the United States and its allies. The causes of the Cold War included the competing desires to have dominant influence in Europe, as well as the fundamental dispute between communist versus capitalist economic systems.

Each leader came to the Yalta Conference with an agenda. U.S. president Franklin D. Roosevelt needed Soviet help in battling Japan in the naval wars of the Pacific. England's Winston Churchill sought democratic elections in Eastern Europe. And Soviet premier Joseph Stalin wanted Eastern Europe as a Soviet sphere of influence, arguing that the Soviet Union's national security depended on its hegemony in the region.

At the conference, Stalin agreed to allow free elections in the region, but he later broke that promise. In response, former British prime minister Churchill

International Monetary Fund (IMF)
The institution charged with regulating monetary relationships among nations, including establishment of exchange rates for major world currencies; established in 1944 by the Bretton Woods Agreement.

World Bank
The international financial institution created by the Bretton Woods Agreement of 1944 and charged with lending money to nations in need.

World Trade Organization (WTO)
The organization created in 1995 to negotiate, implement, and enforce international trade agreements.

Cold War
The political, ideological, and military conflict that lasted from 1945 until 1990 between communist nations led by the Soviet Union and Western democracies led by the United States.

warned Americans in a 1946 speech that the Soviets were dividing Europe with an "Iron Curtain." Churchill's characterization was accurate, because Stalin's brutal dictatorship, combined with the force of the Soviet Red Army, would install a communist government in every Eastern European nation. When Stalin also refused to cooperate in the planned cooperative allied occupation of Germany, the result was the division of Germany into separate zones, one administered by the Soviet Union and the other three by the United States, Great Britain, and France. In 1947, when the Soviets backed communist guerrillas who were attempting to take over Greece and Turkey, U.S. president Harry Truman (1945–1953) committed the United States to "support free people who are resisting attempted subjugation by armed minorities or by outside pressures."[13] This policy—the United States's foreign policy commitment to assist efforts to resist communism—was called the **Truman Doctrine.**

U.S. Efforts to Contain Communism: Korea, Cuba, and Vietnam

The Truman Doctrine reflected the ideas of George F. Kennan, the State Department's Soviet expert at the time. Specifically, Kennan advocated the principle of **containment,** the policy of preventing the spread of communism, mainly by providing military and economic aid as well as political advice to beleaguered countries that were vulnerable to communist takeover. Kennan argued: "It is clear that the main element of any United States policy toward the Soviet Union must be that of a long-term vigilant containment of Russian expansive tendencies."[14] The idea of containment would spur the United States to fight in two protracted wars, the Korean War and the Vietnam War, to contain communism.

THE KOREAN WAR, 1950–1953 The first military effort the United States engaged in to check the spread of communism occurred in 1950. In June of that year,

Truman Doctrine
Articulated by President Harry Truman, a foreign policy commitment by the United States to assist countries' efforts to resist communism in the Cold War era.

containment
The Cold War–era policy of preventing the spread of communism, mainly by providing military and economic aid as well as political advice to countries vulnerable to a communist takeover.

North Korea, with the backing of Stalin and the Soviet Union, invaded South Korea in an attempt to reunify the Korean peninsula under communism. During that summer, the United States sent in forces as part of a UN force to help the South Koreans repel the attack. The defensive strategy quickly succeeded, but by October the United States changed military strategy. Instead of merely containing the spread of communism, the United States sought to reunify North and South Korea—and, in doing so, to depose the communists from North Korea. But as U.S. and South Korean forces edged north, they also came closer and closer to the North Korea-China border.

That October, China, wary of a potential invasion, came to the aid of fellow communists in North Korea. The two countries' combined forces repelled the UN forces back to the 38th parallel, the original border between North and South Korea. Over the next two years, U.S. forces (as part of the UN contingent), North and South Koreans, and Chinese soldiers would continue to do battle, with very little territory changing hands. When an armistice was reached in July 1953, the border established was the 38th parallel—exactly what it had been before the war—although a demilitarized zone (DMZ) was created.

The Korean War marked an escalation and expansion of the Cold War. Not only was the war the first occasion in which the two superpowers clashed militarily, but it also brought the Cold War outside the boundaries of Europe. Significantly, the outbreak of the Korean War also gave rise to the concept of **limited war**—a combatant country's self-imposed limitation on the tactics and strategy it uses, particularly its avoidance of the deployment of nuclear weapons. The idea of limited war would set the stage for subsequent conflicts.

limited war
A combatant country's self-imposed limitation on the tactics and strategy it uses, particularly its avoidance of the use of nuclear weapons.

THE CUBAN MISSILE CRISIS, 1962 Another tactic of U.S. foreign policy during the Cold War was brinkmanship, a term coined by John Foster Dulles, the secretary of state under President Dwight D. Eisenhower (1953–1961). In essence, **brinkmanship** meant fooling the enemy by going to the edge (the brink), even if the party employing brinkmanship had no intention of following through to its logical conclusion.

brinkmanship
The Cold War–era practice of fooling the enemy by going to the edge (the brink), even if the party using the brinkmanship strategy had no intention of following through.

The Cuban Missile Crisis in October 1962 turned out to be a perfect example of brinkmanship, even though that was not the intention of President John F. Kennedy (1961–1963). Reacting to Soviet premier Nikita Khrushchev's decision to put ballistic missiles in Cuba, Kennedy imposed a naval blockade around that island nation 94 miles off the coast of Florida, and warned the Soviet Union to withdraw its missiles, or else—never specifying what he meant by "or else." Although this confrontation seemed like brinkmanship, it was no bluff; rather, it was an act of bravado that could easily have led to nuclear war. Luckily for the United States and the rest of the world, the Soviets backed down, withdrew their missiles, and entered a period of improved relations with the United States.[15]

domino theory
The principle that if one nation fell to communism, other nations in its geographic vicinity also would succumb.

THE VIETNAM CONFLICT, 1965–1975 The United States' involvement in the war in Vietnam was motivated in large part by policymakers' acceptance of the **domino theory,** the principle that if one nation fell to communism, other nations in its geographic vicinity would also succumb. As described by President Eisenhower, "You have broader considerations that might follow what you would call the 'falling domino' principle. You have a row of dominoes set up, you knock over the first one, and what will happen to the last one is the certainty that it will go over very quickly. So you could have a beginning of a disintegration that would have the most profound influences."[16]

And so, the United States again sought to contain the spread of communism in Southeast Asia. Although Vietnam was not of particular strategic importance to the United States, it represented the second "domino" in the faraway region. U.S. involvement in Vietnam started in the late 1950s, and by 1963, the United States became enmeshed in an all-out ground, naval, and air war there. The United States supported the South Vietnamese against the North Vietnamese in the decade-long civil war that would take the lives of almost 60,000 U.S. soldiers and at least 3 million Vietnamese soldiers and civilians. On April 29, 1975, when the South Vietnamese capital, Saigon, fell to the North Vietnamese Vietcong forces, the event marked the first military failure by the United States in its efforts to contain communism.

Détente: A Thaw in the Cold War Chill

Richard M. Nixon (1969–1974) was elected to the presidency in 1968, largely on his promise to end the war in Vietnam. Although several years would pass before the war actually ended, Nixon's approach to the top foreign policy issues of the day marked a departure from that of his predecessors. Specifically, the **Nixon Doctrine** emphasized the responsibility of U.S. allies to provide for their own national defense and security and sought to improve relations with the two communist world powers, the Soviet Union and China. As early as 1970, his administration sought *détente,* or the easing of tensions between the United States and its communist rivals. In keeping with this idea, the Nixon administration normalized diplomatic relations with China and began a series of nuclear arms control talks that would occur throughout the 1970s. Critics of the Nixon Doctrine argued that President Nixon's approach to foreign policy was accommodationist—that it sought the easy solution and ignored the moral and philosophical implications of improving relations between the Western democracies and their communist rivals.

Nixon Doctrine
Policy emphasizing the responsibility of U.S. allies to provide for their own national defense and security, aimed at improving relations with the communist nations, including the Soviet Union and China.

détente
The easing of tensions between the United States and its communist rivals.

>> The United States supported the South Vietnamese against the North Vietnamese in the decade-long civil war that took the lives of almost 60,000 U.S. soldiers, who are memorialized on the Vietnam War Memorial in Washington, D.C. Three million Vietnamese soldiers and civilians also died in the conflict. Here, a veteran looks for the name of a fallen comrade.

Orhan Cam/Shutterstock.com

Part of the motivation for *détente* was the recognition that any escalation of tensions between the superpowers would increase the probability of nuclear war. Since the early 1960s, the United States and the Soviet Union had engaged in a nuclear arms race in which each country attempted to surpass the other's nuclear

mutual assured destruction (MAD)
The doctrine that if one nation attacked another with nuclear weapons, the other would be capable of retaliating and would retaliate with such force as to ensure mutual annihilation.

capability. According to the doctrine of **mutual assured destruction (MAD),** if one nation attacked another with nuclear weapons, the other would be capable of retaliating, and *would* retaliate, with such force as to ensure mutual annihilation. The goal of the arms race (which would continue through the 1980s) was first-strike capability, meaning that each nation sought the ability to use nuclear weapons against the other nation and to eliminate the possibility of that nation's retaliating in a second-strike attack.

deterrence
The idea that nations would be less likely to engage in nuclear war if adversaries each had first-strike capability.

Many foreign policymakers in both the United States and the Soviet Union believed in the power of **deterrence,** the idea that nations would be less likely to engage in nuclear war if the adversaries each had first-strike capability. But Nixon and his primary foreign policy adviser, Henry Kissinger (who served first as Nixon's national security adviser and then as his secretary of state), sought negotiations with the Soviets that would dampen the arms race.

strategic arms limitation talks (SALT talks)
Discussions between the United States and the Soviet Union in the 1970s that focused on cooling down the nuclear arms race between the two superpowers.

SALT I AND SALT II In 1972, the United States and the Soviet Union concluded two and a half years of **strategic arms limitation talks (SALT talks)** that focused on cooling the superheated nuclear arms race between the two superpowers. The resulting treaty, SALT I, limited the two countries' antiballistic missiles and froze the number of offensive missiles that each nation could have. The SALT II treaty set an overall limit on all strategic nuclear launchers and limited the number of missiles that could carry multiple independently targeted reentry vehicles (MIRVs) with nuclear warheads.

Later in 1979, however, the Soviet Union invaded Afghanistan, sparking a new round of U.S.-Soviet tensions. In response, President Jimmy Carter withdrew the SALT II treaty from consideration for ratification by the Senate. Nevertheless, Carter announced (as did his successor, Ronald Reagan) that the United States would abide by all the terms of SALT II as long as the Soviet Union complied as well. During his one term in office, Carter also sought to engage the world in a campaign for human rights, while attempting to convert the vast U.S. military apparatus to peacetime functions—a policy known as **defense conversion.**

defense conversion
President Jimmy Carter's attempt to convert the nation's vast military apparatus to peacetime functions.

The Reagan Years and Soviet Collapse

Ronald Reagan's presidency (1981–1989) marked a pivotal time in U.S.-Soviet relations. On the one hand, the Reagan administration pushed for a *reduction* in missiles and nuclear warheads, not merely a limitation on increases. Because of this new direction, Reagan named these arms reduction talks the **strategic arms reduction talks (START talks).** Despite this overture, the Reagan administration was passionate in the pursuit of a ballistic missile defense system, called the **strategic defense initiative (SDI, or "Star Wars").** In protest of the development of this system, the Soviet Union walked out of the START meeting in 1983. The two superpowers would return to the table in 1985, after Reagan won reelection with a resounding victory.

strategic arms reduction talks (START talks)
Talks between the United States and the Soviet Union in which reductions in missiles and nuclear warheads, not merely a limitation on increases, were negotiated.

strategic defense initiative (SDI, or "Star Wars")
A ballistic missile defense system advocated by President Ronald Reagan.

In 1987, the United States and the Soviet Union signed the Intermediate-Range Nuclear Forces Treaty (INF), the first agreement that resulted in the destruction of nuclear weapons. It eliminated an entire class of weapons—those with an intermediate range of between 300 and 3,800 miles. A pathbreaking treaty, the INF shaped future arms control talks. It provided for reductions in the number of nuclear weapons, established the principle of equality because both nations ended up with the same number of weapons (in this case, zero), and, through the establishment of on-site inspections, provided a means of verifying compliance.

In retrospect, many analysts credit the Soviet Union's eventual collapse to President Reagan. During his tenure, Reagan ratcheted up the rhetoric with his many speeches referring to the Soviet Union as "the Evil Empire." Under his administration, the U.S. defense budget also doubled, with much of the expenditure going toward the SDI. The Soviets reacted with fear and a surge in spending. These developments all came at a time when the Soviet Union was dealing with unrest in 15 republics that eventually would secede. The last straw, however, was the country's troubled economy, because to compete with the U.S. ballistic missile system, the Soviet Union had to increase its military budget to the point where its economy collapsed—and with it, its government.

Post-Soviet Times: The United States as Solo Superpower in an Era of Wars

The START talks, which had resumed in 1985, resulted in a long-awaited agreement that reduced the number of long-range strategic nuclear weapons to 3,000 for each side. In 1991, the agreement was signed by U.S. president George H. W. Bush and Soviet president Mikhail Gorbachev, whose tenure had ushered in the ideas of *glasnost* (openness) and *perestroika* (economic restructuring) in the Soviet Union. That same year, the Soviet Union broke apart, and Russia democratically elected its president, Boris Yeltsin. Upon Yeltsin's election, in another series of talks called START II, Yeltsin agreed to even deeper cuts in nuclear weapons. The START II agreement of 1992 between the superpowers was fully implemented in 2003 and significantly decreased the likelihood of a massive nuclear attack.

Defining U.S. Foreign Policy

THEN

(1984)
The Cold War was the defining feature of U.S. foreign policy.

The United States and the Soviet Union competed as the two world superpowers.

The arms race resulted in unprecedented military spending.

NOW

U.S. foreign policy is being reshaped with ongoing crises in the Middle East and Asia, and a resurgence in the aggressiveness of Russia.

A rapidly changing global context means that the United States competes for its world power status, along with China, Russia, and the European Union.

Military spending increased with new ships for the U.S. Navy, funding for a fighter-jet program, and increased missile-defense spending being prioritized.

NEXT

WHAT'S NEXT?

- What new realities will shape U.S. foreign and national defense policy?

- Will the United States continue as the world's only superpower? How will a superpower be defined in the future? Will the term refer to military or economic might or a combination of these (and/or other) factors?

- What impact will continued military spending have on the U.S. and global economy?

THEN

NATO Members 1960

NOW

NATO Members 2020

>> During the Cold War, Europe was divided between nations in the NATO alliance and those in the Warsaw Pact. The fall of the Berlin Wall and the disintegration of the Soviet Union meant a shift in alliances, and several former Warsaw Pact nations are now members of NATO. Today NATO remains a collective security alliance that seeks to deter Russian encroachment in Eastern Europe. When we consider which countries have been added to NATO since 1960, what can we understand about shifting world power? How different is foreign policy now than during the Cold War?

As a result of the breakup of the Soviet Union, a whole new order emerged in Eastern Europe, with the Balkan nations of Latvia, Lithuania, and Estonia reasserting their independence and an additional 15 former Soviet republics establishing independent states. These sweeping changes meant a changed role for NATO, which in 1999 expanded to include Poland, Hungary, and the Czech Republic in the organization, over the objections of Russia. In 2004, another seven countries in central and Eastern Europe—Estonia, Latvia, Lithuania, Slovenia, Slovakia, Bulgaria, and Romania—joined NATO. Five years later, in 2009, Albania and Croatia also became members of the collective security alliance, in which each member nation pledges protection should any member of NATO be attacked.

The 1990s proved to be a watershed era in global relations in both Asia and Europe. In Asia, China emerged as a world power and has continued to increase its influence on the world stage. In Europe, the Maastricht Treaty, signed in 1992, paved the way for the formation of the European Union (EU). The European Union is a political and economic alliance that prioritizes peace in Europe based on economic cooperation and stability. What started out as an economic union between six nations has grown into an enormous single market in which citizens of the 28 member states can move freely between states, and all members use a single currency, the euro. While Great Britain voted in 2016 to exit the EU (the so-called Brexit vote), there has been relatively little fallout from that decision, as other European nations did not follow suit.

The 1990s also proved to be a novel time in U.S. foreign relations. For the first time in over half a century, the United States was without an enemy, and it found itself the world's lone superpower. The tumult following the collapse of communism ushered in an era of wars—many of them fueled by long-standing ethnic rivalries or disputes—and the creation of new borders and new nations. By the start of the new century, 14 wars were going on around the globe. Some, such as the decades-long conflict in Northern Ireland, now seem to be resolved. Others seemed intractable, such as the conflict in the Middle East over the Palestinian question. Still others, such as the tribal wars in Africa, were all too often manipulated by foreign interests and by corrupt indigenous leaders who were reluctant to give up their power. And other events—such as fighting that erupted between UN and U.S. forces against Somali militia fighters loyal to warlord Mohamed Farrah Aidid in 1993; the 1998 attacks on U.S. embassies in Nairobi, Kenya, and Dar es Salaam, Tanzania; and the 2000 suicide bombing of the U.S. Navy guided missile destroyer USS *Cole* in the port of Aden, Yemen—were harbingers of clashes to come. It was as if a giant hand had lifted a rock at the end of the Cold War, freeing long-submerged problems to crawl out and presenting new challenges for U.S. foreign policymakers as the United States assumed its role as the world's leader.

■ U.S. Foreign Policy in the 21st Century

U.S. foreign policymakers' challenges in the 1990s pale in comparison with those they have faced since the terrorist attacks of September 11, 2001. The incidents on that day have profoundly defined and determined recent American foreign policy.

The Bush Doctrine: A Clash of Civilizations

One prism for viewing the September 11 attacks is that posited by political scientist Samuel P. Huntington. He asserts that "the clash of civilizations will be

clash of civilizations thesis
Samuel Huntington's idea that bitter cultural conflict will continue and escalate between modern Western democracies and fundamentalist Islamic states.

the battle lines of the future."[17] Huntington's **clash of civilizations thesis** asserts that bitter cultural conflict will continue and escalate between modern Western democracies, whose culture emphasizes values rooted in democracy and capitalism, and fundamentalist Islamic states, where traditional values grounded in religious beliefs dominate. Huntington, whose thesis remains controversial, argues that the ideological divisions that characterized the 20th century—the clash between communism and democratic capitalism, for example—will be replaced by an older source of conflict: cultural and religious identity. Huntington initially posited his ideas in 1993, and his theories seemed particularly relevant during the 1990s when ethnic and religious warfare broke out in Bosnia and in parts of Africa. After September 11, 2001, Huntington's neoconservative theory appears to have significantly shaped the foreign policy of both George W. Bush and Donald Trump.

Huntington's clash of civilizations thesis provides one explanation of *why* contemporary U.S. foreign policy has focused on the areas that it has. President George W. Bush himself articulated his views on the *how* of that policy's implementation. According to the **Bush Doctrine,** the United States has a responsibility to further the spread of democracy and create a global order that ensures the security of the United States and its allies, even if it means that the United States acts alone. This unilateral action, according to the Bush Doctrine, is both justifiable and feasible. The Bush Doctrine also asserted that the United States should use its role as the world's only remaining superpower to spread democracy and to create conditions of security that will benefit itself and its allies.

Bush Doctrine
The argument, articulated by President George W. Bush, that unilateral action directly targeted at an enemy is both justifiable and feasible.

WAR IN AFGHANISTAN The United States's first response to the 9/11 attacks was based on the connection of Osama bin Laden and the al-Qaeda terror network to the masterminding and execution of those attacks. For several years before the September 11 attacks, the fundamentalist Taliban regime in Afghanistan had allowed al-Qaeda training camps to operate in that country. In retaliation for the terror strikes, in late 2001 the United States, a coalition of allies, and anti-Taliban rebels from within Afghanistan attacked the training camps and the Taliban government itself. Within weeks the Taliban government fell.

The multilateral forces worked to create first an interim government in Afghanistan and then, in 2004, a democratically elected government. Attacks from Taliban insurgents continue, and about 13,000 American troops were stationed in Afghanistan in 2020. Toppling the Taliban regime proved easier than creating peace in Afghanistan, where government officials and everyday citizens who participate in civic life are routinely targeted by terrorist organizations, including the Taliban, Haqqani Network, and ISIS.

WAR IN IRAQ After the Taliban's fall, President Bush set his sights on changing another regime: that of Iraq's Saddam Hussein. During the presidency of Bush's father, George H.W. Bush (1989–1993), the United States had gone to war with Iraq when that country invaded Kuwait, an ally of the United States. During the younger Bush's 2003 State of the Union address, the president claimed that Iraq possessed weapons of mass destruction and said that the Iraqis were attempting to purchase the components of nuclear weapons. In the ensuing weeks, the Bush administration made a case for going to war with Hussein's regime to both the UN Security Council and the American people. In doing so, Bush introduced the concept of **preventive war,** the strategy of waging war on countries regarded as threatening to the United States in order to avoid future conflicts.

preventive war
The strategy of waging war on countries that are regarded as threatening in order to avoid future conflicts

The concept of preventive war represents a shift in policy from responding to attacks to anticipating attacks. The idea of preventive war is in part an outgrowth of the drastically altered nature of warfare. The biological, chemical, and nuclear weapons of today can cross borders with far deadlier efficiency than troops, ships, or aircraft. In addition, U.S. enemies no longer declare themselves as openly as they did before. The national defense policymakers who advocate preventive war thus argue that the only way to defend the country against these various new threats is to invade *before* the fact, in hopes of deterring another attack.

The invasion of Iraq in March 2003 was initially successful in toppling Saddam Hussein's regime. Despite insurgency violence that prevented peace from taking root, elections were finally held in 2004 and 2005, and power officially passed to an elected government. In the face of continued violence, the Bush administration enacted a military surge policy, resulting in the addition of more than 20,000 troops in Baghdad and Al Anbar Province. The surge strategy was credited with temporarily quelling much of the insurgent violence in these areas. Unfortunately, violence greatly increased in the ensuing years, yielding multiple civilian and military casualties.

Nation building in Iraq proved troublesome—far more so than the rebuilding of Japan after World War II, for example. There, U.S. general Douglas MacArthur undertook the task of reconstructing the nation and creating a system of democratic self-governance. It took four years, but when MacArthur left for duty in Korea, Japan was as close to democracy as any Far Eastern country. Japan's feudal aristocracy was abolished, the country had a new constitution that empowered the legislature to make laws, civil liberties and collective bargaining were guaranteed, the legal equality of the sexes was established, and citizens had been given the right of *habeas corpus* (a petition that allows a prisoner to go to a court where a judge will determine whether he or she is being held illegally). MacArthur also suspended banks that had financed the war, destroyed (at least temporarily) the giant monopolies, and refused to allow "war profiteers" to invade Japan at the expense of local businesses.

>> In the United States's crosshairs for over a decade, Osama bin Laden, mastermind of the September 11, 2001, terror attacks, was caught and killed in this house in Abbottabad, Pakistan, in 2011. The terror attacks, and the U.S. response to them, have been the defining feature of U.S. foreign policy since they occurred.

Aqeel Ahmed/AP Images

Fifty years later, as the United States sought to rebuild Iraq's war-torn infrastructure and feed its people after toppling Hussein's regime, a powerful insurgency thwarted American efforts. Unlike MacArthur, the U.S. military had allowed widespread looting in the early days of the occupation, including the looting of munitions warehouses. These munitions later helped to arm the insurgents, including ISIS, who waged battle in Iraq's deadly civil war. Also unlike MacArthur, who had some familiarity with Japanese culture, few commanders knew either the Arabic language or Iraqi culture and rituals. Even fewer knew how to stem the war profiteering of the multinational corporations that had also "invaded" the country, making millions off the reconstruction of Iraq's infrastructure.

The Obama Doctrine: A More Conciliatory Approach to Foreign Policy

Throughout his tenure both as a candidate and as president, Barack Obama used language that seemed to reject Huntington's clash of civilizations thesis, which was instrumental in shaping Bush administration policy. Based on his rhetoric, President Obama had clearly rejected the idea that the United States and Islamic nations were destined to clash, and he instead sought to build bridges between the United States and the Muslim nations. Nowhere is this in greater evidence than in Iran, where the Obama administration negotiated a halting of that country's nuclear program. Nonetheless, many observers were surprised at the similarities between the Obama and Bush administration policies, despite the change in rhetoric. For example, some analysts say that the success of President Bush's "surge strategy" in Iraq was the guiding principle behind President Obama's troop surge in Afghanistan, with Obama hoping that such a strategy would pave the way for a withdrawal of U.S. forces from Afghanistan, which, though a key tenet of his campaign promise in 2008, did not occur during his eight years in office. Others remark on President Obama's failure to close military prisons at Guantánamo Bay (see "Thinking Critically"), and still others point to his continuation of drone attack programs, in which unmanned combat air vehicles carried out attacks abroad on people and other targets deemed a threat to the United States.

The Trump Doctrine: America First

From the earliest stages of his presidency—indeed, even during the course of his presidential campaign—it was apparent that President Trump fundamentally disagreed with Obama's foreign policy doctrine. In some instances, Trump has seemed to embrace Huntington's clash of civilizations thesis, most demonstrably by demonizing Muslims through his rhetoric.[18] Take, for example, an exchange between Trump and CNN host Anderson Cooper, who asked whether there is "a war between the west and radical Islam or between the west and Islam itself." Trump replied, "Well, it's radical, but it's very hard to define. It's very hard to separate because you don't know who is who."[19] The president's repeated efforts through executive orders to ban all citizens of predominantly Muslim countries from entering the United States also suggested an adherence to Huntington's thesis. The federal courts rejected two such efforts as discriminatory, while the third ban, which also barred citizens from North Korea and leaders and their families from Venezuela, was challenged in the U.S. Supreme Court, which ruled the ban constitutional in a 5-4 decision.

In 2020, Trump's strategy in navigating the tricky waters of Middle East politics was subjected to strong criticism and scrutiny from both within the United States and abroad when, as previously discussed, he unilaterally decided to assassinate Iranian Major General Qassim Suleimani, near the Baghdad airport in Iraq. This assassination unified Iranians in a public outcry and a hard-line stance against the United States. But because the attack took place on Iraqi soil, it also resulted in a

Do the Geneva Conventions Apply When Terrorists Have So Drastically Altered the Rules of War?

THE ISSUE: The Geneva Conventions are a set of four treaties signed in Geneva, Switzerland, in 1949, in the aftermath of World War II. The conventions established standards for the protection of humanitarian concerns under international law. They apply to injured or ill members of the armed forces, prisoners of war, and civilians. Article 13 of the Third Geneva Convention, which specifically guides the treatment of prisoners of war, states that "prisoners of war must at all times be humanely treated. Any unlawful act or omission by the Detaining Power causing death or seriously endangering the health of a prisoner of war in its custody is prohibited, and will be regarded as a serious breach of the present Convention. In particular, no prisoner of war may be subjected to physical mutilation or to medical or scientific experiments of any kind which are not justified by the medical, dental or hospital treatment of the prisoner concerned and carried out in his interest. Likewise, prisoners of war must at all times be protected, particularly against acts of violence or intimidation and against insults and public curiosity. Measures of reprisal against prisoners of war are prohibited."*

Beginning in 2002, military authorities at the U.S. naval base at Guantánamo Bay in Cuba have detained about 775 "enemy combatants." Captured primarily in Afghanistan, these individuals were transported to Guantánamo for questioning. Although authorities in the Bush and Obama administrations have released 90 percent of the prisoners, about 41 remain, with President Trump signing an executive order in 2018 to keep the facility open, saying "In the past, we have foolishly released hundreds and hundreds of dangerous terrorists only to meet them again on the battlefield."** As designated enemy combatants, the prisoners have not enjoyed the legal rights granted to individuals charged with a crime in the United States. The detainees have no legal rights to a lawyer, a trial, or *habeas corpus*.

YES: The Geneva Conventions clearly apply in this situation. As many human rights organizations, including Amnesty International, argue, the detention of prisoners at Guantánamo amounts to a violation of the Geneva Conventions. Specifically, as these critics cite, there have been emphatic allegations of torture by individuals who have been released. Furthermore, the indefinite nature of the detentions— combined with the captors' acknowledged practices of sleep deprivation and constant light exposure, plus the disrespect of the Muslim religion on the part of some—constitutes the abuse of their human rights in violation of the Geneva Conventions. The moral high ground usually occupied by the United States is at stake, and if the United States does not grant these prisoners rights that are consistent with the Geneva Conventions, our own soldiers will be at risk of having their rights denied when they are captured by enemy forces.

WHAT DO YOU THINK?

1. Are the prisoners held at Guantánamo different from the prisoners of war held in other wars? If so, how?

2. Are the Geneva Conventions, drafted soon after the conclusion of World War II, still applicable in the post-9/11 world, in which terrorism is such an urgent problem in international affairs?

3. How does the context of actions including the brutal murder of civilians, journalists, and aid workers by terror groups such as ISIS shape your views of adhering to the Geneva Convention?

*You can read the rules and explore other topics at this International Committee of the Red Cross site: www.icrc.org/ihl.nsf/7c4d08d9b287a421412567390 03e636b/6fef854a3517b75ac125641e004a9e68.

**www.npr.org/sections/thetwo-way/2018/01/31/ 582033937/trump-signs-order-to-keep-prison- at-guantanamo-bay-open.

NO: The Geneva Conventions do not apply when the rules of engagement of war have changed so drastically. The Bush administration convincingly argued that the Geneva Conventions apply only to "prisoners of war" (POWs) and not to "unlawful combatants." Because the nature of the war on terror and of the tactics used by terrorists is in stark contrast to accepted international conventions of war, the treatment of combatants in that war should also vary. The Supreme Court has thus far agreed with the Bush administration's assessment that holding enemy combatants is legal.***

OTHER APPROACHES: The Geneva Conventions do not apply to detainees at Guantánamo because they are not conventional enemy combatants, but the detainees should be afforded their human rights. In times like these, when international terrorist organizations do not follow centuries-old rules of engagement in warfare, the United States cannot follow antiquated rules and expect to keep its citizens safe. Therefore, detention can prevent further terrorist attacks if potential terrorists are prevented from carrying them out. Nevertheless, the detainees are entitled to humane treatment and to a hearing before an impartial judge to determine if they are truly a threat.

***_Hamdi v. Rumsfeld_, 542 U.S. 507 (2004).

rebuke from Iraq, with Prime Minister Adel Abdul Mahdi condemning the attack as "an outrageous breach to Iraqi sovereignty" and demanding the removal of U.S. troops from his country.[20] Ironically, General Suleimani was a leader of the strategy to increase Iranian influence in Iraq, and his assassination—which the U.S. intended as a move to hurt the Iranians—served to strengthen pro-Iranian sentiment in Iraq, and it also appears to have expedited the United States' exit from Iraq, which was one of Suleimani's long-term goals.

In other areas of the world, President Trump's foreign policy viewpoint often seemed disjointed. At times, he antagonized long-standing allies while flattering heads of state whose interests may be contrary to those of the United States, including North Korea's leader Kim Jong-un, Russian president Vladimir Putin, and Chinese president Xi Jinping. Trump also has demonstrated a willingness to defy both political wisdom and his own political and business allies in order to implement unpopular policies he believes will help save American jobs. Such was the case in enacting a series of tariffs on imported goods, a policy that promises to present challenges for U.S. foreign policymakers in the future.

Future Challenges in American Foreign Policy

The volatility and complexity of events in the global arena show no sign of abating. In the foreseeable future and beyond, U.S. foreign policymakers will undoubtedly continue to face a number of pressing issues, including foreign trade policy. And among the most urgent are the ongoing, acute threat of further terrorism directed at domestic and foreign targets and the continued concern over Russia's attempt to expand its influence. Other issues that promise to remain a fixture on the U.S. foreign policy agenda in the years to come include problems related to the environment, human rights, and technology.

Environmental and Health Issues

The COVID-19 pandemic demonstrated the deep vulnerability nations face in protecting public health, and it forced policymakers to grapple with difficult questions concerning global health issues. Our globally integrated society means that health issues cannot be confined within a nation's border. Similarly, environmental concerns are worldwide challenges by their very nature, and these issues promise to remain on the U.S. foreign policy agenda well into the future. Prevention of pandemics is certain to be at the top of policymakers' priorities going forward, as will environmental concerns like climate change, greenhouse gas emissions, enormous world consumption of fossil fuels, deterioration of the oceans, worldwide deforestation, and ongoing air and water contamination.

Trade Policy

Calling it a "horrible deal," as a candidate, Donald Trump railed against the Trans-Pacific Partnership. The TPP, negotiated during the Obama administration, was a trade agreement among 12 countries that border the Pacific Ocean, including the United States, Australia, Brunei, Canada, Chile, Japan, Malaysia, Mexico, New Zealand, Peru, Singapore, and Vietnam. The nations—which represent about 40 percent of global economic production—sought to encourage trade among the countries by cutting tariffs. The long-term goal was to eventually create closer economic ties among the partners and perhaps even create a unified market that could negotiate more favorable trading terms with countries outside the TPP (including the European Union). A shorter-term purpose was to strengthen the United States's trading position in the Asian-Pacific region, in the hopes that stronger economic ties with the TPP member states would curtail some of China's growing influence in that region. The agreement would have eliminated about 18,000 separate tariffs imposed by the various members. Under the agreement, tariffs on U.S.-manufactured goods and nearly all American agricultural products would have been ended immediately. The deadline for ratification by all its member states was February 2018, but President Trump rejected the partnership and thus killed the deal.

In an effort to protect American jobs, President Trump imposed tariffs on imported steel, aluminum, washing machines, and solar panels. The tariffs were targeted at China, but the Trump administration faced blowback from European and North American allies, who both argued for exemptions based on previously negotiated trade deals and threatened retaliatory tariffs if the exemptions were not granted. In response to the new tariffs, China also imposed tariffs on 128 U.S. products, making items like strawberries, oranges, and American-made wine more expensive in the vast Chinese market.[21]

The Trump administration responded in kind, imposing new taxes on Chinese televisions, batteries, and other manufactured goods, making those products more expensive to the American consumer. This tit-for-tat trade retaliatory policy resulted in a global trade war, as tariffs increased to about 20 percent on selected goods. It also forced President Trump to reconsider his position on the Trans-Pacific Partnership, in that increasing U.S. influence through favorable trading conditions in the Asian-Pacific market could provide needed stability in the demand for U.S.-produced goods, given the uncertainty surrounding trade relations with China.

The Ongoing Threat of Terrorism

As the terrorist attacks of 9/11 tragically demonstrated, foreign affairs can be unpredictable. Nonetheless, U.S. foreign policymakers are certain to confront some clear challenges in the years to come. First among these is the continued threat of terrorism. As a tactic, terrorism has proven enormously effective in accomplishing the goals of the attackers. Specifically, it breeds terror—disrupting economies, creating instability, and acting as a polarizing force.

The increasing availability of chemical and biological weapons to nations as well as terror groups also promises to create a tough challenge for U.S. and other foreign policymakers. The potential, enormous damage of these weapons of mass destruction cannot be underestimated.

Russian Expansion and Influence

For decades, Russian expansionism seemed like a threat from the past. But in March 2014, Russian troops moved onto the Crimean Peninsula and annexed the area that had been under control of Ukraine. In the aftermath, large numbers of Russian troops moved onto the border with Ukraine, stirring fears that the nation, under the rule of Vladimir Putin, would continue its push. Fears were also raised in Eastern European nations, especially in the Balkan states of Latvia, Lithuania, and Estonia, which had been overtaken by the Soviets in the 1940s. The specter of Russian aggression is troublesome to foreign policymakers in the United States who recognize that the United States' role in NATO, the regional security organization, would necessitate the use of U.S. troops (likely as part of NATO forces) should a member of the NATO alliance be attacked. In 2016, the United States began repurposing old Warsaw Pact military facilities in Poland as missile defense bases to demonstrate that NATO would defend Eastern European allies in the event of an attack, while reassuring Russia that the facility was for defense purposes only. Although they do not involve Russian troops, allegations that individuals connected to Putin interfered in the 2016 U.S. presidential election and continue to use technology to foment divisions within the United States present the possibility of perhaps a more insidious form of aggression.

Nuclear Proliferation

Not all challenges to come are new, however. The continued proliferation of nuclear weapons presents a serious problem to foreign policymakers throughout the world. Figure 13.2 shows that eight nations have a declared nuclear weapons capability, including India and Pakistan, and another, Israel, has the undeclared potential. The fact that dangerous weapons of mass destruction are in such wide distribution increases the likelihood of their use—either accidentally or intentionally.

Technology's Potential in Foreign Affairs

Although uncertainty hovers over much of what's next in the foreign policy arena, one certainty is that the impact of technology—as a tool in how governments monitor and track citizens throughout the world, in how leaders conduct foreign policy, and in how citizens work to influence the policies and institutions of government—will continue to increase.

Consider, for example, the use of aggregate data provided by cell phone providers in Great Britain and used to predict the spread of the COVID-19 virus during the pandemic. Or consider that law enforcement relied on social media to

Declared nuclear capability
United States
Russia
China
India
Pakistan
Britain
France
North Korea

Undeclared capability
Israel

Seeking capability
Syria

Gave up
Iran
Belarus
Ukraine
Kazakhstan
South Africa

Ended
Brazil
Argentina
Algeria
Libya
Sweden
Iraq
South Korea
Taiwan

FIGURE 13.2 ◼ **The Nuclear Club** What, if anything, do most or all of the countries that gave up or ended their nuclear programs have in common, either among themselves or with the countries that have nuclear capability? What do most or all of the countries that have nuclear capability—either declared or undeclared—have in common? What conclusions can you draw about these commonalities?

Photo: F_/E1/Getty Images

find violators of Italy's nationwide lockdown. In addition, consider that technology has transformed not only how nations communicate with each other, but also how non-state actors can harness the power of social media to communicate directly with policymakers and private citizens. Video technologies increasingly enable nongovernmental organizations, cyber-journalists, and others to make compelling cases directly to individuals. It also allows terror cells to radicalize individuals, turning private citizens into lone wolf terrorists. Technology also is increasingly being relied on as a tool by private citizens, lobbying their governments for favored foreign policies, while governments are using technology in unprecedented ways to monitor the actions of their citizens as well as their adversaries and allies.

Technology also is being used as a tool for those seeking to foster democracy. In 2019, protesters, many of them students, took to the streets of Hong Kong protesting an extradition. The protesters relied on technology to disseminate their message to the world. They also covered their faces to prevent facial-recognition technology from identifying them. The likelihood is great that technology will play an increasingly prevalent role—sometimes for good, other times with negatives effects—in shaping new democracies, checking the authority and policies of governments, and providing a means for cross-national movements.

Conclusion: Thinking Critically About What's Next in Foreign Policy and National Security

In retrospect, the development of the United States's foreign policy over time seems to have followed a natural progression as the nation itself grew and changed. The nation's initial isolationism, spawned by a healthy suspicion of foreign powers and their motives, gave way to international relations in the limited sphere of trade. Then, in both World War I and World War II, the importance of global alliances in helping to shape U.S. foreign policy became evident. With the end of World War II, the United States emerged as a superpower whose foreign policy came to be defined largely by its relations with its chief rival in the global arena, the Soviet Union. After the collapse of the Soviet empire in the 1990s, the foreign policy arena was murky as U.S. and world policymakers searched for a new prism through which to view the nations of the world. Could policymakers have anticipated the threat of terrorism that was to come? And could anyone have predicted that a global pandemic would so drastically alter foreign policy context in just a matter of weeks?

In the wake of the COVID-19 pandemic, policymakers will continue to grapple with the question of how future pandemics can be prevented, particularly in light of the intermeshed global society in which we live, where disease can travel as quickly as the fastest airliner. But lessons from the past point to the fact that oftentimes, while policymakers prepare for one threat, another one materializes.

History also points us to evidence that our global context can change in the blink of an eye. On September 11, 2001, a shaken president and his aides scrambled to respond appropriately to the unforeseen and unprecedented terrorist attacks on U.S. soil. They asked the same question that the millions of Americans who watched the unbelievable events unfold on television asked: Why? Ultimately, the administration's responses to the terrorist strikes showed that significant cultural and political differences separate the United States and the other Western democracies on the one hand, and fundamentalist non-Western states that harbor terrorists on the other hand. The attacks crystallized perceptions both among U.S. policymakers and in the general public that no longer could the terrorist states be viewed simply as potential threats or as insignificant to U.S. interests. Do those perceptions remain widely held by the public and policymakers today?

Challenges facing U.S. foreign policymakers in the next several years are particularly acute, given their unpredictability. Uncertainties surrounding the post-COVID 19 global economy and foreign trade policy will likely continue to be factors in international relations. And the randomness of terrorism confounds policymakers and other experts and prevents them from making accurate predictions and determining adequate modes of defense. Nonetheless, given the high stakes of another potential attack, the threat of terrorism—and the imperative to prevent it—clearly will remain a defining characteristic of U.S. foreign policy in the decades to come.

References

1. Saul K. Padover, ed., *Wilson's Ideals* (Washington, DC: American Council on Public Affairs, 1942), 108.

2. www.vox.com/world/2018/1/8/16850116/trump-pakistan-suspend-aid.

3. www.whitehouse.gov/wp-content/uploads/2018/02/budget-fy2019.pdf.

4. https://fas.org/sgp/crs/row/pakaid.pdfs.

5. "Dodd Assesses Efforts by U.S. to Increase Economic, Diplomatic, Political Pressure on Iran," March 21, 2007.

6. Secretary of State Colin L. Powell, remarks to the United Nations Security Council, February 5, 2003.

7. Alex Chadwick and Mike Shuster, "U.S. Links to Sadaam During Iran-Iraq War," September 22, 2005.

8. See, for example, James Risen, *State of War: The Secret History of the CIA and the Bush Administration* (New York: Free Press, 2006).

9. "President Dwight D. Eisenhower's Farewell Address (1961)," www.ourdocuments.gov/doc.php?flash5true&doc590.

10. www.thebureauinvestigates.com/projects/drone-war.

11. Roger H. Davidson, "Invitation to Struggle: An Overview of Legislative-Executive Relations," *Annals of the American Academy of Political and Social Science* 499 (1988): 1, 9–21.

12. Article 5 of the North Atlantic Treaty, Washington, D.C., April 4, 1949.

13. President Harry S. Truman's address before a joint session of Congress on March 12, 1947.

14. George F. Kennan, writing under the pseudonym "X," "Sources of Soviet Conduct," *Foreign Affairs,* July 1947: 25.

15. Graham T. Allison and Philip Zelikow, *Essence of Decision: Explaining the Cuban Missile Crisis,* 2nd ed. (New York: Longman, 1999).

16. President Eisenhower's News Conference, April 7, 1954, *Public Papers of the Presidents*, 1954, p. 382.

17. Samuel P. Huntington, "The Clash of Civilizations?" *Foreign Affairs* 72, no. 3 (Summer 1993): 22–49.

18. www.vox.com/policy-and-politics/2017/11/29/16714788/trump-retweet-britain-first-islamophobia.

19. www.brookings.edu/blog/markaz/2017/01/04/what-does-it-mean-to-be-at-war-with-radical-islam-on-the-attractions-and-dangers-of-a-vague-term/.

20. https://www.nytimes.com/2020/01/03/world/middleeast/us-iraq.html

21. http://fortune.com/2018/04/02/china-tariffs-128-us-products/.

CHAPTER 13 WRAP-UP

■ Key Terms

▌ Multiple Choice Questions

1. Which of the following best describes American public opinion on U.S. foreign policy?
   A. Engaged
   B. Uninformed
   C. Influential
   D. Knowledgeable

2. One explanation for the tension between the president and Congress over war making authority is that
   A. According to the Constitution, Congress should take the lead in military action
   B. A declaration of war is always required for military intervention
   C. Congress has the authority to immediately recall troops as it sees fit
   D. Under the War Powers Act, the president must submit to certain congressional checks on his authority

3. Current challenges to U.S. foreign policy include all of the following EXCEPT
   A. Technology driving foreign policy
   B. Nuclear proliferation
   C. Rising deficits
   D. Terrorism

4. Which of the following is an accurate comparison of the Nixon and Bush Doctrines?

Nixon Doctrine	Bush Doctrine
A. Preemptive war is justified to protect the interests of the U.S.	Détente
B. Emphasizes the responsibility of U.S. allies to provide for their own national defense and security	Unilateral action directly targeted at an enemy is justifiable and feasible
C. The U.S. has a responsibility to spread democracy and create global order	Nuclear arms control
D. Nuclear proliferation is required for a strong defense	Deterrence

5. A policy of preventing the spread of communism mainly by providing military and economic aid was known as
   A. Rapprochement
   B. Deterrence
   C. Brinkmanship
   D. Containment

6. Which of the following best reflects U.S. influence over NATO in recent years?
   A. A failure to deter Russia's invasion of Ukraine in 2014
   B. Allowing Russia to become a voting member of NATO with veto authority
   C. Inability to effectively prevent China's expansion of contested islands in the South China Sea
   D. Refusal to send peace-keepers to protect non-governmental organization aid workers

7. United States' membership in current international organizations includes which of the following?
   I. The Warsaw Treaty Organization
   II. SEATO
   III. The International Monetary Fund
   IV. The World Bank

   A. I only
   B. IV only
   C. III and IV only
   D. II, III, and IV only

8. Which of the following is an accurate formal and informal power of the president in foreign policy?

	Formal power	Informal power
A.	Executive agreements	Negotiate treaties
B.	Chief diplomat	Executive order
C.	Commander in chief	Issue proclamation
D.	Executive agreement	Head the military

9. Which of the following is true about the War Powers Act (WPA)?
   A. The WPA has contributed to U.S. military victories abroad
   B. The WPA attempted to curb presidential power in the area of foreign policy
   C. The WPA significantly limits the president's foreign policy-making power
   D. The WPA is frequently invoked to end military operations

10. A Republican president with a conservative ideology is most likely to take which of the following policy approaches?
   A. Decrease tariffs so that foreign goods are more competitive in the U.S.
   B. Increase deportations of illegal immigrants
   C. Forgive debt owed to the U.S. by developing nations
   D. Open dialogue between the U.S. and all foreign nations

■ Free Response Questions

Quantitative Analysis

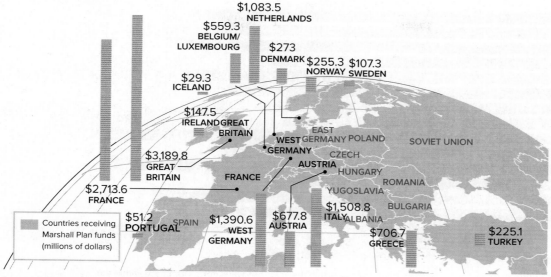

$1,083.5
NETHERLANDS

$559.3
BELGIUM/
LUXEMBOURG

$273
DENMARK $255.3 $107.3
NORWAY SWEDEN

$29.3
ICELAND

$147.5
IRELAND GREAT
BRITAIN

$3,189.8
GREAT
BRITAIN

$2,713.6
FRANCE

EAST
WEST GERMANY POLAND
GERMANY
CZECH
AUSTRIA
HUNGARY
YUGOSLAVIA
ROMANIA
BULGARIA

SOVIET UNION

Countries receiving
Marshall Plan funds
(millions of dollars)

$51.2 SPAIN $1,390.6 $677.8
PORTUGAL WEST AUSTRIA
GERMANY

$1,508.8
ITALY ALBANIA

$706.7
GREECE

$225.1
TURKEY

Source: CNN, Cold War 3/24, Marshall Plan.

Use the information graphic above to answer the questions.

A. Identify the country receiving the greatest amount of aid under the Marshall Plan.

B. Describe a similarity or difference in the recipients of Marshall Plan Aid by country or region, as illustrated in the information graphic, and draw a conclusion about that similarity or difference.

C. Explain how the Marshall Plan exemplified containment.

Concept Application

> When peaceful, pro-democracy protesters in Libya were the targets of a violent response from Libyan dictator Moammar Gadhafi, President Obama launched airstrikes against Gadhafi. The president's decision to use the military came after the UN Security Council passed a resolution that authorized military intervention in Libya. However, the president's action was met with opposition from Republicans in Congress led by Speaker of the House John Boehner (R-OH), and some Democrats.

After reading the scenario, respond to A, B, and C below:

A. In the context of the scenario, describe a power Congress has in war-making authority.

B. In the context of the scenario, explain how the use of congressional power described in Part A can be affected by its interaction with the president.

C. In the context of the scenario, explain how the interaction between Congress and the president is affected by the War Powers Act.

Quantitative Analysis

Timeline of Covid-19 Dispersion and Government Responses

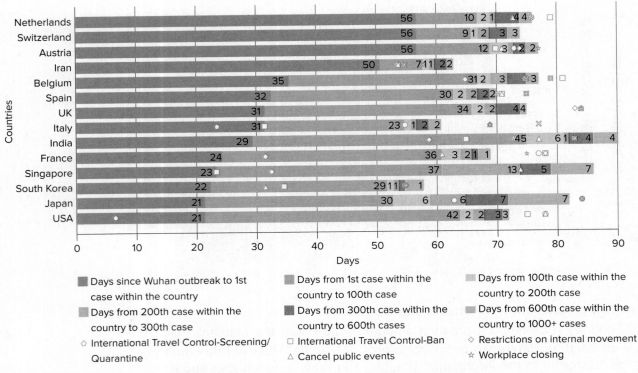

Source: Brookings. https://www.brookings.edu/2020/04/02/the-early-days-of-a-global-pandemic-a-timeline-of-covid-19-spread-and-government-interventions/

A. Identify how the U.S. response to COVID-19 varied from other countries' responses.
B. Describe a similarity in the U.S. response to the responses by other countries on the graph.
C. Explain what the U.S. response as shown on the graph indicates about U.S. policymaking.

As you read the chapters in the American Political Ideologies and Beliefs unit, you were asked to consider the following questions:

- **What are the ways in which political scientists organize and display data? What are limitations of data and data presentations?**

- **What are the relationships among demographic characteristics and political beliefs/behaviors? What are the implications of the trends?**

- **How do ideologies shape policy outcomes, and what are the implications of how ideologies shape outcomes, considering ideological breakdown in the US?**

Let's examine a little of what we read about in response to each of the questions.

What are the ways in which political scientists organize and display data? What are limitations of data and data presentations?

We examined illustrative examples of concepts in the text displayed in pie charts, bar graphs, tables, and infographics. The way data is displayed can highlight its features. Bar graphs for example tend to be easier to read than charts, because they allow the reader to quickly compare data visually. See the figure below from the Political Socialization chapter which reports frequency of attendance at religious services by Republican and Democratic candidates. The bar graph format allows the reader to easily identify which of the two political parties' candidates attend religious services once a week or more, a few times a month, few times a year, or never, by looking at the colored bars. The same information in a numeric chart would be more tedious to read.

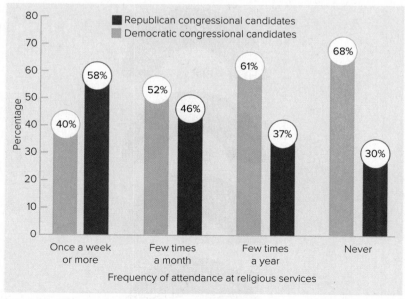

Source: https://www.pewresearch.org/fact-tank/2018/11/07/how-religious-groups-voted-in-the-midterm-elections/

All data have limitations, which refer to information related to data that is not included in the data. What are limitations to the data above? We can find several limitations to this dataset. We don't know what the relationship is between ideology and religious service attendance, nor do we know the relationship between incumbents and religious services, nor do we know whether religious service attendance for congressional candidate varies by religious denomination.

What are the relationships among demographic characteristics and political beliefs/behaviors? What are the implications of the trends?

We learned from the reading in this unit that demographic characteristics of individuals are associated with both political beliefs and behaviors, and that some associations are stronger than others. For example, African Americans make up the strongest voting demographic for the Democratic Party, with approximately 90% of African Americans voting consistently Democratic over time. Hispanics also vote consistently Democratic (except for Cubans who vote Republican), while most Republican support comes from whites. The infographic below shows candidate support for Trump v. Biden by race. Like a bar graph, this infographic is easy to read but also has several limitations. Regardless of the limitations, it will be useful for candidates for office and the public to use this information to identify implications. For example, advisors to the presidential candidates may use this data to identify their core base of supporters and to understand where the gaps of support in their campaign are. One limitation of this data is that it does not identify any aspect of political behavior by demographic. We don't know if the respondents in this dataset are likely to vote or will not vote in the election, making the data not an indicator of potential election outcome. While African Americans vote overwhelmingly Democratic, in many elections the voter turnout rate among African Americans has been low.

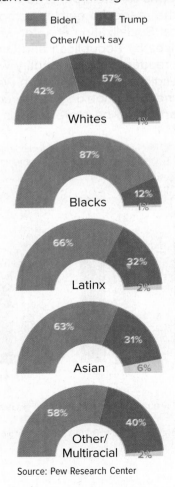

Source: Pew Research Center

Data displayed in line graphs like the one we examined in Chapter 10 are useful to show trends in change over time. The data we just examined was limited because neither dataset showed change over time. In the dataset below, we can see change over time in party identification among men and women. The gender gap refers to the differences between men and women in ideology. The line graph below demonstrates an increasing gender gap over time, and is another datapoint that may be considered by both the Biden and Trump campaigns.

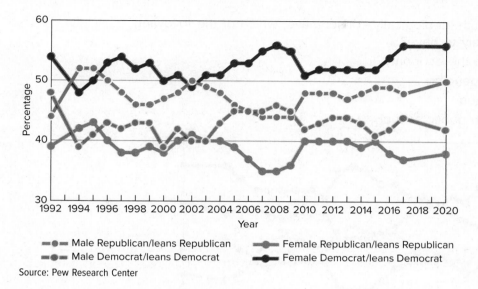

Source: Pew Research Center

How do ideologies shape policy outcomes, and what are the implications of how ideologies shape outcomes, considering ideological breakdown in the U.S.?

We learned from the policy-making chapters that ideology shapes views on public policies, with liberals being more likely to view the government as a positive agent of social welfare, and conservatives being more likely to support market forces when it comes to improving overall economic welfare. For example, Democrats supported the Affordable Care Act passed under Obama and Republicans opposed it. The Affordable Care Act passed when Obama had a Democratically controlled Congress without a single Republican vote. Congress has become increasingly partisan, meaning most members of Congress vote strictly with their party, so it seems in recent years that in order to pass watershed policy, the president and the Congress must be from the same political party, and can depend on the opposing party to act in loyal opposition. This dynamic is a change from earlier decades, such as in the Reagan presidency, when it was more common for the political parties to work together on policy through negotiation and compromise. To make matters more complex, most Americans are not ideologically far to the left or the right – most Americans are moderate, yet members of Congress seem to be more extreme in their behavior while governing than the populations they represent.

■ Multiple Choice Questions

1. When a child's parents are both ideologically conservative, which of the following attitudes is the child most likely to have?

A. Favor government role in the economy

B. Favor reducing military spending

C. Favor ending legal abortion

D. Favor ending all prayer in public school

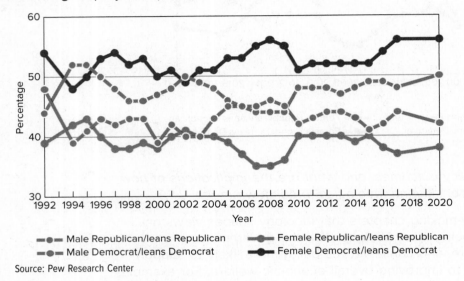

Source: Pew Research Center

Use the data above to answer questions 2 and 3.

2. Which of the following is an accurate statement about the information in the graph?

A. The gender gap is widest when comparing male Republicans to female Democrats

B. The gender gap is narrowest when comparing male Republicans to female Republicans

C. The economy causes the gender gap to widen

D. The gender gap is widening over time

3. Based on the information in the line graph, which of the following is the most likely implication of the gender gap for presidential campaigns?

A. Democrats increasingly rely on women as a voting block

B. Democratic women are likely to contribute more money than men to political campaigns

C. Women are more likely to vote in presidential elections than men

D. Women are more likely to demonstrate for equal rights than men

4. Which of the following is an element of a scientific poll?

    A. Benchmark poll

    B. Tracking poll

    C. Random sample

    D. Exit poll

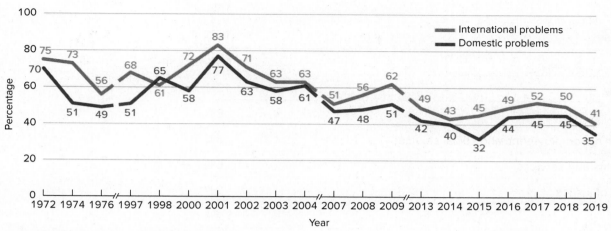

Source: Jeffrey M. Jones "Trust in Government," Gallup.

5. Which of the following is an accurate statement about the information in the line graph?

    A. Trust in and confidence in government varies by political party, with Republicans being more trusting and Democrats being less trusting

    B. COVID-19 caused Americans to lack trust in government for both domestic and international issues

    C. Trust in government to handle international and domestic programs has decreased over time

    D. Presidential approval trends coincide with trends in trust and confidence in government

6. Based on the information in the line graph, which of the following is the most likely implication of levels of trust and confidence in government?

    A. Low levels of trust and confidence in government cannot be changed

    B. Americans are losing trust in government overall

    C. Changes in trust in domestic problems affect changes in trust in international problems

    D. Changes in trust in government do not have an impact on leaders' ability to govern effectively

TABLE 12.1 ■ Percentage of FY 2019 Total Expenditures ($4.5 trillion) by Functions (rounded to the nearest percentage point)

Social Security	24%
Medicare	15%
National defense	15%
Health	13%
Income security	12%
Net interest	8%
Education, training, employment, and social services	3%
Veterans benefits and services	5%
Administration of justice	2%
Transportation	2%
International affairs	1%
Natural resources and environment	1%
Community and regional development	1%
General science, space, and technology	1%
Agriculture	1%
General government	1%
Energy	<1%
Commerce and housing credit	−1%
Undistributed offsetting receipts	−2%

Source: Office of Management and Budget, *Historical Tables*, "Table 3.1—Outlays by Superfunction and Function: 1940–2025." Percentages calculated by author.

7. Based on the above table, which of the following was the highest percentage of FY 2019 expenditures?
   A. Social Security
   B. Medicare
   C. National Defense
   D. Health

8. Which of the following can be concluded from the information in the table above?
   A. Agriculture is the lowest of all government spending
   B. Entitlement spending puts pressure on all other government spending
   C. Defense and health combined spending is lower than entitlement spending in FY 2019
   D. Transportation spending needs to increase in FY 2020

9. Which of the following accurately compares liberal and conservative policy preferences?

	Liberal	Conservative
A.	Increase minimum wage	Pro-choice on abortion
B.	Government intervention to promote the public good	Market approach to economic welfare
C.	Increase regulations on owning firearms	Increase regulations to promote a clean environment
D.	End the death penalty	Open borders

10. A libertarian reviewing policy preferences of Democrats and Republicans would likely agree with which of the following?
   A. Democrats' more lenient border position and Republicans' end the death penalty position
   B. Republicans' belief that there should be an increase in regulations on owning firearms and Democrats' belief that the minimum wage should be increased
   C. Democrats' pro-choice position and Republicans' free market position
   D. Democrats' desire to increase tariffs on foreign goods and Republicans' position on no minimum wage

11. Presidential policy-making abilities are strongest in which of the following areas?
   A. Health care policy
   B. Environmental policy
   C. Foreign policy
   D. Entitlement policies

12. Which of the following is the strongest agent of political socialization?
   A. The media
   B. Peer groups
   C. Church affiliation
   D. The family

13. Which of the following describes a difficulty presidents often face in the policy-making process?
   A. A Congress dominated by the opposing party that is reluctant to enact his or her legislative proposals
   B. A Supreme Court eager to review each proposal in advance of becoming law to screen for unconstitutional bills
   C. Governors opposed to implementing the policy
   D. A bureaucracy that refuses to carry out the law

14. In a public opinion poll of a representative sample of populations, over 1,000 people were asked to answer yes or no in response to the statements below.

(Form A) When a person has a disease that cannot be cured, do you think doctors should be allowed by law to end the patient's life by some painless means if the patient and his or her family request it?

(Form B) When a person has a disease that cannot be cured and is living in severe pain, do you think doctors should or should not be allowed by law to assist the patient to commit suicide if the patient requests it?

For Form A, 70% of respondents agreed. For Form B, 51% of respondents agreed. Which of the following most likely accounts for the different results?

   A. The questions were not open ended
   B. There were no respondents in the sample with experience with assisted suicide
   C. The sample size was not large enough to be reliable
   D. The questions contained a different wording.

15. Which of the following is true about the Affordable Care Act?
   A. It provided health insurance to all Americans
   B. It is a Medicare for all plan
   C. It provided subsidies for the low income to purchase insurance
   D. It required individuals to forfeit their employer-based plans

16. Which of the following was true about the passage of the Affordable Care Act?
   A. It was declared unconstitutional by the U.S. Supreme Court
   B. It passed with bipartisan support
   C. All Democrats in Congress voted for the ACA
   D. It narrowly passed the legislature

17. Which of the following allows the president to act unilaterally in foreign policymaking?
   A. Treaties
   B. Lawmaking
   C. Executive agreements
   D. Signing statements

18. Which of the following describes how the Constitution outlines foreign policymaking?
   A. Shared responsibility between the executive and legislative branches
   B. Presidential dominance over foreign policymaking
   C. Senate dominance over foreign policymaking
   D. The description of foreign policymaking is absent in the Constitution

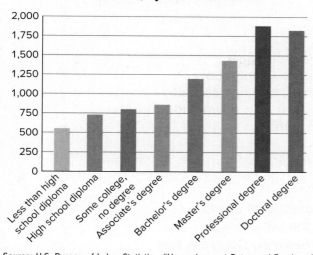

Median Weekly Earnings for Full-Time Workers, by Education Level

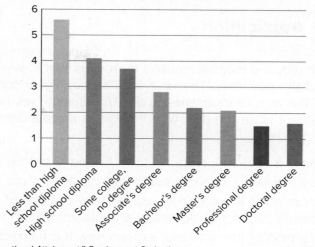

Unemployment Rate for Persons 25 years and over, by Education Level

Source: U.S. Bureau of Labor Statistics, "Unemployment Rates and Earnings by Educational Attainment," Employment Projections, September 4, 2019.

Use the graphs above to answer questions 19 and 20.

19. Which of the following describes the information in the bar graphs above?

    A. Low levels of education have correlated with higher rates of unemployment

    B. A college degree or higher is required for most professions

    C. People with a doctorate are less likely to be employed than people with other degrees

    D. More people get doctoral degrees than other degrees

20. Which of the following is a likely implication of the information in the bar graphs above?

    A. Education expenses are not likely to be supported because they contribute to the national debt

    B. Education spending has bipartisan support

    C. The information in this graph may encourage government leaders to pursue policies that support higher education

    D. The information in this graph is likely to be used by anti-government activists to discourage government spending on education

▌Free Response Questions

Concept Application

There is a global pandemic caused by a virus that is wreaking havoc on public health and the economy. The virus is airborne, highly contagious, and has caused deaths in the tens of thousands in the U.S. Businesses have been shut down and unemployment is on the rise, with no end to the pandemic in sight.

After reading the scenario, respond to A, B, and C below:

A. Describe a power Congress could use to address the scenario.

B. In the context of the scenario, explain how the use of congressional power described in part A can be affected by its interaction with the presidency.

C. In the context of the scenario, explain how the interaction between Congress and the presidency can be affected by linkage institutions.

Data Analysis

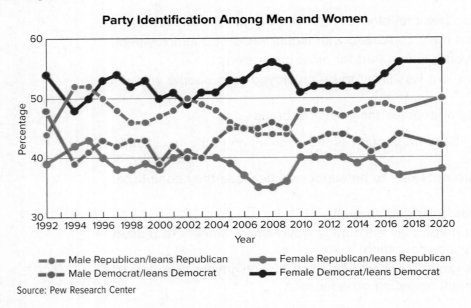

Party Identification Among Men and Women

Source: Pew Research Center

Use the information in the graphic to answer the questions.

A. Identify a trend in the line graph above.

B. Describe a similarity or difference in the identification by party as illustrated in the line graph above and draw a conclusion about that similarity or difference.

C. Explain how the information shown in the graphic demonstrates the gender gap.

Argumentation

Develop an argument about whether presidents should use poll data to inform foreign policy decisions.

In your essay, you must:

- Articulate a defensible claim or thesis that responds to the prompt and establishes a line of reasoning

- Support your claim with at least TWO pieces of accurate and relevant information:

    - At least ONE piece of evidence must be from one of the following foundational documents:

        — *Federalist* No. 10

        — The U.S. Constitution

    - Use a second piece of evidence from another foundational document from the list or from your study of public opinion polling

- Use reasoning to explain why your evidence supports your claim/thesis

- Respond to an opposing or alternative perspective using refutation, concession, or rebuttal

016
Heights

POLITICAL PARTICIPATION

In this unit on Political Participation, we will explore the varied ways that people communicate their priorities and opinions to government policymakers. Through political participation, citizens offer their voice and contribute to democratic governance. Participation is integral to democratic societies, as the foundation of government rests on the will of the people. The ways in which people communicate their will varies: some may take to the streets and organize a #BlackLivesMatter protest. Others might join an interest group—from the National Rifle Association to the Sierra Club—that represents their views. And the myriad ways in which people are involved in campaigns, from contributing campaign funds to candidates, to volunteering on a campaign, to attending a candidate rally or debate, to voicing their views of a particular candidate in the media, to voting are all ways in which people can influence government and politics, and influence the decision made in the policy making process. In this unit, we will examine the institutions—called "linkage institutions" that facilitate people's participation in their government, including political parties, interest groups, campaigns and elections, and the mass media.

Increasingly, and spurred on by the COVID-19 pandemic, many people are relying on technology as a medium to participate in political life, whether that is by subscribing to political influencer YouTube channel, Snapchatting with a candidate for local office, or following an elected leader or hash-tagged movement on Instagram. Technology has transformed all of the linkage institutions: campaign use big data to microtarget voters, while political parties use technology to rapidly conduct voter outreach operations. But in the wake of the 2020 elections and the pandemic, technology has also changed the single most important way we communicate our views to policymakers: through voting. In recent times, states have adjusted voting systems, including facilitating near-universal vote by mail elections. These changes have spawned a backlash, with some states attempting to tighten voter laws, making it more difficult for voters to cast their ballots. As the United States grapples with these and other issues, the proliferation of both online and brick-and-mortar groups and organizations, along with the sweeping transformation of the methods in which people can voice their views using technology, participating in the political life of our communities, states, and nation has never been easier.

■ What is Political Participation?

Big Ideas

AP Big Ideas will help you critically engage with what you read in the following chapters. As you go through this unit, think about how each of these questions is addressed by each chapter, and how these ideas are connected throughout the unit.

- **Why do some people choose to participate in government while others do not?**

- **How does your social network affect your political beliefs?**

- **Why might you join a political party? Why might you choose not to?**

- **How does who you are affect whether you participate or not?**

Before we can answer these questions, we need to ask what *is* political participation? Political participation includes any of the numerous ways that people communicate their priorities and opinions to political leaders and government policymakers. Voting, calling an elected official, participating in a lawful demonstration, joining an interest group or political party, and making a campaign contribution are all examples of legitimate forms of political participation in a democratic system and actions that take place daily. There is really no limit to the nature and forms of political participation a citizen can engage in—political participation can be as small as joining a neighborhood watch group and as large as organizing a political action committee (PAC) that donates millions of dollars toward political advertising.

Today, how Americans participate politically is undergoing drastic change, spurred by the political climate in the United States, by the transformative impact of technology, and by the effect of the COVID-19 pandemic on how people participate. When thinking about why, we should consider *what factors influence the nature and degree of political participation?* How do considerations such as political ideology, ability to see results, structural barriers, and demographics influence the kind and intensity of political participation?

Skills and Practices

As you read through the following chapters, consider how the skills of description, analysis, comparison, and causation help you to make sense of the information. By the end of this unit, you should be able to answer questions such as:

- **What is political participation and what forms does it take?**

- **How do we measure political participation? How does the U.S. compare to other countries, and what kinds of similarities or differences in demographics and history might explain those comparisons?**

- **How has the history of U.S. politics shaped political participation in the present?**

- **How might understanding these factors impact efforts to increase political participation?**

Campaigns, Elections, and Voting

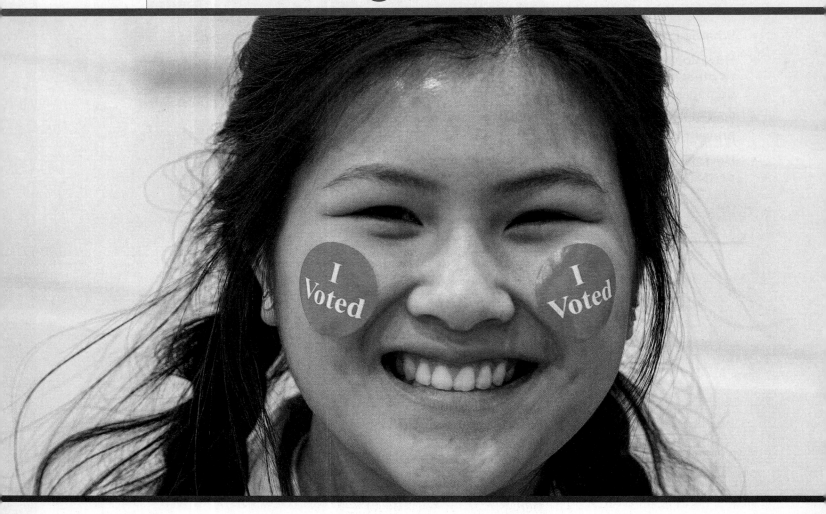

Kerem Yucel/AFP/Getty Images

THEN

Political party–dominated campaigns and grassroots activism were deciding factors in how people voted.

NOW

Candidate-centered campaigns rely on a mix of free social media to communicate with voters, paid professionals, and costly media buys to refine their messages to voters.

NEXT

How will new technologies drive how people vote and how campaigns are run?

How can government, candidates, and voters protect the electoral system from voter suppression, fraud, and corruption?

How will changes in the campaign finance system, including the advent of super PACs, affect how campaigns are waged?

■ Chapter Introduction

The 2020 presidential election was an election like no other. At one point, 29 Democrats vied for their party's nomination. During the Democratic primary, the struggle that initially emerged in 2016 between the moderate standard-bearers of the party versus the upstart progressives again emerged as a theme, but this time, the standard-bearer, 77-year-old former Vice President Joe Biden, not only won the nomination, but he also succeeded in ousting incumbent Republican President Donald Trump from the White House.

The campaign styles of the two septuagenarians could not have been more different. Biden, a Democrat whose working-class roots had defined his political stances and priorities, had a career-long history of sometimes stumbling when speaking off the cuff. Throughout the campaign, Biden remained scripted and on-message. Trump, one of the most divisive political figures in modern history, was beloved or reviled depending on which voter you were talking to. Trump's political success largely had come about by burning the script and riffing at 2 a.m. on Twitter, and this was how he conducted his campaign. He succeeded in rallying his cadre of loyal supporters.

But this election was not just about the candidates, because, more than ever, the context of the election mattered. Throughout the primary season, the conventions, the general election campaign, and finally through the period of early voting and then Election Day, the United State was ravaged by a global pandemic that altered the course of the presidential campaign. Biden conducted most of his campaign events virtually from his campaign compound in Delaware. In spite of the pandemic, Trump held in person campaign rallies, even after he himself was hospitalized after battling COVID-19. While the candidates campaigned, states scrambled to figure out how to facilitate voting in a time when routine aspects of balloting—standing in line in a confined space, touching voting machines, the presence of typically-elderly election workers—presented public health threats. Though not quite seamless, states succeeded in migrating to mail-in balloting, enabling voters to cast their ballots at home.

The aftermath of Joe Biden's victory was another historic touchpoint in U.S. history, a nation in which the peaceful transition of power has remained a cornerstone since George Washington voluntarily left the presidency to ensure that the transition could become routinized. In the face of his loss, Trump and his supporters attempted to discredit the legitimacy of the election, despite a glaring lack of evidence of fraud. With legal challenges to the election unsuccessful, an unruly mob of supporters gathered in Washington, D.C. on Jan. 6, 2021, the day that Congress would certify Joe Biden's election. Bent on preventing that certification, the crowd stormed the Capitol, resulting in the injury of over 140 people and five deaths. The insurrection marked a bleak chapter in history, but late in the evening of Jan. 6th, Congress reconvened in the vandalized Capitol, and in the early morning hours of Jan. 7th, certified the election of Joe Biden as president and Kamala Harris as vice president. Biden and Harris would go on to take their oaths of office in a peaceful inauguration on Jan. 20.

A key takeaway from the 2020 elections is that rules matter, and today throughout the United States, we see disagreement—much of it based in ideological differences—over what the rules should be. For example, in the aftermath of the 2020 elections, some states, including Georgia, have sought to make voting more difficult by decreasing the number of polling places in urban areas, for example, or by decreasing the number of days during which early voting can occur. Other states, like New Jersey, for example, have codified protections to ensure greater access to the ballot. Similarly, in the area of campaign finance, we see efforts by some to curb the influence money has in politics, while other seek to protect the ability of those with money to spend resources to influence election outcomes, arguing that doing so is equivalent to free speech. In these situations, conservatives argue election security outweigh the desire to increase participation and that campaign contributions should be unrestricted in democratic societies. On the other hand, liberals assert that increasing access to balloting, and encouraging voter turnout is fundamental democratic values, and that, given the history of obstacles placed before Black voters seeking to exercise their right to vote, the United State has a special obligation to ensure that all voters have equal access to the ballot, regardless of race or where they live. Liberals also tend to point out that the size of campaign contributions presents an unequal playing field in a society that purports to advocate for equality of opportunity.

The Importance of Fair, Independent Elections

In January 2017, a jointly issued report by the Central Intelligence Agency, the Federal Bureau of Investigation, and the National Security Agency stated with "high confidence" that the Russian government had conducted a sophisticated campaign to influence the 2016 presidential election. According to a declassified version of the report, Russian President Vladimir Putin ordered the effort both to damage Hillary Clinton's presidential campaign and to undermine the U.S. democratic process. "Putin and the Russian government developed a clear preference for President-elect Trump," stated the report.[1] Russia denied the allegations, but in the ensuing months, executives from Facebook testified before Congress, stating that at least 120 fake Russian-backed Facebook pages created 80,000 posts that 29 million Americans received directly, as did countless others who saw the posts through user shares, likes, and follows.[2] Facebook was not alone: By January 2018, Twitter had removed 50,258 accounts that had posted automated tweets about the 2016 election and were linked to Russia. Twitter turned over details to congressional investigators who looked into Moscow's interference with the U.S. election, but the posts reached more than 677,775 Americans before the election.[3]

Why Election Meddling Matters

Throughout U.S. history, individuals, organizations, and campaigns have attempted to influence how the American people think. From *The Federalist Papers*, which

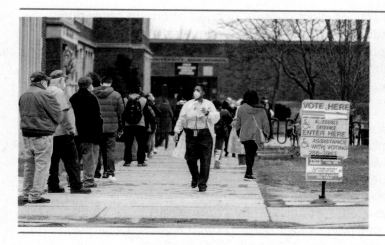

≫ In April 2020, as the COVID-19 pandemic raged, the state of Wisconsin faced criticism that voting had been hampered in Milwaukee, the most Democratic area of the state. Here, an election worker hands out masks to waiting voters.

Sara Stathas/*The Washington Post*/Getty Images

sought to convince Americans that the U.S. Constitution should be ratified, to YouTube videos advocating for Mitch McConnell's reelection to the U.S. Senate in 2020, the art of influencing voters has been part of political life. But in 2016, the evidence that Russia meddled in the U.S. election—and is still attempting to influence public opinion and foment political strife in the United States[4]—is cause for serious concern. Of utmost importance is the issue of national sovereignty— that nations have the right of self-rule without any interference from outside. Fundamental to democracies is that the will of the people is supreme, and the concept of popular sovereignty—that the people rule themselves by creating governments—means that governments are created with consent of the governed. But meddling by a foreign government, particularly one whose interests are often at odds with those of the United States, poses a challenge to popular sovereignty and the supremacy of the will of the people being governed. As Ben Franklin noted, "In free governments, the rulers are the servants and the people their superiors and sovereigns."[5]

Intentional Efforts at Voter Suppression

In 2020, complaints emerged that in some states, efforts were being made to suppress voter turnout in the wake of the COVID-19 pandemic, which altered how elections could and should take place. For example, in April, as the pandemic raged, the state of Wisconsin faced criticism that voting had been hampered in Milwaukee, the most Democratic area of the state. Specifically, Democratic Governor Tony Evers had tried to make it easier for people to vote, including by providing every voter with an absentee ballot and moving the date of the election. However, despite the state being under a stay-at-home order, Republican state legislative leaders blocked these efforts. In Milwaukee, the number of polling stations was decreased from 180 to 5, creating long lines for voters and, in many cases, an inability to socially distance, the effect of which was to suppress Democratic turnout.

Like historical efforts at voter suppression, the Milwaukee situation particularly affected voter participation by African American, Latinx, and Asian American voters who would, on the whole, be more likely to support Democratic candidates.

For example, in the 2016 elections, some voters decried efforts to tamp down voter participation in communities of color, noting antiquated voting machines and a reduced number of polling locations. Indeed, analysis by the Pew Charitable Trust indicated that nearly a thousand polling places have been closed across the United States since the 2016 election, many of them in southern black communities.[6]

In some places, allegations of intentional voter suppression have tainted the electoral process. For example, a report by the Associated Press detailed how Georgia Secretary of State Brian Kemp, who was also running as a Republican for governor in 2016, had suspended more than 50,000 voter registrations.[7] A disproportionate number were the registrations of African Americans, who constitute 32 percent of the state's population but were almost 70 percent of the suspended applications. A coalition of civil rights groups filed a lawsuit to prevent enforcement of the suspensions in the 2018 and 2020 elections.[8]

Political Participation as an Expression of the Will of the People

The act of voting embodies the expression of the will of the people, a nearly sacred concept that has evolved significantly from its origins in ancient Greece. Campaigns, elections, and voting are fundamental aspects of the civic engagement of Americans and are important both for the polity as a whole and for the individuals who participate.[9] They ensure that the government is representative of the people and responsive to their needs. Representative governments, which are the product of individuals' political engagement, tend to be more stable and to make decisions that best reflect the needs and the will of the people who elect them.

Direct forms of political participation such as voting, volunteering on a campaign, and running for office are of keen interest to political scientists and scholars of civic engagement. Many scholarly analysts have noticed an overall decrease in levels of political participation. As discussed in Chapter 16, political scientist Robert Putnam argues that the United States is seeing a decline in its social capital, the social networks and reciprocal relationships characteristic of a community or a society. Some scholars have challenged Putnam's assertion that social capital has declined. They point out that new forms of social capital have arisen in the form of online social networks, instant messaging, and Internet activism to replace the traditional social networks that Putnam studied. Others point to the cyclical nature of political involvement and argue that in modern times, candidate-centered campaigns—particularly ones that evoke high levels of voter passion and participation, including the 2008 and 2020 elections—mark the ebb and flow of political participation and social capital. Despite these differing views, consensus exists that civic participation is essential and that among its most important forms is electoral political participation.

Australian ballot
A secret ballot prepared by the government, distributed to all eligible voters, and, when balloting is completed, counted by government officials in an unbiased fashion, without corruption or regard to individual preferences.

■ The Act of Voting

The process of voting begins when a voter registers to vote. Voting registration requirements vary greatly from state to state. Some states require registration months in advance of an election; others allow voters to register on the day of voting. In the United States, the voters use an **Australian ballot**, a secret ballot prepared by the government, distributed to all eligible voters, and, when balloting is completed, counted by government officials in an unbiased fashion, without corruption or regard to individual preferences. Because the U.S. Constitution guarantees the states the right to conduct elections, the mechanics and methods of voting vary widely from state to state. Some states use touch-screen technology; others employ computer-based ballots or punch cards that are counted by computers. Still other states use traditional lever ballots, in which voters pull a lever to register their vote for a particular candidate. Despite those differences, all ballots are secret ballots.

Although secret ballots are the norm today, that was not always the case. From the days of the early republic through the 19th century, many citizens exercised their right to vote using oral votes cast in public or written votes witnessed by others; some made their electoral choices on color-coded ballots prepared by the political parties, which indicated which party the voter was supporting.

The 2000 Election and Its Impact

In the 2000 presidential election between Democrat Al Gore and Republican George W. Bush, an enormous controversy erupted over the voting in Florida. Because of the closeness of the electoral vote, the outcome of the Florida election turned out to be pivotal. But the tallies in that state's election were in question, not only because of the narrow difference in the number of votes won by each candidate, but also because of the voting process itself, which was marred by voting irregularities caused by poorly designed ballots that forced election officials to begin a tedious process of hand-counting ballots. In the end, the U.S. Supreme Court had the final say. On December 12, 2000, the Court halted the hand counting of ballots in Florida, with the Court's majority ruling that the differing standards of hand-counting ballots from one county to the next and the absence of a single judicial officer charged with overseeing the hand counts violated the equal protection clause of the Fourteenth Amendment to the U.S. Constitution. The ruling meant that George W. Bush, who was leading in the count, was certified the winner of the Florida race, thus securing that state's 25 Electoral College votes, and tipping him over the 270 votes necessary to win the presidency.

Indignation surrounding the 2000 election resulted in federal policy changes to how state elections were conducted. The key policy revision came through the passage of the Help America Vote Act of 2002 (HAVA). HAVA allocated $650 million to assist states in changing from punch card ballots to electronic voting systems and set a deadline of 2005 for states to comply. Most states implemented the election reforms required by HAVA, but many experienced difficulties with electronic-only voting systems, compelling some to adopt systems that created a traceable paper backup system. By 2020 eight states—Texas, Louisiana, Tennessee, Mississippi, Kansas, Indiana, Kentucky, and New Jersey—had electronic voting without any form of backup paper balloting.[10]

Types of Ballots

Two types of ballots are most commonly used in general elections in the states today (Figure 14.1). The first, the **party-column ballot**, organizes the candidates by party so that all of a given party's candidates for every office are arranged in one column. The opposing party's candidates appear in a different column.

party-column ballot
A ballot that organizes the candidates by political party.

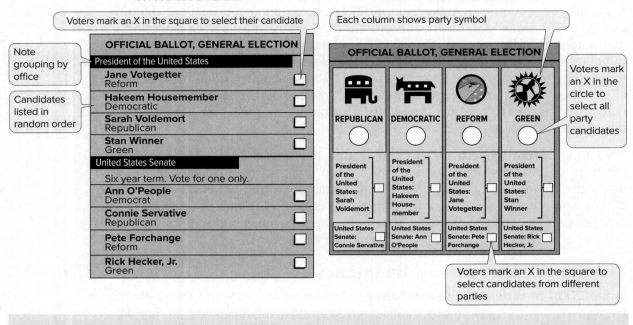

OFFICE-BLOCK BALLOT

Voters mark an X in the square to select their candidate

Note grouping by office

Candidates listed in random order

OFFICIAL BALLOT, GENERAL ELECTION

President of the United States

Jane Votegetter
Reform

Hakeem Housemember
Democratic

Sarah Voldemort
Republican

Stan Winner
Green

United States Senate

Six year term. Vote for one only.

Ann O'People
Democrat

Connie Servative
Republican

Pete Forchange
Reform

Rick Hecker, Jr.
Green

PARTY-COLUMN BALLOT

Each column shows party symbol

Voters mark an X in the circle to select all party candidates

OFFICIAL BALLOT, GENERAL ELECTION

REPUBLICAN | DEMOCRATIC | REFORM | GREEN

President of the United States: Sarah Voldemort

President of the United States: Hakeem Housemember

President of the United States: Jane Votegetter

President of the United States: Stan Winner

United States Senate: Connie Servative

United States Senate: Ann O'People

United States Senate: Pete Forchange

United States Senate: Rick Hecker, Jr.

Voters mark an X in the square to select candidates from different parties

FIGURE 14.1 Office-Block and Party-Column Ballots

party line voting
To vote for every candidate of a given party for every office.

coattail effect
The phenomenon by which candidates running for lower-level offices such as city council benefit in an election from the popularity of a top-of-ticket nominee.

office-block ballot
A type of ballot that arranges all the candidates for a particular office under the name of that office.

The impact of a party-column ballot is twofold: First, party-column ballots increase voters' tendency to vote the "**party line**," that is, to vote for every candidate of a given party for every office. Second, because they increase the tendency to vote the party line, party-column ballots also increase the **coattail effect**, the phenomenon whereby *down-ballot candidates* (candidates who are running for lower-level offices, such as city council) benefit from the popularity of a top-of-ticket nominee. Often, the composition of city councils, county legislatures, and even state legislatures changes because of a coattail effect from a popular presidential or gubernatorial candidate. Because party-column ballots strengthen political parties, parties tend to favor this type of ballot, which is the most commonly used ballot in the United States.

Another type of general election ballot is the **office-block ballot**, which arranges all candidates for a particular office under the name of that office. Office-block ballots are more likely to encourage ticket splitting, where-by voters "split their ticket"—that is, divide their votes—between candidates from different parties.[11] Because office-block ballots deemphasize political parties by breaking up the party line, the parties do not tend to favor them.

Voting by Mail

Because of the outbreak of COVID-19 in 2020, sweeping changes occurred in the number of states that permitted voters to vote by mail. States were faced with the public health risk associated with gathering large numbers of people in an enclosed space and having to disinfect voting machines touched by the public. Moreover, many poll workers are retirees, likely to be more vulnerable if infected with the virus. In response, some states moved elections to all vote by mail. However, the transition was not seamless, as the move increased demands on county, state, and federal bureaucracies charged with creating, printing, mailing, delivering, and counting mailed-in ballots.

Before the pandemic, states had been gradually adopting mail-in voting, as they attempted to increase voter participation by making voting more convenient. Historically, **absentee voting**, in which voters cast their ballots in advance by mail, was allowed only when disability, illness, school, work, service in the armed forces, or travel prevented voters from casting a ballot in their voting precincts. Every state has a provision that allows some voters—the elderly, the infirm, or those traveling—to vote via absentee ballot. To cast a traditional absentee ballot, an individual must typically apply (before a specific state-designated deadline) to vote by absentee in the county where he or she usually votes and is then mailed a ballot. The voter then votes and mails back the ballot. The absentee ballots are counted and added to the votes cast in the voting precincts. Requirements for absentee ballots vary from state to state. Before COVID-19, one-third of the states required voters to have an excuse to cast an absentee ballot, but those structures changed rapidly in 2020.

absentee voting
The casting of a ballot in advance by mail in situations where illness, travel, or other circumstances prevent voters from voting in their precincts.

≫ The process of voting varies from state to state, but in 2020, the voting booth was a rarity, as most states relied on mail-in balloting due to the COVID-19 pandemic. In every state, however, a ballot is prepared by the government, distributed to all eligible voters, and counted by government officials in an unbiased fashion. In your view, would voters be more likely to vote in person or by mail-in ballot?

Eduardo Munoz Alvarez/AFP/Getty Images

The first experiment with statewide vote by mail occurred in Oregon in 1996. In a special election there, where officials had predicted a turnout of less than 50 percent, more than 66 percent of voters cast their ballots. This experiment brought another benefit: It saved taxpayers more than $1 million. Oregon decided to continue the practice in the presidential elections and has regularly seen voter turnout rates that exceed the national average. Oregon has now taken the drastic step of abandoning voting in polling places on Election Day.

Since that time, the practice of enabling citizens to cast their ballots by mail—often before Election Day—has become much more widespread. In Oregon, Washington State, Colorado, and parts of Utah and California, all voters are sent mail ballots automatically. In 34 states plus the District of Columbia, any registered voter can cast a ballot in person during a designated period before Election Day. States vary in how long they allow early voting, with some states holding balloting for 4 days, others up to 45 days. Most states with early voting require that polling places—usually government offices—be open at least one weekend day, enabling those who work long hours to cast their ballots.

Voting by mail offers obvious advantages. When voting becomes easier, more people participate. Further, increased participation may bring to office candidates who are more representative of the will of the people because more people had a say in their election. And if elections are conducted by mail exclusively (that is, without the option of in-person voting), states can save money, as they no longer have to pay to print and mail sample ballots, buy and maintain voting machines, and train and pay poll workers.

Some scholars, however, have criticized both the vote-by-mail and early voting trends. One important criticism is that early voting means that people vote before the final days of the campaign, thus casting their ballots before some additional last-minute information might be revealed about a candidate. Voting by mail could also increase the chance that a ballot might not be counted, an outcome that would be less likely to occur at a polling place. For example, in marking a ballot, if a voter selected too many candidates for a particular office (an "overvote"), that ballot would not count, but this is less likely to occur at a polling place because the electronic voting machines would prevent the error. Also, some contend that vote by mail increases chances of vote fraud. Even though states take measures to ensure the principle of "one person, one vote," voting by mail presents opportunities for corruption. For example, voting at the polls requires a face-to-face encounter, but voting by mail does not, so ballots could be stolen from individuals' mailboxes or intercepted after voters have mailed them.

Voting by mail also may eliminate the privacy associated with voting in recent times. With mail balloting, the vote occurs in a less controlled setting, and the voter might feel pressured by others to select a particular candidate. In contrast, booth voting affords privacy and secrecy that go far toward ensuring that the votes cast behind the curtain reflect the individual voter's will.

As witnessed in the 2020 elections, another disadvantage of vote by mail is cost, particularly when states also offer in-person voting. And that year, states that switched exclusively to vote-by-mail balloting because of COVID-19 scrambled to pay for printing, mailing, and processing ballots at the last minute.

Finally, voting by mail may undermine feelings of civic engagement by eliminating a source of psychological rewards for voters. Going to a polling place, signing the voting registry, entering the voting booth, and casting your vote can elicit feelings of patriotism, civic pride, and fulfillment of civic responsibility—the sense that you are doing your duty to help ensure the election of the best-qualified candidates. Although the results may be the same with voting by mail, some evidence suggests that voting by mail does not bring with it the same sense of civic satisfaction that voting at a polling place confers.

■ Running for Office: The Choice to Run

The reasons that individuals become political candidates vary almost as much as the individuals do. Yet four types of motivation are generally in play when a person decides to declare a candidacy:

- Sense of civic responsibility—the feeling on the candidate's part that he or she bears an obligation to serve.

- Sense of party loyalty—of filling the need for parties to run viable candidates.

- Interest in increasing the candidate's name recognition and stature in the community, often for business reasons.

- Personal goals and, in particular, interest in electoral politics and office holding as a career.

Some people believe they have an obligation to put their experience, knowledge, and skills to work for the greater good of the community or country. Often these civically motivated people become politically involved out of concerns about specific issues. For example, 2018 saw a record number of scientists seeking congressional seats, many as part of a "pro-science resistance" spawned in response to what they perceive as an attack on scientific information and reasoning by the federal government.[12] Eleven scientists were elected that year—a record number—and in 2020 three more, including astronaut Mark Kelly, sought to follow in their footsteps.

Sometimes an individual may choose to run for office out of a sense of party duty. The candidate may run as a "sacrificial lamb" for a seat he or she has little chance of winning, mainly with the intent to ensure that the party offers an alternative to the favored candidate. Some people run for office because of the heightened stature that a candidacy brings to their "regular" careers, through either name recognition or networking opportunities.

Other people are motivated to run for a particular office as their career. Holding office is what they do—and because of the advantages of incumbency, once elected, many remain in office for years. Other candidates run for office because of political ambitions. For example, a town council member who aspires to serve in the state legislature might run for county commissioner even if she thinks she will not win because she realizes that running a viable campaign might help her in a later bid for the statehouse.

Many candidates, of course, run for office for a combination of reasons. They might believe, for example, that they have a responsibility to serve their country *and* that they have something valuable to contribute.

Formal Eligibility Requirements

Article I of the U.S. Constitution specifies some minimum criteria for those seeking election to federal office:

- **President.** A candidate for the presidency must be a natural-born citizen. Naturalized citizens, who are born citizens of another country and then choose to become American citizens such as Ileana Ros-Lehtinen (R-Fla.), a member of the House of Representatives and a native of Cuba, cannot run for president. Presidential candidates also must be at least 35 years old. The youngest person elected president was 43-year-old John F. Kennedy, but Theodore Roosevelt, who assumed the presidency after William McKinley's assassination, was the youngest to hold the office, at age 42. A presidential candidate also must have been a resident of the United States for 14 years by the time of inauguration.

- **Vice president.** A vice presidential candidate, like a contender for the presidency, must be a natural-born citizen and must be at least 35 years old; he or she must not be a resident of the same state as the candidate for president with whom he or she will serve. John Breckinridge, elected vice president in 1856 at age 35, was the youngest person to win the office.

- **U.S. senator.** A candidate for the Senate must have citizen status of at least 9 years, must be at least 30 years old when taking office, and must be a resident of the state from which he or she is elected. Currently the youngest person serving in the Senate is Jon Ossoff (D-Ga,), born in 1987 and sworn into the Senate at age 33 in 2021.

- **U.S. representative.** A candidate for the House of Representatives must be a citizen for at least 7 years, must be at least 25 years old when taking office, and must be a resident of the state from which he or she is elected. Representative Madison Cawthorn (R-N.C.), born in 1995, was elected in 2020 and sworn into office at age 25. He is the youngest member of the House.

Typically, a state's constitution determines the minimal qualifications for the governorship and the state legislature, and these vary from state to state. In general, state requirements address the same issues as federal guidelines—citizenship, age, and residency.

Informal Eligibility Requirements

In addition to the legal eligibility requirements prescribed by the federal and state constitutions, informal eligibility criteria—that is, the characteristics that voters expect officeholders to have—help to determine who is qualified to run for a particular office. By and large, the eligibility pool for elected office depends on the office—and so although your car mechanic might be considered a good candidate for your town council, he would not likely meet the informal eligibility criteria to be elected president of the United States.

Generally speaking, the higher and more prestigious the political office, the greater the informal eligibility requirements are. On the local level, particularly in smaller communities, an individual would be considered eligible to run for town council if he or she was liked and respected in the community, had lived in the community long enough to know the voters, and was gainfully employed, a homemaker, or retired.

Farther up the political office ladder, state legislative candidates in most states are expected to have some kind of professional career. Still, there is a great deal of variation from state to state, and certainly nonprofessionals occupy many state legislative seats. State legislatures tend to be dominated by lawyers and business professionals, occupations that offer the prestige to be considered part of the informal eligibility pool and that allow enough flexibility to facilitate campaigning and legislative work.

>> Informal qualifications for Congress vary according to the political culture in the district. Openly gay members of Congress are a rarity. Mark Takano (D-Ca.), first elected in 2012, is the first openly gay person of color to be elected to the U.S. House of Representatives.

Interpret: How have electoral politics around LGBTQ+ people changed in the last two decades? Does being an openly gay or trans person impact how candidates conduct campaigns, or how voters perceive them?

Bill Clark/CQ Roll Call/Getty Images

The informal eligibility requirements for federal office are even more stringent. Voters expect candidates for the House of Representatives, the U.S. Senate, and the presidency to have higher qualifications than candidates for state and local offices. Among most congressional constituencies, candidates for federal office would be viewed as "qualified" to hold office if they had been elected to office, had a college degree, had considerable professional and leadership experience, and had strong communication skills. But informal qualifications vary according to the political culture in a district, with some districts favoring a particular religious affiliation, ethnicity, or other characteristic. Traditionally, in races for the U.S. Senate and the presidency, the popular press examines the minutest details of candidates' professional and educational backgrounds. For example, sometimes it is not enough that candidates are college graduates; where they went to college, whose university is more prestigious, and who had the higher grade point average are all fodder for the media and political pundits. But 2016 marked a watershed year in defining the appropriate informal eligibility requirements for a presidential candidate. When Donald Trump announced his candidacy for the Republican presidential nomination, many party insiders dismissed the celebrity candidate as not having what it takes to be president. Trump had never been elected to office, had suffered serious ups and downs in his business ventures, and was known to most of the United States as star of the reality television show *The Apprentice*. But Trump's celebrity, and his brash personality, attracted a cohort of voters perhaps weary of the predictable professional politicians who could check off all the boxes of "informal eligibility requirements," and Trump went on to win not only the GOP nomination, but also the presidency itself.

■ Elections in the United States

Every state holds at least two types of elections. A *primary election* comes first and determines the party's nominees—those who will run for office. In presidential elections, in most states, nominees are chosen when voters go to the polls and select a candidate's slate of delegates to the national party convention. For most political offices, there is little or no competition in the primary election. But in presidential and gubernatorial primary elections, vigorous contention is often the rule, particularly within the out-of-power party. House and Senate primary elections that lack an incumbent candidate (that is, one who has been elected to that office before) are also often highly competitive as many candidates attempt to win their party's nomination.

In a **general election**, the parties' nominees run against each other, and, in all but presidential elections, voters decide directly who should hold office because the person with the most votes wins. (Presidential elections are determined by the Electoral College, discussed later in this chapter.) The degree of competition in general elections depends on a number of factors, including the presence of and the strength of incumbency, the degree of party competition, and the level of the office. In recent times, presidential elections have been brutally competitive, as have been certain gubernatorial races and many congressional contests in which no incumbent is seeking reelection. Some communities, particularly big cities, may also experience intense competition for office in general elections.

general election
An election that determines which candidates win the offices being sought.

Deciding the Nomination: Caucuses and Primaries

In a primary election, voters decide which nominees the political parties should run in the general election. But *which* voters decide varies greatly from state to state. In some states, only registered party members are eligible to vote in primary elections, whereas in other states, any registered voter can vote in any party's primary, and in North Dakota, voters are not even required to register.

In U.S. presidential primaries, voters do not vote directly for the candidate whom they would like their party to nominate. Instead, the popular vote determines which candidate's delegates will attend the party's nominating convention and vote for that party's nominee. This system of selecting delegates through a caucus or primary differs from the system used in the 19th and first part of the 20th centuries, when party leaders selected the presidential nominee with little or no input from the rank-and-file party members.

The two major U.S. parties made reforms to the earlier delegate-selection process after the 1968 Democratic National Convention in Chicago. In attempting to address the concerns of anti–Vietnam War activists who had protested the nomination of pro-war candidate Vice President Hubert Humphrey, the Democratic National Committee appointed the McGovern-Fraser Commission (named after its co-chairs), which recommended a series of reforms to the delegate-selection process. The reforms, many of which both the Democratic Party and the Republican Party adopted, significantly increased the influence of party primary voters and caucus attendees. Voters could now select delegates to the national conventions, a power previously restricted to the party elite. The reforms also included provisions that would ensure the selection of a more representative body of delegates, with certain delegate slots set aside for women, minorities, union members, and young party voters. These slots roughly correspond with the proportion of support the party receives from those groups.

caucus
A meeting of party members held to select delegates to the national convention.

CAUCUSES In deciding who a party's nominee should be, as mentioned, some states hold **caucuses**—meetings during which party members choose the delegates. In a caucus, registered members of a local party gather, discuss the candidates, and vote for the candidate whom they want to have their party's nomination. In both parties, the purpose of the caucus vote is to select delegates to attend a county convention; each caucus sends a certain number of delegates, based on the population it represents. The delegates at the county convention in

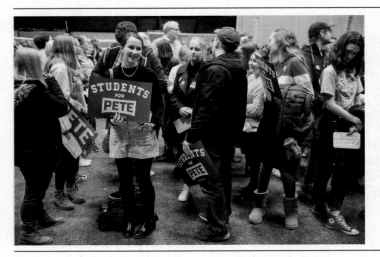

>> The 2020 Iowa caucuses—where Democrats gathered to begin the process of choosing their presidential nominee—were the subject of much controversy. Mismanaged technology used to conduct the election and miscommunication by party officials delayed and marred the results.

Jeremy Hogan/Echoes Wire/Barcroft Media/Getty Images

turn select delegates to go to the congressional district state convention, and those delegates in turn choose the delegates who go to the national convention.

Both political parties have urged states to move away from the caucus system—a structure that was very common historically—and use instead a primary election, which is administered by government officials rather than party leaders. Several states, including Nevada, Hawaii, Maine, Kansas, and Iowa, retain the caucus structure, but Iowa's caucuses are the best-known because they are the first of all the presidential-nomination selection contests to be held every election year. In 2020, the Iowa caucus came under heavy scrutiny when technological glitches meant that certified results were not available for weeks. In the end, Democratic presidential candidate Mayor Pete Buttigieg of South Bend, Indiana, received one more vote than Sen. Bernie Sanders (D-Vt.). However, the caucus results were moot, as both Buttigieg and Sanders dropped out of the race within weeks of the caucus. The technical difficulties experienced in 2020 led many to speculate that political parties would increase pressure on states to switch to a primary system in 2024.

TYPES OF PRIMARY ELECTIONS In an **open primary** election, any registered voter can vote in any party's primary, as can independent voters not registered with a party. In the 20 states[13] with an open presidential primary, parties' ballots are available in the voting booth, and the voter simply selects privately or publicly one on which to register his or her preferences.

In a **closed primary** election, voting in a party's primary is limited to members of that party. In some states, voters must declare their party affiliation well in advance of the primary election—sometimes as many as 60 days before. In other states, voters can declare their party preference at the polling place on the day of the election. Such restrictions on who can vote in a party's primary originated in the parties' maneuvering to have the strongest candidate nominated. For example, if a popular incumbent president were running unopposed in a primary election, members of the president's party might choose to vote in the other party's primary as a way of scheming to get a weak candidate nominated. A closed primary aims to thwart that strategy.

PRESIDENTIAL PRIMARIES The states determine the timing of primary elections. Historically, states that held their presidential primaries earlier in the year had a greater say in determining the nominee than did states with later primaries. The reason is that candidates tended to drop out if they did not win primaries, did not meet media expectations, or ran out of funds. (See "Thinking Critically.") In general, past presidential primaries gave great sway to the agricultural states because many of the more urban states' primaries fell later in the season. **Super Tuesday** is the day in early March on which the most presidential primary elections take place, many of them in southern states. Super Tuesday had been the fruit of a successful effort in 1988 by several southern and rural states to hold their primaries on the same day so as to increase their political importance and allow expression of southern voters' political will.[14]

General Elections

In a general election, voters decide who should hold office from among the candidates determined in the primary election. Most general elections, including presidential elections, are held on the first Tuesday after the first Monday in

open primary
A type of primary in which both parties' ballots are available in the voting booth, and the voters simply select one on which to register their preferences.

closed primary
A type of primary in which voting in a party's primary is limited to members of that party.

Super Tuesday
The Tuesday in early March on which the most primary elections are held, many of them in southern states.

Should the United States Have a National Primary?

THE ISSUE: The party primary process that selects each party's nominee for president was a hot-button issue in the 2020 presidential race. Historically, the primary system focused enormous attention on the states of Iowa, where the first caucus is held, and New Hampshire, where the first party primary takes place. In these states, voters have had the opportunity to gain a deep familiarity with all the candidates seeking the parties' nominations. But critics of the system have charged that these two states' political cultures do not reflect that of the vast majority of Americans. Indeed, given that the party's nominees were effectively chosen by early April, before several of the most populous states (including California and New Jersey) had even held their primaries, many questioned the democratic nature of a primary structure that effectively disenfranchised a segment of the population. Many citizens have asked, "Is this any way to begin electing a president?"

Should states matter when it comes to selecting the parties' nominees? One potential solution to the skewed emphasis on various states is to hold a national primary so that party members throughout the country can choose their nominees on the same day. People have voiced arguments for and against the idea of a national primary.

YES: Having a national primary will help the parties because it will ensure that the nominee chosen in each case is the best candidate for the party. With the shift to a national primary, states that currently have late primaries will no longer be forced to accept a nominee chosen by party members who might be very different from themselves. Furthermore, if more people have a say in choosing their party's nominee, voter turnout might rise in both the primary and the general election. Holding a national primary also will shorten the election season, so that voters will be less fatigued by the length of the campaign.

NO: The primary system ensures that small, agricultural states have a voice in national politics. In the general election, smaller states are overshadowed because the Electoral College, which is based on state population, determines the winner. The current primary and caucus system enables voters in those states to analyze the candidates thoroughly, without the noise and distraction that would come with a large-scale, media-saturated national primary. And because the voters in states such as Iowa and New Hampshire are, after all, party members, they naturally understand that a large part of their responsibility is to select the nominee best equipped to win the general election.

OTHER APPROACHES: Some have suggested the idea of holding regional primaries instead of one national primary, with a different region holding its primary election first in each presidential election year so that no region would have the influence that Iowa and New Hampshire now enjoy. Each region would include a mix of large and

WHAT DO YOU THINK?

1. Do you believe that we should have a national primary? Explain.

2. What impact would a national primary have on your home state's say in the nomination process? How will small states fare compared with large states? Rural compared with urban?

3. What influence do you think a national primary or regional primaries would have on voter turnout? What effect might either type of primary have on how presidential campaigns are waged? Would money be more or less important? Why?

small states and urban and rural areas. Candidates would need to campaign throughout each region in turn rather than the entire country, thus allowing them to focus their efforts more than they would be able to with one national primary, and with three or four regional primaries, the campaign season would still be shortened significantly, thus eliminating voter fatigue.

November. But because the states schedule and oversee elections, you might find that your gubernatorial election, state legislative election, or town council election occurs at a different time of the year.

General elections for Congress and most state legislatures feature a winner-take-all system. That is, the candidate who receives the most votes wins that office (even if that total is not a majority, or even if an opponent receives only one vote fewer than the victor). Thus, a member of the U.S. House of Representatives or Senate can be elected with less than a majority of the votes in his or her district, particularly when three or more candidates are seeking that seat.

Because electoral law varies from state to state, and counties and municipalities within those states have their own structures of governance, less common kinds of elections are possible and are used in some locales. For example, some states require a runoff election when no candidate receives the majority of the votes cast. In a **runoff election**, if no candidate receives more than 50 percent of the vote, several of the top vote-getters (usually the top two) run in another, subsequent election. Typically, the field of candidates is winnowed down until one candidate receives the requisite 50 percent plus one vote. Runoff elections often occur in *nonpartisan* municipal elections, in which candidates do not run on a party label.

runoff election
A follow-up election that is held when no candidate receives the majority of votes cast in the original election.

Owing to advances in technology, runoff elections can occur immediately in some states when needed. In an **instant runoff election**, a computerized voting machine simulates the elimination of last-place vote-getters. How does this system work? In an instant runoff, voters rank candidates in order of preference (first choice, second choice, and so on). If any candidate garners more than 50 percent of all the first-choice votes, that candidate wins. But if no candidate gets a majority of first-choice votes, the candidate in last place is eliminated electronically. The voting machine computer then recalculates the ballots, using the second-choice vote for those voters who voted for the eliminated last-place finisher; in effect, every voter gets to choose among the candidates remaining on the ballot. This process is repeated until a candidate who receives more than 50 percent of the votes emerges. Today's voting machines allow this process to take place instantly.

instant runoff election
A special runoff election in which the computerized voting machine simulates the elimination of last-place vote-getters.

Referendum, Initiative, and Recall

Whereas primary elections and general elections select an individual to run for and serve in office, other kinds of elections are held for the purpose of deciding public policy questions. Although no national mechanism allows all Americans to vote for or against a given policy proposal, citizens can directly decide policy questions in their states by referendum or initiative.[15]

A **referendum** is an election in which voters in a state can vote for or against a measure proposed by the state legislature. Frequently, referenda concern matters such as state bond issues, state constitutional amendments, and controversial pieces of legislation. For example, in 2020, voters in New Jersey were asked to vote on whether they wanted to legalize adult-use marijuana. An **initiative**, sometimes called an initiative petition, is a citizen-sponsored proposal allowed in 24 states that can result in new or amended legislation or a state constitutional amendment. Initiatives differ from referenda in that they are typically propelled to public vote through the efforts of citizens and interest groups.[16] The initiative process usually requires that 10 percent of the number of the voters in the previous election in that state sign a petition agreeing that the **proposition**, or proposed measure, should be placed on the ballot. In 2020, many organizations sought to have questions put on the ballot concerning a wide variety of issues, including measures to protect the LGBTQ community from discrimination, to create nonpartisan redistricting processes, and to legalize marijuana. However, these organizations faced the enormous obstacle of trying to gather signatures when most states had ordered people to stay at home because of the COVID-19 pandemic. Some groups successfully pushed for electronic signature provision; others were forced to wait until 2021.

A third type of special election, the recall, differs from referenda and initiatives in that it is not concerned with policy-related issues. Rather, the **recall** election allows voters to cut an officeholder's term of office short. Recall elections are typically citizen-sponsored efforts that demonstrate serious dissatisfaction with a particular officeholder. Concerned citizens circulate a petition, and, after they gather the required number of signatures, an election is held to determine whether the official should be thrown out of office.

The Nature of Political Campaigns Today

Campaigns today are different from the campaigns of the 1980s or even the early 1990s. The main reasons for the changes are the professionalization of campaign staffs; the dramatically expanded role of the media, the Internet, and social media and digital technologies; and the changing nature of campaign finance driven by candidates' ever-rising need for funding to keep pace with the unprecedented demands of contemporary campaigning.[17]

The Professionalization of Political Campaigns

One of the most significant changes in the conduct of campaigns is the rise in prominence of **campaign consultants**, paid professionals who specialize in the overall management of political campaigns or an aspect of campaigns, such as fund-raising or advertising. Previously, volunteers who believed in the party's ideals and in the candidate ran most campaigns. In contrast, professional consultants dominate modern campaigns for federal offices, many state offices, and some municipal offices. Typically, these advisers receive generous compensation for their services. Although professional consultants may not be as dedicated to a single candidate as earlier grassroots volunteers were, these strategists are typically committed to seeing their candidate elected and often are quite partisan, usually working only for candidates of one party throughout their careers.

THEN

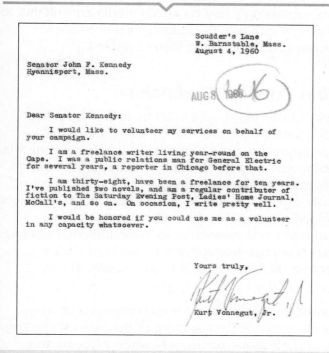

```
                                    Scudder's Lane
                                    W. Barnstable, Mass.
                                    August 4, 1960

Senator John F. Kennedy
Hyannisport, Mass.

                          AUG 8 1960

Dear Senator Kennedy:

     I would like to volunteer my services on behalf of
your campaign.

     I am a freelance writer living year-round on the
Cape.  I was a public relations man for General Electric
for several years, a reporter in Chicago before that.

     I am thirty-eight, have been a freelance for ten years.
I've published two novels, and am a regular contributor of
fiction to The Saturday Evening Post, Ladies' Home Journal,
McCall's, and so on.  On occasion, I write pretty well.

     I would be honored if you could use me as a volunteer
in any capacity whatsoever.


                              Yours truly,


                              Kurt Vonnegut, Jr.
```

NOW

Source Analysis In 1960, campaigns, even those for the presidency, relied primarily on political party organizations and cadres of volunteers, including celebrities like famed author Kurt Vonnegut, who told then-senator Kennedy, "On occasion, I write pretty well." Now, campaigns are highly professional, with the labors of a campaign divided among many hired consultants and technology driving participation among voters. Here, Senator Cory Booker's (D.-N.J.) website directs individuals on how to donate, keep informed, or volunteer on the campaign.

Letter: Kurt Vonnegut Jr. Copyright Trust; *website:* Source: corybooker.com

One of the top jobs in a political campaign is that of **campaign manager**, a professional whose duties include a variety of strategic and managerial tasks. Among these responsibilities may be the development of the overall **campaign strategy**, the blueprint for the campaign, which includes a budget and fund-raising plan, an advertising strategy, and staffing objectives. Once the campaign strategy is set, the campaign manager often hires and manages the office staff; selects the campaign's theme, colors, and slogan; shapes the candidate's image; and creates a **GOTV**—get out the vote—strategy. Another crucial campaign professional is the pollster, who conducts focus groups and polls that help develop the campaign strategy by identifying the candidate's strengths and weaknesses and revealing what voters care about.

campaign manager
A professional whose duties comprise a variety of strategic and managerial tasks, from fund-raising to staffing a campaign.

campaign strategy
The blueprint for the campaign, including a budget and fund-raising plan, an advertising strategy, and a staffing plan.

GOTV
Get out the vote.

finance director

A professional who works with candidates in identifying likely contributors to the campaign and arranges events and meetings with donors.

media consultant

A professional who brings the campaign message to voters by creating handouts and all forms of media ads.

Other professionals round out the candidate's team. A **finance director** works with the candidate to identify likely contributors, sits through hours and hours of "call time"—the time dedicated to phoning potential donors and asking for campaign contributions—and arranges fund-raising events and meetings with donors. Policy directors and public relations consultants help to develop the candidate's stance on crucial issues and to get the candidate's positions out to the voters, and a **media consultant** brings the campaign message to voters by creating handouts and brochures, as well as newspaper, radio, and television promotions. And now campaigns increasingly rely on social media consultants to bring the campaign to voters through YouTube, Facebook, Twitter, Snapchat, e-mail campaigns, web-based advertising, and blogs (see Chapter 17).[18]

The Media: Transforming Political Campaigns

Today, with the presence everywhere of the media in all its forms—television, Internet news sites, blogs, Twitter, radio, podcasts, newspapers, magazines—citizens' access to information is unprecedented. Whereas our ancestors had far fewer sources of news—word of mouth and the printed newspaper dominated for most of American history—people today can choose from a wide range of information sources and a bounty of information. Today, 24-hour news channels such as Fox News, CNN, and MSNBC compete with Internet news outlets, satellite radio programming, and news text messages to grab audience attention, while candidates attempt to spin coverage through the creation of videos available on their YouTube channels. But not all of the information in this bombardment is accurate.

Given the abundance of information disseminated today, engaged citizens have a greater responsibility to be discerning consumers of the news, including coverage of campaigns, voting, and elections particularly when it seems that Americans are intentionally being exposed to false information originating from foreign-sponsored trolls. They cannot be passive listeners and spoon-fed watchers of news as it is dished out on blogs or Facebook, or by daily newspapers, nightly newscasts, and the occasional weekly or monthly periodical. Vivé Griffith, at the University of Texas at Austin's Think Democracy Project, writes: "The challenge for the contemporary citizen is to be more than an audience member. Voters have unprecedented opportunities to access information and, at the same time, myriad ways to see issues obscured. An informed polity is essential to a democracy, and it can be difficult to sort through whether our media-saturated world ultimately serves to make us more or less informed."[19] We consider media coverage of elections, campaigns, and voting in detail in Chapter 18.

Revolutionizing the Campaign: New Technologies

New technologies have dramatically changed the conduct of political campaigns in recent years, and further developments promise to force campaigns to continue to evolve and adapt as technology generates new and faster ways to communicate and interact. Through Zoom Town Halls, texting, tweeting, Instagram, YouTube, and webchatting, candidates can use technologies to communicate with voters, mobilize supporters, and interact with the media. The Internet is among the most valuable and powerful new tools used by candidates. It serves as an efficient means by which office seekers can communicate with potential supporters, contributors, and the media. Candidates'

How Political Campaigns Have Changed in the Past 40 Years

THEN

1980s
Many campaigns were managed and staffed by volunteers.

Grassroots activism was the norm in all but the largest campaigns.

Money was a crucial consideration in campaigns, but grassroots activism demanded fewer financial resources.

NOW

Campaigns are increasingly managed professionally by "guns for hire" and often have an extensive staff dedicated to setting strategy, fund-raising, and managing social media campaigns and traditional media relations.

Netroots activism—political activism driven by tweets, blogs, Snapchat, Instagram and Facebook posts, and candidates' websites—is overshadowing traditional grassroots campaign efforts.

Money rules the day in most campaigns, but technology is increasingly leveling the campaign playing field.

NEXT

- Will campaigns continue to be dominated by professional staffers? Why or why not?

- Given the extent of technologically driven activism during the 2020 campaigns, does traditional grassroots activism still have a role in future campaigns? Explain.

- How can the Internet change the need for money in political campaigns?

---

websites and profiles provide a readily available forum where the electorate can find out about candidates' experiences, policy positions, and priorities. Voters can use this information to make more informed decisions in the voting booth. In addition, the Internet is a powerful fund-raising tool. In discussing the growth of campaign fund-raising on the Internet, Eli Pariser, founder of MoveOn.org's Peace Campaign, noted that "candidates are wasting their time with rubber-chicken donors,"[20] an allusion to donors who contribute to candidates by paying to attend campaign dinners.

Using e-mail and instant messaging, campaigns can communicate quickly with the media, both informing them of positive campaign developments and spinning negative developments in the best possible light for the candidate. Through campaign blogs, candidates can also supplement the information available in more traditional news media outlets. Internet communities and social networking sites also provide powerful tools for campaigns and important mechanisms for individuals' political engagement.

■ Presidential Campaigns

To many Americans, presidential campaigns epitomize the democratic process. In presidential election years, nonstop campaigning affords ample opportunities for the public to learn about the candidates and their positions. Campaigns also provide avenues for participation by the people—for example, by debating candidates' views on Twitter, by volunteering in or contributing to candidates' campaigns, or by voting. Although these opportunities for citizen engagement are especially abundant during a presidential election, they arise well before that time, because potential candidates typically position themselves years in advance of a presidential election to secure their party's nomination and to win the general election.

Party Conventions and the General Election Campaign

Political parties hold conventions in presidential election years to select their party's nominee for president of the United States. As discussed in Chapter 5 and as reviewed earlier in this chapter, the delegates to the national conventions are chosen by citizens in each state who vote in their parties' primary elections or who participate in party caucuses. Eligible incumbent presidents (who have served only one term) are nearly always nominated again, and the nominee of the opposing party is often determined by the primary results. After the conventions are over and the nominees have been decided (typically by late August or early September of the election year), the nominees and their vice presidential running mates begin their general election campaigns. Usually, the parties' choice of nominee is a foregone conclusion by the time of the convention.

The Electoral College

The votes tallied on Election Day determine which presidential candidate's slate of electors will cast their ballots in each state, in accordance with state law. There are 538 electors in the Electoral College because the number of electors is based on the number of members of Congress—435 in the House of Representatives, 100 in the Senate—plus 3 electors who represent the District of Columbia. A presidential candidate needs a simple majority of votes (270) to win. Note that a candidate need not win the popular vote in order to win the Electoral College and thus the presidency, but in most elections, the Electoral College exaggerates the winner's margin of victory (rather than reverses the popular outcome). In 2020, Joe Biden won the popular vote by over seven million votes, and won the Electoral College 306 to 232, as shown in Figure 14.2.

On the Monday following the second Wednesday of December, the slates of electors chosen in each state meet in the state capitals and cast their electoral votes. The results are then announced in a joint session of Congress in early January. In most presidential elections, however, the winner is known on election night, because analysts tabulate the outcome in each state and predict the electoral vote. The winner takes the oath of office as president in inaugural ceremonies on January 20.

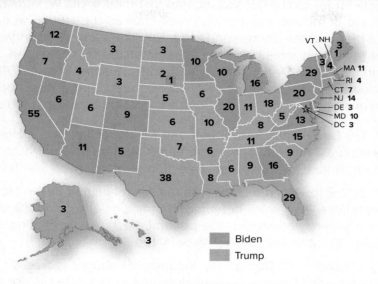

FIGURE 14.2 ▪ **The 2020 Electoral College Vote** In what areas of the country did Donald Trump get much of his support? Where did Joe Biden win? Which candidate won the most populous states?

Congressional Elections

The timetable for congressional elections reflects the framers' views of the differing nature of the House of Representatives and the Senate. House members, as public servants in the legislative body that the framers conceived as closer to the people, are elected every two years, in even-numbered years (2020, 2022, and so on). But the framers also sought to check the power of the people, who they believed could be irrational and unruly, and so members of the Senate originally were chosen by state legislators. Ratification of the **Seventeenth Amendment** to the Constitution in 1913 shifted the election of senators to popular election within the states. Senators serve six-year terms, which are staggered so that one-third of the Senate is elected every two years. Thus, in any given congressional election year, 33 or 34 members of the Senate are up for election. Usually, the two senators from a given state will not be elected in the same cycle, unless the death or resignation of a sitting senator requires a special election. As we saw in Chapter 2, the Constitution requires that the number of seats in the House of Representatives awarded to each state be based on that state's population and that each state have two U.S. senators. On average, a successful campaign for a seat in the House of Representatives cost over $1.6 million in 2018. That is a veritable bargain compared with the price tag for a successful bid for the U.S. Senate, which averaged over $10 million that year. Compare this with the annual salary of $174,000 that rank-and-file members of the House and the Senate collect.

Seventeenth Amendment
A constitutional amendment from 1913 that shifted the election of senators to a popular election within the states.

Incumbency

The status of already holding office—known as *incumbency*—strongly influences a candidate's ability to raise money and is probably the most important factor in determining success in a congressional campaign. The most recent year in which a comparatively large number of incumbents lost their seats was 2018, when "only" 91 percent of incumbents seeking reelection to the House won, while 83 percent of their Senate counterparts did. But like many election years with atypically low reelection rates, 2018 was characterized by some stark differences between Republican and Democratic incumbents. Specifically, the 2018 election was largely viewed as a mandate on President Trump, and a disproportionate number of incumbent Republicans in Congress lost their reelection bids:

- In 2018, 176 Democratic incumbents ran for reelection in the House of Representatives. While two were defeated in primaries, no incumbent Democratic House member lost reelection in the general election.

- In 2018, 202 Republican incumbents ran for reelection in the House of Representatives. Two were defeated in their primaries, and 30 incumbent Republicans were defeated in the general election, constituting 16 percent of U.S. House Republicans who were defeated.

- In the U.S. Senate, 23 Democratic incumbents sought reelection. Of these, four senators—or 17 percent—were defeated in the general election.

- In the U.S. Senate, five Republican incumbents sought reelection, and one senator—or 20 percent—was defeated in the general election.

But historically, 96 percent of incumbent members of the House of Representatives running for reelection win, as do 93 percent of their Senate counterparts. These outcomes may indicate what *individual* members of Congress are doing right: representing their own constituencies effectively, engaging with their constituents, and listening to and addressing their needs. But voters typically think about Congress in terms of *a whole*, rather than individuals, viewing it as a body that is overwhelmingly composed of "other people's" representatives, who do not reflect their views.[21] Thus the voting public frequently attacks Congress as a collective entity, and typically has a negative perception of Congress as a whole. Indeed, in recent years, Congress's approval rating typically has hovered at about 22 percent.

Why do incumbents so often win reelection? Several factors make it more likely that someone already in office will be returned to that office in a reelection bid:

- **Stronger name recognition.** Having run for election before and served in government, incumbents tend to be better known than challengers are.

- **Easier access to media coverage.** Media outlets routinely publicize the activities of elected congressional officials, rationalizing that they are covering the institution of Congress rather than the individuals. Non-incumbent challengers face an uphill battle in trying to get coverage of their campaigns.

- **Redistricting that favors the incumbent party.** Often, after reapportionment, district lines are drawn to benefit the incumbent officeholder's political party, thus making it likely that the incumbent will retain the seat.

- **Franking.** The privilege of sending mail free of charge is known as **franking**. Federal law allows members of Congress free mailings to every household in their state or congressional district. These mailings make it easy for

franking
The privilege of sending mail free of charge by members of Congress.

members of Congress to stay in touch with their constituencies throughout their tenure in office.

- **Campaign contributions.** Political action committees and individuals are interested in supporting candidates who will be in a position to help them once the election is over. Because donors are aware of the high reelection rates of incumbent candidates, incumbents garner an enormous proportion of contributions, sometimes as much as 80 percent in any given congressional election year.

- **Casework.** When an incumbent personally helps constituents solve problems with the federal bureaucracy, the resulting loyalty and good word-of-mouth reputation help to attract support for that candidate during a run for reelection.

- **Incumbent quality.** Incumbents have been tested by voters and, at some point, have earned a plurality of the voters' stamp of approval. While not every incumbent is more qualified than his or her opponent, incumbents often possess a minimal skill set that not every challenger has.

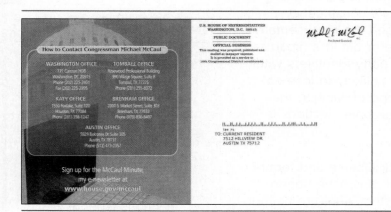

>> A piece of franked mail from a congressional office. Note the signature of the sending member of Congress, which serves as a postage stamp.

H.S. Photos/Alamy Stock Photo

Thus incumbency is a powerful obstacle for outsiders who seek to unseat an elected member of Congress. Despite the incumbency advantage, in each congressional election, many individuals challenge incumbent members of Congress, often doing so knowing that the odds are stacked against them but believing in giving voters a ballot choice. Others run because they seek to bring attention to a particular issue or to shape the policy agenda—or sometimes because they simply underestimate the power of incumbency.

Reapportionment and Redistricting

Sometimes the advantages of incumbency can be diminished, as in election years after reapportionment and redistricting. **Reapportionment** is the reallocation of seats in the House of Representatives on the basis of changes in a state's population since the last census. Every 10 years, in years ending in zero (2020, 2030, and so on), the federal government counts the number of people in the country as a whole. If the census indicates that a state's population has changed significantly, that state may gain or lose seats in the House of Representatives. **Redistricting,** the redrawing of congressional district boundaries within a state, is based on the reapportionment from the census (see "Argumentation: Thinking Critically").

reapportionment
Reallocation of seats in the House of Representatives to each state based on changes in state populations since the last census.

redistricting
The redrawing of congressional district boundaries within each state, based on the reapportionment from the census.

Are Congressional Elections "Rigged" Through Gerrymandering?

THE ISSUE: In earlier times, redistricting occurred when the lines of a congressional district were redrawn to accommodate population changes. This process typically created a greater number of competitive congressional districts, and House members typically had to temper partisan impulses to placate the sizable proportion of his or her constituency that identified with the opposing party.

Today, with the widespread use of computer-driven mapmaking technology, congressional seats can be configured to ensure a "safe seat"—one in which the party identification of the majority of a district's voters makes it likely that a candidate from that party will win an election. Thus, representatives from many of these safe seats can act in a partisan manner with impunity. Many times, a strong majority (but not all) of the member's constituency agrees with the representative's partisan stance, and the representative has little incentive to represent a moderate stance or act in a bipartisan fashion. The effect of this lopsided distribution of party identifiers within congressional districts is that the majority party is unlikely to lose an election, and the party in the minority has little hope of winning the seat, leading some to ask if the system of congressional elections is rigged through the process of gerrymandering.

YES: Democrats, including former President Barack Obama and former Attorney General Eric Holder, contend that Republicans have rigged the redistricting system, creating congressional districts that are neither fair nor compact, but ensure that Republicans are elected to a majority of seats. They charge that Republicans (who control the majority of state legislatures, which determine the redistricting process) have hijacked the congressional redistricting system: Democrats say, "We're . . . feeling that our political system is unfair, and our votes don't count the way they should. The gerrymandering of congressional and legislative districts locks in a Republican majority and locks out the voters."*

NO: Republicans assert that the fact that their success demonstrates a calculated strategy to win state legislative seats in states where the legislature has control over the redistricting process. "As the 2010 Census approached, the RSLC began . . . formulating a strategy to keep or win Republican control of state legislatures with the largest impact on congressional redistricting. . . . That effort, the REDistricting Majority Project (REDMAP), focused critical resources on legislative chambers in states projected to gain or lose congressional seats in 2011 based on Census data. . . . Controlling the redistricting process in these states would have the greatest impact on determining how both state legislative and congressional district boundaries would be drawn. Drawing new district lines in states with the most redistricting activity presented the opportunity to solidify conservative policymaking at the

WHAT DO YOU THINK?

1. Why does the congressional redistricting process matter?

2. Was it fair for Republicans to target state legislative elections (spending millions of dollars) with the goal of controlling redistricting but not advising voters as to this goal? Do you agree with the Democratic strategy to combat the Republicans at the state legislative level? Why or why not?

3. What factors could put Democrats at a disadvantage in attempting to reconfigure the system in the 2021 elections?

*Source: National Democratic Redistricting Committee

**Source: Redistricting Majority Project

state level and maintain a Republican stronghold in the U.S. House of Representatives for the next decade."**

OTHER APPROACHES: Some analysts argue that the redistricting system is skewed in favor of Republicans, but that they won that advantage fair and square by developing a strategy to target state legislative seats that would determine congressional redistricting. And now the Democrats have formed the National Democratic Redistricting Committee, chaired by former Attorney General Eric Holder, to build a targeted, state-by-state strategy to help Democrats sway the 2021 redistricting process—evidence that parties see state legislative elections as the new redistricting battleground. Thus, according to this argument, nothing is inherently unfair about congressional redistricting.

Because the composition of a given congressional district can change as a result of reapportionment and redistricting, this process can mitigate the influence of incumbency. Frequently, the greatest shifts in the composition of the House of Representatives occur in election years ending in 2 (2002, 2012, and so on), when the first elections take place that incorporate the changes from reapportionment and redistricting. When a state loses a seat, the result is that an incumbent member of Congress is likely to lose a seat. When a state gains a seat, a new member of Congress can be elected to the open seat.

Gerrymandering

In many states, the goal of congressional redistricting is to protect House incumbents. The redrawing of congressional boundaries for the purpose of political advantage is a form of **gerrymandering**, the practice of drawing legislative district boundaries to benefit an incumbent, a political party, or some other group. The term was coined in reference to Massachusetts governor Elbridge Gerry after a district shaped like a salamander was created to favor his party in 1811. The Then/Now feature illustration shows the first gerrymander.

gerrymandering
The drawing of legislative district boundaries to benefit an incumbent, a political party, or another group.

Most forms of gerrymandering are legal. In 2020, the Supreme Court ruled that federal courts cannot blanketly determine whether partisan-gerrymandered election maps violate the Constitution, thus paving the way for both parties to focus their energies on creating partisan-gerrymandered districts, and without much threat that the Supreme Court will hear future challenges. Those who would prefer a less partisan, more neutral system had hoped that the Court would rule partisan gerrymanders unconstitutional, but the 5–4 decision left the regulating process to Congress and state legislative bodies.

The 2020 decision followed a 1986 U.S. Supreme Court ruling that a gerrymandering plan is unconstitutional only when it eliminates the minority party's influence statewide.[22] Because of the strict standards, only one partisan gerrymandering plan filed after the 1990 census was successfully challenged. Scholars believe that this ruling, along with changes in how congressional district maps are drawn, explains increased partisan voting in the House of Representatives.

THEN

NOW

THE GERRY-MANDER.

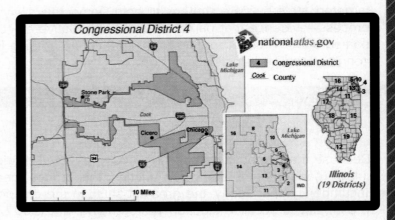

>> The term *gerrymander* originated from this cartoon of a Massachusetts electoral district. To some, the district looked like a salamander. Soon it was christened a "Gerry-mander," after Massachusetts governor Elbridge Gerry, a signer of the Declaration of Independence and the politician who approved redrawing district lines for political advantage. What point does this famous historical cartoon of 1812, representing Massachusetts legislative districts, make about the nature of a gerrymander? Gerrymandering remains a practice today, as seen in Illinois's fourth congressional district. What are your own views on the practice?

Historical cartoon: Bettmann/Getty Images; *Congressional district:* Source: U.S. Department of the Interior

Increased Partisanship and Congressional Redistricting

In earlier times, redistricting occurred through a simple redrawing of the lines of a congressional district to accommodate population changes. But today, with the widespread use of computer-driven mapmaking technology, congressional seats can be configured to ensure a "safe seat"—one in which the party identification of the majority of a district's voters makes it likely that a candidate from a given party will win election. Sometimes, for example, more than 60 percent of a district's population identifies with one political party.

The effect of this lopsided distribution of party identifiers within congressional districts is that there is little risk that the majority party will lose an election, and little hope that the party in the minority will win the seat. Thus, representatives from many of these safe seats can act in a partisan manner with impunity. Many times, a strong majority (but not all) of the member's constituency agrees with the representative's partisan stance, and the representative has little incentive to represent a moderate stance or act in a bipartisan fashion. In contrast, when congressional districts were more competitive, a House member typically would have to temper partisan impulses to placate the sizable proportion of his or her constituency that identified with the opposing party. Otherwise, the member would risk alienating constituents and encouraging potential opponents to run. Today, that is no longer the case, and it appears that Republicans in the House of Representatives have become more conservative and their Democratic counterparts have become increasingly liberal. Consequently, House members are less likely to compromise or to be moderate in their positions in negotiating issues with the opposition. This increasing polarization is likely one additional reason why the public views Congress as an institution negatively, but individual incumbents, who represent the majority view within a district, are viewed favorably and nearly always reelected.

Majority-Minority Districts

While partisan gerrymandering tends to protect the status quo, another form of gerrymandering is sometimes relied upon to help ensure that a diversity of voices are elected to the House of Representatives. State legislatures have attempted to address the issue of racial imbalance in the House of Representatives by constructing a kind of gerrymander called a majority-minority district. A **majority-minority district** is composed of a majority of a given minority community—say, African Americans—and the creators' intent is to make it likely that a member of that minority will be elected to Congress (see "Analyzing the Sources"). In 1991, a lawsuit filed by a group of white voters in North Carolina challenged the state's congressional district map, claiming that the two "majority-minority" districts constituted a racial gerrymander that violated the equal protection clause of the Fourteenth Amendment. In the 1993 decision in *Shaw v. Reno*, the Supreme Court agreed, ruling that race cannot be the predominant factor in creating districts. The effect of the ruling is that racial gerrymandering is legal unless the state legislature redrawing the district lines creates majority-minority districts at the expense of other redistricting concerns. Typically, those concerns include preserving the geographic contiguity of districts, keeping communities within one legislative district, and reelecting incumbents.

While proponents of majority-minority districts argue that their creations lead to the election of larger numbers of minority representatives, others argue that consolidating minority populations into a majority-minority district (a practice known as "packing") sometimes dilutes the influence of communities of color that, if not packed into a single district, may be able to exert influence and elect representatives of color in multiple districts. Others argue that too much diffusion of communities of color between multiple congressional districts—a practice known as "cracking"—makes it more difficult for communities of color to exert influence in the congressional politics of the district.

majority-minority district
A legislative district composed of a majority of a given minority community—say, African Americans—the intent of which is to make it likely that a member of that minority will be elected to Congress.

Shaw v. Reno
A 1993 Supreme Court decision ruling that race cannot be the predominant factor in creating a district, but can be legal if other concerns of redistricting are protected.

Mapping Majority-Minority Districts

The number of majority-minority districts in the United States has grown significantly in recent years. Many minority representatives are elected to districts in which racial or ethnic minorities are not a majority, but the ethnic and racial makeup of a district can contribute to the electoral success of a candidate of color. This figure shows that today, 113 districts in 26 states have an ethnic or a racial minority in the majority.

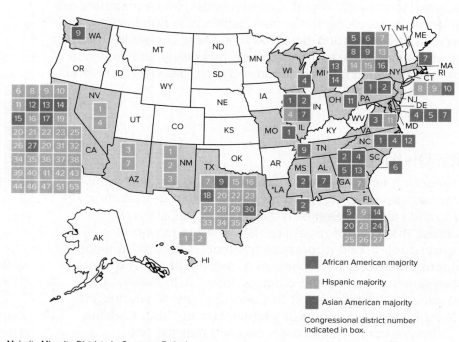

Majority-Minority Districts in Congress Today*

*In some congressional districts, combinations of racial and ethnic minorities create a majority-minority district. In those districts, the largest minority population is identified.

Source: P. Bell and D. Wasserman, "Since 1982, Minority Congressional Districts Have Tripled," *National Journal,* April 13, 2012.

Practice Analytical Thinking

1. Which states have the most majority-minority districts?

2. Which racial or ethnic group has the most majority-minority districts?

3. Compare the location of majority African American districts to Hispanic districts. Which group is more dispersed? Which is more concentrated? Why do you think this is the case?

Who Votes? Factors in Voter Participation

Not all people are equally likely to participate in the process of voting for the president or other government officials. Yet of all the forms of political participation, the act of voting has been analyzed perhaps more than any other.[23] Scholars such as Angus Campbell, Philip E. Converse, Warren Miller, and Donald Stokes have examined what factors influence who votes and how voters decide.[24] They and others have analyzed how characteristics such as education level, income, age, race, and the degree of party competitiveness in a given election influence whether a person will vote.[25] Of course, in considering demographic characteristics such as voter age and income level, we must remember that these are merely generalizations.

Education Level—The Number-One Predictor of Voting

Historically, an individual's level of education is the best predictor of whether that person will vote. Typically, as education increases, so, too, does the likelihood of voting, with measurable differences even among those who have attended but not graduated from college and those who have graduated from college.

The Age Factor

During any presidential campaign, you will hear much about age as a factor in the likelihood of voting. Despite campus-focused initiatives by presidential campaigns, young adults are less likely to vote than are Americans who are middle aged and older, though youth participation has increased in recent years.[26] In 2008, Barack Obama's candidacy brought out young voters in record-breaking numbers—their highest turnout since 18-year-olds were granted the right to vote in 1972. In both 2008 and 2012, the youth vote was key in electing Obama, with young Americans overwhelmingly propelling him to victory. But since that time, candidates of both political parties—Hillary Clinton and Donald Trump in 2016 and Donald Trump and Joe Biden in 2020—struggled to attract young voters. But Figure 14.3, which plots the percentage of people in various age groups who voted in recent presidential elections, illustrates a historic trend: As Americans age, they are more likely to vote. There are numerous reasons young people do not vote. Among 18- to 24-year-olds, the reason most often cited is that they were too busy or had a schedule conflict, but members of this age group are also more likely to report that they forgot to vote or were out of town. Age also is related to mobility—young people might move when they leave for college or to start a new job, and mobility depresses voter turnout.

Race, Ethnicity, and Voter Participation

In both the 2016 and 2020 presidential campaigns, race and ethnicity became pivotal issues. During the early stages of his 2016 campaign, Donald Trump increased the probability that race would become a wedge issue by refusing to disavow white supremacists who supported his campaign.[27] Trump also managed to offend many Latinx voters with his pejorative characterization of Mexican immigrants: "What can be simpler or more accurately stated? The Mexican Government is forcing their most unwanted people into the United States. They are, in many cases, criminals, drug dealers, rapists, etc."[28] His rhetoric alienated other

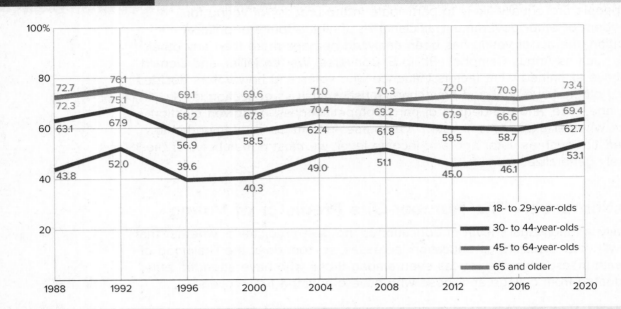

FIGURE 14.3 ▪ **Age and Voting in Presidential Elections** For which age group is the percentage of people voting traditionally the highest? For which age group is the voting percentage lowest? In which years did all age groups' turnout increase? When did young people's increase?

Source: United States Census Bureau.

voters, particularly first-generation Americans, for instance: "The United States has become a dumping ground for Mexico and, in fact, for many other parts of the world."[29]

When Joe Biden selected Sen. Kamala Harris, the daughter of Jamaican and Indian immigrants, as his running mate in 2020, race re-emerged as a focal point in presidential politics. It solidified Biden's support among women in general, but among women of color in particular, and appealed to many younger voters for whom diversity is an important factor. For Biden, the hope was that Harris's nomination would energize the electorate as had the candidacy of his former running mate, Barack Obama. With Barack Obama on the ballot, African American turnout surpassed that of whites (see "Analyzing the Sources"), a trend that was years in the making. But while turnout by African American voters remained high in 2016, it was not at the record-setting pace Obama had been able to generate. Participation by Latinx, who many thought would be mobilized in 2016, also dropped. Nonetheless, Latinx are viewed as an important constituency because they make up an expanding proportion of the population that is becoming increasingly likely to vote. In 2020, high voter turnout in swing states among Black and Latinx voters was pivotal in delivering a victory to Joe Biden.

Income—A Reliable Predictor of Voting

Besides education, income is one of the best predictors of whether an American will vote.[30] Typically in recent presidential election years, U.S. citizens with the

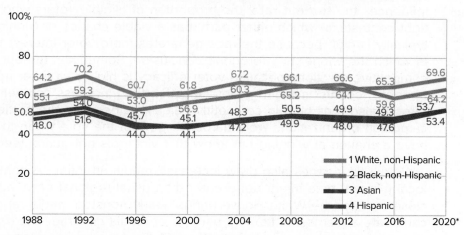

EXPLORING RACE AND VOTING
Voter turnout rates in presidential elections, 1988–2020

*2020 based on election estimates at time of publication.

Note: Hispanics are of any race. For the years 1988 through 2008, whites, blacks, and Asians include only non-Hispanics. For 2012 and 2016, blacks and Asians include Hispanics. Data for non-Hispanic Asians were not available in 1988.

Source: United States Census Bureau.

Practice Analytical Thinking

1. In general, what has been the trend with regard to voter turnout among Black voters and white voters over time?

2. What has been the trend among Hispanics and Asian Americans? In your view, why has participation by members of these groups differed from that of Black and white Americans?

3. From these data, we see a significant occurrence in 2012. Can you identify this event? Why might this have occurred?

lowest income level have had voter turnout levels of 50–60 percent, whereas those with the highest income level have had turnout levels above 85 percent.[31] As income increases, so does the likelihood of voting.

The reasons for the close correlation between income and likelihood of voting are complex.[32] One possibility is that people with lower incomes are less likely than higher-income earners to believe that the government listens to people like them. Another factor may be that individuals with lower incomes have less leisure time in which to learn about candidates and issues and even to vote. State voting registration laws also may impede participation because individuals with unstable housing may face obstacles in determining where their polling places are, or even in finding transportation to the polls. Further, in contrast to American voters, European voters are often mobilized—by class-based trade unions and by the parties themselves—to vote on the basis of their economic interests. In the United

States, the lowest-income workers are less likely to be members of organized labor unions and thus are less likely to be mobilized to vote on the basis of their own economic interests.

Party Competitiveness and Voter Turnout

turnout rate
The proportion of eligible voters who actually voted.

Finally, researchers have found that party competitiveness in elections also influences the **turnout rate**, the proportion of eligible voters who actually voted. In tight contests, in which either party has a viable chance of winning, voter turnout typically is high because the race generates more voter interest than an election in which the winner is a foregone conclusion. Sometimes turnout is high in competitive elections because voter efficacy is higher—a voter may believe that her vote "counts" more in a close election than in a less competitive race. Voter turnout also runs high in competitive elections because the parties and other campaign organizations work harder to get out the vote when they think they have a chance at winning but know that victory is not guaranteed.

Competitive races also draw increased media attention. A tightly competitive local mayoral race might get greater than usual regional news attention, and a close race for the White House brings nearly nonstop media reports and candidate advertisements. The barrage of media coverage increases public awareness and may also boost voter efficacy by conveying the message that every vote counts.

■ How Voters Decide

prospective voting
A method of evaluating candidates in which voters focus on candidates' positions on issues important to them and vote for the candidates who best represent their views.

retrospective voting
A method of evaluating candidates in which voters evaluate incumbent candidates and decide whether to support them based on their past performance

When deciding for whom they will vote, some voters evaluate candidates on the basis of their positions on issues and then cast their ballots for those who best represent their views. Called **prospective voting**, this method of candidate evaluation focuses on what the candidates will do in the future. A more common form of candidate evaluation is **retrospective voting**, in which a voter evaluates an incumbent candidate on the basis of whether the incumbent's past decisions and actions are satisfactory to the voter.[33] If they are satisfactory, the voter will likely support the incumbent. If not, the voter will be disposed to support the incumbent's opponent. The prevalence of an incumbency advantage in election outcomes indicates that many voters have a favorable view of the decisions and actions of incumbent candidates for most offices.[34]

The most important factor that plays into how a voter decides on a candidate and perceives specific candidates, however, is the voter's party identification. Other influential determinants include those specific to a given election, such as candidates' attributes and the effectiveness of the candidates' campaigns.

Major Factors in Voter Decision Making

Often a significant determinant of why people vote the way they do, policy priorities are to a certain extent aligned with party identification (or, even more generally, with ideology), because the political parties usually embrace differing viewpoints on issues. National issues that top the list of concerns among voters have remained consistent over many years and include several domestic policy matters, such as immigration reform, the health of the economy, education, crime, health care, and Social Security.

But how do voters decide which party and which candidate to support at the polls, based on the issues? First and foremost, an issue must be **salient** to voters—that is, it must resonate with them and reflect something that they care deeply about, an issue they are willing to base their vote on.[35] The ability of voters to cast an issue-based vote increases when candidates differ in their positions on an issue.

Incumbency, the situation of already holding an office or an official position, as we have seen, is also a key factor influencing how people vote. Because an incumbent is a "known commodity" with demonstrated experience to serve in office, voters are much more likely to vote for incumbents than for their challengers. Thus, for most offices, incumbents are much more likely to be reelected than are their challengers. But incumbency is also an influence in presidential elections, gubernatorial and state legislative elections, and probably even your local city council elections. Incumbents have notable advantages over challengers—namely, greater name recognition, a track record that voters can evaluate, and access to campaign contributions that help them to get their message out.

Campaign Influences on Voter Choice

As we have seen, parties and candidates conduct campaigns to influence voters' choices at the polls. Campaigns today vary a great deal in how they are waged. Whereas a candidate for a small town's board of selectmen might knock on the door of every voter in the community, a U.S. Senate or gubernatorial candidate might spend most of his or her time raising money to pay for expensive television and radio advertisements, while a presidential candidate might take to Twitter to get his or her views directly to voters. But generally, the lower the level of office, the greater the likelihood that the candidate will rely on grassroots activism.

Trends in modern campaigns, including a far deeper reliance on paid professional staffers, and the prevalence of the savvy use of social media and traditional media as tools for communicating with voters, are catapulting the costs of campaigns sky-high. Voter choices are also affected by increasingly negative campaigns, one outcome of the modern political campaigns' reliance on paid professionals. Outside consultants typically have far fewer qualms about "going negative" than do activists in the all-community volunteer-run campaigns that were more typical of earlier times.

Consultants use negative campaign tactics for a simple reason: Research shows that the approach sways voter opinion.[36] Although the candidates themselves often prefer to accentuate a positive message that highlights their background, experience, and qualifications, paid campaign consultants generally do not hesitate to sling the mud. Once a candidate establishes name recognition and credibility with voters, many consultants believe highlighting the opponent's negative qualities and actions is an effective campaign strategy.

But the effect of negative campaigning is not limited merely to swaying voters from one candidate to another. Research by political scientists shows that negative campaigning can suppress voter turnout in several ways. For example, Shanto Iyengar and Jennifer A. McGrady note that negative advertising may suppress voter turnout among the attacked candidate's supporters.[37] Other political scientists' research shows that negative campaigning undermines the democratic process by decreasing civic engagement among all voters. According to these findings, the electorate becomes disenchanted with the candidates

salient
In relation to a voting issue—having resonance, being significant, causing intense interest.

incumbency
The situation of already holding the office that is up for reelection.

(about whom voters get a barrage of negative information), with the campaigns (because campaigns serve as the primary messengers for delivering negative information about opponents), or with the entire electoral process that facilitates this negativity. Some voters view negative campaigning as being completely at odds with their idealized conception of the democratic process, and this belief may discourage them from voting.

■ Why Some People Do Not Vote

Negative campaigning is one reason some people do not vote, but political scientists have proposed several others. Lack of civic engagement on the part of voters underlies many of these ideas. Other reasons have to do with the nature of campaigns and the structure of elections.

Lack of Efficacy

Some voters do not vote because they do not participate in civic affairs, either locally or at the national level. Many of these nonvoters lack efficacy.[38] They do not believe that the government listens to people like them or that their vote actually matters in determining the outcome of elections and the business of government.[39]

Scholars have determined that individuals who lack efficacy exist across the social and economic spectrums but that poorer people are more likely than better-off individuals to feel that the government does not listen to people like them. While it is a common notion that people are alienated from politics or think that the government does not listen to their concerns, a study estimated that only about 9 percent of the U.S. population feels that way.[40] This same survey indicated that people lacking efficacy—a group that the study called the "disaffecteds"—typically had a low level of educational attainment and were less likely to follow current events than more engaged citizens.

Voter Fatigue and Negative Campaigns

Another explanation for why some Americans do not vote stems from the nature of political campaigns. In the United States, campaigns tend to be long-drawn-out affairs. For example, presidential campaigns typically last for more than a year, with some candidates positioning themselves three or four years in advance of an election. Contrast that with many parliamentary systems, including Germany's, in which an election must be held within 60 days of the dissolution of parliament because of a "no confidence" vote of the chancellor (similar to a prime minister). Some scholars say that the lengthiness of the campaigns leads to **voter fatigue**, the condition in which voters simply grow tired of all candidates by the time Election Day arrives, and may thus be less likely to vote.

voter fatigue
The condition in which voters grow tired of all candidates by the time Election Day arrives, and may thus be less likely to vote.

American journalist and humorist Franklin Adams commented that "elections are won by men and women chiefly because most people vote against somebody rather than for somebody."[41] The prevalence of negative campaigning compounds the phenomenon of voter fatigue. Even the most enthusiastic supporters of a candidate may feel their advocacy withering under the unceasing mudslinging that occurs in many high-level campaigns. And so, although evidence shows that negative advertising is effective in swaying voters' opinions, sometimes such advertising also succeeds in suppressing voter turnout by making voters less enthusiastic about voting.

The Structure of Elections

Political scientists also cite the structure of U.S. elections as a reason more Americans do not vote. For years, voting rights activists claimed that the registration requirements in many states were too complicated and discouraged people from voting by making it too difficult to register. However, that theory was negated when turnout failed to increase significantly after Congress passed the National Voter Registration Act in 1993, which allows people to register when interacting with many government agencies, including when they apply for a driver's license.

Critics of the structure of elections also point to their frequency.[42] In the United States, the number of elections varies from municipality to municipality, and local government charters may call for more than four elections for municipal offices alone. Although most federal offices require only two elections (a primary and a general), these elections are not always held in conjunction with state, county, and municipal elections.

How elections are conducted also affects voter participation. Most general elections are held on a weekday, and research shows that holding elections on weekends or over a two-day period instead, or establishing a national voting holiday, would increase voter turnout by ensuring that voters had ample opportunity to cast their ballots.[43] And now, as states move to vote-by-mail balloting, offering voters the convenience of casting their ballots by mail rather than having to go to a polling place on a designated day, turnout has increased.

Rational Choice Theory

A final explanation as to why some people do not vote is rooted in rational choice theory—the idea that individuals will consider both how much they care about the outcome of an election and the likelihood that their vote will be important in influencing its outcome.[44] This theory states that some individuals decide that the "costs" of voting—in terms of the time, energy, and inconvenience required to register to vote, to become informed about candidates and elections, and actually to vote—are not worth the effort when compared with the expected "benefits," or what the voters could derive from voting.

In light of these cumulative "costs," it is perhaps surprising that so many people choose to vote.[45] One explanation for why they do is that most voters report that they derive psychological rewards from exercising this citizen's right—feelings of being civically engaged, satisfied, and patriotic. But when the costs associated with voting increase too much, turnout drops; more people choose not to vote when voting becomes too inconvenient. This drop-off occurs, for example, when municipalities shorten voting hours and during inclement weather.

The Consequences of Nonvoting

From a civic engagement perspective, nonvoting is both a symptom and a result of a lack of civic involvement on the part of individuals.[46] Your friend might not vote because she is not civically engaged—because she feels that she has little to contribute and that the government does not listen to "people like her" anyway. But by not voting, she perpetuates this lack of efficacy by remaining outside the process rather than staking a claim to what is rightfully hers: the idea that every individual has the right to a voice in the composition and priorities of the government. Only by becoming civically engaged—learning about the candidates, discussing issues, and voting—can she break the cycle of inefficacy. Voting will make her pay more attention to campaigns, candidates, and issues.

Beyond the effects of nonvoting on individuals, low voter turnout affects the polity (see Chapter 1). When relatively few people vote in a given election, the outcome is likely to represent the will of only that subset of the electorate who voted. The process becomes cyclical: These nonvoters who disagree with the outcome conclude that the government does not represent them, they feel less efficacious, and they are less inclined to vote in the future.

Moreover, some scholars assert that democracies with low voter turnout are more likely to generate threats to their own well-being.[47] In democracies with low turnout, these scholars say, charismatic, popular political figures may rise to power and become authoritarian leaders. Corruption, too, can be a problem in low-turnout democracies where government officials might feel relatively unconcerned about the disapproval of disgruntled constituents.

Other researchers, however, contend that nonvoting is not a big problem, especially in cases where large numbers in the electorate are relatively uninformed about candidates and issues.[48] A number of scholars in this camp argue that participation by the uninformed is undesirable, because it may lead to drastic changes in government. Opponents of this view counter that because of political parties' role in selecting candidates, the menu for voter choice is actually quite limited in most elections. Those who argue that nonvoting does not matter also ignore the fact that voting tends to produce more engaged citizens who, because they vote, feel a duty to be informed and involved.

Other scholars who claim that low voter turnout is not a problem argue that low voting rates are simply a function of people's satisfaction with the status quo: Their nonvoting simply means that they do not seek change in government. This argument, however, does not explain why lower turnout is most likely to occur in populations that are least likely to be satisfied with their situation. For example, people with lower incomes are much less likely to vote than those with higher incomes. Whatever the reason—a lack of efficacy as argued by some, satisfaction as argued by others—nonvoters' best chance of having their views reflected in the policy process is to articulate them through voting.

■ Money and Politics

Money—lots of it—is essential in electoral races today. Money and the modern campaign are inextricably linked because of the importance of costly media advertising in modern campaigns.[49] Federal regulations require any group that contributes to candidates' campaigns to register as a political action committee (PAC), and these organizations are subject to constraints in the amount of money that they can contribute to candidate campaigns. But today, as discussed in Chapter 8, in the wake of the Supreme Court ruling *Citizens United v. Federal Election Commission* in 2010, these regulations are being circumvented through the use of new classifications of organizations that allow unlimited contributions and little donor transparency. While the influence of money in electoral politics goes back a long time, as do the efforts to regulate it,[50] so too do the efforts of reformers who have attempted to limit the influence of money on political campaigns for almost as long as campaigns have existed.

Early Efforts to Regulate Campaign Finance

Efforts to limit the influence of money started after a scandal that erupted during the administration of President Warren Harding (1921–1923). In 1921, the president transferred oil reserves at Teapot Dome, Wyoming, from the Department of the Navy to the Department of the Interior. The following year, Harding's secretary of the interior leased the oil fields without competitive bidding. A Senate investigation into the deal revealed that the lessee of the fields had "loaned" the interior secretary more than $100,000 in order to win political influence. The interior secretary was convicted and sentenced to a year in prison and a $100,000 fine. Dubbed the Teapot Dome scandal, this sordid affair led Congress to try to limit the influence of money on politics through legislation.

The Federal Corrupt Practices Act of 1925 sought to prevent future wrongdoing. This act aimed to regulate campaign finance by limiting campaign contributions and requiring public disclosure of campaign expenditures, and it was one of the first attempts at campaign finance regulation. But because the act did not include an enforcement mechanism, it was a weak attempt to fight corruption, and candidates found numerous loopholes in the law.

The Political Activities Act of 1939, also known as the Hatch Act, marked another congressional attempt to eliminate political corruption. With the growth of the federal bureaucracy as a result of the New Deal programs of President Franklin D. Roosevelt, several scandals had emerged, demonstrating the problems that could arise when government employees took an active role in politics. The Hatch Act banned partisan political activities by all federal government employees except the president, the vice president, and Senate-confirmed political appointees. The act also sought to regulate the campaign finance system by limiting the amount of money a group could spend on an election and placing a $5,000 cap on contributions from an individual to a campaign committee. Although the Hatch Act was more effective than the Federal Corrupt Practices Act of 1925, it also contained a significant loophole: Groups that wanted to spend more than the legislated limit of $3 million simply formed additional groups.

In 1971, Congress passed the Federal Election Campaign Act (FECA), the most significant attempt at overhauling the nation's campaign finance system. The law was sponsored by Democrats in Congress who were concerned about the enormous fund-raising advantage the Republicans had had during the 1968 presidential election. This law placed considerable limitations on both campaign expenditures and campaign contributions, and it provided for a voluntary tax-return check-off for qualified presidential candidates. This provision enables you, when filling out your federal income tax return, to contribute three dollars, which will go toward the matching funds that qualified presidential candidates receive.

In 1974, FECA was amended to place more stringent limitations on individual contributions and to limit expenditures by PACs, and it revamped the presidential election process by restricting spending and providing public financing for qualified candidates who abided by the limits. The act also required public disclosure of contributions and expenditures by all candidates for federal office. Most important, the act created an enforcement mechanism in the Federal Election Commission (FEC), the agency charged with enforcing federal campaign finance laws.

The Court Weighs In: Money = Speech

In the subsequent, highly significant Supreme Court case *Buckley v. Valeo* (1976), however, the plaintiffs contended that placing limitations on the amount an individual candidate could spend on his or her own campaign violated First Amendment protections of free speech. The Court agreed, ruling that "the candidate . . . has a First Amendment right to engage in the discussion of public issues and vigorously and tirelessly to advocate his own election."[51] This ruling paved the way for the subsequent explosion in the formation of PACs by recognizing political expenditures as a protected form of speech and removing limits on overall campaign spending, on personal expenditures by an individual candidate, and on expenditures not coordinated with a candidate's campaign and made by independent interest groups.

INTERPRETING IMAGES

© N. Y. "Tribune."

>> A *New York Tribune* cartoon titled "The First Good Laugh They've Had in Years" depicts the Democrats' jubilation over the Teapot Dome scandal of 1921, which saddled Republicans with a reputation for corruption. The scandal led Congress to try to limit the influence of money on politics.

Interpret: How are Democrats and Republicans represented with animals? Is there anything you can discern about class or regional identity for each party in the 1920s? How have those changed over the last century? What kinds of history are helpful to know in order to interpret a cartoon like this one?

Bettmann/Getty Images

In its *Buckley* ruling, the Court boldly overturned the limitations on expenditures that to that point had been written into law. After the ruling, the number of political action committees shot up dramatically. Today, over 5,800 organizations raise and spend money to influence federal elections. Many of those PACs were formed by corporations that do business with the federal government and by associations whose members' livelihoods are significantly affected by federal regulations, including defense contractors, agricultural producers, and government employee unions. The ballooning of the number of PACs over time is indicative of the increased power that PACs have wielded in campaigns for federal office since 1980.

The Bipartisan Campaign Reform Act of 2002

Throughout the 1980s and 1990s, campaign finance reform was a perennial topic in presidential campaigns, and candidates roundly criticized the role of "special interests" in politics. But members of Congress had little to gain from reforming the system that had brought them to office.

Then in 2002, the world's largest energy-trading company and one of the nation's biggest corporations, Enron, collapsed after an internal accounting scandal, leaving in its wake furious stockholders, employees, and retirees whose financial health depended on the company. Investigations revealed extensive corporate fraud, including accounting improprieties that had enabled corporate leaders to lie about profits and debt. Investigations also revealed that Enron had contributed nearly $4 million to state and federal political parties in **soft money contributions** for "party-building activities," such as voter registration drives and later generic campaign advertising. Public indignation at the scandal flared, leading to the passage of the McCain-Feingold Act.

soft money contributions money donated to political parties where the purpose is not to promote a specific candidate; it is mostly unregulated, and with no cap.

The McCain-Feingold Act, formally known as the Bipartisan Campaign Reform Act (BCRA) of 2002, banned nearly all soft money contributions, although PACs can contribute up to a total of $10,000 to state, county, or local parties for voter registration and GOTV drives. The law also increased individual contribution limitations (shown in Table 14.1) and regulated some independent expenditure advertising.

One aspect of the McCain-Feingold Act that became the subject of a series of legal challenges was a ban on independent issue ads that aired close to elections. In many campaigns, groups would target candidates with advertisements critical of their issue positions. In 2003, Senator Mitch McConnell (R-Ky.), an opponent of the act, and a variety of groups affected by the new law (including the National Rifle Association and the California State Democratic Party) filed *McConnell v. the Federal Election Commission*.[52] The suit alleged that McCain-Feingold was a violation of the plaintiffs' First Amendment rights because the act prohibited airing these ads 30 days before a primary election and 60 days before a general election. The Supreme Court at first upheld the ban, but then reversed itself in another 5–4 decision. In 2007's *Federal Election Commission v. Wisconsin Right to Life, Inc.*,[53] the justices held that advertising within the 30- and 60-day windows could not be prohibited, thus paving the way for its extensive use in the 2008 presidential race.

The Court Weighs In (Again): The Birth of Super PACs

The 1976 Supreme Court ruling in *Buckley v. Valeo* eventually would be the basis of the ruling in *Citizens United v. FEC* that paved the way for super PACs. The year 2010 saw one of the most dramatic episodes in U.S. campaign finance history, with the Supreme Court's decision in the *Citizens United* case. According to this ruling, corporations and labor unions are entitled to the same First Amendment protections to freedom of speech that individuals enjoy. The impact of the *Citizens United* decision has enormously increased the importance of money in politics, as corporations and labor unions now recognize the uncontestable influence that they may have in federal elections. The controversial 5–4 decision was hailed by

TABLE 14.1 ■ Contribution Limitations by Donor and Campaign Recipients Under the Bipartisan Campaign Finance Reform Act, 2020 Cycle

Amount Donors May Give	RECIPIENTS				
	Candidate or Candidate Committee per Election	National Party Committee per Calendar Year	State, District, And Local Party Committee per Calendar Year	Any Other Political Action Committee per Calendar Year	Additional National Party Committee Accounts
Individual	$2,800	$35,500	$10,000 (combined limit)	$5,000	$106,500 per account
National Party Committee	$5,000	No limit	No limit	$5,000	No limit
State, District, and Local Party Committee	$5,000 (combined limit)	No limit	No limit	$5,000 (combined limit)	No limit
PAC (Multi Candidate)	$5,000	$15,000	$5,000 (combined limit)	$5,000	$45,000 per account
PAC (Not Multi Candidate)	$2,800	$35,500	$10,000 (combined limit)	$5,000	$106,500 per account
Candidate Committee	$2,000	No limit	No limit	$5,000	No limit

Source: Federal Election Commission, "Contribution Limits For 2019–2020."

conservatives as a victory for free speech rights and was decried by liberals as an avenue by which corporations could increase their stranglehold on politics and the policy process.

Super PACs and Independent Expenditures

Because expenditures are protected from limitations, many PACs now use independent expenditures to spend unlimited sums for or against political candidates.[54] **Independent expenditures** are outlays, typically for advertising that supports or opposes a candidate, that are uncoordinated with a candidate's campaign. These monies come from **super PACs**, which are political organizations that are ostensibly independent of any particular campaign but that use contributions from individuals, corporations, and labor unions to spend unlimited sums on them, thereby influencing the outcomes of elections. Although limits are imposed on the amounts that super PACs can contribute to a candidate, they can spend as much as they want on advertisements and mailings, supporting (or working against) candidates for federal office. This tactic is legal if these expenditures are not coordinated with the candidates' campaigns—that is, the campaign cannot discuss or be involved in creating independent expenditure ads. Until 2010, these ads could not "expressly advocate" for a particular candidate by using terms such as "Vote for . . ." or "Elect . . . ,"[55] but the Court's decision in *Citizens United*

independent expenditures
Outlays by PACs and others, typically for advertising for or against a candidate, but not coordinated with a candidate's campaign.

super PACs
Political organizations that use contributions from individuals, corporations, and labor unions to spend unlimited sums independent from the campaigns, yet influencing the outcomes of elections.

Campaign donations to candidates for elected office by special interest groups escalated throughout the 1990s. In an effort to limit the role of money in congressional elections, Sens. John McCain (R-AZ) and Russ Feingold (D-WI) sponsored the Bipartisan Campaign Finance Reform Act of 2002. The law banned soft money contributions—unlimited donations made to political parties. It also limited advertising by unions and corporations on behalf of congressional candidates, and restricted how political parties could spend money to benefit candidates. Sen. Mitch McConnell (R-TN) joined with the National Rifle Association and other organizations in a lawsuit that argued that provisions of BCRA violated First Amendment free speech protections. But in the landmark 2003 Supreme Court case *McConnell v. FEC,* the Court disagreed, ruling that neither the soft money ban nor the limits on advertising constitute First Amendment violations.

>> Senators John McCain (left) and Russell Feingold (right) collaborated on a bipartisan overhaul of campaign finance laws.

Source: Douglas Graham | Credit: Chip Somodevilla/Getty Images.

A. Identify the clause of the First Amendment that is common to *McConnell v. FEC* and *Citizens United v. FEC.*

B. Identify differences between the facts of the two cases and explain how the decisions by the Supreme Court in the two cases were different.

C. Explain how the ruling in the *Citizens United* case could be limited in the future.

---

eliminated those restrictions. The impact of the *Citizens United* decision could be seen in the 2020 presidential campaign: During the primary season alone, nearly 2,400 super PACs had organized and raised and spent more than $1 billion.

Circumventing the Rules: Dark Money, 527s, and 501(c)4s

Loopholes in the campaign-finance law became apparent with the emergence of new forms of political groups, organizations that spend so-called **dark money**, which are funds given to nonprofit organizations through an anonymous donation and spent to influence elections. These expenditures are characterized as "dark money" because the organizations that spend the funds are not required to disclose their donors. Two kinds of nonprofits typically spend dark money. The first, **501(c)4s**, are organizations operated exclusively to promote social welfare, including lobbying or engaging in political campaigning. Such nonprofits go largely unregulated by the FEC, and their activities are not subject to the transparency requirements that interest groups and campaign organizations are. In contrast, a **527**, named after the section of the IRS tax code that regulates such organizations, is a tax-exempt group that raises money for political activities. If a 527 engages

dark money
Funds given to nonprofit organizations through an anonymous donation and spent to influence elections.

501(c)4s
Nonprofit organizations operated exclusively for the promotion of social welfare, including lobbying or engaging in political campaigning.

527
A tax-exempt group that raises money for political activities, much like those allowed under the soft money loophole.

only in activities such as voter registration, voter mobilization, and issue advocacy, it has to report its activities only to the government of the state in which it is located or to the IRS. Disclosure to the FEC is required only if a 527 engages in activities expressly advocating for the election or defeat of a federal candidate, or if it participates in electioneering communications. Such dark money groups can contribute unlimited anonymous sums to independent expenditure super PACs. In 2018, dark money groups spent over $750 million—an increase of over $500 million from 2016—to influence the outcome of federal elections through voter registration and mobilization efforts and through ads that, though purportedly issue-based, typically criticized a candidate's record.

Conclusion: Thinking Critically About What's Next in Campaigns, Elections, and Voting

The nature of political campaigns in the United States has continuously evolved, but the changes in recent decades have been especially dramatic. An era in which political parties and grassroots activism dominated campaigns has given way to the present-day realities where money, media, and mavens of strategy are key forces in shaping campaigns, which have grown increasingly candidate and technology centered. Prominently driving the changes are the simultaneous *decrease* in political party clout and *increase* in the need for money—money to pay for the small army of professional staffers that run the campaigns; and money to cover the expensive media buys that candidates, especially those running for national and state office, heavily depend on for communicating with the electorate. Increasingly, this money is being raised outside the regulated campaign finance system, with wealthy donors circumventing federal election reporting requirements by contributing to 527s, 501(c)4s, or super PACs, whose influence in federal campaigns is growing.

Recently, outside, foreign interests intent on undermining U.S. democracy have meddled in U.S. elections, using technology to misinform and foment division within the country. But technology can also bring the politics of electoral campaigns back to the grassroots—now perhaps more appropriately called the netroots. Campaigns and candidates can communicate with voters through media such as Twitter, Facebook, YouTube, Zoom, Snapchat, e-mail, and instant messaging—all exciting alternatives to high-priced "campaigning-as-usual"—and these were tactics that many candidates and voters became accustomed to in 2020.

■ References

1. www.dni.gov/files/documents/ICA_2017_01.pdf.

2. www.c-span.org/video/?436362-1/facebook-google-twitter-executives-testify-russias-influence-2016-election.

3. www.theguardian.com/technology/2018/jan/19/twitter-admits-far-more-russian-bots-posted-on-election-than-it-had-disclosed.

4. http://thehill.com/policy/technology/358025-thousands-attended-protest-organized-by-russians-on-facebook.

5. http://teachingamericanhistory.org/convention/debates/0726-2/.

6. Matt Vasilogambros, "Polling Places Remain a Target Ahead of November Elections." Pew Trusts. Sept. 4, 2018. www.pewtrusts.org/en/research-and-analysis/blogs/stateline/2018/09/04/polling-places-remain-a-target-ahead-of-november-elections

7. http://www.wabe.org/voting-rights-become-a-flashpoint-in-georgia-governors-race.

8. Gregory Krieg, "Civil Rights Groups Sue Georgia Republican Brian Kemp over 53,000 'Pending' Voter Registrations," CNN.

9. V. O. Key, *The Responsible Electorate* (Cambridge, MA: Harvard University Press, 1966).

10. https://www.brennancenter.org/our-work/analysis-opinion/voting-machine-security-where-we-stand-six-months-new-hampshire-primary.

11. John F. Bibby, *Politics, Parties, and Elections in America* (Belmont, CA: Wadsworth, 2000), 253.

12. www.washingtonpost.com/news/speaking-of-science/wp/2018/03/04/2018-is-the-year-of-scientists-running-for-congress/?utm_term5.368bc9a42563.

13. Alabama, Arkansas, Georgia, Illinois, Indiana, Michigan, Mississippi, Missouri, New Hampshire, North Dakota, Ohio, South Carolina, Tennessee, Texas, Vermont, Virginia, and Wisconsin have open primaries; Massachusetts, North Carolina, and Oklahoma allow unaffiliated or independent voters to vote in either party's primary.

14. Barbara Norrander, *Super Tuesday: Regional Politics and Presidential Primaries* (Lexington: University of Kentucky Press, 1992).

15. Thomas E. Cronin, *Direct Democracy: The Politics of Initiative, Referendum, and Recall* (Cambridge, MA: Harvard University Press, 1999).

16. David Broder, *Democracy Derailed: Initiative Campaigns and the Power of Money* (New York: Harvest Books, 2001).

17. Pippa Norris, ed., *Politics and the Press: The News Media and Their Influences* (Boulder, CO: Lynne Rienner Publishers, 1997).

18. See, for example, Matthew Dowd, "Campaign Organization and Strategy," in *Electing the President 2004: An Insider's View,* ed. Kathleen Hall Jamieson (Philadelphia: University of Pennsylvania Press, 2006).

19. Vivé Griffith, "The Influence of Media in Presidential Politics," Think Democracy Project, University of Texas at Austin.

20. Dan Morain, "Small Democratic Donors Have an Online Pal," *Los Angeles Times.*

21. Richard F. Fenno Jr., Home Style: House Members in Their Districts (New York: Longman, 2002).

22. Davis v. Bandemer, 478 U.S. 109 (1986).

23. Norman H. Nie, Sidney Verba, and John R. Petrocik, *The Changing American Voter* (Cambridge, MA: Harvard University Press, 1976).

24. Angus Campbell, Philip Converse, Warren Miller, and Donald Stokes, *The American Voter* (New York: Wiley, 1960).

25. Jan Leighley and Jonathan Nagler, "Who Votes Now? And Does It Matter?" (paper presented at the 2007 annual meeting of the Midwest Political Science Association, Chicago).

26. Norman H. Nie, Jane Junn, and Kenneth Stehlik-Barry, *Education and Democratic Citizenship in America* (Chicago: University of Chicago Press, 1996).

27. www.cnn.com/videos/politics/2016/02/28/sotu-tapper-donald-trump-full-interview.cnn.

28. www.washingtonpost.com/news/fact-checker/wp/2015/07/08/donald-trumps-false-comments-connecting-mexican-immigrants-and-crime/.

29. www.businessinsider.com/donald-trumps-epic-statement-on-mexico-2015-7#ixzz3fF897EIH.

30. Jan E. Leighley and Jonathan Nagler, "Socioeconomic Class Bias in Turnout, 1964–1988: The Voters Remain the Same," *American Political Science Review* 86 (1992): 725–736.

31. The Annenberg National Election Study (ANES), "Voter Turnout 1948–2004."

32. Kim Nguyen and James Garand, "The Effects of Income Inequality on Political Attitudes and Behavior" (paper presented at the 2007 annual meeting of the Midwest Political Science Association, Chicago).

33. Pippa Norris, "Retrospective Voting in the 1984 Presidential Election: Peace, Prosperity, and Patriotism," *Political Studies* 35 (1987): 289–300.

34. Daniel M. Shea, *Campaign Craft: The Strategies, Tactics, and Art of Political Campaign Management* (Westport, CT: Praeger, 1996).

35. Nie, Verba, and Petrocik, *The Changing American Voter.*

36. Samuel Kernell, "Presidential Popularity and Negative Voting," *American Political Science Review* 71 (1977): 44–66.

37. Shanto Iyengar and Jennifer A. McGrady, *Media Politics: A Citizen's Guide* (New York: W. W. Norton, 2006).

38. Warren E. Miller, "Disinterest, Disaffection, and Participation," *Political Behavior* 2 (1980): 7–32.

39. E. E. Schattschneider, *The Semi-Sovereign People* (New York: Holt, Rinehart, and Winston, 1960).

40. Pew Research Center for People and the Press, "Beyond Red versus Blue: Profiles of the Typology Groups," 2005.

41. Franklin Pierce Adams, *Nods and Becks* (New York: McGraw-Hill Publishers, 1944), p. 56.

42. Sebastian Garmann, "Election Frequency, Choice Fatigue, and Voter Turnout," *European Journal of Political Economy* 47 (2017): 19–35.

43. Caitlyn Bradfield and Paul Johnson, "The Effect of Making Election Day a Holiday: An Original Survey and a Case Study of French Presidential Elections Applied to the US Voting System," *Journal of Political and International Studies* 34 (2017): 19.

44. Anthony Downs, *An Economic Theory of Democracy* (New York: Harper, 1957).

45. Barbara Norrander and Bernard N. Grofman, "A Rational Choice Model of Citizen Participation in High and Low Commitment Electoral Activities," *Public Choice* 57 (1988): 187–192.

46. Sidney Verba and Norman H. Nie, *Participation in America: Political Democracy and Social Equality* (New York: Harper & Row, 1972).

47. Arend Lijphart, "Compulsory Voting Is the Best Way to Keep Democracy Strong," *The Chronicle of Higher Education,* October 18, 1996, B3–4.

48. Ruy A. Teixeira, "Just How Much Difference Does Turnout Really Make?" *The American Enterprise,* July/August 1992, 52–59.

49. Gary Jacobson, *Money and Congressional Elections* (New Haven, CT: Yale University Press, 1980).

50. David Adamany, "Money, Politics and Democracy," *American Political Science Review* 71 (1977): 289–304.

51. *Buckley v. Valeo,* 424 U.S. (1976).

52. *McConnell v. Federal Election Commission,* 540 U.S. 93 (2003).

53. *Federal Election Commission v. Wisconsin Right to Life, Inc.,* 551 U.S. (2007).

54. See Anthony Corrado, Thomas E. Mann, Dan Ortiz, Trevor Potter, and Frank Sorauf, *Campaign Finance Reform: A Sourcebook* (Washington, DC: Brookings Institute, 1997).

55. *Federal Election Commission v. National Conservative PAC,* 470 U.S. 480 (1985).

Key Terms

Multiple Choice Questions

1. Which of the following scenarios is an accurate comparison of open and closed primaries?

Open Primary	Closed Primary
A. Facilitates the choosing of the party's strongest nominee	May result in a weak nominee
B. Typically has multiple restrictions on who can vote	Results in crossover voting and possible raiding
C. Allows independent voters to participate	Permits only Republican voters to choose nominees for both parties
D. Any registered voter may vote in any party's primary	Only registered party members may participate

2. Which of the following scenarios is an accurate comparison of primaries and caucuses?

Primary	Caucus
A. The most common way of selecting presidential nominees	Only utilized in states with small populations
B. Meetings of party members who openly show support for candidates	Voters determine which candidate's delegates will attend the party's nominating convention
C. Closed to registered party members only	Open to all registered party members
D. Limited to presidential contests only	Tend to turn into riots as activists are crowded into small rooms to debate the candidates

3. All of the following are reasons why people do not vote EXCEPT:
   A. Low levels of political efficacy
   B. Ballot/voter fatigue
   C. Rational abstention thesis
   D. A lack of funds for poll taxes

4. A voter who decides how to vote based on whether their economic situation has improved because of the incumbent candidate's actions while in office is engaging in
   A. Hypothetical voting
   B. Retrospective voting
   C. Prospective voting
   D. Rational voting

5. *Buckley v. Valeo* (1976) and *Citizens United v. Federal Election Commission* (2010) are based on which constitutional clause?

    A. Free exercise clause

    B. Establishment clause

    C. Freedom of speech clause

    D. Due process clause

6. For which age groups is the percentage of people voting consistently the highest?

    A. 18- to 29-year-olds

    B. 30- to 44-year-olds

    C. 45- to 64-year-olds

    D. 65 and older

7. All of the following are possible reasons why younger people tend not to vote as frequently as older Americans EXCEPT

    A. Lower education levels

    B. Too busy

    C. Forgot to vote

    D. More mobility

■ Free Response Questions

SCOTUS Comparison

After the 2010 Census, the Republican-controlled Wisconsin legislature drew a voting district map that would bolster and solidify Republican-held congressional seats in the state. The redistricting plan was passed in the state assembly and signed by the governor in 2011.

Opponents of the plan challenged the plan as an unconstitutional partisan gerrymander. In the ensuing case, *Gil v. Whitford* (2018) the Supreme Court was asked to decide whether the plan systematically diluted the voting strength of Democratic voters statewide. Ultimately, the Court did not decide on the question of whether partisan gerrymandering had occurred because they deemed the plaintiffs lacked standing to bring forth a suit. However, in her dissent, Justice Kagan stated that partisan gerrymandering "injures enough individuals and organizations in enough concrete ways . . . that standing requirements, properly applied, will not often or long prevent courts from reaching the merits of cases like this one."

A. Identify the constitutional clause that is common to both *Gil v. Whitford* (2018) and *Shaw v. Reno* (1993).

B. Based on the constitutional clause identified in part A, explain why the facts of *Gil v. Whitford* (2018) led to a different holding in *Shaw v. Reno* (1993).

C. Explain an action Congress could take to limit the ruling in *Gil v. Whitford*.

Argumentation

Develop an argument in which you decide whether low voter turnout harms democracy.

In your essay, you must:

- Articulate a defensible claim or thesis that responds to the prompt and establishes a line of reasoning.

- Support your claim with at least TWO pieces of accurate and relevant information:

  - At least ONE piece of evidence must be from one of the following foundational documents:

    — The Constitution of the United States (including the Bill of Rights and subsequent amendments)
    — *Letter from a Birmingham Jail*
    — Brutus I

- Use a second piece of evidence from another foundational document from the list or from your study of the electoral process

- Use reasoning to explain why your evidence supports your claim/thesis

- Respond to an opposing or alternative perspective using refutation, concession, or rebuttal

Quantitative Analysis

State Laws Governing Early Voting Options

Legend:
- Early Voting (EV)
- In-Person Absentee
- All-mail with EV Options
- Enacted EV, but not yet implemented

Source: National Conference of State Legislators. https://www.ncsl.org/research/elections-and-campaigns/early-voting-in-state-elections.aspx

Use the map above to answer the questions.

A. Identify the most common method of voting.

B. Describe a similarity or difference in voting methods, as illustrated in the information graphic, and draw a conclusion about that similarity or difference.

C. Explain how voting methods as shown in the information graphic demonstrate the principle of federalism.

675

Chapter
15 | Political Parties

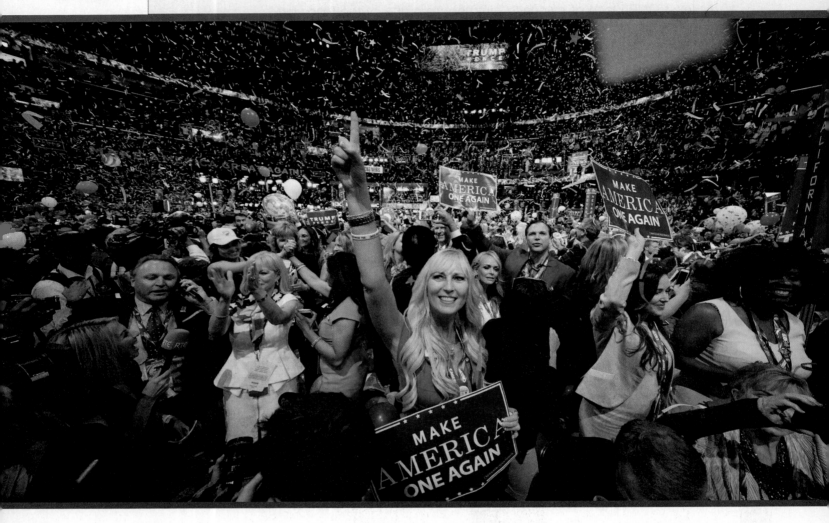

THEN

Political parties relied on patronage and voter loyalty to become powerful entities in American politics.

NOW

The United States seems deeply divided, with rampant partisan rancor.

NEXT

Will the dominance of the Democratic and Republican Parties continue?

Will moderates continue to feel the pressure from the more ideological wings of their parties?

How will digital technologies further shape parties' strategies and expand their reach—and change the membership of parties?

■ Chapter Introduction

In this chapter, you will explore the role of the political party as a linkage institution, or conduit connecting people to the government. Political parties differ from other linkage institutions (such as interest groups) because the main goal of a political party is to get a candidate elected with their party label. Only two major political parties in American politics today are successful in getting candidates elected: the Democratic and Republican Parties. In this chapter, you will explore some of the reasons why our two-party system persists.

The first EU that frames this reading is: *Widely held political ideologies shape policy debates and choices in American policies.* The Democratic Party (referred to as D or DEM in the AP U.S. Government CED) platforms generally align more closely to liberal ideological positions, and the Republican Party (referred to as R or GOP in the AP U.S. Government CED) platforms generally align more closely to conservative ideological positions. Liberal ideologies tend to view personal privacy—areas of behavior where government should not intrude—as extending further than conservative ideologies do, except in arenas involving religious and educational freedom); conservative ideologies favor less government involvement to ensure social and economic equality; and libertarian ideologies disfavor any governmental intervention beyond the protection of private property and individual liberty. The AP U.S. Government curriculum also requires you to know about the Libertarian party, which, while it has been largely unsuccessful at getting members to win congressional seats, has been important in informing the position of many conservative members of Congress who seek to limit government intervention into people's lives.

The second EU that frames this reading is: *Political parties . . . provide opportunities for participation and influence how people relate to government and policy makers.* The political parties play a critical role in the electoral process by educating their members, mobilizing (encouraging) their members to vote, recruiting new candidates for office, and managing their candidate's campaigns. Within the government the political party provides leadership roles and can facilitate (or obstruct) the lawmaking process through teamwork.

The role of the political party in supporting candidates for office has changed in recent years, and today, political campaigns tend to be candidate centered, meaning that while in previous eras, political parties were the most important component of a campaign, today expensive campaigns dominated by paid professional focused on a specific candidate's attributes often takes center stage over partisan or ideological differences.

In recent years, both political parties have been challenged by factionalism: within the past decade, Republicans have faced pressure both from conservatives within their party (a faction called the Tea Party) and by a brand of Republican who identifies primarily as a supporter of President Trump; Democrat continue to face pressure from the progressive left wing of their party. And both parties have had to overcome the new playing field that has emerged as new technologies have changed how political parties operate.

Often, people wonder why the Democrats and the Republicans continue to dominate in the United State. In this chapter we will explore the structural obstacles that make it difficult for other parties to gain traction, including the structure of elections in the United States, and the structure of our government.

As you read about political parties in our democracy, consider the following questions.

- *Why, in a country that is so diverse in demographic background and has so many beliefs and ideologies, are there only two viable choices in our elections?*

- *Will the changes to both the political parties and to the nature of campaigns mean that the political party lacks meaning, or will the political party change and remain important?*[1]

▋ Are Political Parties Today in Crisis?

Democratic Party (DEM)
U.S. political party that currently aligns more closely to liberal ideological positions

Republican Party (GOP)
U.S. political party that currently aligns more closely to conservative ideological positions

political party
An organization of ideologically similar people that recruits, nominates, and elects party members to office in order to control the government.

In the United States today, two major political parties—the **Democratic** and the **Republican Parties**—dominate the political landscape. Generally speaking, a **political party** is an organization of ideologically similar people that nominates and elects its members to office in order to run the government and shape public policy. Parties identify potential candidates, nominate them to run for office, campaign for them, organize elections, and govern.

Historically, political parties have performed important functions, discussed later in this chapter. Since the founding of the United States, it has not been uncommon for one political party to dominate the political landscape temporarily, such as when Democrats controlled national politics during the tenure of Franklin D. Roosevelt or when Republicans did the same during the Reagan years. The popularity of one or the other major political parties ebbs and flows over the decades. However, in recent years, both political parties have struggled to win the approval of the American people, though from Figure 15.1, we can see that Republican Party approval increased dramatically during the Trump presidency, though it dipped drastically in the last months of the Trump presidency as the COVID-19 pandemic raged unabated.

An Evolving Democratic Party

The 2020 election meant a continuation of the struggle within the Democratic Party. The challenge was to balance the pragmatic needs of the moderates, who sought to retain their majority by keeping seats they had picked off in traditionally Republican districts, against the demands of progressives, who sought bolder solutions to the United States's most pressing problems. Since 2018, when a large group of new Democrats were elected to the House of Representatives, obvious tensions have highlighted the political and generational divide between the moderate wing of the Democratic Party, led by Speaker Nancy Pelosi (D-Ca.), and a newly elected band of progressives pressuring for change and pushing the party to the left. Pelosi has led House Democrats for more than 17 years, both as Speaker of the House and House Minority leader.

During her most recent tenure as Speaker, Pelosi has acted as protector of the moderates, particularly offering policy and political cover to the large number of

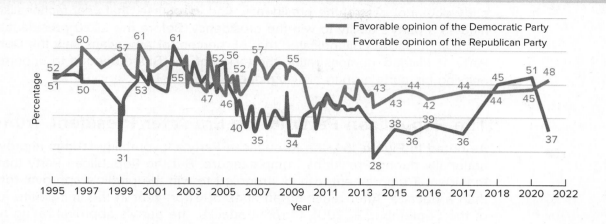

FIGURE 15.1 ■ The People's Opinion of Democrats and Republicans The figure shows the percentage of survey respondents who had a favorable view of the Republican and Democratic Parties between 1997 and 2020. What is the general trend with regards to party favorability ratings? Look at particular high and low points for each political party. What events may have caused people's favorable opinions of the parties to increase or decline?

Source: Gallup, "Party Images," 2020.

"frontline" Democrats—those who won House seats in traditionally Republican districts. Throughout her career, she has won notable policy successes that have furthered the Democratic agenda, most notably the Affordable Care Act in 2010. But for some members elected in 2018, Pelosi's leadership style, one that relies on compromise and seeks to ensure that Democrats continue to have a majority in the caucus, has not been progressive enough. In particular, Pelosi has gone head to head with "the Squad," Representatives Alexandria Ocasio-Cortez (D-N.Y.), Ilhan Omar (D-Minn.), Rashida Tlaib (D-Mich.), and Ayanna Pressley (D-Mass.), who have sometimes used their massive social media presence to voice these differences. Indeed, tensions between the factions became so tense in 2019 that the no-nonsense Pelosi publicly chastised them, saying, "You got a complaint? You come and talk to me about it. But do not tweet about our members and expect us to think that that is just okay."[2]

This factionalism within the Democratic Party could also be seen in 2016. At that time, Hillary Clinton, the front-runner in her party's presidential primary, faced formidable opposition from the left wing of her party with the candidacy of U.S. Senator Bernie Sanders (D-Vt.), who characterizes himself as a democratic socialist. Clinton was viewed as the moderate standard-bearer, but Sanders managed to attract support within the party, particularly among young Americans, who constituted the core of his constituency. Sanders conveyed his dissatisfaction with Clinton to his supporters, contributing to her failure to win the support of many rural white voters without a college degree, and the decision by some Sanders supporters to either vote for Donald Trump or not vote at all, so great was their dissatisfaction with Clinton and the Democratic Party.[3]

Historically, we know that factionalism within a party runs rampant when that party does not control the presidency. And, of course, that very factionalism hinders a party's ability to win the presidency. Before the 2020 presidential election, a Gallup poll indicated that 65 percent of Americans saw the Democratic Party as divided, demonstrating the task that Joe Biden needed to undertake in unifying his party around his candidacy.[4]

The Republican Party in the Era After President Trump

As noted in Figure 15.1, the Republican Party's favorability ratings improved nationally during President Trump's tenure. But the Republican Party that President Trump inherited had struggled to win the public's approval for more than a decade. After reaching an apex of 61 percent in the immediate aftermath of the September 11, 2001, terrorist attacks, the party's approval rating has hovered between 35 percent and 45 percent. Before Trump's election, the Republican Party faced crippling factionalization. The party struggled with the increasing levels of conservatism espoused by voters, members of Congress, and presidential candidates. Members of the **Tea Party movement**—a grassroots, conservative protest movement that opposed government actions, including economic stimulus spending and health care reform—argued that smaller government should be the main goal of the modern Republican Party, similar to the viewpoints of libertarians. They flexed considerable muscle to prevent the more moderate members of their party from compromising. Trump's election and eventual dominance as leader of the GOP stifled that form of ideologically driven dissent within the party, and by early 2020, 56 percent of Americans viewed the Republican Party as unified.[5]

Before his campaign for the Republican nomination, President Trump had historically backed Democratic candidates and supported liberal causes, but as president, he successfully worked with members of the Tea Party in Congress. Still, conservatives' increased strength there, particularly in the House of Representatives, prompted the resignation and retirements of several moderate Republicans leading into the 2018 congressional mid-term elections. In some congressional districts held by Republicans, anti-Trump sentiment was enough to spook incumbents and force retirements.[6] In particular, President Trump's use of derogatory rhetoric to disparage various groups—including women, Latinos, and Muslims—was seen as a rejection of the **big tent principle,** a strategy in which a political party seeks to build a broad coalition among individuals with wide-ranging beliefs, backgrounds, and priorities. Iconic Republican campaign strategist Karl Rove supported the concept of the Republican Party as a big tent and credited this strategy for President George W. Bush's 2004 victory, a win that saw evangelicals and many deeply religious African American voters supporting Bush's candidacy. Donald Trump's ability to forge a new Republican coalition composed of working-class white voters—from union-industrial areas of the Midwest and the rural South—may be the harbinger of a new era in GOP politics.

Although the Republicans have faced significant challenges in satisfying the American people, in general, both political parties have witnessed an overall decline in favorability over the past two decades. In fact, part of the reason

Tea Party movement
A grassroots, conservative protest movement that opposed recent government actions, including economic stimulus spending and health care reform.

big tent principle
A strategy in which a political party seeks to build a broad coalition among individuals with wide-ranging beliefs, backgrounds, and priorities.

for the overall decline stems from the increasing divide between Democrats and Republicans nationally. This growing schism is particularly evident among members of Congress, who, in general, tend to be more ideologically extreme than in decades past. This is a consequence of the process of congressional elections (discussed in greater detail in Chapter 14), which relies on increasingly sophisticated technology to create congressional districts dominated by one political party. This one-party dominance in districts facilitates the election of more extreme ideological members of Congress, who do not have to appeal to moderate constituents or those of the opposing party. As political scientists Marc Hetherington and Thomas Rudolph assert, this increasing polarization has meant that in the general population, Democrats and Republicans increasingly do not like each other, and this dislike results in lower levels of trust in government institutions.[7] With increased polarization, disdain, and distrust, members of Congress—and even presidential candidates—have little incentive to moderate their views, behave civilly, work with the other party, or compromise.

■ Parties Today and Their Functions

Political scientists agree that parties can be distinguished from other political organizations, such as interest groups and political action committees, through four defining characteristics.

First, political parties run candidates under their own label, or affiliation. Most candidates who run for office are identified by their party affiliation. Running a candidate under the party label requires party functions such as recruiting candidates, organizing elections, and campaigning.[8] And political parties typically are the only organizations that regularly run candidates for political office under the party label on a ballot.

>> Tom Perez served as chair of the Democratic National Committee from 2017 to 2021. Perez's primary job was to represent "loyal opposition" to the Republicans.

Evan El-Amin/Shutterstock

Second, unlike interest groups, which hope to have individuals sympathetic to their cause elected but which typically do not want to govern, *political parties seek to govern*. Political parties run candidates hoping that they will win a majority of the seats in a legislature or control the executive branch. Such victories enable the party to enact a broad partisan agenda.

A *third* defining characteristic is that *political parties have broad concerns, focused on many issues*. The major parties in the United States are made up of

platform
The formal statement of a party's principles and policy objectives.

coalitions of different groups and constituencies who rely on political parties to enact their agendas. That is to say, if we were to look at a party's **platform**—the formal statement of its principles and policy objectives—we would find its stance on all sorts of issues, including war, abortion rights, environmental protection, and the minimum wage. These positions are one articulation of the interests of that party's coalition constituencies. Typically, interest groups have narrower issue concerns than parties do, and some focus on only a single issue. For example, we know that the National Rifle Association opposes governmental controls on gun ownership, but what is this interest group's position on the minimum wage? On labeling foods with GMOs? Chances are high that the NRA does not have positions on those matters because its concern is with the single issue of gun ownership.

Finally, political parties are quasi-public organizations that have a special relationship with the government. Some functions of political parties overlap with governmental functions, and some party functions facilitate the creation and perpetuation of government (running elections, for example). The resulting special status subjects political parties to greater scrutiny than private clubs and organizations.

How Parties Engage Individuals

Political scientists who study the nature of Americans' civic engagement recognize that political parties represent one of the main channels through which citizens can make their voices heard. A fixture in the politics of American communities large and small, parties today are accessible to virtually everyone.

Historically, political parties excluded various groups from participating. For example, in many states, women were shut out of party meetings until the mid-20th century.[9] African Americans were formally excluded from voting in Democratic primaries in the South until the U.S. Supreme Court banned the practice in 1944, though it took decades before the party complied with that decision.[10] But in recent times, political parties have increasingly embraced and championed diversity. Evidence of outreach to diverse constituencies can be seen today. Although President Trump faced criticism for his rhetoric aimed at diverse constituencies, in general both parties have, to varying extents, attempted to court women, ethnic and racial minorities, and young voters, providing an important avenue for those traditionally excluded from political life to gain valuable experience as party activists, campaign volunteers, and informed voters. This increasingly diverse participation has also contributed to the parties' health, because it has caused them to recognize that to be successful, candidates must reflect the diverse identities and interests of voters.

What Political Parties Do

As we have seen, by promoting political activity, political parties encourage civic engagement and citizen participation and in that way foster democracy. Parties provide a structure for people to participate in **grassroots organizing**—that is, engaging in tasks that involve direct contact with potential voters, including volunteering on and contributing to party-run campaigns, volunteering in party headquarters, and running for office. Today, much of that organizing occurs online, but parties continue to perform this essential function. For example, leading up to the 2020 presidential election, Democratic and Republican activists registered, canvassed, and mobilized voters. They focused much of their efforts on important

grassroots organizing
Tasks that involve direct contact with voters or potential voters.

>> Historically, political parties excluded various groups, including women. Today, however, both Democrats and Republicans court the support and votes of various constituencies, including women. Here, members of the Active Republican Women's Club of Las Vegas show off the care packages they assembled for soldiers deployed overseas.

Interpret: How is women's political participation portrayed in photos? Can you compare this photo to others of women taking political action in this book? How might these portrayals impact the viewer and their perception of women in politics?

AB Forces News Collection/Alamy Stock Photo

swing states in the presidential race and on competitive elections for the U.S. Senate and House, particularly in open-seat races—districts where no incumbent was seeking reelection and where grassroots organizing efforts were viewed as crucial in determining the outcome of the election.

Political parties also grease the wheels of government and ensure its smooth running. Nearly all legislatures, from town councils to Congress, consist of a majority party, the party to which more than 50 percent of the elected legislators belong, and the minority party, to which fewer than 50 percent of the elected legislators belong. Thus, if five of the nine members of your town council are Republicans and four are Democrats, the Republicans are the majority party and the Democrats are the minority party. The majority party elects the legislature's leaders, makes committee assignments, and holds a majority on those committees.

On the local level, a political party's ability to promote citizen participation varies with its relative influence within the community. Viable political parties— those that effectively contest and win some elections—are more effective at promoting citizen participation than weak political parties. A party that typically is in the minority in a local government—on the town council, in the county legislature—will find it more difficult to attract volunteers, to bring people out to fund-raisers, and to recruit candidates. It follows naturally that parties that are better at attracting public participation are more likely to win elections.

By serving as a training ground for members, political parties also foster effective government. This role of parties is particularly important for groups that traditionally have not been among the power brokers in the government. Historically, African Americans, Latinos, and women have gained valuable knowledge and leadership experience in party organizations—by volunteering on party-run campaigns, assisting with candidate recruitment, or helping with fund-raising endeavors—before running for office.[11] Party credentials established by serving the party in these ways can act as a leveling device that can help make a newcomer's candidacy more viable.

Perhaps most important, political parties promote civic responsibility among elected officials and give voters an important "check" on those elected officials.

Think, for example, about the 2022 congressional midterm elections: undoubtedly, these elections will partially be a mandate on the president's performance in office, even though his name is not on the ballot. This is typical in midterm elections. For example, in 2018, voters who viewed President Trump's tenure favorably were more likely to vote for Republican congressional candidates, while those who perceived his administration negatively were more likely to support Democratic candidates. When an elected leader, particularly a chief executive, is the crucial player in enacting an important policy, the existence of political parties enables voters to hold party members responsible even if that particular elected official is not running for reelection. The system thus provides a check on the power of elected officials, because it makes them aware that the policy or position they take may be unpopular and may have long-lasting repercussions.

Historically, political parties also have fostered cooperation between divided interests and factions, building coalitions even in the most divisive of times; though, as previously discussed, this task is proving increasingly difficult given the growing polarization of political parties. Civic engagement researchers point out that political parties' work in building coalitions and promoting cooperation among diverse groups often occurs away from the bright lights of the media-saturated public arena, where the parties' differences, rather than their common causes, often are in the spotlight.

The Responsible Party Model

responsible party model
Political scientists' view that a function of a party is to offer a clear choice to voters by establishing priorities or policy stances different from those of rival parties.

Historically, according to one theory, political parties have also made government more effective and have provided important cues for voters. The **responsible party model,** developed by E.E. Schattschneider, posits that a party tries to give voters a clear choice by establishing priorities or policy stances different from those of the rival party or parties. Because a party's elected officials tend to be loyal to their party's stances, voters can readily anticipate how a candidate will vote on a given set of issues if elected and can thus cast their vote according to their preferences on those issues.

■ The Three Faces of Parties

American political parties perform their various functions through three "faces," or spheres of operation.[12] The three components of the party include the party in the electorate, the party organization, and the party in government (see Figure 15.2).

The Party in the Electorate

party in the electorate
Individuals who identify with or tend to support a party.

All the individuals who identify with or tend to support a particular party make up the **party in the electorate.** Several factors influence which party an individual will identify with, including personal circumstances, demographic characteristics like race and religion, as well as the party's history, ideology, position on issues of importance to the voter, and candidates.[13]

party identifiers
Individuals who identify themselves as a member of one party or the other, usually by registration.

MEASURING THE PARTY IN THE ELECTORATE The term **party identifier** refers to an individual who identifies himself or herself as a member of one party or another; party identifiers typically are measured by party registration. In most states, party registration is a legal process in which a voter formally selects affiliation with one political party. This declaration of affiliation often occurs when a

FIGURE 15.2 ■ **The Three Faces of Parties**

Creativeye99/iStock/Getty Images

person registers to vote; the prospective voter selects his or her party identification by filling out a voter registration form or party declaration form. Depending on the state, a voter may select the Democratic or the Republican Party, a variety of third parties, or no party. When a voter does not select a party, he or she is technically an unaffiliated voter, but often analysts refer to such a voter as an **independent.**

People's party identification sometimes does not match their actual voting preferences. When we refer to the party in the electorate, we also consider those individuals who express a tendency to vote for one party or a preference for that party.

independent
A voter who does not belong to any organized political party; often used as a synonym for an unaffiliated voter

DETERMINING WHO BELONGS TO EACH POLITICAL PARTY Although we commonly speak in terms of which groups affiliate with and "belong to" each of the political parties, those are just generalizations, with many exceptions. In general, each political party counts specific demographic groups as part of its base of support. A party will often draw party activists and leaders from the ranks of this bloc of individuals who can be counted on for support.

Although whites, men, and people with some college education are naturally found in both parties, they are more likely to be Republicans. For the Democrats, key voting blocs traditionally have included African Americans, women, young people, and people with no college education. Hispanics, a demographic group that is increasing in importance, have traditionally leaned Democratic, though over the years some Hispanics—particularly Cuban Americans and deeply religious Hispanics—were more likely to identify with Republicans. Individuals with a college degree or more are divided evenly between the two parties. Social class also plays a role in party preference. The working class is largely Democratic; the upper-middle class is largely Republican; and the middle class, by far the largest class in the United States, is divided between the two parties. But the best predictor of a person's party identification is his or her ideology. People who identify themselves as conservative are much more likely to be Republicans; people who identify themselves as liberal are much more likely to be Democrats. (See the discussion of ideology in Chapter 1.)

WHY DO PEOPLE BELONG TO THEIR PARTY? In examining who belongs to each political party, it is natural to wonder why people identify with one over the other. It's also interesting to note whether their reasons for supporting one over the other are similar or different.

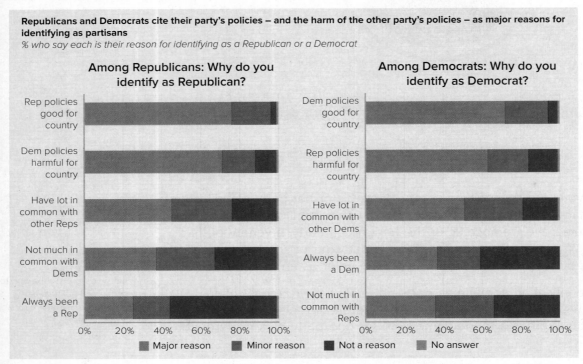

Republicans and Democrats cite their party's policies — and the harm of the other party's policies — as major reasons for identifying as partisans
% who say each is their reason for identifying as a Republican or a Democrat

Source: Pew Research Center. www.pewresearch.org/fact-tank/2018/03/29/why-do-people-belong-to-a-party-negative-views-of-the-opposing-party-are-a-major-factor/

Practice Analytical Thinking

1. What is the biggest reason that partisans of both parties give for identifying with their party? What is the second most important reason?

2. Which party members are most likely to cite loyalty (having always been a member of that party) as a major reason for choosing their party?

3. Explain the differences you see about why Republicans and Democrats identify with their party.

DIFFERENCES BETWEEN DEMOCRATS AND REPUBLICANS We can trace to the 1930s some of the differences—in both ideologies and core constituencies—between today's Democrats and Republicans. That was the era of the Great Depression, a time of devastating economic collapse and personal misery for people around the world. President Franklin D. Roosevelt's drive to expand the role of government by providing a safety net for the most vulnerable in society has remained part of the Democratic agenda to this day. During the latter half of the 20th century, the

Democratic agenda centered on pressing for civil rights for African Americans, equal rights for women, and the expansion of social welfare programs. Evidence of Democrats' continued commitment to a government-provided safety net can be seen in the passage of the Affordable Care Act, which reformed the nation's health care system. Today, key components of the Democratic agenda include economic recovery programs; immigration reform, particularly passage of a policy that would provide a path to citizenship for so-called dreamers, undocumented immigrants who arrived in the United States as children; gay and transgender rights; and issues concerning reproductive justice, including access to safe and legal abortion services.

Traditionally, Republicans have embraced the idea of smaller government that performs fewer social welfare functions. In modern times, this position is manifested in the Republicans' opposition to the Affordable Care Act. Republicans traditionally have also supported measures that protect business and business owners. For many Republicans today, a key stance is advocacy of a stronger governmental role in regulating traditional moral values. Because of this stance, a solid voting bloc within the Republican Party comprises conservative Christians, sometimes called the Christian Right or the Religious Right, who agree with the Republicans' pro-life position on abortion (which includes support for increased regulation of abortion) and appeals for a constitutional amendment banning gay marriage. Republicans also support measures that protect business and business owners. They generally support a decreased role for the federal government, particularly with respect to the economy and social welfare issues, including staunch opposition to Obamacare, and a corresponding larger role for state governments.

It is not surprising that the base constituencies of the parties are drawn from the groups that each party's platform favors. The base of the Democratic Party prominently includes women, the majority of whom, since 1980, have voted for the Democratic presidential nominee. Since Franklin D. Roosevelt's New Deal social welfare policy during the 1930s, African Americans have been an important voting bloc within the Democratic Party, and this support for the Democratic Party among African Americans was shored up during Obama's presidency. Other ethnic minorities, including Latinos and Asian Americans, also tend to support the Democratic Party (as described in Chapter 10). The base of the Republican Party prominently includes many small-business owners; citizens who identify themselves as being very religious; upper-middle-class voters; and under President Trump, rural voters who have not attended college.[14]

>> Latinx are an increasingly important demographic group, as their number of eligible voters grows and their participation rates increase. While many Latinx, including Congresswoman Veronica Escobar (D-Tex.), are staunchly Democratic, the traditional moral values espoused by the Republican Party resonate with many religious members of this population.

Chip Somodevilla/Getty Images

TABLE 15.1 ■ In What Areas Should the Government Play a Major Role? Differences and Similarities Among Democrats and Republicans

PERCENT WHO SAY GOVERNMENT SHOULD PLAY A MAJOR ROLE			
	Republican/ Lean Republican	Democrat/ Lean Democrat	Republican-Democrat Difference
Ensuring access to health care	39%	86%	47%
Helping people get out of poverty	44	80	36
Protecting the environment	45	80	35
Ensuring access to quality education	57	89	32
Setting workplace standards	51	75	24
Ensuring basic income for 65+	58	71	13
Strengthening the economy	73	76	3
Maintaining infrastructure	69	76	7
Ensuring safe food and medicine	83	92	9
Responding to natural disasters	86	90	4
Keeping the country safe from terrorism	92	98	6
Managing the immigration system	78	86	8

Source: Pew Research Center, "Government Gets Lower Ratings for Handling Health Care, Environment, Disaster Response," Pew Research Center, Washington, DC (November, 2015).

Today, the two political parties have a few similarities. For instance, both parties are perceived as equally adept at keeping the country prosperous. And from Table 15.1, we see that identifiers in both political parties agree on certain policy areas where they want to see the government playing a major role. Among these are managing the immigration system (though we would expect stark differences in how partisans would like to see this done), keeping the country safe from terrorism, and responding to natural disasters.

Nonetheless, some differences exist between Democrats and Republicans. Democrats are much more likely to see income inequality as a central problem in the United States, and Republicans are more likely to identify the federal budget deficit as an important issue.[15] And there are sizable party-based differences in the proportion of Democrats and Republicans who think the government should play a major role in specific policy areas. For example, in Table 15.1, we see that Republicans and Democrats disagree about the issue of ensuring access to health care, with only 39 percent of Republicans and those who lean Republican saying the government should play a major role in ensuring access, while 86 percent of Democrats and Democrat leaners say it should. Another major policy area in which Republicans and Democrats disagree relates to helping people get out of poverty, where 44 percent of Republicans and Republican leaners say the government should play a major role, contrasted with 80 percent of Democrats and Democrat leaners.

The Party Organization

Thomas P. "Tip" O'Neill (D-Mass.), Speaker of the House of Representatives from 1977 until 1987, is often quoted as having said, "All politics is local." In no case is that statement truer than it is for American political parties.

Party organization refers to the formal party apparatus, including committees, headquarters, conventions, party leaders, staff, and volunteer workers. In the United States, the party organization is most visible at the local level. Yet county and local parties tend to be loosely organized—centered predominantly on elections—and may be dormant after election season passes.[16] Except during presidential elections, state and local political parties typically function quite separately from the national party. Although the number of individuals who actually participate in the party organization is quite small when compared with the party in the electorate, on the local level, political parties offer one of the most accessible means for individuals to participate in politics.

With respect to political power, county and local parties are the most important components of a party organization. Theoretically, political parties' organization resembles a pyramid (see Figure 15.3), with a broad base of support at the bottom and power flowing up to a smaller group at the state level and then to an even smaller, more exclusive group at the national level.[17] In reality, the national committees of both major U.S. political parties exist separately from the committees of the state and local parties (see Figure 15.4), and real political power can usually be found at the local or county party level, as we will see in the following discussion.

party organization
The formal party apparatus, including committees, headquarters, party leaders, conventions, staff, and volunteer workers.

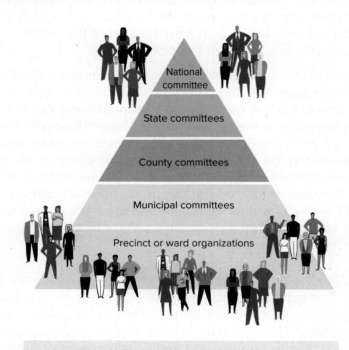

National committee

State committees

County committees

Municipal committees

Precinct or ward organizations

FIGURE 15.3 ■ **Theoretical Structure of Political Parties: A Hierarchical Model of Party Organizations**

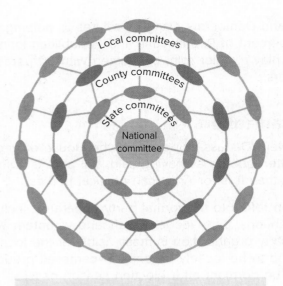

FIGURE 15.4 ■ **Modern Structure of Political Parties: Power Diffused Through Many Party Organizations**

NATIONAL PARTIES Every four years, political party activists meet at a national convention to determine their party's nominee for the presidency. At these conventions, the delegates also adopt rules and develop a party platform that describes the party's policy priorities and positions on issues.

The national party committees (the Democratic National Committee, or DNC, and the Republican National Committee, or RNC) are the national party organizations charged with conducting the conventions and overseeing the operation of the national party during the interim between conventions. The national committee elects a national chair, who is often informally selected by the party's presidential nominee. The national chair, along with the paid staff of the national committee, oversees the day-to-day operations of the political party.

The role of the national chair depends to a large extent on whether the party's nominee wins the presidency. If the party's nominee is victorious, the national chair has a less prominent role because the president serves as the most public representative of the party. If the party's nominee loses, however, the national chair may take on a more public persona, serving as the spokesperson for the **loyal opposition**—voicing the out-of-power party's objections to the policies and priorities of the government in power. In recent years, regardless of whether the party's nominee has won or lost, one of the most important roles of the national chair has been to raise funds. Money donated to the national parties is often redirected to the state and local parties, which use it to help contest elections and mobilize voters.

STATE PARTIES Both national parties have committees in each state (the California State Democratic Committee, for example) that effectively *are* the party in that state. State committees act as intermediaries between the national committees and county committees. Typically, state committees are made up of a few members from each county or other geographic subdivision of a given state.

Historically, state parties were important because of their role in the election of U.S. senators, who until 1913 were elected by their states' legislatures. Since the ratification of the Seventeenth Amendment in that year, the voters of each state have directly elected their senators by popular election.

Later in the 20th century, state political parties began a rebound of power, partly because of the U.S. Supreme Court's decision in *Buckley v. Valeo* (1976). In this case, the Court ruled that political parties are entities with special status because their functions of educating and mobilizing voters and contesting elections help to ensure the smooth functioning of democracy.[18] This ruling created the so-called **soft money loophole,** through which the political parties could raise unlimited funds for party-building activities such as voter registration drives and get-out-the-vote (GOTV) efforts, although contributions to specific candidates were limited. The Court's decision strengthened the influence of the state parties, which the national parties often relied on to coordinate these efforts. The Bipartisan Campaign Reform Act of 2002 eliminated the soft money loophole, but until that time state parties were strengthened by their ability to channel those contributions to political parties. (See Chapter 14 for further discussion of soft money.)

soft money loophole
The Supreme Court's interpretation of campaign finance law that enabled political parties to raise unlimited funds for party-building activities such as voter registration drives and get-out-the-vote (GOTV) efforts.

COUNTY AND LOCAL PARTIES County committees consist of members of municipal, ward, and precinct party committees. The foot soldiers of the political parties, county committees help recruit candidates for office, raise campaign funds, and mobilize voters. The importance of a given county committee's role depends largely on whether its candidates are elected and whether its party controls the government. Party success tends to promote competition for candidates' slots and for seats on the county committee.

In most major cities, ward committees and precinct committees dominate party politics. Because city council members are often elected to represent a ward, ward committees are a powerful force in city politics, providing the grassroots organization that turns voters out in city elections. Precinct committees (a precinct is usually a subdivision of a ward) also help elect city council members.

Besides fund-raising, county and local political parties still play key roles in shaping both community engagement and individual participation in the political process, as they have done historically. During election season (in most places, from the end of August through the first week in November), county and local parties recruit and rely on volunteers to perform a host of functions, including creating and maintaining electronic databases of supporters' contact information, answering phones in party headquarters, registering voters, coordinating mailings, doing advance work for candidates, compiling lists for GOTV efforts, supervising door-knocking campaigns, and staffing phone banks to remind voters to vote on Election Day.

The Party in Government

When candidates run for local, state, or national office, their party affiliation usually appears next to their names on the ballot. After an elected official takes the oath of office, many people do not think about the official's party affiliation. But in fact, the **party in government**—the partisan identifications of elected leaders in local, county, state, and federal government—significantly influences the organization and running of the government at these various levels.

party in government
The partisan identifications of elected leaders in local, county, state, and federal government.

In most towns, the party identification of the majority of the members of the legislative branch (often called the *city council* or *town council*) determines who will serve as the head of the legislature (sometimes called the *president of city council*). And in most towns, the president of city council hails from the majority party. In addition, paid professional positions such as city solicitor (the town's lawyer), town planner, and city engineer are often awarded on the basis of the support of the majority of council. Even though the entire council votes on appointments, the minority party members often defer to the majority, since appointments typically are viewed as a privilege of winning a majority. Other appointments might include positions on voluntary boards such as a town planning or zoning board.

On the state level, the party in government plays a similarly prominent role in organizing government work. Typically, state legislatures are organized around political parties, with leadership roles in each legislative chamber being determined by the majority party. Seating assignments and committee assignments are made by the majority party leadership and are based on a legislator's party affiliation. Figure 15.5 illustrates the partisan breakdown of state legislatures. In each state, the party with a majority in the legislature (shown in the figure) also has a majority on the legislature's committees, which decide the outcome of proposed legislation. Parties moreover are important in the executive branch of state government, since state governors typically appoint party loyalists to key positions in their administrations. Depending on the appointment powers of the governor, which vary from state to state, a governor may also appoint party members to plum assignments on state regulatory boards. In states where the governor appoints the judiciary, the governor also frequently selects judicial nominees from his or her own political party.

Parties perform a similar role in the federal government. Presidents draw from party loyalists to fill cabinet and subcabinet appointments and typically appoint federal judges from their own political parties. Congress is organized based on the party affiliation of its members. When representatives or senators refer to a colleague "on the other side of the aisle," they are referring to a member of the other political party, since congressional Democrats and Republicans sit across the aisle from one another. As in state legislatures, the party with the majority in Congress essentially runs the legislative branch. From its ranks comes the

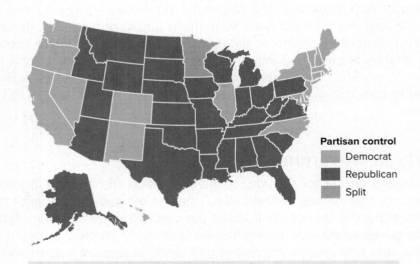

Partisan control
Democrat
Republican
Split

FIGURE 15.5 ■ **Partisan Control of State Legislatures**

Source: "Partisan composition of state legislatures." Ballotpedia. https://ballotpedia.org/Partisan_composition_of_state_legislatures.

congressional leadership, including the Senate majority leader, the Speaker of the House of Representatives, and the House majority leader (see Chapter 4).

DIVIDED GOVERNMENT A party's power has limits. Probably the most important check comes from the opposition party, which can openly criticize the party in power and sometimes succeed in obstructing policy initiatives. During some of their years in office, Presidents Barack Obama, Bill Clinton, and George W. Bush faced **divided government,** the situation in which one party controls both houses of Congress and the other party holds the presidency.[19] Because Democrats took control of the House in 2019, President Trump faced **truncated government,** meaning that one chamber of Congress is controlled by the same party that controls the White House, while the other chamber is controlled by the other party. Presidents Barack Obama, George W. Bush, and Bill Clinton also faced truncated government during their tenures. In 2019, however, the muscle Democrats were able to flex in the House was particularly notable in the charges of impeachment they brought against President Trump.

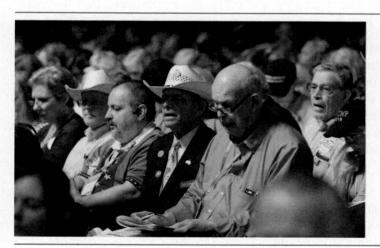

≫ The party organization includes loyalists on the local, state, and national levels. Here, loyal Texas Republican delegates hold a voice vote on a provision of their state party's platform at a statewide convention.

LM Otero/AP Images

■ Political Parties in U.S. History

Modern Americans' divided opinions of political parties would not be surprising to the founders, who viewed political parties with suspicion.[20] Thomas Jefferson said, "If I could not go to heaven but with a party, I would not go there at all." That sentiment was shared by George Washington, who warned of "the baneful effects of the spirit of party."[21] Despite those reservations, political parties began to emerge in the United States during the debate over ratification of the Constitution (with both Washington and Jefferson instrumental in their creation). Those who advocated ratification and a strong central government were called Federalists, and those who opposed ratification and favored states' rights were called Anti-Federalists. Thus began the first party system in the United States. **Party system** refers to the number and competitiveness of political parties in a polity[22]— for example, a government may have a two-party system in which one party is ascending in power. As we will see, the demarcation of party systems typically occurs in hindsight, when social scientists recognize points where there has been **realignment,** a shift in party allegiances or electoral support.[23]

Although these shifting allegiances have played a pivotal role in shaping the context of politics since the country's early days, the founders generally believed that parties threatened the stability of the fledgling democracy.[24] Most thought that political parties enabled individuals and groups to pursue self-serving interests that were often contrary to the common good. Some of the founders argued that parties discouraged independence in thought and action. Some thought that parties exacerbated conflicts and disagreements among the people rather than building consensus. Yet their formation and continued evolution testifies to their important role in achieving political and policy goals for their members.[25]

The First Party System: The Development of Parties, 1789–1828

In 1788, George Washington was elected president, but the consensus surrounding his election proved short-lived. Washington deeply opposed the idea of political parties and ruled during an era without formal parties. But he recognized that despite his popularity, he needed legislators who would push his initiatives through Congress. Washington's secretary of the Treasury and close ally Alexander Hamilton gathered legislators into a loosely knit party, the Federalists, that favored a strong national government.

Thomas Jefferson, secretary of state during Washington's first term (1789–1793), feared a strong central government, and he and his backers opposed Hamilton's Federalists. But Jefferson's primary concern was that the new government should succeed, and so, despite his opposition, he remained in Washington's cabinet during the president's first term. When Jefferson later resigned his secretarial post, in 1793, many of those who shared his apprehensions about a strong central government remained in Congress.

Although Jefferson lost to Federalist John Adams in the 1796 presidential election, he paved the way for his future electoral success by building a base of support—including partisan groups in the states and newly established political newspapers—that allowed him to get his message out.[26] This direct communication with voters marked a significant step in the civic development of the U.S. electorate. The strategy was effective: Jefferson won election to the presidency in 1800 over Adams, and Adams's defeat marked the end of the Federalist Party. Jefferson was reelected in 1804, and both of his elections demonstrated the important function that political parties would play in elections.[27] His supporters became known as Jeffersonian Republicans; later, Democratic-Republicans. The modern descendants of the Democratic-Republicans today are called Democrats.

The Jeffersonian Republicans' effective campaign tactics of communicating with voters, along with the absence of well-organized opposition, resulted in their continued dominance from 1815 to 1828. Historians call those years the Era of Good Feelings, largely because of the widespread popular support for Democratic-Republican presidents James Madison (1809–1817), James Monroe (1817–1825), and John Quincy Adams (1825–1829).

The Second Party System: The Democrats' Rise to Power, 1828–1860

By 1828, some dissension among the Jeffersonian Republicans was becoming apparent. Members of the party, including the charismatic military general and politician Andrew Jackson (1829–1837) of Tennessee, chafed at the elitism of the party and the era. The Jacksonian Democrats—the name for the new coalition that

Jackson formed—emphasized leadership through merit rather than birth.[28] They espoused **populism,** a philosophy supporting the rights and empowerment of the masses, particularly in the area of political participation, and the **spoils system,** in which political supporters were rewarded with jobs (from the phrase "to the victor go the spoils"). The Jacksonian Democrats succeeded in mobilizing the masses, sweeping Jackson to victory in the presidential election of 1828.[29] Political parties had become the medium through which many Americans were politicized, and in 1828, for the first time, more than 1 million Americans cast their ballots in the presidential contest.

Jackson's populism marked a critical step in opening up the civic life of the polity to many new groups of citizens who had not been involved in politics previously.[30] It redefined not only who was eligible to succeed as political leaders, but also who should be eligible to participate in the selection of those leaders. Historian Richard P. McCormick noted that the Jacksonian Democrats extended voting rights to all white adult males, changed the mechanism for selecting presidential electors to popular elections by voters instead of by the state legislatures, and increased the importance of the party convention, in effect giving party members more say in candidates' selection. And although women would not gain the right to vote until 1920, the Jacksonian era saw the formal beginnings of the women's suffrage movement with the formation of the two major women's suffrage organizations and the advent of the Seneca Falls Convention (1848) in support of expanded rights for women.[31]

During the 1830s, southern plantation owners and northern industrialists became concerned about the impact the Democrats' populism would have on economic elites.[32] Their mutual interests crystallized in the formation of the Whig Party in 1836, which succeeded in electing William Henry Harrison (1841) as president. Upon Harrison's death, he was succeeded by his vice president and fellow member of the Whig party, John Tyler (1841–1845).[33] But the era of the Second Party System ultimately was defined by the long-standing effects that Jacksonian principles would have on U.S. politics—namely, through the politicization of a previously excluded mass of citizens, many of whom had been initiated into the rites of full citizenship and others of whom had begun the struggle to win recognition of their status as full citizens.[34]

The Third Party System: The Republicans' Rise to Power, 1860–1896

In the 1850s, slavery became the primary concern for both the Whigs and the Democrats.[35] This highly charged issue divided the Whig Party into proslavery and abolitionist factions, and the party consequently faded away.[36] In its place, a new antislavery party, the Republicans (also called the Grand Old Party, or "GOP"), took shape in 1854 and gained the support of abolitionist Whigs and northern Democrats.[37] The victory of the Republican presidential nominee, Abraham Lincoln, in the election of 1860 marked the beginning of a period of dominance of the antislavery Republicans, which continued even after the Civil War.[38] During this time, the Republican Party enjoyed strong support from newly enfranchised African American voters. Although many African Americans in the South were still prevented from exercising their right to vote through threats, intimidation, and tactics such as the white primary (see Chapter 9), African Americans in the North widely voted Republican. They would remain strong supporters of the "party of Lincoln" for decades.

populism
A philosophy supporting the rights and empowerment of the masses as opposed to elites.

spoils system
The practice of rewarding political supporters with jobs.

political machines
Big-city organizations that
exerted control over many
aspects of life and lavishly
rewarded supporters.

patronage
The system in which a party
leader rewarded political
supporters with jobs or
government contracts in
exchange for their support of
the party.

During this time, political parties grew very strong, and political machines came to dominate the political landscape. A **political machine** was both a corrupt and a useful organization that dominated politics around the turn of the 20th century, particularly in cities. Each political machine was headed by a "boss," whose power rested on a system of patronage. A party leader used **patronage** as a device to reward political supporters—rather than individuals who might demonstrate greater merit or particular competence—with jobs or government contracts. In exchange, those receiving patronage would vote for the party and might be expected to volunteer on a campaign or kick back some of their wages to the party.

INTERPRETING IMAGES

>> As depicted, after President Abraham Lincoln signed the Emancipation Proclamation in 1863, it meant that for decades after his presidency, African Americans would remain an important Republican Party constituency, loyal to "the party of Lincoln."

Interpret: What is the intention behind this picture? How is it meant to portray Lincoln and the others? Do you recognize any other figures in the picture? What narrative does the picture present, and how does that square with what you know about the historical context?

Bettmann/Getty Images

Although political machines were known for corruption, they did accomplish some good. Richard Croker was political boss of Tammany Hall, New York City's Democratic Party political machine, from 1886 until 1902. He explained: "Think of what New York is and what the people of New York are. One half are of foreign birth. . . . They do not speak our language, they do not know our laws. . . . There is no denying the service which Tammany has rendered to the Republic, there is no such organization for taking hold of the untrained, friendless man and converting him into a citizen. Who else would do it if we did not?"[39]

On that score, Croker was right. At the time, political machines provided the vital service of socializing a generation of immigrants to democracy and to the American way of political life. Some machines, including Tammany Hall, generated widespread political participation, and some allowed the participation of women.[40] Political machines helped integrate immigrants into the social, economic, and political fabric of the United States, usually by awarding jobs for loyalty to the party. And in an era when the federal government had not yet become a large-scale provider of social services, urban political machines also provided a safety net for the injured, the elderly, and widows.

The Fourth Party System: Republican Dominance, 1896–1932

The 1896 presidential election between populist Democrat William Jennings Bryan and Republican William McKinley (1897–1901) marked the beginning of a new era in party politics. Bryan appealed widely to Protestants, southerners, midwesterners, and rural dwellers who were suspicious of Catholic, ethnic, working-class immigrants in the urban Northeast. McKinley emphasized economic growth and development and garnered support from industrialists, bankers, and even working-class factory workers, who saw his backing of business as being good for the economy. McKinley won the election handily, his victory ushering in an era of Republican dominance in presidential politics that would last until the election of 1912.

INTERPRETING IMAGES

THE CURIOUS EFFECT OF CLEAN LINEN UPON
THE DEMOCRATIC PARTY

>> **Interpret:** In this cartoon by the famous 19th-century caricaturist and cartoonist Thomas Nast, what does the tiger represent? What point is the cartoonist making about the "clean linen" the tiger is wearing?

H.S. Photos/Alamy Stock Photo

That year, Theodore Roosevelt (1901–1909), who had succeeded McKinley as president in 1901 after the latter's assassination, and who had been elected president in his own right as a Republican in 1904, ran in the presidential election as a Progressive. The Progressive Party advocated widespread governmental reform and sought to limit the power of political bosses. The Republicans' split between William Howard Taft's regular Republicans and Roosevelt's Progressives powered Democrat Woodrow Wilson to the presidency with only 42 percent of the popular vote.

As Wilson's Democratic administration ended up enacting many of the Progressive Party's proposals, the power of the urban political machines declined. For example, recorded voter registration and secret ballot laws were passed, the direct party primary was established, and civil service reform was expanded. The national leaders who spearheaded those measures designed them to take political power out of the bosses' hands and give it to the electorate.

After Wilson's two terms, the Republicans continued to enjoy the support of business elites and the industrial working class. They also benefited from the backing of the many African Americans in the northern cities who continued to support the party of Lincoln, and of women voters, many of whom had been activists in the Progressive movement. With this widespread and diverse support, the Republicans retained control of the presidency throughout the 1920s.

THEN

NOW

>> The original Progressives sought a wide variety of reforms, including an end to child labor. Today, progressives, including these Youth Climate Strike protesters, advocate for policies such as the Green New Deal. Overall, progressive groups put pressure on the existing parties to enact their policy priorities.

(Left): PhotoQuest/Getty Images; (Right): Justin Sullivan/Getty Images

The Fifth Party System: Democratic Dominance, 1932–1968

When the stock market crashed in 1929, the economy entered the deep downturn that history remembers as the Great Depression. In the election of 1932, a broad constituency responded to the calls of the Democratic candidate, Franklin D. Roosevelt, for an increased governmental role in promoting the public welfare. Roosevelt pressed tirelessly for a **New Deal** for all Americans, a broad program in which the government would bear the responsibility of providing a safety net to protect the most disadvantaged members of society.

New Deal
Franklin D. Roosevelt's broad social welfare program in which the government would bear the responsibility of providing a safety net to protect the most disadvantaged members of society.

New Deal coalition
The group composed of southern Democrats, northern city dwellers, immigrants, the poor, Catholics, labor union members, blue-collar workers, African Americans, and women who elected Franklin D. Roosevelt to the presidency four times.

A new alignment among American voters swept "FDR" into presidential office. In fact, the **New Deal coalition**—the name for the voting bloc comprising traditional southern Democrats, northern city dwellers (especially immigrants and the poor), Catholics, unionized and blue-collar workers, African Americans, and women—would elect Roosevelt to the presidency an unprecedented four times.[41]

The era of the Fifth Party System significantly opened up party politics and civic activity to a widening spectrum of Americans. Notably for African Americans and women, Roosevelt's elections marked the first time that they had been actively courted by political parties, and their new political activism—particularly in the form of voting and political party activities—left them feeling they had a voice in their government.

Vice President Harry Truman assumed the presidency on Roosevelt's death in 1945 and was elected in his own right in 1948, but subsequent Democrats were unable to keep Roosevelt's coalition together. Republican Dwight Eisenhower won the White House in 1952 and again in 1956. And although Democrats John F. Kennedy and Lyndon Johnson held the presidency through most of the 1960s, the events of that decade wreaked havoc on the Democratic Party, with deep divisions opening up over the Vietnam War and civil rights for African Americans.[42]

A New Party System?

Until Donald Trump's election, many political scientists expected the trend of Democratic dominance established in the Fifth Party System to continue. But because the recognition of party systems often requires the advantage of hindsight, political scientists are still seeking to determine whether the era that began when Richard Nixon was elected president in 1968 can be considered a separate party system. Republican dominance of the presidency between 1968 and 2008, including the presidencies of presidents Nixon, Ford, Reagan, George H.W. Bush, and George W. Bush, coupled with increasing support of the Republican Party by Southern whites and the increasing activism of conservative Christians in the party, gives support to the claim that a new party system has emerged. Also backing this claim is the support President Trump was able to muster from among rural white voters, particularly those who have not attended college and who live in industrial states.

Additional characteristics of this new party system, according to scholars, include *intense party competition*, in which the two major U.S. political parties have been nearly evenly matched and neither one has dominated, and *divided government*, where a president of one party has to deal with a Congress of the other. This fierce partisan competitiveness is clearly apparent in the outcomes of recent national elections. In particular, the 2000 presidential election demonstrated the ferocious rivalry of the two parties, with a presidential election so close that the outcome was in question for weeks after the voting had ended. That year, voters also evenly divided the Senate, electing 50 Democrats and 50 Republicans. And in 2016, we saw one presidential candidate—Hillary Clinton—win the popular vote, while another won the presidential election through the Electoral College.

The Party System Today: In Decline, in Resurgence, or a Post-Party Era?

Given the various historical changes to the U.S. political party system that we have examined, many political scientists have inquired into what the impact of those changes will be. Do the changes signify an end to party control in American politics? Or can political parties adapt to the altered environment and find new sources of power?

The Party's Over

Some scholars argue that changes in the political environment have rendered today's political parties essentially impotent to fulfill the functions that parties

Party Politics in Flux

THEN

1889
Powerful political parties were in their heyday, and party bosses ruled the cities with an iron fist.

Elected officials toed the party line, because they depended on the party for their office.

The patronage system was in high gear, and political parties derived enormous power and loyalty from the recipients of jobs and lucrative contracts.

NOW

The era of party politics in the United States is over, according to some scholars.

A merit-based civil service system has largely replaced patronage, and parties are weakened because of a decline in the number of loyal members.

Dissatisfaction with both political parties by most Americans means that elected officials sometimes break with their party and its leaders to attract the public's support.

NEXT

- How are advancing technologies likely to change political parties and their operations in the future? Will these weaken or strengthen the parties? Explain.

- How do parties today help voters evaluate candidates? Will they still perform this function in the future? Will the nature of this process change? Explain.

- Will political parties be able to ensure voters that independent candidates will act consistently with their stated principles in the future?

---

performed during stronger party systems. In 1982, political scientist Gary Orren wrote: "In a world in which political scientists disagree on almost everything, there is remarkable agreement among the political science profession that the strength of American political parties has declined significantly over the past several decades."[43] Although some political scientists would subsequently challenge Orren's perspective, many still agree with him.

These theorists note several key factors that have contributed to party decline. Some argue that the elimination of political patronage through the requirement of civil service qualifications for government employees has significantly hurt parties' ability to reward loyal followers with government jobs. Patronage jobs still exist, but most government positions are now awarded upon an applicant's successful performance on a civil service exam that is designed to measure qualifications based on objective criteria. Whereas the recipients of patronage jobs were among the most loyal party members in previous decades, party loyalty has decreased as political parties have lost a significant amount of control in the awarding of jobs.

Other political scientists emphasize the government's increased role over time in providing social welfare benefits as a contributor to the decline of political parties. Because of President Franklin D. Roosevelt's New Deal and further expansion of the government's role as the key provider of social services, the parties typically no longer perform that function. Thus, changing times have brought the elimination of another source of party loyalty.

primary election
An election in which voters choose the party's candidates who will run in the later general election.

Primary elections—elections in which voters choose the party's candidates who will run in the later general election—also have decreased parties' power by taking the control of nominations from party leaders and handing it to voters. In the past, the parties acted as gatekeepers to political nominations. When a party machine anointed nominees at nominating conventions, those nominees became indebted to the party and typically responded with loyalty if they got elected. But today's candidates are less likely to owe their nomination to the party: Instead, in many cases they have fought for and won the nomination by taking their campaign directly to primary voters. Such was the case in 2016, when Donald Trump faced a Republican Party structure that was largely opposed to his nomination. He effectively took his case to primary voters and succeeded in winning the nomination despite efforts to stymie his candidacy by some within the elite of the Republican Party establishment.

Changes in the mass media have also meant a drastically decreased role for political parties. In their heyday, political parties were one of the most important providers of news. Parties published so-called penny papers that reported information to the public. Today, political parties may still provide some information to voters at election time, but most voters rely on other, independent media outlets— including social media, newspapers, television, radio, and Internet news sources— rather than exclusively partisan sources. Take, for example, Donald Trump's 2016 bid to win the Republican nomination for president. Trump entered the race with little support from the party establishment, and indeed, many of his supporters were either new to the Republican Party or new to politics in general. Trump used the traditional media wisely, and media outlets, recognizing that the celebrity candidate attracted large ratings, willingly chronicled his every move. But Trump also relied extensively (and famously) on social media (including the occasional 2 a.m. tweet). Trump's ability to communicate with and mobilize his supporters without relying on the party apparatus demonstrates the ability of candidates to work around the traditional party methods of getting information out to supporters.

The rise in candidate-centered campaigns has also weakened political parties. Candidate-centered campaigns, in which an individual seeking election, rather than an entire party slate, is the focus, have come about because of changes in the parties' functions, the advent of direct primaries, trends in the mass media that have shifted the focus to individual office-seekers, and the 2010 U.S. Supreme Court's decision in *Citizens United v. Federal Election Commission*,[44] which found that the free speech clause of the First Amendment prohibits the government from restricting the amount of money corporations, labor unions, and other organizations can spend on political and election-related communications. This decision paved the way for the explosion of campaign spending by independent groups. Candidate-centered campaigns also must rely more heavily on paid professional campaign workers (instead of party volunteers), making it necessary for contributors to support individual candidates rather than political parties.

These challenges to the ability of political parties to perform their traditional functions, and indeed, the changing nature of the parties themselves, have led some political scientists to conclude that the era of party rule is ending. Other players, they say—including interest groups, candidate-based organizations, and the media—will come to assume the roles traditionally performed by political parties.

The Party's Just Begun

Pointing to the pervasiveness of political discourse, as well as heightened interest and turnout in several recent presidential primaries and general elections, other political scientists strongly disagree that U.S. parties' prime has passed.[45] While conceding that political parties' functions have changed, these theorists observe that parties have proved themselves remarkably adaptable. When the political environment has changed in the past, political parties have responded by assuming different functions or finding new avenues by which to seed party loyalty. According to this view, the parties' ability to rebound is alive and well.

These scholars also argue that the continued dominance in the United States of two political parties—through decades of threats to their survival—has demonstrated a strength and a resilience that are likely to prevail. Today's Republicans, the party of Lincoln, have endured the assassinations of party leaders, the Great Depression, the four-term presidency of popular Democrat Franklin D. Roosevelt, and the Watergate scandal during the Nixon presidency. Today's Democrats are the same party that opposed suffrage for African Americans in the aftermath of the Civil War, and that survived internal divisions over civil rights through the 1960s, to become strong supporters of African American rights in recent decades. The Democrats too have endured assassinations and scandals and have weathered Republican control of the White House for all but 20 years since 1968. Both political parties have remained remarkably competitive despite the challenges to their success.

Scholars who argue that the two main U.S. political parties are once again rebounding cite the lack of viable alternatives to the two-party system. Yes, third parties garnered increased attention in some recent presidential elections, but the present-day party system has not seen the emergence of a strong, viable third party with a cohesive ideology that has attracted a significant portion of the vote in more than one election. And civic education scholars agree that third parties have served an important function by encouraging the political participation of people who are disenchanted with the current two-party system. They also acknowledge, however, the continued dominance of the two main parties in creating opportunities for civic engagement within communities.

A Post-Party Era?

Whether one views U.S. political parties as in decline or rebounding, the evidence demonstrates that the responsible party model (discussed earlier) is not as strong as it once was. Some scholars argue that, as a nation, we are entering a post-partisan era in which political parties are continually decreasing in their importance in national politics but that retain a role as loose organizing structures in government. These scholars see **dealignment,** the phenomenon in which fewer voters support the two major political parties and instead self-identify as independent, as a notable characteristic of this post-partisan era.[46] Others view the increasing trend toward supporting candidates from both parties **(ticket splitting)** or from other parties as evidence of this phenomenon.

One characteristic that lends credence to the assertion of a post-partisan era is the growing importance of candidate-centered politics. The rise of **candidate committees,** organizations that candidates form to support their individual election as opposed to the party's slate of candidates, is one reflection of how politics has become increasingly candidate centered. Candidate committees compete with political parties in many arenas. They raise and spend money, organize campaigns, and attempt to mobilize voters. One effect of their enhanced influence has been that elected officials, particularly members of Congress, are less indebted to their parties than in previous eras and thus sometimes demonstrate less party loyalty when voting on bills in the legislature.

dealignment
The situation in which fewer voters support the two major political parties, instead identifying themselves as independent, or splitting their ticket between candidates from more than one party.

ticket splitting
The situation in which voters vote for candidates from more than one party.

candidate committees
Organizations that candidates form to support their individual election.

Whether or not the United States is entering a post-partisan era, we do know that the rise of candidate committees and the increase in ticket splitting mean that parties are less useful to voters as they assess candidates, because the differences between Republican and Democratic candidates may dissipate in the face of constituent opinion. Yet most Americans disagree: A recent Gallup poll indicated that nearly two-thirds of those surveyed believe that there are important differences between the Democratic and the Republican parties.[47] And the research of some scholars, including David Karol, Hans Noel, John Zaller, and Marty Cohen, indicates that, in most recent election years, party elites, including elected officials and former elected officials, have increased their control in selecting party presidential nominees, suggesting a potential revival of the importance of parties as players in politics today.[48]

■ Two-Party Domination in U.S. Politics

Since the ratification of the Constitution in 1787, the United States has had a two-party system for all but about 30 years in total. This historical record stands in marked contrast to the experience of the many nations that have third parties.[49] A **third party** is a political party organized as opposition or an alternative to the existing parties in a two-party system. Many countries even have multi-party systems.

The United States's two-party system has had two contradictory influences on people's civic engagement. On the one hand, the dominance of only two strong political parties through most of American history has made it easy for individuals to find avenues for becoming civically engaged. Further, at various historical points, political parties have worked for the outright extension of political rights to groups that were excluded from politics, although often with the foremost aim of bolstering their core supporters. On the other hand—the dominance of just two political parties that tend to be ideologically moderate discourages the political participation of some people, particularly those who hold more extreme ideological positions.

Although the grip of the United States's two-party system is frustrating to people who support a greater diversity of parties, the reasons for the two-party system are numerous and difficult to change.

The Dualist Nature of Most Conflicts

Historically, many issues in the United States have been dualist, or "two-sided." For example, the debate over ratification of the U.S. Constitution found people with two basic opinions. On one side, the Federalists supported ratification of the Constitution, which created a federal government that separated powers among three branches and shared power with state governments. They were opposed by the Anti-Federalists, who campaigned against ratification of the Constitution, supported stronger states' rights, and wanted to see states and individuals enjoy greater protections. This split provided the initial structure for the two-party system, and a multitude of issues followed that format.

Political scientists Seymour Martin Lipset and Stein Rokkan asserted that the dualist nature of voter alignments or cleavages shapes how political parties form. In particular, these alignments or cleavages concern the character of the national fabric (for example, whether religious ideals or secular notions should prevail),

2017 Bundestag Election Results

Provisional result

CDU/CSU	SPD	Die Linke	Grüne	FDP	AfD

50% of seats

		% of votes	+/- %	% of seats*
CDU/CSU	Conservatives	32.9	-8.6	34.7
SPD	Social democrats	20.5	-5.2	21.6
Die Linke	Radical left	9.2	+0.6	9.7
Grüne	Greens	8.9	+0.5	9.4
FDP	Pro-business	10.7	+6	11.3
AfD	Populist right	12.6	+7.9	13.3

* Guardian calculation. Parties with less than 5% vote share do not normally get seats in parliament.

Source: The Guardian. "German elections 2017: full results". https://www.theguardian.com/world/ng-interactive/2017/sep/24/german-elections-2017-latest-results-live-merkel-bundestag-afd

In sports, the rules of the game can determine the winning team. In politics, the rules of the elections determine the outcome.

Why do other countries have many parties that win seats in their legislature, while the U.S. has only two? We can answer this question by examining how our congressional election rules compare to the legislative election rules in countries with many parties holding seats in the legislature, such as the German Bundestag (their legislature). Germany allows citizens to cast two votes—one for a member to represent their district, and other for a party. The vote for the party is called a proportional representation system. In this system, the political parties are represented in proportion to the percentage of the vote that they receive (and are not tied to a district, they serve at large). In the proportional representation system, a party must receive at least 5 percent of the vote to be granted a seat. Contrast the proportional representation system to the single-member district winner-take-all-system in the U.S. Parties winning small percentages of the vote do not win districts, therefore, they do not win seats. If the United States instituted proportional voting rules, how might that change our system to be inclusive of more political parties? As a point of comparison, by some estimates, polls consistently indicate the Libertarian Party at about 10% support nationwide or more, yet the Libertarians rarely win congressional seats. With 435 seats in our national legislature, if we had more proportional voting rules, the Libertarians could win about 43/44 seats!

Practice Analytical Thinking

1. In examining the names of the parties winning seats in the Bundestag, which U.S. political party would you think each would most closely associate with?

2. Given our electoral system, is it rational for voters to avoid voting for third party candidates?

3. If our rules were different, how might voting behavior towards third parties change?

DATA ANALYSIS COMPARATIVE

The state of Maine has a strong independent streak and has elected several independent candidates to political offices over the years. Maine has two congressional districts and it is common for Maine to have independent candidates run for office. Let's examine a recent congressional election result in Maine to see how well the third party and independent candidates performed.

| District | Democratic | | Republican | | Others | | Total | | Result |
	Votes	%	Votes	%	Votes	%	Votes	%	
District 1	201,195	58.8%	111,188	32.5%	29,670	8.7%	342,053	100.0%	Democratic Hold
District 2	142,440	50.6%	138,931	49.4%	0	0.00%	281,371	100.0%	Democratic Gain
Total	343,635	55.1%	250,119	40.1%	29,670	4.8%	623,424	100.0%	

Note: in 2018, Maine instituted ranked choice voting for the first time for each of its congressional districts which requires a majority to win, and if no candidate receives a majority the ranked choice is used to determine the winner. The ranked choice voting process was only used in one of the two congressional districts.

Source: Office of the Clerk, U.S. House of Representatives. "Statistics of the Congressional Election from Official Sources for the Election of November 6, 2018." February 28, 2019. https://history.house.gov/Institution/Election-Statistics/Election-Statistics/.

Data Analysis Questions

1. What percent of the vote did third parties/independents receive in Maine's 2018 elections? How many seats did the candidates receive?

2. In the German Bundestag elections in the previous feature, what party received a similar percentage of the votes to the percentage you identified in question 1? How many seats did that party receive?

3. In Germany, the party you identified won seats, while in Maine, the third party did not. Why is this the case?

and they are determined by function (business versus agrarian interests, for example).[50] These cleavages shaped party formation during the 19th century, when the dualist nature of conflict continued to be in evidence in public affairs. Some states wanted slavery; other states opposed "the peculiar institution" of human bondage. In some states, commercial and industrial interests dominated; in other states, agricultural interests held the reins of power. Immigrants, often Catholics, controlled the politics of some states, whereas native-born Protestants held sway in others.

By the 20th century, the dualist conflict had become more ideological. Some Americans agreed with President Franklin D. Roosevelt's plan to help lift the country out of the Great Depression by significantly increasing the role of government in people's everyday lives. Others opposed this unprecedented expansion of the federal government's power. In later decades, debates over civil rights and women's rights demonstrated the continued dualist nature of conflict in American society and culture, a point underscored in later debate centering on gay rights. During President Obama's tenure, an ideologically centered dualist debate concerned the Patient Protection and Affordable Care Act of 2010, or

Obamacare, with many conservatives arguing that the federal government was overstepping its function in mandating and providing mechanisms for health care coverage, while many liberals assert that it is the federal government's responsibility to ensure what they claim is a basic right. Today, the national debate on immigration reform continues to provide evidence of the dualist nature of much of American political discourse, with conservatives taking a hard-line approach to enforcing current immigration laws, while liberals advocate for reform that allows a path to citizenship for undocumented immigrants living in the United States and for allowing more legal immigration.

The Winner-Take-All Electoral System

In almost all U.S. elections, the person with the most votes wins. If a competitor gets just one vote fewer than the victor, he or she wins nothing. If a third party garners a significant proportion of the vote in congressional elections nationwide but does not win the most votes in any given district, the party will not win any seats in Congress.

winner-take-all system
An electoral system in which the candidate who receives the most votes wins that office, even if that total is not a majority.

Compare the **winner-take-all system** with the proportional representation system found in many nations. In a proportional representation system, political parties win the number of parliamentary seats equal to the percentage of the vote each party receives. So, for example, if the Green Party were to capture 9 percent of the vote in a country's election, it would get nine seats in a 100-member parliament. In a proportional representation system, the 19 percent of the vote that Reform Party candidate Ross Perot won in the 1992 U.S. presidential election would have given the Reform Party about 85 seats in the House of Representatives!

proportional representation
An electoral system in which political parties win the number of parliamentary seats equal to the percentage of the vote each party receives.

In nations with **proportional representation,** third parties (which we consider in more detail later in the chapter) are encouraged, because such parties can win a few seats in the legislature and use them to further their cause and broaden their support.[51] In addition, in proportional representation systems, third parties sometimes form a *coalition*, or working union, with a larger party so that the two together can control a majority of a legislature. And so, for example, the Green Party that won nine seats in Parliament in the preceding example might form a coalition with another party that had received 42 percent of the vote, together forming a majority government. In this way, a third party can get members appointed to key positions as a reward for forming the coalition. Consequently, societies with proportional representation systems can sometimes be more inclusive of differing points of view, because even those winning a small proportion of the vote achieve representation, and that representation can be pivotal in the formation of coalitions.

Continued Socialization to the Two-Party System

Another reason the two-party system dominates in the United States is that party identification—like ideology, values, and religious beliefs—is an attribute that often passes down from one generation to the next. Hence, many an individual is likely to be a Democrat or a Republican because his or her parents were one or the other. Many people first learn about government and politics at home. Around the dinner table, a child may have heard her parents rail against Donald Trump's incendiary rhetoric or complain about the numerous scandals surrounding Hillary Clinton. Having become socialized to their household's political culture, children are likely to mimic their parents' views.

Even children who do not share their parents' political outlook or who grow apart from it over time (as commonly occurs during the college years) have been socialized to the legitimacy of the two-party system—unless, of course, their parents routinely criticized both Democrats and Republicans or voiced dissatisfaction with the two-party system.

Election Laws That Favor the Two-Party System

At both the federal and the state levels in the United States, election laws benefit the two major parties because they are usually written by members of one of those parties. Although some local governments mandate nonpartisan elections, in most cities and towns, getting on the ballot typically means simply winning the party's nomination and collecting a state-specified number of signatures of registered party members on a nominating petition. Usually, the party organization circulates this petition for a candidate. Third parties have a much steeper climb to get their candidates in office—sometimes, just getting a candidate's name on the ballot is a serious challenge. Scholars of civic engagement point to the structural impediments to the formation of third parties as key to the low level of civic engagement on the part of individuals who are dissatisfied with the two-party system. Facing seemingly insurmountable structural obstacles to the formation of successful third parties, some Americans shy away from political engagement.

■ Third Parties in the United States

As we have seen, the absence of viable U.S. political parties beyond the Democrats and the Republicans is a source of frustration for some Americans, and many Americans feel that the Democratic and Republican political parties do not do an adequate job of representing the American people. At different times, the proportions of conservatives, liberals, and moderates vary in their likelihood of agreeing that a third party is needed. According to pollsters, this difference may reflect the respondents' opinions of the effectiveness of their party at representing their views. For example, at high points in Donald Trump's presidency, conservatives would have been less likely to say a third party was needed, and the same would hold true for liberals during the Barack Obama presidency.

One of the most significant obstacles to the formation of a viable third party is that people who are dissatisfied with the two dominant parties fall across the ideological spectrum. In general, about 60 percent of Americans say they think a third party is needed, but these individuals differ as to what that party should stand for. Indeed, the group most likely to support the creation of a third party is independents. As shown in Figure 15.6, in recent years, nearly four out of five independents see the need for a third party, while fewer than half of individuals who identify as Democrats or Republicans do. Thus, although many Americans are dissatisfied with the current parties, a third party would have difficulty attracting enough support from among these diversely dissatisfied party members.

Because of the differing ideological viewpoints of those who agree a third party is needed, third parties have had little success in contesting elections. Ralph Nader was an influential candidate in 2000, not because he netted a sizable proportion of votes but because the 3 percent that he did win was enough to

DATA ANALYSIS | EVALUATING THE FACTS

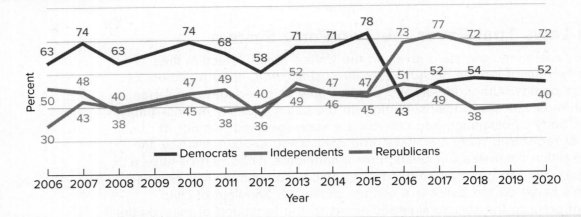

FIGURE 15.6 ■ **Support for a Third Party by Party Identification** This graph presents responses to the following question: "In your view, do the Republican and Democratic parties do an adequate job of representing the American people, or do they do such a poor job that a third major party is needed?" In general, what has been the recent trend regarding Republican and Democratic support for a third party? Why do you think this is the case? Why would Independents be more likely to support a third party? In your view, given these data, is there ample support to sustain a third party?

Source: Gallup, "Majority in U.S. Need for Third Party," 2018.

change the outcome of that razor-close election. Other third-party candidacies have proved influential because of their role in focusing attention—particularly the attention of the victorious candidate—on an issue that might not otherwise have been addressed.[52] Such was the case in 1912 when Progressive Party candidate Theodore Roosevelt ran against Woodrow Wilson. Although he lost the election, Roosevelt succeeded in shaping public opinion so that Wilson felt compelled to enact part of the Progressives' national agenda, including sweeping changes to the nation's child labor laws.

Nonetheless, third parties have played, and continue to play, an influential role in American electoral politics. Indeed, occasionally even the threat of forming a third party is enough to send tremors through the dominant parties, as was the case in the months leading up to the 2016 presidential election, when Republicans feared that Donald Trump, who was running in the Republican presidential primaries, would run as an Independent in the general election. During early primary campaigning, Republicans believed that an Independent Trump candidacy would mean that he would siphon votes from the Republican nominee, leading to a victory by the Democrat, a scenario that in fact had unfolded in 1992. The chairman of the Republican National Committee, Reince Priebus, convinced Trump to sign a "loyalty pledge" stating that Trump would support whoever the party's nominee was. Trump created a loophole to the pledge, saying he would abide by it "only if Republicans treated him fairly." In the end, the loyalty pledge was moot, as Trump himself went on to become the Republican Party nominee.

Types of Third Parties

Third parties have existed in the United States since the early 19th century. Over the nation's history, third parties typically have fallen into one of three general categories: issue advocacy parties, ideologically oriented parties, and splinter parties.

ISSUE ADVOCACY PARTIES Formed to promote a stance on a particular issue, many issue advocacy parties are short-lived. Once the issue is dealt with or fades from popular concern, the mobilizing force behind the party disintegrates. An example is today's United States Marijuana Party, which advocates the legalization of marijuana as well as libertarian views on most issues. The difficulty faced by such parties are exemplified by the struggle of the Green Party, which promotes environmental protection as a primary issue, to become a mainstream party. In the 2000 presidential election, the Green Party sought to win 5 percent of the vote in order to automatically qualify for federal matching funds in the 2004 campaign. It fell short, however, capturing only 3 percent of the vote, and then faded from the national electoral arena.

IDEOLOGICALLY ORIENTED PARTIES The agenda of an ideologically oriented party is typically broader than that of an issue-oriented party. Ideologically oriented parties are structured around an *ideology*—a highly organized and coherent framework concerning the nature and role of government in society (see Chapter 10). Such parties have broad views about many different aspects of government. For example, the **Libertarian Party,** which holds the ideological position that government should not interfere with individuals' social, political, and economic rights, advocates a very limited role for government: no guarantees of minimum wages or other forms of governmental regulation of the economy, including environmental regulation; no governmental interference in individuals' privacy; the legalization of prostitution and drugs; and the elimination of major governmental bureaucracies, including the Central Intelligence Agency, the Internal Revenue Service, and the Federal Bureau of Investigation.

Libertarian Party
U.S. political party holding the ideological position that government should not interfere with individuals' social, political, and economic rights

Another ideologically oriented party is the Socialist Party, which lies at the other end of the ideological spectrum from the Libertarian Party. The Socialist Party, formed in 1901, is one of the longest-standing ideologically oriented parties in the United States. Socialists believe that government should play a large role in ensuring economic equality for all people.

SPLINTER PARTIES A splinter party is a political party that breaks off, or "splinters," from one of the two dominant parties. Often a group splinters off because of intraparty (internal, or within the party) disagreement on a particular issue. In 1948, a group of southern Democrats who opposed the Democratic Party's support of civil rights for African Americans splintered from the Democratic Party to form the States' Rights Party, which quickly became known as the Dixiecrat Party. The party called itself the States' Rights Party because it claimed that Congress had no power to interfere with the administration of laws made by the states. It used that claim to retain the policies that created a system of racial segregation in the South. Although the States' Rights Party was a separate, formal organization, many southern Democratic elected officials and party leaders who agreed with the States' Rights Party's platform supported its views from within the Democratic Party.

The Impact of Third Parties

Despite the difficulties associated with sustaining support in American electoral politics, third parties have important effects in the political arena. First, third

"You can try but it's pretty small in here...the water's going cold and the good soap is gone."

Bruce Bolinger/CartoonStock

There are many reasons why third parties have difficulty winning elections in the United States. Many voters just won't vote for a third party because they know it is extremely unlikely that they will win, and therefore, consider a vote for a third party to be a wasted vote. In addition to voter attitudes, there are rules in our system that make it difficult for third parties to emerge and survive, including the single member district winner-take-all-rule and state rules limiting ballot access for third parties. For a third party to be on the ballot, they must petition the state and have a number of signatures required by the state. Each state has different signature requirement rules, so a presidential candidate attempting to gain ballot access would have to follow each state's rules, making it extraordinarily challenging to be on the ballot in all states.

While it is difficult for third party candidates to be on the ballot, third parties can be an asset to the political process for several reasons. For one, they can force ideas into the debate between the two parties that may not be discussed otherwise. They can provide an outlet for voter discontent with the two more established political parties.

In the cartoon above, the author is mocking the role of third parties in American politics. What are the main ideas of the cartoonist? What evidence exists to support the cartoonist's claims? What electoral rules in American politics are most relevant to the cartoonist's claims?

parties provide a release valve for dissatisfied voters. People who are disgruntled with the two major parties can join or form another political party. This has been the case with the Tea Party, which has channeled the energy of staunch conservatives who view the mainstream Republican Party as too moderate. And while a third party's chances of electoral success are not great, such parties provide a mechanism for like-minded people to come together to try to effect change. At the national level, third parties were a release valve for discontented voters in several elections, as shown in Figure 15.7.

Second, although U.S. third parties usually do not win elections, they can influence electoral outcomes. For example, given the closeness of the 2000 presidential race, many Democrats believe that Green Party candidate Ralph Nader caused Democrat Al Gore to lose the election. They reason that Nader voters would have been more likely to vote for the liberal Gore than for the conservative George W. Bush if Nader had not been a candidate. In a state such as Florida, where the electorate was divided evenly, Nader's candidacy in fact could have changed the outcome of that state's balloting and thus the results of the national election as well. Of course, many third-party advocates claim that supporters of a third-party candidate may not have voted at all if their party had not been on the ballot.

In U.S. history, third-party presidential candidates have won more than 10 percent of the vote seven times, the latest being in 1992, when Independent Party candidate H. Ross Perot captured 19 percent of the vote. As Figure 15.7 illustrates, in five of those seven cases, the incumbent party's presidential nominee lost the presidency. Thus, third parties tend to help the major out-of-power party win election.

Finally, third parties put a variety of issues on the national political agenda. When a third party, especially an issue-oriented third party, draws attention to an issue of concern, sometimes government officials respond to that concern even if the third party fails in its election bid. In some such cases, the issue has not previously been given priority, and the attention the third party draws to it creates a groundswell of political pressure that forces action. In other cases, policymakers might act to address the issue in order to woo the supporters of the third party who have expressed that particular issue concern.

Historically, the two major parties' co-option of issues that were first promoted by third parties has sometimes contributed to the demise of third parties. For example, as we have seen, the Progressives' presidential candidate, Theodore Roosevelt, lost to Democrat Woodrow Wilson in 1912, but Wilson enacted many elements of the Progressive Party's platform, including antitrust regulations, corporate law reforms, and banking regulations. Lacking a unique platform, and with comparatively little electoral success, the Progressives faded away.

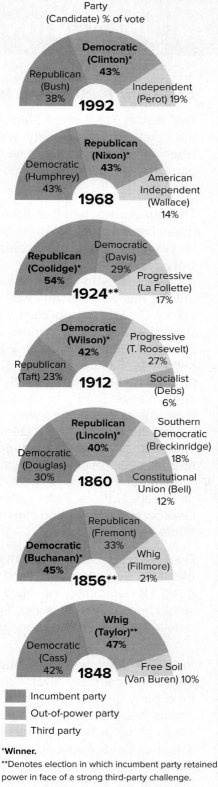

Party
(Candidate) % of vote

Democratic (Clinton)* 43%
Republican (Bush) 38%
Independent (Perot) 19%
1992

Republican (Nixon)* 43%
Democratic (Humphrey) 43%
American Independent (Wallace) 14%
1968

Republican (Coolidge)* 54%
Democratic (Davis) 29%
Progressive (La Follette) 17%
1924**

Democratic (Wilson)* 42%
Republican (Taft) 23%
Progressive (T. Roosevelt) 27%
Socialist (Debs) 6%
1912

Republican (Lincoln)* 40%
Democratic (Douglas) 30%
Southern Democratic (Breckinridge) 18%
Constitutional Union (Bell) 12%
1860

Democratic (Buchanan)* 45%
Republican (Fremont) 33%
Whig (Fillmore) 21%
1856**

Whig (Taylor)** 47%
Democratic (Cass) 42%
Free Soil (Van Buren) 10%
1848

■ Incumbent party
■ Out-of-power party
■ Third party

*Winner.
**Denotes election in which incumbent party retained power in face of a strong third-party challenge.

FIGURE 15.7 ■ Third Parties Help the Out-of-Power Party

Are Third Parties Bad for the United States?

THE ISSUE: The United States's political culture and electoral structure predispose the country to a two-party system. Historically, two parties have dominated, and when third parties have emerged, they have either been subsumed by the dominant parties or simply disappeared when their primary issue of concern was no longer relevant.

The question of whether third parties are bad or good for American democracy dates back almost as far as the democracy itself. But the question has modern implications. In the 2016 campaign, two third-party candidates, the Libertarian Party's Gary Johnson and the Green Party's Jill Stein attracted the attention and support of many voters who were not satisfied with the major parties' nominees. The fear among many Democrats was that Stein would draw from potential supporters of Hillary Clinton; Republicans were wary that Johnson would siphon off votes from Donald Trump. Many pundits argued that third-party candidates have played the role of spoiler during the 2010, 2012, and 2014 congressional elections, when Tea Party candidates challenged Democrats and Republicans for seats in the U.S. House of Representatives and the U.S. Senate. In some races, critics charged that conservative Tea Party candidates who had won primaries against mainstream candidates were weaker general election candidates, and paved the way for some Democratic victories. In other races, Tea Party candidates who ran as independents may have siphoned votes from Republicans, resulting in a stronger Democratic showing. Similar arguments were made in 1992, when pundits charged Reform Party candidate H. Ross Perot with taking votes away from Republican George H. W. Bush and thus ushering Democrat Bill Clinton into the White House.

Do third-party candidacies hurt American democracy by skewing elections away from the third party's major party rival? Or are they good for democracy because they bring out voters who otherwise would have stayed at home and because they help ensure that issues of crucial concern to the electorate get on the national agenda?

YES: The presence of third-party candidates on a ballot means that the major political party—Democratic or Republican—that is closest to the third party in ideology and in base of support will be hurt. This effect occurs because if the third-party candidate were not on the ballot, many of his or her supporters would vote for the candidate (Democratic or Republican) who is ideologically closest to the third-party candidate. Thus, that major party candidate is at a disadvantage, because the third-party candidate essentially siphons off or splits the vote for the major party candidate. Democracy is subverted, because often a candidate wins who is least appealing to the majority of voters (that is, those who voted for the losing major party candidate and those who voted for the third-party candidate). As a result, people are highly dissatisfied with both the political process and elected officials.

WHAT DO YOU THINK?

1. Do you think third parties help or hurt American democracy? Why?

2. What kind of third party do you think would be successful in winning elections?

3. Are you satisfied with how the Democratic and Republican Parties are performing their jobs? How might an individual's perspective on the current state of political parties affect their evaluation of whether third parties are bad for the United States?

NO: Only through third parties and third-party candidacies can voters get the national agenda they desire. Tea Party candidates have successfully framed the national political agenda, and their prioritization of their key values—including a limited role of government—has attracted many voters who previously had been apathetic to the two-party system. Without third parties to spearhead such conversations of democracy, many more people will be turned off by and disaffected from the political process.

OTHER APPROACHES: Third parties are a mixed blessing for the United States. Proponents of third parties are correct in asserting that they provide a safety valve for participation by those dissatisfied with the status quo. Third parties have been effective at getting specific policy concerns on the national agenda, even though frequently that has occurred because one of the major parties co-opts a third party's key issue. But supporters of third parties should realize that the electoral politics in the United States is structured to ensure the perpetuation of the two-party system and that, by supporting a third-party candidate, they run the risk of spoiling the chances of their preferred major party candidate.

New Ideologies, New Technologies: The Parties in the 21st Century

American political parties and their priorities have changed dramatically in recent years. Global events such as the COVID-19 pandemic and its aftermath, the rise of international and domestic terrorism and multifront wars, and the impact of the Internet and cellular technologies have partly driven the changes. Within the Republican and Democratic parties, the changes have reflected an ideological boomerang from an era when a party was defined by its position on social welfare policy, to a time when global issues were central, and back and forth. Today, the economic aftermath of COVID-19 and a bevy of other economic issues, including job creation in the United States' industrial economy, dominate the national agenda. Democrats and Republicans take distinct positions on these and other issues. And while much emphasis today is placed on the differences between the Democrats and the Republicans, many citizens see shades of "purple" between the reds and the blues (see Figure 15.8).

Republicans Today: The Establishment, President Trump, and the Tea Party

The emergence and success of Donald Trump's 2016 presidential candidacy took many Republicans by surprise. And his solid popularity among Republicans unified the party. Among those who look at the long game, though, many wonder about the Republican Party in a post-Trump era, given that the recent success of the party has been so grounded in the brand of Trump's personality. Will future Republicans be able to replicate the kind of personality-based loyalty Trump has created? This question is particularly important given what Trump's tenure will leave behind. Many within his party remain unconvinced that Trump's rhetoric,

In General, Do You Believe . . .

	YES	NO
That government should play a more active role in ensuring individuals' well-being?	☐	☐
That government should actively promote equality in the workplace through affirmative-action programs?	☐	☐
That tax cuts are among the best ways to spur economic growth?	☐	☐
That the government should regulate gun ownership?	☐	☐
That U.S.-targeted international terrorism is linked to the Arab-Israeli conflict and that fighting terrorism should include furthering the peace process there?	☐	☐
That government should work to reduce income inequality through tax and wage policies, including increases to the minimum wage?	☐	☐
That marriage should be defined as a heterosexual union?	☐	☐
That women should have the right to an abortion?	☐	☐
That the government should promote economic growth and job creation with tax, legal, and labor policies that businesses advocate?	☐	☐
That the government should aggressively protect the environment, even if it means more government regulations for industries?	☐	☐
That immigration policy should include a provision granting amnesty for undocumented foreign nationals currently living in the United States?	☐	☐

FIGURE 15.8 ■ **Are You Red, Blue, or Purple?** News commentators use the terms "red" and "blue" to refer to Republicans and Democrats, respectively. Although the basis for an individual's political ideology is complex (see Chapter 1), party identification in the United States often reflects differences in viewpoint on several key issues. Do you know what each party stands for? Do you know which party best represents your views? Take this brief quiz to find out which party you lean toward. Of course, before voting for candidates of that party or even counting yourself as a party identifier, you should further investigate the positions of the parties and the positions of the candidates. The websites listed at the end of the chapter are a good place to start.

Clipboard: Kyoshino/iStock/Getty Images

which often targeted groups that some party members were trying to bring into the GOP fold, is helpful to the future prospects of the Republican Party. For example, Trump's derogatory comments aimed at Mexicans and his mantra of "Build That Wall" (between the United States and Mexico as a mechanism to staunch the flow of undocumented immigrants) are viewed as harmful in the context of attracting Latinx—the fastest-growing voter demographic—into the Republican Party. Others have fretted over inconsistencies in his policy positions, which sometimes seemed to repudiate long-held beliefs within the party.[53] Party leaders fear that these positions might alienate groups that have been core constituents of the Republican Party, including business leaders, members of the military, and veterans, though his appeal to working-class white voters did breathe new life into the Republican Party.

Moderate establishment Republican leaders also seek to fend off attacks and heal wounds caused by divisions between staunchly conservative activists and more moderate members of the party. Conservatism is nothing new to the Republican Party, but the election of Barack Obama in 2008 fueled the flames of a grassroots movement that began growing in communities across the United States. Outraged by what they saw as excessive spending by the administration and the Democrats in Congress, and particularly incensed during the debates concerning health care reform, conservative activists formed the Tea Party movement. The moniker is a reference to the colonial era, when colonists dumped tea into Boston Harbor to protest taxes imposed by the British Crown, an action that contributed to the American Revolution.

A Battle for the Soul of the Democratic Party Today

Today, we continue to see tension among Democratic Party factions. During the 2020 presidential election, much of this tension centered on the divide between the moderate views held by Democratic nominee Joe Biden and some of the more progressive members of the party, who had hoped to not only reflect the views of more liberal voters within the party, but also push the nation's policy agenda to the left. Some of these differences are borne out by a generational divide in which some Millennial voters support a more liberal stance, while some older Democrats support more moderate views. We see the divide reflected in Congress, with much of the party establishment firmly planted in the moderate camp, resisting efforts to move policy and their party to the left, knowing that doing so would hurt their own electoral chances in more moderate congressional districts. But the Democrats have solidified in their opposition to President Trump's legislative agenda, uniformly criticizing his administration's policies, including their stance on immigration, the elimination of state and local tax credits over a certain threshold, and his foreign policy, particularly regarding North Korea and China. Democrats also were unified in their support of impeaching Trump and have been critical of the president's personality and social media presence.

Changing Both Parties: New Technologies

The ways in which party members and voters give and get information, as well as the methods by which parties campaign, have changed drastically in recent years. These changes are discussed in greater detail in Chapter 18, but today a key technological development is the use of "big data" by political parties to target potential supporters. Companies such as NGP VAN, which works with Democrats, and Aristotle, which works with Republicans, have databases containing information not only on every voter in the United States, but even on individuals they hope they can convince to become voters and support one party or the other.

Some data come from information sources openly available to the public, such as a registered voter's age, address, and years in which the voter cast a ballot. But that public information is supplemented with private information purchased by the data companies, For example, are you a member of the National Rifle Association? If so, the Republicans would know that, because the NRA sells their lists to data companies, thus enabling the Republican Party to provide you with information about pro–Second Amendment Republican candidates. Many companies, including CVS, grocery stores, "big box" stores, and newspaper and magazine subscription services, sell their data to companies like NGP VAN and Aristotle. The parties then supplement these databases themselves. For example, a Republican pollster might telephone and ask you what the most important issue in the campaign is, or how likely you are to support a particular candidate. This information is then analyzed and can be used to target you if you are a likely supporter of a particular candidate the party supports.

In addition to this (perhaps alarming) use, technology is changing how political parties connect with potential supporters, as more and more people in the electorate are finding information about issues on the Internet and via their cell phones. Both of the political parties communicate with their supporters and potential supporters using social media. Relying on a medium unheard of only a decade ago, both the Democrats and Republicans use YouTube (their respective channels are The Democrats and GOP) not just to disseminate information, but also to create a dialogue with Americans.

During the 2020 campaign, both the national Democrats and Republicans used their websites to drive supporters to Joe Biden's and Donald Trump's campaigns, encouraging them to contribute and volunteer for these efforts. Both offered downloadable apps that allowed supporters to link their social networking pages and to raise funds by linking the campaigns' sites to their own websites, and this availability has democratized the party process. Partisan activism is no longer limited to individuals who can attend meetings. Whole new forms of Internet activism have emerged. People with access to the Internet can chat, organize, plan, lobby, raise funds, contribute, and mobilize without leaving their desks.

Conclusion: Thinking Critically About What's Next in American Political Parties

Despite the cynicism with which people often view them, political parties are a vital institution for the civic engagement of Americans and are essential to democracy. For many citizens, political parties are the gateway to political participation. For others, they provide cues that guide decisions at the ballot box. The role of parties in teaching individuals essential skills that may lead to elective office, in recruiting candidates, in contesting elections, and in governing—all these valuable functions often do not get the recognition they deserve.

Despite the comparative low esteem in which the two major U.S. political parties are currently held and the significant challenges they face in satisfying their divergent groups of constituents, they both have demonstrated enormous adaptability over time. But the cultural and structural forces that perpetuate the two-party system show little sign of relenting. And although the prospect of a third party provides rich fodder for political pundits who speculate about their importance, in electoral terms third parties have demonstrated very little ability to win elections. Instead, third parties commonly advocate issues that eventually are co-opted by one or both of the major parties, and they sometimes play the role of spoiler in elections.

In the future, the parties will be challenged to adapt. In particular, they will need to adjust continually to new circumstances, as technology changes how the party organizations identify, organize, mobilize, and communicate with the party in the electorate, as well as how the party in government governs. The contemporary faces of the two major parties demonstrate their continuing evolution and responsiveness to their identifiers and constituents.

References

1. E. E. Schattschneider, *Party Government* (New York: Farrar & Rinehart, 1942), 1.

2. https://www.washingtonpost.com/politics/outright-disrespectful-four-house-women-struggle-as-pelosi-isolates-them/2019/07/10/a33c63a8-a33f-11e9-b7b4-95e30869bd15_story.html.

3. https://www.npr.org/2017/08/24/545812242/1-in-10-sanders-primary-voters-ended-up-supporting-trump-survey-finds.

4. https://news.gallup.com/poll/24655/party-images.aspx.

5. Ibid.

6. www.pbs.org/wgbh/frontline/article/whats-driving-republican-retirements-from-congress/.

7. Marc J. Hetherington and Thomas J. Rudolph, *Why Washington Won't Work: Polarization, Political Trust, and the Governing Crisis* (Chicago: University of Chicago Press, 2014).

8. L. Sandy Maisel and Kara Z. Buckley, *Parties and Elections in America,* 4th ed. (Lanham, MD: Rowman & Littlefield, 2004).

9. Jo Freeman, *A Room at a Time: How Women Entered Party Politics* (New York: Rowman & Littlefield, 2000).

10. Ibid.

11. Melanie Gustafson, Kristie Miller, and Elisabeth Israels Perry, *We Have Come to Stay: American Women and Political Parties, 1880–1960* (Albuquerque: University of New Mexico Press, 1999).

12. V. O. Key, *Politics, Parties, and Pressure Groups* (New York: Thomas Y. Crowell, 1964).

13. Seymour Martin Lipset and Stein Rokkan, *Party Systems and Voter Alignments* (New York: Free Press, 1967).

14. Geoffrey Layman, *The Great Divide: Religious and Cultural Conflict in American Party Politics* (New York: Columbia University Press, 2002).

15. Jeffrey M. Jones, "Economy Is Paramount Issue to U.S. Voters," February 29, 2012.

16. Walter Dean Burnham, *Critical Elections and the Mainsprings of American Politics* (New York: W. W. Norton, 1997).

17. John Aldrich, *Why Parties? The Origin and Transformation of Party Politics in America* (Chicago: University of Chicago Press, 1995).

18. *Buckley v. Valeo,* 424 U.S. 1 (1976).

19. Regina Dougherty, "Divided Government Defines the Era," in *America at the Polls: 1996,* ed. Regina Dougherty, Everett C. Ladd, David Wilber, and Lynn Zayachkiwsky (Storrs, CT: Roper Center for Public Opinion Research, 1997).

20. Richard Hofstadter, "A Constitution against Parties: Madisonian Pluralism and the Anti-Party Tradition," *Government and Opposition* 4 (1969): 345–366.

21. Jefferson and Washington, quoted in Richard Hofstadter, *The Idea of a Party System: The Rise of Legitimate Opposition in the United States, 1780–1840* (Berkeley and Los Angeles: University of California Press, 1969), 2, 123.

22. Richard Hofstadter, *The Idea of a Party System: The Rise of Legitimate Opposition in the United States 1780–1840* (Berkeley: University of California Press, 1970).

23. James L. Sundquist, *Dynamics of the Party System: Alignment and Realignment of Political Parties in the United States* (Washington, DC: Brookings, 1983).

24. Everett C. Ladd, *American Political Parties* (New York: W. W. Norton, 1970).

25. David R. Mayhew, *Electoral Realignments: A Critique of an American Genre* (New Haven, CT: Yale University Press, 2002).

26. William Nisbet Chambers, *Political Parties in a New Nation: The American Experience, 1776–1809* (New York: Oxford University Press, 1963).

27. Lance Banning, *The Jeffersonian Persuasion: Evolution of a Party Ideology* (Ithaca, NY: Cornell University Press, 1978).

28. Richard L. McCormick, *The Party Period and Public Policy: American Politics from the Age of Jackson to the Progressive Era* (New York: Oxford University Press, 1986).

29. Jules Witcover, *Party of the People: A History of the Democrats* (New York: Random House, 2003).

30. Lee Benson, *The Concept of Jacksonian Democracy* (Princeton, NJ: Princeton University Press, 1961).

31. Aileen Kraditor, *The Ideas of the Woman Suffrage Movement, 1890–1920* (New York: W. W. Norton, 1981).

32. Eric Foner, *Free Soil, Free Labor, Free Men: The Ideology of the Republican Party Before the Civil War* (New York: Oxford University Press, 1995).

33. William E. Gienapp, *The Origins of the Republican Party, 1852–1856* (New York: Oxford University Press, 1987).

34. Witcover, *Party of the People.*

35. McCormick, *The Party Period and Public Policy.*

36. Joel H. Silbey, *The Partisan Imperative: The Dynamics of American Politics Before the Civil War* (New York: Oxford University Press, 1985).

37. Lewis L. Gould, *Grand Old Party: A History of the Republicans* (New York: Random House, 2003).

38. Paul Kleppner, *The Third Electoral System, 1853–1892: Parties, Voters, and Political Cultures* (Chapel Hill: University of North Carolina Press, 1979).

39. Quoted in A. James Reichley, "Party Politics in a Federal Polity," in *Challenges to Party Government,* ed. John Kenneth White and Jerome M. Mileur (Carbondale: Southern Illinois University Press, 1992), 48.

40. Kristi Anderson, *After Suffrage* (Chicago: University of Chicago Press, 1996), 30.

41. John Petrocik, *Party Coalitions: Realignment and the Decline of the New Deal Party System* (Chicago: University of Chicago Press, 1981).

42. David G. Lawrence, *The Collapse of the Democratic Majority: Realignment, Dealignment, and Electoral Change from Franklin Roosevelt to Bill Clinton* (New York: Westview, 1997).

43. Gary Orren, "The Changing Styles of American Party Politics," in *The Future of American Political Parties: The Challenge of Governance,* ed. Joel L. Fleishman (Englewood Cliffs, NJ: Prentice Hall, 1982), 31.

44. *Citizens United v. Federal Election Commission,* 558 U.S. _____ (2010).

45. The basis for this argument can be found in Larry J. Sabato and Bruce Larson, *The Party's Just Begun: Shaping Political Parties for America's Future,* 2nd ed. (New York: Longman, 2001).

46. Edward G. Carmines, John P. McIver, and James A. Stimson, "Unrealized Partisanship: A Theory of Dealignment," *Journal of Politics* 49 (1987): 376–400. Page 297

47. "Party Images," www.gallup.com/poll/24655/Party-Images.aspx.

48. David Karol, Hans Noel, John Zaller, and Marty Cohen, "Polls or Pols? The Real Driving Force behind Presidential Nominations," *Brookings Review* 21, no. 3 (2003): 36–39.

49. Arend Lijphart, *Electoral Systems and Party Systems: A Study of Twenty-Seven Democracies, 1945–1990* (New York: Oxford University Press, 1994).

50. Lipset and Rokkan, *Party Systems and Voter Alignments.*

51. Maurice Duverger, *Political Parties* (New York: Wiley, 1951).

52. Steven J. Rosenstone, Roy L. Behr, and Edward H. Lazarus, *Third Parties in America,* 2nd ed. (Princeton, NJ: Princeton University Press, 1996).

53. www.npr.org/programs/all-things-considered/2018/01/30/581798328.

Key Terms

Multiple-Choice Questions

1. Which of the following is NOT a function of political parties?
   A. Recruiting candidates for office
   B. Writing party platforms for presidential elections
   C. Selecting key members of the White House staff
   D. Raising money for congressional races

2. Which of the following generalizations about the party in the electorate are true?
   A. There are more registered Republicans than Democrats
   B. They are key players in the day to day operation of political parties
   C. Independents are unaffiliated with either party but often vote partisan
   D. More Americans identify as Republicans than Democrats.

Questions 3 and 4 are based on the graphic below.

Opinion of the Two Parties

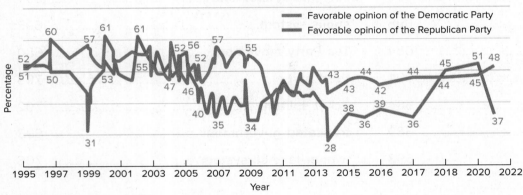

Source: Gallup, "Party Images," 2020.

3. Which of the following accurately describes the information based on the graph above?
   A. Favorable opinions of both Democrats and Republicans are increasing over time
   B. Favorable opinions of both Democrats and Republicans are decreasing over time
   C. When one party's favorability increases, the other's tends to decrease.
   D. More Americans are becoming independent of both political parties

4. Based on the data presented in the graph, which of the following statements are true?
   A. In general, people have a more favorable view of the Democratic Party than the Republican Party.
   B. Republican presidents from 1995–2018 were very unpopular
   C. Both parties' favorability tends to increase and decrease simultaneously.
   D. In general, people have a more favorable view of the Democratic Party than the Republican Party.

Questions 5 and 6 are based on the graphic below.

Modern Structure of Political Parties

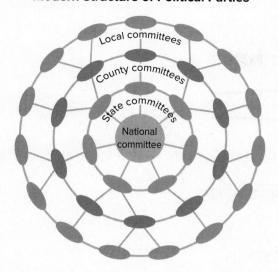

5. The graphic above represents which defining feature of political party organization in the U.S.?

   A. Power flows from the national committee down to the state and local committees

   B. The relative unimportance of county committees in the presidential election process

   C. Largely independent organizations at the state and local level that function independently from the national committee

   D. Power is concentrated with the national committee

6. According to the text, which of the following is the most important component of the party organization?

   A. National committee

   B. State committees

   C. County and local committees

   D. Regional committees

7. Which of the following scenarios is an accurate comparison of the Democratic and Republican Parties?

Democrats	Republicans
A. Expansion of civil rights	Expansion of safety net programs
B. Favors government spending on social welfare programs	Favors government spending on defense
C. Strong state governments	Strong central government
D. Pro-life	Pro-choice

Use the data in the following table to answer questions 8 and 9.

Need for a Third Party

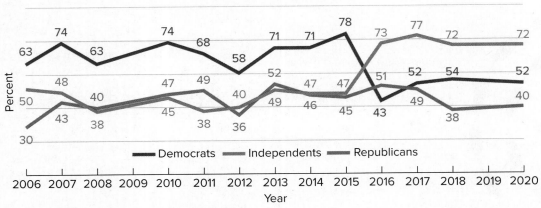

Source: Gallup, "Majority in U.S. Need for Third Party," 2018.

8. Which of the following best describes a trend in the line graph above?

A. Over time, Republicans are becoming more conservative

B. Independents are between Democrats and Republicans when it comes to support for a third party

C. Over time, Independents have surpassed Democrats and Republicans in support for a third party

D. Democrats are consistently less likely to support a third party than Republicans

9. Which of the following is an accurate conclusion based on a comparison of the trends in the line graph above and your knowledge of political parties?

A. Even when favorability of a third party is high, it is difficult for third parties to emerge and survive

B. Trends in support for a third party are likely to lead to multiple parties being competitive in upcoming elections

C. Trends in support for a third party are not a reflection on trends in support for the two major political parties

D. There is no relationship between third party support and support for Democratic and Republican Parties

10. What is a key reason why the two-party system persists in the United States?

A. The single member district winner-take-all system makes it difficult for third parties to compete

B. Federal laws restrict third parties from being able to register and run a candidate under their label

C. Third parties lack access to publicity because they are not allowed to run television advertisements

D. Only two parties accurately represent the views of Americans

▌Free Response Questions

Quantitative Analysis

Party Switchers

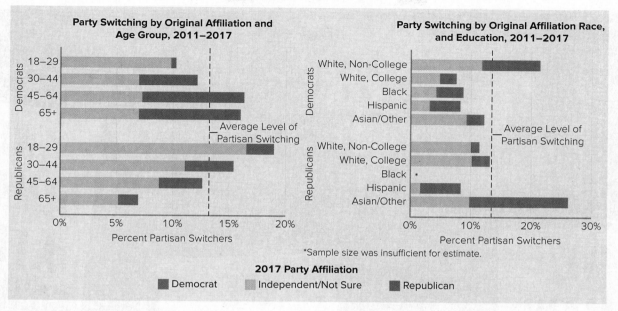

Source: "Why do people belong to a party? Negative views of the opposing party are a major factor." Pew Research Center. March 29, 2018.
www.pewresearch.org/fact-tank/2018/03/29/why-do-people-belong-to-a-party-negative-views-of-the-opposing-party-are-a-major-factor/

Use the information graphic above to answer the questions.

A. Identify the most common type of party affiliation to which voters switch.

B. Describe a similarity or difference in partisan switching, as illustrated in the information graphic, and draw a conclusion about that similarity or difference.

C. Explain how partisan switching as shown in the information graphic demonstrates the principle of party realignment.

Concept Application

> WASHINGTON—A flurry of last-minute moves by the House, Senate and White House late Monday failed to break a bitter budget standoff over President Obama's health care law, setting in motion the first government shutdown in nearly two decades. The Obama administration and the Republican-controlled House had come close to failing to finance the government in the past but had always reached a last-minute agreement to head off a disruption in government services.
>
> —*Washington Post, September 30, 2013*

After reading the scenario, respond to A, B, and C below.

A. During this time, President Obama faced truncated government. Define this concept, and explain how it differs from divided government.

B. In the context of the scenario explain how divided and truncated government serves to "check" the executive.

C. Given what you know about Republican priorities, why would Republican House members have fought to prevent President Obama's health care law from being passed?

Mark Wilson/Staff/Getty Images

THEN

Individuals joined voluntary organizations to achieve goals of value to their members and to influence the direction of society and government.

NOW

Interest groups and social movements continue to be important vehicles that citizens use to persuade government to act in their interest, and technology has now transformed the tactics these groups use.

NEXT

Will digital fund-raising, organizing, and web-based activism strengthen the clout and efficacy of interest groups?

Will young people continue to form and participate in groups to convey their opinions and priorities?

Will digital group activism have unintended negative consequences?

∎ Chapter Introduction

Political parties and interest groups are organizations which connect people to the government and are referred to in AP U.S. Government & Politics as linkage institutions. Individuals who have a position on a public policy matter may participate in the political process through joining an interest group and engaging in activities sponsored by the group.

Both parties and interest groups link people to the government, but the two types of organizations have different goals: the goal of a political party is to get candidates running on the party label elected to office, and in legislatures, to elect controlling majorities. The goal of interest groups is to influence government policies to the benefit of the group's members. The Enduring Understanding is: *Political parties, interest groups, and social movements provide opportunities for participation and influence how people relate to government and policy-makers.*

The U.S. system of government provides multiple opportunities for citizens to access government and attempt to influence policy. On both the federal and state level, citizens can join interest groups who will influence policy makers. Interest groups accomplish this by engaging in a range of activities, including protesting, lobbying, get out the vote drives, fundraising, and advertising. In addition to accessing lawmakers, interest groups may also attempt to influence government policy through the courts. An interest group may hire attorneys and press litigation, depending on the issue. Attorneys can write *amicus curiae* (friend of the court) briefs as outside parties attempting to sway the outcome of a case. It is often through an interest group that a citizen may interact with an elected official. For example, groups like the National Education Association sponsor large citizen lobbying events in which educators may visit with their elected officials to discuss education policy matters in hopes of having influence.

The U.S. Constitution does not specifically mention interest groups, but the framers of the Constitution were aware of the role interest groups would play in a free society. in *Federalist* No. 10 *James Madison* discussed "the mischiefs of faction (interest groups)." Interest groups were potentially mischievous in Madison's view because of the nature of interest groups to be self-interested, rather than concerned about the public good. Madison argued that it was in human nature to form groups and asserted that the Constitution could not prevent factions (interest groups) from forming, because to prevent interest groups would be to destroy liberty. The First Amendment to the U.S. Constitution protects the right of interest groups to assemble and protects the rights of free expression. Our democratic system is predicated on the assumption that people will express their interests through groups. Big Idea 3 in the AP US Government and Politics course states: *Popular sovereignty, individualism, and republicanism are important considerations of U.S. laws and policy making and assume citizens will engage and participate.*

In the United States, we have more interest groups per capita than any other country—Americans seem to like joining groups. Today, the proliferation of interest groups is partly due to the ease of forming or joining a group using new technologies. Many traditional interest groups now rely on a cadre of supporters on Facebook, Instagram, or Twitter to perform some on their functions.

The ways in which interest groups interact with citizens, policymakers, and those charged with implementing policy is the focus of Big Idea 4: *Multiple actors and institutions interact to produce and implement possible policies.* Interest groups are just one of many actors in the U.S. political process that interact with multiple policymakers at the federal and state levels of government.

■ The Value of Interest Groups

interest group
An organization that seeks to achieve goals by influencing government decision making.

The 19th-century French historian and writer Alexis de Tocqueville, author of the influential work *Democracy in America*, dubbed Americans "a nation of joiners" in 1835, and his analysis still rings true today.[1] Indeed, estimates indicate that about 80 percent of all Americans belong to some kind of voluntary group or association, although not every group is an **interest group.**[2] The key role that interest groups would play in politics was foreseen by the founders—James Madison acknowledged the idea that people with similar interests would form and join groups to prompt government action. He believed that the only way to cure "the mischiefs of faction" was by enabling groups to proliferate and compete with one another.[3]

social capital
The relationships that improve our lives by giving us social connections to solve problems, communicate, and interact with government.

Yet some contemporary scholars argue that Americans today are increasingly staying at home. Political scientist Robert Putnam, author of *Bowling Alone: The Collapse and Revival of American Community*, found a marked decrease in the number of people who belong to interest groups and other types of clubs and organizations. These organizations, Putnam argues, are essential sources of **social capital,** the relationships that improve our lives by giving us social connections with which to solve common problems. Putnam demonstrates that social capital improves individual lives in very concrete ways: People with a greater number of social ties live longer, happier, and healthier lives. But social capital also improves communities, and even larger polities, because it stimulates individuals to communicate and interact with their governments. Efficacy increases, because when people are engaged and communicate with government officials, government responds by meeting their needs more effectively. This response in turn creates

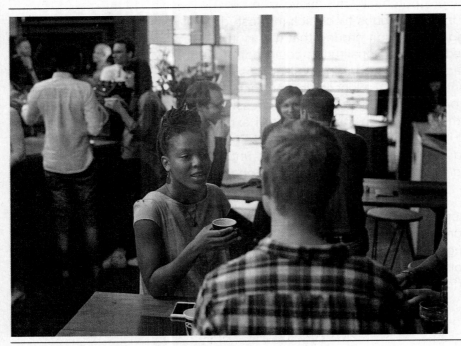

>> Can a conversation over a matcha green tea latte create social capital? People may not be joining gardening clubs, but are they really less connected than in the past? Does technology foster stronger social bonds?

Mariusz Szczawinski/Alamy Stock Photo

the feeling among individuals that government listens to people like them. And when government responds, it becomes more likely that those affected will try to influence government decisions again.[4]

However, Putnam's work was written 20 years ago, while the Internet was blossoming but social media had not yet emerged as an important tool for modern social relationships. Thus, his work does not analyze the social capital that may be derived from participation in online civic engagement and activism. Critics of Putnam's work have also noted that although the number of people belonging to the kinds of groups he analyzed may be declining, people are engaged in other types of groups and clubs and enjoy various forms of group recreation.[5] For example, you probably are not a member of a gardening club like those that Putnam researched. (But if you are, good for you!) Yet you likely belong to an online community such as Instagram or Snapchat. Such communities facilitate social relationships and may even provide the opportunity for participants to solve community problems. And although people may be less likely to entertain friends and relatives in their homes today (another activity Putnam measured), they are more likely to socialize with friends and relatives over meals in restaurants. So even if Putnam is correct in his analysis that we are no longer socially engaged the way Americans used to be, we may still be engaged—but through different channels and in different settings.

How Group Participation Has Changed in the United States

THEN

(1960s)
Individuals joined bowling leagues, civic associations, and community service organizations.

Many people entertained and socialized a great deal at home.

Groups used traditional activities to communicate their interests to policymakers, including letter writing and lobbying.

NOW

People join virtual communities and use social networking sites to keep in touch with others who share their personal and public interests.

People are more likely to visit with friends and relatives in restaurants, cafés, and other public settings, as well as online through "virtual visits," like FaceTiming and Snapchatting.

Groups rely on traditional activities but also increasingly use social media, including Twitter, to communicate with members, to fund-raise, and to lobby policymakers.

NEXT

- What new media technologies and strategies might shape how interest groups organize and mobilize members in the future?

- Are there *negative* consequences to relying on the Internet as an organizing tool? What obstacles will some Internet-based organizations face in mobilizing their supporters around a given issue?

- In what ways will technology change how policymakers are influenced in the future?

Political scientist E.E. Schattschneider has written: "Democracy is a competitive political system in which competing leaders and organizations define the alternatives of public policy in such a way that the public can participate in the decision-making process."[6] One of the key types of competitive organizations Schattschneider was describing is interest groups. Schattschneider and other political scientists study and assess the value that interest groups provide in American democracy. This value centrally includes interest groups' usefulness in channeling civic participation—serving as a point of access and a mechanism by which people can connect with their governments. Political scientists also explore interest groups, on the one hand, as valuable avenues by which people can influence the policy process and, on the other hand, as resources for policymakers. In this section, we consider various perspectives on the role of interest groups in a democracy, the diverse value that interest groups confer, and the drawbacks of interest groups.

Interest Groups and Civic Participation

Scholars who study civic engagement acknowledge the significant ways in which interest groups channel civic participation. Interest groups afford a way for people to band together to influence government as a *collective force*. Interest groups also seek to involve *individuals* more actively in the political process by encouraging them to vote and to communicate their views one-on-one to their elected officials. In addition, interest groups assist in the engagement of *communities* by providing a forum through which people can come together and form an association. Importantly, too, interest groups offer an alternative means of participation to individuals who are disenchanted with the two-party system, or with the status quo in general. By taking part in interest groups, individuals, acting together, perform important roles in the polity not only by communicating their viewpoints to policymakers but also by providing a medium that other people can use to express their opinions.

Pluralist Theory versus Elite Theory

An interest group can represent a wide variety of interests, as in the case of the National Association for the Advancement of Colored People (NAACP), a century-old civil rights organization that continues today to advocate for a wide variety of policies, including voting rights, economic equality, and criminal justice reform. Alternatively, an interest group can restrict itself to a narrower focus, as does the Society for the Preservation and Encouragement of Barbershop Quartet Singing. But how one views the role that interest groups play shapes the perception of the representative democracies in which the groups exist. For example, scholars who support **pluralist theory** emphasize how important it is for a democracy to have large numbers of diverse interest groups representing a wide variety of views.[7] Indeed, pluralists view the policy-making process as a crucial competition among diverse groups whose members attempt to influence policy in numerous settings, including agencies in the executive branch of government, Congress, and the courts.[8] Pluralists believe that interest groups are essential players in democracy because they ensure that individual interests are represented in the political arena even if some individuals opt not to participate. Like some of the founders, pluralists argue that individuals' liberties can be protected only through a proliferation of groups representing diverse competing interests, so that no one group dominates.

pluralist theory
A theory that holds that policy making is a competition among diverse interest groups that ensure the representation of individual interests.

Pluralists believe, moreover, that interest groups provide a structure for political participation and help ensure that individuals follow the rules in participating in civic society. Following the rules means using positive channels for government action rather than extreme tactics such as assassinations, coups, and other forms of violence. Pluralists also stress that groups' varying assets tend to counterbalance one another. And so, although an industry association such as the American Petroleum Institute, an interest group for the oil and natural gas industry, may have a lot of money at its disposal, an environmental group opposing the industry, such as Greenpeace, may have a large membership base from which to launch grassroots activism.

Proponents of **elite theory** dispute some claims of pluralist theory. In particular, elite theorists point to the overwhelming presence of elites as political decision makers. According to elite theory, a ruling class composed of wealthy, educated individuals wields most of the power in government and also within the top universities, corporations, the military, and media outlets. Elite theorists claim that despite appearances that the political system is accessible to all, elites hold disproportionate power in the United States. They also emphasize that elites commonly use that power to protect their own economic interests, frequently by ensuring the continuation of the status quo. And so, although non-elites represented by interest groups may occasionally win political victories, elites control the direction of major policies. But elite theorists posit that there is mobility into the elite structure; they emphasize that (in contrast to the situation in aristocracies) talented and industrious individuals from non-elite backgrounds can attain elite status in a democracy, often through education. This mobility, they say, gives the political system an even greater façade of accessibility.

elite theory
A theory that holds that a group of wealthy, educated individuals wields most political power.

Although these theories offer competing explanations for the role and motivation of interest groups in the United States, many political scientists agree that aspects of both theories are true: elites do have disproportionate influence in policymaking, but that power is checked by interest groups. Undisputed is that interest groups are an essential feature of American democracy and provide an important medium through which individuals can exercise some control over their government.

Key Functions of Interest Groups

Many Americans join interest groups, and yet interest groups have a generally negative reputation. For example, it has been said of many a politician that he or she is "in the pocket of the special interests." This statement suggests that the politician is not making decisions based on conscience or the public interest but instead has been "bought." This notion is closely linked to the ideas held by elite theorists, who argue that elites' disproportionate share of influence negatively affects the ability of the average person to get the government to do what she or he wants it to. Yet despite the criticisms frequently leveled by politicians, pundits, and the populace about interest groups' efforts to influence government, these groups serve several vital functions in the policy-making process in the United States:

- *Interest groups educate the public about policy issues.* Messages from interest groups abound. For example, thanks to the efforts of organizations such as Mothers Against Drunk Driving (MADD), most people are aware of the dangers of drinking and driving. In educating the public, interest groups often provide a vehicle for civic discourse, so that genuine dialogue about policy problems and potential solutions is part of the national agenda.

- *Interest groups provide average citizens with an avenue of access to activism.* Anyone can join or form an interest group. Although wealthy and well-educated people are most likely to do so, interest groups can speak for all kinds of people on all kinds of issues. Historically in the United States, interest groups have been significant forces for advocates of civil rights for African Americans,[9] as well as for supporters of equal rights for women.[10] Consider, for example, the diverse interests that have come together under the label of "progressive" groups. These groups include organizations such as #Resist, Working Families, Women's March, Progressive Women, and many others, and they advocate for a wide variety of policies, including Medicare for All, the Green New Deal, workers' rights, gender equality, and social justice through marijuana legalization. And all have successfully channeled the passionate energy of their members to rally for their collective causes.[11]

- *Interest groups mobilize citizens and stimulate them to participate in civic and political affairs.* Some people are "turned off" by politics because they feel that elected officials do not represent their views. In these cases, interest groups, with their typically narrower area of focus, can sometimes fill the void. Interest groups, particularly grassroots organizations that foster community identity among individuals who had previously felt they lacked a voice in government, encourage civic and political participation. Today, groups that advocate for racial equality; immigrant rights; and rights for gays, lesbians, and transgender people all nurture participation among individuals who previously felt excluded from the political process. Moreover, large national interest groups may spawn community involvement by encouraging the formation of local chapters of larger interest groups.

- *Interest groups perform electoral functions.* By endorsing and rating candidates and advertising their positions, interest groups provide voters with cues as to which candidates best represent their views. Interest groups also mobilize campaign volunteers and voters. These activities facilitate informed civic participation. For example, before the 2020 elections, the Republican-oriented interest group the American Conservative Union rated members of Congress, enabling voters to learn which members are the most conservative; at the same time, Democratically aligned groups, including Democracy for America, used sophisticated get-out-the-vote software to turn Democratic voters out for Democratic candidates.

- *Interest groups provide information and expertise to policymakers.* The private sector often has greater resources than the public sector and can be a source of meaningful data and information for policymakers on pressing social issues. Sometimes, interest group "experts" might include celebrities, who, through their status, not only provide information to legislators, but also increase public awareness of their issue. Indeed, some research indicates that when legislators are insulated from the interest group environment, they are less likely to revise policies already on the books.[12]

- *Interest groups can protect the common good.* The federal government is structured so that only one individual (the president) is elected from a national constituency. Interest groups can work to protect the nation's interest as a whole, rather than just the needs of a specific constituency. For example, in the months leading up to the Flint, Michigan, water crisis, several interest groups, including the Flint-based Coalition for Clean Water, the American Civil Liberties Union of Michigan, and the Natural Resources Defense Council, petitioned the federal Environmental Protection Agency to investigate Flint's water, as elevated lead levels were found both in the water supply and in blood tests performed on the city's children. They pressured for a declaration of a state of emergency in the city and surrounding county, which allowed the Federal Emergency Management Agency to provide up to $5 million in aid to provide clean water for the city's residents and improve the city's water infrastructure.

- *Interest groups are an integral part of the government's system of checks and balances.* Interest groups often "check" one another's influence with competing interests, and they can similarly check the actions of policymakers. And so, for example, while labor-oriented interest groups advocate for an increase in the federal minimum wage, business groups, including industry associations and the Chamber of Commerce, lobby against such legislation.

The Downside of Interest Groups

Despite the valuable functions of interest groups, certain criticisms of these organizations are valid. Interest groups do contribute to the appearance of (and sometimes the reality of) corruption in the political system. Indeed, there are various criticisms of the "interest group state." Former president Jimmy Carter (1977–1981) bemoaned the influence of special interests, saying that they are "the single greatest threat to the proper functioning of our democratic system," and former president Ronald Reagan charged that interest groups are "placing out of focus our constitutional balance."[13]

Another criticism is that interest groups and their **political action committees (PACs),** entities whose specific goal is to raise and spend money to influence the outcome of elections, have made money a vital force in American politics. (See Chapter 14 for a detailed discussion of PACs.) By contributing large sums of money to political campaigns, interest groups' PACs make campaigns expensive and often lopsided; candidates without well-stuffed campaign war chests have a difficult, if not impossible, task in challenging those who receive large PAC contributions. Money also changes the nature of campaigns, making them less engaging for citizens on a grassroots level and more reliant on the mass media. These concerns have been exacerbated by a 2010 U.S. Supreme Court ruling that enables corporations and labor unions to spend money freely on political ads supporting or targeting candidates for federal office and allows corporations and unions to buy advertisements even in the last days of political campaigns. Critics say these rule changes are increasing the importance of money in political campaigns and are enabling corporations to exert greater influence over the electoral process.

political action committee (PAC)
An entity whose specific goal is to raise and spend money to influence the outcome of elections.

Interest groups, moreover, are faulted for strengthening the advantages enjoyed by incumbents. Most interest groups want access to policymakers, regardless of these elected officials' party identification. Realizing that the people already in office are likely to be reelected, interest groups use their resources disproportionately to support incumbent candidates. Doing so increases incumbency advantage even further by improving the odds against a challenger.

Finally, although the option to form an interest group is open to any and all activists and would-be activists, elites are more likely to establish and to dominate interest groups than are non-elites. This fact skews the policy process in favor of elites. Interest group activism is much more prominent among the wealthy, the white, the upper middle class, and the educated than among the poor, the nonwhite, the working class, and the less educated. Although in recent years, Internet-based interest groups have been particularly effective in attracting young people and others not traditionally drawn to such organizations, many of the most effective national interest groups remain dominated by traditional interest group populations.

■ Who Joins Interest Groups, and Why?

People are not all equally likely to join or form interest groups, and this reality has serious consequences for the ability of interest groups to represent everyone's views. Political scientists agree that income and education tend to be the best predictors of interest group membership. That said, enormous diversity exists in the types of people who choose to join or form interest groups. Even the meaning of "belonging" to these groups varies a great deal. Among both online and traditional interest groups, a small cadre of individuals may be highly active, while a large number are passive but counted as members despite their less-active roles. For example, a member of an Internet-based interest group may play a highly active role—communicating with other members regularly, attending rallies and other campus events, and taking concrete actions such as signing an Internet petition and participating in a protest. Others may limit their activity to reading the regular e-mails from the group but may only occasionally participate in events. Or, they may be members in name only. And nearly every group has a contingent of "members" who signed up mainly for the free T-shirt or umbrella.

Patterns of Membership

Interest group participation is related to four demographic characteristics: income, social class, education, and race. But these characteristics are increasing related to the types of interest groups individuals participate in. Indeed, while the interest group arena historically had been dominated by white individuals with higher levels of income and education, the increasing prominence of online interest groups (many of which may also rely on offline strategies) means that, increasingly, young, less-affluent African Americans and Latinx are forming and joining interest groups.

TRADITIONAL INTEREST GROUPS When we examine patterns of membership of traditional "brick-and-mortar" interest groups, we see that people with higher incomes are more likely to participate than those with lower incomes. Also, many surveys show that those who identify themselves as upper-middle or middle class are more likely to join these kinds of interest groups than those who self-identify as lower-middle or working class. Similarly, higher education levels are a strong predictor of traditional interest group participation.

Income and Education as Predictors of Membership Individuals with higher levels of education and income have dominated traditional interest groups for several reasons, and as we shall see, some of these reasons are interconnected. For example, wealthier people have more disposable income to spend on membership dues for organizations. They are also likely to have occupations in which interest group activity is useful (or even required, as in some professional fields such as the law). Doctors and lawyers, for example, are likely to be members of professional associations such as the American Medical Association and the American Bar Association. These organizations give incentives for membership, such as accreditation of qualified professionals, and also attempt to influence government policy on members' behalf. Workers such as teachers and tradespeople are likely to belong to labor unions, while executives in business and industry are likely to be members of industry-specific and general business organizations that advocate on behalf of their members.[14] All these professional associations, labor unions, and business organizations are types of interest groups.

Educational attainment also has a strong influence on whether a person will join an interest group. Individuals with higher education levels are more likely to be informed about issues and more willing to invest the time and energy in joining an interest group that represents their views. They may also be more likely to understand how important interest groups are in shaping public policy.

Interest Group Participation and Social Class Differentiating the influence of income from that of class can be difficult when examining the impact of social class on the likelihood of joining an interest group. But in general, people who identify themselves as working class are less likely to have been socialized to participate in traditional interest groups, with the important exception of labor unions, which historically have been most likely to organize working-class occupations. As we considered in Chapter 10, an important predictor of political participation (and interest group participation, specifically) is whether a person learns to take part and join from a young age. If your mother participated in your town's historical preservation society, and your father attended meetings of the local Amnesty International chapter, you are likely to view those behaviors as "what people do" and do them yourself. If you come from a working-class family, you are generally less likely to see your parents engage in these participatory behaviors, rendering you similarly less likely to participate. Although scholars trace much of the lack of participation of working-class people to how they are socialized, the overlapping occurrence of working-class status and lower income is also a factor.[15] Working-class people may not be able to afford membership dues or have access to child care that would allow them to attend meetings. Or they may simply lack the leisure time to participate.

MODERN EQUALITY AND RIGHTS MOVEMENTS Over the past years, several **social movements**—large, often informal groups of individuals or organizations striving for a broad, common goal that is frequently centered on significant change to the social or political order—have emerged in the United States. As discussed in Chapter 9, the women's rights movement and the civil rights movement of the 1960s established a framework for the successful transformation of the social and political order. Today, we see several groups relying on time-tested strategies while also forging new pathways to pressure for change, including the Black Lives Matter movement. And for decades, activists in the gay rights movement have relied on protest, lobbying, public education, and judicial redress (that is, lawsuits) to win rights for gay, lesbian, and transgender Americans. The successes seen by the gay rights movement, as well as the increasing prominence of celebrity transgender individuals, has empowered an increasingly active transgender rights movement. In the past several years, immigrant rights groups have also relied on a wide range of tactics to pressure politicians for immigration reform.

social movement
Large, often informal groups of individuals or organizations striving for a broad, common goal, frequently centered on significant change to the social or political order.

These groups, which tend to be loosely organized, have thrived in an era in which the Internet facilitates the organization and mobilization of large numbers of like-minded people. Without a formal membership base and without a hierarchical leadership structure, these groups have resonated particularly with individuals who, typically, are less likely to join traditional interest groups: the young, the poor, African Americans and Latinx, and working-class individuals.

While social movements clearly resonate with many people who agree with the need to change the social and political order in one way or another, in examining online civic participation the evidence suggests that one demographic characteristic remains an important determinant of participation: A recent study surveyed 19- to 23-year-olds and found that those who were college students were more than twice as likely to join a politically motivated interest group as their age-group peers who did not attend college.[16]

Motivations for Joining Interest Groups

Some people may join an interest group for the benefits they can gain. Others may gravitate to a group sponsoring a particular cause. Still others may become members of a group for the simple reason that they want to meet new people. Recognizing that individuals have various motivations for joining, interest groups typically provide a menu of incentives for membership.

solidary incentive
The motivation to join an interest group based on the companionship and the satisfaction derived from socializing with others that it offers.

SOLIDARY INCENTIVES Some people join interest groups because they offer **solidary incentives**—the feeling of belonging, companionship, friendship, and the satisfaction derived from socializing with others. Solidary incentives are closely linked to Robert Putnam's idea of social capital: Both solidary incentives and social capital are related to the psychological satisfaction derived from civic participation. For example, your friend might join the Sierra Club because she wants to participate in activities with other people who enjoy hiking or care deeply about wilderness protection. Your uncle might join the National Rifle Association because he likes to compete in shooting contests and wants to get to know others who do the same.

purposive incentive
Motivation to join an interest group based on the belief in the group's cause from an ideological or a moral standpoint

PURPOSIVE INCENTIVES People also join interest groups because of **purposive incentives;** that is, because they believe in the group's cause from an ideological or a moral standpoint. Interest groups pave the way for people to take action with like-minded people. And so, you might join People for the Ethical Treatment of Animals (PETA) because you strongly object to animal abuse and want to work with others to prevent cruelty to animals. A friend who is passionately pro-life might join the National Right to Life Committee, whereas your pro-choice cousin might join NARAL Pro-Choice America (formerly the National Abortion Reproductive Rights Action League).

economic incentive
Motivation to join an interest group because the group works for policies that will provide members with material benefits.

ECONOMIC INCENTIVES Many people join interest groups because of material or **economic incentives;** that is, they want to support groups that work for policies that will provide them with economic benefits. Sometimes these groups advocate for tangible, concrete items. For example, the National Association of Police Organizations lobbies Congress concerning many appropriations measures that could affect its membership, including bills that would provide or increase funding for Community Oriented Policing Services (COPS) programs, bulletproof vests, and overtime pay for first responders to disasters.

Nearly all corporate and labor interest groups offer economic incentives to their members. They sometimes do so by advocating for policies that support business or labor in general, such as policies focused on the minimum wage, regulations concerning workplace conditions, and laws governing family leave or health coverage.

Other interest groups offer smaller-scale economic benefits to members. Many Americans over age 50 join AARP (formerly the American Association of Retired Persons) because of the discounts members receive on hotels, airfares, and car rentals. Other organizations provide discounts on health insurance, special deals from merchants, or low-interest credit cards. Most people join and remain in interest groups for a combination of reasons, purposive incentive, economic benefits, or even social connections.

■ How Interest Groups Succeed

Given that interest groups attempt to influence all kinds of policies, why are some interest groups better than others at getting what they want? Political scientists agree on various factors that influence whether an interest group will succeed. These factors include the interest group's *organizational resources*, the tools it has at its disposal to help achieve its goals, and its *organizational environment*, the setting in which it attempts to achieve those goals.

Organizational Resources

The effectiveness of interest groups in influencing government policy often depends on the resources these groups use to sway policymakers.[17] Interest groups rely on two key types of resources: membership, the people who belong to a given group; and financial resources, the money the group can spend to exert influence.

HOW MEMBERSHIP AFFECTS SUCCESS A large membership enhances an interest group's influence because policymakers are more likely to take note of the group's position. The sheer number of a group's membership is often an important factor in forcing policymakers, the media, and the public to pay attention to an issue. Among the largest U.S. interest groups is the AARP, which boasts a membership of over 38 million people. This vast size gives the organization incredible clout and historically has made policymakers unwilling to take on any issue that would unleash the wrath of AARP's formidable membership. For example, for years many economic analysts have suggested increasing the age at which people become eligible to receive Social Security. They reason that the average life span has risen significantly since the eligibility age was set and that people are working longer because they remain healthier longer. But this potential policy solution has long simmered on the back burner. Indeed, Congress has not tackled the issue of raising the retirement age since 1983, when it phased in a small increase—from 65 to 67—in the age at which an individual could collect full Social Security retirement benefits over 22 years. The reason? Politicians in Congress and the White House have not wanted to incur the disapproval of the AARP's members, who would widely oppose increasing the eligibility age and might respond by voting unsympathetic officials out of office.

But size is not the only important aspect of an interest group's membership. The *cohesion* of a group, or how strongly unified it is, also matters to participants and to policymakers.[18] For example, the Human Rights Campaign (HRC) lobbies for federal legislation to end discrimination on the basis of sexual orientation and provides research to elected officials and policymakers on issues of importance to people who are gay, lesbian, bisexual, transgender, or queer. The HRC has a membership of more than 3 million people, but because the organization limits its advocacy to issues affecting gay, lesbian, bisexual, transgender, and queer people, it is an extremely cohesive association.

Another significant aspect of an interest group's membership is its *intensity*. Intensity is a measure of how strongly members feel about the issues they are targeting. Some organizations may reach an intense crescendo of activism but may find it difficult to sustain that level of intensity. But certain kinds of organizations, including pro-life interest groups such as the National Right to Life Committee, environmental groups such as Greenpeace and the Sierra Club, and animal rights groups such as People for the Ethical Treatment of Animals (PETA), are known for sustaining high levels of intensity. These organizations are more adept at attracting new members and younger members than are older, more entrenched kinds of groups. These newer, youthful members are a significant force behind the persistence and intensity of these groups.

The *demographics* of a group's membership also may increase its success. Members who know policymakers personally and have access to them mean greater influence for the group.[19] Other demographic attributes also matter. Members who are well educated or affluent tend to have more influence. Policymakers perceive these attributes as important because the group's membership is more likely to lobby and to contribute financial resources on behalf of the organization's cause. But today, geographically dispersed members are becoming an increasingly important interest group demographic, as technology enables individuals around the country to have quick input in the policy process.[20] Increasingly, this use of technology in lobbying policymakers means younger citizens are becoming more effective at articulating their concerns to them.

HOW FINANCIAL RESOURCES AFFECT SUCCESS For an interest group, money can buy power.[21] Money fuels the hiring of experienced and effective staff and lobbyists, who communicate directly with policymakers, as well as the undertaking of initiatives that will increase the group's membership. Money also funds the raising of more money.[22] For example, the Business Roundtable represents the interests of 150 chief executive officers of the largest U.S. companies, including American Express, General Electric, IBM, and Verizon. In 2016, it spent over $16 million lobbying the president, Congress, and several cabinet departments for policies that would benefit its member corporations, their shareholders, and their member corporations' 10 million employees.[23] Issues of concern to the Business Roundtable include policies such as Securities and Exchange Commission rules, laws concerning corporate ethics, and immigration reform. Many critics believe that the financial resources of an organization will play an even greater role in determining the group's success in the future because of new campaign finance rules that allow unlimited expenditures by business and labor.

Sometimes interest groups form a political action committee (PAC) to shape the composition of government; that is, they contribute money to the campaigns of favored candidates, particularly incumbents who are likely to be reelected.[24]

>> Intensity is a measure of how strongly members feel about the issues they are targeting. Some organizations, including the National Rifle Association, are known for sustaining high levels of intensity, which helps them pressure policymakers to enact components of their agenda. These organizations are more adept at attracting new members and younger members, such as former NRA spokeswoman Dana Loesch.

Olivier Douliery/Abaca Press/Sipa USA/AP Images

Interest groups representing the economic concerns of members—business, industry, and union groups—generally tend to have the greatest financial resources for all these activities.[25]

Organizational Environment

The setting in which an interest group attempts to achieve its goals is the *organizational environment*. Key factors in the organizational environment include its leadership and the presence or absence of opposition from other groups.[26]

LEADERSHIP Strong, charismatic leaders contribute to the influence of an interest group by raising public awareness of the group and its activities, by enhancing its reputation, and by making the organization attractive to new members and contributors. Thomas Donohue became leader of the U.S. Chamber of Commerce in 1997, when he vowed to "build the biggest gorilla in town."[27] Since that time, Donohue, known in Washington, D.C., for his straight talk and assertive leadership, has transformed the organization that represents many of the nation's businesses into an enormously powerful force. Today, the U.S. Chamber of Commerce employs more than 170 lobbyists and spends over $100 million annually lobbying policymakers,[28] making it the largest interest group in the nation in terms of its expenditures and financial resources.

OPPOSITION The presence of opposing interest groups can also have an impact on an interest group's success. When an interest group is "the only game in town" on a particular issue, policymakers are more likely to rely on that group's views. But if groups with opposing views are also attempting to influence policy, getting policymakers to act strongly in any one group's favor is more difficult. Consider this example: Hotel Employees and Restaurant Employees International Union supports increasing the minimum wage, but the National Restaurant Association, which advocates for restaurant owners, opposes a minimum wage hike, arguing that the higher wage would cut into restaurant owners' profits or limit its members' ability to hire as many employees. In the face of such opposing

THEN

NOW

>> In the traditional approach to fundraising, interest groups and candidates met face to face, often with donors attending swanky events, like this one (left) that Bill Clinton hosted. Today, interest groups use platforms, including ActBlue, to raise money online, increasing the role small donors play in politics.

photo: Wilfredo Lee/AP Images; *ad:* Source: Actblue.com

interests, policymakers are often more likely to compromise than to give any one group exactly what it wants.

In addition to opposition, competition influences interest group success.[29] Research indicates that when a group faces an environment in which other groups with similar agendas are forming, competition may damage the older, more established groups, at least initially.[30] One study concluded that if the established groups can withstand the initial challenge, their chances of survival are high.[31]

Although each of these factors—organizational resources and the organizational environment—influences how powerful an interest group will be, no single formula determines an interest group's clout. Sometimes an interest group has powerful advocates in Congress who support its cause. Other times, a single factor can prove essential to an interest group's success.

▮ Types of Interest Groups

A wide variety of political interest groups try to exert influence on virtually every type of policy question, from those concerning birth (such as the minimum hospital stay an insurance company must cover after a woman gives birth) to matters related to death (such as what funeral home practices should be banned by the government). Despite the broad range of issues around which interest groups coalesce, political scientists generally categorize interest groups by what kinds of issues concern them and who benefits from the groups' activities.

Economic Interest Groups

When economic interest groups lobby government, the benefits for their members can be direct or indirect. In some cases, the economic benefits flow directly from the government to the interest group members, as when an agricultural interest group successfully presses for *subsidies,* monies given by the government to the producers of a particular crop or product, often to influence the volume of production of that commodity. In other instances, economic interest groups lobby for or against policies that, though not directly benefiting their members, have an indirect impact on the interest group's membership.

CORPORATE AND BUSINESS INTERESTS Large corporate and smaller business interest groups are among the most successful U.S. pressure groups with respect to their influence on government. These groups typically seek policies that benefit a particular company or industry. For example, the Motion Picture Association of America (MPAA) lobbies policymakers (often by hosting prerelease screenings of films and lavish dinner receptions) with the goal of securing the passage of anti-piracy laws, which protect the copyrights of their films.

Certain industries have their own stand-alone organizations, such as the newly formed National Cannabis Industry Association, which encourages marijuana retailers to join the organization this way: "banding together with your fellow

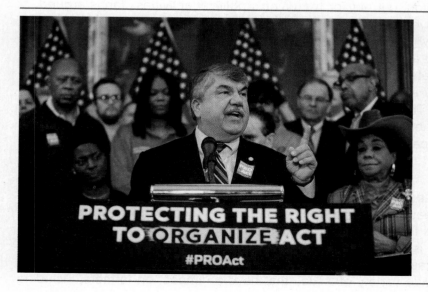

>> Among the most important economic interest groups are organized labor unions, including the AFL-CIO, an umbrella organization comprised of many labor unions that is headed by Richard Trumka. The AFL-CIO advocates for workers' rights across many sectors.

Samuel Corum/Stringer/Getty Images

business people and entrepreneurs in the only unified, coordinated, and industry-led effort to change federal law increases the power of our new industry."[32]

Like corporate interest groups, labor interest groups include both national labor unions and umbrella organizations of unions. During the 1950s and 1960s, nearly 35 percent of all U.S. workers were union members. By 1983, membership had decreased to about 20 percent, and today about 11 percent of all U.S. workers belong to unions, many of whom are public-sector employees, including teachers, police officers, and firefighters. Today, only 7 percent of private-sector employees are union members.[33] In part, this decline stems from changes in the U.S. economy, with many highly unionized manufacturing jobs being replaced by less unionized service-sector jobs. At the same time, some labor unions are rebounding in the era of the gig economy, organizing workers in the rideshare and bikeshare sectors, among others. However, given the overall drop in union membership, for a while labor interest group influence appeared to be waning. Nevertheless, more recently, in the face of proposed Trump administration policies that unions perceive as potentially hurtful to their members, cohesion within labor unions has increased. This was particularly true during the COVID-19 pandemic, when unions of teachers and other public-sector workers fought for policies to protect their rank-and-file members.

umbrella organizations
Interest groups that represent collective groups of industries or corporations.

Labor, industry, and business groups also commonly advocate for policies using **umbrella organizations,** which are interest groups representing groups of labor unions or of industries. The AFL-CIO, an umbrella organization made up of more than 50 labor unions, is among the nation's most powerful interest groups. Examples of umbrella business organizations include the Business Roundtable and the U.S. Chamber of Commerce.

public employee unions
Labor organizations comprising federal, state, and municipal workers, including police officers and teachers.

Damaging to the ability of unions to organize was the 2018 U.S. Supreme Court case *Janus V. United States*, when Mark Janus, a child support specialist who works for the Illinois Department of Healthcare and Family Services, declined union membership. Under Illinois law, Janus is permitted to decline membership in the American Federation of State, County, and Municipal Employees, which is a **public employee union,** made up of federal, state, and municipal workers. But Janus and others who declined were still required by law to pay an "agency fee," which was to cover expenses associated with negotiating contracts and administering the union, but not for the union's political activities. Janus argued that all public employee spending is linked with the union's political purposes and that he and others who disagree with the union's positions should not have to subsidize its political activities. The Court agreed, saying that as "the compelled subsidization of private speech seriously impinges on First Amendment rights, it cannot be casually allowed," essentially ending compelled union dues for public employees.[34] The impact of the decision will have a widespread effect on the strength of public employee unions, which are among the most unionized workforces, with 35 percent of all governmental employees belonging to a labor union.[35]

AGRICULTURAL INTERESTS The largest agricultural interest group today is the American Farm Bureau Federation (AFBF), which grew out of the network of county farm bureaus formed in the 1920s. With more than 5 million farming members, the AFBF is one of the most influential interest groups in the United States, primarily because of its close relations with key agricultural policymakers. It takes stands on a wide variety of issues that have an impact on farmers, including subsidies, budget and tax policies, immigration policies that affect farm workers, energy policies, trade policies, and environmental policies.

In addition to large-scale, general agricultural interest groups such as the AFBF, an industry-specific interest group represents producers for nearly every crop or commodity in the agricultural sector. Think of the growing prevalence of commodities once rare in the American diet. Often, products come into favor through the efforts of interest groups, including those of the American Kale Association and the California Avocado Commission.

TRADE AND PROFESSIONAL INTERESTS Nearly every professional occupation— doctor, lawyer, engineer, chiropractor, dentist, accountant, and even video game developer—has a trade or professional group that focuses on its interests. These interest groups take stands on a variety of policy matters, many of which indirectly affect their membership.

Public and Ideological Interest Groups

Public interest groups typically are concerned with a broad range of issues that affect the populace at large. These include social issues such as the environmental causes of food safety, clean air and clean water, as well as economic issues such as Social Security reform and revision of the federal tax structure. Examples of public interest groups include End Citizens United, the National Taxpayers Union, Common Cause, and Sierra Club. Usually, the results of the efforts of a particular public interest group's advocacy cannot be limited to the group's members; rather, these results are **collective goods** (sometimes called *public goods*)—outcomes that are shared by the general public. For example, if an organization like Food and Water Watch succeeds in their goal of getting a law passed that would require food manufacturers to label foods with genetically modified ingredients (GMOs), everyone shares from the benefit of being aware of what ingredients are in the foods they purchase and consume. Specifically, it is impossible to make this information a privilege restricted only to Food and Water Watch members.

collective goods
Outcomes shared by the general public; also called *public goods*

The nature of collective goods—the fact that they cannot be limited to those who worked to achieve them—creates a **free rider problem,** the situation whereby someone derives a benefit from the actions of others. You are probably familiar with the free rider problem. Suppose, for example, that you form a study group to prepare for an exam, and four of the five members of the group come to a study session having prepared responses to essay questions. The fifth member shows up but is unprepared. The unprepared group member then copies the others' responses, memorizes them, and does just as well on the exam. The same thing happens to interest groups that advocate for a collective good. The group may work hard to improve the quality of life, but the benefits of its work are enjoyed by many who do not contribute to the effort.

free rider problem
The phenomenon of someone deriving benefit from others' actions.

Economist Mancur Olson asserted in his **rational choice theory** that from an economic perspective, it is not rational for people to participate in a collective action designed to achieve a collective good when they can secure that good without participating. So, in the study group example, from Olson's perspective, it is not economically rational to spend your time preparing for an exam when you can get the benefits of preparation without the work. Of course, taking this idea to the extreme, one might conclude that if no one advocated for collective goods, they would not exist, and thus free riders could not derive their benefit. In addition,

rational choice theory
The idea that from an economic perspective it is not rational for people to participate in collective action when they can secure the collective good without participating.

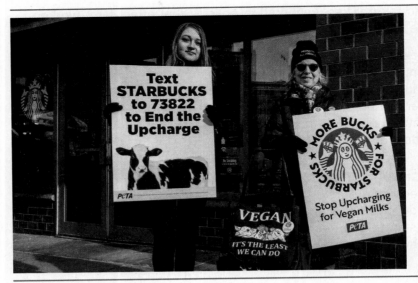

>> Some interest groups rely on confrontational tactics, which attract media attention and sway public opinion. PETA is one interest group known for doing so, as in the protest shown here, where PETA members called attention to the upcharge Starbucks charges for vegan milk products.

Gabriele Holtermann-Gorden/Sipa USA/AP Images

rational choice theory ignores the intangible benefits individuals may receive from collective action, including the solidary incentives discussed earlier in this chapter.

CONSUMER INTERESTS In 2020, the House Financial Services Committee heard testimony from the National Consumer Law Center (NCLC) about the problem of "rent-a-bank" schemes. In these scenarios, some rogue banks make loans that would violate laws in many states, but they evade these laws by claiming to state regulators that they are "service providers only." They then quickly sell these loans to evade state interest-rate caps, and they charge borrowers exorbitant interest rates. The NCLC and other consumer groups urged Congress to pass legislation to protect people from these predatory lenders. The role of consumer interest groups such as NCLC is to hold businesses that provide goods and services to the public accountable. The first consumer interest group was Public Citizen, founded in 1971 by activist Ralph Nader. In the 1970s and 1980s, these organizations lobbied primarily—and successfully—for changes in automotive design that would make cars safer. One result was the mandatory installation of harness safety belts in rear seats, which then typically had only lap belts. Today, consumer interest groups advocate for a wide variety of issues, including food safety, fair pricing of pharmaceuticals, commercial airline fliers' rights, and protection from predatory lending practices.

ENVIRONMENTAL INTERESTS Many groups that advocate for the protection of the environment and wildlife and for the conservation of natural resources came about as a result of a broader environmental movement in the 1970s. Some environmental groups, such as People for the Ethical Treatment of Animals (PETA) and Greenpeace, use confrontational tactics, including protests outside retail establishments. In 2020, for example, PETA mobilized protests around the country at local Starbucks, attempting to persuade the company from up-charging for non-dairy milk in its products. The confrontational protest tactic also has the advantage of attracting media attention, which serves to increase public awareness.[36] Other groups, such as the Environmental Defense Fund, forge partnerships with corporations to research solutions to environmental problems and then persuade the government to provide market incentives for these solutions.

RELIGIOUS INTERESTS For a long time, organized religions in the United States were essentially uninvolved in politics, partly because they were afraid of losing their tax-exempt status by becoming political entities. But formal religions increasingly have sought to make their voices heard, usually by forming political organizations separate from the actual religious organizations. Today, religious interests are among the most influential interest groups in U.S. politics.

In the early stages of their activism, Christian organizations typically were most politically effective in the Republican presidential nomination process, when the mobilization of their members could alter the outcome in low-turnout primaries. During the 1970s, several conservative Christian organizations, most notably the Moral Majority, became a force in national politics. The Moral Majority helped to elect Ronald Reagan, a Republican, to the presidency in 1980 and was instrumental in shaping the national agenda of the Reagan years, particularly regarding domestic policy. In 1989, another conservative Christian organization, the Christian Coalition, took shape, emphasizing "pro-family" values[37] and becoming a pivotal player in presidential elections. During the 2000 election, the organization was an important supporter of George W. Bush's candidacy for the presidency, and with his election, the group's influence grew considerably. These groups also play a role in Republican primaries.

The Christian Coalition and other religious groups—including Pax Christi USA (the national Catholic peace movement), B'nai B'rith (an interest group dedicated to Jewish interests), and the Council on American-Islamic Relations (CAIR, a Muslim interest group)—also advocate for the faith-based priorities of their members. But religious groups do not all function in the same way: while many Evangelical Christian groups tend to be conservative, other faith-based groups are often less ideological, and instead center their activism around measures that would protect members of their faith. For example, in 2020, leaders of B'nai B'rith called for the creation of an office on Antisemitism, to be housed at the Department of Justice. And many religious organizations have become increasingly active in state and local politics in recent years, by running slates of candidates for local school boards, for example, or by spearheading efforts in state legislatures to pass bills supported by the faith-based groups.

Foreign Policy Interests

In the United States, interest groups advocate for specific foreign policies and foreign governments, as well as international corporations based abroad, vigorously pressing for U.S. policies beneficial to them. Often a foreign government benefits from the efforts of an interest group made up of U.S. citizens of the foreign nation's heritage. Indeed, one of the more influential interest groups lobbying for foreign concerns is the U.S.-based American Israel Public Affairs Committee (AIPAC), which has 100,000 members. AIPAC lobbies the U.S. government for pro-Israel foreign policies.[38] Sometimes interest groups of expatriates advocate for policies that they feel will improve the conditions in their country of origin. The Cuban American National Foundation, made up largely of Cuban Americans, works to influence Congress to adopt measures that it believes will promote democracy in Cuba, and has been successful in its efforts to convince policymakers to normalize relations with the communist nation.

Foreign nationals are banned from contributing money to political campaigns, but foreign entities do lobby the U.S. government, particularly through domestically owned subsidiaries. Often, international corporations lobby for favorable trade policies. For example, for years Chinese businesses—many of them subsidized by the Chinese government—spent millions of dollars to influence trade and other U.S. policies to their advantage.[39] These businesses enjoyed particular success with the congressional U.S.-China Working Group because many of the 60 members represent congressional districts that depend on China for trade, including rural districts where agricultural goods are exported to China. With the imposition of tariffs on China by President Trump, the group sought to pass the Trade Authority Protection Act, which would allow Congress to review trade actions by presidential administrations.[40]

■ Interest Group Strategies

Interest groups use two kinds of strategies to advance their causes. *Direct strategies* involve actual contact between representatives of the interest group and policymakers. *Indirect strategies* use intermediaries to advocate for a cause or generally to attempt to persuade the public, including policymakers, to embrace the group's position.

Direct Strategies to Advance Interests

Groups often opt for direct strategies when they seek to secure passage or defeat of a specific piece of legislation. These strategies include lobbying, entering into litigation to change a law, and providing information or expert testimony to decision makers.

LOBBYING, ISSUE NETWORKS, AND IRON TRIANGLES Interest groups hire professionals to **lobby,** or to communicate directly with, policymakers on the interest groups' behalf. President Ulysses S. Grant (1869–1877) coined the term *lobbyist* when he walked through the lobby of the Willard Hotel in Washington, D.C., and commented on the presence of "lobbyists" waiting to speak to members of Congress.

lobby
To communicate directly with policymakers on an interest group's behalf.

Today, lobbying is among the most common strategies that interest groups use, and the practice may include scheduled face-to-face meetings, "buttonholing" members of Congress as they walk through the Capitol, telephone calls, and receptions and special events hosted by the interest groups. The professional lobbyists whom interest groups hire are almost always lawyers, and their job is to cultivate ongoing relationships with members of Congress (and their staff) who have influence in a specific policy area. In many situations, lobbyists help navigate access to these policymakers for industry and interest group members.

Interest groups have learned that one of the most effective ways of influencing government is to hire as lobbyists former government officials, including cabinet officials, members of Congress, and congressional staffers. Because these ex-officials often enjoy good relationships with their former colleagues and have an intimate knowledge of the policy-making process, they are particularly effective in influencing government. Frequently, this practice creates an **issue network,** the fluid web of connections among those concerned about a policy and those who create and administer the policy.

issue network
The fluid web of connections among those concerned about a policy and those who create and administer the policy.

Similarly, an interest group's effectiveness often depends on it having close relationships with the policymakers involved in decisions related to the group's causes. During the rough-and-tumble policy-making process, the interaction of mutual interests among a "trio" comprising (1) members of Congress, (2) executive departments and agencies, and (3) organized interest groups is sometimes referred to as an **iron triangle,** with each of the three players being one side of the triangle (see Figure 16.1). Take, for example, the relationship among (1) members of Congress who represent agricultural states; (2) an executive department, such as the Department of Agriculture; and (3) an interest group that lobbies for farming interests, such as the American Farm Bureau. The relationships among these individuals—all of whom are experts in and concerned about agricultural matters—constitutes an iron triangle. But their power comes not only from their common concern with farming; it also comes from long-term relationships in which, for example, retired members of Congress might go work for a farming interest group, or a former congressional staff member might take a position with an executive department. And so, this interconnected web of individuals grows to become a powerful issue network.

Although each side in an iron triangle is expected to fight on behalf of its own interests, constituents, or governmental department, the triangle often seeks a policy outcome that benefits all parts of the triangle. Often this outcome occurs because of close personal and professional relationships that develop as a result of the interactions among the sides in an issue-based triangle. (See Chapter 7 for further discussion of the role of iron triangles in policymaking.)

LITIGATION BY INTEREST GROUPS Sometimes interest groups challenge a policy in the courts. For example, a 2010 U.S. Supreme Court case that resulted in a drastically altered political landscape for campaign funding came as the result

iron triangle
The interaction of mutual interests among members of Congress, executive agencies, and organized interest groups during policymaking.

FIGURE 16.1 ■ **Iron Triangle** Who are the players in an iron triangle? How do interest groups benefit from their iron triangle relationships? Why do you think the triangular relationship has been described as "iron"?

Citizens United v. Federal Election Commission
Supreme Court ruling stating that corporations and labor unions are entitled to the same First Amendment free speech protections that individuals enjoy, resulting in drastically increased spending through super PACs by corporations and labor organizations.

of a lawsuit filed by an interest group. In **Citizens United v. Federal Election Commission,** the interest group Citizens United argued that federal bans on corporate and union expenditures to promote or target candidates for federal office violated the organizations' right to free speech. A 5–4 majority of Supreme Court justices agreed with the interest group and lifted the ban, ruling that the First Amendment's protection of free speech—previously applicable only to individuals—applies to political advertising and the communications of corporations, labor unions, nonprofits, and other organizations.[41] Today, another interest group, American Promise, is advocating for a constitutional amendment that would overturn *Citizens United.*[42]

By litigating, interest groups can ensure that laws passed by legislatures and signed by executives are in keeping with current constitutional interpretation. By bringing their causes before the courts, they also can shape policy and encourage enforcement by executive agencies.

PROVIDING INFORMATION AND EXPERT TESTIMONY Interest groups are one of the chief sources of information for policymakers. Interest groups have the resources to investigate the impact of policies. They have access to data, technological know-how, and a bevy of experts with extensive knowledge of the issues. Most interest groups provide information to policymakers, and policymakers understand that the information received is slanted toward the group's interest. But if competing interest groups supply information to policymakers, then policymakers can weigh the merits of the various sets of information.

Sometimes interest groups use celebrities as "experts" to testify, knowing that they will attract greater attention than most policy experts—for example, in 2019 comedian Jon Stewart testified before the House Judiciary Committee concerning "The Need to Reauthorize the September 11th Victim Compensation Fund."

Indirect Strategies to Advance Interests

Reaching out to persuade the public that their position is right, interest groups rely on citizens as grassroots lobbyists, and they engage in electioneering. These two activities are examples of indirect strategies that interest groups use to pursue their public policy agendas. Indirect tactics are likely to be ongoing rather than targeted at a specific piece of legislation, although that is not always the case.

PUBLIC OUTREACH Interest groups work hard—and use a variety of strategies—to make the public, government officials, their own members, and potential members aware of issues of concern and to educate people about their positions on the issues. Some interest groups focus solely on educating the public and hope that through their efforts people will be concerned enough to take steps to have a particular policy established or changed. Thus, the groups promote civic engagement by informing individuals about important policy concerns, even if the information they provide is skewed toward the group's views. The groups also encourage civic discourse by bringing issues into the public arena. Often, they do so by mounting advertising campaigns to alert the public about an issue. Consider, for example, the use of the hashtag #MeToo, a phrase that embodied the sentiments of many women protesting the treatment of women who had been sexually assaulted, harassed, or discriminated against in the workplace. On Twitter, Instagram, and other social media outlets, #MeToo became a shorthand rallying cry of a social movement.

Sometimes interest groups and corporations engage in **climate control,** the practice of using public outreach to build favorable public opinion of the organization or company. The logic behind climate control is simple: If a corporation or an organization has the goodwill of the public on its side, enacting its legislative agenda or getting its policy priorities passed will be easier because government will know of, and may even share, the public's positive opinion of the organization. For example, when Walmart encountered opposition to the construction of its superstores in communities across the country, it relied on public relations techniques, particularly advertising, to convince people that Walmart is a good corporate citizen. As critics complained about Walmart's harmful effects on smaller, local merchants, the firm's ads touted Walmart's positive contributions to its host communities. When opponents publicized the company's low-wage jobs, Walmart countered with ads featuring employees who had started in entry-level positions and risen through the ranks to managerial posts. These ads were viewed both by policymakers (municipal planning board members, for example) and by citizens, whose opinions matter to those policymakers.

Other groups, especially those without a great deal of access to policymakers, may engage in protests and civil disobedience to be heard. Sometimes leaders calculate that media attention to their actions will increase public awareness and spark widespread support for their cause.

ELECTIONEERING Interest groups often engage in the indirect strategy of **electioneering**—working to influence the election of candidates who support their issues. All the tactics of electioneering are active methods of civic participation. These techniques include endorsing particular candidates or positions and conducting voter-registration and get-out-the-vote drives. Grassroots campaign efforts often put interest groups with large memberships, including labor unions, at an advantage.

Campaign contributions are considered a key element of electioneering. The importance of contributions puts wealthier interest groups, including corporate and business groups, at an advantage. Figure 16.2 shows the breakdown of contributions by incumbency status. From this figure, we see that incumbent candidates have a significant edge in raising money from political action committees. The data indicate that most PACs recognize that incumbents—who are most likely to win reelection—are best situated to look after their interests following the election.

The issue of party affiliation also matters to PACs. Business PACs and individuals with business interests make up the largest sources of revenue for political candidates and tend to favor Republicans over Democrats. Labor groups and individuals associated with them give overwhelmingly to Democratic candidates, but they contribute a great deal less money than do business PACs. Ideologically driven PACs and individuals are nearly evenly divided between Democrats and Republicans.

Interest groups also commonly use the tactics of endorsements and ratings to attract support for the candidates whom they favor and to reduce the electoral chances of those whom they do not (see "Analyzing the Sources"). Through endorsements, an interest group formally supports specific candidates and typically notifies its members and the media of that support. An endorsement may also involve financial support from the interest group's PAC. With the technique of rating candidates, the interest group examines candidates' responses to a questionnaire issued by the group. Sometimes a group rates members of

climate control
The practice of using public outreach to build favorable public opinion of an organization.

electioneering
Working to influence the election of candidates who support the interest group's issues.

FIGURE 16.2 ▪ **Incumbents and Challengers** In 2020, 438 incumbent members of the House and Senate ran against 1,341 challengers, while 529 candidates ran for open seats. Incumbents received more than half of the funds donated, though by a lower margin than in many years.

Source: Center for Responsive Politics, "2020 Election Overview," 2020.

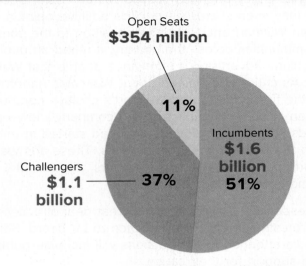

Open Seats
$354 million

11%

Incumbents
$1.6 billion 51%

Challengers
$1.1 billion

37%

Contributions to 2020 Congressional Candidates

Disproportionately, incumbents receive the lion's share of campaign contributions, while challengers often struggle to raise even a few thousand dollars. Interest groups and political action committees typically funnel their contributions to incumbents who support the group's issue stance, recognizing that over 90 percent of House and Senate incumbents are likely to be reelected, and return to the seat of power where decisions impacting the interest group or PAC are being made.

Quantitative Analysis

Use the information in the graphic above to answer the questions.

A. Thinking about the events leading up to the 2020 elections, including the impeachment of President Trump in the House but the failure to convict in the Senate, why might challengers in 2020 have fared a bit better than in a typical election year?

B. Compare the proportion of contributions to the number of candidates in that category. When considering the number of candidates in each category, which type of candidate was the best funded? The worst?

C. The figure only takes into account money raised by candidate committees. What other sources of financial support would candidates also receive? Would candidates be equally likely to receive these additional categories of support?

Congress on the basis of how they voted on measures important to the group. The ratings of a liberal interest group, such as Americans for Democratic Action (ADA), or a conservative interest group, such as American Conservative Union (ACU), can serve as an ideological benchmark.

Evaluating Interest Group Strategies

The accompanying table shows the ratings of members of Congress from the state of Florida from two interest groups that are concerned with the abortion issue. Interest groups rate legislators and candidates based on their public statements, their voting behavior on key issues (if applicable), and sometimes their responses to interest group surveys about their positions on relevant issues.

Interest Group Ratings of Florida Legislators

District		Party	Planned Parenthood Action Fund	National Right to Life Committee
Senator	Marco Rubio	Republican	0%	100%
Senator	Rick Scott	Republican	0	100
Florida—1	Matt Gaetz	Republican	0	100
Florida—2	Neal Dunn	Republican	0	100
Florida—3	Ted Yoho	Republican	0	100
Florida—4	John Rutherford	Republican	0	100
Florida—5	Al Lawson Jr.	Democrat	100	0
Florida—6	Michael Waltz	Republican	0	100
Florida—7	Stephanie Murphy	Democrat	100	0
Florida—8	Bill Posey	Republican	0	100
Florida—9	Darren Soto	Democrat	100	0
Florida—10	Val Demings	Democrat	100	0
Florida—11	Dan Webster	Republican	0	100
Florida—12	Gus Bilirakis	Republican	3	100
Florida—13	Charlie Crist	Democrat	100	0
Florida—14	Kathy Castor	Democrat	100	0
Florida—15	Ross Spano	Republican	0	100
Florida—16	Vern Buchanan	Republican	3	100
Florida—17	Greg Steube	Republican	0	100
Florida—18	Brian Mast	Republican	0	100
Florida—19	Francis Rooney	Republican	0	100
Florida—20	Alcee Hastings Sr.	Democrat	100	0
Florida—21	Lois Frankel	Democrat	100	0
Florida—22	Ted Deutch	Democrat	100	0
Florida—23	Debbie Wasserman Schultz	Democrat	100	0
Florida—24	Frederica Wilson	Democrat	100	0
Florida—25	Mario Diaz-Balart	Republican	3	92
Florida—26	Debbie Mucarsel-Powell	Democrat	100	0
Florida—27	Donna Shalala	Democrat	100	0

Sources: Planned Parenthood Action Fund, National Rights to Life Committee.

According to their ratings sheets, "National Right to Life Committee (NRLC) is the nation's largest pro-life organization, with 50 state affiliates and approximately 3,000 local affiliates nationwide. NRLC works through legislation and education to protect those threatened by abortion, infanticide, euthanasia, and assisted suicide."

"The [Planned Parenthood] Action Fund engages in educational and electoral activity, including legislative advocacy, voter education, and grassroots organizing to promote the Planned Parenthood mission. Planned Parenthood Federation of America, Inc., (PPFA) is the nation's leading provider and advocate of high-quality, affordable health care for women, men, and young people, as well as the nation's largest provider of sex education. With over 650 health centers across the country, Planned Parenthood organizations serve all patients with care and compassion, with respect and without judgment. Through health centers, programs in schools and communities, and online resources, Planned Parenthood is a trusted source of reliable health information that allows people to make informed health decisions."

In general, the National Right to Life Committee is recognized as the nation's leading pro-life interest group, while Planned Parenthood is recognized as a leading pro-choice interest group.

Practice Analytical Thinking

1. Why is it important to understand what the interest groups' perspective is when evaluating their ratings? Why does this perspective matter?

2. Describe the relationship between the two groups' ratings of legislators.

3. Explain the relationship between the interest groups' ratings and the legislators' political party affiliation.

Interest Groups, Politics, and Money: The Influence of Political Action Committees

The influence of money on politics is not a recent phenomenon. Louise Overacker, one of the first political scientists to do research on campaign finance, wrote this in 1932: "Any effective program of control must make it possible to bring into the light the sources and amounts of all funds used in political campaigns, and the way in which those funds are expended."[43] Years later, Congress saw the wisdom of Overacker's analysis and enacted regulations stipulating that a group that contributes to any candidate's campaign must register as a political action committee (PAC). For that reason, most interest groups form PACs as one arm of their organization, although federal law now permits corporations and labor unions to use their financial resources to purchase advertisements for federal campaigns directly.

Whereas an interest group pursues a group's broad goals by engaging in a variety of activities, its PAC raises and spends money to influence the outcome

Should Super PACs Enjoy Unlimited Free Speech?

THE ISSUE: Super PACs were enormously important in the 2020 congressional elections, and their presence has been felt in the U.S. political arena since they initially emerged on the political scene in 2012. Super PACs are a special form of political action committee that raises unlimited amounts of money from individuals (or a single individual donor) and then spends unlimited amounts in political races. Unlike traditional PACs, they may not contribute directly to the candidates they are supporting, and they must report their independent expenditures to the Federal Election Commission (FEC). The legal path for the creation of Super PACs was paved in the 2010 D.C. District Court of Appeals decision *SpeechNow.org v. Federal Election Commission*. Some argue that Super PACs represent an important tool of free speech. Others say they constitute merely another avenue for the wealthy to dominate the electoral process. In your view, should Super PACs (and the donors behind them) enjoy unlimited free speech, including unlimited political advertising?

YES: Some free speech proponents argue that the ruling has increased the amount of information available to voters. Under previous regulations, free speech advocates argue, the contribution limitations to PACs restricted "the individuals' freedom of speech by limiting the amount that an individual can contribute to SpeechNow and thus the amount the organization may spend."* Brad Smith, former chairman of the FEC and founder and chair of the Center for Competitive Politics, argued in favor of the decision: "The rise of independent expenditure groups made possible by the *SpeechNow* ruling has increased the information available to voters and increased the number of competitive races."** Many conservatives also argue that organizations consist of individuals who form associations and that the Constitution protects not only free speech but also freedom of association.

NO: Critics of the decision argue that it facilitates unmitigated corporate influence in political campaigns. Giving organizations protected rights that individuals enjoy, like free speech, detracts from the protection of individual human rights. Some critics argue that enabling these organizations to spend freely to influence campaigns has a detrimental effect on campaigns, which should be a competition of ideas and candidates rather than which candidate has the support of large Super PAC war chests. Others argue against Super PACs, believing that they increase the clout of enormously wealthy individuals who enjoy more than their fair share of influence through their ability to spend unlimited sums.

OTHER APPROACHES: In light of the *SpeechNow* ruling, voters need to be increasingly skeptical of claims made by organizations about

---

WHAT DO YOU THINK?

1. Are you aware of any advertising or information campaigns sponsored by Super PACs in the 2020 election? Do you know who was responsible for funding those ad campaigns?

2. Do you believe that enabling Super PACs to purchase unlimited independent expenditure ads is a protected right?

3. How can average Americans get their opinions about candidates heard? How can they find out whether allegations made by Super PACs are accurate?

---

*Federal Election Commission, "*SpeechNow.org v. FEC Case Summary*," 2010, www.fec.gov/law/litigation/speechnow.shtml#summary.

**Center for Competitive Politics, "*SpeechNow.org v. FEC*—Protecting Free Speech for the Last 2 Years," 2012.

political candidates. In effect, these Super PACs are only as powerful as average Americans enable them to be, and their influence can be countered through the formation of opposing groups comprising individuals who share a viewpoint. The availability of technology provides a medium for average citizens both to get information and to form groups with like-minded people, thus potentially mitigating the effect of the influence of Super PACs.

of an election. Typically, it will do so by contributing to candidates' campaigns. Funding campaigns helps an interest group in various ways. For one thing, it establishes the interest group as a formal supporter of one or more candidates. And, importantly, campaign contributions are a door opener for an interest group's lobbyists. For a lobbyist, access to policymakers is crucial, and campaign contributions provide a means of contact and help to ensure that a phone call will be returned or an invitation responded to, even if the policymaker does not support the group's position on every issue.

Table 16.1 lists the PACs that contribute the most money to U.S. campaigns and highlights the party their contributions favor. As the table illustrates, labor groups tend to support Democrats, whereas many traditional business and corporate PACs favor Republicans. (See "Thinking Critically" for more information on Super PACs.) In addition, PACs, particularly those formed by economic interest groups,

ARGUMENTATION | THINKING CRITICALLY

Develop an argument that takes a position on whether Super PACs should enjoy unlimited free speech.

In your essay, you must:

- Articulate a defensible claim or thesis that responds to the prompt and establishes a line of reasoning

- Support your claim with at least TWO pieces of accurate and relevant information:

    - At least ONE piece of evidence must be from one of the following foundational documents:

        — *Federalist* No. 10

        — *Federalist* No. 51

        — The U.S. Constitution

    - Use a second piece of evidence from another foundational document from the list or from your study of interest groups

TABLE 16.1 ■ Top PAC Contributors to Candidates, 2019–2020

PAC Name	Total Amount	Percent to Democrats	Percent to Republicans
Operating Engineers Union	$1,989,000	79%	21%
Credit Union National Assn	1,891,000	54	46
Honeywell International	1,886,000	55	45
National Beer Wholesalers Association	1,859,500	52	48
Sheet Metal, Air, Rail & Transportation Union	1,826,250	91	9
Raytheon Technologies	1,826,000	44	56
American Crystal Sugar	1,738,500	52	48
Comcast Corp.	1,736,700	46	54
National Air Traffic Controllers Association	1,724,600	67	33
National Assn of Realtor	1,715,195	53	47

Source: The Center for Responsive Politics. OpenSecrets.org

overwhelmingly favor incumbents. PACs' powers-that-be know that incumbent candidates are likely to be reelected, and thus the PACs support their reelection bids. As we examined in Chapter 14, interest groups rely on PACs to channel their support to candidates that espouse their views.

Conclusion: Thinking Critically About What's Next for Interest Groups

Interest groups are powerful vehicles by which individuals can join forces and collectively persuade policymakers to take legislative action on their goals. As such, interest groups play a strong role in the policy-making process. Throughout U.S. history and continuing today, the prevalence of interest groups is testimony to people's desire to influence the pathways of their society and government.

Interest groups have the potential to be one of the great leveling devices in U.S. politics. They are organizations that enable ordinary people to influence policy through collective action and organization. Although not all Americans are equally likely to join and form interest groups, these groups represent an avenue of participation open to all, and with enough variety in tactics and strategies to offer appealing means of civic participation to a broad spectrum of the population. Particularly today, with the Internet providing a highly accessible medium for participation, interest groups give individuals the opportunity to increase their own social capital—to improve their lives and the life of their community by making government more responsive to their needs and concerns and by increasing the effectiveness of the public policy-making process.

Although opinions differ about the role and the value of interest groups in U.S. politics, their influence in policy making is unquestioned. Thus, interest groups offer enormous potential for people who wish to become civically engaged. The abundance of groups for virtually every cause (and the ability of anyone to form his or her own group) means that like-minded individuals can work together to ensure that government policy represents their views. How does the number of groups available today differ from decades past? What is the result of that difference in terms of potential members?

Today, through the Internet and other digital technology, interest groups can provide individuals with instantly accessed information and organizational tools. Advances in computing, telephone communications, and television have opened the doors to participation in politics and government in ways that were undreamed of a few decades ago. Thanks to technology, the potential exists for interest groups to reach new and ever-widening audiences. As we have seen, however, the potential audience, at least in the present day, excludes many members of the working class, who may not have been socialized to take part in groups and who may lack the time and means to access computer technology. This lack of access poses a challenge to some interest groups, because they rely ever more heavily on digital recruiting, communicating, organizing, and fund-raising, and likely will continue to depend on these methods in the future.

References

1. Alexis de Tocqueville, *Democracy in America: The Complete and Unabridged Volumes I and II* (1835–1840; New York: Bantam, 2000), 51.

2. Everett Carll Ladd, *The Ladd Report* (New York: Free Press, 1999).

3. *Federalist no. 10,* Publius (James Madison), 1787.

4. Robert D. Putnam, *Bowling Alone: The Collapse and Revival of American Community* (New York: Touchstone, 2000).

5. Claude S. Fischer, "Bowling Alone: What's the Score?" *Social Networks* 27 (May): 155–167.

6. E. E. Schattschneider, *The Semi-Sovereign People* (New York: Holt, Rinehart, and Winston, 1960), 132.

7. Earl Latham, *The Group Basis of Politics* (Ithaca, NY: Cornell University Press, 1952).

8. David B. Truman, *The Governmental Process* (New York: Knopf, 1951).

9. Hugh Davis Graham, *The Civil Rights Era: Origins and Development of National Policy, 1960–1972* (London: Oxford University Press, 1990).

10. Sidney Verba, Kay Schlozman, and Nancy Burns, *The Private Roots of Public Action: Gender, Equality, and Political Participation* (Cambridge, MA: Harvard University Press, 2001).

11. Joshua Zeitz, " Progressives Should Read Progressive History—So They Don't Blow It This Time," Politico, June 1, 2019, https://www.politico.com/magazine/story/2019/06/01/progressives-history-227037.

12. https://www.womensmarch.com/welcome3/.

13. Quoted in Mark P. Petracca, *The Politics of Interests* (Boulder, CO: Westview, 1992), 347.

14. Julie Greene, *Pure and Simple Politics: The American Federation of Labor and Political Activism, 1881–1917* (New York: Cambridge University Press, 1998).

15. Elizabeth Sanders, *Roots of Reform: Farmers, Workers, and the American State, 1877–1917* (Chicago: University of Chicago Press, 1998).

16. Sharon E. Jarvis, Lisa Montoya, and Emily Mulvoy, *The Civic Participation of Working Youth and College Students: Working Paper 36* (Austin, TX: The Annette Strauss Institute for Civic Participation, and CIRCLE, the Center for Information and Research on Civic Learning and Engagement, 2005).

17. James Q. Wilson, *Political Organizations* (New York: Basic Books, 1973).

18. Jeffrey Berry, *The Interest Group Society,* 3rd ed. (New York: Longman, 1997).

19. Martin J. Smith, *Pressures, Power and Policy: Policy Networks and State Autonomy in Britain and the United States* (Pittsburgh, PA: University of Pittsburgh, 1994).

20. Nina Hall, "Innovations in Activism in the Digital Era," in *The Governance Report 2017,* The Hertie School of Governance (Oxford: Oxford University Press, 2017).

21. Herbert Alexander, *Money in Politics* (Washington, DC: Public Affairs Press, 1972).

22. Frank Sorauf, *Money in American Elections* (New York: Little, Brown, 1988).

23. OpenSecrets.org, www.opensecrets.org/lobby/clientsum.php?id=D000032202.

24. Frank Sorauf, *Inside Campaign Finance: Myths and Realities* (New Haven, CT: Yale University Press, 1992).

25. Gary C. Jacobson, *Money in Congressional Elections* (New Haven, CT: Yale University Press, 1980).

26. Allan J. Cigler and Burdett A. Loomis, *Interest Group Politics* (Washington, DC: CQ Press, 1991).

27. Danny Hakim, "Big Tobacco's Staunch Friend in Washington: U.S. Chamber of Commerce," *The New York Times,* October 9, 2015.

28. Open Secrets, www.opensecrets.org/lobby/clientissues.php?id=D000019798&year=2015.

29. Donald P. Haider-Markel, "Interest Group Survival: Shared Interests versus Competition for Resources," *Journal of Politics* 59 (1997): 903–12.

30. Virginia Gray and David Lowery, "Life in a Niche: Mortality Anxiety Among Organized Interests in the American States, *Political Research Quarterly* 50 (1997): 25–47.

31. Anthony J. Nownes and Daniel Lipinski, "The Population Ecology of Interest Group Death: Gay and Lesbian Rights Interest Groups in the United States, 1945–98," *British Journal of Political Science* 35 (2005): 303–19.

32. https://thecannabisindustry.org/join-now/.

33. U.S. Bureau of Labor Statistics, www.bls.gov/news.release/union2.nr0.htm.

34. *Janus v. American Federation of State, County, and Municipal Employees,* Council 31, No. 16-1466, 585 U.S. _____

35. U.S. Bureau of Labor Statistics, "Union Members Summary," January 20, 2016.

36. Lucy G. Barber, *Marching on Washington: The Forging of an American Political Tradition* (Los Angeles: University of California Press, 2002).

37. Christian Coalition of America, "About Us," www.cc.org/about_us.

38. Jeremy M. Sharp, *U.S. Foreign Aid to Israel,* Congressional Research Service, June 10, 2015.

39. Samuel Wagreich, "Lobbying by Proxy: A Study of China's Lobbying Practices in the United States 1979-2010 and the Implications for FARA." (2013): 130-159.

40. Ibid.

41. *Citizens United v. Federal Election Commission,* 558 U.S. 310 (2010).

42. https://www.americanpromise.net/who-we-are/the-28th-amendment/.

43. Louise Overacker, *Money in Elections* (New York: Macmillan, 1932), 3.

Key Terms

▌ Multiple-Choice Questions

1. Which of the following supports James Madison's theory in *Federalist* No. 10 that factions ensure representation of competing interests?

A. Factionalism

B. Pluralism

C. Elitism

D. Hyperpluralism

2. Which of the following best describes the concept of elite theory?

A. A multiplicity of interests will naturally balance each other out

B. Far too many interest groups are at play and create a system of hyperpluralism

C. Affluent, well-educated individuals who are leaders in business, academia, and the military exert disproportionate influence in government

D. The poor form coalitions that overwhelm the interests of other Americans

Questions 3 and 4 refer to the illustration below.

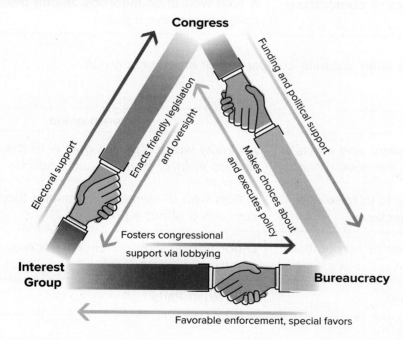

3. The illustration above represents which of the following strategies used by interest groups to advance their interests?

A. Grassroots lobbying

B. Issue networks

C. Iron triangle

D. Litigation

4. Which of the following is an example of one of the exchanges described in the illustration on the previous page?

   A. A PAC makes a donation to a Senate candidate that has a favorable record on policies concerning the PAC

   B. A member of Congress votes to support legislation opposed by an interest group

   C. The NAACP lobbies Congress to cut the budget of the Justice Department

   D. The House Agriculture Committee holds a hearing to investigate wrongdoing by the Department of Agriculture

5. Which of the following scenarios is an accurate comparison of a PAC and an interest group?

PAC	Interest group
A. An entity that recruits, nominates, and elects members to office to control the government	A grassroots conservative protest movement that opposes economic stimulus spending
B. An informal group striving for a broad, common goal	Labor organization comprising federal, state, and municipal workers
C. An entity whose specific goal is to raise and spend money to influence elections	An entity whose specific goal is to get legislation passed in favor of the group's policies
D. Groups representing industries or corporations	A fluid web of connections among those concerned about a policy

6. Which of the following scenarios is an accurate comparison of an interest group and a political party?

Political party	Interest group
A. An entity that recruits, nominates, and elects members to office to control the government	An entity whose specific goal is to get legislation passed in favor of the group's policies
B. An entity whose specific goal is to raise and spend money to influence elections	A fluid web of connections among those concerned about a policy
C. Groups representing industries or corporations	Labor organization comprising federal, state, and municipal workers
D. The National Rifle Association	Libertarian Party

7. Which of the following best represents the U.S. Supreme Court's ruling in *Citizens United v. FEC* (2010)?

    A. Restrictions on individual contributions did not violate the First Amendment

    B. Not all political speech is protected by the First Amendment

    C. Federal bans on corporate and union expenditures violated an organization's right to free speech

    D. Aggregate spending limits on campaign contributions by individuals are unconstitutional

8. The National Rifle Association publishes a voter guide for its members that describes candidates' positions on the Second Amendment. Which of the following roles is the interest group fulfilling?

    A. Linkage institution

    B. Fundraiser

    C. Logrolling

    D. Free-rider

9. Which of the following represents an iron triangle?

    A. Congressional committee, federal agency, lobbying group

    B. Congress, the president, and executive agencies

    C. The Supreme Court, state judiciaries, and attorneys

    D. Governor, state legislature, and local government

10. How might an interest group attempt to influence a federal agency?

    A. Through rulemaking

    B. By writing *amicus curiae* briefs

    C. Through litigation in state courts

    D. By introducing legislation

■ Free Response Questions

SCOTUS Comparison

In the aftermath of Watergate, Congress attempted to restore public faith by reducing corruption in political campaigns by imposing restrictions on contributions to candidates running for political office. The Federal Election Campaign Act of 1971 limited the amount an individual could contribute to a political campaign, and placed limits on campaign expenditures.

In the ensuing case *Buckley v. Valeo* (1976), the Supreme Court upheld the limits on hard money contributions, determining that the limits enhanced the "integrity of our system of representative democracy" by guarding against corruption and bribery. However, the Court struck down the portion of the law that limited expenditures, ruling that campaign expenditures constitute speech, and therefore cannot be limited.

A. Identify the constitutional clause that is common to both *Buckley v. Valeo* (1976) and *Citizens United v. Federal Election Commission* (2010).

B. Based on the constitutional clause identified in part A, explain how the decision in *Citizens United v. Federal Election Commission* (2010) extended the decision in *Buckley v. Valeo* (1976).

C. Explain an action citizens could take to limit the ruling in *Citizens United*.

Argumentation

Develop an argument in which you decide whether factions (interest groups) promote or threaten democracy.

In your essay, you must:

- Articulate a defensible claim or thesis that responds to the prompt and establishes a line of reasoning.

- Support your claim with at least TWO pieces of accurate and relevant information:

  - At least ONE piece of evidence must be from one of the following foundational documents:

    - The Constitution of the United States (including the Bill of Rights and subsequent amendments)
    - *Federalist* No. 10
    - Brutus I

- Use a second piece of evidence from another foundational document from the list or from your study of linkage institutions

- Use reasoning to explain why your evidence supports your claim/thesis

- Respond to an opposing or alternative perspective using refutation, concession, or rebuttal

Concept Application

Recently, public employee unions—comprising federal, state, and municipal workers—have wrestled with governors who have challenged the terms of the public employee contracts, including salaries, pensions, and benefits. Republican governor of Wisconsin Scott Walker succeeded in limiting public employees' collective bargaining rights, but some observers have argued that these strategies may have resulted in a backlash that is serving to energize union employees.

After reading the scenario, respond to A, B, and C below:

A. Describe a tactic unions could use to address the situation outlined in the scenario.

B. In the context of the scenario, explain how interest groups such as unions can influence lawmakers for more favorable outcomes.

C. In the context of the scenario, explain how the interaction between interest groups, Congress, and the bureaucracy can be affected by the iron triangle.

THEN

The relationship between the media and consumers was one-way.

NOW

Technology has created a two-way relationship between the media and consumers, involving the exchange of a seemingly limitless amount of information of varying quality, targeted to specific audiences.

NEXT

Will the abundance and the reach of the media overload people with information?

Will some people continue to select media sources that serve only to confirm their views?

Will new technologies continue to change the nature of the news business?

▌Chapter Introduction

If you are like most Americans and indeed like multitudes of people across the globe, the media are a fixture in your daily life. You may wake and check Snapchat before you even get out of bed. You may scroll through Instagram while brushing your teeth, watch cable news over breakfast, and listen to a podcast each morning when commuting to school or work. In the evening, you may watch YouTube videos of televised news stories concerning the latest international crisis. You may receive real-time news updates on your cell phone or visit Internet news sites and blogs regularly. As a citizen of the 21st century, you are bathed in a sea of news and information. While once people had to seek out news and information, today, they are inundated with it, and they must develop the skills needed to distinguish the reliable from the unreliable.

The media serves as one of several linkage institutions studied in AP U.S. Government and Politics. A linkage institution is an informal mechanism connecting citizens to the government. Like all linkage institutions, the media facilitates a relationship between the people and their government. But unlike political parties and interest groups which may require action on the part of the people, all individuals are likely to consume some media. The media acts as a linkage institution in several ways. First, the media educate the public about various policy issues.—in doing so, the media shapes public opinion. The media—through increasingly two-way communication, facilitates political participation by providing a venue for individuals to articulate their views. The media also serve to inform policymakers, who are likely to access many of the same forms of news that the average person relies on.

Due to the increased availability of unverifiable news (aka "fake news") it is increasingly important in our democracy that citizens have the ability to determine if the information they are receiving is accurate. Studies of media consumption indicate that people tend to gravitate to news that reinforces their pre-existing views. This gravitation occurs when people read news articles posted by like-minded friends on social media and watch news programs that conform to their own ideological bias.

The rapidly increasing demand for media and political communication outlets from ideologically diverse audiences have led to debates over media bias and the impact of partisan news sites.

What is the result of the massive amount of information in the media, both reliable and unreliable? Is the tendency of people to consume news that conforms to their own bias increasing ideological polarization in the United States? The AP U.S. Government Enduring Understanding for the media asserts: *The various forms of media provide citizens with political information and influence the ways in which they participate politically.* In The Media chapter, you will learn how the media continuously shapes the ways we receive information and the ways we participate in the democratic process.

▌The Modern Media

At one time, it was easy to recognize the media: newspapers, television news, and cable news networks, to name a few. But defining the media today is trickier: Do tweets from your mayor, Instagrams from your roommate, or Facebook posts from your mom count as media? Although many observers regard the **media**

media
Tools used to store and deliver information or data.

simply as tools used to store and deliver information or data (in which case, all the preceding communications would be considered media), we must differentiate between media outlets that distribute unverifiable or opinion-based information and those that disseminate verifiable information.

The media exist in various forms today, including print media such as newspapers and magazines; electronic media, which traditionally means radio and television; and **new media,** sources of information including Internet websites, blogs, social networking sites such as Snapchat, Facebook, and Twitter, photo- and video-sharing platforms such as Instagram and YouTube, and apps—and the cellular and satellite technologies that facilitate their use. In previous eras, media consumers often accepted what was broadcast or printed as fact, but today one must be a critical consumer of information. Just because information appears on social media, a blog, or even hundreds of blogs or reputable websites does not necessarily mean that information is accurate. How can today's media consumers be certain the information they are receiving is accurate? One good method is to rely on media outlets with a track record of providing solid information and adhering to journalistic standards. Another is to check sources independently: Today, the Internet has made it possible to verify some information simply by clicking on a hotlink to the original sources. More and more, news organizations will come to rely on "citizen journalists," increasing the probability that unscrupulous individuals will distribute false information widely. Thus, today's media consumers must exercise a high level of caution when reading, listening, and viewing.

new media
Sources of information—including Internet websites, blogs, social networking sites such as Facebook and Twitter, photo- and video-sharing platforms such as Instagram and YouTube, and apps—and the cellular and satellite technologies that facilitate their use.

■ The Political Functions of the Media

In the United States today, the media in all forms—including print, television, radio, and new media—fulfill several key functions. Much of what the media do revolves around entertaining us, whether that means playing *Fortnite,* watching *Stranger Things*, or reading an article on Buzzfeed. But the media perform important political functions as well and are a vital element of our democracy. Specifically, the media perform these political functions:

- Provide political information.

- Help us to interpret events and policies and influence agenda setting in the national political arena.

- Provide a forum for political conversations.

- Socialize children to the political culture.

Providing Information

One long-standing function of the mass media is to serve up a steady diet of news and information to readers, viewers, and listeners. Indeed, the media, particularly the electronic media, are the primary source of information for most individuals. In its role of providing political information, the media has often been criticized for focusing attention on which candidate is ahead in the polls. Dubbed **horse race journalism,** the tendency of the media to accentuate popularity and poll numbers over substance has meant that qualifications, policy platforms, and issue stances are often given short shrift. But today the quantity of information available—on blogs, websites, and cable television stations—surpasses the volume available at any other time in history. Coverage includes everything from weather watches, to sports

horse race journalism
the tendency of the media to accentuate popularity and poll numbers over substance

scores, to the latest legislative developments on Capitol Hill, to serious analysis of top domestic policy issues and international problems. From this steady diet arises the problem of information overload—the constant availability of news information to the point of excess, which may cause media consumers to ignore, dismiss, or fail to see the significance of particular events. Media critics especially fault the television networks for injecting entertainment into news shows. They dub this combination **infotainment** (a hybrid of the words *information* and *entertainment*). More recent is the trend of uniting comedy with political content, as in *Saturday Night Live*'s "Weekend Update" and *Full Frontal with Samantha Bee,* both of which interpret news events with a comedic slant. But the merging of our informational and entertainment worlds could best be seen through the 2016 presidential candidacy of Donald Trump: Known to the American public primarily for his role on the reality television show *The Apprentice*, Trump was catapulted to the national stage when his celebrity brand attracted enough attention through his expert use of the media to win over sizable contingents of supporters—eventually, enough to win him the Republican nomination for president and then the presidency.

Interpreting Matters of Public Interest and Setting the Public Agenda

Besides reporting information, the media help people to comprehend and interpret matters of public interest and to make informed decisions about public policies (see "Analyzing the Sources"). Political scientist Shanto Iyengar asserts that this process often begins with the media **framing**—setting a context that helps people understand important events and matters of shared interest. The media also help shape the **public agenda**—public issues that most demand the attention of government officials. Such was the case with the issue of gun violence in the United States, which has generated significant media coverage in recent years, both nationally and within states. In doing so, the media engaged in **priming**—using their coverage to bring particular policies on issues to the public agenda, a common tactic used in shaping the public agenda.

Providing a Forum for Conversations About Politics

Although the media have provided an often lively forum for conversations about politics, the prominence of this role has reached new heights in the Internet era. Historically, information flowed from the media—which through the years have included everything from the political broadsides and leaflets of colonial times to modern newspapers, radio news, and television programming—to the people. The people then formed opinions based on what they read, heard, and saw. This historical one-way tradition typically featured little give-and-take between media sources and their consumers. A notable exception has been the **letter to the editor,** in which a reader responds to a newspaper story, knowing that the letter might be published in that paper. The advent of talk radio gave listeners one of their first regular opportunities to express their views publicly. Television took note, and call-in shows became common fare on cable television stations.

But no other medium has expanded the ability of people to communicate their views to the degree that the Internet has. Today, blogs provide an ideal forum for online conversations about issues, inviting an ongoing dialogue between blog hosts and posters. Discussion boards (even those that are "nonpolitical") are filled with political discussion and opinions. The comment section following an online newspaper article has become the new water cooler around which opinions are voiced. And social networking sites such as Facebook and Twitter provide an easily accessible

infotainment
A hybrid of the words *information* and *entertainment*; news shows that combine entertainment and news.

framing
The process by which the media set a context that helps people understand important events and matters of shared interest.

public agenda
The public issues that most demand the attention of government officials.

priming
Bringing certain policies on issues to the public agenda through media coverage.

letter to the editor
A letter in which a reader responds to a story in a newspaper, knowing that the letter might be published in that paper.

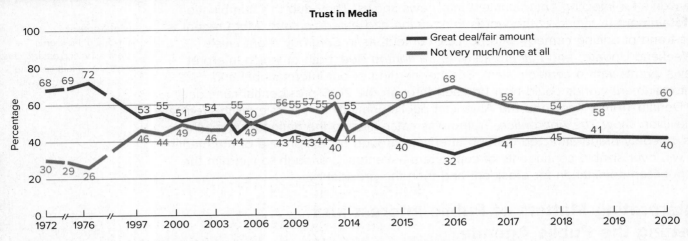

Trust in Media

Source: Gallup Poll, "Americans' Trust in Mass Media Edges Down to 41%." https://news.gallup.com/poll/267047/americans-trust-mass-media-edges-down.aspx

Confidence in the Media

The Gallup Organization has asked the following question in surveys since 1972: "In general, how much trust and confidence do you have in the mass media—such as newspapers, TV, and radio—when it comes to reporting the news fully, accurately, and fairly: a great deal, a fair amount, not very much, or none at all?"

This graph illustrates survey respondents' views on that question, showing survey data at various times between May 1972 and September 2020. You can see that considerable changes have occurred in people's assessment of news organizations in this period.

Practice Analytical Thinking

1. Describe the trend during the 1970s concerning people's confidence in the media, citing specific data from the figure.

2. What has been the trend since 2001 regarding Americans' confidence in the media?

3. What do the latest data indicate concerning the issue of confidence in the media? Why do you think this is the case?

4. What do the data say about the overall trends with regards to people's confidence in the media?

5. What factors could have contributed to the changes in people's assessment of the media over time? Explain.

means by which people can communicate facts, eyewitness accounts, and opinions. David Weinberger, a Democratic marketing consultant and Internet adviser, describes this phenomenon: "Think of it as conversation space. Conversation is the opposite of marketing. It's talking in our own voices about things we want to hear about."[1]

>> Cenk Uygur and Ana Kasparian are co-hosts of *The Young Turks* (TYT), a liberal news and opinion show on YouTube that has generated large viewership, combining a television-like news show format with an Internet-based distribution platform.

Joe Scarnici/Stringer/Getty Images

Socializing Children to Political Culture

The media also socialize new generations to the political culture. For young children, television programming remains an important medium for both entertainment and socialization, whether watched on television or streamed on phones, tablets, or laptops. The shows children watch play an important role in socializing them to important cultural values. Shows such as *Sesame Street* and *Sanjay and Craig* send powerful messages about the value of diversity in society. Young children's shows also subtly instruct watchers on the value of patriotism and of specific civic behaviors. TV programming for older children similarly takes on political issues. A series of episodes of *SpongeBob SquarePants* depicts Bikini Bottom's first presidential election, in which SpongeBob's best friend, Patrick Starfish, runs against Crustacean Party candidate Larry the Lobster.

Even television and radio programs not specifically aimed at youth often reinforce democratic principles and practices. What is *The Voice* if not a televised election? And when the tribe speaks on *Survivor*, they do so through the process of voting. Talk radio and television call-in programs rest on the assumption that individuals' opinions matter and that they have the right to voice them. These kinds of programming may not directly spur a particular political behavior on the part of viewers. Nonetheless, television and other forms of media that we often think of as pure entertainment frequently reinforce and legitimize dominant American political values, including the value of participating in civic society in a democracy.

The Press and Politics: A Historical View

The sheer volume of information available through the media today makes the media's influence in our times beyond dispute. Historically, too, the media have played an essential role in setting the political agenda and shaping public policy. The power of the media was evident even in pre-Revolutionary times, when, for example, newspaper owners and readers rallied against the Stamp Act's (1765) imposition of taxes on newspapers and other kinds of legal documents. Newspaper publishers sympathetic to the colonists' cause of ejecting Great Britain from American shores used their "power of the pen" to arouse public opinion, and they strongly supported the patriot cause throughout the Revolution. Taking sides in an internal conflict was a new role for the press, one that would sow the seeds of future media influence on the country's domestic and foreign policy. The early history of media development also raised issues that continue to create conflict about the media's role in society.

The Early Role of the Press

Great leaders learned early how intimately their careers were linked to favorable press coverage and influence. From the 1790s to the 1830s, the press served primarily as a vehicle for the leaders of political parties, who expressed their opinions through newspapers known to reflect their particular viewpoints in reporting the news. The circulation of these newspapers was small, but so was their audience; most people could not read and write and did not vote.

By the 1830s, the environment had changed. For openers, the average American was now able to read. New technology made possible the **penny press**—newspapers that sold for a penny. The field of **journalism,** the practice of gathering and reporting events, flourished. Circulation increased, and the working class became interested in what the newspapers had to offer. Another reason newspapers reduced their price was the advent of advertising; newspaper owners figured out that if they sold advertising, they could increase both their profits and their papers' circulation. The 1830s was the first time advertising became part and parcel of the newspaper business, and although pressures from advertisers sometimes affected coverage and editorial opinion, few readers noticed that practice, and even fewer challenged it.

Over time, the influence of advertising grew exponentially. Although today's major newspapers do not openly change their editorial opinions to please their advertisers, occasionally advertisers flex their muscles, as General Motors did when it withdrew its advertising from the *Los Angeles Times* after the newspaper recommended the firing of the company's CEO.[2]

Yellow Journalism and Muckraking

Throughout the last part of the 19th century, newspapers competed vigorously with one another for ever-greater shares of readership. Publishers found that stories about sex, gore, violence, and government corruption sold papers faster than reports about garbage collection and school budgets. Well-known publishers William Randolph Hearst and Joseph Pulitzer established their reputations and their fortunes at that time, Hearst with the *New York Journal American* and Pulitzer with the *New York World*. Along with Hearst and Pulitzer, at the beginning of the 20th century came the practice of yellow journalism, so named after the yellow ink used in the "Yellow Kid" cartoons in the *New York World*. The term **yellow journalism** has come to signify an irresponsible, sensationalist approach to news reporting and is used to this day to criticize certain elements of the press.

The most famous example of the impact of yellow journalism came with both Hearst's and Pulitzer's support of the United States's entry into the Spanish-American War (1898). This conflict is sometimes referred to as "the newspaper war" because of the major role of the press in President William McKinley's decision to invade Cuba and later the Philippines. Influenced by reports of Spanish cruelty toward the Cubans during and after the Cuban independence movement, public sentiment in the United States strongly favored Cuba. Hearst and Pulitzer, followed by other newspapers across the country, fanned the flames of war with sensational and lurid anti-Spanish stories, dwelling on the brutality of the Spanish toward Cuban rebels. The precipitating event, the explosion of the U.S. battleship *Maine* in Havana harbor in February 1898, may or may not have

penny press
Newspapers that sold for a penny in the 1830s.

journalism
The practice of gathering and reporting events.

yellow journalism
An irresponsible, sensationalist approach to news reporting, so named after the yellow ink used in the "Yellow Kid" cartoons in the *New York World*.

>> Yellow journalism can influence the national policy agenda. When the battleship *Maine* exploded in Havana harbor in February 1898, newspaper coverage significantly molded public opinion, and in turn Congress declared war on Spain. Can you think of examples of recent media coverage of events that have influenced public opinion?

Bettmann/Getty Images

been due to a Spanish torpedo, according to recent evidence. But press reports, accompanied by the cry "Remember the *Maine,*" galvanized the public and Congress. The president responded to the intensifying pressures, and Congress declared war on Spain in April. The press and the public had guided public policy.

Hard on the heels of the Spanish-American "newspaper war" came the era of **muckraking,** an about-face that placed journalists in the heroic role of exposing the dark underbelly of government and industry. The most famous of the muckrakers included Ida Tarbell, who exposed the oil industry in a series of articles running from 1902 to 1904 in *McClure's* magazine; Lincoln Steffens, who published *The Shame of the Cities* in 1904; and Upton Sinclair, whose novel *The Jungle* (1906) revealed the horrors of the meat-processing industry, leading to passage of the Pure Food and Drug Act and later to the establishment of the Food and Drug Administration.[3]

muckraking
Criticism and exposés of corruption in government and industry by journalists at the turn of the 20th century.

A Widening War for Readership

Yellow journalism died down after World War I, and newspapers entered a period that, at least on the surface, valued objectivity. Newspapers increasingly found themselves competing with the new media of the time that were just coming into being: radio stations from 1920 to 1950; television from the 1940s to 1980; and from then on, the explosion of today's new media. This increased competition has had several effects on the newspaper industry. First, for over a decade, print newspaper readership had steadily declined, particularly the audience for printed local newspapers, though in the aftermath of the 2016 election, the largest American newspapers, including *The New York Times* and *The Wall Street Journal*, saw an uptick in subscriptions. However, the additional subscriptions were not enough to counteract the overall decline seen by newspapers across the country, as shown in Figure 17.1. In response, newspaper publishers have adapted to the changes in how individuals get their news, and many have consolidated and increased their digital presence, offering digital-only formats or publishing printed editions only on Sundays. Newspapers continue in their effort to solve the challenge they face due to declining print-ad revenue. Increasingly, that solution has meant that online advertising is generating a greater portion of

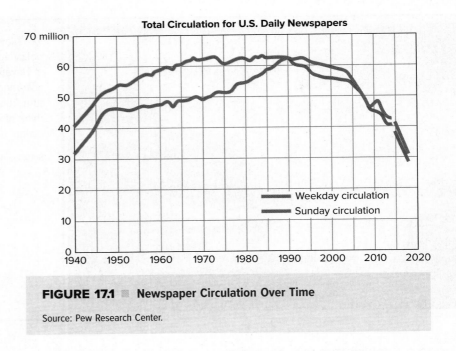

Total Circulation for U.S. Daily Newspapers

Weekday circulation
Sunday circulation

FIGURE 17.1 ■ **Newspaper Circulation Over Time**

Source: Pew Research Center.

digital paywall
The practice of limiting access to a website unless users pay a fee or purchase a subscription.

newspapers' revenue. And some newspapers are profiting by providing information to readers via the Internet using a **digital paywall**—the practice of limiting access to a website unless users pay a fee or purchase a subscription.

Beyond changing platforms, sources of revenue, and readership, the newspaper industry has changed as society has changed. Gone are the grand urban headquarters that housed newspapers—and anchored entire downtown areas—of days gone by. Today, many city newspapers have relocated to the cheaper real estate of the suburbs, with smaller newsrooms that rely on telecommuting reporters. Large cities are now likely to have smaller weekly publications targeted to specific demographic audiences—women, people of color, and members of the LGBTQ community, for example—and to publish foreign-language newspapers appealing to diverse newcomers to the United States, such as Mexican, Brazilian, Vietnamese, Iranian, Nigerian, and Russian immigrants.

Increasing Diversity in Newsrooms

As the industry has changed, so too has the human face of the newsroom. First, there are fewer faces in the newsroom, as the long-term trend of declining revenue led many newspapers to reduce their reporting staff. Second, Figure 17.2 shows that in 2018, almost one-third of newsrooms increased their gender diversity, but 21 percent of newsrooms became less diverse in terms of gender. Other research shows that among younger journalists, we are likely to see more diversity and that many online publications are more diverse than media outlets based in the print legacy.

Another measure of how modern newsrooms have changed along with American society is the proportion of racial and ethnic minority journalists working at newspapers. Data indicate that minority journalists are much more likely to be employed at larger-circulation newspapers, with African Americans, Latinx, and Asian Americans constituting over one-fifth of the journalists at papers with a circulation of 250,000 to 500,000. That proportion is nearly as high at the largest-circulation newspapers and steadily tapers off among newspapers with a circulation of less than 250,000.

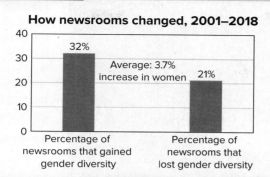

How newsrooms changed, 2001–2018

32% — Percentage of newsrooms that gained gender diversity

Average: 3.7% increase in women

21% — Percentage of newsrooms that lost gender diversity

FIGURE 17.2 ■ **Newsroom Employment by Gender** In the past, "newsmen" were in fact men. What does the graph indicate about women's employment in today's newsrooms?

Source: American Society of News Editors

The Media Go Electronic: The Radio and Television Revolutions

It is impossible to overemphasize the transformative impact of the early electronic media. From the time of the first U.S. radio broadcasts in the early 1920s, radio allowed listeners to hear news in real time. That immediacy marked a drastic change from the standard, delayed method of receiving news, which was by reading the morning and evening editions of newspapers, plus the occasional "extra edition" published when important breaking news warranted it. Radio also altered the relationship between politicians—particularly presidents—and their constituents, because it enabled listeners to hear the voices of their elected leaders. Television further revolutionized that relationship by making it possible for people to see their leaders (though initially only in black and white).

How Radio Opened Up Political Communication

Radio was the first electronic medium that brought people into direct contact with their leaders. Beginning in the 1920s, radios became a fixture in American living rooms, and families who could not afford a radio of their own would often spend evenings at the homes of friends or neighbors who could.

FDR'S FIRESIDE CHATS Franklin D. Roosevelt was the first politician to realize the value of radio as a device for political communication—and to exploit that value. As governor of New York (1928–1932), Roosevelt faced a Republican state legislature hostile to many of his liberal social welfare programs. To overcome the opposition, Roosevelt used radio addresses to appeal directly to his constituents, who would then lobby the legislators for his policies. Indeed, after some of Roosevelt's radio addresses, legislative offices were flooded with letters from constituents asking lawmakers to support a particular policy.

By the time Roosevelt became president in 1933, he had grasped the importance of radio as a tool for communicating directly with the people. FDR

>> President Franklin D. Roosevelt was recognized as a master political communicator. Using the newest technology of his time available, Roosevelt relied on a folksy, conversational tone and the medium of radio to bring his message to the people. How does a politician's ability to communicate successfully with the people influence his or her governing?

Bettmann/Getty Images

fireside chats
President Franklin D. Roosevelt's radio addresses to the country.

often began his radio addresses to the country—his **fireside chats**—with the greeting, "Good evening, friends," highlighting the personal relationship he wished to cultivate between himself and his listeners. (You can listen to many of Roosevelt's fireside chats in MP3 format from the Vincent Voice Library at Michigan State University.) Through these folksy fireside chats, Americans learned about presidential initiatives on the banking crisis, New Deal social welfare programs, the declaration of war on Japan after that nation's attack on Pearl Harbor, and the progress of U.S. forces during World War II. In all, Roosevelt had 30 fireside chats with Americans over his 12 years as president.

TALK RADIO: TALKING THE POLITICAL TALK Radio began to emerge from the shadows of television in the 1970s and 1980s. Those decades brought a renaissance of sorts for radio, as the medium saw tremendous growth in **talk radio**—a format featuring conversations and interviews about topics of interest, along with call-ins from listeners. As many AM station owners switched to an all-talk format in those years, music programming migrated to the FM band.

talk radio
A format featuring conversations and interviews about topics of interest, along with call-ins from listeners.

In 1987 the Federal Communications Commission (FCC), the U.S. government agency that regulates interstate and international communications by radio, television, wire, satellite and cable, repealed the **fairness doctrine,** which had required stations holding broadcast licenses to present both sides of controversial issues of public importance and to do so in a manner that was honest, fair, and balanced. Since the law's repeal, partisan radio programming has grown dramatically. Today, listeners tend to tune in to radio hosts who share—many say, reinforce—the listeners' existing opinions, and they interact with these hosts through call-in opportunities.

fairness doctrine
The requirement that stations holding broadcast licenses present both sides of controversial issues of public importance and do so in a manner that was honest, fair, and balanced.

Television and the Transformation of Campaigns and Elections

Although radio predates television, TV nonetheless has been the centerpiece of U.S. home entertainment for a long time. Television began to make a mark on the American scene in the 1940s, when small TV sets—their screens flecked with static snowflakes—hit the market. Its effect on the world of politics cannot be

THEN

NOW

≫ In the first-ever televised presidential debate in 1960, the importance of being telegenic emerged as an important quality for candidates. John Kennedy came across as handsome, relaxed, and articulate, while Richard Nixon, despite having a strong command of the issues, was viewed as appearing nervous and sinister. By 2020, being television savvy had become a necessary trait for presidential candidates, including both Donald Trump and Joe Biden.

Kennedy/Nixon: Bettmann/Getty Images; *Trump/Biden:* Win McNamee/Getty Images

overstated. Suddenly, being **telegenic,** or looking good on TV, became almost mandatory for serious political candidates. It is likely that President Abraham Lincoln's handlers would have marched him straight to a cosmetic surgeon to have the giant mole on his cheek removed. Richard Nixon might have won the presidency in 1960 had it not been for his nervous demeanor and the "five o'clock shadow" on his face that made him look sinister in the first-ever televised presidential candidate debates that year. In appearance and demeanor, his opponent, the handsome, relaxed, and articulate John F. Kennedy won the debate hands down, even though in hindsight most analysts agree that Nixon "won" the debate on its verbal merits. Since that election, the effective use of television has been a necessity for high-ranking elected office.

Today, people are as likely to watch cable television as they are to watch ABC, CBS, or NBC, the original three networks that dominated the United States's national political life for more than a half-century, and they are less likely to watch television at all than Americans two or three decades ago. One measure of these changes is viewership of nightly network news broadcasts on ABC, CBS, and NBC, which plummeted between 1992 and today. Significantly, nightly news network viewership strongly correlates with age, with the youngest

telegenic
The quality of looking good on TV.

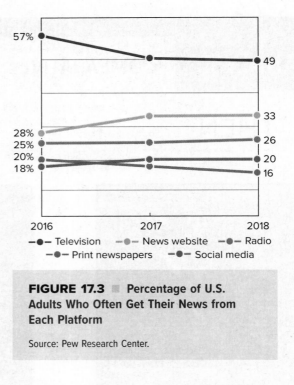

FIGURE 17.3 Percentage of U.S. Adults Who Often Get Their News from Each Platform

Source: Pew Research Center.

Americans being least likely to watch the news. But even among the oldest Americans, viewership has steeply declined as the result of the skyrocketing competition from cable channels and the ability to learn about the latest happenings in real time on a computer or phone.

How Americans Use the Media to Get Political Information

As cable news channels such as CNN, MSNBC, and FOX News have increased their viewing audience, it is no wonder the word *broadcasting* has spawned the term **narrowcasting:** the practice of aiming political media content at specific segments of the public, divided according to political ideology, party affiliation, or economic interests. This winnowing of audiences has led to **media segmentation,** the breaking down of the media in general according to the specific audiences they target. Examples of segmented media include Black Entertainment Television (BET); the U.S.-based Spanish-language television network Telemundo; and the Lifestyle Network, which includes the Food Network and HGTV. Through media segmentation, advertisers can hone their advertising to the tastes of their targeted markets.

But media segmentation is only partially responsible for the decline of television networks. Since 2010, the proportion of Americans relying on digital news sources has increased, while those relying on traditional sources, particularly print newspapers, has declined. The trend can be seen in Figure 17.3: Today, increasing numbers of Americans get their news online. Indeed, more American adults are getting their news from online sources, including news websites and social media platforms (53 percent combined), than from television (49 percent). And although in total, television and radio still dominates, Figure 17.4 shows that in the future, based on where the younger generations are getting their news, online news sources will dominate.

narrowcasting
The practice of aiming media content at specific segments of the public.

media segmentation
The breaking down of the media according to the specific audiences they target.

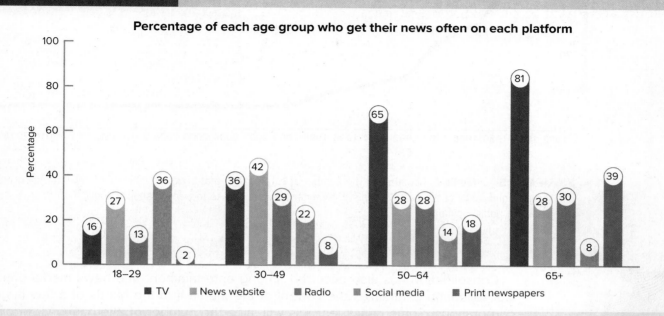

Percentage of each age group who get their news often on each platform

■ TV   ■ News website   ■ Radio   ■ Social media   ■ Print newspapers

FIGURE 17.4 ■ **Where Americans Get Their News Varies by Age** Younger Americans—Millennials and Gen Z-ers—are the most likely groups to get their news from social media sites, but older Americans still rely on TV. What are the biggest differences between generations in how they get their news? Which group is most likely to get their news from news websites? How do you predict these groups will get their news in the next five years? Why is the online audience for news likely to grow in the future?

Source: Pew Research Center.

▮ Media Consolidation

Technology has changed the business of news. Today, our expectations of news outlets have increased. No longer will the afternoon paper delivered to your doorstep by a bicycle-riding paperboy suffice. Today's "newspapers" are media outlets: We expect them to tweet us updates, and we "like" them on Facebook. We are increasingly likely to read them on a tablet rather than in print form. And as our expectations of the role of the media have changed, so too have the businesses that **are** the media.

Today, corporations are increasingly likely to be universal providers of all our digital needs. Thus, **consolidation** occurs—the phenomenon of large corporations buying smaller ones so that there are fewer and fewer companies providing products. Apple is notoriously committed to controlling the user media experience from start to finish and so has created partnerships with various media outlets that distribute their content via Apple's product. In doing so, it has gobbled up several smaller companies, including the voice-recognition platform Siri. Facebook, too, has entered into agreements with technology corporations, such as the messaging service WhatsApp and the photo-sharing platform Instagram, and with media outlets, including News Corporation's *The Wall Street Journal* and also *The Washington Post* and *The Guardian*.

consolidation
The phenomenon of large corporations buying smaller ones so that there are fewer and fewer companies' products available.

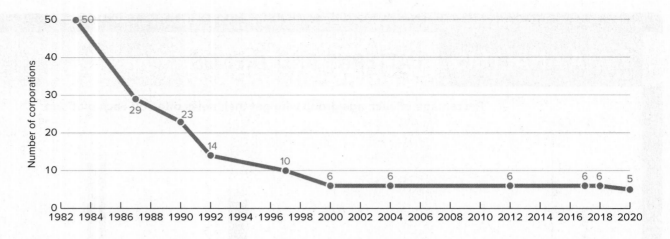

FIGURE 17.5 ■ **Media Consolidation** The number of corporations that bring the majority of news to Americans has shrunk significantly in the past 35 years. How might the fact that so few corporations control the news we receive affect public opinion?

Consolidation has also occurred among entertainment and news media outlets. Consolidation centralizes the control of the media into the hands of a few large corporations. Some critics fear this will stifle the number of alternative viewpoints that are presented to the American public. The number of corporations responsible for supplying the majority of news to Americans has shrunk from 50 in 1983 to five today, as shown in Figure 17.5. The five media giants are Comcast, Walt Disney (which bought 21st Century Fox in 2019), AT&T (which owns Time Warner), Viacom, and CBS Corporation. Some observers believe these five giants could disproportionately affect public opinion and public policy by allowing corporate interests to influence how the news is reported. Media consolidation, however, is countered by a proliferation of media sources, including newer entities such as Netflix, which not only distribute content developed by others but also create original content.

The Proliferation of News Sources and Greater Scrutiny

In the mid-20th century, rural communities could not receive broadcast signals from the big cities. As a result, hundreds of cable television systems sprang up around the country. In the early 1970s, commercial satellites enabled the advent of satellite networks. Media entrepreneurs established many new, nonbroadcast networks—Home Box Office (HBO) in 1975, followed by others in the 1980s, such as CNN, ESPN, and MTV. Then in the 1990s, another technological revolution created profoundly more diverse sources of news and information—the Internet.

The Cell-Phone Watchdogs

The rise of cable stations and the Internet has fundamentally changed politics by increasing the number of sources from which Americans can get their news. This trend results not only in narrowcasting but also in greater scrutiny of government

How Technology Has Changed How We Get Information

THEN

(1960s)
Three television networks—ABC, NBC, and CBS—provided all the nightly news.

Network television programming matured and revolutionized how the media entertained and provided information.

Television accentuated a new set of candidate qualities—including being telegenic—that had not mattered much in earlier political campaigns.

NOW

Americans are increasingly likely to get their news from digital sources, including websites, podcasts, and social networking sites.

Digital cable technology and new delivery methods—including Internet television sites like Hulu and Netflix and Internet music-streaming sites like Spotify—are revolutionizing entertainment and information-getting.

Omnipresent cell phone cameras mean that candidates must consistently display the qualities that make them appealing to voters, lest their mistakes be caught in a YouTube moment.

NEXT

WHAT'S NEXT?

- How will the content of television change in the next several years? What factors might influence how television content is changing?

- Is there a downside to the new pervasiveness of television and other electronic media for candidates? For voters? If so, what?

- What new media technologies will shape the evolution of television in the future?

---

officials and public policy. Things happen now in the time it takes to swipe a phone, and politicians and government officials, including police, are aware of the ever-present cell phone video cameras chronicling their every move for YouTube posterity. Indeed, some contend that the presence of cell phones, with their ability to chronicle the use of excessive force by police officers—including in the killing of George Floyd—propelled the social movement demanding criminal justice reforms. As Americans watched these viral videos, many felt they could no longer deny the need for reforms.

The portability of cellular technology has also contributed to Americans' consumption of news. Using our smartphones, we always have access to news outlets, and this access has increased our consumption of news, including "long form" news—not just the 280-character tweet or a brief Facebook posting but real news coverage, analysis, debate, and discussion. In fact, one study found that smartphones and tablets increased traffic on major newspaper websites by 9 percent.[4] Simultaneously, the timeframe of "news" also has changed. The adage that a "week is an eternity in politics" has become an understatement in the age of the Internet and the 24-hour news cycle.

Blogs: The New Penny Papers?

Technology has changed the format and content of written news as well. Today blogs have become an important component of how individuals communicate and convey information and how media outlets keep us informed. Because blogs are typically written from a subjective point of view, their authors less frequently adhere to professional journalism standards. So, like the penny papers of early American times, blogs offer the opportunity for political viewpoints to infiltrate a medium whose primary standard was once neutrality. Blogging has increased enormously in the past five years, a trend that is likely to continue. Blogs are playing an increasingly important role not just in providing a platform for citizen journalists but also in shaping the agenda of the traditional media establishment. It is not uncommon for bloggers to "break" a story that then becomes a firestorm in the traditional media. Chapter 18 offers further discussion of the increasingly important role that blogs are playing in the American political arena.

▋ Biased Media?

Media critics today are everywhere. All of them claim that both print and electronic media exhibit bias in their reporting, in their selection of what issues to cover, and in favoring one side of an issue (or one politician) over another. One of the most common complaints is that the media have an ideological bias.

The Question of Ideological Bias

A long-standing complaint is that the media evidence a liberal bias. For example, President Trump often jibed at the "liberal media," calling it "so dishonest, so disgusting,"[5] and claiming the media's bias makes the president's job harder.

The Republicans' criticism of the "liberal media" is not a new charge. In 1964, former president Dwight D. Eisenhower, in his address to the Republican National Convention, condemned a liberal media bias: "My friends, we are Republicans. If there is any finer word in the field of partisan politics, I have not heard it. So let us particularly [scorn] the divisive efforts of those outside our family, including sensation-seeking columnists and commentators, who couldn't care less about the good of our party."[6] Many conservatives point to studies indicating that a majority of newsroom reporters identify themselves as liberal or Democrat. Conservatives charge that the ideological bent of journalists carries through to the topics covered and to the perspectives of the stories.

But in recent years, greater attention has been paid to the role that the "conservative media" plays in shaping U.S. politics. Conservative talk-show hosts, including many aired on FOX News, have been important in shaping Republican party politics. Indeed, writing for CNN, Brian Rosenwald and Michael Smerconish argue that Donald Trump's and Ted Cruz's ability to outlast their Republican rivals for the 2016 GOP presidential nomination can be attributed to the influence of the "conservative media" in politics. "Over the course of the last three decades, these media personalities have surpassed party officials and even elected representatives in their influence, ascending to exalted status atop Republican leadership. Yet, they prioritize goals seemingly at odds with good governance, and often, even the party's sole purpose for existence," Rosenwald and Smerconish write.[7]

Numerous studies conducted by various political scientists, including C. Richard Hofstetter, Michael J. Robinson, and Margaret A. Sheehan, refute the idea that print journalists' personal viewpoints tinge the content of the news in a liberal way.[8] Indeed, studies suggest that most news stories take the form of a debate, with the journalist presenting the various sides of an issue and leaving the conclusion to the reader's interpretation. But increasingly, changes in the nature of the mass media have led to increasingly vocal charges that cable news stations and newer media outlets, particularly talk radio and the blogosphere, are ideologically biased, with some favoring a liberal bias and others taking a conservative slant.

The Issue of Corporate Bias

Media critics also argue that another form of bias has emerged as a result of the corporate structures that dominate the news industry, altering what is considered news and how that news is covered.[9] Corporate bias—and the desire to attract, keep, and please an audience—produces skewed programming. Will corporate conglomerates be willing to report on situations that may put themselves and their advertisers in a negative light? How does the drive for profits influence what is in the news? Are viewers being fed "news" that is not particularly newsworthy? There is no doubt that profits influence the media to cover the kinds of stories that viewers and readers want. In particular, violence dominates most local news programming, so much so that the principle of "if it bleeds, it leads" now extends into the first 15 minutes of many local news broadcasts. Fires; political, sports, and sex scandals; and celebrity-heavy news are also powerful audience attractors.

Regulation of the Media: Is It Necessary?

The government regulates and controls the ownership of radio and television stations through the independent regulatory agency known as the Federal Communications Commission (FCC). Founded in 1934 by Congress, the FCC regulates interstate and international communications by radio, television, wire, satellite, and cable throughout the United States.

Most of the FCC's rules have concerned ownership, such as the number of outlets a network may own. Some regulations, however, govern the content of radio and television programming, attempting to ensure that "decent" content— an ambiguous term, according to many broadcasters—is on the airwaves (see "Thinking Critically").

Other FCC regulations, however, concern how media providers operate. For example, in 2016, the FCC sought a rule change that would require video providers, including Comcast and DISH network, to open their video feeds by enabling other companies to manufacture cable or satellite ("set-top") boxes used by their subscribers. Gale Ann Hurd, a producer of television's *The Walking Dead*, argued in a *USA Today* opinion piece that reducing the security options would encourage piracy of licensed video: "[L]et me explain why the FCC's proposal would spell disaster for those of us who are trying to figure out how to keep making the movies and TV shows audiences love. And I'm not talking about just

Should Network Television Be Subject to Stricter Regulations Than Cable and the Internet Are?

THE ISSUE: In 1978, the U.S. Supreme Court ruled that the Federal Communications Commission should have the power to regulate the content that broadcasters provide. In *Federal Communications Commission v. Pacifica Foundation*,* the Supreme Court asserted that regulating content served to protect children from indecent material, since broadcasted content in television and radio had become permanent fixtures in most homes in the United States. The Court also justified regulation because the networks relied on public airwaves to broadcast their content and because giving the FCC broad authority would protect individuals from unwanted speech in their private homes.

The case initially stemmed from a lawsuit filed by a father whose son had heard comedian George Carlin's routine called "Filthy Words" (also known as the "seven words you can never say on television"). He complained to the FCC, which fined Pacifica Foundation, the entity that owned the radio station that broadcast the comedy bit. After the ruling, content deemed indecent by the FCC (including Carlin's filthy words) was bleeped out or edited from broadcasts. In 2012, the Supreme Court ruled in *Federal Communications Commission v. Television Stations, Inc.* concerning fines issued by the FCC for the "single use of vulgar words" on the FOX television network. During the 2002 and 2003 Billboard Music Awards, Cher and Nicole Richie used obscene words and the network was fined by the FCC. FOX challenged the fines in court. The Court invalidated the fines and ruled that while the regulations at the time did not cover "fleeting expletives," the FCC's regulations do not violate the First Amendment because the FCC is regulating on behalf of the public interest. The FCC has since amended broadcasting rules to encompass fleeting expletives.

YES: The FCC should continue to have broad authority over the regulation of television content since the same circumstances that held true in 1978 remain a reality for many Americans today. Television networks provide a "safe haven" for children and other individuals who do not wish to be bombarded with the indecency that is prevalent in cable television and online. Removing regulations or failing to penalize violators will mean a degeneration of the quality of the content available on network television. In addition, the public nature of the airwaves means that the content provided by broadcasters should meet common standards of decency that would be acceptable to most Americans.

NO: Current FCC regulations impinge on the First Amendment free speech rights guaranteed by the Constitution. They create a structure in which cable television programming, the Internet, and newspapers are not held to the same standards as radio and television, rendering radio and television less competitive. This differential stymies free speech by individuals communicating through regulated media. In addition, the standards enforced by the FCC reflect the values of a

WHAT DO YOU THINK?

1. Do you believe that the Federal Communications Commission should regulate decency on broadcast television? Why or why not?

2. Do such regulations stifle free speech? Do the same criteria the Court cited in 1978 apply today? Why or why not?

3. Do you think that the Supreme Court has an obligation to voice an opinion on the matter of indecency rules? Why or why not?

bygone era. Moreover, technological changes in American homes allow for parental control. Televisions now have V-chips, which allow parents to control content, and most cable subscribers also have parental control capability.

OTHER APPROACHES: The FCC's current policy is ambiguous because it does not provide broadcasters with concrete guidelines as to what is indecent and what is permissible. The creation of such guidelines would enable broadcasters to create compliant programming and work within a predictable framework. In addition, broadcasters operate without a reliable guide as to what the commission would find offensive.

the actors and the producers. Hundreds of thousands of crewmembers across the country will be out of jobs, too. Studios and networks can't keep making content if they stop receiving revenue from legitimate sources," Hurd argued.[10]

Media also are regulated by the Telecommunications Act of 1996, which opened the communications markets to telephone companies. This sweeping law allowed competition in the communications industry. It presented new (often confusing) options for consumers, as individual companies began to offer a suite of services, from local and long-distance telephone service, to Internet access, to cable and satellite television.

With the combination of all of these services provided by single companies, large corporate conglomerates have increasingly gained control of the media. These firms exert a powerful influence over what news the average American sees and reads on a given day. The advent of these media titans has given rise to concerns about whether this type of control will deter balanced reporting of the news and unbiased presentations of issues. In addition, public conversations about our democracy are questioning whether the relative lack of competition (because there are so few competitors) means that a valuable check on what the media do and how they do it has been lost.

Conclusion: Thinking Critically About What's Next for the Media

The surge in the number and the variety of media outlets—along with the changes in the nature of the media and in people's interactions with them—have affected politics and government in many ways. Once defined as a one-way relationship, the relationship between the media and consumers has evolved in unforeseen ways. Even the nature of the "old media" has changed, although many people would ask whether the change has been for the better. On the one hand, narrowcasting and the resulting segmentation of media markets, a central feature of media growth, might raise the comfort level of many people who no longer have to throw soft objects at their television sets in protest but can instead pick and choose what they watch. On the other hand, media segmentation also limits the exposure of many people to new ideas. Like gated communities, segmented media are also segregated media, detached environments that expose people only to viewpoints with which they agree, thus cordoning them off from society and from many of its problems. Segmented media also confuse genuine political participation with mere ranting. After all, sounding off on a radio talk show is much easier and more entertaining than attending a zoning board meeting to fight urban congestion or becoming civically engaged in other ways.

While the number of media sources and platforms available to consumers continues to proliferate, we know that consolidation is now characteristic of the business of media. So, although we may rely on an ever-increasing number of different news outlets, these outlets are owned and operated by a shrinking number of global media conglomerates, giving those corporations nearly unprecedented power in controlling the information available to consumers. This consolidation of the business of media is offset by the proliferation of other new technologies, including the advent of citizen journalism and blogging, that have diversified the sources of information available to media consumers. Nonetheless, we can anticipate even greater levels of consolidation and convergence in the future.

Can we predict the future of the media by examining the past and the present? Certainly, we can foretell increasing transparency because of the pervasive nature of today's media and the steady trend in that direction, but we cannot predict the forms media will take. What we can guarantee is continued change in the forms and usage of media and steadily increasing access to information. Will this expanding access overload people with information? It appears that many of us are developing new skills to cope with the abundance of information, much in the way that our grandparents may have developed the skill of skimming a newspaper, selecting only those stories that mattered to them. The question remains as to whether we will select only information that confirms what we already think. One trend is clear: The ever-increasing volume of information and the speed of its delivery will yield an abundance of both poor-quality and high-quality information that media consumers will need to evaluate in their efforts to get accurate information.

▮ References

1. David Weinberger, www.hillwatch.com/ PPRC/Quotes/Internet_and_Politics.aspx.

2. On April 7, 2005, General Motors pulled its advertising from the *Los Angeles Times* after columnist Dan McNeil, who covers the automotive trade for the newspaper, published several columns critical of GM, including one that chastised the company for pushing gas-guzzling SUVs rather than pursuing hybrid technology and another that called for the "impeachment" of two of the company's top executives.

3. New editions of all of these works are available: Tarbell (New York: Norton, 1969); Steffens (New York: Sangamore Press, 1957); and Sinclair (Cambridge, MA: B. Bentley, 1971).

4. Pew Research Center, *2012 State of the News Media.*

5. https://twitter.com/realDonaldTrump/ status/764867963845484545.

6. Dwight D. Eisenhower, Republican National Convention Speech, July 14, 1964.

7. Brian Rosenwald and Michael Smerconish, "Ted Cruz and Donald Trump: Signs of Conservative Media's Grip on GOP," *CNN,* February 3, 2016.

8. C. Richard Hofstetter, *Bias in the News: Network Television Coverage of the 1972 Election Campaign* (Columbus: Ohio State University Press, 1976); Michael J. Robinson and Margaret A. Sheehan, *Over the Wire and on TV: CBS and UPI in Campaign '80* (New York: Russell Sage Foundation, 1983).

9. Michael Parenti, *Inventing Reality: The Politics of the Mass Media* (New York: St. Martin's Press, 1986).

10. Gale Ann Hurd, "Stop Piracy Apocalypse: 'Walking Dead' Producer," *USA Today,* April 12, 2016.

■ Key Terms

Multiple Choice Questions

Questions 1 and 2 are based on the graph below.

Total Circulation for U.S. Daily Newspapers

Source: Pew Research Center.

1. Which of the following trends is depicted on the graph regarding newspaper circulation over time?
   A. Weekday circulation of newspapers has remained unchanged
   B. Sunday circulation of newspapers has continued to increase over time
   C. Weekday and Sunday circulation of newspapers is in decline
   D. Weekday and Sunday circulation will increase again in the future as Americans move away from television for news

2. All of the following are reasons for the decline in newspaper circulation EXCEPT:
   A. Newspapers are no longer affordable
   B. The introduction of cable news
   C. The accessibility of news and information on the internet
   D. The emergence of talk radio as a forum for political information

3. The term issue framing refers to the media's providing of a contextual setting specifically designed to
   A. Allow a political party to leverage its message to undecided voters
   B. provide the public with important information that allows people to form opinions on public policy
   C. Message U.S. foreign policy objectives to its allies over matters of international concerns
   D. Equalize coverage of all political points of view as mandated by law

4. Which of the following best accounts for why the media are often referred to as the fourth branch of government?
A. The media have quasi-legal authority over Congress
B. The media have great influence over Executive Branch appointments
C. The media act as a watchdog over the three branches checking their actions
D. The media have been able to blackmail the government by reporting on scandals

5. The media act as a linkage institution in that they serve as an agent of political
A. Socialization
B. Activism
C. Philosophy
D. Efficacy

6. All of the following are true about ideological bias and the media EXCEPT
A. News outlets are more segmented than ever
B. Talk radio in particular has a strong reputation for bias
C. Most journalists identify as liberal
D. Television news broadcasters today are more likely to inject personal opinion

7. Which of the following is true about media consolidation?
A. The number of alternative viewpoints may be stifled
B. Media coverage has become less politicized and more neutral
C. More attention is being paid to the media than ever before
D. Newspaper readership across the United States has decreased

8. Which of the following best explains how the media's role as a linkage institution has been transformed in recent decades?
A. Citizens are influenced by a handful of media conglomerates including 24-hour news and network news
B. Advances in media have transformed how people routinely acquire political information
C. There is so much news to consume, that the average American shies away from reading news stories
D. The media's role as a linkage institution is diminishing because of lack of trust in the reliability of news stories

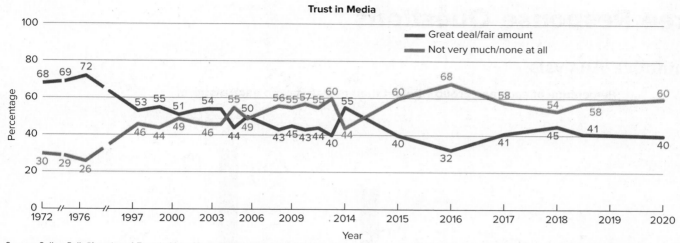

Trust in Media

Source: Gallup Poll, "Americans' Trust in Mass Media Edges Down to 41%." https://news.gallup.com/poll/267047/americans-trust-mass-media-edges-down.aspx

9. The trend in the chart above can be best explained by which of the following?

A. Increase in fake news

B. Increase in partisanship

C. Decrease in respect for the military

D. Decrease in popularity of the president

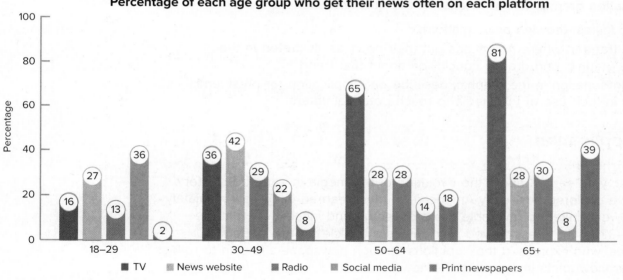

Percentage of each age group who get their news often on each platform

■ TV   ■ News website   ■ Radio   ■ Social media   ■ Print newspapers

Source: Pew Research Center.

10. If you were using the data in the table above to advise a candidate on how to improve standing with the elderly demographic in his or her reelection campaign, which of the following ad strategies would you recommend targeting?

A. Television

B. News websites

C. Radio

D. Social media

Free Response Questions

Quantitative Analysis

Percentage of each age group who get their news often on each platform

Source: Pew Research Center.

Use the information graphic above to answer the questions.

A. Identify the fastest-growing news platform.
B. Describe a trend in where Americans get their news as illustrated in the information graphic, and draw a conclusion about that trend.
C. Given the information in the graphic, describe one implication for presidential candidates in their use of the media to reach potential voters.

Concept Application

In this chapter, you learned about the evolution of the media in early U.S. history. Specifically, we explored how early-American "leaders learned early how intimately their careers were linked to favorable press coverage and influence. From the 1790s to the 1830s, the press served primarily as a vehicle for the leaders of political parties, who expressed their opinions through newspapers known to reflect their particular viewpoints in reporting the news."

Later, in the late 1800s, we learned of the effect of yellow journalism, the irresponsible, sensationalist approach to news. But by the turn of the 20th century, journalists had become muckraking heroes who exposed the dark underbelly of government and industry.

A. Compare today's social media climate to the politician-oriented press of early America.
B. Which media outlets today are most likely to engage in yellow journalism? What, in general, is their goal? How do they compare with the original "yellow journalists?"
C. Are there modern muckrakers? Which type of media outlet most likely encourages journalists to investigate wrong-doing?

Argumentation

Develop an argument that explains whether the increase in media outlets in recent decades facilitates or impedes competitive presidential elections in the U.S.

In your essay, you must:

- Articulate a defensible claim or thesis that responds to the prompt and establishes a line of reasoning

- Support your claim with at least TWO pieces of accurate and relevant information:

    - At least ONE piece of evidence must be from one of the following foundational documents:

        — Article I of the U.S. Constitution

        — The First Amendment to the U.S. Constitution

    - Use a second piece of evidence from another foundational document from the list or from your study of the electoral process and the media

- Use reasoning to explain why your evidence supports your claim/thesis

- Respond to an opposing or alternative perspective using refutation, concession, or rebuttal

THEN

Technology had little influence on politics.

NOW

Technology is the most important tool for participation in democracies—shaping how citizens get information, how campaigns are run, how candidates behave, how voters vote, and how governments provide services.

NEXT

Will people use technology as the great equalizer to facilitate participation in our democratic system?

Will campaigns use increasingly sophisticated microtargeting mechanisms and "big data" to deliver better information to voters?

Will democracies succeed in preventing foreign powers from using technology to interfere with elections?

Biden for President/Getty Images

∎ Chapter Introduction

"For most of our existence, we focused on all the good that connecting people can bring. As Facebook has grown, people everywhere have gotten a powerful new tool to stay connected to the people they love, make their voices heard, and build communities and businesses. . . . But it's clear now that we didn't do enough to prevent these tools from being used for harm as well. That goes for fake news, foreign interference in elections, and hate speech, as well as developers and data privacy. We didn't take a broad enough view of our responsibility, and that was a big mistake. It was my mistake, and I'm sorry." So began Facebook CEO Mark Zuckerberg's 2018 testimony before the House Committee on Energy and Commerce. He appeared at the committee hearing after it was revealed that Cambridge Analytica, which worked with Donald Trump's 2016 campaign, had acquired the Facebook profiles of 87 million U.S. citizens and used the data to build a software program to predict and influence voters. At the heart of the scandal—and of Zuckerberg's testimony— are both a necessity and an onerous responsibility: While tech companies strive to meet the growing demand to connect individuals in new ways, they must also protect users' privacy and ensure content that is not intentionally harmful.

The value of technology in political and civic life can't be underestimated: It enables candidates to communicate directly with constituents, governments to connect directly with citizens, parties and other organizations to inform and mobilize voters, and citizens themselves to debate and discuss issues online. During the COVID-19 pandemic in 2020, technology rose to the forefront as the key medium by which businesses stayed afloat, students attended classes, citizens remained informed and engaged, voters participated in elections, and indeed, how friends and family members nurtured their bonds. Digital technology has rapidly transformed our social, economic, and personal lives, but earlier kinds of technology have created similar, though more gradual, change before. Just over a half century ago, the advent of television changed the nature of political and economic life in the United States in many ways. For one, it changed the characteristics essential for candidates to succeed. In addition, television advertising changed how campaigns were run and how voters were kept informed of issues.

From the start, some Internet innovators hoped new technologies might usher in an age of better democratic governance. The founder of the World Wide Web, Tim Berners-Lee (who created the first successful communication between a hypertext transfer protocol [http] client and a server using the Internet) stated that "greater openness, accountability, and transparency in government will give people greater choice and make it easier for individuals to get more directly involved in issues that matter to them."[1] Berners-Lee's vision for the Internet is directly related to the AP US Government Enduring Understanding, *The various forms of media provide citizens with political information and influence they ways in which they participate politically.* Berners-Lee's vision for the Internet has occurred, but it has been accompanied by unanticipated outcomes that pose serious threats to democracies, and these threats must be addressed.

The Modern Technological Revolution: The Internet and Cellular Technology

The modern media revolution began with the birth of the Internet. As a medium of communication, a source of news and information, and a tool for political engagement and grassroots organizing, the Internet has had an incalculable—and a global—impact on the way people interact. Today, 90 percent of American adults use the Internet. In addition, the hardware of modern technology—the Internet, smartphones, and other cellular devices—is revolutionizing how politics is done in the United States. This transformation is being facilitated not only by the devices we use, but also by the platforms, software, and apps that these devices use. Of particular importance in politics are **social networking sites,** which enable users to construct a profile, specify other users with whom they share a connection, and view others' connections.[2]

> **social networking sites**
> Platforms that enable users to construct a profile, specify other users with whom they share a connection, and view others' connections.

The modern media revolution continues today as cellular technology makes the Internet portable and constantly available. Thus, we spend so much time on the Internet because we can—using cellular technology, we can Snapchat while waiting for the bus, check Instagram while in line at the grocery store, or blog while eating lunch in the cafeteria (but of course we would *never* text in class . . .). The convenience and power of the combination of these technologies have enormous implications for how politics takes place now and how politics will happen in the future as access to cell phones continues to increase. Today, 81 percent of all American adults own a smartphone, more than double the rate of ownership in 2012.[3] And since 96 percent of Americans own some kind of mobile phone today, the number of smartphone owners is likely to increase as contracts on standard phones expire and prices of smartphones drop.[4]

Who Uses the Internet?

Even in an age when Internet usage is nearly universal, groups still differ in the extent to which they do and do not use technology. The term for this unequal access to computer technology is the **digital divide.** Historically, one of the largest sources of the digital divide has been income: Poorer people were less likely to have access to new technologies. Today, however, the chief condition fueling the digital divide is age. Still, other demographic factors, including region, income, education, and race, also play a role in predicting whether an individual will use technology, as shown in Table 18.1. Indeed, among certain populations—those aged 18–29, those with a household income over $75,000, and those with a college degree—Internet usage today is essentially universal (with 100 percent, 98 percent, and 98 percent of those populations, respectively, using the Internet).[5]

> **digital divide**
> Unequal access to computer technology.

Historically, the digital divide was also based in geography, with rural areas having less access to swift online connections. But today that gap is shrinking, with 85 percent of rural residents using the Internet, compared with 91 percent of urban residents.[6] Disabilities can also contribute to a digital divide. Today, 89 percent of Americans use the Internet, but Internet use shrinks to 77 percent among adults living with a disability that interferes with daily life, a group that constitutes about 19 percent of the U.S. population.[7]

Although the digital divide is less about income than ever before, even today, affluent individuals are more likely to have smartphones, unlimited data plans, computers, and high-speed Internet connections than are other people. Access to high-speed Internet service even in the world's most affluent democracies can be

TABLE 18.1 ▪ Who Uses the Internet?

ALL ADULTS	90%	**EDUCATION LEVEL**	
SEX		Less than high school	71
Men	90	High school grad	84
Women	91	Some college	95
RACE/ETHNICITY		College +	98
White (Non-Hispanic)	92	**HOUSEHOLD INCOME**	
Black	85	Less than $30,000	82
Hispanic	86	$30,000–$49,999	93
Asian American*	97	$50,000–$74,999	97
AGE GROUP		$75,000+	98
18–29	100	**COMMUNITY TYPE**	
30–49	97	Urban	91
50–64	88	Suburban	94
65 +	73	Rural	85

In general, what demographic groups are most likely to be Internet users? What factors might prevent less likely populations from using the Internet?

*Data for Asian Americans is from 2014 and includes only "English speaking Asians," according to the Pew Research Center.

Source: Pew Research Center.

expensive,[8] and in the developing world, access to technology is nearly always limited. Where information technology is relatively broadly available, as in the United States, several political scientists, including Matthew Hindman[9] and Laura McKenna, argue that access to the Internet produces unequal benefits politically. McKenna notes that "those with lower levels of political capital are lost in a sea of facts, distracted by online poker and joke e-mails, and may be simply not interested in reading political content . . . [while] those who avail themselves of superior political resources on the Internet accelerate their political skills."[10] But evidence indicates that as the use of cellular technology increases (and becomes cheaper) and free Wi-Fi service becomes more widely available, the income-based digital divide will shrink even further. The geographic digital divide, by which residents of rural areas lack access to wired broadband technology, also is changing because of greater availability of Internet access through cellular (wireless) technology, even in many remote regions.

Internet usage today is skewed toward highly educated, high-income earners. But because of the propensity for young people to use the Internet, and because of the increasing use of smartphones, Internet usage is likely to be nearly universal in the future.

Yet, despite the fact that some Americans do not own computers or have online access, the Internet has broadly transformed life in the United States in general and political life specifically. Technology has changed the structure of how information is communicated, how political participation occurs, and how governments govern. As political scientist Michael Cornfield noted: "I can't think of anything except kissing babies that you can't do online."[11] (Today, candidates probably do that by FaceTiming.) In any case, the influence of the Internet has been both positive and negative, and it continues to evolve.

New Forms of Community

Internet technology also facilitates the formation of virtual communities. These networks of interested participants, although different from their IRL (in-real-life) counterparts, share features with those real-world groups.[12] Many blogs, for example, have community leaders, regular contributors, expert commentators, and participants with established roles. Blogs promote civic engagement and participation by disseminating information, exposing readers to the viewpoints of others, providing a forum allowing bloggers to share their own views, serving as a venue for the formation of online communities that can foster feelings of efficacy among participants, and channeling activism, both virtual and real.

virtual communities
Online networks where individuals perform as leaders, information and opinions can be shared, and strategies can be planned, priorities organized, and roles assigned.

Facebook, Instagram, and other social networking sites also create **virtual communities,** online networks—of friends, fans, and groups—where individuals perform as leaders, information and opinions can be shared, and strategies can be planned, priorities organized, and roles assigned. Clay Skirky's *Here Comes Everybody* chronicles why some online entities—including flashmobs and Wikipedia—effectively create organizational structure and channel participation, while others flounder.[13] And the success that individuals enjoy in virtual roles may spill over into real-life behaviors in political organizations. For example, much research indicates that the use of social media sources increases civic engagement and participation in the real world,[14] although some social network users are no more likely to participate in politics than are users of other media.[15] Furthermore, online groups perform many of the same positive civic functions as offline groups, specifically in terms of mobilizing political participation (although not in terms of increasing political knowledge).[16] In many ways, social networking sites undertaking political work closely resemble the in-real-life groups that preceded them and also spur activism that may not have been possible through offline groups.

>> Demographic factors, including income, education, race, and age, play a role in predicting whether an individual will use technology. But because of the propensity for young people to use the Internet, and because of the increasing use of smartphones, Internet usage is likely to be nearly universal in the future.

Mario Tama/Getty Images

Technology Now: Changing How Candidates Campaign and Citizens Participate

The prevalent use of technology in campaigns today, particularly in the wake of the ongoing COVID-19 epidemic during the 2020 presidential election, makes it appear that technology has been the *modus operandi* for decades. The reality, however, is that it has been just a little more than a decade—Barack Obama's first campaign for president in 2008—that an election was considered a watershed in terms of technology use. Dubbed the Web 2.0 election, then-Senator Obama consistently had the advantage, creating a user-friendly website where supporters could access up-to-the-minute campaign news (including links to stories about the candidate and the campaign in the popular media), review talking points, download campaign posters and flyers, make computer-assisted phone calls to undecided voters in swing states, and map out door-to-door canvassing operations in their area.[17] Obama's campaign relied on social media to reach young voters, boasting more Facebook friends than his opponent, Senator John McCain, by a 5-to-1 margin. The Obama campaign and its supporters posted twice as many videos to his official YouTube channel,[18] which bested McCain's in the number of subscribers by an 11-to-1 margin.[19] As the campaign heated up, this vast social network helped to spin news and deflate opposition messages. Finally, new cellular technologies and software platforms provided for a sophisticated get-out-the-vote effort on Election Day, with many "armchair activists" relying on their computers and telephones to encourage turnout. Obama's success made campaign organizers, political candidates, and the media realize how crucial it is to leverage emerging technology to create strategic advantages.

Since that game-changing campaign, technology has continued to transform how American politics happens. Technology has changed not only how campaigns are run, but also how we receive information and how governments provide services. Perhaps lost in all this, and yet of great importance, is technology's promise: Cellular technology and the Internet hold the potential of serving as a means by which people can exercise control over their democracy. And because of the differences in how generations use technology, it holds the greatest promise for younger people. Communications scholar Howard Rheingold argues that the digital media in particular serve as a key avenue through which young people can use their "public voice" to consume and share information.[20] This information is available immediately at any time of the day or night. Since the information superhighway is no longer a one-way street, it provides greater

>> Shrinking the digital divide for the visually impaired: With the RAY app, users who are visually impaired can navigate all phone features with eyes-free operation, thus enabling communication with friends, family, and colleagues. Technology is increasingly making it easier for all people to participate in the civic life of their communities.

Project Ray

opportunities for political conversations, debates, and reactions. It is also increasingly serving as a platform through which communities that influence political life come together and exert influence.

Politics on Demand

Nightly newscasts—once the main method by which Americans got their news—now seem quaint, as information is transmitted instantaneously to our cell phones via the Internet. News websites—including those of all the network and cable news stations, plus sites maintained by Internet service providers—give Internet users access to news stories when they want them instead of at predetermined times. And **news aggregators,** services such as *Google News* and *Apple News,* compile all the stories we want from various outlets, including news headlines, blogs, and podcasts, in one location so that we can consume information quickly. Immediate, on-demand access to political information is a recent phenomenon. Most Americans report that they follow the news using, on average, four different devices or technologies[21] and a variety of ways to connect to the Internet. These users can selectively search for specific information or sign up for alerts to keep informed about public issues that matter to them, building their knowledge base at a finger's click. Moreover, many contemporary news outlets, such as magazines and radio programs, make available downloadable podcasts that give individuals even greater access to reports on social issues, policy initiatives, and politics.

YouTube provides a compelling example of how the evolving Internet has worked to provide on-demand and real-time information. This website, which debuted in February 2005 and is now owned by Google, allows individuals to post and watch original videos. The success of the YouTube experiment would have been inconceivable in a world of dial-up Internet connections that was the norm not too long ago. Today, 500 hours of video are uploaded to YouTube every minute by its 2 billion unique users. More video is uploaded to YouTube in one month than has been broadcast by the three television networks in the past 60 years. YouTube reaches more people just on mobile devices in the United States than any television network does, and people watch 5 billion videos each day.[22]

One way the behemoth of YouTube is affecting political life in the United States is by furnishing an unprecedented amount and variety of on-demand data concerning candidates and elections. Today it is standard practice for candidates to have their own YouTube channels that provide original content (including biographic videos and longer advertisements than would appear on television). But the political impact of the Internet is not limited to the United States, or even to democracies. Indeed, 80 percent of YouTube views come from outside the United States. The interactivity embodied in viewing, commenting, and posting has revolutionized civic discourse globally. Indeed, the Internet has made the world smaller, enabling the global spread of news and information and exerting an influence on national politics that was unheard of before.

Technological Tools: Paving the Two-Way Communication Street

In its early years, the Internet functioned in much the same way that traditional media formats, such as newspapers and periodicals, functioned: It provided a convenient but "one-way" means for people to get information at times determined by the publishers. As **bandwidth**—the amount of data that can travel through a transmission medium in a given time period—has increased, so, too, has the sophistication of web content, as well as the venues and formats that serve as information sources. In the early 1990s, when Tim Berners-Lee invented hypertext and researchers at the University of Illinois introduced the first graphic web browser, Mosaic, Internet users could e-mail, post, and access text files and even communicate via rudimentary bulletin boards. Yet accessing a single page with graphics or photos could take well over a minute. By the mid-1990s, however, businesses and venture capitalists recognized the commercial potential of the World Wide Web. Cable supplanted dial-up modem-driven access and thus expanded bandwidth. Start-up companies and IT giants raced to develop hardware and software products that allowed for the exchange of text, voice, images, and videos in new ways. Cell phone towers sprang up around the world as these devices evolved to provide laptop functionalities. Within just a few years, instant messaging, voicemailing, and posting images, audio, videos, and text had become built into the pattern of 21st-century communication.

As a result, communication is a two-way street, no longer mediated by media outlets. Governments, candidates, their organizations, grassroots organizations, interest groups, and political parties use technology to communicate directly with individuals, and vice versa. And as we first saw in the 2016 presidential election, the openness of the medium of communication has exposed a key vulnerability: as authentic organizations use social media to reach individuals, so too can those who seek to undermine and disrupt democracy, as we discuss later in this chapter. Nonetheless, civic participation has been facilitated by the rise of these forms of communication, which enable conversations about information rather than just information reception. The Internet has also created a hybrid between producers and consumers of news, as many individuals simultaneously consume and produce information in the forms of videos, postings, and websites.

SOURCE ANALYSIS   ANALYZING VISUAL SOURCES

CartoonStock.com

>> President Trump used Twitter more than any other president that preceded him. Occasionally his tweets had typographical errors. One tweet by Trump, "Covfefe" was deleted by Trump six hours later but became an Internet sensation with jokes and speculations as to its meaning. Trump acknowledged it was a mistype of the word "coverage." Trump's frequent use of Twitter to spread his political message enabled him to have a presence among young voters and the public at large but was also criticized for lacking caution. What is the message of the cartoonist here? What are positive and negative consequences of Twitter for American presidents?

Mark Hill/CartoonStock

The Future of Facebook

THEN

(2004)
It was called "The Facebook."

It had 1 million users.

Users posted on a Facebook wall.

Fewer than 800 college networks were part of the Facebook.

Source: Facebook Investor Relations

NOW

It's just Facebook. (And it owns Instagram.)

It has over 2 billion active daily users around the world.

Users post on a Timeline.

Seventy percent of all Americans use Facebook.

NEXT

- How can Facebook ensure that platform users do not intend harm to democracies?

- How might Facebook and Instagram be used as political tools by activists and campaigns in the future?

- What does Facebook's expansion internationally mean for its political utility?

---

blogosphere
The community of bloggers.

Another tool that establishes a new "two-way street" of political communication is the **blogosphere**—the community, or social network, of bloggers. Increasing numbers of people are as likely to subscribe to popular blogs such as *Daily Kos*, *ThinkProgress*, and *RedState* as they are to local or national newspapers. Using blog platforms like Tumblr or Reddit, anyone can blog, and the number of blogs increases enormously each year, with some observers estimating that 1 million blogposts are created each day.[23] As the number has multiplied, their variety and credibility have increased. Research indicates that there is enormous crossover between the blogosphere and traditional media outlets, with many traditional media outlets increasingly providing blogs written by professional journalists.

Blogs provide immediate distribution of information to large numbers of users, spreading news and energizing supporters more rapidly than any other medium. Blogs, like the partisan penny papers that were a specialized medium of information in early American times, also enable people to select sources of information that mimic and confirm their own views.[24] And those who participate online tend to be among the most active citizens in offline forms of engagement as well.

New Campaign Strategies and Modes of Political Participation

Technology has changed the nature of political participation and of political campaigns through the introduction of new strategies that give candidates advantages and enable new modes of political participation.

E-CAMPAIGNING While e-campaigning was an inevitable trend for political candidates, the continuation of the COVID-19 epidemic in the middle of the 2020 U.S. presidential and congressional races kept candidates from running traditional in-person "retail" campaigns, in which candidates interact with voters directly, and pushed them into the digital space. Today, it is common to open up Facebook and see a sponsored page available from your member of Congress or a candidate for other political office. Due to increasingly sophisticated software that recognizes our location, preferences, priorities, opinions, and Internet habits, we are often targeted for political ads. But social media platforms are not the only places where candidates advertise. Increasingly, Google is **remarketing**—that is, targeting Google political ads based on the cookies a user dropped on other websites. So, for example, say during the 2020 congressional election, you visited U.S. Senator John Cornyn's (R-Tex.) campaign website and then read the *Houston Chronicle* online. You may have then seen a Google ad soliciting support for John Cornyn on your screen because when selling ads to campaigns and other organizations, Google recognizes that based on your Internet behavior, you're more likely to contribute to or support causes you have demonstrated an interest in through your online behavior.

Among the first to understand the value that information technology held for political campaigns was Jesse Ventura, a former professional wrestler who served as the governor of Minnesota from 1999 to 2003. He represented the Reform Party, founded in 1995 and supported by people who were disillusioned with what they saw as the corruption and ineffectiveness of the two major parties. Ventura credited the Internet with opening up the political process by enabling grassroots mobilization through **e-campaigning**, the practice of mobilizing voters using the Internet, which allowed an outsider like him to be elected governor. Winning half of the under-30 vote, Ventura conducted the first stage of his campaign without any physical headquarters. Armed with a large e-mail list, he collected pledges of support that short-circuited the traditional doorbell ringing and telephone calls that go with the territory when running for office. His tactics gave him the final surge of voters that he needed to win. Ventura's victory foreshadowed the power of the Internet as a political campaign tool.

The potential of the Internet as a force in political campaigns came into sharp focus again in 2004, when liberal Democrat Governor Howard Dean of Vermont used the Internet extensively for recruiting volunteers and raising money. Dean's efforts proved so successful that other candidates quickly followed his strategy. By the 2008 campaign, every major presidential candidate had a staff of website designers, Internet campaign managers, and blog managers. Today, the tech side of campaigns sometimes overshadows the boots-on-the-ground campaigns taking place in each of the states.

But the rapid expansion of Internet technology also has made it more difficult for presidential campaigns (and administrations) to manage the news.[25] In a pattern established during the campaign, White House staffers often were flummoxed with President Trump's seeming unwillingness to stay "on message" and his ability to ignite firestorms by personally tweeting out incendiary comments. And the omnipresent nature of technology means that campaigns and elected officials must be aware of the always-handy cell phone, with camera and audio recording devices constantly at the ready. Regarding the phenomenon of "going viral," Patrick Healy of *The New York Times* wrote that a "clip may have been trivial, but the brief episode surrounding it illustrated how visual and audio technologies like video streaming have the potential to drive political news in unexpected directions, and how White House candidates are aggressively

remarketing
Targeting political Google ads based on the cookies that a user drops on other websites.

e-campaigning
The practice of mobilizing voters using the Internet.

monitoring and trying to master them."[26] The omnipresent nature of technology also must give candidates pause about behaviors they engaged in even before running for office: In 2005, when Donald Trump bragged to Billy Bush, then of *Access Hollywood*, using vulgar terms about kissing and groping women, that "when you're a star, they let you do it," he certainly could not have imagined that the conversation would be recorded on a hot mic and obtained by the media nearly a decade later as he was pursuing a bid for the presidency.

Although many eschew Twitter as a "toxic" medium, it offers one of the most effective means for immediate distribution of information to large numbers of people, currently boasting 330 million monthly active users who tweet over 500 million messages of 280 or fewer characters each day. And although Twitter has comparatively fewer users than Facebook, it is enormously important among political operatives and many activists—a fact borne out by the important role Donald Trump's use of Twitter had in propelling him to the presidency. While many candidates might view Twitter as a component of their campaign, for Trump it was the centerpiece, a mechanism by which he generated fast, widespread, and unfettered attention. In describing the medium, Trump explained, "I can let people know that they were a fraud. I can let people know that they have no talent, that they didn't know what they're doing. You have a voice."[27] Trump's use of Twitter—including outrageous statements, defended immediately by an army of supporters who generated enormous social media attention that was then covered by the mainstream media— proved a game changer in the practice of presidential campaigns. But when Trump repeatedly used Twitter to make false claims that the 2020 election was "rigged" and had been "stolen" from him, Twitter banned Trump for life from the platform.

Research indicates that in addition to the important role Twitter plays among political consultants and activists, it plays a significant role in shaping public opinion. Researchers Fei Xiong and Yun Liu ran 6 million tweets through a computer algorithm and discovered that the diffusiveness that characterizes initial public opinion on an issue evolves and consolidates quickly, often through

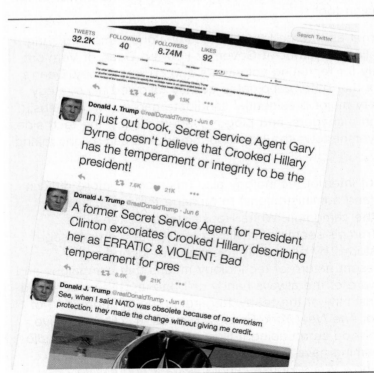

≫ During his 2016 run for president, Donald Trump's use of Twitter—sometimes effective, sometimes damaging to his campaign—demonstrated the rapidly evolving role of technology in political campaigns. And during Trump's 2020 race, he tweeted, without evidence, that casting ballots by mail allows for voter fraud. Twitter placed fact-checking warnings on several of these tweets.

Source: Twitter

endorsements of large groups, which are most effective at swaying opinions. Despite the evolved consensus, small segments of Twitter users who hold minority views may not change, but for candidates and elected officials, it is crucial to act early in order to forge the consensus view, as once public opinion solidifies around an issue on Twitter, it is difficult to change. Thus, **promoted tweets**—that is, targeted advertising—found on a Twitter page that target Twitter users based on whom they follow and who follows them may be an effective tool for candidates and elected officials to shape opinion.

BIG DATA AND MICROTARGETING One of the hallmarks of today's technology is that it allows candidates and other organizations to rely on information derived from **big data,** or large data sets collected from numerous sources (including virtual assistants like Siri, Alexa, and OK Google, online searches, purchases tracked through rewards programs, location tracking, and social media use) that through computational analysis can indicate individual patterns, associations, preferences, and opinions. Candidates can then **microtarget**—that is, use data-mining techniques to track individual voter preferences so they can tailor messages in various forms to generate support, contributions, and votes. For example, NationBuilder is a platform that mines Internet data and enables a candidate, political party, interest group, or other organization to use that mined data to create lists of potential supporters based on their online profiles. Using social networking platforms, organizations can then target these individuals and try to garner their support.

Other programs use surveys to determine voter priorities and preferences and then, based on the potential supporters' responses, campaign canvassers can access already-prescribed talking points to convince potential supporters to vote for their candidate or join their cause. They can even access compelling videos targeted at the respondents on a smartphone or an iPad. Using a smartphone, a canvasser can immediately sign up residents for text or e-mail subscriptions. Once back at headquarters, the canvasser will sync the phone with databases that will track the voter for years and update his or her preferences and concerns.

DIGITAL CAMPAIGNS Candidates can also benefit or suffer from digitally based campaigns. With one click, you can influence how someone you know thinks about a political leader, sometimes creating a **cyber cascade**, which occurs when an electronic document "goes viral" or becomes widely distributed digitally through e-mail, social networking, or video sharing.[28] Today, people who are unsure about the accuracy of claims made on social media or in e-mails can be assisted by such fact-checking websites as Snopes.com and Politifact.com, but many people repost or forward hoax e-mails without checking. Digital campaigns are not always damaging or inaccurate, though.[29] Sometimes social media and e-mail provide a quick means by which those with a common interest, from the environment to school funding, can keep informed about issues and be advised when action is necessary. Groups will often post or e-mail "action alert" messages asking members to contact government officials to pass a particular piece of legislation or to join a protest against a government official or another organization.

From the early days of the Internet, individuals used chain e-mails to garner support and communicate with policymakers. Today, using the Internet site Change.org, any individual can create an **e-petition,** an online petition used as a tool to garner support for a position or cause.

promoted tweets
Targeted advertising found on a Twitter page that targets Twitterers based on whom they follow and who follows them.

big data
Large data sets collected from numerous sources that through computational analysis can indicate individual patterns, associations, preferences, and opinions.

microtarget
Data-mining techniques that facilitate the tracking of individual voter preferences so that tailored messages in various forms can be used to generate support, contributions, and votes.

cyber cascade
What occurs when an electronic document becomes very widely distributed digitally through e-mail, social networking, or video sharing.

e-petition
An online petition used as a tool to garner support for a position or cause.

MACRO-PROTESTING The #MeToo movement, discussed in Chapter 9, provides an example of the power of social media to foster macro-protests. The hashtag became a rallying cry, as women throughout the United States shared their experiences of being sexually harassed in the workplace and lobbied for changes in workplace policies, the enforcement of sexual harassment laws, and the dismissal of serial predators. But what started as a viral hashtag became a much larger social movement, with women advocating for changes to policy in real life. This macro-protesting generated enormous media coverage in traditional news outlets and in online news sites and blogs and created a groundswell of Internet information-sharing and activism through Facebook and Twitter.

E-MOBILIZATION Some organizations have been particularly effective at advocating for candidates and policy changes, or compelling individual actions, by using the Internet to mobilize like-minded individuals. One of the earliest, most influential groups was MoveOn.org, a liberal organization spawned by two Silicon Valley tech entrepreneurs who were frustrated with the partisan bickering surrounding President Bill Clinton's impeachment hearings. On September 18, 1998, the two started an e-petition to "Censure President Clinton and Move On to Pressing Issues Facing the Nation." The petition netted hundreds of thousands of signatures.[30] Today, MoveOn.org has 7 million members, and nearly 1.6 million people "like" it on Facebook. The organization circulates electronic petitions, endorses candidates, and uses traditional advertising to sway public opinion and generate support for candidates.

HACKTIVISM In an era in which everything from our photos of Grandma's last visit to our bank accounts is stored electronically, hackers hold considerable power. **Hacktivism** is the authorized or unauthorized use of or destruction of electronic files in pursuit of a political or social goal. One of the best-known hacktivist groups is a loosely organized collection of individuals called Anonymous. These unidentified individuals collaborate, often in denial-of-service attacks, which prevent targeted servers from functioning by overloading them. For example, in 2015, French members of Anonymous announced a hacking operation against the terror group ISIS following the coordinated attacks in Paris in November of that year. A translation of the video states, "Anonymous from all over the world will hunt you down. You should know that we will find you and we will not let you go."[31] In other acts of hacktivism, the group hacked the United Nations website in 2020 and created a webpage for Taiwan, whose seat at the United Nations was taken in 1971 by the People's Republic of China. It also crippled the mail servers and websites of Monsanto, a biotech giant that supplied Agent Orange to the U.S. government during the Vietnam War and currently produces genetically modified seeds. They also took down over 40 child pornography sites and published the names of hundreds of individuals associated with these sites. Anonymous supported WikiLeaks, a website that released millions of secret government documents. During the 2016 presidential campaign, Hillary Clinton was the subject of a WikiLeaks attack when the organization published e-mails that indicated the Clinton campaign and the Democratic National Committee had worked in tandem against primary challenger U.S. Senator Bernie Sanders (I-Vt.). In the wake of the scandal, the chair of the DNC, Debbie Wasserman Schultz, was forced to resign, and considerable speculation mounted that WikiLeaks would release an "October surprise," a tactical release of information that many speculated would be damaging to Hillary Clinton's presidential bid in the weeks leading in to the November general election. As hackers join forces, they resemble social movements undertaking protests in the real world, yet they have a much wider reach as they wreak havoc or work for the betterment of society.

hacktivism
The authorized or unauthorized use of or destruction of electronic files in pursuit of a political or social goal.

Technology Now: Revolutionizing How Governments Work

Governments use technology more broadly than any other entity. Indeed, the roots of most technological innovation stem from government needs, particularly in the defense and national security arenas. For example, the Internet was developed by the Defense Advanced Research Projects Agency in late 1969 so

CIA ✓
@CIA

Follow

We can neither confirm nor deny that this is our first tweet.

↩ Reply 🔁 Retweet ★ Favorite ••• More

RETWEETS FAVORITES
302,266 188,572

10:49 AM - 6 Jun 2014

» Interpret: How does Twitter allow government agencies to do more effective public relations? What critiques might there be of tweets like the one above?

Source: twitter.com/CIA

that researchers from the U.S. Department of Defense could share information with one another and with defense researchers and scientists in other government agencies and in academia. But today, this technology has grown from its cloak-and-dagger past to represent the most important mechanism by which governments are communicating with and serving their citizens. This phenomenon, known as **e-Government,** is defined as "the employment of the Internet . . . for delivering government information and services to the citizens."[32] By using e-Government, practitioners hope that technology will enable governments to offer their services to citizens efficiently and cost-effectively. E-Government also should increase **transparency,** meaning that citizens will have more and better information about governmental processes as well as services. For example, the Federal Election Commission and state election law agencies have portals that allow citizens to learn about the sources of campaign contributions that elected officials and candidates for office accept.

e-Government
Employment of the Internet for delivering government information and services to the citizens.

transparency
Ability of citizens to have more and better information about governmental processes as well as services.

Today, governments at all levels are using cutting-edge technology to transform the way they operate. In 2020, during the COVID-19 pandemic, necessity compelled governments to use technology to both communicate with citizens and provide services to an entire nation subject to shelter-in-place orders. Almost overnight, reliance on technology became the norm. But this posed a steep learning curve for some, as both individuals and governmental agencies were forced to build a proverbial jet plane while flying it in order to immediately replace in-person communication and delivery of governmental services with digital solutions. Take, for example, the U.S. Congress in March 2020, with up to 200 members participating in conference calls as they tried to create policy during the onset of the pandemic. As Rep. Katie Porter (D-Calif.) described that process in its infancy, "So the most common repeated message from leadership wasn't, 'We're all going to be OK,' it was, 'You might have to unmute your phone.' So there's a real need for Congress to improve our technological capacity, improve our procedures."[33]

Due to these swift changes, many technological structures and habits developed in the wake of the pandemic will remain. For example, once people file their income tax returns online, renew their drivers' license through their state's portal, or use

THEN

NOW

>> In 1976, Apple Computer was founded by Steve Jobs (left), Steve Wozniak (right), and Ronald Wayne (not pictured) in the garage of Jobs's parents. Today, Apple has revolutionized how we communicate, work, and play.

Computer: Sal Veder/AP Images; *iPhone X:* ViktoriyaFivko/Shutterstock

the digital resources available at their local library, they are likely to continue to do so, and so demand for online services will likely continue to increase.

The pandemic generated a variety of governmental responses to the crisis via online services. For example, on the federal level, coronavirus.gov provided a platform for the Centers for Disease Control and Prevention, the Federal Emergency Management Agency, and the White House to provide live updates, information on social distancing, and health-related information. Benefits.gov provided a clearinghouse for information for those who had lost their jobs and needed health care, help for their family, or support for their small businesses. During the height of the crisis, states offered residents updates on the disease via text messages, and they increased the use of technology to, for example, process massive numbers of unemployment claims and facilitate all vote-by-mail elections. Local governments, too, played a pivotal role in providing information, particularly in the areas hardest hit by the pandemic, by reminding residents about public health guidelines, encouraging enforcement, and disseminating information about the availability of local support services.

Increased use of such practices may sometimes help governments rein in spending. For example, the Alabama Department of Conservation and Natural Resources implemented a program that enabled hunters and fishermen to obtain their licenses through an online licensing process, at an estimated cost savings of $200,000 annually.[34] But, as was seen during the coronavirus pandemic, evidence also indicates that technological innovation can be costly. This is because governments often attempt to integrate **legacy systems**—that is, the old way of doing things, either in paper form or using outdated computer systems—while also using the new, more efficient technologies.[35]

In more mundane circumstances, local governments also are using technology to improve the quality of services to residents through smartphone apps. For instance, the geolocation app **Foursquare** uses the iPhone's built-in GPS, or global positioning system (which determines your location using satellite-based radio navigation), to display civic attractions in your area as well as to broadcast your location to your friends. You can even use Foursquare to report a pothole in New York City. Soon governments will also use such programs to provide direct services to residents and visitors. For example, you may be able to search nearby restaurants by health-department grade, enabling you to pass up the sushi restaurant with a C grade in favor of walking the four blocks to its A-rated competitor.

Government leaders, too, rely on technology to help them better communicate more routine messages with their residents. For example, local and state police departments often use text messages, tweets, and Facebook posts to inform citizens about traffic delays or weather advisories. Such communication tools also may alert residents to potential natural disasters, including hurricane, flood, or tornado warnings, and Amber Alerts (regarding missing children) are broadcast to cell phone subscribers. Governments also use the Internet for the more routine business of governing: Open Public Meetings Act notifications; bid alerts for public contracts; minutes of public meetings; video streams of state legislative meetings or city council meetings; texts of adopted laws, policies, or regulations; campaign finance disclosure reports; and even job openings are readily available online.

What Is the Impact of Technology on Political Life?

We know that technology is changing how we participate in the political life of our communities, states, nation, and world. On the whole, these changes signify greater access to information and influence by everyday people. Nonetheless, technology affects political life negatively as well.

Technology Is a Powerful Tool for Protesters and Activists

In May 2020, the world watched as George Floyd lay on the street in Minneapolis, an officer's knee on his neck, with Floyd begging for his life for eight minutes and forty-six seconds. We know this because a bystander captured it on a cell phone. Technology has the power to allow the world to bear witness, and it provides a check on those who would abuse their authority.

That governments can no longer control the use of technology was demonstrated during the 2019 pro-democracy protests in Hong Kong. Because protesters feared that the Chinese government would crack down on them if they used traditional, traceable social media platforms like Facebook and Instagram, they instead relied on messaging apps that offer end-to-end encryption like Signal, and they also relied

legacy systems
The old way of doing things, either in paper form or using outdated computer systems.

Foursquare
Geolocation app that uses an iPhone's built-in GPS to display attractions in your area.

on Telegram, a cloud-based messaging app in which messages can "self-destruct." Organized primarily through these apps, millions of protesters gathered to oppose an extradition agreement that would have allowed Hong Kong residents charged with crimes to be sent to mainland China for trial. As another means of defeating technology, the protesters wore masks and other disguises, fearing that the Beijing government would use facial-recognition technology to identify them and charge them with "rioting"—a crime that carries a 10-year prison sentence. These anonymous, technologically organized protests came to symbolize push-back against mainland China and the demands by Hong Kong's youth to retain their limited autonomy. And after months of massive protests, the extradition plan was scrapped.

Also, consider the 2014 case of ISIS insurgents in Iraq who were battling their way toward Baghdad. There, the government attempted to thwart the rebels' use of social media sites by denying access to Twitter and Facebook, which they were using to communicate. But, as noted in the Hong Kong example, it is becoming increasingly difficult for governments to control access to modern technology. In Iraq, insurgents instead relied on fiber-optic lines and satellite links from Turkish, Jordanian, and Iranian telecommunications companies. Whether pro-democracy protesters or Islamic insurgents, technology provides an enormous tool for the masses, and increasingly this tool is outside the reach of government. The implication for this is twofold: Technology in the hands of some may foster the development of democracies; in the hands of others, it can be used to manipulate or overturn democratic governments.

In democratic societies, technology can also be an equalizer for candidates and for political and community groups. Before information technology, the cost of running a campaign or organizing a group could be prohibitive, but new technology sometimes now means that mobilizing can become much more affordable. Campaign mailers, lawn signs, or informational brochures might be out of reach for some candidates or groups. But today, for some candidates seeking local or state office, technology has revolutionized campaign costs, in some cases eliminating the need for prohibitively expensive network television advertising. Although some forms of technology can be pricey for campaigns, civic organizations, interest groups, and other groups, networking through social media can provide a cost-effective and efficient means of reaching out to like-minded citizens.

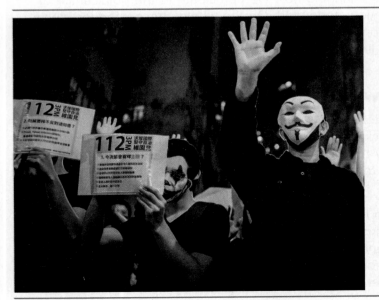

≫ In Hong Kong, democracy activists defied a law banning face coverings, and in this way, they prevented police from using facial recognition technology to identify and prosecute the protesters.

Anthony Wallace/AFP/Getty Images

Technology has put the power to communicate into the hands of the masses and, in many circumstances, taken it outside the reach of government control or manipulation. That reality was demonstrated in the United States when the Russian government, through the activities of hackers, interfered with the 2016 elections. Thus, some viewed the 2016 election as a wake-up call to both secure state election processes and assess the risks presented by social media platforms via which those seeking to undermine democratic processes can quickly and intentionally spread false information.

Technology Increases the Amount of Political Information Available

Earlier in this chapter, we discussed the phenomenon of the on-demand news cycle. Technology has shrunk the news cycle, and candidates and organizations need to be constantly at the ready to spin events to their favor. So although officials may still attempt to manipulate the cycle (by timing announcements to garner more or less news coverage, depending on whether it is good or bad news), the reality is that today elected officials and government agencies are less capable of controlling the news cycle than in decades past. That said, the changing nature of the news makes it more susceptible to manipulation by those who seek to disrupt civic life. In addition, the advent of citizen journalism in the form of blogs, YouTube, and social networking means that relatively obscure events—gaffes or poignant moments—may go viral at any turn and create a whirlwind of unanticipated media coverage (positive or negative) for an official or a candidate.

Finally, as a result of new technology, individuals, and particularly young people, are more interested in political news, even though they may generally lack a depth of knowledge about current events given the nature of the information they receive. This is particularly true of our shrinking global environment. Not so long ago, it would take time for news reports to emerge from hotspots around the world. Today, we are able to watch governments being overthrown live on our iPhones. Individuals may be glued to minute-by-minute coverage of an international crisis, yet these reports often do not explain the context of those events or provide in-depth analysis as to why these situations are unfolding.

What's Next: How Technology Will Continue to Transform the Political Landscape

The effect that today's technology has had on political life was unimaginable a generation ago. We know that nearly all aspects of the political landscape are being transformed, including how we register to vote, how we contribute to candidates, how we are mobilized by campaigns, and how grassroots organizing and fund-raising take place. So, although we can barely speculate about some of the ways that technology will transform political life in the generations to come, there are some very clear trends that we can say with certainty will prove to be political game-changers.

One of the most important transformative tools for politics is in the palm of your hand. Smartphone apps will continue to facilitate increasingly sophisticated targeting operations and to help candidates and other organizations create voter profiles that track voter concerns and opinions of candidates, thus facilitating enormously strategic get-out-the-vote efforts. Moreover, candidates, political parties, and interest groups are likely to invest great sums to manipulate the social media environment in favor of their candidate or their cause, using **bots**

bots
computer programs or computers designed to perform automatic repetitive or malicious actions

and other means similar to those Russian operatives used to influence the 2016 presidential election. In the future, it is likely that smaller, wearable (even implantable) devices will transform our political, social, and economic lives by altering our real-life perceptions. Imagine, for example, the experience of going on a blind date 25 years from now: Will our glasses perform facial recognition and immediately scour the Internet for the date's social networking profile, work history, past purchases, and so on?

Decades ago, campaigns were transformed by television advertising. Suddenly a new set of candidate characteristics became mandatory, including the ability to present well on television, and campaigns had to develop expertise in media strategy. Campaign television advertising also increased negativity in campaigns, and negative charges could be spread to wider audiences than through older means of reaching voters. In the future, new strategies will emerge as paramount, as video advertisements on such outlets as YouTube and Hulu increasingly replace television ads. With fewer people watching television, and fewer still watching television in real time (a necessity for ad viewing), greater numbers of political advertisements will be seen on new IT venues. Because the length of a YouTube user session is just 15 minutes,[36] in all likelihood campaign ads will shrink to become mini sound bites that appear before videos. Decades ago, many television ads were 60 seconds long. Then 30-second ads became more common. Now, 15-second video ads appear before feature videos that have been targeted by campaigns as having viewers who will likely be sympathetic to the candidate's or group's message.

But also changing the nature of political advertising will be data-driven Internet advertising that capitalizes on technology to build better databases for campaigns. By collecting cookies from sites that constituents use, companies can strategically target their candidate- and issue-based advertising. Increasingly, these ads will be nonstatic: By asking viewers to click through to the campaign's website, campaigns can drop cookies to examine viewership and offer opportunities to sign up for e-mail lists, follow on Twitter, friend on Facebook, or otherwise collect identifying information about viewers.

Another area of politics affected by technological change is the move away from in-person balloting. As the COVID-19 virus roared across the United States in 2020, state after state faced the challenge of enabling voters to cast their ballots remotely. Many states converted entirely to vote-by-mail systems, but in the future, all states will likely pursue the goal of secure online balloting. Although election policy expert Roy Saltman asserts that Americans have long perceived technology as a natural way to expand the participating franchise,[37] evidence shows that, in the future, new technologies will particularly transform how military service members and citizens living abroad will be enfranchised. This will prove increasingly important for countries with high numbers of educated citizens living abroad, including India,Turkey, and other diaspora.

The Downside of Technology in Politics

The positive effects of information technology are undeniable, but technology also presents a series of challenges both to users and to society. As technology grows more sophisticated, privacy issues are becoming critical.[38] And with such an abundance of information readily available, one key challenge for those who rely on the Internet is the problem of evaluating the accuracy of information. Another is the threat of cyber attacks that can potentially upend communication, commerce, and governmental operations, including those related to security. Finally, balancing free speech rights while protecting the rights of individuals who face physical threats or threats to their reputations is another issue with which modern societies are struggling.

Election Infiltration

In the wake of the 2016 election, the U.S. intelligence community—including the Central Intelligence Agency, the Federal Bureau of Investigation, and the Director of National Intelligence—concluded that top Russian officials concocted and implemented a covert plan to influence the outcome of the U.S. elections. The Russians used various strategies: First, they hacked internal communications from Hillary Clinton's campaign and the Democratic National Committee and released them to the public. Also, using bots, they created an elaborate social media structure designed to foment dissension and division within the American electorate and to undermine Clinton's campaign (see "Analyzing the Sources"). Take one day in 2016: On May 21, Russian **trolls** operating out of a "troll farm" in St. Petersburg, Russia, used Facebook pages to organize both an anti-Islam protest and a pro-Islam counterprotest at the same location in Houston. All told, almost 15,000 targeted Facebook users viewed the fake Russian Facebook pages, "Stop Islamization of Texas" and "Save Islamic Knowledge."

trolls
those who deliberately harass or antagonize others online by posting inflammatory or offensive content, with the intention to disrupt

The allegations against the Russians were investigated by U.S. special counsel Robert Mueller, who also investigated whether anyone associated with Donald Trump's presidential campaign unwittingly or intentionally colluded with the Russians. Mueller filed charges against 13 Russian nationals and three Russian entities for perpetrating an illegal "information warfare" scheme to disrupt the 2016 presidential election and assist the candidacy of President Donald Trump.

But just as the U.S. intelligence community agreed that Russia interfered with the 2016 U.S. presidential election, they also agreed that what happened in 2016 was not an isolated incident and that the tactical mission of undermining the democratic process in which citizens elect government leaders in a fair and free method was an intentional, consistent strategy. Evidence suggested that Russia attempted to interfere with various European elections as well and had also set its sights on the 2020 U.S. presidential election. In February of that year, the U.S.

Trolling for Votes

In the 18 months leading up to the 2016 presidential election, about 126 million Americans saw Facebook content that included ads and posts generated by Russian operatives. Using bots, the Russians sought to influence the outcome of the election and foment divisions and dissent among the American people. Using Facebook's advertiser tools, the Russians targeted Americans based on their self-professed "likes"—algorithms that indicate users' political preferences—and demographic characteristics including age, sex, and geography.

Source: BM (Facebook event)

Source: Being Patriotic (Facebook event)

Practice Analytical Thinking

1. Why would Russian operatives seek to create divisions within the American electorate?

2. In the wake of the 2016 disinformation campaign, Facebook changed its advertising policy for the 2020 elections. Today, what are the obstacles to preventing such covert disinformation attacks? Are these obstacles present on all forms of social media?

3. How can social media users protect themselves from being the target of disinformation campaigns?

intelligence community briefed members of the House Intelligence Committee on their investigation, concluding that Russia was interfering in the 2020 election. The intelligence community separately assessed that Russia viewed President Trump favorably.[39] Moreover, during the presidential race, evidence suggested that Russia's tactics had changed from creating social media content that would foment division to relying on trolls to amplify organically created posts highlighting division and conspiracy theories.[40]

Cyber Threats

Increasingly, cyber threats—that is, the possibility that a nation or group might intentionally do damage to the technological or financial infrastructure—are a reality. For example, using the international bank messaging system Swift (the Society for Worldwide Interbank Financial Telecommunication), a super-secure network that banks use to authorize payments from one account to another, hackers have succeeded in pulling off digital heists that eventually could threaten a nation's economy. In one such heist, hackers stole $81 million from Bangladesh's central bank in a planned and well-organized attack; when banking officials attempted to contact the Bangladesh bank to alert it about the breach, it was a weekend in Bangladesh. By the time the Bangladeshi bankers discovered the missing funds, it was a weekend in the United States. The attack eventually was linked to a hacking group called "Lazarus," based in North Korea, which has attacked, or has attempted to attack, banks in Costa Rica, Ethiopia, Gabon, India, Indonesia, Iraq, Kenya, Malaysia, Nigeria, Poland, Taiwan, Thailand, and Uruguay. In addition, the U.S. Justice Department indicted seven hackers it claimed attacked U.S. banks' public websites numerous times and also broke into the computer facility at a dam in Rye, New York, allegedly to disrupt the dam's operation. The individuals indicted are associated with the government of Iran. This is the first case in which state-sponsored individuals have been charged with hacking with an intent to disrupt the U.S. economy.

State-sponsored cyber threats typically involve efforts to learn about financial and infrastructure systems, in case that information could be used to further the state's goals (militarily, economically, or politically). Sometimes cyber threats are retaliatory. But whether launched for information-gathering purposes or seeking to do damage, such threats to the U.S. technological structure will likely continue to be a great risk as rogue states and disgruntled groups continue to grow more technologically sophisticated.

Domestic Surveillance, Data Breaches, and Other Privacy Issues

Today, we see that the roots of technological innovation continue to shape how governments use technology. In June 2013, a series of newspaper articles around the world described a domestic surveillance operation being conducted by the U.S. National Security Agency (NSA). A former CIA employee, Edward Snowden, leaked information that revealed that the NSA had been monitoring the actions of Americans on U.S. soil, including collecting metadata of phone communications, e-mail traffic, and other Internet communications. The NSA's domestic surveillance program began under the George W. Bush administration, and Snowden held off on whistleblowing in the hopes that President Obama would end the program after being elected. Snowden was disappointed when Obama continued and then expanded the program, so Snowden leaked documents revealing the extent of the United States's domestic surveillance program. Among the revelations was the fact that the NSA and 16 other spying agencies, working with a $56 billion "black budget,"[41] conducted a multitude of operations, including:

- Compelling U.S. telecommunications corporations, including Verizon, to provide information on a daily basis concerning telephone calls both within the United States and between the United States and other nations.[42]

- Monitoring the location of cell phones and tracking 5 billion records each day.[43]

- Using cookies acquired by Google to identify and locate targets for government hacking.[44]

- Monitoring foreign communications traffic occurring over Microsoft, Google, Yahoo!, Facebook, PalTalk, YouTube, Skype, AOL, and Apple through a secret NSA program named PRISM,[45] while copying metadata flowing from Yahoo! and Google across fiber-optic cables[46] through a program called MUSCULAR.

- Searching e-mails, online chats, and "nearly everything a typical user does on the Internet" using XKeyscore,[47] a top-secret data-mining analytical tool.

- Infiltrating multiplayer video games, including Xbox Live, World of Warcraft, and Second Life, in collaboration with its British counterpart, Government Communications Headquarters (GCHQ), in an effort to catch real-life terrorists.[48]

>> Edward Snowden, a computer specialist who worked for the Central Intelligence Agency and the National Security Agency (NSA), released classified documents in 2013 that revealed that the NSA had engaged in a vast array of domestic surveillance tactics.

Laurence Topham/Guardian/eyevine/Redux

Snowden, who was both hailed as a hero whistleblower and reviled as a traitor to his country, feared for his own life as well as the lives of the journalists with whom he entrusted his information. He currently lives in Russia, where he has temporary asylum, though he has stated that he would like to repatriate back to the United States, hoping the felony espionage charges that await him will eventually be resolved or that he will someday be granted a presidential pardon.

Today, government surveillance of our use of technology means that not just our communications can be monitored but also our whereabouts, our physical appearance, our habits, our associations with others, and even—to the extent that our Google search history indicates our interests—our thoughts. We live in an era in which society is attempting to balance the value that technology brings with the protection of individuals' rights. Today, privacy concerns center on the tools that law enforcement and other government officials have at their disposal to monitor individuals and their locations. But corporations also can access an enormous volume of material—from our grocery shopping habits to the kinds of apps we buy for our phones—and the challenges that our society faces will escalate with new technological innovations. Most people concerned with the issue of government surveillance agree that increased technological developments—through encryption and other surveillance-blocking mechanisms—hold the greatest promise in the potential to protect our privacy. But there is increased concern that these mechanisms will also be used by terrorists and others who would use the privacy protections offered by these new technologies to do harm.

Edward Snowden ✓
@Snowden

+ Follow

Can you hear me now?

RETWEETS   LIKES
120,601   122,793

9:00 AM - 29 Sep 2015

» Edward Snowden, who has nearly 4 million Twitter followers, follows only the National Security Agency, the agency Snowden's whistleblowing documents revealed as conducting domestic surveillance. At left is his tweet to the NSA.

Interpret: Compare this with the earlier tweet from the CIA. How has Twitter changed the ways that Americans interact with government? Who is the audience for these tweets? Does the public nature of Twitter change the way that citizens, government agencies, and political figures communicate?

Source: twitter.com/Snowden

The NSA was granted broad powers by the Foreign Intelligence Surveillance Act (FISA) Amendments passed in 2008, which forced U.S. telecommunications companies to provide information to the NSA as part of its domestic surveillance program. But unlike traditional law enforcement agencies, which have been overseen by the courts (which, for example, might produce a warrant if there is probable cause), NSA's domestic surveillance program lacked oversight. The NSA asserts that such oversight—whether by Congress or the courts—would render the program less effective. This argument has resonated when discussing foreign targets abroad, but after Edward Snowden's revelation that the NSA was spying on U.S. citizens in the United States, there was significant public outcry about these practices, which many Americans perceive as a violation of their Fourth Amendment rights. In 2015, Congress approved and President Obama signed the USA Freedom Act, a significant rollback of NSA powers, banning the agency from collecting and storing Americans' telephone dialing records unless expressly granted that legal authority by a court order.

The increasing prevalence of cloud computing, whereby files are stored on remote servers rather than on users' personal hard drives, means that our information may be more vulnerable to misuse by corporations, government officials, and hackers than if we stored our data privately. For example, web-based e-mail services (Gmail, Outlook, Yahoo!, and so on), certain word processing and spreadsheet programs (such as those stored on a Google Drive), and photo storage applications (Picasa, Snapfish) hold our information "in the cloud." Although these sites strive to protect users' privacy, the sheer volume of information available may lead to vulnerabilities as a result of both intentional damage through hacking and unintentional potential damage through technological glitches.

» Edward Snowden revealed that the National Security Agency, headquartered in Fort Meade, Maryland, has engaged in extensive efforts to monitor the activities, communications, and whereabouts of Americans living in the United States.

Handout/NSA/Getty Images

Fake News and the Issue of Accuracy

The explosion of the Internet into politics has also opened up a Pandora's box of misinformation. Unlike newspapers, magazines, and television networks, where editors and fact-checkers are responsible for ensuring accuracy, the Internet is almost entirely unmonitored. The problem of misinformation is compounded when the president himself communicates directly to the people using social media and spreads inaccurate information, whether unwittingly or intentionally. Consider, for example, the statements President Trump made in only eight weeks during the initial outbreak of the COVID-19 pandemic in the United States:

- "No, not at all. We have it totally under control. It's one person coming in from China, and we have it under control. It's going to be just fine." (January 20, 2020)

- "We're going to be pretty soon at only five people. And we could be at just one or two people over the next short period of time. So we've had very good luck." (February 26, 2020)

- "No, I'm not concerned at all. No, I'm not. No, we've done a great job." (March 7, 2020)

- "The Fake News Media and their partner, the Democrat Party, is doing everything within its semi-considerable power (it used to be greater!) to inflame the CoronaVirus situation, far beyond what the facts would warrant. Surgeon General, 'The risk is low to the average American.'" (March 9, 2020)

- "This is a pandemic. I felt it was a pandemic long before it was called a pandemic. All you had to do is look at other countries; I think now it's in almost 120 countries all over the world. No, I've always viewed it as very serious. There was no difference yesterday from days before." (March 20, 2020)

In presidencies past, of course, a president might have misspoken, engaged in hyperbole, or simply gotten his facts wrong. Today, however, with the presence of live news feeds, social media, and a traditional media, the capacity to fact-check every statement is strained, which means that "alternate facts" are fed to the American people, who may accept them as fact because of the source of the information, the prestige of the office, and the medium by which they have been conveyed. It is rational, for example, that when the president of the United States tells you that he is not concerned, you yourself would be reassured and also not concerned that a global pandemic would soon be ravaging the nation.

In political campaigns, misinformation can be devastating, and once a damaging charge is sounded, it is often almost impossible to unring that bell, even if the allegations are false. For example, a long-standing issue that dogged President Obama throughout his first term in office was that several Internet sites, including the Drudge Report,[49] questioned his U.S. citizenship. The allegations followed the president from the early days of his 2008 presidential campaign until he released the long-form copy of his birth certificate in April 2011. Indeed, some "hybrid news sites," including Newslo, pepper fact-based news stories with outlandish fictions and enable readers to "Show Facts" or "Hide Facts." One Newslo story that was published (and was subsequently shared over the Internet as true) was the claim that Donald Trump had suggested dropping nuclear bombs on Mexico if it refused to build his proposed wall separating the nation from the United States. While Trump did propose the wall, he never proposed using nuclear weapons to compel Mexico to comply with his plan.

Sophisticated technology enables the creation of "deepfake videos" which are videos that make a person appear to say or do something they never said or did. It has become easier than ever to create these artificial videos. In May 2020, a deepfake video of House Speaker Nancy Pelosi slowed down her speech and appeared to make her slur her words. This video was an effort by Pelosi's political opponents to discredit her. In a feud with Speaker Pelosi, President Trump tweeted the video to his supporters suggesting that she was stammering during a news conference. The video received over 2.5 million views.

Under the right set of circumstances, deepfakes can influence voters. Anyone can make a deepfake to discredit a political opponent during a campaign, including foreign nationals. Deepfakes are a form of misinformation in politics—they are essentially the dissemination of a lie. There is no current government policy on deepfakes, but some social media organizations such as Facebook have attempted to detect and remove deepfakes before they go viral. Social media companies have the right to police their own sites, but it is more challenging for the government to address this type of speech. The First Amendment was designed to protect all speech, especially political speech. While libel and slander are not necessarily protected speech, the government may not be able to ban deepfakes, and individuals would need to rely on litigation to attempt to protect themselves. Citizens who want to make informed choices will need the tools to evaluate the content, which may also be very challenging.

Critical Thinking

1. How does President Trump's tweet of the deepfake video demonstrate the presidential power to use the bully pulpit?

2. What was the potential impact of President Trump's use of the video?

3. How might citizens educate themselves to recognize deepfakes?

4. Are you concerned about the role of deepfake videos in political campaigns? Why or why not?

5. What actions can be taken to address the problem of deepfakes spreading misinformation in the political process, and who should take those actions?

Sources: https://www.brookings.edu/blog/techtank/2019/06/03/deepfakes-social-media-and-the-2020-election/

https://www.cbsnews.com/news/doctored-nancy-pelosi-video-highlights-threat-of-deepfake-tech-2019-05-25/

The sheer volume of information available online can in itself create a problem. To become and remain accurately informed, voters and other individuals must develop the critical thinking skills needed to discern what information is valuable (and sometimes rely on online fact-checking sites like Snopes.com to validate claims that seem outlandish). Consumers of information also need to consider the sources of information and determine the sources' biases or perspectives. In short, devoid of a trusted source of information, we should treat many claims made on the Internet with a healthy dose of skepticism.[50]

A Tool for Terrorists: Recruiting, Communicating, Operationalizing

Tashfeen Malik and Syed Farook, a married couple who were the parents of a six-month-old baby and who had been radicalized by the terror group ISIS, killed 14 people and seriously injured 22 others when they fired on a gathering of Farook's colleagues in San Bernardino, California, in 2015. Malik and Farook were later killed in a gun battle with police. In the aftermath, law enforcement authorities sought access to Farook's iPhone, believing that information on it could lead investigators to other potential targets the couple may have identified, to contacts with the terror group ISIS and to other United States–based terror cells. Apple, which had manufactured the phone, argued that it did not have the capability to override the four-digit password protection the phone had. The federal government sued Apple, and U.S. Magistrate Judge Sheri Pym ruled in favor of the Federal Bureau of Investigation's request for Apple to disable a security feature that would wipe out data on Farook's iPhone if investigators trying to access it made more than 10 incorrect password attempts. Apple challenged the ruling, and while the case was wending its way through legal channels, the FBI recovered the phone's information. It did so by hiring so-called grey hat hackers, those who exploit small glitches in companies' operating systems and sell them sometimes to the government, sometimes to the companies themselves. While the solution provided to the FBI would work on only a small number of iPhones, the issue of whether tech companies should assist governments in their attempts to get information that might thwart criminal activities, including terrorist attacks, remains a controversial one. Law enforcement officials argue that hardware-related security measures prevent them from accessing information about a wide variety of illegal activity, including issues related to illegal drug distribution, human trafficking, and potential terror plots.

But hardware is not the only obstacle for law enforcement officials: In light of revelations about the reliance of terror cells on encrypted messaging systems like WhatsApp, Telegram, and Signal, government officials in both the United States and Europe have increased calls for regulation, with Britain and France at various points entertaining the idea of banning encryption technologies. But the tech industries, especially Apple CEO Tim Cook, have fought back, arguing, for instance, that Apple's encryption technology in its iMessaging system protects consumers from cyber criminals. Other supporters of encryption note that the technology also has the ability to protect pro-democracy activists from authoritarian governments that would persecute those advocating for democracy without the protection that encryption provides.

Technology platforms, particularly social media sites, have proved to be an important recruiting and organizational tool for terrorists. By their very nature, social media sites encourage discourse across a wide spectrum of populations, and because they are open to everyone, they have been used to radicalize individuals sympathetic to their cause. In recognition of that reality, Twitter announced the suspension of 125,000 accounts associated with promoting terrorist acts, primarily related to ISIS, as well as the intent to step up efforts to review accounts connected to extremism so that they could be deactivated more quickly: "Like most people around the world, we are horrified by the atrocities perpetrated by extremist groups. We condemn the use of Twitter to promote terrorism and the Twitter Rules make it clear that this type of behavior, or any violent threat, is not permitted on our service."[51]

Despite the efforts by Twitter and other social media platforms, widespread evidence exists that ISIS continues to recruit and reach out to potential members—sometimes young people living in Western democracies—by relying on social media.[52]

Twitter and other tech companies including Facebook and YouTube are facing increasing criticism that the sites facilitate terrorism by providing a platform that extremists can use to attract sympathizers and communicate and organize attacks. Such a process was described in the *New York Times* podcast "The Caliphate," in which journalist Rukmini Callimachi interviews a Canadian former ISIS recruit who describes the role Twitter and Instagram played in his recruitment.[53] But because these sites are primarily platforms for the constant flow of user-generated content, regulation is difficult and relies on users themselves to flag inappropriate content so that site reviewers can determine whether the postings are appropriate.

Fomenting Polarized Partisanship and Extremism

Information technology can foment increased extremism domestically. The Internet makes selective exposure—the phenomenon of individuals choosing to read or view information that enforces their already-held beliefs while rejecting sources that provide contradictory views—quite easy. This lack of exposure to contradictory sources of information means that people's views—even the most extreme—will only be confirmed and reinforced. The lack of contradictory information may steer people to more-polarized ideological viewpoints, as the moderate, compromising views are eschewed by those relying on partisan information. This phenomenon is particularly problematic when foreign nations or other organizations intentionally spawn hatred, dissent, and extremism. Some research indicates that this scenario has increased political polarization in the United States and has fostered the adoption of more extremist political viewpoints.[54]

The Internet has also contributed to the decline in civility in political discourse in the United States. In describing the political climate regarding threats to presidential candidates, Secret Service director Mark Sullivan noted that "historically, it's the same issues we've always had and the same things people are upset about.

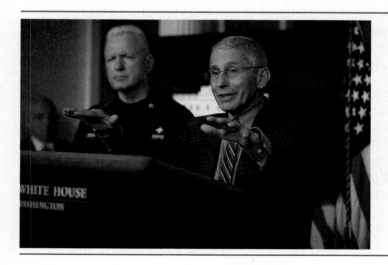

>> Anthony Fauci (right), director of the National Institute of Allergy and Infectious Diseases, became the face of the U.S. government's COVID-19 response during President Trump's nightly news conferences. When Fauci earned a reputation for correcting misstatements made by Trump, he faced extremist backlash online and received death threats.

Chip Somodevilla/Getty Images

There are just a lot more venues for people to put it out there, including the Internet."[55] Such was the case in March 2020 with Anthony Fauci, the top U.S. infectious-diseases expert who guided the government's response to the corona-virus pandemic. Fauci was one of a few members of the Trump administration to correct President Trump's public misstatements, following which he faced death threats, which forced the government to step up his security protection.

But threats need not only be physical: Some bloggers and anonymous message-board posters seek to destroy their opponents' reputations. The nature of the Internet means that lies and slanderous accusations can often be leveled with no consequence to the poster. As noted earlier, sometimes the claims—made via e-mail messages, Facebook postings, and/or tweets—are quite sophisticated and seem believable.

The Dominance of "Big Tech"

Another concern is the disproportionate influence "big tech" plays in our everyday lives, and the potentially corrupting influence technology companies *could* have. Arguing that "big tech has become way too powerful," former Secretary of Labor Robert B. Reich notes that the "most valuable intellectual properties are platforms so widely used that everyone *else* has to use them, too. Think of standard operating systems like Microsoft's Windows or Google's Android; Google's search engine; Amazon's shopping system; and Facebook's communication network. Google runs two-thirds of all searches in the United States. Amazon sells more than 40 percent of new books. Facebook has nearly 1.5 billion active monthly users worldwide. This is where the money is. . . . Sure, big platforms let creators showcase and introduce new apps, songs, books, videos and other content. But almost all of the profits go to the platforms' owners, who have all of the bargaining power."[56] Reich argues that tech monopolies have become economic and political powerhouses that have effectively controlled how markets are regulated (or not), thus ratcheting up their power even more by controlling the competitive environment.

The Internet and Free Speech

Part of the political conundrum faced by Americans is the desire to balance free speech rights with the ability of government to protect those whose person or reputation may be threatened by someone's speech. The rise of the Internet has overwhelmed our guarantees of free speech, with the volume and content of speech growing faster than society's ability to digest their impact. In parts of Europe, for example, hate speech on the Internet is forbidden and carefully regulated; in the United States, it is not. As a result, a large number of hate sites register their domains in the United States, where they can operate freely and spew their venom throughout the world without fear of government interference.

The United States is deeply wedded to the principle, refusing to regulate the Internet or any other vehicle of free speech. Throughout the nation's history, speech of all kinds has been protected, with periodic exceptions for sedition in wartime, as well as for child pornography and hate speech in peacetime. Americans have great tolerance for language and believe that fringe groups can flourish freely in a democracy without risking tears in the fabric of society. But as the threat of terrorism grows, many citizens expect lawmakers to do whatever is necessary—including setting limits on free speech—to curb violence spawned by the prevalence of hate on the Internet.[57]

Regulation of the Internet: Is It Necessary?

When Noah Kravitz left his job as an editor and videoblogger at PhoneDog, a company that reviews cell phones and other electronics, he took his Twitter account and his 17,000 followers with him. The U.S. District Court in Northern California was asked to decide whether the account and the followers are Kravitz's or whether they are legally comparable to a customer list and thus the possession of PhoneDog. The case offers another example of how technology has presented an abundance of disputes with which the law has yet to keep up. The Internet raises issues that could not have been foreseen by the framers of the U.S. Constitution. Some issues concern contract law; others, privacy rights; yet others, freedom of speech, the press, and assembly. Take, for example, freedom of the press: The framers had to be concerned only with print media when they guaranteed this freedom, one of the fundamental liberties they ensured in the Bill of Rights. As media evolved into formats such as radio and television, government created a regulatory structure to govern them as well. But technology has outpaced the government's ability to regulate certain forms of electronic media, including the Internet and cellular technology.

Take, for example, the question of control over the business of the media (see "Thinking Critically"). The issue, a controversial one, centers on **net neutrality:** the idea that Internet traffic—e-mail, websites, videos, and phone calls—should flow through the Internet pipeline without interference or discrimination by those who own or are running the pipeline. *Should* these broadband behemoths be able to use their market power to control information or to favor certain clients online? Critics charge that congressional passage of legislation supporting the service providers would destroy the neutrality and openness of the Internet. Tim Berners-Lee, the inventor of the World Wide Web, says: "The neutral communications medium is essential to our society. . . . It is the basis of democracy, by which a community should decide what to do."[58] President Obama agreed, and after a period of public comment during which over 4 million Americans voiced their views on net neutrality, in 2015 the Federal Communications Commission voted to preserve the open Internet, by adopting regulations in three key areas. First, the FCC prohibited broadband providers from blocking lawful content, services, applications, or devices. The regulations also banned providers from slowing down specific services or applications (a practice called *throttling* in the broadband industry). The third area of regulation prevented providers from isolating Internet traffic based on who is sending or receiving data, what the data is, or whether the content is viewed as competitive to the providers' own content. So, for example, under these regulations, Comcast (a broadband provider) would have been prohibited from blocking or throttling Netflix (so that Comcast subscribers would be forced to rely on Comcast's on-demand video service) or isolating content that Netflix provides. In 2017, President Trump's appointee as FCC chairman, Ajit Pai, announced a rollback of the net neutrality order, though changes dragged because of pending lawsuits regarding the rule changes. Following a ruling by the U.S. Court of Appeals for the D.C. Circuit, which largely upheld the net neutrality rollback, the FCC initiated a court-mandated review by the agency to evaluate the effect of the decision.

net neutrality
The idea that Internet traffic should flow through the Internet pipeline without interference or discrimination by those who own or are running the pipeline.

Should We Regulate the Internet Infrastructure?

THE ISSUE: The technological revolution has brought ongoing, exponential growth in Internet traffic. As rising numbers of people turn to the Internet for more and more uses—from viewing videos online to sending pictures to Grandma, and from buying gifts and personal items to calling friends and relatives—the volume of information that the Internet's broadband infrastructure must transmit is becoming overwhelming. The owners of that infrastructure—corporate giants such as AT&T, Verizon, and Comcast—are seeking legislation and pursuing lawsuits that would allow them to charge companies that produce high volumes of traffic. In effect, this legislation would set up a two-tiered system of broadband access, in which one tier is an "express lane" with tolls and the other is an older, slower lane with free access. One problem is that many of today's services (video streaming, for example) require the faster access to make them effective. Several Republican members of Congress have sponsored measures that would create a two-tiered system, but in 2015, the Federal Communications Commission voted by a 3-to-2 margin for regulations that would preserve the open Internet, a decision that FCC chairman Ajit Pai reversed. Industry leaders and some members of Congress supported Pai's rollback of net neutrality.

YES: We need a two-tiered system of broadband access. The telecommunications titans in command of the Internet infrastructure argue that in order to keep up with the increasing demand for broadband space, they will continually have to expand and improve the system. These improvements cost money, and companies should be able to pass the costs and benefits on to their customers. Corporate advocates of a two-tiered system of broadband access also are interested in providing premium-quality broadband service to their own clientele. Thus, for example, Verizon wants to ensure that its Internet subscribers (rather than the subscribers of its competitors) have high-quality access to the broadband infrastructure technology that Verizon owns, so that its subscribers do not get caught in an Internet traffic jam.

NO: "Fast Lane" services would hurt both businesses and consumers. The FCC adopted regulations for Preserving a Free and Open Internet, stating that providers must have transparency of network management practices, not block lawful content, and not unreasonably discriminate in transmitting lawful network traffic. A broad coalition of businesses and interest groups, including savetheinternet.com, oppose measures that would enable broadband providers to charge for their services. These entities also include such firms as Microsoft, Google, eBay, and Yahoo! and powerful citizen organizations such as the American Association of Retired Persons (AARP).

It is the very accessibility of the Internet that has fostered strong business growth. Start-ups such as YouTube and Vonage Internet phone service are examples of ventures that might not have been able to compete and survive in a tiered broadband system. A paying system could prevent future Internet business development.

WHAT DO YOU THINK?

1. Should the FCC or Congress accept or reject proposals to create a for-fee fast lane for Internet traffic? Why? Or do you think that the marketplace should determine which services get faster access to broadband lines? If so, why would the latter be preferable?

2. What effect could the creation of a two-tiered Internet structure have on Internet business development? On national security?

3. Should the federal government help to defray the costs of improvements to the Internet infrastructure? Why or why not?

OTHER APPROACHES: Tax dollars should be used to expand the Internet infrastructure. Without essential maintenance and expansion, the Internet infrastructure will be incapable of keeping up with soaring demand. In addition, the security of the infrastructure is crucial to continued business activity and corporate financial growth, as well as to national economic health. Broadband availability is a national security issue, because if law enforcers, airports, hospitals, nuclear power plants, and first responders do not have adequate or immediate access to the information they need to perform their jobs, human lives are at risk. Because of these critical financial and security implications, a tax or user fee could be instituted that would pay for Internet infrastructure improvements.

Conclusion: Thinking Critically About What's Next in Politics and Technology

Technology has revolutionized how politics happens in the United States, and it is revolutionizing political life throughout the world. One of the most remarkable characteristics of the technological revolution has been the swiftness of the transformation it has propelled. Though the Internet is only 30 years old, it has spawned earth-shattering changes in our political lives and indeed throughout society. And although there remains a digital divide both within and outside the United States, that divide is shrinking domestically. Because of cellular technology and increasing access to the Internet, information technology represents one of the most powerful tools in helping people communicate with government officials, secure political information, and participate in the political life of their communities, states, and country.

Whether through traditional websites, blogging, social media, or politically specific technological platforms, technology has transformed political life by making information more easily available. But the sheer volume of information means that consumers must be wary of the information they receive and aware of concerted efforts to misinform and to foster divisions.

In particular, social media has opened up a host of opportunities for political communication and participation, but also has exposed a vulnerability enabling those who would do democracy harm to infiltrate. In addition to providing avenues of communication between constituents and elected officials, among candidate or issue supporters, and between governments and the people they serve, technology is providing more efficient and cost-effective means by which governments can provide services. In the future, technology will become a more integrated and essential part of our lives, having sweeping implications for how campaigns, governments, and citizens use technology in political life.

References

1. "Ordnance Survey Offers Free Data Access," *BBC News*, April 1, 2010.

2. D. M. Boyd and N. B. Ellison, "Social Network Sites: Definition, History, and Scholarship," *Journal of Computer-Mediated Communication* 13 (2007), article 11.

3. Mobile Fact Sheet, June 12, 2019, www.pewresearch.org/internet/fact-sheet/mobile/.

4. www.pewinternet.org/fact-sheet/mobile/.

5. Pew Research Center, "Internet/Broadband Fact Sheet."

6. Ibid.

7. Susannah Fox, "Americans Living with Disability and Their Technology Profile," Pew Internet and American Life Project, January 21, 2011; and Monica Anderson and Andrew Perrin, "Disabled Americans Are Less Likely to Use Technology," Pew Research, April 4, 2017.

8. Mark Wheeler, *Politics and the Mass Media* (Oxford: Blackwell, 1997), 228.

9. Matthew Hindman, *The Myth of Digital Democracy* (Princeton, NJ: Princeton University Press, 2009).

10. Laura McKenna, "The Internet and American Politics: Where the Politically Rich Get Richer and the Politically Poor Get Perez Hilton," presented at the annual meeting of the American Political Science Association, Toronto, Canada, 2009.

11. Michael Cornfield, *Politics Moves Online: Campaigning and the Internet* (New York: The Century Foundation, 2004).

12. Howard Rheingold, *The Virtual Community: Homesteading on the Electronic Frontier* (Cambridge, MA: MIT Press, 2000).

13. Clay Skirky, *Here Comes Everybody* (New York: Penguin, 2008).

14. See Josh Pasek, Eian More, and Daniel Romer, "Realizing the Social Internet: Online Social Networking Meets Offline Civic Engagement," *Journal of Information Technology and Politics* 6 (2009): 197–215.

15. See Jody C. Baumgartner and Jonathan S. Morris, "MyFaceTube Politics: Social Networking Websites and Political Engagement of Young Adults," *Social Science Computer Review* 28 (2009): 24–44; and Weiwu Zhang, Thomas J. Johnson, Trent Sletzer, and Shannon Bichard, "The Revolution Will Be Networked: The Influence of Social Networking Sites on Political Attitudes and Behaviors," *Social Science Computer Review* 28 (2010): 75–92.

16. Jessica T. Feezell, Meredith Conroy, and Mario Guerrero, "Facebook Is . . . Fostering Political Engagement: A Study of Online Social Networking Groups and Offline Participation," presented at the annual meeting of the American Political Science Association, Toronto, Canada, 2009.

17. Terri L. Towner and David A. Dulio, "The Web 2.0 Election: Voter Learning in the 2008 Presidential Campaign," in *Techno Politics in Presidential Campaigning: New Voices, New Technologies, and New Voters,* ed. John Hendricks and Lynda Lee Kaid (New York: Routledge, 2008).

18. Pew Research Center Journalism Project's Staff, "McCain vs. Obama on the Web," September 15, 2008.

19. Ibid.

20. Howard Rheingold, "Using Participatory Media and Public Voice to Encourage Civic Engagement," in *Civic Life Online: Learning How Digital Media Can Engage Youth,* ed. Lance W. Bennett, The John D. and Catherine T. MacArthur Foundation Series on Digital Media and Learning (Cambridge, MA: MIT Press, 2008).

21. American Press Institute, "How Americans Get Their News," March 17, 2014.

22. https://www.omnicoreagency.com/youtube-statistics/.

23. Aaron Barlow, *The Rise of the Blogosphere* (New York: Praeger, 2007).

24. Christine Gibbs Springer, "Mastering Strategic Conversations," *PA Times* (September 2006).

25. See Howard Kurtz, *Spin Cycle—How the White House and the Media Manipulate the News* (New York: Simon & Schuster, 1998).

26. Patrick Healy, "To '08 Hopefuls, Media Technology Can Be Friend or Foe," *The New York Times,* January 31, 2007, A15.

27. Michael Barbaro, "Pithy, Mean, and Powerful: How Donald Trump Mastered Twitter for 2016," *The New York Times,* October 15, 2015.

28. Cass Sunstein, *Republic.com* (Princeton, NJ: Princeton University Press, 2001), 83.

29. Andrew Paul Williams and Evan Serge, "Evaluating Candidate E-Mail Messages in the 2008 U.S. Presidential Campaign," in *Techno Politics in Presidential Campaigning: New Voices, New Technologies, and New Voters,* ed. John Hendricks and Lynda Lee Kaid (New York: Routledge, 2001).

30. David Karpf, *The MoveOn Effect: The Unexpected Transformation of American Political Advocacy* (New York: Oxford University Press, 2012).

31. https://www.youtube.com/watch?v=BAUZnDIWu2I.

32. United Nations Department of Economic and Social Affairs, "United Nations E-Government Survey 2010."

33. https://www.nytimes.com/spotlight/on-politics?campaign_id=56&emc=edit_cn_20200401&instance_id=17261&nl=on-politics-with-lisa-lerer®i_id=39742264&segment_id=23558&te=1&user_id=eec3acb3794bae9028ccc48980b5b067

34. NIC Core Services, "Outdoor Licensing," www.egov.com/Solutions/CoreServices/Pages/Outdoor.aspx.

35. Dana Gardner, "Staying on Legacy Systems Ends Up Costing IT More," www.zdnet.com/blog/gardner/staying-on-legacy-systems-ends-up-costing-it-more/3231.

36. Lev Grossman, "The Beast with a Billion Eyes," *Time* (January 30, 2012).

37. Roy Saltman, *The History and Politics of Voting Technology* (New York: Palgrave Macmillan, 2008).

38. Daniel Solove, *The Digital Person: Technology and Privacy in the Information Age* (New York: New York University Press, 2004).

39. www.cnn.com/2020/02/23/politics/intelligence-briefer-russian-interference-trump-sanders/index.html.

40. https://www.npr.org/2020/02/22/808536024/troll-watch-russian-interference-in-2020.

41. Barton Gellman and Greg Miller, "'Black Budget' Summary Details U.S. Spy Network's Successes, Failures and Objectives," *The Washington Post,* August 29, 2013. Page 389

42. Glenn Greenwald, "NSA Collecting Phone Records of Millions of Verizon Customers Daily," *The Guardian,* June 5, 2013.

43. Barton Gellman and Ashkan Soltani, "NSA Tracking Cellphone Locations Worldwide, Snowden Documents Show," *The Washington Post,* December 4, 2013.

44. "NSA Signal Surveillance Success Stories," *The Washington Post.*

45. Barton Gellman and Laura Poitras, "U.S., British Intelligence Mining Data from Nine U.S. Internet Companies in Broad Secret Program," *The Washington Post,* June 6, 2013.

46. Barton Gellman and Ashkan Soltani, "NSA Infiltrates Links to Yahoo, Google Data Centers Worldwide, Snowden Documents Say," *The Washington Post,* October 30, 2013.

47. Glenn Greenwald, "XKeyscore: NSA Tool Collects 'Nearly Everything a User Does on the Internet,'" *The Guardian,* July 31, 2013.

48. James Ball, "Xbox Live Among Game Services Targeted by US and UK Spy Agencies," *The Guardian,* December 9, 2013.

49. "Book to Reveal Obama's 'True' Identity?" *Drudge Report,* April 20, 2011, http://drudgereport.com/flash7.htm.

50. Cass Sunstein, Republic.com (Princeton, NJ: Princeton University Press, 2001).

51. Twitter, "Combating Violent Extremism," February 5, 2018.

52. See Rukmini Callimachi, Chapter 2, "The Recruit," in the podcast *The Caliphate,* www.nytimes.com/interactive/2018/podcasts/caliphate-isis-rukmini-callimachi.html.

53. https://www.nytimes.com/2018/09/20/podcasts/caliphate-transcript-chapter-two-recruitment.html

54. Thomas E. Mann and Norman J. Ornstein, *It's Even Worse Than It Looks: How the American Constitutional System Collided with the New Politics of Extremism* (New York: Basic Books, 2012).

55. Donna Leinwand Leger, "Internet Creates Wider Venue for Political Incivility, Threats," *USA Today,* February 2, 2012, p. 6A.

56. Robert B. Reich, "Big Tech Has Become Way Too Powerful," *The New York Times,* September 15, 2015.

57. Sunstein, *Republic.com 2.0.*

58. Ibid.

■ Key Terms

∎ Multiple-Choice Questions

1. Internet access has come to replace bowling leagues as a means of developing
A. Collective security
B. Social capital
C. Social welfare
D. Virtual capacity

2. Which of the following statements about e-campaigning is true?
A. E-campaigning relies primarily on raising online campaign contributions
B. E-campaigning mostly avoids use of social networking sites such as Facebook
C. Barack Obama avoided the use of e-campaigning during the 2008 election
D. Former governor Jesse Ventura successfully pioneered the use of grassroots

3. Which of the following factors is the chief cause fueling the current digital divide?
A. Income
B. Age
C. Gender
D. Region

4. Which of the following is a consequence of the explosion of the Internet into politics?
A. Lack of accuracy
B. It is used as a tool for terrorists
C. Fomenting polarized partisanship and extremism
D. All of the above

5. From which of the following sources do Americans get the majority of their news?
A. Newspapers
B. Radio
C. Internet
D. Television

6. Which of the following is true about the Internet and the First Amendment?
A. Broad First Amendment protections have allowed hate speech on the Internet to proliferate
B. Selective exposure has led individuals into a state of information overload
C. First Amendment protections have made it virtually impossible to track terrorists
D. Widespread prosecution for libel has had a chilling effect on Internet political blogs

7. All of the following are new technologies used in modern political campaigns EXCEPT

    A. e-campaigns

    B. microtargeting

    C. cyber campaigning

    D. hacktivism

8. Which of the following has provided greater opportunity for the president to use the bully pulpit in recent years?

    A. Social media

    B. National news broadcasts

    C. The military

    D. Executive orders

9. The rise of the independent media outlets has had which of the following effects on political parties?

    A. The role of the party in supporting candidates has been weakened

    B. The political party label is more important in determining election outcomes

    C. The national party spotlight has increased

    D. Candidates increasingly seek third party labels

10. Which of the following groups is more likely to use social media to get information about political candidates?

    A. African Americans

    B. Hispanics

    C. 65 years old and above

    D. 18- to 21-year-olds

▪ Free Response Questions

Argumentation

Develop an argument that takes a position that social media has improved or hindered a fair national campaign process.

In your essay, you must:

- Articulate a defensible claim or thesis that responds to the prompt and develops a line of reasoning

- Support your claim with at least TWO pieces of accurate and relevant information:

  - At least ONE piece of evidence must be from one of the following foundational documents:

    — The U.S. Constitution

    — *Federalist* No. 78

    — Brutus 1

  - Use a second piece of evidence from another foundational document from the list or from your study of politics and technology

- Use reasoning to explain why your evidence supports your claim/thesis

- Respond to an opposing or alternative perspective using refutation, concession, or rebuttal

Quantitative Analysis

Who Uses the Internet?

ALL ADULTS	90%	**EDUCATION LEVEL**	
SEX		Less than high school	71
Men	90	High school grad	84
Women	91	Some college	95
RACE/ETHNICITY		College +	98
White (Non-Hispanic)	92	**HOUSEHOLD INCOME**	
Black	85	Less than $30,000	82
Hispanic	86	$30,000–$49,999	93
Asian American*	97	$50,000–$74,999	97
AGE GROUP		$75,000+	98
18–29	100	**COMMUNITY TYPE**	
30–49	97	Urban	91
50–64	88	Suburban	94
65 +	73	Rural	85

In general, what demographic groups are most likely to be Internet users? What factors might prevent less likely populations from using the Internet?

*Data for Asian Americans is from 2014 and includes only "English speaking Asians," according to the Pew Research Center.

Source: Pew Research Center.

A. Identify a group that uses the Internet at a high rate.
B. Describe a pattern in the information graphic and draw a conclusion about the pattern.
C. Explain how Internet use may affect strategy for candidates running for political office.

Concept Application

President Trump actively used Twitter during his presidency, sometimes tweeting several times a day. With over 87 million followers, analysts believed Trump's tweets had wide-ranging ripple effects. The president used Twitter to announce policy, criticize the press, to dismiss selected presidential appointees, and to energize his base during the election, seeming to prefer this medium over holding formal press conferences. When Trump tweeted that transgender individuals should not serve in the military, this caused a crisis in the LGBQT+ community. When Trump tweeted about the economy, this affected global markets, and when Trump tweeted about foreign leaders, this affected diplomacy.

After reading the scenario, respond to A, B, and C below:

A. Explain how the scenario described above illustrates e-Government.
B. In the context of the scenario, explain the consequences of e-Government.
C. In the context of the scenario, explain how social media serves as a linkage institution.

At the beginning of this unit, we asked you to consider the following Enduring Understanding (EU): *What factors influence the nature and degree of political participation?* Specifically, we asked that you consider the following questions in the context of the reading:

- **How do salient issues, such as those motivating the BLM movement, influence the nature and degree of political participation? Similarly, how can a crisis such as the COVID-19 pandemic change how much attention people pay to the presidential election?**

- **What structural barriers to voter participation prevented Blacks from voting? To what extent are there still barriers to voter participation?**

- **Is BLM improving political efficacy or is BLM so intense in part because of the sense that Black Americans historically and today lack efficacy?**

Salient issues can increase or decrease political participation, depending on the issue and circumstances. When participation increases, it is often channeled through linkage institutions. When participation decreases, it is often due to structural barriers. In the chapter on interest groups, you read that interest groups help groups of people organize to attempt to influence government as a collective force. In the chapter on political socialization, you read that political scientists have noticed patterns in political participation and in voting by demographic characteristic. In the chapter on campaigns and elections, you learned that there were recent efforts to suppress African American voters in some states in spite of the ratification of the Twenty-Sixth Amendment abolishing the poll tax and the passage of the Voting Rights Act of 1965. These structural barriers have deep implications for African American attitudes and political participation.

Recent news reports suggest that the COVID-19 crisis diverted attention away from the presidential election before the presidential campaign was in full swing, only to later produce historically high turnout rates when the election arrived.

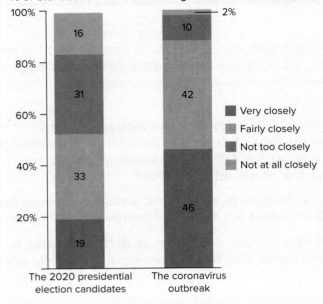

U.S. PUBLIC IS PAYING FAR LESS ATTENTION TO THE 2020 ELECTION THAN TO THE CORONAVIRUS OUTBREAK

% of U.S. adults who are following news about each topic ...

Legend:
- Very closely
- Fairly closely
- Not too closely
- Not at all closely

The 2020 presidential election candidates:
- 19 (Not at all closely)
- 33 (Not too closely)
- 31 (Fairly closely)
- 16 (Very closely)

The coronavirus outbreak:
- 46 (Not at all closely)
- 42 (Not too closely)
- 10 (Fairly closely)
- 2% (Very closely)

Source: Survey of U.S. adults conducted April 20-26, 2020.

Source: Pew Research Center. https://www.pewresearch.org/fact-tank/2020/05/22/americans-are-following-news-about-presidential-candidates-much-less-closely-than-covid-19-news/.

In the presidential election of 2020, turnout rates hit a 50-year high. At the time of this publication, a reported 66% of the eligible voting age population participated in the election. President Trump received over 74 million votes, more than he received in 2016 and the highest number a losing candidate has ever received. Biden received over 81 million votes, the highest number a winning candidate has ever received. Many attribute the high turnout to the availability of early voting and mail-in voting in many states, modifications states made due to COVID-19.

There have traditionally been high levels of political participation and voting among well-educated citizens (those with a college degree or higher) and among older generations (those 65 and older). Voter turnout has been traditionally lower among the young (18- to 21-year-olds) and lower among African American and Latinx voters overall when compared to other demographic groups. It will take some time for exit polls to report on the demographics of the voters of 2020, but early indicators suggest that neither Trump nor Biden made inroads with the opposing party. Rather, turnout was high among traditional Democratic and Republican voters. Trump had a majority of white votes, and African Americans, Latinxs, and Asian Americans voted strongly for Biden. Early reports also suggest that Black voters in key cities helped deliver the election for Biden, and that BLM leaders helped boost African American turnout, indicating that perhaps BLM is improving Black efficacy.

▌Multiple-Choice Questions

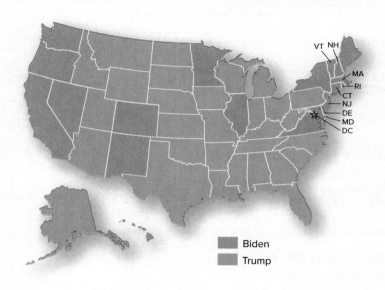

Biden
Trump

1. Using the map above, which of the following best explains why Donald Trump defeated Hillary Clinton in the 2016 presidential election?

   A. Trump won in all swing states

   B. Trump won more popular votes than Clinton

   C. Trump won in more electoral-rich states than Clinton

   D. Trump dominated the West and Northeast

2. Which of the following is an accurate comparison of the goals of interest groups and political parties?

	Interest group goals	Political parties' goals
A.	Win elections under a label	Mobilize voters
B.	Influence policy	Win elections
C.	Promote a big tent	Organize governing policy
D.	Label candidates	Promote a big tent

Hypothetical Statewide Congressional Election Results

Party	Percent of the Vote won	Seats
A	51%	6
B	40%	5
C	8%	0

3. Which of the following best explains why Party C did not win a congressional seat?

A. No one voted for Party C

B. Party C did not represent mainstream political ideals

C. The winner-take-all-rule discriminated against Party C

D. The election was held using proportional rules

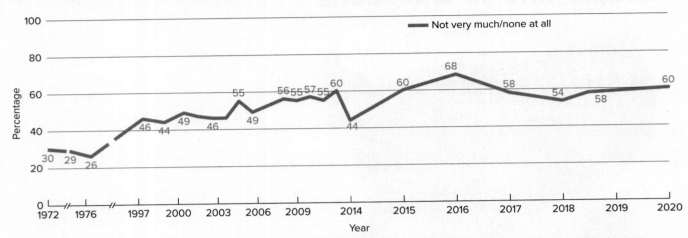

Source: Gallup Poll, "Americans' Trust in Mass Media Edges Down to 41%." https://news.gallup.com/poll/267047/americans-trust-mass-media-edges-down.aspx

4. Which of the following best describes a trend in the graph above?

A. Confidence in the media in the U.S. is consistently high

B. Confidence in the media has declined over time

C. Confidence in the media has fluctuated in recent decades

D. Confidence in the media is inversely related to trends in trust and confidence in government

5. Based on your knowledge of U.S. Government, which of the following best correlates with the trend above?

A. Increase in new media

B. Increasing confidence in government

C. Increasing civic engagement

D. Decreasing political participation

© N. Y. "Tribune."

Bettmann/Getty Images

6. Which of the following cases is most closely related to the topic of the cartoon above?

A. *Shaw v. Reno* (1993)

B. *Baker v. Carr* (1962)

C. *Citizens United v. Federal Election Commission* (2010)

D. *McDonald v. Chicago* (2010)

7. Which of the following is the best example of a candidate-centered campaign strategy?

A. A candidate emphasizes the ideals of his or her party platform

B. A candidate situates his or her political image to appeal directly to grassroots voters

C. A candidate reviews fund-raising strategy to resist large donations

D. An incumbent candidate for re-election casts an unpopular vote on policy for the greater good

8. An unemployed citizen is voting in an upcoming election. This citizen believes the incumbent candidate did not work hard enough to stimulate job growth and as a result, will vote against the incumbent. What type of voting model best explains this scenario?

A. Rational choice voting

B. Retrospective voting

C. Prospective voting

D. Party line voting

9. Which of the following types of elections is most likely to result in an ideological candidate?

A. Open primaries

B. Closed primaries

C. Presidential election

D. Congressional election

10. Which of the following accurately pairs the legal protection in the Constitution with the group it expanded suffrage to or protected?

	Constitutional Amendment	
A.	**Fifteenth Amendment**	Women
B.	**Nineteenth Amendment**	African Americans
C.	**Twenty-Fourth Amendment**	Latinos
D.	**Twenty-Sixth Amendment**	18- to 21-year-olds

11. An interest group lacks fund-raising ability. Which of the following is the most likely strategy the interest group will utilize to influence policy?

A. TV advertising

B. Grassroots mobilization

C. PAC contributions

D. Lobbyist pressure on senators

12. When a member of the Farm Bureau networks with members of the U.S. Department of Agriculture and the Congressional Committee on Agriculture to ensure farm subsidy policy continues, which of the following has occurred?

A. Iron triangle

B. Free rider

C. Horserace journalism

D. Interest group mobilization

Congressional Election Results

Candidate	Percent of vote won
A	66%
B	34%

13. Which of the following is likely to be true of the candidates in the election above?

A. Candidate A is a member of a third party

B. Candidate B won more electoral votes

C. Candidate A is the incumbent

D. Candidate B was not well supported by the national party

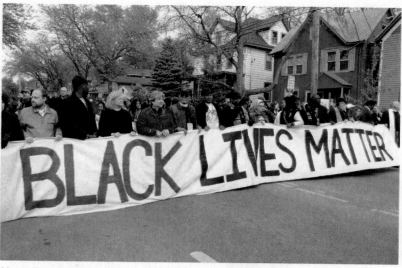

AAraujo/Shutterstock

14. What political strategy is being utilized in the photo above?

    A. Electioneering

    B. Grassroots mobilization

    C. Free rider

    D. Lobbying

"Our democracy works best when everyone's voice is heard, and no one's voice is drowned out. But five years ago, a Supreme Court ruling allowed big companies – including foreign corporations – to spend unlimited amounts of money to influence our elections. The Citizens United decision was wrong, and it has caused real harm to our democracy. With each new campaign season, this dark money floods our airwaves with more and more political ads that pull our politics into the gutter. It's time to reverse this trend. Rather than bolster the power of lobbyists and special interests, Washington should lift up the voices of ordinary Americans and protect their democratic right to determine the direction of the country that we love."

President Obama, State of the Union Address

Source: Obama, Barack. "Statement from the President." National Archives and Records Administration, January 21, 2015. https://obamawhitehouse.archives.gov/the-press-office/2015/01/21/statement-president.

15. Which of the following is the main idea of the passage above?

    A. Ordinary Americans should exercise their right to vote

    B. Campaign contributions corrupt the political process

    C. Dark money violates the First Amendment

    D. Our elections are dominated by foreign corporations

16. A critic of Obama's statement above would most likely use which of the following in their argument?

    A. First Amendment right to free speech

    B. Second Amendment right to bear arms

    C. Fourth Amendment protection from illegal searches

    D. Fifth Amendment right to due process of law

1 Potential supporter visits candidate site

2 CampaignGrid checks voter vault and drops cookie on supporter's browser

3 Visitor leaves site and continues to browse Web

5 Ads drive supporter back to candidate site

4 CampaignGrid serves ads to voter across the Grid Network

Contextual ad placement drives performance

17. Which of the following can be concluded about grid targeting displayed in the information graphic above?

A. Companies can strategically target their advertising to identify specific voters

B. Potential voters who visit a candidate's website end up voting for the candidate

C. Political advertising increases voter turnout

D. Campaign grid technique is no more likely to change voter minds than traditional advertising

18. Which of the following may be a direct impact of the phenomena described in the information graphic above?

A. People are more likely to vote due to targeted advertising

B. People are likely to receive advertisements from candidates whose websites they visited

C. People are more likely to use the Internet than other forms of media to research political candidates

D. People are more likely to be informed about the policy positions of all candidates

Use the following table to answer questions 19 and 20.

Who Uses the Internet?				
ALL ADULTS	90%			
SEX		**EDUCATION LEVEL**		
Men	90	Less than high school	71	
Women	91	High school grad	84	
RACE/ETHNICITY		Some college	95	
White (Non-Hispanic)	92	College +	98	
Black	85	**HOUSEHOLD INCOME**		
Hispanic	86	Less than $30,000	82	
Asian American*	97	$30,000–$49,999	93	
AGE GROUP		$50,000–$74,999	97	
18–29	100	$75,000+	98	
30–49	97	**COMMUNITY TYPE**		
50–64	88	Urban	91	
65 +	73	Suburban	94	
		Rural	85	

In general, what demographic groups are most likely to be Internet users? What factors might prevent less likely populations from using the Internet?

*Data for Asian Americans is from 2014 and includes only "English speaking Asians," according to the Pew Research Center.
Source: Pew Research Center.

19. What is the main idea of the table above?
   A. Lack of access to technology will limit an individual's information
   B. Regional differences influence Internet use
   C. There is a digital divide by demographic group
   D. Education is the primary cause of the digital divide

20. Which of the following is true, based on the data above?
   A. African Americans are less likely to use the Internet than other demographic groups
   B. Women use the Internet ten percent less than men
   C. People with less than a high school diploma are less likely to use the Internet than other demographic groups
   D. Lower-income individuals are more likely to use the Internet than those with an income of $75,000 or more

■ Free Response Questions

Concept Application

(The novel coronavirus led to stay-at-home orders by many governors in the United States to stop the spread of the virus.)

During the first two months of the COVID-19 pandemic, states and localities implemented their own guidelines about which businesses could stay open and which could close. Many restaurants, nail salons, retail stores, and others were forced to lay off staff, leading to 36 million unemployment claims by May 2020.

When workers could start returning to work, many saw reduced hours and smaller paychecks while still risking contracting the virus. Yet if they continued to stay home, they could not claim unemployment benefits.

After reading the scenario, respond to A, B, and C below:

A. Describe a power Congress could use to address the scenario.
B. In the context of the scenario, explain how the use of congressional power described in part A can be affected by its interaction with the presidency.
C. In the context of the scenario, explain how the interaction between Congress and the presidency can be affected by linkage institutions.

Quantitative Analysis

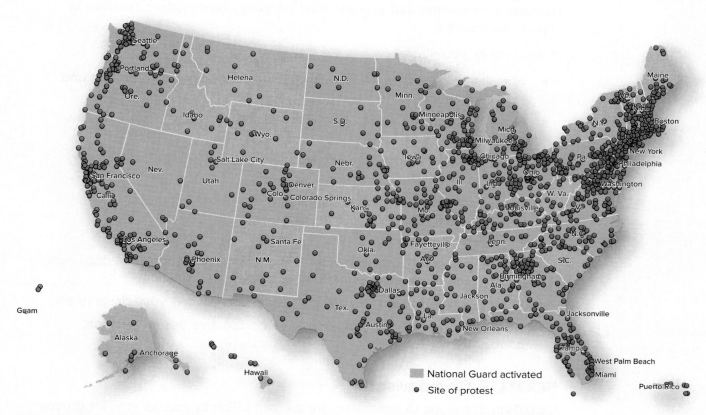

Source: USA Today. https://www.usatoday.com/in-depth/graphics/2020/06/03/map-protests-wake-george-floyds-death/5310149002/.

Use the information graphic above to answer the questions.

A. Describe the protests in the United States as displayed in the graphic.

B. Describe a pattern in protests displayed in the graphic.

C. Explain how the First Amendment to the U.S. Constitution facilitates protests and describe a government barrier to protest in the U.S.

Argumentation

Develop an argument that explains how campaign contributions facilitate or impede democracy.

In your essay, you must:

- Articulate a defensible claim or thesis that responds to the prompt and establishes a line of reasoning
- Support your claim with at least TWO pieces of accurate and relevant information
  - At least ONE piece of evidence must be from one of the following foundational documents:
    - Declaration of Independence
    - The U.S. Constitution
    - *Federalist* No. 10
  - Use a second piece of evidence from another foundational document from the list or from your study of political participation
- Use reasoning to explain why your evidence supports your claim/thesis
- Respond to an opposing or alternative perspective using refutation, concession, or rebuttal

SCOTUS Comparison

Campaign donations to candidates for elected office by special interest groups escalated throughout the 1990s. Concerned about the excess influence of special interests and in an effort to curb campaign donations by them, the Bipartisan Campaign Reform Act of 2002, sponsored by Senator McCain (R-AZ) and Senator Feingold (D-WI) was passed. The law banned unrestricted soft money donations made directly to political parties, limited advertising by unions, corporations, and non-profit organizations on behalf of candidates, and restricted political parties' use of funds for advertising on behalf of candidates. Senator McConnell (R-TN), a longtime proponent of allowing freedom in campaign contributions, joined with the National Rifle Association and others to challenge the limits in court, and their case ultimately reached the Supreme Court. In *McConnell v. FEC* (2003), the Supreme Court held that neither the soft money ban nor the limits on advertising were in violation of the First Amendment.

A. Identify the clause of the First Amendment that is common to *McConnell v. FEC* and *Citizens United v. FEC*.
B. Identify differences between the facts of the two cases and explain how the decisions by the Supreme Court in the two cases were different.
C. Explain how the ruling in the *Citizens United* case could be limited in the future.

■ Section I: Multiple Choice Questions

Questions 1 & 2 refer to the graph below.

% of U.S. adults who are following news about candidates for the 2020 presidential election ...

Note: Whites and blacks include non-Hispanics; Hispanics can be of any race.

Source: Pew Research Center. https://www.pewresearch.org/fact-tank/2020/05/22/americans-are-following-news-about-presidential-candidates-much-less-closely-than-covid-19-news/

1. Which of the following statements is reflected in the data in the chart?
    A. A higher percentage of people with some college are following the election very closely when compared to those who are college grads
    B. A higher percentage of people in older age brackets are following the election very closely
    C. A higher percentage of women are following the election very closely when compared to men
    D. Republicans are following the election more closely than Democrats

2. Which of the following is a potential consequence of the trend illustrated in the chart?
    A. Women will be more likely to vote than men
    B. Individuals with less education will be more involved in the election than other voters
    C. Older voters will be more knowledgeable about the issues in the election
    D. Republicans will be more likely to vote on Election Day while Democrats will be more likely to vote early

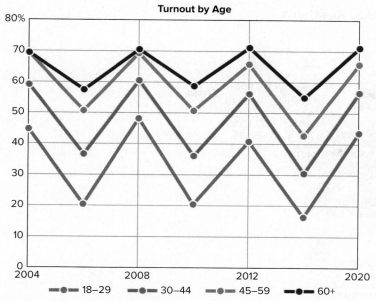

Turnout by Age

Legend: 18–29 · 30–44 · 45–59 · 60+

Source: United States Elections Project.

3. Which of the following is reflected in the line graph above?

A. Voter turnout has consistently declined over time

B. When young voters are energized, they vote at high rates

C. People over 60 consistently vote at higher rates than younger voters

D. Voter turnout between the ages of 30 and 44 is declining

4. Which of the following is a potential consequence of the information in the line graph above?

A. Candidates for office will likely attempt to appeal to older voters

B. On average, voter turnout rates will remain at about 50% for all elections

C. Higher voter turnout will favor Democrats

D. Republican candidates for office will attempt to increase voting among young people

Thousands of Governments Serve U.S. Residents

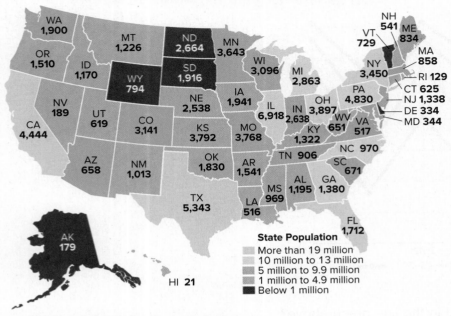

Number of Local Governments in Each State

Sources: U.S. Census Bureau, "2017 Census of Governments."; U.S. Census, "2019 Census Estimates".

5. Which of the following describes the information presented in the map?

   A. All citizens have equal access to lawmakers

   B. New Mexico has fewer lawmakers per capita than any other state

   C. Alaska has more lawmakers per capita than any other state

   D. The number of local lawmakers varies by state

6. The information presented in the map above is a consequence of which of the following principles?

   A. Due process of law

   B. Equal protection under the law

   C. Federalism

   D. Separation of powers

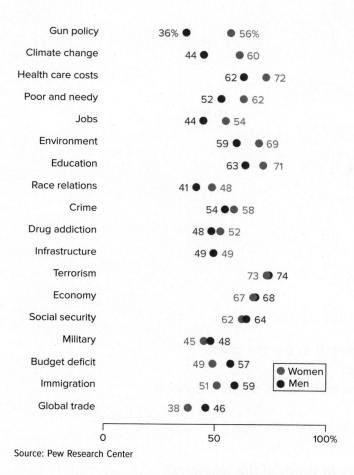

Gun policy   36% ●   ● 56%
Climate change   44 ●   ● 60
Health care costs   62 ●   ● 72
Poor and needy   52 ●   ● 62
Jobs   44 ●   ● 54
Environment   59 ●   ● 69
Education   63 ●   ● 71
Race relations   41 ●   ● 48
Crime   54 ●● 58
Drug addiction   48 ●● 52
Infrastructure   49 ● 49
Terrorism   73 ● 74
Economy   67 ● 68
Social security   62 ●● 64
Military   45 ●● 48
Budget deficit   49 ●   ● 57
Immigration   51 ●   ● 59
Global trade   38 ●   ● 46

● Women
● Men

0   50   100%

Source: Pew Research Center

7. Which of the following is reflected in the data in the chart above?
  A. Global trade and immigration are top priorities for women
  B. Health care and care for the poor/needy are top priorities for women
  C. Men place a higher priority on gun policy than women
  D. Women place a higher priority on immigration than men

8. The data in the chart above supports which of the following?
  A. There is gender gap in the electorate on most issues
  B. Men and women are divided on all issues
  C. Men are more likely to vote Republican than women
  D. Women are more likely to disagree with both political parties

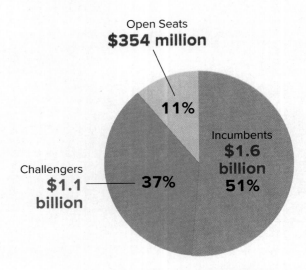

Open Seats
$354 million

11%

Incumbents
$1.6 billion
51%

Challengers
$1.1 billion

37%

**Contributions to 2020
Congressional Candidates**

Sources: The Center for Responsive Politics. OpenSecrets.org

9. Which of the following describes information presented in the pie chart?
  A. Open congressional seats are the least funded
  B. Current holders of political office receive more than half of all contributions from PACs
  C. PACs contribute more in campaign donations than individuals
  D. Challengers are the best funded candidates

10. The information in the pie chart leads most directly to which of the following?
  A. Lack of competition in the electoral process
  B. Decrease in cost of political campaigns
  C. Inflationary effects of political advertising
  D. Increase in new candidates for public office

Questions 11–13 relate to the passage below.

Excerpt from: Opening the Third Century of American Federalism: Issues and Prospects

By Daniel Elazar

Strong forces for centralization continue to operate in the American federal system; however, especially since the election of President Ronald Reagan in 1980, countervailing forces have worked to promote decentralization and even restore noncentralization in the federal system. . . . The potential for greater noncentralization is being reinforced by changing socioeconomic conditions that place a greater emphasis on networks of relationships rather than on traditional hierarchies.

. . . By its decisive actions in so many fields, the Reagan administration demonstrated that it was still possible to take hold of the reins of government and begin to reverse seemingly irreversible trends, including the at least seventy-year-long thrust toward greater government permeation of society. Yet fulfilling Reagan's promise to strengthen the state within that system, and thereby strengthen the system as a whole, has not been easy.

. . . Especially during the first postwar generation (194-76), there was an environmental basis for centralization. . . . The civil rights revolution led to substantial federal intervention in the legal and educational systems.

Elazar, Daniel J. "Opening the Third Century of American Federalism: Issues and Prospects." The Annals of the American Academy of Political and Social Science 509 (1990): 11-21.

11. Which of the following summarizes the author's main argument?
A. The national government is the strongest level of government in the U.S.
B. State governments have reasserted themselves in the power structure
C. Centralization is a continuing trend in the U.S.
D. State governments know what is best for the people

12. Which of the following provisions of the Constitution supports the author's argument?
A. First Amendment
B. Tenth Amendment
C. Due process clause
D. Equal protection clause

13. Based on the text, which of the following would the author most likely agree with?
A. Policy innovations are best when they occur at the state level
B. Overburdensome national government power persists
C. The civil rights movement provided opportunities for state innovation
D. Environmental policy was handled appropriately by the national government

Federalist No. 68 by Alexander Hamilton (Excerpt):

...[T]he Executive should be independent for his continuance in office on all but the people themselves . . . This...will also be secured, by making his election to depend on a special body of representatives, deputed by the society for the single purpose of making the important choice.

All these advantages will happily combine in the plan devised by the convention; which is, that the people of each State shall choose a number of persons as electors, equal to the number of senators and representatives of such State in the national government, who shall assemble within the State, and vote for some fit person as President. Their votes, thus given, are to be transmitted to the seat of the national government, and the person who may happen to have a majority of the whole number of votes will be the President. But as a majority of the votes might not always happen to centre in one man, and as it might be unsafe to permit less than a majority to be conclusive, it is provided that, in such a contingency, the House of Representatives shall select out of the candidates who shall have the five highest number of votes, the man who in their opinion may be best qualified for the office.

The process of election affords a moral certainty, that the office of President will never fall to the lot of any man who is not in an eminent degree endowed with the requisite qualifications. Talents for low intrigue, and the little arts of popularity, may alone suffice to elevate a man to the first honors in a single State; but it will require other talents, and a different kind of merit, to establish him in the esteem and confidence of the whole Union, or of so considerable a portion of it as would be necessary to make him a successful candidate for the distinguished office of President of the United States.

Hamilton, Alexander. "Federalist No. 68: The Mode of Electing The President." New York Packet, 1788. Library of Congress. https://guides.loc.gov/federalist-papers/text-61-70#s-lg-box-wrapper-25493455.

14. Which of the following is the main idea of the passage?
- A. Under the Constitution, the choice of president will be made by qualified individuals
- B. The president should be independent of the people
- C. The presidential election may not always be by a majority
- D. Only talented individuals will have a chance at being elected to the presidency

15. Which of the following is inconsistent with the author's concern?
- A. Media calculation of national popular votes
- B. Electors being bound to vote based on state popular vote
- C. The states winner-take-all rule
- D. The calculation of the number of electors by state

16. Based on the text, which of the following would the author most likely agree with?
- A. The importance today for a presidential candidate to win electoral votes
- B. The calculation of popular votes
- C. The heavy emphasis in presidential elections on swing states
- D. The role of the media in announcing the outcome of the presidential election

Questions 17–18 relate to the political cartoon below.

Paul Snover/CartoonStock

17. Which of the following best describes the message in the political cartoon?
   A.   Federal and local government power is shared
   B.   The federal government has gained too much power over local government
   C.   Local government powers are protected in the U.S. Constitution
   D.   Local government needs support from the federal government

18. Which of the following principles is most relevant to the topic of the cartoon?
   A.   Separation of powers
   B.   Checks and balances
   C.   Federalism
   D.   Due process of law

Questions 19–20 relate to the political cartoon below.

Ron Hauge/CartoonStock

19. Which of the following describes the message in the cartoon above?

A. The federal government spends money freely

B. Banks need to be regulated by Congress

C. Banks need to be taxed by the federal government

D. Direct payments to individuals will stimulate the economy

20. Which of the following policies is most directly linked to the main idea of the cartoon above?

A. Supply-side economics

B. Keynesian economics

C. Fiscal policy

D. Monetary policy

Questions 21–22 refer to the image below.

Leila Navidi/Star Tribune/ASSOCIATED PRESS

21. Which of the following describes what is taking place in the image above?

A. Lobbyists are gathering prior to meeting with lawmakers

B. Citizens are waiting to hear the results of a court case

C. An interest group is staging a political advertisement

D. Members of a social movement are lawfully demonstrating in support of a cause

22. Which of the following forms of democracy is illustrated in the image above?

A. Participatory democracy

B. Pluralist democracy

C. Elite democracy

D. Majoritarian democracy

23. Which of the following is an accurate comparison of the two court cases?

	Engel v. Vitale	**Wisconsin v. Yoder**
A.	Incorporated the First Amendment to state governments	Involved members of the Jehovah's Witnesses faith attempting to freely practice their religion
B.	Was a case that pertained to freedom of speech	Was a case that pertained to free exercise of religion
C.	Decided that state-sponsored prayer violated the establishment clause	Decided that removing children from public school after the 8th grade for religious reasons was protected by the free exercise clause
D.	Led to removal of teacher-led prayer in school	Led to removal of religious clubs sponsored by the school

24. Which of the following is an accurate comparison of conservative and liberal views concerning economic policy?

	Conservative	Liberal
A.	Government spending should be reduced to stimulate the economy	Government spending stimulates the economy during economic downturns
B.	Fiscal policy should be used to stimulate the economy	Monetary policy should be used to stimulate the economy
C.	The minimum wage should be raised	Raising the minimum wage will increase unemployment
D.	Tax cuts should only be provided to the middle class	Tax cuts on the wealthy will stimulate the economy

25. Which of the following accurately compares the House of Representatives with the Senate?

	House of Representatives	Senate
A.	Six-year terms	Two-year terms
B.	Try articles of impeachment	Write articles of impeachment
C.	Limits on debates	Allows filibusters
D.	Represent states at large	Represent narrow constituencies

26. Which of the following is an accurate comparison of interest groups and political parties?

	Interest Groups	Political Parties
A.	Represent broad interests	Represent narrow interests
B.	Participate in get-out-the-vote efforts	Strong national, top-down organization
C.	Provide a label for candidates for office	Participate in fund-raising activities
D.	Goal: influence government	Goal: get elected to government

27. Which of the following accurately compares a national government responsibility with a state government responsibility?

	National Government	State Government
A.	Foreign relations	Treaties
B.	Sales tax	Income tax
C.	Military	Education
D.	Education	Marriage

28. An interest group would like the voting age to be lowered to 16. Which of the following actions should the interest group take to maximize their efforts to achieve this policy objective?

   A.   Lobby the U.S. Congress to request a change to the voting age

   B.   File litigation to challenge the 18-year-old minimum voting age

   C.   Petition local governments to lower the voting age to 16

   D.   Request the president issue an executive order changing the voting age

29. A high school student wears a T-shirt to school expressing anti-government beliefs and is suspended by the school administration. The family of the student challenges the suspension. How is this case likely to be resolved?

   A.   The school will be required to rescind the suspension, so long as the student was not disruptive

   B.   The student will need to perform community service before returning to school

   C.   The school will need to prove there was a clear and present danger to justify the suspension

   D.   The student suspension will be upheld and the student will be allowed to return to school after the suspension

30. In the Smith family, the parents are very active politically, vote Democratic and send their two children to public school. Which of the following is likely to be true?

   A.   Both Smith children will be politically apathetic

   B.   One of the two Smith children will favor the Republican Party

   C.   The Smith children will vote Democratic when of voting age

   D.   The Smith children will be politically socialized in public school

31. An interest group attempts to influence government policy to make schools more equitable through lobbying Congress but is not successful. Which of the following alternatives is most attractive to the interest group?

   A.   Lobbying judges

   B.   Litigation

   C.   Publishing newspaper articles

   D.   Calling for school board resignations

32. Which of the following is a legitimate action a state legislature can take to undermine the campaign of an incumbent member of Congress?

   A.   Redraw the district lines to favor an opponent

   B.   Give campaign contributions to the challenger

   C.   Request that the Supreme Court count ballots

   D.   Ask the governor to publicly discredit the member of Congress

33. Members of the U.S. House of Representatives Committee on Homeland Security is concerned about the security of the U.S.-Mexico border. Which of the following is an action the committee can take to address the concern?

   A.   Hold a hearing and subpoena high-level officials in the Department of Homeland Security to testify

   B.   Impound funds for border facilities until the problems are addressed

   C.   Place a referendum on the ballot in each state to increase spending on border security

   D.   Appoint a new secretary of the Department of Homeland Security

34. A member of the House introduced a bill to reform the Affordable Care Act, but it has been in committee for 36 days and is unlikely to make it to the floor. Which of the following can the member pursue to have a chance of getting the bill to the floor for a vote?

A. Cloture

B. Request immediate review by the Rules Committee

C. File a discharge petition

D. Logroll

35. Based on previous rulings, the Supreme Court is likely to view a case concerning affirmative action in which of the following ways?

A. Admission quota is in violation of the equal protection clause

B. The due process clause allows all affirmative action programs to stand

C. Affirmative action is allowed in cases of race and gender but not nationality

D. States can pursue affirmative action but the national government cannot

36. Which of the following is the most efficient way for a president to carry out a policy?

A. Issue a signing statement

B. Issue an executive order

C. Hold an oversight hearing

D. Require state governments to carry out the policy

37. A member of Congress votes with her district on tax issues but votes her conscience on bills related to the federal budget. Which of these voting models is the member following?

A. Delegate

B. Trustee

C. Politico

D. Bi-partisan

38. Changes in political news in recent years has led to which of the following?

A. Uncertainty over the credibility of news sources and information

B. A more liberal media

C. Fewer choices of where to access news stories

D. An increase in Americans watching the network news

39. Which of the following was a result of the *Citizens United v. Federal Election Commission* (2010) case?

A. Candidates for office began to rely more on individual campaign contributions

B. Foreign governments began to increase campaign contributions

C. Spending by corporations on political campaigns increased

D. Third party campaigns became more competitive

40.

Party of candidate	Electoral Votes	Popular Votes
Republican	304	63,980,160
Democrat	227	65,845,063
Libertarian	0	4,488,931
Green	0	1,457,050

Which of the following scenarios produced the presidential election results above which awarded the Republican candidate the presidency?

A. The Republican candidate won the popular vote narrowly in electoral vote-rich states
B. The Democrat won the most votes and the presidency
C. The Libertarian candidate was the spoiler for the Republican candidate
D. Neither the Green Party nor the Libertarian Party won votes

41. Which of the following points supports the argument that the Electoral College facilitates democracy?
A. The Electoral College gives a voice to small states
B. The Electoral College supports the one-man one-vote idea
C. The Electoral College results represent the will of the people
D. The Electoral College gives a voice to third party candidates

42. Which of the following is a reason why interest groups are linkage institutions?
A. They support candidates running for public office
B. They provide voters with information about government
C. They support cross-party dialogue on policy issues
D. They provide talking points to federal bureaucrats testifying before congressional oversight committees

43. Which of the following is a barrier to third parties winning congressional seats?
A. Lack of proportional representation
B. Cumbersome requirements to register to form a new party
C. Inability of third parties to advertise
D. Lack of dissenting views towards the two major political parties

44. Which of the following form an iron triangle?
A. Congress, the presidency, and the Supreme Court
B. State legislatures, congressional committee, and federal government agency
C. Congressional committee, federal government agency, and interest group
D. President, foreign leader, and interest group

45. Congress writes an automobile safety law and requests the U.S. Department of Transportation write the supporting regulations. The DOT proceeds to write regulations that Congress views as overly cumbersome for the automobile industry. Which of the following gives the DOT the ability to do this?

A. Bureaucratic oversight

B. Administrative discretion

C. Executive orders

D. Signing statements

46. Congress writes an automobile safety law and requests the U.S. Department of Transportation write the supporting regulations. The DOT proceeds to write regulations that Congress views as overly cumbersome for the automobile industry. Which of the following actions would be the next step for Congress to control the bureaucracy?

A. Hold a hearing

B. Issue an executive order

C. Begin litigation

D. Begin a public relations campaign to discredit the bureaucracy

47. An election is coming up, and John Smith is deciding how to cast his ballot. He believes the Republican candidate is less likely to raise taxes, so that is the candidate he chooses. What voting model explains John's voter behavior?

A. Rational choice

B. Retrospective voting

C. Prospective voting

D. Party line

48. Which of the following is true of Libertarian ideology?

A. They tend to agree with Democrats on social issues and Republicans on economic issues

B. They tend to advocate for increased government regulation in the environment

C. The ideology is successful in winning congressional districts in small states

D. Libertarian ideology is the newest third party in the U.S.

49. Which of the following arguments would a conservative likely make regarding health care policy?

A. The Affordable Care Act provides competition in the health care market

B. Medicare is cost effective

C. Health care policy should be left to state governments

D. Health care should be a public good

50. Which of the following is true about how justices view affirmative action?

A. Some view that the Constitution is colorblind, while others believe it only forbids racial classifications designed to harm minorities

B. Justices have universally affirmed most affirmative action programs

C. Justices at the state level support affirmative action in state universities, while justices at the federal level have struck down most race-based programs

D. Justices view affirmative action as part of the living Constitution

51. Which of the following is true about the right of privacy?

    A.   *Roe v. Wade* was the first Supreme Court ruling to express a right of privacy

    B.   The right of privacy is explicitly stated in the U.S. Constitution

    C.   The Court has interpreted the due process clause to encompass a right of privacy

    D.   *Roe v. Wade* does not specifically mention the word *privacy*

52. The Supreme Court has applied parts of the Bill of Rights to state governments. This process is known as which of the following?

    A.   Incorporation

    B.   *Stare decisis*

    C.   Judicial review

    D.   *Amicus curiae*

53. *McDonald v. Chicago* ruled which of the following?

    A.   The Second Amendment's right to keep and bear arms applied to state government

    B.   The Second Amendment did not encompass personal firearms

    C.   The due process clause requires individuals to have the right to self-defense

    D.   The state government cannot regulate personal firearm use

54. A student is suspended for making a political statement, but the school system's legal team advises the school to reverse the suspension. Which of the following is most directly related to this ruling?

    A.   The substantial disruption test resulting from the *Tinker v. Des Moines* case

    B.   *Engel v. Vitale's* limitations on school discipline

    C.   *Wisconsin v. Yoder's* protections of students

    D.   The clear and present danger test resulting from the *Schenck v. U.S.* case

55. A recent poll reports that over half of respondents support the use of the death penalty to deter crime. Which of the following would indicate the poll is credible?

    A.   The poll reported a sampling error

    B.   The poll was conducted via volunteer participation from a social media inquiry

    C.   The poll had a small sample size

    D.   The poll was conducted online

56. Which of the following was a main idea expressed in Martin Luther King, Jr.'s *Letter from Birmingham Jail*?

    A.   Citizens of all races have a right to a speedy trial

    B.   The right to protest injustices is fundamental

    C.   The African American right to vote should be protected

    D.   Prison conditions in the U.S. are unjust

■ Section II: Free Response

Concept Application

Starting in the fall of 2019 and continuing into 2020, Dr. Helen Y. Chu, an infectious disease expert, and her team at the University of Washington were collecting nasal swabs in the Seattle area for their research project on the flu. Once the first U.S. case of coronavirus was confirmed, Chu and her team repeatedly requested that state and federal government officials allow them to repurpose their tests for monitoring the new disease. Eventually, Washington State's epidemiologist contacted the chief of the national Centers for Disease Control and Prevention's (CDC) epidemiology and prevention branch, requesting that Chu's study be used to test for the coronavirus. The CDC's National Center for Immunization and Respiratory Disease responded that the national Food and Drug Administration (FDA) would have to approve this request. The FDA replied that it could not give approval because Chu's lab was not certified as a clinical lab, but rather as a research lab. The lab could apply to the Centers for Medicare and Medicaid for reclassification; however, that process could take months.

After reading the scenario, respond to A, B, and C below:

A. Describe a power Congress could use to address the problem outlined in the scenario.
B. In the context of the scenario, explain how the use of congressional power described in Part A can be affected by its interaction with the presidency.
C. In the context of the scenario, explain how the interaction between Congress and the presidency can be affected by federalism.

Quantitative Analysis

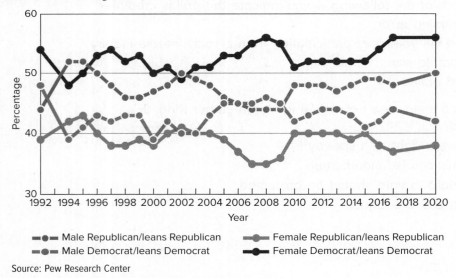

Source: Pew Research Center

Use the line graph to answer the questions.

A. Identify a trend in party identification.
B. Describe a similarity or difference in party identification by gender, and draw a conclusion about that similarity or difference.
C. Explain how party identification as shown in the line graph is related to ideology.

SCOTUS Comparison

In 2015, Tyson Timbs received approximately $73,000 from a life insurance policy when his father passed away. He spent $42,000 of that money on a Land Rover. After his father's death, Timbs, who was addicted to opioids, began to use heroin. Eventually, Timbs pled guilty to one count of dealing in a controlled substance and one count of conspiracy to commit theft. He was sentenced to six years with the first year on home detention and the next five on probation, and the Land Rover was seized as part of the civil forfeiture. He also was ordered to pay court costs and other fees totaling just over $1,000. The trial court found for Timbs, stating the forfeiture was "grossly disproportional to the gravity (seriousness) of the offense," because the Land Rover was worth over four times the maximum fine for the crime of $10,000. The Indiana Court of Appeals agreed with the trial court's decision. However, the Indiana Supreme Court reversed the decision and wrote, "the Supreme Court has never held that States are subject to the Excessive Fines Clause" and, for that reason, upheld the seizure. Timbs asked the Supreme Court of the United States to hear his case, and the Court granted review.

The issue argued before the U.S. Supreme Court was: Is the Eighth Amendment's excessive fines clause incorporated against the states under the Fourteenth Amendment? The Court held that the Eighth Amendment's excessive fines clause is incorporated against the states by the Fourteenth Amendment's due process clause.

A. Identify the constitutional issue that is common to both *Timbs v. Indiana* and *McDonald v. Chicago*.

B. Based on the constitutional issue identified in part A, explain why the facts of *Timbs* led to a holding similar to the holding in *McDonald v. Chicago*.

C. Describe an action that state prosecutors who disagree with the holding in *Timbs* could take to limit its impact.

Argumentation

Develop an argument that explains which of the three models of congressional representation—delegate, trustee, or politico—best achieved the founders' intent for the democracy.

In your essay, you must:

- Articulate a defensible claim or thesis that responds to the prompt and establishes a line of reasoning.

- Support your claim with at least TWO pieces of accurate and relevant information:

    - At least ONE piece of evidence must be from one of the following foundational documents:

        — *Federalist* No. 10

        — The U.S. Constitution

    - Use a second piece of evidence from another foundational document from the list or from your study of congressional representation.

- Respond to an opposing or alternative perspective using refutation, concession, or rebuttal.

Guidelines for Answering the Concept Application, Quantitative Analysis, and SCOTUS Comparison Questions

When answering any of these questions, make sure to label your responses a, b, and c, according to the prompt, and answer the question in complete sentences.

For any scenario question, answer the question *in the context of the scenario* which means you'll need to apply what is asked in the scenario itself each time referencing the scenario is requested. For the quantitative analysis question, make sure to reference the data in the prompt when answering the question. For the SCOTUS question, you'll need to identify the commonality between the required Supreme Court case and the case described in the prompt.

For all three of these questions (Concept Application, Quantitative Analysis, and SCOTUS), focus on the task verbs in the question. For example, if the question is asking to "identify," then you should provide specific information, but if the question is asking to "describe," you'll want to elaborate and provide more information. Always, always, be sure to answer the full question.

Guidelines for Answering the Argumentation Essay

You will write in essay format when responding to this question, and follow the format and order of the essay prompt, beginning your essay with a thesis that takes an explicit position answering the prompt and establishing a line of reasoning (do NOT attempt to argue both sides in the thesis) (paragraph 1).

Two pieces of evidence will be needed to be provided to support the thesis, and you should write one short (approximately 3 sentence) paragraph for each piece of evidence. When selecting evidence to defend the thesis/line of reasoning, think carefully about what you choose. To answer this question well, you'll need to be knowledgeable about the 9 required foundational documents because a short selection of these will be provided as choices to support the thesis. There is a set of evidence you can use in support of one side or another side, depending on what the question asks, so do not assume that any item in the list of evidence can be used for either side (paragraphs 2 and 3).

Next, you'll want to acknowledge the opposing position and refute or concede the opposing point of view (paragraph 4). One way to address the other side is to say the following: "Some may disagree with this thesis and claim . . . to be true. However, this view is short-sighted because of . . . "

The generic rubrics below will help you understand how readers will evaluate your answers to the Free Response Questions on the AP Exam.

∎ Concept Application

Scoring Criteria	Scoring guidelines w/acceptable examples for each criterion (Total: 3 pts)
Describe a political institution, behavior, or process connected with the scenario (0–1 point)	
Explain how the response in part (A) affects or is affected by a political process, government entity, or citizen behavior as related to the scenario (0–1 point).	
Explain how the scenario relates to a political institution, behavior, or process in the course (0–1 point)	

∎ Quantitative Analysis

Scoring Criteria	Scoring guidelines w/acceptable examples for each criterion (Total: 4 pts)
Identify or describe the data in the quantitative visual (0–1 point)	
Describe a pattern, trend, or similarity/difference as prompted in the question (0–1 point) and draw a conclusion for that pattern, trend, or similarity/difference (0–1 point).	
Explain how specific data in the quantitative visual demonstrates a principle in the prompt (0–1 point)	

◼ SCOTUS Comparison

Scoring Criteria	Scoring guidelines w/acceptable examples for each criterion (Total: 4 pts)	
Identify a similarity or difference between the two Supreme Court cases, as specified in the question (0–1 point)		
Provide prompted factual information from the specified required Supreme Court case (0–1 point), and explain how or why that information from the specified required Supreme Court case is relevant to the non-required Supreme Court case described in the question (0–1 point)		
Describe or explain an interaction between the holding in the non-required Supreme Court case and a relevant political institution, behavior, or process (0–1 point)		

▋ Argument Essay

Scoring Criteria	Scoring guidelines w/acceptable examples for each criterion (Total: 6 pts)	
Articulate a defensible claim or thesis that responds to the question and establishes a line of reasoning (0–1 point)	Position A	Position B
Describe one piece of evidence that is accurately linked to the topic of the question (1 out of 3 points)*; use one piece of specific and relevant evidence to support the argument (2 out of 3 points); use two pieces of specific and relevant evidence to support the argument (3 out of 3 points) *One piece of evidence will come from a required foundational document.	Position A	Position B
Explain how or why the evidence supports the claim or thesis (0–1 point)		
Respond to an opposing or alternate perspective using refutation, concession, or rebuttal that is consistent with the argument (0–1 point)	Position A	Position B

GLOSSARY

22nd Amendment Limits presidential terms to two.

501(c)4s Nonprofit organizations operated exclusively for the promotion of social welfare, including lobbying or engaging in political campaigning.

527 A tax-exempt group that raises money for political activities, much like those allowed under the soft money loophole.

A

absentee voting The casting of a ballot in advance by mail in situations where illness, travel, or other circumstances prevent voters from voting in their precincts.

administrative adjudication The process by which agencies resolve disputes over the implementation of their administrative rules.

administrative discretion The authority delegated to bureaucrats to use their expertise and judgment when determining how to implement public policy.

administrative rule making The process by which an independent commission or agency fills in the details of a vague law by formulating, proposing, and approving rules, regulations, and standards that will be enforced to implement the policy.

adversarial judicial system A judicial system in which two parties in a legal dispute each present its case and the court must determine which side wins the dispute and which loses.

advice and consent The Senate's authority to approve or reject the president's top appointments and negotiated treaties.

agency review Part of the committee or subcommittee process of considering a bill, wherein committee members ask executive agencies that would administer the law for written comments on the measure.

agenda setting The determination by Congress of which public issues the government should consider for legislation.

agents of socialization The individuals, organizations, and institutions that facilitate the acquisition of political views.

ambassadors Official representatives of the United States in host nations.

American dream The belief that in the United States hard work and persistence will reap a financially secure, happy, and healthy life, with upward mobility.

amicus curiae **brief ("friend of the court" brief)** A legal brief, filed by an individual or a group that is not a party in the case; it is written to influence the Supreme Court's decision.

Anti-Federalists Individuals who opposed ratification of the Constitution because they were deeply suspicious of the powers it gave to the national government and of the impact those powers would have on states' authority and individual freedoms.

appellate jurisdiction Judicial authority to review the interpretation and application of the law in previous decisions reached by another court in a case.

appropriation law A law that gives bureaucracies and other government entities the legal authority to spend money.

approval ratings The percentage of survey respondents who say that they "approve" or "strongly approve" of the way the president is doing his job.

Article I courts Courts created by Congress under constitutional authority provided in Article I that help administer and resolve conflicts over specific federal legislation.

articles of impeachment Charges against the president during an impeachment.

associate justice Title of the eight Supreme Court justices who are not the chief justice.

attentive public The segment of voters who pay careful attention to political issues.

attitudinal model Judicial decision-making model that claims judicial decision making is guided by policy and ideological preferences of individual judges.

Australian ballot A secret ballot prepared by the government, distributed to all eligible voters, and, when balloting is completed, counted by government officials in an unbiased fashion, without corruption or regard to individual preferences.

authoritarianism System of government in which the government holds strong powers but is checked by some forces.

authorization law A law that provides the plan of action to address a given societal concern and identifies the executive branch unit that will put the plan into effect.

B

bad tendency test A test established by the Supreme Court in *Gitlow v. New York* determining that any speech with the likelihood of inciting crime or disturbing the public peace can be silenced.

balance of power system A system of international alliances that, in theory, would balance the power of one group of nations against the power of another group and thus discourage war.

balanced budget A budget in which the government's expenditures are equal to or less than its revenues.

balanced ticket The selection of a running mate who brings diversity of ideology, geographic region, age, gender, race, or ethnicity to the slate.

ballot measure A proposed piece of legislation, a constitutional amendment, or some other policy proposal placed on the Election Day ballot for voters to approve or reject.

bandwidth The amount of data that can travel through a network in a given time period.

bench memo Written by a justice's law clerk, a summary of the case, outlining relevant facts and issues presented in the case documents and briefs, that may also suggest questions to be asked during oral arguments.

bench trial A trial in which the judge who presides over the trial decides on guilt or liability.

beyond a reasonable doubt The standard of proof the government must meet in criminal cases; the government must convince the judge or the jury that there is no reasonable doubt that the defendant committed the crime.

bicameral legislature Legislature comprising two parts, called *chambers*.

big data Large data sets collected from numerous sources that through computational analysis can indicate individual patterns, associations, preferences, and opinions.

big tent principle A strategy in which a political party seeks to build a broad coalition among individuals with wide-ranging beliefs, backgrounds, and priorities.

bill A proposed piece of legislation.

Bill of Rights The first 10 amendments to the Constitution, which were ratified in 1791, constituting an enumeration of the individual liberties with which the government is forbidden to interfere.

Black Codes Laws passed immediately after the Civil War by the former Confederate states that limited the rights of "freemen" (people formerly enslaved).

block grant A grant-in-aid for a broadly defined policy area, whose funding amount is typically based on a formula.

blogosphere The community of bloggers.

brinkmanship The Cold War–era practice of fooling the enemy by going to the edge (the brink), even if the party using the brinkmanship strategy had no intention of following through.

Brown v. Board of Education of Topeka This 1954 Supreme Court decision ruled that segregated schools violated the equal protection clause of the Fourteenth Amendment.

budget authority The authority provided by law for agencies to spend government funds.

budget deficit More money spent than collected through revenues.

budget reconciliation The annual process of rewriting authorization legislation to comply with the expenditure ceiling and revenue floor of the concurrent budget resolution for the upcoming fiscal year.

budget surplus Money left over after all expenses are paid.

bully pulpit The ability of presidents to speak out and be listened to by voters.

bureaucracy The collection of all executive branch organizations in a government.

bureaucratic structure A large organization with the following features: a division of labor, specialization of job tasks, hiring systems based on worker competency, hierarchy with a vertical chain of command, and standard operating procedures.

bureaucrats Non-elected government employees hired to implement public policy; public administrators; public servants.

Bush Doctrine The argument, articulated by President George W. Bush, that unilateral action directly targeted at an enemy is both justifiable and feasible.

business regulation Government rules, regulations, and standards directed at preserving competition in the marketplace.

C

cabinet The group of experts chosen by the president to serve as advisers on running the country.

campaign consultant A paid professional who specializes in the overall management of political campaigns or an aspect of campaigns.

campaign manager A professional whose duties comprise a variety of strategic and managerial tasks, from fund-raising to staffing a campaign.

campaign strategy The blueprint for the campaign, including a budget and fund-raising plan, an advertising strategy, and a staffing plan.

candidate committees Organizations that candidates form to support their individual election.

candidate-centered campaign A campaign in which the individual seeking election, rather than an entire party slate, is the focus.

capital budget A budget that accounts for the costs and revenues for expensive building and purchasing projects from which citizens will benefit for many years and for which governments can borrow money.

capitalism An economic system in which the means of producing wealth are privately owned and operated to produce profits.

casework Personal work by a member of Congress on behalf of a constituent or group of constituents, typically aimed at getting the government to do something the constituent wants done.

cash transfer The direct provision of cash (in forms including checks, debit cards, and tax breaks) to eligible individuals or to providers of goods or services to eligible individuals.

categorical formula grant A grant-in-aid for a narrowly defined purpose, whose dollar value is based on a formula.

categorical project grant A grant-in-aid for a narrowly defined purpose for which governments compete with each other by proposing specific projects.

caucus A meeting of party members held to select delegates to the national convention.

centralized federalism Intergovernmental relations in which the national government imposes its policy preferences on state and local governments.

cert memo Description of the facts of a case filed with the Supreme Court, the pertinent legal arguments, and a recommendation as to whether the case should be taken, written by one of the justices' law clerks and reviewed by all justices participating in the pool process.

***certiorari* petition** A petition submitted to the Supreme Court requesting review of a case already decided.

charter The constitution of a local government.

checks and balances A system in which each branch of government can monitor and limit the functions of the other branches.

chief justice The leading justice on the Supreme Court, who provides both organizational and intellectual leadership.

chief of staff Among the most important staff members of the White House Office (WHO); serves as both an adviser to the president and the manager of the WHO.

citizens Members of the polity who, through birth or naturalization, enjoy the rights, privileges, and responsibilities attached to membership in a given nation.

Citizens United v. Federal Election Commission Supreme Court ruling stating that corporations and labor unions are entitled to the same First Amendment protections that individuals enjoy, resulting in drastically increased spending through super PACs by corporations and labor organizations.

civic engagement Individual and collective actions designed to identify and address issues of public concern.

civil disobedience Active, but nonviolent, refusal to comply with laws or governmental policies that are morally objectionable, while accepting the consequences of violating these laws.

civil law The body of law dealing with disputes between individuals, between an individual and corporations, between corporations, and between individuals and their governments over harms caused by a party's actions or inactions.

civil liberties Constitutionally established guarantees that protect citizens, opinions, and property against arbitrary government interference.

civil rights The rights and privileges guaranteed to all citizens under the equal protection and due process clauses of the Fifth and Fourteenth Amendments; the idea that individuals are protected from discrimination based on characteristics such as race, national origin, religion, and sex.

civil servants Bureaucrats hired through a merit-based personnel system and who have job protection.

clash of civilizations thesis Samuel Huntington's idea that bitter cultural conflict will continue and escalate between modern Western democracies and fundamentalist Islamic states.

clear and probable danger test A standard established in the 1951 case *Dennis v. U.S.* whereby the government could suppress speech to avoid grave danger, even if the probability of the dangerous result was relatively remote; replaced by the imminent lawless action (incitement) test in 1969.

climate change A pattern of significant changes in regional and/or global temperature, precipitation, wind patterns, and other measures of climate that occur over several decades.

climate control The practice of using public outreach to build favorable public opinion of an organization.

closed primary A type of primary in which voting in a party's primary is limited to members of that party.

cloture A procedural move in which a supermajority of 60 senators agrees to end a filibuster.

coattail effect The phenomenon by which candidates running for lower-level offices such as city council benefit in an election from the popularity of a top-of-ticket nominee.

Cold War The political, ideological, and military conflict that lasted from 1945 until 1990 between communist nations led by the Soviet Union and Western democracies led by the United States.

collective defense The concept that allied nations agree to defend one another in the face of an invasion.

collective goods Outcomes shared by the general public; also called *public goods.*

collective security The idea that peace could be achieved if nations agreed to collectively oppose any nation that attacked another country.

collegial court A court made up of a group of judges who must evaluate a case together and decide on the outcome; compromise and negotiation take place as members try to build a majority coalition.

commander in chief The president's role as supreme officer in charge of the country's armed forces

commerce clause Article I clause that delegates to Congress the power to regulate interstate and international commercial interactions.

commercial speech Advertising statements that describe products.

commission A form of local government that is more common in county and township governments than in other general-purpose governments and for which voters elect a body of officials who collectively hold legislative and executive powers.

common law Judge-made law grounded in tradition and previous judicial decisions, instead of in written law.

concurrent budget resolution A document approved by the House and the Senate at the beginning of their budget processes that establishes binding expenditure ceilings and a binding revenue floor as well as proposed expenditure levels for major policy categories.

concurrent powers Basic governing functions that are exercised by the national and state governments independently, and at the same time, including the power to make policy, raise revenue, implement policies, and establish courts.

concurring opinion A judicial opinion agreeing with the majority decision in the case but disagreeing with at least some of the legal interpretations or conclusions reached in the majority opinion.

confederal system A government structure in which several independent sovereign states agree to cooperate on specified policy matters by creating a central governing body; each sovereign state retains ultimate authority over other governmental matters within its borders, so the central governing body is not a sovereign government.

confederation A union of independent states in which each state retains its sovereignty, that is, its ultimate power to govern, and agrees to work collaboratively on matters the states expressly agree to delegate to a central governing body.

conference committee A bicameral, bipartisan committee composed of legislators whose job is to reconcile two versions of a bill.

conflict of interest In the case of public servants, the situation in which they can personally benefit from a decision they make or an action they take in the process of doing their jobs.

congressional oversight The process by which the legislative branch "checks" the executive branch to ensure that the laws Congress has passed are being administered in keeping with legislators' intent.

Connecticut Compromise The compromise between the Virginia Plan and the New Jersey Plan that created a bicameral legislature with one chamber's representation based on population and the other chamber having two members for each state (also known as the *Great Compromise*).

consent of the governed The idea that, in a democracy, the government's power derives from the consent of the people.

conservatism An ideology that emphasizes preserving tradition and relying on community and family as mechanisms of continuity in society.

consolidation The phenomenon of large corporations buying smaller ones so that there are fewer and fewer companies' products available.

constitution Document that presents the mission of the government, the fundamental principles that will guide the government's operations, and the foundational structures and procedures by which the government operates to fulfill its mission.

constitutional law The body of law that comes out of the courts in cases involving the interpretation of the Constitution.

constitutionalism Government that is structured by law, and in which the power of government is limited.

consumer price index (CPI) The most common measure of inflation, it gauges the average change in prices over time of a "market basket" of goods and services including food, clothing, shelter, fuel, transportation costs, and selected medical costs.

containment The Cold War–era policy of preventing the spread of communism, mainly by providing military and economic aid as well as political advice to countries vulnerable to a communist takeover.

continuing resolution An agreement of the House and Senate that authorizes agencies not covered by approved appropriation laws to continue to spend money within their previous budget year's levels.

contracting-out Also called *outsourcing*; a process by which the government contracts with a private for-profit or nonprofit organization to provide public services, such as disaster relief, or resources needed by the government, such as fighter planes.

contributory cash-transfer program (social insurance program) A program paid for with tax revenues collected specifically for it.

cooperative federalism Intergovernmental relations in which the national government supports state governments' efforts to address the domestic matters reserved to them.

Council of Governments (COG) A regional agency composed of representatives from several local governments who share resources to address one or more mutual problems.

council-manager (commission-administrator) A form of general-purpose local government found in many counties and the majority of cities; it is composed of an elected body with legislative and executive powers whose members hire a professional manager to oversee the government's day-to-day operations.

council-mayor (council-executive) A form of general-purpose local government comprising (1) a legislative body elected by voters and (2) an independently elected chief executive.

country desk The official operation of the U.S. government in each country that has diplomatic ties to the United States.

county government A general-purpose local government created by states to assist them in implementing policy in geographic subdivisions of the state.

court of last resort The highest court in a court system.

courts of appeal Courts with authority to review cases heard by other courts to correct errors in the interpretation or application of law.

criminal due process rights Safeguards for those accused of crime; these rights constrain government conduct in investigating crimes, trying cases, and punishing offenders.

criminal law The body of law dealing with conduct so harmful to society as a whole that it is prohibited by statute, and is prosecuted and punished by the government.

cult of the robe The trappings of judicial office (robe, high bench, no filming, private deliberations) that separate the judicial branch from the elected bodies to make it appear to be outside partisan politics.

cyber cascade What occurs when an electronic document becomes very widely distributed digitally through e-mail, social networking, or video sharing.

D

dark money Funds given to nonprofit organizations through an anonymous donation and spent to influence elections.

de facto segregation Segregation maintained by practice.

de jure segregation Segregation mandated by law.

dealignment The situation in which fewer voters support the two major political parties, instead identifying themselves as independent, or splitting their ticket between candidates from more than one party.

debt ceiling The legal borrowing limit for the national government.

defense conversion President Jimmy Carter's attempt to convert the nation's vast military apparatus to peacetime functions.

deficit spending Government expenditures costing more than is raised in taxes, during the budget year, leading to borrowing and debt.

democracy Government in which supreme power of governance lies in the hands of its citizens.

demographics The study of populations in terms of race, sex, educational attainment and other characteristics.

department One of 15 executive branch units responsible for a broadly defined policy area and whose top administrator (secretary) is appointed by the president, is confirmed by the Senate, and serves at the discretion of the president.

depression A long-term and severe recession.

deregulation The reduction or elimination of government rules and regulations (laws) that businesses and industries must follow.

descriptive representation The attempt to ensure that governing bodies include representatives of major demographic groups—such as women, African Americans, Latinas, Jews, and Catholics—in proportions similar to their representation in the population at large.

détente The easing of tensions between the United States and its communist rivals.

deterrence The idea that nations would be less likely to engage in nuclear war if adversaries each had first-strike capability.

devolution The process whereby the national government returns policy responsibilities to state or local governments.

digital divide Unequal access to computer technology.

digital paywall The practice of limiting access to a website unless users pay a fee or purchase a subscription.

Dillon's rule The ruling articulated by Judge John Forrest Dillon in 1868 that local governments are creatures of the state that created them, and they have only the powers expressly mentioned in the charters written and approved by the state and those necessarily implied by the formally expressed powers.

diplomacy The conduct of international relations, particularly involving the negotiation of treaties and other agreements between nations.

direct democracy A structure of government in which citizens discuss and decide policy through majority rule.

direct provision A policy tool whereby the government that creates a policy hires public servants to provide the service.

direct subsidy A cash transfer from general revenues to particular persons or private

companies engaged in activities that the national government believes support the public good.

director of national intelligence (DNI) The person responsible for coordinating and overseeing all the intelligence agencies within the executive branch.

discharge petition A special tactic used to extract a bill from a committee to have it considered by the entire House.

discretionary jurisdiction The authority of a court to select the cases it will hear from among all the cases appealed to it.

discretionary spending Payment on programs for which Congress and the president must approve budget authority each year in appropriation legislation.

dissenting opinion A judicial opinion disagreeing both with the majority's disposition of a case and with their legal interpretations and conclusions.

district courts The federal trial courts with mandatory jurisdiction.

divided government The situation that exists when Congress is controlled by one party and the presidency by the other.

divine right of kings The assertion that monarchies, as a manifestation of God's will, could rule absolutely without regard to the will or well-being of their subjects.

doctrine of *stare decisis* From the Latin for "let the decision stand," a common-law doctrine that directs judges to identify previously decided cases with similar facts and then apply to the current case the rule of law used by the courts in the earlier cases.

domestic policies Policies addressing the problems, needs, and relations of people residing within the country's borders.

domino theory The principle that if one nation fell to communism, other nations in its geographic vicinity also would succumb.

double jeopardy The trying of a person again for the same crime that he or she has been cleared of in court; barred by the Fifth Amendment.

dual court system The existence of 50 independently functioning state judicial systems, each responsible for resolving legal disputes over its state laws, and one national judicial system, responsible for resolving legal disputes over national laws.

dual federalism The initial model of national and state relations in which the national government takes care of its enumerated powers while the state governments independently take care of their reserved powers.

dual sovereignty A system of government in which ultimate governing authority is divided between two levels of government, a central government and regional governments, with each level having ultimate authority over different policy matters.

due process The legal safeguards that prevent the government from arbitrarily depriving citizens of life, liberty, or property; guaranteed by the Fifth and Fourteenth Amendments.

E

e-campaigning The practice of mobilizing voters using the Internet.

e-Government Employment of the Internet for delivering government information and services to the citizens.

e-petition An online petition used as a tool to garner support for a position or cause.

earmark A designation within a spending bill that provides for a specific expenditure.

economic boom Rapid economic growth.

economic incentive Motivation to join an interest group because the group works for policies that will provide members with material benefits.

economic policy A collection of public policies that affect the health of the economy, which includes taxing and spending policies (fiscal policy), monetary policy, regulatory policy, and trade policy.

economy A system for producing, selling, buying, and using goods and services.

efficacy Citizens' belief that they have the ability to achieve something desirable and that the government listens to people like them.

electioneering Working to influence the election of candidates who support the organization's issues.

Electoral College The name given to the body of representatives elected by voters in each state to elect the president and the vice president.

elite theory A theory that holds that a group of wealthy, educated individuals wields most political power.

emergency powers Broad powers exercised by the president during times of national crisis.

Engel v. Vitale The Supreme Court banned formal teacher- or adminstrator-led prayer in public elementary or secondary schools as a violation of the establishment clause of the First Amendment.

entitlement program A program for which the government guarantees benefits to all who meet the eligibility criteria.

enumerated powers The powers of the national government that are listed in the Constitution.

environmental racism The term used to describe the higher incidence of environmental threats and subsequent health problems in lower-income communities, which frequently are also communities dominated by people of color.

equal protection clause The Fourteenth Amendment clause stating that no state shall "deny to any person within its jurisdiction the equal protection of the laws."

essential services Public services provided by state and local governments on a daily basis to prevent chaos and hazardous conditions in society.

establishment clause The First Amendment clause that bars the government from passing any law "respecting an establishment of religion"; often interpreted as a separation of church and state but this is increasingly challenged.

exclusionary rule The criminal procedural rule stating that evidence obtained illegally cannot be used in a trial.

executive agreement An international agreement between the United States and other nations, not subject to Senate approval and in effect only during the administration of the president who negotiates the agreement.

executive budget The budget document and budget message that explains the president's fiscal plan.

Executive Office of the President (EOP) The offices, councils, and boards that help the president to carry out his day-to-day responsibilities.

executive order The power of the president to issue orders that carry the force of law.

executive privilege The right of the chief executive and members of the administration to withhold information from Congress or the courts, or the right to refuse to appear before legislative or judicial bodies.

exit polls Polls conducted at polling places on Election Day to project the winner of an election before the polls close.

expressed powers Presidential powers enumerated in the Constitution.

extradition The return of individuals accused of a crime to the state in which the crime was committed upon the request of that state's governor.

F

fairness doctrine The requirement that stations holding broadcast licenses present both sides of controversial issues of public importance and do so in a manner that was honest, fair, and balanced.

federal courts of appeals (circuit courts) Federal courts with mandatory, appellate jurisdiction.

federalism The U.S. government structure of two levels of governing, involving both national and state governments.

federal system A governmental structure with two levels of government in which each level has sovereignty over different policy matters and geographic areas; a system of government with dual sovereignty.

Federalists Individuals who supported the new Constitution as presented by the Constitutional Convention in 1787.

feminization of poverty The phenomenon of increasing numbers of unmarried, divorced, and separated women with children living in poverty.

fighting words Speech that is likely to bring about public disorder or chaos; the Supreme Court has held that this speech may be banned in public places to ensure the preservation of public order.

filibuster A procedural move by a member of the Senate to attempt to halt passage of a bill, during which the senator can speak for an unlimited time on the Senate floor.

finance director A professional who works with candidates in identifying likely contributors to the campaign and arranges events and meetings with donors.

fireside chats President Franklin D. Roosevelt's radio addresses to the country.

fiscal federalism The relationship between the national government and state and local governments whereby the national government provides grant money to state and local governments.

fiscal policy Government spending and taxing and their effect on the economy.

fiscal year (FY) The 12-month accounting period for revenue raising and spending, which for the national government begins on October 1 and ends on September 30 of the following year.

food insecurity The situation in which people have a limited or an uncertain ability to obtain, in socially acceptable ways, enough nutritious food to live a healthy and active life.

foreign service officers The diplomatic and consular staff at U.S. embassies abroad.

Foursquare Geolocation app that uses an iPhone's built-in GPS to display attractions in your area.

framing The process by which the media set a context that helps people understand important events and matters of shared interest.

franking The privilege of sending mail free of charge by members of Congress.

free exercise clause The First Amendment clause prohibiting the government from enacting laws prohibiting an individual's practice of his or her religion; often in contention with the establishment clause.

free rider problem The phenomenon of someone deriving benefit from others' actions.

free trade policy The elimination of tariffs and nontariff trade barriers so that international trade is expanded.

full faith and credit clause The constitutional clause that requires states to comply with and uphold the public acts, records, and judicial decisions of other states.

G

gender gap The measurable difference in the way women and men vote for candidates and in the way they view political issues.

general election An election that determines which candidates win the offices being sought.

general-purpose government A government providing services in numerous and diverse policy and functional areas to the residents living within its borders.

generational effect The impact of an important external event in shaping the views of a generation.

gerrymandering The drawing of legislative district boundaries to benefit an incumbent, a political party, or another group.

Gideon v. Wainwright The Supreme Court determined that the Sixth Amendment's guarantee to the right of counsel requires that the government provide an attorney for people who cannot afford to hire one.

Gitlow v. New York The Supreme Court decision establishing the **bad tendency test**, which determines that any speech with the likelihood of inciting crime or disturbing the public peace can be silenced.

global economy The worldwide economy created by the integration and interdependence of national economies.

global warming The rising temperature of the earth as a result of pollution that traps solar heat, keeping the air warmer than it would otherwise be.

GOTV Get out the vote.

government The institution that creates and implements policy and laws that guide the conduct of the nation and its citizens.

government corporation An executive branch unit that sells a service and is expected to be financially self-sufficient.

government subsidy A tax break or another kind of financial support that encourages behaviors the government deems beneficial to the public good.

grandfather clause A clause exempting individuals from voting conditions such as poll taxes or literacy tests if they or their ancestors had voted before 1870, thus sparing most white voters.

grant-in-aid (intergovernmental transfer) The transfer of money from one government to another government that does not need to be paid back.

grassroots organizing Tasks that involve direct contact with voters or potential voters.

greenhouse effect The heating of the earth's atmosphere as a result of humans' burning of fossil fuels and the resultant buildup of carbon dioxide and other gases.

gross domestic product (GDP) The total market value of all goods and services produced by labor and properties within a country's borders during a specified time period.

H

habeas corpus An ancient right that protects an individual in custody from being held without the right to be heard in a court of law.

hacktivism The authorized or unauthorized use of or destruction of electronic files in pursuit of a political or social goal.

hate crime A crime committed against a person, property, or society, in which the offender is motivated, in part or in whole, by his or her bias against the victim because of the victim's race, religion, disability, sexual orientation, or ethnicity.

healthy economy According to economists, an economy experiencing an increase in its gross domestic product (GDP), low unemployment rate, and low inflation rate.

hearings Sessions held by committees or sub-committees to gather information and views from experts.

hegemony A form of imperial geographic dominance.

heightened scrutiny test (intermediate scrutiny test) The guidelines used most frequently by the courts to determine the legality of sex-based discrimination; on the basis of this test, sex-based discrimination is legal if the government can prove that it is substantially related to the achievement of an important public interest.

Holocaust The genocide perpetrated by Adolf Hitler and the Nazis of 6 million Jews, along with political dissidents, Catholics, homosexuals, individuals with disabilities, and Roma.

home rule Power delegated by a state government to its citizens to formulate and adopt their municipal and county government charters and to determine the extent of those governments' powers and responsibilities as long as they comply with state and national law.

home rule charter A local government constitution written and approved by citizens following state-mandated procedures, including a referendum.

honeymoon period A time early in a new president's administration characterized by optimistic approval by the public.

hopper A wooden box that sits on a desk at the front of the House of Representatives, in which House members place bills they want to introduce.

horizontal federalism The state-to-state relationships created by the U.S. Constitution.

House majority leader The leader of the majority party, who helps the Speaker to develop and implement strategy and who works with other members of the House of Representatives.

House minority leader The leader of the minority party, whose job mirrors that of the majority leader but without the power that comes from holding a majority in the House of Representatives.

household income The total pretax earnings of all residents over the age of 15 living in a home.

housing insecurity The situation in which people have limited or uncertain ability to obtain, in socially acceptable ways, affordable, safe, and decent-quality permanent housing.

Human Development Index (HDI) A UN-created measure to determine how well a country's economy is providing for a long and healthy life, educational opportunity, and a decent standard of daily living.

I

imminent lawless action test (incitement test) A standard established in the 1969 *Brandenburg v. Ohio* case, whereby speech is restricted only if it goes beyond mere advocacy, or words, to create a high likelihood of immediate disorder or lawlessness.

impeachment The power of the House of Representatives to formally accuse the president (and other high-ranking officials, including the vice president and federal judges) of crimes.

imperial presidency A term coined by Arthur Schlesinger to describe the modern executive branch and the enormous powers the office has gained through assertion, the size of the bureaucracy, and the presence of staff loyal to an individual president.

implied powers The powers of the national government that are not enumerated in the Constitution but that Congress claims are necessary and proper for the national government to fulfill its enumerated powers in accordance with the necessary and proper clause of the Constitution.

impressment During the early 19th century, the forcible removal of merchant sailors from U.S. ships on the spurious grounds that the sailors were deserters from the British Navy.

in-kind assistance A cash transfer in which the government pays cash to those who provide goods or services to eligible individuals.

income inequality The gap in the proportion of national income held by the richest compared to that held by the poorest.

incumbency The situation of already holding the office that is up for reelection.

independent A voter who does not belong to any organized political party; often used as a synonym for an unaffiliated voter.

independent administrative agency An executive branch unit created by Congress and the president that is responsible for a narrowly defined function and whose structure is intended to be protected from partisan politics.

independent expenditures Outlays by PACs and others, typically for advertising for or against a candidate, but not coordinated with a candidate's campaign.

independent regulatory commission An executive branch unit outside of cabinet departments, responsible for developing standards of behavior within specific industries and businesses, monitoring compliance with these standards, and imposing sanctions on violators.

indexed benefit A government benefit with an automatic cost-of-living increase based on the rate of inflation.

indirect democracy Sometimes called a *representative democracy,* a system in which citizens elect representatives who decide policies on behalf of their constituents.

individualistic political culture The view that the decision to take part in government is an individual choice and those who choose to participate determine the purpose of government and personally benefit from their participation.

inflation The decreased value of money as evidenced by increased prices.

infotainment A hybrid of the words *information* and *entertainment*; news shows that combine entertainment and news.

inherent characteristics Individual attributes such as race, national origin, religion, and sex.

inherent powers Presidential powers that are implied in the Constitution.

initiative A citizen-sponsored proposal allowed in 24 states that can result in new or amended legislation or a state constitutional amendment.

inspectors general Political appointees who work within a government agency to ensure the integrity of public service by investigating allegations of misconduct by bureaucrats.

instant runoff election A special runoff election in which the computerized voting machine simulates the elimination of last-place vote-getters.

instructed delegate model A model of representation in which legislators, as representatives of their constituents, should vote in keeping with the constituents' views, even if those views contradict the legislators' personal views.

interest group An organization that seeks to achieve goals by influencing government decision making.

intergovernmental relations (IGR) The interactions of two or more governments (national, state, and local) in their collective efforts to provide goods and services to the people they each serve.

intermestics The influence of domestic interests on foreign policy.

International Monetary Fund (IMF) The institution charged with regulating monetary relationships among nations, including establishment of exchange rates for major world currencies; established in 1944 by the Bretton Woods Agreement.

intersectionality The experience of multiple forms of oppression (based on race, gender, class, sexual orientation, or sexual identity) simultaneously.

interstate compacts Agreements between states that Congress has the authority to review and reject.

interventionism A foreign policy characterized by a nation's willingness to participate and intervene in international situations, including another country's affairs.

invidious discrimination Occurs when a class of people are treated in a manner that is malicious, hostile, or damaging.

iron triangle The interaction of mutual interests among members of Congress, executive agencies, and organized interests during policy making.

ISIS The Islamic State in Iraq and Syria, a radical international fundamentalist terror organization.

isolationism A foreign policy characterized by a nation's unwillingness to participate in international affairs.

issue network The fluid web of connections among those concerned about a policy and those who create and administer the policy.

J

Jim Crow laws Laws requiring the strict separation of racial groups, with whites and "non-whites" required to attend separate schools, work in different jobs, and use segregated public accommodations, such as transportation and restaurants.

joint committee A bicameral committee composed of members of both chambers of Congress.

joint referral The practice, abolished in the 104th Congress, by which a bill could be referred to two different committees for consideration.

journalism The practice of gathering information and reporting events.

judicial activism An approach to judicial decision making whereby judges are willing to strike down laws made by elected officials as well as step away from precedents.

judicial federalism State courts' use of their state constitutions to determine citizens' rights, particularly when state constitutions guarantee greater protections than does the U.S. Constitution.

judicial independence Insulating judges from the need to be accountable to voters or elected officials so that they can make impartial decisions based on the law.

judicial restraint An approach to judicial decision making whereby judges defer to the democratically elected legislative and executive branches of government.

judicial review Court authority to determine that an action taken by any government official or governing body violates the Constitution; established by the Supreme Court in the 1803 *Marbury v. Madison* case.

jury trial A trial in which a group of people selected to hear the evidence presented decides on guilt or liability.

K

Keynesian economics The theory that recommends that during a recession the national government increase its spending and decrease taxes, and during a boom, cut spending and increase taxes.

L

laissez-faire The hands-off stance of a government in regard to the marketplace.

law A body of rules established by government officials that bind governments, individuals, and nongovernment organizations.

lead committee The primary committee considering a bill.

League of Nations A representative body founded in the aftermath of World War I to establish the collective security of nations.

legacy systems The old way of doing things, either in paper form or using outdated computer systems.

legal model Judicial decision-making model that focuses on legal norms and principles as the guiding force in judicial decision making, including existing precedents, relevant constitutional and statutory law, and the lawmakers' intent.

legitimacy A quality conferred on government by citizens who believe that its exercise of power is right and proper.

***Lemon* test** A three-part test established by the Supreme Court in the 1971 case *Lemon v. Kurtzman* to determine whether government aid to parochial schools is constitutional; the test is also applied to other cases involving the establishment clause.

letter to the editor A letter in which a reader responds to a story in a newspaper, knowing that the letter might be published in that paper.

libel False written statements about others that harm their reputation.

liberalism An ideology that advocates change in the social, political, and economic realms to better protect the well-being of individuals and to produce equality within society.

libertarianism An ideology whose advocates believe that government should take a "hands off" approach in most matters.

liberty The most essential quality of American democracy; it is both the freedom from governmental interference in citizens' lives and the freedom to pursue happiness.

life term (life tenure) Judicial appointment that will last until the judge dies.

limited government Government that is restricted in what it can do so that the rights of the people are protected.

limited war A combatant country's self-imposed limitation on the tactics and strategy it uses, particularly its avoidance of the use of nuclear weapons.

literacy test A test to determine eligibility to vote; it was designed so that few African Americans would pass.

living Constitution View that legal interpretation of the Constitution can and should adapt to changing social customs and norms.

living wage A wage high enough to keep workers and their families out of poverty and to allow them to enjoy a basic living standard.

lobby To communicate directly with policymakers on an interest group's behalf.

logrolling The practice of members of Congress agreeing to vote for a bill in exchange for their colleague's vote on another bill.

loyal opposition A role that the party out of power plays, highlighting its objections to policies and priorities of the government in power.

M

majority rule The idea that in a democracy, only policies with 50 percent plus one vote are enacted, and only candidates that win 50 percent plus one vote are elected.

majority whip The go-between with the majority leadership and party members in the House of Representatives.

majority-minority district A legislative district composed of a majority of a given minority community—say, African Americans—the intent of which is to make it likely that a member of that minority will be elected to Congress.

mandate Clauses in legislation, including legislation that establishes grants-in-aid programs, that direct state and local governments to comply with national rules, standards, and other legislative directives.

mandatory jurisdiction The requirement that a court hear all cases filed with it.

mandatory spending Government spending for debt and programs whose budget authority is provided in legislation other than annual appropriation acts; this budget authority is open ended, obligating the government to pay for the program whatever the cost, every year.

manifest destiny The idea that it was the United States' destiny to spread throughout the North American continent; used to rationalize the expansion of U.S. territory.

Marbury v. Madison The 1803 Supreme Court case that established the power of judicial review, which allows the Court to strike down laws passed by the other branches that it views to be in conflict with the Constitution.

marketplace of ideas A concept at the core of the freedoms of expression and press, based on the belief that true and free political discourse depends on a free and unrestrained discussion of ideas.

markup The process by which the members of legislative committees "mark up" a bill with suggested language for changes and amendments.

Marshall Plan The U.S. government program that provided funds necessary for Western European countries to rebuild after World War II.

matching funds requirement A grant requirement that obligates the government receiving the grant to spend some of its own money to match a specified percentage of the grant money provided.

McCulloch v. Maryland The 1819 case that established that the necessary and proper clause justifies broad understandings of enumerated powers.

McDonald v. Chicago This Supreme Court decision requires the states to guarantee their own citizens the Second Amendment's protection of an individual's right to own guns.

means-tested benefit A benefit for which eligibility is based on having an income below a government-specified amount, typically based on a percentage of the poverty guideline.

media Tools used to store and deliver information or data.

media consultant A professional who brings the campaign message to voters by creating handouts and all forms of media ads.

media segmentation The breaking down of the media according to the specific audiences they target.

median household income The middle of all household incomes—50 percent of households have incomes less than the median and 50 percent have incomes greater than the median.

merit selection process A process for selecting judges in which a nonpartisan committee nominates candidates, the governor or legislature appoints judges from among those candidates to a short term of service, and then the appointed judges face a retention election at the end of the short term.

merit-based civil service A personnel system in which bureaucrats are hired on the basis of the principles of competence, equal opportunity (open competition), and political neutrality; once hired, these public servants have job protection.

microtarget Data-mining techniques that facilitate the tracking of individual voter preferences so that tailored messages in various forms can be used to generate support, contributions, and votes.

minority whip The go-between with the minority leadership, whose job mirrors that of the majority whip but without the power that comes from holding a majority in the House of Representatives.

Miranda rights A criminal procedural rule, established in the 1966 case *Miranda v. Arizona,* requiring police to inform criminal suspects, on their arrest, of their legal rights, such as the right to remain silent and the right to counsel; these warnings must be read to suspects before interrogation.

monarchy Government in which a member of a royal family, usually a king or queen, has absolute authority over a territory and its government.

monetarism The theory that says the government's proper economic role is to control the rate of inflation by controlling the amount of money in circulation.

monetary policy The body of Federal Reserve actions aimed at adjusting the amount of money (coin, currency, and bank deposits) in the economy to maintain a stable, low level of inflation.

Monroe Doctrine President James Monroe's 1823 declaration that the Americas should not be considered subjects for future colonization by any European power.

moralistic political culture The view that the purpose of government is to serve the public good, including providing for those who are disadvantaged, and that all citizens should participate in government.

muckraking Criticism and exposés of corruption in government and industry by journalists at the turn of the 20th century.

multilateral Many-sided; having the support of numerous nations.

municipal government Self-governing general-purpose government—including city, borough, and town governments—created by states to provide goods and services within a densely populated area.

mutual assured destruction (MAD) The doctrine that if one nation attacked another with nuclear weapons, the other would be capable of retaliating and would retaliate with such force as to ensure mutual annihilation.

N

narrowcasting The practice of aiming media content at specific segments of the public.

national debt The total amount of money the government owes to all the individuals and groups that loaned it money.

national security advisor The assistant to the president for national security affairs, advisor to the president on national security policy, and administrator over the day-to-day operations of the National Security Council.

National Security Council (NSC) Consisting of top foreign policy advisers and relevant cabinet officials, this is an arm of the Executive Office of the President that the president consults on matters of foreign policy and national security.

natural law The assertion that standards that govern human behavior are derived from the nature of humans themselves and can be applied universally.

natural rights The rights possessed by all humans as a gift from nature, or God, including the rights to life, liberty, and the pursuit of happiness (also called *unalienable rights*).

naturalization The process of becoming a citizen by means other than birth, as in the case of immigrants.

necessary and proper clause (elastic clause) A clause in Article I, Section 8, of the Constitution that gives Congress the power to do whatever it deems necessary and constitutional to meet its enumerated obligations; the basis for the implied powers.

net neutrality The idea that Internet traffic should flow through the Internet pipeline without interference or discrimination by those who own or are running the pipeline.

New Deal Franklin D. Roosevelt's broad social welfare program in which the government would bear the responsibility of providing a safety net to protect the most disadvantaged members of society.

New Deal coalition The group composed of southern Democrats, northern city dwellers, immigrants, the poor, Catholics, labor union members, blue-collar workers, African Americans, and women who elected Franklin D. Roosevelt to the presidency four times.

New Jersey Plan The proposal presented in response to the Virginia Plan by the less populous states at the Constitutional Convention, which called for a unicameral national legislature in which all states would have an equal voice (equal representation), an executive office composed of several people elected by Congress, and a Supreme Court whose members would be appointed by the executive office.

new media Sources of information—including Internet websites, blogs, social networking sites such as Facebook and Twitter, photo- and video-sharing platforms such as Instagram and YouTube, and apps—and the cellular and satellite technologies that facilitate their use.

New York Times v. U.S. In this decision, the Supreme Court found that prior restraint of the press—prohibiting publication—violated the First Amendment's protection of freedom of the press.

news aggregators Services that compile in one location news we want from various outlets.

NIMBY ("not in my backyard") syndrome A pattern of citizens' behavior in which people are not inspired to participate in politics until a government action or inaction threatens them directly.

Nixon Doctrine Policy emphasizing the responsibility of U.S. allies to provide for their own national defense and security, aimed at improving relations with the communist nations, including the Soviet Union and China.

noncontributory program A program that benefits a targeted population and is paid for by a portion of the general revenue collected from all taxpayers.

nonpartisan election An election in which the candidates are not nominated by political parties and the ballot does not include party affiliations.

nontariff trade barriers Business and social regulations as well as government subsidies aimed at creating a competitive advantage in trade.

normal trade relations (NTR) status The international trade principle holding that the least restrictive trade conditions (best tariff rates) offered to any one national trading partner will be offered to every other nation in a trading network (also known as *most favored nations*).

North Atlantic Treaty Organization (NATO) An international mutual defense alliance formed in 1949 that created a structure for regional security for its 15 member nations.

nuclear option A maneuver exercised by the presiding officer in the Senate in which a standard rule of the Senate is overridden.

nullification A legal theory that state governments have the authority to invalidate national actions they deem unconstitutional.

O

obscenity Indecent or offensive speech or expression.

Office of Management and Budget (OMB) The office that creates the president's annual budget.

office-block ballot A type of ballot that arranges all the candidates for a particular office under the name of that office.

oligarchy Government in which an elite few hold power.

ombudsperson A role in which an elected or appointed leader acts as an advocate for citizens by listening to and investigating complaints against a government agency.

open primary A type of primary in which both parties' ballots are available in the voting booth, and the voters simply select one on which to register their preferences.

operating budget A budget that accounts for all the costs of day-to-day government operations and covers such items as salaries and benefits, utilities, office supplies, and rent.

ordinary scrutiny test (rational basis test) On the basis of this test, sex-based discrimination is legal if it is a reasonable means by which the government can achieve a legitimate public interest.

original jurisdiction Judicial authority to hear cases for the first time and to determine guilt or liability by applying the law to the facts presented.

originalism (textualism) View that the law should be interpreted based on how it was publicly understood when written.

P

partisan election An election in which candidates are nominated by political parties and the ballot lists each candidate's political party affiliation.

partisan federalism The phenomenon of preference for state or national government action (hence, preference for dual federalism, cooperative federalism, or centralized federalism) depending on policy substance and partisan makeup of government at the other levels.

party identifiers Individuals who identify themselves as a member of one party or the other.

party in government The partisan identifications of elected leaders in local, county, state, and federal government.

party in the electorate Individuals who identify with or tend to support a party.

party organization The formal party apparatus, including committees, party leaders, conventions, and workers.

party system The categorization of the number and competitiveness of political parties in a polity.

party-column ballot A ballot that organizes the candidates by political party.

patronage The system in which a party leader rewarded political supporters with jobs or government contracts in exchange for their support of the party.

patronage system A personnel system in which the chief executive officer (CEO) can appoint whomever he or she wants to top bureaucratic positions, without the need for open competition for applicants; those hired through patronage typically serve at the pleasure of the CEO who hired them.

payroll taxes Taxes employers deduct from workers' paychecks that pay for social insurance programs including Social Security and Medicare.

penal code The compilation of a state's criminal law—legislation that defines crime—into one document.

penny press Newspapers that sold for a penny in the 1830s.

platform The formal statement of a party's principles and policy objectives.

Plessy v. Ferguson 1896 Supreme Court ruling creating the separate but equal doctrine.

plum book A publication that lists the top jobs in the bureaucracy to which the president will appoint people through the patronage system.

plural executive system A state and local government structure in which the citizens elect more than two people to top positions in the executive branch of government.

pluralist theory A theory that holds that policy making is a competition among diverse interest groups that ensure the representation of individual interests.

pocket veto A special presidential veto of a bill passed at the conclusion of a legislative session, whereby the president waits 10 days without signing the bill, and the bill dies.

police powers The states' reserved powers to protect the health, safety, lives, and properties of residents in a state.

political action committee (PAC) An entity whose specific goal is to raise and spend money to influence the outcome of elections.

political culture The people's collective beliefs and attitudes about government and political processes.

political engagement Citizen actions that are intended to solve public problems through political means.

political ideology An integrated system of ideas or beliefs about political values in general and the role of government in particular.

political machines Big-city organizations that exerted control over many aspects of life and lavishly rewarded supporters.

political party An organization that recruits, nominates, and elects party members to office in order to control the government.

political socialization The process by which we develop our political values and opinions.

politically uncontrollable spending Spending on programs that are so popular that elected officials are not willing to change the laws that authorize the programs for fear of the effect on their reelection prospects.

politico A hybrid model of representation in which legislators vote in keeping with constituents' views on important or high-profile matters but rely on the trustee model for more mundane matters.

politics The process of deciding who gets benefits in society and who does not.

politics-administration dichotomy The concept that elected government officials, who are accountable to the voters, create and approve public policy, and then competent, politically neutral bureaucrats implement the public policy.

poll tax A fee for voting; levied to prevent poor African Americans in the South from voting.

popular referendum Process by which voters may petition the government to demand a vote of the electorate to approve or reject a new law passed by the legislature.

popular sovereignty The theory that government is created by the people and depends on the people for the authority to rule.

population In a poll, the group of people whose opinions are of interest and/or about whom information is desired.

populism A philosophy supporting the rights and empowerment of the masses as opposed to elites.

pork barrel Legislators' appropriations of funds for special projects located within their congressional districts.

poverty The condition of lacking the income sufficient to purchase the necessities for an adequate living standard.

poverty guidelines A simplified version of the U.S. Census Bureau's poverty thresholds developed each year by the Department of Health and Human Services; used to set financial eligibility criteria for benefits.

poverty rate The proportion of the population living below the poverty line as established by the national government.

poverty thresholds The U.S. Census Bureau's annually updated set of income measures (adjusted for family size) that define who is living in poverty.

precedents Previous cases with similar facts that judges identify for use in a new case they are deciding; judges apply the legal principles used in the precedent cases to decide the legal dispute they are currently resolving.

preemption The constitutionally based principle that allows a national law to supersede state or local laws.

preponderance of evidence The standard of proof used in civil cases; the evidence must show that it is more likely than not that the accused caused the harm claimed by the complainant.

president pro tempore Also called *president pro tem;* theoretically, the chair of the Senate in the vice president's absence; in reality, an honorary title, with the senator of the majority party having the longest record of continuous service being elected to the position.

press secretary The president's spokesperson to the media.

preventive war The strategy of waging war on countries that are regarded as threatening in order to avoid future conflicts.

primary election An election in which voters choose the party's candidates who will run in the later general election.

priming Bringing certain policies on issues to the public agenda through media coverage.

prior restraint A form of censorship by the government whereby it blocks the publication of news stories viewed as libelous or harmful.

privileges and immunities clause The Constitution's requirement that a state extend to other states' citizens the privileges and immunities it provides for its citizens.

progressive tax A tax that takes a larger percentage of the income of wealthier taxpayers and a smaller percentage of the income of lower-income taxpayers.

progressives A faction within the Democratic party who emphasize the need for societal reform that results in greater economic and social equality.

promoted tweets Targeted advertising found on a Twitter page that targets Twitterers based on whom they follow and who follows them.

property Anything that can be owned.

proportional (flat) tax A tax that takes the same percentage of each taxpayer's income.

proportional representation system An electoral structure in which political parties win the number of parliamentary seats equal to the percentage of the vote the party receives.

proposition A proposed measure placed on the ballot in an initiative election.

prospective voting A method of evaluating candidates in which voters focus on candidates' positions on issues important to them and vote for the candidates who best represent their views.

protectionist trade policy The establishment of trade barriers to shelter domestic goods from foreign competition.

public agenda The public issues that most demand the attention of government officials.

public diplomat An individual outside government who promotes his or her country's interests and thus helps to shape international perceptions of the nation.

public employee unions Labor organizations comprising federal, state, and municipal workers, including police officers and teachers.

public goods Goods whose benefits cannot be limited and that are available to all.

public opinion The public's expressed views about an issue at a specific point in time.

public opinion poll A survey of a given population's opinion on an issue or a candidate at a particular point in time.

pure capitalist economy An economy in which private individuals and companies own the modes of producing goods and services, and the government does not enact laws aimed at influencing the marketplace transactions that distribute those goods and services.

purposive incentive Motivation to join an interest group based on the belief in the group's cause from an ideological or a moral standpoint.

push polls A special type of poll that both attempts to skew public opinion about a candidate and provides information to campaigns about candidate strengths and weaknesses.

 Q

quota sample A method by which pollsters structure a sample so that it is representative of the characteristics of the target population.

R

rally 'round the flag effect The peaks in presidential approval ratings during short-term military action.

random sampling A scientific method of selection in which each member of the population has an equal chance of being included in the sample.

ratification The process by which constitutions and constitutional amendments are formally confirmed, thereby becoming law

rational choice theory The idea that from an economic perspective it is not rational for people to participate in collective action when they can secure the collective good without participating.

realignment A shift in party allegiances or electoral support that propels a political party to majority status.

reapportionment Reallocation of seats in the House of Representatives to each state based on changes in state populations since the last census.

recall A special election in which voters can remove an officeholder before his or her term is over.

recession An economic downturn during which unemployment is high and the production of goods and services is low.

Reconstruction era The time after the Civil War between 1866 and 1877 when the institutions and infrastructure of the South were rebuilt.

red tape Bureaucratic rules and procedures that are viewed as inefficient, dehumanizing, and requiring tedious paperwork.

redistricting The redrawing of congressional district boundaries within each state, based on the reapportionment from the census.

redlining An illegal practice in which banks or insurance companies refuse or limit loans, mortgages, or insurance within specific geographic areas, often inner-city neighborhoods.

referendum An election in which voters in a state can vote for or against a measure proposed by the state legislature.

regime change The replacement of a country's government with another government by facilitating the deposing of its leader or leading political party.

regional security alliance An alliance typically between a superpower and nations that are ideologically similar in a particular region.

regressive tax A tax that takes a greater percentage of the income of lower-income earners than of higher-income earners.

regulated capitalist economy (mixed economy) An economy in which private ownership of the modes of production dominates and the government enacts policies to influence the health of the economy.

remarketing Targeting political Google ads based on the cookies that a user drops on other websites.

report A legislative committee's explanation to the full chamber of a bill and its intent.

representative bureaucracy A bureaucracy in which the people serving resemble the larger population whom they serve in demographic characteristics such as race, age, ethnicity, sex, religion, and economic status.

republic A government that derives its authority from the people and in which citizens elect government officials to represent them in the processes by which laws are made; a representative democracy.

reserved powers The matters referred to in the Tenth Amendment over which states retain sovereignty.

responsible party model Political scientists' view that a function of a party is to offer a clear choice to voters by establishing priorities or policy stances different from those of rival parties.

retention election A noncompetitive election in which an incumbent judge's name is on the ballot and voters decide whether the judge should be retained.

retrospective voting A method of evaluating candidates in which voters evaluate incumbent candidates and decide whether to support them based on their past performance.

right to privacy The right of an individual to be left alone and to make decisions freely, without the interference of others.

Roe v. Wade The Supreme Court decision that expanded the right of privacy to include a woman's right to have an abortion, balanced by the state's concern to protect the health of the woman and the potential of human life

Roosevelt Corollary The idea, advanced by President Theodore Roosevelt, that the United States had the right to act as an "international police power" in the Western Hemisphere to ensure stability in the region.

Rule of Four Practice by which the Supreme Court justices determine if they will hear a case if four or more justices want to hear it.

rule of law Belief that a country should be governed by consistently applied and legitimately adopted policies and statutes, not by the will of an individual.

Rules Committee One of the most important committees in the House, which decides the length of debate and the scope of amendments that will be allowed on a bill.

runoff election A follow-up election that is held when no candidate receives the majority of votes cast in the original election.

S

safety net programs A collection of public policies aimed at ensuring that citizens' basic physiological needs are met.

salient In relation to a voting issue—having resonance, being significant, causing intense interest.

sampling error Also called *margin of error*, a statistical calculation of the difference in results between a poll of a randomly drawn sample and a poll of the entire population.

sanctions Penalties that halt economic exchanges.

Schenck v. U.S. Established the **clear and probable danger test** whereby the government may silence speech or expression when there is a clear and present danger that this speech will bring about some harm that the government has the power to prevent.

select committee A congressional committee created to consider specific policy issues or address a specific concern.

selective incorporation The process by which, over time, the Supreme Court applied those freedoms that served *some* fundamental principle of liberty or justice to the states, thus rejecting total incorporation.

Senate majority leader The most powerful position in the Senate; the majority leader manages the legislative process and schedules debate on legislation.

Senate minority leader The leader of the minority party in the Senate, who works with the majority leader in negotiating legislation.

senatorial courtesy A custom whereby the Senate will not confirm a presidential nominee if the nominee is opposed by one (or both) senators from the nominee's home state.

Senior Executive Service (SES) A unique personnel system for top managerial, supervisory, and policy positions offering less job security but higher pay than the merit-based civil service system.

seniority system The system in which the member with the longest continuous tenure on a standing committee is given preference when the committee chooses its chair.

separate but equal doctrine Established by the Supreme Court in *Plessy v. Ferguson,* it said that separate but equal facilities for whites and nonwhites do not violate the Fourteenth Amendment's equal protection clause.

separation of powers The Constitution's delegation of authority for the primary governing functions among three branches of government so that no one group of government officials controls all the governing functions.

shadow bureaucrats People hired and paid by private for-profit and nonprofit organizations that implement public policy through a government contract.

Shaw v. Reno A 1993 Supreme Court decision ruling that race cannot be the predominant factor in creating districts, but can be legal if other concerns of redistricting are protected.

signing statement A written message that the president issues upon signing a bill into law.

slander False verbal statements about others that harm their reputation.

social capital Relationships that improve our lives in many ways by social connections.

social contract An agreement between people and their leaders in which the people agree to give up some liberties so that their other liberties are protected.

social contract theory The idea that individuals possess free will, and every individual is equally endowed with the God-given right of self-determination and the ability to consent to be governed.

social movement Large, often informal groups of individuals or organizations striving for a broad, common goal, frequently centered on significant change to the social or political order.

social networking sites Platforms that enable users to construct a profile, specify other users with whom they share a connection, and view others' connections.

social regulation Government rules, regulations, and standards aimed at protecting workers, consumers, and the environment from market failure.

socialism An ideology that advocates economic equality, theoretically achieved by having the government or workers own the means of production (businesses and industry).

soft money loophole The Supreme Court's interpretation of campaign finance law that enabled political parties to raise unlimited funds for party-building activities such as voter registration drives and get-out-the-vote (GOTV) efforts.

Solicitor General The person appointed to represent the federal government in all appeals before the Supreme Court.

solidary incentive The motivation to join an interest group based on the companionship and the satisfaction derived from socializing with others that it offers.

Speaker of the House The leader of the House of Representatives, chosen by the majority party.

special-purpose government A government providing one service or function for residents living within its borders.

spoils system The practice of rewarding political supporters with jobs.

standing committee A permanent committee in Congress, with a defined legislative jurisdiction.

standing to sue The legal right to bring lawsuits in court.

stare decisis See *doctrine of* stare decisis.

statutory powers Powers explicitly granted to presidents by congressional action.

strategic arms limitation talks (SALT talks) Discussions between the United States and the Soviet Union in the 1970s that focused on cooling down the nuclear arms race between the two superpowers.

strategic arms reduction talks (START talks) Talks between the United States and the Soviet Union in which reductions in missiles and nuclear warheads, not merely a limitation on increases, were negotiated.

strategic defense initiative (SDI, or "Star Wars") A ballistic missile defense system advocated by President Ronald Reagan.

strategic model Judicial decision-making model that states that the primary guide for judges is their individual policy preferences; however, their preferences are tempered by their consideration of institutional factors, as well as concern over the legitimacy of the court system.

stratified sampling A process of random sampling in which the national population is divided into fourths and certain areas within these regions are selected as representative of the national population.

strict scrutiny test Guidelines the courts use to determine the legality of suspect classification based discrimination; on the basis of this test, discrimination is legal if it is a necessary means by which the government can achieve a compelling public interest.

strong mayor An elected municipal government executive who holds the powers traditionally delegated to elected chief executives (veto power, power to formulate the budget, and power to appoint many executive branch officials).

subcommittee A subordinate committee in Congress that typically handles specific areas of a standing committee's jurisdiction.

substantive representation Assumption that a government official will best serve the concerns of the racial, ethnic, gender, or other group to which he or she belongs.

sunset clause A clause in legislation that sets an expiration date for an authorized program or policy unless Congress reauthorizes it.

sunshine laws Legislation that opens up government functions and documents to the public.

super PACs Political organizations that use contributions from individuals, corporations, and labor unions to spend unlimited sums independent from the campaigns, yet influencing the outcomes of elections.

Super Tuesday The Tuesday in early March on which the most primary elections are held, many of them in southern states.

superpowers Leader nations with dominating influence in international affairs.

supply-side economics The theory that advocates cutting taxes and deregulating business to stimulate the economy.

supremacy clause A clause in Article VI of the Constitution that states that the Constitution and the treaties and laws created by the national government in compliance with the Constitution are the supreme law of the land.

supreme law of the land A clause in Article VI, by which the U.S. Constitution's ultimate authority is established; the clause states that all laws made by governments within the United States must comply with the Constitution.

suspect classifications Distinctions based on race, religion, and national origin, which are assumed to be illegitimate.

symbolic representation Diversity among government officials as a symbol, an indication, that our democracy, our government by and for the people, is functioning appropriately by offering equal opportunity to influence government by becoming a government official.

symbolic speech Nonverbal "speech" in the form of an action such as picketing, flag burning, or wearing an armband to signify a protest.

T

take care clause The constitutional basis for inherent powers, which states the president "shall take Care that the Laws be faithfully executed."

talk radio A format featuring conversations and interviews about topics of interest, along with call-ins from listeners.

tariff A special tax on imported goods paid by the importer.

tax base The overall *wealth* (income and assets of citizens and corporations) that the government can tax to raise revenue.

tax expenditures (also, *tax breaks* or *loopholes*) Government financial incentives that allow individuals and corporations to pay reduced taxes, to encourage behaviors that promote the public good.

Tea Party movement A grassroots, conservative protest movement that opposed recent government actions, including economic stimulus spending and health care reform.

telegenic The quality of looking good on TV.

The Federalist Papers A series of essays, written by James Madison, Alexander Hamilton, and John Jay, that argued for the ratification of the Constitution.

third party A party organized in opposition or as an alternative to the existing parties in a two-party system.

Three-Fifths Compromise The negotiated agreement by the delegates to the Constitutional Convention to count each slave as three-fifths of a free man for the purpose of representation and taxes.

ticket splitting The situation in which voters vote for candidates from more than one party.

time, place, and manner restrictions Regulations regarding when, where, or how expression may occur; must be content neutral.

Tinker v. Des Moines The Supreme Court decision protecting the political speech of school children in public schools as long as it does not interfere with the educational process.

tort Situation when a person's body or property is harmed by another person's negligence or other wrongful act, other than the violation of a contract.

total incorporation The theory that the Fourteenth Amendment's due process clause requires the states to uphold *all* freedoms in the Bill of Rights; rejected by the Supreme Court in favor of selective incorporation.

totalitarianism System of government in which the government essentially controls every aspect of people's lives.

township A unit of government that serves people living outside municipalities, in rural areas where the population is more dispersed than in areas served by municipal governments.

tracking polls Polls that measure changes in public opinion over the course of days, weeks, or months by repeatedly asking respondents the same questions and measuring changes in their responses.

trade policy A collection of tax laws and regulations that support the country's international commerce.

traditionalistic political culture The view that the purpose of government is to maintain the status quo and that participants in government should come from the society's elite.

transgender Individuals whose gender identity does not match the sex they were assigned at birth.

transparency Ability of citizens to have more and better information about governmental processes as well as services.

trial court Court with original jurisdiction in a legal dispute that decides guilt or liability based on its understanding of the facts presented by the two disputing parties.

Truman Doctrine Articulated by President Harry Truman, a foreign policy commitment by the United States to assist countries' efforts to resist communism in the Cold War era.

truncated government The situation that exists when one chamber of Congress is controlled by the same party that controls the White House, while the other chamber is controlled by the other party.

trustee model A model of representation in which a member of the House or the Senate follows his or her own conscience when deciding issue positions.

turnout rate The proportion of eligible voters who actually voted.

U

U.S. Code A compilation of all the laws passed by the U.S. Congress.

U.S. Supreme Court The court of last resort for conflicts over the U.S. Constitution and national laws; in addition to its appellate jurisdiction, the Court has limited original jurisdiction.

umbrella organizations Interest groups that represent collective groups of industries or corporations.

unanimous consent An agreement by every senator to the terms of debate on a given piece of legislation.

unicameral legislature A legislative body with a single chamber.

unitary system A governmental system in which one central government is *the* sovereign government and it creates other, regional governments to which it delegates some governing powers and responsibilities; however, the central government retains ultimate authority (sovereignty).

United Nations (UN) An international body established in 1945 in order to prevent future wars by achieving collective security and peace.

United States v. Lopez Case in which the U.S. Supreme Court ruled the national Gun-Free School Zones Act unconstitutional and affirmed that state governments have the right to establish gun-free school zones.

V

veto The president's rejection of a bill, which is sent back to Congress with the president's objections noted.

Virginia Plan The governmental structure proposed by the Virginia delegation to the Constitutional Convention, which consisted of a bicameral legislature (Congress), an executive elected by the legislature, and a separate national judiciary; state representation in Congress would be proportional, based on state population; the people would elect members to the lower house, and members of the lower house would elect the members of the upper house.

virtual communities Online networks where individuals perform as leaders, information and opinions can be shared, and strategies can be planned, priorities organized, and roles assigned.

voter fatigue The condition in which voters grow tired of all candidates by the time Election Day arrives, and may thus be less likely to vote.

W

waivers Exemptions from particular conditions normally attached to grants.

War Powers Act A law that limits presidential use of military forces to 60 days, with an automatic extension of 30 additional days if the president requests such an extension.

Warsaw Pact A regional security structure formed in 1955 by the Soviet Union and its seven satellite states in Eastern Europe in response to the creation of the North Atlantic Treaty Organization (NATO).

Watergate During the Nixon administration, a scandal involving burglaries and the subsequent cover-up by high-level administration officials.

weak mayor An elected municipal government executive who holds few, if any, of the powers traditionally delegated to elected chief executives.

weapons of mass destruction (WMDs) Nuclear, chemical, and biological weapons.

whistleblower A bureaucrat or private party who discloses to the government mismanagement, fraud, waste, corruption, or threats to public health and safety.

White House counsel The president's lawyer.

White House Office (WHO) The office that develops policies and protects the president's legal and political interests.

white primary A primary election in which a party's nominees for general election were chosen but in which only white people were allowed to vote.

winner-take-all system An electoral system in which the candidate who receives the most votes wins that office, even if that total is not a majority.

Wisconsin v. Yoder Case in which the Supreme Court found that an individual's interest in the free exercise of religion outweighs the state's interest in requiring education after the eighth grade.

Works Progress Administration (WPA) A New Deal program that employed 8.5 million people at a cost of more than $11 million between 1935 and 1943.

World Bank The international financial institution created by the Bretton Woods Agreement of 1944 and charged with lending money to nations in need.

World Trade Organization (WTO) The organization created in 1995 to negotiate, implement, and enforce international trade agreements.

writ of *certiorari* Latin for "a request to make certain"; issued by a higher court, this is an order for a lower court to make available the records of a past case it decided so that the higher court can review the case.

Y

yellow journalism An irresponsible, sensationalist approach to news reporting, so named after the yellow ink used in the "Yellow Kid" cartoons in the *New York World*.

INDEX

Page numbers followed by *f* indicate figures; *t* indicate tables; *italicized* page numbers indicate photos and illustrations.

shadow bureaucrats, 293
Shaw v. Reno, 655
Shays, Daniel, 54
Shays Rebellion, 54
Sheehan, Margaret A., 779
Shelby County v. Alabama, 400
Sherman, Roger, 62
Sierra Club, 734
signing statement, 201, 202
Silent Spring (Carson), 536
Sinclair, Upton, 512, *513,* 769
sites, for social networking, 472, 647, 727,
    764, 765, 777, 792, *792,* 794
sketches for courts, *262*
Skirky, Clay, 794
slander, 352
slavery, *14*
    civil rights and, 387–394, 394*f*
    conflict and compromise over, 59–62
    history of, 387–394
    opposition to, 388
    politics of, 695
Small Business Administration (SBA), 532
Smeal, Eleanor, 457–458, *458*
Smerconish, Michael, 778
Smith, Adam, 496
Smith Act of 1940, 348
Smithson, James, *300*
Smithsonian Institution, 298, 300, *300*
SNAP (Supplemental Nutrition Assistance
    Program), 532, 551
Snapchat, 9, 23, 763
Snapfish, 813
Snopes, 13
Snowden, Edward, 811–813
soccer, *581*
social capital, 632, 726–727
social class, 733
social contract theory, 18
social insurance program, 545
socialism
    components of, 24*t*
    libertarianism and, 26–27
    New Deal as, 687, 698
    Socialist Party, 709
socialization, 15
social media, 604–605
    for communication, 821
    diplomacy and, 580
    forms, 763
    as presidential influence tool, 221–222
    and privacy, 363
    usage by Donald Trump, 221, 269
social media, impact on electoral politics, 9
social movements, 733–734
social networking sites, 792
social policy, 527
social regulation, 301, 511, 512–514
Social Security, 314, 532
    history of, 545–546
    politics of, 527
    retirement program, 505
    Social Security Act, 122
    Social Security Administration, 247, 305
    taxes for, 545
social security, 527
Social Security Act (1935), 122
Social Security Administration, 247, 305
Social Security Disability Insurance
    (SSDI), 545
society
    conflict in, 165
    social capital, *726,* 726–727
    social contract, 18
    social movements, 733–734
soft money loophole, 691
Soleimani, Qassim, 607
Solicitor General, 254
solidary incentives, 734
Sons of Liberty, 47, 48
South Dakota, 134
South Dakota v. Dole, 134
Southern Christian Leadership Conference
    (SCLC), 397
"Southern Manifesto," 269
South Korea, 591–592

sovereign territory, 14, 46
sovereignty
    conflicts over, 139
    theory of, 110
Spain, 15
Speaker of the House, 106, 107, 174, 693
spending caps, 506, 507
spending policy, 504–505
splinter parties, 709
spoils system, 694
SpongeBob SquarePants (TV show), 767
sports, *350, 609*
SSDI (Social Security Disability
    Insurance), 545
SSI (Supplemental Security Income),
    445–446, 545
Stalin, Joseph, 349, 590, *591,* 592
Stamp Act (1765), 48
standing committees, 170
standing to sue, 389
Stanton, Edwin, 227
Stanton, Elizabeth Cady, 404, 406
stare decisis doctrine, 244–245, 269
START (strategic arms reduction)
    talks, 594
Star Wars, 564
State Children's Health Insurance
    Program, 552
states
    authority for, 95, 100
    citizens and, 94
    civic engagement for, 635
    commerce for, 121–122
    constitutions for, 245
    feminism in, 405, *406*
    government and, 95, 113*f*
    interstate compacts, 119
    as laboratories of democracy, 124–125
    militias for, 54
    national government obligations to, 123, 124*t*
    powers delegated to, 118–119, 118*f*
    sovereignty, 117–119, 118*f*
    state parties, 690–691
    States' Rights Party, 709
    U.S. and, 97
States' Rights Party, 709
state-to-state relations, 66
    as horizontal system, 119–120
    policy for, 94–95
    politics of, 70–71
statistics
    for gender, 30*f*
statutes, 245–246
statutory powers, 216
Steffens, Lincoln, 769
Stein, Jill, 712
Stokes, Donald, 667
Stone, Lucy, 405
Stone, Roger, 269
Stowe, Harriet Beecher, 388
strategic arms limitation talks
    (SALT talks), 594
strategic arms reduction talks (START
    talks), 594
strategic defense initiative (SDI), 594
strategic model, 262
Strategic Petroleum Reserve, 541
strategies
    campaign, 645
    for candidates, 798–802, *800*
    indirect strategies, 746–748
    for interest groups, 749–750
    for politics, 798–802, *800*
stratified sampling, 469
strict scrutiny test, 386
strict separation of church and state, 355–356
structure
    of elections, 663
    of executive branch, 64
    of federal court system, 251–253
    of government, 23, 284–287, 285*t,* 286*f*
    of judicial branch, 66
    of legislative branch, 63
    of republics, 52
student loans, forgiveness program for,
    543–544

Student Non-violent Coordinating
    Committee (SNCC), 397
subcommittees, 170, 171
subsidies
    direct, 532
    government, 515
substantive representation, 256
success, 735–738
succession, for presidents, 212–214, 213*t*
suffrage, 404–407, *406*
Sullivan, Mark, 817
sunset clause, 309
Sunshine Act of 1976, 307
sunshine laws, 311
    Government in the Sunshine Act, 307
    ideology of, 306
Superfund law, 539
supermajorities, 172
super PACs, 628, 667–670, 751–752
superpowers, 587–597, 588*f, 591, 593*
Super Tuesday, 641
Supplemental Nutrition Assistance Program
    (SNAP), 532, 551
Supplemental Security Income (SSI)
    program, 445–446, 545
supply-side economics, 496, 500, 502, 504
supremacy clause, 43, 56, 67–69, 96, 116
Supreme Court
    ACA for, 180, 260, 302, 687
    audio recording, *262*
    authority for, 251
    Barron v. Baltimore, 341
    Baze v. Rees, 367
    Bostick v. Clayton County, Georgia, 413
    Bowers v. Hardwick, 413
    Bradwell v. Illinois, 405, 409
    Brandenburg v. Ohio, 349
    Brown v. Board of Education of Topeka, 264,
        269, 395, 417
    Buckley v. Valeo, 666, 667, 691
    Burwell v. Hobby Lobby, 359
    campaign finance for, 666
    censorship for, 780–781
    Chaplinsky v. New Hampshire, 352
    checks and balances for, 266–267
    *Citizens United v. Federal Election
        Commission,* 270, 352, 664, 669,
        701, 746
    commerce for, 121–122
    Constitution amendments interpreted
        by, 74–75
    Constitution (U.S.) and, 633
    decision making for, 260*f*
    discrimination for, 385–387
    District of Columbia v. Heller, 265, 344
    diversity, 255
    Dred Scott v. Sandford, 389
    Engel v. Vitale, 358
    facts for, 260–261
    *Federal Communications Commission v.
        Television Stations, Inc.,* 780
    *Federal Election Commission v. Wisconsin
        Right to Life, Inc.,* 667
    free speech for, 349–351
    functions, 259–263
    Furman v. Georgia, 366–367
    gender in, 405
    general welfare for, 122–123
    gerrymandering for, 653
    Gibbons v. Ogden, 121–122, *122*
    Gideon v. Wainwright, 366
    Gitlow v. New York, 342, 348
    Griswold v. Connecticut, 359–360
    ideology of, 253
    imminent lawless action test, 349
    incitement test, 349
    interpretation of Constitution, 120–123
    Lawrence v. Texas, 362, 413
    Ledbetter v. Goodyear Tire & Rubber,
        263, 267
    Lemon v. Kurtzman, 356
    lobbying and, 731
    Mapp v. Ohio, 364
    Marbury v. Madison, 66, 241–242, 245,
        250, 263
    Massachusetts v. Mellon, 134

*McConnell v. the Federal Election
    Commission,* 667
McCulloch v. Maryland, 109, 121
McDonald v. Chicago, 344
Mendez v. Westminister, 416
Miller v. California, 352
    for minorities, 682
Minor v. Happersett, 405
Miranda rights, 365, 366*t*
Near v. Minnesota, 342, 354
New York Times v. U.S., 354
Obergefell v. Hodges, 260, 362, 413
Plessy v. Ferguson, 169, 392, 393
    powers for, 121–123
    preferential treatment standard, 356
    presidents and, 181
Reed v. Reed, 409
    representative democracy for, 85
    Roberts Court, 253, 271*t,* 278*t*
Roe v. Wade, 361, *362,* 410
    Rule of Four, 260
Schenck v. U.S., 347
Shelby County v. Alabama, 400
    sketches for, *262*
South Dakota v. Dole, 134
    super PACs for, 751–752
Texas v. Johnson, 351
Tinker v. Des Moines, 350
Torrey Dale Grady v. North Carolina, 365
    trends in, *357*
*United States v. Curtiss-Wright Export
    Corp.,* 217
United States v. Lopez, 122–123
United States v. Richard M. Nixon, 218, 225
United States v. Virginia, 409
United States v. Windsor, 413
U.S. v. Eichman, 351
U.S. v. O'Brien, 350, 351
Van Orden v. Perry, 357
Virginia v. Black, 352
Wisconsin v. Yoder, 359
    work, citizens' approval of, 268
supreme law of the land, 116
surge strategy, 473, 599, 600
surveillance, 811–813
    Foreign Intelligence Surveillance Act
        (1978), 252, 813
    PRISM, 812
Survivor (TV show), 341, 453, *453,* 767
suspect classifications, 386
Swift messaging, 811
symbolic representation, 256
symbolic speech, 349–351
Syria
    air strikes in, 573
    ISIS, 573
systems
    adversarial judicial system, 247
    balance of power system, 585
    confederal, 111
    dual court, 242–243, 243*f*
    federal court system, 251–253
    fifth party system, 698–699
    first party system, 694
    fourth party system, 696–697, *697*
    government, 112*f*
    horizontal, 119–120
    legacy systems, 805
    legal model, 261
    Merit System Protection Board, 293
    party system, 693
    patronage system, 288
    proportional representation system,
        704, 706
    second party system, 694–695
    seniority system, 170
    spoils system, 694
    Swift messaging, 811
    third party system, 695–696, *696*
    two-party system, 703–707
    unitary, 110
    winner-take-all system, 706

Taft, William Howard, 697
Takano, Mark, *638*
take care clause, 215